Leading Issues in
Economic Development

Leading Issues in Economic Development

FOURTH EDITION

GERALD M. MEIER
Stanford University

New York   Oxford
OXFORD UNIVERSITY PRESS
1984

Copyright © 1964, 1970, 1976, 1984 by Oxford University Press, Inc.

Library of Congress Cataloging in Publication Data
Main entry under title:

Leading issues in economic development.

Includes index.
1. Economic development.   I. Meier, Gerald M.
HD82.L3273   1984   338.9   83-19372
ISBN 0-19-503415-5 (pbk.)

Printing (last digit):   9 8 7 6

Printed in the United States of America

For Daniel

PREFACE TO THE FOURTH EDITION

The overriding objective of this fourth edition of *Leading Issues in Economic Development* remains the same as stated in the first edition—to present a new kind of course book that will bring some order to the diffuse subject of economic development without sacrificing a variety of viewpoints and different perspectives. The evolution of the subject confirms my belief that it can best be studied in a manner different from the usual approaches of either a textbook or a book of readings. Development practitioners must operate in an imperfect, second-best world, and development economists cannot yet claim that their subject constitutes a self-contained discipline. I believe that the student's most sensible introduction to economic development is through a study of several "leading issues" that are at present a major preoccupation of both development economists and development practitioners.

This new edition reflects the current development mood of stock-taking and reassessment. It focuses on an appraisal of development experience and the reinterpretation of development thought in order to highlight future policy options. After four decades of struggling against poverty, the international development community is asking what has gone right? What has gone wrong? And still we must be concerned with future efforts to lessen the pain of poverty suffered by two-thirds of mankind. But we must also put the future of the development movement in perspective by building on the lessons of development experience. From that experience, there should emerge fresh thinking on the leading issues in economic development.

I have chosen to concentrate on a relatively few issues that are now of central concern to development professionals. On each of these strategic issues, I have brought to bear a variety of materials that should be read together. To provide additional direction and cohesion, I have written a substantive commentary through a series of connecting text Notes. In some instances, I have introduced a Note to treat a topic more concisely than could be done through separate readings; in other instances, a Note is designed to cover a topic that is not yet adequately treated in the literature, or to tie one issue with another.

Even more than in earlier editions, I want to emphasize the importance of the interrelatedness of the readings on each issue—taken as a set—rather than any one particular reading. Each selection acquires added significance through its contextual position, and the materials are enhanced by their very combination. This is especially true for the interrelations among the various materials that deal with analysis, policy implications, and the lessons of development experience. The major focus is on the analytical core of the subject. At the same time, the analysis is made as policy-oriented as possible. And the materials can be readily supplemented by country cases and empirical studies.

The changes in this edition are extensive. I have introduced new chapters. I have also extensively modified all the earlier chapters, replacing many of the older selections with new selections that emphasize more current topics. I have tried to strengthen the entire book by eliminating the merely descriptive or wordy selections of previous editions and by including new selections that will deepen the student's understanding of fundamental economic principles and of empirical relationships. I have added more of my own Notes and revised the Notes contained in previous editions.

This edition also introduces Comments and Exhibits. The Comments are intended primarily to elaborate on selections, to raise questions, or to suggest additional readings on a topic that is not adequately covered in this book. The Exhibits present charts and tables that give more empirical content to the subject.

I wish to express my appreciation to the authors and publishers who have granted permission to use excerpts from articles, books, and other publications for which American or foreign copyrights exist. Specific acknowledgment is given with each selection. Some parts of the original versions of the selected materials have been (silently) omitted out of consideration for relevancy and to avoid repetition. In some cases, tables and diagrams have been renumbered; in other cases, footnotes have been omitted, while others have been renumbered.

As in previous editions, many of the revisions in this edition have been inspired by my students at Stanford University and by lecture audiences in developing countries. Their challenging questions and incisive observations have meant much to me. I hope this volume will prove of value to another generation of students concerned with the future of the developing world. This hope has sustained me through the laborious process of preparing this new edition.

My thanks are also due to Timothy Quey, Sridhar Moorthy, and Srikant Datar who relieved me of many library chores. And a very special acknowledgment is due Pat Sharp who has taken the roughest of copy and, with remarkable good humor and admirable efficiency, has guided the manuscript from handwritten scrawls through the word processor to the printer. Without the speedy imprint of her skills, this new edition would have been postponed indefinitely.

Finally, I wish to acknowledge the assistance I received while a Visiting Professor at the Economic Development Institute of the World Bank as well as the advice of Bruce F. Johnston, Walter P. Falcon, Derek Healey, and Paul P. Streeten—and the entire profession of development economists whose writings have contributed to this volume.

January 1984   G.M.M.
Stanford, California

CONTENTS

ACRONYMS

ASEAN	Association of South East Asian Nations
C-20	Committee of Twenty
DAC	Development Advisory Committee of OECD
ECA	Economic Commission for Africa
ECLA	Economic Commission for Latin America
ECOSOC	Economic and Social Council
FAO	Food and Agriculture Organization
G-24	Group of Twenty-four
GAB	General Arrangements to Borrow
GATT	General Agreement on Tariffs and Trade
GNP	Gross national product
IBRD	International Bank for Reconstruction and Development
IDA	International Development Association
IDB	Inter-American Development Bank
IFC	International Finance Corporation
ILO	International Labour Organisation
IMF	International Monetary Fund
ITO	International Trade Organization
LDCs	Less developed countries
MDCs	More developed countries
MTN	Multilateral trade negotiations
NICs	Newly industrializing countries
NIEO	New International Economic Order
ODA	Official Development Assistance
OECD	Organization for Economic Co-operation and Development
OPEC	Organization of Petroleum Exporting Countries
SDRs	Special drawing rights
UN	United Nations
UNCTAD	United Nations Conference on Trade and Development
UNDP	United Nations Development Program
UNESCO	United Nations Educational, Scientific and Cultural Organization
WFC	World Food Council
WFP	World Food Program
WHO	World Health Organization

**Leading Issues in
Economic Development**

CHAPTER I

The Development Record

We are concerned in this book with the future standard of living for 70 percent of the world's population—the poverty-ridden peoples in the less developed countries (LDCs) of Asia, Africa, and Latin America. Two centuries after the Industrial Revolution, most of the world is still poor. The need to accelerate the development of the poor countries remains, in the words of the recent President of the World Bank, Robert McNamara, "the central historical event of our times."

We examine the major analytical and policy issues raised by the challenges to accelerate economic growth rates, eradicate absolute poverty, reduce inequality, and create more productive employment opportunities. These challenges now require the international community to reassert the development priority and reshape development policies.

The World Bank emphasizes that the failure to achieve a minimum level of income above the "poverty line" has kept some 40 percent of the people in the LDCs in the condition of "absolute poverty"—a condition of life so degraded by disease, illiteracy, malnutrition, and squalor that it denies its victims the basic human necessities. The persistence of absolute poverty, despite respectable achievements in rates of growth in gross national product (GNP), is now of more concern than that of relative poverty, or a "widening gap" between the rich and poor countries. With the increase in the world's population, the number of people in absolute poverty below minimum standards of nutrition, health, shelter, and education has grown and is now of the order of 800 million.

A major theme of this book is the emphasis on discovering and promoting those positive forces that raise real income per head, improve employment opportunities, and achieve a wider distribution of the gains from development.

These forces of development are not, however, readily identifiable. After disappointments in the record of development, economists can no longer rely on simple causal relationships that emphasize development planning, capital accumulation, and foreign aid. The forces of development are too complex, subtle, and insufficiently known to yield to any simple formula.

One way of recognizing that a wide range of development forces must be identified is to realize at the outset that the development process encompasses more than the economic theory of production. Empirical studies of the sources of growth in output in a number of countries have demonstrated that much of the increase in aggregate production over a long period cannot be explained by an increase in only the standard physical inputs of the factors of production. A large part of the increase in total output remains to be attributed to some "unexplained residual factor" in the economy's aggregate production function. In historical studies of several presently advanced countries, the "residual factor"—the unisolated source of growth—is left to account for 50 percent or more of the increase in total output. This residual has been called a "measure of our ignorance" of the determinants that create a rise in productivity—the complex of little understood forces that cause output per unit of utilized resources to rise.[1]

A fundamental question is: What are the other sources of growth that can be identified in the catchall of the "residual," and introduced as inputs that are amenable to policy promotion? Another theme of this book, therefore, is the need to proceed beyond a narrow economic theory of production to a broader interpretation that requires attention to "efficiency" in the utilization of inputs as well as a wider understanding of an economy's "learning process."

An additional theme is that national development must now occur within the international context of coexisting rich and poor countries. Capital, technology, knowledge, values, and institutions are more readily transferable from rich to poor countries than ever before. There may, however, be drawbacks as well as advantages in being a latecomer to development, and the late-developing country is increasingly aware of the need for "appropriate" transfers. There is now a more imaginative search for means by which to raise the social benefit-cost ratio of these transfers to the developing countries.

At the same time, the greater interdependence between the more developed countries (MDCs) and the less developed countries (LDCs) gives the LDCs new negotiating strategies for designing trade, investment, and international monetary arrangements. The LDCs have assumed an enhanced role in shaping the emergence of a new international economic order to replace the old Bretton Woods system. The contentions of the United Nations Conference on Trade and Development (UNCTAD) and the criticisms of the General Agreement on Tariffs and Trade (GATT) and the International Monetary Fund (IMF) must receive serious attention because the future of national development will be closely related to reforms in international trade and monetary arrangements—a new Bretton Woods II.

The time has also come for a reassessment of development planning and policymaking. Many have become disenchanted with centralized, detailed planning as it has been practiced in some LDCs. But even for the "lighter" type of framework planning, indicative planning, sectoral planning, the simpler monetary and fiscal policies, or only project evaluation—even for these less ambitious policies, the quality of policymaking must be raised. More efficient public-sector management is of the essence. The analysis of what policies are needed, the choice of policy instruments, and the methods of implementation must all be improved. Intimately related to improvement in policymaking is the role to be assigned to the market price system and decentralized decision making. The removal of price distortions and the use of the market as an instrument of policy are aspects of this theme of improving the quality of development policymaking.

To begin the pursuit of these several themes, this first chapter attempts to reach a clearer understanding of the meaning of economic development. The objectives of development are examined and certain misconceptions of development clarified in section I.A. The selections in section I.B. then consider different measurements of economic development and various

---

[1] Moses Abramovitz, "Resource and Output Trends in the United States Since 1970," *American Economic Review,* May 1956, pp. 11–14.

dimensions of poverty. Some of these selections reflect the shift from viewing poverty as inadequacy of means—for example, inadequate income—to viewing poverty as unsatisfactory results, such as low expectation of life and low levels of literacy. The recent emphasis on "basic human needs" is considered in selection I.B.3. Other selections explore the question of who benefits from development. Particular attention is given to the inequality of the "inverted-U hypothesis" (I.B.4) and the possible tradeoff between growth and equity (I.B.5).

Turning to an examination of country performance over the past three or four decades, section I.C. outlines some successful development strategies; summarizes some of the empirical evidence on growth, absolute poverty, and distribution (I.C.1); and evaluates the development performance of a number of countries—South Korea (I.C.2), Brazil (I.C.3), Sub-Saharan Africa (I.C.4), and China (I.C.5).

Our emphasis is on the disappointments in the development record: the low growth performance of the poorest countries, the unanticipated high rate of population growth, the weakness of the agricultural sector, the huge number in absolute poverty, and the pervasive underutilization of labor.

Considering these disappointments in the development record, the final Note (section I.D) in the chapter outlines the strategic policy issues that now confront the developing countries—issues to be analyzed in subsequent chapters. Unless these issues are resolved, the development effort will remain stalled, and the policy changes necessary to regain the development momentum and allow the LDCs to reach their potential will not be forthcoming. Such a loss will be all the more tragic when it is realized that forecasts for the year 2000 indicate that there will be four times as many people in the developing world than in the industrialized world. And with each year that the development effort stagnates, the severity of future problems only intensifies.

I.A. OBJECTIVES OF DEVELOPMENT—NOTE

Dissatisfaction with the results of the development effort over the past three decades has led to a refocusing of strategy to meet the future problems of development. The growth of GNP is no longer regarded as the main objective or index of development—but no single criterion can be readily substituted. To the dismay of the purist, but not to the surprise of the development practitioner, it is difficult to give one precise meaning to "economic development." Perhaps it is easier to say what "economic development" is *not*.

At the outset it should be recognized that economic development is not equivalent to the total development of a society: it is only a part—or one dimension—of general development. We usually focus on the nation-state as the unit of development, but "national development" is a term that encompasses, at a minimum, social and political development, as well as economic development, in the building of national identity. Depending on the orientation of one's discipline, it is also possible to consider other types of development—for example, legal or administrative. The interrelationships among these various types of development are extremely important. A major question implicit in our entire subject is how sociocultural and political development contribute to economic development and are, in turn, determined by it. It will be apparent that much more interdisciplinary study is needed to determine how economic and noneconomic forces interact.

It is also necessary to caution against equating economic development with either "economic independence" or "industrialization." As a result of their colonial history and newly acquired political independence, many poor countries have expressed discontent with their "dependence" on export markets and foreign capital. Such "dependence" is often interpreted as synonymous with "foreign domination" or "exploitation"—to be avoided now by import-substitution policies and restrictions on the inflow of private foreign capital. The emphasis on national independence through "inward-looking" policies and the advocacy of policies to avoid "foreign domination" become part of an ideology that might be called the "economics of discontent." But the "economics of discontent" should not be confused with the economics for development. National independence and the process of national consolidation may be called, as it is in India, "emotional integration";[1] but this is not to say that this noneconomic objective also contributes to economic development. "Inward-looking" policies are most likely to run counter to economic development, as is argued more fully in Chapter VIII.

Another aspect of the economics of discontent is the poor country's protest against being a primary-producing country. Industrialization tends to be viewed as a superior way of life; rich countries are believed to be rich because they are industrialized; and poor countries are believed to be poor because they are primary-producing. Whether an industrial society enjoys a superior way of life is, however, a noneconomic question. The relevant economic question for a poor country is whether agricultural development or industrial development is now the appropriate strategy for accelerating the country's economic development.

Economic development is not to be equated simply with industrialization for several reasons. First, the concentration of a large percentage of production in the primary sector is in itself not a cause of poverty: the cause is the low productivity in agriculture. A poor country's high ratio of agricultural population to total population is also more appropriately viewed as a consequence, rather than a cause, of poverty. Whenever the agricul-

[1]Gunnar Myrdal, *Asian Drama,* New York, 1968, pp. 53, 722–3.

5

tural population is poor, the nonagricultural population serving the agricultural population tends to be relatively small in size and also at a low standard of living. When the rural sector is prosperous, the nonrural sector tends to be large and also prosperous.[2]

Second, progress in industrialization is highly dependent on agricultural development. Without the necessary support of improvements in primary production, the policies of industrialization will be severely handicapped. In Chapter VII we examine the essential ways in which the rate of industrialization depends on surmounting the limitations of the agricultural bottleneck.

Third, economic development is much more than the simple acquisition of industries. It may be defined as nothing less than the "upward movement of the entire social system";[3] or it may be interpreted as the attainment of a number of "ideals of modernization," such as a rise in productivity, social and economic equalization, modern knowledge, improved institutions and attitudes, and a rationally coordinated system of policy measures that can remove the host of undesirable conditions in the social system that have perpetuated a state of underdevelopment.[4]

These views also imply that economic development involves something more than economic growth. Development is taken to mean growth plus change; there are essential qualitative dimensions in the development process that may be absent in the growth or expansion of an economy through a simple widening process. This qualitative difference is especially likely to appear in the improved performance of the factors of production and improved techniques of production—in our growing control over nature. It is also likely to appear in the development of institutions and a change in attitudes and values.

If we turn from what economic development is not, and attempt to consider its meaning more directly, we immediately encounter ambiguities because the ideal of economic development tends to be associated with different policy goals. The phenomena that one chooses to denote as "economic development" are very much a matter of what one values as the economy's policy goals. And any definition of development inevitably becomes a "persuasive definition," implying that development—as so defined—is a desirable objective.

Although requiring careful interpretation, perhaps the definition that would now gain widest approval is one that defines economic development as the *process* whereby the *real per capita income* of a country increases over a *long period* of time—subject to the *stipulations* that the number below an "absolute poverty line" does not increase, and that the distribution of income does not become more unequal. We emphasize *process* because this implies the operation of certain forces in an interconnected and causal fashion. In the following chapters we examine the process of economic development as a form of progressive action—a working-out of certain principal forces that reveal the inner structure or "logic" of an economy's development. To interpret development in terms of a process involving causal relationships should prove more meaningful than merely to identify development with a set of conditions or catalog of characteristics. If our interest in the development of a poor country arises from our desire to remove mass poverty, then we should also emphasize as the primary goal a rise in *per capita* real income rather than simply an increase in the economy's real national income, uncorrected for population change. For, if the criterion were only an increase in real national income, then it would be possible for aggregate output to rise without a per capita improvement in living standards. Population growth may surpass the

[2]For an elaboration of primary production as only an associative—rather than causative—characteristic of poverty, see S. Kuznets, *Economic Change,* New York, 1953, pp. 222–5; J. Viner, *International Trade and Economic Development,* Oxford, 1953, p. 50; G. M. Meier and R. E. Baldwin, *Economic Development,* New York, 1957, pp. 315–16.

[3]Myrdal, *Asian Drama,* p. 1869.

[4]C. E. Black, *The Dynamics of Modernization,* New York, 1966, pp. 55–60.

growth of national output or run parallel with it; the result would be falling, or at best constant, per capita income, and we would not consider this as economic development.

We also stress a *long period* of time because what is significant from the standpoint of development is a sustained increase in real income—not simply a short-period rise such as occurs during the upswing of the business cycle. The underlying upward trend over decades—at least two or three decades—is the stronger indication of development. From this standpoint, a five-year development plan is only the start of the development process, and it remains to be seen whether there is the power to sustain the process so that per capita real income continues to rise over the longer period. There is a vital distinction between *initiating* development and the more difficult task of *sustaining* development over the longer run.

Although the increase in real income per head can be adopted as the primary goal, it has also become common to interpret economic development in terms of a number of subgoals or particular categories of the overall primary objective. Thus, a certain distribution of income is another policy objective. A diminution in economic inequality is a generally stated objective of development plans. Most students of development would also undoubtedly qualify the primary goal by requiring that the absolute number of people below a minimum level of real income should also diminish at the same time that real per capita income rises. Otherwise it is conceivable that if there is population growth, the numbers of those living below a poverty line may actually have grown while there has been a rise in the average income of the population as a whole. When a dual economy exists—with a division between the modern money economy and the traditional indigenous economy—it is also possible for all of the increase in total income to occur in the modern economy,[5] and income per head

might still rise even though there had been no change in the indigenous economy. Judgment on the distribution of income is thus an integral part of the development problem.

A few of the many possible other subgoals may be the specification of a minimum level of consumption, a certain composition to the consumption stream, a maximum level of unemployment that will be tolerated, avoidance of marked disparities in the prosperity and growth of different regions within a country, diversification of the economy, and the attainment of the "ideals of modernization."

Owing to this variety of policy objectives, the emphasis on various dimensions of economic development will vary at different times and in different countries. We should, therefore, beware of interpreting economic development as meaning economic progress or an increase in economic welfare. An increase in real per capita income is not by itself a sufficient condition. Per capita real income is only a partial index of economic welfare because a judgment regarding economic welfare will also involve a value judgment on the desirability of a particular distribution of income. All observers would not, therefore, definitely say that economic welfare has increased even if per capita income has risen, unless the resultant distribution of income is also considered desirable.

Economic welfare poses not only the question of distributive justice. There are also the prior questions of what is the composition of the total ouput that is giving rise to an increase in per capita real income, and how this output is being valued. Whether a larger total output corresponds to individual preferences—let alone the more difficult test of collective choice—depends as much on what is produced and its quality as it does on the quantity produced. The valuation of the output may also be biased insofar as it is valued by market prices. These prices become the equivalent of weights, but they have been affected by the distribution of income: with a different distribution of income, prices would be different, and both the composition and value of the national output would also be different. Market prices will also have limited

---

[5]The problem of dualistic development is discussed fully in Chapter III.

value insofar as they do not reflect external diseconomies or social costs.

If such considerations of the composition of aggregate output, its valuation, and its distribution make it difficult to equate economic development with economic welfare, it is all the more unreasonable to claim that economic development means an increase in social welfare in general. Economic welfare is but a part of social welfare, and even if in the course of a country's development all the conditions necessary to promote economic welfare have been satisfied, this need not also mean that social welfare has been promoted. For the process of development has a profound impact on social institutions, habits, and beliefs, and it is likely to introduce a number of sources of tension and discord. Some aspects of human welfare might suffer if relations that were once personal become impersonal, the structure and functions of the family change, the stability in one's way of life is disrupted, and the support and assurance of traditional values disappear. Tensions also arise when the inequalities in income distribution, both among individuals and among regions in the developing country, tend to increase; when development creates "open unemployment" as well as employment; and when the pressures of excessive urbanization occur. In a fundamental sense, discords arise from the contrasts between the modern and the backward—from the superimposing of modern functions on traditional institutions.

In sum, even though it is conventional to begin with an increase in per capita real income as the best available overall index of economic development, we abstain from labeling this an increase in economic welfare, let alone social welfare, without additional considerations of various subgoals and explicit recognition of the value judgments regarding at least the composition, valuation, and distribution of the expanded output. The student of development must adopt such a cautious approach as a result of the strictures of welfare economics and the need for clarity on value premises in social research.

Even more, the policymaker must adopt such an approach because in many countries it has become only too painfully apparent that despite growth in aggregate output there can still be a larger number of people below the poverty line, rising unemployment, and greater income inequality. The quality of development is completely masked if the policymaker does not pierce the aggregate measure of GNP and consider its composition and distribution.

Development economists no longer worship at the altar of GNP, but concentrate more directly on the quality of the development process. In the words of an official for the government of Pakistan, "the problem of development must be defined as a selective attack on the worst forms of poverty. Development goals must be defined in terms of progressive reduction and eventual elimination of malnutrition, disease, illiteracy, squalor, unemployment, and inequalities. We were taught to take care of our GNP because it would take care of poverty. Let us reverse this and take care of poverty because it will take care of the GNP. In other words, let us worry about the *content* of GNP even more than its rate of increase."[6]

Years before the start of the United Nations' first Development Decade, Professor Viner had offered a similar warning that should have received more attention. He stated that:

While the supplementing of data as to economic aggregates by *per capita* averages provides additional and often essential information . . . even this does not suffice for some purposes. Let us suppose, for instance, that a country which has embarked on a programme of economic development engages in periodic stock-taking of its progress, and finds not only that aggregate wealth, aggregate income, total population, total production, are all increasing, but that *per capita* wealth, income, production, are also all increasing. All of these are favourable indices, but even in combination do they suffice to show that there has been "economic

[6]Mahbub ul Haq, "Employment and Income Distribution in the 1970's: A New Perspective," *Pakistan Economic and Social Review*, June–December 1971, p. 6.

progress," an increase in economic "welfare," rather than retrogression?

Suppose that someone should argue that the one great economic evil is the prevalence of a great mass of crushing poverty, and that it is a paradox to claim that a country is achieving economic progress as long as the absolute extent of such poverty prevailing in that country has not lessened or has even increased? Such a country, nevertheless, might be able to meet all the tests of economic development which I have just enumerated. If its population has undergone substantial increase, the numbers of those living at the margin of subsistence or below, illiterate, diseased, undernourished, may have grown steadily consistently with a rise in the average income of the population as a whole. . . .

Were I to insist, however, that the reduction of mass poverty be made a crucial test of the realization of economic development, I would be separating myself from the whole body of literature in this field. In all the literature on economic development I have seen, I have not found a single instance where statistical data in terms of aggregates and of averages have not been treated as providing adequate tests of the degree of achievement of economic development.[7]

Long after Viner's warning, Hollis Chenery introduced the World Bank's influential study on *Redistribution with Growth* with this statement:

It is now clear that more than a decade of rapid growth in underdeveloped countries has been of little or no benefit to perhaps a third of their population. Although the average per capita income of the Third World has increased by 50 percent since 1960, this growth has been very unequally distributed among countries, regions within countries, and socio-economic groups. Paradoxically, while growth policies have succeeded beyond the expectations of the first Development Decade, the very idea of aggregate growth as a social objective has increasingly been called into question.[8]

This questioning has become common among development policymakers. If there have been misconceptions during the past decades of development, the future of development calls for a basic reconsideration of the meaning of development and a fundamental redirection of development policy. Instead of settling for any aggregate, or even per capita, index of "development," many now advocate that direct attention be given to the achievement of "first things first"—to the achievement of better nourishment, better health, better education, better living conditions, and better conditions of employment for the low-end poverty groups in the poor countries of the world. Instead of seeking "development" as an end, we might better view it as a means—as an instrumental process for overcoming persistent poverty, absorbing the surplus labor, and diminishing inequality. To help illuminate this process is the intention of this book.

[7]Jacob Viner, *International Trade and Economic Development,* Oxford, 1953, pp. 99–100.

[8]Hollis Chenery et al., *Redistribution with Growth,* London, 1974, p. xiii.

Comment

The term "economic development" is subject to various interpretations. The relationship between development and welfare was considered early by W. A. Lewis in *The Theory of Economic Growth* (1955), in an appendix. The extension of the meaning of development beyond GNP or GNP per capita is advocated by Dudley Seers; see his paper "What Are We Trying to Measure," *Journal of Development Studies* (April 1972); and "The Meaning of Development" in David Lehmann (ed.), *Development Theory* (1979).

Seers states:

The questions to ask about a country's development are: What has been happening to poverty? What has been happening to unemployment? What has been happening to inequality? If all three of these central problems have been growing worse, it would be strange to call the result "development," even if per capita income had soared. This applies, of course, to the future too. A "plan" which conveys no targets for reducing poverty, unemployment and inequality can hardly be considered a "development plan." [Lehmann, ed., *Development Theory,* p. 12]

Indicators of infant mortality, life expectancy, and basic literacy have been used as the components of a composite "Physical Quality of Life Index" (PQLI) that measures performance in meeting the most basic needs of people. This composite indicator of poverty is designed to measure results, not inputs such as income. The rationale for the PQLI is explained in detail by Morris David Morris, *Measuring the Condition of the World's Poor* (1979).

For the less developed countries, "economic development" involves a process of emerging from poverty. Concepts of poverty, however, are subject to various interpretations. Normally, both *absolute* and *relative* deprivation are essential ingredients of a common understanding of poverty. Absolute deprivation relates to the denial of basic needs (see I.B.3). Relative deprivation relates to interpersonal gaps in the income distribution within the poor country and also to the international gaps in standards of living. Nonincome factors captured by the PQLI are important, but so are income and consumption statistics and distribution—sensitive methods of aggregation by which to obtain an overall poverty index. For example, see Amartya Sen, "Levels of Poverty Policy and Change," *World Bank Staff Working Paper* No. 401 (July 1980).

Intercountry comparisons of levels of income are often misleading when such comparisons are made by converting the incomes of the various countries into a common currency, say the U.S. dollar, through the use of official exchange rates. These nominal exchange rates do not reflect the relative purchasing powers of different currencies, and thus errors are introduced into the comparisons. Studies by Irving Kravis and his associates have attempted to adjust international comparisons for the real purchasing power parities of national currencies. See I. B. Kravis, A. Heston, and R. Summers, *World Product and Income: International Comparisons of Real Gross Domestic Product* (3 volumes: 1975, 1978, 1982); "Real GDP per Capita for More Than One Hundred Countries," *Economic Journal* (June 1978); and "International Comparison of Real Product and its Composition: 1950–1977," *Review of Income and Wealth* (March 1980).

EXHIBIT I.1. The Level of GNP and Population of Developing Countries in 1980 and the Growth of Real GNP and GNP per Capita, 1970–80[a]

Countries	1980		1970–80 Real Growth Rate (%)		1980 GNP Million US $[b]
	GNP/ CAP US $	Population (millions)	GNP/ CAP	GNP	
LLDCs					
Afghanistan	170	15.94	1.3	3.9	5,000
Bangladesh	120	90.20	−0.3	2.6	11,490
Benin	300	3.53	0.6	3.5	1,120
Bhutan	80	1.30	−0.1	2.1	110
Botswana	910	0.80	11.7	14.3	780
Burundi	200	4.10	0.9	3.0	880
Cape Verde	300	0.32	3.8	5.9	90
Central African Rep.	300	2.29	0.5	2.7	730
Chad	120	4.46	−5.0	−3.1	500
Comoros	300	0.35	−2.1	1.6	100
Ethiopia	140	31.47	0.8	3.0	4,080
Gambia	250	0.60	1.6	4.7	160

EXHIBIT I.1. (*Continued*)

Countries	1980 GNP/CAP US $	1980 Population (millions)	1970–80 Real Growth Rate (%) GNP/CAP	1970–80 Real Growth Rate (%) GNP	1980 GNP Million US $[b]
Guinea	290	5.43	0.1	3.1	1,480
Guinea-Bissau	160	0.79	0.3	1.9	140
Haiti	270	5.10	2.3	4.0	1,400
Laos	110	3.43	−2.0	−0.5	360
Lesotho	390	1.34	7.4	10.0	570
Malawi	230	5.95	3.2	6.1	1,490
Maldives	260	0.15	0.2	3.2	40
Mali	190	6.94	1.8	4.5	1,420
Nepal	140	14.29	−0.2	2.1	2,030
Niger	330	5.32	−0.2	2.7	1,810
Rwanda	200	5.10	0.6	3.4	1,050
Somalia	380	3.91	1.4	3.7	1,520
Sudan	470	18.37	0.4	3.1	7,640
Tanzania	260	18.14	0.2	3.7	4,860
Uganda	280	13.20	−4.4	−1.6	10,230
Upper Volta	190	5.73	−0.8	0.8	1,140
Western Samoa	850	0.16	3.1	4.1	130
Yemen	460	5.81	3.5	5.4	4,010
Yemen, Dem.	430	1.90	6.4	8.9	1,000
Totals and averages	**210**	**276.33**	**0.2**	**2.9**	**67,350**
LICs–LLDCs					
Angola	470	7.08	−6.5	−4.3	2,880
Bolivia	570	5.57	1.5	4.1	5,790
Burma	180	33.31	2.4	4.6	5,580
Djihouti	480	0.35	−4.4	3.5	170
Egypt	580	39.77	4.8	7.0	25,300
El Salvador	590	4.54	−1.1	1.8	3,330
Equatorial Guinea	460	0.36	2.8	5.1	170
Ghana	420	11.68	−2.3	0.7	15,360
Honduras	560	3.69	0.6	4.0	2,420
India	240	673.21	1.3	3.4	173,310
Indonesia	420	146.24	4.5	7.0	64,420
Kampuchea	110	6.40	0.3	−0.7	730
Kenya	420	15.87	2.1	5.7	6,850
Liberia	520	1.86	0.1	3.4	1,000
Madagascar	350	8.71	−1.9	0.6	3,210
Mauritania	320	1.63	−1.2	1.6	510
Mayotte	230	0.05	2.3	5.2	10
Mozambique	270	10.47	−3.6	−1.1	2,810
Pakistan	300	82.17	1.6	4.8	25,050
St. Helena	440	0.01	–	–	–

EXHIBIT I.1. (*Continued*)

Countries	1980 GNP/ CAP US $	1980 Population (millions)	1970–80 Real Growth Rate (%) GNP/ CAP	GNP	1980 GNP Million US $[b]
St. Vincent	520	0.11	−0.6	1.4	60
Sao Tome and Principe	490	0.11	0.3	2.2	60
Senegal	450	5.66	−0.9	1.6	2,600
Sierra Leone	270	3.47	−1.4	1.2	970
Solomon Islands (Br.)	460	0.23	1.2	4.7	130
Sri Lanka	270	14.82	3.0	4.7	4,100
Togo	410	2.48	0.4	2.8	1,010
Tokelau Islands	550	0.00	–	–	–
Tonga	480	0.10	0.9	2.4	50
Turks and Caicos Islands	470	0.01	−1.5	–	–
Tuvalu	550	0.01	−2.8	–	–
Vanuatu (N. Hebrides)	520	0.12	−1.1	2.5	60
Vietnam, Soc. Rep.	190	54.05	0.5	2.3	10,110
Zaire	220	28.29	−2.2	0.5	5,340
Zambia	560	5.77	−2.6	0.4	3,560
Totals and averages	**290**	**1,168.20**	**1.6**	**3.9**	**366,920**
China	290	976.74	2.8	4.6	283,250
MICs					
Anguilla	630	0.01	1.5	–	–
Antigua	1,270	0.08	−1.1	0.2	100
Bahamas	3,300	0.24	−2.0	1.1	800
Bahrain	5,560	0.42	1.1	8.3	2,260
Barbados	3,040	0.25	3.0	3.5	800
Belize	1,080	0.15	3.7	5.7	160
Bermuda	11,230	0.06	2.0	3.3	660
Brunei	11,890	0.22	5.7	11.4	2,620
Cameroon	670	8.44	3.1	5.4	5,840
Cayman Islands	2,890	0.02	−1.9	3.5	50
Chile	2,160	11.10	2.1	3.9	27,170
Colombia	1,180	26.67	3.6	6.0	32,520
Congo	730	1.54	0.1	2.6	1,160
Cook Islands	1,090	0.02	3.6	2.5	20
Costa Rica	1,730	2.21	2.6	5.1	4,850
Cuba	730	9.86	−1.2	0.2	7,180
Cyprus	3,580	0.62	1.9	2.2	2,100
Dominica	620	0.08	−2.6	−1.1	50
Dominican Republic	1.140	5.44	3.7	6.7	6,480
Falkland Islands	3,800	0.00	5.8	5.8	10
Fiji	1,850	0.63	3.5	5.5	1,190
Gibraltar	5,080	0.03	3.3	4.4	150
Grenada	690	0.11	−0.5	1.1	80

EXHIBIT I.1. (*Continued*)

Countries	1980 GNP/CAP US $	1980 Population (millions)	1970–80 Real Growth Rate (%) GNP/CAP	1970–80 Real Growth Rate (%) GNP	1980 GNP Million US $[b]
Guadeloupe	3,870	0.33	4.6	4.7	1,270
Guatemala	1,110	7.01	2.9	5.8	7,810
Guiana, French	2,880	0.06	1.0	3.2	180
Guyana	690	0.79	−0.2	0.8	560
Israel	4,500	3.88	1.7	4.5	2,030
Ivory Coast	1,150	8.64	0.9	6.6	10,170
Jamaica	1,030	2.19	−4.5	−3.0	2,400
Jordan	1,010	3.24	4.3	8.0	3,380
Kiribati	730	0.06	0.1	1.8	40
Lebanon	1,890	2.66	6.0	6.8	5,400
Macao	2,030	0.31	12.9	15.5	640
Malaysia	1,670	13.44	5.5	7.9	22,700
Malta	3,470	0.34	10.3	10.9	1,240
Martinique	4,640	0.33	4.3	4.1	1,510
Mauritius	1,060	0.96	4.1	5.6	970
Montserrat	1,910	0.01	3.6	2.8	20
Morocco	860	20.18	2.8	5.9	17,690
Nauru	5,300	0.01	6.6	6.6	40
Netherlands Antilles	4,290	0.26	1.4	2.9	1,160
New Caledonia	7,000	0.15	−3.5	−0.4	1,050
Nicaragua	720	2.67	−2.6	0.7	1,050
Nigeria	1,010	84.73	4.7	7.3	91,990
Niue Island	1,100	0.00	7.2	–	–
Oman	4,380	0.89	3.5	6.8	4,550
Pacific Islands (U.S.)	920	0.13	−2.5	–	120
Panama	1,730	1.83	2.1	4.4	3,190
Papua New Guinea	780	3.01	0.3	2.6	2,430
Paraguay	1,340	3.06	5.7	8.8	4,320
Peru	930	17.63	0.2	3.0	18,420
Philippines	720	47.88	3.6	6.4	35,920
Polynesia, French	6,530	0.15	1.5	4.1	970
Reunion	3,830	0.53	0.2	2.0	2,010
St. Kitts-Nevis	920	0.05	2.4	3.2	50
St. Lucia	850	0.12	2.0	4.2	110
St. Pierre and Miquelon	1,630	0.01	–	–	10
Seychelles	1,770	0.07	4.4	6.9	120
Surinam	2,840	0.35	5.5	4.9	1,040
Swaziland	680	0.56	3.4	6.1	400
Syria	1,340	8.98	4.4	8.2	12,390
Thailand	670	46.45	4.1	6.6	32,200
Trinidad and Tobago	4,370	1.17	3.8	5.2	5,440
Tunisia	1,310	6.35	5.9	8.2	8,440

EXHIBIT I.1. (*Continued*)

Countries	1980 GNP/ CAP US $	1980 Population (millions)	1970–80 Real Growth Rate (%) GNP/ CAP	1970–80 Real Growth Rate (%) GNP	1980 GNP Million US $[b]
Turkey	1,460	45.36	2.5	5.1	59,110
Uruguay	2,820	2.92	2.8	3.2	9,740
Virgin Islands (Br.)	2,100	0.01	−2.6	–	30
Wallis and Futuna	990	0.01	−2.0	–	10
Zimbabwe	630	7.40	−0.6	2.8	4,710
Totals and averages	**1,150**	**415.35**	**3.0**	**5.6**	**476,250**
NICs					
Argentina	2,390	27.74	0.9	2.5	142,030
Brazil	2,050	118.67	6.3	8.6	230,450
Greece	4,520	9.33	4.1	4.7	42,210
Hong Kong	4,210	5.11	6.3	9.1	21,760
Korea, Rep.	1,520	38.45	6.1	6.1	57,670
Mexico	2,130	67.46	2.3	5.4	162,650
Portugal	2,350	9.84	2.3	3.6	23,750
Singapore	4,480	2.39	7.4	8.9	10,380
Spain	5,340	37.38	2.6	3.7	207,250
Taiwan	2,160	17.65	7.4	9.5	40,210
Yugoslavia	2,620	22.33	5.2	6.2	71,930
Totals and averages	**2,540**	**356.33**	**3.8**	**5.8**	**1,010,280**
OPEC					
Algeria	1,920	18.92	2.5	5.9	39,730
Ecuador	1,220	8.36	4.5	8.0	10,890
Gabon	4,440	0.66	2.3	3.6	3,410
Iran	1,940	38.13	−0.1	2.9	83,480
Iraq	3,020	13.07	9.4	13.2	39,040
Kuwait	22,840	1.35	2.0	8.3	30,650
Libya	8,640	2.98	−2.9	1.1	30,540
Qatar	26,080	0.23	2.7	10.4	6,650
Saudi Arabia	11,260	8.96	8.7	13.6	117,580
United Arab Emirates	30,070	0.89	3.1	16.4	27,060
Venezuela	3,630	14.93	1.4	4.8	60,720
Totals and averages	**3,760**	**108.48**	**3.8**	**7.3**	**449,750**
Total LDC and averages	**750**	**3,301.43**	**3.2**	**5.5**	**2,653,800**

Source: OECD, *Development Co-Operation 1982 Review,* Paris, 1982, pp. 254–6.

Note: LICs:　Low-income countries (per capita income in 1980 under $600).
　　　 LLDCs: Least-developed countries.
　　　 MICs:　Middle-income countries (per capita income in 1980 exceeding $600).
　　　 NICs:　Newly industrializing countries.

[a]World Bank and Secretariat estimates.

[b]At current prices and exchange rates, not comparable to data in other columns.

I.B. INDICATORS OF DEVELOPMENT

I.B.1. Measuring Development*

So long as economists were willing to assume the possibility of unrestricted transfers among income groups, they found no conflict in principle between the objectives of distribution and growth. Once it is recognized that large-scale transfers of income are politically unlikely in developing countries, however, it becomes necessary to evaluate the results of any development policy in terms of the benefits it produces for different socio-economic groups. While this idea has been accepted in the recent literature of project evaluation, it has found little reflection in the methodology of macroeconomic planning and policy formulation.

An index of economic performance reflecting these objectives can be developed as follows. Assume a division of society into N socio-economic groups, defined by their assets, income levels, and economic functions. For purposes of policy analysis, it is necessary to distinguish several poverty groups such as small farmers, landless laborers, urban underemployed, and others according to the similarity of their responses to policy measures. In order to illustrate the problem of evaluation, we will classify merely by income size into ordinally ranked percentile groups.

Assuming a division by income level into quintiles, the rate of growth of income of each group, g_i, can be taken to measure the increase of its social welfare over the specified period. The rate of increase in welfare of the society as a whole can therefore be defined as a weighted sum of the growth of income in all groups:

$$G = w_1g_1 + w_2g_2 + w_3g_3 + w_4g_4 + w_5g_5 \quad [1]$$

where G is an index of the growth of total social welfare and w_i is the weight assigned to group i.[1]

A summary measure of this type enables us to set development targets and monitor development performance not simply in terms of growth of GNP but in terms of the distributional pattern of income growth. The weights for each income class reflect the social premium on generating growth at each income level; they may be set according to the degree of distributional emphasis desired. As the weight on a particular quintile is raised, our index of the increase in social welfare reflects to a greater extent the growth of income in that group. Thus if we were only concerned with the poorest quintile we would set $w_5 = 1$ and all other $w_i = 0$, so that growth in welfare would be measured only by g_5. This approach is closely related to the more formal approach to welfare choices using explicit social welfare functions to measure improvements in welfare.

In these terms the commonly used index of performance—the growth of GNP—is a special case in which the weights on the growth of income of each quintile are simply the income share of each quintile in total income. The shortcomings of such an index can be seen from the following income shares for the

---

*From Montek S. Ahluwalia and Hollis B. Chenery, "The Economic Framework," in *Redistribution with Growth,* joint study by World Bank's Development Research Center and Institute of Development Studies at the University of Sussex, Oxford University Press, 1974, pp. 38–43, 48–9. Reprinted by permission.

[1]This measure can be applied either to the income or the consumption of each group. When applied to income, the weight assigned should take account of the contribution made by each group to the financing of investment and government expenditure. For long-run simulations of policy an index based on consumption only is preferable.

different quintiles, which are typical for underdeveloped countries:

Quintiles	1	2	3	4	5	Total
Share in Total Income	53%	22%	13%	7%	5%	100%

The combined share of the top 40 percent of the population amounts to about three-quarters of the total GNP. Thus the rate of growth of GNP measures essentially the income growth of the upper 40 percent and is not much affected by what happens to the income of the remaining 60 percent of the population.

An alternative welfare principle that has considerable appeal is to give equal social value to a one-percent increase in income for any member of society. On this principle, the weights in equation [1] should be proportional to the number of people in each group and would therefore be equal for each quintile. Thus a one-percent increase in income in the lowest quintile would have the same weight in the overall performance measure as a one-percent increase in income for any other quintile, even though the absolute increment involved is much smaller for the lowest quintile than for the others.

When we use the growth of GNP as an index of performance, we implicitly assume that a dollar of additional income creates the same additional social welfare regardless of the income level of the recipient.[2] Given the typical income shares of the different quintiles, it follows that a one-percent growth in income in the top quintile is given almost eleven times the weight of a one-percent growth in the lowest quintile (in the preceding example) because it requires an absolute increment which is eleven times as great. In contrast to the GNP measure, the equal weights index gives the same weight to a one-percent increase in income in the lowest quintile as it does to a one-percent increase in the highest quintile. In this case a dollar of additional income in the lowest quintile is valued at eleven times a dollar of additional income in the highest quintile.

Many individuals (and some countries) may wish to define social objectives almost exclusively in terms of income growth of the lowest groups, placing little value upon growth in the upper-income groups beyond its contribution to national savings and investment. The welfare implications of such a "poverty weighted" index are stronger than those underlying either the rate of growth of GNP or the "equal weights" index, since it would be a welfare function based primarily on the lower-income groups.

Weighted indexes of the sort discussed above provide a very different evaluation of performance in many countries than is obtained from conventional measures. This can be illustrated using data for the fourteen developing countries for which we have observations at two points in time. The numerical results presented here are subject to the limitations of the data and are essentially "illustrative" to show the potential usefulness of weighted growth indexes in evaluating performance. They are not presented as definitive assessments of country experience.

Table 1 shows the difference in estimates of welfare increments based on three different weighting systems: shares of each quintile in GNP (giving the rate of growth of GNP); equal weights for each quintile; and "poverty weights" of 0.6 for the lowest 40 percent, 0.3 for the next 40 percent, and 0.1 for the top 20 percent.[3] The following differences can be observed among the countries when comparing GNP growth with the other two indexes.

(i) In four countries (Panama, Brazil,

---

[2]This statement has to be qualified to allow for the higher savings of the upper-income recipients and their greater contribution to future growth. In a more complete analysis, the increase in social welfare can be measured by the weighted growth of consumption rather than income.

[3]In terms of weights for unit increments, these weights imply that a dollar of income accruing to the bottom 40 percent is worth 33 times a dollar accruing to the top 20 percent, instead of 11 times as with equal weights.

TABLE 1. Income Distribution and Growth

| Country | Period | 1. Income Growth | | | II. Annual Increase in Welfare | | | III. Initial Gini Coefficient |
		Upper 20%	Middle 40%	Lowest 40%	(A) GNP Weights	(B) Equal Weights	(C) Poverty Weights	
Korea	1964–70	10.6	7.8	9.3	9.3	9.0	9.0	.34
Panama	1960–69	8.8	9.2	3.2	8.2	6.7	5.6	.48
Brazil	1960–70	8.4	4.8	5.2	6.9	5.7	5.4	.56
Mexico	1963–69	8.0	7.0	6.6	7.6	7.0	6.9	.56
Taiwan	1953–61	4.5	9.1	12.1	6.8	9.4	10.4	.55
Venezuela	1962–70	7.9	4.1	3.7	6.4	4.7	4.2	.52
Colombia	1964–70	5.6	7.3	7.0	6.2	6.8	7.0	.57
El Salvador	1961–69	4.1	10.5	5.3	6.2	7.1	6.7	.53
Philippines	1961–71	4.9	6.4	5.0	5.4	5.5	5.4	.50
Peru	1961–71	4.7	7.5	3.2	5.4	5.2	4.6	.59
Sri Lanka	1963–70	3.1	6.2	8.3	5.0	6.4	7.2	.45
Yugoslavia	1963–68	4.9	5.0	4.3	4.8	4.7	4.6	.33
India	1954–64	5.1	3.9	3.9	4.5	4.1	4.0	.40

Note: The rates of growth of income in each income group were calculated as follows: income shares were applied to GNP (constant prices) to obtain the income of each group in each year. The growth rate is the annual compound growth rate estimated from the two endpoint income estimates for each income group. GNP series are from the World Bank data files. Equal weights imply a weight of 0.2, 0.4, and 0.4 for the three income groups while poverty weights are calculated by giving weights of 0.1, 0.3, and 0.6, respectively.

Mexico, and Venezuela), performance is worse when measured by weighted indexes. In these countries the data show that relative income distribution worsened over the period considered; i.e., growth was disproportionately concentrated in the upper-income groups. The indexes giving greater weight to the growth of income in lower-income groups are therefore lower than the rate of growth of GNP.

(ii) In four countries (Colombia, El Salvador, Sri Lanka, and Taiwan), the weighted indexes are higher than GNP growth. In these countries the data show that distribution improved over the period; i.e., the growth of incomes in lower-income groups was faster than that in higher-income groups.

(iii) In five countries (Korea, the Philippines, Yugoslavia, Peru, and India) the use of weighted indexes does not alter the GNP measurement of growth to any great extent. In these cases the data show that distribution remained largely unchanged and all income classes grew at about the same rate. In general the extent to which a weighted index of growth diverges from the growth rate of GNP and the direction of divergence are measures of the extent and direction in which growth is distributionally biased.

It is important to note that the proposed index is a measure of the *increase* in welfare rather than of total welfare. Increasing equality is indicated by a weighted growth rate in excess of GNP growth and increasing inequality by the opposite difference. The measure cannot be used to compare performance among countries without allowing for their initial distribution of income. For example, Table 1 shows inequality increasing in both Brazil and India, but in India the starting point was a relatively equal distribution in 1954 while in Brazil distribution was already quite unequal in 1960.

We recognize that the use of such indexes for evaluation of performance will be severely limited by the initial lack of accurate data. For the present they are perhaps more valuable as analytical devices to be used in redefining the objectives of development strategy. They help to clarify both the statement of distributional objectives and the limits of acceptable trade-offs between growth and income distribution. In particular, the use of welfare indexes emphasizes the importance of increasing the rates of growth of income in the poverty groups instead of focusing on the static picture of income inequality.

TOWARD A THEORY OF DISTRIBUTION AND GROWTH

The preceding section suggests that the objective of distributive justice is more usefully conceived of as accelerating the development of the poorer groups in society rather than in terms of relative shares of income. As a way of implementing this approach, we can visualize the role of the state as using available policy instruments (including the allocation of investment in physical and human capital) so as to maximize a welfare function of the type just described. State intervention of this sort requires both an analysis of the determinants of income in poverty groups and of the linkages between the incomes of different groups. The fact of income linkages is crucial for any analysis of distributional problems since they impose important constraints on policy. Thus tax-financed transfers from the rich to the poor may raise the income of the poor but, if they reduce savings and capital accumulation by the rich, they may in time lead to lower income in the poorer groups. An analysis of these interactions requires an integration of growth and distribution theory.

Distribution of Income and Capital

Existing theories of income distribution are of only limited value in establishing an analytical framework for comprehensive governmental action because they are somewhat narrowly focused on the functional distribution of income between labor and capital. Most theories conceive the central problem of income distribution as the determination of the levels of employment and remuneration of the factors of production, usually grouped into capital and labor. They differ mainly in their assumptions about market behavior and the way in which wages and product prices are determined. Neoclassical theory assumes competitive equilibrium in all markets and thus derives factor returns from pure production relationships and demand patterns, given factor supply conditions. At the other extreme, the classical and Marxist wage theory that forms the basis for most dual economy models assumes relatively fixed real wages with all surplus value appropriated by the owners of capital.

The inadequacy of existing theories for our purposes arises less from the lack of consensus as to the determinants of the functional division of income than from the omission of other aspects of the problem. The available evidence on the nature of poverty in underdeveloped countries shows that half of the poor are self-employed and do not enter the wage economy. Most wage-earners are already in the middle-income groups, so that policies affecting the split between wages and profits mainly concern the upper end of the distribution.

The principal element that is missing from existing theories is an explicit treatment of the distribution of the various forms of assets.[4] A more general statement would recognize that the income of any household is derived from a variety of assets: land, privately owned capital, access to public capital goods, and human capital embodying varying degrees of skills.

We distinguish four basic approaches to the problem of raising the welfare of the low-income groups: (i) *Maximizing GNP growth* through raising savings and allocating resources more efficiently, with benefits to all groups in society. (ii) *Redirecting investment* to poverty groups in the form of education, access to credit, public facilities, and so on.

---

[4]Recognition of the importance of asset distribution is common to neoclassical theorists as well as to Marxists, but it has not been incorporated in empirical models.

(iii) *Redistributing income* (or consumption) to poverty groups through the fiscal system or through direct allocation of consumer goods.
(iv) *A transfer of existing assets* to poverty groups, as in land reform. In most countries some elements of each of these approaches will be applicable, depending on the initial economic and social structure.

The advantages and limitations of each strategy will vary with the circumstances of each country, and an assessment of these considerations is necessarily a matter of detailed study. Nevertheless, it is useful to consider some broad characteristics of each strategy in a relatively pure form. The general conclusions from the analysis can be summarized as follows:

(i) Maximizing the growth of GNP involves some measures that benefit all groups, as well as others—such as favoring high-savings groups through lower income taxes or wage-restraint policies—in which there is a conflict with distributional objectives. Because of the relatively weak income linkages between the poverty groups and the rest of the economy, their growth tends to lag until the expansion of employment creates a shortage of unskilled labor and hence an upward pressure on wage rates. Although—as suggested by Table 1—the poor may be better off even in this case than with slower GNP growth, the welfare effects of a maximal growth strategy can almost always be improved by adding transfers.

(ii) As compared to maximal growth of GNP, increased investment in the physical and human assets of the poverty groups is likely to require some sacrifice of output in the short run because returns on investment in human capital take longer to develop. Even so, the welfare index will be higher because these investments lead to income growth in target groups which have higher welfare weights. While this strategy has a short-run cost to the upper-income groups, in the longer run they may even benefit from the "trickle up" effects of greater productivity and purchasing power of the poor.

(iii) General transfers of income in support of consumption can also raise the weighted welfare index in the short run, but they have too high a cost in terms of foregone investment to be viable on a large scale over an extended period. Nevertheless, some direct consumption supplements for specific target groups (child nutrition, maternal health services) are a necessary supplement to an investment-oriented strategy, since they are the only way to alleviate some types of absolute poverty.

(iv) Political resistance to policies of asset redistribution makes this approach unlikely to succeed on any large scale in most countries. However, in areas such as land ownership and security of tenure, some degree of asset redistribution is an essential part of any program to make the rural poor more productive. Beyond this essential minimum, a vigorous policy of investment reallocation in a rapidly growing economy may well be a more effective way of increasing the productive capacity of the poor than redistribution from the existing stock of assets, which is likely to have a high cost in social and political disruption.

(v) In the longer term, population policy can have an important influence on both the distribution of incomes and the level of consumption in the poverty groups. Our simulations show a tendency of income distribution to worsen with population growth above 2.5 percent per year, while with more optimistic assumptions it tends to improve. There is considerable demographic evidence that investments in the health, education, and economic growth of the poverty groups may also contribute to a reduction of fertility and hence indirectly to better income distribution.

Particular emphasis should be given to directing public investment to raise the productive capacity and incomes of the poor. There is a strong analogy between this strategy and an international strategy of assisting investment in poor countries. In both cases transfers of resources that increase productive capacity and lead to greater self-support in the future are more efficient as well as more attractive to donors than continuing subsidies for consumption.

I.B.2. Dimensions of Poverty*

It is difficult to measure the extent of poverty. To begin with, absolute poverty means more than low income. It also means malnutrition, poor health and lack of education—and not all of the poor are equally badly off in all respects. There is also room for disagreement about where to draw the line between the poor and the rest, and about the correct way to calculate and compare incomes and living standards at different times and in different places.

To compound these difficulties, the data are inadequate. Household surveys, if they exist, sometimes underrepresent the poor. Very few follow the fortunes of individuals and families through time, or disaggregate the household to examine the well-being of women, children and the elderly. Nor is direct observation necessarily a reliable basis for generalization, especially in the countryside, where many of the poor are beyond the gaze of the casual visitor to villages and rural development projects—away from the roads, away from the markets and project sites, or on the outskirts of the villages.

Despite all this, no one seriously doubts that a very large number of people are extremely poor. Taking as the cutoff a level of income based on detailed studies of poverty in India, the number of people in absolute poverty in developing countries (excluding China and other centrally planned economies) is estimated at around 780 million. In 1975, about 600 million adults in developing countries were illiterate; and only two-fifths of the children in these countries currently complete more than three years of primary school. In 1978, 550 million people lived in countries where the average life expectancy was less than 50 years, 400 million in countries where the average annual death rate of children aged one to four was more than 20

per 1,000—20 times that in the industrialized countries.

Nor is there any serious disagreement about who the poor are. Half of the people in absolute poverty live in South Asia, mainly in India and Bangladesh. A sixth live in East and Southeast Asia, mainly in Indonesia. Another sixth are in Sub-Saharan Africa. The rest—about 100 million people—are divided among Latin America, North Africa and the Middle East. With the partial exception of Latin America (where about 40 percent are in the towns) the poor are primarily rural dwellers, overwhelmingly dependent on agriculture—the majority of them landless (or nearly landless) laborers. Some minority groups—for example, the Indians in Latin America and the scheduled castes in India— are also overrepresented among the poor. And there is a tendency for absolute poverty in particular places, families and social groups to persist from generation to generation.

THREE DECADES OF POVERTY REDUCTION

In aggregate, however, considerable progress has been made in reducing the incidence of poverty over the past 30 years (see Figure 1). Progress would have been greater still but for the dramatic growth of population, which has doubled the number of people in the developing world since 1950 and has begun to slow down—though as yet slightly—only since the mid-1960s.

Since 1950 income per person in the developing world has doubled. But in low-income countries, the average increase has been half that, and in both low- and middle-income countries the incomes of the poor have grown more slowly than the average. The *proportion* of people in absolute poverty in developing countries as a group is estimated to have fallen during the past two decades (though probably not in Sub-Saharan Africa in the 1970s). But because population

*From *World Bank Development Report, 1981,* Oxford University Press, 1981, pp. 33–6. Reprinted by permission.

Income

GNP per Person[a] (1980 dollars)	1950	1960	1980
Industrialized countries	3,841	5,197	9,684
Middle–income countries	625	802	1,521
Low–income countries	164	174	245

Average annual growth (percent)	1950–60	1960–80
Industrialized countries	3.1	3.2
Middle–income countries	2.5	3.3
Low–income countries	0.6	1.7

[a]Excludes all centrally planned economies.

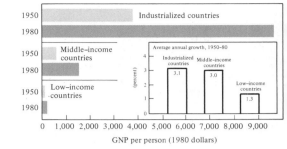

Health
Life Expectancy at Birth (years)

	1950	1960	1978	Increase, 1950–78
Industrialized countries	66.0	69.4	73.5	7.5
Middle–income countries	51.9	54.0	61.0	9.1
Low–income countries	35.2	41.9	49.9	14.7
Centrally planned economies[c]	62.3	67.1	69.9	7.6

[a]Includes Bulgaria, Czechoslovakia, German DR, Hungary, Poland, Romania, USSR.
[b]Includes Albania, Cuba, North Korea, Mongolia.
[c]Excludes China.

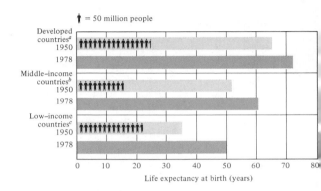

Education
Adult Literacy Rate (percent)

	1950	1960	1975
Industrialized countries	95	97	99
Middle–income countries	48	54	71
Low–income countries	22	29	38
Centrally planned economies	.97	98	99

[a]Excludes centrally planned economies.

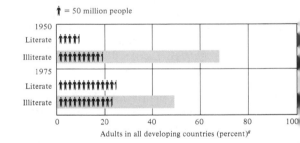

Population
Average Annual Percentage Growth

	1950–60	1960–70	1970–80
Industrialized countries	1.2	1.0	0.7
Middle–income countries	2.4	2.5	2.5
Low–income countries	1.9	2.5	2.3
Centrally planned economies	1.9	1.7	1.3

[a]Includes Bulgaria, Czechoslovakia, German DR, Hungary, Poland, Romania, USSR.
[b]Includes Albania, Cuba, North Korea, Mongolia.
[c]Includes China.

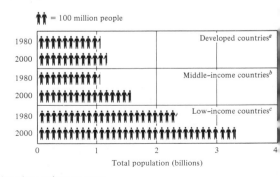

FIGURE 1. Three decades against poverty.

has grown, the *number* of people in absolute poverty has increased.

There has also been progress in education. The proportion of adults in developing countries who are literate is estimated to have increased over the past three decades from about 30 percent to more than 50 percent; the proportion of children of primary-school age enrolled in school rose from 47 percent in 1960 to 64 percent in 1977. These advances have been shared by most countries and religions, including those that initially were furthest behind, such as Sub-Saharan Africa. But the quality of schooling remains low in many countries; and because of population growth, there has been an increase of about 100 million in the absolute number of illiterate adults since 1950.

The most striking advances against poverty have been in health. Average life expectancy in middle-income developing countries has risen nine years over the past three decades. In low-income countries, the increase has been even greater—15 years. But even though infant mortality rates (which are a major determinant of life expectancy) have fallen substantially in developing countries since 1950, there now are so many more children born that the absolute number of infant deaths probably has not declined.

Another way of viewing the progress of the past three decades is to compare the developing with the industrialized countries. The gap in income per person between them has widened, even in proportional terms (though in the case of the middle-income countries only slightly). But the gaps in education and health have narrowed—by 15 percentage points in adult literacy and five years in life expectancy.

Poverty and Growth

Most poor people live in poor countries. Whether absolute poverty is measured by low income, low life expectancy or illiteracy, there is a strong correlation between the extent of poverty in a country and its GNP per

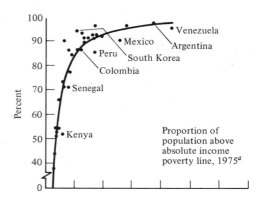

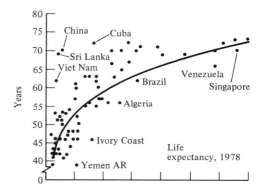

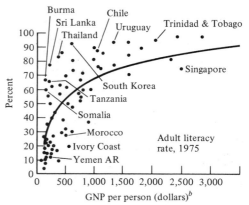

[a] Absolute income poverty line is income of 45th percentile in India.
[b] Refers to year specified in each section of figure, expressed in the prices of that year.

FIGURE 2. National income and national poverty.

person (see Figure 2). This suggests that the solution to poverty is economic growth. There is a great deal of truth in this proposition, but it needs to be carefully qualified.

First, comparing countries, the relation between the extent of their absolute poverty and the level of GNP per person is (as the dispersion of points in Figure 2 shows) far from perfect. Because of differences in income distribution, the proportion of the population below the poverty line in 1975 was more than twice as high in Colombia as in South Korea, even though the average incomes of the two countries were close. Sri Lanka is a low-income country, yet the life expectancy of its people approaches that of the industrialized countries. Some middle-income countries, such as Morocco and the Ivory Coast, have literacy rates below those of the average low-income country.

Second, looking at changes over time within particular countries, the connection between growth and poverty reduction over periods of a decade or two appears inexact. There is general agreement that growth, in the very long term, eliminates most absolute poverty; but also that some people may (at least temporarily) be impoverished by development—as when a tenant farmer is displaced by his landlord's tractor or a shoemaker by mass-produced shoes. Because

relevant data are sparse and unreliable, however, it remains a matter of dispute how consistently growth over comparatively short periods has reduced the proportion of the population in absolute poverty.

What is clear is that different countries have had different experiences. The proportion below the absolute poverty line apparently has not fallen in some slow-growing countries (including rural India betwen 1956 and 1974) or in some periods in faster-growing countries. But it appears to have fallen markedly over the past 25 years in several fast-growing countries (including Thailand and Yugoslavia) and in some slower-growing ones (including Costa Rica and Sri Lanka). The association between economic growth and improvements in education and health has also been imperfect.

Third, the connection between economic growth and poverty reduction goes both ways. Few would dispute that the health, education and well-being of the mass of people in industrialized countries are a cause, as well as a result, of national prosperity. Similarly, people who are unskilled and sick make little contribution to a country's economic growth. Development strategies that bypass large numbers of people may not be the most effective way for developing countries to raise their long-run growth rates.

Comment

There is not yet a refined theory to explain the determinants of inequality in relative income shares. Besides Kuznets' evidence, some partial hypotheses and empirical evidence are presented by I. Adelman and C. T. Morris, *Economic Growth and Social Equity in Developing Countries* (1973); Felix Paukert, "Income Distribution at Different Levels of Development," *International Labour Review* (August–September 1973); Shail Jain, *Size Distribution of Income: A Compilation of Data* (1975); A. K. Sen, *On Economic Inequality* (1973); W. R. Cline, "Income Distribution and Development," *Journal of Development Economics* (February 1975); Jeffrey Williamson, "Regional Inequality and the Process of National Development: A Description of the Patterns," *Economic Development and Cultural Change* (1965).

The empirical basis for statements about trends in income distribution is still weak. For the debate over income distribution in Latin America, see A. Fishlow, "Brazilian Size Distribution of Income," *American Economic Review* (May 1972); Richard Webb, "Government Policy and the Distribution of Income in Peru, 1963–1973" (1974); Joel Bergsman, "Income Distribution and Poverty in Mexico," *World Bank Staff Working Paper* No. 395 (June 1980).

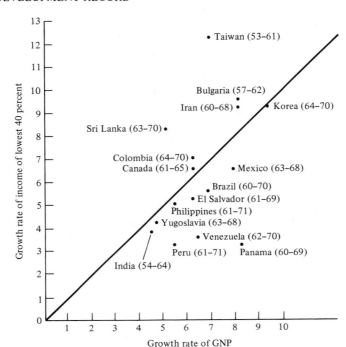

EXHIBIT I.2. Growth and the Lowest 40 Percent

Countries above the 45 degree line are countries in which the income share of the lowest 40 percent increased over the period so that the estimated rate of growth of income for this group is higher than for the economy as a whole. Countries below the 45 degree line are countries in which the relative income shares of the lowest 40 percent declined.

Comment

The Gini coefficient is a single measure of relative poverty and the most frequently encountered in studies of income distribution. It is based on a curve fitted to percentile shares (see Table 1), which was developed by Lorenz and, not surprisingly, named after him—the Lorenz curve. Figure 1 illustrates this curve and a Gini coefficient that flows from it.

The vertical axis measures the percentage of income going to income recipients, who are arrayed in percentiles on the horizontal axis. Income recipients are ordered from the poorest to the richest, moving from left to right. Thus in Figure 1, *OX* percent of the population (the poorest group) receives *a* percent of the income, and so on, giving the Lorenz curve, *L*. Complete equality would occur only if *a* percent of the population receive *a* percent of the income, as indicated by the curve of complete equality, *E*. The curve of perfect inequality is *OGH*, with a right angle at *G*. This curve represents the case where one person has 100 percent of the income.

The shaded area in the figure, enclosed by the theoretical line of equality, *E*, and the observed Lorenz curve, *L*, is known as the concentration area (or area of inequality). The Gini coefficient is the ratio of this area to the total area under the line of equality. The simplest computation of the Gini proceeds by taking the sum of the areas under all trapezoids, such as *WXYZ*, and subtracting this from the area under *E* to give the concentration area. The required ratio then follows. As a measure of income concentration, the Gini coefficient ranges from 0 to 1—the larger the coefficient, the greater the inequality. Thus 0 represents perfect equality and 1 represents perfect inequality.

For problems of data analysis, see Shail Jain, *Size Distribution of Income* (1975) and Nanak Kakwani, *Income Inequality and Poverty* (1980).

For an illuminating application of the methodology of Gini coefficient analysis, see John C. H. Fei, Gustav Ranis, and Shirley W. Y. Kuo, *Growth with Equity: The Taiwan Case* (1979).

TABLE 1. Percentile Distributions for Households in Brazil, 1970

Population Decile	Percentage of Income
First	1.2
Second	1.8
Third	2.7
Fourth	3.5
Fifth	4.6
Sixth	6.0
Seventh	7.9
Eighth	10.8
Ninth	16.0
Tenth	45.5
	100.0

Source: Shail Jain, *Size Distribution of Income* (1975).

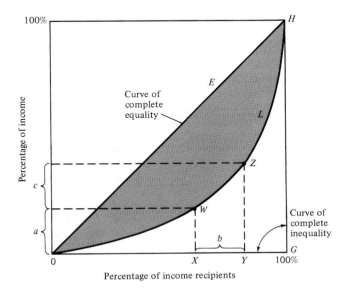

FIGURE 1. The Lorenz curve.

I.B.3. A Basic Needs Yardstick*

The disappointment with GNP per head and its growth has led to greater emphasis on employment and redistribution. But it was soon seen, on the one hand, that unemployment in the sense in which the term is used in the developed countries was not the problem in the developing countries and that, on the other hand, redistribution from growth yielded only very meager results. Furthermore, it is clear that mass poverty can coexist with a high degree of equality, and reductions in absolute poverty are consistent with increases in inequality. The concern has shifted to the eradication of absolute poverty, particularly by concentrating on basic human needs. Meeting these needs in nutrition, education, health, and shelter may be achieved by various combinations of growth, redistribution of assets and income, and restructuring of production. It is the composition of production and its beneficiaries, rather than indices of total production or of income distribution, that have become the principal concern. This new focus on meeting basic human needs requires an indicator or a set of indicators, therefore, by which deprivation can be judged and measured, and policies directed at its alleviation and eradication can be initiated and monitored.

Whether social indicators should reflect inputs or results depends on their purpose. For performance testing there is something to be said for the approach of choosing indices that measure results or outputs, since these are closer to what we are trying to achieve. Furthermore, measures of inputs can introduce biases toward certain patterns of meeting needs which may not be universal. For instance, a country with fairly acceptable health standards should not be encouraged to acquire the same number of doctors as one

with serious health problems. We are back with the problem of "regrettable necessities," which should not be counted as final goods or as social achievements. Moreover, the number of doctors does not measure the distribution of these doctors and medical services, or the degree of their specialization. Resources may be deployed in inefficient ways, failing to benefit the poor. Measures such as infant mortality and life expectancy, however, indicate the degree to which basic needs have been fulfilled, rather than the resources expended. Likewise, literacy measures the effectiveness of the educational system, and is, in principle, a better indicator than the number of students enrolled or the student/teacher ratio. In general, output measures are better indicators of the level of welfare and basic needs achievement. Moreover, most outputs are also inputs. Health, education, and even nutrition are valued not only in their own right, but also because they raise the productivity of present and future workers, though higher productivity is valued because it contributes to a better life.

Input measures, such as doctors or hospital beds per 1000 or enrollment rates in schools, on the other hand, also have their uses. They may reflect government intention, commitment, and efforts to provide public services. For purposes of assessing policies and monitoring performance, both sets of indicators are necessary. Input measures are useful indicators of resources devoted to certain objectives (though these can be misdirected). To the extent to which we know how to link inputs to results, i.e., have a "production function," we can trace the connections between means and ends. Even where we do not have knowledge of a "production function" (e.g., linking expenditure on family planning to a decline in the fertility rate), the combination of input and output measures presents the raw material for research into the causal links between the two, particularly since, in a social system of interdependent variables, so many outputs are also inputs. In addition, where output measures cannot be readily

*From Norman Hicks and Paul Streeten, "Indicators of Development: The Search for a Basic Needs Yardstick," *World Development,* Vol. 7, 1979, pp. 568, 571–2, 577–9; Paul Streeten et al., *First Things First,* Oxford University Press, 1981, pp. 35–7. Reprinted by permission.

found, it might be necessary to fall back on measures of inputs as useful proxies.

The current discussion of basic needs oriented development focuses on the alleviation of poverty through a variety of measures other than merely redistribution of incremental output. Such a focus supplements attention to *how much* is being produced, by attention to *what* is being produced, in *what ways,* for *whom,* and with what *impact.* Obviously, the rapid growth of output will still be important to the alleviation of poverty, and GNP per head remains an important figure. What is required, in addition, are some indicators of the composition and beneficiaries of GNP, which would supplement the GNP data, not replace them. The basic needs approach, therefore, can be the instrument for giving the necessary focus to work on social indicators.

As a first step, it might be useful to define the best indicator for each basic need. At present, the essential basic needs are considered to cover six areas: nutrition, basic education, health, sanitation, water supply and housing, and related infrastructure. This list is not exhaustive, nor do all needs listed have the same status. It is intended to be illustrative. A limited set of core indicators covering these areas would be a useful device for concentrating efforts. Once defined, however, this set could then serve as a call for the collection of more adequate, standardized, comparable international statistics, and thus help focus data gathering efforts on only the most important indicators. It is not clear that, because there are six basic needs, there need be only six core indicators. It may be that more than one indicator will be necessary to measure adequately progress in any one area of basic needs. Nevertheless, the basic needs concept serves as a useful device for integrating efforts of data gathering and analysis.

Once defined, these core basic needs indicators would have the potential for important policy analysis relating, for instance, to international comparisons of performance and relative aid levels. Such indicators would be a more useful guide to the relative "gap" between rich and poor countries, and offer a different view on the speed with which this gap

was widening or narrowing. They would be useful in understanding which countries were meeting their basic needs, and how their policies are related to the growth of output, trade, investment, infrastructure, etc. Not enough is being done internationally to improve the capacity of developing countries to identify, collect, and issue better primary data on a regular, systematic and comparable basis. Such data collection can be costly, but a substantially greater effort seems to be justified.

The problem of selecting the appropriate index in each field is best taken up by technical experts in each sector. To give an indication, however, of the indicators which might be included, the following have been identified as a preliminary set:

Health:	Life expectancy at birth
Education:	Literacy
	Primary school enrollment (as percent of population aged 5–14)
Food:	Calorie supply per head or calorie supply as a percent of requirements
Water supply:	Infant mortality (per thousand births)
	Percent of population with access to potable water
Sanitation:	Infant mortality (per thousand births)
	Percent of population with access to sanitation facilities
Housing:	None

The core indicators identified here attempt to follow the philosophy of the paper in stressing measures of results, rather than inputs. Infant mortality is assumed to be a good indicator of the availability of sanitation and clean water facilities because of the susceptibility of infants to water-borne diseases. Furthermore, data on infant mortality are generally more readily available than data on access to water. While literacy is a good general measure of progress in education, the percent of the relevant age group enrolled in primary school is included to measure country effort. Input measures have also been identified for water supply and sanitation as supplementary measures. It has not been possible, however, to identify a satisfactory measure of housing needs. The only readily available indicator is people per room, but this really does not capture much of the quality of housing, only the number of rooms, which in turn is a very rough index of crowding. Ideally, these indicators should be supplemented by data about distribution of calories per head, etc.

If an acceptable system of weights could be developed, it might be possible to combine the core indicators into a composite basic needs index. The chances of an acceptable system of weights being developed, however, are extremely small. Despite considerable research on composite indices, no one has come close to developing a rational weighting system. It is difficult even to suggest directions for further research. (Some may question the desirability of such a composite index, even if it could be constructed.)

Instead of attempting to develop a composite index of basic needs, a useful alternative may be to narrow the range of indicators from six to one or two, which correlate highly with basic needs development. This approach would serve the need of those who desire a single number for making quick judgments on social performance, without introducing the problems of weighted composite indices. The prospects for doing this are considerably enhanced by the fact that many of the so-called "basic needs" are, in fact, inputs rather than ultimate goals. Certainly nutrition, water supply, and sanitation are valued because they improve the health status of the population. To a more limited extent, this is also true of housing and education. All of these can be considered to be inputs into the health "production function." They may be valued for reasons other than their influence on health status, but a high association between the various core indicators can be traced to their impact on health. Therefore, it could be argued that some measure of health, such as life expectancy at birth,

would be a good single measure of basic needs. In a sense, life expectancy is a kind of weighted "composite" of progress in meeting physiological basic needs. It has the advantage of capturing the impact on individuals, not only of non-market factors but also of income net of taxes, transfer payments, and social services, without raising all the difficulties of income per head measures, such as the appropriate unit (individual, household, or family), the appropriate magnitude (capital, consumption, income), the appropriate set of prices (market prices, international prices), what to value as final goods, and what as costs, etc. . . .

INCOME APPROACH VERSUS BASIC NEEDS

The income approach recommends measures that raise the real incomes of the poor by making them more productive, so that the purchasing power of their earnings, together with the yield of their subsistence production, enables then to acquire the basic needs basket. There can be no doubt that efforts to make the poor more productive and their activities more remunerative are central to all poverty-oriented development strategies. And some features of the basic needs approach were contained in the earlier approaches. The basic needs approach in the narrow sense, however, regards the income-orientation of earlier approaches as incomplete and partial, for seven reasons.

1. Some basic needs can be satisfied only, or more effectively, through public services (education, health, water, sanitation), through subsidized goods and services, or through transfer payments. These services call for progressive taxation, for indirect taxation of luxury goods, for ensuring that the poor have access to the services, and for a system of checks against abuse. The provision of public services is, of course, not a distinctive feature of the basic needs approach. But the approach is distinguished by its emphasis on investigating why these services have so often failed to reach the groups for

whom they were intended, or were claimed to be intended, and why they have often reinforced inequalities in the distribution of private income. By redesigning these services, the basic needs approach ensures that they do reach the poor.

2. There is some evidence that consumers (both poor and rich) are not always efficient, especially in optimizing nutrition and health, and especially in the case of subsistence farmers who become cash earners. Additional cash income is sometimes spent on food of lower nutritional value than that previously consumed (as when polished rice is substituted for coarse grains, or rice for wheat) or on items other than food.

3. The manner in which additional income is earned may affect nutrition adversely. Female employment may reduce breast feeding and therefore the nutrition of babies, even though the mother's income has risen. More profitable cash crops may replace "inferior" and cheaper crops, such as millets, that are grown for home use; or dairy farming, though it creates employment, may divert land from cheaper but more nutritious maize. The human energy costs of producing a cash crop that replaces subsistence agriculture may be so great in relation to wages that the dependent members of the family are systematically deprived of adequate nutrition. In such a situation more food would mean lower levels of nutrition. Hydroelectric dams and irrigation or drainage schemes, while raising incomes, can contribute to the spread of water-borne diseases, such as malaria, onchocerciasis, and schistosomiasis. In some cases, the extra costs of preventing these diseases are more than offset by the additional returns from the project. But in other cases, the fate of the victims has no bearing on the project.

Both reasons 2 and 3 raise difficult and controversial questions about free choice and society's right to intervene, and about effective methods of aiding choice and strengthening and reaching the weak.

4. There is maldistribution within households, as well as between households; women and children tend to have a lower proportion of their needs met than do males. In many societies women also carry the heaviest work load, so that it cannot be argued that food is distributed according to effort.

5. A substantial proportion of the destitute are sick, disabled, aged, or orphaned; they may be members of households or they may not. Their needs can be met only through transfer payments or public services since, by definition, they are incapable of earning. This group has been neglected by the income and productivity approach to poverty alleviation and employment creation. Of course, the problems of implementation are particularly difficult. Even some quite affluent societies have not been successful in eradicating the poverty of their handicapped, and societies with very meager resources have a much more difficult task.

6. The income approach has paid a good deal of attention to the choice of technique but has neglected to provide for appropriate products. Many developing societies import or produce domestically oversophisticated products that meet excessive needs transferred from relatively high-income, high-saving economies. This has frustrated the pursuit of a basic needs approach by catering to the demand of a small section of the population or by preempting an excessive slice of the low incomes of the poor. An essential feature of the basic needs approach is to choose appropriate final products and produce them by appropriate techniques, thereby giving rise to more jobs and a more even income distribution, which in turn generates the demand for these products. This goal cannot necessarily be fully achieved by a redistribution of income and reliance on market responses (though foreign trade is not ruled out).

7. As already mentioned, the income approach neglects the importance of nonmaterial needs, both in their own right and as instruments of meeting some material needs more effectively, at lower cost, and in a shorter period. This point becomes particularly relevant if the nonsatisfaction of nonmaterial needs (such as participation) increases the difficulty of meeting basic needs more than that of achieving income growth.

Comment

The literature of basic needs is now extensive. Most notable is Paul Streeten et al., *First Things First* (1981), which contains an extensive bibliography. Other studies are the International Labour Organization's *The Basic Needs Approach to Development* (1977); Paul Streeten and Shahid Javed Burki, "Basic Needs: Some Issues," *World Development* (March 1978); Paul Streeten, "Basic Needs: Premises and Promises," *Journal of Policy Modeling* (January 1979); Norman Hicks, "Growth vs. Basic Needs: Is There a Trade-Off?" *World Development* (November/December 1979); Frances Stewart, "Country Experience in Providing for Basic Needs," *Finance & Development* (December 1979); Shahid Javed Burki and Mahbub ul Haq, "Meeting Basic Needs: An Overview," *World Development* (February 1981); Jorge Garcia-Bouza, *A Basic Needs Analytical Bibliography* (OECD Development Centre, 1980).

For critiques of the basic needs approach, see T. N. Srinivasan, "Development, Poverty and Basic Human Needs: Some Issues," *Food Research Institute Studies* (1977) and Sidney Dell, "Basic Needs or Comprehensive Development" *CEPAL Review* (1978). Dell argues that there are difficulties of concept, of measurement, and of implementation in using "basic needs" as an operational tool for planning. Three issues are raised: (1) a trade-off between higher rates of growth and basic needs; (2) the rate at which any particular level of basic consumption should be approached over time; (3) whether the basic needs strategy implies a pattern of labor-intensive rural development instead of large-scale industrial growth.

Comment

The correlations between GNP per head, indicators of basic needs, and the components of the PQLI are generally high, but by no means perfect. For individual countries, there are deviations in the rankings that are worth pursuing for insights into policy issues. For a discussion of these correlations—and why per capita GNP cannot serve as a surrogate for the other indicators of poverty—see Morris David Morris, *Measuring the Condition of the World's Poor* (1979), pp. 52–6; Norman Hicks and Paul Streeten, "Indicators of Development: The Search for a Basic Needs Yardstick," *World Development* (June 1979), pp. 572–5; and A. K. Sen, "Levels of Poverty: Policy and Change," *World Bank Staff Working Paper* No. 401 (1980).

I.B.4. The Inverted-U Hypothesis*

The pathbreaking work in this area is that of Kuznets (1955).[1] Measuring inequality by the income shares of various quintiles, Kuznets compared India, Ceylon, Puerto Rico, the United Kingdom, and the United States and observed greater inequality in the devel-

oping countries. Some of his data are given in Table 1. Kuznets explains the difference between less-developed and developed countries this way:

The former have no "middle" classes: there is a sharp contrast between the preponderant proportion of the population whose average income is well below the generally low countrywide average, and a small top group with a very large relative income excess. The developed countries, on the other hand, are characterized by a much more gradual rise from low to high income shares, with

*From Gary S. Fields, *Poverty, Inequality and Development*, Cambridge University Press, 1980, pp. 60–7, 70–1. Reprinted by permission.

[1]Simon Kuznets, "Economic Growth and Income Inequality," *American Economic Review,* March 1955, pp. 1–28.

TABLE 1. Relative Inequality in Various Countries in about 1950

	Income Share (%)		Ratio
Country/Date	Poorest 60%	Richest 20%	Richest 20% Poorest 60%
India (1949–50)	28	55	1.96
Ceylon (1950)	30	50	1.67
Puerto Rico (1948)	24	56	2.33
United States (1950)	34	44	1.29
United Kingdom (1947)	36	45	1.25

Source: Kuznets, 1955, pp. 201.

substantial groups receiving more than the high countrywide income average, and the top groups securing smaller shares than the comparable ordinal groups in underdeveloped countries. [1955, p. 22]

Viewed from this perspective, the variations in inequality reflect real differences across countries in participation in the "advanced" or "modern" sectors of the economy.

A few years later, Kravis (1960) presented evidence on patterns of inequality in eleven countries.[2] Taking the United States as a standard for comparison, he found higher inequality than that of the United States in Italy, Puerto Rico, El Salvador, and Ceylon; comparable inequality to that of the United States in Great Britain, Japan, and Canada; and less inequality than in the United States in Denmark, the Netherlands, and Israel. Thus, like Kuznets, Kravis found that less-developed countries had relatively greater inequality than did more-developed countries.

At about that same time, Oshima (1962) suggested that inequality increases up to and through the semideveloped stage and declines once a country is fully developed.[3] But this speculation was not tested, owing to data limitations.

The pattern of greater relative income inequality in less-developed countries than in the developed countries was confirmed for eighteen countries in a subsequent paper by Kuznets (1963).[4] His findings include:

1. The shares of the upper income groups are distinctly larger in the less-developed countries (LDCs) than in the more-developed countries (DCs).
2. Although the shares of the lowest-income groups in some LDCs are lower than in some DCs, the differences are much narrower than for the shares of the upper-income groups.
3. It follows from (1) and (2) that the shape of the income distribution curve is different in LDCs than in DCs.

These findings are depicted in Figure 1. Finding (1) is illustrated in the upper right corner; finding (2) in the lower left. At either end of the income distribution, the Lorenz curve for the typical LDC lies below that for the typical DC. On the likely assumption that the two curves do not intersect in the middle, it would follow that the Gini coefficient of inequality would be greater in LDCs than in DCs. The data show an average Gini coefficient of .44 for the LDCs covered by the data; .37 for the DCs.[5]

On that evidence, Kuznets was led to the view that the *level* of economic development

[2]Irving B. Kravis, "International Differences in the Distribution of Income," *Review of Economics and Statistics,* November 1960, pp. 408–16.

[3]Harry Oshima, "The International Comparison of Size Distribution of Family Incomes with Special Reference to Asia," *Review of Economics and Statistics,* November 1962, pp. 439–45.

[4]Simon Kuznets, "Quantitative Aspects of the Economic Growth of Nations: VIII, Distribution of Income by Size," *Economic Development and Cultural Change,* January 1963, pt. 2, pp. 1–80.

[5]Ibid., p. 17.

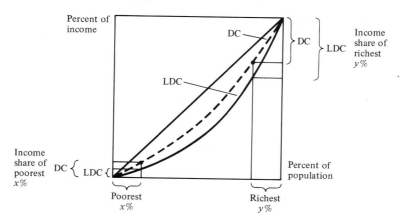

FIGURE 1. Patterns of relative inequality in developed countries (DC) and less-developed countries (LDC).

(as measured by gross national product per capita) is a major determinant of the extent of income inequality in a country. The specific nature of that dependence has come to be known as the *inverted-U hypothesis,* which states that relative income inequality rises during the early stages of development, reaches a peak, and then declines in the later stages. Much research effort has gone into attempts to confirm or refute the inverted-U pattern.

One line of research has regarded the hypothesis dynamically, testing it by measuring relative inequality at several points in the course of a given country's economic development. Kuznets himself assumed that LDCs had greater inequality in their earlier stages of development, because everyone was thought to be more or less the same, that is, equally poor. No data were availabe to test this speculation. Even today, for only a handful of less-developed countries are there data on the distribution of income at several points in time. Economists have had to perform indepth analyses of individual countries to test the inverted-U hypothesis. This motivation appears explicitly in a number of studies of growth and distribution, for instance, in the work of Fei, Ranis, and Kuo (1978, p. 17) on Taiwan.[6] They write:

[6]John C. H. Fei, Gustav Ranis, and S. W. Y. Kuo, "Growth and the Family Distribution of Income by Factor Components," *Quarterly Journal of Economics,* February 1968, pp. 17–53.

The key question that is raised again and again is whether or not the beginnings of rapid growth in the developing economy must necessarily be associated with a worsening distribution of income [meaning here increasing relative inequality, not absolute immiserization].... The careful examination of even one successful counter-example to any such "historical necessity" should prove useful in its own right. But beyond that, a fuller understanding of some of the underlying causal relationships ... will hopefully provide us with some policy relevant conclusions concerning the precise conditions under which "things do not have to get worse before they get better."

The other way of viewing the inverted-U hypothesis is as a cross-sectional statement, whereby countries at intermediate stages of development are thought to have more unequal distributions of income than do richer or poorer countries. Such a pattern is generally supported by Kuznets' studies from the 1950s and 1960s. More recently, several new and more comprehensive data sets have been compiled, which give further credence to the inverted-U pattern. Some of the major studies are reviewed here.

In the late 1960s and early 1970s, Adelman and Morris gathered new data for forty-three developing countries. Their 1973 book presented considerable evidence on the correlates of relative income inequality.[7] By

[7]Irma Adelman and Cynthia Taft Morris, *Economic Growth and Social Equity in Developing Countries,* Stanford, Calif.: Stanford University Press, 1973.

means of analysis of variance, they found six factors to be important in explaining variations in relative income inequality, one of which was the level of economic development. We will return to the correlates of inequality later in this section.

A short while later, Paukert (1973) refined Adelman and Morris's estimates.[8] He discarded information that he thought to be particularly unreliable, added some new countries where good data had recently become available, and presented summary information on the size distribution of income in fifty-six countries. The Gini coefficients and gross domestic product per capita are presented in Table 2. For each of several alternative relative inequality measures, Paukert found that inequality begins at a comparatively low level, reaches a peak in countries with per capita incomes of $301–$500, and then diminishes at higher incomes. Thus the inverted-U pattern is reconfirmed.

Most recently, new intercountry evidence has been reported by Chenery and Syrquin[9] and Ahluwalia[10] at the World Bank, and by Lydall[11] for the International Labour Office. Using updated data compiled by Jain[12] for sixty-two countries, these authors also found the inverted-U pattern in the cross-sectional studies.

In summary, the cross-section data on income inequality at different stages of devel-

[8]F. Paukert, "Income Distribution at Different Levels of Development: A Survey of Evidence," *International Labour Review,* August–September 1973, pp. 97–125.

[9]Hollis Chenery and Moises Syrquin, *Patterns of Development, 1950–1970,* New York: Oxford University Press, 1975.

[10]Montek Ahluwalia, "Dimensions of the Problem," in Hollis B. Chenery et al. (eds.), *Redistribution with Growth,* New York: Oxford University Press, 1974, pp. 3–37; "Income Distribution and Development: Some Stylized Facts," *American Economic Review,* May 1976a, pp. 128–35; "Inequality, Poverty and Development," *Journal of Development Economics,* Vol. 3, 1976b, pp. 307–42.

[11]Harold B. Lydall, "Income Distribution during the Process of Development," International Labour Office, *World Employment Programme Research Working Paper* No. 52, February 1977.

[12]S. Jain, *Size Distribution of Income: A Compilation of Data,* Washington, D.C.: World Bank, 1975.

opment reveal two patterns: higher inequality on the average in the less-developed countries than in the developed countries; and within the less-developed countries, lower average inequality in the very poorest countries than in the less poor ones. Let us now explore further the relationship between income inequality in a country and the level of its economic development.

ON THE INEVITABILITY OF THE INVERTED U

The evidence on relative inequality patterns presented in the last section was disturbing to many development economists. The prevailing view as recently as 1975 was that income distribution must get worse before it gets better. Considerable pessimism was expressed over the supposed trade-off between growth and income equality. Some were even skeptical about the welfare implications of the development process itself.

There are two immediate problems with this inference. One is that the conclusion is based on cross-section data rather than on analysis of historical trends over time. For this reason, Adelman and Morris, for example, in the introduction to their book, use words like "preliminary," "exploratory," and "tentative" to describe their efforts. But having voiced these words of caution, they and others like them proceed to conclusions about the process of economic development by viewing countries at different stages of development. Making inference from cross-section data about dynamic growth processes is a well-established practice pioneered at Harvard and practiced by many over the last two decades. The maintained assumption of such analyses is that currently developing countries will follow much the same patterns in their development experiences as are found in the cross section. This assumption requires a leap of faith that many, myself included, are hesitant to make.

A second problem with the inverted U is that we are dealing with averages among *groups* of countries and not, for the most part, with the information on individual

TABLE 2. Gini Coefficient of Inequality and Gross Domestic Product per Capita

Country and Level of GDP per Head	Gini Ratio	GDP per Head in 1965 (U.S. $)	Country and Level of GDP per Head	Gini Ratio	GDP per Head in 1965 (U.S. $)
Under $100			Jamaica (1958)	.56	465
Chad (1958)	.35	68	Surinam (1962)	.30	424
Dahomey (1959)	.42	73	Lebanon (1955–60)	.55	440
Niger (1960)	.34	81	Barbados (1951–2)	.45	368
Nigeria (1959)	.51	74	Chile (1958)	.44	486
Sudan (1969)	.40	97	Mexico (1963)	.53	441
Tanzania (1964)	.54	61	Panama (1969)	.48	490
Burma (1958)	.35	64	Group average	.494	426.9
India (1956–7)	.33	95			
Madagascar (1960)	.53	92	*$501–$1,000*		
Group average	.419	78.3	Republic of South		
			Africa (1965)	.58	521
$101–$200			Argentina (1961)	.42	782
Morocco (1965)	.50	180	Trinidad and Tobago		
Senegal (1960)	.56	192	(1957–8)	.44	704
Sierra Leone (1968)	.56	142	Venezuela (1962)	.42	904
Tunisia (1971)	.53	187	Greece (1957)	.38	591
Bolivia (1968)	.53	132	Japan (1962)	.39	838
Ceylon (Sri Lanka)			Group average	.438	723.3
(1963)	.44	140			
Pakistan (1963–4)	.37	101	*$1,001–$2,000*		
South Korea (1966)	.26	107	Israel (1957)	.30	1,243
Group average	.468	147.6	United Kingdom		
			(1964)	.38	1,590
$201–$300			Netherlands (1962)	.42	1,400
Malaya (1957–8)	.36	278	Federal Republic of		
Fiji (1968)	.46	295	Germany (1964)	.45	1,667
Ivory Coast (1959)	.43	213	France (1962)	.50	1,732
Zambia (1959)	.48	207	Finland (1962)	.46	1,568
Brazil (1960)	.54	207	Italy (1948)	.40	1,011
Ecuador (1968)	.38	202	Puerto Rico (1963)	.44	1,101
El Salvador (1965)	.53	249	Norway (1963)	.35	1,717
Peru (1961)	.61	237	Australia (1966–7)	.30	1,823
Iraq (1956)	.60	285	Group average	.401	1,485.2
Philippines (1961)	.48	240			
Colombia (1964)	.62	275	*$2,001 and Above*		
Group average	.499	244.4	Denmark (1963)	.37	2,078
			Sweden (1963)	.39	2,406
$301–$550			United States (1969)	.34	3,233
Gabon (1960)	.64	368	Group average	.365	2,572.3
Costa Rica (1969)	.50	360			

Source: Paukert, 1973, Table 6.

countries themselves. Figure 2 presents Paukert's data. In Figure 2, the individual data are indicated by asterisks and averages for each income class by large dots. Even casual inspection suggests much more variation in relative inequality *within* countries grouped by gross domestic product per capita than *between* them. That is, level of income is only an imprecise predictor of income inequality in a country.

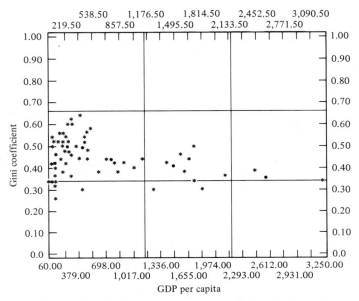

FIGURE 2. Gini coefficient and gross domestic product per capita, 56 countries. Computed from data in Paukert, 1973, pp. 114–15.

Before regarding the inverted-U pattern as inevitable, even in the cross section, we need to know how well the inverted U fits the data. To explore this question, let us work directly with the individual country data rather than with the grouped data. By means of multiple regression analysis, we may determine (1) whether an inverted U is the appropriate characterization of the relationship between inequality and level of income, and (2) whether any particular pattern of inequality change over time is inevitable. On both accounts, the evidence suggests that income distribution need *not* get worse before it gets better.

These empirical findings need to be evaluated carefully. The evidence *does* show the highest relative inequality in the group of lower-middle-income countries than elsewhere. However, this pattern is far from inevitable. Concerning the inevitability issue (the view that income distribution *must* get worse before it gets better), we should note how little of the variance in relative inequality is explained by income level. At most one-fourth of the intercountry variation in inequality is explained by income level. This means, very simply, that the inverted U *is* avoidable.

In the perspective of the overall economic development literature, it should not be too surprising to find that income level fails to provide a satisfactory explanation for the degree of inequality in a country. These results are consistent with the writings of many leading development economists (e.g., Fei and Ranis, 1964;[13] Kuznets, 1966;[14] and Adelman and Morris, 1973)[15] who have been saying that the income distribution is determined as much or more by the *type* of economic development and the policies followed in a given country as by the *level* of development. One can hope, therefore, that appropriate public policy can be designed so as to avoid a deterioration in the relative distribution of income and to effect an improvement in the economic status of the poor.

[13]J. C. H. Fei and G. Ranis, *Development of the Labor Surplus Economy,* Homewood, Ill.: Irwin, 1964.

[14]Simon Kuznets, *Modern Economic Growth,* New Haven: Yale University Press, 1966.

[15]Adelman and Morris, *Economic Growth and Social Equity in Developing Countries,* 1973.

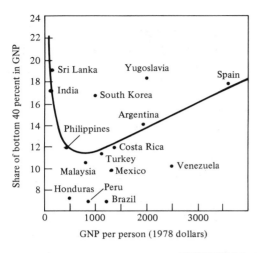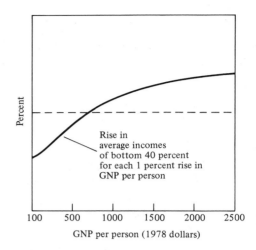

EXHIBIT I.3. Income of Poorest Groups

This pattern is described by the Kuznets curve, which demonstrates that the incomes of the poorest 40 percent of the population normally grow more slowly than the average until income per person reaches a range of $700 or $900. Beyond this range, the incomes of poorer groups tend to grow faster than the average. Thus the distribution of income typically is less unequal in developed countries than in developing countries.

I.B.5. Growth-Distribution Tradeoffs*

Concepts of progress in most developing countries are heavily conditioned by their colonial past. Many of them express their objectives in terms of "catching up" with the advanced industrial societies and pattern their economies on this model. This tendency is reinforced by political objectives in countries that wish to acquire military power and influence.

One drawback to the emphasis on growth is that its benefits have usually been concentrated on the modern sectors of the economy, and increasing inequality of incomes has

often led to political tensions. An alternative view of progress focuses more on achieving an equitable society and reducing poverty, with growth regarded as a necessary but by no means sufficient condition.

The postwar experience of relatively rapid growth in developing countries has provided a rich body of data on this set of relations that is only now being analyzed. Since there is relatively little established theory to guide this analysis, the collection of data and the formulation of hypotheses have gone hand in hand. Although substantial progress has been made in understanding the economic forces at work, the results to date are largely speculative and fall considerably short of the needs of policymakers. This article explores some of the implications of the prevalent

*From Hollis B. Chenery, "Poverty and Progress—Choices for the Developing World," *Finance & Development*, June 1980, pp. 26–30. Reprinted by permission.

views of progress in developing countries in the light of the information available on the results.

CONCEPTS OF PROGRESS

Catching Up

The material success of the industrialized West has been a powerful incentive to the rest of the world to adopt elements of Western experience that are conducive to accelerated growth. The success of countries with different historical backgrounds and economic and political systems has served to reinforce this objective.

The concept of catching up with the industrial leaders is a product of the Industrial Revolution and its outward spread from Western Europe. This concept both provides a goal for social action and suggests a means by which this goal can be achieved. The technology and forms of economic organization created by the advanced Western countries have provided the means for accelerated growth for countries in all parts of the world. Nations following this model have differed primarily in their choice of the economic and social elements to be incorporated in their societies.

The prototype of a successful process of catching up is Japan, whose economic structure and income level in 1910 were not significantly different from those of the poor countries today. Econometric estimates of the sources of Japanese growth suggest that the process of borrowing technology from more advanced countries is now virtually completed and that Japan is likely to attain the income level of the United States by 1990 (Jorgensen and Nishimizu, 1978).

The Japanese example has had a powerful effect on Taiwan, Korea, Singapore, Thailand, and other countries of East Asia. All of these economies are now growing considerably faster than those of the advanced countries and some may be able to complete the transformation from a state of underdevelopment to one of maturity in less than the 60 years taken by Japan.

Several of these East Asian countries provide modern approximations to the earlier idea of progress as a process in which "good things come in clusters." Unlike most developing countries, the benefits of growth have been widely distributed in Japan, Taiwan, Singapore, and Korea, and the incomes of the poor have grown almost as fast as those of the rich. Postwar governments have been growth minded and authoritarian but not very repressive, and these countries have ranked high on most indicators of social progress. In more typical cases growth has been achieved at the expense of increasing the concentration of wealth and income, however, and the poor have benefited much less.

Equity

Although the more equitable sharing of income features prominently among the political objectives of virtually all governments, it is taken much less seriously in practice than is the objective of rapid growth. Even though widespread government intervention in production and income distribution is justified largely on the grounds of reducing poverty, in fact most studies show that on balance the effects of government revenue collection and expenditure in developing countries favor the upper-income groups rather than the poor.

A few developing countries have, however, gone beyond the endorsement of equitable growth and have adopted policies designed to achieve it. Notable examples include the People's Republic of China, Cuba, India, Israel, Sri Lanka, Tanzania, and Yugoslavia. Although their social goals vary with the form and extent of government control of the economy, there is a common emphasis on providing a minimum level of income to the poorest groups. In the more extreme socialist formulations, greater equality is considered a goal in itself, even if it is achieved with an adverse impact on efficiency—that is, lowering the incomes of the rich rather than raising those of the poor.

A pioneering attempt to reconcile the objectives of growth and the alleviation of poverty in an operational framework was made in 1962 by the Perspective Planning Division of the Indian Planning Commission (Srinivasan and Bardhan, 1974). This approach was based on a formulation in which the rate of poverty reduction in India was determined by the growth of the national income, while the extent of redistribution considered feasible was based on the experience of other countries. This approach has been refined in the concept of "redistribution with growth" (Ahluwalia and Chenery, 1974), which forms the basis of the comparative analysis in the following section. If the idea of a feasible limit to the redistribution that can be achieved with a given set of institutions is accepted, the conflict between growth and distribution is reduced.

A further refinement in the concept of poverty alleviation has been achieved by shifting from the use of income as a measure of poverty to physical estimates of the inputs required to achieve minimum standards of nutrition, health, shelter, education, and other essentials. These indicators of basic needs provide a way of evaluating the effectiveness of any set of policies designed to reduce poverty (Streeten, 1979). The "basic needs" approach focuses particularly on the distribution of education, health, and other public services as a necessary element of policies designed to raise productivity and to alleviate poverty. This is an area in which some of the more effective socialist societies, such as the People's Republic of China, showed marked improvement.

Formulating Social Objectives

The social goals of developing countries—and of international bodies representing them—tend to be stated in political terms that confuse ends and means and ignore the different dimensions of progress. For example, the goal of catching up with more advanced countries is a poor proxy for improving welfare because it often leads to emphasis on heavy industry and other policies that concentrate growth in the modern sectors of the economy. Similarly, many of the goals announced by international agencies, such as

the attainment of given levels of nutrition, education, shelter, or industry, are misleading because they ignore the need to achieve a balance among the several dimensions of social progress.

The economist's answer to this problem is to replace a set of separate objectives by a social welfare function that defines the goal of a society in utilitarian terms as the increase in a weighted average of income or consumption of its members over time. Although the national income is one such average, the typical income distribution gives a weight of over 50 percent to the rich (the top 20 percent) and less than 5 percent to the poor (the bottom 20 percent). If the growth of aggregate national income is used as a goal, it therefore implies giving 10 to 20 times as much weight to a 1 percent increase in the incomes of the rich as to a 1 percent increase in those of the poor (Ahluwalia and Chenery, 1974).

In principle, any set of weights could be applied to the income or consumption of different groups to remedy this bias. One possibility is to give equal weight to a given percentage increase in the income of each member of society, which is the equivalent of weighting by the population in each group. A more extreme welfare function, which corresponds to the announced goals of a few socialist societies, concentrates entirely on raising the incomes of the poor and gives social value to increasing other incomes only to the extent that they contribute to this objective.

Although there is no scientific way to determine the appropriate welfare function for any given society, the concept is useful in bringing out potential conflicts in the idea of progress and in deriving alternative measures of performance. It will be used for this purpose in the following section.

EXPERIENCE WITH DISTRIBUTION

Perceptions of the nature of progress have evolved considerably as a result of the varied experience of the postwar period. Many of the early postcolonial governments set forth optimistic objectives that now seem highly oversimplified. However, there has also been a notable willingness to learn from experience in countries with varying ideologies. Equity-oriented countries such as the People's Republic of China, Cuba, Sri Lanka, and Tanzania have found it necessary to give greater attention to economic efficiency and growth, while some of the leading exponents of rapid growth—Brazil, Mexico, Thailand, Turkey—are now taking poverty alleviation more seriously.

Although scholarly interest in these relations has expanded rapidly in recent years, the statistical measures needed to test and refine hypotheses are only now becoming available. Twenty-five years ago, Simon Kuznets addressed the question: "Does inequality in the distribution of income increase or decrease in the course of a country's economic growth?" Although his answer was based on evidence for only a handful of countries and was labeled "perhaps 5 percent empirical information and 95 percent speculation," it has provided the starting point for empirical work in this field (Kuznets, 1955). Kuznets hypothesized that the distribution of income tends to worsen in the early phases of development and to improve thereafter. This "U-shaped curve" hypothesis has been subsequently verified in several cross-country studies based on samples of 50 or 60 developing countries (Ahluwalia, 1976).

There are several reasons for the earnings of middle-income and upper-income groups to rise more rapidly than those of the poor in the early stages of growth. Development involves a shift of population from the slow growing agricultural sector to the higher-income, more rapidly growing modern sector. In this process inequality is first accentuated by more rapid population growth in rural areas and ultimately reduced by rising wages produced by more rapid absorption of labor in the modern sector (Frank and Webb, 1977). The more capital-intensive type of development strategy followed by Mexico or Brazil absorbs less labor and produces greater concentration of income, while the more labor-intensive forms of Taiwan and

Korea distribute the benefits of modernization more widely. A number of other factors, such as the greater demand for skilled than for unskilled labor and the concentration of public expenditure in urban areas, also contribute to growing inequality in many countries.

My present concern is with the broader aspects of the relations between growth and distribution. How universal is the tendency toward less equal distribution in developing countries? Does it lead to an absolute decline in welfare for some groups? What kinds of policies have served to offset these tendencies? Is social conflict an inevitable concomitant of economic advance? Although none of these questions can be answered with great confidence, the average relationships and the variety of individual experience can be brought out by combining the available cross-country and time-series evidence for the postwar period.

The average relationship between rising income and its distribution is best shown by estimates of the Kuznets curve from data for all countries having comparable measures in some recent period (Ahluwalia, Carter, and Chenery, 1979). Although the variation in income shares was computed separately for each quintile, the general phenomenon is depicted in Figure 1 by considering only two groups: the rich (upper 40 percent) and the poor (lower 60 percent). As national income rises from the lowest observed level to that of the middle-income countries, the share received by the poor declines on average from 32 percent to 23 percent of the total. In a hypothetical country following this average relationship, 80 percent of the increase in income would go to the top 40 percent of recipients.

The relationship between the income growth of different groups and that of the whole society can be brought out more clearly by expressing it in terms of the per capita income of each group. This is done in Figure 1, which plots the per capita income of the poor against that of the rich. Since the income level "Y" of the society is a weighted average of the two groups "a and b" ($Y =$

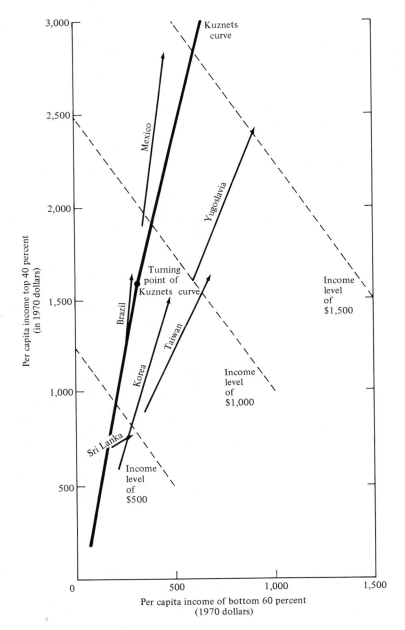

FIGURE 1. The Kuznets curve with country observations.

$.4Y_a + .6Y_b$), the downward sloping straight lines define given levels of per capita income. Points on these lines indicate different distributions, and a growth process with a constant distribution is represented by a straight line through the origin, as in the case of Yugoslavia. A line deviating toward the vertical axis indicates growing inequality, as in the case of Mexico or Brazil. Growing equality is shown by Sri Lanka and Taiwan.

The Kuznets curve shown in Figure 1 consists of two segments: a phase of worsening distribution up to an income level of about $800 (of constant purchasing power) and a phase of improving distribution thereafter. In the first phase the per capita income of the rich grows from about $300 to $1,600 while that of the poor increases from about $100 to $300. For the poorest 20 percent, the rate of growth is considerably less. Since an increase in national income of this magnitude may take 40 or 50 years even with the relatively rapid growth rates recently experienced in developing countries, in the typical country the very poor cannot look forward to an annual increase of much more than 1 percent— even though the economy is growing at two or three times that rate. Furthermore, there is nothing automatic about the improvement in distribution above $800, as shown by Mexico and Brazil.

Tradeoff between Growth and Equity

Although acceptable time-series data are only available for a dozen or so countries, they indicate a considerable variation around this average relation. Table 1 gives selected measures of overall growth and of the share going to the lower 60 percent for countries having observations for a decade or more. They are divided into three groups according to the share of the increment in income going to the poor. The five good performers show over 30 percent of the increment going to the bottom 60 percent, while the three poor performers show less than 20 percent. Whether distribution is getting better or worse is indicated by comparing these increments to the initial distribution and by the ratio of the

growth of the per capita income of the poor to the national average in the last column.

This information, together with less complete data on other countries, provides a basis for describing the following patterns of growth and distribution observed in the developing world:

- *Growth-oriented pattern,* illustrated by Brazil and Mexico.
- *Equity-oriented, low growth,* illustrated by Sri Lanka.
- *Rapid growth with equity,* illustrated by Taiwan, Yugoslavia, and Korea.

These cases illustrate the main types of deviation from the average pattern that can be observed in the 12 countries of Table 1; India, Turkey, the Philippines, and Colombia follow the average relations of the Kuznets curve.

These examples suggest the following observations on the relationship between income growth and social welfare in developing countries. First, a small group of countries has achieved rapid growth with considerable equity. In addition to Taiwan, Korea, and Yugoslavia, this group includes Israel, Singapore, and perhaps the People's Republic of China. The policies underlying this successful performance vary from primary reliance on market forces in Taiwan, Korea, and Singapore to substantial income transfers and other forms of intervention in Yugoslavia and Israel. Second, substantial tradeoffs between growth and equity are illustrated by the other cases. Although Sri Lanka has grown much less rapidly than Mexico or Brazil, the poor have done considerably better in the former case. Cuba presents an even more extreme tradeoff, since the welfare of the poor has risen despite a continuous fall in the nation's per capita income since 1960 (Seers, 1974).

Only in the few cases where economic growth has been both rapid and fairly equitably distributed is it possible to make unambiguous comparisons among countries— or among different development strategies for a single country. In other cases it is necessary to define some properties of a social welfare function to make such comparisons.

TABLE 1. Changes in Income and Its Distribution

Country	Income Level[a]				Distribution			Growth Rates (In percent)		
	Initial Year	Increments			Percentage Share of Bottom 60 Percent			Total	Bottom 60 Percent	Ratio of Bottom 60 Percent to Total
		Total	Top 40 Percent	Bottom 60 Percent	Initial Year	Final Year	Increase Incremental			
Good Performers										
Taiwan (1964–74)	562	508	758	341	36.9	38.5	39.5	6.6	7.1	1.1
Yugoslavia (1963–73)	1,003	518	822	316	35.7	36.0	36.5	4.2	4.3	1.0
Sri Lanka (1963–73)	388	84	58	101	27.4	35.4	51.3	2.0	4.6	2.3
Korea (1965–76)	362	540	938	275	34.9	32.3	31.1	8.7	7.9	0.9
Costa Rica (1961–71)	825	311	459	212	23.7	28.4	33.6	3.2	5.1	1.6
Intermediate Performers										
India (1954–64)	226	58	113	21	31.0	29.2	25.8	2.3	1.6	0.7
Philippines (1961–71)	336	83	155	35	24.7	24.8	25.0	2.2	2.3	1.0
Turkey (1963–73)	566	243	417	128	20.8	24.0	27.9	3.6	5.1	1.4
Colombia (1964–74)	648	232	422	106	19.0	21.2	24.0	3.1	4.3	1.4
Poor Performers										
Brazil (1960–70)	615	214	490	31	24.8	20.6	15.5	3.1	1.2	0.4
Mexico (1963–75)	974	446	944	114	21.7	19.7	18.0	3.2	2.4	0.8
Peru (1961–71)	834	212	435	63	17.9	17.9	17.9	2.3	2.3	1.0

Source: Ahluwalia, Carter, and Chenery, 1979, table 5.

[a]Measured by per capita income expressed in 1970 U.S. dollars of constant purchasing power.

To take two extreme cases from Table 1, the incomes of the poor have grown nearly four times as fast over a decade in Sri Lanka as in Brazil, while the opposite is true of the incomes of the rich. Since the latter receive greater weight in the national income, per capita income has grown 50 percent faster in Brazil; conversely a population-weighted index of welfare increases 50 percent faster for Sri Lanka. Even this limited sample therefore demonstrates that judgments about economic progress cannot be separated from social and ethical postulates.

REDUCING WORLD POVERTY

Attempts to extend the concept of material progress to a global scale run up against more acute problems of equity than the national issues described above. Although most governments recognize their national income as one dimension of national welfare, no one has suggested that global income has much relevance to an assessment of global welfare. Instead political and economic efforts of international institutions are increasingly focused on the reduction of poverty and other aspects of equity as objectives that command the support of people of widely varying political views.

In recent years considerable efforts have been made to establish measures of poverty based on standards of nutrition, health, shelter, education, and other essentials. Conservative estimates set the proportion of the world's population that falls below a poverty line based on such minimum standards at between 20 and 25 percent. Although this proportion has declined somewhat in the past 30 years, the overall increase in the world's population has meant that the absolute number of people below this poverty line has continued to grow and is currently of the order of 800 million.

In technical terms the reduction or even elimination of world poverty seems deceptively easy. If resources could be shifted to satisfying the needs of poverty groups efficiently, it would only require a reallocation of 2 to 3 percent of the world's output per annum from 1980 onward to meet the identifiable costs of eliminating poverty by the year 2000 (Streeten and Burki, 1978). Since three-fourths of the world's poor live in very poor countries, however, the annual cost of eliminating poverty in these countries is more meaningfully stated as equal to about 15 percent of their gross national product (GNP), even if expenditures could be designed to serve only the target groups. In the light of the distributional experience outlined in the previous section, the problem is seen to be vastly more difficult.

Some of the principal constraints to a more realistic attempt to reduce global poverty include:

1. The multiple objectives of nation–states, among which the alleviation of poverty is usually subordinated to a variety of nationalistic goals.
2. The limited scope for resource transfers in the existing international economic order. Official development assistance from the industrialized countries has declined from 0.50 percent of their GNP in 1960 to 0.35 percent or less since 1970. Transfers from the Organization of Petroleum Exporting Countries (OPEC), while substantial, do not offset the negative effects of higher oil prices on the growth of the oil importing developing countries.
3. Rapid growth of population, which will double in the next 35 years even though the rate has started to decline.

What are the possibilities of more rapid progress in the face of these and other constraints? In an attempt to compare approaches to poverty alleviation, Ahluwalia, Carter, and Chenery have simulated income growth and the numbers of absolute poor over the next 20 years for a large sample of developing countries (Ahluwalia, Carter, and Chenery, 1979, tables 3 and 9). If the trends of the past 20 years—a period of relatively rapid growth of income—continue, the number of absolute poor in 2000 would be at about the same level as in 1960. This represents rapid progress in one sense, since the proportion of the poor would fall from 50 percent to 20 percent of the population of developing countries. However, since this result would be achieved only by a reduction in absolute poverty in middle-income countries that offsets the rising numbers in the very poor countries, it is not a long-term solution.

The reduction in poverty will have to come from one of three sources: improved distribution, accelerated growth, or a more rapid decline in population growth. Improved distribution is particularly important in many middle-income countries, such as those in Latin America (where income is quite unequally distributed), but some acceleration of growth is essential in the poor countries of Africa and South Asia. Although there are some short-term tradeoffs between growth and distribution, in the longer term it is more likely that all three types of policy will be mutually reinforcing. Even within restrictive limits to capital transfers, the industrial countries can considerably improve the outcome by giving greater priority to poverty alleviation in allocating aid among countries (Edelman and Chenery, 1977).

These projections lead to the conclusion that, although the elimination of poverty is much more difficult than is sometimes suggested, it remains a plausible goal for international policy. One of the principal means to this end would be accomplished if the tendency of the poor to lag behind the higher-income groups in the process of development could be eliminated. There is increasing acceptance of the idea that international efforts should be more directly focused on reducing poverty in order to offset this tendency of the international system. Enough examples of how this result can be accomplished have been cited in economic systems ranging from socialist to free enterprise to suggest that it is a feasible objective.

This conclusion leaves several fundamental issues unresolved. To what extent should poverty alleviation replace the principle of self-help as a guide to international action? To achieve this objective, will it not be necessary to establish enforceable standards of performance to assure that the benefits actually reach the poverty groups? The new emphasis on poverty alleviation does not resolve these old dilemmas in the field of international economic cooperation. It may even accentuate them.

References

M. S. Ahluwalia, "Inequality, Poverty and Development," *Journal of Development Economics,* Vol. 3, September 1976, pp. 307–42.

M. S. Ahluwalia, N. Carter, and H. Chenery, "Growth and Poverty in Developing Countries," Ch. 11 in H. Chenery, *Structural Change and Development Policy,* Oxford, Oxford University Press, 1979.

M. S. Ahluwalia and H. Chenery, "The Economic Framework," in H. Chenery et al. *Redistribution with Growth,* Oxford, Oxford University Press, 1974.

J. Edelman and H. Chenery, "Aid and Income Distribution," in *The New International Economic Order: The North–South Debate,* J. N. Bhagwati, (ed.), Cambridge, Mass., M.I.T. Press, 1977.

C. R. Frank and R. C. Webb (eds.), *Income Distribution and Growth in the Less Developed Countries,* Princeton, N.J., Princeton University Press, 1977, chapter 2.

D. Jorgensen and M. Nishimizu, "U.S. and Japanese Economic Growth, 1952–74: An International Comparison," *Economic Journal,* Vol. 88, December 1978, pp. 707–26.

Simon Kuznets, "Economic Growth and Income Inequality," *American Economic Review,* Vol. 45, March 1955, pp. 1–28.

Pitambar Pant, "Perspective of Development (1961–1976): Implications of Planning for a Minimum Level of Living," reprinted in T. N. Srinivasan and P. K. Bardhan, *Poverty and Income Distribution in India,* Statistical Publishing Society, Calcutta, India, 1974.

Dudley Seers, "Cuba" in Chenery et al., *Redistribution with Growth,* Oxford, Oxford University Press, 1974.

Paul Streeten, "Basic Needs: Premises and Promises," *Journal of Policy Modeling 1,* 1979, pp. 136–46.

Paul Streeten and Shahid Javed Burki, "Basic Needs: Some Issues," *World Development,* Vol. 6, March 1978, pp. 411–21.

I.C. COUNTRY PERFORMANCE

I.C.1. Twenty-Five Years of Development*

Any attempt to evaluate the post-1945 development experience needs first to recognize the change in objectives over this period. In recent years, there has been a sharp shift in emphases. It is now considered that maximization of the gross national product (GNP) per capita is too narrow an objective; aims related to the reduction of poverty also need to be considered, such as improving income distribution, increasing employment, and fulfilling basic needs.

GROWTH IN GNP PER CAPITA

Up to 1950 there had been little serious thought about the growth and development prospects of what were then called the "backward areas." The few people who had given the matter some thought did not have high

*From David Morawetz, "Twenty-five Years of Economic Development," *Finance & Development,* September 1977, pp. 10–13. Reprinted by permission.

hopes. After all, the industrialized countries, in their long period of economic growth unparalleled in human history, had managed to increase per capita income by only about 2 percent per annum. There was no reason to expect that the so-called "underdeveloped countries," many of which had experienced no growth for millenia, would do any better.

The GNP per capita of the developing countries grew at an average of 3.4 percent per annum during 1950–75, or 3.0 percent if the People's Republic of China is excluded (see Table 1). This was faster than either the developed or the developing nations had grown in any comparable period prior to 1950, and exceeded both offical goals and private expectations.

This high average rate masks a wide diversity of performance. On the one hand, nine countries, with a combined 1975 population of about 930 million people, grew at an average rate of 4.2 percent or better for the full period (Table 2), while a second group of nine countries with 220 million people grew

TABLE 1. GNP per Capita and Its Growth Rate, by Regions, 1950–75

Region	Population 1975 (in millions)	GNP per Capita		
		In 1974 Dollars		Growth Rate 1950–75 (in percent per annum)
		1950	1975	
Africa	384	170	308	2.4
China, People's Rep. of	820	113	320	4.2
East Asia	312	130	341	3.9
Latin America	304	495	944	2.6
Middle East	81	460	1,660	5.2
South Asia	830	85	132	1.7
Developing countries[a]	2,732	160	375	3.4
Developed countries[b]	654	2,378	5,238	3.2

[a]If the People's Republic of China is excluded, the line for developing countries reads: 1,912, 187, 400, 3.0
[b]All OECD members except Greece, Portugal, Spain, and Turkey.

45

TABLE 2. GNP per Capita and Its Growth Rate, Selected Countries, 1950–75

Country	Population 1975 (in millions)	GNP per Capita		
		In 1974 Dollars		Growth Rate 1950–75 (in percent per annum)
		1950	1975	
Eight most populous countries				
China, People's Rep. of	820	113	320	4.2
India	610	95	139	1.5
Indonesia	132	103	169	2.0
Brazil	307	373	927	3.7
Bangladesh	79	105[a]	103	−0.6[b]
Nigeria	75	150	287	2.6
Pakistan	69	86[a]	131	3.2[b]
Mexico	60	562	1,092	2.7
Nine fastest-growing countries[c]				
Libya	2	786[d]	4,675	7.4
Iraq	11	283	1,180	5.9
China, Rep. of	16	224	817	5.3
Korea	34	146	504	5.1
Iran	34	384	1,321	5.1
Hong Kong	4	470	1,584	5.0
Jamaica	2	376	1,185	4.7
Israel	3	1,090	3,287	4.5
China, People's Rep. of	820	113	320	4.2
Nine slowest-growing countries[c,e]				
Rwanda	4	119	81	−1.6
Burundi	4	117	91	−1.0
Upper Volta	6	99	87	−0.5
Madagascar	9	195	180	−0.3
Central African Empire	2	202	212	0.2
Bolivia	6	244	290	0.7
Chile	11	596	700	0.7
Ghana	10	354	427	0.7
Honduras	3	272	322	0.7

Source: World Bank.

[a]1960.

[b]1960–75.

[c]Countries with population of 1 million or more.

[d]Real growth rates (and hence estimated 1950 GNP per capita figures) for oil exporting countries depend heavily on the choice of base years in calculation of constant price national accounts. For example, in 1950 prices, Libya's 1950 GNP per capita was probably less than $100.

[e]Excluding Cambodia (growth rate, −1.4 percent), Vietnam (0.5 percent), and the Lao People's Democratic Republic (0.3 percent).

at between 3 and 4 percent. On the other hand, the large, poor countries of South Asia and many countries in Africa, with a total of some 1.1 billion people, grew in per capita income terms by less than 2 percent per annum between 1950 and 1975. That is to say, although it is true that for some 33 percent of the people of the developing world per capita income roughly trebled during the past twenty-five years, it is also true that for another 40 percent the increase during the same period in measured per capita income has been only one or two dollars per year.

The increasing disparity between richer and poorer developing countries can be seen from two different perspectives. At the regional level, in 1950 the average per capita income of the richest regions (Latin America and the Middle East) was five or six times that of the poorest (South Asia); whereas by 1975 the multiple for the Middle East over South Asia had risen to 13, while that for Latin America was seven. At the individual country level, the ranking of 80 developing countries by GNP per capita remained remarkably stable between 1950 and 1975, while the absolute disparity between the richest and the poorest developing countries increased by a factor of about three. Note, though, that the relationship between initial regional per capita income and subsequent regional growth rate is by no means consistent: Latin America, initially rich, grew relatively slowly, while the People's Republic of China and East Asia, initially poor, grew quickly (Table 1). Similarly, at the country level, the correlation between the initial GNP per capita and the subsequent growth rate is weak.

POVERTY REDUCTION

A major problem with using growth in average per capita income as the sole index of development is that it grants equal importance to each extra dollar of income, whether it is earned by a rich or a poor person. Ideally, one would like to measure growth in weighted per capita income, where each extra dollar is multiplied by the social wel-fare weight attached to its recipient. The welfare weights would presumably be heavier for the poor than for the rich, and may also vary by location, occupation, or other criteria. Unfortunately, since there is seldom agreement on the precise welfare weights to be applied to different income recipients, the ideal cannot usually be calculated in practice. For this reason, interest has recently returned to various second-best, partial welfare indicators, which may be used in conjunction with data on average per capita income to examine the extent to which growth has improved the economic condition of the poor. Some of these supplementary indicators relate to employment, others to income distribution, and a third set to fulfillment of basic needs.

Most people in developing countries work within the family or are self-employed in agriculture, services, and informal industry, where the concept of a "job" is much less clear than in the formal sector. Furthermore, in the absence of unemployment compensation, only the relatively well-off can afford to be openly unemployed. Therefore, in most developing countries, the employment problem expresses itself more in terms of underemployment—working too few hours or with excessively low productivity—than in open unemployment.

What has been happening to rates of underemployment in developing countries over time? We do not know, and, what is more, it may not be possible to know. A meaningful "percentage of underemployment" is by definition almost impossible to estimate.

The only data maintained over a period which *are* available are on unemployment in a small number of countries for the period between 1960 and 1974. These data are deficient for two principal reasons. They do not measure the concept that is needed, which is unemployment *plus* underemployment. And even what they do measure, they do not always measure accurately or consistently. For example, Indian labor force surveys often place urban open unemployment at around 3 percent. But after making a series of simple and apparently quite reasonable adjustments, David Turnham concludes in *The Employ-*

ment Problem of the Less Developed Countries (OECD, 1971), that the true rate may be closer to 6 to 9 percent.

For what they are worth, the data which are available for nine countries in Latin America, three countries in East Asia, and one nation each in Africa and the Middle East show no clear trend toward a worsening of open unemployment. In most of these countries, open unemployment fluctuated around a fairly constant trend, while in Korea and the Republic of China it clearly declined. But note that no appropriate data are available for the poor, heavily populated South Asian countries, and that nothing at all can be said with certainty about the trend in underemployment.

INCOMES OF THE POOR

Increasing employment is not an objective in itself. Rather, what is wanted is to raise the incomes of the poor, both relative to those of the rich and in absolute terms.

In quite a large number of countries the share of the poorest people in GNP seems to have either increased or at least remained fairly constant over time. This group includes fast-growing, market-oriented countries like Iran, Israel, Korea, the Republic of China, and Singapore, as well as countries which have consciously concerned themselves with income distribution like the People's Republic of China and the slower-growing Sri Lanka. It also includes Costa Rica, El Salvador, and possibly Colombia. By contrast, in a second, also quite large, group, including Argentina, Brazil, India, Mexico, Panama, Peru, the Philippines, and Puerto Rico, the share of the poorest people seems to have declined over time.

There seems to be no clear relationship between the rate of economic growth and either (1) the degree of income inequality at a point in time, or (2) the trend of inequality over time. Fast growers include both equal and unequal societies which have been growing more, and less, unequal. The same is true also of slow growers.

Are there countries in which the poor have experienced an absolute worsening in their situation over time? Unfortunately, the available data do not allow an unambiguous answer to this question. Among the largest developing countries, only in the People's Republic of China and possibly Mexico do the poor seem to have clearly become better off. In Bangladesh, Brazil, India, Indonesia, and Pakistan the matter is in dispute, with alternate sets of evidence—and sometimes even a single set of evidence—yielding different conclusions to different investigators.

BASIC NEEDS

In terms of poverty reduction, even better incomes are only a means to an end. The ultimate goal is access of the poor to the goods and services required to fulfill their basic needs: food, health care, education, and the like.

The amount of food available per capita seems to have increased relatively little in developing countries since 1950. The problem does not seem to be basically one of supply. The existing "calorie deficit" (representing the level below minimum nutritional needs), 25 million tons, represents no more than 2 percent of current world production of foodgrains. The main problem seems to be one of effective demand—how to get purchasing power to the undernourished. Distribution is an obstacle, too. Even when large supplies of food are available in one area, distant and scattered rural communities often do not receive their share.

Health standards, however, in the developing countries have improved significantly over the past twenty-five years, if life expectancy is taken as the best single indicator of national health levels. Life expectancy, the average life span of people in the developing countries, has increased in the past two decades by as much as it rose in a century in the industrialized nations. Today, average life expectancy in the developing countries stands at 50 years, a level attained in Western Europe only at the beginning of this century. The increases mainly reflect a sharp drop in infant mortality rates, and provide one of the strongest available indications that real standards of living have risen on a broad front in the developing world since 1950. The increases in life expectancy were due more to these general improvements in living conditions than to more closely defined medical improvements. Nevertheless, there was also considerable progress in medical services especially in control of communicable diseases. By 1975 smallpox and plague had been virtually eradicated, while malaria—which seemed to have been controlled by 1966 but subsequently rebounded—and cholera undoubtedly kill fewer people today than they did in 1950.

In education, too, significant progress has been achieved. Between 1950 and 1970 the number of pupils in primary schools in developing countries trebled, reaching 200 million. During the same period, the number of students in secondary and tertiary education increased sixfold, reaching 42 million and 6 million, respectively. The increases in attendance rates are equally remarkable if viewed in percentage terms, and were widely shared throughout Africa, Asia, and Latin America. The proportion of developing country adults who are literate, which stood at about 40 percent in 1960, had risen to 50 percent by 1970, although, again, there are disparities among individual countries.

MANY ROADS, MANY QUESTIONS

What can be learned from the experience of the past twenty-five years and what are some of the questions suggested by it? Clearly, there is more than one feasible route to equitable growth and development. Some countries have succeeded by pursuing market-oriented, outward-looking strategies, relying on entrepreneurial skills (Hong Kong, Korea, the Republic of China) or physical resources (oil exporting countries) as the keys to growth. By contrast, the People's Republic of China has followed a socialist, inward-looking strategy based on considerable natural resources, ideology, and highly effective social organization.

Does this mean that each country can se-

lect its own socioeconomic system from the full menu of choices? Or do large, poor countries which wish to eradicate poverty necessarily have to follow a route like that of the People's Republic of China? What about small trade-dependent economies: Do they have any realistic option other than to follow the Republic of China-Korea route? A number of smaller countries—Burma, Cuba, North Korea, Sri Lanka, and Tanzania, to name a few—have tried to follow basic needs-oriented paths; to what extent have they succeeded? In general, is it possible to follow a strategy oriented toward income equality and toward the fulfillment of basic needs without closing off the economy from foreign trade as the People's Republic of China and some of the smaller socialist countries have done? If the economy is not closed off, how can talented people be prevented from leaving (other than by distorting the domestic income distribution) and how can the generation and adaptation of technology be fostered?

Some countries seem to have been successful in leaving day-to-day decision making to lower-level local management, in spite of strongly centralized political and economic systems. By contrast, in a number of countries in which the central government got itself involved in detailed decision making at a micro level—whether by production- and import-licensing in a market-oriented system or by detailed planning and programming in a socialized one—the result was often an initiative-stifling combination of red tape, bureaucratic delays, and arbitrary decisions.

Whatever the underlying political philosophy, a decentralized system of decision making relies heavily for success on the response of the local-level functionaries to centrally determined incentives. In a market-oriented system these functionaries are the entrepreneurs and managers; in a socialized one they are the local officials. Many developing countries (the striking exceptions being some African countries) seem to have an abundant supply of petty entrepreneurs—small traders and "informal sector" producers—but only in a few cases are there significant numbers of larger-scale operators. What are the factors that determine the growth of medium-scale to large-scale entrepreneurship? And what kind of policy intervention can help to foster it? Although something is already known on the subject, more work might also profitably be done on the ways in which socialized systems have succeeded (and failed) in the parallel task of motivating local officials to take initiatives and make socially appropriate decisions.

GROWTH AND POVERTY

Although it is true that some of the poorest people in some developing countries may have become worse off in absolute terms since 1950, the blame for this state of affairs can hardly be laid on economic growth. Countries in which many poor people have, or may have, become worse off include at least as many fast growers as slow growers. For poor, heavily populated nations like Bangladesh, India, Indonesia, and Pakistan, *only* long-term, sustained growth of per capita income, equitably distributed, offers the majority of the people any hope of economic advancement.

Many of the countries which experienced rapid, equitably distributed growth between 1950 and 1975 began the period with relatively equal asset and income distributions; many of those that experienced rapid, inequitably distributed growth began with sharply unequal distributions. This suggests that the *initial* distribution of assets and incomes may be an important determinant of the *trend* in inequality. Such a hypothesis makes some intuitive sense. People who own assets—whether physical or human capital—are best placed to profit once growth begins. Furthermore, both historical and simulative evidence suggest that the most powerful determinant of income distribution

is the underlying structure of the economy; once growth is taking place, it seems to be difficult to effectively redistribute income through the use of "marginal" instruments such as taxation and public employment.

These combined observations have potentially powerful implications: in particular, if equality is to be a short- to medium-term goal, it simply may not be possible to "grow first and redistribute later." Rather, it may be necessary to tackle asset redistribution as a first priority by whatever means are at hand.

POLITICS AND EXPECTATIONS

The historical experience suggests that political stability of whatever ilk may be an important and underrated determinant of economic growth. Most of the countries which grew fastest during the period were stable, many of the slowest growers conspicuously were not. Bolivia provides an interesting example in this regard. To oversimplify the case: up to 1970 Bolivia had had 184 governments in 146 years, and its growth rate for 1950–70 was one of the slowest in the developing world. Then a period of unusual political stability began—and after a short period the growth rate accelerated significantly.

There also seems to be a tendency for expectations to rise in step with development performance. "Upper-limit" projections have been surpassed, "almost unmeetable challenges" have been met; yet everywhere there is dissatisfaction. It might be useful to bear in mind that first-round successes (health improvements, the Green Revolution) very often lead to second-round problems (population explosion, worsening of rural income distribution), and that even in the best of cases, development is a long, slow process measured in generations rather than decades.

Comment
By viewing development as a set of interrelated changes in the structure of an economy, several studies have attempted to measure these structural changes and to provide an empirical basis for models of development. Outstanding quantitative analyses of changes in the economic structure of LDCs are: Hollis Chenery and Moises Syrquin, *Patterns of Develop-*

ment, 1950–1970 (1975) and Hollis Chenery, *Structural Change and Development Policy* (1970). These studies try to establish testable links between empirically derived development patterns and the deductive results of development theory.

Intercountry and intertemporal comparisons of economic structure are expected to yield more or less regular or "normal" patterns of changes in economic structure as per capita income increases. Chenery and Syrquin examine 10 types of structural characteristics that provide the dependent variables of the statistical analysis: investment, government revenue, education, domestic demand, production, foreign trade, labor allocation, urbanization, demographic transition, and income distribution. Ordinary least squares regressions specify all the structural characteristics as a function of per capita GNP, population, net resource inflow, and a time trend. The regression results are used to present the normal variation in the different measures of economic structure with changes in per capita income between $100 and $1,000 (at 1964 prices). Most of the processes can be described by S-shaped curves, having asymptotes at low and high levels of income. The periods of more rapid change, however, occur at different levels of income for different processes. Cross-section patterns are also compared with time series experience.

Comment

The statistical record of country performance can be documented from World Bank reports for individual developing countries; World Bank's *World Development Report* (annual); United Nations *Economic Surveys* of the regional commissions; *Annual U.N. Yearbooks on National Accounts, Demography, Trade;* and the *Annual Report and World Economic Outlook* of the International Monetary Fund.

The statistics should be interpreted in light of Simon Kuznets, "Problems in Comparing Recent Growth Rates for Developed and Less Developed Countries," *Economic Development and Cultural Change* (January 1972), and the references to Kravis and his associates (cited on p. 10).

EXHIBIT I.4. Basic Indicators

	Population (millions) Mid-1981	Area (thousands of square kilometers)	GNP per Capita		Average Annual Rate of Inflation (percent)		Adult Literacy (percent) 1980	Life Expectancy at Birth (years) 1981
			Dollars 1981	Average Annual Growth (percent) 1960–81	1960–70	1970–81		
Low-income economies	**2,210.5 t^a**	**31,020 t**	**270 w^b**	**2.9 w**	**3.5 m^c**	**11.2 m**	**52 w**	**58 w**
China and India	**1,681.5 t**	**12,849 t**	**280 w**	**3.5 w**	**—**	**—**	**56 w**	**61 w**
Other low-income	**529.0 t**	**18,171 t**	**240 w**	**0.8 w**	**3.3 m**	**11.6 m**	**40 w**	**50 w**
1 Kampuchea, Dem.	—	181	—	—	3.8	—	—	—
2 Bhutan	1.3	47	80	0.1	—	—	—	45
3 Lao, PDR	3.5	237	80	—	—	—	44	43
4 Chad	4.5	1,284	110	−2.2	4.6	7.4	15	43
5 Bangladesh	90.7	144	140	0.3	3.7	15.7	26	48
6 Ethiopia	32.0	1.222	140	1.4	2.1	4.1	15	46
7 Nepal	15.0	141	150	0.0	7.7	9.3	19	45
8 Burma	34.1	677	190	1.4	2.7	10.7	66	54
9 Afghanistan	16.3	648	—	—	11.9	5.0	20	37
10 Mali	6.9	1,240	190	1.3	5.0	9.7	10	45

EXHIBIT I.4. (*Continued*)

	Population (millions) Mid–1981	Area (thousands of square kilometers)	GNP per Capita		Average Annual Rate of Inflation (percent)		Adult Literacy (percent) 1980	Life Expectancy at Birth (years) 1981
			Dollars 1981	Average Annual Growth (percent) 1960–81	1960–70	1970–81		
11 Malawi	6.2	118	200	2.7	2.4	10.3	25	44
12 Zaire	29.8	2,345	210	−0.1	29.9	35.3	55	50
13 Uganda	13.0	236	220	−0.6	3.2	41.2	52	48
14 Burundi	4.2	28	230	2.4	2.8	11.6	25	45
15 Upper Volta	6.3	274	240	1.1	1.3	9.5	5	44
16 Rwanda	5.3	26	250	1.7	13.1	13.4	50	46
17 India	690.2	3,288	260	1.4	7.1	8.1	36	52
18 Somalia	4.4	638	280	−0.2	4.5	12.6	60	39
19 Tanzania	19.1	945	280	1.9	1.8	11.9	79	52
20 Viet Nam	55.7	330	—	—	—	—	87	63
21 China	991.3	9,561	300	5.0	—	—	69	67
22 Guinea	5.6	246	300	0.2	1.5	4.6	20	43
23 Haiti	5.1	28	300	0.5	4.0	10.0	23	54
24 Sri Lanka	15.0	66	300	2.5	1.8	13.1	85	69
25 Benin	3.6	113	320	0.6	1.9	9.4	28	50
26 Central African Rep.	2.4	623	320	0.4	4.1	12.6	33	43
27 Sierra Leone	3.6	72	320	0.4	—	12.2	15	47
28 Madagascar	9.0	587	330	−0.5	3.2	10.6	50	48
29 Niger	5.7	1,267	330	−1.6	2.1	12.2	10	45
30 Pakistan	84.5	804	350	2.8	3.3	13.1	24	50
31 Mozambique	12.5	802	—	—	—	—	33	—
32 Sudan	19.2	2,506	380	−0.3	3.7	15.9	32	47
33 Togo	2.7	57	380	2.5	1.3	8.9	18	48
34 Ghana	11.8	239	400	−1.1	7.6	36.4	—	54
Middle-income economies	**1,128.4** *t*	**41,108** *t*	**1,500** *w*	**3.7** *w*	**3.0** *m*	**13.1** *m*	**65** *w*	**60** *w*
Oil exporters	506.5 *t*	15,036 *t*	1,250 *w*	3.8 *w*	3.0 *m*	13.8 *m*	58 *w*	57 *w*
Oil importers	621.9 *t*	26,072 *t*	1,670 *w*	3.7 *w*	3.0 *m*	13.0 *m*	72 *w*	63 *w*
Lower middle-income	**663.7** *t*	**19,302** *t*	**850** *w*	**3.4** *w*	**2.8** *m*	**11.1** *m*	**59** *w*	**57** *w*
35 Kenya	17.4	583	420	2.9	1.6	10.2	47	56
36 Senegal	5.9	196	430	−0.3	1.7	7.9	10	44
37 Mauritania	1.6	1,031	460	1.5	2.1	9.0	17	44
38 Yemen Arab Rep.	7.3	195	460	5.5	—	15.6	21	43
39 Yemen, PDR	2.0	333	460	—	—	—	40	46
40 Liberia	1.9	111	520	1.2	1.9	8.9	25	54
41 Indonesia	149.5	1,919	530	4.1	—	20.5	62	54
42 Lesotho	1.4	30	540	7.0	2.7	10.5	52	52
43 Bolivia	5.7	1,099	600	1.9	3.5	23.0	63	51
44 Honduras	3.8	112	600	1.1	2.9	9.1	60	59
45 Zambia	5.8	753	600	0.0	7.6	8.4	44	51
46 Egypt	43.3	1,001	650	3.5	2.6	11.1	44	57
47 El Salvador	4.7	21	650	1.5	0.5	10.8	62	63
48 Thailand	48.0	514	770	4.6	1.8	10.0	86	63
49 Philippines	49.6	300	790	2.8	5.8	13.1	75	63

EXHIBIT I.4. (*Continued*)

	Population (millions) Mid–1981	Area (thousands of square kilometers)	GNP per Capita		Average Annual Rate of Inflation (percent)		Adult Literacy (percent) 1980	Life Expectancy at Birth (years) 1981
			Dollars 1981	Average Annual Growth (percent) 1960–81	1960– 70	1970– 81		
50 Angola	7.8	1,247	—	—	—	—	—	42
51 Papua New Guinea	3.1	462	840	2.5	4.0	8.6	32	51
52 Morocco	20.9	447	860	2.4	2.0	8.2	28	57
53 Nicaragua	2.8	130	860	0.6	1.8	14.2	90	57
54 Nigeria	87.6	924	870	3.5	4.0	14.2	34	49
55 Zimbabwe	7.2	391	870	1.0	1.3	10.1	69	55
56 Cameroon	8.7	475	880	2.8	4.2	10.6	—	50
57 Cuba	9.7	115	—	—	—	—	95	73
58 Congo, People's Rep.	1.7	342	1,110	1.0	5.9	11.8	—	60
59 Guatemala	7.5	109	1,140	2.6	0.3	10.4	—	59
60 Peru	17.0	1,285	1,170	1.0	10.4	34.3	80	58
61 Ecuador	8.6	284	1,180	4.3	6.1	14.1	81	62
62 Jamaica	2.2	11	1,180	0.8	4.0	16.8	90	71
63 Ivory Coast	8.5	322	1,200	2.3	2.8	13.0	35	47
64 Dominican Rep.	5.6	49	1,260	3.3	2.1	9.1	67	62
65 Mongolia	1.7	1,565	—	—	—	—	—	64
66 Colombia	26.4	1,139	1,380	3.2	11.9	22.4	81	63
67 Tunisia	6.5	164	1,420	4.8	3.6	8.2	62	61
68 Costa Rica	2.3	51	1,430	3.0	1.9	15.9	90	73
69 Korea, Dem. Rep.	18.7	121	—	—	—	—	—	66
70 Turkey	45.5	781	1,540	3.5	5.6	32.7	60	62
71 Syrian Arab Rep.	9.3	185	1,570	3.8	2.6	12.0	58	65
72 Jordan	3.4	98	1,620	—	—	—	70	62
73 Paraguay	3.1	407	1,630	3.5	3.1	12.4	84	65
Upper middle-income	**464.7** *t*	**21,806** *t*	**2,490** *w*	**4.2** *w*	**3.0** *m*	**18.6** *m*	**76** *w*	**65** *w*
74 Korea, Rep. of	38.9	98	1,700	6.9	17.5	19.8	93	66
75 Iran, Islamic Rep. of	40.1	1,648	—	—	−0.5	20.1	50	58
76 Iraq	13.5	435	—	—	1.7	—	—	57
77 Malaysia	14.2	330	1,840	4.3	−0.3	7.4	60	65
78 Panama	1.9	77	1,910	3.1	1.6	7.6	85	71
79 Lebanon	2.7	10	—	—	1.4	14.6	—	66
80 Algeria	19.6	2,382	2,140	3.2	2.7	13.4	35	56
81 Brazil	120.5	8,512	2,220	5.1	46.1	42.1	76	64
82 Mexico	71.2	1,973	2,250	3.8	3.5	19.1	83	66
83 Portugal	9.8	92	2,520	4.8	3.0	17.0	78	72
84 Argentina	28.2	2,767	2,560	1.9	21.4	134.2	93	71
85 Chile	11.3	757	2,560	0.7	33.0	164.6	—	68
86 South Africa	29.5	1221	2,770	2.3	3.0	12.8	—	63
87 Yugoslavia	22.5	256	2,790	5.0	12.6	19.4	85	71
88 Uruguay	2.9	176	2,820	1.6	51.1	60.2	94	71
89 Venezuela	15.4	912	4,220	2.4	1.3	12.5	82	68
90 Greece	9.7	132	4,420	5.4	3.2	14.8	—	74
91 Hong Kong	5.2	1	5,100	6.9	2.4	18.4	90	75
92 Israel	4.0	21	5,160	3.6	6.2	45.5	—	73

EXHIBIT I.4. (*Continued*)

	Population (millions) Mid–1981	Area (thousands of square kilometers)	GNP per Capita Dollars 1981	GNP per Capita Average Annual Growth (percent) 1960–81	Average Annual Rate of Inflation (percent) 1960–70	Average Annual Rate of Inflation (percent) 1970–81	Adult Literacy (percent) 1980	Life Expectancy at Birth (years) 1981
93 Singapore	2.4	1	5,240	7.4	1.1	5.2	83	72
94 Trinidad and Tobago	1.2	5	5,670	2.9	3.2	18.7	95	72
High-income oil exporters	**15.0 *t***	**4,012 *t***	**13,460 *w***	**6.2 *w***	**—**	**18.2 *m***	**32 *w***	**57 *w***
95 Libya	3.1	1,760	8,450	4.7	5.2	17.3	—	57
96 Saudi Arabia	9.3	2,150	12,600	7.8	—	24.3	25	55
97 Kuwait	1.5	18	20,900	−0.4	—	18.2	60	70
98 United Arab Emirates	1.1	84	24,660	—	—	—	56	63
Industrial market economies	**719.5 *t***	**30,935 *t***	**11,120 *w***	**3.4 *w***	**4.3 *m***	**9.9 *m***	**99 *w***	**75 *w***
99 Ireland	3.4	70	5,230	3.1	5.2	14.2	98	73
100 Spain	38.0	505	5,640	4.2	8.2	16.0	—	74
101 Italy	56.2	301	6,960	3.6	4.4	15.7	98	74
102 New Zealand	3.3	269	7,700	1.5	3.6	12.9	99	74
103 United Kingdom	56.0	245	9,110	2.1	4.1	14.4	99	74
104 Japan	117.6	372	10,080	6.3	5.1	7.4	99	77
105 Austria	7.6	84	10,210	4.0	3.7	6.1	99	73
106 Finland	4.8	337	10,680	3.6	6.0	12.0	100	75
107 Australia	14.9	7,687	11,080	2.5	3.1	11.5	100	74
108 Canada	24.2	9,976	11,400	3.3	3.1	9.3	99	75
109 Netherlands	14.2	41	11,790	3.1	5.4	7.6	99	76
110 Belgium	9.9	31	11,920	3.8	3.6	7.3	99	73
111 France	54.0	547	12,190	3.8	4.2	9.9	99	76
112 United States	229.8	9,363	12,820	2.3	2.9	7.2	99	75
113 Denmark	5.1	43	13,120	2.6	6.4	10.0	99	75
114 Germany, Fed. Rep.	61.7	249	13,450	3.2	3.2	5.0	99	73
115 Norway	4.1	324	14,060	3.5	4.4	8.8	99	76
116 Sweden	8.3	450	14,870	2.6	4.3	10.0	99	77
117 Switzerland	6.4	41	17,430	1.9	4.4	4.8	99	76
East European nonmarket economies	**380.8 *t***	**23,422 *t***	**—**	**—**	**—**	**—**	**99 *w***	**72 *w***
118 Albania	2.8	29	—	—	—	—	—	70
119 Hungary	10.7	93	2,100	5.0	—	2.9	99	71
120 Romania	22.5	238	2,540	8.2	−0.2	—	98	71
121 Bulgaria	8.9	111	—	—	—	—	—	73
122 Poland	35.9	313	—	—	—	—	98	73
123 USSR	268.0	22,402	—	—	—	—	100	72
124 Czechoslovakia	15.3	128	—	—	—	—	—	72
125 German Dem. Rep.	16.7	108	—	—	—	—	—	73

Source: World Bank, *World Development Report, 1983*, pp. 148–9.

[a] Indicates a total (*t*).

[b] Indicates a weighted average (*w*).

[c] Indicates a median value (*m*).

EXHIBIT I.5. Population, GNP, and GNP per Capita: Shares, Relationships, and Growth, 1955–1980

Country group	Share in World Population		Share in World GNP[a]		Per Capita GNP in Current Prices as Percentage of U.S. GNP		Per Capita GNP in Constant 1980 Dollars	
	1953	1980	1955	1980	1955	1980	1955	1980
All developing countries	68.1	73.6	20.7	21.5	4.5	6.4	340	730
Low-income	44.7	47.1	8.1	4.8	2.7	2.2	160	260
China	22.0	22.2	4.7	2.5	3.2	2.5	160	290
India	14.4	15.2	2.2	1.6	2.3	2.2	170	260
Other	8.3	9.7	1.2	0.7	2.1	1.7	140	190
Middle-income	23.4	26.5	12.6	16.7	8.1	13.7	700	1,580
Major exporters of manufactures	7.1	7.3	5.1	7.7	10.7	22.9	1,050	2,650
Other oil importers	6.7	8.0	3.8	4.0	8.4	10.9	600	1,260
Oil exporters	9.6	11.2	3.7	5.0	5.8	9.7	500	1,120
High-income oil exporters	0.2	0.3	0.1	1.4	8.1	95.8	4,900	11,080
Industrial nonmarket economies	12.4	10.7	8.6	12.4	10.4	25.0	940	2,880
Industrial market economies	19.3	15.4	70.6	64.8	54.7	91.8	4,940	10,610
Europe	9.2	6.5	26.6	27.9	43.2	92.8	4,640	10,720
Japan	3.3	2.6	2.4	9.5	11.0	77.9	1,600	9,010
United States	6.0	5.1	40.3	23.7	100.0	100.0	7,030	11,560
World	100.0	100.0	100.0	100.0	14.9	21.7	1,320	2,510

Source: *World Development Report, 1982.*
[a]Evaluated at current prices and exchange rates.

EXHIBIT I.6. Growth of Population, GNP, and GNP per Capita (annual growth rates in percentages)

Indicator	1960–70	1970–75	1975	1976	1977	1978	1979(P)
Population							
Developing countries							
Low income: Asia and Pacific	2.4	2.3	2.2	2.2	2.1	2.1	2.3
Africa south of Sahara	2.5	2.7	2.7	2.7	2.7	2.8	2.9
Middle income: Africa south of Sahara	2.6	2.8	2.8	2.8	2.7	2.9	2.7
North Africa and Middle East	2.6	2.5	2.7	2.8	2.9	2.9	2.9
Asia and Pacific	2.8	2.5	2.5	2.4	2.5	2.1	2.2
Latin America and Caribbean	2.8	2.7	2.7	2.7	2.7	2.7	2.7
Europe	1.4	1.6	1.6	1.6	1.6	1.6	1.6
Total	2.4	2.4	2.4	2.4	2.3	2.3	2.5
Capital surplus oil exporters	3.0	3.3	3.5	3.5	3.5	3.6	3.2
Industrialized countries	1.0	0.9	0.8	0.5	0.6	0.6	0.5
Centrally planned economies	1.8	1.5	1.4	1.3	1.2	1.1	1.2

EXHIBIT I.6. (*Continued*)

Indicator	1960–70	1970–75	1975	1976	1977	1978	1979(P)
Gross National Product (GNP)							
Developing countries							
Low income: Asia and Pacific	3.9	3.6	7.6	4.0	6.2	5.8	4.0
Africa south of Sahara	4.2	3.4	−0.6	2.4	2.9	0.1	2.8
Middle income: Africa south of Sahara	4.8	5.6	1.3	5.2	2.5	3.2	4.7
North Africa and Middle East	4.9	6.2	8.0	11.6	7.3	7.2	4.0
Asia and Pacific	7.9	7.7	5.0	10.7	8.3	9.8	7.7
Latin America and Caribbean	5.6	7.1	3.2	4.9	4.3	4.8	5.6
Europe	6.9	6.2	2.1	3.5	3.8	3.4	3.7
Total	5.6	6.1	3.6	5.3	4.9	5.0	5.0
Capital surplus oil exporters	9.9	9.3	12.2	10.2	7.3	5.6	8.3[a]
Industrialized countries	5.1	3.3	−0.8	5.3	3.7	3.7	3.5
Centrally planned economies	—	6.1	6.0	4.0	5.4	4.8	3.2
Gross National Product (GNP) per capita							
Developing countries							
Low income: Asia and Pacific	1.5	1.3	5.3	1.8	4.0	3.6	1.7
Africa south of Sahara	1.8	0.7	−3.2	−0.3	0.2	−2.7	−0.1
Middle income: Africa south of Sahara	2.2	2.7	−1.4	2.3	−0.2	0.3	1.9
North Africa and Middle East	2.2	3.6	5.2	8.6	4.4	4.3	1.1
Asia and Pacific	5.0	5.1	2.4	8.1	5.4	7.6	5.4
Latin America and Caribbean	2.8	4.3	0.5	2.1	1.5	2.1	2.8
Europe	5.4	4.5	0.5	2.0	2.2	1.9	2.1
Total	3.1	3.6	1.2	2.9	2.5	2.6	2.5
Capital surplus oil exporters	6.7	5.8	8.4	6.6	3.8	2.2	4.3[a]
Industrialized countries	4.0	2.4	−1.6	4.7	3.1	3.0	3.0
Centrally planned economies	—	4.5	4.5	2.6	4.2	3.7	2.0

Source: World Bank.
P = Preliminary.
[a]Excludes Iran.

I.C.2. Korea*

Focusing on Korea, we see that her rapid growth dates from about 1963. Few observers at that time were optimistic about Korea's economic prospects, and for apparently good

*From Joel Bergsman, "Growth & Equity in Semi-Industrialized Countries," *World Bank Staff Working Paper* No. 351, 1979, pp. 22–32. Reprinted by permission.

reasons. Korea's separation from Japan and the North–South partition after World War II left South Korea a poor agricultural half-economy. The North had about half the manufacturing sector and almost all the good mines, and more importantly almost all the electric power generation capacity. After five years of independence came the Korean War, which lasted from 1950 to 1953, and devastated the South. Sixty percent of the cultivated land was laid waste, most of the limited industrial capacity was destroyed, and over one-quarter of the population were homeless refugees. Per capita income in 1953 was about $196 (1976 prices), and manufacturing was only 9 percent of GNP.[1]

Over the next ten years, from 1953 to 1963, Korean policy aimed at reconstruction, defense, and increased private consumption. U.S. aid was heavily relied on; from 1953 through 1958 aid averaged 15 percent of GNP.[2] Import-substituting industrialization in nondurable consumer goods led manufacturing growth of 11 percent per year, while agriculture was somewhat neglected and grew at about 2.5 percent per year. GNP grew at 4.6 percent per year during 1954–58, but during 1959–62 growth slowed to 3.4 percent per year[3] as the import substitution possibilities in consumer nondurable goods were exhausted, agriculture did poorly, and economic and political instability further reduced investment and growth. The industrial growth that did occur in the 1950s did, nevertheless, further increase Korea's stock of both physical and human capital.

Looking back we can see that there were some important bright spots in this mostly bleak picture of Korea in the early 1960s. Behind the shattered economy and the low-income level was a society that has an egalitarian ethos and situation, and was open to advancement by merit, with a population that was relatively well educated and achievement oriented. Two land reforms (in 1947 and 1950) and the destruction wrought by the war of 1950–53 had left almost all Koreans equally poor by 1953. This poverty was, however, the result of the preceding chaotic events; in human resources Korea was far richer than the abnormally low-income level

suggested. Widespread education was vigorously promoted by United States advisors after World War II, and continued strong in the 1953–63 decade—the literacy rate rose from 30 to over 80 percent,[4] and school attendance at all levels increased dramatically. By 1965, Korea had achieved a level of human resources above the level expected for a country with three times its GNP per capita (Harbison and Myers, pp. 31ff; cited in Adelman and Robinson p. 41).

A new military government took office in 1961. During its first year in office the strategy of Korea's growth was changed to export-oriented industrialization, a path it has followed ever since.[5] The government chose not to carry import substitution back to intermediate goods, capital goods, and consumer durables, but rather to promote continued growth of output of consumer nondurables, through export markets. While the motives of decision makers can never be completely known, participants in the process suggest that the most important factor in this turnaround was a need to earn foreign exchange. Exports had averaged a miniscule 2 percent of GNP during the 1950s, and the foreign aid that was paying for the rest of imports (11 percent of GDP) was clearly not going to keep flowing forever. Opportunities for more import substitution were seen as unprofitable, and there were no natural resources to export. So the chosen alternative was to export manufactures.

The turnaround in trade incentives was not sharp and immediate. Some measures to promote exports had already been taken in the late 1950s. In the 1961–64 period, progress was far from continuous. Devaluations were neutralized by inflation. Import liberalization was partly reversed in 1963. Special export subsidy schemes were installed, modified, and replaced by others. But in 1964 and 1965 an effective and long-lasting package was implemented by the newly elected government

[1]Edward S. Mason, Dwight H. Perkins, Kwang Suk Kum, David C. Cole, and Mahn Je Kim, *The Economic and Social Modernization of Korea: 1945–1975*, draft, 1978, chapter IV, p. 2.

[2]David Cole and Princeton Lyman, *Korean Development: The Interplay of Politics and Economics*, Harvard University Press, 1971, p. 165.

[3]Mason et al., table IV-1.

[4]Irma Adelman and Sherman Robinson, *Income Distribution Policy in Developing Countries: A Case Study of Korea*, Stanford University Press, 1978, p. 41.

[5]Mason et al., chapter IV, p 6.

of President Park Chung Hee. A sharp devaluation was supported by restrictive monetary and fiscal policies, and subsequently inflation was compensated for by devaluations. Quantitative restrictions on imports were eased, although tariffs rose. Producers for export could import raw materials free of duty, were exempted from all indirect taxes and paid reduced rates of income tax on profits earned by export, received low-interest loans, and were granted other subsidies as well. Korean producers had easy access to purchased inputs at world market prices and quality, and received world market prices for their export sales. At the same time, reduction in protection in the domestic market meant that profits were higher for exports than for domestic sales. This package continues in force, with some modifications, today.

Three other important sets of measures complemented the new trade policies. First, interest rates were raised dramatically. They reached about 10 to 20 percent in real terms during the first few years[6] and remain higher than in most other semi-industrialized countries (SICs). This sharp rise in interest rates was followed by increased flows of personal savings through financial intermediaries, providing an important source of noninflationary financing for the boom that was underway. Second, the President and the government were strongly committed to economic growth, perhaps in large part to compete with the Korean Democratic Republic to the North. As an illustration of this commitment, the President personally took part in the export promotion drive. He held monthly meetings to review achievements, to revise targets (upwards; actual exports almost always exceeded targets), and to direct the government to solve problems and ease the path for exporters.

The final, and crucial, part of the success story was the well-educated labor force that was available to work at relatively low wages.

The results were amazing. Exports rose from 3.3 percent of GNP in 1960 to 48 percent in 1977. Manufactured exports rose 51 percent per year (at current prices), from 1 percent of value added in manufacturing to 96 percent in the same period. In fact, the increase in manufactured exports accounted *directly* for 25 percent of the increase of manufacturing output during 1960–66, and for 46 percent during 1966–73. For all exports, the increase was 13 percent of the increase in GNP during 1960–66 and 35 percent during 1966–73.

Using input-output linkages to estimate direct and indirect effects combined, Kubo and Lewis (1978)[7] estimated that import substitution accounted for 21 percent of Korea's growth in total gross production during 1955–63, and none during subsequent periods. Export growth accounted for an estimated 10 percent in 1955–63, 22 percent in 1963–70, and 56 percent in 1970–73. In the last period export growth was even more important than growth in domestic demand, which is very unusual. Thus Korea is an extreme example of export led growth. And this growth was also amazing: GDP grew by 9.3 percent per year from 1960 through 1977. Agricultural output grew at 4.7 percent per year, and industry at over 17 percent per year. Aided by a decline in population growth (from 3 percent per year around 1960 to about 1.7 percent in the mid-1970s), per capita GDP in 1977 prices rose from $244 in 1960 to $820 U.S. dollars in 1977—an average annual increase of 7.4 percent.

Since the early 1960s the government's stable and strong commitment to economic growth and its pragmatic competence have been important contributors to growth. Neither conflicting goals nor inept management have been allowed to restrain actions needed for growth. Decisions are taken quickly, and if they don't work they are changed. Private-sector activities are regulated in the first instance by generalized price incentives, but particular firms that don't perform are said to find that they run into trouble with tax ex-

---

[6]Mason et al., chapter VIII, p. 47.

[7]Y. Kubo and J. Lewis, "Sources of Industrial Growth in Three Asian Countries," draft, September 19, 1978.

aminers or banks. (Financial intermediaries in Korea are controlled by the government.) Policies and targets are set by the government, but private businessmen are consulted both before and after the decisions are taken and, as already noted, the decision is changed if the desired results are not following. Many public-sector enterprises yield a profit (as they typically do not in other SICs) because they are supposed to and because when they don't their management is replaced. Many observers think that an important factor for private-sector growth (which has, after all, been the overwhelming source of GDP growth) in Korea has been the knowledge that government is committed to help, and the fact that the government does help to achieve increased output and increased exports, at or very near to internationally competitive costs.

But while a commitment to growth by a stable and competent government was important, the crucial aspect seems to have been the *combination* of policies and comparative advantage, together with favorable conditions in world markets. Korea's policies to export manufactures and to keep her labor cheap were the perfect complements to her lack of natural resources, modest internal market, but well-educated and willing labor force and her talents for management and organization.

Korea's record of rapid income growth is all the more interesting because of her simultaneous near-elimination of absolute poverty. Thus Korea's income distribution is among the more equal in the developing world—although it apparently has been getting less equal in the 1970s. The poorest 40 percent of all households received an estimated 16.9 percent of the national total in 1976, and the ratio of the top 20 percent share to the bottom 20 percent share was only 8 to 1. These were among the most egalitarian values measured for any LDC. Data from 1963 to 1970 show at most a small increase in inequality—remarkable in view of the rapid and highly capitalistic nature of growth during that time. The latest data (1976) show sharper increases in inequality,

but still place Korea among the more egalitarian SICs.

The overall low degree of inequality was the result of low inequality for both rural and urban incomes separately and a relatively small difference between rural and urban incomes. These were in part the result of deliberate policy designed to achieve such a goal (land reform, maintaining agriculture's terms of trade), and in part a result of certain initial conditions combined with the type of growth that took place. For Korea there was no trade-off between growth and equity; to the contrary, the same conditions and policies that produced the growth also maintained the egalitarian distributions.

Our simplified interpretation of the mechanics of that process is shown in Figure 1. We can start from the results on the bottom of the figure and trace the mechanism back to its proximate causes. The equality within the rural sector is easy to understand. The two land reforms of 1947 and 1949 gave land to virtually every rural family and established a ceiling of approximately 3 hectares on holdings. The result was that almost every family had a very small farm. This equality was maintained by: (a) continued enforcement of the 3 hectare ceiling; (b) the slowdown of population growth; and (c) the rapid absorption of labor by industry—10.7 percent per year from 1963 to 1975, one of the highest rates ever recorded in any country. These factors prevented both a reconcentration of holdings and the reformation of a large group of landless agricultural workers.

The reasons for equality within the urban sector are more complex. Before the analysis, a qualification as to fact is in order: the urban surveys on which this analysis is mostly based do not cover families with incomes above about $5,000 U.S. dollars per year.[8] Analysis of car ownership, income tax returns, and casual observation suggest that a small but growing percentage of urban families has been receiving very high incomes. Even so, the estimates of overall inequality through the early 1970s are low compared to other

[8]Mason et al., chapter XII, p. 3.

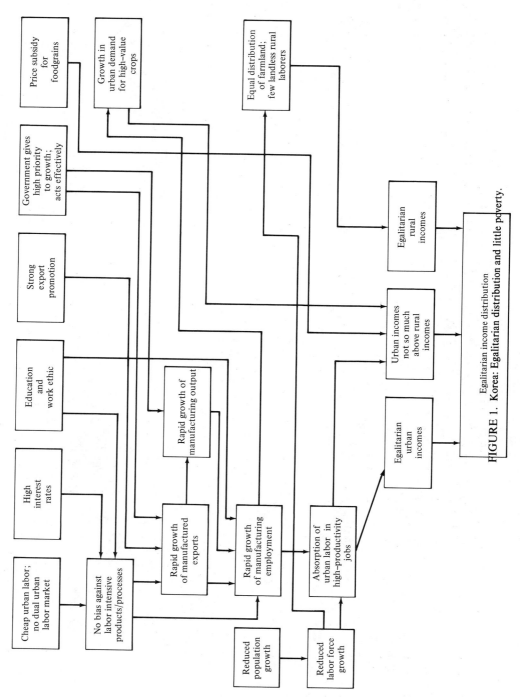

FIGURE 1. **Korea: Egalitarian distribution and little poverty.**

countries. More recently, estimated inequality has increased.

The low degree of urban poverty—the relatively high share of income received by the urban poor—had its proximate cause in the very rapid absorption of labor in higher productivity sectors and occupations. Mining and manufacturing absorbed 38 percent of the total employment increase during 1963–75. Workers did not have to become landless rural laborers, or urban shoe-shine boys, car guarders, etc., in any significant number because better jobs were available. This good performance on the creation of productive jobs was in turn the result of rapid growth in output, absence of bias against labor-intensive products or processes, and a highly educated and achievement-oriented population, willing to work very long hours under highly disciplined conditions. Korea has no effective union pressures, and no effective minimum wage. Real wages have risen slightly faster than value added per worker for the economy as a whole—7 and 6.1 percent per year, respectively. In manufacturing, real wages rose about 9 percent per year. But at least until the late 1970s wages remained low compared to productivity, and the absence of market restrictions resulted in less of the urban dualism so common in many other countries (from Brazil and Mexico to the United States!), where those workers who can get jobs in oligopolistic, high productivity, and/or unionized sectors do very well while others subsist in what has come to be called the "secondary" labor market, characterized by high turnover, low earnings, and little chance for advancement.

The third element of Korea's egalitarian distribution was the relatively small gap between urban and rural average incomes. The ratios of average rural to urban family incomes of 0.6 to 0.8 in Korea (except in bad crop years) compare favorably to countries at the other extreme such as Mexico with a ratio around 0.4 (1975 survey) or Brazil around 0.3.[9] Korea's small urban-rural income differential is also reflected in her very low ratio of value added per worker in industry to value added per worker in agriculture. This aspect of Korea's relative equality has three proximate causes. First and foremost, the rapid absorption of labor in modern urban activities that has prevented the formation of a large pool of poverty-stricken landless rural laborers. Second, government purchase of rice and barley at high prices, the rapid growth in demand for vegetables and other high-value cash crops in urban markets (caused by income gains), and the rapid shift of labor out of agriculture (which is the other side of the rapid labor absorption in industry) have kept farm prices in line with farmers' costs—whereas in many other LDCs farm output prices have fallen relative to input prices. Third, Korea's farmers are mostly literate and achievement oriented, and with government help they have enormously high productivity per hectare, comparable to Japan. Korea has no important backward rural regions, as are found in all of the SICs that still have a significant amount of absolute poverty.

Note that it was the same policies and social characteristics that promoted manufactured exports and efficient growth elsewhere in the economy that also promoted rapid labor absorption and hence helped to maintain the egalitarian income distribution.

Like almost all other SICs, Korea has *not* engaged in much redistribution of *income* through taxation. What equality there is results mainly from equality in before-tax income.

[9]Carlos Geraldo Langoni, *Distribuicao de Renda e Desenvolvimento Economico do Brasil*, Editora Expressao e Cultura, 1973, tables A.1.10 and A.1.12.

Comment

Much attention has been given to the "success stories" of the Asian foursome—Taiwan, South Korea, Singapore, and Hong Kong. Excellent studies are Walter Galenson (ed.), *Economic Growth and Structural Change in Taiwan* (1979); John C. H. Fei, Gustav Ranis, and Shirley W. Y. Kuo, *Growth with Equity: The Taiwan Case* (1979); Larry E Westphal, "The

Republic of Korea's Experience with Export-Led Industrial Development," *World Development* (March 1978); Larry E. Westphal, "The Private Sector as Principal Engine of Development: Korea," *Finance & Development* (June 1982); D. C. Cole and P. N. Lyman, *Korean Development: The Interplay of Politics and Economics* (1971); I. Adelman and S. Robinson, *Income Distribution Policy in Developing Countries: A Case Study of Korea* (1978); Edward S. Mason et al., *The Economic and Social Modernization of the Republic of Korea, 1945–75,* (1979); Bela Balassa, *The Newly Industrializing Countries in the World Economy* (1981), essays 15–18.

I.C.3. Brazil*

Up to now, Brazil's extraordinary economic progress—which led to real growth rates of 8.5 percent a year between 1965 and 1980—has sprung from a strategy to build an economy modeled on those of the Western industrial nations. This approach which has been followed by many other middle-income countries, usually with less success, has brought material well-being to a considerable portion of the population. But serious social problems persist. Malnutrition, high infant mortality, and lack of access to basic public services are still experienced by a large proportion of Brazilians.

PATTERN OF GROWTH

Despite Brazil's rapid rate of population increase, per capita gross domestic product (GDP) growth over the past 15 years has been impressive, averaging 5.7 percent. With a gross national product (GNP) equivalent to over US$230 billion (roughly $1.940 per capita) in 1980, Brazil's economy is now the world's tenth largest, roughly on a par with that of the People's Republic of China or Canada. Brazil is now the third largest agricultural exporter and the tenth largest producer of automotive vehicles.

A hint of vulnerability in the country's eco-

*From Peter T. Knight and Ricardo Moran, "Bringing the Poor into the Growth Process: The Case of Brazil," *Finance & Development*, December 1981, pp. 22–4. Reprinted by permission.

nomic performance has been its lagging primary energy production, which has grown at a rate one fourth less than that of energy consumption between 1967 and 1980 (see Table 1). The shortfall has been made up by increasing imports of petroleum and, to a much lesser extent, coal. Since 1973, petroleum-fueled growth has been maintained only at the cost of massive foreign borrowing and accelerating inflation. By 1980, petroleum imports, accounting for 83 percent of domestic petroleum consumption, absorbed almost 50 percent of total export earnings. Servicing the foreign debt required another 60 percent. Meanwhile domestic savings rates fell in both the private and public sectors. Incentives to save were eroded as interest rates increasingly lagged behind inflation over the past five years. Thus Brazil has become highly dependent on continued capital inflows and petroleum imports.

The style of Brazilian growth was an immediate outcome of the major national goal to build in Brazil a "modern" economy. Development projects often utilized the most up-to-date technologies as soon as they could be brought to Brazil. Exchange rate policy, fiscal incentives, and subsidized credit reduced the cost of capital goods, while the use of labor was taxed. With its large domestic market, Brazil was able to follow a strategy of import-substituting industrialization longer and more successfully than most other countries that have taken this route and has

TABLE 1. Growth of the Brazilian Economy, 1965–80

	1965	1980	Annual Average Rate of Change (in percent) 1965–80
Population *(in millions)*	81	119	2.6
Real GDP *(1970 prices)*	100	338	8.5
Real GDP per capita	100	231	5.7
General price index, domestic supply	100	7339	33.2
Total exports *(1970 prices)*	100	390	9.5
Total imports *(1970 prices)*	100	432	10.2
Agricultural production	100	172	3.7
Industrial production	100	400	9.7
Automotive vehicle production *(in thousands)*	185	1165	13.0
	In Million Metric Tons Petroleum Equivalent		
	1967	1980[a]	1967–80
Primary energy production	40	77	5.2
Primary energy consumption	51	122	6.8
Primary energy imports	11	44	11.0

Sources: Fundacåo Getúlio Vargas, *Conjuntura Econòmica,* December 1978, and February 1980; Fundacåo Instituto Brasileiro de Geografia e Estatistica, *Censo Demografico do Brasil 1980, Resultados Preliminares;* Instituto Brasileiro de Geografia e Estatistica, *Anuario Estatistico do Brasil, 1967;* Ministry of Mines and Energy, *National Energy Balance,* 1978.

[a]1980 figures are estimates based on projections for 1980 in *National Energy Balance, 1978,* and adjusted using 1980 trade data.

even been able to expand rapidly its exports of manufactures.

But this development strategy has required increasing amounts of investment to produce an additional unit of output. The incremental capital output ratio averaged 2.9 over the period 1965–70 and 3.0 for 1970–75. But by 1975–79 it had risen to an average of 3.9. Plant expansion often involved a high degree of automation. Capital-intensive and high-technology industries—such as petrochemicals, aircraft, and nuclear power—absorbed large amounts of capital and led to rapid increases in the demand for skilled labor that helped raise the salaries of skilled technical and managerial personnel to levels at or above those paid in much richer countries. They have not, however, created as many jobs for the unskilled.

DISTRIBUTION; EMPLOYMENT

The available evidence suggests that to some degree growth benefited the poor. Gains in absolute income levels appear to have been widespread. The distribution of consumer durables illustrates the extent of trickle-down, which has been facilitated by a rapid expansion of consumer credit. In 1976 almost 76 percent of Brazilian homes had a radio, 47 percent had a television, and 42 percent had a refrigerator. Even among the poorest third of the rural households, located mainly in the rural Northeast, Brazil's poorest region, 52 percent had a radio (although very few had either a television or refrigerator).

But the gains of the rich have been immeasurably larger than those of the poor, reflecting persistently high levels of income inequality. Available estimates suggest that, for the last 20 years or so, the richest 10 percent of families have been receiving over 50 percent of the income, while the poorest 40 percent have received well under 10 percent. Not only is the income received by the poorest 40 percent of families a very small share of the total but also the absolute amounts of income received by the households are meager. Data from the 1978 National Household Sample Survey show that in 1978 about 43 percent of Brazilian families had a total income (including income in kind) equivalent to less than about $216 per month in today's prices (or about $47 monthly per family member). Such low incomes received by so many households largely explain why life expectancy and infant mortality in Brazil are comparable to those in countries with much lower average incomes.

The large differences in the incomes earned by different population groups are reflected in correspondingly large differences in the amenities available to them in different parts of the country. In 1970, the latest year for which sufficiently detailed data are available, life expectancy at birth in the industrialized southern regions of Brazil was roughly comparable to that in many developed countries; the average life expectancy of the lowest income group in the urban areas of the central northeast states, however, at 40 years, was about the same as Ethiopia's average—a country with a per capita GNP about one-eighth of Brazil's. While average life expectancy in the Northeast increased 26 percent between 1960 and 1976, faster than for Brazil as a whole, a Northeastern child born in the latter year could still expect to live eight years less than the average Brazilian child. Data on health, nutrition, water supply, sanitation, and education tell a similar story, though rates of improvement have been quite fast in some areas, particularly water supply. (See Table 2.) Despite substantial progress over the past two decades and despite high numbers of physicians, hospital beds, educational opportunities, and so on, relative to the population—which allow Brazil to compare favorably with other countries in its income class—the quality and distribution of these services are uneven. Residents of the Southeast are generally much better supplied than those of other regions—particularly of the poverty-ridden Northeast; urban areas are much better supplied than rural areas.

To accelerate improvement in the economic welfare of the neglected groups in Brazil will require a concerted effort by the authorities to extend basic services and to redistribute incomes. The surest way for the authorities to redistribute incomes is to make more jobs available to the poor and underskilled. Rapid population growth during the past decades assures that the potential labor force will continue to grow between 2.5 and 3.0 percent until the end of the century. If the trend toward increasing labor force participation rates continues, the rate of job creation will have to increase even faster.

Over the period 1960–78, rapid economic growth expanded the number of jobs paying more than one 1970 "minimum wage" (or about $76 per month in today's prices) almost twice as fast as the working age population but roughly 30 percent slower than GDP. By 1978 such jobs were held by about half the employed labor force compared with one-third in 1960. Jobs paying more than one minimum wage held by low-skilled workers (those with four or less years of schooling), however, increased about one-third as fast as those held by workers with five or more years of formal education, 40 percent as fast as GDP, and only slightly faster than the working age population. Between 1973 and 1976, total employment of adults (aged 20 and above) outside the agricultural sector increased at 4.4 percent per year while GDP growth averaged 8.1 percent. All this information suggests that, unless Brazil's economic development strategy is altered, minimum growth rates of GDP on the order of 5 to 7 percent will be necessary in the 1980s to avoid growing social tension due to inadequate creation of jobs paying more than the minimum wage, a rather low standard that is not enough even to feed a family of five adequately except in a few rural areas of Brazil

TABLE 2. Selected Social Indicators, 1960 and 1978

	1960		1978	
	Brazil	Northeast	Brazil[a]	Northeast
	Years			
Life expectancy at birth[b]	52	42	61	53
	Deaths of infants aged 0–12 months per thousand live births			
Infant mortality[b]	123	169	89	122
	In percent of total population			
Population with access to general water networks	21	5	52	28
Population living in homes with any sanitary device (latrine, septic tank, flush toilet, and so on)	49	24	75	42
Adult literacy rate	60	40	76	56
	In percent of population aged 7–14 years			
Students in grades 1–8	57	36	94	79
	In percent of all children aged 0–17 years			
Children with second or third degree malnutrition[c]	n.a.	n.a.	21	30

Sources: Knight, Moran, et al., 1979; Fundacåo Instituto Brasileiro de Geografia e Estatistica, *Pesquisa Nacional por Amostra de Domicilios 1978;* Instituto Brasileiro de Geografia e Estatistica, *Censo Demografico do Brasil, 1960;* and United States National Academy of Sciences Committee on Population and Demography, Panel on Brazil, *Preliminary Report, 1979.*

[a]Brazil data for 1978 excludes the rural areas of the North and Center West regions, roughly 5 percent ot total population.

[b]Estimates centered on the end of 1957 and of 1973, derived from data in the 1960 demographic census and 1976 National Household Sample Survey, the latter excluding rural areas of the North and Center West regions.

[c]75 percent or less of normal body weight.

(given prevailing dietary habits), much less meet other needs.

Brazil's serious balance of payments problems, a less favorable international environment, rising energy costs, and the need to bring down the rate of inflation suggest that the sustainable rate of GDP growth in the 1980s will be in the lower half of this range. Unexpected difficulties could reduce it further. If Brazil is to continue or accelerate its social progress under these difficult conditions, a development strategy is required that increases employment generated per unit of new investment, reduces imports per unit of additional output, increases the proportion of children from low-income families obtaining the higher skills that more than four years of schooling provide, and raises the productivity and well-being of the poor through improving their health. Since decreased infant mortality, higher educational status of mothers, and increased participation of women in the labor force are known to reduce fertility, such a strategy could also help slow population growth even in the absence of an official family planning program.

A NEW STRATEGY

Many elements of such a strategy are contained in Brazil's Third National Development Plan for the years 1980–85, major objectives of which are to improve income distribution and accelerate the growth of income and employment while fighting inflation and achieving equilibrium in the balance of payments. The idea is to alter the profiles of investment and consumption, to slow imports and energy use, while creating more jobs and giving more people the opportunity to do them. The essence of the strategy is to accelerate the expansion of basic public services (through the state sector) and of basic wage goods (through the private sector).

I.C.4. Sub-Saharan Africa*

During the past two decades economic development has been slow in most of the countries of Sub-Saharan Africa. When, in the mid-1970s, the world economy experienced inflation and recession, nowhere did the crisis hit with greater impact than in this region.

The picture is not uniformly bleak. There are signs of progress throughout the continent. Vastly more Africans are in schools, and most are living longer. Roads, ports, and new cities have been built and new industries developed. Technical and managerial positions, formerly occupied by foreigners, are now held by Africans. Of the 45 countries in the region, nine posted annual growth rates of over 2.5 percent per capita between 1960 and 1979.

But for most African countries, and for a majority of the African population, the record is grim and it is no exaggeration to talk of crisis. Slow overall economic growth, sluggish agricultural performance coupled with rapid rates of population increase, and balance-of-payments and fiscal crises—these are dramatic indicators of economic trouble.

Between 1960 and 1979, per capita income in 19 countries grew by less than 1 percent per year, while during the last decade, 15 countries recorded a *negative* rate of growth of income per capita. And by the end of the 1970s, economic crises were battering even high-growth countries like Kenya, Malawi, and Ivory Coast—where per capita GNP growth had averaged an annual 2.7 percent between 1960 and 1979—compelling them to design programs, supported by the World Bank, to restructure their economies. Output per person rose more slowly in Sub-Saharan Africa than in any other part of the world, particularly in the 1970s, and it rose more slowly in the 1970s than in the 1960s (see Table 1).

The tragedy of this slow growth in the African setting is that incomes are so low and access to basic services so limited. Per capita income was $329 in 1979 (excluding Nigeria) and $411 when Nigeria is included. Death rates are the highest in the world and life expectancy is the lowest (47 years). Fifteen to twenty percent of the children die by their first birthday, and only 25 percent of the population have access to safe water. Of the 30 countries classified by the United Nations Conference on Trade and Development (UNCTAD) as the poorest in the world, 20 are African. Of the 36 countries listed in the World Bank's *World Development Report 1981* as "low income" (a per capita income of less than $370), almost two-thirds are African.

The economic crisis is especially evident in agriculture, and is reflected in output figures. Export crop production stagnated over the

*From World Bank, *Accelerated Development in Sub-Saharan Africa,* 1981, pp. 2–6. Reprinted by permission.

TABLE 1. Sub-Saharan Africa and the World: Basic Data

Countries	Population (millions) Mid–1979	GNP per Capita Average Annual Growth Rate (percent)		Per Capita Growth 1970–79 (percent)		Adult Literacy Rate (percent) 1976	Life Expectancy at Birth (years) 1979	Death Rate of Children Aged 1–4 (per thousand) 1979
		1960–70	1970–79	Agri-culture	Volume of Exports			
Sub-Saharan Africa	343.9	1.3	0.8	−0.9	−3.5	28	47	25
Low-income	187.1	1.6	−0.3	−1.1	−4.5	26	46	27
Nigeria	82.6	0.1	4.2	−2.8	−2.8	n.a.	49	22
Other middle-income	74.2	1.9	−0.5	−0.4	−3.5	34	50	22
South Asia[a]	890.5	1.5	1.5	0.0	0.6	36	52	15
All developing	3,245.2	3.5	2.7[b]	0.1	−1.5	57	58	11
Low-income	2,260.2	1.8	1.6[b]	0.1	−3.1	50	57	11
Middle-income	985.0	3.9	2.8[b]	0.6	1.9	72	61	10
All industrialized	671.2	4.1	2.5[b]	0.2	5.2	99	74	1

Source: World Bank data files.

[a]Bhutan, Bangladesh, Nepal, Burma, India, Sri Lanka, and Pakistan.

[b]1970–80.

past two decades. A 20 percent increase in production registered during the 1960s was wiped out by a decline of similar proportions in the 1970s. Consequently, Africa's share of the world market dwindled. As for food crops, while data are uncertain, they leave no doubt about general tendencies. Total food production rose by 1.5 percent per year in the 1970s, down from 2 percent in the previous decade. But since population was rising rapidly—by an annual average of 2.5 percent in the 1960s and 2.7 percent in the 1970s—food production per person was stagnant in the first decade and actually declined in the next. Imports of food grains (wheat, rice, and maize) soared—by 9 percent per year since the early 1960s—reinforcing food dependency. Food aid also increased substantially. Since 70 to 90 percent of the population earns its income from agriculture, the drop in production in this sector spelled a real income loss for many of the poorest.

The deterioration in agriculture and other internal and global factors led to widespread balance-of-payment crises in the 1970s. Cur-rent account deficits in the region as a whole rose from a modest $1.5 billion in 1970 to $8 billion in 1980. External indebtedness climbed from $6 billion to $32 billion between 1970 and 1979, and debt service increased from 6 to 12 percent of export earnings in the same period. Foreign exchange reserves, which were comfortable in 1970, fell sharply. In 1970, reserves could cover only two months' imports and by 1980 reserves had fallen even lower. Fiscal pressures also intensified in many countries, as indicated by declining real budgetary allocations for supplies and maintenance, growing imbalances between salary and nonsalary spending, and difficulties in financing local and recurrent costs of externally funded development projects.

The crises that evolved in much of the region are particularly disturbing since, during the period from 1960 to 1974, world trade and the world economy in general expanded rapidly, and many less-developed countries elsewhere experienced relatively high growth rates. Now, against a backdrop of global economic recession, the outlook for all less-developed nations—but especially for the Sub-Saharan region—is grim. Although cyclical factors may push prices of some African exports up from their low levels of the recent past, mounting energy costs, slow growth in the industrial countries (which translates into diminished markets for the developing world), and reduced growth of international trade (factors that have plagued the global economy for the last half decade) will make renewed African growth difficult.

In sum, past trends in African economic performance and continued global recession together explain the pessimistic projections for African development in the 1980s. The *World Development Report 1981,* under its most optimistic set of assumptions about the expansion of the world economy, forecasts virtually no growth in per capita income for the continent in this decade[1]; under less favorable assumptions, a negative rate of growth (-1.0 percent per year) is projected for the poorest nations in the region.

These prospects and their political, social, and economic implications are not acceptable either to the countries concerned or to the international community. There is an urgent need to understand what has gone wrong and what must be done—by African governments themselves and the concerned international community—to assure a better future for Africa's people.

SOURCES OF LAGGING GROWTH

Africa's disappointing economic performance during the past two decades reflects, in part, internal constraints based on "structural" factors that evolved from historical circumstances or from the physical environment. These include underdeveloped human resources, the economic disruption that accompanied decolonization and postcolonial consolidation, climatic and geographic fac-

[1]World Bank, *World Development Report 1981,* New York, Oxford University Press, 1981, table 1.1.

tors hostile to development, and rapidly growing population.

Growth was also affected by a set of external factors—notably adverse trends in the international economy, particularly since 1974. These include "stagflation" in the industrialized countries, higher energy prices, the relatively slow growth of trade in primary products, and—for copper and iron-ore exporters—adverse terms of trade.

The internal "structural" problems and the external factors impeding African economic growth have been exacerbated by domestic policy inadequacies, of which three are critical. First, trade and exchange-rate policies have overprotected industry, held back agriculture, and absorbed much administrative capacity. Second, too little attention has been paid to administrative constraints in mobilizing and managing resources for development; given the widespread weakness of planning, decision making, and management capacities, public sectors frequently become overextended. Third, there has been a consistent bias against agriculture in price, tax, and exchange-rate policies.

NEW PRIORITIES AND ADJUSTMENTS IN POLICY

A reordering of postindependence priorities is essential if economic growth is to accelerate. During the past two decades most African governments rightly focused on political consolidation, on the laying down of basic infrastructure (much of it tied to the goal of political integration), and on the development of human resources. Relatively less attention was paid to production. Now it is essential to give production a higher priority—without neglecting these other goals. Without a faster rate of production increase, other objectives cannot be achieved, nor can past achievements be sustained. Three major policy actions are central to any growth-oriented program: (1) more suitable trade and exchange-rate policies; (2) increased efficiency of resource use in the public sector; and (3) improvement in agricultural policies.

EXHIBIT I.7. Indexes for 18 Low-Income African Countries[a]

	1960–70	1970–77	1977–80
Population growth rate	2.5	2.7	2.9
GDP: growth rate p.a.[b]	4.1	2.9	2.8
Investment as percent of GDP[c]	18	16	16
Savings as percent of GDP[c]	12	11	16
Exports: growth rate p.a.[b]	6.2	−3.3	2.3
Imports: growth rate p.a.[b]	6.7	−2.6	−5.3
Resource gap as percent of GDP[c]	2.7	5.3	7.2
Export price index[c]	70	100	110
Import price index[c]	89	100	162
Terms of trade index[c]	79	100	68
Current account deficit as percent of GDP[c]	1.8	3.0	5.4
Debt service as percent of exports[c]	6.4	9.0	18.2
Incremental capital—output ratio	4.3	6.0	5.9
Current account deficit[c] (million $ current prices)	249	923	2,258
Gross disbursement of term loans[c] (million $ current prices)	423	1,561	3,024
Gross disbursement of concessional loans[c] (million $ current prices)	241	939	1,672
Debt service[c] (million $ current prices)	220	569	1,351

Source: World Bank.

[a]Benin, Burundi, Central African Republic, Chad, Ethiopia, Guinea, Kenya, Lesotho, Madagascar, Malawi, Mali, Niger, Rwanda, Somalia, Tanzania, Uganda, Upper Volta, Zaire.

[b]In constant prices.

[c]For terminal year.

I.C.5. China *

Three broad categories of reasons help explain why China has accomplished what it has. First, the Chinese Communist Revolution was fought in the name of and to a large extent by the poor. Revolutions, of course, have been fought in the name of many causes only to see the causes betrayed when the revolution succeeded. But in China a number of concrete steps were taken, particularly in rural areas, to ensure that the interests of the poor majority would dominate decision mak-

*From Dwight H. Perkins, "The Central Features of China's Economic Development," in Robert F. Dernberger (ed.), *China's Development Experience in Comparative Perspective*, Harvard University Press, 1980, pp. 121–33, 138–9, 146–7. Reprinted by permission.

ing in certain key areas. In most nations, in contrast, it is the rich or the more educated and organized "middle class" that dominates decision making, and it is reasonable to presume that giving the poor a major share of power would make a difference. In fact, several key features of the Chinese experience, in rural areas at least, can be understood only in these terms.

To say that the Chinese put the poor in command does not imply that all organizations in China were run by people of poor peasant origins. The key point is that cooperatives and communes were run by such people. The Politburo and other centers of power, in contrast, were manned by people of diverse origins. Even these higher-level power centers, however, saw the former poor as the main base of their political support.

Second, China has a particular authoritarian political system. Just being authoritarian does not distinguish China's politics from that of a few other less developed countries. But China is an authoritarian nation with a difference. The degree of political control over daily activities in China, whether economic or social, is far more thoroughgoing than in all but a handful of other less developed nations. The economic aspects of this phenomenon show how development is affected. China has been able to institute a system of centralized planning more complete than that in any other less developed nation except possibly North Korea. It is not that other nations have no interest in instituting a similar system; but most know that if they tried, they would bring their economies grinding to a halt. The Chinese economy has slowed down, but it has not ground to a halt, and it is worth attempting to understand why. Part of the reason, it appears, is that China's people had acquired enough experience to make the new system work. They acquired this experience over decades and even centuries; it was not an instantaneous addition in 1949.

Third, like all nations, China has its own peculiar resource and factor endowment. Much of this endowment is a reflection of China's great size in land mass and people. Equally important is that crops can be grown on only a small proportion of China's surface. China, in a very fundamental way, is a land-short nation.

Elements other than these three, of course, have also played some role in shaping China's economic development. Marxist-Leninist ideology is an important example. But the term "putting the poor in command" covers some of the essential ground of that ideology and does so with a simple clarity that cannot be achieved by reference to the many works of Marx and Lenin, not to mention Mao Tse-tung.

There are many features of China's economy that distinguish that economy from others, but several stand out. To begin with, China's economy is socialist to a degree not found in many other nations in the less developed or non-Communist world. Private ownership is confined in the main to personal household effects, much rural housing (and a little urban housing), individual savings deposits, and the right to farm small private plots equivalent to about 5 to 7 percent of the total arable land. The land in these private plots is not privately owned; only the rights to farm some small piece of land can be said to be private.

Industry, even a firm with only a few workers, is owned by the state or collectively by rural communes and brigades. Much the same is true of commerce, banking, and transport. There are small private rural markets where farmers sometimes trade the produce of their private plots, and individuals may contract to do repairs on private homes in their spare time. But these activities are a tiny fraction of the total spectrum of industry and commerce in China. In agriculture the private sector is larger than in industry because it has so far proved impossible efficiently to collectivize much vegetable and hog raising, household handicrafts, and the like. Still, three-quarters or more of farm output is handled collectively.

Only a relatively small proportion of Chinese industry is controlled soley by central planners in Peking. Even large modern plants producing precision products for national markets are placed formally under provincial and city planning authorities or under joint province-central control. Smaller plants and those producing for more localized markets are placed under planning authorities at the district and county level. . . .

At all levels, county, province, and center, planner control is exercised directly and not through manipulation of the market. Each enterprise receives a series of targets (gross value output, cost, employment, profits, and so forth) from the planners at their level. The process involves three stages and negotiation between planners and enterprise managers. Initially the planners propose broad targets, and the factory replies with what it thinks it can do to meet these targets. The center (or

TABLE 1. China's Gross Domestic Product, Selected Years (in billions of 1957 yuan)

Year	Industrial Value Added (M+)	Agricultural Value Added (A)	Services (S)	GDP
1952	20.79	35.59	17.47	73.85
1957	38.16	44.72	21.80	104.68
1962	50.15	35.30	22.84	108.29
1965	72.60	49.10	28.94	150.64
1970	106.79	59.96	37.15	203.90
1974	152.80	67.09	46.35	266.24

TABLE 2. Sectoral Shares in GDP

Year	Industry (M+)	Agriculture (A)	Services (S)	GDP
1952	.282	.482	.237	1.000
1957	.365	.427	.208	1.000
1962	.463	.326	.211	1.000
1965	.482	.326	.192	1.000
1970	.524	.294	.182	1.000
1974	.574	.252	.174	1.000

province or county) then attempts to achieve consistency between what each enterprise can do and sends the final targets back to the enterprise. The enterprise is then expected to guide its actions to surpass those targets.

Agriculture is not subject to as rigorous control by plans as industry. Plans exist, of course, and they influence which crops are planted where. But the degree of control is much looser than in industry, and plans are often backed by general controls such as price manipulation rather than physical targets enforceable by law. Because agricultural production teams are cooperatives whose members divide their net income among themselves, prices have a significant influence on decisions. Planning in agriculture, as a result, is much less complex than that in industry.

A second key feature of China's economic development is that its highly complex system works reasonably well. We do not yet have enough data to say whether China's economic system is more or less efficient than that of, say, India, Japan, or the Soviet Union. But we know that China's economy has grown and that the most complicated sector in both engineering and planning terms, namely the modern producer goods industry, has grown much more rapidly than the other sectors.

Estimates of Chinese GDP, the shares of agriculture, manufacturing, and services and growth rates are presented in Tables 1 to 3. Different assumptions would lead to slightly different results; but all the data in these tables (except services) were derived from offi-

TABLE 3. Chinese Growth Rates, in 1957 Prices (in percentages)

Period	Industry	Agriculture	GDP
1952–1957	12.9	4.7	7.2
1957–1965	8.4	1.2	4.7
1965–1970	8.0	4.1	6.2
1970–1974	9.4	2.8	6.9
1952–1974	9.5	3.4	6.2
1957–1974	8.5	2.4	5.6

cial Chinese publications or releases, and there is an increasing degree of consensus among people working on the Chinese economy that the official data, if used with care, are the best available.

Several distinguishing features of China's economy are immediately apparent from the estimates in Tables 1 to 3. First, China's gross domestic product has grown at a rate of about 6 percent a year for over two decades. Different estimation procedures might bring this rate down to 5 percent, but in either case the rate is well above the percentage increase in China's population, which is about 2 percent and falling. Not many nations have done as well for such a sustained period. A number have grown at faster rates in recent years, but only a few have matched China's longevity.

China's GDP, as a result, has risen to nearly four times the level of 1952 when the post-1949 development effort began. Per capita GDP has more than doubled.

Another aspect of this development in China has been the degree to which growth has been concentrated in the industrial sector. The share of industry (and transport) has risen steadily from about a quarter of GDP to over half. Agriculture, in contrast, has managed to stay only a bit ahead of population growth, and its share has declined steadily as a result. In the course of economic growth the share of industry always rises and that of agriculture falls, but the pace at which these changes have occurred in China is more pronounced than in most other developing nations. Within industry, the producer goods sector has grown more rapidly than the consumer goods sector. Machine building, in particular, has increased at a very rapid rate.

A third distinguishing characteristic of Chinese development has been the ability of the nation to mobilize fully its resources for growth. The rising share of the producer goods sector is one aspect of this phenomenon. As national product has increased, China has succeeded in holding the rise in personal consumption to modest levels. Government consumption, mainly in the form of military expenditures necessitated by the 1960 break with the Soviet Union, rose

sharply in the 1960s; despite this rise there is little doubt that China's investment rate (gross domestic capital formation as a percentage of GDP) has increased to a very high level. Precise estimates are not available, but indirect methods of estimation indicate that China's current rate of gross domestic capital formation has reached or passed 25 percent of GDP and is still rising.

Even more dramatic has been China's ability to mobilize its labor force for development. Although there is a continuing debate in the economics literature whether "surplus labor" exists anywhere in the world, few would dispute that the adult population of most less developed nations is not fully employed throughout the year. Within most cities in the less developed world there are large numbers of overtly unemployed. In rural areas unemployment is disguised and seasonal, but extensive.

In China, in contrast, both urban and rural populations are hard at work throughout the entire year. Much of this activity is in occupations of very low productivity. Peasants carrying dirt from a nearby mountainside to build a dam or a small addition to the cultivated acreage are doing back-breaking labor in exchange for often only modest increases in farm output. Many rural people, one suspects, would choose leisure time if they were free to do so. Whether voluntarily or not, China has succeeded in mobilizing billions of man-days of labor from a labor pool that in most less developed nations would have remained idle.

China has also fully mobilized its agricultural land resources. There is no area in China comparable to parts of Latin America where land that could be used to grow crops is slated for low productivity activities such as grazing. . . .

A fourth characteristic of Chinese economic development, the one that currently receives the most attention, is the Chinese effort to narrow the inequalities in income in both urban and rural areas. Great attention, however, has not led to much effort to measure the degree of inequality that exists in China today. The one major work on the sub-

TABLE 4. Changes in the Distribution of Rural Income, 1930s to 1952

Income Category	Farm Income			Total Income		
	Percentage Share		Change in Share	Percentage Share		Change in Share
	1930s	1952		1930s	1952	
Top 10%	26.0	21.6	−4.4	24.4	21.6	−2.8
Top 20%	42.7	35.1	−7.6	42.0	35.0	−7.0
2nd 20%	23.8	21.3	−2.5	23.9	21.3	−2.6
3rd 20%	16.3	17.5	+1.2	14.9	17.4	+2.5
4th 20%	11.4	14.8	+3.4	13.2	15.0	+1.8
Bottom 20%	5.8	11.3	+5.5	6.0	11.3	+5.3
Bottom 10%	1.8	5.1	+3.3	2.5	5.1	+2.6

Source: C. Robert Roll,"The Distribution of Rural Income in China: A Comparison of the 1930's and the 1950's," Doctoral dissertation, Harvard University, 1974, p. 76.

ject, on rural incomes only, is that of C. Robert Roll. His estimates, presented in Table 4, reveal that the land reform of the early 1950s during which landlordism was effectively eliminated from rural China led to a substantial redistribution of income. The incomes of the top 20 percent of the population were reduced by nearly one-fifth, and those of the bottom 40 percent were raised by roughly 50 percent.

The redistribution of Chinese income did not stop in 1952, but was given another boost in the cooperative movement of 1955–56. At that time all the peasants in a given co-op (which was frequently coterminus with a village) pooled their land, thus eliminating income inequalities due to differences in the size and quality of individual landholdings within the cooperative. In 1958–59 cooperatives were pooled into communes, thereby temporarily eliminating inequality caused by differences in landholdings between cooperatives within a single commune. The transfer down to the production team as the basic accounting unit, however, brought the situation back to that of 1957. In fact, the average production team today is much smaller than the old cooperative, but significant amounts of income are generated at the brigade and commune level as well.

There are two other major sources of in-

equality in rural areas. Income within the team is determined by the number of work points earned by family members; thus a family with more and better workers has a higher income. Far more important sources of inequality are the remaining differences between teams in the amount and the quality of their land. Land quality, of course, is determined not only by the properties of the soil but also by proximity to roads, electricity, urban markets, and the like.

How large are these remaining sources of inequality, and have they been reduced over the years? Unfortunately, only speculation is possible because no serious quantitative study of the subject has yet been made. As Roll demonstrates, there is little doubt that remaining between-region differences in income are substantial.

The situation in urban areas is somewhat similar. A major redistribution of income and assets took place in the 1950s through the socialization of industry and commerce and the elimination of most property incomes. The closed nature of Chinese society, notably the lack of free emigration, meant that China could keep highly skilled personnel (other than those who had already fled) without paying salaries competitive with those in the West. The eight-grade wage system determined the incomes of most workers and employees. The eight-grade system was similar throughout the country and between regions except for minor variations due to cost of living differentials, hardship allowances, and the like.

There have been few changes in the nature of this system since 1956. The roughly three-to-one differential between grades 1 and 8 has been altered little if at all. Greater worker equality since 1956, therefore, could only have come about through promotions that significantly changed the distribution of workers in the grades, but we know next to nothing about any such changes. There has also been some rise in the free services provided to the workers (health, housing, and so forth), and these tend to be provided on the basis of need.

Technicians and cadres are paid according to scales other than the eight-grade system. Such wages can reach levels ten times that of the bottom of the eight-grade system. There is some evidence of creeping equality in these incomes, however. The wages of older technicians are not being lowered, but as they retire, they are replaced by younger people who are paid much lower salaries. If this process continues, one suspects that within a decade or two few people will be earning more than twice the top of the eight-grade system.

Finally, there is the difference in income between urban and rural areas. Work by Roll, however, suggests that this differential may not have been very great in the 1950s when allowance is made for differences in the cost of living. Whatever the precise magnitude of the disparity, rising farm purchase prices have contributed to an increase in average rural incomes while average wages have changed little. The greater provision of urban services, on the other hand, may tend to widen the gap, although recent efforts to promote rural health work in the opposite direction.

The fifth and final distinguishing characteristic of Chinese economic development to be discussed here is the Chinese effort to minimize the nation's dependence on external assistance and foreign trade. China's limited dependence on external financial assistance is the easiest to document. Estimates of China's balance of trade are presented in Table 5. The balance of trade is an imperfect guide to capital flows into and out of a country, but in China's case a considerable body of additional information supports the view that China's balance of trade reflects in a rough way the direction and magnitude of Chinese external capital movements.

Beginning modestly in 1973 and in a major way in 1974, China borrowed abroad on an intermediate-term basis (up to five years) to finance a rapid expansion in imports of new plants in chemicals, steel, and other key sectors. Up to the mid-1970s it is fair to say that China depended on foreign financial aid on

TABLE 5. China's Foreign Trade, 1950–1974 (in millions of U.S. dollars)

Year	Exports	Imports	Trade Balance
1950	620	590	30
1951	780	1,120	−340
1952	875	1,015	−140
1953	1,040	1,255	−215
1954	1,060	1,290	−230
1955	1,375	1,660	−285
1956	1,635	1,485	150
1957	1,615	1,440	175
1958	1,940	1,825	115
1959	2,230	2,060	170
1960	1,960	2,030	−70
1961	1,525	1,490	35
1962	1,525	1,150	375
1963	1,570	1,200	370
1964	1,750	1,470	280
1965	2,035	1,845	190
1966	2,210	2,035	175
1967	1,945	1,950	−5
1968	1,945	1,820	125
1969	2,030	1,830	200
1970	2,050	2,240	−190
1971	2,415	2,305	110
1972	3,085	2,835	250
1973	4,895	4.975	−80
1974[a]	6,515	7,490	−975

Source: Nai-Ruenn Chen, "China's Foreign Trade, 1950–74," China: A Reassessment of the Economy, Washington, D.C., U.S. Congress, Joint Economic Committee, 1975, p. 645.

[a]Preliminary.

either concessionary or commercial terms to a lesser degree than any other less developed country that has achieved a sustained period of economic growth. Nations such as Burma may also have eschewed foreign assistance for long periods, but they have failed to grow as well. In per capita terms, aid to China never passed $2 in total and averaged under $0.50 a year throughout the early 1950s and zero thereafter.

An analysis of the degree of China's dependence on foreign trade is far more complex than an appraisal of the role of external financial assistance. The appropriate methodology would involve estimating China's GNP in the absence of foreign trade or some substantial part of that trade. Data limitations make such an analysis impossible. One is left, therefore, with the task of attempting to judge whether China's ratio of foreign trade to GNP is unusually low and whether Chinese imports appear to consist of items essential to the proper functioning of the economy. Even these inadequate measures can be dealt with only superficially here.

Estimating China's ratio of foreign trade (exports plus imports) to GDP is difficult because the Chinese trade data available outside China are calculated in U.S. dollars while Chinese GDP figures are in yuan. Either the former must be converted into yuan or the latter into dollars, but at what exchange rate? At the official 1974 exchange rate which floated around 1.95 yuan to the dollar, the 1974 trade ratio was 11 percent. Similar procedures for 1970 lead to an estimate for that year of only 6 percent. But it is unclear whether the higher percentage in 1974 reflects a real increase in the share of trade or simply a rise in the prices of traded goods that was more rapid than the revaluation of the yuan relative to the dollar. Until an updated purchasing power parity comparison is made, we shall have to defer judgment. For purposes of this analysis a ratio of 10 percent is used as indicative of China's "typical" trade level.

Have the commodities imported by China played a key role in China's economic development? Here the answer is a clear yes.

From the beginning the People's Republic has cut all nonessentials from its import bill. In the 1950s over 90 percent of all imports were producer goods, and these provided much of the key equipment for the first and second five-year plans. In the 1960s the share of grain in imports rose to significant levels, but the purpose of these imports was to relieve pressure on and hence encourage the grain surplus areas to produce. In the 1970s, with the accelerated investment program in industry, there has been a renewed surge of complete plant imports.

There is no question that China in 1976 is far less dependent on imported producer goods than it was in the 1950s. China's machine-building capacity now provides most domestic requirements, whereas in the early 1950s virtually all machinery had to be imported. Yet it is equally clear that where certain types of advanced technology are involved (petro-chemicals, and so forth) China must still import to expand capacity. In many respects, therefore, China's current dependence on imports is more like that of nations with much higher per capita incomes than the "typical" less developed country. By rapidly expanding its producer goods sector, China can now continue to expand in many directions with domestic equipment. Few if any other nations with per capita incomes below $300 (or $1000) can make that statement. On the other hand, China is far more dependent on imports of high technology than the industrially most advanced nations: the United States, the Soviet Union, Japan, West Germany.

Thus it is incorrect to say that China's economic development has proceeded solely on the basis of China's own efforts. It is right to say that China has provided a far higher proportion of its own development investments (in both financial and physical terms) than most other less developed nations in the world today.

A low foreign trade ratio and a high investment rate also go a long way toward explaining China's overall development strategy. In brief, a nation that cannot rely heavily on imports is forced to follow something approximating a (supply-side) balanced growth strategy. To begin with, there must be balance between agriculture and industry. Single-minded pursuit of growth in one sector to the exclusion of the other quickly generates import requirements far beyond the nation's capacity to pay. Within industry as well there must be a degree of balance. If China obtained all its mid-1970s steel needs of 25 million plus tons from imports, that item alone would cost China around U.S. $6–$7 billion, an amount equal to its entire import bill in 1974.

Thus the principal policy options open to Chinese planners were between a high and a low rate of investment and, within the consumption sector, between government (mainly military) and private consumer goods. Given these decisions and assuming some degree of consumer sovereignty over private consumption goods, the remaining options available to planners were severely limited. If one removes the assumption of consumer sovereignty over the consumer goods mix, the range of options increases slightly although much less so in a poor country than in a rich one. Chinese planners, for example, could raise the rate of growth in agriculture from say 2.5 percent to 3.5 percent a year, but they could not let it fall much below 2.5 percent for long without causing major economic and political difficulties.

Saying that Chinese planners' options are limited given a low trade ratio and a high rate of investment is not the same thing as saying that China's development strategy will be identical to that of any other nation with comparable trade and investment ratios. China's factor endowment also plays an important role, particularly in determining the relative performances of industry and agriculture. The most significant part of China's factor endowment is its shortage of cultivable land. China is a land-short nation in two basic ways. First, there has been little or no net expansion in China's cultivated acreage since the 1950s largely because the costs of developing currently uncultivated land are prohibitive. Second, Chinese grain yields per

hectare, particularly in areas suitable for rice, are comparable to the highest yields achieved anywhere in the world, including Japan. Further breakthroughs depend crucially on scientific advances such as the development of new plant varieties and on large-scale investment in water conservancy in north China. Food output can be expanded by increases in inputs of labor and items such as chemical fertilizer, but the return to these inputs is falling and in many cases is already very low. Expansion on a major scale will come instead through methods that take time (scientific breakthroughs) and are extremely expensive (for example, control of the Yellow River).

If the analysis that lies behind these statements is correct, then China's rapid industrial development and much slower development in agriculture, one of the key characteristics of China's post-1949 economic performance, can be explained in part by China's factor endowment. In the absence of a severe shortage of land in both of the senses mentioned before, current high rates of investment in Chinese agriculture would have achieved much more dramatic results. Whether Chinese planners would have chosen to achieve higher agricultural growth rates or alternatively to shift investment funds in agriculture to other sectors cannot be known. But with a different factor endowment they would at least have had that chance.

China's revolution created political conditions that made possible major shifts in economic policy. With the poor in command in rural areas, cooperatives and communes could be formed with little disruption of the economy, and these collective units could in turn mobilize labor and resources to begin transforming the countryside. In the cities revolutionary political change also eased the processes of replacing privately controlled industry and commerce with state-owned firms and of introducing rationing of necessities.

But China's revolution was only part of the reason for the post-1949 government's ability to choose from a wide range of economic policy options. The political triumph of the poor had little to do with China's ability to introduce a centralized system of planning and management on the Soviet model. Of central importance was that China had the personnel to administer such a system. Those people were available because of a Chinese heritage of emphasis on education and experience with a complex commercial economy. China's authoritarian heritage, reinforced by the power of the Chinese Communist party, also opened key options to policymakers, notably in the area of increased taxes and the potential for a high rate of investment.

On the other hand, China's size and land-short factor endowment dictated certain strategies by limiting other kinds of options. A major shift in investment funds toward agriculture in the early 1960s managed to keep farm output growing faster than population, but not fast enough to alter sectoral development with a pronounced industrial producer goods emphasis. Similarly, limited dependence on foreign trade has been turned into a political virtue, but China's size has more to do with this degree of independence than any set of deliberate policies.

Comment

In considering various country studies, we should ask whether the success stories (or failures) are the result of favorable (or unfavorable) initial conditions, internal factors, or external factors. It is also instructive to ask whether the specific institutions and programs of the success stories are transferable to other developing countries.

For discussion of the relevance of China's experience for other countries, see Robert F. Dernberger and Francoise Le Gall, "Is the Chinese Model Transferable?" in Robert F. Dernberger (ed.), *China's Development Experience in Comparative Perspective* (1980). Also instructive are D. B. Keesing, "Economic Lessons from China," *Journal of Development Economics* (March 1975); Joint Economic Committee, Congress of the United States, *Chinese Economy Post-Mao: A Compendium of Papers* (1978); Doak Barnett, *China's Economy in Global Perspective* (1981); Chu-yuan Cheng, *China's Economic Development* (1982).

EXHIBIT I.8. Poverty and Human Development in China

Country and Country Group	GNP per Person (dollars) 1979	Annual Population Growth Rate (percentage) 1970–79	Adult Literacy (percentage) 1976	Net Primary School Enrollment (percentage) 1975 or 1977	Life Expectancy at Birth (years) 1950[a]	1979
China	260	1.9	66[b]	93[b]	[36]	64
Sri Lanka	230	1.7	85	62	[55]	66
India	190	2.1	36	64	[38]	52
Indonesia	370	2.3	62	66	[35]	53
Low-income countries	210	2.3	39	56	[37]	51
Middle-income countries	1,420	2.4	72	71	[48]	61
Industrial countries	9,440	0.7	99	94	67	74

Source: *World Bank Development Report, 1981*, p. 101.

[a]Most 1950 data are estimated.

[b]1979.

I.C.6. Poverty Elimination and Entitlements*

Each economic and political system produces a set of entitlement relations governing who can have what in that system.[1] Ultimately poverty removal is a matter of entitlement raising. There are both aggregative and distributive influences on the determination of entitlements, and while balanced growth might work through the former, institutional arrangements affecting the "division of the cake" work through the latter. The precise characterization of entitlement relations will, of course, vary with the nature of the economy and society,[2] but some distinguished cases are easy to identify.

For a market economy, the determining variables of entitlements can be broadly split into (i) ownership vector (e.g., the land, capital or labour power which a person owns), and (ii) exchange entitlement *mapping* (e.g., for each ownership bundle the set of alternative bundles of commodities any one of which the person can acquire through production or trade). The ownership vector for a particular group may be enhanced either through overall increase (e.g., capital accumulation), or through asset redistribution (e.g., land reform). These influences on entitlements through ownership changes are rather more palpable and tend to be more often discussed. Entitlement raising through improving the exchange entitlement mapping is a bit more complex to analyze, but may be no less important. It includes such diverse

factors as, say, guaranteeing better terms of trade for poor peasants, or ensuring employment at a living wage, or providing social security protections.

The method of removing poverty used in South Korea and Taiwan is one of guaranteeing employment at a tolerable wage, and this has been possible by a very fast expansion of these economies using labor-absorbing production processes. In contrast, the level of unemployment in Sri Lanka is high, and the wages, especially of estate workers, quite low. There the guarantee of basic entitlements has not come *through* the market, but outside it, in the form of a direct right against the state.

The constrast is not, of course, a pure one. Some social security provisions do exist in Taiwan, and to a lesser extent in South Korea. Similarly, in Sri Lanka even the pre-tax "gross" distribution of income is not as unequal as in some developing countries. But the crucial and distinctive features of entitlement enhancement in the two types of economies are different. In Taiwan and South Korea the social services only rather marginally improve what is provided by a buoyant labor market. Sri Lanka's rather "middling" performance in market-based entitlements is vastly improved by public policy of distribution and social service.

More importantly, there is an important similarity between the two strategies, which superficially might look poles apart. Ultimately, poverty removal must come to grips with the issue of entitlement guarantees. The two strategies differ in the *means* of achieving this guarantee. While one relies on the successfully fostered growth and the dynamism of the encouraged labour market, the other gives the government a more *direct* role as a provider of provisions. The similarities can be seen more clearly if we look at the distributional pattern through which these means work to guarantee entitlement.

It is not easy to obtain internationally com-

---

*A. K. Sen, "Levels of Poverty: Policy and Change," *World Bank Staff Report* No. 401, July 1980, pp. 53–65. Reprinted by permission.

[1]A. K. Sen, "Real National Income," *Review of Economic Studies,* Vol. 43, 1976; "Starvation and Exchange Entitlement: A General Approach and Its Application to the Great Bengal Famine," *Cambridge Journal of Economics,* Vol. 1, 1977; "Famines," *World Development,* Vol. 8, 1980a; and *Poverty and Famines: An Essay on Entitlement and Deprivation,* Clarendon Press, Oxford, 1981.

[2]Sen, 1980b, chapters 1 and 5–10 and appendixes A and B.

TABLE 1. Comparisons of Relative Equalities of Income Distribution

Country	Relative Share of Bottom 20%	Relative Share of Bottom 40%	Relative Share of Bottom 60%	Relative Share of Bottom 80%	Borda Score
Taiwan 1971	8.7	21.9	38.5	60.8	4.0
Sri Lanka 1969–70	7.5	19.2	34.7	56.6	10.0
Yugoslavia 1973	6.5	18.4	36.0	60.0	11.0
India 1964–65	6.7	17.2	31.5	51.1	17.0
South Korea 1976	5.7	16.9	32.3	54.7	18.0
Argentina 1970	4.4	14.1	28.2	49.7	25.5
Chile 1968	4.4	13.4	27.2	48.6	27.5
Philippines 1970–71	3.7	11.9	25.1	46.1	34.0
Costa Rica 1971	3.3	12.0	25.3	45.2	37.5
Turkey 1973	3.4	11.4	23.9	43.4	42.0
Mexico 1977	2.9	10.3	23.5	45.5	45.5
Venezuela 1970	3.0	10.3	23.2	46.0	45.5
Malaysia 1970	3.3	10.6	22.8	43.5	46.5
Peru 1972	1.9	7.0	18.0	39.0	59.5
Honduras 1967	2.3	7.3	15.3	32.2	60.0
Brazil 1972	2.0	7.0	16.4	33.4	60.5

Source: Calculated from table 24 of the *World Development Report, 1979.*

parable income distribution data, but to get some broad idea Table 1 presents income distributional data for 16 countries taken from the *World Development Report 1979*. (These are all the countries with income per head less than $3,000 for which such data are given.) The incomes in question are of "total disposable household income," net of taxes.

The *World Development Report 1979* gives the data in the form of shares of each *successive* quintile. For ready comparison of parameters of inequality, these have been presented here in the form of *cumulative* aggregates, i.e., the shares of the bottom 20 percent, bottom 40 percent, bottom 60 percent and bottom 80 percent, respectively.

The most satisfactory method of comparison with these data is the so-called "Lorenz dominance." Country A Lorenz-dominates country B in terms of equality of income distribution if compared with country B, country A has at least as high an income share for *each* x percent poorest population, and a strictly higher share for some x percent poorest population. When Lorenz dominance holds between two distributions of income, many interpretable conclusions can be drawn, and in general this may be regarded as the most satisfactory method of comparing the income distribution of two countries. On the other hand, this is a demanding criterion, and very often neither country Lorenz-dominates the other in a pairwise comparison.

Lorenz domination yields a partial ordering of "clear" rankings, but given its incompleteness, some less demanding method of ranking has to be chosen to supplement Lorenz comparison if completeness is sought. A simple method of doing this—surprisingly little used in empirical comparisons—is to follow Borda's method of rank-order scoring, giving points equal to the rank value of each country in each criterion of comparative ranking. This produces a complete ordering based on all the criteria taken together in terms of lowness of the sum of ranks (Borda scores).

Both the Lorenz and Borda methods of ranking the 16 countries in Table 1 have been used, and the results are represented in the form of two Hasse diagrams (with descending lines representing superiority of the higher placed country vis-à-vis the lower). The partial ordering of Lorenz dominance given by Hasse Figure 1 is subsumed by the complete ordering of Borda ranking in Hasse Figure 2. Interestingly enough, the countries which were commended for their performance in poverty removal and longevity extension come very much at the top of these rankings. Countries which were separated out for disappointing performance in terms of poverty removal commensurate with their income, viz., Brazil, Peru and Mexico, also figure here towards the bottom of the two rankings.

Poverty removal and related features, including longevity enhancement, are ultimately dependent on a wide distribution of effective entitlements, and this—for any given level of per capita income—would tend to be reflected in the low level of inequality in the distribution of income. At this *immediate* level of explanation, in terms of entitlements and income distributions, Yugoslavia, Sri Lanka, Taiwan and South Korea have much in common despite their widely different political systems and economic strategies. At the remoter level the explanations differ; Taiwan and South Korea rely on high employment at a reasonable wage as an instrument, while Sri Lanka leans on security outside the market mechanism. At a still remoter level, the former pair of countries have profited from the strategy of export expansion, while Sri Lanka has not used such a strategy, nor is Yugoslav planning especially export oriented. Learning from the experience of Taiwan or Korea need not take the form of seeing virtues in export expansion irrespective of the nature of the country, and indeed the remoter we move in the chain of explanation, the more conditional, in general, the explanation becomes.

The specific nature of the economic problems faced by these countries to which their economic strategies responded has often tended to be ignored. But on these specificities, the remoter explanations may substantially depend. Consider, for example, the strategy of relatively free trade with absent *or* refunded import duties, used by Taiwan. The necessity of such a policy for export expansion in the Taiwanese context has been explained admirably by Maurice Scott (1979):[3]

Taiwan has very few mineral resources and strictly limited agricultural resources. It could only prosper, and has in fact prospered, by exporting what effectively are labor and capital services. These services, however, have mainly taken the form of adding value to imported materials rather than being services pure and simple (as are tourism,

[3]M. Scott, "Foreign Trade," in W. Galenson (ed.), *Economic Growth and Structural Change in Taiwan,* Ithaca, Cornell University Press, 1979.

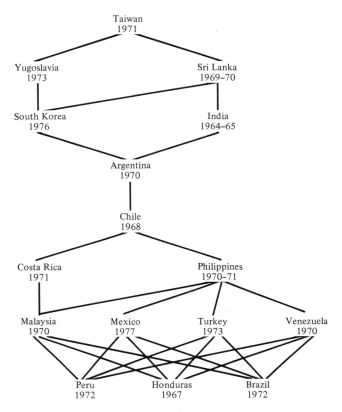

FIGURE 1. Hasse diagram showing partial order of Lorenz dominance.

banking, transportation, and the like). Thus the most important single condition for an export "take-off" was access by manufacturers to imported materials, components, and capital equipment at world prices. For a typical manufacturer in one of Taiwan's export industries . . . materials account for around 65 to 70 percent of the selling value of output, capital altogether receives a further 5 to 12 percent of selling value, and, of this, over half can be attributed to costs of plant machinery, vehicles, and stocks of materials. Hence, the total percentage of selling value represented by the cost of materials or equipment might be around 70 to 75 percent or even more for a typical exporter. If his exports are sold at world prices, without benefit of any subsidy, he must be able to buy these materials and equipment at or close to world prices if the export is to be profitable. A 40 percent tax on materials and equipment would wipe out, not merely all potential profit, but also all potential wages, fuel costs, or payment for other bought-in services (advertising and other selling costs, rent of buildings and land, and so forth), and a much smaller tax, say 10 percent, would make many exports totally unprofitable.

Under the circumstances the compelling advantages of Taiwan's policy regarding imports are clear enough, but these may or may not be shared by other countries with different economic characteristics (e.g., larger economies, greater mineral resources, less skill of the kind needed for export expansion in the present world markets, etc.). Similar discriminating analysis can be done with other instruments, e.g., high savings rate, social welfare delivery systems, and there is need for caution in reading lessons from success stories.

FIGURE 2. Hasse diagram showing complete order of Borda scores of relative equality.

The ways of achieving widespread entitlements differ, and while different economic strategies have things in common both in terms of ultimate consequences as well as in underlying causation, the precise combination of instruments and policies varies tremendously with the conditions in different economies. In a somewhat stylized form Figure 3 brings out such contrasts. Roughly path *a* tries to capture the causal mechanism in South Korea and Taiwan; path *c* that in Sri Lanka; and paths *b* and *c* that in Yugoslavia. It is common to all these strategies that low poverty in the form of high longevity and low proportion of population below the poverty line are brought about by a widespread distribution of entitlements, but beyond this immediate link there are sharp differences in the way such entitlement delivery is made. There is similarity also in the role ultimately played by calculated and determined public policy. But while the Korean-Taiwanese causal mechanism goes through industrial expansion with exports expanding much faster, employment-oriented fast growth, achievements in total income enhancement and in income distribution, the Sri Lankan path goes through social welfare programmes, public distribution systems, achievements in income distribution and in non-income advantages (e.g., in people having better health when the income subsidy comes in the form of food, medical provisions, etc.). The Yugoslav experience fits neither since it is somewhat similar to the Korean-Taiwanese strategy of high growth with good distribution, but differs from it in not having export expansion noticeably faster than the growth of national product and in having a more developed social security system.

It is only natural that "lessons" will be sought from the experience of those countries which have been unusually successful in poverty elimination. But the lessons to be drawn have to concentrate on understanding the *functional roles* of various instruments rather than on blind imitation of the instruments themselves. Other countries can learn much from the experience of success stories if the

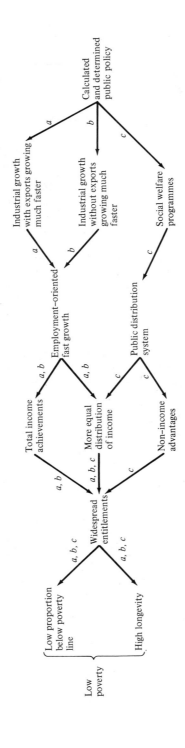

FIGURE 3. Consequential links and levels of explanation.

a – South Korea and Taiwan.
b – Yugoslavia.
c – Sri Lanka and Yugoslavia.

causal mechanisms are fully studied and re-moter causes distinguished from the less re-mote ones. To what extent, say, fast growth is possible with export industries taking the lead, is a question that can be answered for any particular country only by looking at the details of its economic circumstances. The same applies to the possibility of delivering provisions through social welfare programs. Neither of these circumstantial conditionalities renders the experience of the successful countries unproductive for policy formulation, but blind imitation may well have counter-productive consequences.

Comment

Numerous forecasts have been made for the prospects of developing countries in the decades ahead. For the decade of the 1980s, most assessments point to lower growth rates, greater numbers of poor, and scarcer and more expensive food and energy. Together with much higher populations, the problems of development are expected to become more severe.

For a range of forecasts, see the World Bank's *World Development Report 1981; The Global 2000 Report to the President of the United States;* Wassily Leontief, *The Future of the World Economy* (1977); *Interfutures: A Study of the World Economy* sponsored by OECD; and the Brandt Commission's *North/South: A Program for Survival* (1980).

Some of these reports are summarized by Shahid Javed Burki in "The Prospects for the Developing World: A Review of Recent Forecasts," *Finance & Development* (March 1981).

Table 1 shows World Bank projections for various country groups in a low and high range of growth possibilities.

TABLE 1. Past and Projected Growth of GDP, 1960–1995 (*average annual percentage change*)

Country Group	1960–73	1973–80	1980–82	1982–85	1985–95 Low	1985–95 Central	1985–95 High
All developing countries	6.0	4.7	1.9	4.4	4.7	5.5	6.2
Low-income							
Asia	4.6	5.4	4.1	4.5	4.5	4.9	5.3
Africa	3.5	1.4	0.5	2.9	2.7	3.3	3.9
Middle-income							
Oil importers	6.3	5.2	1.2	4.5	4.4	5.7	6.9
Oil exporters	7.0	3.7	1.7	4.0	5.3	5.7	5.8
Industrial countries	5.1	2.5	0.4	3.0	2.5	3.7	5.0

Source: World Bank, *World Development Report, 1983*, p. 27.

I. D. LEADING ISSUES—NOTE

From the preceding discussion of the development record, three overriding questions emerge: (1) What have been the constraints on the *potential* rates of development in the LDCs? (2) Why have the *actual* rates of development been below the potential rates in most of these countries? and (3) What policies in a strategy of development can now raise growth rates, eradicate absolute poverty, reduce inequality, and provide more productive employment opportunities? These questions will dominate much of the analysis throughout this book.

The disappointments that have been experienced in the development record now call for correction of the errors of omission and commission in development thought and for a reappraisal of policy options. Contrary to the optimistic views of development economists in the 1950s and 1960s, the actual development performance has been disappointing in several respects. Although some countries have grown markedly, the poorest of the poor countries have grown the least. Population growth has been higher than expected because of the fall in mortality rates and a lag in the decline of fertility rates. As emphasized above, the benefits of growth have not trickled down, and despite high growth rates in per capita income, the numbers in absolute poverty have increased in many poor countries. So too have rates of unemployment and underemployment risen in several countries. The problem of inequality in the distribution of income has also intensified in some countries. Furthermore, the agricultural sector has lagged, or even stagnated, in many countries. The transfer of resources from rich to poor countries has diminished.

Many of the readings in subsequent chapters consider whether the development process is now encountering increasingly severe—or even intractable—difficulties. It will become apparent that there is a divergence of views on whether the limitations to development are to be located mainly within the economies of the LDCs or whether external obstacles to development are to be blamed. There are also differing conclusions on whether the obstacles are best removed by promotion of the market mechanism or by comprehensive central planning.

Behind the disappointments in the statistical record lie five major constraints that have limited the attainable rate of development in most of the less developed world. One major constraint stems from the low level of savings. The inability to mobilize sufficient domestic resources, or to supplement domestic resources with external resources, has continued to inhibit development. An increase in the ratio of savings to national income is still imperative in most of the LDCs. It is, however, disturbing that the rate of increase of capital formation has slowed down in many countries, and it is indeed questionable whether in many LDCs the domestic savings rate and capital inflow are now sufficiently high to sustain a satisfactory rate of development. Problems associated with the savings constraint are examined in Chapters IV and V.

Another bottleneck relates to the agricultural sector. Agriculture constitutes a large share of the GDP of developing countries, and agricultural commodities account for a considerable part of the value of their total exports. Agricultural development is therefore essential for economic growth, accumulating capital through savings and taxation, and earning foreign exchange. It must also support and complement industrial development by providing food for a growing nonagricultural labor force, raw materials for industrial production, and a growing home market for domestic manufacturers. The development record has demonstrated a close association between the agricultural performance and the overall growth rate of developing countries: in the "high-growth" developing countries the average rates of increase in agricultural production have been considerably higher than in the slower-growth countries.

For the majority of developing countries, however, agriculture has been a problem sector. A major restraint on the development rate has been the slow growth of their agricultural output in general and of food crops in particular. In almost one-half of the developing countries, food production per head was lower at the end of the 1970s than a decade earlier. In many LDCs, the demand for food has grown faster than food production, and an increasing number of LDCs have become net importers of food. The neglect of the agricultural sector has been pervasive, and it underlies problems created by the population explosion, unemployment and underemployment, inequality, and absolute poverty. In Chapter VII, we stress the important role of agricultural improvements in the development process, and we examine the interactions between the industrial and agricultural sectors.

As distressing as the lagging performance of the agricultural sector, and not unrelated to it, is the lag in the export sector. The foreign exchange constraint—or the deterioration in the capacity to import—is an acute limitation on the size of development plans. The ratio of value of exports from LDCs to total world exports has declined. At the same time, development programs have stimulated the demand for imports. It is also contended that for structural reasons the demand for imports rises more rapidly than national product and also exceeds the rate of increase in exports. The import demand by LDCs has thus risen more than their capacity to import based on export earnings. And since the early 1970s, the stagnation of the world economy and the slowing down of world trade have contrasted with the buoyancy of overseas markets during the 1950s and 1960s. A new export pessimism has set in. Compounding the difficulties, the net inflow of foreign capital has slowed down, debt servicing of amortization and interest on public foreign debt has risen markedly, and income payments of

dividends and profits on private direct foreign investment have grown, so that in many countries the import surplus that can be supported by external financial resources has also diminished. The oil crisis has had severe balance-of-payments repercussions for many LDCs. Except for some oil-exporting countries and a very few other exceptional developing countries, the foreign exchange constraint has persisted as a severe limitation on a country's development program by making it impossible to fulfill import requirements. The problems of mobilizing external resources are discussed in Chapter V; the related notion of a "widening trade gap"—and its policy implications with respect to import substitution and export promotion—is considered in Chapter VIII.

Another major constraint is connected with the need for human-resource development. The policy issues relating to the need for social development are now critical. It has become increasingly apparent that an improvement in the quality of human life cannot be simply awaited as an ultimate objective of development but must instead be viewed as a necessary instrument of development. Even more necessary than an increase in the quantity of productive factors is the need to improve the quality of people as economic agents. If development is growth *plus* change, and change is social and cultural as well as economic, then the qualitative dimensions of development become extremely significant in terms of human-resource development. Without such change, the process of development will not become self-sustaining.

This qualitative change requires a greater emphasis on investment in human capital and on measures to modify social and cultural values. Recognizing that the problem of controlling population growth has now reached serious dimensions through most of the underdeveloped world, many would also argue that population control policies are essential to foster a rise in the standard of living in many poor countries. Unless this is done, it will be all the more difficult to improve the quality of the population, and the potential for development will not be realized.

Finally, another lesson of experience is the need to overcome organizational, staffing, and logistical bottlenecks if public policy measures are to be effectively implemented. The quality of national economic management has become of crucial importance. On the basis of the success stories and failures in development experience, it can be said that a poor country is poor because of inappropriate policies. In developing countries, the pursuit of appropriate policies, stability of government, strong commitment to development goals, and capacity for efficient public management are essential even if the other constraints on the attainable rate of development are relaxed. Only then can the actual rate of development approach more closely the potentially attainable rate.

Although we do not minimize the significance of noneconomic factors in the process of modernization, we emphasize in this book the strategic economic policy issues connected with a relaxation of the savings, agricultural, foreign exchange, human-resource, and organizational constraints.

These constraints—multiple in number and both internal and external to the developing country's economy—aggravate the problem of development. The problem is all the more complicated by the question of tradeoffs that involve growth, employment, and equity. Is there a conflict between increasing output and increasing employment? Given that capital is a scarce resource, is the type of production that economizes on the use of capital per unit of output consistent with maximizing employment? Or does output have to be sacrificed in providing more employment? The conflict lies not so much with the relationship between current output and current employment, but with the relationship between current employment and the growth rate of employment and output in the future.

Another troublesome tradeoff is between output and equity. Does social justice have to be sacrificed for greater output? Or is it possible to achieve what might be termed "efficient equity"—that is, an improvement in equity together with an increase in output? Does this also hold in intertemporal terms? In other words, is it possible to have both greater equity and greater output in the present period and in future periods as well? Or is it more probable that a country can have greater equity and greater output in the future only if it endures greater inequality in the present?

Various perspectives on the development record and development theories, to which we now turn, may begin to illuminate these issues.

CHAPTER II

Development Perspectives

Against the background of the development record, we may now consider the interplay between experience and changes in hypotheses about the development process. In the early postwar period of development planning, a development theory was only too often misread as if it provided a recipe for successful development, and access to the teachings of modern economics was thought to bestow some new magical quality. Since the disillusioning experience of postwar development efforts, however, a reaction has set in against such a naive approach. In the LDCs, modern economics is losing its mystique and policymakers are seeking more relevant analyses. If we emphasize the constraints on development, we must ask just what is the relevance of economic theory and history in understanding how these constraints might be relaxed.

It might be thought that we must depart radically from "Western economics" and introduce a completely different system of economic thought in order to reach a fuller understanding of development problems. After all, economic analysis has matured in the more advanced industrial nations, and the problems that have preoccupied economists' attention in these countries might be considered to have little pertinence for less developed economies. In this vein, one could argue for new approaches in economic theory to fit the problems and interests of poor countries.

The evolution of development economics has not, however, proceeded in this direction. Instead of becoming a new subdiscipline, quite distinct from traditional economics, theoretical foundations of development economics have increasingly relied on the fundamental principles of mainstream economics—the neoclassical economics of resource allocation, international trade theory, and the macroeconomics of monetary and fiscal policies. But the application of these principles and the derivation of policy proposals have had to change as the conditions of developing countries altered.

Changes in the perception of the development process can be traced through the selections in this chapter.

If we are to appreciate fully the variety, complexity, and pervasiveness of development problems, we must be aware of their historical dimension. Historical perspective is one of the best safeguards against taking a superficial view of these problems. Section II.A, therefore, considers the relevance of historical experience in contributing to our understanding of the sources of development. It does so, in part, by focusing on Professor Rostow's provocative application of a stage approach to the course of development. As a grand historical thesis, Rostow's analysis of stages of growth had especially strong appeal during the 1960s in the less developed countries. But it received substantial criticism, and some of these critiques deserve equal attention for their concern with those historical factors neglected by Rostow.

Basic to Rostow's original analysis, in *Stages of Economic Growth,* was his sketch of a dynamic theory of production that emphasized the composition of investment and the growth of particular sectors in the economy. This theory of production allowed Rostow to identify certain "leading sectors," the growth of which is thought to be instrumental in propelling the economy forward. Rostow also indicated that a sequence of optimum patterns of investment can be postulated from a set of optimum sectoral paths determined by the level of income and population, by technology, by the quality of entrepreneurship, and by the empirical fact that deceleration is the normal optimum path of each sector. The actual course of investment, however, generally differs from these optima inasmuch as they are influenced not only by private choices, but also by the politics of governments and the impact of wars. Nonetheless, Rostow believes that, at any period of time, leading sectors can be identified, and the changing sequence of leading sectors plays an important role in Rostow's stages of growth. The sequence of stages suggests, in turn, that a succession of strategic choices is open to societies, and that political and social decisions about the allocation of resources are made in terms beyond the usual market processes. Of Rostow's five stages of growth, the most relevant for poor countries at present are the first three—the "traditional society," the emergence of the "preconditions for take-off," and the "take-off."

Other selections in section II.A criticize Rostow's stage theory and suggest different viewpoints for attempting to draw some conclusions regarding the correspondence and variation between past and present efforts at development. The Note on "Future Development in Historical Perspective" (II.A.4) places special emphasis on some of the differences between past and present cases of development—differences that give rise to problems that will receive extensive consideration in subsequent chapters.

The changes in development thought over the past two or three decades are brought out by the selections in section II.B. A general survey of contrasting perceptions of development is offered by Streeten (II.B.1) who indicates that from an initial concentration on growth, development economists moved to stressing the creation of employment, and then to the redistribution of benefits to the poor, and more recently to an emphasis on basic human needs. The evolution of the methodology of structural analysis is discussed by Chenery (II.B.2). Some of the economist's advances in understanding of the development process are summarized by Ranis (II.B.3). Turning to the more specific practice of development modeling, Tinbergen summarizes the state of the art (II.B.4).

In section II.C, we consider some alternative perceptions outside the mainstream. Among alternative analyses, the Marxist view (II.C.1) and "dependencia" school of thought (II.C.2) are most prominent.

The chapter ends with a Note that examines the relevance and realism of an "Economics *for* Development" to be used by the development practitioner (II.D).

II.A. HISTORICAL PERSPECTIVES

II.A.1. Rostow and Marx—Note

It has always been tempting to search for regularities in history, and many writers have adopted a uni-directional view of development in terms of some pattern of stages. As summarized by Professor Kuznets, "a stage theory of long-term economic change implies: (1) distinct time segments, characterized by different sources and patterns of economic change; (2) a specific succession of these segments, so that *b* cannot occur before *a*, or *c* before *b*; and (3) a common matrix, in that the successive segments are stages in one broad process—usually one of development and growth rather than of devolution and shrinkage. Stage theory is most closely associated with a uni-directional rather than cyclic view of history. In the cyclic view the stages are recurrent; in a uni-directional view, a stage materializes, runs its course, and never recurs. Even in the process of devolution and decline, the return to a level experienced previously is not viewed as a recurrence of the earlier stage."[1]

The central question raised by Kuznets is: How can such a simple design be a summary description or analytic classification of a vast and diverse field of historical change sufficiently plausible to warrant the formulation and persistence of many variants?

At one extreme, Adam Smith referred to the sequence of hunting, pastoral, agricultural, commercial, and manufacturing stages. At the other, Karl Marx related Hegel's thesis, antithesis, and synthesis to the Marxian stages of feudalism, capitalism, and socialism. Most recently, Professor Walt Rostow attempted to generalize "the sweep of modern economic history" in a set of stages of growth, designated as follows: the traditional society; the preconditions for take-off; the take-off; the drive to maturity; the age of high mass-consumption.[2]

The "take-off" is meant to be the central notion in Rostow's schema, and it has received the most critical attention. The take-off is interpreted as "a decisive transition in a society's history"—a period "when the scale of productive economic activity reaches a critical level and produces changes which lead to a massive and progressive structural transformation in economies and the societies of which they are a part, better viewed as changes in kind than merely in degree." The take-off is defined "as requiring all three of the following related conditions":

1. a rise in the rate of productive investment from, say, 5% or less to over 10% of national income (or net national product);
2. the development of one or more substantial manufacturing sectors, with a high rate of growth;
3. the existence or quick emergence of a political, social, and institutional framework which exploits the impulses to expansion in the modern sector and the potential external economy effects of the take-off and gives to growth an on-going character.[3]

Of the earlier proponents of stages, only Marx commands Rostow's explicit attention. Indeed, Rostow presents his analysis as an alternative to Marx's theory of modern history. Describing his system as "A Non-Communist Manifesto," Rostow poses his five stages of growth against Marx's stages of feudal-

[1]Simon Kuznets, "Notes on Stage of Economic Growth as a System Determinant," in Alexander Eckstein (ed.), *Comparison of Economic Systems,* Berkeley, 1971, p. 243.

[2]W. W. Rostow, "The Stages of Economic Growth," *Economic History Review,* August 1959; *The Stages of Economic Growth,* Cambridge, 1960; *The Economics of Take-Off Into Sustained Growth,* London, 1963.

[3]Rostow, *The Stages of Economic Growth,* pp. 36–40.

ism, bourgeois capitalism, socialism, and communism.

We can recognize some broad similarities between Rostow's analysis and Marx's sequence. Both are audacious attempts to interpret the evolution of whole societies, primarily from an economic perspective; both are "explorations of the problems and consequences for whole societies of building compound interest into their habits and institutions";[4] and both recognize that economic change has social, political, and cultural consequences.

From other viewpoints, however, there are fundamental differences. The basic Marxian problems of class conflicts, exploitation, and inherent stresses within the capitalist process find no place in Rostow's analysis. Nor does Rostow reduce the complexities of man to a single economic dimension. Rostow recognizes that, in terms of human motivation, many of the most profound economic changes must be viewed as the consequence of noneconomic human motives and aspirations. Instead of limiting human behavior to simply an act of maximization, Rostow interprets net human behavior "as an act of balancing alternative and often conflicting human objectives in the face of the range of choices men perceive to be open to them."[5] Rostow allows for the different facets of human beings, and interprets the total performance of societies as an act of balance in the patterns of choice made by individuals within the framework permitted by the changing setting of society. Rostow insists that although his "stages-of-growth are an economic way of looking at whole societies, they in no sense imply that the worlds of politics, social organization, and of culture are a mere superstructure built upon and derived uniquely from the economy."[6] On the contrary, what most concerns Rostow is how societies go about making their choices and balances: "the central phenomenon of the world of post-traditional societies is not the

economy—and whether it is capitalist or not—it is the total procedure by which choices are made."[7] Marx's assumption that a society's decisions are merely a function of who owns property is therefore rejected as inaccurate; instead it is maintained that "one must look directly at the full mechanism of choice among alternative policies, including the political process—and indeed, the social and religious processes—as independent arenas for making decisions and choices."[8]

The implications of this broader view of human motivation become especially significant when Rostow's interpretation of post-traditional societies is contrasted with Marx's account of the post-feudal phase. Thus, Rostow concludes that his account of the break-up of traditional societies is

based on the convergence of motives of private profit in the modern sectors with a new sense of affronted nationhood. And other forces play their part as well, for example the simple perception that children need not die so young or live their lives in illiteracy: a sense of enlarged human horizons, independent of both profit and national dignity. And when independence or modern nationhood is at last attained, there is no simple, automatic switch to a dominance of the profit motive and economic and social progress. On the contrary there is a searching choice and problem of balance among the three directions policy might go: external assertion; the further concentration of power in the centre as opposed to the regions; and economic growth.[9]

This approach may have more immediate relevance for the problems now confronting many underdeveloped countries than Marx's narrower view that political behavior is dependent on economic advantage, and that the decisions of capitalist societies are made simply in terms of the free-market mechanism and private advantage.

Moreover, as Rostow observes, the Marxian sequence suffers by basing its categories on only one historical case: the case of the British take-off and drive to maturity. Rostow reminds us that Marx had presented his

[4]Ibid., p. 148.
[5]Ibid., p. 149.
[6]Ibid., p. 2.

[7]Ibid., p. 150.
[8]Ibid.
[9]Ibid., p. 152.

whole system before any other society except Britain had experienced the take-off , and instead of revising his categories so as to be more applicable to other cases, Marx merely generalized and projected his interpretation of the British case. A concentration on the British case, however, misses the variety of experience in the evolution of different societies, and makes the Marxian analysis of the "march of history" unduly rigid and artificial. If for no other reason than that it draws upon a far wider range of historical knowledge, and is thereby more comprehensive and less doctrinaire, Rostow's analysis can claim to be a superior alternative to the Marxian sequence.

Nonetheless, if Rostow's thesis is to assert with a high degree of generality that it is able to trace a structure of history in the form of a sequence of stages, then it must also answer a number of criticisms that have commonly been levied against stage-theorists. "Stage-making" approaches are misleading when they succumb to a linear conception of history and imply that all economies tend to pass through the same series of stages. Although a particular sequence may correspond broadly to the historical experience of some economies, no single sequence fits the history of all countries. To maintain that every economy always follows the same course of development with a common past and the same future is to overschematize the complex forces of development, and to give the sequence of stages a generality that is unwarranted. A country may attain a later stage of development without first having passed through an earlier stage, as stages may be skipped, and different types of economies do not have to succeed or evolve from one another. The sequence is also blurred inasmuch as frequently the stages are not mutually exclusive, and characteristics of earlier stages often become mixed with characteristics of later stages. Anyone who attempts to impose upon economic history a one-way course of economic evolution is bound to be challenged, since it is difficult to accept one unique schema as the only real framework in which the facts truly lie; the same facts can be arranged in many patterns and seen from many perspectives.[10] What matters, therefore, is how suggestive and useful Rostow's pattern is in providing answers to our questions as we attempt to make sense out of the past and make the future more predictable. This comes down to the question of the adequacy of Rostow's pattern in helping us isolate the strategic factors which make for change, especially those factors that constitute the necessary and sufficient conditions for determining the transition of an economy from a preceding stage to a succeeding stage.

In this respect, Rostow's efforts are more substantial than those by other proponents of stages. Recognizing how important the search for strategic factors is, Rostow adopts an approach that is more analytical and related to a wider range of issues than any of the approaches of his predecessors. His argument abounds with terms such as "forces," "process," "net result," "inner logic"—all indicative of his desire to present an analytical, not merely a descriptive, set of stages. According to Rostow, the "analytic backbone" of his argument is "rooted in a dynamic theory of production," and he believes that his set of stages reveals a "succession of strategic choices" that confronts a country as it moves forward through the development process. On this basis, perhaps the most illumination can be gained from Rostow's analysis by interpreting each stage as posing a particular type of problem, so that the sequence of stages is equivalent to a series of problems that confronts a country in the course of its development. Rostow's ultimate objective, however, has been to present through his set of stages a theory about economic growth and a means of uncovering both the uniformities and the uniqueness of each nation's experience. To be in a better position to judge how successful Rostow has actually been in fulfilling these claims, we should now consider the following appraisal of his analysis.

[10]Although Rostow gives little attention to the problem, his analysis raises many questions related to basic social theory. In this connection, it is illuminating to consult Isaiah Berlin, *Historical Inevitability,* London, 1954, especially sections 2, 8.

II.A.2. Empty Economic Stages?*

Professor Rostow's bold generalisations ordering the process of economic growth are no less controversial now than they were in 1960 and of no less interest. Scholars and planners continue to wrestle with the same basic problem of economic development, but in a context considerably influenced by Rostow's writings. The appearance of this volume affords us all a valuable opportunity to re-examine and rethink the issues that have evolved in the debate of almost a decade upon the concept of take-off.[1]

THE TWO THEORIES OF TAKE-OFF

Despite frequent clarifications and restatements by Rostow of the concept of take-off in the course of his two essays and liberal participation in the discussion, its underlying duality is not resolved. The implicit recognition that there are indeed two theories of take-off is perhaps one of the most fruitful contributions made by the Conference. At one level the take-off is a sectoral, non-linear, threshold notion. This is the realm of the leading sector, with its forward, backward and spreading effects breathing regular innovation into the heretofore slumbering *corpus economicum*. It is the domain of certain crucial industries, such as those of coal, iron and engineering. Economic growth is viewed as a constant struggle among a succession of activities first accelerating and decelerating.

The other level is highly aggregative. Here the setting is that of the familiar Harrod-Domar model in which the rate of growth of income is the product of an average propensity to save and the inverse of a reasonably stable capital-output ratio. Take-off then

consists of a recognisable discontinuity in the observed growth of income *per capita,* which under these conditions means a sharp increase in the savings rate:

It is . . . useful to regard as a necessary but not sufficient condition for the take-off the fact that the proportion of net investment to national income (or net national product) rises from, say, 5% to over 10%, definitely outstripping the likely population pressure (since under the assumed take-off circumstances the capital output ratio is low) and yielding a *distinct* rise in real output per capita.[2]

The theories, of course, are not mutually exclusive. But neither are they ever integrated into a single framework. The discussion of interindustrial relationships takes for granted the availability of resources and emphasises instead the power of the demand nexus in stimulating growth among complementary activities. Its purpose is the exposition of a mechanism for transmitting autonomous impulses affecting one sector to the economy as a whole. Not only output but also technology is involved. The final objective is a description of how the industrial matrix— its quantities *and* coefficients—undergoes a decisive and discontinuous transformation. The aggregate model takes as its starting-point, on the other hand, the constraint of savings, and hence investment, without which growth cannot attain regularity at high rates. Within an environment where the inducement to invest is the limiting factor, rather than savings, the sectoral approach seems much the more fruitful. The propensity to save is dependent not so much upon consumer decisions as those by entrepreneurs, and the elasticity of resources and automaticity of technological advance is high. Some underdeveloped countries may indeed fit such a mould; Professor Hirschman's writings stress this theme, and in this volume Professor Leibenstein also argues that such a shift

*From Albert Fishlow, "Empty Economic Stages?" *Economic Journal,* Vol. 75, No. 297, March 1965, pp. 112–16, 120–25. Reprinted by permission.
[1]A review of W. W. Rostow, ed., *The Economics of Take-off into Sustained Growth,* Proceedings of a Conference held by the International Economic Association, London, Macmillan & Co. Ltd., 1963.

[2]W. W. Rostow, *The Stages of Economic Growth,* Cambridge, 1960, p. 37.

in emphasis to investment rather than concentration upon savings is desirable.

Yet Rostow fails to elaborate the conditions under which one approach rather than the other yields a more cogent explanation of how growth took root, or how the two are related. This explains why Professor Solow is troubled by the absence of any coherent theory and why Rostow's reply to him is unsatisfactory. By shifting between them in almost random fashion Rostow does the concept of take-off little service. And by not introducing resource constraints and a more adequate discussion of technological diffusion into his sectoral theory he deprives it of a clarity and consistency that the aggregate model does enjoy. Furthermore, the data required to establish the acceleration in income *per capita* and savings proportions are easier to come by than the detailed analyses of individual countries, and Rostow confines himself with infrequent exception to such evidence. Thus, while he frequently protests the neglect of his sectoral approach, the blame resides not only on his critics.

THE USEFULNESS OF THE AGGREGATE APPROACH

The result, then, is that it is the aggregate notion of take-off that has become most bruited about. How well does it perform? Not very, I believe. Despite its elegant simplicity, the conception of growth as a resultant of the savings rate and the aggregate capital-output is singularly inappropriate for a society in transformation. Even if formally correct, it obscures and misleads concerning the fundamental forces at work. The national capital-output ratio lacks behavioural content. Its constancy subsumes complementary changes in other inputs, such as labour and entrepreneurial skills, not to mention technological progress. It excludes the important category of human capital. Its stability is consistent with wide-ranging shifts in industrial composition and investments in which we precisely are interested. And as pointed out above, the savings propensity itself can hardly be regarded as subject to autonomous change. Were the question merely one of history, the observed regularity of the ratio might suffice and causality be regarded more lightly. In a world where take-off has become a goal, and policies are at issue, there can be no such facile resolution, particularly when some of the careful qualifications stated by Rostow are lost in the midst of a widening audience. Professor Cairncross' essay speaks cogently and quite usefully to these matters in more detail, and it is unnecessary to elaborate further here.

Thus, at best the regularity hypothesised by Rostow—the sharp increase in the savings rate and accelerated growth of *per capita* income within the span of a generation—provides us with entrée to the problems of transition rather than its solution. Unfortunately, however, the hard facts of developmental experience cast considerable doubt upon such a convenient and universal order. Drawing upon data for Japan, Sweden, Germany, Britain, Canada and the United States, Professor Kuznets forcefully denies that such discontinuity is common to all. Rather he sketches a picture of economies initially blessed with respectable savings proportions and growth rates, and experiencing gradual increases in both well beyond what have been denoted as the take-off decades. Sometimes, in his zeal, his conclusions overreach his own evidence. For Germany and Japan the available series begin during the supposed take-off; hence the relevant comparison with the earlier magnitudes is excluded. Similarly, for Britain the discontinuity in the annual rate of change of aggregate product understates the break in the *per capita* series after 1785. Moreover, even such a rise in the growth rate of total output as from 0.9% prior to 1770 and 1.5% from 1770 to 1880 should not be dismissed too lightly. Finally, more recently compiled data for countries such as Italy and Denmark appear to fit the original Rostow specification very well indeed.[3]

These amendments to Kuznets' findings are not to argue for the validity of the Rostow

---

[3]Reported in Simon Kuznets, "Long Term Trends in Capital Formation Proportions," *Economic Development and Cultural Change*, Vol. IX, No. 4, Part II, 1961.

conjecture. Still other countries, like Norway, do not conform at all, and recently compiled United States evidence stands in even greater contradiction than that available to Kuznets in 1960. The increase in the share of output devoted to domestic capital formation from the 1830s on appears to be substantially more modest than that observed in other economies: the gross rate starts at 15% in 1834–43, changes little during the *ante bellum* period and increases (in part due to relative price changes) to about 25% in the postwar decades.[4] There is obviously a variety of national experiences to be reckoned with. Some economies may have executed the requisite *saltus* in aggregate terms, while others pursued a more gradual course. (Appropriately enough, Kenneth Berrill finds the same diversity in the dependence upon foreign capital in the course of development.) Since both groups attained the same conversion to economic growth rooted in a modern technology, the Rostow hypothesis must be adjudged of limited merit.

Note also the additional and unfortunate rigidity imposed by enmeshing the take-off within a full-blown stage theory of economic evolution. Like most nineteenth-century conceptions of progress, the path is orderly and monotonic: societies move through each of the stages in succession. But unfortunately excluded by such a hierarchy are many of the most interesting cases—economies that entered well into the transition phase but did not succeed. Some of the nations of Latin America seem to have been so beset. At the end of the nineteenth and beginning of the twentieth century, the pace of development quickened in that part of the world as it did in Russia and Italy, among others. In Mexico, between 1895 and 1910, one set of per capita income estimates places growth at 1.6% annually, or faster than Britain and possibly even Russia during their take-offs.

Nor was it simply exploitation of mineral resources: manufacturing expanded at the salutary rate of 5% per year as well. Again, in Argentina the net national capital formation proportion averaged some 20% in the years 1900–15, with annual growth of product of almost 3%. Much social overhead capital had been accumulated, and in Argentina, at least, much human capital as well.[5] Many of these same features are common to Chile. Yet retrospectively, the anticipated prize of sustained growth did not materialise. Must we then agree that take-off did not occur since "the subsequent periods of stagnation or relapse . . . are clear" (p. 27)? Why not take-off, followed by structural difficulties that left such economies modernised only in certain, but not all, respects?

The unnecessarily narrow Rostow view is imposed by the logic of a stage theory without an endogenous propulsive force. Take-off accordingly must be defined not in terms of the extent and nature of the inner transformation, but the later accomplishment of continuing flight. For only then, precisely by reference to the self-sustained character of subsequent growth, can we be certain take-off has occurred. In turn, the preconditions have been satisfied, since they are specified only as those permitting take-off to occur. The minimum social overhead capital, the rise of a large enough entrepreneurial class, the prior sufficient growth in agricultural productivity, are all ratified. The other, and necessary, way of articulating the three central stages of the global theory is to specify the conditions for moving from one to the other independently of later events; this in turn means a complete theory of social change, including non-economic factors. Rostow, despite even more than customary obeisance to the latter, never successfully integrates them into his analysis, precisely for the reason that the linkage he imposes runs in the opposite temporal direction.

---

[4]These are the estimates of Robert E. Gallman and will appear in his "Gross National Product in the United States, 1834–1909," to appear in Vol. 29 of *Studies in Income and Wealth.*

[5]For Mexico, see *México, Cincuenta Años de Revolución,* Mexico City, 1960, Vol. I, p. 585; for the Argentine data, see Kuznets, "Long Term Trends in Capital Formation Proportions."

The consequence is a non-operational concept. To talk knowingly of countries in the world to-day as in the pre-conditions phase or the midst of take-off is sheer guesswork, unrelated to the theory itself. This is why it is possible (so far) to be right with the assessment of Mexico but wrong with Argentina. In neither instances are objective criteria invoked. The consequence of this counter-temporal linkage is to rob the take-off phase at the same time of its attractiveness as a decisive period—possibly one of many—in the growth of a society and to reduce it to a mechanical construct whose identification within a specific set of years is more to be worried about than an elaboration of its content. . . .

THE SECTORAL VARIANT OF TAKE-OFF

The aggregate approach to take-off has not fared well. It is unable to deliver the universal, endogenous theory of development it promises. But such deserved criticism should not obscure the many insights take-off has to offer at the sectoral level. There its great strength is an explicitly partial orientation emphasising process, and so subject to empirical test. Rostow's various views may be summarized by the following interrelated propositions:

1. Successful industrialisation is unbalanced in the sense that a single, or limited number of industries, is the source from which an initial acceleration ramifies through the economy. There is a consequent discontinuity in production of manufactures.

2. Such leading sectors have three paths of influence upon the economy: forward, lateral and backward linkages, of which the latter route has historically predominated.

3. Certain industries have played the role of leading sector in a number of different countries, notably the railroad.

4. The development of certain subsidiary activities—coal, iron and machinery—is a good index of the extent of industrialisation and the probability of its continuation.

5. Industrial, rather than agricultural, growth affords the initial basis for sustained development.

Now, to be sure, these propositions are by no means proven. Indeed, one can set out many concrete instances in which the Rostow examples purporting to establish one or more of the points is grossly in error. Not the least of these deal with the supposed importance of the railroad in triggering take-off. In the United States, for example, the role played by the railroad before 1860 in developing for the first time a machinery industry is clearly mis-stated. The reason locomotives and other equipment were produced domestically so soon after the introduction of the railway was that machinery firms were already in existence to serve the textile and steamboat interest. Virtually all the locomotive firms grew out of such origins. Nor did their specialised production dominate the industry anything like the mistaken horse-power estimates Rostow cites. Where the unique significance of the railway resides with respect to engineering inputs is in its substantial maintenance requirements. Widely dispersed repair shops training pools of local talent undoubtedly were a significant factor in technological diffusion.

What is more, the entire emphasis upon the industrial consequences following from the backward linkage of railroadisation as being crucial in the United States misses the point. At the time when pig-iron output first underwent apparent rapid increase in the 1840s iron rail demand was an insignificant proportion of the whole. Coal, too, was a minor need for railroad operations in an era of wood-burning engines. Rather what made the rapid projection of the railroad in the 1850s so consequential was the impetus it gave to agricultural expansion. In this and other instances Rostow tends to understate the role of the market, actual and anticipated, in favour of derived demand nexuses. While the latter may to-day be more potent, we should not re-write history in its image. Modernisation may proceed impelled by relative prices as well as by government, and by way of forward linkages as well as backward.

It also follows that yet another proposition closer study may amend and qualify is the extent to which commercial agriculture may serve as a leading sector. Professor Bulhões treats the case of the state of São Paulo in Brazil, where he outlines a sequence leading from expanding coffee production to social overhead investment to industrial diversification. The evolutionary process in this instance contradicts both the Rostow and Gerschenkron emphasis. For new countries, drawing extensively upon immigration and capital imports, and with large land resources, this may be the natural pattern. One may cite the United States, Canada, Australia and New Zealand. Where such a process is arrested, as in Brazil and Argentina, it may cause sustained growth to be much more difficult to achieve than might otherwise be the case. Ungrasped opportunities may exact a continuing toll as a disadvantage of forwardness.

On the other hand, Professor Boserup's comprehensive essay defends what has almost come to be the conventional view that industrialisation proceeds despite agriculture rather than as a consequence of a progressive primary sector. "In the normal course of events, new things do not originate in the agricultural milieu" (p. 205). At best, rising agricultural productivity serves as a precondition for take-off, and some type of institutional reform is required to raise supply elasticities. Within the European and South Asian context of sedentary agriculture, one can find little fault with these conclusions; the principal caveat is the applicability of the results to more recently settled lands.

These limitations are of no matter. Much more detailed research is required before the central tenets of the hypothesis can be fairly evaluated and suitably qualified. That the sectoral variant of take-off both permits and structures such research is testimony to its usefulness. Indeed, Rostow himself in this volume has restated the mechanism in such a way as to further its application. By making more explicit the type of linkages by which leading sectors transmit their impulses he considerably improves upon the earlier version, which tended to stress the observed rate of growth of the leading sector as a measure of significance. The legitimate criticisms of Kuznets, that leadership represents a combination of internal growth, weight within the industrial matrix and the magnitude of other effects, thus are fully met. . . .

With the forward, backward and lateral linkages spelled out in this fashion, Rostow's leading sectors now become virtually the historical analogue of Hirschman's strategy for contemporary unbalanced growth. Certain activities have capacity for greater influence than others because they have more dispersed, or larger, demands upon manufactures as a whole, or some critical subset; other sectors pass along their output not to consumers directly but to other industries for further processing, and so present a potential force from the side of supply; finally, some industries, by virtue of location, or training of a skilled labour force, or demonstration effects, operate beyond interindustrial relationships. Leading sectors presumably possess some critical combination of all three, the first two of which, at least, are subject to well-defined empirical investigation.

There is much to be done to extract the potential gains of this approach. Forward linkages, which are more behavioural in their inducements than the technically determined backward linkages, are yet to be suitably defined. Various proposed measures within the input-output framework, such as the proportion of sales to industrial purchasers versus final demand or more detailed summaries of the inverse matrix of technological coefficients to rank the absorptive consequences of an initial expansion in output, do not fully render the market dimensions of this supply influence.[6] The extent to which backward

---

[6]Albert Hirschman, *The Strategy of Economic Development,* New Haven, 1958, pp. 106–7, uses the sales ratio measure. P. N. Rasmussen, *Studies in Inter-Sectoral Relations,* Copenhagen, 1956, develops an index of sensitivity of dispersion that "expresses the extent to which the system of industries draws upon industry no. *i*" (p. 135).

linkages have been emphasised may reflect the better analytical basis for measuring derived demands as much as their differential importance.

Nor can we ignore the very real data limitations. Complete, disaggregated industrial matrices are not now available, and perhaps never can be, far distant into the past. None the less, in most actual instances relatively few, but significant, interactions are involved. However crude the first historical applications of the leading sector concept inevitably turn out to be, they promise to add a considerable sophistication to our studies of past industrialisations, successes and failures. The input-output apparatus so mobilised distinguishes clearly between the magnitude of direct and indirect effects, and settles the recurrent question raised at this Conference and elsewhere of whether rates of growth or absolute increments are the relevant criteria of the importance of a single industry by placing its contribution in an appropriate multi-sector context.

This comparative-statical framework, however enlightening, does not exhaust the content of initial industrialisation. But neither does it fully render the concept of take-off. Rostow's category of lateral linkages is an attempt to introduce further elements of change into the picture. That such a grouping is too broad and nebulous to serve the needs of empirical research is not to deny his recognition of the problem. In preference to that procedure, it would seem better to retain the input-output context and to interpret the entire array of technical coefficients not as constants but as variables themselves subject to change as a function of changes in output of certain industries or specific coefficients.[7] Not only do we thereby faithfully translate the Rostow emphasis upon productivity change as one of the fundamental influences upon modern growth but we retain the appli-

cability of many of the initial Rostow propositions. Take-off becomes a sectoral joint theory of output change *and* technological diffusion.

So interpreted, the leading sector becomes not only the agent of triggering quantity response in other industries but also of disseminating modern techniques. It therefore is likely to be a new industry itself using advanced technology, a description consistent with the broad contours of historical industrialisations. Corresponding to the discontinuity in industrial production is a threshold level of acceptance of novel methods. Here is where the thrust of non-economic influences should be directed: which social circumstances are barriers and aids to technological change. Once the level of resistance has been overcome, diffusion is assumed to be regular and continual. Industrial growth typically, then, will continue at high levels for backward economies as they absorb better production techniques.

Such a prominent place for technology in the schema reinforces the logical basis for many of the earlier Rostow conjectures concerning the pattern of industrialisation. The physical presence of an industry like machinery—in contrast to dependence upon imports—is indeed a good guide to successful industrialisation. It creates a national vested interest committed to technological progress and obsolescence while at the same time reducing uncertainty by assuring close contact between supplier and user of the new techniques. Where maintenance needs are apt to be crucial, proximity is no small comfort. Needless to say, the portrait of an industrial matrix expanding by initial augmentation of sectors utilising modern technology gives greater weight to the preference for manufactures over agriculture as a vehicle of growth.

Whether these statements suffice or other propositions relating to technological diffusion are substituted, the important point is that productivity increase is afforded an explicit and central position in the hypothesis. This is a great advance beyond the simple capital-accumulation models still current—and un-

---

[7]It is useful in this context to note the identity between a geometric index of productivity change and that obtained from the changing matrix of technical input-output coefficients. See Evsey D. Domar, "On the Measurement of Technological Change," *Economic Journal*, Vol. LXXI, 1961, pp. 709–29.

derlying the aggregate version of take-off itself. Much must be done to implement the approach, both analytically and empirically. Historical initial conditions must be allowed to influence the propositions, thereby softening the claims of universality.[8]

The take-off phase itself must be integrated into later, sustained growth. Are long savings a miniature replay of the initial discontinuity postulated, as Rostow sometimes seems to suggest? How are the initital resource constraints imposed by inadequate capital formation resolved over time in response to industrialisation? How do increases in agricultural productivity become regular, not as a pre-requisite of the industrial surge, but as a resultant? Without a respectable rate of growth of agricultural product, rapid national income advance is almost impossible. Finally, much systematic historical research lies ahead. We do not even know at the present what the role of productivity change was, or is, in the contemporary world in the first stages of industrialisation!

The sectoral variant of take-off thus can serve as the basis for important and relevant research into many still unresolved problems of economic growth.[9] While economic theorists wrestle with the implications of embodied and disembodied technical progress, and empirical workers extend the frontiers of measurement of productivity, it is only appropriate that historians bring to bear accumulated experience upon technological diffusion and its contribution to successful industrialisation.

[8]Recent Latin American experience where rapid increase in the manufacturing sector has not led to continuing growth is an obvious case in point. For Chile, see Marto A. Ballesteros and Tom E. Davis, "The Growth of Output and Employment in Basic Sectors of the Chilean Economy, 1908–1957," *Economic Development and Cultural Change,* Vol. XI, No. 2, 1962, p. 153.

[9]For one related attempt see Hollis B. Chenery, Shuntaro Shishido, and Tsunehiko Watanabe, "The Pattern of Japanese Growth, 1914–1954," *Econometrica,* Vol. XXX, No. 1, 1962, pp. 114–118 especially. Although they fail to carry the analysis of technological change very far, their results illustrate the potential returns from sectoral analysis.

CONCLUDING COMMENT

The appearance of *The Economics of Take-off* marks a turning-point in a debate that has now been carried on for almost a decade. Here for the first time is a systematic confrontation of the take-off hypothesis with a considerable segment of historical experience. The aggregate version of the concept emerges qualified at best: Rostow's readiness to accept any number of amendments is testimony less to the flexibility of the notion than to its failure to fit well the actual diverse paths of development.

The test of the hypothesis afforded by the recent quantitative research upon historical patterns of growth constitutes the principal contribution of the volume. The papers and discussion based less factually have a correspondingly less impact, in no small measure because their relationship to the take-off is more tenuous. Yet despite this progress the Conference achieved in its examination of the discontinuity of modern economic growth, important questions remain. It is for this reason that I have tried to suggest a new focal point for the discussion by differentiating between the aggregate and sectoral approaches to take-off, and to the role technological change plays in the last. Where there is little reason to accept the complete explanation of national income growth Rostow offers, there is good cause to pursue his many suggestions concerning the process by which industrialisation becomes rooted. Rostow, paradoxically, is at his best read as a prospectus rather than as a treatise.

The loss of grandeur in the descent from manifesto to partial hypothesis must not be exaggerated. It is a rare occasion when operational, albeit partial, theories pregnant with potential are put forward. The conception of take-off is just such an event. Professor Clapham, some forty years ago, chided his theoretical colleagues for providing him with empty boxes. Better that historians today recognise the important possibilities of take-off in structuring inquiry than to continue to expound (or to reject out of hand) a grand set of stages that lamentably are sometimes vacant.

Comment

Rostow has extended his analysis in *How It All Began* (1975) and *Why the Poor Get Richer and the Rich Slow Down: Essays in the Marshallian Long Period* (1970).

For a more detailed exposition of Rostow's general thesis, and criticisms levied against it, see the papers presented at the International Economic Association's conference, published in W. W. Rostow et al., *Economics of Take-Off into Sustained Growth* (1963).

Several other critiques deserve special mention: K. Berrill, "Historical Experience: The Problem of Economic 'Take-Off,' " in K. Berrill (ed.), *Economic Development with Special Reference to East Asia* (1964), chapter 7; Henry Rosovsky, "The Take-Off into Sustained Controversy," *Journal of Economic History* (June 1965); P. Baran and E. Hobsbawm, "The Stages of Economic Growth," *Kyklos,* Vol. 14, No. 2 (1961); P. T. Bauer and Charles Wilson, "The Stages of Growth," *Economica* (May 1962); S. G. Checkland, "Theories of Economic and Social Evolution: The Rostow Challenge," *Scottish Journal of Political Economy* (November 1960); E. E. Hagen, *On the Theory of Social Change* (1962), appendix 2; D. C. North, "A Note on Professor Rostow's 'Take-Off' into Self-sustained Economic Growth," *The Manchester School* (January 1958); Goran Ohlin, "Reflections on the Rostow Doctrine," *Economic Development and Cultural Change* (July 1961); G. L. S. Shackle, "The Stages of Economic Growth," *Political Studies* (February 1962). But see Rostow's second edition of *The Stages of Economic Growth* (1971) and *Politics and the Stages of Growth* (1971).

Of special interest is the Festschrift in honor of Rostow, *Economics in the Long View* (1982), edited by C. P. Kindleberger and Guido di Tella.

II.A.3. Economic Backwardness in Historical Perspective*

The map of Europe in the nineteenth century showed a motley picture of countries varying with regard to the degree of their economic backwardness. At the same time, processes of rapid industrialization started in several of those countries from very different levels of economic backwardness. Those differences in points—or planes—of departure were of crucial significance for the nature of the subsequent development. Depending on a given country's degree of economic backwardness on the eve of its industrialization, the course and character of the latter tended to vary in a number of important respects. Those variations can be readily compressed into the shorthand of six propositions.

*From Alexander Gerschenkron, *Economic Backwardness in Historical Perspective*, Cambridge, Mass.: Harvard University Press, copyright, 1962, by The President and Fellows of Harvard College, pp. 353–9. Reprinted by permission.

1. The more backward a country's economy, the more likely was its industrialization to start discontinuously as a sudden great spurt proceeding at a relatively high rate of growth of manufacturing output.[1]

2. The more backward a country's economy, the more pronounced was the stress in its industrialization on bigness of both plant and enterprise.

3. The more backward a country's economy, the greater was the stress upon producers' goods as against consumers' goods.

[1]The "great spurt" is closely related to W. W. Rostow's "take-off" (*The Stages of Economic Growth,* Cambridge University Press, 1960, Chap. 4). Both concepts stress the element of specific discontinuity in economic development; great spurts, however, are confined to the area of manufacturing and mining, whereas take-offs refer to national output. Unfortunately, in the present state of our statistical information on long-term growth of national income, there is hardly any way of establishing, let alone testing, the take-off hypotheses.

4. The more backward a country's economy, the heavier was the pressure upon the levels of consumption of the population.

5. The more backward a country's economy, the greater was the part played by special institutional factors designed to increase supply of capital to the nascent industries and, in addition, to provide them with less decentralized and better informed entrepreneurial guidance; the more backward the country, the more pronounced was the coerciveness and comprehensiveness of those factors.

6. The more backward a country, the less likely was its agriculture to play any active role by offering to the growing industries the advantages of an expanding industrial market based in turn on the rising productivity of agricultural labor.

... [T]he differences in the level of economic advance among the individual European countries or groups of countries in the last century were sufficiently large to make it possible to array those countries, or group of countries, along a scale of increasing degrees of backwardness and thus to render the latter an operationally usable concept. Cutting two notches into that scale yields three groups of countries which may be roughly described as advanced, moderately backward, and very backward. To the extent that certain of the variations in our six propositions can also be conceived as discrete rather than continuous, the pattern assumes the form of a series of stage constructs. Understandably enough, this result obtains most naturally with regard to factors referred to in proposition 5, where quantitative differences are associated with qualitative, that is, institutional, variations. ...

Such an attempt to view the course of industrialization as a schematic stagelike process differs essentially from the various efforts in "stage making," the common feature of which was the assumption that all economies were supposed regularly to pass through the same individual stages as they moved along the road of economic progress. The regularity may have been frankly presented as an inescapable "law" of economic development.[2] Alternatively, the element of necessity may have been somewhat disguised by well-meant, even though fairly meaningless, remarks about the choices that were open to society.[3] But all those schemes were dominated by the idea of uniformity. Thus, Rostow was at pains to assert that the process of industrialization repeated itself from country to country lumbering through his pentametric rhythm. ...

The point, however, is not simply that these were important occurrences which have just claims on the historian's attention. What matters in the present connection is that observing the individual methods of financing industrial growth helps us to understand the crucial problem of prerequisites for industrial development.

The common opinion on the subject has been well stated by Rostow. There is said to be a number of certain general preconditions or prerequisites for industrial growth, without which it could not begin. Abolition of an archaic framework in agricultural organization or an increase in the productivity of agriculture; creation of an influential modern elite which is materially or ideally interested in economic change; provision of what is called social-overhead capital in physical form—all these are viewed as "necessary preconditions," except that some reference to the multifarious forms in which the prerequisites are fulfilled in the individual areas are designed to take care of the "unique" factors in development. Similarly, the existence of a value system favoring economic progress and the availability of effective entrepreneurial groups basking in the sun of social approval have been regarded as essential preconditions of industrial growth.

These positions are part and parcel of an undifferentiated approach to industrial history. But their conceptual and empirical deficiencies are very considerable, even though

[2]See, for example, Bruno Hildebrand, *Die Nationalökonomie, der Gegenwart und Zukunft und andere gesammelte Schriften,* 1, Jena, 1922, p. 357.

[3]See Rostow, *The Stages of Economic Growth,* pp. 118ff.

it is by no means easy to bid farewell to this highly simplified way of viewing the processes of industrialization. It took the present writer several years before he succeeded in reformulating the concept of prerequisites so that it could be fit into the general approach premised upon the notion of relative backwardness. . . .

There should be a fine on the use of words such as "necessary" or "necessity" in historical writings. As one takes a closer look at the concept of necessity as it is appended to prerequisites of industrial development, it becomes clear that, whenever the concept is not entirely destitute of meaning, it is likely to be purely definitional: industrialization is defined in terms of certain conditions which then, by an imperceptible shift of the writer's wrist, are metamorphosed into historical preconditions.[4]

The recourse of tautologies and dexterous manipulations has been produced by, or at any rate served to disguise, very real empirical difficulties. After having satisfied oneself that in England certain factors could be reasonably regarded as having preconditioned the industrialization of the country, the tendency was, and still is, to elevate them to the rank of ubiquitous prerequisites of all European industrializations. Unfortunately, the attempt was inconsistent with two empirical observations: (1) some of the factors that had served as prerequisites in England either were not present in less advanced countries or at best were present to a very small extent; (2) the big spurt of industrial development occurred in those countries despite the lack of such prerequisites.

If these observations are not ignored or shrugged away, as is usually done, they quite naturally direct research toward a new question: in what way and through the use of what devices did backward countries *substitute* for the missing prerequisites? . . . It appears, on the one hand, that some of the alleged prerequisites were not needed in

industrializations proceeding under different conditions. On the other hand, once the question has been asked, whole series of various substitutions become visible which could be readily organized in a meaningful pattern according to the degree of economic backwardness. . . . [I]t is easy to conceive of the capital supplied to the early factories in an advanced country as stemming from previously accumulated wealth or from gradually plowed-back profits; at the same time, actions by banks and governments in less advanced countries are regarded as successful attempts to create *in the course* of industrialization conditions which had not been created in the "preindustrial" periods precisely because of the economic backwardness of the areas concerned. . . .

. . . [T]he area of capital supply is only one instance of substitutions for missing prerequisites. As one looks at the various patterns of substitution in the individual countries, taking proper account of the effects of gradually diminishing backwardness, one is tempted to formulate still another general proposition. The more backward was a country on the eve of its great spurt of industrial development, the more likely were the processes of its industrialization to present a rich and complex picture—thus providing a curious contrast with its own preindustrial history that most often was found to have been relatively barren. In an advanced country, on the other hand, the very richness of its economic history in the preindustrial periods rendered possible a relatively simple and straightforward course in its modern industrial history.

Thus, the concept of prerequisites must be regarded as an integral part of this writer's general approach to the industrial history of Europe. At the same time, it is important to keep in mind the heuristic nature of the concept. There is no intention to suggest that backward countries necessarily engaged in deliberate acts of "substitution" for something that had been in evidence in more advanced countries. Men in a less developed country may have simply groped for and found solutions that were consonant with the

---

[4]It is not surprising, therefore, to see Rostow at one point (p. 49) mix conditions and preconditions of industrial development very freely.

existing conditions of backwardness. In fact, one could conceivably start the study of European industrializations in the east rather than in the west of the Continent and view some elements in English industrial history as substitutions for the German or the Russian way of doing things. This would not be a very good way to proceed. It would make mockery of chronology and would be glaringly artificial. True, some artificiality also inheres in the opposite approach. It is arbitrary to select England as the seat of prerequisites. Yet this is the arbitrariness of the

process of cognition and should be judged by its fruits.

The main advantage of viewing European history as patterns of substitutions governed by the prevailing—and changing—degree of backwardness lies, perhaps paradoxically, in its offering a set of predictabilities while at the same time placing limitations upon our ability to predict. To predict is not to prophesy. Prediction in historical research means addressing intelligent, that is, sufficiently specific, questions as new materials are approached.

Comment

No attempt can be made to do justice to the innumerable historical studies of development. Only a few survey studies can be singled out: R. M. Hartwell, "The Causes of Industrial Revolution: An Essay in Methodology," *Economic History Review,* Vol. 18, No. 1 (1965); Richard A. Easterlin, "Is There a Need for Historical Research on Underdevelopment?" *American Economic Review* (May 1965); Barry E. Supple, "Economic History and Economic Underdevelopment," *Canadian Journal of Economics and Political Science* (November 1961); John C. H. Fei and Gustav Ranis, "Economic Development in Historical Perspective," *American Economic Review* (May 1969), J. Hughes, *Industrialization and Economic History,* New York (1970), part II; J. R. Hicks, *A Theory of Economic History,* London (1969).

An interesting collection of "successful and promising beginnings" of development is contained in Malcolm E. Falkus (ed.), *Readings in the History of Economic Growth,* New York (1968); also, Barry E. Supple (ed.), *The Experience of Economic Growth,* New York (1963).

II.A.4. Future Development in Historical Perspective—Note

"The historian is a prophet looking backwards"—this dictum is apt for the economic historian concerned with development. Rostow's analysis, for instance, presumes that the choices now confronting the poor countries may be revealed in the light of the stages of preconditions and take-off that the currently rich countries experienced in earlier centuries, and that historical perspective may contribute to the formulation of development policy. From this viewpoint, Rostow's analysis may be most instructive for many countries that have not yet passed successfully through the take-off stage: it may point up the similarities and differences between past

and present take-offs, and suggest what policy implications flow from the differences.

With respect to the role of particular sectors of the economy, Rostow observes many problems and patterns familiar from the past. He submits that present take-offs depend, as in the past, on the allocation of resources

to building up and modernizing the three non-industrial sectors required as the matrix for industrial growth: social overhead capital; agriculture; and foreign-exchange-earning sectors, rooted in the improved exploitation of natural resources. In addition, they must begin to find areas of modern processing or manufacture where the application of modern technique (combined with high income-

or price-elasticities of demand) are likely to permit rapid growth-rates, with a high rate of plow-back of profits.[1]

It will be instructive to reconsider these conclusions after reading Chapters VI–IX below, where questions not recognized by Rostow are raised regarding the allocation of investment resources and the role of industrialization.

Further, Rostow believes that for the presently underdeveloped nations, the inner mechanics of the take-off involve problems of capital formation, just as in the past. If their take-offs are to succeed, the underdeveloped countries "must seek ways to tap off into the modern sector income above consumption levels hitherto sterilized by the arrangements controlling traditional agriculture. They must seek to shift men of enterprise from trade and money-lending to industry. And to these ends patterns of fiscal, monetary, and other policies (including education policies) must be applied, similar to those developed and applied in the past."[2]

Again, this interpretation of the take-off should be critically reexamined after reading Chapter IV, below, where a case is made against assigning as much importance to the role of capital accumulation as Rostow does. Rostow also notes some political and sociocultural similarities between past and present take-offs. As in the past, political interest groups range from defenders of the *status quo* to those prepared to force the pace of modernization at whatever cost; there exists the balance between external expression of nationalism in almost every case; above all, "there is continuity in the role of reactive nationalism, as an engine of modernization, linked effectively to or at cross-purposes with other motives for remaking traditionalist society."[3]

Historical cases of successful take-offs also indicate a contemporary catalogue of necessary social change:

... how to persuade the peasant to change his methods and shift to producing for wider markets; how to build up a corps of technicians, capable of manipulating the new techniques; how to create a corps of entrepreneurs, oriented not towards large profit margins at existing levels of output and technique, but to expand output, under a regime of regular technological change and obsolescence; how to create a modern professional civil and military service, reasonably content with their salaries, oriented to the welfare of the nation and to standards of efficient performance, rather than to graft and to ties of family, clan, or region.[4]

On the basis of foregoing similarities, Rostow regards the process of development now going forward in Asia, the Middle East, Africa, and Latin America as analogues to the stages of preconditions and take-off of other societies in earlier centuries. But there are also differences—by way of different kinds of problems now confronting poor countries, and in the manner in which some problems, although similar in kind to those of the past, are now expressed in different degrees of intensity and complexity. Especially significant is the fact that the poor countries now stand in a different relationship to rich countries than was true when the presently rich countries were poor. These differences are extremely important, and they deserve more attention than Rostow gives them. For insofar as most of these differences aggravate the problems of the take-off, they warn against letting the success-stories of past take-offs lull us into too easy an interpretation of the development task. Nor should we equate the LDCs to the early stages of the presently developed countries. The persistence of underdevelopment in the world economy poses some refractory problems that were absent in earlier cases of successful development. If we recognize these differences, we may hesitate to join Rostow in concluding that in the end the lesson of history is that "the tricks of growth are not all that difficult."[5]

In the first place, poor countries are attempting to accelerate their development from a lower economic level than was true for

---

[1]W. W. Rostow, *The Stages of Economic Growth*, Cambridge, 1960, p. 139.

[2]Ibid.

[3]Ibid., p. 140.

[4]Ibid.

[5]Ibid., p. 166.

the presently rich countries at the time of their rapid rates of development. As Kuznets observes,

Output per capita is much lower in the underdeveloped countries today than it was in the presently developed countries at the date of entry—a period rather than a point of time—into modern economic growth, i.e., when growth of per-capita product (with an already high rate of population growth) began to accelerate, the shift toward non-agricultural sectors occurred, modern technology (modern by the times) was adopted, and so forth. However difficult the comparison of per-capita gross product at such distances of time and space, the weight of the evidence clearly suggests that, with the single and significant exception of Japan (the records for which are still to be fully tested), the pre-industrialization per-capita product in the presently developed countries, at least $200 in 1958 prices (and significantly more, in the off-shoots overseas), was appreciably higher than per-capita product in underdeveloped countries in the late 1950s—certainly in most of Asia and Africa, and in a good part of Latin America.

Yet this statistical difference in aggregate output per capita is less important than what it represents. It implies that even today these underdeveloped countries still have such a low product per capita that they are not at the same stage as the presently developed countries were at their initial stage of modern economic growth. This seems to be the case despite access to modern technology and despite the existence of a modern sector within these countries (no matter how small). These underdeveloped countries are either at some earlier stage within the long-term trend of the presently developed countries—in terms of the Western European sequence perhaps at the period of city formation in the early Middle Ages; or, what is far more defensible, they are at some stage in a sequence of long-term growth separate and distinct from that of the Western European cradle of the modern economic epoch and are following a time and phase sequence that may be quite different.[6]

Not only do poor countries now confront the strategic policy issues of development from an absolutely lower level of per capita

income than did the presently developed countries, but their relative positions are also inferior compared with other countries—unlike the position of the early comers to development that entered the industrialization process from a position of superior per capita income relative to other countries. The implications of attempting to develop rapidly from a lower level of per capita income, and from a relative position that entails more pressures of backwardness, should receive a fuller treatment than Rostow's analysis provides.

Gerschenkron's suggestive analysis, outlined above, can provide a more profound understanding of these implications. We should examine, as does Gerschenkron, the processes of industrial development in relation to the degree of backwardness of the areas concerned on the eve of their great spurts of industrialization. Gerschenkron's approach has distinct advantages over Rostow's in maintaining that it is only by comparing industrialization processes in several countries at various levels of backwardness that we can hope to separate what is accidental in a given industrial evolution from what can be attributed to the historical lags in a country's development, and that it is only because a developing country is part of a larger area which comprises more advanced countries that the historical lags are likely to be overcome in a specifically intelligible fashion.[7]

Another fundamental difference is that many of the poor countries have not yet experienced any significant degree of agricultural improvement as a basis for industrialization. The failure to have yet undergone an agricultural revolution makes the present problem of accelerating development far more difficult than it was for the now developed countries when they entered upon their industrial revolutions. It is fairly conclusive that productivity is lower in the agricultural

---

[6]Simon Kuznets, "Notes on Stage of Economic Growth as a System Determinant," in Alexander Eckstein (ed.), *Comparison of Economic Systems,* Berkeley, 1971, pp. 254–5.

[7]Alexander Gerschenkron, *Economic Backwardness in Historical Perspective,* Cambridge, 1962, p. 42. For the application of this general conception of a system of gradations of backwardness to particular countries, see Chaps. 1, 4, 7, 8.

sector of underdeveloped countries than it was in the pre-industrialization phase of the presently developed countries. Although direct evidence of this is unavailable, it is indirectly confirmed by data suggesting that the supply of agricultural land per capita is much lower in most underdeveloped countries today than it was in presently developed countries during their take-off, and that there is a wider difference between per worker income in agricultural and nonagricultural sectors in the underdeveloped countries today than there was in the pre-industrial phase of presently developed countries.

The more severe population pressures in the underdeveloped areas constitute another essential difference. Rates of population increase in these areas are higher than those that generally obtained during the Western cases of development in the past. Even though not all the poor countries are now densely populated, the rate of population growth is, or gives indications of soon becoming, a serious problem for most of them. And, unlike the earlier cases in which population growth was induced by, or at least paralleled, a higher rate of development, the present growth in population is simply the result of the introduction of public-health measures, which lower death rates. These measures act as an autonomous factor, quite unrelated to the rate of internal development. Moreover, unlike the European industrial countries that began lowering their birth rates before their sharpest declines in mortality, the poor countries now will not do so until long after their mortality has reached a modern low level. Given the fact that many poor countries are already experiencing population growth rates that are two to three times higher than those that confronted the currently rich nations when they were in their early phases of development, and that other poor countries may face a population problem in a relatively short time, the need to attain increases in production sufficient to outstrip potential increases in population is now more acute than it ever was in Western countries at the beginning of their industrialization.

Sociocultural and political differences also account for some obstacles to development that are now more formidable than in the past. Unlike the social heritage with which Western countries entered the take-off stage, the social structure and value pattern in many poor countries are still inimical to development. The structure of social relations tends to be hierarchical, social cleavages remain pronounced, and mobility among groups is limited. Instead of allowing individuals to achieve status by their own efforts and performance, their status may be simply ascribed to them, according to their position in a system of social classification—by age, lineage, clan, or caste. A value system that remains "tradition-oriented" also tends to minimize the importance of economic incentives, material rewards, independence, and rational calculation. When the emphasis is on an established pattern of economic life, family obligations, and traditional religious beliefs, the individual may simply adopt the attitude of accepting what happens to exist, rather than attempting to alter it—an attitude of resignation rather than innovation. Within an extended family system or a village community, individuals may resign themselves to accepting group loyalties and personal relationships which remain in a stable and tradition-dominated pattern, assigning little importance to material accomplishments and change. Even though they may have latent abilities, individuals may lack the motivations and stimulations to introduce change; there may not be sufficiently large groups in the society who are "achievement-oriented," concerned with the future, and believers in the rational mastery of nature. The positive value which the traditional way of life still holds for many of the people in a poor country inhibits the necessary orientation toward the future, and change is either resisted or, if accepted, is restricted to fringe areas.

In short, the cultural context in many poor countries may not yet be as favorable to economic achievement as it was in Western countries. This is not, of course, to assume simply that, because the West is developed, Western values and institutions are therefore necessary for development, and that Western cultural patterns must be imported into the poor countries. Many Western values and institutions may be only accidentially associated with Western development, and many values and institutions in poor countries are not obstacles to development. But though the West need not be imitated, some institutional changes and modifications in the value structure are necessary if the inhibiting institutions and values are to be removed. To allow poor countries to enter into the development process with a favorable cultural framework as did the currently developed nations, there must be changes in their cultures so that new wants, new beliefs, new motivations, and new institutions may be created. Until these cultural changes are forthcoming, an acceleration of development will be more difficult to achieve than it was in the past.

If the degree of sociocultural development has been less than what occurred in the past, so too has there been a difference in political development. In many poor countries, the political foundations for developmental efforts are not yet as firm as they were in Western development. Whereas the currently developed countries had already enjoyed a long period of political independence and a stable political framework before their periods of rapid economic development, most of the currently poor countries have only recently acquired a real measure of political independence. Political instability, undifferentiated and diffuse political structures, and inefficient governments are still only too prevalent. In some countries, government leadership has yet to be exercised by groups that do not have vested interests in preserving the *status quo;* in others, there is still a wide gap between the traditional mass and a modern elite which controls the central structures of government and is the main locus of political activity.[8]

All the foregoing differences might be subsumed under a more general observation that it matters a great deal for the course of an individual country's development where that country stands relative to other countries. This has already been alluded to by Gerschenkron for European cases of development. With more direct reference to the problems of the presently poor countries, Professor Streeten has argued persuasively that the fact that advanced industrial societies already exist when countries embark on development, makes a number of important differences to the development prospects of the less developed societies.[9]

On the one side, the coexistence of rich and poor countries now has a number of drawbacks for the less developed countries. A suggestive list follows.[10]

1. The most important difference is that the advanced state of medical knowledge that can be borrowed from rich countries makes it now possible to reduce deaths cheaply and rapidly, without contributing to an equivalent reduction in births—thereby presenting the LDCs with more difficult population problems than the now advanced countries faced in their pre-inustrial phase.

2. Modern technology in rich countries evolved under conditions of labor scarcity and has therefore been designed to save labor in relation to capital. But the transfer of labor-saving technology to LDCs, which is encouraged by attitudes toward modernization and by the prestige of Western technology, tends to aggravate the underutilization of labor in the LDCs.

3. The knowledge of organizations and institutions that prevail in the advanced countries may be ill-adapted to the needs of LDCs. The adoption of the trade union structure, for example, may be inappropriate for conditions of labor surplus. Or public expenditure on social welfare services developed in advanced industrial welfare states may be premature for LDCs. Or large-scale business enterprises may be undesirable in lesser-de-

[8]For a discussion of the difference between Western and non-Western political systems, see G. A. Almond and J. S. Coleman (eds.), *The Politics of the Developing Areas,* Princeton, 1960.

[9]Paul P. Streeten, "The Frontiers of Development Studies: Some Issues of Development Policy," *Journal of Development Studies,* October 1967, pp. 2–24.

[10]Streeten fully elaborates this list and some other differences, ibid., pp. 3–7.

veloped economies. The transfer of inappropriate institutions to the LDCs may impede the development.

4. Technical progress in advanced economies has harmed the trade prospects of the less developed countries that depend on the export of primary products by facilitating the substitution of synthetics for natural products, by reducing the input of raw materials per unit of industrial output, and by shifting demand away from products with a high primary import content.

5. The land-rich or capital-rich countries which at one time served as an outlet for labor surplus countries are no longer receptive to immigration; with accelerated population growth and the intensified underutilization of labor, the development pressures are thus all the greater. At the same time, the scarce resources of capital and skilled individuals are drained off to the rich centers and away from the poor peripheral countries.

Streeten has rightly emphasized that it is this coexistence of rich and poor countries, rather than the international or unintentional exploitation of colonialism or neocolonialism, which can have detrimental effects on development efforts. And he properly concludes that it is this coexistence which sets limits to the ready transfer of the lessons of one historical setting to the entirely different present setting of poor countries vis-à-vis much more advanced countries.

Beyond the coexistence of rich and poor countries, we should also recognize that the attempts of many poor countries to develop simultaneously may also intensify the task for any one of the LDCs. The policies adopted by each country in its effort to develop may hinder the development of another country. Thus the poor countries compete among themselves in attempting to increase their exports, in attempting to attract private capital and skilled services, in attempting to foster industrialization via import-substitution policies, and by way of other restrictive nationalistic policies which have beggar-my-neighbor (usually a poor neighbor) effects.

Although these several differences now aggravate the problem of development, there are some dissimilarities which, on the other side, make the problems less difficult. Some advantages may accrue to presently poor countries from their position of being latecomers to development. Most helpful now may be the ability of the poor countries to draw upon the accumulated stock of knowledge in countries that have already developed. Not only may improved productive techniques and equipment be derived from these countries; more generally, they may benefit from the transference of ideas in the realm of social techniques and social innovation as well as technological. As we have already seen, however, the value of this imitative ability is debatable, since it is still necessary to modify and adapt—not simply imitate—the technological and social innovations within the context of the borrowing country's environment. This problem receives fuller treatment in Chapter V, below. And aside from the requirements of readaptation, there also remains the ultimate difficulty of having change accepted and integrated into the recipient society. We should not, therefore, accept too readily the view that by drawing upon the lessons and experiences of countries that have developed earlier, the latecomers are in a position to telescope the early stages of development.

The existence of many advanced countries that have already reached a high level of development, which was not the case when these same countries were in their preindustrial phase, may now, however, help to ease the development of poor countries by providing a flow of resources from the rich to the poor countries. Never in the past has there been so much international concern with the desirability of increasing trade, technical assistance, private foreign investment, and the flow of public funds as objectives of development policy. But how effective foreign economic assistance may actually prove to be is, of course, another matter. Some judgment on this may be had from Chapter V, below.

Finally, there is now a strong conscious desire for development on the part of national leaders in many countries. The national interest in deliberate and rapid development, the willingness of national authorities to assume responsibility for directing the country's economic development, and the knowledge of a variety of policies that a government can utilize to accelerate development—all these give new dimensions to the role that the State may play in the development of emerging nations. Through governmental action, to a degree unknown in Western development, a more favorable environment for a take-off might be created. Nonetheless, as will be appreciated time and again in subsequent chapters, the mere act of development planning cannot be expected to remove the difficult choices and decisions that must be made to accelerate development.

Depending on how much importance we attach to each of the various differences between past and present conditions, we may reach contrasting conclusions as to whether present conditions are more or less favorable than in the past for the acceleration of development. But in the final analysis, what will decide whether a poor country will succeed is whether its government can implement effectively the possible policies that might make the country's development potential realizable, and whether its people are prepared to bear the costs that accelerated development will necessarily entail. Regardless of whether we interpret conditions in the currently poor countries as being on balance more or less favorable, we must not expect these countries to follow simply the historical patterns of presently developed countries. We must still give due weight to the severity of the particular problems confronting these countries. And we must determine what policies might now be most effective in removing the barriers to development. With the benefit of historical perspective, however, we should be better able to appraise the significance of these present-day development problems and their various policy implications.

II.B. ANALYTICAL PERSPECTIVES

II.B.1. Contrasting Perceptions*

Somewhat oversimplifying, we can identify five recent changes in the perception of the development process. Although the shift in perceptions has been described as "recent," some of these changes go back a considerable time. Indeed, hardly any of the features of the "old" perception were generally accepted at any stage, and qualifications, criticisms and alternative perceptions were put forward almost as soon as the "orthodox" perception had been formulated.

1. The first change between our perception of development until about 1970 and after can be traced to differences of view between the First World and the Third World, and the Right and the Left, although there are all kinds of cross-alignments. The more popular (though not the academic) thinking of the Fifties and Sixties, codified in the Pearson Commission Report, was dominated by W. W. Rostow's doctrine of the stages of growth. This perspective was, partly, superseded in the early 1970s by what has sometimes been called a "dependencia" interpretation of international economic relationships. To illuminate the shift in perceptions from the first of these views to the second, let us review briefly each in turn.

According to Rostow's doctrine, development is a linear path along which all countries travel. The advanced countries had, at various times, passed the stage of "take-off," and the developing countries are now following them. Development "was seen primarily as a matter of 'economic growth,' and secondarily as a problem of securing social changes necessarily associated with growth.

*From Paul Streeten, "Development Ideas in Historical Perspective," in *Toward a New Strategy for Development,* A Rothko Chapel Colloquium, Pergamon Press, New York, 1979, pp. 25–35. Reprinted by permission.

It was taken for granted that organizing the march along the development path was the prime concern of government. . . .

The linear view begged a host of questions about the nature, causes and objectives of development. It tended to focus on constraints or obstacles (particularly lack of capital), the removal of which would set free the "natural" forces making for the steady move toward ever higher incomes.

Applied to the area of international relations, this view calls on the rich countries to supply the "missing components" to the developing countries and thereby to help them break bottlenecks or remove obstacles. These missing components may be capital, foreign exchange, skills or management. The doctrine provides a rationale for international capital aid, technical assistance, trade, private foreign investment. By breaking bottlenecks, rich countries can contribute to development efforts a multiple of what it costs them and thus speed up the development process in underdeveloped countries. Models pointing to gaps between required and available savings or foreign exchange are a rationalization of foreign assistance. The ultimate purpose of aid is to be rid of aid.

This linear or stages-of-growth view has come under heavy fire. It was criticized on logical, moral, historical and economic grounds. Logically, it should have been clear that the coexistence of more- and less-advanced countries is bound to make a difference (for better or worse) to the development efforts and prospects of the less advanced, compared with a situation where no other country was ahead or the distance was not very large. The larger the gap and the more interdependent the components of the international system, the less relevant are the lessons to be learned from the early starters. Morally and politically, the linear view ruled out options of different styles of development. Inexorably, we were all bound to pass through the Rostovian stages, in the words of the famous limerick, like a tram, not a bus. Historically, the view can be criticized as excessively determinist. Economically, it is deficient because it ignores the fact that the propagation of impulses from the rich to the poor countries alters the nature of the development process; that late-comers face problems essentially different from the early starters, and that "late late-comers" again find themselves in a world with a range of demonstration effects and other impulses, both from the advanced countries and from other late-comers, which present opportunities and obstacles quite different from those that England or even Germany, France and Russia, faced in their pre-industrialization phase.

Summarized briefly, it may be thought that too much weight is given to Rostow and to the linear view of the development. The "stages of growth" were criticized from the beginning by Kuznets, Gerschenkron and others. The heavy concentration on physical capital was criticized by Cairncross, Hirschman, and the human capital school of T. W. Schultz. There were many nonlinear theorists, from Schumpeter to Rosenstein-Rodan and Nurkse. The whole debate on balanced versus unbalanced growth does not fit into the linear perception. But it remains true that, though not in academic circles, the Rostow model had a powerful grip on the imagination of policy makers, planners and aid officials and that it was this view that gave rise to a reaction.

Succeeding the linear development perspective in popularity in the early 1970s was a second view, according to which the international system of rich-poor relationships produces and maintains the underdevelopment of the poor countries (the rich "underdevelop" the poor, in André Gunder Frank's phrase). In various ways, malignly exploitative or benignly neglectful or simply as a result of the unintended impact of events and policies in rich countries, the coexistence of rich and poor societies renders the efforts of the poor societies to choose their style of development more difficult or impossible. Certain groups in the developing countries—entrepreneurs, salaried officials, employees—enjoy high incomes, wealth and status and, constituting the ruling class, they perpetuate the international system of inequality and conformity. Not only Marxists but also a growing number of non-Marxists have come to attribute a large part of underdevelopment and of the obstacles encountered in the process of development to the existence and the policies of the industrial countries of the West, including Japan and the Soviet Union.

According to one line of this second view, aid is not a transitional phenomenon to be ended after "take-off," but a permanent feature, like an international income tax. According to a more radical line, aid is itself part of the international system of exploitation, and self-reliant, independent development has to get rid of it.

The conclusion drawn from this perception is that the developing countries should put up barriers between themselves and the destructive intrusions of trade, technology, transnational corporations, and educational and ideological influences, and should aim at "delinking" or "decoupling," at pulling down a bamboo or poverty curtain, at insulating and isolating themselves from the international system.

W. W. Rostow, for the first kind of perception, and André Gunder Frank, for the second, are the popular rather than the academic models. Prebisch, Singer, Myrdal, Hirschman, and Perroux, not to say anything of Marx and List, had long ago developed approaches to development that separated "spread" or "trickle-down" effects from "polarization," "backwash" or "dominance" effects. And many had raised doubts as to whether everything would be fine if all countries only pursued free trade policies and established competitive markets. But probably because of their more careful formulations, the impact of their thinking, important though it was, remained regional—"peripheral," not "mainstream"—and sales of their books did not reach the figures of A. G. Frank's.

Irrespective of whether the "new" perception is true, what matters is that many developing countries see their place in the international system in this way and their perception is a political fact to be reckoned with. This clearly does not mean that the perception should not be subjected to a critical analysis.

The transition between the two perceptions has been overdrawn. Perceptions alternate, points emphasized change and there is no rapid, large-scale conversion. At about the same time that the critics of the international economic order became more vocal, and advocated "delinking," there took place a rebirth of orthodox thinking. The work on effective protection by Johnson, Corden and Balassa, the Organization of Economic Cooperation and Development (OECD) studies of industrialization and trade centering on the work by Little, Scitovsky and Scott, research by the Brookings Institution and the World Bank, and the doctrines of the Chicago School that influenced many Latin American policy makers reflected a recoil against inefficient protectionism and "inward-looking" planning. The conclusions pointed to more "outward-looking" policies. These changing analyses and perceptions alternate and interact.

A reconciliation between the two perceptions (viz., that development can be speeded up by the international "system" and underdevelopment is caused by it) is possible along the following lines. The advanced industrial countries emit a large number of impulses of two kinds: those that present opportunities for faster and better development than would otherwise have been possible, and those that present obstacles to development, those that stunt growth. Arthur Lewis invited us in 1974 to imagine that the developed countries were to sink under the sea in 1984. (He gave us ten years in order to allow time for adjustments. He felt it necessary to add that this was not a recommendation.) He then posed the question: Are the developing countries better off, worse off, or would it make little difference?

The answer to the question neatly separates the adherents of different "paradigms." The upholders of the first "paradigm" would say "worse" (pointing to Korea, Singapore, and Hong Kong as beneficiaries from the international system and Burma and Uganda as losers from "closing themselves off"), those of the second "better," and Sir Arthur thought it would make little difference. But I submit that, whichever answer one is inclined to give, this is not a helpful way of presenting the problem, however useful it is in sorting out ideologies. The developed countries propagate a large number of impulses to the developing countries. Reasonable men may differ about the net balance of these impulses, e.g., whether the exploitation by ruthless transnational companies offsets the availability of a stock of scientific, technological and organizational knowledge, or whether the harm done by the brain drain is greater or less than the benefits from foreign technical assistance, or whether the inflow of grants and loans at concessionary interest rates is counterbalanced by aid-tying and capital flight, etc. The interesting question then is not "Do the developing countries benefit or lose from their coexistence with developed countries?" but, "How can they pursue selective policies that permit them to derive the benefits of the positive forces, without simultaneously exposing themselves to the harm of the detrimental forces?" Looked at in this way, the question becomes one of designing selective policies for aid, trade, foreign investment, transnational companies, technology, foreign education, movements of people, etc.

2. The shift from a linear theory of missing components to some version of a theory of neocolonialism and dependence was accompanied by another change. It amounted to a change in emphasis of what constitutes the meaning and measure of development.

Early thinking and policy making was

dominated by economic growth as the principal performance criterion of development, not so much because growth was regarded as an appropriate objective in itself, but because it was thought either that its fruits would rapidly trickle down to the poor, or that corrective government action could be relied upon to redistribute them, or that inequality and poverty are essential for growth (which, through accumulation by the rich, would first have to create the productive base from which to launch the attack on poverty). But is was soon evident that none of these three assumptions was valid. It became clear that growth in many countries remained concentrated on a narrow enclave of modern, organized, urban industry; that governments often were unwilling or incapable of using taxes and services to offset growing inequalities; and that the concentration of income in the hands of the rich was not a necessary condition of development. (For example, research has disclosed that small farmers with access to improved agricultural technologies save as high a proportion of their incomes as large farmers and are often more efficient in terms of yield per acre.)

The expected absorption of the rapidly growing labor force from the subsistence sector into the modern, industrial sector was considerably slower than expected. Dualism in many countries was marked and prolonged. The golden age of growth with greater equality, ushered in after a period of growing inequality, or by the full absorption of labor from the subsistence sector into the modern sector, seemed, with a few important exceptions, to move into the distant future. This awareness led to a new emphasis on rural development and "employment." It was soon seen, however, that the problem was not "unemployment," which is a Western concept that presupposes modern sector wage employment, labor markets, labor exchanges and social security payments in the form of unemployment benefits. (It has been said that only those relatively well-off can afford to be unemployed.) The problem was rather unremunerative, unproductive work of the poor, particularly of the rural poor. The In-

ternational Labor Office (ILO) Kenya mission suggested the "informal sector" as not just another name for disguised unemployment but as a potentially productive labor force. The new emphasis on the "working poor" led to a concern for redistribution of productive assets as a path to reduced inequality. The relation between the increased concern for equity and conventionally measured economic growth presented a dilemma. On the one hand, it was accepted that in poor societies poverty can be eradicated only through increased production. On the other hand, the growth experience in some countries (though not in all) has shown that growth had reinforced inequalities in income, asset and power distribution which made it more difficult or impossible, both economically and politically, for its benefits to be spread widely. Attention, therefore, shifted to the conditions under which "redistribution with growth" is possible and desirable.

The next step was to realize that what was needed was a more direct and speedier attack on deprivation. Reductions in inequality do not necessarily reduce poverty. It was not just inequality as such that was offensive, but also the fate of the destitute, whether working or incapable of working, whether unemployed, underemployed or unemployable. The objective narrowed down to "meeting basic human needs," which covers not only adequate earning opportunities to purchase the necessities of life, but also access to the provision of public services for education, health and safe water. The progress was from highly aggregated magnitudes like "national income" and "growth rates" to increasingly disaggregated objectives, like different types of employment (e.g., for the young, for recent migrants) and reduced inequality, to meeting highly specific human needs of particular poverty groups.

In focusing on these needs, it became clear that measured income and its growth is only a part of basic needs. Adequate nutrition and safe water at hand, continuing employment, secure and adequate livelihoods for the self-employed, more and better schooling for their children, better preventive medical services, adequate shelter, cheap transport and (but not only) a higher *and* growing level of measured income: some or all of these would figure on the list of urgently felt needs of poor people.

In addition to these specific "economic" objectives, there was now a new emphasis on "nonmaterial" needs that cannot be dispensed, but, in addition to being valued in their own right, may be the conditions for meeting "material" needs, like self-determination, self-reliance, political freedom and security, participation in making the decisions that affect workers and citizens, national and cultural identity, and a sense of purpose in life and work. This was accompanied by attempts to evolve human and social indicators of development that would reflect the extent to which some of these needs were met.

3. A third shift in interest and emphasis was away from the specific economic problems of development and toward the world's common problems and shared constraints: resources and, in particular, energy, the environment and its global pollution, the sea and the sea bed, and world population. The new emphasis was on scarcity and interdependence.

The new emphasis on interdependence was regarded by some as calling for greater solidarity and cooperation ("spaceship earth," "one world"), by others, such as the advocates of *triage* and of the lifeboat philosophy, as calling for partial contracting out of human obligations, and by others again as a shift of attention from positive-sum to zero-sum games. The renewed emphasis after 1972 on scarcities of resources and exhaustion of raw materials extended not only to food, energy and certain metals, but also to some previously free goods, like clean air and clean water, with the resulting concern for environmental protection.

Interdependence does not necessarily point to solidarity; on the contrary, it may give rise to threats, "blackmail," the demand for ransoms, and attempts at isolation. But whatever the response, the fact is that many problems are now global and are shared by all people.

Whereas, with the growing interest in different societies in the Sixties, many had argued that there is no single, universal "science" of economics, applicable from China to Peru, and Dudley Seers wrote on "the economics of the special case," the wheel has now turned full circle and we (with Dudley Seers in the lead) now acknowledge that many of the issues that we had considered as belonging to the poor countries are seen to be universal, of concern to the rich, too. Alienation, pollution and crime can spring from underdevelopment as well as from overdevelopment; "intermediate technology" is just as relevant to high-income societies suffering from unemployment in the face of resource limitations, pollution and alienation from work; all states confront the new phenomenon of the transnational corporation; we are all affected by the energy crisis; there are diseases of affluence as well as diseases of poverty; migration of workers and professionals affects rich and poor countries; there is global experimentation with new lifestyles; there is a heritage common to all mankind and the unexploited resources of the sea and the sea bed can be allocated according to worldwide priorities.

4. A fourth and closely related change is that from a tacitly or explicitly assumed international harmony of interests (which was built into the stages-of-growth model) and positive-sum games, to greater emphasis on actual or potential conflict and zero-sum games. There was much talk of cooperation versus confrontation. The new perception was brought out vividly by the actions of the Organization of Petroleum Exporting Countries (OPEC) and by the Intergovernmental Council of Copper Exporting Countries (CIPEC) as well as similar attempts with bauxite, phosphate and iron ore; by attempts or threats of the developing countries to use bargaining power in other fields with refusals to participate in drug control, or the control of nuclear weapons, or patent conventions; by threats of expropriation or tougher terms for transnational companies; and by the support by a few governments of terrorists and hijackers. As the old harmony has benefited the

haves, the new confrontation was intended to be used to change the rules of the game in favor of the have-nots.

The fact that economists point to potential joint gains from, say, trade liberalization or commodity price stabilization, and thus to positive-sum games does not, of course, mean that governments perceive such policies as in their national interest. Policies are shaped by pressure groups and lobbies and the ubiquity of protection testifies to the power of these interests. On the other hand, developing countries may on occasion have an interest in show-downs rather than negotiations of common interest. There are political advantages in the publicity of such confrontations. In any case, sovereign political power is in its nature a zero-sum game and the added strength of one country is often perceived ipso facto as a defeat for a rival.

At the same time, negotiations do appeal, if not to common interests, at least to common norms and to acceptable rules. Most nations realize that a world in which each nation and group of allied nations exercises to the full its bargaining power to extract maximum concessions from others is a world in which most nations will be worse off. Bargaining must, therefore, appeal not only to national self-interest but also to widely acceptable principles, rules, and norms on which tacit agreement can either be assumed or assumed to be more readily reached than is possible with selfish demands and threats. If bargaining is seen and conducted in this light, its power to disintegrate the world community is greatly weakened, even if the game is, in economic terms, a zero-sum one. Properly used, bargaining can strengthen world cooperation through joint attempts to evolve a more acceptable set of rules and institutions.

5. A fifth change was that from treating the Third World as a homogenous group of countries with common interests to the acknowledgement of the wide variety of experiences, interests and stakes in the world order—in spite of the growth of solidarity of the "Group of 77" at the United Nations

Conference on Trade and Development (UNCTAD) and other international forums. Gaps in income per head opened up more widely within the Third World than between the developed and the developing countries.

The unprecedentedly high average rate of growth of income per head in the developing countries between 1950 and 1975 masked a wide diversity of experience. In Korea, Taiwan, Hong Kong, Singapore, some OPEC countries and the People's Republic of China, income per head rose rapidly and the fruits of this growth were fairly evenly distributed (though the high growth rates for China are crucial and disputed). This group of countries contains about one billion people, or 35 percent of the population of the developing countries.

In a second group of countries, including Pakistan, the Philippines, Thailand, Turkey and many Latin American countries, especially Brazil, containing about 25 percent of the developing world's population, moderate to rapid growth was combined with growing inequality, though it is controversial whether absolute poverty increased.

In a third group of countries, comprising some of the large countries of South Asia (India, Bangladesh) and some of the poorer countries of Africa (incorporating about 40 percent of the developing countries' population) slow growth was probably combined with growing poverty in absolute terms. This group contains some of the largest countries and it remains a disputed issue whether the proportion of absolutely poor increased.

The distribution of the benefits of the commodity boom, especially the oil price rise, and the incidence of the damage done by the world recession were highly uneven and further sharpened differences within the Third World. The hoped-for benefits of the New International Economic Order (NIEO) also are likely to be unequally distributed.

6. The sixth change in the perception of the development process, closely related to the other five changes, is that from abounding optimism about development prospects and the contribution to them by the rich (through

aid, trade and private investment) and by economic analysis, which dominated the Fifties and Sixties, to the deep pessimism of the Seventies. Both optimism and pessimism have their social origins. The optimism of the early decades, as Gunnar Myrdal has pointed out, had its origin not only in the excitement of the discovery of new areas but also in the desire of the governments in the industrial countries to please the new elites in the newly independent countries and to reinforce the view that transfer of capital, skills and technology from rich to poor countries will soon lead to self-sustained growth and thereby get rid of the need for future aid. When faced with the real problems and difficulties of development, which transcended the economic variables—and, at the same time, in their own countries, faced with what has come to be known as "stagflation," together with a host of new problems such as urban ghettoes, student unrest, a growing number of industrial strikes, drug addiction, racial tensions, etc.—the pessimism of the rich countries was a convenient excuse for falling and failing commitments to development cooperation and for contracting out of or for reducing contributions.

Comment

Some of the earlier theories of economic growth—in particular, those of the classical economists, Marx, neoclassicists, and Schumpeter—are reviewed in G. M. Meier and R. E. Baldwin, *Economic Development: Theory, History, Policy* (1957), Part 1. An outstanding interpretation of analyses of economic development in the history of thought is provided by Lord Robbins, *The Theory of Economic Development in the History of Economic Thought* (1968).

After World War II, the subject of "development economics" was formulated in its own right. Investigating issues that went beyond the earlier growth economics of classical economists (Smith, Malthus, Ricardo), a "New Development Economics" began to be formulated by a number of writers. Outstanding contributions were made in the 1940s and 1950s by: Colin Clark, *The Conditions of Economic Progress* (1940); P. N. Rosenstein-Rodan, "Problems of Industrialization of Eastern and Southeastern Europe," *Economic Journal* (June–September 1943); Kurt Mandelbaum, *The Industrialization of Backward Areas* (1945); Raúl Prebisch, "The Economic Development of Latin America and its Principal Problems," *Economic Bulletin for Latin America,* Vol. 7 (1950); P. C. Mahalanobis, "Some Observations on the Process of Growth in National Income," *Sankhya,* Vol. 12, No. 4 (1953); Ragnar Nurkse, *Problems of Capital Formation in Underdeveloped Countries* (1953); Jacob Viner, *International Trade and Economic Development* (1953); Hla Myint, "An Interpretation of Economic Backwardness," *Oxford Economic Papers* (June 1954); W. Arthur Lewis, *The Theory of Economic Growth* (1955); P. T. Bauer and B. S. Yamey, *The Economics of Under-Developed Countries* (1957); Gunnar Myrdal, *Economic Theory and Underdeveloped Regions* (1957); Albert Hirschman, *Strategy of Economic Development* (1958); Jan Tinbergen, *The Design of Development* (1958).

Comment

Several retrospective papers consider the evolution of development thought over the past three or four decades. Most useful in tracing the changing views of development economists are the following: P. P. Streeten, "Development Ideas in Perspective," in *Toward a New Strategy for Development,* A Rothko Chapel Colloquium (1979); Gustav F. Papanek, "Economic Development Theory: The Earnest Search for a Mirage," in Manning Nash (ed.), *Essays on Economic Development and Cultural Change in Honor of Bert F. Hoselitz* (1977); Gustav Ranis, "Development Theory at Three Quarter Century," in Manning Nash (ed.), *Essays on Economic Development and Cultural Change in Honor of Bert F. Hoselitz* (1977); Albert O. Hirschman, "The Rise and Decline of Development Economics," in *Essays in Trespassing* (1981); Fernando Henrique Cardoso, "The Originality of a Copy: CEPAL and the Idea of

Development," *CEPAL Review* (1977); Dudley Seers, "The Birth, Life and Death of Development Economics," *Development and Change,* Vol. 10 (1979); Hans Singer, "Thirty Years of Changing Thought on Development Problem," in *Rich and Poor Countries* (1977), chapter 13; Jere R. Behrman, "Development Economics," in Sidney Weintraub (ed.), *Modern Economic Thought* (1974); Ian Livingstone, "The Development of Development Economics," *ODI Review,* No. 2, 1981; Amartya Sen, "Development Which Way Now?" *Economic Journal* (December 1983).

II.B.2. Structuralist Approach to Development Policy *

Several approaches to the analysis of developing economies have evolved over the past twenty-five years. From a methodological standpoint, they can be grouped under three main headings: neoclassical, neo-Marxist, and structuralist. The first two attempt to adapt systems of thought that were initially formulated for the study of industrial societies to the less developed countries. The structuralist approach attempts to identify specific rigidities, lags, and other characteristics of the structure of developing economies that affect economic adjustments and the choice of development policy.

The initial set of structural hypotheses was formulated in the 1950s by writers such as Paul Rosenstein-Rodan, Ragnar Nurkse, W. Arthur Lewis, Raúl Prebisch, Hans Singer, and Gunnar Myrdal. They explain phenomena such as balance of payments disequilibrium, unemployment, and worsening income distribution on the basis of particular properties of demand and production functions and other specifications of economic behavior. A common theme in most of this work is the failure of the equilibrating mechanisms of the price system to produce steady growth or a desirable distribution of income.

The success of a number of developing countries in accelerating their rates of growth

in the 1960s casts some doubt on the significance of the structural problems that had been identified in the previous decade. However, in the past few years the importance of structural rigidities has been reemphasized by several new phenomena: the limited ability of economies to absorb the growing labor force, the worsening of the income distribution in several developing countries, and—most recently—the disruption to world trade caused by increased oil and food prices, which will require a substantial adjustment in productive structures. In short, development policy again seems to be constrained by a number of structural factors that require a more explicit analysis of the possibilities for short-term adjustment and for longer term changes in the economic structure itself....

METHODOLOGY

The methodology of structural analysis has evolved over the past twenty-five years from a set of rather intuitive hypotheses to models of increasing empirical validity and analytical rigor. This evolution can be summarized in three stages: formulation of hypotheses, empirical testing, and the elaboration of more complete models. This sequence can be illustrated for two of the basic elements of structuralist systems: the concept of a dual economy and the concept of complementarity in demand, which underlies theories of balanced growth.

*From Hollis B. Chenery, "The Structuralist Approach to Development Policy," *American Economic Review, Papers and Proceedings,* May 1975, pp. 310–315. Reprinted by permission.

The concept of a dual economy stems from the observation that development takes place unevenly both within and between sectors of an economy. Although this concept has had many different formulations, the most influential is that of Lewis. He makes three basic assumptions as to the structure of a developing economy: (1) that technology can be divided between capital-using (capitalist) and non-capital-using (subsistence); (2) that the labor supply is elastic at a conventional wage; and (3) that saving is done largely by the recipients of nonwage income (capitalists). These assumptions, or variants of them, have been incorporated in models that explain the acceleration of growth, the allocation of the labor force, and changes in the distribution of income.

The early formulations of concepts of balanced growth by Nurkse and Rosenstein-Rodan also relied on a simple set of structural hypotheses: (1) a generalized version of Engels' law, specifying that consumer demand for food, clothing, shelter, and other major commodity groups is mainly a function of income and little affected by relative prices; (2) a similar assumption as to the limited price elasticity of demand for exports; and (3) in Rosenstein-Rodan's formulation, the importance of economies of scale in overhead facilities and basic industries. The first two assumptions make it necessary to expand output and allocate investment in close relation to the pattern of domestic demand. They also provide an explanation for structural disequilibrium and slow growth in countries that fail to do so.

Both sets of assumptions have in general stood up well to subsequent empirical tests. The acceleration of population growth has probably made the surplus labor assumption more generally valid today than when it was initially formulated for underdeveloped countries. Econometric tests by R. Weisskoff and C. Lluch and A. Powell provide some support for the generalized version of Engels' law underlying the theory of balanced growth, since they show most price elasticities to be less than unity. Among the basic structuralist assumptions listed, only the assumed inelastic demand for exports needs to be seriously qualified.

The third stage of theoretical refinement and policy application has proved more difficult. In the first place, it has been shown that the structural relations posited are not sufficient to lead to some of the policy conclusions suggested in the original formulations. As in the case of the Keynesian assumptions, a more complete formulation of models that can be statistically estimated has proved necessary in order to reach useful policy conclusions. Much current work consists in developing a second generation of models in the structuralist tradition that are designed for statistical application in individual countries, rather than for deriving broad generalizations.

The structuralist approach has had a substantial impact on both internal and external development policies. In both instances it focuses on identifying the consequences of various kinds of structural disequilibria. In domestic policy, the principal phenomena examined have been the effects of surplus labor on resource allocation and more recently the interpretation of worsening income distribution as resulting from a set of disequilibrium conditions. In international policy, analysis has focused on the nature of structural disequilibrium in the balance of payments and its effect on trade and aid policies. The following sections examine some of the relationships between the methodology employed and the policy conclusions reached in these two areas.

INTERNAL DEVELOPMENT POLICY

Unlike the neoclassical assumptions, the structuralist alternatives do not lead automatically to policy conclusions. To produce such conclusions, they must also be embodied in an explicit general equilibrium framework. For this purpose, most analysts have used one of two simple models: either a neoclassical model with particular structural relations added or some version of a linear Leontief input-output model, which excludes most forms of substitution. The neoclassical framework minimizes the effects of the specific rigidities in the economic system, while the input-output system tends to exaggerate them.

Most elaborations of the dual economy and surplus labor concepts have been made in a two-sector neoclassical system, as in the work of J. C. Fei and G. Ranis, L. Lefeber, and A. C. Kelley, J. G. Williamson and R. J. Cheetham. One policy result from this type of model is to determine the shadow price of labor, which can then be used in project evaluation and in establishing the need for labor subsidies. Empirical applications of these models have been limited by the lack of data on different aspects of dualism. It will require some expansion of the two-sector framework before statistical estimation of the underlying structural relations becomes feasible.

The balanced growth hypotheses have been widely used in empirical analysis and are usually incorporated in input-output models which include foreign trade. These are applied to the formulation and testing of development plans, as illustrated in surveys by Chenery (1971) and A. Manne. Apart from its use in country planning, this type of model can also be used to deduce more general propositions through systematically varying the structural parameters and determining a set of solutions based on either simulation or optimization.

This form of sensitivity analysis lends considerable support to some of the conclusions of balanced growth theorists. For example, it is necessary in larger countries to expand agriculture at a rate that is largely determined by the income elasticity of domestic demand for foodstuffs because of the limited possibilities of expanding nonagricultural exports to offset a shortfall. Failure to meet this condition has retarded growth in a number of countries. This conclusion does not apply when industry is disaggregated to individual sectors such as steel or fertilizer, however, in which the optimal investment allocation to sectors having economies of scale is charac-

terized by the alternating pattern of expansion of production and imports described by T. Scitovsky and by Chenery and L. Westphal.

The elaboration of structuralist hypotheses in planning models has also focused attention on the value of flexibility in adapting resource allocation to changing circumstances. This problem does not arise in the neoclassical system, which assumes perfect foresight and a high degree of substitutability. When these assumptions are abandoned, flexibility can be provided by increased exports or capital inflows and by planning some excess capacity in physical and human capital stocks. Although a formal treatment of the benefits of flexibility and the ways of achieving it has not been developed, this is an important problem for developing countries which cannot be analysed in the neoclassical system.

The revival of interest in income distribution has added a new dimension to structural analysis. The traditional approach focuses on the division between wage and nonwage income and is ill suited to developing countries, in which modern sector wage earners are in the middle-income groups. Recent studies by M. S. Ahluwalia have brought out the fact that the bulk of the poorest groups in developing countries are self-employed and largely rural. Their incomes depend more on the availability of land and capital and access to public facilities than on wages. Since each of the main poverty groups—small farmers, landless laborers, urban self-employed—has a different set of productive possibilities and constraints, a new form of structural analysis based on identification of these groups is necessary for distribution-oriented policies.

This recognition of the importance of asset distribution does not necessarily lead to the Marxist conclusion that the redistribution of existing assets is the only alternative. Measures to redistribute increments in income and new asset formation are more likely to be acceptable to the majority of the population and less disruptive of development in most countries. Development strategies based on this approach are elaborated by Ahluwalia and Chenery. The neo-Marxist policy recommendations suffer from the same defects as the neoclassical in that they are implicit in the initial assumptions rather than being derived from an analysis based on empirical estimates of the underlying structural relations.

EXTERNAL POLICY

The conflict among the three analytical approaches is perhaps most acute in the area of external policy. The neoclassical approach tends to exaggerate the benefits of trade in an open economy when it does not explicitly consider the effects of uncertain export prices and the difficulties of shifting resources to meet changing market conditions. Conversely, the neo-Marxist approach exaggerates the costs of "dependence" on external trade and investment and tends to ignore the benefits of the technological transfers that accompany them. The early structuralist views have also proved to be excessively pessimistic as to the possibilities and benefits of nontraditional exports of manufactures and services.

The structuralist concept of development as characterized by rigidities that limit economic adjustments requires an analytical framework in which external policy is more closely linked to domestic resource allocation than does the neoclassical view, which minimizes these restrictions. Attempts to formalize these relationships started from simple two-gap models, which incorporate explicit limits on the rate of increase of domestic saving, investment, and exports. These models were elaborated by including optimizing procedures and shadow prices, the disaggregation of productive sectors, and more explicit treatment of structural change over time, as in the work of Chenery and A. MacEwan, M. Bruno, and S. D. Tendulkar. Experiments with these types of models in a number of countries have led to several general conclusions as to development analysis and policy, the most significant of which are: (1) the enhanced value of increased exports and capital

inflows in bottleneck situations, in which the trade limitation is more restrictive than supplies of capital and skilled labor; (2) a restatement of the empirical basis for assessing comparative advantage over time in relation to the factors limiting development; and (3) clarification of the relation between internal and external constraints in the evaluation of individual investment projects.

During the 1960s a number of countries progressed from an initial strategy of import substitution to the promotion of manufactured exports after they had developed a sufficient industrial base to do so. As countries achieve a more diversified productive structure and reduce their concentration on a few exports, the difference between the neoclassical and structural prescriptions diminishes because some of the constraints that had previously limited growth are no longer significant. An assessment of the experience of some of the industrializing countries that have made this transition—Taiwan, Israel, Korea, Brazil, Mexico—suggests that earlier conclusions as to the high cost of the initial stage of import substitution need to be reexamined in light of the subsequent ability of the country to shift to manufactured exports and break out of the phase of trade limited development. This evaluation suggests that the dichotomy between inward-oriented and outward-oriented policies has perhaps been overdrawn, and that these policies can be more usefully viewed as sequential elements of a strategy designed to bring about changes in the structure of both production and trade.

CONCLUSIONS

The preceding discussion has illustrated the relations between theoretical premises and policy implications in several fields of development. The simplifying assumptions of the models currently in use tend to exaggerate the differences between neoclassical and structuralist prescriptions. As statistically determined relations replace a priori hypotheses, it is predictable that these differences will be reduced. A similar process can be hoped for when neo-Marxist theorists turn their attention to verifying their hypotheses.

Although better knowledge of elasticities of substitution in demand and production would do quite a bit to reduce the conflicts in policy guidance, several real differences in basic concepts remain. Neoclassical policy consists essentially in removing impediments to the functioning of markets so as to make the real world as much like the abstract model as possible. However, it will never be possible to achieve perfect knowledge or instantaneous adjustment to market signals. It is therefore necessary to incorporate these "imperfections" into the model itself. Once this has been done, it will become possible to take account of the existence of internal or external disequilibria and to devise more realistic policies to cope with them. In the theoretical literature, these policies are misleadingly referred to as "second best" in relation to the neoclassical model. It would be more accurate to characterize the model itself as overly simple and "first best" policies as simply unattainable. More attention should be given to improving the realism of basically neoclassical models instead of discarding them in favor of equally oversimplified structuralist formulations.

In minimizing or ignoring the advantages of market adjustments, structuralist (and Marxist) policy prescriptions usually put too much weight on the limited administrative apparatus of developing countries. As A. Hirschman has stressed, this is one of the main limitations to development; it should be allowed for by not seeking too much fine tuning of development policy. Difficulties in implementing a complex set of policies may prove much more costly than the allocative inefficiency of a simpler program that can be more readily carried out.

Finally, it must be recognized that the task of development has been made much more difficult for most countries by the recent changes in the world economy. Virtually every country is currently suffering from more or less serious disequilibria in its economic structure. Despite our desire to give greater weight in development policy to distributional considerations, this cannot be achieved without giving equal priority to adjustments in external trade and capital flows.

References

M. S. Ahluwalia, "Income Inequality: Some Dimensions of the Problem," in H. Chenery et al., *Redistribution with Growth,* London, 1974.

———— and H. Chenery, "A Model of Distribution and Growth," in H. Chenery et al., *Redistribution with Growth,* London, 1974.

M. Bruno, "Optimal Patterns of Trade and Development," *Review of Economic Statistics,* November 1967, Vol. 49, pp. 545–54.

H. Chenery, ed., *Studies in Development Planning,* Cambridge, Mass., 1971.

———— and A. MacEwan, "Optimal Patterns of Growth and Aid: The Case of Pakistan," in I. Adelman and E. Thorbecke, eds., *The Theory and Practice of Economic Development,* Baltimore, 1966.

———— and L. Westphal, "Economies of Scale and Investment Over Time," in J. Margolis, ed., *Public Economics,* London, 1969.

J. C. Fei and G. Ranis, *Development of the Labor Surplus Economy,* Homewood, Ill., 1964.

A. Hirschman, *The Strategy of Economic Development,* New Haven, 1958.

A. C. Kelley, J. G. Williamson and R. J. Cheetham, *Dualistic Economic Development,* Chicago, 1972.

L. Lefeber, "Planning in a Surplus Labor Economy," *American Economic Review,* June 1968, Vol. 58, pp. 343–73.

W. A. Lewis, "Economic Development with Unlimited Supplies of Labor," *Manchester School,* May 1954, Vol. 22, pp. 132–91.

C. Lluch and A. Powell, *International Comparisons of Expenditure and Saving Patterns,* Int. Bank for Recon. and Dev., Res. Cent., dis. pap. no. 2, 1973.

A. Manne, "Multi-Sector Models for Development Planning: A Survey," *Journal of Development Economics,* June 1974, Vol. 1, pp. 43–70.

G. Myrdal, *Economic Theory and Underdeveloped Regions,* London, 1957.

R. Nurkse, *Problems of Capital Formation in Underdeveloped Countries,* Oxford, 1953.

R. Prebisch, "Commercial Policy in the Underdeveloped Countries," *American Economic Review, Papers and Proceedings,* May 1959, Vol. 49, pp. 251–73.

P. Rosenstein-Rodan, "Problems of Industrialization of Eastern and South-Eastern Europe," *Economic Journal,* June-September 1943, Vol. 53, pp. 205–16.

T. Scitovsky, "Growth—Balanced or Unbalanced," in M. Abramovitz et al., *The Allocations of Economic Resources,* Stanford, 1959.

H. W. Singer, "The Distribution of Gains Between Investing and Borrowing Countries," *American Economic Review, Papers and Proceedings,* May 1950, Vol. 40, pp. 473–85.

S. D. Tendulkar, "Interaction Between Domestic and Foreign Resources in Economic Growth: Some Experiments for India," in H. Chenery, ed., *Studies in Development Planning,* Cambridge, Mass., 1971.

R. Weisskoff, "Demand Elasticities for a Developing Economy: An International Comparison of Consumption Patterns," in H. Chenery, ed., *Studies in Development Planning,* Cambridge, Mass., 1971.

II.B.3. Changes in Development Theory *

It is my purpose in this section to trace some of the main advances in our understanding of the development process during the past couple of decades and to relate them, where appropriate, to more recent changes in the objective function articulated by most developing-country spokesmen and aid officials.

Perhaps the most important dimension of conceptual progress, in my opinion, is the growing awareness that the analysis of growth, employment, and distribution must be viewed as integrally of one cloth, with the focus on the existence and size of trade-offs among these objectives. The notion that employment and distributional issues are best treated "after the fact," that is, after all the production/allocation dust has settled, has died hard. There is still a substantial body of theoretical literature which claims that

"trickle-down" is likely to work, and a related body of more policy-tinged expert opinion to the effect that employment and income distribution objectives should be met via "secondary strategies," for example, public-works programs and fiscal redistribution. Trickle-down is still sufficiently respectable to have been the basis of the so-called Prebisch Report, 1970s vintage, calling for higher growth rates in Latin America in order to pull in the unemployed; and the preponderance of work on income distribution and poverty still emphasizes the potential redistributive effects of tax and expenditure policies, nationalization, and public-works programs.

The empirical evidence that has been accumulating, on the other hand, indicates that even if fiscal redistribution, after the fact, were politically and administratively feasible, it would have to assume completely unrealistic proportions to make a real difference. And, turning the problem on its head, it would take an unreasonably large exogenous shift in income distribution to achieve anything meaningful in the way of a more em-

*From Gustav Ranis, "Development Theory at Three Quarter Century," in *Essays on Economic Development and Cultural Change in Honor of Bert F. Hoselitz* (ed. by Manning Nash, University of Chicago Press, 1977), pp. 256–66. Reprinted by permission.

ployment-intensive output mix. Moreover, the advice that an increase in overall growth targets from 5 to 8 percent would solve the unemployment problem is weak on two grounds—it is highly impractical to locate the additional fuel to make the old Model T move that much faster and, perhaps more importantly, even if sufficient natural resources and/or foreign capital could be harnessed, the accompanying income distribution outcomes are not necessarily acceptable. Finally, intrinsic administrative and organizational difficulties, at least in the mixed-economy LDC context, make a solution via major reliance on a massive public-works program highly impractical.

It is for these reasons that I count the gradually growing consensus that these new dimensions of development must be analyzed and solved as an integral part of the old as the most important single step forward. Simply put, we are not in a position to "dethrone the GNP," as has been variously suggested, but rather we must try to place it on an analytically sturdier throne. This means analyzing much more carefully than we have in the past what the meaning of alternative growth paths—or alternative ways of achieving a particular growth rate—might be in terms of the other things we care about.

This, of course, may lead us to the conclusion that a change in the nature of the growth path itself—that is, the way in which output is generated—can give us not only better employment and distribution outcomes but more growth in the bargain. On the other hand, there may be trade-offs among these objectives; and the nature of these trade-offs, that is, the extent to which they are manmade rather than inherent in the basic structure of development, is of great theoretical and policy interest. It is my belief that much of our current and prospective progress rests on this ability to integrate neoclassical or classical growth theory with a rigorous statement of employment and equity considerations.

Among the more important ingredients in our theoretical capacity to deal with this new and broadened view of development is our in-

creased willingness to sector the typical developing economy into meaningful components for purposes of general equilibrium analysis. The literature on economic, social, and technological dualism has a long and distinguished history. But the revival of classical economics after Arthur Lewis's pathbreaking work, and its application to contemporary problems of development, has represented a major analytical advance—permitting us to trace the interactions over time among sectors not homogeneous in structure and/or behavior. More recently, it has been recognized that so-called two-sector models need to be modified by extension to three or four sectors, for example, along the lines of more than one traditional and more than one commercialized sector, with possibly two urban and two rural components emerging. While controversy on this point persists, there are more and more adherents now to the notion that meaningful analysis in development requires breaking the economy down into a few, sometimes heterogeneous, sectors in the dualistic tradition rather than the conventional treatment of many homogeneous sectors in the input/output tradition.

A second and related advance permitting the more meaningful simultaneous analysis of growth, employment, and equity has been in the area of recognizing the importance of typological differences among developing societies. In the immediate postwar period there seemed to be two major prevailing views—one, that every LDC is *sui generis* and that only country-intensive studies were likely to advance our understanding; the other, that a general theory of underdevelopment applicable to all countries was within reach and that, in the meantime, we could behave as if Afghanistan and Argentina had more in common with each other than with any so-called mature economy. In more recent years, we may note a marked convergence between these positions via the acceptance of the notion of halfway houses or subfamilies of LDCs differentiated by such features as size, resource endowment, and other structural as well as, possibly, behavioral characteristics. This trend is exemplified, on the one hand, by the evolving work of Chenery and his associates, which has moved away from homogeneous 50-country samples and toward the attempt to differentiate empirically among different country types; on the other, expositors of development typologies, for example, of the land-surplus and labor-surplus school, have begun to open these models to trade and to more empirical treatment. While this work remains very much in flux, we seem to have growing agreement that it is worthwhile to differentiate countries by size—thus underlining the relative importance of trade—by the extent of dualism or labor surplus—thus assessing the relevance of classical versus neoclassical conditions in agriculture—and by the strength of their natural-resources base—thus determining the quantity of land-based fuel available for the transition effort.

Closely related to this growing acceptance of the usefulness of a typological approach has been the recognition that a fuller explanation of the historical laboratory would have a substantial payoff for advances in development theory. In the forties and fifties, the profession understandably was forced to concentrate on cross-sectional analysis of the less developed world as well as on the history of the now-advanced societies, including western Europe, Japan, and, to a lesser extent, Australia, North America, and other "empty" continents. By now, however, a quarter-century later, sufficient data have accumulated to permit us to look at developing societies in a historical context and to try to isolate meaningful subphases of development. There is no reason to permit the unfortunate "stages-of-growth" controversy linked to the name of W. W. Rostow to inhibit us in this respect any longer. While no historical inevitability connotation is intended, developing societies do seem to move in certain transitional states between the long epoch of open agrarianism and another long epoch of modern growth. One of the more common transitional states is one of dualism, whether of the Lewis/Fei-Ranis or the Jorgensen/Kelley-Williamson type.

Moreover, there are some of us who believe that the dualism subphase may itself be typically characterizable—to analytical advantage—by distinct subphases, including a domestic-market-oriented or primary-import-substitution subphase, followed by either an outer-oriented or export-substitution subphase or the prolongation of domestic-market orientation via a secondary-import-substitution subphase. The identification of such subphases—based on changes in the underlying resource endowment as well as in accommodating changes in the official policy package combining to fundamentally affect domestic as well as trade relations—constitutes, we believe, an essential ingredient in advancing our understanding of development. For example, the extent to which growth, employment, and income distribution objectives of a society are mutually reinforcing or competitive depends very much on the subphase in which a society finds itself—as well as, of course, on the LDC subfamily to which it belongs.

By way of such illustration only, for the labor-surplus economy which moves from primary import to export substitution, for example, Taiwan, we can clearly identify turning points between subphases and note substantial contrasts in the "before and after" performance. During primary import substitution, focused on infant industrial or entrepreneurial protection and fueled by land-intensive exports and foreign capital, we would expect trade-offs to be more pronounced; during export substitution, focused on penetrating international markets by combining maturing entrepreneurial capacity with "unlimited" supplies of labor, we would expect such trade-offs to be substantially reduced, if not altogether eliminated. On the other hand, countries which persevere in secondary import substitution—often combined with some export promotion (i.e., subsidized exportation)—in consumer durable, capital, and intermediate goods will find such trade-offs becoming increasingly severe.

What makes such typology and time-oriented analysis more analytically feasible today than a quarter-century ago is the number of specific advances in our understanding of alternative growth paths. One such advance clearly is a revised view of technology choice and technology change. It has not been all that long that the Eckaus view of essentially fixed proportions, and consequent technological unemployment, was dominant in the LDC literature, with little flexibility in either output or technology mixes. Added to that was the notion making a virtue of capital intensity even in a labor-surplus context, namely, the need for large profit and low wage shares to ensure high saving and low population growth rates.

Substantial differences in the industry-specific technology actually found to be most profitable in developing countries over time, as well as the existence of substantial cross-sectional differences within developing countries for the same industry as one moves across scales, have cast serious doubt on the first proposition. The new conventional wisdom with respect to technology choice is more nearly that while some industries, especially continuous-process industries, are clearly intrinsically not as flexible as others—no matter what the environment—in most industries substantial efficient choice does exist across countries and across scales within countries. This flexibility is most pronounced in the core processes of discrete or batch production, in machine-peripheral activities, as well as with respect to plant-saving possibilities. While "small is not always beautiful"—since it may be inefficient—the conventional wisdom has now swung to the recognition that under less distorted relative price environments, growth and employment at least can be rendered much more compatible—via appropriate technology choices—and that, using the foreign-trade mechanism, appropriate technology choices will also permit a wider range of output mix variability.

The overwhelming burden of the evidence is consistent with the basic notion that, in a developing country which is open and not too large in size, less relative factor and commodity price distortions, along with the reduction of institutional barriers to information, procurement choice, etc., may be expected to produce a substantial increase in employ-ment—in spite of a pronounced dependence on imported machinery in the first instance. There exists, in other words, substantial potential flexibility both in the initial choice of technology from abroad and in the domestic adaptation potential "on top of" such imported technology. Adaptation possibilities may, in fact, be quantitatively more important than the range of shelf technology choice, which is often more heavily constrained and only partially illuminated. Nevertheless, the two acts are closely interrelated in theory and practice; that is, economies which try to borrow ahead of their skill levels will find it more difficult to assimilate what they borrow, quite aside from incurring the higher expense of the initial choice.

It may be well for us to note that the adaptive-technology argument in industry may be more closely related to the situation in agriculture than the profession has yet been willing to acknowledge. For instance, agricultural economists are now coming around to the idea that, while the contribution of international research on new hybrids, etc., has been substantial—and rightly ballyhooed—it has probably been overstated relative to the need for adaptive national research to protect new varieties against disease and ensure the continuity of such "Green Revolutions." Agricultural technology is more of a public than a private good and thus more easily appropriated and diffused. With respect to industrial technology, therefore, we might do well to distinguish between technology proper, where the analogies to the better-understood agricultural sector may hold fairly well—in spite of the lower level of competition and higher level of appropriability—and the product and taste differentiation type of "technology," which is a horse of a different color and not really treated here. These analogies may be especially relevant in light capital goods, cement, brick, and other relatively homogeneous product industries, and at the medium and small-scale end of the spectrum.

The second aforementioned proposition has proven equally doubtful; that is, there is no clear evidence that the admittedly higher saving rates out of a larger profit share are sufficient to overcome the lower absolute levels of output, and profits, resulting from substantial static inefficiency. The posited relationship of technology choice to population growth has never been established. Small wonder that the explanation as to why, in spite of large endowment differentials, technology choices are not, in fact, as dissimilar as we might expect has been shifting elsewhere. If countries do not, in fact, always take full advantage of the potential that exists in terms of known technology shelf choices, this may have more to do with imperfect information channels or the ability of entrepreneurs, due to the existence of monopoly profits, to indulge their engineering preferences—quite aside from the most common explanation, that is, the effect of severely distorted relative factor and commodity prices.

The choice of the direction of technology change, a closely related issue, is still something more of a mystery, because, as in advanced-economy growth theory, we have no analytically sound innovation inducement mechanism on which to base our reflections. Yet most of us do recognize that the Hayami-Ruttan type of inducement mechanism as loosely applied to agriculture is likely to be at work, that is, that labor-surplus economies with expectations of a continuing relative shortage of capital and abundance of labor are more likely to seek labor-using or capital-stretching innovations—just as societies in which capital can be expected to grow secularly faster than labor have shown evidence of increasing the pool of labor-saving innovations. What is admittedly less clear, and a subject of considerable theoretical and practical interest, is whether or not the pool of labor-using innovations, mainly in the form of plant floor rearrangements, the speeding up of machines, etc., is likely to be as easily replenished as the pool of labor-saving innovations in western European and U.S. experience. More likely, additional adaptations of a labor-saving type will require the impetus of additional acts of shelf technology borrowing. In agriculture, we have gradually swung

to the realization, moreover, that as important as international research inputs may have been, for example, in the case of the Green Revolution, it is national adaptive research responses which are going to be crucial in establishing the nature of the employment/output generation nexus immediately and, perhaps more importantly, in determining how self-sustained technology change will ultimately be. In industry, imported technology change is more nearly a privately appropriable commodity in most instances, and we are still less able to disentangle the respective roles of public and private sector R & D and information access in the borrowing and adaptation processes. However, the overall importance, for growth and labor absorption, of the size of the innovational effort apparently increases over time relative to the quality or bias of the innovation.

In summary, there is substantial consensus today that technology change, both in terms of its strength and in terms of its bias, represents perhaps the single most important element in effecting the reduction and possibly the elimination of any trade-off between employment and growth objectives. Actual country experience indicates that there exists a "deviant" minority of labor-surplus developing economies which have, in fact, created an environment conducive to appropriate technology choice and technology change during their export substitution subphase, and have apparently been able to entirely eliminate the conflict between employment and growth. In Taiwan, for example, growth rates accelerated during the 1960s and an unskilled labor shortage replaced labor surpluses by the end of the decade.

While growth and employment are now increasingly viewed as, at least potentially, compatible, there is still a good deal of controversy surrounding the question of growth versus income distribution. In fact, the majority view here clearly holds that, especially as growth first gets under way, "things must get worse before they can get better." The results of Kuznets, and later Oshima, using cross-sectional data, and those of Adelman and Morris employing more sophisticated techniques on a broader set of cross-sectional socioeconomic data, point in the same direction. Most observers seem to have found this evidence persuasive for purposes of prognostication for individual developing countries over time. Kuznets, for example, sees this outcome as a necessary concomitant of increasing levels of profit and rent-fed accumulation, as growth gets under way, plus the effect of shifts in the center of gravity from "more equal" to "less equal" sectors (agriculture to nonagriculture). A. Lewis notes that, while the unlimited supply of labor phase persists and wage rates are held down, the profit share must necessarily rise—tending to a worsening of the distribution of income.

These arguments have been further buttressed by the actual historical experience of a substantial number of contemporary LDCs. Whether we pick the Gini coefficient or McNamara's favorite index relating the proportion of total income accruing to the lowest and highest quartiles, the distribution of income in Mexico, in Brazil, in the Philippines, in fact, in most LDCs, has been worsening over the past decade. Nevertheless, though expert opinion is generally as pessimistic as the historical evidence, we need to reassure ourselves as to whether this record is inevitable in the nature of things—or, once again, man-made and thus just possibly avoidable. Kuznets and Adelman-Morris data, after all, are heavily policy distorted, with most LDCs examined remaining under essentially import-substitution types of policy settings.

What should give us pause is that the old chestnut of an unequal distribution of income required to generate high saving rates is no longer generally accepted. We certainly have examples of countries—outside of the socialist orbit—which, like Japan and Korea, have simultaneously experienced high saving rates and a fairly equal distribution of income. Most significant surely is the actual record of one such economy, for example, Taiwan, which yields not only remarkably low levels of the Gini coefficient (near .3 rather than .5, as for most LDCs) but the avoidance of any but the slightest tendency to rise during the period of fastest growth and employment generation, namely, the 1960s. It is worth noting that even Adelman concedes that South Korea and Taiwan may constitute exceptions to the rule, even though she does not go into the reasons. Our own detailed examination of Taiwan leads us to the conclusion that the inverse U-shaped or Kuznets pattern can be substantially softened and possibly even eliminated, so that even before the commercialization point, when labor surplus disappears, the trade-off between growth and distribution may disappear. Our analysis is based on the effort to decompose the overall Gini into factor Ginis and then linking changes in these Ginis to such growth-relevant phenomena as reallocation under dualism, capital intensity, and innovational bias. While this is not the place to dwell on our findings in detail, our analysis permits us to conclude that a combination of early concentration on agricultural productivity increase, along with rural industrialization in the dual-economy context, can produce this result. This follows basically from the fact that, even as real wages do not rise very much, additional employment opportunities are provided for members of the poorest landless agricultural families.

The profession is clearly still groping toward a consensus on how to analyze distribution and poverty in relation to growth in a largely rural dualistic setting. But this should not deter us from recognizing that a substantial conceptual shift in emphasis has already taken place in a number of important dimensions. Some of these try to incorporate important institutional or noneconomic variables into our analytical framework; others focus heavily on structural and other typological differences among families of LDCs; still others are trying to use large-scale general equilibrium models and sensitivity analysis to help us focus our attention on the important behavioral relations. But what most of these approaches have in common is a continuing deemphasis on the brute forces of capital accumulation and rigid Harrod-Domar-type output relations and an increasing emphasis on the importance of human resources, technology change, and other sources of flexibility in the system.

II.B.4. Development Modeling: State of the Art*

Among the developing countries, India was probably the first to introduce its own planning system, guided by P. C. Mahalanobis, who was impressed very much by the Soviet accomplishments, and took over the habit of drawing up five-year plans. Mahalanobis was the first to introduce the so-called specific capital goods, differentiating between capital goods needed to produce consumer goods and capital goods to produce capital goods. The main use made by him of this concept is to show that, to put it simply, initial restraint on consumption may later bring higher levels of well-being than in the absence of the initial restraint.

Understandably, in developing countries, interest was more concentrated on long-term movements of the economy than in developed countries where short-term movements (especially cyclical) and speculative operations evoked more interest. For any economy, however, short-term fluctuations cannot be fully neglected. In developing economies, they probably are to a larger extent the consequences of crop variations and hence almost random. So, short-term economic models also became a subject for systematic research, as shown by Narasimham.

With an increasing number of former colonies becoming independent, at least formally, the formulation of development policies as part of a government's tasks spread. This was enhanced by institutions, such as the World Bank Group and the International Monetary Fund, which needed a basis of evaluation of the loans extended to developing countries. International co-operation also began to be more institutionalized, as shown by the solemn proclamation, in 1961, of the "Development Decade," later rebaptized as the First D. D. (D. D. I.).

In view of the increasing practical applications of what erstwhile were principles

*From Jan Tinbergen, "Development Modeling: The State of the Art," in *The Pakistan Development Review*, Vol. XIX, No. 2, Summer 1980, pp. 93–98. Reprinted by permission.

only, such as the "Domar—Harrod principle," a number of more concrete and simplifying techniques were proposed, discussed and applied. One of these was planning in stages, where initially three levels were distinguished: the macro, the middle (or meso), and the micro levels. Macro calculations used national totals, such as national income or product, investments, consumption, imports and exports. The next stage referred to sectors or branches of activity in its "functional" version, or provinces in its "geographical" version, which, in the case of a federated nation, might be states. The micro-level of the functional version would be single projects (sometimes enterprises), the subject matter of loan negotiations. (A separate source of information usually resulted from such negotiations.) In the geographical version, either cities or homogeneous regions, possibly river valleys, entered the scene.

Among the sectors, some might receive special attention; for instance, education or educational subsectors. Alternatively, public and private, or formal and informal sectors, had to be kept apart.

A technique that found widespread application is known as input-output analysis, originating from previous concepts of production of goods by goods (Sraffa) and the core also of the Soviet planning system, even if not infrequently in simplified ways, with the emphasis on the "material balances." A refinement of conventional input-output analysis was obtained by a distinction between tradables and nontradables and got the name of semi-input-output analysis (cf. Kuyvenhoven).

Another useful tool of analysis proved to be the two-gap concept. A nation, when looked at as a whole, may be in disequilibrium in the sense that either its savings fall short of the investmest it wants to finance or its exports fall short of the imports it wants to finance. The former gap is indicated as the savings gap, the latter as the trade gap (where trade implies invisibles). In fact, and "ex post" (looking at the figures of past time units), the two are identical and in that sense there is no point in using two words. But, estimated in advance, "ex ante," the two may be different and one appears larger than the other. It is then sometimes called "dominant" and this state of affairs may be an indication of the measures that need to be taken first. The variables that are the subject of such measures are called "adjustors." Their use, and the adjustment process, may be either automatic (part of the "free forces of society") or policy-induced. If more than one adjustor exists, we may even have one or more "degrees of freedom." Several authors have used the tool just mentioned in order to arrive at policy recommendations or even a range of possible policies, where the policy-maker has a choice. An excellent survey of the practice of and experience with planning has been given by Waterston et al.

A last remark to be made in this section is on international models. These became increasingly necessary as a consequence of the task created by the institution of the United Nations Development Planning Committee. This committee came into being as a consequence of the concern, around 1965, in the developing countries that the Development Decade's objectives were not attained. On behalf of the committee's discussions, the U.N. Secretariat prepared a world model, largely inspired by J. L. Mosak, but unfortunately never published it. In all probability, it was the first of its kind. More recently, Leontief et al. made an impressive attempt at constructing various alternatives of a world model. . . .

ASPECTS UNDER DEBATE

. . . [L]et us now discuss how the experiences of the past decades and the new tasks as now understood have their impact on development planning and the models to be used for it. We will discuss this impact under two main headings: (a) the additional variables that must enter into our models, and (b) the new use to be made of planning models.

The additional variables needed for our models will be discussed in succession, without a claim to completeness. To begin with, more social variables are needed and a first example is of figures on income distribution. Although accurate data are hard to get, crude approximations have been estimated for up to sixty developing countries. A crude distinction into quintiles of income distribution will already be useful; for links have to be made with other variables in order to integrate them into the model. An interesting example is given by Bornschier in a sociological model, comparing up to 72 countries in a cross-country study. Another very complex study for one country, Korea, shows what can be undertaken in the socio-economic field for a country known for its wealth of data (Adelman and Robinson). A host of other social data are being collected under the general name of social indicators, which claim an important position in the welfare concept (Levy and Guttman; Scheer).

Another extension of the number of the needed variables relates to the "informal sector." Depending on the type of information needed, some of it will be already part of the official statistics, as handicraft and other small-scale business. Sample surveys are the best known tool to obtain data on the informal sector, and in some countries, e.g., India, there is a vast wealth of them. Yet the general impression is that much remains to be done in this field. For a developed country, such as Britain, novel ideas have been formulated on both the household and the informal (partly illegal) sectors by Gershuny.

Of late, the discussion on appropriate technology has acquired much momentum. As a matter of course, most information has to come from single enterprises, and economists will have to co-operate with engineers. Path-breaking work has been done by Boon, a good deal under the auspices of El Colegio de Mexico, but also by Beyrard, and probably by many consulting engineering firms. Among the United Nations organizations, UNIDO and FAO are the most involved, but twice already a general conference on the subject of science and development (Geneva,

1963 and Vienna, 1979) was organized. The subject is so vast that each sector in each country required its own treatment. While there is much scope for the application of the principle of self-reliance in this field also, one world-wide problem looms large at the horizon of technology, namely the consequences of the introduction of microelectronic devices. Even though inertia will slow down real developments in comparison to those theoretically deduced from what the avant-garde performs, the need for case studies concerning previous generations of electronic devices is strong. In such case studies, important variables to be ascertained are the capital intensity of new processes and the elasticity of demand for their services. If the latter is high, which is by no means impossible, the threat to employment is less, of course, than if that elasticity is low. Some institutions in the field of banking have announced their expectation of no threat to employment, but opinions widely diverge. The impact on comparative costs in developed and developing countries has hardly been put on the agenda for discussion, but, as a matter of course, it should be included.

Some technologies will experience the impact of higher energy prices; these have made feasible, economically speaking, village-level activities such as biogas production (Reddy, Prasad, and Prasad).

Some of the important new variables which must be introduced into development models are of an environmental character. Among them may be the minimum surface under forests, i.e., the surface needed to avoid desertification. For an island such as Java, Indonesia's densely populated central island, this is now becoming a question of life and death; and transmigration of a part of Java's population to Sumatra is one of the most urgent activities to be organized at a much larger scale than heretofore.

This brings us to the category of non-measured variables which have now attracted the attention of model builders. We already mentioned variables concerning the informal sector, and could add the activities of self-reliance, by the "mobilization" of village populations, practised by the Institute of Cultural Affairs, located near Bombay, with affiliations all over the world. Econometricians are accustomed to entering non-measured variables into models with the aid of "proxies"; in a way, social indicators, discussed before, are such proxies for "happiness" or "utility" in economic jargon, the very aim of socio-economic policies.

Let us now turn to the (partly) new use that is going to be made of models.

Newer methodologies for use of econometric models nowadays abound (cf. Nijkamp). One is needed to deal with a major fact of life, namely that policy-makers more often disagree than agree about their aims. Hence all sorts of compromising processes characterize development policies. The problem is more than a century old in economic science and was first tackled by the French economist Cournot in an attempt to describe the attitude of competitors who are few (representing a near-monopoly situation). Several other new methods are tried out, all containing assumptions on how politicians "play their game" (cf. the Theory of Games, due to Von Neumann and Morgenstern).

Another example of the new use made of models is due to Cohen. His method consists in maintaining a sufficient number of degrees of freedom so as to alternatively use the model for maximizing welfare of different groups. Depending on the power shifts which may occur, another group's welfare function may be taken as maximum and so the effects of the power change can be studied.

Again, another way of using models is called interactive multiple-goal planning (Nijkamp and Spronk). In essence, it is a reaction to the way to which policy-makers maximize their objective function. They hardly know what an objective function means, but they do know which of the different situations they prefer. The planning process is given the shape of a dialogue between model-builders and policy-makers. The former show a feasible situation of the economy to the latter and ask them whether they want a change in any of the objective variables or targets. After the policy-maker has suggested a new value for that target, the model-handler tells him what other target has then to be changed (mostly in an unfavourable sense) and whether the change is worth the gain on the first target. Thus the dialogue finishes in a situation which, for the policy-maker, is the best attainable configuration.

References

Adelman, J., and S. Robinson, *Income Distribution Policies in Developing Countries. A Case Study of Korea,* London, Oxford University Press, 1978 (published for the World Bank).

Boon, G. K., *Technology and Sector Choice in Economic Development,* Alphen and Rijn, Sijthoff and Nordhoff, 1978.

Bornschier, V., "Einkommensungleichheit innerhalb von Landern in Komparative Sicht," *Schweiz. Zeitschr. f. Soziologie,* Vol. 4, 1978.

Cohen, S. I., *Agrarian Structures and Agrarian Reforms,* Leiden/Boston, Martinus Nijhoff, 1978.

Gershuny, J. L., *Address to the Dutch Scientific Council of Government Policy,* The Hague, 1979.

Kuyvenhoven, A., Planning with the Semi-Input-Output Method, Leiden/Boston/London, Martinus Nijhoff, 1978.

Leontief, W., et al., *The Future of the World Economy,* New York, Oxford University Press, 1977.

Levy, S., and L. Guttman, "On the Multivariate Structure of Well-being," *Social Indicators Research,* Vol. 2, 1975.

Narasimham, N. V. A., *A Short-Term Planning Model for India,* Amsterdam, North Holland, 1965.

Nijkamp, P., *Multidimensional Spatial Data and Decision Analysis,* New York, Wiley, 1979.

Nijkamp, P., and J. Spronk, "Interactive Multiple Goal Programming," Rotterdam, Centrum voor Bedfijfskundig Onderzoek, Erasmus University, 1978 (Report 7803/A).

Reddy, A. K. N., C. R. Prasad, and K. Krishna Prasad, "Bio-Gas Plants: Prospects, Problems and Tasks," *Economic and Political Weekly,* Vol. IX (Special Number), August 1974.

Scheer, Lore, *Quality of Life,* Vienna, Arbeitsgemeinschaft fur Lebensniveauvergleich, 1977.

Von Neumann, J., and O. Morgenstern, *Theory and Games of Economic Behavior,* Princeton, N.J., Princeton University Press, 1944.

Waterston, A., et al., *Development Planning, Lessons of Experience,* Baltimore, Md., The Johns Hopkins Press, 1965.

II.C. RADICAL PERSPECTIVES

II.C.1. A Marxist View *

What we find, therefore, is a spotty growth record within the Third World capitalist countries, some of them doing well but many foundering and, at best, a lackluster performance in the areas of equity and employment opportunities. We do not find, however, despite such a suggestion from some Marxist analyses, a uniform lack of progress among the LDCs toward industrialization, higher living standards, fairer treatment of peasants and the urban poor, or containment of the population upsurge. In these and other directions, progress has been recorded here and there within this group of countries, even though the general situation is not good.

Where, then, do these considerations leave us with respect to Marxian views about economic development in the Third World?

DIALECTICAL DEVELOPMENT: WEALTH AND POVERTY

I would say that recent experience has supported the Marxist contention that the development process is a dialectical one. This means that development produces not only equilibrium but its opposite, disequilibrium, not only continuities but discontinuities, both social harmonies and social conflicts, balances and imbalances, growth and stagnation, and so on. In this view of economic development, growth contains within it antigrowth forces, which will lead to the inevitable breaking up of the existing state of things, to the transiency of all things. So the development process cannot be a gradual, steady, harmonious movement toward equilibrium, as seen by many advocates of neoclassical doctrine. It cannot be an uninterrupted growth process in which growth is

*From John G. Gurley, "Economic Development: A Marxist View," in K. P. Jameson and C. K. Wilber (eds.), *Directions in Economic Development,* Copyright 1979, University of Notre Dame Press, Notre Dame, Indiana, pp. 201–14. Reprinted by permission.

protected from contamination against external antagonists. For the antagonists are found within the growth process itself.

A particular version of this general Marxist view is the notion that the capitalist accumulation process produces both wealth and poverty. Marx originally formulated this proposition, in the first volume of *Capital,* as the general law of capitalist accumulation. In that work, Marx wrote:

The same causes [that] develop the expansive power of capital, develop also the labor-power at its disposal. The relative mass of the industrial reserve army increases therefore with the potential energy of wealth.... *This is the absolute general law of capitalist accumulation.* Like all other laws it is modified in its working by many circumstances.... This law rivets the laborer to capital more firmly than the wedges of Vulcan did Prometheus to the rock. It establishes an accumulation of misery, corresponding with accumulation of capital. Accumulation of wealth at one pole is, therefore, at the same time accumulation of misery, agony of toil, slavery, ignorance, brutality, mental degradation, at the opposite pole, i.e., on the side of the class that produces its own product in the form of capital.[1]

In this passage, Marx had in mind not only *material* poverty (absolute and relative) at the one pole but the poverty of alienation as well, for he added that "in proportion as capital accumulates, the lot of the laborer, *be his payment high or low,* must grow worse."[2]

This thesis has been accepted by generations of Marxists, though it has often been modified in one way or another, and it has been applied in numerous ways, including applications to problems associated with underdeveloped countries. Marx and Engels paved the way for later analyses by arguing, in a dialectical manner, that European colonial expansion was an inevitable outgrowth of the

[1] Karl Marx, *Capital,* Vol. 1, New York, International Publishers, 1967, p. 644–5.

[2] Ibid., p. 645 (my emphasis).

development of capitalism, that it brutalized and plundered the peoples of the colonized areas and disrupted or destroyed their livelihoods, but that, despite all of this, such expansion was necessary to push many of the backward countries off dead-center so as to implant in them the seeds of capitalist development. Enrichment at one end was inextricably linked to impoverishment at the other. But the impoverishment and the brutality that accompanied it were part of a historical process in which destruction contained construction within it. The construction would be a capitalist one, Marx and Engels believed, in which the bourgeoisie would create progress and wealth at one pole, but at the same time drag masses of people "through blood and dirt, through misery and degradation." This polarization would end only with the demise of the bourgeoisie:

When a great social revolution shall have mastered the results of the bourgeois epoch, the markets of the world and the modern powers of production, and subjected them to the common control of the most advanced peoples, then only will human progress cease to resemble that hideous pagan idol, who would not drink the nectar but from the skulls of the slain.[3]

That is just about as grisly a picture of capitalism and the wealth-poverty dichtomy it fosters as can be found anywhere.

In recent years, Paul Baran has argued that the British, while enriching themselves, "systematically destroyed all the fibres and foundations of Indian society."[4] He supported Nehru's statement that British rule and policy were responsible for the later "tragic poverty of the people."[5] Baran then set out to show how such exploitative relationships characterize the entire structure of world capitalism. In much the same way, Paul Sweezy asserted that "capitalist development inevitably produces development at

one pole and underdevelopment at the other"; a proposition, he emphasized, that "applies not only to the relations between the advanced capitalist countries" and the colonial and semicolonial countries, but also within both of these parts.[6]

This thesis was generalized and carried to its ultimate destination by A. G. Frank, who contended that capitalism had long ago entered every nook and cranny of the satellite world in such a way as to make global capitalism an integrated structure of metropoles and satellites that bound nations, regions, and urban-rural areas into dominant-dependent relationships. A systematic transfer of economic surpluses continually occurred from the base of this world structure—that is, from the millions of workers and peasants—that benefited the metropoles and harmed the satellites throughout the structure, in which a lower metropolis was in turn a satellite of a higher metropolis. Frank claimed that when such exploitative ties were temporarily loosened, such as during wars or depressions involving higher metropoles, a type of development occurred in the satellites; when the ties were later strengthened, underdevelopment was generated. He also asserted that "the greater the wealth [that was] available for exploitation [in the past], the poorer and more underdeveloped the region today; and the poorer the region was as a colony, the richer and more developed it is today."[7]

Samir Amin has most recently analyzed this polarization thesis in greater depth. All peripheral or satellite formations, Amin writes, have four main characteristics: (1) the predominance of agrarian capitalism; (2) a local, mainly merchant bourgeoisie that is dominated by foreign capital; (3) the growth of a large bureaucracy, which substitutes for an urban bourgeoisie; and (4) incomplete proletarianization, which takes the form of masses of poor peasants, urban unemployed, and many marginal workers. These are the

[3]These views can be found in Shlomo Avineri, ed., *Karl Marx on Colonialism and Modernization*, New York, Anchor, 1969, pp. 137–9.

[4]Paul Baran, *The Political Economy of Growth*, New York, Monthly Review Press, 1957, pp. 144–150.

[5]Ibid.

[6]Ibid.

[7]A. G. Frank, *Lumpenbourgeoisie and Lumpendevelopment*, New York, Monthly Review Press, 1972, p. 19.

features of an incomplete and extraverted development of local capitalism, in which the center capital reshapes the periphery into extensions of the center, thereby preventing autocentric development in the periphery and establishing unequal exchange between center and periphery—that is, differences between the returns to labor that are larger than differences between their productivities.[8] The dominance of foreign capital in the periphery, Amin claims, means distorted development toward export activities and excessive development of the tertiary sector and light industry. It also means extreme unevenness of development, the disarticulation of the economy, a development process that is not cumulative, and a strong tendency toward periphery indebtedness to the center.[9]

It is a general consensus, then, among Marxists that capitalism produces polarization, day in and day out. The basic mechanism is that capital utilizes its economic and political dominance to exploit labor throughout the global system by employing for this purpose both plain force and market forces; and that, throughout the structure, big capital dominates small capital.

When it comes to "market forces," however, Marxist theorists appear to be only in the early stages leading to a full formulation of the variety of mechanisms in the capital-accumulation process that generate biformity. Still, there have been some outstanding achievements here. Arghiri Emmanuel has analyzed how increasing inequality between nations is rooted in an unequal exchange that tends to increase over time, so that poor nations become poorer and the rich ones richer. Samir Amin has extended the analysis into processes of biformity within the satellite or periphery countries, as I previously discussed. Also, many notable contributions have been made by economists and others pursuing dependency theory, including Theo-

tonio Dos Santos, Celso Furtado, and F. H. Cardoso. But my impression is that we still fall far short of a full understanding of how market forces, and the values and behavior patterns that support market processes, contribute to polarization of living standards at the various levels of the global capitalist system.

A convincing explanation of this must commence with the fundamental mechanism of exploitation of labor by capital. The explanation would then include the process that makes the reserve army of labor a necessary element of the capitalist mode of production and an analysis of how the expansion of this mode dispossesses and impoverishes previously self-sufficient producers. The explanation would also include an analysis of how the capitalist mode necessarily builds on efficiency, which is often antithetical to equity; of how it builds on specialization, which increases the vulnerability of people and areas to adverse developments; and of how it transfers wealth from poor areas to wealthy ones, via the price mechanism. It would then go on to discuss the values and behavior patterns, engendered and supported by the capitalist mode, which compel individuals to seek success even at the expense of others' welfare and which encourage and reward cheating and extortion of the poor by the rich. Finally, the explanation would show how poverty, once established, feeds on itself—the poor lack capital, information, education, and so on—and how wealth, once established, also feeds on itself.

Marx once said, in discussing the repeal of the Corn Laws in England: "If the free-traders cannot understand how one nation can grow rich at the expense of another, we need not wonder, since these same gentlemen also refuse to understand how within one country one class can enrich itself at the expense of another."[10] Present-day Marxists do understand these things, but they are still several steps away from having a general theory about them.

[8]This is most fully explored in Arghiri Emmanuel, *Unequal Exchange: A Study of the Imperialism of Trade,* New York, Monthly Review Press, 1976.

[9]Samir Amin, *Unequal Development,* New York, Monthly Review Press, 1976, pp. 203, 249–51, 288, 334–64.

[10]Karl Marx, "On the Question of Free Trade," in Karl Marx, *The Poverty of Philosophy,* New York, International Publishers, 1969, p. 223.

CONVENTIONAL DEVELOPMENT: LIFE-CYCLES AND MISTAKES

Conventional development economists, while recognizing poverty, inequalities, and unemployment in the Third World countries, have explanations and remedies for these ills that contain enough truth to be of interest to Marxist theorists. And yet the latter have paid little attention to these orthodox rationalizations.

The principal and most general explanation of the economic ills of the Third World is that they are associated with the particular stage of a life-cycle that the LDCs happen to be in, and so can be outgrown. Thus, as one version of this explanation has it, all countries, provided they are not eternally damned to the inferno, enter a purgatory stage before they go onward and upward to blessedness and earthly paradise. Along this development path, income distribution worsens before it gets better. Population growth gets out of hand before birth rates begin to fall into line with death rates. Countries become chronic debtors before they burst into the heaven of creditors. They go through the hell of hyper-inflation before they develop their economies sufficiently to allow price stabilization. The unemployed pile up in new urban centers before full employment can be enjoyed. And countries might even suffer dictatorship before democracy wins out. Another version of the life-cycle explanation—the straight-line instead of the U-shaped model—is that things start off bad and then get better and better. . . .

These explanations are meant to suggest, of course, that, when one encounters the growing ills of the Third World, one is merely looking at some childhood diseases. With proper care of the kiddies, all will be well later on. In many cases, though, the data themselves are quite underdeveloped and just barely suggest what is so confidently asserted. Moreover, the results rest on cross-section data which are intended to apply to individual countries over time. The dangers of making this leap are so well known as to require no comment from me. Also Marxists would be correct to point out that young socialist countries appear to be immune to most, and perhaps to all, of these diseases. Yet, in each of the examples that I just cited, there is a plausible hypothesis with more or less supporting data that should enlist the attention of Marxists, who, however, are too busy ascribing all ills to capitalism in general to have time to consider the orthodox arguments.

Conventional development economists have another arrow for their bow. The ills of poverty, inequality, and unemployment that one finds in Third World countries, they say, are largely owing to the gross inefficiency with which these economies are run. Their economic managers create the maladies by espousing policies that are almost insane. For example, a host of measures underprice capital and overprice labor: high minimum wage rates, too low a rate of interest, overvalued currency (which makes imported machinery cheap), payroll taxes on employers for their employees, and exemptions from custom duties for imported capital equipment. Each of these measures induces the substitution of capital for labor, thereby exacerbating unemployment, poverty, and income inequalities. The same thing is accomplished when policymakers neglect agriculture, which uses labor-intensive methods, and support heavy industry, which utilizes capital-intensive methods. Other policies, it is said, also interfere with what would be correct relative prices, and the resulting distortions are enough to make anyone sick.

The World Bank has recently set forth a similar explanation of poverty and other bourgeois ills. There has been a poor ordering, the Bank says, of national priorities. A reordering is called for. Instead of policies to foster "growth in general," policies should be redesigned to direct investment to poverty groups in the form of education, access to credit, health care, public facilities, and so on. Thus, the new national priorities should be "growth," as before, but growth in the lower income groups where absolute poverty resides.

Just as in the previous set of arguments,

the intention here is to make one believe that the growing ills one sees in young capitalist economies are not owing to capitalism per se but to the appalling way the economies are managed. If the distortions or improper national priorities were corrected, the argument goes, the economic ills would be cured. In this case, too, there is probably enough truth behind the argument to warrant the attention of Marxists. But even granting this, Marxists must go on to ask, as conventional economists do not, why there is so much inefficiency and ineptness. Does it serve a political purpose? Which class does it help, and how? Or is it simply due to ignorance? Conventional economists believe much too naively that no one wants unemployment or poverty, and so they must arise from lack of knowledge or willpower. Marxists know that such seeming disorders are often beneficial to ruling classes, and hence are no mistakes at all but outcomes of rational policies. While I believe that Marxists are mainly correct about this, it is still true that the inefficiencies and absurdities, willful or not, are well worth studying. Marxists themselves are too prone to assume that all capitalist economies, at whatever stage of development they find themselves, are run with equal efficiency. There is much for Marxists to learn in this area.

CONVENTIONAL DEVELOPMENT: THE POPULATION EXPLOSION

Many conventional economists ascribe the ills of the LDCs in part to the population explosion that is taking place throughout the Third World. It is claimed that this is so unusual in history and so devastating as to account for much of the poverty and inequality that one observes everywhere.

Marxists have assumed that the so-called population problem is meant to divert attention from the real issues, which involve the transformation of the present exploitative economic systems into socialist societies. I think that Marxists are largely correct about this. Underdevelopment—with its low growth rates, high levels of unemployment,

harsh income inequalities, widespread lack of education, the dominance of rural living, and the oppression of females—is closely associated with high birth rates and so with high rates of population growth. Thus, if ruling classes, through their exploitation of working classes and in other ways, generate underdevelopment, the consequence is likely to be high population growth rates, which in turn feed back to lower incomes per capita and more underdevelopment. The overthrow of these ruling classes is a necessary, though not a sufficient, condition for breaking this vicious cycle.

While all of this is largely true, Marxists have not taken adequate account of the reasons for and the consequences of the population explosion that has occurred in recent decades. World population up to 1650 grew by only a small fraction of 1 percent per annum. For the next 300 years the rate crept up toward 1 percent. But in the last two or three decades it has risen to around 2 percent or more—1 percent in the developed countries and 2½ percent in the less developed ones. Between A.D. 1 and 1750, world population rose by 480 million. In the next 200 years, it rose by 1,750 million, and in the last 28 years by the same amount. China and India alone this year will add about 30 million to the world's population, a number that exceeds the *total* national population of 87 percent of the countries of the world.

The major reason for this explosion is the decline in death rates owing to rapid technological advances in modern medicine—especially vaccination against malaria, smallpox, yellow fever, and cholera—and to the spread of modern public health measures. The sharp drop in death rates generated a very high natural rate of increase because both birth and death rates in the LDCs were a percentage point higher than they had been in preindustrial Europe (4½ against 3½ percent). All of this has created serious difficulties for many countries in the Third World, unlike the nineteenth-century experience of western Europe when both death and birth rates declined slowly and together.

Although there is evidence that a new

global demographic transformation is now underway, involving declining birth rates to match the previous drop in death rates, population pressure for many LDCs will remain intense and will retard improvements in living standards for hundreds of millions of people for many years to come. This is a problem that concerns both socialist and capitalist countries. Some countries in both camps have succeeded in recent years in getting their population problems somewhat under control—socialist China as well as capitalist Taiwan and Singapore. Thus there would appear to be some mechanisms within the capitalist mode of production that, to some degree, control population upsurges, and these ought to be more carefully investigated by Marxist development economists than they have been in the past.

THE TESTING OF THEORIES

A serious failing of Marxist development economists lies in their lack of interest in testing theory against the facts. Almost without exception, it has been the conventional economists who have dug out the information on income inequalities, differential growth rates, absolute poverty, unemployment, and the like. Even with these data available, Marxists appear uninterested in them and, instead, remain totally absorbed in more model building. An unfriendly critic would say that Marxists ignore these data because they disprove their theories. A better and more profound explanation is that Marxists are trained to be highly suspicious of surface phenomena and the crude empiricism often used in analyzing these outward manifestations of deeper, underlying realities. Marx prepared the way for this attitude with his analysis of the production and circulation spheres of the accumulation process; in the former, located in the underworld, so to speak, resided the reality of exploitation, while in the latter, located on the surface of everyday life, "equality and freedom" reigned. Surface data, therefore, could badly mislead one, could create fantastic illusions about how the system really operated. Ever

since that brilliant analysis of Marx, his followers have been extremely wary of all such superficial evidence.

But this attitude is wrong. Marx himself used plentiful data in his major work. These "facial expressions" of capitalism are extremely useful to the investigator, so long as he or she is aware of what is really going on underneath it all. Since there are systematic relations between the one world and the other, Marxist theories about the underlying realities can be tested against the surface data with good effect. Indeed, Marxists ought to be in a better position than conventional economists to provide analytical depth to the interpretation of these data.

In any event, Marxists ought to look carefully at what conventional economists call the "success stories" of capitalist economic development and, indeed, at all the evidence that has been so laboriously compiled by the more orthodox economists, no matter how embarrassing it may be. One would not think it necessary to say that, but it is.

SUMMARY OF MARXIST AND ORTHODOX RESPONSES

A large number of non-Marxian LDCs are stagnating. Many, however, are expanding, but, even in these cases, their growth is often accompanied by growing inequities, unemployment, and impoverishment. Orthodox economists look on these "ills" either as childhood diseases or as residues of the past and, hence, either curable with time and patience or capable of being gradually mopped up. Marxists, on the other hand, believe that capitalist development itself creates these so-called ills, day in and day out, along with society's wealth. Furthermore, orthodox economists think that the "ills" are truly social maladies not desired by society, while Marxists are convinced that they often serve a useful function for the ruling classes and hence are results of rational, purposive policies. These are two entirely different ways of looking at the development process. The first suggests reform; the second revolution. Indeed, Marxists believe that the very processes of capitalist accumulation create the revolutionary conditions required for overthrowing capitalism and establishing more humane socialist societies.

In fact, for the better part of this century, capitalism *has* been overthrown in large parts of the world, and Marxism has taken over these areas.

II.C.2. Dependency Theories of Underdevelopment*

The general field of study of the dependency analyses is the development of Latin American capitalism. Its most important characteristic is its attempt to analyse it from the point of view of the interplay between internal and external structures.

There is no doubt that the "father" of this approach is Paul Baran. His principal contribution to the general literature on development (Baran, 1957) continues the central line of Marxist thought regarding the contradictory character of the needs of imperialism and the process of industrialization and general economic development of the backward nations. Thus he affirms at the outset that

What is decisive is that economic development in underdeveloped countries is profoundly inimical to the dominant interests in the advanced capitalist countries (1957, p. 28).

To avoid such development the advanced nations will form alliances with pre-capitalistic domestic elites (who will also be adversely affected by the transformations of capitalist development), intended to inhibit such transformations. In this way the advanced nations would have easy access to domestic resources and thus be able to maintain traditional modes of surplus extraction. Within this context the possibilities of eco-

*Reprinted with permission from *World Development*, Vol. 6, Gabriel Palma, "Dependency: A Formal Theory of Underdevelopment or a Methodology for the Analysis of Concrete Situations of Underdevelopment?," Copyright 1978, Pergamon Press, Ltd., pp. 899–902.

nomic growth in dependent countries would be extremely limited; the surplus they generated would be expropriated in large part by foreign capital, and otherwise squandered on luxury consumption by traditional elites. Furthermore, not only would resources destined for investment thereby be drastically reduced, but so would their internal multiplying effect, as capital goods would have to be purchased abroad. This process would necessarily lead to economic stagnation, and the only way out would be political.

Starting out with this analysis Frank attempts to develop the thesis that the only political solution is a revolution of an immediately socialist character; for within the context of the capitalist system there would be no alternative to underdevelopment (Frank, 1967).

For the purpose of this analysis we may distinguish three levels in Frank's "model of underdevelopment." The first is that in which he attempts to demonstrate that Latin America and other areas in the periphery have been incorporated into the world economy since the early stages of their colonial periods. The second is that in which he attempts to show that such incorporation into the world economy has transformed the countries in question immediately and necessarily into capitalist economies. Finally, there is a third level, in which Frank tries to prove that the integration of these supposedly capitalist economies into the world economy is necessarily achieved through an interminable metropolis—satellite chain, in which the surplus generated at each stage is successively drawn off towards the centre. On account of this he develops a subsidiary thesis:

If it is satellite status which generates underdevelopment, then a weaker or lesser degree of metropolis-satellite relations may generate less deep structural underdevelopment and/or allow for more possibility of local development (Frank, 1967, p. 11).

But as the weakening of the satellite-metropolis network can, according to Frank, *only take place* for reasons external to the satellite economies, of a necessarily transient nature, it follows that there is no real possibility of sustained development within the system. According to this analysis, the only alternative becomes that of breaking completely with the metropolis-satellite network through socialist revolution or continuing to "underdevelop" within it.

In my opinion, the value of Frank's analysis is his magisterial critique of the supposedly dual structure of peripheral societies. Frank shows clearly that the different sectors of the economies in question are and have been since very early in their colonial history linked closely to the world economy. Moreover, he has correctly emphasized that this connection has not automatically brought about capitalist economic development, such as optimistic models (derived from Adam Smith) would have predicted, by means of which the development of trade and the division of labour inevitably would bring about economic development. Nevertheless Frank's error lies in his attempt to explain this phenomenon using the same economic determinist framework of the model he purports to transcend; in fact, he merely turns it upside-down: the development of the "core" necessarily requires the underdevelopment of the "periphery." Thus he criticizes both the alternative proposed by the traditional Latin American left (the possibility of a democratic bourgeois revolution, because in this context the only political solution is a revolution of an immediately socialist character), and the policies put forward by ECLA.

Nevertheless, his critique is not directed towards the real weaknesses in the analysis made by the Latin American left—the mechanical determination of internal by external structures; on the contrary, he strengthens that mechanical determination in his attempt to construct a model to explain the mechanisms through which the expropriation of the surplus takes place. Probably still unduly influenced by his training as an economist at the University of Chicago, he constructs a mechanico-formal model which is no more than a set of equations of general equilibrium (static and unhistorical), in which the extraction of the surplus takes place through a series of satellite-metropolis relationships, through which the surplus generated at each stage is syphoned off.

It is not surprising that his method leads Frank to displace class relations from the centre of his analysis of economic development and underdevelopment. Thus he develops a circular concept of capitalism; although it is evident that capitalism is a system where production for profit via exchange predominates, the opposite is not necessarily true: the existence of production for profits in the market is not necessarily a signal of capitalist production. For Frank, this is a *sufficient* condition for the existence of capitalist relations of production. Thus for Frank, the problem of the origins of capitalism (and therefore the origins of the development of the few and the underdevelopment of the majority) comes down to the origins of the expanding world market *and not to the emergence of a system of free wage labour.*

Although Frank did not go very far in his analysis of the capitalist system as a whole, its origins and development, Immanuel Wallerstein tackled this tremendous challenge in his remarkable book, *The Modern World System: Capitalist Agriculture and the Origins of the European World—Economy in the Sixteenth Century* (1974).

Frank has reaffirmed his ideas in a series of articles published jointly in 1969; a year later he sought to enrich his analysis with the introduction of some elements of Latin American class structure (Frank, 1970).

Frank has been criticized from all sides, and on almost every point in his analysis.

Prominent among his critics is Laclau (1971), who provides an excellent synthesis of Frank's theoretical model, and shows that the only way in which Frank can "demonstrate" that all the periphery is capitalist and has been since the colonial period is by using the concept of capitalism in a sense which is erroneous from a Marxist point of view, and useless for his central proposition, that of showing that a bourgeois revolution in the periphery is impossible. As regards this point then, Laclau concludes that Frank makes no contribution, leaving the analysis exactly where it started.

Robert Brenner (1977) takes Laclau's analysis of Frank (as well as Dobb's critique of Sweezy), and demonstrates how the work of Sweezy, Frank and Wallerstein—brilliantly summarized and analysed by him—are doomed to negate the model put forward first by Adam Smith in *The Wealth of Nations,* Book 1, but

because they have failed . . . to discard the underlying individualistic—mechanist presuppositions of this model, they have ended up by erecting an alternative theory of capitalist development which is, in its central aspects, the mirror image of the "progressist" thesis they wish to surpass. Thus, very much like those they criticize, they conceive of (changing) class relations as emerging more or less directly from the (changing) requirements for the generation of surplus and development of production, under the pressures and opportunities engendered by a growing world market. Only, whereas their opponents tend to see such market-determined processes [the development of trade and the division of labour], as setting off, automatically, a dynamic of economic development, they see them as enforcing the rise of economic backwardness. As a result, they fail to take into account either the way in which class structures, once established, will in fact determine the course of economic development or underdevelopment over an entire epoch, or the way in which these class structures themselves emerge: as the outcome of class struggles whose results are incomprehensible in terms merely of market forces (Brenner, 1977, p. 27).

Thus the way in which Frank uses the concepts "development" and "underdevelopment" seems incorrect from a Marxist point

of view; furthermore, they do not seem useful for demonstrating what Frank attempts to demonstrate.

To summarize, Frank's direct contribution to our understanding of the process of Latin American development is largely limited to his critique of dualist models for Latin America. Nevertheless, his indirect contribution is considerable. By this I mean that his work has inspired a significant quantity of research by others (whether to support or rebut his arguments), in their respective disciplines, particularly in the sociology of development.

The central line of Frank's thought regarding the "development of underdevelopment" is continued, though from a critical point of view, by the Brazilian sociologist Theotonio dos Santos, for whom

the process under consideration [Latin American development] rather than being one of satellization as Frank believes, is a case of the formation of a certain type of internal structures conditioned by international relationships of dependence (1969, p. 80).

Dos Santos distinguishes different types of relations of dependency (essentially colonial, industrial-financial and industrial-technological, the latter having grown up since the Second World War), and consequently distinguishes different kinds of internal structures generated by them. Dos Santos emphasizes the differences and discontinuities between the different types of dependency and between the internal structures which result from them, while Frank himself stresses the continuity and similarity of dependency relations in a capitalist context. In other words, while Frank wishes to emphasize the similarities between economic structures in the times of Cortez, Pizarro, Clive and Rhodes, and between those and the structures typified by the activity of multinational corporations, dos Santos is more concerned with the differences and discontinuities between them.

There is within dos Santos's analysis the beginnings of an interesting attempt to break with the concept of a mechanical determination of internal by external structures which dominated the traditional analysis of the left in Latin America, and which particularly characterized Frank's work. One perceives initially in his analysis the perception not only that both structures are contradictory, but that movement is produced precisely through the dynamic of the contradictions between the two. Nevertheless, as he proceeds in the analysis he re-establishes, little by little, the priority of external over internal structures, separating almost metaphysically the two sides of the opposition—the internal and the external—and losing the notion of movement through the dynamic of the contradictions between these structures. The analysis which begins to emerge is again one typified by "antecedent causation and inert consequences." The culmination of this process is his well-known *formal definition of dependency, which because of its formal nature is both static and unhistorical;* it is found in his 1970 article in the *American Economic Review:*

Dependence is a conditioning situation in which the economies of one group of countries are conditioned by the development and expansion of others. A relationship of interdependence between two or more economies or between such economies and the world trading system becomes a dependent relationship when some countries can expand through self-impulsion while others, being in a dependent position, can only expand as a reflection of the dominant countries, which may have positive or negative effects on their immediate development (1970, pp. 289–90).

Lall (1975) offers an interesting critique of a number of dependency studies. He argues that the characteristics to which underdevelopment in dependent countries is generally attributed are not exclusive to these economies, but are also found in so-called "non-dependent" economies, and that therefore they are properly speaking characteristics of capitalist development in general and not necessarily only of dependent capitalism. He further argues that such analyses are not surprisingly unable to show causal relationships between these characteristics and underdevelopment.

Lall argues that any concept of dependency which claims to be a theory of underdevelopment should satisfy two criteria:

(i) it must lay down certain characteristics of dependent economies which are not found in non-dependent ones;
(ii) these characteristics must be shown to affect adversely the course and pattern of development of the dependent countries (1975, p. 800).

If crucial features of "dependence" can be found in both dependent and "non-dependent" economies, the whole conceptual schema is defective. And if it does not satisfy the second criterion, that is, if particular features of dependency cannot be demonstrated to be casually related to underdevelopment, we would be faced not with a "theory of Latin American underdevelopment" but simply with a catalogue of social, political, economic and cultural indicators, which will not help us to understand the dynamic of underdevelopment in Latin America.

Lall goes on to analyse the principal characteristics commonly associated with dependent economies and concludes that it appears that the technique is

to pick off some salient features of modern capitalism as it affects some less developed countries and put them into a distinct category of dependence (1975, p. 806).

He goes on to consider the possibility that the characteristics associated with the dependent economies could have a particular cumulative effect when occurring together, but finds no conclusive evidence. He concludes then that such a concept of dependency applied

to less developed countries is impossible to define and cannot be shown to be causally related to a continuance of underdevelopment (1975, p. 808).

It is not surprising then that

one sometimes gets the impression on reading the literature that "dependence" is defined in a circular manner: less developed countries are poor because they are dependent, and any characteristics that they display signify dependence (1975, p. 800).

References

Baran, P., 1957, *La Economia Politica del Crecimiento*, Mexico, F.C.E., 1969.

Brenner, R., 1977, "The origins of capitalist development: a critique of neo-Smithian Marxism," *New Left Review*, No. 104, July–August 1977, pp. 25–93.

Dos Santos, Theotonio, 1969, *La dependencia económica y las alternativas de cambio en América Latina*, México, November 1969.

Frank, A. G., 1967, *Capitalism and Underdevelopment in Latin America: Historical Studies of Chile and Brasil*, New York, Monthly Review Press, 1967.

Frank, A. G., 1970, *Lumpenbourgeoisie: Lumpen Development, Dependence, Class and Politics in Latin America*, reprinted, New York, Monthly Review Press, 1972.

Laclau, E., 1971, "Feudalism and capitalism in Latin America," *New Left Review*, May–June 1971, pp. 19–38.

Lall, S., 1975, "Is dependence a useful concept in analysing underdevelopment?" *World Development*, Vol. 2, No. 11, 1975, pp. 799–810.

Wallerstein, I., 1974, *The Modern World System: Capitalist Agriculture and the Origins of the European World—Economy in the Sixteenth Century*, New York, Academic Press, 1974.

Comment

We consider other aspects of dependency theory in connection with foreign investment and multinational corporations in Chapter V. In Chapter VIII, the discussion of international trade as a mechanism of international inequality is also related to dependency theory.

Within the school of dependency, different meanings are accorded to the concept of "dependence," and different analyses are offered to explain underdevelopment as a result of the interplay between internal and external structures.

Variants of dependency theory can be considered in the following works: Paul Baran, *The Political Economy of Growth* (1957); *Dependence and Underdevelopment in the New World and the Old*, special issue of *Social and Economic Studies* (March 1973); Samir Amin, "Underdevelopment and Dependency," *Journal of Modern African Studies*, Vol. 10, No. 4 (1972); Samir Amin, *Unequal Development* (1976); Fernando Henrique Cardoso, "Dependency and Development in Latin America," *New Left Review* (July–August 1972); Cardoso and Enzo Faletto, *Dependency and Development in Latin America* (1979); Andre Gunder Frank, *Capitalism and Underdevelopment in Latin America* (1967); Andre Gunder Frank, *Latin America: Underdevelopment or Revolution?* (1969); Andre Gunder Frank, *Lumpenbourgeoisie and Lumpendevelopment* (1972); C. Furtado, *Development and Underdevelopment* (1976); T. dos Santos, "The Structure of Dependence," *American Economic Review* (May 1970); O. Sunkel, "National Development Policy and External Dependence in Latin America," *Journal of Development Studies* (October 1969); A. Emmanuel, *Unequal Exchange* (1972); I. Wallerstein, "Dependence in an Interdependent World," *African Studies Review*, Vol. 17, No. 1 (1974); Ronald H. Chilcote, "Theories of Dependency: The View from the Periphery," *Latin American Perspectives* (Spring 1974); Enmer L. Bacha, "An Interpretation of Unequal Exchange from Prebisch-Singer to Emmanuel," *Journal of Development Economics*, Vol. 5 (1978); Herald Munoz, ed., *From Dependency to Development* (1981).

Some critical discussions of dependency theory are Sanjaya Lall, "Is 'Dependence' a Useful Concept in Analysing Underdevelopment?" *World Development*, (November/December 1975); P. J. O'Brien, "A Critique of Latin American Theories of Dependency," in I. Oxaal et al., eds., *Beyond the Sociology of Development* (1975); Benjamin J. Cohen, *The Question of Imperialism* (1973); Alec Nove, "On Reading Andre Gunder Frank," *Journal of Development Studies* (April–July 1974); Colin Leys, "Underdevelopment and Dependency: Critical Notes," *Journal of Contemporary Asia* (1977).

A number of country studies contradict the dependency thesis: Robert Kaufman et al., "A Preliminary Test of the Theory of Dependency," *Comparative Politics* (April 1975); David Ray, "The Dependency Model and Latin America: Three Basic Fallacies," *Journal of Inter-American Affairs and World Studies* (February 1973); Patrick J. McGowan, "Economic Dependency and Economic Performance in Black Africa," *Journal of Modern African Studies,* Vol. XIV, No. 1 (1976); Patrick J. McGowan and Dale L. Smith, "Economic Dependency in Black Africa: An Analysis of Competing Theories," *International Organization* (Winter 1978).

II.D. ECONOMICS *FOR* DEVELOPMENT—NOTE

The foregoing selections give credence to Keynes's appraisal that "The theory of economics does not furnish a body of settled conclusions immediately applicable to policy."[1] In few, if any, areas of economic policy does the distance between theory and policy tend to be as great as it is for development problems. The various theories of development discussed in this chapter are ways of thinking systematically about the development process—but in abstract terms and from the outside. They relate to the economics *about* development. This approach, however, is far different from the economics *for* development—the economics that the development practitioner must use in formulating and administering an actual development program in a specific environment. In the administration of a development program, development practitioners cannot rely simply on the analyst's view of development "from the outside." They must apply economic principles to specific problems embedded within the general development process. This they cannot do by merely being knowledgeable about the latest development model.

To improve the quality of policymaking, the literary economist is now being asked to provide more operational concepts and empirical constructs instead of "empty stages of growth" or ambiguous phrases such as "big push" or "balanced growth." The mathematical economist is being asked to be more aware of the limits of mathematical programming in a less developed country. The econometrician is being cautioned to recognize the simplifying assumptions that are necessary to keep econometric models within manageable dimensions.

Moreover, most development economists no longer look for a completely different subdiscipline of development economics that would be in contrast to the use of neoclassical

economics.[2] Many did argue in the 1940s and 1950s that "orthodox monoeconomics" descended from Anglo-Saxon economics and was relevant only for the special case of advanced industrial capitalist economies, not for the less developed countries. But this argument has lost force as experience has demonstrated that the principles of monoeconomics—especially those delimiting efficient resource allocation—cannot be overlooked in any economy.

In reconsidering development policies, however, the development economist must still rethink some basic premises of both price theory and income theory. Price theory has to be extended to consider problems of intertemporal allocation of resources and the implications of prices for the mobilization of resources. A "correct set of prices" is needed not only for allocational objectives during a given period of time, but even more importantly as proper signals and sufficient incentives for the fuller utilization and mobilization of resources over time. The development economist needs to understand more precisely just what is meant by "getting prices right" in this dynamic context.

The major concern of neoclassical economics has been with the short-period analysis of resource allocation. In this analysis, it is assumed that population, "state of the arts," institutions, and supply of entrepreneurship are all given. But the very essence of the development process is that these parameters become variables. What is normally taken as "given" in static analysis must actually be explained when the problem is one of secular change. Economics must be broadened—indeed, must at times become interrelated with

---

[1] J. M. Keynes, "General Editorial Introduction" to *Cambridge Economic Handbooks Series.*

[2] See Albert O. Hirschman, *Essays in Trespassing,* 1981, pp. 1–14. Gunnar Myrdal remains a major exception: "Need for Reforms in Underdeveloped Countries," in S. Grossman and E. Lundberg (eds.), *The World Economic Order: Past and Prospects,* 1981, pp. 501–25.

other disciplines—in order to explain the determinants of population growth, technological progress, institutional change, and increase in the supply of entrepreneurship.

Neoclassical economics must also be extended to incorporate more analysis of distribution issues. Problems of absolute poverty and inequality cannot be downgraded to the small technical problem of efficiency in resource allocation. And a welfare economics that prides itself on avoiding interpersonal comparisons and judgments about the distribution of income must appear anemic compared with the emphasis on basic needs. The task is to integrate neoclassical economics with employment and distribution issues.

The conventional Keynesian type of income theory also leaves the development economist perplexed about the causes of unemployment and what might be effective policies for fuller employment. The investment multiplier of Keynesian economics was first identified as an employment multiplier, and more employment was expected to parallel greater output. But notwithstanding the rise in their investment ratios and growth in GNP, many developing countries have at the same time experienced rising unemployment and underemployment. The unemployment problem may be related to the inappropriate set of prices and to structural phenomena that have been ignored by income theory. As indicated frequently in this book, the unemployment problem in LDCs is not of the Keynesian variety, and the policy implications of income theory have to be modified for LDCs.

Economists in the developing countries are also beginning to realize that in many cases they have neglected solutions to immediate and crucial needs by overreaching—by attempting to use sophisticated techniques of analysis and highly formalized long-range planning models. The vogue for long-term plans to the neglect of a more concentrated effort to improve current policymaking has been decried by Sir Alec Cairncross in these words:

For young mandarins who have returned from the universities of the West, initiated into the abracadabra of input-output analysis, linear programming and other mysteries, the preparation of long-term plans is a very beguiling operation, and one full of intellectual challenge even when the practical outcome may be highly obscure. On the other hand, the short-term management of an economy that is subject to rapid changes in circumstances offers harsher and more restricted choices with little scope for subtlety.[3]

Whether it be the result of the operation of an international "demonstration effect" in governmental policymaking or the dominant influence of intellectuals on planning commissions, there has been in many developing countries an overly keen receptivity for the most refined model, the newest technique, the latest element of expertise. It has, however, become increasingly apparent that the use of the latest technique is likely to be premature, and that the attraction to the highest style analysis may be without practical effect.

As the Hungarian economist Janos Kornai has observed, the implementation of mathematical planning is dependent on the degree of maturity of nonmathematical planning. It is only clear what policy objectives are worth striving for when there has already been established an organized institutional, nonmathematical form of planning. For, as Kornai states,

in a single model only a few hundred relationships and constraints can be considered. But people working in the central planning agencies and lower-level institutions and enterprises "sense" hundreds of thousands of further constraints and relations, and they can give expression to these in their own estimates. Mathematical planning will develop successfully only when it develops as one element of well-prepared and well-oriented institutional planning, connected by many threads with real economic life in developing countries.[4]

The overly refined mathematical approach to planning has displayed three prominent

[3]A. K. Cairncross, *The Short Term and the Long in Economic Planning,* Tenth Anniversary Lecture, Economic Development Institute, Washington, D.C., January 6, 1966, p. 7.

[4]Janos Kornai, "Models and Policy: The Dialogue between Model Building and Planner," in C. R. Blitzer et al. (eds.), *Economy-wide Models and Development Planning,* 1975, chapter 2.

types of bias: a bias toward macromodels in plan formulation to the relative neglect of the microeconomic aspects of planning (ranging from project analysis to the installation of incentives and enlistment of mass participation); a bias toward the quantitative aspects of planning to the relative neglect of other developmental forces that are not quantifiable but are of crucial importance (for instance, many aspects of human resource development and sociocultural and political changes for which data are limited); and a bias toward concentration on the formulation of a development plan without due regard for its implementation.

Although it cannot be gainsaid that problems of underdevelopment are different in degree—and, to some extent, even in kind— from those encountered in developed countries, nevertheless it would be overreacting to conclude that entirely different economic tools and principles are needed to analyze these problems. The progress that has been made in development economics has actually been mainly within the framework of traditional economic analysis. Many tools of traditional economics and many principles of accepted economic theory have proved directly applicable to the problems of poor countries, and some conceptions and techniques can become more useful with some ready-made modifications or extension.

What has become clear, however, is that we must frequently be prepared to depart from traditional assumptions when analyzing problems of development. We must recognize that the premises of accepted economic theory may have to be altered to make the theory more immediately relevant to countries that have a different social system and economic structure from those to which Western economists are accustomed. The task of development economists is made difficult not because they must start afresh with a completely new set of tools or because they confront wholly different problems, but because they must acquire a sense of the different assumptions that are appropriate to analyzing a problem within the context of a poor country. In particular, this calls for special care in identifying different institutional relations,[5] in assessing the different quantitative importance of some variables, and in allowing some elements that are usually taken as "given" to become endogenous variables in development analysis.

When examining the selections of the following chapters, we should therefore be alert to the efforts being made to adapt our conventional way of thinking about economic problems to the particular context of development problems. For some issues, the adaptation is made explicit: the key factors distinguishing the situation in a poor country from that in an advanced economy are recognized, and a new set of assumptions is explicitly adopted; for example, the existence of a subsistence sector, or disguised unemployment, or an unorganized money market may require modification of the usual assumptions of macroanalysis. In other instances, some concepts are introduced out of consideration for the special conditions of poor countries— for instance, "social dualism," the structuralist view of inflation, or noneconomic criteria for investment. Whether they are introduced explicitly or are only implicit, we should be aware that these considerations of the relevance of conventional economic analysis constitute a major theme of this book. This problem of adapting our accepted tools and principles is, in a fundamental sense, an overriding general issue in development economics.

[5]At first sight, it might be thought that behavioral relations are also of a different kind. On closer examination, however, the usual postulates of rationality and the principles of maximization or minimization appear to have quite general applicability. For illustrative evidence, see P. T. Bauer and B. S. Yamey, *The Economics of Under-Developed Countries*, London, 1957, pp. 91–101; W. J. Barber, "Economic Rationality and Behavior Patterns in an Underdeveloped Area: A Case Study of African Economic Behavior in the Rhodesias," *Economic Development and Cultural Change*, April 1960, pp. 237–51; W. O. Jones, "Economic Man in Africa," *Food Research Institute Studies*, May 1960, pp. 107–34.

CHAPTER III

Surplus Labor and Dualistic Development

Having considered in the preceding two chapters the general context of developmental problems and some approaches to their analyses, we are now ready to turn directly to a more detailed examination of the development process. We begin by focusing on an outstanding characteristic of LDCs—that of "dualism." In many LDCs, a modern commercialized industrial sector has developed alongside a traditional subsistence agricultural sector, resulting in what is termed a *dual economy*. Although only relatively few LDCs have yet entered into a Rostovian process of self-sustained growth, most of them do exhibit some elements of modernization in one sector or in parts of their economies. The contrast in economic and social organization between the advanced exchange economy and the backward indigenous economy is one of the most striking—and puzzling—characteristics of a poor country. Professor Kuznets relates the dualism of the domestic economy to the fact that the LDCs are late-developing countries.

It is a crucial characteristic of the presently underdeveloped countries that they *are* underdeveloped while others are much more developed—and this situation has lasted a long enough time to affect markedly the structure of the underdeveloped countries; and also to cover several phases in the changing impact of the developed upon the underdeveloped parts of the world.

This impact, in the broadest terms, is the introduction of a modern component into the structure of the otherwise traditional underdeveloped countries. The magnitude of this component, its specific economic content, and the way in which it was introduced, confined, or encouraged, could and did vary widely. In a territory with colonial status a substantial modern sector often emerged but was organized by Western entrepreneurs of the metropolitan country. In a politically independent underdeveloped country with an export sector oriented toward the developed countries' markets the economic organization was and is quite different from that in a country with domestically oriented agriculture or industry. And in some others, a few members of the native elite educated in some Western lore are participating in administration and attempting to introduce Western elements into what may still be a purely traditional economic society.

Obviously, in the countries that are still underdeveloped, this modern component, even if in existence for a long period, has not expanded sufficiently to shift the country to developed status, and in most cases has not even raised its per-capita product to an intermediate level. Given the long coexistence of developed and underdeveloped economies, it is no exaggeration to argue that a major result of such coexistence in the underdeveloped economies is their dual structure. There are two distinct components, the modern and the traditional; and in marked contrast with the past record of the presently developed countries, the two components continue to perform without the modern one, despite its greater productivity, rapidly outpacing the other. It is the *persistence* of the dual structure and the confinement or limitation of the modern sector that are crucial, for the two have operated simultaneously but for a shorter period in the developed countries also.[1]

If we are to identify the structural relationships involved in the development process, we must understand the dual structure of the modern and traditional, and we must consider how the acceleration of development will entail a higher rate of structural transformation in a developing country. Instead of using an aggregative model, we may gain more insights from the study of interactions among sectors. We therefore explore in this chapter several questions about dualism: What conditions have given rise to a dual economy? In what sense is a dual economy also a labor surplus economy? How can the absorption of the indigenous economy into an expanding modern economy be accomplished?

One explanation of dualism, propounded principally by J. H. Boeke and other Dutch economists in their studies of Indonesian development, emphasized the differing social organizations and cultural contrasts that result in "social dualism." The attention to dualism now centers less on its sociocultural aspects and more on its purely economic features, especially in terms of the effects of a dual economy on the pattern of development. Underemployment is commonly believed to be a dominant feature of densely populated, underdeveloped countries, and the labor force is continually increasing with population growth. It is therefore important to consider how dualism is related to the problem of providing adequate employment opportunities for the currently underemployed workers and for the increase in the labor force.

There has been much confusion over the phenomena of unemployment, underemployment, and disguised unemployment in the traditional sector of a poor country. The selections in section III.A are therefore designed to clarify the effects of a dualistic structure on employment by examining the concept of the "labor surplus economy."

Several models of development have focused on the structural formation of a dual economy (section III.B.). Prominent among these is the Fei-Ranis model of a labor surplus economy, which is characterized by the coexistence of a relatively large and overwhelmingly stagnant subsistence agricultural sector in which institutional forces determine the wage rate, and a relatively small but growing commercialized industrial sector in which competitive conditions shape the labor market. In such a labor-surplus dualistic economy, labor is not scarce, while capital is extremely so. Development therefore requires that "the center of gravity must continually shift towards industry through the continuous reallocation of labor from the agricultural to the industrial sector: the related criterion of 'success' in the development effort is thus a rate of industrial labor absorption sufficiently rapid to permit the economy to escape from the ever-threatening Malthusian trap."[2]

Perhaps most celebrated of the labor surplus models is Sir Arthur Lewis's analysis of "Development with Unlimited Supplies of Labor." The Note on "Intersectoral Relationships in a Dual Economy" (III.B.1) summarizes this model, emphasizing the interaction between an advanced "capitalist" sector and an indigenous "noncapitalist" sector in a developing econ-

---

[1]Simon Kuznets, "Notes on Stage of Economic Growth as a System Determinant," in Alexander Eckstein (ed.), *Comparison of Economic Systems* (1971), pp. 256–7.

[2]John C. H. Fei and Gustav Ranis, *Development of the Labor Surplus Economy* (1964), p. 3.

omy, and indicating how resources can be drawn into the modern exchange system through capital accumulation in the expanding capitalist sector. The Lewis model is helpful in explaining the mechanism by which the proportion of domestic savings in the national income increases during the course of development of a dual economy whose growth is the result of the expansion of capitalist forms of production. As the model explains, growth in the capitalist sector turns on the higher than average propensity to save from profit income, as well as on the rise of the share of profits in the national income in the early stages of development. The noncapitalist sector, in turn, serves as a reservoir from which the expanding capitalist sector draws labor. The model therefore has significant policy implications for labor absorption and for the employment problem—a problem to which we return frequently in subsequent chapters.

Rural-urban migration, as examined in section III.C, is central to the problem of growing urban unemployment. The model by Todaro emphasizes a migration function that hypothesizes that the relevant urban income is the present value of expected earnings (that is, a rational calculation by an individual migrant that allows for the probability of the migrant obtaining urban employment). In a distorted labor market, growing urban unemployment is consistent with equilibrium in this model, and rural-urban migration is assumed to occur until there is equality between the actual rural wage and the expected urban wage. Although the specific character of the probability function for urban employment can be questioned, the migration function is analytically useful in explaining why policies that are devoted only to raising urban labor demand cannot be relied on to reduce urban unemployment.

The high rate of population growth has also been the main cause of the high density of land occupation in the rural areas; this, in turn, has been an underlying factor in the high rate of migration from rural to urban areas in many countries. The accelerated rural-urban labor migration has produced extremely high rates of growth of the active population in urban areas that have far exceeded the growth of urban employment opportunities, culminating in rising levels of urban unemployment. Given the limited employment opportunities in the modern sector of urban areas, an increasing share of the urban labor force has become unemployed or has drifted into the tertiary sector, or what has come to be called the "informal sector." As unemployment and underemployment have been transferred from the rural sector, the absorption of labor in the informal sector has become in many respects an extension into the urban areas of the traditional rural subsistence economy.

As discussed in selection III.C.2, an ILO mission to Kenya has given considerable emphasis to the role of the "informal sector." In almost every area of Kenyan activity, there appears to be a sharp and analytically significant dualism between the protected, organized, large-scale, foreign-influenced, formal sector and the unprotected, unorganized, small-scale, family-based, and essentially self-reliant, informal sector. The mission argued that to infer the growth of total employment, let alone the volume of unemployment, from the growth of formal sector employment can be very misleading. It has become a general phenomenon in the urban areas of the LDCs that during the past three decades the number in the informal sector has increased absolutely and as a proportion of the labor force. The size of urban areas has commonly doubled within a decade, and with such high urban growth rates, unemployment and underemployment have also risen.

We can begin to investigate the problem of labor absorption by considering what has gone wrong with the Lewis model of labor transfer—why urban unemployment has increased and why the labor reservoir in the noncapitalist sector still remains so large after more than three decades of developmental effort since Lewis propounded his model. Section III.D examines how some important conditions of the Lewis model have failed to be fulfilled in reality. Other selections, however, indicate ways by which the explanatory power of the model could be improved. Specifically, it is suggested that the analysis give more attention to the interrelations between the rural and urban sectors, to the existence of an informal (nonmodern, non-capitalist) sector alongside the organized (modern, capitalist) sector in urban areas, and to the need for improving the quality of employment in the informal sector as well as the quantity of employment throughout the economy. Capitalist and noncapitalist subsectors are within both the rural and urban sectors, giving the economy the characteristic of "double dualism." Unemployment and underemployment are not confined to the rural areas, but comparable problems of open unemployment, inadequate incomes, and low productivity have also arisen in urban areas.

Estimates of the magnitude of the employment problem are necessarily imprecise because of the ambiguities in the conceptual meaning of "unemployment" and "underemployment," lack of data, and statistical pitfalls in measurement.

Section III.E outlines various dimensions of the employment problem. This section emphasizes that the employment problem is not one problem but three: (1) the shortage of work opportunities, (2) inadequate incomes from work, and (3) underutilized labor resources. Within each of these categories, different types of unemployment and underemployment can be identified, both visible and "disguised."

An entire set of policies is now needed that will concentrate on employment in the urban informal sector and the rural sector, as well as on demand in the organized urban sector. The underutilized labor reservoir in the traditional sector and open unemployment in the urban area are problems in their own right. Employment problems, however, pervade the economy, and pervasive policies are therefore needed, as emphasized in section III.F. Several of this chapter's selections can be read as a plea for a set of interrelated policy measures rather than partial measures. While some specific policies are discussed in section III.F, subsequent chapters will also relate to the employment problem, especially in connection with the transfer of technology, income distribution, education, and trade expansion. Section III.F analyzes the central question of whether there is a conflict between output and employment. Is maximum production compatible with maximum employment? From a comprehensive analysis of the employment problem, we should become aware that the objectives of greater utilization of labor, diminution of poverty, and improved income distribution are complementary, not competitive objectives.

III.A. THE LABOR SURPLUS ECONOMY

III.A.1. Labor Surplus on the Land*

The concept of surplus farm labor has attracted increasing attention in the underdeveloped countries, especially in Asia. The simplest definition of it implies that some labor could be withdrawn from subsistence farming without reducing the volume of farm output. In technical terms, the marginal productivity of labor is believed to be zero. If this is true, it has some far-reaching implications. But is it true? Is it even conceivable? Some economists have had serious doubts on this score. It must be admitted that the idea of "disguised unemployment," as it is usually called, has sometimes been carelessly formulated and inadequately substantiated.

The subject must be viewed in relation to the general population problem. The crucial fact is that world population has doubled in the last hundred years. About two-thirds of the increase has taken place in the underdeveloped areas, chiefly in Asia, largely through a fall in death-rates. This has been part of the uneven impact of Western civilization on the rest of the world. Now in the poorer countries as a rule the majority of the population works in agriculture to start with, for basic and obvious reasons. Just as food is the major item of consumption in low-income communities, so the struggle for food takes up most of their time and resources. In such countries rapid population growth naturally leads, and in some has already led, to excess population on the land.

Consider for a moment the effects of population growth in a community of peasant cultivators. Numbers are increasing while land, capital and techniques remain unchanged. Alternative employment opportunities may be lacking because of the rigid social structure, and may actually be decreasing because of the decline of traditional handicraft industries due to the competition of imported manufactures.

With the growing pressure of people on the land, farms become smaller and smaller. What is more, farms are divided and subdivided into tiny strips and plots. Accordingly it seems to me that agricultural unemployment in densely populated peasant communities may be said to take at least two basic forms: (1) underemployment of peasant cultivators due to the small size of farms; (2) unemployment disguised through fragmentation of the individual holding. . . .

To the extent that the labor surplus is absorbed—and concealed—through fragmentation, it cannot be withdrawn without bad effects on output unless the fragmentation is reversed and the holdings are consolidated. Over a limited range the marginal productivity of labor might be zero without any such reorganization. It could be zero over a much wider range if the remaining factors of production were appropriately reorganized, which would require for one thing a consolidation of plots. Appropriate reorganization of the other factors of production is clearly a necessary and a reasonable pre-requisite for purposes of policy as well as analysis.

There are a number of empirical studies that tend to confirm this general picture. The evidence can never be entirely satisfactory in a matter such as this where some things, including the weather, would have to be held constant and others subjected to a reorganization which may necessitate a revolutionary change in rural life, bringing inevitably other changes with it. Nevertheless the connection between over-population and fragmentation goes a long way to make the existence of surplus farm labor plausible.

*From Ragnar Nurkse, "Excess Population and Capital Construction," *Malayan Economic Review,* October 1957, pp. 1, 3–5. Reprinted by permission.

On a theoretical view of the matter it is clear that excess population can be so great in relation to land and capital that the marginal productivity of labor is reduced to zero. There are, however, two reasons why some economists have found this idea difficult to accept. First, anyone trained in Western economics would have to ask: Who would employ these people if their product is zero? Or else one might ask: How can these marginal people live, what do they eat, if they really produce nothing?

The answer to the first question is that in many countries the wage-labor system, which Western economists are apt to take for granted, hardly exists. The prevailing condition in subsistence farming is one of peasant family labor.

The answer to the second question—How can they live?—is that they live by sharing more or less equally in the total product of the farm, which includes the product of intramarginal labor and of any land and capital goods the peasants may own. The product from these factors goes into the same pot and the members of the household eat out of that same pot. These institutional arrangements are foreign to the economies of business enterprise, and so the conditions which they make possible may seem paradoxical.

If this sharing of food is considered a little further the ultimate limit to the multiplication of people on the farms becomes starkly plain.[1] If the average total product per person falls below the physical level of subsistence, the outcome is the Malthusian state of starvation cutting down numbers or at least checking their further increase. At the point where this average product equals the physical subsistence level, the marginal product of

labor may well be zero or even negative.[2] Still, it need not be as low as zero. Conversely, if and when labor's marginal product is zero, the average product need not be as low as the physical subsistence level; it may be a little above that level.

In any case, excess population necessarily implies that the marginal product is less than the average. In this state of affairs further population growth brings down the average level of consumption. Why? Because the additional labor contributes less than the average worker previously, and so it pulls down the average product per head. If the average product is as low as we know it to be, it does not seem far-fetched to suppose that in some cases the marginal product of labor may be zero. The upshot of the argument does not, of course, depend on its being exactly zero, although this is a convenient case on which to concentrate the analysis. The essential point is that the marginal workers live, in effect, on a subsidy if their own contribution to output is less than their intake of food and other necessities.

The relationship between total product and total population is illustrated in the accompanying diagram (Figure 1). Average product per head is reflected in the slope of the vector from the origin to any point on the curve. The marginal product is reflected in the slope of the curve itself at any given point. The average product per head reaches a maximum at A (where the angle AOL is

[1]The analysis concentrates on the subsistence farm sector. The reader should bear in mind that even the most backward economy usually contains other sectors also, including export production, commerce, government and even some industrial activity.

[2]Professor J. E. Meade has shown this very clearly in his book, *The Theory of International Economic Policy;* Vol. II, *Trade and Welfare,* issued under the auspices of the Royal Institute of International Affairs, London, Oxford University Press, 1955, chapter 6 and appendix 1.

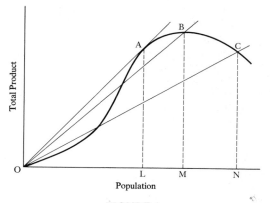

FIGURE 1.

largest) and declines thereafter as population increases further. The marginal product becomes zero at *B* (where the average product measured by the angle *BOM* may still be substantial). If population increases beyond *M*, the marginal product becomes negative and the average product continues to fall. If we suppose that the average product at *N* represents the absolute physical minimum of subsistence, then population cannot increase beyond *N*. This supposition is of course purely arbitrary and illustrative. Actually the physical subsistence level of average product per head may lie, not in the range of negative marginal productivity, but conceivably at *B* or somewhere between *A* and *B* where marginal product is still positive. The diagram merely illustrates the possibilities and does not, of course, tell us what actually happens.

It must be conceded that this view of the matter is essentially that of "optimum population" theory (in the diagram the optimum size of population is *OL*). Now this theory has sometimes been criticized as being an unrealistic exercise in comparative statics. It assumes that nothing changes except the number of people—and, in response thereto, the volume of total product. It abstracts from, and ignores, any connections that may exist between population size on the one hand and, say, the state of techniques or the volume of capital on the other hand. It holds all other things constant. Is this not bound to lead to a distorted view of reality?

The criticism may be perfectly valid with regard to population trends in the Western world. But if we consider Asia over the last hundred years, I am not sure that the objection has much force. I began by saying that the population explosion in Asia, due largely to the fall in death-rates, reflects the *uneven* impact of Western civilization. The point is precisely that while population has doubled, other things such as techniques, capital supplies and cultivable land have remained *too much the same*. Therein lies the whole problem. Of course, there has been some advance in these other things too, but not nearly at the same rate as in population. In Asia there has been nothing like the advance that accompanied population growth in the West. In this state of affairs it seems to me that the "optimum population" approach, questionable though it may be in the West, has a good deal of validity in the East. The economic problem of the East has been largely a consequence of dynamic population growth in an otherwise relatively static environment.

"Optimum population" theory directs attention chiefly to the variation of *average* product as the size of population varies. We have found it at least equally important to consider the *marginal* product. The question might be asked: Why this obsession with the margin? Why not stress the obvious fact of a low general level of productivity? The answer is that the marginal approach is useful here because of the need to take away some labor from current production for work on capital construction.

III.A.2. The Concept of "Disguised Unemployment"*

The term "disguised unemployment" is commonly used to designate a situation in which the removal from a working combination of

*From Jacob Viner, "Some Reflections on the Concept of 'Disguised Unemployment,'" in *Contribuicoes à Análise do Desenvolvimento Econômico*, Livraria Agir Editôra, Rio de Janeiro, 1957. Reprinted by permission.

factors of some units of labor, nothing else of consequence or worth mentioning being changed, will leave the aggregate product of the working combination undiminished, and may even increase it. To say that there is "disguised unemployment" is therefore equivalent to saying that in that working combination the marginal productivity of labor is zero or almost zero and may even be a negative quantity. The "unemployment" may be only metaphorical, since there may be hard work even at the margin, when "unemployed" must mean "unproductively employed." But sometimes it is intended to be realistically descriptive, as when it is used to include seasonal unemployment; in such cases, I do not know what the adjective "disguised" is supposed to mean. I will in this note treat "seasonal unemployment" as a distinct phenomenon not obviously presenting a serious problem and not obviously having any peculiar relationship to agriculture in underdeveloped countries. As I look at the agricultural world with my inexpert eye, it seems to me that agricultural employment is most seasonal, is least continuous, in the temperate zones where agriculture is most "developed" and yields the highest levels of average and marginal product per labor-year.

As an intermittent phenomenon, resulting from the vagaries of weather and human error, zero marginal productivity of labor in agriculture is a commonplace concept. But how can a priori the possibility of zero marginal productivity of employed labor, as a *chronic* phenomenon, be plausibly established? One way that has been suggested is on the assumption that the (average and marginal) technical coefficients of production are constant, so that the addition to a working combination of more units of labor will add nothing to the aggregate product unless additions are made also to the quantities used of all (or of some) of the other factors of production—Pareto's "fixed coefficients," or Frisch's "limitational factors."

I am not aware that anyone has ever given a convincing illustration of a technical coefficient which is "fixed" in a valid economic sense. The plausibility of the idea has resulted, I believe, from the confusion of chemical ingredients of a product, or actual engineering elements in a productive process, with potential economic input-items in a productive process. If iron ore, or coal, were as expensive per ton as gold I am sure that the steel industry would find ways of appreciably reducing the amounts of iron ore, or of coal, it uses to produce a ton of steel of given specific character, even though the chemical constituency of the steel were invariant, and, moreover, it would readily find ways of changing the chemical constituency of a ton of "steel" without reducing its suitability for its ordinary uses, and this not only in the long run but in the very short run. As far as agriculture is concerned, I find it impossible to conceive of a farm of any kind on which, other factors of production being held constant in quantity, and even in form as well, it would not be possible, by known methods, to obtain some addition to the crop by using additional labor in more careful selection and planting of the seed, more intensive weeding, cultivation, thinning, and mulching, more painstaking harvesting, gleaning, and cleaning of the crop. Even supposing that there were such a farm, on which every product had technically and economically fixed ingredients, labor would still have positive marginal productivity unless there were not only fixed technical coefficients of production for all the economically relevant potential products of the farm, but the proportions between the technical coefficients were uniform for all of these products. For if these proportions are different as between different products, then it will always be possible by appropriate change in the product-mix, in the direction of more production of those products whose labor technical coefficients are relatively high, to absorb productively any increment of labor.

Unless one assumes non-economic motivation on the part of employers, there is difficulty also in conceiving why they should hire at any wage-rate additional units of labor beyond the point at which they know the labor will add less in value to the product than the wage-cost, to say nothing of the case where the labor will add nothing to and may even subtract from the product. The employer may, of course, be ignorant as to the facts, but I know of no experience to persuade me that the speculative economist is on such matters better informed than the experienced farmer in immediate touch with reality. This is probably what W. A. Lewis has in mind, although I cannot find that he anywhere explicitly says so, when he concedes that in agriculture "disguised unemployment" occurs only for peasant or self-employed labor, and not for plantation labor.[1] Since there is a good deal of plantation agriculture in underdeveloped countries, this is an important limitation of the applicability of the concept of "disguised unemployment." But it raises its own difficulties. In Brazil, for instance, I take it that agriculture is even in the same localities a mixture of hired labor on plantations, of self-employed labor on owned (or rented?) small farms, and of squatter labor. Should there not be a tendency for equalization of the marginal productivity of labor in all agrarian uses where labor can fairly readily move from one type of use to another? Where there is labor-mobility, marginal productivity of labor must rise substantially above zero in peasant or squatter agriculture or sink to zero or near-zero on the plantations. This would especially be the case . . . if a member of a peasant or squatter family would not lose access to the family supply of food by taking employment on a nearby plantation. When I was in Brazil, I heard of complaints by plantation owners in districts in which there was also peasant and squatter agriculture of "shortage of hands" *(falta de mao)*. I don't see how this can be reconciled with the prevalence of zero marginal productivity of labor, whether on the plantations or for self-employed agricultural labor. . . .

W. A. Lewis has suggested, as an explanation of "disguised unemployment" in agriculture that, when "there are too many persons on too little land" the farmer cannot afford to keep cattle, so that the land gets no manure and land is put under the plough which ought to be left in forest or in fallow; and land is over-cropped, so that fertility is destroyed.[2] . . . Given the situation as Lewis describes it, the *long run* marginal productivity of labor could be zero or negative, but it would be in the long run interest of the owner of the crowded farm not to over-work it. Genuine unemployment on the farm, or employment of the "surplus" labor only on such tasks as would not impair fertility, would in the long run be more profitable than full employment, but the shortsightedness of the owner, or the hunger of his family, might nevertheless trap him into exploiting the short-run marginal productivity of labor, which I would expect to be always positive in a situation such as here described. Lewis concedes that this phenomenon of impairment of soil-fertility through over-crowding would be present only in "over-populated areas," and lists China, India, Japan, Java, Egypt, some countries in the Middle East, Kenya, and some small islands as the only countries in this category. Latin America and Eastern Europe, which many writers have regarded as subject to "disguised unemployment," are thus excluded by Lewis, and, as we have seen, he would exclude also the plantation agriculture of any country.

Ragnar Nurkse has suggested that where "disguised unemployment" prevails in agriculture, it would be desirable to transfer the surplus labor off the farms to produce capital goods, while keeping the consumption of food by the population as a whole constant through taxation or direct controls.[3] This would be relevant for Lewis's type of zero or negative marginal productivity of agricultural labor resulting from loss of fertility of soil through over-crowding and over-cropping. But as I have pointed out, it would not be a solution in the short run, for in the short run transferring labor out of agriculture would, or might, reduce the total output. N. Koestner has objected against Nurkse's argument that it fails to take account of the fact that the urban workingman needs more calories than the idle rural inhabitant.[4] But for Lewis the "disguised unemployed" of agriculture may be working as hard as anyone else, and may in fact need more calories for

[1] *The Theory of Economic Growth,* Homewood, 1955, pp. 326–7. In "Economic Development with Unlimited Supplies of Labour," *The Manchester School,* May 1954, pp. 141–2, the presence of "disguised unemployment" is claimed for hired agricultural labor also, although in lesser degree than for self-employed labor.

[2] *The Theory of Economic Growth,* op. cit., pp. 327–8.

[3] *Problems of Capital Formation in Underdeveloped Countries,* Oxford, 1953, pp. 36 ff.

[4] "Some Comments on Prof. Nurkse's Capital Accumulation in Underdeveloped Countries," *L'Egypte contemporaine,* XLIV, April 1953, p. 9.

farm-work than they would need for factory-work. They are "idle" in the sense only that their work is unproductive. On the other hand, Nurkse does not mention the inevitable and possibly appreciable loss of food involved in deterioration, spoilage, and spillage when the food is consumed in the city instead of on or near the farm where it is produced.

Still another kind—or source—of zero or less marginal productivity of agricultural—or urban—labor can be conceived of, and may even be important in practice, although I have not encountered it in the literature, and it would not be a simple matter, even if it existed, to demonstrate the fact. Suppose that given the "quality" of the labor force and the supplies of other productive resources, the marginal productivity function of labor could be represented, in the familiar manner, by a slowly-descending curve which within the range of observation remains substantially above the zero-productivity level. Suppose, however, that the quantity of food available for the farm family depends wholly on the output of the farm, that the food is shared by all members of the family, and that when it falls below a certain quantity per capita the energy and productive will and capacity of the worker-members of the family decline. It then becomes conceivable that if some of the members of the family, including working-members, were removed from the farm (or if the whole family were removed from the farm, and the farm joined to a similar adjoining farm) and if those removed could no longer draw on the food-resources of the farm, the labor remaining on the farm would acquire a sufficiently higher marginal productivity curve, so that the farm would produce more than it did before when the number of workers was greater. In such a case, much of what has been said about "disguised unemployment" and about appropriate remedies for it would be relevant. Not so, however, Nurkse's proposal of removal of some of the workers off the farms without termination of their dependence, direct or indirect, on the farm for their food. Unless the per capita food consumption on the farm was increased, there would in this case be a re-duction in the total food output of the farm if any of its workers were removed.

Let me now, as my last illustration, suggest the possibility of a special kind of unemployment which is not "disguised" or "hidden," but is open and voluntary. This is the kind of unemployment which would result from a rise in productivity, or in income per time-unit of labor, when the supply curve of labor was of the kind to which many years ago I gave the label of a "rising-backward supply curve." When income per time-unit of labor and aggregate income per laborer both rise, the laborer's relative valuation of marginal units of leisure and of wages per unit of labor may so change as to make a shorter working-day, week, or year attractive even at the cost of a smaller increase in the size of the pay envelope. (For labor paid on a piece-rate basis and for self-employed labor a similar adjustment may occur through reduction in the intensity rather than in the duration of the labor.) The English mercantilists of the eighteenth century thought that this was the usual pattern of behavior of labor, and therefore believed in the inexpediency of high wages. There is no reason why such behavior should be peculiar to agricultural labor, but it may be that it is more likely to be prevalent for habit-ridden rural populations, as an initial response to the availability of choice between higher income or less—or less intensive—labor.

Lewis claims that "disguised unemployment" is not confined to agriculture, but is in underdeveloped countries common also in cities in the form of over-staffed retinues of domestic servants and of over-crowded service occupations where self-employment is the rule.[5] To make plausible the argument that maintenance of a large retinue of domestic servants is a symptom of "disguised unemployment" any more in the city of an underdeveloped country than it would be in London or Paris, one must assume, as Lewis does, that provision of employment for persons who otherwise would be openly unemployed is a major motive of the employers in

[5] *The Manchester School,* May 1954, pp. 141–2.

the underdeveloped countries. Nurkse has claimed that the attractiveness of the consumers' goods of advanced countries to the population of underdeveloped countries operates as a serious barrier both to the development of their own industries and to capital formation.[6] Since industrialization in underdeveloped countries, when not directed otherwise by government, tends to concentrate on consumers' goods of advanced-country types, a shift of taste away from Lewis's type of domestic service to tangible consumers' goods should promote instead of retarding industrialization, although I do not venture to guess whether it would promote or work against "economic welfare."

I refrain from discussing here the appropriateness of the application of the term "underemployment" to agriculture, even to American agriculture, merely to signify either allegedly low-productivity employ-

ment or considerable seasonal unemployment, in the absence of convincing evidence that the employment is not reasonably "productive" when everything relevant to "real income" and to available alternatives is taken into account or that we know how to grow spring wheat or cabbages in an American winter. If we must do without the spring wheat or the cabbages if we are to escape the seasonal unemployment, perhaps it is sensible to reconcile ourselves to its persistence. I find it unhappy semantic usage also to label as "underemployment" and as "disguised unemployment" labor which would be "unnecessary" to maintain product undiminished if "intensity of work per hour" were raised,[7] since this would lead to the conclusion that there was "underemployment" and "disguised unemployment" in the most prosperous American urban industries even when overtime work was common.

[6]*Problems of Capital Formation,* op. cit., Chap. 3.

[7]Chiang Hsieh, "Underemployment in Asia," *International Labour Review,* LXVI, June 1952, p. 709.

III.A.3. Choice of Techniques*

Unemployment is often not "visible." It may be "disguised" as a result of a particular task being performed by more labour than is necessary (given the technique and the productive resources). As Professor Nurkse puts it "the marginal productivity of labour, over a wide range, is zero." Thus labour can be taken away from these occupations without affecting production.

The concept of "disguised unemployment" is actually less simple than it looks, and we must say a few words on it to avoid any possible misunderstanding. We may ask if "marginal productivity of labour, over a wide range, is zero," why is labour being applied at all? Does it not go against rational behaviour? In Figure 1, curve Y gives the relationship between labour and output, given the technique and the supply of other productive

*From A. K. Sen, *Choice of Techniques,* Basil Blackwell, 1960, pp. 13–6. Reprinted by permission.

factors. If OL_2 is the amount of labour that is applied and the marginal productivity becomes zero at point L_1, then L_1L_2 is the relevant range. But what is the point of applying labour beyond L_1?

This confusion arises because of not distinguishing between *labour* and *labourer*. It is.

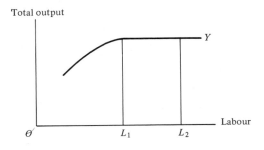

FIGURE 1.

not that too much labour is being spent in the production process, but that too many labourers are spending it. Disguised unemployment thus normally takes the form of smaller number of working hours per head per year; for example, each of three brothers shepherding the sheep every third day. It is thus the marginal productivity of the *labourer*, so to say, that is nil *over a wide range* and the productivity of *labour* may be just equal to zero at the margin. It may also take the form of lower intensity of work with people "taking it easy," e.g., the peasant having time to watch the birds while working. If a number of labourers went away, the others would be able to produce about the same output working *longer* and *harder*. There is no contradiction between disguised unemployment and rational behaviour. In a family-based peasant economy unemployment will naturally put on this disguise. A piece of land that can be cultivated fully by two, may actually be looked after by four, if a family of four working men having no other employment opportunity happens to own it. All this is represented in Figure 2. The south represents the number of labourers, the east the number of labour-hours spent and the north the product. The

marginal product of labour becomes *nil* with OL_1 labour-hours and labour is not applied beyond this point. The working population being OP_2, each puts in tan a hours of work. Tan b represents the "normal" working hours per labourer. So the job can be done by OP_1 labourers keeping normal hours. In this sense P_1P_2 population is surplus. Thus while marginal productivity of *labour* is *nil* at point L_1 only, that of the *labourer* is *nil over the range* P_1P_2. This represents the volume of "disguised unemployment."

A further difficulty with the concept of disguised unemployment is that any shift of labour from the rural area will lead to some reorganization of the techniques of production in that area. The *organization* of production may change considerably and thus the concept of zero marginal productivity, from the point of view of strict theory, becomes difficult to apply. The contrast between a movement *along* the productivity curve and a *shift* of the curve as a result of a change of the supply of other factors of production (e.g., "organization") is relevant in this connection. But actually from the point of view of operational policy these conceptual complications need not be very important. The point is that we are in a position to remove a considerable part of the rural labour force away from the rural area without affecting the rural output appreciably.

A more real difficulty will arise if it is found that at the given supply of capital and land, marginal productivity of labour is not *in fact* nil. In this case, when some of the rural labourers move out, some real investment (and not merely more "organization") is necessary to keep the output constant. The "opportunity cost" of labour can be measured by the amount of investment that has to be put in to keep rural output constant as a labourer moves out. This is a measure of the cost in *stock* terms. In terms of *flow*, the opportunity cost can be measured (*a*) as the amount of alternative rural output sacrificed per year as a result of drawing a labourer away from the rural area, or (*b*) as the amount of alternative output sacrificed per year as a result of putting in the compensatory investment to make good the above loss of rural output rather

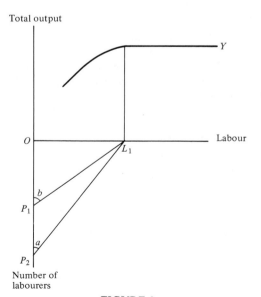

Total output

O

Labour

Number of labourers

FIGURE 2.

than using that amount of investment in some other field.

It is in fact possible that even in some of the so-called "overpopulated" areas scarcity of capital has led to such a substitution of capital by labour that the marginal product of labour is not zero; thus a withdrawal of labour *will* reduce the rural output somewhat. Rural techniques of production in some of the underdeveloped countries are so primitive and labour-intensive that this will not be very surprising. It is, however, likely that in this case a relatively small amount of investment may make good the loss of rural output and the opportunity cost in terms of the necessary increase in the capital *stock* or in terms of the resulting loss of *flow* of alternative output, i.e., in sense (*b*), may be rather small. Thus, while labour in some of these economies may not be "free," it is likely to be cheap—cheaper than the conventionally-measured opportunity cost, sense (*a*), suggests.

III.B. DUAL SECTOR MODELS

III.B.1. Intersectoral Relationships in a Dual Economy—Note

When a dual economy exists, the ultimate question for the country's future development is how the modern exchange sector is to expand while the indigenous sector contracts. This requires an analysis of the interrelationships between the two sectors. Sir W. Arthur Lewis has offered a perceptive analysis of this problem.[1] This note summarizes Lewis's model and assesses its relevance for contemporary problems of development.

Lewis analyzes the process of economic expansion in a dual economy composed of a "capitalist" sector and a "noncapitalist" sector. The capitalist sector is defined as that part of the economy which uses reproducible capital, pays capitalists for the use thereof, and employs wage-labor for profit-making purposes. Capitalist production need not be restricted to manufacturing; it may also be in plantations or mines that hire labor and resell its output for a profit. The capitalist sector may also be either private or public: again, the distinguishing feature of the capitalist sector is the hiring of labor and sale of its output for a profit, which can be undertaken by public enterprise as well as private. The subsistence sector is that part of the economy which does not use reproducible capital and does not hire labor for profit—the indigenous

traditional sector or the "self-employment sector."[2] In this sector, output per head is much lower than that in the capitalist sector; given the available techniques, the marginal productivity of a laborer in agricultural production may be zero as a limiting case. As a result of institutional arrangements, such as the family farm or communal holdings of land, members of the farm labor force consume essentially the average product of the farm's output even though the marginal product of some farm laborers may be well below the average product.

A fundamental relationship between the two sectors is that when the capitalist sector expands, it draws labor from the reservoir in the noncapitalist sector. For countries that have experienced high rates of population growth and are densely populated, it is assumed that the supply of unskilled labor to the capitalist sector is unlimited. Labor is "unlimited" in the sense that when the capitalist sector offers additional employment opportunities at the existing wage rate, the numbers willing to work at the existing wage rate will be greater than the demand: the

[1] W. Arthur Lewis, "Economic Development with Unlimited Supplies of Labor," *The Manchester School*, May 1954, pp. 139–91; "Unlimited Labour: Further Notes," ibid., January 1958, pp. 1–32. "Reflections on Unlimited Labor," in Luis Eugenio Di Marco (ed.), *International Economics and Development, Essays in Honor of Raúl Prebisch*, New York, 1972, pp. 75–96. The analysis has been extended in some respects by Professors Gustav Ranis and J. C. H. Fei, "A Theory of Economic Development," *American Economic Review*, September 1961, pp. 533–65; "Innovation, Capital Accumulation, and Economic Development," ibid., June 1963, pp. 283–313; *Development of the Labor Surplus Economy: Theory and Policy*, Homewood, 1964; "Agrarianism, Dualism, and Economic Development," in I. Adelman and E. Thorbecke (eds.), *The Theory and Design of Economic Development*, Baltimore, 1966.

[2] The characterization of this traditional agricultural sector as the "self-employed" sector is suggested by Kazushi Ohkawa, "Balanced Growth and the Problem of Agriculture—with Special Reference to Asian Peasant Economy," *Hitotsubashi Journal of Economics*, September 1961, pp. 13–25.

Professor Reynolds has also proposed that a four-sector model would be more relevant—with the "traditional sector" divided into the rural sector and the urban trade-service sector, and with both an industry subsector and a government subsector in the "modern sector." The urban trade-service sector employs people with little skill and little initial capital, and there is relative freedom of entry. For a discussion of the different production functions in these four sectors, see Lloyd G. Reynolds, "Economic Development with Surplus Labor: Some Complications," *Oxford Economic Papers*, March 1969, pp. 89–103. Reynolds's urban trade-service sector bears some resemblance to the "informal sector" discussed in selection III.C.2, below.

supply curve of labor is infinitely elastic at the ruling wage. According to Lewis, one condition for this is that the ruling wage of the capitalist sector exceeds the earnings in the noncapitalist sector of those who are willing to transfer themselves. The other condition is that any tendency which the transfer may set in motion for earnings per head to rise in the noncapitalist sector must initially be offset by the effect of increases in the labor force (natural increase, immigration, or greater female participation).[3] A large component of the unlimited supply of labor from the noncapitalist reservoir of labor is composed of those who are in disguised unemployment in agriculture and in other overmanned occupations such as domestic service, casual odd jobs, or petty retail trading. Another source of labor is women who transfer from the household to commercial employment, and the labor force has also grown as a result of the population increase. The large pool of unskilled labor enables new industries to be created or old industries to expand in the capitalist sector without encountering any shortage of unskilled labor.

The wage which the growing capitalist sector has to pay is determined in Lewis's model by what labor earns in the subsistence sector. Peasant farmers will not leave the family farm for wage employment unless the real wage is at least equal to the average product on the land.[4] Capitalist wages, as a rule, will have to be somewhat higher than subsistence earnings in order to compensate labor for the cost of transferring and to induce labor to leave the traditional life of the subsistence sector. (Lewis observes that there is usually a gap of 30 percent or more between capitalist wages and subsistence earnings). At the existing capitalist wages, however, the supply of labor is considered to be perfectly elastic.

This situation is illustrated in Figure 1 where OA represents subsistence earnings, OW the real wage rate in the capitalistic sector, and WS the perfectly elastic supply of

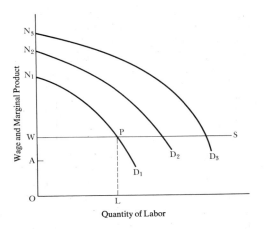

FIGURE 1.

labor. Given a fixed amount of capital at the outset, the demand for labor is initially represented by the marginal productivity schedule of labor, N_1D_1 in Figure 1. If we assume profit maximization, capital will then be applied up to the point where the current wage equals the marginal productivity of labor. If OW is the current wage, the amount of labor employed in the capitalistic sector is OL; beyond L, workers earn whatever they can in the subsistence sector. The total product N_1PLO in the capitalist sector will then be divided between wages in the amount $OWPL$ and the capitalists' surplus or profits in the amount WPN_1.

In tracing the process of economic expansion, Lewis emphasizes that the key to the process is the use of the capitalist surplus. The driving force in the system is generated by the reinvestment of the capitalist surplus in creating new capital. As the capitalist sector expands, labor withdraws from the subsistence sector into wage employment, the surplus then becomes even larger, there is still more reinvestment of profits, and the process continues on progressively absorbing surplus labor from the subsistence sector.

Figure 1 illustrates this process by the outward shift of the demand for labor, from N_1D_1 to N_3D_3 over time. When some of the initial surplus WPN_1 is reinvested, the amount of fixed capital increases, and the schedule of the marginal productivity of

[3]Lewis, "Reflections on Unlimited Labor," p. 77.

[4]Even though the marginal product of labor is zero in disguised unemployment, a member of the extended family shares in the total product and receives approximately the average product.

labor is then raised to the level of say, N_2D_2. Both the capitalist surplus and capitalist employment are now larger. Further investment then raises the marginal productivity of labor to, say, N_3D_3. And so the process continues.

The growth in capitalist profits is crucial in this process, and the share of profits in the national income is of strategic importance. This will be determined by the share of the capitalist sector in the national output and by the share of profits in the capitalist sector. As the capitalist sector expands, and the wage-price ratio remains constant, the share of profits in national income increases. And since the major source of savings is profits, savings and capital formation also increase as a proportion of the national income.

Barring a hitch in the process, the capitalist sector can expand until the absorption of surplus labor is complete, and the supply function of labor becomes less than perfectly elastic. Capital accumulation has then caught up with the excess supply of labor; beyond this point real wages no longer remain constant but instead rise as capital formation occurs, so that the share of profits in the national income will not necessarily continue to increase, and investment will no longer necessarily grow relative to the national income.

In their two-sector model, Professors Ranis and Fei consider disguised unemployment to exist in the agricultural sector when the marginal physical product of labor is less than its average product which is the institutional wage under the extended family system in agriculture. When labor has a marginal product of zero, it is termed "redundant labor." In the Ranis-Fei model the horizontal supply curve to the capitalist sector is then considered to end when the redundant labor force in the agricultural sector is taken up and a relative shortage of agricultural goods appears, so that the terms of trade turn against the capitalist sector that is trading with the agricultural sector. This upward trend in the labor supply curve is later accentuated by a rise in the agricultural real wage traceable to the removal of disguised unemployment and the commercialization of agriculture so that real wages become determined by competitive market forces, not by the non-market institutional average product.[5] When the marginal product is equal in the capitalist and noncapitalist sectors, the analysis then becomes the same as in the usual neoclassical one-sector economy.

In Lewis's model, the expansion process might be cut short, however, by a rise in real wages and a reduction in profits that halts capital accumulation before the excess labor supply is completely absorbed. This may be due to a rise in average product in the subsistence sector because the absolute number of people in this sector is being reduced without a fall in total output, or labor productivity happens to increase in the subsistence sector, or the terms of trade turn against the capitalist sector.

If, for instance, the capitalist sector produces no food, and the demand for food rises as the capitalist sector expands, then the price of food will rise in terms of capitalist products—that is, the terms of trade turn against the capitalist sector. In order to keep the real income of workers constant, capitalists then have to pay out to labor a larger part of their product as wages, thereby reducing their profits.

The possibility that industrialization can be inhibited by a deterioration in the terms of trade for the industrial sector points up the extreme importance of providing an agricultural surplus for consumption in the expanding industrial sector. This is one of several reasons why agricultural output must expand along with industrial development. This problem, together with other relationships between industry and agriculture, will be discussed more fully in Chapters VI and VII below.

It should, of course, be recognized that if the country earns sufficient foreign exchange, the capitalist sector could overcome the agricultural constraint on its further expansion by importing the necessary food and raw materials from overseas instead of being limited by domestic agricultural output. But if export earnings are insufficient, then the failure of exports to keep pace with needed imports will constrain the rate of growth of output.

[5]Ranis and Fei, "A Theory of Economic Development," pp. 539–40.

Although the Lewis model highlights some basic relationships in dualistic development, its applicability has been questioned on several counts. Some critics believe that the model rests on the existence of disguised unemployment in the noncapitalist sector, and they contend this is unrealistic. The strict interpretation of disguised unemployment is that the marginal productivity of labor, over a wide range, is zero—that is, labor is redundant or in surplus and can be withdrawn without any loss of output even if no change in production techniques or use of other productive resources occurs. But the existence of disguised unemployment is not necessary for the expansionary process that Lewis describes; all that the model needs is the fact that supply exceeds demand at the current wage. It is therefore not necessary to say anything about the productivity of marginal units of labor in the reservoir, beyond noting that it must be less than the wage offered by capitalists.

Moreover, although Lewis refers to the zero marginal productivity of labor as a limiting case, he means by this the marginal product of a *man,* not the marginal product of a *manhour.* "For example, in many countries the market stalls (or the handicraft industries) are crowded with people who are not as fully occupied as they would wish to be. If ten percent of these people were removed, the amount traded would be the same, since those who remained would do more trade. This is the sense in which the marginal product of men in that industry is zero. It is a significant sense, and its significance is not diminished by pointing out that the fact that others have to do more work to keep the total product constant proves that the marginal product of manhours is positive."[6]

This interpretation of zero marginal productivity of labor is similar to that offered by A. K. Sen, who distinguishes between the amount of labor and number of laborers.[7]

It is difficult to estimate empirically the amount of surplus labor. Lewis simply states:

[6]Lewis, "Reflections on Unlimited Labor," p. 79.

[7]A. K. Sen, *Choice of Techniques,* Oxford, 1968, pp. 3–5. [See selection III.A.3.]

Nobody denies that in the overpopulated countries handicraft workers, petty traders, dock workers, domestic servants, and casual workers have a lot of spare time on their hands, and that most of them (except the domestic servants) would be glad to exchange extra work for extra income at the current rate. Neither does anybody deny that there is much seasonal unemployment in agriculture. The dispute is confined to the situation on small family farms at the peak of the agricultural season, in some parts of Asia and the Middle East.

I do not believe that the productivity of a man-hour is zero in agriculture, domestic service, petty retailing, handicrafts, or any other part of the noncapitalist reservoir. Nevertheless, I have seen nothing in the now vast literature of underemployment to alter my belief that in India or Egypt one could mobilize a group equal to, say, ten per cent of the unskilled noncapitalist labor force without significantly reducing the output of the noncapitalist sectors from which they were withdrawn.[8]

Another type of underemployment that characterizes some LDCs may, however, create more difficulties for the Lewis analysis. A type of "traditional" underemployment arises when sociocultural determinants of the division of labor between men and women in the traditional sector leave the men underemployed. In some African economies, for instance, it is common practice for the men to clear and prepare the land for cultivation while the women do the routine work of sowing and cultivating. The men are left in surplus supply in agriculture, but they then frequently become migrant laborers in the exchange sector. As temporary immigrants from the traditional sector, they might work in industry or mining on a seasonal basis, or even for a year or two, and then return to their peasant farms.[9] The migration of labor for short periods might have only a negligible effect on agricultural output, but several

[8]Lewis, "Reflections on Unlimited Labor," pp. 81–2.

[9]Informative discussions of migrant labor are presented by Guy Hunter, *The New Societies of Tropical Africa,* Oxford, 1962, pp. 93–101, 191–203; W. J. Barber, *The Economy of British Central Africa,* Stanford, 1961, pp. 71–3; W. Elkan, "Migrant Labor in Africa: An Economist's Approach," *American Economic Review, Papers and Proceedings,* May 1959, pp. 188–97; W. Watson, *Tribal Cohesion in a Money Economy,* Manchester, 1959.

studies have shown that adult manpower cannot be spared from the traditional system of agriculture for more than two or three years without reducing output.[10] This special situation of temporary labor migration does not conform to a precise interpretation of disguised unemployment. It is more enlightening to analyze the labor supply as a case of joint supply whereby workers are being supplied jointly to the advanced sector and the traditional sector over a period of time. An important part of this problem is to determine whether and for how long an individual will offer his labor for wage employment in the wage sector.[11]

The case of a migrant labor force, however, poses special problems that cannot be adquately analyzed in Lewis's model. To make it more relevant for this type of situation, the Lewis model has been modified by Professor Barber in his analysis of the interaction between the indigenous economy and the expanding money economy in British Central Africa.[12]

Another difference is that even if an unlimited supply of unskilled labor is assumed to exist, it is nonetheless generally true that in poor countries skilled labor is in very short supply. Lewis recognizes this problem, but discounts its importance by considering it to be only a temporary bottleneck which can be removed by providing the facilities for training more skilled labor. This will, however, at best involve a time lag, and recent experience in developing countries indicates that the problems of skill formation are not quickly overcome for uneducated and untrained manpower.

A more serious limitation of the Lewis model is that it simply takes for granted the demand side of the investment process. Can we assume, as Lewis does, that a capitalist class already exists? A major obstacle to development in many countries still may be the absence of a capitalist class with the necessary ability and motivation to undertake long-term productive investment. We must confront the problem of how a class of private capitalists is to emerge, or else we must rely at the outset on the presence of foreign capitalists or a class of state capitalists. The analysis of the behavior in the capitalist sector may have to be modified, according to which type of capitalist class exists.

Further, it is assumed that whatever the capitalist sector produces, it can sell; no allowance is made for a problem of aggregate demand. But why should this be true if the output is to be sold within the capitalist sector itself, or if the product is an export good? The remaining alternative—that the capitalist sector sells to the noncapitalist sector—presents a special difficulty. For then productivity must rise in the noncapitalist sector in order to ensure an adequate market for the output of the capitalist sector. But if real wages rise in the noncapitalist sector, the supply-price of labor to the capitalist sector will then be higher, profits will be reduced, and the expansionary process may stop before all the surplus labor is absorbed.

Despite these restrictions on its direct applicability, the Lewis model retains high analytical value for its insights into the role of capital accumulation in the development process. What is clearly of prime significance is the way investment becomes a rising proportion of national income.

Lewis wanted his model to explain rising savings and profit ratios, and he states that "the chief historical example on which the model was based was that of Great Britain where ... net savings seems to have risen from about 5 per cent before 1780 to 7 per cent in the early 1800s, to 12 per cent around 1870, at which level it stabilized. A similar rise is shown for the United States [between the 1840s and 1890s].... Similar changes can be found since the second world war for many less-developed countries such as India or Jamaica."[13]

Along with the expansion of the capitalist

[10]Barber, *Economy of British Central Africa*, pp. 72–3, and other references listed in note 9.

[11]See E. J. Berg, "Backward-Sloping Supply Functions in Dual Economies—The African Case," *Quarterly Journal of Economics*, August 1961, pp. 468–92.

[12]Barber, *Economy of British Central Africa*, pp. 180–8.

[13]Lewis, "Reflections on Unlimited Labor," p. 75.

sector and the rise in investment, the model also indicates that—short of the model's turning points—labor will be continually absorbed from the reservoir of the noncapitalist sector, and that disguised unemployment or underemployment or surplus labor will continually diminish. Despite two Development Decades, however, and rising investment ratios and expansion of the capitalist sectors in most of the LDCs, the persistence of surplus labor remains as acute in these countries as it was when Lewis first presented his model in 1954. A generation later, as we review the Lewis model, we find that the creation of employment is still a major challenge for poor countries. We now turn to that problem— and to some of its manifestations that the Lewis model did not adequately anticipate.

Comment

Lewis responded to criticisms of his first article, "Economic Development with Unlimited Supplies of Labor," in subsequent papers: "Unlimited Labor: Further Notes," *The Manchester School of Economic and Social Studies* (January 1958); "Reflections on Unlimited Labor," in Luis Eugenio Di Marco (ed.), *Essays in Honor of Raúl Prebisch* (1972); "The Dual Economy Revisited," *The Manchester School of Economic and Social Studies* (September 1979).

Other models of a dual economy have been offered by J. C. H. Fei and G. Ranis: "A Theory of Economic Development," *American Economic Review* (September 1961); *Development of the Labor Surplus Economy: Theory and Policy* (1964); "Agrarianism, Dualism and Economic Development," in I. Adelman and E. Thorbecke (eds.), *Theory and Design of Economic Development* (1966); "A Model of Growth and Employment in the Open Dualistic Economy: The Cases of Korea and Taiwan," *Journal of Development Studies* (January 1975). In addition, models have been presented in these papers: D. W. Jorgenson, "The Development of a Dual Economy," *Economic Journal* (June 1961); D. W. Jorgenson, "Surplus Agricultural Labor and the Development of a Dual Economy," *Oxford Economic Papers* (November 1968); D. W. Jorgenson, "Testing Alternative Theories of the Development of a Dual Economy," in I. Adelman and E. Thorbecke (eds.), *Theory and Design of Economic Development* (1966); A. C. Kelley, J. G. Williamson, and R. Cheetham, *Dualistic Economic Development* (1972); A. K. Dixit, "Models of Dual Economies," in J. A. Mirrlees and N. H. Stern (eds.), *Models of Economic Growth* (1973).

III.B.2. Technological Dualism— Note

One of the most important effects of dualistic development is its influence on the pattern of employment. Several writers have suggested that the labor employment problems of a poor country are due to the existence of "technological dualism"—that is, to the use of different production functions in the advanced sector and the traditional sector.[1] In this interpretation, dualism is associated with "structural unemployment" or "technological unemployment"—a situation in which productive employment opportunities are

[1]As an alternative to Boeke's sociological theory of dualism, the theory of technological dualism has been emphasized by Benjamin Higgins, *Economic Development*, New York, 1968 (revised edition), pp. 17–20, 296–305. The theory of technological dualism incorporates the "factor proportions problem," as discussed by R. S. Eckaus, "The Factor Proportions Problem in Underdeveloped Areas," *American Economic Review*, September 1955. Earlier references include Joan Robinson, *The Rate of Interest and Other Essays*, London, 1952, pp. 110–11; M. Fukuoka, "Full Employment and Constant Coefficients of Production," *Quarterly Journal of Economics*, February 1955.

limited, not because of lack of effective demand, but because of resource and technological restraints in the two sectors.

The traditional rural sector is said to have the following characteristics: it is engaged in peasant agriculture and handicrafts or very small industries; the products can be produced with a wide range of techniques and alternative combinations of labor and capital (improved land)—that is, the sector has variable technical coefficients of production; and the factor endowment is such that labor is the relatively abundant factor, so that techniques of production are labor-intensive (in the sense that relatively large amounts of labor and relatively small amounts of capital are used).

In contrast, the modern sector is composed of plantations, mines, oil fields, or large-scale industry; there is either in fact, or entrepreneurs believe there is, only a very limited degree of technical substitutability of factors, so that production is characterized by fixed technical coefficients; and the production processes in this sector are relatively capital-intensive. This situation can be represented by a production function as in Figure 1, where the points a, b, c, etc., denote the fixed combinations of factors—capital (K) and labor (L)—that would be used to produce the outputs q_1, q_2, q_3, etc., irrespective of what the relative factor prices might be.[2] The line OE joining the points a, b, c, etc., represents the expansion path of this sector, and its slope is equal to a constant, relatively capital-intensive factor ratio.

Only when capital and labor are actually available in proportions equal to the fixed capital-labor ratio is it possible that both factors can be fully utilized simultaneously. If

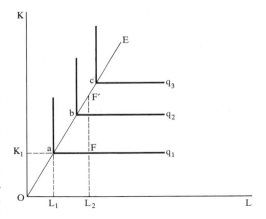

FIGURE 1.

the actual factor endowment is to the right of line OE—say, at point F—there must then be some unemployment of labor in this sector. To produce an output of q_1 the sector will use OK_1 units of capital and OL_1 units of labor; even though OL_2 units of labor are available, the excess supply of labor will have no effect on production techniques and L_1L_2 units of labor will remain in excess supply, regardless of the relative factor prices of capital and labor. Only if the capital stock were to increase in the amount indicated by the length of the dashed line FF' could the redundant labor be absorbed in this sector. Failing a sufficient accumulation of capital, the excess labor supply will simply remain unemployed, or must seek employment in the traditional sector.

It is interesting to note that Marx had a similar view of the problem of unemployment. According to Marx, the amount of employment offered by capitalists depends on the amount of capital in existence, and there is unemployment because there is insufficient capital to employ all the potential available labor. If A represents the total labor available, and N the amount of employment required to work the existing stock of capital at its normal capacity, then $(A - N)$ is Marx's "reserve army of unemployed labor."[3]

[2]Units of capital (K) are measured on the vertical axis, and units of labor (L) on the horizontal axis. The curve q_1 is an isoquant representing a certain level of output; as drawn, the output q_1 can be produced only with the unique combination of factors at point a (OK_1 of capital and OL_1 of labor). The curves q_2, q_3, etc., represent different levels of output, with output increasing along the expansion line OE. Output can be increased, however, only by increasing the use of K and L in the constant proportions given by the slope of OE.

[3]Cf. Robinson, *Rate of Interest*, pp. 110–11, n. 2.

Having in mind the different production functions in the two sectors, we may now summarize the argument that technological dualism has intensified the problem of employment in dual economies. In many countries, the advanced sector was initially developed by an inflow of foreign capital. As foreign enterprises operated under efficient management with modern production techniques, output in this sector expanded. At the same time, however, population was growing—in some cases at a rate considerably in excess of the rate at which capital was accumulating in the advanced sector. And since production processes in this sector were capital-intensive, and fixed technical coefficients were used, this sector did not have the capacity to create employment opportunities at a rate sufficient to absorb the greater labor force. While investment and output expanded in the advanced sector, capital accumulation was nonetheless slow relative to population growth, and labor became a redundant factor in this sector. Entry into the traditional rural sector was then the only alternative open to surplus labor.

As the labor supply increased in the traditional sector, it may have been possible initially to bring more land under cultivation, but eventually land became relatively scarce. Labor increasingly became the relatively abundant factor, and since technical coefficients were variable in this sector, the production process became ever more labor-intensive in the traditional sector. Finally, all available land became cultivated by highly labor-intensive techniques, and the marginal productivity of labor fell to zero or even below: "disguised unemployment" began to appear.[4] Thus, with continuing population growth, the limited availability of capital caused a surplus of labor to arise in the traditional rural sector. Given the labor surplus, there was no incentive in the traditional sector to move along the production function toward higher capital-labor ratios and thereby achieve an increase in output per man.

Further, it is contended that, over the

[4]Higgins, *Economic Development*, p. 330.

longer run, technological progress did not ease this situation. For in the modern sector technological progress favored more capital-intensive techniques, so that it was all the more difficult to increase employment opportunities in this sector as investment and output expanded. At the same time, there was no incentive in the rural sector to introduce labor-saving innovations (even if it were assumed that the technical possibilities were known and the necessary capital was available).

It has also been suggested that the locus of technological progress is such that a capital-intensive invention affects the choice of technique in only those cases in which the cost of labor to capital is high, but not when it is low as in the traditional sector. As Professor Leibenstein argues,[5] this is because the gradual type of technological progress, which, through redesign and general improvement, increases the effectiveness of given types of machines and tools, is more likely to cause a shift of points on the production function in this region of high rather than low capital-labor ratios, such as in the shift from q to q' in Figure 2. In the traditional sector, where the capital-labor ratio is low, there is less likelihood of recognizing opportunities for

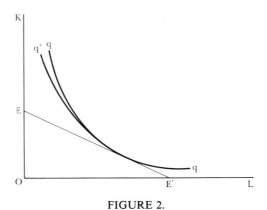

FIGURE 2.

[5]Harvey Leibenstein, "Technical Progress, the Production Function and Dualism," *Banca Nazionale del Lavoro Quarterly Review*, December 1960, pp. 13–15.

gradual inventions and improvements, the scale of operations may not be sufficient to support any new equipment, and there may be a lack of the complementary inputs needed to adopt some type of new capital good. Accordingly, it is maintained that there is little tendency for the isoquants to shift at points with low capital-labor ratios. If the expenditures line EE' in Figure 2 represents the existing ratio of labor cost to capital cost (in this case: relatively low wage rates, as reflected in the slope of EE'), then the shift in the capital-intensive portion of the isoquant has no effect on the choice of technique in the traditional labor-intensive sector.

Although the theory of technological dual-ism indicates why factor endowment and the differences in production functions have resulted historically in the rise of underemployment of labor in the traditional sector, its empirical relevancy can certainly be questioned. Has production in the advanced sector actually been carried on with fixed coefficients? Even if an advanced, capital-intensive process was initially imported, was there subsequently no adaptation to the abundant labor supply? Was technical progress actually labor-saving in the advanced sector? These questions call for empirical studies beyond the highly impressionistic statements contained in the foregoing summary of the theory of technological dualism.

Comment

During the colonial and early postcolonial periods, the concept of "social dualism" received considerable attention. J. H. Boeke and other Dutch economists in their studies of Indonesian development emphasized "the clashing of an imported social system with an indigenous social system of another style." See J. H. Boeke, *Economics and Economic Policy of Dual Societies* (1953). Boeke's analysis, with its conclusion that there is need for a distinctive economic and social theory for underdeveloped countries, is criticized by Benjamin Higgins, "The 'Dualistic Theory' of Underdeveloped Areas," *Economic Development and Cultural Change* (January 1956).

III.B.3. Dualism and Wage Differentials *

We have noted that the level of wages is generally higher in the modern sector than in the traditional sector of the underdeveloped country. How far does this imply the existence of a dualism in the labour market, discouraging the expansion of the modern sector and distorting the allocation of resources in the opposite direction from that caused by financial dualism? Without entering into a detailed enumeration of the possible causes of the wage differentials between the two sec-

*From H. Myint, *Economic Theory and The Underdeveloped Countries,* Oxford University Press, New York, 1971, pp. 331–40. Reprinted by permission.

tors, we may consider them under three heads.

First, there are the wage differences which reflect genuine economic differences in skills, in costs of living, etc. which clearly do not distort the allocation of labour between the two sectors.

Next, there is the less well-recognized fact that in the underdeveloped countries the wage rate in the modern sector reflects the payment to the head of the family to induce him to move with his dependents on a permanent basis to the place of his work, whereas the wage rate in the traditional sector reflects the payment to a single worker on a casual or temporary basis. Now even in the absence of government regulations and trade union pressure, the larger-scale concerns in the modern sector may prefer to pay higher wages to obtain a regular labour force, for at least two reasons. First, the gains in productivity from a stable labour force and a low rate of turnover may more than pay for the higher wage bill. Second, if the concerns are run by foreign entrepreneurs or managers, they do not have the necessary local knowledge and skills in labour relations to cope with the casual type of labour. Indeed, from their point of view the cost of re-adapting their whole system of production and organization to make use of the cheaper casual labour would be much too high and they would be prepared to pay considerably higher wages to obtain a labour force approximately similar to the type of regular labour force they are used to in their own countries. Historically, this can be illustrated by the contrasting labour policies adopted in the development of the textile industry by foreign entrepreneurs in India and by indigenous entrepreneurs in Japan. The former recruited their labour force from adult males, paying them a wage rate sufficient to maintain their dependents; the latter took advantage of the cheaper, but equally efficient, labour of young farm girls available for a few years before they got married.[1] The present-day expansion of the modern manufacturing sector in the underdeveloped countries relies heavily on foreign managers and technical experts, not to speak of the branch factories of international corporations set up to jump the tariff and import controls. Thus we have a pattern of wage policy and labour organization based on a high differential between the ruling wage rate in the regular labour market and that in the unorganized market for casual la-

[1]For a comparative analysis of the labour policies adopted in the development of the textile industry in India and Japan see S. J. Koh, *Stages of Industrial Development in Asia,* University of Pennsylvania Press, 1966, Chs. II and III; see also W. W. Lockwood, *The Economic Development of Japan,* Princeton, 1954, pp. 213–14; for a theoretical analysis of this point, see D. Mazumdar, "Underemployment in Agriculture and the Industrial Wage Rate," *Economica,* November 1959.

bour. How are we to interpret this type of wage differential between the modern and the traditional sector? In so far as the large-scale modern concerns are willing to pay a higher wage rate, voluntarily and without any external pressure, there can be no distortion of resource allocation originating from the labour market. Yet the wage differential is associated with a distinct dualism in industrial organization and may be a sign of managerial rigidity on the part of the modern sector failing to make a more effective use of the abundant supply of casual labour. In so far as this creates a distortion, it is not due to a high wage rate discouraging the expansion of the larger-scale economic units in the modern sector, but due to an insufficient development of the small-scale indigenous economic units which are more likely to be able to take advantage of the abundant supply of casual labour.

Lastly, we have the factors which arbitrarily widen the wage differential between the modern and the traditional sectors and clearly distort the allocation of labour between the two. However, these need to be disentangled from the concept of "disguised unemployment." A familiar argument for the protection of domestic manufacturing industry based on this concept may be summarised as follows. Because of heavy population pressure on existing land, the marginal product of labour in agriculture is reduced to zero. But the income level in the traditional sector is equal not to the marginal product but to the average product of labour on land because of the prevalence of the extended family system sharing the total output among its members. In recruiting labour from the traditional sector the modern sector must pay a wage rate equal to the income level in the traditional sector plus an incentive margin. Thus the modern sector is being penalised by having to pay a wage rate high above the social opportunity cost of labour as measured by its marginal product in agriculture, and in order to correct this distortion the modern manufacturing industry should be given tariff protection.

In order to argue that a person in the traditional sector can enjoy an income equal to the average product of labour even when his marginal product is zero we need, first of all, to assume that his family owns the land and that he is being supported in a state of "disguised unemployment" out of what is, properly speaking, rent from the land. Once we introduce the landlords into the picture, then the income left to the family after paying economic rent must be wage income: i.e., the marginal product of family labour on land must be positive. Even if the family owns the land, the marginal product of labour on the farm will not be zero if there are alternative opportunities of using some part of the family labour elsewhere. Once we introduce some form of market for agricultural labour, the marginal product of labour on the family farm will approximately reflect the wage rate in the neighbourhood. Finally, even in the absence of landlords and a labour market, the marginal product of labour on the family farm will not be zero unless we are prepared to make the highly unrealistic assumption that the marginal disutility of work on the farm is zero. But the notion of the zero marginal product is not needed for the purpose of showing the existence of a distortion in the labour market. All that we need for the purpose is to show that there are certain factors arbitrarily or artificially widening the wage differential between the modern and the traditional sector beyond the extent required to reflect the genuine economic differences in the two sectors.

It is possible to find three such factors. The first consists of the various government regulations on labour and minimum wage rates. These exert a differential effect in that while they can be strictly enforced in the bigger economic units in the modern sectors they are unenforceable for the small economic units in the traditional sector. The second arises from the greater ease with which the urban labour force in the manufacturing sector can organize itself into strong trade unions restricting free entry of labour. The third factor is important in countries which have a prosperous foreign-owned industry such as petroleum or copper. Here the high wage rates which the trade unions are usually able to extract out of the export sector tend to spread, by a series of sympathetic wage rises, into the rest of the modern sector, imposing a heavy burden both on the domestic manufacturing industry and on the public sector. While all these three factors can cause a serious distortion in the allocation of resources, none of them constitutes an argument for special protection of domestic industry. The distortions have to be cured by reforms within the labour market. In particular the third source of distortion is similar to the point we have discussed in connection with "disguised unemployment" in agriculture. Here also the distortion arises from the fact that the rent income which the government should have extracted from the foreign companies in the extractive industries and kept for its own use has been unjustifiably permitted to inflate the wage level in the modern sector above the marginal productivity of labour.

Finally, we may turn to the main argument for domestic industrialization which underlies much of the current writings on economic dualism in the underdeveloped countries. This argument combines the concept of "disguised unemployment" with that of technological dualism and attempts to support the case for the expansion of domestic manufacturing industry, not in terms of deviations from the static optimum but in terms of "dynamic" considerations. Thus it is argued that, given the heavy pressure of population on land, it is no longer possible for the underdeveloped countries to absorb any more labour in agriculture: the only way of absorbing the surplus labour is through the expansion of the manufacturing sector. But the underdeveloped countries are obliged to import modern technology in a ready-made form from the advanced countries: this means that the expansion of the manufacturing sector has to be based on methods of production which are not only capital-intensive but also require capital and labour in fixed proportions.[2] In terms of the static optimum

[2] Cf. R. S. Eckaus, "The Factor-Proportions Problem in Underdeveloped Areas," *American Economic Review*, September 1955.

theory, this pattern of economic development goes against the grain of the factor endowments in the underdeveloped countries, but it is argued that it can be justified on two grounds. First, given the factor disproportionalities and technological rigidities which characterise the dualistic economic structure of the underdeveloped countries, there is really very little scope for smooth and flexible substitutions and adjustments assumed in a neo-classical model of the economic system. Second, the "dynamic" gains from the expansion of the modern manufacturing industry will tend to outweigh the static losses from the distortion in the allocation of resources.

We shall now show that these arguments do not stand up to a critical scrutiny and that they seriously underestimate the scope for the introduction of labour-intensive methods of production both in agriculture and in the manufacturing sector by appropriate domestic economic policies. Even the exponents of the population pressure argument recognise that the underdeveloped countries in Africa and Latin America are not so thickly populated as some of the Asian countries. Thus they tend to use countries such as India or Pakistan as prime examples of agricultural overpopulation. But a broad survey of the Asian agricultural scene is sufficient to cast doubts on the assumption that the agricultural sector in these countries is so saturated with labour that there is no further scope for the introduction of labour-intensive methods along any known lines. As a matter of fact, the highest population densities on land and the smallest-size peasant holdings are to be found in countries such as Japan, Taiwan and Korea. On the other hand, these countries are also outstanding illustrations of how agricultural output can be rapidly increased by intensive methods of farming based on small peasant holdings provided that appropriate economic policies are followed. These include (a) the adequate provision by the government of agricultural inputs, notably the irrigation facilities which enable multiple cropping on the same piece of land, reduce seasonal unemployment and encourage the use of fertil-

isers and improved seeds; and (b) improvements in agricultural credit and marketing. Compared with the genuinely intensive agriculture of Northeast Asia, the agriculture in the so-called overpopulated countries of India and Pakistan may not unfairly be described as an inefficient *extensive* type of farming offering great potentialities for the introduction of labour-intensive methods.[3] In terms of our analysis, the agricultural backwardness of these countries may be attributed to two types of dualism: (a) unequal provision of government economic services to the modern manufacturing sector and to the agricultural sector with some degree of dualism within the agricultural sector itself, created by unequal access to public economic facilities between the larger and the small farmers; and (b) financial dualism, which is a serious obstacle to the adoption of improved methods by small farmers. Thus it is no accident that

in Japan, where the rural and small-scale industrial sectors are more integrated in the organized credit market (more than half of all agricultural credit is provided by financial institutions), interest differentials are much smaller: on the average, interest rates are lower in the traditional sectors, but considerably higher in the fully organized sector, than in India and Pakistan.[4]

Let us now turn to the argument that the scope for substitution of labour for capital is severely limited by the need to adopt modern technology in the manufacturing sector and that, given this technical rigidity, the only method of absorbing surplus labour is to expand the size of the manufacturing sector on a capital-intensive basis. This implicity identifies the manufacturing sector with the larger-scale modern style factories. But in many underdeveloped countries small-scale industries of various types employ by far the largest proportion of the labour and contrib-

---

[3]For two very important recent contributions to this subject, see Shigeru Ishikawa, *Economic Development in Asian Perspective,* Kinokuniya, Tokyo, 1967, Ch. 2 and also charts 2–4; and G. Myrdal, *Asian Drama,* 1968, Vol. I, Ch. 10 and Vol. II, Part V.

[4]G. Myrdal, op cit., vol. III. appendix 8, p. 2095.

ute a substantial proportion of the output of the manufacturing sector.[5] If we define the manufacturing sector to include both its modern segment of the larger-scale economic units and its traditional segment of the small-scale economic units, then one thing becomes clear: even if all the large-scale modern factories operated rigidly on the basis of fixed technical coefficients, there would still be considerable scope for increasing the proportion of labour to capital in the manufacturing sector as a whole by substituting the output of the small-scale economic units for that of the larger-scale units. As we have seen, the possibilities in this direction are greater than generally allowed, for two reasons: first, the modern factories set up for the purpose of import substitution in many underdeveloped countries are predominantly in the field of light consumers' goods which are also produced by the traditional sector; and second, the lower quality of the products of the small-scale industries is compensated for by their cheaper prices. But, as we have shown, this overlap in the range of goods produced by the larger and the smaller manufacturing units is associated with and attributable to the glaringly unequal terms on which capital funds, foreign exchange and economic services provided by the government are made available to the two types of manufacturing industry by the prevailing policy of domestic industrialization. These policies may be said to protect the larger-scale modern factories not only from foreign competition but also from the domestic competition of the small-scale economic units. Thus it would seem reasonable to expect that a reduction in the unequal access to scarce economic inputs between the larger-scale and small economic units would make the latter more competitive and increase their share of the manufacturing output, thereby raising the proportion of labour to capital employed in the manufacturing

sector as a whole. A reduction of economic dualism in this sense would have the effect of encouraging a greater degree of economic specialization between the larger and smaller economic units and thus introduce a new pattern of complementary economic relationships between the two types of manufacturing industry.

Complementary relationships based on vertical linkages between different industries are a familiar theme in development economics. But so far the analysis has been handicapped by confining the concept of complementarity only to the modern segment of the manufacturing sector. Further, given the popularity of the input-output models, complementarity tends to be interpreted in purely technical terms: in terms of fixed technical co-efficients linking up insufficiently disaggregated sectors. When, however, we broaden the concept of complementarity to the possible economic linkages between the larger and smaller industries and apply the older Adam Smithian notions of division of labour and specialization[6] to the situation, we begin to have a richer understanding of the possible complementary relationships within the manufacturing sector which would have the effect of introducing a greater degree of economic flexibility into the domestic economic organization of the underdeveloped countries. With a reduction in dualism, the small economic units may be typically expected to take over a larger share of the output in the light consumers' goods industries while the larger economic units shift into the production of inputs for the small industries. As a matter of fact, the small industries in the underdeveloped countries have shown considerable enterprise in changing over from their traditional materials to new imported materials in such inputs as dyes, yarns, plastics, etc. and this is the reason why they are so handicapped by foreign exchange controls which restrict their access to imports. But the division of labour between the

[5]For quantitative evidence for the importance of small-scale industries in the underdeveloped countries, see S. Kuznets, *Modern Economic Growth: Rate, Structure and Spread*, 1966, table 8.1 and pp. 417–20; also E. Staley and R. Morse, *Modern Small Industries for Developing Countries*, 1965, Ch. 1.

[6]See G. J. Stigler, "The Division of Labour is Limited by the Extent of the Market," *Journal of Political Economy*, June 1951.

larger-scale and the small economic units may take various other patterns: the larger economic units may sub-contract any part of their productive processes to the small economic units; the small economic units may set up repair shops and other servicing activities for the bigger economic units; and so on. In general, given easier access to capital and foreign exchange, the small economic units may be expected to increase their share of economic activities in the manufacturing sector whenever their lower overhead costs and their access to cheap family and casual labour give them a comparative advantage over the larger economic units. These various possibilities are well illustrated by the history of the economic development of Japan, where the small industries have played a very important role. Significantly, the growth of the small industries was greatly facilitated by access to cheap electric power—a reduction of the dualism in the supply of public economic services. W. W. Lockwood describes the development of complementary economic relations between the larger-scale economic units and the small economic units as "a skillful utilization of Japan's limited capital resources and technical experience to employ a large and expanding population in productive pursuits."[7]

[7] W. W. Lockwood, *The Economic Development of Japan*, 1954, p. 211. See also the rest of his Ch. 4.

III.C. RURAL-URBAN MIGRATION

III.C.1. A Model of Rural-Urban Migration*

In this section I would like to set forth briefly a theoretical framework which yields some important insights into the causes and mechanisms of rural-urban migration in tropical Africa. No attempt will be made to describe this model in any great detail since that has been done elsewhere. I believe that the model can usefully serve two purposes: first, to demonstrate why the continued existence of rural-urban migration in the face of rising levels of urban unemployment often represents a rational economic decision from the point of view of the private individual; and second, to demonstrate how such a theoretical framework can be used in an analysis and evaluation of alternative public policies to alleviate the growing urban unemployment problem.

THE INDIVIDUAL DECISION TO MIGRATE: SOME BEHAVIOURAL ASSUMPTIONS

The basic behavioural assumption of the model is that each potential migrant decides whether or not to move to the city on the basis of an implicit, "expected" income maximisation objective. There are two principal economic factors involved in this decision to migrate. The first relates to the existing urban-rural real wage differential that prevails for different skill and educational categories of workers. The existence of large disparities between wages paid to urban workers and those paid to comparably skilled rural labourers has long been recognised as a crucial

factor in the decision to migrate. The increasing divergence between urban and rural incomes has arisen both as a result of the relative stagnation of agricultural earnings (partly as a direct outgrowth of post-war bias toward industrialisation at the expense of agricultural expansion) and the concomitant phenomenon of rapidly rising urban wage rates for unskilled workers. For example, in Nigeria Arthur Lewis noted that "urban wages" are typically at levels twice as high as average farm incomes. Between 1950 and 1963 prices received by farmers through marketing boards in southern Nigeria fell by 25 per cent while at the same time the minimum wage scales of the Federal Government increased by 200 per cent.[1]

In Kenya average earnings of African employees in the non-agricultural sector rose from £97 in 1960 to £180 in 1966, a growth rate of nearly 11 per cent per annum. During the same period the small farm sector of Kenya experienced a growth of estimated family income of only 5 per cent per annum, rising from £57 in 1960 to £77 in 1966. Consequently, urban wages rose more than twice as fast as agricultural incomes in Kenya so that in 1966 average wages in the urban sector were approximately two-and-a-half times as high as average farm family incomes.[2] Moreover, the urban-rural income differential in Kenya in 1968 varied considerably by level of educational attainment. For example, whereas farm income was approximately K£85 in 1968, individuals with zero to four

*Michael P. Todaro, "Income Expectations, Rural-Urban Migration and Employment in Africa," *International Labour Review*, Vol. 104, No. 5, November 1971, pp. 391–5, 411–13, Copyright © International Labour Organisation 1971.

[1] W. Arthur Lewis, *Reflections on Nigeria's Economic Growth*, Paris, OECD Development Centre, 1967, p. 42.

[2] Dharam P. Ghai: "Incomes policy in Kenya: need, criteria and machinery," in *East African Economic Review*, June 1968, p. 20.

years of primary education in urban areas earned on the average K£102, those with five to eight years of primary education earned K£156, while migrants who had completed from one to six years of secondary education earned on the average K£290 per annum in 1968.[3]

The second crucial element, which for the most part has not been formally included in other models of rural-urban migration, relates to the degree of probability that a migrant will be successful in securing an urban job. Without introducing the probability variable it would be extremely difficult to explain the continued and often accelerated rate of migration in the face of sizeable and growing pools of urban unemployed. Arguments about the irrationality of rural peasants who unwittingly migrate to urban areas permeated by widespread unemployment are as ill-conceived and culture-bound as earlier assertions that peasant subsistence farmers were unresponsive to price incentives. The key, in my opinion, to an understanding of the seemingly paradoxical phenomenon of continued migration to centres of high unemployment lies in viewing the migration process from an "expected" or permanent income approach where expected income relates not only to the actual wage paid to an urban worker, but also to the probability that he will be successful in securing wage employment in any given period of time. It is the combination and interaction of these two variables—the urban-rural real income differential and the probability of securing an urban job—which I believe determine the rate and magnitude of rural-urban migration in tropical Africa.

Consider the following illustration. Suppose the average unskilled or semi-skilled rural worker has a choice between being a

[3]For an analysis of the relationship between education and migration in Africa, see Michael P. Todaro: "Education and rural-urban migration: theoretical constructs and empirical evidence from Kenya," paper prepared for the Conference on Urban Unemployment in Africa, Institute for Development Studies, University of Sussex, September 1971, especially pp. 16–30.

farm labourer (or working his own land) for an annual average real income of, say, 50 units, or migrating to the city where a worker with his skill or educational background can obtain wage employment yielding an annual real income of 100 units. The more commonly used economic models of migration, which place exclusive emphasis on the income differential factor as the determinant of the decision to migrate, would indicate a clear choice in this situation. The worker should seek the higher-paying urban job. It is important to recognise, however, that these migration models were developed largely in the context of advanced industrial economies and, as such, implicitly assume the existence of full employment or near-full employment. In a full employment environment the decision to migrate can in fact be predicated solely on securing the highest-paying job wherever it becomes available. Simple economic theory would then indicate that such migration should lead to a reduction in wage differentials through the interaction of the forces of supply and demand, both in areas of out-migration and in points of in-migration.

Unfortunately, such an analysis is not very realistic in the context of the institutional and economic framework of most of the nations of tropical Africa. First of all, these countries are beset by a chronic and serious unemployment problem with the result that a typical migrant cannot expect to secure a high-paying urban job immediately. In fact, it is much more likely that upon entering the urban labour market the migrant will either become totally unemployed or will seek casual and part-time employment in the urban traditional sector. Consequently, in his decision to migrate the individual in effect must balance the probabilities and risks of being unemployed or underemployed for a considerable period of time against the positive urban-rural real income differential. The fact that a typical migrant can expect to earn twice the annual real income in an urban area than he can in a rural environment may be of little consequence if his actual probability of securing the higher-paying job within, say, a one-year period is one chance in five. In such a situation we could say that his actual probability of being successful in securing the higher-paying urban job is 20 per cent, so that his "expected" urban income for the one-year period is in fact 20 units and not the 100 units that the fully employed urban worker receives. Thus, with a one-period time horizon and a probability of success of 20 per cent it would be irrational for this migrant to seek an urban job even though the differential between urban and rural earnings capacity is 100 per cent. On the other hand, if the probability of success were, say, 60 per cent, so that the expected urban income is 60 units, then it would be entirely rational for our migrant with his one-period time horizon to try his luck in the urban area even though urban unemployment may be extremely high.

If we now approach the situation more realistically by assuming a considerably longer time horizon, especially in view of the fact that the vast majority of migrants are between the ages of 15 and 23 years, then the decision to migrate should be represented on the basis of a longer-term, more permanent income calculation. If the migrant anticipates a relatively low probability of finding regular wage employment in the initial period but expects this probability to increase over time as he is able to broaden his urban contacts, then it would still be rational for him to migrate even though expected urban income during the initial period or periods might be lower than expected rural income. As long as the present value of the net stream of expected urban income over the migrant's planning horizon exceeds that of the expected rural income, the decision to migrate is justified.

The mathematical details of our model of rural-urban migration are set forth in the Appendix to this article. For our present purposes, suffice it to say that the model attempts to demonstrate the conditions under which the urban-rural "expected" income differential can act to exacerbate the urban *unemployment* situation even though urban *employment* might expand as a direct result of government policy. It all depends on the re-

lationship between migration flows and the expected income differential as expressed in an "elasticity of migration response" term developed in the Appendix.

Since the elasticity of response will itself be directly related to the probability of finding a job and the size of the urban-rural real income differential, the model illustrates the paradox of a completely urban solution to the urban unemployment problem. Policies which operate solely on urban labour demand are not likely to be of much assistance in reducing urban unemployment since, in accordance with our expected income hypothesis, the growth of urban employment *ceteris paribus* also increases the rate of rural-urban migration. If the increase in the growth of the urban labour force caused by migration exceeds the increase in the growth of employment, the level of unemployment in absolute numbers will increase and the unemployment rate itself might also increase. This result will be accentuated if, for any increase in job creation, the urban real wage is permitted to expand at a greater rate than rural real income. A reduction or at least a slow growth in urban wages, therefore, has a dual beneficial effect in that it tends to reduce the rate of rural-urban migration and increase the demand for labour.

A second implication of the above model is that traditional methods of estimating the "shadow" price of rural labour to the urban sector will tend to have a downward bias if the migration response parameter is not taken into account. Typically, this shadow price has been expressed in terms of the marginal product of the rural worker who migrates to the city to secure the additional urban job. However, if for every additional urban job that is created more than one rural worker is induced to migrate, then the opportunity cost will reflect the combined loss of agricultural production of all those induced to migrate, not just the one who is fortunate enough to secure the urban position. It also follows that whenever there are sizeable pools of the urban unemployed, traditional estimates of the shadow price of urban labour will reflect an upward bias.

APPENDIX

A Mathematical Model of Rural-Urban Migration

Consider the following formulation of the theory of rural-urban migration used in this article. I begin by assuming that individuals base their decision to migrate on considerations of income maximisation and that their calculations are founded on what they perceive to be their expected income streams in urban and rural areas. It is further assumed that the individual who chooses to migrate is attempting to achieve the prevailing average income for his level of education or skill attainment in the urban centre of his choice. Nevertheless, he is assumed to be aware of his limited chances of immediately securing wage employment and the likelihood that he will be unemployed or underemployed for a certain period of time. It follows that the migrant's expected income stream is determined both by the prevailing income in the modern sector and the probability of being employed there, rather than being underemployed in the traditional sector or totally unemployed.

If we let $V(O)$ be the discounted present value of the expected "net" urban-rural income stream over the migrant's time horizon; Y_u, $_r(t)$ the average real incomes of individuals employed in the urban and the rural economy; n the number of time periods in the migrant's planning horizon; and r the discount rate reflecting the migrant's degree of time preference, then the decision to migrate or not will depend on whether

$$V(O) = \int_{t=0}^{n} [p(t) Y_u(t)$$
$$- Y_r(t)] \, e^{-rt} dt - C(O)$$

is positive or negative, where

$C(O)$ represents the cost of migration, and
$p(t)$ is the probability that a migrant will have secured an urban job at the average income level in period t.

In any one time period, the probability of being employed in the modern sector, $p(t)$, will be directly related to the probability π of having been selected in that or any previous period from a given stock of unemployed or underemployed job seekers. If we assume that for most migrants the selection procedure is random, then the probability of having a job in the modern sector within x periods after migration, $p(x)$, is:

$$p(1) = \pi(1)$$
and
$$p(2) = \pi(1) + [1 - \pi(1)] \pi(2)$$
so that
$$p(x) = p(x - 1) + [1 - p(x - 1)] \pi(x)$$
or
$$p(x) = \pi(1) + \sum_{t=2}^{x} \pi(t) \prod_{s=1}^{t-1} [1 - \pi(s)]$$

where

$\pi(t)$ equals the ratio of new job openings relative to the number of accumulated job aspirants in period t.

It follows from this probability formulation that for any given level of $Y_u(t)$ and $Y_r(t)$, the longer the migrant has been in the city the higher his probability p of having a job and the higher, therefore, is his expected income in that period.

Formulating the probability variable in this way has two advantages: (1) it avoids the "all or nothing" problem of having to assume that the migrant either earns the average income or earns nothing in the periods immediately following migration: consequently, it reflects the fact that many underemployed migrants will be able to generate some income in the urban traditional sector while searching for a regular job; and (2) it modifies somewhat the assumption of random selection since the probability of a migrant having been selected varies directly with the time he has been in the city. This permits adjustments for the fact that longer-term migrants usually have more contacts and better information systems so that their expected incomes should be higher than those of newly arrived migrants with similar skills.

Suppose we now incorporate this behaviouristic theory of migration into a simple aggregate dynamic equilibrium model of urban labour demand and supply in the following manner. We once again define the probability π of obtaining a job in the urban sector in any one time period as being directly related to the rate of new employment creation and inversely related to the ratio of unemployed job seekers to the number of existing job opportunities, that is—

$$\pi = \frac{\gamma N}{S - N} \quad (1)$$

where γ is the net rate of urban new job creation, N is the level of urban employment, and S is the total urban labour force.

If w is the urban real wage rate and r represents average rural real income, then the "expected" urban-rural real income differential d is—

$$d = w \cdot \pi - r \quad (2)$$

or, substituting (1) into (2)—

$$d = w \cdot \frac{\gamma N}{S - N} - r \quad (3)$$

The basic assumption of our model once again is that the supply of labour to the urban sector is a function of the urban-rural *expected* real income differential, i.e.—

$$S = f_s(d) \quad (4)$$

If the rate of urban job creation is a function of the urban wage w and a policy parameter a, e.g., a concentrated governmental effort to increase employment through a comprehensive programme of industrial import substitution or, as in the case of Kenya, the 1964 and 1970 Tripartite Agreements to raise employment levels, both of which operate on labour demand, we have—

$$\gamma = f_d(wa) \quad (5)$$

where it is assumed that $\frac{\partial \gamma}{\partial a} > 0$. If the growth in the urban labour demand is increased as a result of the governmental policy shift, the increase in the urban labour supply is—

$$\frac{\partial S}{\partial a} = \frac{\partial S}{\partial d} \frac{\partial d}{\partial \gamma} \frac{\partial \gamma}{ga} \quad (6)$$

Differentiating (3) and substituting into (6), we obtain—

$$\frac{\partial S}{\partial a} = \frac{\partial S}{\partial d} w \frac{N}{S - N} \cdot \frac{\partial \gamma}{\partial a} \quad (7)$$

The absolute number of urban unemployed will increase if the increase in labour supply exceeds the increase in the number of new jobs created, i.e., if—

$$\frac{\partial S}{\partial a} > \frac{\partial(\gamma N)}{\partial a} = \frac{N \partial \gamma}{\partial a} \quad (8)$$

Combining (7) and (8), we get—

$$\frac{\partial S}{\partial d} w \frac{N}{S - N} \cdot \frac{\partial \gamma}{\partial a} > \frac{N \partial \gamma}{\partial a} \quad (9)$$

or—

$$\frac{\partial S/S}{\partial d/d} > \frac{d}{w} \cdot \frac{(S - N)}{S} \quad (10)$$

or, finally, substituting for d—

$$\frac{\partial S/S}{\partial d/d} > \frac{w \cdot \pi - r}{w} \cdot \frac{(S - N)}{S} \quad (11)$$

Expression (11) reveals that the absolute level of unemployment will rise if the elasticity of urban labour supply with respect to the expected urban-rural income differential, $\frac{\partial S/S}{\partial d/d}$ (what I have called elsewhere the "migration response function") exceeds the urban-rural differential as a proportion of the urban wage times the unemployment rate, $\frac{S - N}{S}$. Alternatively, equation (11) shows that the higher the unemployment rate, the higher must be the elasticity to increase the level of unemployment for any expected real income differential. But note that in most developing nations the inequality (11) will be satisfied by a very low elasticity of supply when realistic figures are used. For example, if the urban real wage is 60, average rural real income is 20, the probability of getting a job is .50 and the unemployment rate is 20 per cent, then the level of unemployment will increase if the elasticity of urban labour supply is greater than .033, i.e., substituting into (11) we get—

$$\frac{\partial S/S}{\partial d/d} = \frac{.50 \times 60 - 20}{60} \times .20 = .033$$

Clearly, much more needs to be known about the empirical value of this elasticity coefficient in different African nations before one can realistically predict what the impact of a policy to generate more urban *employment* will be on the over-all level of urban unemployment.

Comment

The key question of what determines rural-urban migration can be explored further in studies that set forth probabilistic job search models and in empirical investigations of migration functions. Field studies and econometric analyses indicate the importance of the economic motive in the decision to migrate. Econometric estimates of migration functions have also demonstrated that the probability of urban employment, independent of the differences in actual rural and urban wages, contributes significantly to the explanation of variance among time periods and subgroups of the rural population in rates of urban migration.

See J. R. Harris and M. Todaro, "Migration, Unemployment and Development: A Two-Sector Model, *American Economic Review* (March 1970); J. Bhagwati and T. N. Srinivasan, "On Reanalyzing the Harris-Todaro Model," *American Economic Review* (June 1974); A. G. Blomquist, "Urban Job Creation and Unemployment in LDCs: Todaro vs. Harris and Todaro," *Journal of Development Economics* (March 1978); M. B. Levy and W. J. Wadycki, "Education and the Decision to Migrate: An Econometric Analysis of Migration in Venezuela," *Econometrica* (March 1974); L. Yap, "The Attraction of the Cities: A Review of the Migration Literature," *Journal of Development Economics* (September 1977); Derek Byerlee, "Rural-Urban Migration in Africa," *International Migration Review* (Winter 1974); J. Stiglitz, "Alternative Theories of Wage Determination and Unemployment in LDCs," *Cowles Foundation Discussion Paper* (1973); H. Joshi and V. Joshi, *Surplus Labor and the City: A Study of Bombay* (1976); D. Mazumdar, "The Rural-Urban Wage Gap, Migration and the Wage Gap," *Oxford Economic Papers* (1976); J. Connell et al., *Migration from Rural Areas* (1976); Richard H. Sabot (ed.), *Migration and the Labor Markets in Developing Countries* (1982), with an extensive bibliography covering both analytical and empirical studies of an econometric and descriptive character. For a review of theory, evidence, methodology, and research priorities, see Michael Todaro, *Internal Migration in Developing Countries* (1976).

EXHIBIT III.1. Urban Population, Major Areas and Regions, 1950–2000 (thousands)

	1950	1960	1970	1975	1980	1990	2000
World total	724,147	1,012,084	1,354,357	1,560,860	1,806,809	2,422,293	3,208,028
More developed regions	448,929	572,730	702,876	767,302	834,401	969,226	1,092,470
Less developed regions	275,218	439,354	651,481	793,558	972,408	1,453,067	2,115,558

Source: United Nations, *Patterns of Urban and Rural Population Growth,* ST/ESA/Ser. A/68.

EXHIBIT III.2. Net Rural to Urban Migration in Selected Countries, 1950–1970

	Number (thousands)		As Percentage of Urban Growth	
	1950–1960	1960–1970	1950–1960	1960–1970
Low-income countries				
Nepal	36	241	56.3	81.4
Uganda	123	287	80.9	80.2
Cambodia	123	252	53.5	76.8
Tanzania	153	314	76.9	64.7
Pakistan	2,464	3,524	57.9	56.1
Indonesia	2,476	3,486	53.5	48.6
Kenya	185	189	62.9	48.0
Burma	311	403	40.1	35.6
Sri Lanka		211		33.7
India	3,971	4,630	22.0	18.2
Middle-income countries				
Ivory Coast	265	566	84.4	77.2
Ghana	594	959	68.9	66.6
Korea	3.647	3,540	92.3	63.8
Zambia	193	315	65.9	59.8
Uruguay	392	352	66.9	58.1
Malaysia	729	1,020	63.6	54.2
Tunisia	267	311	59.2	53.7
Algeria	727	952	61.5	51.4
Bolivia	83	99	48.3	46.3
Morocco	695	968	52.9	46.2
Nigeria	1,677	2,759	45.3	45.0
Venezuela	1,263	1,451	55.2	43.4
Chile	811	855	46.8	43.2
Columbia	1,432	1,840	48.6	40.8
Peru	590	708	38.0	40.4
Guatemala	218	305	52.8	39.0
Brazil	6,345	8,360	48.3	37.1
Thailand	371	552	35.8	33.4
Taiwan	673	841	30.1	27.5
El Salvador	41	57	29.5	24.5
Mexico	2,833	3,803	31.0	24.3
Argentina	742	843	28.5	20.6
Paraguay	25	34	15.7	13.6

Source: Lyn Squire, *World Bank Staff Working Paper* No. 336, p. 55.

III.C.2. The Informal Sector*

The problem with employment is that the statistics are incomplete, covering a major part of wage-earning employment and some self-employment in the larger and more organised firms but omitting a range of wage earners and self-employed persons, male as well as female, in what we term "the informal sector."

The popular view of informal-sector activities is that they are primarily those of petty traders, street hawkers, shoeshine boys and other groups "underemployed" on the streets of the big towns. The evidence suggests that the bulk of employment in the informal sector, far from being only marginally productive, is economically efficient and profit-making, though small in scale and limited by simple technologies, little capital and lack of links with the other ("formal") sector. Within the latter part of the informal sector are employed a variety of carpenters, masons, tailors and other tradesmen, as well as cooks and taxi-drivers, offering virtually the full range of basic skills needed to provide goods and services for a large though often poor section of the population.

Often people fail to realise the extent of economically efficient production in the informal sector because of the low incomes received by most workers in the sector. A common interpretation of the cause of these low incomes (in comparison to average wage levels in the formal sector) has been to presume that the problem lies within the informal sector; that it is stagnant, non-dynamic, and a net for the unemployed and for the thinly veiled idleness into which those who cannot find formal wage jobs must fall. It is hardly surprising that this view should be widespread, for academic analysts have often encouraged and fostered such an interpretation. Further, from the vantage point of central

*From ILO Mission, *Employment, Incomes, and Equality: A Strategy for Increasing Productive Employment in Kenya,* Geneva, 1972, pp. 5–8, 503–8. Copyright 1972, International Labour Organisation, Geneva.

Nairobi, with its gleaming skyscrapers, the dwellings and commercial structures of the informal sector look indeed like hovels. For observers surrounded by imported steel, glass and concrete, it requires a leap of the imagination and considerable openness of mind to perceive the informal sector as a sector of thriving economic activity and a source of Kenya's future wealth. But throughout the report we shall argue that such an imaginative leap and openness of mind is not only necessary to solve Kenya's employment problem, but is entirely called for by the evidence about the informal sector. There exists, for instance, considerable evidence of technical change in the urban informal sector, as well as of regular employment at incomes above the average level attainable in smallholder agriculture. The informal sector, particularly in Nairobi but to varying degrees in all areas, has been operating under extremely debilitating restrictions as a consequence of a pejorative view of its nature. Thus there exists an imminent danger that this view could become a self-fulfilling prophecy.

Later we explain how employment in the informal sector has grown in spite of obstacles and lack of outside support: the evidence suggests that employment has probably increased a good deal faster in the informal than in the formal sector. It is therefore impossible to judge how the employment problem has changed merely from the data on employment in the formal sector.

Our analysis lays great stress on the pervasive importance of the link between formal and informal activities. We should therefore emphasise that informal activities are not confined to employment on the periphery of the main towns, to particular occupations or even to economic activities. Rather, informal activities are the way of doing things, characterised by—

1. ease of entry;
2. reliance on indigenous resources;
3. family ownership of enterprises;

4. small scale of operation;
5. labour-intensive and adapted technology;
6. skills acquired outside the formal school system; and
7. unregulated and competitive markets.

Informal-sector activities are largely ignored, rarely supported, often regulated and sometimes actively discouraged by the Government.

The characteristics of formal-sector activities are the obverse of these, namely—

1. difficult entry;
2. frequent reliance on overseas resources;
3. corporate ownership;
4. large scale of operation;
5. capital-intensive and often imported technology;
6. formally acquired skills, often expatriate; and
7. protected markets (through tariffs, quotas and trade licenses).

Our strategy of a redistribution from growth aims at establishing links that are at present lacking between the formal and the informal sectors. A transfer of incomes from the top income groups to the working poor would result in new types of labour-intensive investments in both urban and rural areas. This should not only generate demand for the products of the informal sector but also encourage innovations in labour-intensive techniques in this sector. The various policies which we recommend in other parts of the report are intended to reduce risk and uncertainty on the part of those employed in the informal sector and to ensure a dynamic growth of this large segment of the Kenyan economy.

Unemployment is often analysed as simply the result of the first type of basic imbalance, between a rapidly growing labour force and a more slowly growing number of job opportunities. If population, it is said, grows at 3.3 per cent as in Kenya, and enumerated wage-earning employment grows—as in Kenya since 1964—at 1.9 per cent, increasing un-

employment results.[1] And as long as the divergent growth rates continue, the prospect of growing unemployment in the future seems inevitable. Economic growth even at Kenya's recent rates of 6 to 7 per cent is no protection, it is argued, since inappropriate technologies and rising wages increase productivity so rapidly that growth is robbed of its power to increase the number of jobs faster than the labour force. Although this explanation has sometimes been used in Kenya, it should by now be clear why we have found it seriously deficient, and in some respects seriously misleading, as the main explanation of the Kenyan situation. It ignores the fact that the bulk of the population works on the land, not in wage-earning jobs. It depends crucially on the statistics of the growth of enumerated employment in the formal sector, whereas—as we stated earlier—enumerated employment ignores a large and apparently growing amount of employment in the "informal sector." Thirdly it focuses too exclusively on jobs, instead of on opportunities for earning a reasonable income.

But apart from these weaknesses, the explanation just discussed analyses the situation exclusively in terms of over-all imbalances, giving no weight to imbalance between the structure of skills and aspirations of the labour force and the structure of incentives and incomes from work. It pays no attention to the variations in the incidence of employment problems seasonally, regionally, by age or by sex.

There are also marked contrasts between the relative security and income levels of those with wage-earning jobs in the bigger firms and those self-employed in the informal sector. These sharp inequalities inevitably create strong ambitions to migrate to the towns, to strive for higher education, to search for a job. As long as extreme imbalances persist, so will unemployment, since large differentials will always attract a mar-

[1]The imbalance is even greater if one compares growth rates of the urban population or of the number of school leavers with the growth of enumerated employment.

gin of job seekers to hover in the towns, near the chances of the good jobs, in the hopes of snapping one up. This explains why the analysis of inequality is fundamental to the explanation of employment problems in Kenya.

But unemployment is not only the result of imbalance in differentials and opportunities. Even with perfect equality, unemployment could arise. Fast rates of population growth, of urbanisation and school expansion inevitably make it more difficult to absorb the growing labour force and reduce the time that might otherwise be available for structural adjustments. Here a second set of imbalances arise—dynamic imbalances relating to the structure of economic growth in the economy and to the constraints upon it. Rapid growth is needed, but rapid growth can itself generate imbalances which will frustrate its continuation—most notably a shortage of foreign exchange, of domestic savings, of skills and entrepreneurship, of demand or of the political support needed to keep the system workable. For this reason our report is not merely concerned with alleviating unemployment, poverty and gross inequality, but with economic growth on a pattern which can be sustained in the future, and which generates wider and more productive employment opportunities in the process. . . .

THE RELATION BETWEEN THE FORMAL AND INFORMAL SECTORS

The process of economic transformation and growth in Kenya has been marked by growing inequalities in the distribution of wealth and income among Africans. The usual explanation is the traditional-modern division of the economy, in which the westernised modern sector is the source of dynamism and change and the traditional sector slowly withers away. This view does not correspond to the reality of Kenya; we reject it for that reason, and because it ignores the dynamism and progressive elements indigenous to the Kenyan economy. We have considera-

ble evidence to refute a view that attributes the sources of economic and social change almost exclusively to outside forces.

Furthermore, the traditional-modern analysis focuses only on the positive effects of the westernisation of the Kenyan economy and ignores the negative effects. In particular, it ignores inter-sectoral dynamics, which are the key to the employment problem. The accumulation of wealth in a small part of the modern sector is the consequence of the concentration of political power in that sector, and has given rise to the development of an impoverished and economically deprived modern sub-sector. The slums of Nairobi, Mombasa and to a lesser extent other urban areas are completely modern and due to the differences of wealth and income between different sectors of the economy. These differences draw migrants towards the concentrations, and bring about the modernisation of almost the entire economy, but not the spread of wealth. Because of the slow growth of high-wage employment, migration to urban areas by income seekers has led to the growth of a low-income periphery. This low-income sector is peripheral both literally and figuratively. In Nairobi it sprang up, and continues to grow, just outside the borders of the wealthy urban zone, to supply goods and services to the fortunate few inside that zone and to its own population. Figuratively, it is peripheral in that it has only fortuitous and restricted access to the sources of wealth.

Characteristics and Dynamics of the Informal Sector

We describe these two urban sectors as being the "formal" and the "informal" sector. This designation is not intended to contribute to an academic proliferation of labels; we merely seek an analytical terminology to describe a duality that avoids the bias against the low-incomes sector inherent in the traditional-modern dichotomy. Both sectors are modern; both are the consequence of the urbanisation that has taken place in Kenya over the last 50 years. We might have used the terms "large-scale" and "small-scale," but those terms are purely descriptive and tell us nothing about why one sector is large-scale and the other is small-scale. An explanation of this is central to explaining and solving the employment problem in Kenya. One important characteristic of the formal sector is its relationship to the Government. Economic activities formally and officially recognised and fostered by the Government enjoy considerable advantages. First, they obtain the direct benefits of access to credit, foreign exchange concessions, work permits for foreign technicians, and a formidable list of benefits that reduce the cost of capital in relation to that of labour. Indirectly, establishments in the formal sector benefit immeasurably from the restriction of competition through tariffs, quotas, trade licensing and product and construction standards drawn from the rich countries or based on their criteria. Partly because of its privileged access to resources, the formal sector is characterised by large enterprise, sophisticated technology, high wage rates, high average profits and foreign ownership.

The informal sector, on the other hand, is often ignored and in some respects helped and in some harassed by the authorities. Enterprises and individuals within it operate largely outside the system of government benefits and regulation, and thus have no access to the formal credit institutions and the main sources of transfer of foreign technology. Many of the economic agents in this sector operate illegally, though often pursuing similar economic activities to those in the formal sector—marketing foodstuffs and other consumer goods, carrying out the repair and maintenance of machinery and consumer durables and running transport, for example. Illegality here is generally due not to the nature of the economic activity but to an official limitation of access to legitimate activity. Sometimes the limitations are flouted with virtual abandon, as in the case of unlicensed *matatu* taxis; sometimes the regulations are quite effective. The consequence is always twofold: the risk and uncertainty of earning a livelihood in this low-income sector are magnified, and the regulations ensure a high quality of services and commodities for the wealthy few at the expense of the impoverished many.

The formal-informal analysis applies equally well to the agricultural sector. The parallels are obvious and striking. The division between favoured operators with licences and those without in urban areas is reproduced in agriculture between those who grow tea and coffee with official sanction and those who do so illegally. Similarly, with other agricultural products such as beef, there are those whose wealth enables them to conform to and benefit from standards officially laid down, while others can make a livelihood only by contravening the regulations. In the agricultural sector extension services take the place of the industrial estates and of loans from the Industrial and Commercial Development Corporation in the urban areas: farmers whose wealth and income allow them to conform to bureaucratic criteria benefit. Perhaps the most striking rural-urban parallel is with illegal rural squatters, who move unofficially on to land scheduled for resettlement and face a continual danger of eviction. Their similarity to urban squatters is obvious—both are irresistibly drawn to real or perceived sources of wealth, despite legal restrictions of access.

In the Introduction to this report we considered the characteristics, other than relation to the Government, that distinguish the informal sector from the formal. These characteristics of the informal sector, both agricultural and non-agricultural, result in low incomes for those who work in it. A natural consequence of these low incomes is that monetary exchanges within the informal sector are different in quality from those in the formal sector. A most important consequence of a low income is the primacy of risk and uncertainty. The loss a small farmer or a small entrepreneur can bear is disproportionately smaller than that which can be borne by a wealthy operator, particularly when the former has no access to institutionalised sources of credit. As a consequence, the entrepreneur in the informal sector must act continually to protect himself against risk. Accordingly he establishes semi-permanent relations with suppliers and buyers, frequently at the expense of his profits. For the same reason he may be hesitant to innovate, particularly in agriculture, for he cannot take the chance of failure. These characteristic behavioural responses are not inherent in the informal sector; they are adaptive responses to low income.

As pointed out in our report, a rate of increase of employment in the formal sector high enough to reduce the relative size of the informal sector seems to us to be beyond the bounds of possibility for the foreseeable future. An absolute reduction is much less likely still. On the basis of any reasonable calculation, the urban informal sector in 1985 will include a larger proportion of the urban labour force than it does today. We do not view this inevitable development with dismay, for we see in the informal sector not only growth and vitality, but also the source of a new strategy of development for Kenya. The workshops of the informal sector can provide a major and essential input for the development of an indigenous capital goods industry, which is a key element in solving the employment problem. The informal sector is not a problem, but a source of Kenya's future growth. In addition, it is in its workshops that practical skills and entrepreneurial talents are being developed at low cost. Many of its enterprises are inefficient technically and economically, and will disappear in the process of growth; but this applies equally to the formal sector, where tariff and quota protection, access to capital goods below world market prices and other restrictions on competition perpetuate gross operating inefficiencies that go hand in hand with sophisticated technology.

Despite the vitality and dynamism we see in the informal sector, we do not delude ourselves that it will develop successfully under present conditions. Although it has the potential for dynamic, evolutionary growth, under the existing nexus of restrictions and disincentives, the seeds of involutionary growth have been sown. Unlike the determinants of growth of the formal sector, the determinants of growth of the informal sector are largely external to it. The relevant question is not whether the informal sector is inherently evolutionary or involutionary, but what policies should be followed to cause evolutionary growth. Irrespective of policy changes, the informal sector will grow in the next 15 years. If policy continues as at present, the growth will be involutionary and the gap between the formal and informal sectors will widen. The employment problem will then be worse.

A Model of Inter-sectoral Flows

The purpose of this section is to identify the major factors determining employment in the informal sector. The model used is a simple identity rather than a behavioural model. The points may seem self-evident, but we feel it is useful to make them, because linkages between the small-scale, informal sector and other sectors of the economy have generally been ignored.

From the writings of economists on urban areas in poor countries it appears that the criterion authors use for dividing the urban economy is not the modernity of activities but their enumeration in government labour force surveys.[2] The relation between the two urban sectors implicit in this analysis can be

[2] "A more meaningful distinction than that of employed-underemployed-unemployed is between those employed in establishments employing five or ten workers which are usually covered in annual labour surveys . . . and the rest of the labour force. The larger establishments . . . can generally be characterised as modern-sector establishments, as opposed to the smaller-scale establishments which are better characterised as traditional. Employees in traditional establishments are generally underemployed under most definitions of the term, while modern sector employees can be thought of as fully employed. . . ." Charles R. Frank, Jr., "The problem of urban unemployment in Africa," in R. G. Ridker and H. Lubell (eds.), *Employment and unemployment problems of the Near East and South Asia*, Delhi, Vikas, 1971, pp. 785–6.

called the "residual" model. The residual model is based on the presumption that the informal sector is a reservoir of unemployment and marginally productive activity into which those who cannot obtain paid jobs in the formal sector sink, barely making ends meet by begging, hawking or embarking on petty crime. In short, the activities in this sector are seen as providing no economic service or commodity. The demand for labour in the sector is presumed to be static. Popular though this view is, we do not feel that it is particularly useful. It asserts *a priori* a characteristic of the informal sector (unemployment) that can be determined only empirically. The mechanism of the residual model can be summarised briefly. The informal or "traditional" urban sector has a static demand for labour, or a demand for labour that is quite income-inelastic.[3] Therefore, an increase in the number of persons seeking a living in the informal sector (for example, after a reduction of employment in the formal sector) merely drives down average earnings in that sector; and if average earnings are at subsistence level, the influx presumably results in unemployment. A further prediction of this type of model when it incorporates a rural sector is that if average earnings in the urban informal sector are not below those in rural areas, migration will result. Facts mentioned in the first part of the report cast doubt on this last prediction for Kenya.

This view of the informal sector ignores linkage effects and product substitution, which we feel are at present quite significant in Kenya, and should be strengthened in the future. To identify these linkages we use a four-sector model of the economy, which distinguishes between smallholder agriculture, the informal (non-agricultural) sector, the private formal sector and the government sector. The outputs of these sectors are X_1, X_2, X_3 and X_4 respectively. The output of the informal (non-agricultural) sector is by defi-

nition given by the following input-output row:

$$X_2 = a_{21}X_1 + a_{22}X_2 + a_{23}X_3 + a_{24}X_4 + X_{2F} \quad (1)$$

The symbol a indicates input-use coefficients, and X_{2F} is the final demand for informal-sector output. From our observations and reading in Kenya we can make up a list of the most important goods and services supplied by the informal sector to itself and the other three sectors.

Using sector	Goods and services supplied
1. Agriculture	Grain-grinding, building materials, transport, marketing, repair and maintenance.
2. Informal	Furniture for commercial use, tools, transport, repair and maintenance.
3. Private formal	Marketing and distribution, transport, furniture, repair and maintenance.
4. Government	Construction, furniture, transport.
5. Final demand	Clothing, prepared food, furniture, repair and maintenance.

In our report we have discussed in detail the ways of increasing the final demand for informal-sector products and strengthening linkages between the informal and other sectors. Here we restrict ourselves to a discussion of the most important parameters of identity (1) above. The strategy we have suggested for Kenya would have the effect in time of strengthening the linkages of the informal sector and fostering a dynamic growth of its final demand; this implies a shift in the composition of output from relatively capital-using to relatively labour-using production processes. In short, we foresee the production of certain types of commodities and services with more labour for a given level of output. This will not occur, of course (indeed, the reverse will occur), unless the

---

[3]This, of course, is also an empirical question, and the assumption of a low income elasticity of demand is rather arbitrary. The over-all income elasticity of demand for the output of the informal sector, for example, is sensitive to the distribution of income.

present development strategy is radically altered.

Identity (1) can be solved for informal-sector output as follows:

$$X_2 = \frac{1}{1 - a_{22}} (a_{21}X_1 + a_{23}X_3$$
$$+ a_{24}X_4 + X_{2F}). \qquad (2)$$

If we assume the capital stock of the informal sector to be constant, then a change in X_2 production is—$\Delta L_2 \dfrac{\Delta X_2}{\Delta L_2}$, where $\dfrac{\Delta X_2}{\Delta L_2}$ is, at the limit, the marginal product of labour in the informal sector. This allows us to write (2) in terms of employment:

$$\Delta L_2 = \frac{1}{1 - a_{22}} \frac{\Delta L_2}{\Delta X_2} [\Delta(a_{21}X_1$$
$$+ a_{23}X_3 + a_{24}X_2 + X_{2F})]. \qquad (3)$$

While extremely simple, (3) is useful in analysing the growth of employment in the informal sector.

It is obvious that an increase in any X will increase employment in the informal sector if none of the input coefficients is zero. For a given increase in total output, the effect on employment in the informal sector is determined by the values of the coefficients and the composition of the increase in output in terms of $X_1, X_2, \ldots X_{2F}$. The effect of the recommendations in the main report is—

1. to increase the size of the coefficients; and
2. to shift the composition of future increases in output toward the sectors where the coefficients are highest.

Even if steps are taken to induce the private formal sector and the Government to shift purchases of inputs toward sector 2, there are significant technological and consumer taste influences militating against success. The extent of potential linkages between sector 2 and sectors 3 and 4 (parameters a_{23} and a_{24}) is strongly related to the nature and pace of technical change occurring outside Kenya. This, in turn, is related to the choice of products, particularly in sector 3. Sector 3 products, which require sophisticated technology for quality reasons (and constantly undergo labour-saving technical change), are unlikely to provide much scope for subcontracting or for intermediate inputs supplied by small producers. Thus the choice of products must be determined either through the redistribution of income or through direct restrictions. In addition, active measures must be taken to increase the technical capacity of the informal sector to supply inputs.

The model used here needs to be elaborated along behavioural lines, and an attempt must be made to estimate the parameters. Data are lacking, though we have made very rough calculations, based on arbitrary but moderate assumptions, that indicate that the present situation in sectors 1, 2 and 3 and shifts in government purchases within the present structure of public demand imply an intermediate demand for sector 2 output of almost £70 million. This very rough calculation indicates that there is considerable scope for employment in the informal sector in Kenya. Further, we feel that this model, with an attempt to estimate its parameters, represents a more fruitful approach to an understanding of the informal sector than the analysis underlying the residual model.

Comment

The concept of the informal urban sector was first introduced by Keith Hart, with the distinction between wage and self-employment as the essential difference between the formal and informal sectors; see Keith Hart, "Informal Income Opportunities and Urban Unemployment in Ghana," *Journal of Modern African Studies* (March 1973). As noted in the preceding selection, the ILO identifies the informal sector by a variety of other characteristics. For analytical purposes, it may be most incisive to define the informal sector as simply that sector in which the return to labor, whether or not it be in the form of wages, is determined by forces of demand and supply.

For studies of the informal sector, see Dipak Mazumdar, "The Urban Informal Sector,"

World Development, (August 1976); T. W. Merrick, "Employment and Earnings in the Informal Sector in Brazil," *Journal of Developing Areas* (1975); J. Weeks, "Policies for Expanding Employment in the Informal Urban Sector of Developing Economies," *International Labour Review* (January 1975); Stephen Guisinger and Mohammed Irfan, "Pakistan's Informal Sector," *Journal of Development Studies* (July 1980); Peter Lloyd, *The 'Young Towns' of Lima: Aspects of Urbanization in Peru* (1980). Several studies by the International Labour Office on urban development and employment also relate to the informal sector in Abidjan (1967), Calcutta (1974), Sao Paulo (1976), Jakarta (1976), Bogota (1978), and Lagos (1978). See also "Third World Migration and Urbanization: A Symposium," *Economic Development and Cultural Change* (April 1982).

III.D. GROWTH WITHOUT EMPLOYMENT—NOTE

Although Lewis's two-sector model did not so intend it, the capitalist sector in his model has, in practice, become identified with industry or the urban sector, while the noncapitalist sector has become identified with agriculture or the rural sector. It may be more perceptive, however, to recognize that in actuality a "double dualism" has arisen within the poor country. Not only is there rural-urban dualism, but also within each of the two sectors there are two subsectors that might be termed the "organized" and "informal" subsectors. The organized subsector in the urban sector is composed of wage earners in formal employment, is characterized by modern management and modern techniques of production, and is protected by governmental policies.

As noted in selection III.C.2, the informal subsector, in contrast, is composed of the self-employed and small-scale traditional crafts and services, all unprotected by governmental policies. In the informal subsector we find the hawkers, porters, shoeshine boys, but also the small-scale craftsmen, small retail traders, own-account workers, and unpaid family workers. Employment opportunities in the informal subsector are created by supply: necessity drives people to work in every conceivable way. Workers in the informal subsector may actually be working long hours at extremely difficult physical labor, but their productivity is very low, and their meager income is variable and frequently shared with others. With the extensive rural-urban migration, and the incapacity of the urban organized subsector to absorb the migration, the informal subsector of the city has acted as a sponge for the surplus labor. In most LDCs the number in the urban informal subsector has risen not only absolutely but also as a proportion of the total labor force. In urban centers, such as Calcutta or Bombay, it is estimated that one-half or more of the workforce is in the informal subsector.

In the rural sector a similar subdivision is evident. The organized sector comprises plantations, estates, and mines with modern management, advanced techniques of production, and wage employment. Widespread, however, is the informal subsector in which production is still of the traditional subsistence variety with production for household consumption.

Many development plans have been premised with objectives of transferring resources out of agriculture to the industrial urban sector and achieving a marked decline in the relative size of the agricultural labor force. An early belief of development planning was that the process of industrialization could provide a substantial growth of employment opportunities in the modern urban sector. And yet, one of the most perplexing—and serious—problems now confronting many developing countries is their growing level of urban unemployment and underemployment in the modern industrial sector. Perplexing—because levels of unemployment and underemployment have risen despite a rise in the rate of investment and an expansion in output. Serious—because this intensifies social resentment and political unrest.

As elaborated in Chapter I, the increase in the absolute number of unemployed and underemployed questions whether development is actually occurring. Unemployment, underemployment, low productivity employment, and the "working poor" are all aspects of the employment problem. The problem is not confined to one sector, but pervades the entire economy.

Although we may wish for more refined statistics,[1] a number of studies have emphasized the broad dimensions of the problem:

[1]For some problems of statistical coverage and a discussion of statistical methods, see Edgar O. Edwards (ed.), *Employment in Developing Nations*, 1974, passim; David Turnham, *The Employment Problem in Less Developed Countries* (1971): Erik Thorbecke, "The Employment Problem: A Critical Evaluation of Four ILO Comprehensive Country Reports," *International Labor Review*, May 1973.

industrial employment has lagged behind growth in industrial output, behind growth of the urban population, and even behind the general growth rate of population. Only a portion of the annual increase in the urban labor force has been absorbed in the urban organized subsector.

In numerous developing countries, despite creditable rates in aggregate growth, it is not uncommon for the rate of *open* unemployment (not disguised unemployment or underemployment) in major urban areas to be as high as 15 to 20 percent. Even worse, the rates of urban unemployment in the age group of 15–24 are generally about double the rates of unemployment among the urban labor forces as a whole.[2]

The number of underemployed is considerably greater than those in open unemployment. Underemployment can be either visible or invisible underemployment. Those in visible underemployment would work more hours if the employment opportunity were available. Those in invisible underemployment are working, but at low productivity occupations that are below a cutoff point in productivity or earnings.

The labor utilization problem in a developing economy is chronic and in large part a problem of underemployment. This suggests that the Keynesian unemployment model that focuses on short-term cyclical unemployment of an open character, caused by a deficiency of aggregate demand, does not fit the less developed country.

Furthermore, it indicates that the actual course of industrialization has deviated considerably from Lewis's model of development with unlimited supplies of labor. As we saw in selection III.B.1, the essence of the Lewis model is that wages in the modern sector are based on the average product of labor in the traditional rural sector, but are somewhat higher—for unskilled labor, normally about 50 percent above the income of subsistence farmers—in order to attract labor into the modern sector and compensate for the higher cost of urban living and any nonpecuniary disadvantages. At this higher wage rate,

Lewis believed that "this brings the modern sector as much labor as it wants without at the same time attracting much more than it can handle."[3] Furthermore, the model postulates that wage rates should not rise with increasing productivity, but instead that capital formation and technical progress in the capitalist sector should raise the share of profits in the national income. To the extent that the profit ratio rises, there should then be capital-widening investment in the industrial sector, so that the demand for labor continues to rise and more industrial workers are employed at a constant real wage. Finally, after the surplus labor is absorbed, wages begin to rise.

In actuality, however, the real income gap between the modern and rural sectors has been much greater than allowed for in the Lewis model. The wage rate in the modern sector has been higher than that needed to cover the cost of transfer and the higher urban costs of living. And the differential above rural income has widened. The wage level in the industrial sector has risen in spite of open unemployment and before the surplus labor of the rural sector has been absorbed. It has also continued to rise in many of the LDCs, although the average product in agriculture may have been even stagnant in some economies. Instead of Lewis's suggested 50 percent differential, the average real wage for workers outside of agriculture has commonly been two to three times greater than the average family income in the traditional sector.

Most importantly, the inflow of labor to the modern sector has actually been "more than it can handle": contrary to what is to be expected from the Lewis model, an exceedingly high rate of unemployment and underemployment has materialized in the modern sector. Those formerly in disguised unemployment in the rural sector have, in effect, transferred into visible unemployment and underemployment in the modern sector.

[2] See Edwards, *Employment in Developing Nations*, p. 13.

[3] W. A. Lewis, *Development Planning*, London, 1966, pp. 77–8, 92. Also W. A. Lewis, "Unemployment in Developing Areas," in A. H. Whiteford (ed.), *A Reappraisal of Economic Development*, Chicago, 1967, p. 5.

The reasons for this can be found in some of the actual deviations from the conditions of the Lewis model and in some structural distortions that have been perpetuated by inappropriate policy measures.

The rate of urbanization has indeed been high. The amenities and public services of the urban area are attractive in themselves to labor from the rural sector. But the strongest inducement has been the widening income difference between urban wages and rural income at the same time as rural employment opportunities have not expanded. Fundamentally, it can be submitted that the employment problem in the urban area has been the result of a premature increase in the industrial wage level combined with a premature reduction in agricultural employment.[4] To a lesser extent, but still significantly in some countries, labor has been released from the very labor-intensive indigenous handicraft industries that cannot compete with the growth in new manufacturing activities. "Rationalization" of labor practices in the tertiary sector has also tended to increase the supply of labor to the urban industrial sector.

As already noted, the urban wage level has not been controlled by real earnings in agriculture. Urban wages have commonly risen to two to four times higher than agriculture earnings. Urban wages have risen independently through the wages policies of the government and trade unions.[5] Trade union pres-

[4]In Africa, the unemployment among school leavers is one indication of this. Not only are there school leavers within the city, but also those who attend schools in villages reject the traditional occupations on the land and migrate to the cities in search of wage-paid jobs. See A. Callaway, "Education Expansion and the Rise of Youth Unemployment," in P. C. Lloyd et al. (eds.), *The City of Ibadan*, Cambridge, 1968, pp. 197–209.

[5]Lewis did recognize the effects of minimum wages and union action as being among the various possibilities that could cause the process of absorbing surplus labor from agriculture to come to a premature halt; see W. A. Lewis, "Economic Development with Unlimited Supplies of Labor," *The Manchester School of Economic and Social Studies*, May 1954, pp. 172–3. But the model is allowed to run its course without this restraint coming into effect.

In his *Development Planning*, however, Lewis does concentrate more on the resultant unemployment; see pp. 76–87.

sures have increased in many countries, and labor-supported governments have shown some sympathy to such pressures. Moreover, the monopolistic structure of many product markets has facilitated the passing on of higher wages in the form of higher prices. In several countries, union pressure in crucial sectors of the economy—for instance, in the oil, copper, and bauxite industries—has been instrumental in setting a pattern of wage increases in other sectors.

More significantly, governmental policies have been directly instrumental in raising urban wages. The public sector is frequently the largest sector of wage employment and also the only sector that is highly organized. Wages in the public sector have risen rapidly and have commonly acted as the base for a wider pattern of wage increases.

In newly independent countries, the salary scales are still basically those that were paid to expatriates during the earlier colonial period; but this scale does not now conform to the utilization of the domestic supply of labor, and it puts undue pressure on the wage structure. Nor can the heightened expectations from the extension of education be fulfilled. Furthermore, minimum wage regulation has been influential in raising urban wages and in having a great impact on the total wage structure in a developing country. The minimum wage in a dominant industry is frequently negotiated with the government on a basis of "an ability to pay" criterion; but this wage tends to spread through other industries. The increase in the minimum wage will have considerable effect in raising the whole wage scale since the wages being received by most of the unskilled workers are at or near the current minimum wage. The generalization of a minimum wage may then become highly unrealistic because it is oblivious to conditions of supply and demand in the labor market, living standards in the traditional sector, and the effects on the wage structure as a whole. Workers who were only marginally useful—but nonetheless employed at the lower wage—become redundant when the minimum wage rises.

Minimum wage policies for unskilled labor have the effect of making the skilled-unskilled wage differential too narrow, as has happened in many African and Asian countries. Market forces of supply and demand are left to determine wages for skilled labor, but demand rises only slowly so that the market-determined wage for skilled labor also tends to rise slowly. If governments then insist that unskilled wages should increase independently of demand and supply conditions in the unskilled labor market, there is a likelihood that unskilled wages will increase faster than skilled wages, and that relatively low-wage labor will become overvalued.

In default of adequate profit taxation or other tax policy, governments have also found it convenient in effect to "tax" companies—especially foreign companies— through wage increases. The government's policy of encouraging higher wages may initially be directed only at foreign companies in order to prevent "excess" profit repatriation and to raise the share of income for domestic factors. But the demonstration effect of higher wages in the foreign enterprises also causes a spread of higher wages to other enterprises.

At the same time as government policies have supported urban wage increases, no particular attention has been given to the level of agricultural wages. The result has been a widening gap between the urban and agricultural wage levels. Such a large differential has served to attract the disguised unemployed from the rural sector to the urban sector, but it has simultaneously kept industrial labor overpriced. Moreover, the differential between urban and rural wages has proceeded to widen in face of the substantial and growing urban unemployment and underemployment. With the rising expectational wage, it has become increasingly difficult to absorb the excess supply of labor.

Although the Lewis model envisages sufficient capital-widening investment in the industrial sector to absorb the labor inflow, the actual result has been a substitution of capital for labor in the modern organized sector. Contrary to the model, wage rates in many of the LDCs have actually risen more rapidly than productivity. Real wages have risen at rates comparable to those in the advanced industrial countries. But whereas in the industrial countries real wages have increased roughly in line with average national productivities, the rise of wages in the developing countries often implies an increase considerably faster than that in real national product per capita.

The consequence of this has been the use of more capital-intensive production methods, either through the introduction of labor-saving machinery in response to rising wages or through improvement in personnel and production management practices that have trimmed the labor requirements per unit of output.

Capital-intensive methods of production have also been subsidized by other price distortions—especially through too low a rate of interest and too low a price for foreign exchange. When interest rates in the urban sector do not reflect the true scarcity of capital, a bias is imparted to capital-intensive production methods. This is often intensified by inflation which lowers the real rate of interest below the nominal rate, possibly even to a negative real rate. So too is there a bias toward more advanced production techniques when the LDC's currency is overvalued in terms of foreign currency, and the true cost of importing machinery is hence undervalued. Governments have also lowered the relative price of producers' equipment by such measures as allowing duty-free importation of equipment, a preferential exchange rate, and making available foreign exchange for servicing loans from overseas machinery suppliers. When domestic enterprises are protected by tariffs and import quotas, the pressure to economize on capital is also less than it would be in more competitive markets.

It is most significant that the strategy of industrialization via import substitution has dominated the expansion of the industrial-urban sector. In Chapter VIII, we examine in some detail the policies used to promote the home replacement of imported final goods. At this point, we need only recognize that the attempt to industrialize via import substitution has generally been accompanied by inflation and an overvalued exchange rate. These policies have resulted in a distorted price structure in many LDCs: too low a rate of interest in the urban sector, too low a rate for foreign exchange, and too high a level of urban wages.

The capital-intensive bias is also supported by a number of other measures. Employers tend to seek means of reducing their labor requirements when the government uses wage policies as a substitute for social legislation by requiring family allowances, pensions, licensing and health measures, or other fringe benefits bordering on social insurance. Officially required fringe benefits and wage supplements may commonly amount to as much as 30 to 40 percent of the basic wage. When the employers are foreign enterprises, they are also likely to be simply imitating the advanced techniques of production known in the advanced country—techniques which are appropriate for the factor supply of the advanced country but not for the labor surplus of the less developed country.

Contrary to the Lewis model, the expansion of the modern industrial sector has also tended to slow down in many LDCs. Being based on import substitution, the industrial sector might be expected to have initially a substantial rate of growth as imports are replaced. But this may be a once-for-all expansion with little subsequent reinvestment—unless the home market continues to grow, or the process of import substitution can proceed on from the final stages of production down through the production process to the replacement of intermediate goods; or the import-replacement industry is able to gain a competitive advantage in export markets. Such opportunities for the continual expansion of the modern sector have not materialized, and the capital-widening investment of the Lewis model with an ever-expanding demand for surplus labor has not been sustained.

At the same time as domestic policies have had the effect of subsidizing capital-intensive import-substitution industries, they have implicitly imposed a levy on domestic agriculture. This has gone against an expansion in labor-intensive agricultural output and a rise in rural employment.

For these various reasons the employment problem has become a central problem of development.

Comment

Lewis later recognized the unemployment problem and stated that

The most important ingredient in employment policy is to prevent too large a gap opening up between wages in the modern and earnings in the traditional sectors. So long as the traditional sector is not disturbed by a large income gap, it can hold and provide for all the people whom the modern sector is not yet ready to employ. . . .

Other ingredients are: measures to prevent excessive capital intensity; avoidance of an overvalued currency; adequate expenditure on developing the countryside; curbing the growth of a few large towns, in favor of developing more numerous small urban centers; and a population policy. . . . Deliberate action to substitute labor for machinery, in accordance with shadow pricing, even if confined to the public sector would go a long way towards eliminating open unemployment (Lewis, *Development Planning* 1966, p. 83).

III.E. MEASUREMENT OF THE "UNEMPLOYMENT EQUIVALENT"—NOTE

If there is not one employment problem but many, there must be various approaches to the measurement of unemployment, and the relevant approach must depend on the particular problem or policy question at hand. It has already been emphasized, however, that the employment problem in LDCs cannot be interpreted as simply a Keynesian type of involuntary unemployment. A pervasive problem is that of the "working poor"—those who actually work long hours but earn only a low income below a poverty line. The disguised unemployed constitute another major dimension of the employment problem. Beyond measures of "open involuntary unemployment" it is just as important—if not more so—to have measures of the "underemployed" and "disguised unemployed."

We might usefully think of a range of unemployment, beginning at one extreme with open unemployment in the urban area, defined as "zero hours work and zero income." Beyond this extreme, we can apply four major criteria for determining whether a person may be called unemployed or underemployed: (1) the time criterion, (2) the income criterion, (3) the willingness criterion, and (4) the productivity criterion.[1] Thus, we may call a person unemployed or underemployed if either: (1) by the time criterion, he is gainfully occupied during the year for a number of hours (or days) less than some number of normal or optimal hours (or days) defined as full employment hours or days; or (2) by the income criterion, he earns an income per year less than some desirable minimum; or (3) by the willingness criterion, he is willing to do more work than he is doing at present—he may either be actively searching for more work or be available for more work if it is offered on terms to which he is accustomed; or

[1]These criteria are presented by Raj Krishna, "Unemployment in India," *Economic and Political Weekly,* March 3, 1973, p. 475.

(4) by the productivity criterion, he is removable from his present employment in the sense that his contribution to output is less than some normal productivity, and therefore his removal would not reduce output if the productivity of the remaining workers is normalized with minor changes in technique or organization.

Another study also emphasizes that there are several dimensions of underutilization of labor:

In addition to the numbers of people unemployed, many of whom may receive minimal incomes through the extended family system and therefore not rightly classified with the very poor, it is also necessary to consider the dimensions of (1) time (many of those employed would like to work more hours per day, per week or per year), (2) intensity of work (which brings into consideration matters of health and nutrition), and (3) productivity (lack of which can often be attributed to inadequate, complementary resources with which to work). Even these are only the most obvious dimensions of effective work, and factors such as motivation, attitudes, and cultural inhibitions (as against women, for example) must also be considered. Our discussions have thrown up the following forms of underutilization of labor, which may indicate the diversity of the phenomenon but which further study will probably show to be incomplete:

1. *Open unemployment*—both voluntary (people who exclude from consideration some jobs for which they could qualify, implying that they have some means of support other than employment) and involuntary.
2. *Underemployment*—those working less (daily, weekly, or seasonally) than they would like to work.
3. *The visibly active but underutilized*—those who would not normally be classified as either unemployed or underemployed by the above definitions, but who in fact have found alternative means of "marking time," including
   a. *Disguised underemployment.* Many people seem occupied on farms or employed in government on a full-time basis even though the

services they render may actually require much less than full time. Social pressures on private industry also may result in substantial amounts of disguised underemployment. If available work is openly shared among those employed, the disguise disappears and underemployment becomes explicit.

b. *Hidden unemployment.* Those who are engaged in "second choice" nonemployment activities, perhaps notably education and household chores, primarily because job opportunities are not (i) available at the levels of education already attained, or (ii) open to women, given social mores. Thus, educational institutions and households become "employers of last resort." Moreover, many of those enrolled for further education may be among the less able, as indicated by their inability to compete successfully for jobs before pursuing further education.

c. *The prematurely retired.* This phenomenon is especially apparent, and apparently growing, in the civil service. In many countries, retirement ages are falling at the same time that longevity is increasing, primarily as one means of creating promotion opportunities for some of the large numbers pressing up from below.[2]

Different estimates of "unemployment" will be possible according to which criterion or various combinations of the different criteria are applied. A gross measure of the employment problem might be termed the "unemployment equivalent"—that is, the sum of those in open unemployment plus a measure of the "equivalent" of the underemployed. Conventional measures underestimate both the size of the labor force and the amount of unemployment. In addition to the "involuntary unemployed" (those conventionally defined as "seeking work at the existing wage rate"), there are many others who are not seeking work because they estimate that the probability of finding employment is too low, or they lack skill qualifications, or they suffer from malnutrition or ill health. Even more, there is a part of the labor force that may be actually employed but only for a limited time in part employment or seasonal employment. There is also a large portion of the labor force that constitutes the "working poor." Finally there are those who, while working, are unproductive: they are "underemployed," and they constitute part of the "labor reserve" that could through effective policy measures be allowed to work more hours or more productively. Just what these policy measures might be is the concern of much of the remainder of this book. The essential point here is that a labor reserve does exist, and that because of the underutilization of labor this reserve exceeds the conventional measures of "unemployment."

[2]Edgar O. Edwards (ed.), *Employment in Developing Nations,* New York, 1974, pp. 10–11.

Comment

A review of several studies that attempt to measure the amount of unemployment and underemployment can illuminate the different concepts of "unemployment" and indicate statistical difficulties in measurement. See Gunnar Myrdal, *Asian Drama,* (1968), part 5, appendix 6; Richard Jolly et al. (eds.), *Third World Employment* (1973); P. P. Streeten, "A Critique of Development Concepts," *European Journal of Sociology,* Vol. 11, No. 1 (1970); Edgar O. Edwards, *Employment in Developing Nations* (1974); S. Paglin, "Surplus Agricultural Labor and Development: Facts and Figures," *American Economic Review,* (September 1965); E. Kritz and J. Ramos, "The Measurement of Urban Underemployment," *International Labour Review* (January–February 1976); Peter Gregory, "Employment, Unemployment, and Underemployment in Latin America," *Statistical Bulletin of the OAS* (October–December 1980); David Turnham, *The Employment Problem in Less Developed Countries,* OECD Development Center Studies (1971).

III.F. EMPLOYMENT STRATEGIES

III.F.1. Output and Employment Trade-offs *

Neither of the objectives, maximum output and maximum employment, are unambiguous. The output objective is ambiguous because output at any time consists of a heterogeneous collection of goods. Types of employment, in duration—daily, weekly and seasonally—in effort and by regions, etc. also differ. In addition, both output and employment occur over time. Current levels of output and employment may influence future levels. Weighting therefore both intra- and inter-temporally is crucial to the *definition* of the objectives. However, we shall begin by ignoring these ambiguities and assume that our sole concern is with current levels of output and employment, and that maximizing current levels automatically leads to achievement of future objectives, or put more formally, that maximizing current levels of output and employment is equivalent to maximizing the present value of the entire streams of output and employment over time. We shall also begin by assuming that there is a single index for output and employment.

CONFLICTS RESULTING FROM SCARCE COMPLEMENTARY FACTORS OF PRODUCTION

We can then rephrase the question and ask: is maximum current production compatible with maximum employment? On the face of it, the answer seems to be an obvious "yes." More men must surely be able to produce more. It is hard to picture conditions in which it is impossible to find anything useful to do for extra hands.

*From F. Stewart and P. P. Streeten, "Conflicts between Output and Employment Objectives," in R. Robinson and P. Johnston (eds.), *Prospects for Employment Opportunities in the 1970s*, HMSO, 1972, pp. 367–73, 375–8, 381–4. Reprinted by permission.

At a given time, with a given stock of capital equipment (inherited from the past), the employment of more men on that equipment is likely to increase output, though it could be that, as a result of the reorganization of the work, of less efficient production methods used, of people standing in one another's way or of a fall in efficiency for some other reason, the extra workers do not add to, or even subtract from, production. However, the choice facing a country is not simply a question of employing additional men with the existing capital stock but of the type of new equipment to install, and in this decision about the nature of new investment there can be a conflict between output and employment. Given that the total funds available for new investment are limited, using the funds for equipment to employ people in one way will inevitably mean *not* using the same funds for some other equipment which may involve *less* employment but might also produce more output. Maximizing output involves using scarce resources as efficiently as possible. If capital is the scarce resource, it involves minimizing the capital-output ratio. The type of production this requires may be, but need not be, consistent with maximizing employment.

Suppose in the textile industry the minimum capital-output ratio is associated with fairly modern style industry. If £100,000 is available for investment in textiles, if the capital-output ratio is 2.5, and if the capital cost per work place for this type of factory is £1000 (assuming a firm degree of utilization of capacity), then investing all funds in this modern factory will involve extra employment of 100 and extra output of £40,000. An alternative way of investing the funds might be to introduce hand-spinning. Suppose for this the capital-output ratio was 5.0 and the cost per work place £100; then the extra output resulting from using the funds for hand-spinning would be £20,000 and the extra employment generated 1000. In this case there is a fairly dramatic conflict between employment and output maximization. It should be noted that this conflict (which is a fairly realistic one if one examines actual figures for costs, etc. in the textile industry)[1] arises because the more labour-intensive method in the sense of the method which uses a lower capital-labour ratio or shows lower cost per work place, actually involves *more capital per unit of output* than the capital-intensive method. Some theoretical models assume this can never happen. It would be true that it could not, if all techniques of production were invented and developed simultaneously, since the labour-intensive methods which use more capital would never be developed. But in fact methods of production are developed over an historical period with the more labour-intensive methods generally originating from an earlier period. One reason why this sort of situation develops is the existence of economies of scale; as machinery has been adapted for larger-scale production the capital costs in relation to output have tended to fall, so that for large-scale production the later and more capital-intensive methods tend to economize on capital in relation to output. For small-scale production the older machinery may remain efficient.[2] Implicit in this example is the assumption that there is a specific level of employment associated with each technique, and thus that it is sensible to talk of a "cost per work place." In fact, the

[1]Bhalla (1964), suggests that the capital-output ratio (including working capital as well as fixed capital) using factory methods in cotton spinning is about three quarters of that using the hand Ambar Charkha methods. Bhalla's analysis of rice-pounding (1965), suggests a similar conflict here; the technique which maximizes employment (or has the lowest cost per work place), the pestle and mortar, requires nearly twice the capital per unit of value added compared with the large sheller machine. The latter requires investment per work place of about 100 times as great as the former.

[2]The importance of scale in determining the efficient range of production possibilities is emphasized by many empirical studies, including Boon (1964); Strassmann (1968).

number of people employed with any given machine may vary. . . .

So long as output is responding positively to additional workers the level of employment associated with a given machine will depend partly on the level of wages. Even where output is invariant with respect to employment the actual employment associated with given machinery may depend partly on real wages since managerial effort may be substituted for employment as real wages rise. Thus the employment level associated with any given machine may not be independent of the wage rate. In the examples above some wage level is implicitly assumed in associating each machine with a unique output and employment level. A range to represent output and employment at different wage levels would have been a more realistic representation. If one assumes that continuous variations in output are associated with continuous variations in employment for each machine, but that there is diminishing marginal product as employment is increased, one is back in a neo-classical world where there are variable factor proportions and any amount of capital (or any machine) may be associated with any level of employment. In this neo-classical world the limit to employment is set by the real wages workers demand. There can be no conflict between output and employment because every type of machine can be associated with any amount of employment. Thus if the modern factory methods were employed in spinning, the extra 900 workers could be employed in the factory and would each add to output. At least as much employment and more output could result from choice of the factory alternative. We do not believe that this is a realistic assumption. Though some variation in employment is possible with any given machine, there comes a point at which the machine is operating at its maximum pace, when additional workers do not increase output. There is thus a limited range of employment possibilities associated with each machine, which means that there can be a conflict between output and employment. Put in another way, for any positive real wage there comes a point at which it is no longer worth while employing extra workers with a particular machine. This point may be reached at lower employment level and a higher output level for one machine than for another. In this case there is a conflict between output and employment, which is independent of any institutional or other lower limit on the level of real wages.

Just as some economists assume that such a conflict between output and employment cannot arise, others assume not only that it has arisen in the past, but also that it necessarily must arise. The capital-intensive methods of production, it is claimed, will always involve lower capital costs per unit of output (and higher costs per work place) than the labour-intensive methods.[3]

This position is as extreme as the other. There is considerable evidence that in many industries, and in many processes, the more labour-intensive methods also save capital per unit of output.[4] In these cases maximizing employment and output are consistent. Probably of more significance is the possibility of devoting research and development (R and D) efforts to the labour-intensive methods (in the sense of low capital cost per work place) so that they become efficient as compared with capital-intensive methods. Present possibilities reflect the fact that almost all R and D is concentrated on producing methods suitable for the developed world, in which labour is scarce; the labour-intensive methods currently available are generally the products of earlier and less sophisticated science and technology. . . .

[3]See, for example, Kaldor (1965), pp. 28–9: "There is no question *from every point of view* of the superiority of the latest and more capitalistic technologies" (our italics). Similar emphasis on the overall superiority of capital-intensive techniques is found in Amin (1969), pp. 269–92.

[4]A. K. Sen suggests that in cotton weaving the capital-output ratio is the lowest for the most labour-intensive technique, the fly shuttle hand loom, and highest, nearly 2½ times as big, for the automatic power loom (again including working capital). Evidence for the existence of a range of efficient techniques in a number of industries below a certain critical scale of output is also contained in Boon (1964).

REASONS FOR PREFERRING EMPLOYMENT TO OUTPUT

If a conflict between maximizing current output and employment were inevitable, why should we wish to sacrifice output to employment? Four possible answers occur to us, though others might think of additional reasons. First, employment creation and the consequential wage payments may be the only mechanism by which income can be redistributed to those who would otherwise remain unemployed. With an efficient fiscal system, taxation combined with unemployment relief, free social services and other forms of assistance to the unemployed could be used as an engine of redistribution. In an underdeveloped society, loyalty to the extended family may induce the employed wage earner to share his wages with his often large extended family. But if neither fiscal system nor family provide a systematic channel of redistribution, job creation may have to be used for this purpose. Production will then be sacrificed for better distribution and, as a means to this, greater employment.

Second, unemployment is demoralizing. To feel unwanted, not to be able to make any contribution, lowers a man's morale and makes him lose his self-respect. The preservation of self-respect is worth sacrificing some production. As Barbara Ward has said, "of all the evils, worklessness is the worst"— clearly not only and even not mainly because, and if, it lowers national product. It is worth sacrificing production to reduce this evil.

Third, it might be thought that work is intrinsically good, whatever its impact on morale, self-respect and other subjective feelings. The Puritan ethic may commend job creation as valuable irrespective of its contribution to production. Puritanism played a valuable part in making desirable the necessary but unpleasant sacrifices which promoted the industrial revolution in Britain. Whether this ethic, where it has been adopted in the developing world (and it is notable that most Puritan-like statements tend to come from expatriates) should be encouraged and where it has not been adopted should be promoted, if it leads to a situation which impedes rather than speeds up development by requiring the adoption of inefficient techniques to compensate for the masochistic value placed on work, is another question. Other aspects of Puritanism are certainly conducive to development; to the extent that Puritanism is a package deal, this aspect may have to be accepted along with the rest.

Fourth, there are obvious political disadvantages and dangers in widespread unemployment and non-employment. This is an important reason for valuing employment since, in so far as anyone does, it is the politicians who lay down "the objective function" of society. Political instability may, in any case, eventually endanger output levels and growth. . . .

The desire for employment which is so apparent in many countries cannot be entirely divorced from the desire for higher incomes. Many of those seeking urban employment are looking for work *at the going wages* in the organized industrial sector, where wages are generally considerably higher than incomes obtainable elsewhere. Discussion of the need for rural employment opportunities to reduce the underutilization of labour normally takes place in the context of the need to create opportunities for increasing incomes through fuller labour utilization. Again the need is for incomes as much as for work. It is unlikely that the unemployed, or those scratching a living in the rural areas, would be prepared to suffer some loss in *their* incomes for the sake of more work. What is wanted is increased opportunities to work *and* earn higher incomes. Because both work and higher incomes are required it is difficult to disentangle the two. Clearly, the desire for redistribution of income is of prime importance. To achieve this redistribution, employment opportunities may be needed but the sacrifice, or trade-off involved may be of the income of the better-off for the sake of that of the worse-off, rather than of output for the sake of employment. However, it can be argued that it is not just a question of income redistribution but of providing a chance to *earn,* not simply receive, the higher incomes.

These are the only reasons we can think of as to why the employment objective might conflict with the output objective, and sacrifice of output to employment, *properly defined,* is justified. But what are the proper definitions? As argued in the first paragraph, objectives are ambiguous. Two types of ambiguity are relevant. First, national product consists of a heterogeneous collection of goods, "of shoes, and ships and sealing wax, of cabbages" (and possibly of the services of kings) and it accrues to different people, in different regions, with varying needs. In putting all these together we must use a system of weighting the different items and different sets of weights may lead to contradictions. One set may give the impression that we are sacrificing product for employment, another may not.

Another ambiguity arises because both production and employment occur in time and stretch into the future. An infinite number of time profiles within any horizon that we care to consider can be drawn up. Any profile for either of our two objectives that lies all the way below another profile of the same objective can be dismissed as inefficient. But in order to choose between those that intersect at some moment of time, we must make additional choices in the light of our policy objectives. What if 5 per cent less employment now gives us 15 per cent more employment in two years' time? What if a rise of 10 per cent in employment now prevents us from employing an additional per cent of a vastly larger labour force in 10 years and after? We must turn to the problems of *weighting* and *timing.*

WEIGHTING: TIME

Another serious ambiguity arises from the fact that sacrifices now may yield gains in the future. We must consider two opposite sets of circumstances: first, where less production and more employment now lead to more production later than would otherwise have been possible; second, where less employment and more production now lead to more employment later than would otherwise have been possible.

In order to illustrate the first case, let us return to the situation where men were demoralized by unemployment. We then regarded self-respect and high morale as ends in themselves. But we may also regard them as necessary for the continued employability of men. If men remain unemployed for long, their skills as well as their attitudes deteriorate and they are incapable of producing as much later. This situation cannot be remedied by unemployment assistance, for it is only on the job that ability to work and motivation are maintained. Just as machines sometimes have to be kept going in order to prevent attrition or rust, so workers and teams of workers have to be kept busy to prevent them from becoming rusty or apathetic. Current employment, even where there is nothing to show for it, can be regarded as a form of investment—human maintenance—which prevents future deterioration of productivity. In addition men's productive capacity, their ability to work, their initiative and organizational ability and their concentration may not merely be maintained but may actually be increased by working. This form of learning by working means that the greater current employment opportunities, the greater is future productive capacity.

The second case works in the opposite direction and is possibly the most important way in which an apparent conflict between employment and output arises. Here we maximize production in the short run, even though it means tolerating now more nonemployed, because the extra production enables us to generate more jobs later than would otherwise have been possible. If there is a current conflict between output and employment, it must be remembered that output is useful not only for itself, but can be used to generate more employment.

The inter-temporal "trade-off" between employment now and employment tomorrow arises because, by tolerating more unemployment now for the sake of producing more, we can provide the men (and their children) with more jobs later. This is only partly a matter of investment, i.e., producing now the machines, or resources with which to buy the machines, that will give jobs tomorrow. A greater volume of food which provides better nutrition for the workers and their children, of health measures and of certain forms of education can also contribute to greater employment (and fuller labour utilization) in the future. The point leads once again to income distribution, but this time not valued independently as desirable, but as instrumental to faster growth. The choice between maximum employment and maximum output reduces to one between jobs now or later, because more output can promote more, and more effective, employment in the future. To raise employment means sacrificing not only output now (and, on our assumption, the rate of growth of output) but also the rate of growth of employment. This means that at some future date the level of employment will be lower than it would otherwise have been. To go back to the example discussed earlier, suppose in each case, modern factory and hand spinning wheel, 20 per cent of income generated is saved. The factory solution will involve £8000 investment available in the next year, while the hand wheel alternative will involve £4000. The divergence will get greater in subsequent years. The factory alternative will lead to an annual growth in income (and assuming the same £1000 a work place technology is adopted, in employment) of 8 per cent per annum while the hand spinning wheel alternative will lead to 4 per cent annual growth in output and employment. (This ignores the impact of extra consumption on growth.) Figure 1 illustrates the possibilities. . . .

As to the right choices, a good deal will depend upon our time horizon and on certain future developments. As far as employment is concerned, the life span of one generation and perhaps its children will be relevant, but few societies would be prepared to tolerate widespread unemployment over two generations to improve the job prospects of their

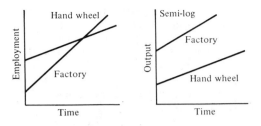

FIGURE 1.

great-grandchildren. This is not only because we show less concern for our great-grandchildren, but also because we may rightly hope that their prospects will improve for other reasons, such as the development of more appropriate technologies, improvements in motivation, administration, education, etc. Given the time horizon, we might say that, on the other hand, the richer society of tomorrow can look better after its unemployed and to be unemployed then will be a smaller hardship. On the other hand, with present trends of growth of the labour force in less developed countries and likely opportunities for jobs, the total number of unemployed is increasing rapidly. While the lot of a given number of unemployed will therefore be better in the future and the burden of maintaining them lighter, the number to be looked after will be larger. In the more distant future, however, we may assume that population control will have become effective or new scope for migration will have opened up. In view of all this, it seems right to discount future jobs and to give more weight to more jobs now and in the near future.

On balance it seems that the discount rate that we should apply to employment may be less than the one we apply to output. The main argument for applying a discount rate to output is that the marginal utility of income is less for a richer society. This does not apply in the same way to employment—i.e., the value of extra employment generated does not decline as the level increases—though increasing *incomes* per head may make employment in the future less important as a means of income redistribution. On the other hand, the contrasts between those

employed and those not employed and the accompanying resentment may work the other way. Poverty in the midst of affluence is worse than plain poverty widely shared. This, and the question of numbers, suggests that it may be correct to give greater relative weight to future as against current employment than to future as against current output.

Planners must know not only their preferences between the present and the future, for both output and employment, but also what opportunities there are for trade-offs. Conflicts between current levels of growth rates of output and employment may arise either because growth rates are determined by savings rates (or, more generally, developmental expenditure rates), savings rates by income distribution and income distribution by employment levels, or because growth rates are determined by the allocation of a given savings ratio between sectors and this allocation has different effects on employment.

It is common to assume in this context that a capital-intensive technique leads to a higher savings ratio for the same income level than a labour-intensive technique. On this assumption, lower employment now can give faster growth of both output and employment. Those who make this assumption (Sen, 1968; Little and Mirrlees, 1968) assume:

1. That a higher proportion of profits is saved than of wages (at its most extreme this assumption is that all profits are saved, all wages consumed); and that consumption makes no contribution to future growth;

2. That wage rates do not depend on techniques;

3. That the government is incapable of securing the savings ratio it desires by taxing wage earners and generating adequate public savings or using inflation to reduce real wages.

Since the growth rate is the product of the savings ratio and the output/capital ratio, the effect on the growth rate of raising the savings ratio by increasing the capital-intensity of technique adopted will depend on the consequences for the output/capital ratio.

TECHNICAL PROGRESS

Until now we have ignored technical progress and assumed that output and employment grow at the same rate if a single technique is chosen and adhered to over time. In practice technical possibilities available increase over time. Generally technical progress takes a form which involves increasing labour productivity, so that the rate of growth of employment is less than the rate of growth of output. This phenomenon—output increasing faster than employment—has been observed in many developing countries. The precise form that technical progress takes will affect the terms of any conflict between output and employment.

If technical progress is disembodied, affecting existing capital equipment as much as new and therefore unrelated to the rate of investment, and if it increases the labour productivity associated with techniques of varying capital intensity to the same extent, then the technique which maximizes the rate of growth of output will be the same as the technique which maximizes the rate of growth of employment, though the latter will be lower than the former. If technical progress is embodied, affecting only new investment, the greater the rate of investment, the greater the increase in labour productivity. Hence, for any increase in growth rate, resulting from an increase in the investment ratio, there will be a less than proportionate increase in the rate of growth of employment. Similarly, if labour productivity is positively related to the scale of production, measures which speed up the growth of output (whether they be investment or other means) will increase the growth of employment less than proportionately. Relationships of this type have been observed for developing countries, though the relationship appears less strong than for developed countries (Oherlihy, 1970). Since the growth in output remains bigger than the associated growth in labour productivity, the technique which increases the growth rate of output will also increase the growth of employment, but the gains in terms of growth of *employment*, will be less than the gains in terms of growth of *output*.

Technical developments are likely to affect some techniques more than others. In particular, research, development and use of techniques in the developed countries are virtually confined to techniques of high, and increasing, capital-intensity. Thus for these techniques labour productivity, and often capital productivity as well, may rise over time, while the more labour-intensive techniques may be unaffected by technical progress. The labour-intensive techniques may therefore become inferior over time and their use may involve a sacrifice of output as compared with the later techniques.

However, for labour-intensive techniques various improvements are likely to result from their widespread use, including a fall in their cost simply as a result of economies of scale in their production. Labour-intensive techniques are also often easier to produce in the developing countries, because they are often of simpler design and more (in number) are required in a particular country so that some of the economies of scale may be exploited. Current relative costs and efficiency of different techniques may therefore fail to reflect potential relative costs after technical progress through use has been realized. They may also fail to take into account the differing possibilities for local production and repair of the different techniques. This means that current possibilities may understate the likely implications for output of labour-intensive techniques; the conflict between employment and output may therefore be less in reality than at first appears.

THE PRODUCT-MIX

So far we have assumed the composition of consumption goods to be determined and have varied only the techniques of producing them and the allocation of investment between sectors. If different consumption goods require different proportions of labour and capital, we can raise the level of employment without varying the techniques of producing any product by enlarging the share of labour-intensive products at the expense of capital-intensive products. If there are opportunities for international trade on favourable terms, this is an obvious solution. If, however, a changing composition involves changing the products consumed at home, the question is whether, with a proper system of weighting, losses in consumers' welfare would arise. If the labour-intensive products are also those largely demanded by the poor, we have already seen that a fall in output may be an optical illusion and that the weights derived from a more equal income distribution might show a rise. There may also be external diseconomies of consumption or buying as a result of created wants or of habits. If a product is wanted (a) because others buy it or (b) because it was bought in the past or (c) wants are created through advertising, and if these features are peculiar to the capital-intensive products, its elimination may lead to smaller welfare losses (in cases (b) and (c) after a time) than the expenditure values would indicate or it may lead to welfare gains.

The scope for changing the consumers' product-mix in a labour-intensive direction is generally considered somewhat limited, apart from possibilities of international trade, by the need for a reasonable balance in the composition of demand. We cannot expect people to consume all food and no clothes for example, or to have more haircuts at the expense of bicycles. But the conclusions drawn from this, in terms of the narrow scope for product substitution, arise partly from a mistaken definition of product. Any given need may be fulfilled by a number of different products: nylon or cotton shirts fulfil the need for clothing, wooden houses, mud huts, reinforced concrete multi-storey buildings fulfil the need for shelter. While maintaining a reasonable balance in terms of needs (cloth-

ing, housing, shelter, etc.), there is considerable scope for substitution towards more labour-intensive products for the fulfilment of each need. The possibilities of concentrating more on labour-intensive products to fulfil each need may therefore extend the scope for using the product-mix to increase employment opportunities.

References

Amin, S. (1969), "Levels of remuneration, factor proportions, and income differentials with special reference to developing countries," in A. Smith (ed.), *Wage Policy Issues in Economic Development*, Macmillan.

Bhalla, A. S. (1964), "Investment allocation and technological choice—a case of cotton spinning techniques," *Economic Journal*, Vol. 4, pp. 611–22.

———, (1965), "Choosing techniques: hand pounding vs. machine-milling of rice: an Indian case," *Oxford Economic Papers*, Vol. 17, pp. 147–57.

Boon, G. K. (1964), *Economic Choice of Human and Physical Factors in Production*, North Holland.

Kaldor, N. (1965), in R. Robinson (ed.), *Industrialization in Developing Countries*, Cambridge University Press.

Little, I. M. D., and Mirrlees, J. (1968), in *Manual of Industrial Project Analaysis in Developing Countries*, Vol. 2, p. 42.

Oherlihy, C. St. J. (1970), "Wages and employment," Meeting of Directors of Development Training and Research Institutes, ILO (mimeo).

Sen, A. K. (1968), *Choice of Techniques*, Blackwell.

Strassmann, W. P. (1968), *Technological Change and Economic Development*, Cornell University Press.

EXHIBIT III.3. Gross Domestic Investment per New Labor Market Entrant, 1975

	Gross Domestic Investment/ GDP (percent)	Gross Domestic Investment (millions of U.S. dollars)	Percent Rate of Labor Force Growth 1974–75	Increase in Labor Force 1974–75 (thousands)	Gross Domestic Investment per Labor Force Entrant
Ethiopia	10.5	278	2.0	234	1,190
Bangladesh	6.1	563	1.6	402	1,400
Burma	10.5	376	1.6	203	1,850
Tanzania	21.3	543	2.4	152	3,570
Pakistan	15.6	1,718	2.5	479	3,590
Zaire	33.9	745	1.9	199	3,740
Sri Lanka	16.4	434	2.5	116	3,740
India	22.0	18,352	2.0	4,619	3.970
Kenya	19.6	617	2.6	132	4,680
Indonesia	19.0	6,756	2.2	1,003	6,740
Thailand	26,8	3,837	2.9	536	7,160
Ghana	10.6	556	2.1	76	7,320
Korea	26.8	5,121	3.0	562	9,110
El Salvador	20.1	370	3.3	40	9,250
Columbia	17.3	2,325	3.2	237	9,810
Senegal	15.5	316	1.7	32	9,900
Cameroon	21.4	467	1.4	32	10,850
Philippines	31.1	4,908	2.7	410	11,970
Egypt	27.3	3,394	2.5	257	13,210
Morocco	23.6	1,875	2.8	125	15,000
Nigeria	28.9	7,766	2.1	507	15,320
Peru	18.6	2,617	3.0	132	19,820
Turkey	22.7	8,049	1.8	302	26,650
Brazil	25.1	31,194	2.9	966	32,300
Syria	31.4	1,654	2.6	48	34,460
Mexico	28.8	22,764	3.3	550	41,390
Iran	29.8	16,266	2.6	237	68,630
Algeria	57.4	7,809	2.8	102	76,560
Argentina	21.4	10,589	1.2	118	98,740
Yugoslavia	33.0	10,214	1.3	125	81,720
United States	15.4	231,800	1.7	1,555	149,070
Japan	32.5	158,457	1.4	796	199,070
France	22.5	75,588	1.3	287	263,370

Source: Compiled by T. King and quoted in Nancy Birdsall, *Population and Poverty in the Developing World,* draft, February 15, 1980, p. 40.

III.F.2. Technology and Employment*

We shall use the term *local technology sector* (or L-sector) to describe those techniques in the old-style traditional sector and the new-style informal sector; and *foreign technology sector* (or F-sector) to describe those techniques in the sector using technology developed recently in the advanced countries.

We may discuss three types of analysis that have been put forward to explain the employment problems of underdeveloped countries: distorted factor prices, the factor proportions problem, and inappropriate technologies.

"DISTORTED" FACTOR PRICES

These form the central pivot of much neo-classical analysis of unemployment in underdeveloped countries. The argument is that there exists some "natural" or "undistorted" set of factor prices—wage rates, interest rates, and prices of investment goods—which would reflect the opportunity cost of the various resources, and which would ensure full employment of all resources. Un- or under-employment is then attributed to various market imperfections distorting the factor prices and thus preventing full employment of resources. For example, trade unions and government wage regulation interfere in the labour market, pushing up wages above their natural rate; subsidies on investment, designed to increase the rate of investment, artificially cheapen it. Similarly, overvalued exchange rates maintain real wages above the natural rate, and the costs of imported investment goods below the natural rate. Figure 1 illustrates the situation. There is assumed to be an infinite choice of techniques of varying labour and investment intensity, allowing any investment rate to be associated

with any rate of employment. Full employment of resources would occur with price line, PP', given limited investment resources Oi, and labour supply OL. But distortions of the kind mentioned result in the actual price line of DD'. Given limited investment resources, Oi, unemployment uL results. The solution to the problem is clear: "Let the endowment speak," as one author has put it. Factor prices should be changed, or factor use subsidised/taxed to bring them into line with "undistorted" full employment prices.

A fundamental objection to this approach is the assumption made about the nature of technological choice—both as to the range of techniques assumed, and to the critical determinants of choice. The discussion of technological choice [see selection III.B.2] demonstrated the unrealism, in most cases, of the neo-classical assumption of a wide range of available techniques of varying labour and capital intensity to produce any given product, while it also suggested that the relative price of capital and labour was only one among a number of determinants of the choice of technique.

A second objection is the assumption that wages paid may be freely varied without affecting labour efficiency necessary for its

*Frances Stewart, *Technology and Underdevelopment*, 2nd edition, 1978, pp. 46–50, by permission of Macmillan, London and Basingstoke.

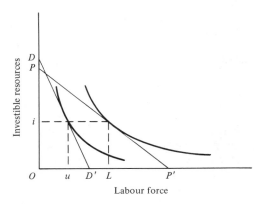

FIGURE 1.

working. The labour force has to be well fed, healthy, punctual and clothed. The sort of wages required to get "undistorted" factor prices are often well below the sort of level necessary—and are therefore inconsistent with modern technology. Here we are primarily concerned with the analysis of the employment situation on which this type of approach is based. It is assumed—normally implicitly—that only the modern sector counts in terms of employment, and the rest of the population are more or less equivalent to unemployed. Thus the factor price distortions referred to as *the* central problem are the factor prices ruling in the modern sector. Outside the modern sector there is no question of the factor endowment not speaking. Incomes from work are very low, interest rates high. In the traditional sector, activities are as labour-intensive as the technology and human willingness to work permits. But the full employment that is aimed for is the employment of everyone in the F-sector. By ignoring the rest of the economy the approach may be counterproductive. Reductions in wage rates in the F-sector may increase employment there. But it may also reduce employment opportunities in the traditional/ informal sectors by a greater extent, since the lower wage rates will enable the F-sector to undercut the L-sector. Any switch in production from the L-sector to the F-sector tends to reduce total employment opportunities because of the greater labour-intensity activity in the L-sector. Expansion of the F-sector may also increase the rate of open unemployment through increasing the chance of acquiring a modern sector job and hence the incentive to switch jobs. This may be offset by a sufficient reduction in wage-rates, reducing the reward for securing such a job, But if the change were achieved by subsidies on the employment of labour, rather than changes in wage-rates, this offsetting would not occur.

By concentrating entirely on the modern sector, the approach may thus produce counterproductive solutions. Only if the modern sector could really be expanded to absorb the total labour force does it offer the possibility of a solution rather than an accentuation of the problem of poverty as well as unemployment. However, trends over time . . . combined with the character of F-technology . . . rule out the possibility of total F-sector absorption for many underdeveloped economies.

THE FACTOR-PROPORTIONS PROBLEM

The starting position of this analysis of the employment situation is that the neo-classical assumption of a range of technological possibilities is incorrect. Assuming complete technological fixity, with a unique ratio of investment to employment, then changing factor prices will have no effect on employment. Technological possibilities are not then represented by a smooth curved isoquant as in Figure 1, but by rigid proportions shown by a straight ray from the origin as in Figure 2. For any given amount of investment, say, OK, a unique amount of employment, Ou, will be generated, irrespective of factor prices. Thus total employment is determined by the rate of investment. Unemployment results if, given the ratio of investment to employment, the rate of investment falls below that level necessary to ensure full employment. In the diagram with investment OK, unemployment uL results. Since technology in the modern sector is developed in advanced countries for their factor proportions . . . it is likely that it will be too investment-intensive for full employment in underdeveloped countries.

In so far as there is more than one good and/or more than one process, factor proportions may not be rigidly determined, but free to vary according to the ratio in which different goods are produced (or processes used), and the factor proportions associated with the alternative goods/processes. However, the range of production possibilities may still be too narrow to allow full employment. This is shown in Figure 2b where, if the more labour-intensive techniques are adopted, unemployment ML none the less results.

The rigid factor proportions theory suggests two possible solutions to the problem:

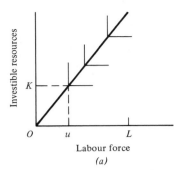
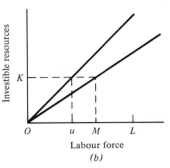

OL is total labour supply

FIGURE 2.

one, expansion of investible resources to encompass as many as possible of the unemployed; *two,* modification of the modern technology in a labour-intensive direction so as to fit with the availability of resources in underdeveloped countries.

The rigid factor-proportions theory is similar to the "distorted" prices in concentrating entirely on the modern sector, and assuming that anyone outside the sector is virtually unemployed. As with the distorted prices theory, the suggested solution may actually increase open unemployment as the F-sector expands and the chance of getting a job increases. Again, the strategy is only feasible if the investment rate can be increased and/or the technology sufficiently adapted to encompass the whole of the labour force.

ALTERNATIVE TECHNOLOGIES

Whereas the two previous approaches concentrate entirely on the F-sector, aiming to extend it to cover the whole economy, the alternative technology approach is concerned to improve the productivity and work opportunities of the L-sector, as well as modifying technology in the F-sector. The "distorted" factor price approach and the fixed factor proportions approach both assume that underdevelopment prevails in the L-sector and can only be eliminated by expanding the F-sector. In contrast, the alternative technology approach views activities in the L-sector as just as legitimate as those in the F-sector, and

sees the solution to the problem as improving opportunities there rather than the full-scale takeover by the F-sector. While measures of underemployment are highly relevant to the first two approaches, because they show the extent of the necessary expansion in the F-sector, they are irrelevant to the alternative technology approach. What is relevant to this approach is an examination of incomes, work and the technology in both sectors, and the interrelationship between the two, without any attempt to define people as *underemployed.*

The different approaches may be illustrated by returning to the previous representation. In Figure 3, the shaded area shows the direction of change suggested by the approaches. Figure 3*a* shows "distorted factor prices" and rigid technology solutions. Both involve an expansion of employment in the F-sector (in the distorted factor price case to be achieved by modifying factor prices, in the rigid factor proportions by modifying F-technology and increasing investment), and a reduction in average productivity in the F-sector (in the distorted factor prices case through inducing a changed selection of techniques in the sector as a result of the modified factor prices, in the rigid factor proportions through new technological developments in the F-sector). In both cases, open unemployment remains more or less the same since the effect of somewhat reduced average rewards is offset by increased F-employment opportunities. Figure 3*b* shows the alternative

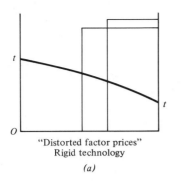
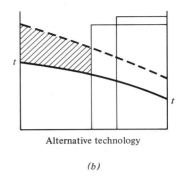

"Distorted factor prices"
Rigid technology

(a)

Alternative technology

(b)

FIGURE 3. Alternative technological strategies.

technology solution. It is two-pronged, involving an increase in employment in the F-sector and a reduction in its labour productivity, like the other approaches, to be achieved by modification of technology in that sector; but it also involves raising productivity in the L-sector. The gap between the sectors is reduced and the consequence is that open unemployment may be reduced since there is a reduced incentive to switch between the sectors, with the greater productivity of the L-sector.

III.F.3. Policy Implications—Note

Although this chapter has outlined some dimensions of the employment problem and has suggested broad strategies of employment creation, we are left with numerous specific policy questions that need to be clarified. It might first be thought that the malfunctioning of labor markets is a major cause of the employment problem. But empirical studies of labor market performance indicate that labor markets actually work reasonably well, with rational responses to incentives.[1] Frequently unemployment is sector specific because of segmented labor markets. An excess supply of labor may appear in one sector (for example, in bauxite mining in Jamaica), while a shortage of labor exists in another sector (sugar cane cutting). Labor may decide to forgo low-income employment opportunities and queue for the few high-income jobs available in a segmented labor market. Although market imperfections do exist (minimum wage laws, trade unions), it is not plausible to argue that, if only these imperfections were removed, wages would be reduced and then unemployment and underemployment would disappear. Policies other than the removal of labor distortions are required.

Policies designed for increasing the efficiency of labor markets are of limited significance compared with other major employment policies that focus on raising the demand for labor through greater output and higher output-elasticity of demand for labor, while easing the supply side of the problem through a slowing down in the hitherto fast growth of the labor force. Not labor market

[1]A. Berry and R. H. Sabot, "Labor Market Performance in Developing Countries: A Survey," *World Development,* November-December 1978, pp. 1199–1249; with extensive bibliography. See also Lyn Squire, "Labor Force, Employment, and Labor Markets in the Course of Development," *World Bank Staff Working Paper* No. 336, June 1979.

imbalance, but the entire set of development policies that affect the demand and supply sides of the labor problem should be of concern. Thus, all the remaining chapters will concentrate on the formulation of a set of employment policies by relating to the mobilization and allocation of investment resources, agricultural development, industrialization programs, and trade strategy.

At this point, however, it may be useful to offer some general principles underlying possible policy options for the better utilization of labor. Their validity will then be explored in greater detail in subsequent chapters.

a. If urban unemployment is to be reduced, policy measures must reduce the rural-urban drift. To this end, a reduction of urban-rural real income differentials would be most helpful; but this is probably the most difficult objective to achieve. According to the Todaro model of labor migration, the larger the gap between urban and rural nominal wages, the higher must be the urban unemployment rate before migration in excess of job opportunities ceases. As long as urban wages rise more rapidly than average rural incomes, rural-urban migration will continue in spite of rising levels of urban unemployment. All policies that would redress the imbalance between urban and rural income levels would therefore be desirable—urban wage restraint, adjustment of minimum wage rates, revision of the tax structure, a comprehensive national income and wages policy.

A number of institutional and political considerations, however, militate against the efficacy of these policies, and it is not realistic to expect any strong downward pressure on urban wages. An effective "wages policy" has proved difficult in the developed—let alone newly developing—countries.

b. If it is difficult to institute a "wages policy" that would increase urban employment, it is all the more important to emphasize the "supply side" of the problem. When the urban sector cannot absorb the inflow of labor from the rural sector, special consideration must be given to policies that will remove the causes of the rural "supply push" and help contain the labor force in rural areas. Urban problems are in a fundamental sense rural problems: urban "pull" must be offset by lessening the "push" through rural development.

The modern sector must avoid producing what can be produced in the rural sector—e.g., village handicraft employment should not be displaced if this entails the wasteful use of capital in the modern sector to produce an output which could be produced equally well by surplus labor. It is to be recalled that in Japan's case of successful development, both agriculture and village industry became more labor-intensive. There may also be a considerably greater scope for rural-based industry involving simple technology and the processing of agricultural materials.

Beyond this, however, a full-scale program of rural development is needed to absorb and retain large amounts of manpower. If the rural to urban migration is to be reduced, it is necessary to modify policies that have turned the terms of trade against the agricultural sector. Ceiling prices on foodstuffs, export taxes or restrictions on primary products, and tariff protection on industrial inputs and consumer goods have acted as disincentives to agricultural producers while they have artificially increased the urban-rural differential.

Efforts should also be made to disperse to the rural sector some of the amenities and public services now concentrated in urban areas. Readier access to such services as public utilities, health, education, and entertainment in the rural areas may amount to an increase in the rural social wage, and diminish the attractions of the city.

Of greatest consequence will be the type of strategy pursued for developing the agricultural sector. As elaborated in Chapter VII, the most important factor influencing a developing country's ability to absorb a growing labor force into productive employment is whether a labor-using, capital-saving type of approach to agricultural development is followed (as in Japan and Taiwan). For most developing countries, the employment potential in rural modernization can be greater than that of the modern urban sector—provided that the countries avoid implicit taxation of agriculture and "unduly labor displacing" measures in agriculture.

c. If the previous strategy of industrialization via import substitution has resulted in "urban bias"—that is, distortions that favor the urban, import-substituting, modern sector at the expense of the rural sector,[2] then in the future the promotion of nontraditional exports may allow a strategy of industrialization via export substitution that creates more employment, among other advantages. Chapter VIII discusses various policies—notably those connected with trade policy and foreign investment—that are needed to make export substitution effective.

The distortions in the price structure also create divergences between domestic and international prices that inhibit the country's exports. To the extent that the comparative advantage of the country lies in labor-intensive commodities, the employment-intensity of trade can be raised by "getting prices right" and by establishing an efficient commodity composition of exports.

d. More effort is also needed to devise a range of technological choices that are superior to the country's indigenous traditional technology but are not as advanced and labor-saving as are the modern machines and equipment that have been imported from advanced industrial countries. As discussed in Chapter V, the transfer of "appropriate" technology has important consequences for employment in both the urban industrial sector and the rural agricultural sector.

The choice of a more labor-intensive production technique may, of course, conflict with other investment criteria—in particular, the maximum absorption of labor may yield only a low return per unit of capital and not maximize the future rate of growth in output.

The crucial consideration is the emphasis on devising new technology that is "capital-stretching" in an efficient way—that is, the labor-intensive equipment should raise the labor/capital ratio without also raising the capital/output ratio. A more appropriate technology would in effect retain the essential quality of the tool element in physical equipment without the superfluous labor-saving appendages of the advanced technology of industrial countries.

To lessen the bias toward relatively capital-intensive techniques, it is again necessary to stress the removal of factor price distortions. Given that there is a positive elasticity of substitution of labor against capital,[3] it would become less profitable to use capital-intensive technologies if interest rates were increased, foreign exchange became more expensive in terms of home currency, and the increases in urban wages were restrained.

e. As long as labor is induced to migrate from the rural sector and the manufacturing sector cannot absorb labor in sufficient quantities, it will be necessary for labor to seek employment in the tertiary sector. Labor has done so in many of the LDCs, and employment in services and commerce has actually risen more rapidly than in other sectors.

From the standpoint of providing an employment outlet, it is therefore advisable not to promote too rapid an increase in efficiency in employment practices in the service sector. As remarked by Professor Galenson,[4] the pushcarts should not be too readily replaced by the supermarket; the bicycles by the trucks; a casual but large labor force by a permanent and stable but smaller labor force. The inefficient use of labor in the tertiary sector will not, of course, have the undesirable cost effects that would occur if this were done in the import-replacement or export sectors. In the production of nontradable commodities it may therefore be important to be unimportant about seeking the least cost combination of factors when this would displace labor.

[3]For a careful empirical study that suggests that considerable substitution possibilities exist in a number of manufacturing industries, see Howard Pack, "The Employment-Output Trade-Off in LDCs—A Microeconomic Approach," *Oxford Economic Papers*, November 1974.

[4]W. Galenson, "Economic Development and the Sectoral Expansion of Employment," *International Labour Review*, January–June 1963, pp. 505–19.

[2]Michael Lipton, "Urban Bias and Rural Planning," in Paul Streeten and Michael Lipton (eds.), *The Crisis of Indian Planning*, London, 1968, pp. 89–95.

Emphasizing that "Asian countries will be forced to develop the labor-intensive sectors if jobs are to be created for the increasing waves of youngsters coming into the labor market," Oshima has stated that

the nonagricultural labor-intensive sector is very large, perhaps engaging two-thirds to three-fourths of the nonagricultural labor force. It is a sector that provides employment using the least amount of capital, in terms of capital efficiency uses the less scarce type of capital and saving, requires material inputs which are domestically produced, utilizes labor not appropriate for modern industries, and produces goods of the traditional type, consumed by lower-income families located in various parts of the country instead of being concentrated in the cities. It is an excellent complement to modern industrialization for underdeveloped countries where modern types of inputs and factors are scarce—whether these be capital and savings, skills, infrastructure, inputs, etc.[5]

An illustrative OECD study calculated that on average in the developing countries the manufacturing sector employs 20 percent of the labor force, and the unemployment rate and underemployment rate together average 25 percent. The increase in labor productivity is assumed to be 2.5 percent a year. In order to absorb an increase in the labor force growing at 3 percent a year (a conservatively low estimate), industrial production would have to increase at the exceptional rate of 18 percent a year—a rate beyond the achievement of any LDC. To eradicate within a decade the existing rural and urban unemployment and underemployment it would have to increase by 30 to 35 percent a year. Not surprisingly, the report concludes: "Thus eradication of general underemployment through the development of industrial employment is a practical impossibility in the medium term."[6]

f. If open unemployment persists and its unfavorable social and political repercussions

are to be avoided, the government will itself have to provide employment opportunities. On public work projects, or elsewhere in the public sector, labor may then be receiving a wage greater than its marginal product. Thus, there comes about in the public sector a situation similar to the disguised unemployment that exists in agriculture (in the sense of the real wage being greater than the marginal product of labor). But if it is decided that labor should not remain unnecessarily idle, then in a labor surplus economy the labor will have to be used even to the point where its social marginal product becomes zero.

g. Finally, more attention must be given to the "supply side" of the problem in terms of population control policy and the "outputs" of the country's educational system. Growth in the labor force is a derivative of the population growth rate and the labor participation rate. But since there is about a 15-year lag between a decline in the birth rate and a decline in the labor force entry rate, any deceleration of population growth can only have long-run effects and is not a relevant instrument for short-term policy. Investment in human capital may, however, influence employment more readily. In this connection, some relevant points will be noted in Chapter IX on human-resource development.

From even this summary listing of policy implications, it should be apparent that employment policies make sense only within the context of an overall development strategy. An integrated set of employment policies has to provide for the mobilization and allocation of domestic and foreign resources so as to achieve more labor-intensive output growth, investment in human capital, a more labor-intensive industrialization program, an agricultural program that is itself labor-absorbing and also contributory to industrialization, access to more appropriate technology, and the slowing down of population growth.

The range of policies extends from measures that can be instituted immediately to other measures that can take effect only in the long run. With respect to employment in Africa, for example, Todaro has proposed the following short-run policies: (1) the elimina-

---

[5]Harry T. Oshima, "Labor-Force 'Explosion' and The Labor-Intensive Sector in Asian Growth," *Economic Development and Cultural Change,* January 1971, p. 178.

[6]Quoted in Jonathan Power, "Why Going Back to the Land Is the Only Hope for the Third World," *The London Times,* October 18, 1974, p. 18.

tion of present factor-price distortions, (2) the establishment of a "dual" wage structure through the use of wage subsidies in some combination with a policy of wage restraint, (3) the immediate creation of new types of employment opportunities through various voluntary agreements, and (4) the restriction of excess emigration through the use of moral exhortation to return to the land, the adoption of forced controls on the movement of people, or the establishment of urban labor exchanges to regulate and control the process of job placement. The most important medium-term strategies include (1) the estab-lishment of a comprehensive incomes policy, (2) the acceleration of rates of industrial and urban output growth, and (3) the intensification of efforts to stimulate agricultural and rural development. Long-run policies would include the establishment and maintenance of an effective program to limit rapid population growth, and efforts to plan for the eventual development of domestic labor-intensive capital goods industries.[7]

[7]Michael P. Todaro, "Income Expectations, Rural-Urban Migration and Emloyment in Africa," *International Labour Review*, November 1971, pp. 396, 402, 407.

Comment

Some three decades after Sir Arthur Lewis formulated his dual sector model, development economists recognize that the nature and causes of the employment problem have changed, and so too must strategies and policies to provide additional employment opportunities and more effective utilization of labor resources. Instead of concentrating on an expansion of modern-sector jobs, much more attention is being given to improvement in productivity and the utilization of labor outside the modern large-scale sector. But, as emphasized in the foregoing selections, there is no unique "employment problem" in LDCs; instead, there is a syndrome of problems that require for their solution the coordinated pursuit of a number of policies affecting prices, the level of investment, technological change, the foreign trade sector, the agricultural sector, the informal sector, government expenditure, education, and training. All the chapters in this book therefore have some bearing on the employment problem, and they should be read with their implications for employment policy in mind.

Employment policies are considered in more detail in the following works: Paul Bairoch, *Urban Unemployment in Developing Countries* (1976); Mark Blaug, *Education and the Employment Problem in Developing Countries* (1976); H. Bruton, "Economic Development and Labor Use: A Review" *World Development* (December 1973); H. Chenery et al., *Redistribution with Growth* (1974); ILO series of studies on employment strategies for Colombia (1973), Ceylon (1974), Kenya (1977), Iran (1973), Philippines (1974), Sudan (1978); J. Mouly and E. Costa, *Employment Policies in Developing Countries* (1974); A. K. Sen, *Employment, Technology and Development* (1975); Lyn Squire, *Employment Policy and Developing Countries* (1982); Guy Standing, *Labour Force Participation and Development* (1978); Frances Stewart (ed.), *Work, Income, and Inequality: Payments Systems in the Third World* (1982); Frances Stewart, "Employment Policies," in Robert Cassen and Margaret Wolfson (eds.), *Planning for Growing Populations* (1978).

CHAPTER IV

Mobilizing
Domestic
Resources

Even though labor may be abundant, the output of an LDC remains limited by a shortage of capital. It is widely recognized that the LDCs must make additional efforts to mobilize and achieve effective use of their internal resources. The mobilization of domestic resources— along with the mobilization of external resources (to be discussed in the next chapter)—requires policies to facilitate the process of capital accumulation. Many economists emphasize capital accumulation as the major factor governing the rate of development. Professor Rostow, for example, specifies a rise in the rate of productive investment to over 10 percent of national income as a necessary requirement for a country's take-off.

Similarly, in presenting his model of a dual economy, Sir Arthur Lewis contends that

The central problem in the theory of economic development is to understand the process by which a community which was previously saving and investing 4 or 5 per cent of its national income or less, converts itself into an economy where voluntary saving is running at about 12 to 15 per cent of national income or more. This is the central problem because the central fact of economic development is rapid capital accumulation (including knowledge and skills with capital).[1]

The discussion of technological dualism (III.B.2) also implied that development requires primarily large amounts of capital investment, especially in the underdeveloped sector.

Certainly there has been no tendency among development economists to underestimate the importance of capital. On the contrary, it has been stressed so much that a reaction has set in, and there is a strong counterview that the role of capital has received excessive attention to the neglect of other essential components of the development process. The materials in section IV.A present opposing views on the legitimacy of emphasizing capital as the key variable determining the rate of development. Since capital-output ratios have figured promi-

---

[1]W. Arthur Lewis, "Economic Development with Unlimited Supplies of Labour," *The Manchester School,* May 1954.

nently in the discussion of capital accumulation, the Note on capital output ratios clarifies various interpretations of the capital-output ratio, and at the same time levies a number of criticisms that restrict the use of a capital-output ratio in practice (selection IV.A.2).

To the extent that an increase in the rate of investment is necessary or desired, a developing country must mobilize the required savings. The Note in section IV.B focuses on this issue by outlining the various sources of capital formation. In examining these sources, we should assess each source of capital formation from the wider standpoint of how its contribution to the flow of resources for developmental purposes can be intensified.

Of increasing interest are the problems of financial development—the manner in which financial institutions and financial policies may help overcome the shortage of capital and influence a country's pattern of development. Economic theory has been generally conducted in "real" terms, such as national product in physical units, production functions, and capital-output ratios. And yet, for an understanding of the process of development we must consider how the financial superstructure and the real infrastructure interact, and what are the effects of such interaction on development.

The selections in section IV.C ask some basic questions about the contribution of financial development to economic development. What are the alternative techniques available to each country for mobilizing its economic surplus and channeling capital flows? What are the relationships between finance and the rate and pattern of development? These general questions should help to place in perspective the empirical studies of particular financial institutions or the financial development of individual countries.

It is especially important to consider the need for more efficient capital markets to improve the quantity and quality of capital formation. "Financial repression" is characteristic of inefficient capital markets and the consequence is the substitution of direct, microeconomic measures that distort prices and the allocation and mobilization of resources.

Although much of the discussion in this chapter is designed to indicate various ways of mobilizing resources for developmental expenditures without causing inflation, many countries have in practice desired a higher rate of investment than could be maintained by non-inflationary sources of finance. Recourse to the substitute method of monetary expansion and credit creation has become common. Increased spending of an inflationary sort is therefore an important issue of development policy. On this issue, however, there are marked differences of opinion regarding the causes and consequences of inflation.

We try in section IV.D to sort out these differences and reach some assessment of the effects of inflation in LDCs. To do this, we examine in analytical terms the main forces and consequences of inflation. Why are the LDCs so prone to inflation? How might inflation be stopped? Would it do more harm than good to stop inflation in a developing country?

Against the background of this general analysis, we also give specific attention to the problem of inflation in Latin America. The selections in this section center on the issues between the traditional "monetarist" view of inflation and the contrasting "structuralist" view. Different interpretations of the causes of inflation lead naturally to divergent conclusions on policies for curbing inflation. While the orthodox prescription has been to restrain demand by the exercise of monetary and fiscal discipline, this policy is criticized by "structuralists" as being concerned with only the "propagating" factors of inflation or the "symptoms" instead of the underlying real structural causes. In contrast, the structural position looks to the supply side of the problem and stresses the need for social and economic reforms to correct basic structural imbalances.

There is no denying that underdeveloped countries are especially prone to inflationary pressures, and that the policies available to an underdeveloped country for effectively controlling inflation are more limited than those in an advanced country. What remains controversial, however, is whether these inflationary pressures encourage or inhibit development. This issue is discussed in section IV.D with arguments presented both in favor of and against the method of development through inflation.

Besides the usual points advanced in favor of inflation, consideration is given to the following special contentions: inflation permits the employment of underemployed workers; monetary or credit expansion is necessary to allow the "development authorities" to bid resources away from consumption; in the early stages of inflation, the "money illusion" may induce factors of production to work more intensively; the period of inflation may be short, since it will increase investment which, in turn, will expand total output, and a large portion of the increment in output may then be saved and taxed to offset the rise in investment; and none of the alternative methods of financing a rise in investment is any less free of hardships.

As for the case against inflation, the following arguments are especially persuasive: inflation has harmful effects on the efficient allocation of resources, being particularly detrimental in creating distortions in investment patterns; balance of payments pressures result from the adverse impact on exports, the spillover into imports, and the discouragement of foreign investment; the volume of resources available for domestic investment may actually fall as voluntary savings decline and incentives are diminished; and the government lacks the power to constrain the inflation and prevent the pressures from becoming progressively severe.

IV.A. THE ROLE OF CAPITAL

IV.A.1. Capital Accumulation and Development*

The general rate of development is always limited by shortage of productive factors. If any one scarce factor associated with under-development should be singled out, it would be capital. The final goal of development programming is, therefore, to find the best way of breaking the vicious circle between capital shortage and under-development and to design the most efficient and optimum rate of capital accumulation.

It would be an over-simplification, of course, to regard economic development as a matter of capital accumulation alone. Other things are needed in addition, such as entrepreneurship and training of workers and public administrators. Yet these are seldom possible without some increase in the stock of capital. Therefore capital accumulation may very well be regarded as the core process by which all other aspects of growth are made possible.

Capital increases by investment, and more investment necessitates more savings or foreign assistance. Foreign assistance, if not in the form of grants, means some burden in the future. The extent to which foreign loans can be serviced and repaid will ultimately depend on what can be saved at home in the future. Domestic savings are, therefore, the more reliable source of investment to break the vicious circle of poverty and under-development. But domestic savings can be increased only by a sacrifice in consumption which has to be compared with the future increases in consumption it promises. Investment, moreover, yields different results, depending on the industries in which it is made. In order, therefore, for the government of an under-developed country to design an appropriate

*From United Nations, ECAFE, *Programming Techniques for Economic Development.* Report of the First Group of Experts on Programming Techniques, Bangkok, 1960, pp. 8–13. Reprinted by permission.

plan for development, it must be informed of the quantitative aspects of savings and investment, and their effects on production and consumption.

These quantitative aspects are of crucial importance in determining the most desirable rate of development. It is important, for one thing, particularly when population is growing rapidly, to estimate the rate of development that would be needed to bring about an improvement in *per capita* income or a high rate of employment for the growing work force. Another element which may play a role in estimating a minimum rate of development is the necessity to give a certain minimum size to some projects in order that they are at all economically sound. In some industries where so-called "indivisibilities" play a role, there are such minimum sizes of projects. For the country as a whole, this may mean that only a "big push," as it has been called, can really help to start the process of development. Although this may produce results which appear ambitious in the light of current efforts, it provides a fair indication of the tasks involved in the planning effort.

Whatever the initial approach, there are some useful concepts which should be borne in mind in planning the rate of development. These concepts may conveniently be described in terms of investment. There is, first, the concept of a *minimum rate of investment,* which measures the rate needed to prevent *per capita* income from falling in the face of population growth. A rate of investment somewhat above this minimum is the lowest target at which any plan should aim, even though this may involve a heavy effort when population is growing rapidly. For some countries this may be a rate that can be easily attained on the basis of an effort which does not require any fundamental policy decisions, any changes in attitudes or behaviour patterns, or any improvements in techniques, skills and methods of business or public administration. For these countries, the minimum rate of investment is clearly too low, and is useful only for reference.

A second concept of use in this context is that of a *practical maximum rate of investment*. In theory a maximum rate of investment may refer to a level of capital accumulation which involves saving and investing at least all income above, say, a subsistence level. Clearly, such a maximum is of no practical significance. A practicable maximum may, therefore, be determined differently in the light of the extent to which the population would be willing to accept austerity now, so as to enjoy a higher standard of living in the future. The planner must form his best judgment as to what this practical maximum would be. The rate just defined above is the one to be determined by an evaluation of people's potential propensity to save.

A third concept is that of the highest rate of investment consistent with *absorptive capacity*. Absorptive capacity depends on natural resources, taxes, the labour supply, the level of labour, technical and managerial skills, entrepreneurial capacity, the efficiency of public administration, the extent of "technology-mindedness" of the population, and so on. Such capacity sets a limit to the amount of efficient investment physically possible, and although it can itself be increased through further investment, it does effectively limit the rate of development possible, particularly in the short run. Maximum absorptive capacity may, of course, permit of a higher rate of investment than that allowed by the ability of the population to save. In this case, it would be the role of an ideal international policy to fill the gap and to raise investment to the highest level consistent with absorptive capacity. On the other hand, where absorptive capacity is below the practicable rate of savings, both national and international policies should be directed towards raising such capacity. These policies would then constitute the initial phase of a long-term plan.

Thus, one of the logical ways to start planning the general rate of economic development is first to estimate the amount of domestic savings and capital imports that could be expected with no change in economic policies; then to calculate the rate of growth that this level of savings and investment would provide; and finally to compare it with the desired rate of growth. Usually, the ratio of saving to income is fairly stable over long periods of time, and these saving-income ratios are lower in under-developed countries (under 10 per cent) than in higher advanced countries (about 15 per cent). Any empirical estimation of this ratio must start with the observation of the rates of savings experienced by the country in the recent past. The estimates may be based on data for incomes and the savings of households, business and government, or domestic investment *minus* capital imports. It may also be possible to base the estimates on the experiences of comparable countries, keeping in mind the differences in income levels.

After estimating the current rate of savings, the crucial question will be what amount of net national output may be expected from the investment to be made on the basis of the estimated savings. A number of studies have been made on the amount of capital required to increase output by one unit per annum in each sector of the economy and for a national economy as a whole. This amount is called the "capital-output ratio," or "capital coefficient." . . .

Although the capital-output ratio is usually calculated as the "average" capital-output ratio, what really matters is the "marginal" or "incremental" capital-output ratio: we need information on the capital required to *increase* the national output. If we want to increase output by 20 and estimate the capital-output ratio as 4, then the required addition to the capital stock, to be provided by new investment, is 80. Evidently the figure 4 in this example stands for the "incremental capital-output ratio."

Given estimates of the current rate of savings and the capital-output ratio, the rate of economic growth, in terms of national output, could be projected in the following way. If the current level of national output is

TABLE 1. Rate of Economic Growth in Terms of National Output

National Output (1)	Saving Ratio (2)	Saving (3)	Investment (4)	Capital-Output Ratio (5)	Increase in National Output (6)
1,000	0.06	60	60	4	15

$$\text{Growth rate (G)} = \frac{(6)}{(1)} = \frac{15}{1,000} = \frac{(2)}{(5)} = \frac{0.06}{4} = 0.015$$

1,000, and the saving ratio is 0.06, domestic savings would be 60, which may be invested to generate the increased national output. [See Table 1]. With a capital-output ratio of 4, this amount of savings and investment could generate an increase in national output of 15, not more. An increase in national output of, say, 20 will not be possible, because the amount of investment required for this purpose is 80, which exceeds the current savings of 60. Hence, the increase in output warranted by the savings of 60 is 60 ÷ 4 = 15, which gives the growth rate of 1.5 per cent in national output. The rate of growth in national output can thus be calculated by dividing the saving ratio by the capital-output ratio.

This method of projecting the future level of national output can be checked by other ways of forecasting, e.g., extrapolation of past figures, If the projected national income shows a lower growth rate than actual income did in the past, it may be that the saving ratio has been underestimated or the capital-output ratio overestimated. If the ratios are right, a slowing down of economic growth must be expected. Another check would be to divide the projected national output by the numbers in the active labour force, to obtain an index of the average productivity of labour in the future. If this index does not rise as much as the past trend, the estimates of parameters should again be reconsidered. If they are correct, inefficiency or unemployment must be expected in the future, unless measures are taken to prevent them.

The rate of growth of an economy will be somewhat less than shown by the preceding calculations, if the gestation period of the investment envisaged is large. The calculation above tacitly assumes that capital created by the investment in one period can be used productively in the following period. If, however, the gestation period of some investment project is longer than one year, say three years, then capital available for productive use will not increase before three years. At that time, the level of national income will be higher, and hence the rise in production, as a percentage of total national income, is somewhat less. This means that the extension of the gestation period has the same effect as the decline in the saving ratio, or the increase in the value of the capital-output ratio. If this is the case, then the rate of economic growth computed in the preceding way must be adjusted downward. Needless to say, a lengthening of this time lag has further adverse effects, owing to the additional postponement of the fruits of investment.

If such projections of current trends show no significant rise in the people's standard of living, there is a definite need to increase the growth rate of national output. Suppose that the expected population increase is 1.5 per cent a year, the saving ratio 6 per cent, and the capital-output ratio 4. This will leave the standard of living unchanged, and represents the minimum rate of investment as defined [above]. If the *per capita* national income must increase by, say, 2 per cent a year, the national income must increase by 1.5 + 2.0 = 3.5 per cent every year. This means that, with the same capital-output ratio, the saving ratio must be increased from 0.06 to 0.14, requiring a considerable adjustment in policy measures. If such a sudden rise in the saving ratio is difficult to achieve, the targets for improvements in living standard must be lowered to what was called ... the practical maximum rate of investment.

IV.A.2. Criticisms of the Capital-Output Ratio—Note

A capital-output ratio is frequently employed to estimate the amount of investment needed to achieve a certain rate of growth in income. This was done explicitly in ECAFE's calculations of capital requirements (IV.A.1). A definite causal relationship between the growth of capital and of output, however, cannot be as readily assumed as the foregoing selection would imply. And it is misleading to suppose that the whole of any increase in output is due simply to capital accumulation.

Many conceptual difficulties and statistical pitfalls surround the derivation and use of capital-output ratios. Even after it is decided which of the several possible definitions of "capital" and "output" are best to use, and some solution to the problem of valuation is accepted, there still remain ambiguities. It is first necessary to distinguish between the average and the marginal capital-output ratio. The average ratio is the value of the total stock of capital divided by total annual income; the marginal—or incremental—ratio for the entire economy is the value of the addition to capital (net investment) divided by the addition to income (net national income). The marginal ratio need not, of course, equal the average ratio, and even though any change in the average ratio may be expected to be slow, the marginal ratio can vary a great deal more.

In framing a development plan, it is common practice to calculate the amount of additional capital required to produce a one unit increase in annual output at the margin. For this purpose, a marginal capital-output ratio is used. Net investment is estimated over the plan-period; the increase in net output (or income) is estimated between the year before the plan-period and the last year of the plan. All measurements are made at the same price level. The use of a marginal capital-output ratio in this fashion has been inspired to a large extent by the Harrod-Domar theory of growth, which relates a country's rate of growth of income to its savings-income ratio and marginal capital-output ratio.[1] The Harrod-Domar analysis, however, relates to an advanced economy, and it seeks an answer to the question of how much national income would have to grow to induce sufficient investment to maintain this rate of growth in income. For a poor country, the relevant problem is not that of sustaining a certain rate of growth, but rather the prior task of initiating or generating a higher growth rate in the first place.

Moreover, it is important to be clear whether all other productive factors that must cooperate with capital are also assumed to increase when capital increases. In an advanced economy an adequate supply of cooperant factors is likely to exist. The institu-

[1]Evsey Domar, "Expansion and Employment," *American Economic Review,* March 1947, pp. 34–5; "The Problem of Capital Formation," *American Economic Review,* December 1948, pp. 777–94; "Economic Growth: An Econometric Approach," *American Economic Review, Papers and Proceedings,* May 1952, pp. 479–95; R. F. Harrod, "An Essay in Dynamic Theory," *Economic Journal,* March 1939, pp. 14–33; *Towards a Dynamic Economics,* London, 1948; W. J. Baumol, *Economic Dynamics,* New York, 1951, Chap. 4.

tional, political, and social prerequisites for development also already exist. When using the marginal capital-output ratio under these conditions, it is reasonable to make a *mutatis mutandis* assumption that the supply of other necessary factors is forthcoming. But in a poor country where the cooperant factors tend to be in short supply, and the other prerequisites for development may not yet exist, it is not legitimate to consider an increase in capital as a sufficient condition for an expansion in output. Even though investment may be a necessary condition, an increase in output may still not be produced unless other conditions are also fulfilled along with the increase in capital supply. Since an expansion in output depends on many factors of which capital formation is only one, greater output may require changes in other factors along with an increase in capital. Or output may even increase independently of investment. Even if we accept the assumption that there is a fixed relationship between capital and output as determined by technical factors, it does not follow that we can infer from this relationship that only capital is needed to increase output. We must also consider explicitly the effect of other variables on output—for example, the supply of trained manpower, entrepreneurship, institutional arrangements, attitudes, etc. To ignore these other variables or simply to assume that accommodating changes occur, and then to attribute all of the output-increment to investment, is to take a too mechanical—and too easy—view of the changes that are necessary for an increase in output.

On the other hand, exclusive attention to a capital-output ratio may exaggerate the need for investment, insofar as output may be increased by changes in other factors without requiring a sizeable amount of investment, or even any additional capital. If, for instance, unutilized capacity exists, it is possible to raise output with the fuller utilization of the existing capital stock or without requiring much more capital. Or there may be considerable opportunity to raise output by applying better methods of production to existing plant. To avoid taking either an overoptimistic view of what can be accomplished by capital accumulation alone, or an overpessimistic view of how much investment is needed, we should guard against a too simple use of capital-output ratios.

For the purpose of clearly recognizing the changing circumstances that may occur when additions to the capital stock are made, it is helpful to distinguish between the "net marginal capital-output ratio" and the "adjusted marginal capital-output ratio."[2] The net ratio interprets the marginal capital-output ratio as net of any changes in other factors; it considers the capital-output ratio with a *ceteris paribus* assumption—the supplies of all other factors are held constant. The adjusted ratio, however, refers to what the capital-output ratio would be if it were adjusted to a given specific increase in the supply of other factors; it assumes that investment is accompanied by changes in other output-yielding variables. For a given increment in output, the net marginal capital-output ratio is higher than the adjusted marginal capital-output ratio. Capital requirements will therefore be underestimated if they are initially based on an adjusted marginal capital-output ratio, but the other output-yielding factors do not actually accommodate themselves to the growth of capital as expected.

In calculating capital requirements, a development plan usually concentrates on an overall or global capital-output ratio for the entire economy. But this ratio depends on capital-output ratios in the various sectors of the economy, with the overall ratio being an average of the sectoral ratios, weighted by the increases in sectoral outputs. Since the overall ratio will be affected by the changing composition of output and investment among the several sectors, it is essential to analyze the capital-output relationships at the sectoral level.

Recognizing the problems raised above, W. B. Reddaway has offered a summary of what needs clarification when considering a

---

[2]Such a distinction is suggested by Harvey Leibenstein, *Economic Backwardness and Economic Growth,* New York, 1957, p. 178.

marginal capital-output ratio for a sector. He states that it would be desirable to divide the increase in output for a sector between two dates into these components.[3]

Output. (i) Increase due to better methods applied to old plant, involving little or no net capital expenditure (called P for progress). (ii) Changes due to fuller (or lower) utilization of old plant, as a reflection of changes in demand (called D). (iii) Changes due to introduction of double-shifts, etc. (S). (iv) Changes due to better weather (W). (v) Changes of the kind for which a certain relationship between capital and output may reasonably be assumed as "given" by technical factors—at least if we assume a fixed number of shifts, fairly full utilization, and no shortage of labor; the bringing into use of new steel mills is a good example. If the capital cost of these is x and the capital-output ratio in a new mill is r, then the increase in annual output $= x/r$.

Investment. Investment in the period will consist of x, plus any capital expenditure designed to save labor without increasing output (M for "modernization") and plus (or minus) an adjustment for the difference between expenditure on construction in the period and completion (L for "lag").

Observed Capital-Output Ratio. If we work from historical statistics (or from figures for future years included in a plan) the traditional marginal capital-output ratio for a sector is then equal to

$$\frac{x + M + L}{\dfrac{x}{r} + P + D + S + W}$$

If we consider only the first term in the numerator and the first term in the denominator—ignoring changes in M, L, P. D, S, and W—we are then using the capital-output ratio in an oversimplified way. Only if these other changes are small relative to x and x/r can the marginal capital-output ratio be considered approximately equal to r. But this is to treat the ratio as if it were simply a technical relationship applicable to a new plant; in practice, the actual ratio is likely to differ from r, depending on the values of the other terms in the above ratio.[4] Although M, D, S, and W may be relatively small, P will not be insignificant if there are large opportunities for increasing output by methods which involve negligible amounts of investment, and L will not be small if much of the period's investment goes into projects that are not completed during the period. When P is significant, the observed marginal capital-output ratio will be lower than if simply r is estimated; and when L is significant, because new investment projects take a long time to complete and considerable construction is started in the period, then the observed ratio will be higher than simply r. These considerations caution us against assuming that the marginal ·capital-output ratio is constant, even at the sectoral level.

At the aggregate level, the difficulties are compounded. Even in the simplest (but most special) of cases—namely, production coefficients fixed in all sectors and relatively small values for all the other variables that might affect output—the overall marginal capital-output ratio will still not be fixed, since sectoral output may vary with changes in demand. More generally, the overall ratio will vary according to a number of conditions, some of which may allow only a small additional income to be generated when more capital is accumulated, while others may contribute to a large increment in output. Thus, the following conditions will tend to make the capital-output ratio high: the sectoral pattern of investment is biased toward heavy users of capital, such as public utilities, public works, housing, industry rather than agriculture, and heavy industry rather than light industry; there is excess capacity in the utilization of capital; other resources are limited, and capital is substituted for these limitational factors; capital is long-lived; the rate of technological and organizational progress is low; and investment is for completely new

[3]W. B. Reddaway, *The Development of the Indian Economy,* Homewood, 1962, pp. 207–8.

[4]Ibid., pp. 208–9.

units of production rather than simply for extensions of existing plant.

In contrast, the marginal capital-output ratio will be lower when the composition of output is biased toward labor-intensive commodities, the average life of capital is shorter, the rate of technological and organizational progress is high, and when some capital expenditure allows fuller use of previously unutilized capacity, increases the productivity of labor, allows capital-saving innovations, opens up new natural resources, or permits the realization of economies of scale.

From such considerations, we must conclude that the marginal capital-output ratio is unlikely to be constant over time. A projected ratio must be estimated over the period for which investment requirements are being calculated, and it may then turn out that there is a wide discrepancy between the actual ratio and the projected ratio.

IV.A.3. The Place of Capital in Economic Progress*

Capital occupies a position so dominant in the economic theory of production and distribution that it is natural to assume that it should occupy an equally important place in the theory of economic growth. In most of the recent writings of economists, whether they approach the subject historically (e.g., in an attempt to explain how the industrial revolution started) or analytically (e.g., in models of an expanding economy) or from the side of policy (e.g., in the hope of accelerating the development of backward countries), it is the process of capital accumulation that occupies the front of the stage. There is an unstated assumption that growth hinges on capital accumulation, and that additional capital would either promote or facilitate a more rapid rate of economic development even in circumstances which no one would describe as involving a shortage of capital.

Yet there seems no reason to suppose that capital accumulation does by itself exercise so predominant an influence on economic development. In most industrialized communi-

*From A. K. Cairncross, "The Place of Capital in Economic Progress," in L. H. Dupriez (ed.), *Economic Progress,* Papers and Proceedings of a Round Table held by the International Economic Association, Louvain, 1955, pp. 235, 236–7, 245–8; Cairncross, *Factors in Economic Development,* George Allen and Unwin, London, 1962, pp. 111–14. Reprinted by permission.

ties the rate of capital accumulation out of savings is equal to about 10 per cent of income. If one were to assume that innovation came to a standstill and that additional investment could nevertheless yield an average return of 5 per cent, the consequential rate of increase in the national income would normally be no more than ½ per cent per annum. We are told that the national income has in fact been rising in such communities at a rate of 2–3 per cent per annum. On this showing, capital accumulation could account for, at most, one-quarter of the recorded rate of economic "progress." Nor were things very different in the nineteenth century. . . .

Even this way of putting things exaggerates the rôle of capital in economic development. For the yield on additional capital would rarely be as high as 5 per cent if there were not a discrepancy between the existing stock of capital and the stock appropriate to the existing state of technique. If innovation in the broadest sense of the term were at a standstill, accumulation would continue until the rate of interest fell to a point at which saving ceased. The sole object of accumulation in those circumstances would be to take advantage of the progressive cheapening of capital in order to introduce more roundabout methods of production, not to keep pace with current developments in technique.

Ordinary observation suggests, however, that the scope for investment *in industry* to take advantage merely of lower rates of interest, once the long-term rate is below 5 per cent, is extremely limited, although there may be a good deal more scope in other directions where capital charges form an unusually high proportion of the final cost (e.g., in the erection of dwelling-houses, public buildings and the like).

The contribution of capital to economic progress is not, however, confined to the usufruct of additional capital assets, similar to those already in existence. It embraces three distinct processes. First, a greater abundance of capital permits the introduction of more roundabout methods of production or, to be more precise, of a more roundabout pattern of consumption. This covers the freer use of capital instruments in the production of a given product, the use of more durable instruments, and a change in the pattern of consumption in favour of goods and services with relatively high capital charges per unit cost. Secondly, the accumulation of capital is a normal feature of economic expansion, however originating. This is the process normally referred to as widening, as opposed to deepening, the structure of production. It may accompany industrialization, or any change in the balance between industries that makes additional demands on capital; or it may accompany an extension of the market associated with population growth, more favourable terms of trade, or the discovery of additional natural resources. Thirdly, additional capital may be required to allow technical progress to take place. It may either finance the discovery of what was not known before or more commonly, the adaptation of existing knowledge so as to allow of its commercial exploitation through some innovation in product, process or material.

Now of these three, the first is generally of subordinate importance; it is unusual for capital accumulation, unassisted by other factors, to bring about a rapid increase in income. The second, which also abstracts from any change in technology, accounts for nearly all the capital accumulation that has taken place in the past; forces making for rapid increase in income may be largely nullified unless they are reinforced by a parallel increase in capital. It is to the third, however, that one must usually look—at least in an advanced industrial country—for the main influences governing the rate of growth of real income per head. Whatever may have been true in the past, it is now technical innovation—the introduction of new and cheaper ways of doing things—that dominates economic progress. Whether technical innovation, in the sectors of the economy in which it occurs, makes large demands on capital is, however, very doubtful. Many innovations can be given effect to in the course of capital replacement out of depreciation allowances, which, in an expanding economy, may be fully as large as net savings. Others may actually reduce the stock of capital required. Existing buildings and existing machines can often be modified so as to allow most of the advantages of the new techniques to be gained. It is economic expansion, far more than technological change, that is costly in capital. . . .

Given that the national income is increasing, whether under the influence of technical progress, population growth, or some other factor, there is good reason to expect that additional capital will be required in some important sectors on a comparable scale. Habits of thrift—a phrase that must now be stretched to include not only the practices of corporations in adding to reserves but the propensities of Finance Ministers—appear to admit of capital accumulation at a rate of about 2½ per cent per annum, and this has in recent years been close to the rate of growth of income. Provided, therefore, that the capital requirements of industry—the main sector left out of account—are also increasing at this rate, the capital-income ratio will remain constant and the whole of the country's thrift will be effectively mobilized. There can be no guarantee, however, that industry's requirements will in fact mount at this rate, even in the long run. In the short run, for reasons that are familiar, the whole process of capital accumulation may be thrown out of gear.

Now the significant feature of this argument is that it hinges far more on the indirect than on the direct demand for capital. It assumes that technical progress operates largely in independence of capital accumulation and that capital is needed, not in order to allow innovation to be made but in order to consolidate the improvements in income that innovation brings about. Moreover, it implies that if, at any time, the process of innovation creates a bulge in the demand for capital, it should be possible to adapt the pattern of investment so as to accommodate the high-yielding requirements of industry by displacing part of the larger, but less remunerative, requirements of house-building, stock-building, and so forth.

It is hardly necessary to show that this implication may be mistaken. Public policy may maintain the demand for capital in the sectors capable of compression or the capital market may be so organized that industry is unable to draw capital from the sources that finance other forms of accumulation. But unless the bulge is a very large and consistent one it is doubtful whether innovation need suffer greatly.

The effect of technical progress is generally to widen the divergence between the actual stock of capital and the stock consistent with the full exploitation of current worker opportunities. Some part of the additional capital will be needed to finance the innovations in the sectors of the economy in which they arise; some will be linked with the innovations directly, either because associated industries are offered a wider market or because social capital has to be provided in an area where it has become insufficient; some will be linked indirectly, in the way already outlined, because the increased expenditure of consumers will give rise to a derived demand for capital. Now it is common to find that, particularly with a major advance in technique, the influence which it exerts on the scope for eventual capital accumulation is far more profound than its immediate impact on the current flow of capital formation. There is generally a chain reaction, strung out through time, one physical asset being wanted only after another has been created. Although the full consequences may be entirely foreseeable, development does not work up to its full momentum until a whole series of changes have occurred: an extension of capacity here, an application of the new technique there; a shift of location in one industry, a building up of new attitudes in another. The introduction of the steam engine, for example, brought into existence a large reservoir of projects that trickled out into capital formation all through the nineteenth century: the stock of capital appropriate to existing technique was far above the existing stock both because the steam engine was capable of wide application and because many industries that themselves made no use of it (such as bridge-building) were transformed in scale or (like agriculture and many pursuits ancillary to it) in location.

Moreover, because the chain reaction takes time and the innovation is, *ex hypothesi,* a profitable one, the process is to a large extent self-financing. If there is a spate of such innovations, interest and profits are likely to show some response and a corresponding shift in the ratio of savings to income will ease the heavier burden of finance. It may happen, however, that the situation is not regulated in this way: interest rates may be sticky upwards as well as downwards. The probable outcome will then be a series of spurts in investment, followed by periods of indigestion. . . .

A variant of this situation is one in which there has been a considerable lag behind the known opportunities for the fruitful use of capital at existing rates of interest. A country may fail to make use of technical knowledge available elsewhere and suddenly become alive to the possibilities of applying that knowledge. At that stage its capital requirements will increase discontinuously and the additional capital which it requires before bumping up against the limits of technical advance may be very large. It appears to be this situation that is in the minds of those who assume that the injection of additional capital into a country's economy will almost automatically speed up its economic progress. Sometimes the argument is framed more specifically in terms of a shift of employment from agriculture to industry, with a large net gain in productivity from the shift, and the large capital investment needed to accomplish it operating as a brake.

This is a complex situation and it may exist in some underdeveloped countries. But it is by no means obvious that additional capital, whether borrowed from abroad or accumulated through the exertions of surplus labour in the countryside, would by itself suffice to start off a cycle of industrialization. The problem is often one of organization quite as much as of capital creation: of training managements and men; of creating new attitudes towards industrial employment; of taking advantage of innovations that need little capital and using the resulting gains to finance investment elsewhere.

On the whole, there is a greater danger that the importance of capital in relation to economic progress will be exaggerated than that it will be underrated. How many successful firms, looking back over their history, would single out difficulty of access to new capital as the major obstacle, not to their growth, but to the adoption of the most up-to-date technique? How many countries in the van of technical progress have found themselves obliged to borrow abroad? It is where there has been a lag, where technical progress has been too slow, that capital is called upon to put matters right. No doubt where capital is plentiful, more risks can be taken and development is speeded up, so that rapid development and rapid capital accumulation go together. But the most powerful influence governing development, even now, is not the rate of interest or the abundance of capital; and the most powerful influence governing capital accumulation, even now, is not technical progress. . . .

There is general agreement that, in all countries, the process of economic growth and capital accumulation are closely interconnected. It was in terms of this interconnection that the earliest theories of economic development were formulated; and in the work of modern economists, output is still assumed to be limited by capital, whether there is abundant labour or not. A high rate of capital formation usually accompanies a rapid growth in productivity and income; but the causal relationship between the two is complex and does not permit of any facile assumption that more capital formation will of itself bring about a corresponding acceleration in the growth of production.

In industrial countries this is only too obvious. Capital formation may assume forms, such as house-building or an addition to liquid stocks, that are unlikely to add very perceptibly to productivity although they may yield a sufficient return to make them worth while. If all capital formation were of this character, or represented an enlargement of the capital stock with assets broadly similar to those already in existence, it would be hard to account for the rates of growth actually recorded. A moment's reflection will show that even an average return of 10 per cent to capital in a country saving 10 per cent of its income annually would raise income by no more than 1 per cent per annum.[1] Similarly, efforts to impute the recorded expansion in industrial production to the additional labour and capital contributing to it invariably leave a large unexplained residual.[2] It is necessary, therefore, to take account of other influences, such as technical progress and improvements in social and economic organization, which may operate through investment, or independently of it, so as to raise the level of production. These influences, if they take effect uniformly throughout the economy in competitive conditions, will tend to swell the national income without raising the average return to capital, the extra output slipping

[1] This point is developed in my "Reflections on the Growth of Capital and Income," *Scottish Journal of Political Economy*, June 1959. See also the comments by E. Lundberg, "The Profitability of Investment," *Economic Journal*, December 1959.

[2] See, for example, W. B. Reddaway and A. D. Smith, "Progress in British Manufacturing Industries in the Period 1948–54," *Economic Journal*, March 1960, and O. Aukrust, "Investment and Economic Growth," *Productivity Measurement Review*, February 1959.

through to the consumer, the wage-earner or the government.

How far it is correct to attribute an expansion in output to high investment, when high investment is only one of the factors at work is necessarily debatable. It would certainly be legitimate if capital formation was lagging behind, and finance could be identified as a bottleneck in the process of expansion. It might also happen that the rate of technical advance was itself controlled by the scale of investment, not merely because capital formation was the means by which new techniques were adopted but also because high investment created an atmosphere favourable to experimentation and innovation. There is undoubtedly some tendency for all the symptoms of rapid growth to show themselves simultaneously. But there is no invariable dependence of growth on a high rate of capital formation and it is easy to imagine circumstances in which efforts to increase capital formation may actually slow down the progress of the economy.

Moreover there is some justification for turning the causal relationship the other way round. If income is growing fast, investment opportunities are likely to be expanding correspondingly fast, so that the growth in income draws capital accumulation along behind it. The biggest single influence on capital formation is market opportunity, and many types of capital accumulation are likely to be embarked upon only when income is booming. If capital formation does not respond, its failure to do so will certainly act as a drag on the expansion in output. But there is no reason why it should bring it to a halt, and, given a re-arrangement of the investment pattern, income might grow a long way before the shortage of capital became acute. In the meantime the rapid growth in income, particularly if it were accompanied by high profits, would be likely to generate additional savings and so mitigate any symptoms of capital shortage that manifested themselves.

All this presupposes that a spurt in income could precede an acceleration of investment, and that capital formation is subordinate to other elements in the process of growth.

These suppositions are not altogether extravagant. Technical progress does not always involve high net investment: indeed it may permit of a *reduction* in the stock of capital or an expansion in output without any comparable investment. A change in the pattern of investment could also, by enforcing the continued use or overloading of old types of plant, make possible a far more rapid construction of those newer types which bear the fruits of technical progress in greatest abundance.

Attempts are sometimes made to settle the issue by citing the apparent constancy of the capital-income ratio and deducing from this the "neutrality" of technical progress. But the capital-income ratio is affected by many things other than technical progress: the distribution of consumers' expenditure between capital-intensive and labour-intensive products; indivisibilities in past investment—for example, in the transport and communication network; changes in the pattern of trade; investment in social assets such as roads, schools, and hospitals to which no income is imputed; and so on. Even if these influences, too, are neutral and if the capital-income ratio does remain constant—and neither of these assumptions seems well-founded—the fact that capital and income grow at the same rate tells us nothing about the causes of growth in either. There is no reason at all why one should rule out the suggestion that the same circumstances that favour rapid growth of income are also favourable to a rapid growth of investment.

This may seem a rather arid and irrelevant issue: arid, because if capital requirements must keep pace with the growth of income that is all we need to know for practical purposes; irrelevant, because the issue relates to experiences in industrial rather than preindustrial countries. But when it is so commonly urged that countries will be able to take-off if only they are provided with sufficient capital from outside, the issue seems neither arid nor irrelevant. For this thesis assumes the very causal relationship that is in dispute.

EXHIBIT IV.1. Structure of Demand

	Distribution of Gross Domestic Product (percent)											
	Public Consumption		Private Consumption		Gross Domestic Investment		Gross Domestic Saving		Exports of Goods and Nonfactor Services		Resource Balance	
	1960[a]	1981[b]	1960[a]	1981[b]	1960[a]	1981[b]	1960[a]	1981[b]	1960[a]	1981[b]	1960[a]	1981[b]
Low-income economies	8 w	11 w	78 w	74 w	19 w	24 w	18 w	21 w	7 w	9 w	−1 w	−3 w
China and India	—	—	77 w	74 w	21 w	26 w	20 w	25 w	4 w	8 w	−1 w	−2 w
Other low-income	10 w	11 w	81 w	84 w	12 w	14 w	10 w	7 w	15 w	12 w	−2 w	−7 w
1 Kampuchea, Dem.	—	—	—	—	—	—	—	—	—	—	—	—
2 Bhutan	—	—	—	—	—	—	—	—	—	—	—	—
3 Lao, PDR	—	—	—	—	—	—	—	—	—	—	—	—
4 Chad	13	—	82	—	11	—	5	—	23	—	−6	—
5 Bangladesh	6	8	86	90	7	17	8	2	10	7	1	−15
6 Ethiopia	8	15	81	81	12	10	11	4	9	13	−1	−6
7 Nepal	—	c	—	92	—	14	—	8	—	—	—	−6
8 Burma	c	c	89	83	12	24	11	17	20	9	−1	−7
9 Afghanistan	c	—	87	—	16	—	13	—	4	—	−3	—
10 Mali	12	26	79	80	14	16	9	−6	12	18	−5	−22
11 Malawi	16	10	88	80	10	22	−4	10	21	22	−14	−12
12 Zaire	18	16	61	59	12	33	21	25	55	36	9	−8
13 Uganda	9	c	75	97	11	3	16	3	26	1	5	(.)
14 Burundi	3	16	92	79	6	19	5	5	13	9	−1	−14
15 Upper Volta	10	15	94	96	10	16	−4	−11	9	13	−14	−27
16 Rwanda	10	17	82	75	6	23	8	8	12	12	2	−15
17 India	7	10	79	70	17	23	14	20	5	7	−3	−3
18 Somalia	8	—	86	—	10	—	6	—	13	—	−4	—
19 Tanzania	9	14	72	78	14	22	19	8	31	14	5	−14
20 Viet Nam	—	—	—	—	—	—	—	—	—	—	—	—
21 China	c	c	76	72	23	28	24	28	4	9	1	(.)
22 Guinea	—	19	—	67	—	11	—	14	—	34	—	3
23 Haiti	c	c	93	99	9	13	7	1	20	14	−2	−12
24 Sri Lanka	13	7	78	81	14	28	9	12	44	31	−5	−16
25 Benin	16	13	75	89	15	35	9	−2	12	31	−6	−37
26 Central African Rep.	19	13	72	90	20	9	9	−3	23	26	−11	−12
27 Sierra Leone	—	11	—	91	—	13	—	−2	—	17	—	−15
28 Madagascar	20	16	75	77	11	15	5	7	12	13	−6	−8
29 Niger	9	9	79	76	13	27	12	15	9	22	−1	−12
30 Pakistan	11	11	84	82	12	17	5	7	8	12	−7	−10
31 Mozambique	—	—	—	—	—	—	—	—	—	—	—	—
32 Sudan	8	c	80	100	12	13	12	(.)	16	9	(.)	−12
33 Togo	8	17	88	68	11	31	4	15	19	25	−7	−16
34 Ghana	10	11	73	85	24	6	17	4	28	4	−7	−2

EXHIBIT IV.1. Structure of Demand (*Continued*)

	Distribution of Gross Domestic Product (percent)										
	Public Consumption		Private Consumption		Gross Domestic Investment		Gross Domestic Saving		Exports of Goods and Nonfactor Services		Resource Balance	
	1960[a]	1981[b]	1960[a]	1981[b]	1960[a]	1981[b]	1960[a]	1981[b]	1960[a]	1981[b]	1960[a]	1981[b]
Middle-income												
economies	11 *w*	14 *w*	70 *w*	66 *w*	20 *w*	25 *w*	19 *w*	22 *w*	17 *w*	23 *w*	−1 *w*	−3 *w*
Oil exporters	11 *w*	15 *w*	70 *w*	61 *w*	18 *w*	26 *w*	19 *w*	24 *w*	21 *w*	23 *w*	1 *w*	−2 *w*
Oil importers	11 *w*	14 *w*	70 *w*	69 *w*	21 *w*	25 *w*	19 *w*	21 *w*	15 *w*	23 *w*	−2 *w*	−4 *w*
Lower middle-income	10 *w*	13 *w*	76 *w*	68 *w*	15 *w*	25 *w*	14 *w*	19 *w*	15 *w*	23 *w*	−1 *w*	−6 *w*
35 Kenya	11	21	72	63	20	25	17	16	31	25	−3	−9
36 Senegal	17	22	68	83	16	17	15	−5	40	29	−1	−22
37 Mauritania	25	29	71	62	38	38	4	9	15	49	−34	−29
38 Yemen Arab Rep.	—	20	—	101	—	44	—	−21	—	6	—	−65
39 Yemen, PDR	—	—	—	—	—	—	—	—	—	—	—	—
40 Liberia	7	21	58	62	28	18	35	17	39	51	7	−1
41 Indonesia	12	11	80	66	8	21	8	23	13	28	(.)	2
42 Lesotho	17	26	108	163	2	21	−25	−89	12	13	−27	−110
43 Bolivia	7	10	86	77	14	13	7	13	13	13	−7	(.)
44 Honduras	11	14	77	68	14	24	12	18	22	32	−2	−6
45 Zambia	11	28	48	57	25	23	41	15	56	36	16	−8
46 Egypt	17	19	71	64	13	30	12	17	20	34	−1	−13
47 El Salvador	10	15	79	75	16	12	11	10	20	31	−5	−2
48 Thailand	10	12	76	65	16	28	14	23	17	25	−2	−5
49 Philippines	8	8	76	67	16	30	16	25	11	19	(.)	−5
50 Angola	—	—	—	—	—	—	—	—	—	—	—	—
51 Papua New Guinea	28	26	71	63	13	28	1	11	16	38	−12	−17
52 Morocco	12	*c*	77	92	10	23	11	8	24	21	1	−15
53 Nicaragua	9	21	79	73	15	24	12	6	24	21	−3	−18
54 Nigeria	6	12	87	65	13	29	7	23	15	25	−6	−6
55 Zimbabwe	11	18	67	67	23	22	22	15	—	—	−1	−7
56 Cameroon	—	7	—	71	—	21	—	22	—	32	—	1
57 Cuba	—	—	—	—	—	—	—	—	—	—	—	—
58 Congo, People's Rep.	23	12	98	50	45	32	−21	38	21	62	−66	6
59 Guatemala	8	8	84	81	10	17	8	11	13	17	−2	−6
60 Peru	9	13	64	73	25	19	27	14	20	17	2	−5
61 Ecuador	11	15	78	61	14	26	11	24	16	22	−3	−2
62 Jamaica	7	*21*	67	*67*	30	*16*	26	*12*	34	*50*	−4	−4
63 Ivory Coast	10	18	73	62	15	27	17	20	37	34	2	−7
64 Dominican Rep.	13	8	68	78	12	24	19	14	24	18	7	−10
65 Mongolia	—	—	—	—	—	—	—	—	—	—	—	—

EXHIBIT IV.1. Structure of Demand (*Continued*)

	Distribution of Gross Domestic Product (percent)											
	Public Consumption		Private Consumption		Gross Domestic Investment		Gross Domestic Saving		Exports of Goods and Nonfactor Services		Resource Balance	
	1960^a	1981^b	1960^a	1981^b	1960^a	1981^b	1960^a	1981^b	1960^a	1981^b	1960^a	1981^b
66 Colombia	6	8	73	68	21	28	21	24	16	12	(.)	−4
67 Tunisia	17	15	76	62	17	31	7	23	20	42	−10	−8
68 Costa Rica	10	15	77	60	18	28	13	25	21	44	−5	−3
69 Korea, Dem. Rep.	—	—	—	—	—	—	—	—	—	—	—	—
70 Turkey	11	11	76	70	16	25	13	19	3	11	−3	−6
71 Syrian Arab Rep.	—	22	—	69	—	24	—	9	—	18	—	−15
72 Jordan	—	30	—	86	—	41	—	−16	—	54	—	−57
73 Paraguay	8	7	76	74	17	29	16	19	18	7	−1	−10
Upper middle-income	**12** *w*	**15** *w*	**67** *w*	**65** *w*	**22** *w*	**25** *w*	**21** *w*	**24** *w*	**18** *w*	**23** *w*	**−1** *w*	**−1** *w*
74 Korea, Rep. of	15	12	84	66	11	26	1	22	3	39	−10	−4
75 Iran, Islamic Rep. of	10	—	69	—	17	—	21	—	19	—	4	—
76 Iraq	18	—	48	—	20	—	34	—	42	—	14	—
77 Malaysia	11	21	62	53	14	32	27	26	54	53	13	−6
78 Panama	11	21	78	56	16	29	11	23	31	40	−5	−6
79 Lebanon	10	—	85	—	16	—	5	—	27	—	−11	—
80 Algeria	15	16	60	45	42	37	25	39	31	34	−17	2
81 Brazil	12	*c*	67	81	22	20	21	19	5	9	−1	−1
82 Mexico	6	15	76	62	20	25	18	23	10	13	−2	−2
83 Portugal	11	16	76	77	19	27	12	8	17	27	−7	−19
84 Argentina	9	15	70	62	22	26	21	23	9	7	−1	−3
85 Chile	9	13	79	75	14	22	12	12	14	18	−2	−10
86 South Africa	9	13	64	50	22	29	27	37	30	36	5	8
87 Yugoslavia	19	15	49	56	37	32	32	29	14	23	−5	−3
88 Uruguay	9	13	79	75	18	15	12	12	14	15	−6	−3
89 Venezuela	14	14	53	56	21	25	33	30	32	30	12	5
90 Greece	12	18	77	66	19	25	11	14	9	20	−8	−11
91 Hong Kong	7	8	87	68	18	30	6	24	82	111	−12	−6
92 Israel	18	36	68	59	27	20	14	5	14	43	−13	−15
93 Singapore	8	10	95	57	11	42	−3	33	163	212	−14	−9
94 Trinidad and Tobago	9	*c*	61	60	28	30	30	40	37	45	2	10
High-income oil exporters	—	**21** *w*	—	**22** *w*	—	**26** *w*	—	**58** *w*	—	**69** *w*	—	**32** *w*
95 Libya	—	26	—	26	—	34	—	48	—	60	—	14
96 Saudi Arabia	—	23	—	18	—	26	—	59	—	68	—	33
97 Kuwait	—	15	—	39	—	17	—	46	—	71	—	29
98 United Arab Emirates	—	11	—	17	—	28	—	72	—	78	—	44

EXHIBIT IV.1. Structure of Demand (*Continued*)

	Distribution of Gross Domestic Product (percent)										
	Public Consumption		Private Consumption		Gross Domestic Investment		Gross Domestic Saving		Exports of Goods and Nonfactor Services		Resource Balance	
	1960[a]	1981[b]	1960[a]	1981[b]	1960[a]	1981[b]	1960[a]	1981[b]	1960[a]	1981[b]	1960[a]	1981[b]
Industrial market economies	15 w	17 w	63 w	61 w	21 w	22 w	22 w	21 w	12 w	20 w	1 w	−1 w
99 Ireland	12	22	77	62	16	30	11	16	32	63	−5	−14
100 Spain	7	12	72	70	18	20	21	18	10	17	3	−2
101 Italy	13	18	62	63	25	21	25	19	14	27	(.)	−2
102 New Zealand	11	17	68	60	23	25	21	23	22	29	−2	−2
103 United Kingdom	17	22	66	58	19	17	17	20	21	28	−2	3
104 Japan	8	10	59	58	33	31	33	32	11	15	(.)	1
105 Austria	13	18	59	56	28	26	28	26	25	42	(.)	(.)
106 Finland	13	18	58	55	30	28	29	27	23	34	−1	−1
107 Australia	10	17	65	60	29	26	25	23	15	15	−3	−3
108 Canada	14	20	65	55	23	25	21	25	18	28	−2	(.)
109 Netherlands	13	18	62	61	27	18	29	21	48	58	2	3
110 Belgium	13	20	69	66	19	18	18	14	33	65	−1	−4
111 France	13	16	62	67	23	21	25	17	15	22	2	−4
112 United States	17	18	64	64	18	19	19	18	5	10	1	−1
113 Denmark	13	28	62	56	26	16	25	16	32	36	−1	(.)
114 Germany, Fed. Rep.	14	21	57	56	27	23	29	23	19	30	2	(.)
115 Norway	13	19	59	47	30	26	28	34	41	48	−2	8
116 Sweden	16	30	60	52	25	19	24	18	23	31	−1	−1
117 Switzerland	9	13	62	63	29	26	29	24	29	37	(.)	−2
East European nonmarket economies	—	—	—	—	—	—	—	—	—	—	—	—
118 Albania	—	—	—	—	—	—	—	—	—	—	—	—
119 Hungary	c	10	74	61	28	30	26	29	—	39	—	−1
120 Romania	—	—	—	—	—	33	—	—	—	28	—	(.)
121 Bulgaria	—	—	—	—	—	—	—	—	—	—	—	—
122 Poland	—	—	—	—	—	—	—	—	—	—	—	—
123 USSR	—	—	—	—	—	—	—	—	—	—	—	—
124 Czechoslovakia	—	—	—	—	—	—	—	—	—	—	—	—
125 German Dem. Rep.	—	—	—	—	—	—	—	—	—	—	—	—

Source: World Bank, *World Development Report, 1983*, pp. 156–57.

[a]Figures in italics are for 1961, not 1960.

[b]Figures in italics are for 1980, not 1981.

[c]Separate figures are not available for public consumption, which is therefore included in private consumption.

w Indicates a weighted average.

(.) Indicates a nil amount.

IV.B. SOURCES OF CAPITAL FORMATION—NOTE

Whether it be financed from internal sources or external, by noninflationary or inflationary means—the accumulation of capital in any developing economy requires the mobilization of an economic surplus. If investment is to increase, there must be a growing surplus above current consumption that can be tapped and directed into productive investment channels. The different ways of financing capital formation will entail different institutional arrangements (for example, the plowing back of industrial profits into investment would imply a different institutional framework from that of financing through taxation by the state). It should be recognized, however, that the process of capital formation involves three essential steps: (1) an increase in the volume of real savings, so that resources can be released for investment purposes; (2) the channeling of savings through a finance and credit mechanism, so that investible funds can be collected from a wide range of different sources and claimed by investors; and (3) the act of investment itself, by which resources are used for increasing the capital stock.

The first requirement—an increase in the volume of real savings—is of fundamental importance if a higher rate of investment is to be achieved without generating inflation. This crucial step of mobilizing savings should not be confused, however, with the monetary financing of investment. The significance of financial institutions lies in their making available the means to utilize savings. As one study of the role of financial institutions concludes:

> However poor an economy may be there will be a need for institutions which allow such savings as are currently forthcoming to be invested conveniently and safely, and which ensure that they are channelled into the most useful purposes. The poorer a country is, in fact, the greater is the need for agencies to collect and invest the savings of the broad mass of persons and institutions within its

borders. Such agencies will not only permit small amounts of savings to be handled and invested conveniently but will allow the owners of savings to retain liquidity individually but finance long-term investment collectively.[1]

Although the existence of a more developed capital market and financial intermediaries will aid in the collection and distribution of investible funds, they in no way lessen the need for real saving. The rate of investment which it is physically possible to carry out is limited by saving, and a "shortage of capital"—in the sense of a shortage of real resources available for investment purposes—cannot be solved merely by increasing the supply of finance. Indeed, it is comparatively easy to introduce institutional arrangements to increase the supply of finance, and a lack of finance need not persist as a serious bottleneck. Once a sizeable class of savers and borrowers come into being, financial intermediaries are likely to appear, and lending institutions are readily created. But the creation of new financial institutions is no substitute for the necessary performance of real saving.

It is therefore important to be clear on the various sources from which the necessary savings can be mobilized to provide the wherewithal for capital expenditure. From internal sources, an increase of savings may be generated voluntarily through a reduction in consumption; involuntarily through additional taxation, compulsory lending to the government, or inflation; or, finally, by the absorption of underemployed labor into productive work. From external sources, the financing of development may be met by the investment of foreign capital, restriction of consumption imports, or an improvement in the country's terms of trade.

An increase in voluntary saving through a

---

[1] Edward Nevin, *Capital Funds in Underdeveloped Countries,* London, 1961, p. 75.

self-imposed cut in current consumption is unlikely when the average income is so low. At best, it can be hoped that when income rises, the marginal rate of saving may be greater than the average rate. Instead of relying on voluntary saving, the government will normally have to resort to "forced" saving through taxation, compulsory lending, or credit expansion. The efficacy of credit expansion and its resultant inflationary consequences are discussed in section IV.D.

Issues of taxation can be analyzed from two different perspectives—that of incentives or that of resources. If, as in supply-side economics, one believes that a lack of adequate incentives inhibits investment and growth, then the tax system should be improved through the granting of additional concessions of various kinds. If, however, insufficient investment and low growth are attributed to a lack of resources, then the tax system should be designed to increase resources available for investment through additional taxation.

Emphasizing the shortage of resources in an LDC, rather than inadequate incentives, Kaldor has stated:

The importance of public revenue from the point of view of accelerated economic development could hardly be exaggerated. Irrespective of the prevailing ideology or the political color of particular governments, the economic and cultural development of a country requires the efficient and steadily expanding provision of a whole host of non-revenue-yielding services—education, health, communications systems, and so on, commonly known as "infrastructure"—which require to be financed out of government revenue. Besides meeting these needs, taxes or other compulsory levies provide the most appropriate instrument for increasing savings for capital formation out of domestic sources. By reducing the volume of spending by consumers, they make it possible for the resources of the country to be devoted to building up capital assets. . . .
Ruling out inflation as a deliberate instrument, it may be asked: What are the most appropriate taxes that can be relied on for maximum revenue? The question does not admit of any general answer in the widely varying conditions of "underdeveloped" countries. The only feature that is common

to them is that they all suffer from a shortage of revenue. This is partly because they have a low "taxation potential"—which may be defined as the maximum proportion of the national income that can be diverted for public purposes by means of taxation. But more important is the fact that the taxation potential in such countries is rarely fully exploited.[2]

A country's "taxation potential" depends on a variety of conditions—the level of per capita real income, the degree of inequaltiy in the distribution of income, the relative importance of different sectors in the economy (cash crops, subsistence agriculture, mining, foreign trade), the political leadership, and administrative powers of the government. It is generally true that in the lagging LDCs the actual ratio of tax revenue to national income is less than in the more progressively developing countries and is less than their tax potential. In many countries it might be possible to increase the tax effort and approach closer to the tax potential—especially if more effective systems of progressive taxation were to be designed that recognized the inequality in the distribution of income, the taxable capacity of the agriculture sector, and the rising share of industrial and commercial wealth as development proceeds. The saving that is forced by additional taxation, however, will be less than the additional tax revenue to the extent that there is a restriction in private voluntary saving instead of a fall in consumption by the full amount of the tax.

To assess the tax performance of a developing country, we should go beyond a static index, such as the ratio of tax revenue to national income, and introduce more dynamic concepts such as "tax elasticity" and "tax effort." The "tax elasticity" indicates the income-elasticity of the tax system: if the marginal rate of taxation exceeds the average rate, there will be an automatic increase in the ratio of tax revenue to national income as income rises. The "tax effort" measures the

[2]Nicholas Kaldor, "Taxation for Economic Development," *Journal of Modern African Studies,* Vol. 1, No. 1, 1963, p. 7; also, Kaldor, "Will Underdeveloped Countries Learn to Tax?" *Foreign Affairs,* January 1963.

political and administrative efforts to increase effective tax rates or the coverage of the tax system.[3]

There is only narrow scope in a poor country for the practice of compulsory saving through the practice of compulsory purchase of nonnegotiable government bonds. Of greater practical significance may be the operation of state marketing boards which have a statutory monopoly over export crops. These boards may compel native producers to save by purchasing the native's produce at prices below world prices.

Finally, another internal source of saving is represented by the "investible surplus" of underemployed labor. If this "investible surplus" is utilized in productive activity, the national output would be increased, and the required savings might be generated from the additional output. It should also be noted that the direct formation of capital through the use of underemployed labor can be obtained by what is termed the "unit multiplier" method.[4] If labor does have zero productivity in agriculture, it can be withdrawn and put to work on investment projects (construction, irrigation works, road building, etc.) without a drop in agricultural output. Most of the payment of the additional wages will be directed towards foodstuffs, and agricultural income will rise. The higher income may then be taxed, and the tax revenue can finance the investment project. If taxes are levied in an amount equivalent to the additional wage-bill, there will be no change in consumption but income will have risen by the amount of the investment. When the investment projects are completed there will be an increase in output, and some of this increase in income may also be captured through taxation. How much scope there is for this method of direct investment in kind

depends on the ease with which labor can be attracted to investment projects, the degree to which labor can form capital directly without requiring additional investment expenditure, the absence of an adverse effect on agricultural output, and the capacity to offset the investment with taxation.

When we look to external sources of financing development, the capital assistance provided by foreign economic aid and the private investment of foreign capital are of most importance. The next chapter examines the contribution of foreign aid and private foreign investment. [See sections V.A and V.D.] Some contribution may also come from a restriction of consumption imports. Provided that there is not simply a switch in expenditure from imports to domestic consumption, the level of savings will then rise. Imports of capital goods can then be increased, and this will represent a genuine addition to the rate of capital formation: the increase in the flow of investment goods imported is, in this case, matched by an increase in the flow of domestic income saved. If, however, consumers increase their domestic spending when they cannot import, then resources will be diverted from domestic capital production in favor of the increased domestic consumer spending, and the increase in imports of investment goods will be offset by reduced domestic investment. An increase in saving is therefore necessary if the restriction of consumption imports is to result in an increase in total net capital formation.[5]

A similar analysis applies to changes in the terms of trade. When export prices rise, the improvement in the country's commodity terms of trade makes it possible for the country to import larger quantities of capital goods. But again, this source of capital formation will not be fully exploited unless the increment in domestic money income due to the increase in export proceeds is saved. If the extra income merely increases consumer spending on home produced or imported

[3]For a fuller discussion, see Richard M. Bird, "Assessing Tax Performance in Developing Countries: A Critical Review of the Literature," in J. Toye (ed.), *Taxation and Economic Development*, 1978, pp. 33–61.

[4]James S. Duesenberry, "Some Aspects of the Theory of Economic Development," *Explorations in Entrepreneurial History*, Vol. 3, No. 2, December 1950, pp. 65–7.

[5]Cf. Ragnar Nurkse, *Problems of Capital Formation in Underdeveloped Countries,* Oxford, 1953, pp. 111–16.

goods, the opportunity for new saving is lost. The extra resources made available by the improvement in the terms of trade must be withheld from consumption and directed into investment.[6] Either a corresponding increase in voluntary saving or in taxation is necessary to give the country a command over additional imports of investment goods.

A special word should be added about consumption and capital formation. We have implied above that present consumption is at the expense of future output; as usually stated, it is believed that restraints on consumption are needed to divert resources from the production of more consumer goods to capital accumulation. But is this always true? Can a case be made that—in the context of a developing country—an increase in current consumption may actually lead to an expansion in future production?

When the level of living is as low as it is in an LDC, the distinction between consumption and investment becomes overdrawn insofar as private consumption may well have a positive marginal productivity. The reason is not that consumption will augment resources, but that a rise in consumption may improve labor quality and efficiency and hence allow better use to be made of the existing labor resources. The consumption of health-improving goods should improve the ability to work and increase the intensity of work. The greater consumption of foodstuffs that aid nutrition is especially significant. For it has now been established by medical scientists that improper food, especially a diet low in protein, can in itself impair the physical and mental development of children from birth.[7]

In an empirical study of the impact of components of "labor quality" on the growth of output, Professors Galenson and Pyatt have demonstrated that an increase in con-

sumption may improve labor quality. The components of labor quality examined are calories per head, investment in dwellings, higher education, health indicators, and social security benefits. Of these various components, better diet is shown to have the greatest impact on labor productivity and growth of output.[8]

Certain policy implications follow from the view that private consumption may be productive. In its efforts to raise the community's marginal rate of saving, the government should put more emphasis on taxation and on business saving through profits rather than on individual saving through a curtailment of consumption. But there should at the same time be an improvement in the pattern of consumption so that it might contribute as directly as possible to increasing efficiency. What is needed is a selective increase in consumption. Luxury consumption, for instance, should be taxed, and the import-replacement of consumer goods should be limited insofar as this policy has become suboptimal. There should, however, be an increase in consumption that favors the rural population if this will help overcome the agricultural bottleneck. In this connection, we should note Professor Myint's observation that "incentive consumer goods" can be a useful means of encouraging peasants to enter the money

[6]Ibid., pp. 97–103.

[7]*Pre-School Malnutrition: Primary Deterrent to Human Progress,* National Academy of Sciences, National Research Council, Washington, D.C., 1966; N. S. Scrimshaw, "Infant Malnutrition and Learning," *Saturday Review,* March 16, 1968, pp. 64–8. See further, IX.B, below.

[8]W. Galenson and G. Pyatt, *The Quality of Labour and Economic Development in Certain Countries,* ILO, Geneva, 1964, pp. 15–19, 87–8.

Another study has shown that, in the rural areas of Asia, an insufficiency of calories may take the form of inadequate work effort after the peak season. See Harry T. Oshima, "Food Consumption, Nutrition, and Economic Development in Asian Countries," *Economic Development and Cultural Change,* July 1967, pp. 390–91. Cf. also, F. A. O., *Nutrition and Working Efficiency,* Rome, 1962; Gunnar Myrdal, *Asian Drama,* New York, 1968, pp. 1912–19. But see Elliott J. Berg, "Major Issues of Wage Policy in Africa," in A. M. Ross (ed.), *Industrial Relations and Economic Development* London, 1966, pp. 190–96. Professor Berg argues that under conditions of migrant labor and a joint family system, higher income does not necessarily lead to better nutrition. He also contends that better nutrition is not sufficient to improve individual efficiency unless there are also present the necessary motivation and essential cooperant factors with labor.

economy: a rise in the aspiration to consume these goods may lead to the sale of a food surplus and may encourage better methods of production that will increase the food surplus in the future.[9]

In its most general terms, the principle that consumption can be productive raises the complex problem of specifying criteria for intertemporal efficiency in consumption, and then shaping policy instruments to meet

[9]Hla Myint, *The Economics of the Developing Countries,* London, 1964, pp. 88.

these criteria. If we take the largest view, this brings us to the very frontier of multisectoral intertemporal models where we should attempt to interrelate an optimal consumption policy with an optimal capital policy. The problem of the total amount of investment that can be made in the future then becomes a function of investment allocation and the pattern of consumption in the present period. We need not be overwhelmed at this point by the complexities of such a model, but we will return in Chapter X to the problem of optimal investment allocation.

Comment

Reviews of the theoretical and empirical literature on savings rates in LDCs are provided by R. Mikesell and J. Zuiser, "The Nature of the Savings Function in Developing Countries," *Journal of Economic Literature* (March 1973); H. S. Houthakker, "On Some Determinants of Saving in Developed and Underdeveloped Countries," in E. A. G. Robinson (ed.), *Problems in Economic Development* (1965); G. S. Laumos and P.S. Laumos, "The Permanent Income Hypothesis in an Underdeveloped Economy," (September 1976).

The role of the government as saver raises problems of taxation and the relative merits of alternative fiscal policies in developing countries. These problems can be examined in the following works: R. M. Bird and O. Oldman (eds.), *Readings on Taxation in Developing Countries,* 3rd ed. (1975); R. M. Bird, *Taxation of Agricultural Land in Developing Countries* (1974); John F. Due, *Taxation and Economic Development in Tropical Africa* (1963); John F. Due, *Indirect Taxation in Developing Countries* (1970); A. R. Prest, *Public Finance in Underdeveloped Countries,* 2nd ed. (1972); U. K. Hicks, *Development Finance* (1965); R. J. Cheliah, *Fiscal Policy in Underdeveloped Countries* (1970); Nicholas Kaldor, *Indian Tax Reform* (1956); A. M. Martin and W. A. Lewis, "Patterns of Public Revenue and Expenditure," *The Manchester School of Economic and Social Studies* (September 1956); U. Tun Wai, "Taxation Problems and Policies of Underdeveloped Countries," *IMF Staff Papers* (November 1962); H. P. Wald, *Taxation of Agricultural Land in Underdeveloped Economies* (1959); R. S. Thorn, "Evolution of Public Finances during Economic Development," *The Manchester School of Economic and Social Studies* (January 1967); Donald R. Snodgrass, "The Fiscal System as an Income Redistributor in West Malaysia," *Public Finance* (1974); Charles E. McLure, "Taxation and the Urban Poor in Developing Countries," *World Development* (March 1977); J. F. J. Toye (ed.), *Taxation and Economic Development* (1978).

Noteworthy research on tax issues and empirical studies of tax trends in developing countries have been undertaken by the Fiscal Affairs Department of the International Monetary Fund and reported in various issues of *IMF Staff Papers.*

The appropriateness of different taxes for developing countries is often judged with reference to such criteria as (1) fruitfulness of revenue sources, (2) effects on resource allocation, (3) contribution to equity, and (4) ease of administration. For an empirical study of these criteria, see International Monetary Fund, *Taxation in Sub-Saharan Africa,* Occasional Paper No. 8 (October 1981).

EXHIBIT IV.2. Forty-Seven Developing Countries: Tax Ratios 1969–71 and 1972–76

| Country | Taxes as Percent of GNP | | Ranking 1969–71 |
	1972–76	1969–71	
Iran	32.7	21.6	(6)
Guyana	31.7	23.4	(3)
Zambia	30.8	31.3	(1)
Zaire	27.2	29.4	(2)
Venezuela	23.1	20.4	(7)
Malaysia	22.5	19.3	(11)
Trinidad and Tobago	21.9	17.7	(17)
Tunisia	20.7	21.7	(5)
Ivory Coast	20.6	19.8	(8)
Senegal	20.2	18.1	(14)
China, Republic of	19.9	17.8	(15)
Kenya	19.2	14.4	(12)
Jamaica	1910	19.4	(10)
Tanzania	18.9	13.9	(24)
Sudan	18.9	18.2	(13)
Morocco	18.6	17.8	(15)
Chile	18.4	19.6	(9)
Egypt	18.1	19.2	(12)
Brazil	18.1	22.9	(4)
Sri Lanka	17.9	17.7	(17)
Indonesia	16.3	10.0	(39)
Turkey	16.2	15.6	(20)
Singapore	15.7	13.2	(28)
Ghana	14.2	15.8	(19)
Peru	14.0	14.2	(23)
Thailand	13.9	12.4	(32)
India	13.9	13.4	(25)
Costa Rica	13.6	13.1	(30)
Korea	13.6	15.4	(21)
Argentina	13.3	13.4	(25)
Mali	12.9	13.2	(28)
Togo	12.4	11.3	(34)
Ecuador	12.0	13.4	(25)
Bolivia	11.8	8.2	(43)
Colombia	11.6	12.5	(31)
Honduras	11.5	11.3	(34)
Pakistan	11.4	8.8	(41)
Upper Volta	11.3	10.3	(38)
Lebanon	10.2	11.2	(36)
Philippines	10.1	9.1	(40)
Ethiopia	10.1	8.6	(42)
Rwanda	0.0	7.9	(44)
Burundi	9.3	11.4	(33)
Paraguay	8.8	10.9	(37)
Mexico	8.6	7.1	(46)
Guatemala	8.1	7.9	(44)
Nepal	5.4	4.4	(47)
Average	16.1	15.1	

Source: *IMF Staff Papers,* March 1979, p. 130

IV.C. FINANCIAL DEEPENING

IV.C.1. Financial Structure and Economic Development*

During economic development, as their incomes per capita increase, countries usually experience more rapid growth in financial assets than in national wealth or national product.[1] During the past century and a half, this has been true for the United States. Financial assets there were only about one-half the level of national wealth in the early 1880's, but they have been considerably larger than real wealth in recent years. Financial assets have grown much faster than gross national product in the United States: the ratio increased from about unity at the beginning of the last century to 4.5 now.

Japan has had a similar experience. There the ratio of financial assets to real wealth rose from pehaps 10 percent in 1885 to over 150 percent in recent years. In the Soviet Union, this ratio moved up from 10 percent in 1928 to 35 percent a few years ago. Financial growth in excess of real growth is apparently a common phenomenon around the world.

In somewhat rougher outline, this same picture is revealed by comparison among countries at any moment of time. Countries that are poor in income per capita generally have very low ratios of financial to real wealth. The present ratio in Afghanistan and Ethiopia, for instance, is probably little higher than 10 or 15 percent, comparable to the Japanese ratio in 1885 but lower than the ratio in the United States 150 years ago. The ratio is somewhat higher, from 30 to 60 per-

cent, in more prosperous countries such as Argentina, Brazil, Guatemala, Mexico, the Republic of Korea, Venezuela, and Yugoslavia. India, though less developed than most of these countries, has a financial ratio of around 35 percent. In still more highly developed countries, the proportion of financial to real wealth often lies in the range of 80 to 100 percent. France, Israel, West Germany, and several other countries are in this range. However, the Soviet Union has a low financial ratio for its income per capita, about 35 percent, while Japan (150 percent), Switzerland (over 200 percent), and the United Kingdom (215 percent) have exceptionally high ones.

At the present time, national stocks of financial assets vary from 10 to more than 200 percent of national real wealth. As the foregoing examples suggest, differences in income per capita go a long way toward explaining this variety of financial experience. The United States does have a higher financial ratio than France, France than Mexico, and Mexico than Afghanistan. Over time, for any one country as its income per capita increases, financial assets rise relative to national real wealth.

REASONS FOR SECULARLY RISING FINANCIAL RATIOS

The relationship between growth in financial assets and growth in real wealth and income per capita may be analyzed in various ways. For example, financial development depends on division of labor that is feasible only in the context of real development. Again, financial development depends on conditions of demand for and supply of financial assets that are sensitive to real development. We consider each of these approaches in this section.

---

*From John G. Gurley and Edward S. Shaw, "Financial Development and Economic Development," *Economic Development and Cultural Change,* Vol. 15, No. 3, April 1967, pp. 257–65, 267–8. Reprinted by permission.

[1]The measurements we use for relative growth in financial assets, tangible assets, and income are based consistently on nominal values except when deflated values are mentioned explicitly. Financial assets include all intangible assets—claims against both nonfinancial spending units (primary securities) and financial institutions (indirect securities). . . .

Finance and self-sufficiency are antonyms: Robinson Crusoes do not accumulate debt and financial assets. Finance is associated with division of labor in three senses: (1) division of labor in production that involves exchange of factor services and outputs implies lending and borrowing. In primitive market economies, these financial transactions are in kind. Subsequently, the diseconomies of finance-in-kind induce monetization. It seems to be the general rule that the pace of monetization exceeds the pace of real growth in diminishing degree. There is everywhere a limit, in terms of real wealth and income per capita, beyond which the stock of means of payment grows in step with wealth and income or even less rapidly. When money payments are ubiquitous, the ratio of money to income or of money to wealth hovers near to its secular peak.

In the United States, the ratio of the money supply to gross national product was only 7 percent in 1805. It doubled by 1850 and doubled again by 1900. Thereafter, the money-income ratio has shown no strong trend up or down: it is still around 30 percent. A similar pattern appears in cross-section comparisons. On the basis of data for 70 countries since World War II, one observes that the money-income ratio varies from approximately 10 percent or less in the poorest countries to 20 percent in countries with gross national product per capita of about $300. Then the rise in the ratio is retarded, though it continues to 30 percent and a little more.

(2) Finance is associated with division of labor between saving and investment. Where it is one sector in the community that releases factors of production from consumer goods industries and another sector that absorbs such factors into accumulation of real capital, financial assets and debt accumulate in both monetary and nonmonetary form. The rate of accumulation depends on the mix of techniques for transferring savings to investment.

This division of labor leads to issues of primary securities by ultimate borrowers (investors) and to acquisitions of financial assets by ultimate lenders (savers). In between lie the markets on which primary securities are bought and sold. During the growth process, the division of labor between saving and investing becomes more intricate, and this institutional evolution implies more rapid accumulation of primary debt and financial assets than of real wealth. Financial accumulation falls into step with real accumulation when the institutional evolution approaches its limit. Similarly, factor inputs of the financial sector increase more rapidly for a time than inputs of other sectors, but balanced growth of inputs comes eventually.

Primary security issues approximate 1 or 2 percent of gross national product in the poorer countries. The ratio generally lies within the range of 10 to 15 percent in wealthier countries. A similar contrast emerges from data for the United States: the issues-income ratio was apparently small during the early years of the nineteenth century, but it rose to more than 10 percent by the close of the century, and there it remains. During the nineteenth century in the United States, the stock of primary securities more than doubled relative to national wealth and income, and then changed little after 1900.

(3) There is division of labor in a third sense that promotes growth in both quantity and variety of financial assets. Specialization develops between saving and ownership of primary securities. Financial intermediaries solicit savings, paying a deposit rate for them, and assume responsibility for savings allocation, charging a primary rate of interest to ultimate borrowers. The spread between the primary rate and the deposit rate compensates for factor costs and risks in intermediation. This spread shrinks during financial development. In combination with shifts in savers' tastes among financial assets, the relative rise in the deposit rate induces layering of indirect debt upon primary debt and growth in total financial assets of savers relative to national income and wealth.

There are countries which develop a comparative advantage in intermediation. They import primary securities and export indirect debt, earning the spread between the primary rate of interest and the deposit rate. Countries with a comparative disadvantage in intermediation prefer smaller factor inputs for the domestic financial sector. Exporters of intermediation have relatively high and rising ratios of total financial assets to income and wealth, but their portfolios of indirect financial assets follow a rising trend.

Stocks of nonmonetary indirect financial assets, including both domestic and foreign claims, rise almost without let-up during the development process. They were a negligible fraction of gross national product in the United States at the beginning of the nineteenth century. They rose almost continuously from that time, reaching 35 percent of gross national product by 1900 and 60 percent in the last few years. Cross-section data have very much the same story to tell: time and savings deposits, which comprise the bulk of nonmonetary indirect assets, are only 1 or 2 percent of gross national product in the poorest countries, 10 percent in countries with national products per capita of about $300 to $400, and 40 or 50 percent in the richer nations.

We have seen that financial assets accumulate as income and wealth grow. Our suggestion is that such accumulation reflects division of labor in production, saving and investment, and intermediation. Specialization in the use of productive factors generates a rising stream of income and a rising stock of both real and financial wealth.

The coincidence and interaction of real and financial growth can be explained also in terms of supply and demand conditions on real and financial markets. The income elasticity of savings is greater than unity at low levels of income, and the savings elasticity of demand for financial assets *en masse* seems to remain above unity as income rises. Though the secular decline in the real rate of interest that accompanies development tends to depress saving, trends in both explicit and implicit returns on financial assets and particularly on indirect financial assets stimulate portfolio demands. These trends can be attributed to technological change, to economies of scale, and sometimes to regulatory controls on markets for financial assets. Briefly, both income and price phenomena associated with real development stimulate finance.

The retroactive impact of finance upon the real world need not be explored carefully here. Anything that the financial sector does to accelerate savings, improve their allocation to investment, and economize costs in transmitting savings to investment implies an increase both in its own flows and stocks of financial assets and in flows and stocks of real output.

There are degrees and kinds of differences in national financial systems that cannot be explained by differences in income and wealth. . . .

ALTERNATIVE TECHNIQUES FOR MOBILIZING THE ECONOMIC SURPLUS

The principal reason for dissimilar financial structure at given national levels of income and wealth is that there are alternative techniques for mobilizing the economic surplus—for eliciting savings and allocating them to investment. The financial technique, or the debt-asset system, is only one method. Each of the other techniques is a substitute for it.

In its full detail, the list of alternative processes for putting saving to the service of selected investment is very long. However, the list may be compressed into two major classes: processes of internal finance and processes of external finance. In the former, the investor draws on his own savings. In the latter, the investor draws on the savings of others.

Internal finance itself comprises two principal techniques: self-finance and taxation. In self-finance, savings are put at the investors' disposal by adjustments in relative prices on commodity and factor markets and on markets for foreign exchange. The taxation technique employs taxes and other nonmarket alternatives to channel savings to the state for either governmental or private investment. Within external finance, the debt-asset system is the technique for mobilizing domestic savings. In addition, savings from abroad may be supplied by gift or loan, on the initiative of either private or governmental sources.

We condense the long list of alternative processes to four: self-finance and taxation, as internal finance processes; the debt-asset system and foreign aid, as external finance processes. This section has to do mainly with internal finance, but there are first a few comments on external finance to bring out the contrast between processes.

External Finance

The debt-asset system for mobilizing domestic savings depends upon and encourages division of labor between savers and investors, as well as between savers and intermediaries. It belongs in the context of decentralized decision-making, of market organization, of dependence upon relative prices to guide economic behavior. Market rates of interest, as one class of relative prices, bear a heavy responsibility for the rate and direction of investment.

The issue and accumulation of government debt is a component of the debt-asset system. It draws private savings through security markets and intermediaries to both private and governmental uses. The stock of government debt has a role to play in portfolio diversification that affects deeply the performance of the debt-asset system.

Internal Finance

The processes of internal finance—self-finance and taxation—are substitutes for the debt-asset system. Each of them involves more centralization of decision-making, less specialization between savers and investors. Each of them leads to a less elaborate financial structure.

Self-finance. The processes of self-finance involve adjustment in terms of trade on commodity, factor and foreign-exchange markets—"opening the scissors," as Paul Baran would have said, of relative prices to the advantage of an investing sector, forcing involuntary savings upon other sectors. These adjustments in relative prices may be imposed by government, socialist or capitalist, at a stable price level. They may be induced by government through inflation of the price level. They may be imposed by private investors with monopoly power on some commodity or factor market. The processes of self-finance can operate through socialist central planning, monopoly or state-directed capitalism, or inflation. . . .

Socialist extraction of savings depends upon prices paid and received by state enterprise, to a lesser extent upon taxation, and in minor degree upon accumulation by private savers of financial claims, including money, against the state. Private solicitation of savings for investment in private capital, including consumer durables, is unimportant, though expansion of consumer credit is to be anticipated. Allocation of savings according to plan can be achieved by simple transfers to state enterprise on the records of the state bank.

Socialist centralism foregoes most of the division of labor that we have stressed as one basis for relatively high finance-income ratios. Saving and investment are generated principally within the state sector, so that market transfers of savings at explicit rates of interest are as unnecessary as they are distasteful in socialist doctrine. Demand for financial assets in other sectors is depressed by constraints on personal income and wealth. It is depressed, too, because the state undertakes to supply various services for which people save in capitalist societies, because private bequests are minimized, and because reduced private risks imply reduced precautionary portfolios. Under these circumstances of demand and supply, there is little occasion for markets in either primary or indirect securities. Moreover, because of pressure for internal development, there has not been significant accumulation by socialist societies of financial claims abroad, and there has been no industry of financial intermediaries to export its services.

The process of socialist centralism reduces the dependence of economic units on a financial structure; contact is made less through financial markets and financial institutions and more through planning bureaus and other central coordinating devices; the order of the day is internal finance and balanced budgets, not external finance and the issue of new securities. The theory and design of socialist society are incompatible with relatively high ratios of financial assets to income and wealth.

Manipulation of the terms of trade between agriculture and industry, whether under socialism or capitalism, is a case of self-finance. It has been the socialist view that a preindustrial society could not mobilize its surplus effectively without collectivization of peasant farming. Only then could prices of agriculture be reduced relatively for the benefit of industrial investment. Or, as one knows from American experience, the scissors can be opened in the farmer's behalf to increase his savings for his investment in agricultural capital.

Factor prices are an obvious target for techniques of self-finance. Peasant migration to the city depresses real wage rates and raises real profit rates, with the consequence that industry has access to flows of new finance for its own capital. Controls on rates charged by public utilities under foreign ownership can extract involuntary savings from abroad.

Overvaluation of domestic currency on the foreign exchanges may transfer real income from an exporting sector, with taste for imports of consumption goods or of foreign financial assets, to an importing sector that is accumulating plant and equipment. Depending upon relevant elasticities of demand and supply, overvaluation can also appropriate foreign savings for domestic use.

Inflation is a technique of self-finance. Because of its impact on relative prices, relative incomes, and relative wealth positions, inflation appeals to "structuralists" as a temporarily necessary alternative in some retarded societies where relative prices tend to move perversely for purposes of growth and where

other techniques of mobilizing and allocating savings are underdeveloped. In the theory of structuralism, stagnation is the alternative if inflation is not used to generate savings among spending units with investment opportunities. The "cost-push" variant of structuralist doctrine accepts inflation as a corrective for relative-price distortions that tend to reduce the flow of savings into the retained earnings of business and its self-financed capital formation. Inflation is a second-best "income policy" to prevent dissipation of savings through consumption or underemployment. It is inferior, the argument goes, to productivity ceilings on factor prices, but it is preferable to stagnation.

Inflation in prospect affects anticipated relative yields on various types of wealth, financial and real, reducing real rates of return on assets with the more inflexible nominal rates and raising real prospective returns on assets with more flexible nominal rates. The inevitable result is to change rates of saving, allocation of savings, and channels by which savings flow. Self-finance gains at the expense of debt-asset finance. Foreign aid through intergovernmental loans and gifts may gain if inflation reduces domestic saving of the recipient country below a target level of investment. The channels that lose are debt-asset finance and also taxation, unless tax rates happen to be progressive to inflation.

Inflation transfers net worth as well as income. It taxes such forms of financial wealth as money balances, assessing creditors for the benefit of debtors, public or private. If the result is to depress the wealth position of savers and the debt position of investors below preferred levels, a temporary acceleration of saving, investment, and debt-asset finance can ensue. Needless to say, this result does not follow for gross inflation that is expected to continue.

Self-finance is centralist. It has been common in precapitalism, before the decentralizing evolution of commodity, factor, and financial markets. It is inherent in anti-capitalism, or socialism. Even in the general context of capitalism, there occur changes in the socioeconomic structure that involve reversion to self-finance. Degeneration in processes of debt-asset finance reduces saving and investment, but it can also divert funds into the channels of self-finance. Self-finance may increase if business firms combine to avoid encounters, as Baran puts it, with "the restraining hand of financial institutions." Cooperative credit among, say, consumers or farmers has been at times a way of detaching relatively small, homogeneous groups from reliance on broader security markets. The *mujin* and *kye* of the Far East, "traditional" credit institutions, are illustrations of cooperative saving-investment processes that border on both self-finance and the debt-asset system.

Taxation.   The tax technique is a variant of internal finance, a way of mobilizing the economic surplus that implies centralized decision-making. While it is true that there are taxes which work to the benefit of debt-asset finance, there can be a structure of taxation which depresses demand for financial assets, displaces issues of securities by investors and intermediaries, and makes securities markets superfluous. The receipted tax bill is a substitute for the financial asset in spending units' portfolios.

CRITERIA FOR CHOICE AMONG ALTERNATIVE SAVING-INVESTMENT TECHNIQUES

We have defined four technologies or processes of eliciting and allocating savings: self-finance, taxation, debt-asset, and foreign aid. We have suggested that differences in the ratio of financial assets to income and wealth, between countries and between times for any one country, may reflect differences and changes in choice between the debt-asset technology and the others. In the present section, we consider some criteria for choice among the four technologies.

The objective of public policy regarding the saving-investment process, we assume, is to maximize the capital value of anticipated real consumption. Given a social discount rate, the technology or combination of technologies for eliciting and allocating saving is best which implies highest consumer welfare, counting government among consumers. The optimal consumption stream has the qualities of equity and stability that conform to a social welfare function.

The contribution of each saving-investment technology to consumer welfare has a positive (gross yield) component and a negative (factor cost) component, and the difference is the net yield of the technology. Additional real resources applied to a saving-investment technology may raise rates of saving and investment, the nation's capital stock, and hence the future flow of consumption. The gross yield of these real resources is the capital value of the economy's anticipated gross additions to its consumption stream. Factor cost is the capital value of the stream of final goods that could have been produced by the real resources if they had not been diverted to a saving-investment technology. The net yield is the difference between these two capital values.

We suggest that there is an optimal combination of saving-investment technologies for each economy in each phase of its development. This optimal combination has been attained when no gain in net yield can result from shifting factor inputs between technologies. Then no transfers of resources between technologies can advance the possibility frontier of anticipated consumption. If the optimal combination varies with the aggregate of factor inputs into all saving-investment technologies, one may wish to define the best combination more narrowly, as that which prevails when net yield is zero at the margin for all technologies. . . .

Bias and Evolution in Choice Between Technologies

Economic development is marked by iterative probing for the optimal combination of saving-investment technologies. The search is guided in part by principle and prejudice, in part by foreign example, by trial and error, and even by rational analysis. The combinations and permutations of technology are so numerous that no two countries are likely to follow the same probing sequence or, specifically, to reach the same ratio of financial assets to tangible wealth at any given level of real wealth or income per capita.

The probing sequence is most deeply affected by the economy's choice between self-finance with central planning and technologies that are compatible with decentralized decision regarding saving and investment. This is a choice between Left and Right. Advocates of either can design imposing proof that it is cheaper in resource inputs, more effective in eliciting and allocating savings, less vulnerable to instability in the consumption stream, and more compatible with the ethics of equity.

As the socialist sees decentralized finance, it is exorbitantly expensive in marble columns, bank presidents, and energy consumed in managing portfolios. It elicits too little in savings, because monopoly finance does not pay savers enough, because decentralized decisions pay too little attention to the consumer welfare of succeeding generations, or because savers do not measure accurately the rewards to saving. It allocates savings badly—on ostentation, on consumer durables, on military capital. Its allocation is biased by indifference to externalities of private investment, by hostility to public goods,

by undervaluation of human capital. It is inherently unstable in the short run: variance in the future consumption stream is high. It reeks of inequity. Needless to say, the capitalist's view of socialist central planning is no less emphatic, using the same criteria of capitalized yield and cost.

As development proceeds, these blacks and whites of choice between technologies appear to shade off to greys of varying intensity. The probing process everywhere seems to lead toward a mixture of self-finance under central planning and decentralized processes. At the margin, neither black nor white has a long life expectancy. If we dared to suggest a Law of Financial Development, it would be this: each economy begins its development by intensive exploitation of a saving-investment technology that is chosen for historical, political, social, or perhaps economic reasons, and then, as this technology produces a diminishing net yield, experiments with alternative technologies that are marginally superior in terms of their capitalized returns and costs. Whatever the first choice may be, it is tilled intensively until there is obvious advantage in trying the extensive margin that involves a mix of processes for eliciting and allocating savings. Along the extensive margin, a socialist society may tolerate market as well as shadow rates of interest, and a capitalist society may put up with some centralized self-finance.

IV.C.2. Organized and Unorganized Money Markets*

The size of an organized money market in any country may be indicated by either or

*From U Tun Wai, "Interest Rates in the Organized Money Markets of Underdeveloped Countries," *International Monetary Fund Staff Papers,* Vol. 5, No. 2, August 1956, pp. 249–50, 252–3, 255, 258, 276–8; "Interest Rates Outside the Organized Money Markets of Underdeveloped Countries," ibid., Vol. 6, No. 1, November 1957, pp. 80–83, 107–9, 119–25. Reprinted by permission.

both of the following ratios, although neither measurement is perfect: the ratio of deposit money to money supply and the ratio of the banking system's claims (mostly loans, advances, and bills discounted) on the private sector to national income. . . .

The ratio of deposit money to money supply actually measures banking development of the money market. However, to the extent that the development of commercial banking is synonymous with the development of the money market, this ratio may be used as an indicator of the growth of a money market. In most underdeveloped countries, there are hardly any lending agencies of importance other than commercial banks. There are no discount houses or acceptance houses, and savings institutions (including life insurance companies) are in the early stages of development. . . .

Both ratios might be expected to be low in an underdeveloped country and high in a developed one. The ratio of deposit money to money supply should be higher in a more developed country because, with economic development, there is also development of the banking system. . . .

The structure of interest rates in the organized money markets of underdeveloped countries is usually more or less the same as in the developed ones. The short-term rate of interest is generally much below the long-term rate, as indicated by the spread between the government treasury bill rate and the government bond yield; the rate at which bills of exchange are discounted is also lower than the rate at which loans and advances are granted.

The lowest market rates are usually the call loan rates between commercial banks. The next lowest are those paid by commercial banks on short-term deposits, followed by the government treasury bill rate. Then come the rates at which commercial banks discount commercial paper, varying according to the type of security and the date of maturity. In most countries, especially in Asia, the government bond yield comes next, followed by the lending rates of commercial banks. . . .

In general, the level of interest rates in underdeveloped countries, even in organized money markets, is higher than in the more developed countries. The more notable difference between the two groups of countries, however, is that the range of interest rates is generally much wider in underdeveloped countries. The volume of loans granted at relatively low rates in an underdeveloped country is not very important, as only limited amounts of financial assets are available to serve as collateral for lending at low rates. It is usually the foreign business firms with longer experience and larger capital which are able to borrow at the lower rates. Most of the indigenous firms have to pay the higher rates; this is especially true where foreign banks occupy an important position in the banking system. . . .

In spite of the small direct dependence of commercial banks on the central banks for funds, the latter are able to influence market rates by changes in the bank rate because of their economic, and at times their legal, position in the domestic money market, with wide powers for selective credit control, open market operations, and moral pressures.

The general expectation is that the long-term trend of interest rates in underdeveloped countries, at least in the organized markets, should be downward. Generally speaking, in these countries the banking systems and with them the money markets are likely to develop at a faster rate than the other sectors of the economy. The long-term supply of loanable funds therefore tends to increase more rapidly than the long-term demand. Where, for one reason or another, the growth of banking has been restricted or the banking system subjected by law to many restrictions, including controls on interest rates and of the purposes for which loans may be granted (as in a number of countries in Latin America), the long-term trend of interest rates may, however, not be downward. . . .

In [the above] examination . . . of the interest rate structure and the lending practices of organized money markets in underdeveloped countries, . . . it was shown that these differed much less than might have been expected from those prevailing in most developed countries. In underdeveloped countries, however, unorganized money markets also play a very important role, and any study of credit conditions in these countries that is to be adequate must be extended to cover the unorganized as well as the organized markets. Efforts have often been made to repair the deficiencies of the unorganized markets by government action designed to stimulate the development of cooperative credit or to provide credit through agricultural banks, etc.; it is convenient to include these government-sponsored institutions in a study of unorganized money markets in general.

Interest rates in the unorganized money markets of underdeveloped countries are generally very high in relation both to those in the organized money markets and to what is needed for rapid economic development. These high interest rates are caused by a disproportionately large demand for loanable funds coupled with a generally inelastic and limited supply of funds. The large demand stems from the special social and economic factors prevalent in the rural areas of underdeveloped countries. The low level of income leaves little surplus for saving and for the accumulation of capital for self-financing of agricultural and handicraft production. The uncertainty of the weather, which affects crop yields and incomes, causes an additional need for outside funds in bad years. A significant portion of the demand for loanable funds in rural areas is for financing consumption at levels much higher than are warranted by the low income of the peasant. . . .

The supply of loanable funds in the unorganized money markets is very limited and inelastic because the major source is the moneylender, and only very small quantities are supplied by indigenous bankers and organized institutions, such as cooperative credit societies and land mortgage banks. The moneylender in most cases is also a merchant or a landlord and therefore is willing to lend only at rates comparable with what he could earn by employing his capital in alternative uses which are often highly profitable. The lenders in the unorganized money markets do not have the facilities for mobilizing liquid funds available to commercial banks in organized markets and therefore the supply of funds is rather inflexible. Since the unorganized money markets are generally not closely connected with the organized money markets, there is little possibility of increasing the supply of loanable funds beyond the savings of the lending sector of the unorganized money markets. The limited supply of

loanable funds indeed reflects the general shortage of capital in underdeveloped countries.

The disadvantages of the high rates of interest in the unorganized money markets are well known and include such important effects as "dead-weight" agricultural indebtedness, alienation of land from agriculturalists to moneylenders and the agrarian unrest that is thus engendered, and a general slowing down of economic development. . . .

The organized money markets in underdeveloped countries are less fully integrated than the money markets in developed countries. The unorganized money markets in underdeveloped countries are even more imperfect, and indeed it is questionable whether the existing arrangements should be referred to as "markets." They are much less homogeneous than the organized markets and are generally scattered over the rural sector. There is very little contact between the lenders and borrowers in different localities. The usual textbook conditions for a perfect market are completely nonexistent: lenders and borrowers do not know the rates at which loans are being transacted in other parts of the country; the relationship between borrower and lender is not only that of a debtor and creditor but is also an integral part of a much wider socioeconomic pattern of village life and rural conditions.

In unorganized money markets, moreover, loans are often contracted and paid for not in money but in commodities; and the size of the average loan is very much smaller than in the organized money markets. Both borrowers and lenders in the two markets are often of quite different types. In the organized money markets, the borrowers are mainly traders (wholesale and retail) operating in the large cities and, to a less extent, manufacturers. Agriculturalists rarely account for a significant portion of demand except in those underdeveloped countries where export agriculture has been developed through plantations or estates. In the unorganized money markets, the borrowers are small agriculturalists, cottage industry workers, and some retail shopkeepers. The lenders in the organized money markets consist almost exclusively of commercial banks. In the unorganized markets, the suppliers of credit consist of a few financial institutions, such as cooperatives, private and government-sponsored agricultural banks, indigenous bankers, professional moneylenders, large traders, landlords, shopkeepers, relatives, and friends. Proper records of loans granted or repaid are usually not kept, and uniform accounting procedures are not adopted by the different lenders. Loans are granted more on a personal basis than in the organized money markets, and most of the loans granted by the moneylenders and by other noninstitutional sources are unsecured beyond the verbal promise of the borrower to repay.

The unorganized money market may be divided into three major parts: (1) a part in which the supply is dominated by indigenous bankers, cooperatives, and other institutions, and the demand by rural traders and medium-sized landlords; (2) a part in which the demand originates mainly from small agriculturalists with good credit ratings, who are able to obtain a large portion of their funds from respectable moneylenders, traders, and landlords at high but reasonable rates of interest, i.e., rates that are high in relation to those prevailing in the organized money market but not exorbitant by the standards of the unorganized money market; (3) a part in which the demand originates from borrowers who are not good credit risks, who do not have suitable collateral, and who in consequence are driven to shady marginal lenders who charge exorbitant rates of interest. . . .

Many explanations have been offered for the high interest rates that generally prevail in unorganized money markets. One theory is that interest rates are high there because they are determined by custom and have always been high. This might be called the theory of the customary rate of interest. . . .

The theory of customary rates is not satisfactory, however, because it does not explain how or why the custom of high rates developed. The true explanation has to be found in the economic and social conditions of underdeveloped countries, which cause the demand for loanable funds to be large in relation to the available supply. Some writers tend to explain the high rates of interest in terms of demand factors while others emphasize supply.

The demand for funds, in relation to the supply, is large because the average borrower in the unorganized money market has a very low income and therefore has no surplus funds to finance his business operations. The majority of the cultivating tenants—one of the most important groups of potential borrowers—have to borrow money not only for investment in land, cattle, etc., and for working capital to make purchases of seeds and fertilizers, but also for their minimum basic necessities of food, shelter, and clothing.

On the supply side, there is a general shortage of capital in underdeveloped countries and an inadequate level of domestic savings. Also, the small amount of domestic savings is not channeled effectively into the unorganized money market because of the absence of proper financial and credit institutions which not only would integrate the organized and unorganized money markets but also would facilitate the mobilization of savings in the rural areas. . . .

The difference in the levels of interest rates between the organized and unorganized money markets stems partly from the basic differences between the sources of supply of funds in the two markets. In an organized money market, facilities for the expansion of credit are open to the commercial banks, which have the use of funds belonging to depositors. These banks are therefore able to charge relatively low rates of interest and yet make satisfactory profits for the shareholders. On the other hand, moneylenders in an unorganized money market have little influence on the supply of funds at their disposal and, furthermore, their supply price tends to be influenced by the alternative uses to which their funds can be put.

A number of institutional factors are also responsible for high rates of interest in unorganized money markets. The size of the loan is usually small and thus the fixed handling charges are relatively high. Defaults also tend to be larger in unorganized money markets. These higher defaults are due not so much to a lower standard of morality and willingness to repay debts as to the fluctuations in prices and incomes derived from agricultural products, which reduce the ability of the agriculturalists to repay debts at inopportune times. . . .

Another general factor causing high rates of interest is experience in regard to inflation. While this is probably of importance in many Latin American countries, it hardly seems relevant for prewar colonial territories which, by their rigid currency exchange standards, had maintained fairly stable conditions but still had high interest rates in the unorganized money markets. The large development programs in most underdeveloped countries, however, constitute possible inflationary pressures and may be considered as a factor in maintaining high rates of interest.

The list of causes of high interest rates could be extended to include other social and economic factors in underdeveloped countries—even to fairly remote factors, such as the system of land tenure which prevents land from being used as collateral. A general statement, however, is that interest rates in the unorganized money markets of underdeveloped countries are high because the economy is underdeveloped and the money market unorganized. . . .

Any program to bring down interest rates in unorganized money markets must be comprehensive and should be guided by the principle that interest rates can be lowered only by reducing the demand for loanable funds as well as by increasing the supply. . . .

A reduction in borrowing for productive purposes may not be desirable, especially as the amount of self-financing which can take its place is negligible. Such borrowing can be reduced in the long run only through an increase in savings from higher agricultural output and income. It is not sufficient that the ability of the farmer to save be increased. The willingness to save must also be created. The problem of cheap agricultural credit is inseparable from the whole problem of agricultural development, including such measures as increasing the use of fertilizers and proper seeds; making available adequate marketing facilities, including proper grading, transportation, and storage of crops; and providing an efficient agricultural extension service. . . .

Even if it is true that the cure for high rates of interest is to be found more on the demand side than on the supply side, the supply of credit should also be increased. Supply should be increased in such a way that legitimate credit needs are met at cheaper rates without encouraging borrowing for consumption. This can be achieved by increasing the supply of institutional credit while at the same time taking steps to discourage borrowing from noninstitutional lenders. In this connection, it could be argued that legislation regarding moneylenders which has had the effect of drying up noninstitutional credit may be a blessing in disguise—although in a manner different from that intended by legislators.

Increasing the supply of institutional credit is a difficult problem, but the efforts of governments have had a fair degree of success. One problem is that of getting the commercial banks to lend more to agriculture. This problem cannot be solved merely by opening more branches, because even at present agriculturalists who are fairly close to the big cities are as isolated from the organized money market as others living some distance away from the cities. The opening of more bank branches is desirable, but the branches' business will as likely as not be confined to financing local retail and wholesale trade.

One way of inducing the organized financial institutions to lend more to agriculture is by making agriculturalists more creditworthy and generally reducing the risks of lending by lessening the impact of some of the natural calamities (floods, plant and animal diseases); improving the human factor, i.e., reducing carelessness and increasing honesty; reducing the uncertainties of the market through crop insurance, stabilized agricultural prices, etc. The lenders might also take certain steps, such as spreading loans between different types of borrower and region and supervising the use of loans for productive purposes.

IV.C.3. Demand-Following or Supply-Leading Finance*

Typical statements indicate that the financial system somehow accommodates—or, to the extent that it malfunctions, it restricts—growth of real per capita output. For example,

It seems to be the case that where enterprise leads finance follows. The same impulses within an economy which set enterprise on foot make owners of wealth venturesome, and when a strong impulse to invest is fettered by lack of finance, devices are invented to release it . . . and habits and institutions are developed.[1]

Such an approach places emphasis on the demand side for financial services; as the economy grows it generates additional and new demands for these services, which bring about a supply response in the growth of the financial system. In this view, the lack of financial institutions in underdeveloped countries is simply an indication of the lack of demand for their services.

We may term as "demand-following" the phenomenon in which the creation of modern financial institutions, their financial assets and liabilities, and related financial services is in response to the demand for these services by investors and savers in the real economy. In this case, the evolutionary development of the financial system is a continuing consequence of the pervasive, sweeping process of economic development. The emerging financial system is shaped both by changes in objective opportunities—the economic environment, the institutional framework—and by changes in subjective responses—individual motivations, attitudes, tastes, preferences.

The nature of the demand for financial services depends upon the growth of real output and upon the commercialization and monetization of agriculture and other traditional subsistence sectors. The more rapid the growth rate of real national income, the greater will be the demand by enterprises for external funds (the saving of others) and therefore financial intermediation, since under most circumstances firms will be less able to finance expansion from internally generated depreciation allowances and retained profits. (The proportion of external funds in the total source of enterprise funds will rise.) For the same reason, with a given aggregate growth rate, the greater the variance in the growth rates among different sectors or industries, the greater will be the need for financial intermediation to transfer savings to fast-growing industries from slow-growing industries and from individuals. The financial system can thus support and sustain the leading sectors in the process of growth.

The demand-following supply response of the growing financial system is presumed to come about more or less automatically. It is assumed that the supply of entrepreneurship in the financial sector is highly elastic relative to the growing opportunities for profit from provision of financial services, so that the number and diversity of types of financial institutions expands sufficiently; and a favorable legal, institutional, and economic environment exists. The government's attitudes, economic goals, and economic policies, as well as the size and rate of increase of the government debt, are of course important influences in any economy on the nature of the economic environment. As a consequence of real economic growth, financial markets develop, widen, and become more perfect, thus increasing the opportunities for acquiring liquidity and for reducing risk, which in turn feeds back as a stimulant to real growth.[2]

The demand-following approach implies that finance is essentially passive and permissive in the growth process. Late eighteenth

*From Hugh T. Patrick, "Financial Development and Economic Growth in Underdeveloped Countries," *Economic Development and Cultural Change,* Vol. 14, No. 2, January 1966, pp. 174–7. Reprinted by permission.

[1] Joan Robinson, "The Generalization of the General Theory," in *The Rate of Interest and Other Essays,* London, 1952, pp. 86–7.

[2] Cf. W. Arthur Lewis, *The Theory of Economic Growth,* London, 1955, pp. 267–86.

and early nineteenth century England may be cited as a historical example. In fact, the increased supply of financial services in response to demand may not be at all automatic, flexible, or inexpensive in underdeveloped countries. Examples include the restrictive banking legislation in early nineteenth century France, religious barriers against loans and interest charges, and Gerschenkron's analysis of the abortive upswing of Italian industrial development in the 1880's "mainly, it is believed, because the modern investment bank had not yet been established in Italy."[3] In underdeveloped countries today, similar obstacles, together with imperfections in the operation of the market mechanism, may dictate an inadequate demand-following response by the financial system. The lack of financial services, thus, in one way or another restricts or inhibits effective growth patterns and processes.

Less emphasis has been given in academic discussions (if not in policy actions) to what may be termed the "supply-leading" phenomenon: the creation of financial institutions and the supply of their financial assets, liabilities, and related financial services in advance of demand for them, especially the demand of entrepreneurs in the modern, growth-inducing sectors. "Supply-leading" has two functions: to transfer resources from traditional (non-growth) sectors to modern sectors, and to promote and stimulate an entrepreneurial response in these modern sectors. Financial intermediation which transfers resources from traditional sectors, whether by collecting wealth and saving from those sectors in exchange for its deposits and other financial liabilities, or by credit creation and forced saving, is akin to the Schumpeterian concept of innovation financing.

New access to such supply-leading funds may in itself have substantial, favorable expectational and psychological effects on entrepreneurs. It opens new horizons as to possible alternatives, enabling the entrepreneur to "think big." This may be the most significant effect of all, particularly in countries where entrepreneurship is a major constraint on development. Moreover, as has been emphasized by Rondo Cameron,[4] the top management of financial institutions may also serve as entrepreneurs in industrial enterprises. They assist in the establishment of firms in new industries or in the merger of firms (the advantages of economies of scale may be more than offset by the establishment of restrictive cartels or monopolies, however), not only by underwriting a substantial portion of the capital, but more importantly by assuming the entrepreneurial initiative.

By its very nature, a supply-leading financial system initially may not be able to operate profitably by lending to the nascent modern sectors.[5] There are, however, several ways in which new financial institutions can be made viable. First, they may be government institutions, using government capital and perhaps receiving direct government subsidies. This is exemplified not only by Russian experience in the latter half of the nineteenth century, but by many underdeveloped countries today. Second, private financial institutions may receive direct or indirect government subsidies, usually the latter. Indirect subsidies can be provided in numerous ways. Commercial banks may have the right to issue banknotes under favorable collateral conditions; this technique was more important in the eighteenth and nineteenth centuries (national banking in Japan in the 1870's; wildcat banking in the United States) than it is likely to be in present underdeveloped countries, where this right is reserved for the central bank or treasury. Nonetheless, modern equivalents exist. They include allowing private financial institutions to create deposit money with low (theoretically, even negative)

[3]Alexander Gerschenkron, *Economic Backwardness in Historical Perspective—A Book of Essays,* Cambridge, 1962, p. 363. See also Chapter 4.

[4]Rondo Cameron, "The Bank as Entrepreneur," *Explorations in Entrepreneurial History,* Series 2, Vol. I, No. 1, (Fall 1963), pp. 50–5.

[5]Except in the extreme case where inherent profit opportunities are very high, and supply-leading stimulates a major entrepreneurial effort.

reserve requirements and central bank rediscount of commercial bank loans at interest rates effectively below those on the loans. Third, new, modern financial institutions may initially lend a large proportion of their funds to traditional (agricultural and commercial) sectors profitably, gradually shifting their loan portfolio to modern industries as these begin to emerge. This more closely resembles the demand-following phenomenon; whether such a financial institution is supply-leading depends mainly on its attitude in searching out and encouraging new ventures of a modern nature.

It cannot be said that supply-leading finance is a necessary condition or precondition for inaugurating self-sustained economic development. Rather, it presents an opportunity to induce real growth by financial means. It thus is likely to play a more significant role at the beginning of the growth process than later. Gerschenkron implies that the more backward the economy relative to others in the same time period (and the greater the forced-draft nature of the economic development effort), the greater the emphasis which is placed on what I here term supply-leading finance.[6] At the same time, it should be recognized that the supply-leading approach to development of a country's financial system also has its dangers, and they should not be underestimated. The use of resources, especially entrepreneurial talents and managerial skills, and the costs of explicit or implicit subsidies in supply-leading development must produce sufficient benefits in the form of stimulating real economic development for this approach to be justified.

In actual practice, there is likely to be an interaction of supply-leading and demand-following phenomena. Nevertheless, the following sequence may be postulated. Before sustained modern industrial growth gets underway, supply-leading may be able to induce real innovation-type investment. As the process of real growth occurs, the supply-leading impetus gradually becomes less im-portant, and the demand-following financial response becomes dominant. This sequential process is also likely to occur within and among specific industries or sectors. One industry may initially be encouraged financially on a supply-leading basis and as it develops have its financing shift to demand-following, while another industry remains in the supply-leading phase. This would be related to the timing of the sequential development of industries, particularly in cases where the timing is determined more by governmental policy than by private demand forces.

Japan between the 1870's and the beginning of World War I presents an excellent example of the sequence of supply-leading and demand-following finance. A modern banking system was created in the 1870's, subsidized by the right to issue banknotes and by government deposits. These banks, in the absence of large-scale industrial demand for funds, initially concentrated their funds on financing agriculture, domestic commerce, and the newly important foreign trade. However, they also became the locus for much of the early promotional and entrepreneurial talent which initiated the industrial spurt beginning in the mid-1880's, especially in railroads and in cotton textiles (at first import-competing, and later export-oriented). The banks also became an early important source of industrial funds, albeit *via* an indirect route. The modern financial system thus was not only created in advance of Japan's modern industrialization, but, by providing both funds and entrepreneurial talent on a supply-leading basis, contributed significantly to the initial spurt. By the mid-1890's, the emphasis apparently moved from supply-leading to demand-following in the financing of the textile and other consumer goods industries. On the other hand, the financing of most heavy manufacturing industries continued on a supply-leading basis perhaps until World War I, with a considerable portion of external funds provided through the long-term loans of special banks established at government initiative and utilizing government funds. . . .

[6]Op. cit.

IV.C.4. Financial Repression and Liberalization*

Most developing countries have formal plans for industrial development, public infrastructure such as roads and utilities, the future course of education, foreign trade, agriculture, and so on. Yet planners typically do not set targets for, or even assess achievements in, the financial sector. Unfortunately, regulation rather than development is the usual emphasis.

However, no other sector in market-oriented economies is more important for promoting indigenous entrepreneurship. Nascent business firms and artisans in cities or small farmers in the countryside do not function efficiently unless they can borrow or lend freely on a quid pro quo basis. Only then is it possible to have broadly based development, with new technologies being widely introduced, to reflect accurately the social scarcity of capital throughout the economy. . . .

THE BANKING SYSTEM AND LOANABLE FUNDS

In developing countries, open markets for primary securities are usually insignificant. This situation does not constitute a distortion but merely reflects the low level of per capita income and the resulting low level of individual saving and investment. Information is insufficient for small farmers or merchants to be able to issue their own notes or publicly traded shares. Small-scale investors cannot issue bonds, common stock, mortgages, trade bills, and so forth in an organized securities market for purchase in significant quantities by household savers. They and other small savers are precluded from doing so by uncertainty about the debt instruments of fledgling entrepreneurs—by the absence of accounting

*From Ronald I. McKinnon, "Financial Policies," in John Cody et al. (eds.), *Policies for Industrial Progress in Developing Countries,* London, Oxford University Press, 1980, pp. 93–9, 102–5, 110–14. Reprinted by permission. Copyright 1980 by the World Bank.

systems and their unknown default potential. These savers, in any event, cannot easily diversify their portfolios. Only a small and inadequate number of moneylenders, pawnbrokers, and village storekeepers can extend limited credit directly to worthy private borrowers.

The absence of open markets in primary securities means that the monetary system has a much more important role as an intermediary between savers and investors. Private financial savings in developing countries are largely currency and deposits—claims on central banks, commercial banks, and near banks such as savings and loan associations, *financieras* (development banks), postal savings depositories, and so on. These banking intermediaries issue liquid short-term deposits whose nominal value is virtually guaranteed by the state, a great advantage to small savers. This guarantee arises because society must have a stable means of payment. The provision of money to provide these services has long been recognized as one of the major attributes of sovereignty. It was accepted as a state responsibility long before the development of banks which, as they evolved, tended to take it over. Consequently the supervision of banks has been accepted as a government responsibility in most countries.

Institutional relationships among central banks, commercial banks, building societies, development of investment banks, agricultural credit banks, and so forth can vary a great deal from one country to another because of different economic circumstances and regulatory practices. Many of the differences are not critical for the efficient overall operation of a bank-based capital market. Initially, therefore, consider a situation in which the balance sheets of all organized banking units in an economy are consolidated into "Monobank." Monobank collects all checking (demand) and interest-bearing time deposits from, and also issues coins and currency to, the nonbank public, private households and firms. Monobank's balance sheet, when all interbank claims and liabilities are netted out, is shown in Table 1.

In an economy, three distinct roles can be distinguished for the banking system that are often complementary but sometimes in conflict: (1) the traditional monetary role: providing a stable unit of account, store of value, and means of payment in the economy; (2) the financial intermediation role: bringing private savers together with public and private investors; (3) fiscal support for the government: a source of revenue to the exchequer, to be allocated in parallel with tax proceeds, possibly for consumption purposes or transfer payments.

In mobilizing resources for economic development, the intermediary role of the banks under (2) above is extremely important because open markets for primary securities are not substantial and are highly illiquid. Money in the form of currency and demand deposits, and quasi money in the form of time and savings deposits are, on the other hand, highly liquid. Being legal tender in an otherwise fragmented and illiquid capital market, money yields almost instant purchasing power for goods and services outside of subsistence agriculture. Acceptance of interest-bearing time deposits is officially regulated to ensure their safe convertibility into the means of payment.

Thus in many poor countries the banking system is virtually the only financial means of attracting voluntary private savings on a large scale. It has the potential to promote investment in two important ways: (1) Through the issue of currency (central bank), demand deposits (commercial banks), or time deposits (savings banks), credits can be extended to investing enterprises in the private or public sector, as represented by the left-hand side of Monobank's balance sheet. (2) Less obviously, the banking system can promote *self-financed* saving-investment *within* industrial firms and family-owned farms. In the less developed economy, most small enterprises and potential new ones do not have easy access to outside credits, even from the banking system. But new innovative investments to buy machinery or hire workers require substantial discrete outlays of cash at separated points in time. To finance these outlays, small-scale entrepreneurs accumulate bank deposits or stash currency under their mattresses before making their investments. Thus the economic attractiveness of building up and holding cash balances—as represented by the right-hand side of Monobank's balance sheet—is itself important for self-financed capital accumulation in the less developed economy. Here the term "finance motive" is used to refer to the desire of investor-savers to hold real cash balances.

Given this important dual role of the banking system in financing new investment, how can achievements in the financial sector be assessed empirically as industrialization proceeds and per capita income grows?

One way is to devise a rough statistical measure of the flow of loanable funds through Monobank, which is equivalent to the banking system as a whole. Take M_2 to be a broad definition of the banking system's liabilities, as represented in Table 1 by the right-hand side of Monobank's balance

TABLE 1. The Monobank Balance Sheet

Assets	Liabilities
Loans to private borrowers	Coin and currency
Government bonds	Demand deposits
Net claims on foreigners	Time deposits (interest bearing)
	Net worth (capital subscription)
Total assets = Total liabilities	

sheet,[1] less the net worth of private banks. To what extent can data on the stock of money, as measured by the ratio M_2 to gross national product (GNP), be an adequate measure of the *flow* of loanable funds in a typical developing country?

First, the M_2/GNP ratio is indicative of the absolute size of the banking system that reinvests, in potentially new directions, funds from old loans that have matured. It also measures the stock of liquidity available for self-financed investments.

Second, the flow of current saving of households and firms shows up in part as changes in the assets and liabilities of Monobank. In particular, the increase in the *real* stock of money is a measure of the realized net private financial saving in the prototypical developing country without open markets in primary securities. The flow of private saving in monetary form that is eroded by inflation—part of the inflation tax collected by the government—is omitted from this measure. However, increases in the ratio of M_2/GNP provide an indication of real additions to the ongoing loanable funds capacity of the banking system. . . .

INTEREST CEILINGS AND FINANCIAL REPRESSION

It is easy to persuade small savers to keep a minimum level of highly liquid "working" cash balances within the banking system; these consist mainly of coin and currency and perhaps demand deposits. Beyond these basic working balances, small savers will increase their money holdings relative to their incomes only if the menu of interest-bearing passbook savings, time deposits, and possibly certificates of deposit of longer maturity are made attractive. In part, this requires a physical infrastructure of banking facilities and easily accessible services—such as post offices often provide throughout the country. At the bottom line, however, small savers will

substantially augment their real cash balance holdings only if the real interest yield is adequate. Indeed, if initially most of the population is poor, a significantly high yield on longer-term deposits of the order of 8 or 9 percent—after adjusting for ongoing inflation—may well be necessary to encourage a spurt in financial saving such as that enjoyed by Taiwan.

The basic problem is, of course, that banks can pay a high yield to depositors only if they are earning an even higher yield on their loan portfolio. As a practical matter, this is rarely the case, as the semi-industrialized and industrializing countries portrayed in Table 2 have a long history of imposing both direct and indirect ceilings on the interest rates that can be charged on loans from the banking system. Depositors then necessarily receive a low yield—which can be highly negative after allowing for price inflation. Potential depositors respond by strictly limiting their saving in financial forms, thus giving rise to financial repression. . . .

A repressed system may have two other associated features. First, where there are excess credit demands, an unorganized financial sector—sometimes called the extra-bank market because it may operate illegally—is maintained and even stimulated. Private borrowers outside the supervision of the organized financial system can offer higher returns to depositors and other lenders and use the resulting funds to cover the demands of borrowers who are prepared, or forced, to pay higher interest rates than prevail in the organized sector. Because this unorganized market is unable to provide the legal guarantees provided to depositors and others in the organized system, the supply price of credit to this market tends to include a default risk that depositors and others would not demand in the organized market. Hence there is a "default spread" in such markets. Paradoxically, it leads to an overall rise in the cost of credit resulting from legal restrictions designed to lower this cost.

Second, lenders in the organized market may be stimulated to lend indirectly to the

---

[1]As distinct from M_1, which consists only of coin and currency and demand deposits.

TABLE 2. Bank Loanable Funds in Typical Semi-industrialized and Industrializing Developing Countries (ratio of M_2 to GNP)

Country	1960	1965	1970	1975	Mean 1960–75
Latin America					
Argentina	0.245	0.209	0.267	0.168	0.222
Brazil	0.148	0.156	0.205	0.164	0.168
Chile	0.123	0.130	0.183	0.099	0.134
Colombia	0.191	0.204	0.235	n.a.	0.210
Mean ratio of M_2/GNP for four Latin American countries: 0.184					
Asia and the Middle East					
India	0.283	0.262	0.264	0.295	0.276
Philippines	0.186	0.214	0.235	0.186	0.205
Sri Lanka	0.284	0.330	0.275	0.255	0.286
Turkey	0.202	0.223	0.237	0.222	0.221
Mean ratio of M_2/GNP for four Asian-Middle Eastern countries: 0.247					

n.a. Not available.

Source: IMF, *International Financial Statistics*, various issues. M_2 is defined as money plus quasi money plus deposits outside commercial banks. M_2 is a stock tabulated as of June 30 for each calendar year, whereas GNP is the flow of output for that year.

unorganized market. While admittedly "formal" loans are only rarely made openly to "curb markets," many wholesalers, retailers, and other traders receiving bank loans in effect act as moneylenders to customers without direct access to bank credit. In the best of circumstances, where an unorganized market evolves, a dual financial system develops in which transaction costs are duplicated and a nepotistic credit system is encouraged outside organized and supervised institutions. Monopoly rents accrue to financial entrepreneurs who skim off the spread between market and regulated interest charges.

The financial reforms in Taiwan in the 1950s and Korea in the 1960s included at least a partial freeing of interest rates. Opening the organized flow of capital to market pressures served to relegate the informal markets to insignificant importance. While formalizing credit flows through the organized banking sector was not the only cause of the rapid industrialization of both countries after the monetary reforms, its allocative effects did contribute to this progress.

Malaysia is another example of a country in which freely operating financial markets contributed to rapid industrial growth. . . .

INFLATION AND THE FINANCIAL SYSTEM

The distortive effects of inflation are well known. If monetary profits can be achieved by the stockpiling of commodities as hedges against inflation, there will be a shift from productive physical investment to sterile commodity hoarding. Any inhibition of physical investment will bear most heavily on new types of investment that are likely to appear more risky (even though the potential of increased profits accompanies the increased risks).

Similarly, with prospective inflation, there is the probability that expected domestic currency profits can be gained from holding foreign exchange and other low-yielding foreign assets when the inevitable exchange depreciation is undertaken. Equally important, firms become reluctant to borrow abroad, and thus to incur debts in foreign exchange.

This is another manifestation of net capital outflow from the economy. Such prospective profits, moreover, shift the relative private returns between foreign and domestic investment to the disadvantage of the latter.

Perhaps most important, prospective inflation increases the riskiness associated with all investment decisions. As the expected general level of prices rises, the potential range of future prices widens. If prices are expected to rise by something like 5 percent in the next year, there may be a general level of expectation that they will settle within the 4 to 6 percent range. If the general level of increase is expected to be something like 50 percent, this range may become 40 to 60 percent. It is not impossible that the increased uncertainty may make this range 30 to 70 percent. The effects of this increased uncertainty will not be spread evenly over all investments. They will bear most heavily on those investments that take a long time to mature, because the price level will be more uncertain as the maturity date approaches. A characteristic of highly inflationary economies is that private investors will undertake only projects with a very short time horizon.

Aside from these and other general inhibiting effects on industrial diversification and other innovations to which attention has frequently been directed, inflation has certain direct consequences for the operation of the financial system. For example, the repression problem can be aggravated by inflation. A prospective increase in prices will alter the prospective relative values of financial assets and consumption, unless the returns on financial assets rise to compensate for their prospective decline in terms of constant prices. That is, inflation will lead to a reduction in the flow of funds to the financial system unless the nominal deposit rate of interest is allowed to rise at least as much as the expected increase in prices.

Concurrently, the anticipated constant price cost of credit will decline. If funds borrowed today can be used to purchase goods that may be more expensive tomorrow, the price limit that borrowers will place on credit will rise. In the simplest terms, if today's borrowings can be repaid in tomorrow's depreciated currency, the true cost of borrowing is the interest cost minus the currency depreciation over the period of the loan.

The market-clearing rate of interest will rise if it is expected that prices will rise. While the inflation surcharge may be greater or less than the expected rate of inflation, it will always be positive. If institutional rates are limited by law or convention, the market-clearing rate may be pushed above the institutional rate, with the repressive effects discussed earlier. If the credit markets are already repressed by usury restrictions, inflation will greatly aggravate the consequent problems. Clearly a 5 percent ceiling on the interest rate paid to passbook savers is much more repressive when inflation rises from zero to 20 percent a year. A deposit rate of interest of 25 percent may be necessary to prevent the M_2/GNP ratio from falling. . . .

In the short run, and within limits, inflation may encourage a reconstitution of the constant price value of convenience assets (demand deposits and currency) that will stimulate their acquisition and therefore give rise to the increase in the savings ratio that has been observed in many countries in recent years. This is the current form of the "inflation-forced-savings" phenomenon. However, the limits on this process are very specific. After a point, nonfinancial assets become effective convenience assets, and the allocative role of the financial system largely disappears. The banking system may continue to provide minimal transaction balances, but not other convenience assets such as savings and time deposits.

Inflation has led to some flexibility in interest rates over time, and in a few cases the monetary value of convenience assets and of institutional assets have been indexed to "live with inflation." In a hierarchy of policies, however, indexing is clearly not the first-best answer to the problems of inflation. It introduces an additional element of uncertainty and therefore, at least in subjective terms, an additional cost in an already uncertain world. Indexation may alleviate some of the costs of inflation, but it cannot eliminate them all.

IV.D. INFLATION AND ITS EFFECTS

IV.D.1. Effects of Inflation*

Governments are tempted to obtain resources by printing money or creating credit, because of the political resistance which they encounter if they raise taxes instead. The results depend on how much money is created, how long inflation continues, what the money is used for, how people react, and how well the economy is managed.

MATCHING RESOURCES

An increase in the supply of money will not raise prices if it is limited to matching an increase in output or in the demand for money. There are two cases where a limited increase in the supply of money will not raise prices.

First, the amount of goods and services to be exchanged against money increases continuously. Population is increasing; productivity is increasing; and the monetized sector of the economy is increasing at the expense of the subsistence sector. For these reasons alone the supply of money could increase by, say, 30 to 40 per cent in a decade without prices increasing.

Secondly, an increase in the quantity of money will not raise prices if there are idle resources capable of producing increased amounts of the kinds of goods on which the money would be spent. Idle labour is not enough; there must also be idle factories and idle land capable of producing more consumer goods in immediate response to demand. This is the situation in industrial countries during a trade depression. It is not the case in underdeveloped countries, and is not therefore relevant to their problems.

In several underdeveloped countries (especially in Asia and the Middle East) unemployed labour exists which could be used

productively without any significant drain on other currently used resources. It could not work in factories, because there are no idle factories; or produce agricultural products, because there is very little idle cultivable land. But it could be used to build roads, to drain swamps, to dig irrigation canals, to rehabilitate eroded lands, to build houses with local woods or clays, and other useful ways which require no machines and employ only locally available materials. (Ever since the Pharaohs we have known that construction requires very little physical capital.) Such works can increase the productive capacity of the country, especially by making it possible to cultivate more land. The obstacle is that the workers, when paid for their labour, spend most of the money on consumer goods. They produce capital goods, but demand consumer goods. Hence the prices of consumer goods tend to rise. If they were producing consumer goods of the kind they demand there would be no increase in prices, but the resources required for producing more of such goods (industrial equipment, cultivable land) do not exist.

The effect of inflation in these circumstances is to redistribute consumer goods; the previously employed get less while the previously unemployed get more. Inflation is thus a substitute for taxation, used to finance investment in the absence of voluntary savings.

EFFECT ON INVESTMENT

Some writers seem to deny that inflation can increase investment, but this position is not tenable. To analyse the problem correctly one must distinguish between the primary objective of inflation and its secondary consequences. The primary objective is normally achieved; if money is created for expenditure on investment projects, investment increases.

*From W. Arthur Lewis, *Development Planning*, George Allen & Unwin Ltd., London, 1966, pp. 130–38. Reprinted by permission.

What these writers are denying is that, if money is created for other primary purposes, investment will increase as a secondary consequence.

Most inflations occur in wartime, to enable the Government to get more resources for making war. This purpose is achieved. The normal purpose of peacetime inflation is to enable the Government to have more civil servants or soldiers than it could pay out of the proceeds of taxes alone. This objective also is normally achieved. Very rarely has a Government used inflation to create productive capacity—to build factories or to reclaim agricultural land, for example. (The USSR in the 1930s is one such case.) On the other hand, it is quite common for commercial banks to create credit to finance investment by private capitalists. There is no reason to doubt that if the purpose of creating money is to spend it on creating productive capacity, this purpose will be achieved.

Money which is created for other purposes does not have the primary effect of increasing investment. Does it have this secondary effect? It will if the increase in prices redistributes income in favour of people who are particularly prone to save and invest; otherwise it will not. The argument about the secondary effects on investment therefore turns on analyzing the effect of rising prices on income distribution.

The immediate effect of an inflation is to increase profits, since prices rise faster than costs. This is not necessarily the ultimate effect. Wage earners and consumers resent the price increase, and take steps to try to keep their money incomes rising as fast as prices. They may succeed, or they may not. If they fail, the share of profits in the national income increases. This is normally expected to increase investment, but whether it does so depends on the psychology of those who get the profits. The capitalists who save and invest in plant and equipment tend to follow conservative price policies, under the influence of cost accountants. A large part of inflationary profits goes to get-rich-quick capitalists, and are used rather for speculation in commodities and in foreign exchange. Hence

inflation need not result in any large increase in investment if this was not its primary purpose.

Inflation will normally have some positive effect on investment, since the expectation of rising prices makes it profitable to acquire durable assets. But the pattern of investment may be grossly distorted in response to distortion of prices. An inflation raises domestic prices relatively to world prices. This discourages exports and import substitution. Thus investment is diverted from these important sectors into lines which are not affected by world competition. Investment of the kinds which could ease the balance of payments diminishes, in favour of investment in commercial and luxury building. To avoid this consequence requires either increasingly elaborate controls and subsidies to exports, or else frequent devaluation of the currency.

EFFECT ON PRICES

Suppose the Government prints money, and uses it to finance capital formation: how long will the inflation continue? Prices cease to rise in one of two circumstances. Either, if the inflation changes the distribution of income in such a way that the Government is able to continue financing capital formation without printing more money; or, if as a result of the capital formation, an extra output of consumer goods begins to keep pace with the extra flow of money.

The effect on the distribution of income depends on the public's reaction. At the start, the prices of consumer goods rise faster than wages, in favour of profits. Take first the simplest case: suppose that the public accepts the change; i.e., suppose that the distribution of income is altered permanently in favour of profits. Part of the profits will flow to the Government automatically through the income tax. If the profit-makers also use the rest of their profits to buy newly-issued Government bonds, prices will cease to rise, since the Government can finance continued capital formation, merely by issuing more bonds, and without printing any more money. This simple outcome is unlikely. The profit-makers will use only part of their net profits to buy Government bonds, so the Government will have to issue some more money. And in any case, the public will not simply accept an increase of prices, without trying to secure higher incomes; so wages will start to chase prices in a cumulative spiral.

The course of the inflation also depends on how quickly the new capital becomes productive, and how productive it is. If the money has been used to reclaim land and settle farmers on it, their increased output will check the rise of prices when it reaches the market. Also, the public is more likely to accept an unfavourable change in distribution which is offset by an increase in real consumption per head. This is a most important difference between the creation of money, say, to pay Government employees, and the use of such money to finance the creation of new resources which will increase commodity output.

Theoretically, an inflation can peter out either because of a permanent shift to taxes and savings, which flow to the original investors and so enable the new investment level to be held without additional new money; or because there is an increased flow of consumer good output which catches up with the increased money supply. If neither of these does the trick, prices will continue to rise. The reaction of the public then depends on the length of time during which this goes on. If the monetary tap is turned on for a couple of years, to finance some particular project, and then turned off again, prices may have ceased to rise before the public is sufficiently well organized to take protective measures. This is what happens in inflations caused by the creation of bank credit to finance private investment; the tap is turned on for two or three years, but before the public gets a chance to believe that prices will now rise continuously, the monetary authorities step in and turn it off again.

If the tap is not turned off, and prices continue to rise, the reaction of the public will also be influenced by the effectiveness of the Government in moderating the more obvious consequences of the inflation. Prices of goods which enter into the cost of living of the general population are more crucial than others; if these prices can be controlled, wage demands can be moderated. The increase in prices creates a shortage of foreign exchange; if the use of foreign exchange can be controlled effectively, and evasion avoided, priority needs can be met. Investment is distorted; export industries are discouraged; instead funds are put where prices are expected to rise most, including into stocks and real estate. An effective licensing of investment is difficult, but becomes necessary if the pattern of the economy is not to be grossly distorted. Governments differ in the efficiency with which they can operate such administrative controls, and populations vary widely in their willingness to co-operate.

SPIRAL INFLATION

No matter how efficient the Government may be, if the inflation is large enough (the rise in prices exceeding, say, 5 per cent per annum) and goes on for long enough (say, more than four years) it is likely to spiral. The public tumbles to what is happening and insists on taking protective measures. Wage and salary earners arrange for their incomes to rise as fast as prices. Each price increase is followed by an increase in wages; this raises costs, so prices increase again; and so on. This process can go on indefinitely, if the rate of inflation is held steady; some countries have had price increases averaging 20 per cent per annum for more than 50 years.

However, an "equilibrium" inflation of this kind serves no useful purpose. An inflation is useful only so long as the cost of living rises faster than the average expenditure on consumption, for this gap is what permits an increase in capital formation. Once the stage is reached where wages and prices are rising at the same rate, the inflation ceases to be useful. If the Government persists in trying to transfer resources through monetary expansion, it will have to expand the money supply at an accelerating rate, with prices rising faster and faster. This is the way of hyper-inflation. This cannot go on for very long, since no population will tolerate it for long.

Spiral inflations are not only useless, but are also difficult to stop. Wage and salary earners have grown accustomed to getting regular pay increases to catch up with price increases. At any point in time that a decision to stop the inflation is taken, some incomes are due for a rise. If they do not get it, there is unrest; whereas if they do get it, but employers are prohibited from passing on the increase, there will be some unemployment. Investors have grown used to profits accruing from a continuously augmented supply of money. Once the monetary supply is stabilized, a number of enterprises cease to be profitable, and employment is cut. Hence an inflation cannot be stopped without a temporary crisis in investment and employment. The crisis need not be long; six to eighteen months is normal. But those who will lose oppose the adoption of measures which would stop the inflation, and if they are sufficiently powerful, they can prevent a Government from putting an end to inflation. Some Latin American countries have had persistent inflation for so many decades that they are now probably incapable of living in any other way, unless there are major changes in the balance of political forces.

ALTERNATIVE TO TAXES

Thus the course and effects of an inflation cannot be predicted without knowing its circumstances; what the money is being used for; whether a permanent shift to profits is possible; whether the Government can maintain effective controls; and how public opinion will react. One can say at once that most underdeveloped countries would be unwise to launch upon an inflationary course because they could not control it. But one cannot rule out the possibility that some of the better organized societies can safely finance some capital formation by the creation of money.

Given the desire to accelerate capital formation, the practical alternative to the creation of money is the levying of higher taxes.

This too is likely to have some inflationary effects. For any attempt to reduce the share of consumption in national income, or to redistribute consumption at the expense of large groups, is certain to be unpopular whether it is done by increasing the supply of money or by increasing taxes. Inflation and an increase in indirect taxation both have the same immediate effect: an increase in prices; and direct taxes tend to be even more unpopular. Whatever the method of financing, the public will most probably react by demanding higher wages or income, so any method is capable of starting a price-wage spiral.

The fact is that an increase in the ratio of capital formation to national income is almost always accompanied by some increase in prices, however it may be financed. Even if the increase is financed by genuine savings, a rise in wages in profitable industries may provoke sympathetic increases in prices throughout the economy; or expansion may come up against crucial bottlenecks. If the increase in capital formation is financed from taxes, the public may resist changes in consumption patterns and start a cost-push spiral. It is not true that an increase in the price level always accelerates capital formation; but it is true that in most economies where the ratio of capital formation is accelerating, prices will be found to be rising. (Whether the ratio is high or low is not the point; the emphasis is on acceleration.)

Though taxation may also raise prices, it is nevertheless from the economic point of view greatly superior to inflation as a source of finance for capital formation. First, its effect on prices is likely to be much smaller. Secondly, the discipline of controlling the money supply is easier to maintain if the Government is not committed to using inflation as a means of acquiring resources. Once the tradition of monetary discipline is lost, Governments take to inflation like ducks to water, and financial control disappears. Thirdly, the incidence of taxation can be controlled more fairly and efficiently than the incidence of inflation. And fourthly, inflation is not so dangerous to the balance of payments, or so distorting to the pattern of investment. Continuous price inflation, moving domestic costs out of line with world prices, can be a major source of economic stagnation.

The idea that it is politically easier to mobilize resources through inflation than through taxation is probably spurious. For a Government which is capable of using inflation intelligently is probably equally capable of mobilizing resources through taxation; since if it is courageous, popular and efficient enough to enforce the measures which control inflation (and to stop it before it spirals) it is presumably equally capable of levying and collecting the necessary taxes. The situation may well be that countries which could use inflation safely do not need it; and those which need it cannot use it without getting into more trouble than it is worth; but political analysts may find some marginal cases.

SUMMARY

1. The supply of money can be increased as fast as the supply of goods without raising prices. An increase in the monetary sector relative to the subsistence sector also makes possible an increased supply of money to match increased demand.

2. An increase in the supply of money will immediately stimulate a greater output of consumer goods in an industrial country suffering from a trade depression. It will not generally have this effect in an underdeveloped country.

3. If the primary purpose of creating money is to finance increased capital formation, this purpose is likely to be achieved. The secondary effects of inflation on investment cannot be predicted with certainty. Some net increase is probable; considerable distortion is also probable, since inflation discourages investment in export industries and import substituting industries, and favours sectors not subject to world competition, such as luxury construction.

4. The degree of inflation will depend on the willingness of the general public to accept the redistribution of income which inflation causes; if the public is not willing, the inflation may spiral. The longer the inflation continues, the more effective the public becomes in evading its consequences, and therefore the greater the chance of its spiralling.

5. The degree of inflation also depends on the purpose of the inflation. If its purpose is to create quick-yielding productive capacity, the resulting flow of consumer goods holds prices in check; the public is also more likely to accept an unfavourable change in distribution which is offset by an increase in real consumption per head.

6. In an underdeveloped country inflation is merely a substitute for taxation. From the economic point of view it is an inferior substitute.

7. It may be easier politically to start an inflation than to tax; but the measures which control inflation, maximize its usefulness and minimize its disadvantages are no easier to adopt or administer than would be an increase in taxation.

IV.D.2. Inflation and Development Policy*

The first question to be discussed is whether the mobilization of an economy's resources

*From Harry G. Johnson, "Is Inflation the Inevitable Price of Rapid Development or a Retarding Factor in Economic Growth?" *Malayan Economic Review*, Vol. 11, No. 1, April 1966, pp. 22–8. Reprinted by permission.

by development policy inevitably involves inflation. It is contended here that some degree of inflation—but a moderate degree only—is the logical concomitant of efficient economic mobilization. The argument rests on two propositions. One is that so long as inflation proceeds at a rate low enough not to disturb seriously the general confidence in the stability of the value of money its effects are primarily to redistribute incomes, and to do so to an extent that does not involve serious social consequences, rather than to produce significant misallocations of resources, such as those which occur when people come to expect inflation and seek to protect themselves from it by holding goods instead of money and by using political means to safeguard their real incomes. The other proposition is that, owing to the various rigidities and immobilities characteristic of any economy, but paticularly of underdeveloped economies, upward movements of wages and prices can help to reallocate labour and resources and to draw labour out of traditional or subsistence sectors into the developing sectors of the economy. It is important to note that this proposition, like the first, presumes a general expectation of stability in the value of money, as a precondition for the offer of higher wages and prices to serve as an inducement to mobility.

The second proposition implies that some inflationary pressure in the economy will assist the task of mobilizing resources for development; the first implies that such inflationary pressure will not introduce offsetting distortions causing significant real losses to the economy as a whole, but will instead mainly involve transfers of income within the economy, the social consequences of which will be small enough to be acceptable. Efficient policy-making will therefore involve arriving at a trade-off between the mobilizing and redistributive effects of inflation that will involve some positive rate of inflation. The indicated optimum rate of inflation is likely to be significantly higher for an underdeveloped than for an advanced economy for two reasons: first, the sophisticated financial system of an advanced economy provides many more facilities for economizing on the use of money in face of expected inflation; and second, the superior mobility of resources of an advanced economy implies that the increase in total output achievable by inflationary means is relatively much smaller. Thus one might expect that whereas "tolerable" price stability

in an advanced economy is frequently defined as a rate of inflation of no more than one to two per cent a year, the tolerable degree of stability for an underdeveloped economy might be in the range of a four to six per cent annual rate of price increase. (Harberger has suggested that a 10 per cent annual rate of inflation represents the outside limit of inflation justifiable by this line of argument.)[1] This analysis, of course, relates to purely domestic considerations and ignores the balance-of-payments or exchange-rate implications of internal price trends.

The foregoing remarks relate to the question of inflation as a consequence or aspect of economic development policy, and to the argument that some degree of inflation is the necessary price of rapid development. It has been argued that a modest rate of inflation is a logical part of an efficient development policy, in the sense that the "price" may purchase gains in efficiency of resource allocation and utilization that outweigh the costs. The argument now turns to the second problem raised by the question, the effectiveness or otherwise of inflationary financing of development programmes.

The main theoretical arguments for inflationary development policies derive from two systems of economic thought, the Keynesian theory of income and the quantity theory of money. The Keynesian approach to the question (which derives from the Keynes of the *Tract* and the *Treatise* as much as from the Keynes of the *General Theory*) argues that inflation will promote growth in two ways: by redistributing income from workers and peasants, who are assumed to have a low marginal propensity to save, to capitalist entrepreneurs, who are assumed to have a high marginal propensity to save and invest; and by raising the nominal rate of return on investment relative to the rate of interest, thus promoting investment. Neither of these arguments, however, is either theoretically

[1] Arnold C. Harberger, "Some Notes on Inflation," in Werner Baer and Isaac Kerstenetzky (eds.), *Inflation and Growth in Latin America,* Homewood, Ill.: Irwin, 1964.

plausible or consistent with the facts, at least so far as sustained inflationary processes are concerned. Both rest on the arbitrary and empirically unsupported assumption that entrepreneurs realize that inflation is occurring, whereas the other members of the economy do not, or at least do not realize it fully. As to the first, the theoretical prediction is that all sectors of the economy the prices of whose services are upwards-flexible will come to anticipate inflation, so that no significant redistributions of income will take place; this prediction accords with the mass of the available evidence. As to the second, the theoretical expectation is that free-market interest rates will rise sufficiently to compensate holders of interest-yielding assets for the expected rate of inflation; this expectation also accords with the mass of the available evidence. This argument for inflation, therefore, is valid only under two possible sets of circumstances: first, in the early stages of an inflationary development programme, while the mass of the population (especially the workers and the savers) still has confidence in the stability of the value of money; and second, when inflationary financing is accompanied by governmental policies of holding down the wage and interest costs of business enterprise. Such policies would generate distortions in the allocation of resources, which might offset any benefits to growth from the inflationary policy; in particular, the contrary view has been argued that inflation will discourage the supply of saving for investment.

The quantity theory approach, on the other hand, adopts the more realistic assumption that in a sustained inflationary process the behavior of all sectors of the economy will become adjusted to the expectation of inflation, and that consequently the effect of inflation will be, not to redistribute income from workers or savers to capitalist entrepreneurs, but to redistribute it from the holders of money balances—who are the only losers from an inflation that is anticipated—to the monetary authorities who issue money the real value of which steadily depreciates. Inflation imposes an "inflationary tax" on holdings of money, which consists in the real resources that the

holders of money have to forego each period in order to restore the real value of their money holdings. The presence of this tax, in turn, encourages the public to attempt to evade the tax by reducing their holdings of money, shortening payments periods, holding inventories of goods instead of cash, and so forth; these efforts involve a waste of real resources and a reduction of real income, representing the "collection cost" of the inflationary tax. On the other hand, the real resources collected by the inflationary tax are available for use in the development programme; and if they are used for investment, the inflationary policy may accelerate economic growth. It should be noted, however, that in the transitional stages of an inflationary development policy, or in the process of acceleration of such a policy, whatever contribution to growth there is may be outweighed by the increased waste of resources produced by the increase in the inflationary tax.

In practical experience, resort to the inflationary tax as a method of financing economic development is generally prompted by the inability of the developing country to raise enough revenue by taxation and by borrowing from the public to finance its development plans, either as a result of the low income and taxable capacity of the economy, or more commonly as a result of inability to command the necessary political consensus in support of the necessary sacrifices of current income. Unfortunately, the same characteristics of underdevelopment that limit the capacity to finance development by orthodox fiscal methods also place rather narrow limits on the possibility of financing development by inflation. In particular, underdevelopment implies a relatively smaller use of money than is common in advanced countries, and therefore a relatively smaller base on which the inflationary tax can be levied.

Before discussing this point in detail, it is appropriate to refer to a related question that figured large in the development literature of about a decade ago, the question of the extent to which development can be financed by monetary expansion without producing inflationary consequences. The answer, clearly, is that such financing can be safely pursued up to the limit set by the growth of demand for money consequent on the expected growth of the economy at stable prices, plus the growth of demand for money associated with the monetization of the subsistence sector (where relevant), minus the portion of the growth in the money supply that must be created against private debt. The magnitude of the resources that can be made available for financing development by this means, however, depends on the magnitude of the absolute increase in the money supply permitted by these factors or, to put it another way, on the rate of growth of the demand for money, the ratio of money to income, and the portion of the additional money that can be used to finance public spending. Thus, for example, with a rate of growth of demand for money of 6 per cent, half of which can be used to finance public spending, the budget deficit financed by monetary expansion would be 3 per cent of the initial money supply. If the ratio of money supply to national income were in the neighborhood of two-fifths, as is common in advanced countries, this would make 1.2 per cent of national income available for development investment; if, on the other hand, the ratio of money supply to national income were in the lower neighborhood of one-fifth, as is common in underdeveloped countries, only one half of one per cent of national income would be available for development investment.[2] The difference in the order of magnitude of the money-to-income ratio explains both why budget deficits in underdeveloped countries are more frequently associated with inflation, and why in such countries inflationary financing of developent is more frequently resorted to, than in advanced countries.

In the same way as it limits the scope for non-inflationary deficit financing of development, the restricted use of money in underdeveloped countries limits the extent to

which inflation can make resources available for economic development through the inflationary tax. Ignoring the possibilities of non-inflationary financing by monetary expansion due to the growth and monetization of the economy, the yield of the inflationary tax as a proportion of national income will be the product of the money-to-income ratio, the rate of inflation, and the proportion of the increase in the money supply captured for financing development. Thus, with the assumed money-to-income ratio of one-fifth and an assumed capture rate of one-half, a 10 per cent rate of inflation would secure 1 per cent of national income for the development programme, and so on. The money-to-income ratio, however, is not insensitive to the rate of inflation, but is on the contrary likely to decrease appreciably as the rate of inflation rises, thereby setting limits to the possibilities of development finance by these means. Further, it should be noted that insofar as development financing depends on a growth of demand for money resulting from monetization of the economy, inflation is likely to reduce that growth by inhibiting monetization, so further reducing the net amount of resources gathered for development finance through inflation. . . .

The circumstances in which inflation is resorted to in underdeveloped countries, however, are far from the most favorable conceivable, and their inflations are extremely likely to proceed in such a way, and to be accompanied by such other economic policies, as to exercise a serious retarding influence on economic growth. Specifically, inflationary financing may impede growth in three major ways, each contrary to the assumptions of the inflationary tax model.

In the first place, contrary to the assumption that prices throughout the economy adjust freely to inflation, the government of a developing country employing inflationary development policies is likely to be under strong political pressure to protect important sectors of the community from the effects of inflation, through control of food prices, rents, urban transport fares, and so on. Such controls inevitably distort the allocation of

[2]The illustrative numbers used are derived from J. J. Polak, "Monetary Analysis of Income Formation and Payments Problems," *International Monetary Fund Staff Papers,* November 1957, Table on p. 25.

resources within the economy, and particularly their allocation to private investment in growth. Fixing of low prices for food inhibits the development of agricultural production and the improvement of agricultural technique; control of rents, on the other hand, may unduly foster the construction of new housing to accommodate those who cannot find rent-controlled housing or to enable landlords to evade rent controls. All these policies tend to promote urbanization, which involves expenditure on social overhead and may increase the numbers of the urban unemployed. Moreover, control of prices of food, and particularly of fares on state-owned transport facilities, may involve the state in explicit subsidies on the one hand and budget deficits on the other, so that the proceeds of the inflationary tax are wasted in supporting the consumption of certain sections of the population rather than invested in development. Such phenomena are widely observable in the underdeveloped countries of the world. (They are also observable in advanced countries, but the latter can easily afford the wastes of resources involved.)

Second, contrary to the assumptions of the inflationary tax model, inflation typically does not proceed at a steady and well-anticipated rate, but proceeds erratically with large politically-determined variations in the rate of price increase. These variations in the rate of inflation divert a great deal of the effort of private business into forecasting and speculating on the rate of inflation, or hedging against the uncertainties involved. They also destroy the possibility of rational calculation of small margins of profit and undermine the incentives to strive constantly to reduce costs and improve performance, which striving is the key to the steady increase of productivity in the industrially advanced nations.

Finally, the inflationary tax model assumes either a closed economy or a country on a floating exchange rate system. In reality, countries—especially underdeveloped countries—are exposed to competition in and from the world economy, yet they display a strong propensity to maintain fixed exchange rates and to defend them to the limit of their exchange reserves, borrowing powers, and ability to use exchange controls. In this kind of setting inflation introduces a progressive tendency toward exchange rate overvaluation, balance-of-payments difficulties, and resort to increasing protectionism, which in turn results in the diversion of resources away from export industries and toward high-cost import-substituting industries, and a consequent loss of economic efficiency. While the appearance of growth may be generated by the establishment of import-substitute industries, the reality may be lost in misallocation of resources produced by protectionism and the inefficiency of exchange control procedures. Moreover, eventually the increasing overvaluation of the currency is likely to force a devaluation, coupled with a monetary reform involving drastic domestic deflation. This experience, in addition to the immediate disturbing effects of deflation in interrupting the growth of the economy, has the long-run effect of damaging the stability and confidence of expectations on which the process of investing in the growth of the economy depends.

To summarize, this paper has argued the following propositions. First, an efficient development policy should plan on some modest degree of inflation as a means of more fully mobilizing the economy's resources; in this limited sense, inflation is an inevitable price of rapid development. Second, while a policy of financing development by deliberate inflation has strong attractions theoretically and politically, the possibilities of stimulating economic development by these means are quite limited. Third, inflationary development policies in practice are unlikely to achieve this stimulating effect, but on the contrary likely to retard economic growth, by distorting the allocation of resources and wasting the inflation-gathered development resources on consumption, by increasing uncertainty and reducing incentives for innovation and improvement, and through their balance-of-payments effects by fostering the inefficiencies of protectionism and exchange control.

IV.D.3. Monetarism and Structuralism in Latin America*

The controversy between "monetarists" and "structuralists" in Latin America has been exaggerated beyond all bounds. While rather virulent in theoretical disquisitions, it narrows down substantially when practical policy recommendations have to be formulated.

One cruel fact that the structuralists must face, when entrusted with policy responsibilities outside the academic wards, is that structural adjustments inevitably take a long time, while the combat to inflation, if it is to succeed, needs fairly quick, visible results; and those can be obtained much more expeditiously (though often at the cost of painful side effects) through the demand side—via monetary and fiscal policies—than through the supply side (unless foreign aid is available in unlimited amounts). I do not, of course, deny that the purely monetary or fiscal solution may not be durable or consistent with stable growth unless adjustments are also made on the supply side. The truth is, that in the short run, all structuralists when entrusted with policy-making responsibilities become monetarists, while all monetarists are, in the long run, structuralists. Thus, we might jocosely define a monetarist as a structuralist in a hurry and a structuralist as a monetarist without policy-making responsibility.

Let us try to determine at this stage what the controversy is not. It is not a quarrel between those economists and policy-makers who recognize the existence of structural rigidities and those who do not. All recognize that structural problems do exist. It is not a controversy between those who favor economic growth and development and those who do not. It is not a debate between those who advocate an economic policy which permits the economy to grow and those who ad-

*From Roberto de Oliveira Campos, "Economic Development and Inflation with Special Reference to Latin America," in OECD, *Development Plans and Programmes*, OECD Development Center, Paris, 1964, pp. 129–37. Reprinted by permission.

vocate a restrictive monetary policy in an attempt to hold down the money supply and keep prices absolutely constant.

The basic controversy lies in the tendency of economists of the structuralist persuasion to view monetary expansion and inflation as an unavoidable feature of structural change and economic growth in Latin America; and correlatedly to claim that the attempt to avoid monetary expansion and inflation will only hamper structural changes and economic growth. If other descriptions are needed, one might say that the structuralists would hold that the permissiveness of the monetary and fiscal policy of the monetary authorities is simply a reflection of exogenous factors, particularly the decline in import capacity, while the monetarists would hold that this fatalistic result is not inevitable, and that inflation cannot be blamed exclusively or even predominantly on "exogenous" factors, but rather on the "policies of inaction" pursued by most of the Latin American governments.

Another "spurious" presentation of the controversy is to take the view that monetarists in Latin America are slavishly following monetary tenets of classical liberalism, by adhering strictly to the quantity theory in money and banking, to free trade views in matters of international trade, to non-intervention doctrines insofar as government activities are concerned, and generally by ascribing lower priority to development than to stabilization and by neglecting the special problems of structural under-employment or unemployment in underdeveloped countries. . . .

THE MONETARIST VIEW ON INFLATION AND GROWTH

Apart from a small current of thought that approaches the question of inflation and development from the viewpoint of value judgments, and that, by questioning the social advantage of inflation-financed development, tends to ascribe high social priority to stabilization, the bulk of the monetarists in Latin America appear to recognize the social priority of development, while insisting that continued and stable growth can best be attained in an environment of monetary stability. Their position can be thus summarized:

1. The only possible contributions of inflation to growth derive:

a. From the forced saving mechanism, through which the decline in real wages due to rising prices and the wage lag would increase investible profits. Thus inflation would act as a disguised taxation on consumers and savers to the benefit of investors;

b. From the assumption that the pressure of inflationary demand would permit a fuller utilization of manpower and resources, while conversely the attempt to combat inflation by wiping out excess demand might bring employment and resource-utilization down to the level permitted by bottleneck factors;

c. From the assumption that inflation would stimulate bold entrepreneuriship and reward investors at the expense of conservative savers or rentiers.

Against these supposed advantages, the monetarists raise a formidable number of qualifications: (i) the forced savings device can act only temporarily for discontinuous inflation, but has its efficacy lowered or destroyed when inflation is chronic and becomes a part of the expectation of wage earners, who devise defense mechanisms to prevent a decline in real wages. It is true that in dual societies, in which because of institutional factors real wages in some urban industries are set above the limit of marginal productivity, it is possible, because of the continuous migration of under-employed rural labor to the city, and given the relative rigidity of factoral proportions of labor and capital in modern technology, to depress the real urban wage for protracted periods; this, however, only prolongs a little bit the usefulness of the forced savings mechanism but does not guarantee its continuity; (ii) such transfer of resources as may take place from consumers to the government or to investors

may be offset by luxury consumption of the entrepreneurial group, by the lower efficiency of government investments or by bottlenecks in the import capacity; (iii) while inflation encourages the adventurous entrepreneur, it tends to discourage risk-taking in basic enterprises of a long maturation period.

2. Inflation discourages the inflow of foreign capital and renders more difficult the absorption of financing from foreign governments and institutional organizations.

3. Inflation tends to impair the qualitative composition of investments. It discourages investments in basic industries and infrastructural services which are either price-controlled or require long gestation periods, or both. It weakens or prevents the creation of credit and capital markets and stimulates speculative investments in inventories.[1]

4. The structural thesis exaggerates the two basic alleged rigidities: the inelasticity of the food supply and the inelasticity of exports. The reasoning of the structuralists starts from the premise of a total sectoral incompressibility of prices, so that any upward price pressure would result in a rise in the general price level. Thus the pressure of population growth and rising urban incomes would tend to raise, through a chain-reaction mechanism, first the price of agriculture goods, secondly the general price level and thirdly wages, thus creating an inflationary spiral of a structural nature. Similarly, the inelasticity of world demand for primary export would tend to lower the export capacity below import requirements for growth, rendering necessary an accelerated process of import substitution. But, at least initially, import substitution tends to be inflationary because of the relative inefficiency of the new industries during the learning period, this cost pressure being aggravated by the need for exchange devaluations in an attempt to restore external balance. The monetarists would argue that the alleged structural in-

[1]These results need not necessarily occur. For a different view, see Werner Baer, "Inflation and Economic Efficiency in Brazil," paper presented at the Rio de Janeiro Conference on Inflation and Development, January, 1963.

elasticity of food supplies is often not structural at all. It stems frequently from the fact that the administrative control of food prices, designed to protect the urban consumer, cuts off the agricultural producer from price and market stimuli, so that the inelasticity of food supply, rather than being an inherent structural characteristic, may be a distortion induced by administrative controls. While in some cases the structure of land tenure would prevent in any event the diffusion of market incentives, thus rendering structural reform a precondition for increasing food production, this situation occurs only rarely. As to industrial import substitution, while it is not denied that it carries a built-in inflationary pressure, at least if the industrial expansion takes place at constant cost, the cost-push arising therefrom has been grossly exaggerated. Thus, assuming that imports for a typical underdeveloped country represent 10 per cent of national product, that real income is rising at 6 per cent per annum, that exports are stationary and that the income-elasticity of demand for imported products equals 2, and finally, that the needed customs protection for the national substitutes is 100 per cent—all of those factors would not entail a price increase above 1.2 per cent per annum, a margin vastly surpassed in the inflated economies of Latin America.

CRITICISM OF THE MONETARIST APPROACH

The monetarist approach has curiously enough been attacked from two conflicting vantage points. It is argued, on the one hand, that it is too strong because controls will restrain investment, generating unemployment and losses in real output, thus not only aggravating the supply problem but also arousing political instability. Some argue, on the other hand, that it is too weak, because without the leverage of fiscal policies it does not really control excess demand nor go to the heart of structural and institutional problems.

Four points may be readily granted. The *first* is that the only meaningful interpretation of the monetarist approach is that it encompasses not only the use of traditional monetary weapons—the efficacy of which is by definition very limited in the rather primitive financial markets characteristic of the less developed countries—but also of fiscal policies. The *second* is that the effectiveness of monetary weapons, *stricto sensu,* is considerably greater in the case of *demand inflation* than of *cost inflation.* This is particularly true if the problem is that of a wage spiral, where the reduction of the quantity of money may stop the rise in prices but *only* at the expense of employment. The *third* point is that monetary tools, as distinct from fiscal policies, are inappropriate when the problem is to curb consumption (which can only be achieved via fiscal policies), the effectiveness of monetary restraints being greater if the objective is to restrain investment.

The *fourth* point is the asymmetrical effect of monetary policies; through a combination of quantitative and qualitative credit controls it is possible to orient a selective expansion of certain economic sectors but much harder to enforce a selective restriction of undesirable sectors.

The net upshot of these observations is that monetary weapons, though an indispensable ingredient in anti-inflationary programmes, have to be used in a prudent combination with fiscal policies. The shortcomings to their application arise not only from asymmetrical effects—they affect investment more than consumption, their efficiency is greater in reducing demand than costs—but from the limited organization and responsiveness of money and credit markets in the less developed countries. Fiscal policies, particularly when designed to curb luxury consumption by taxation of wealthier groups so as to raise the marginal tax rate above the average rate, have undoubtedly a fundamental role to play in anti-inflation programmes.

The applicability of monetary policies depends, of course, on the speed desired in checking inflation and on the degree of flexibility of the wage pattern and labor organisation. The latter factor is a major determinant of the possibility of utilization of credit controls without untoward unemployment effects.

THE "STRUCTURALIST" VIEW

The "structuralist" school stresses the "structural vulnerability" of Latin American economies to inflation because of two alleged basic rigidities.

The first one is the slow and unstable rate of export growth, which is held to be chronically inadequate to support the needed rate of development; the sluggish growth rate makes necessary a continuous and sharp effort of import substitution, creating a cost-push because of the substitution effort itself; the instability of the growth rate in turn creates occasional contraction of government tax revenues arising from exports, precisely when government expenditures need to be increased to offset the depressant effect of the stagnation or recession of the export sector; finally, the secular trend towards deterioration of the trade of primary products creates an additional complication, further limiting the potentialities of growth of the export income, and reinforcing the trend toward periodical exchange rate devaluation.

The second one is the inelasticity of agricultural production, due largely to defective patterns of land tenure which decrease the responsiveness of food production to price stimuli.

The cost-push in Latin American economies would thus come from a fourfold direction: cost of import substitution, rise in agricultural prices, deterioration of the terms of trade and exchange rate devaluation.

Fortified with those tenets, the structuralists proceed to inveigh against what they call the "orthodox" monetary policies advised by the International Monetary Fund, which in their view do not go to the heart of the problem—structural change—and have depressant effects, manifested in a decrease in the level of investment, in the contraction of the private sector due to the incompressibility of the public sector and in the deflationary effects of unemployment and the wage lag.

Thus stability is achieved only at the expense of growth.

CRITICISM OF THE STRUCTURALIST APPROACH

While the structuralists are very articulate in their diagnosis of Latin American inflation and in their strictures on monetarism, they are far less explicit on practical policy recommendations. These do not go usually beyond the expression of pious hopes for structural changes, which because of their long-run nature are not serviceable recipes for the short-run cure of inflation.

The structuralist tends therefore to advocate gradualism in anti-inflationary programmes and to postulate an increase in foreign aid and international financing as major factors in helping to buy time for the needed structural changes.

One of the most cogent and articulate criticisms of the structuralist interpretation of Latin American inflation has been put forward by Arthur Lewis in his "Closing remarks at the Conference on Inflation and Development in Latin America," convened in January, 1963 in Rio de Janeiro.

Lewis' initial and important contribution is to stress the difference between *self-liquidating* and *spiral inflation,* the first being relevant and the second irrelevant for economic development. Through *self-liquidating* inflation limited policy objectives can be attained, such as altering permanently the distribution of income in favor of investment. The *spiral* inflation, in turn, does not serve any growth objective but is rather a political phenomenon, arising from tensions in the society.

The *first* stricture of Lewis is to question the alleged inevitable sluggishness of the export sector of primary producing countries. He mentions that between 1950 and 1960, the quantum of trade in primary products grew by 6 per cent, only slightly under the rate of growth of manufactured exports, which was 7 per cent. While Lewis is right in excoriating the excessive importance attributed by the structuralist school to the "structural" sluggishness of the export sector in Latin America, he dismisses altogether too glibly the trade problem, which is real. In particular, he overlooks the fact that:

a. Part of the statistical expansion of exports of primary products in the last decade did not come from the underdeveloped countries but from the industrialized countries. The latter expanded their export of primary products by 57 per cent while the former by only 14 per cent. Thus not only world trade in manufactures expanded at a faster rate, but the lion's share of primary exports was taken by the industrialized countries themselves. Latin American exports were also greatly affected by a price decline since 1953. While world trade grew in volume by 50 per cent between 1953 and 1960, raw material prices declined by 7 per cent. Brazil expanded its volume of exports by 20 per cent in the above period, while unit prices fell by 37 per cent.

b. The trade experience with which Professor Lewis is most familiar is that of the sheltered trade area of the British Commonwealth countries. But Latin America was for all practical purposes, until the recent creation of LAFTA, an unsheltered trade area, and the GATT report on "Trends in International Trade" presents conclusive evidence that trade within sheltered areas has been expanding at a substantially faster rate than the trade of unsheltered areas.

Just as Professor Lewis appears to minimize unduly the importance of the decline in the import capacity of Latin America, the "structuralists" of ECLA overestimate its explanatory and causal role in the process of inflation. As Professor Grunwald has pointed out, despite a decline in the export quantum over the last decade, the Latin American countries managed to maintain or even to increase their import quantum by depletion of exchange reserves and/or increase in international indebtedness.[2]

[2]Grunwald, "Invisible Hands in Inflation and Growth," p. 11, paper submitted to the Rio de Janeiro Conference on Inflation and Development, January, 1963. [W. Baer and I. Kerstenetzky (eds.), *Inflation and Growth in Latin America*, Homewood, 1964.]

It is true that this does not quite solve the problem, particularly in those countries where the decline in export activity requires compensatory government policies for domestic expansion, or where fiscal revenues are greatly dependent on export taxation. But the brunt of the argument is taken. The two main weaknesses of the structuralist view on trade are then:

a. that some of the sluggishness in the export growth is not really structural but results plainly from the failure to exploit, because of overvalued exchange rates, export opportunities that may still exist;

b. the import quantum has been maintained, on the average, for Latin America, despite the decline in export revenues, so that there has been no inflationary decrease in the availability of import goods.

The *second* stricture of Professor Lewis concerns the wage push. He tends to deny any special characteristic to the Latin American wage scene, as compared to other underdeveloped regions more successful in controlling inflation; he also writes off the wage spiral in Latin America as simply a political problem, resulting from the low degree of sympathy of trade unions for their governments. It is impossible to deny, however, that there are vast differences between Latin America and other underdeveloped regions of Africa or Asia in a number of respects. There is less surplus labor in Latin America, the degree of labor organisation is greater, there is more responsiveness to Western consumption habits and less passivity in claiming social benefits. Even within Latin America, there are substantial regional differences, the difficulty of preventing a wage spiral being directly related to the degree of labor union organisation, which seems greater in the Argentine and Chile, much lower in Mexico, Peru and Colombia, while Brazil holds an intermediate position.

The *third* stricture of Professor Lewis concerns the alleged rigidity of agricultural production. He is right in pointing out that pressure on food supplies is not peculiar to the underdeveloped countries of Latin America and that structuralists underestimate the possibility of corrective adjustments by increasing the propensity to export or by reducing the propensity to import.

What might be said by way of conclusion is that the basic flaws in the structuralist argument seem thus to lie in that:

a. no separation is made between autonomous structural rigidities and induced rigidities resulting from price or exchange controls or mismanaged government intervention;

b. the quantitative importance of the cost-push generated by import substitution, or by losses in import capacity through the decline in terms of trade, is greatly exaggerated; while those factors might account for a moderate inflationary pressure, they are of little use to explain the massive and chronic inflation in Latin America.

Comment

An excellent guide to the literature on the "structuralist school" is contained in Dudley Seers, "A Theory of Inflation and Growth in Under-developed Countries Based on the Experience in Latin America," *Oxford Economic Papers* (June 1963). For additional readings on inflation in Latin America, the following may be consulted: Werner Baer, "Inflation and Economic Growth: An Interpretation of the Brazilian Case," *Economic Development and Cultural Change* (October 1962); Werner Baer, "The Inflation Controversy in Latin America: A Survey," *Latin American Research Review* (Winter 1967); Werner Baer and I. Kerstenetzky (eds.), *Inflation and Growth in Latin America* (1964); David Felix, "Structural Imbalances, Social Conflict, and Inflation," *Economic Development and Cultural Change* (January 1960); David Felix, "An Alternative View of the 'Monetarist'–'Structuralist' Controversy," in A. O. Hirschman (ed.), *Latin American Issues* (1961); G. Maynard, "Inflation and Growth: Some Lessons to be Drawn from Latin American Experience," *Oxford Economic Papers* (June 1961); Celso Furtado, "Industrialization and Inflation," *International Economic Papers,* Vol. 12 (1967); Rosemary Thorp, "Inflation and the Financing of Economic Development," in Keith Griffin (ed.), *Financing Development in Latin America* (1971).

The structuralist and monetarist explanations of inflation are also discussed, together with a review of the theoretical and empirical evidence on inflation in LDCs, in C. H. Patrick and F. I. Nixson, "The Origins of Inflation in LDCs: a Selective Review," in M. Parkin and G. Zis (eds.), *Inflation in Open Economies* (1976).

General aspects of the problem of inflation in LDCs are also examined in the following: E. M. Bernstein and I. G. Patel, "Inflation in Relation to Economic Development," *IMF Staff Papers* (November 1952); Bent Hansen, *Inflation Problems in Small Countries* (1960); G. S. Dorrance, "Rapid Inflation and International Payments," *Finance & Development* (June 1965); A. P. Thirwall, *Inflation, Savings and Growth in Developing Economies* (1974); P. J. Drake, *Money, Finance and Development* (1980); W. R. Cline et al., *World Inflation and the Developing Countries* (1981); M. J. Flanders and A. Razin (eds.), *Development in an Inflationary World* (1981); Harvey Leibenstein, *Inflation, Income Distribution and X-Efficiency* (1980); Anand G. Chandavarkar, "Monetization of Developing Economies," *IMF Staff Papers* (November 1977); Peter S. Heller, "Impact of Inflation on Fiscal Policy in Developing Countries," *IMF Staff Papers* (December 1980).

IV.D.4. Causes and Consequences of Inflation*

According to the structuralist view, there will exist at any given time some sectors which are under-utilised and suffering from inadequate demand co-existing with others experiencing excess demand and rising prices. Because of poor information flows, shortages of entrepreneurial and capital resources, policy biases and other factors making for small elasticities of supply, large disequilibria will be necessary before economic forces respond to break the bottlenecks. Because of downward stickiness, rising prices in excess demand sectors will not be offset by falling prices in the excess supply sectors and there will thus be a continuous (but not very rapid) upward movement in the general price level. The agricultural sector is likely to be important in this context, with its small short-run elasticities of supply and its tendency in many countries to lag behind the expansion of the remainder of the economy. A heavy cost would be imposed in terms of reduced output and growth if total demand were held to such low levels that prices were stable even in the low-elasticity sectors. At least at moderate rates of inflation, a trade-off is thus postulated between growth and inflation; a society that gives priority to growth must be willing to tolerate the inflation that comes with it.

Many economists accept the validity of this argument and of the view that governments should allow aggregate demand persistently to exert mild pressure on available resources, as a stimulus to investment. Some have gone further positively to advocate inflationary deficit financing by the government as a means of accelerating growth. The essence of this case is that this demand inflation will redistribute income in ways which raise saving and investment. Company profits (and self-financed investment) will go up as firms find themselves able to raise prices without

corresponding increases in costs. The government budget, so it is argued, will also benefit, in the form of revenue from the 'inflation tax', which is the loss of real purchasing power imposed by rising prices on holders of money balances. So long as companies and the government have larger marginal propensities to save than the groups in society whose real incomes fall, total saving and investment will be increased. And if investment is the binding constraint on the growth of the economy, the rate of growth will accelerate.

In opposition to this, there are others who argue that inflation is more likely to hamper growth. Far from encouraging saving, rising prices penalise it by eroding its real value. Inflation, it is further argued, tends to distort the composition of investment in favour of quick-yielding, perhaps speculative, projects while discouraging long-term investments in research or heavy industry. Moreover, inflation, the greater price instability that accompanies it and the expectation of counter-measures by the government will be imperfectly anticipated, thus increasing uncertainty and making forward planning more difficult. This will deter some investment altogether and reduce the productivity of the investments which do occur. In the extreme case, hyperinflation results in a flight out of money, a breakdown in the allocative efficiency of the economy, severe bottlenecks, dysfunctional changes in the distribution of income, and retarded growth.

However, it is argued, probably the most potent way in which inflation can harm growth is through its effect on the balance of payments. If (a) inflation at home is faster than the general rate of world inflation and (b) the exchange rate is fixed or imperfectly flexible, then excess demand at home will spill over into additional imports, and export production costs will rise without compensating increases in world prices. The balance of trade will thus be weakened and the economy may encounter a foreign-exchange constraint.

*From Tony Killick, "Inflation in Developing Countries: An Interpretative Survey," *ODI Review 1*, 1981, pp. 4–6, 8–11, 13–15. Reprinted by permission.

These various arguments conflict in every way except one: they all treat growth as the dependent and inflation as the independent variable, with causality running from the latter to the former. It is, however, possible to reverse this hierarchy, to argue that inflation will be a diminishing function of the real growth of the economy. Growth expands the supply of goods and services which, if not accompanied by equal increases in demand, can absorb previously existing pressures of excess demand. The growth of real incomes will increase the demand for money balances relative to money supply, which will diminish any excess supply of money and excess demand for goods.

There is thus a wide range of viewpoints on the likely connections between inflation and growth, yielding quite different hypotheses and policy implications. It is, nevertheless, possible to suggest a limited degree of consensus within the profession. This would postulate an inverted-U-shaped relationship between inflation and growth. At one end of the inflationary spectrum, it is suggested, there would be general agreement that there is some "safe," low range of inflation which will be positively associated with growth because it will stimulate capacity utilisation and investment or, more negatively, because the policies needed to avoid it would slow down the expansion of the economy. It is also in this range that the growth of output will have its most noticeable effects in moderating inflationary pressures. At the other end of the spectrum, there would probably be wide acceptance that very rapid inflation is harmful to growth, for reasons already outlined. If there is an inverted-U relationship, it implies the existence of an optimal rate of inflation, above which it becomes increasingly important for the government to take corrective action.

However, only a limited consensus is claimed. Most would probably agree that single-figure inflation is in the "safe" range; and that rates of above, say 25 per cent are likely to hamper the growth of output. The remaining disagreement is about the effects of inflation within the notional range of 10 per cent to 25 per cent—but it is in that range that much inflation occurs!

It should, in principle, be possible to establish the nature of the relationship in question through econometric testing. There are, however, a number of complicating factors. First, there are many influences on the growth of an economy besides the behaviour of the price level—influences which are difficult to capture adequately in regression models. Second, the inverted U-shaped relationship is non-linear and is thus not well suited to testing by the techniques of linear regression. Third, it is possible for various of the influences summarised earlier to be at work simultaneously but tending to cancel each other out: the top of the inverted-U may be roughly horizontal over a range of inflation values and this would result in weak correlations. Finally, there are difficulties in interpretation, about the direction of causality between inflation and growth.

It is therefore unsurprising that few empirical studies of the growth-inflation relationship have arrived at strong statistical results. . . . Nevertheless, some studies have produced evidence consistent with the inverted-U hypothesis—results which are not individually strong but which collectively do assume some substance. . . .

Since the growth of an economy is likely to be strongly influenced by the rates of saving and investment, an alternative approach to the study of the influence of inflation is to measure its effect on these variables. Here too the evidence is not strong, with most results having unsatisfactory levels of significance. . . .

So far the discussion has related exclusively to the connections between price movements and economic growth. But it is no longer necessary to argue that growth is only one aspect of economic development. We must pay attention to the impact of inflation on the structure of the economy, on poverty and on the distribution of income, although the evidence is tentative. Take first the impact on productive structure.

It is intuitively plausible to think that accelerating inflation will be associated with increased *relative* movements of prices within the economy. For one thing, there are liable to be considerable differences in the supply elasticities of different sectors. Indeed, Hirschman is among those who have advocated the use of inflation to stimulate output by providing large incentives for fresh investments in low-elasticity sectors. We are not aware of any direct evidence on the behaviour of relative prices during inflation in developing countries, but there is evidence from America that changes in relative prices are a positive function of the general rate of inflation.

Changing relative prices are likely to induce changes in the composition of output if they are of a more than transitory nature. Whether inflation persistently biases prices in favour of particular sectors is not clear and Spraos has suggested, on the basis of theoretical considerations, that the outcome will be crucially influenced by whether the problem is one of demand or cost inflation. In the case of cost inflation, he suggests that relative prices will shift systematically in favour of manufacturing; demand inflation will shift relative prices in favour of primary production, of which foodstuffs is likely to be the most important component. From a different standpoint, the structuralist school claims a persistent tendency for final food prices to rise relative to the general level, although they have supply bottlenecks and anti-agricultural policy biases in mind, rather than general excess demand. There is, in fact, some evidence of a bias towards agriculture. For example, the median inflation rate for the 70 developing countries covered by [a recent study] was 6.9 per cent p.a., while the median rate for food items alone was 8.4 per cent. On alternative assumptions about the weight of food in the total index, this implies that food prices rose 35 per cent to 50 per cent faster than non-food items.

Any tendency for food prices to outstrip the general price level will also influence *distributional* consequences of inflation, and the same is true of other ways in which the price level interacts with the productive structure. More generally, the incidence of gains and losses will depend upon the nature of the inflationary process; and upon the abilities of different groups in society to anticipate inflation and protect themselves against it. It is difficult to generalise but if we take the case of demand inflation, with supply elasticities in foodstuffs production lower than for most other goods and a fixed exchange rate, then the *gainers* are likely to include (a) the producers and distributors of foodstuffs; (b) those who derive their incomes from profits (because final selling prices rise faster than costs when there is demand inflation); and (c) distributors of imported goods (because buoyant demand conditions and a foreign exchange constraint will result in a scarcity premium on such goods). The *losers* from this type of situation will include (d) the economically inactive (the unemployed, housewives, the aged); (e) the urban poor; (f) other members of the urban wage-labour force; and (g) exporters (faced with rising costs and a fixed exchange rate).

If this is accepted as a likely outcome, then it seems more likely than not that inflation will increase inequalities, with the urban poor being especially vulnerable, although this conclusion would need to be modified if smallholder food farmers were substantial beneficiaries.

THE CAUSES OF INFLATION

There is much controversy, and a large accompanying literature, on the causes of inflation in LDCs. We can make a beginning by exploring the relative importance of external and domestic forces, for the global nature of inflation has become evident in recent years and some analysts have emphasised the inflationary effects of rising import prices. On the basis of cross-country data, however, it is difficult to believe that rising import prices could directly explain more than a modest part of LDC inflation. Remember that LDC imports are typically equivalent to about 20 per cent of GDP, so that the direct impact of a 10 per cent increase in import prices should only be to add about 2 per cent to the general price level. If we confine ourselves to impact effects, even the large import price rises of the post-1973 years could only account statistically for a moderate increase in the inflation rate.

Even more persuasive, however, is the fact that at all times LDC inflation rates have been faster than the rate of increase in import prices. . . .

It could, no doubt, be countered that the impact effects of rising import prices are magnified by the resulting attempts of wage-earners and others to protect their living standards, so that even a modest initial impact could lead to a large and continuing inflation. It is doubtful, however, whether such powerful propagation mechanisms exist in more than a minority of LDCs. We should also remember the finding reported above of a negative correlation between inflation and openness. While the behaviour of import prices no doubt contributed importantly to the accelerated inflation of 1973–79, even for this period it is evident that there were also powerful domestic forces at work. We therefore turn to consider the relative importance of the various possible domestic sources of inflation. A good deal of the relevant literature has already been surveyed by the present writer elsewhere and it is a useful short-cut to reproduce the main conclusions below, before going on to consider further evidence. These were as follows:

1. Both supply and demand factors contribute to an on-going inflation. This makes it difficult to establish the initiating cause.
2. There is, in any case, no reason for thinking that the initiating force will be the same for all countries, or at different times in a single country.
3. Although import prices do have an inflationary influence, the cost-push model fails to provide an adequate explanation of the initiation of inflation in most LDCs.
4. Structural considerations help to explain why LDCs are generally more prone to inflation than industrial countries. But the inflationary effects of structural disequilibria are unlikely to be large in most circumstances and they cannot explain widely varying inflation experiences among LDCs, nor the initiation of rapid inflations experienced in a few of them.
5. Expansion of the supply of money more rapidly than the growth in demand for it is sufficient to initiate inflation and essential to keep inflation going. This was probably the initiating force in at least some high-inflation countries. However, the impact of rising prices on the general public is limited to the extent that production and consumption still occur outside the monetised part of the economy. . . .

[A summary analysis of cross-country and individual-country studies is omitted.]

The balance of the evidence . . . points rather firmly to monetary expansion as the chief proximate source of inflation. If this is accepted, it has implications for the causes of the balance-of-payments difficulties also common among LDCs, for the excess demand generated by monetary expansion will increase the demand for imports and exportables in addition to pulling up domestic prices. Given government reluctance to depreciate the currency in line with increases in domestic prices and costs relative to those of the outside world, inflation tends to result in over-valued currencies, which reduces the incentives to export and to produce local import-substitutes. Acceptance of the proposition that inflation frequently has roots in the monetary system thus lends support to the IMF view that a high proportion of countries' foreign-exchange difficulties have domestic origins.

But some important qualifications are necessary. First, while the available published evidence does lean towards monetarist explanations, there is by no means unanimity and there are no grounds for believing that inflationary processes are uniform between countries. One difficulty is that the structuralist argument does not lend itself easily to statistical testing, which may bias results in favour of alternative hypotheses. More fundamentally, the monetary factor can only offer a superficial explanation, which is why we have called it a "proximate" source of inflation.

Always assuming governments to have control over monetary aggregates (although they may not), we are left with the question why governments allow money supply to expand so fast as to produce unwanted inflation and payments difficulties.

The answer is probably that effective measures to halt the monetary expansion are at least as unpopular as inflation and foreign-exchange shortages themselves. Cutting back on government spending, imposing credit restrictions, increasing taxation are all measures liable to worsen unemployment in economies already characterised by much unemployment; to reduce private consumption in countries with already low living standards; and to reduce public-sector investment in a situation of capital scarcity.

It is also likely that those who gain from inflation (or who would suffer most from attempts to control it) are among the politically more powerful members of society, for the business community can expect profit margins to widen with demand inflation but to narrow during periods of demand restraint. The government itself is likely to stand among the gainers. Even if government expenditures often move ahead of tax receipts in response to inflation the government will still benefit from the lower real cost of servicing the domestically-owned public debt and from the "inflation tax." Treasury officials may thus be ambiguous about anti-inflation measures, and they are a group of key importance. On the other side, the welfare costs of inflation tend (a) to be diffused across the general consuming public but (b) to be particularly concentrated on groups possessing little political clout—the urban poor and various categories of economic dependents. Governments have to weigh the diffused and ambiguous unpopularity of allowing inflation against the often more sharply focussed unpopularity of, and resistances to, countermeasures. Inflation may cause less social disharmony (and lose less popular support) than its alternatives, which helps to explain why governments are so rarely willing to pursue anti-inflation policies successfully for more than temporary interludes.

Even if the monetarist explanation is accepted, therefore, the management of inflation is not just a technical matter of regulating money supply and it is for reasons of this kind that there is a growing literature offering socio-political explanations of inflation. Economic stabilisation measures thus involve highly political judgements and the sensitivity of the issues helps explain why governments find it hard to pursue successful stabilisation or to accept the demand management policies urged upon them by the IMF.

Comment

The structuralist view of instability, in the form of open or repressed inflation, has been increasingly criticized by newer views on financial repression. Monetary mismanagement, both in the form of excessive growth of the money supply and erroneous selective credit policies, holds institutional interest rates (particularly deposit rates of interest) below their market equilibrium. This financial repression not only fails to overcome structural deficiencies but actually exacerbates them. In contrast, it is argued that the rise in real interest rates that results from the simultaneous introduction of a financial stabilization plan and the liberalization of portfolio and interest rate regulations should promote growth. Going beyond monetarists who only take into account the necessary restriction of the money supply, the proponents of liberalization to overcome financial repression advocate financial reforms that raise real interest rates and improve the process of financial intermediation.

The long-run negative relationship between inflation and growth in financially repressed economies has been analyzed by the following: Ronald I. McKinnon, *Money and Capital in Economic Development* (1973); E. S. Shaw, *Financial Deepening in Economic Development* (1973); Maxwell J. Fry, "Saving, Investment, Growth and the Cost of Financial Repression," *World Development* (April 1980); Vicente Gablis, "Structuralism and Financial Liberalization," *Finance & Development* (June 1976); Vicente Gablis "Financial Intermediation and Economic Growth in LDCs,' *Journal of Development Studies* (January 1977); Warren L. Coats and Deena R. Khatkhate (eds.), *Money and Monetary Policy in LDCs* (1980).

For a good survey, see Maxwell J. Fry, "Analyzing Disequilibrium Interest-Rate Systems in Developing Countries," *World Development* (December 1982).

Comment

Stabilization programs to reduce the rate of domestic inflation and to correct unsustainable balance-of-payments deficits have become a central policy issue for many developing countries and for the IMF. The IMF's criteria of loan "conditionality" have aroused considerable controversy. See, for example, Sidney Dell and Roger Lawrence, *The Balance of Payments Adjustment Process in Developing Countries* (1980); Thomas Reichmann and Richard Stillson, "Experience with Programs of Balance of Payments Adjustment: Stand-by Arrangements in the Higher Credit Tranches," *IMF Staff Papers* (June 1978); Joseph Gold, *Conditionality* (1979); Manuel Guitian, *Fund Conditionality: Evolution of Principles and Practices* (1981); John Williamson (ed.), *IMF Conditionality* (1983).

An excellent account of various stabilization programs is provided by William R. Cline and Sidney Weintraub (eds.), *Economic Stabilization in Developing Countries* (1981). Some conclusions of that study are: (1) inflation has proved more difficult to deal with than balance-of-payments problems; (2) both international and domestic factors caused stabilization problems in the 1970s, unlike the 1950s and 1960s when the absence of external shocks meant that most stabilization difficulties were the result of domestic causes; (3) even in the 1970s, however, the evidence from the country studies attributes greater weight to internal than to external causes for stabilization programs; (4) another common pattern is that stabilization prospects are affected by the government's credibility and therefore by the success or failure of past attempts; and (5) it is clear that early action is crucial to successful stabilization with minimum adjustment cost to real economic growth.

The recent experience with stabilization programs in Latin America in light of traditional and monetarist models of inflation and the exchange rate is reviewed critically by Rudiger Dornbusch, "Stabilization Policies in Development Countries: What Have We Learned?" *World Development* (September 1982). Also relevant are Rosemary Thorp and Lawrence Whitehead (eds.), *Inflation and Stabilization in Latin America* (1979); and Jere Behrman and James A. Hanson (eds.), *Short-Term Macroeconomic Policy in Latin America* (1979).

See also Andrew D. Crockett, "Stabilization Policies in Developing Countries: Some Policy Considerations," *IMF Staff Papers* (March 1981); John Odling-Smee, "Adjustment with Financial Assistance from the Fund," *Finance & Development* (December 1982).

The response to external shocks is examined by Bela Balassa et al., *The Balance of Payments Effects of External Shocks and of Policy Responses to These Shocks in Non-OPEC Developing Countries* (1981).

CHAPTER V

Mobilizing Foreign Resources

The overriding concern of this chapter is how to improve the process of transferring resources from rich to poor countries—whether this transfer be in the form of public financial aid, loans from private foreign banks, private foreign investment, or a nonmonetary transfer of managerial and technical knowledge. This is not only a matter of a greater amount of resources; there is now also concern over the "appropriateness" of the transfers from the developed to the less developed countries. In view of the redefinining of development objectives, it is now important that the transfers to the poor countries contribute to more employment and greater equality. It cannot simply be assumed that the stock of resources and the stock of knowledge that now exist in the developed countries are in this sense "appropriate" for the late developing countries.

Section V.A focuses on issues that are of the most analytical and policy interest in the transfer of foreign aid. Public financial aid—that is, concessional finance, or the "grant equivalent" in the capital inflow—has a twofold function. It supplements the LDC's low domestic savings, and hence helps fill the resources gap or "saving gap," and also provides additional foreign exchange and thereby helps fill the "foreign exchange gap." The "two-gap analysis" of the role of external aid is also significant in indicating that one gap may be greater than another *ex ante:* if, for example, the foreign exchange gap is greater than the saving gap, foreign aid becomes the means of permitting the required imports, so that the full saving potential can be realized and resources will not be left underutilized because of an import bottleneck. The necessary identity of the savings-investment and export-import gap *ex post* is brought about by a process of adjustment.

In terms of policies, we should recognize the costs of aid to the donor countries as well as the benefits received through aid by the recipient countries. There is considerable controversy over the contribution that aid makes to development; some economists dissent from the conventional view by arguing that, as an instrument of development, aid is generally of limited value—let alone an indispensable instrument—because it cannot substantially affect the basic factors that are needed to promote the material progress of the people in the aid-receiving countries. Others, however, emphasize the need to improve the quality of the aid relationship—not only from the standpoint of the more conventional "performance criteria," but now also in the context of meeting the needs of target poverty groups, redistribution, and employment. The more socially oriented measure of "performance" associated with the redefinition of development objectives raises some difficult questions for redirecting aid policy.

The related problem of debt servicing has become of increasing concern in view of the large expansion in external public indebtedness by the developing countries during the 1970s—especially to commercial banks. Although the commercial banks operated as efficient international financial intermediaries in recycling petrodollars through syndicated Eurocurrency loans to the LDCs, the large accumulation of debt—much of it of short or medium maturity—has raised fears of a liquidity crisis, if not one of solvency, for debtor nations. Analysis of a country's creditworthiness is therefore of crucial importance, as discussed in the Note on "External Debt and Country Risk Analysis" (section V.B).

If the real amount of resource flows through financial aid has diminished, it is important to discover alternative means of providing aid. One alternative is related to the current demands for international monetary reform. Differences of opinion now exist as to whether proposals for an increase in international liquidity should also provide a link to development finance. The Note on "The International Monetary System and Development Finance" (section V.C) discusses this issue. Other measures of providing aid through trade policy will be noted in Chapter VIII.

The discussion in section V.D is concerned with policy measures that a developing country might take to obtain a more substantial contribution to its development program from private foreign capital. To assess the potential contribution of private foreign investment, the Note on the "Benefits and Costs of Private Foreign Investment" (V.D.1) first outlines the benefits and costs of various forms of private foreign investment, viewed in terms of the recipient country's development program. As an agent of private foreign investment, the multinational enterprise merits special consideration. Against this conceptual background, we might better appraise the nature of the bargaining process between host countries and foreign investors.

In the final section (V.E), we explore further the possibility of securing a more effective transfer of managerial and technical knowledge to the LDCs. The technology that has been imported from developed countries may have an excessive capital bias, be inappropriate for the recipient country's factor endowment, and aggravate the problems of unemployment and inequality. While the recipient country may want a technology that raises the labor-capital ratio, it wants to avoid at the same time an increase in the capital-output ratio: efficient capital-stretching innovations are needed. This is not only a matter of new research and development (R&D) efforts devoted to the requirements of a new technology. The problem of technology transfer is of a much more far-reaching nature—ranging over issues that extend from the composition of an "appropriate" product mix to various policies of bargaining over the terms and conditions of technology importation.

V.A. PUBLIC FINANCIAL AID

V.A.1. Calculation of Capital Requirements*

The word "requirements" is used in this context as indicating a need for a transfer of goods and services in order to achieve certain targets; these may be target rates of growth for the economies as a whole, or they may be target rates of investment, although, where this is so, investment is normally thought of as being the means by which rates of growth of income are increased. The basic idea, however, is that such estimates of capital inflow or capital requirements shall be related to a generally recognizable and agreed aim, and that this aim should include the transformation of the recipient economy in such a way as to increase permanently its ability to contribute to economic welfare. They are not normally regarded as subsidies to current consumption, although such capital flows may include such subsidies within a suitable framework of foreign aid.

TWO APPROACHES

There are two possible approaches to making such estimates and both are based on the idea that increased income and wealth depend fundamentally upon the application of more capital, either to increase output directly when used in combination with local resources, or indirectly when the use of such capital will lead to a more effective use of other resources.

The first approach is to make an overall estimate of the uses that are made of the output of goods and services, with particular reference to the share that is allocated to consumption and the share that is allocated to investment. It is then argued that the future growth of the economy depends on a suitable

*From E. K. Hawkins, "Measuring Capital Requirements," *Finance & Development*, Vol. 5, No. 2, 1968, pp. 2–5. Reprinted by permission.

increase in the share of goods and services allocated to investment. An attempt is made to estimate the effect upon the future growth of income of any additional investment so as to be able to assess how much capital is needed to achieve a given rate of growth. This is then compared with the estimated ability of the economy to make available such a share of resources. (In other words, how much saving can an economy at a particular stage of development carry out?) The difference between these two estimates will then give some indication of the required size of the capital inflow from abroad.

Such estimates are made without any consideration of the specific form that the investments are likely to take. By contrast, the second approach builds up such an overall estimate from below by a detailed study, on a project-by-project or a sector-by-sector basis, of the need for capital. An examination is then made of the possible sources of such capital locally, and a discrepancy will thus emerge between the needs for the development of all the projects under consideration and the resources which can be made available. This difference is the required capital inflow from overseas, the counterpart of which can be the estimate reached by the first approach mentioned.

These two approaches are different not only in their nature, but in their provenance. The first approach corresponds to the various calculations of capital requirements which have been made in the last 20 years by the United Nations and by the U.S. Government. The second approach is, generally speaking, the one followed by the World Bank in producing the estimates which have been developed in recent years by its own thinking on the subject.

There is a further important difference, however, in the manner in which this subject has been treated by other international organizations and the way in which it has been viewed by he World Bank Group. Estimates made outside the Bank have all been concerned with the requirements aspect of capital inflows. They begin by specifying a target rate of growth which is to be the aim of the developing country and then proceed to estimate the amount of capital which would be needed to reach that target. In the estimates made by the World Bank Group no explicit target is used; instead, the estimates emerge from a multidimensional examination of the economy in question and represent the amount of capital which the Bank feels might be used in an effective way in the future, provided that certain levels of economic performance are achieved and suitable policies are followed by the country concerned. . . .

THE "TWO-GAP" APPROACH

Attention is also focused, however, on what is thought to be a more important limitation on development: a possible shortage of foreign exchange, as a result of which countries may be unable to acquire from abroad the goods and services necessary for promoting domestic development. This approach has become known as the "two-gap" approach because it operates in two dimensions; while continuing to argue that development is a function of investment it also holds that such investment, which requires domestic savings, is not sufficient to ensure that development takes place. It must also be possible to obtain from abroad the goods and services that are complementary to those available at home. In most developing countries the structure of the economy is so simple that it can produce only a limited range of products when relying solely on domestic sources. In these circumstances an act of saving, by itself, even though it releases resources for investment purposes, may not make available the correct kind of resources. In physical terms a country may be unable to produce the cement, steel, or machinery which go into the various projects required to raise income in the future, although it may be able to make the necessary savings by cutting down on consumption. Unless these savings can be used to pur-

chase the necessary goods and services from overseas no progress can be made.

Estimates made as a result of this approach start from certain basic relationships which are generally accepted as holding true for all countries. The usages of modern national accounting are designed to express the fact that the amount that can be invested in any country is identical with the amount that is saved; that is to say, only those goods and services which are not consumed can be deployed to increase future income through investment. At the same time, if these resources are to be supplemented from abroad, such a flow of resources will appear in this accounting framework as an excess of imports over exports. It will, in fact, always appear twice, first as the difference between investment and the amount that can be saved within the economy and second as an equal excess of imports and services over exports of goods and services.

THE FOUR IMPORTANT MAGNITUDES

Calculations of capital requirements proceed on the basis of projections of the four important magnitudes: savings, investments, exports, and imports. A target rate of growth is specified, and then the amount of additional capital that will be required in order to reach that target rate of growth is estimated. This gives a figure for capital requirements which can be compared with the likely availability of domestic savings. At the same time it is possible to make projections of the likely behavior of exports and imports. The former will depend on the supply of goods and services available, or likely to be available, for export from the domestic economy, the state of the world markets, and the economic health of the developed countries which are the markets for such exports. A similar estimate can be made for import requirements. All these projections (which are of course capable of such subdivision) can be made independently of one another, and it follows that there is very little likelihood that such independent projections will all arrive at an answer which satisfies the basic accounting relationship already referred to above. Projected investments may well exceed projected savings; projected imports, on the other hand, may exceed the projected exports by a different amount. However, national income accountancy demonstrates that the excess of investment over savings must necessarily be equal to the excess of imports over exports and this must hold true at all points of time. It follows that there is something inconsistent about the projections that have been made independently. The two-gap method, therefore, is essentially a way of ensuring that inconsistencies, which may be *implicit* in other ways of making projections, are brought out into the open.

Estimates of capital requirements made by this method, therefore, yield not one, but two figures for consideration. . . . The use of this approach requires either that the projections include the necessary changes in the structure and the behavior of the economy which will make the two estimates consistent with each other, or that a decision has to be made that the larger of the two gaps will be the more significant and will be taken as the required capital inflow from abroad.

A "THREE-PHASE" APPROACH

A variant on the approach has also been followed by . . . Hollis B. Chenery and Alan M. Strout, who, in a study[1] prepared for the U.S. Agency for International Development (AID), employed a three-phase approach, where an attempt was made to specify in quantitative terms the constraint on development arising from the limiit of absorptive capacity.[2] This work has had a considerable

[1]Hollis B. Chenery and Alan M. Strout, "Foreign Assistance and Economic Development," *American Economic Review,* September 1966.

[2]Absorptive capacity covers all the ways in which the ability to plan and execute development projects, to change the structure of the economy, and to reallocate resources is circumscribed by the lack of crucial factors, by institutional problems, or by unsuitable organization. Not only the structure of the economy but also the utilization of its existing capacity will have an important bearing on a country's absorptive capacity. Cf. J. H. Adler, *Absorptive Capacity: The Concept and Its Determinants,* Brookings Institution, Washington, 1965.

influence on discussions of the subject. In their study, various constraints—a savings constraint, the foreign exchange constraint, and the limitation of absorptive capacity—come into operation for a particular developing economy at various stages of its growth. They focus special attention on two aspects: first, the savings behavior of the economy concerned, or its ability to refrain from consumption and allocate additional resources to investment; and second, the question of absorptive capacity, viewed, in this instance, as a performance factor. In other words, if absorptive capacity is increasing over the years, it can be regarded as a measure of the improved economic performance of the country concerned, and of its ability to make better use of capital from abroad. In their work they spelled out the operation of these three constraints in terms of three different stages of development. An interesting feature of this study is its extensive coverage on a country basis, since the model was applied to 50 developing countries and totals obtained for a spectrum of different assumptions.

This three-phase approach can be useful for expository purposes, but it can only be an approximation to the real life problems of many developing countries where the three constraints often coexist and interact with one another. It has been found, for example, that the limitations of absorptive capacity may apply only to particular sectors of the economy, while other parts of the economy are able to absorb more capital than can be obtained from local sources of savings. This coexistence of the various constraints on development is in many ways a central characteristic of an underdeveloped country.

One limitation of all the approaches detailed above is precisely that they operate at a highly aggregate level. Any aggregative approach of this kind treats all units of investment as if each were adding to a volume of capital which is homogeneous. In practice this is only true of the monetary units in which capital and investment are measured. It is convenient to measure investment and capital in monetary terms, but the money values often only hide the significance of the specific nature of the investment item. Cement once incorporated into a highway cannot be used for other purposes; steel once built into a building must yield additional wealth in that form, otherwise the investment will have been wasted. It is the underlying importance of this aspect of development which emphasizes the project and sector approach to the measurement of capital requirements.

Comment

Some fundamental theoretical formulations of the foreign exchange constraint, two-gap analysis, and foreign capital requirements are presented in the following studies: R. McKinnon, "Foreign Exchange Constraints in Economic Development," *Economic Journal* (June 1964); H. Chenery and I. Adelman, "Foreign Aid and Economic Development: The Case of Greece," *Review of Economics and Statistics* (February 1966); H. Chenery, I. Adelman, and A. MacEwan, "Optimal Pattern of Growth and Aid: The Case of Pakistan," *Pakistan Development Review,* Summer 1966; H. Chenery, I. Adelman, and A. Strout, "Foreign Assistance and Economic Development," *American Economic Review* (September 1966); J. Vanek, *Estimating Foreign Resource Needs for Economic Development* (1967); John Adler (ed.), *Capital Movements and Economic Development* (1967); A. Sengupta, "Foreign Capital Requirements for Economic Development," *Oxford Economic Papers* (March 1968); H. J. Bruton, "The Two Gap Approach to Aid and Development: Comment," *American Economic Review* (June 1969); D. Lal, "The Foreign Exchange Bottleneck Revisited," *Economic Development and Cultural Change* (July 1972); Vijay Joshi, "Saving and Foreign Exchange Constraints," in Paul P. Streeten (ed.), *Unfashionable Economics* (1970), pp. 111–133.

V.A.2. Growth-and-Debt Stages*

In discussing the ability of countries to service external debt, it is essential to distinguish among different categories of debt. A particular debt will or will not be serviced on schedule depending on the terms of other loans contracted to finance the country's total resource gap. It is, therefore, best to look at the total blend of capital entering a country and consider the blend most suitable to the country's present and prospective position. For this purpose, one may distinguish the following categories of official capital provided to developing countries:

(a) Concessionary financing, almost exclusively public, including loans with interest of 3 per cent or less and grants.

*From Barend A. De Vries, "The Debt Bearing Capacity of Developing Countries—A Comparative Analysis," *Banca Nazionale del Lavoro Quarterly Review,* March 1971, pp. 12–18. Reprinted by permission.

(b) "Conventional" loans, with interest above 3 per cent but more typically between 5 and 8 per cent or higher and maturities over 10 years, including privately placed bonds, IBRD and regional development bank loans.

(c) Export or commercial credits, provided to finance export trade of industrial countries, with a variety of terms centering around 5–8 per cent interest (depending on the extent of subsidy provided) and maturities depending on the value of the contract and the characteristics of the project for which the goods are used, but usually 10 years or less.

(d) Eastern European credits (characterized by low interest, about 2½ per cent, and relatively short maturities, 10 years or less).

The "strongest" countries will be able to finance their capital needs with predominantly hard loans—i.e. mostly with "conventional" loans or export credits. The weaker a country's ability to service loans, the softer must be the blend, i.e. the greater its concessionary component.

The factual analysis in the present paper is based on data about grants and loans, with maturities over one year, provided by "donor" governments or guaranteed by recipient governments. Assessment of countries' debt bearing capacity must, however, also cover short-term credits and, more generally, the flow of finance from private creditors (industrial firms or banks) to private debtors without government guarantee and including short-term (mostly commercial) loans. They may at times bulk large in the capital flow to individual countries. Commercial credits when excessive (or in arrears) have, at times, been consolidated into longer-term public debt. In addition, the assessment must consider the role played by private investment. The "servicing" of private investment does not proceed according to the same kind of schedules as used for loan capital, but nevertheless imposes a long-term claim on the economy which must be taken into account in analysing the country's balance of payments prospects.

PRINCIPAL DEVELOPMENT STAGES

The successive stages of development can be characterized by countries' dependence on foreign capital, the level of debt contracted and the level of income achieved. In the early stage of development countries tend to have a relatively small dependence on external capital. They may even have a resource surplus, being mostly exporters of primary products, while the rest of the economy and society is left undeveloped. Since the amounts to be financed are small, external debt is also small. As development gathers momentum, the external resource need—the "gap"—increases and, after perhaps many years, reaches a peak. The gap will start to decline after the country has made certain critical achievements, which will depend on its development strategy, its resource base, geo-

graphical location, etc. Examples of these achievements are the production of a sufficient range of import substitutes, overcoming stagnation in traditional export markets and development of new export products and markets, and mobilization of sufficient domestic resources to finance its own investments. As the gap starts to decline, the debt contracted to finance it will continue to rise as long as new debts are needed to cover the resource gap. In fact, the debt continues to rise even after the gap turns into a surplus and as long as the surplus is less than the interest needed to pay debts outstanding. Once the surplus is large enough to cover interest on outstanding debt the country will be able to start reducing its debts.

In the sequence of growth-and-debt stages described, a basic assumption is that income rises in subsequent phases, i.e., the capital mobilized domestically and borrowed abroad is effectively used to increase output. The more effective the use of capital the quicker the country will be able to reduce its gap. Accordingly, it will be possible to distinguish subsequent phases in which first the gap, next the debt and finally the income level increases. In the later phases the gap declines first and next the debt, while the income level continues to rise. This sequence of events results in the following phases.

Phase	Gap	Debt	Income
I A	Low	Low	Low
II A	High	Low	Low
III A	High	High	Low
III B	High	High	Middle
IV A	Low	High	Middle
V	Low	Low	High

In the sequence of phases countries are depicted as evolving, over a period of years, a stronger basic balance of payments position as measured by the relative extent of its dependence on external capital. It should not be denied, of course, that payments positions may be subject to considerable short-term fluctuation or that, regardless of income level, countries may follow policies which greatly affect their dependence on outside capital. The basic question is whether the country's policies promote growth and reduce its longer term dependence on external assistance. The gap may be kept small by direct controls which may be harmful to growth. Empirical evidence does not conclusively suggest that long-term development proceeds according to the sequence presented. Various factors may, in fact, help countries to accelerate their move from one stage to another or may explain why countries do not neatly fit into any of the phases presented:

(a) The debt burden may remain "low" because the country has received loans on predominantly soft terms. On the other hand, an unfavorable debt structure may increase the debt burden even while the resource gap and the income level are still low.

(b) A successful export orientation makes it possible to reach middle level income without developing a large resource gap.

(c) Private investment finances a substantial portion of the resource gap and enables the country to keep down the debt burden. A number of countries manage to finance a substantial portion of a relatively large resource gap with private capital and thus have at present a low public external debt burden. . . .

Against the background of the growth-and-debt sequence one can derive two basic criteria for determining a country's ability to service debt:

(a) The more "developed" the country, the greater its debt bearing capacity: as the country approaches the end of the sequence, its need for external capital is reduced relative to its own resources and its ability to service debt improves.

(b) The more effective its policies are in moving toward the next "phase" of the sequence, the greater its ability to service loans.

Clearly, debt servicing capacity will tend to be greatest in the last phase. In this phase countries may be able to finance their external capital needs on hard terms even though their growth policies may not in all cases be very effective. Next in line would be countries which have reached the higher income level while their debt is still relatively high.

For remaining phases the second consideration is critical. In the earlier development phases a slow growth rate may require a very low average interest rate if countries' debt repayment capacity is not continuously and progressively to fall short of their debt obligations.[1]

---

[1]In long-term debt-and-growth anaylsis a critical question is whether the debtor country can reach a point at which its "savings surplus" increases faster than the interest on its debt. If, over the longer term, interest increases faster than the savings available to repay debt, the country's debt will increase continuously. The interest rate at which this explosive debt situation occurs, the so-called critical interest rate, can be derived from the country's growth parameters (growth of product, the marginal savings rate and the capital output ratio). The slower the growth rate, the lower the marginal savings rate, and the less productive its capital investment the lower is the critical interest rate.

EXHIBIT V.1. Total Flow of Resources from DAC Countries by Major Categories

	1970	1971	1972	1973	1974	1975	1976	1977	1978	1979	1980	1981
					(a) Net Current Prices ($ billion)							
Official Development Assistance	6.9	7.6	9.2	9.1	11.6	13.8	14.0	15.7	20.0	22.8	27.3	25.6
Grants by private voluntary agencies	0.9	0.9	1.0	1.4	1.2	1.3	1.4	1.5	1.7	2.0	2.4	2.0
Nonconcessional flows	8.1	8.9	10.0	11.9	9.7	29.7	30.6	34.3	48.9	50.6	45.7	60.4
Total flow of resources	15.9	17.4	20.2	22.4	22.5	44.8	46.0	51.5	70.6	75.4	75.4	88.0
					(b) 1981 Prices and Exchange Rates ($ billion)							
Official Development Assistance	17.8	18.4	20.1	17.7	20.5	21.1	20.8	21.6	23.9	24.1	26.5	25.6
Grants by private voluntary agencies	2.3	2.2	2.2	2.7	2.1	2.0	2.1	2.1	2.0	2.1	2.3	2.0
Nonconcessional flows	20.9	21.6	21.8	23.2	17.1	45.4	45.4	47.1	58.3	53.5	44.3	60.4
Total flow of resources	41.1	42.2	44.1	43.7	39.7	68.5	68.2	70.7	84.2	79.8	73.1	88.0
					(c) As Percent of GNP							
Official Development Assistance	0.34	0.34	0.36	0.29	0.34	0.36	0.33	0.33	0.35	0.35	0.38	0.35
Grants by private voluntary agencies	0.04	0.04	0.04	0.04	0.04	0.04	0.03	0.03	0.03	0.03	0.03	0.03
Nonconcessional flows	0.41	0.40	0.38	0.38	0.28	0.77	0.74	0.73	0.86	0.79	0.63	0.83
Total flow of resources	0.79	0.78	0.78	0.72	0.65	1.17	1.10	1.09	1.24	1.17	1.04	1.21

Source: OECD, *Development Cooperation,* 1982 Review of Members of the Development Assistance Committee (DAC), Paris, November 1982, p. 177.

EXHIBIT V.2. Official Development Assistance from OECD Members

OECD	Amount (millions of U.S. dollars)									
	1960	1965	1970	1975	1977	1978	1979	1980	1981	1982
101 Italy	77	60	147	182	198	376	273	683	666	820
102 New Zealand	—	—	14	66	53	55	68	72	68	65
103 United Kingdom	407	472	500	904	1,114	1,465	2,157	1,852	2,194	1,794
104 Japan	105	244	458	1,148	1,424	2,215	2,685	3,353	3,171	3,023
105 Austria	—	10	11	79	108	154	131	178	313	361
106 Finland	—	2	7	48	49	55	90	110	135	144
107 Australia	59	119	212	552	400	588	629	667	649	882
108 Canada	75	96	337	880	991	1,060	1,056	1,075	1,189	1,185
109 Netherlands	35	70	196	608	908	1,074	1,472	1,630	1,510	1,473
110 Belgium	101	102	120	378	371	536	643	595	575	497
111 France	823	752	971	2,093	2,267	2,705	3,449	4,162	4,177	3,991
112 United States	2,702	4,023	3,153	4,161	4,682	5,663	4,684	7,138	5,782	8,302
113 Denmark	5	13	59	205	258	388	461	481	403	415
114 Germany, Fed. Rep.	223	456	599	1,689	1,717	2,347	3,393	3,567	3,181	3,163
115 Norway	5	11	37	184	295	355	429	486	467	566
116 Sweden	7	38	117	566	779	783	988	962	919	987
117 Switzerland	4	12	30	104	119	173	213	253	237	251
Total	4,628	6,480	6,968	13,847	15,733	19,992	22,821	27,264	25,636	27,919

EXHIBIT V.2. Official Development Assistance from OECD Members (*Continued*)

OECD	Amount (as percentage of donor GNP)									
	1960	1965	1970	1975	1977	1978	1979	1980	1981	1982
101 Italy	.22	1.0	.16	.11	.10	.14	.08	.17	.19	.24
102 New Zealand	—	—	.23	.52	.39	.34	.33	.33	.29	.28
103 United Kingdom	.56	.47	.41	.39	.45	.46	.52	.35	.44	.38
104 Japan	.24	.27	.23	.23	.21	.23	.27	.32	.28	.29
105 Austria	—	.11	.07	.21	.22	.27	.19	.23	.48	54
106 Finland	—	.02	.06	.18	.16	.16	.22	.22	.28	.30
107 Australia	.37	.53	.59	.65	.42	.55	.53	.48	.41	.57
108 Canada	.19	.19	.41	.54	.50	.52	.48	.43	.43	.42
109 Netherlands	.31	.36	.61	.75	.86	.82	.98	1.03	1.08	1.08
110 Belgium	.88	.60	.46	.59	.46	.55	.57	.50	.59	.59
111 France	1.35	.76	.66	.62	.60	.57	.60	.64	.73	.74
112 United States	.53	.58	.32	.27	.25	.27	.20	.27	.20	.27
113 Denmark	.09	.13	.38	.58	.60	.75	.77	.74	.73	.77
114 Germany, Fed. Rep.	31	.40	.32	.40	.33	.37	.45	.44	.47	.48
115 Norway	.11	.16	.32	.66	.83	.90	.93	.85	.82	1.01
116 Sweden	.05	.19	.38	.82	.99	.90	.97	.79	.83	1.02
117 Switzerland	.04	.09	.15	.19	.19	.20	.21	.24	.24	.25

	National Currencies									
101 Italy (billions of lire)	48	37	92	119	175	319	227	585	757	1,109
102 New Zealand (millions of dollars)	—	—	13	54	55	53	66	74	78	86
103 United Kingdom (millions of pounds)	145	169	208	409	639	764	1,018	797	1,091	1,027
104 Japan (billions of yen)	38	88	165	341	382	466	588	760	699	753
105 Austria (millions of schillings)	—	260	286	1,376	1,785	2,236	1,751	2,303	4,985	6,158
106 Finland (millions of markkaa)	—	6	29	177	197	226	351	410	583	694
107 Australia (millions of dollars)	53	106	189	422	361	514	563	586	565	870
108 Canada (millions of dollars)	73	104	353	895	1,054	1,209	1,237	1,257	1,425	1,462
109 Netherlands (millions of dollars)	132	252	709	1,538	2,229	2,324	2,953	3,241	3,768	3,933
110 Belgium (millions of francs)	5,050	5,100	6,000	13,902	13,298	16,880	18,852	17,400	21,350	22,708
111 France (millions of francs)	4,063	3,713	5,393	8,971	11,139	12,207	14,674	17,589	22,700	26,230
112 United States (millions of dollars)	2,702	4,023	3,153	4,161	4,682	5,663	4,684	7,138	5,782	8,302
113 Denmark (millions of kroner)	35	90	443	1,178	1,549	2,140	2,425	2,711	2,871	3,458
114 Germany, Fed. Rep. (millions of deutsche marks)	937	1,824	2,192	4,155	3,987	4,714	6,219	6,484	7,189	7,675

EXHIBIT V.2. Official Development Assistance from OECD Members (*Continued*)

OECD	National Currencies									
	1960	1965	1970	1975	1977	1978	1979	1980	1981	1982
115 Norway (millions of kroner)	36	79	264	962	1,570	1,861	2,172	2,400	2,680	3,653
116 Sweden (millions of kronor)	36	197	605	2,350	3,491	3,538	4,236	4,069	4,653	6,201
117 Switzerland (millions of francs)	17	52	131	268	286	309	354	424	466	510
	Summary									
ODA (billions of U.S. dollars, nominal prices)	4.63	6.48	6.97	13.85	15.73	19.99	22.82	27.26	25.63	27.92
ODA (as percentage of GNP)	.51	.49	.34	.36	.33	.35	.35	.38	.35	.39
ODA (billions of U.S. dollars, constant 1980 prices)	16.41	20.19	18.15	21.60	21.91	24.09	24.89	27.26	25.82	28.37
GNP (trillions of U.S. dollars, nominal prices)	.90	1.30	2.00	3.90	4.70	5.70	6.50	7.20	7.30	7.24
ODA deflator	.28	.32	.38	.64	.72	.83	.92	1.00	.99	.98
	Net Bilateral Flow to Low-Income Countries (as percentage of donor GNP)									
101 Italy	.03	.04	.06	.01	.02	.01	.01	.01	.02
102 New Zealand	—	—	—	.14	.04	.03	.02	.02	.01
103 United Kingdom	.22	.23	.15	.11	.11	.15	.16	.11	.13
104 Japan	.12	.13	.11	.08	.06	.07	.11	.11	.06
105 Austria	—	.06	.05	.02	.01	.01	.02	.11	.02
106 Finland	—	—	—	.06	.06	.04	.06	.08	.08
107 Australia	—	.08	.09	.10	.07	.08	.09	.07	.06
108 Canada	.11	.10	.22	.24	.13	.17	.13	.11	.31
109 Netherlands	.19	.08	.24	.24	.33	.34	.30	.35	.12
110 Belgium	.27	.56	.30	.31	.24	.23	.28	.26	.21
111 France	.01	.12	.09	.10	.07	.08	.08	.09	.10
112 United States	.22	.26	.14	.08	.03	.04	.03	.03	.03
113 Denmark	—	.02	.10	.20	.24	.21	.26	.27	.16
114 Germany, Fed. Rep.	.13	.14	.10	.12	.07	.07	.08	.07	.25
115 Norway	.02	.04	.12	.25	.30	.39	.34	.28	.09
116 Sweden	.01	.07	.12	.41	.44	.37	.40	.33	.28
117 Switzerland	—	.02	.05	.10	.05	.08	.06	.08	.06
Total	.18	.20	.13	.11	.07	.09	.09	.09	.07

Source: World Bank, *World Development Report,* 1983, p. 182.

EXHIBIT V.3. Non-Oil-Developing Countries: Balance-of-Payments Summaries, 1973–1983 (in billions of U.S. dollars)

	1973	1974	1975	1976	1977	1978	1979	1980	1981	1982	1983
All non-oil developing countries											
Exports (f.o.b.)	85.5	118.0	117.4	139.6	175.0	200.7	258.6	326.8	344.1	329.6	350.5
Imports (f.o.b.)	−95.8	−151.3	−158.3	−166.8	−200.2	−238.1	−309.9	−401.1	−423.7	−381.8	−392.0
Trade balance	−10.3	−33.3	−40.8	−27.0	−25.3	−36.6	−51.3	−74.3	−79.6	−52.2	−41.4
Net services and private transfers	−1.0	−3.7	−5.5	−5.6	−3.7	−4.7	−9.7	−14.7	−28.1	−34.6	−26.4
Balance on current account	−11.3	−37.0	−46.3	−32.6	−28.9	−41.3	−61.0	−89.0	−107.7	−86.8	−67.8
Net official transfers	5.5	8.7	7.1	7.5	8.2	8.2	11.6	12.5	13.8	13.2	13.1
Net capital inflows	16.0	29.4	35.1	33.1	30.2	49.0	62.0	75.0	83.4	41.4	58.6
Overall balance	10.2	1.1	−4.1	8.0	9.5	16.0	12.6	−1.4	−10.6	−32.2	4.0

Source: IMF, *World Economic Outlook, 1983*, p. 188.

EXHIBIT V.4. Non-Oil-Developing Countries: Financing of Current Account Deficits and Reserve Accretions, 1973–1983[a]

	1973	1974	1975	1976	1977	1978	1979	1980	1981	1982	1983
					In billions of U.S. dollars						
Current account deficit	11.3	37.0	46.3	32.6	28.9	41.3	61.0	89.0	107.7	86.8	67.8
Increase in official reserves	10.4	2.7	−1.7	13.0	12.5	17.4	12.6	4.5	2.1	−7.1	7.2
Total	21.7	39.7	44.6	45.6	41.4	58.7	73.6	93.5	109.8	79.7	75.0
Financed by											
Non-debt-creating flows, net	10.3	14.6	11.8	12.6	14.4	17.9	23.9	24.1	28.0	25.1	24.2
Long-term capital from official sources, net	4.9	6.8	11.7	10.5	11.4	13.8	13.3	17.6	23.0	19.5	23.8
Long-term capital from private sources	6.8	11.3	15.4	17.5	13.2	23.4	23.2	29.6	39.7	21.5	40.3
Other financing flows, net	−0.3	7.0	5.7	5.0	2.4	3.6	13.2	22.2	19.1	13.6	−13.4
Distribution of financing flows					In percent						
Non-debt-creating flows, net	47.5	36.8	26.5	27.6	34.8	30.5	32.5	25.8	25.6	31.5	32.3
Official long-term capital, net	22.6	17.1	26.2	23.0	27.6	23.6	18.1	18.9	21.0	24.5	31.8
Private long-term capital, net	31.3	28.5	34.5	38.4	31.9	39.9	31.6	31.7	36.2	27.0	53.7
Other financing flows, net[b]	−1.4	17.6	12.8	11.0	5.8	6.2	18.0	23.8	17.4	17.1	−17.9

Source: IMF, *World Economic Outlook, 1983*, p. 197.

[a]Excludes data for the People's Republic of China prior to 1977.

[b]Includes private short-term capital flows, exceptional financing, net use of Fund credit, and errors and omissions.

V.A.3. Adverse Repercussions of Aid*

Official Western aid has now gone to the Third World for about thirty years, more than a human generation. Over this period major deficiencies, even startling anomalies, have become apparent. These untoward results might not matter much if the policy had served to promote the well-being of the peoples of the Third World, but it has not done so. Only exceptionally and in the most propitious circumstances can aid promote or accelerate economic advance, and then merely to a minor extent.

The effects of foreign aid have been quite different. It is foreign aid that has brought into existence the Third World (also called the South). It thus underlies the so-called North-South dialogue or confrontation. *Foreign aid is the source of the North-South conflict, not its solution.* The paramount significance of aid lies in this very important, perhaps momentous, political result.

A further pervasive consequence of aid has been to promote or exacerbate the politicization of life in aid-receiving countries. This major result has gravely damaged the interests of the West and the well-being and prospects of the peoples of Third World countries.

The money spent by the West in no way measures these crucial sequelae of aid. Whatever percentage of their national incomes aid represents, the donor governments cannot wash their hands of the consequences of their so-called caring.

THE CREATION OF "NORTH" AND "SOUTH"

What is there in common between, say, Thailand and Mozambique, Nepal and Argentina, India and Chad, Tuvalu and Brazil,

*From Peter Bauer and Basil Yamey, "Foreign Aid: What is at Stake?" *The Public Interest,* Summer 1982, pp. 53–55, 57–61, 63, 67–69. Reprinted by permission.

Mayotte and Nigeria? Public and political discussion nowadays envisages the world as one-third rich—the West—and two-thirds poor or even hungry—the "Third World" or "South." In this picture, extreme poverty is the common feature of the Third World.

This is altogether misleading. There is a continuous range of incomes in the world, both between countries and within them, making the line of division between rich and poor countries quite arbitrary. One could say that the world is two-thirds rich and one-third poor, or one-tenth rich and nine-tenths poor, or choose any other two fractions which add up to one. The size of the celebrated gap between rich countries and poor countries (i.e., the difference in their average incomes) depends on the placement of the arbitrary line of division. The picture is also misleading in that many groups or societies in the Third World—expecially in the Far East, the Middle East, Southeast Asia, and Latin America—are richer than large groups in the West.

Nor is the Third World stagnant. In recent decades many Third World countries have grown rapidly, as for instance have South Korea, Taiwan, Thailand, Malaysia, Singapore, Jordan, Guatemala, Venezuela, Colombia, Brazil, Kenya, and the Ivory Coast. Indeed, in so far as global aggregation and averaging of incomes and growth rates make any sense at all, both total and *per capita* incomes in the Third World as a whole have, since 1950, grown no less fast than in the West, and probably have grown faster.

It is, of course, hardly sensible to lump together and average incomes of the very different societies of the Third World or South, which comprise some two-thirds of mankind. These societies live in widely different physical and social environments, display radically different attitudes and modes of conduct, and their governments pursue very different policies.

But the diverse components of the Third World do indeed share one characteristic.

This is not poverty, stagnation, exploitation, brotherhood, or skin colour; it is the receipt of foreign aid. *The concept of the Third World and the policy of official aid are inseparable. Without foreign aid there is no Third World.* Official aid provides the only bond joining together its diverse and often antagonistic constituents. This has been so ever since practically all of Asia, Africa, and Latin America came to be lumped together in the late 1940's, as the underdeveloped world, and thereafter known successively as the less-developed world, the non-aligned world, the developing world, the Third World, and now the South. These expressions never made any sense except in that they denoted a collectivity of aid recipients. . . .

AID AND ECONOMIC GROWTH

Although the case for official transfers is largely taken for granted, various arguments or rationalizations are often advanced. These are addressed primarily to audiences not yet firmly committed.

The central argument for foreign aid has remained that without it Third World countries cannot progress at a reasonable rate, or cannot progress at all. But not only is foreign aid patently not required for development, it is, in actual fact, much more likely to obstruct it than to promote it.

It diminishes the people of the Third World to suggest that, although they crave material progress, unlike the West they cannot achieve it without external doles. Of course, large parts of the Third World made rapid progress long before foreign aid—witness Southeast Asia, West Africa, and Latin America. The emergence of hundreds of millions of people, both in the South and in the West, from poverty to prosperity has not depended on external gifts. Economic achievement has depended, as it still does depend, on people's own faculties, motivations, and ways of life, on their institutions and on the policies of their rulers. In short, economic achievement depends on the conduct of people, including governments. External donations have never been necessary for the develop-

ment of any country, anywhere. There are, of course, a number of Third World countries or societies which have not progressed much in the postwar period. This lack of progress reflects factors which cannot be overcome by aid, and are indeed likely to be reinforced by it.

Governments or businesses in the Third World that can use capital productively can borrow at home and abroad.[1] This is also true for governments borrowing to spend on the so-called infrastructure, i.e., on facilities which do not yield a directly appropriable return. If spending on infrastructure is productive, it increases taxable capacity so that the governments can readily service the borrowed capital. It follows that the absolute maximum contribution of foreign aid to development, in the sense of the growth of the national income, is the avoided cost of borrowing, i.e., interest and amortization. As a percentage of the national income for large Third World countries, this maximum contribution is at best minute, and is far too small to register in the national income statistics. For India in recent years, the contribution of aid would have been at best on the order of one-quarter to one-half of 1 percent of recorded gross domestic product.

The maximum benefit from foreign aid is thus a modest reduction in the cost of investible funds—a resource which is *not* a major independent factor in economic development. It is evident on reflection that the volume of investible funds is not a critical determinant of economic progress, for, if it were, countless poor individuals and societies could not have advanced rapidly in a very short period, as they have done both in the West and in the Third World. The relative unimportance to material progress of the volume of investible funds has been confirmed by much recent research, including that of Simon Kuznets, Ed-

[1]Where the political survival of a newly-created country is widely doubted, it may not be able to raise capital even if it can use capital productively. These apparent exceptions to the rule that development does not depend upon external aid are plainly irrelevant to the case for global transfers to the Third World.

ward Denison, Moses Abramovitz, and Sir Alec Cairncross.[2] It is economic achievement that produces assets and money; it is not assets and money which produce economic achievement.

However, suppose that, contrary to the results of reflection and observation, the volume of investible funds was a critical determinant of economic advance. If it were, then those actions of many Third World governments which restrict the inflow of foreign private capital—a course of action made easier by receipts of aid—would be evidence that these governments gave a low priority to economic development. The same applies also to the practice of several governments, including those of India and Nigeria, of in effect passing on to other governments part of the aid they themselves receive.

Any benefit from the reduction of the cost of investible funds is likely to be small. It is also likely to be much more than offset by the adverse repercussions of official aid. And these repercussions are brought about by amounts of aid which, while small in relation to the national income of recipient countries, are nevertheless often a *significant* part of their government revenues and of foreign exchange receipts. These are the relevant magnitudes in assessing the principal repercussion of these transfers, because aid goes to governments and it increases both the revenues and the external balances at their direct disposal. . . .

[2]According to Kuznets, the contribution of the increase in material capital (both reproducible and nonreproducible) to the increase of per-capita income over long periods in major developed countries was limited, "ranging from less than a seventh to not much more than a fifth" (S. Kuznets, *Postwar Economic Growth,* Cambridge: Harvard University Press, 1964, p. 41). Much more important were improved efficiency in the use of resources and the movement of resources from less productive to more productive sectors. See also P. T. Bauer, *Dissent on Development* (London and Cambridge, Mass.: Harvard University Press, 1971), ch. 2, and *Equality, the Third World and Economic Delusion* (London and Cambridge, Mass.: Harvard University Press, 1981), ch. 14.

HOW AID CAN INHIBIT DEVELOPMENT

The adverse repercussions of official aid operate precisely on the personal, social, and political factors which determine economic development.

Most importantly, aid increases the money, patronage, and power of the recipient governments, and thereby their grip over the rest of society. It thus promotes the disastrous politicization of life in the Third World. . . . When social and economic life is extensively politicized, people's livelihood or even their economic and physical survival comes to depend on political and administrative decisions. This result promotes conflict, especially in the multiracial societies of most Third World countries. This sequence diverts energy and attention from productive activity to the political arena; and the direction of people's activities is necessarily a crucial determinant of economic performance.

There are further untoward implications and repercussions of foreign aid which are far from trivial. Aid enables governments to pursue policies which patently retard growth and exacerbate poverty, and there is a long list of such policies. These include persecution of the most productive groups, especially minorities, and sometimes also their expulsion; restraints on the activities of traders and even the destruction of the trading system; restriction on the inflow of foreign capital, enterprise, and skills; voluntary or compulsory purchase of foreign enterprises (which deprives the country of skills very helpful to development, besides absorbing scarce capital); forced collectivization; price policies which discourage food production; and, generally, the imposition of economic controls which restrict external contacts and domestic mobility, and so retard the spread of new ideas and methods.

Aid also is apt to bias development policy towards unsuitable external models. Familiar examples include steel and petrochemical complexes and official airlines. Moreover, in some instances the adoption of external prototypes has gone hand in hand with attempts at more comprehensive modernization, including attempted transformation of people's mores, values, and institutions. Such policies can have dangerous, even explosive, consequences (as in Iran).

Aid also impairs the international competitiveness of economic activities in the recipient countries by helping to create or maintain overvalued exchange rates or to increase the domestic money supply.[3] (These adverse effects could be offset if the transfers greatly enhanced the productivity of resources, but this is extremely improbable.) Foreign aid also makes it easier for governments to pursue imprudent financial policies. Unless aid is increasingly forthcoming, these policies lead to disruptive domestic inflation and to balance of payments difficulties, which in turn are apt to engender a crisis atmosphere and a flight of capital. This sequence encourages the imposition of specific controls, with adverse economic, social, and political results.

It would be naive to suppose that adverse policies would cease in the absence of aid. What is pertinent is that aid makes it easier to pursue and continue these policies. This is the case because, while it does little or nothing to promote development, aid can relieve immediate shortages, especially of consumer goods and of imports. This makes it easier for governments to conceal temporarily from their populations the worst effects of the damaging policies.

BETWEEN AID AND THE POOR: THIRD WORLD RULERS

Foreign aid does not go to the pitiable figures we see on aid posters or in aid advertisements—it goes to their rulers. The policies of these rulers who receive aid are sometimes directly responsible for conditions such as those depicted. This is notably so in parts of Africa and Southeast Asia. But even where this is not so the policies of the rulers, including their patterns of public spending, are determined by their own personal and political interests, among which the position of the

poorest has very low priority.[4] Indeed, to support rulers on the basis of the poverty of their subjects does nothing to discourage policies that lead to impoverishment. Many Third World governments have persecuted and even expelled the most productive groups, such as the Chinese in Vietnam and Indonesia, or the Asians in East Africa. On the criterion of poverty, such governments then qualify for more aid, because incomes in their countries have been reduced.

These anomalies or paradoxes are obscured when it is suggested that giving money to the rulers of poor countries is the same as giving it to poor, even destitute people. Giving money to governments is certainly not the same thing as helping the poor. On the contrary: Western aid to Third World governments, especially in Asia and Africa, has extensively supported disastrous economic policies, which have greatly aggravated the lot of the poorest. . . .

Many people think that world-wide redistribution from rich to poor through foreign aid is a natural extension of domestic redistribution through progressive taxation. But international transfers effected by foreign aid differ radically from internal transfers effected by progressive taxation (whatever the case for the latter). Aid goes from government to government. Unlike progressive taxation, aid transfers are in no way adjusted to the personal circumstances of taxpayers and recipients. Many taxpayers in donor countries are far poorer than many people in recipient countries, in which aid largely benefits the powerful and the relatively well-off rather than the poor.

Redistributive taxation postulates basic similarities of conditions, and therefore of requirements, within its area of operation. Globally, these requirements differ widely. The meaning of riches and poverty depends

---

[3]This effect of aid is discussed in Hans O. Schmitt's "Development Assistance: A View from Bretton Woods," *Public Policy*, Fall 1973.

[4]This political reality has been recognized by others. Governments "genuinely committed to improving the material standards of life of the mass of their population" are "rare in the Third World." C. H. Kirkpatrick and F. I. Nixson, "The North-South Debate: Reflections on the Brandt Commission Report," *Three Banks Review* (London, September 1981), p. 39.

crucially on people's requirements, and thus on physical and social living conditions. This is obvious for physical conditions, notably climate. But it applies also to social conditions, including customs and values.

Unlike progressive taxation within a country, global redistribution relies on international income comparisons. These are subject to very large biases and errors. They greatly understate the relative incomes of large Asian and African countries compared to the West. . . .

RESHAPING AID POLICY

Foreign aid cannot achieve its declared objectives and has far-reaching damaging political and economic results. Yet it will not be terminated promptly because of existing commitments and because of the vested interests behind it both in the government and the market sectors, in the donor as well as in the recipient countries. Can the worst effects of aid be mitigated by changes in its method of operation?

To begin with, it may help a little if aid were to take forms which made it possible to identify its costs and possibly its benefits. This rules out indirect methods of aid such as commodity agreements. Not only are their results perverse, but their overall impact cannot be assessed. And such schemes are not subject to any public budgetary control.

There may be some advantage in avoiding soft loans in favour of outright grants. The latter avoid problems of measurement and of the confusion between gifts and loans. Aid should also take the form of direct grants from donor government to recipient government rather than of payments to multilateral organizations to be allocated to the ultimate recipients. Such direct grants permit a modicum of control by the elected representatives of the taxpayers in the donor countries, i.e., the real donors. The more distant the relationship between the supplier of funds and their user, the more likely that they will be used ineffectively. Attempts to extend the multilateral component of aid should be resisted; so also should attempts be resisted to make aid more automatic by the introduction

of international taxation, as proposed for instance in the recent Brandt report.

But these proposed reforms would make little difference in practice unless the granting of aid were made deliberately discriminating. Aid would have to be concentrated carefully on governments whose domestic and external policies were most likely to promote the general welfare of their peoples, and notably their economic progress. Aid would have to go to governments which tried to achieve this end by effective administration, the performance of the essential tasks of government, and the pursuit of liberal economic policies. At present, many aid recipient governments neglect even such basic tasks as maintaining public security, while nevertheless trying to run closely controlled economies. Selective allocation of aid along these lines would reduce its propensity to politicize life, and thereby it would reduce the extent and intensity of political conflict. It would also promote prosperity in the recipient countries, to the limited extent that external donations can do so.

Relief of need, especially humanitarian relief of poverty in the Third World, should be left to voluntary agencies, notably to nonpoliticized charities. They are already active in this field. They could do much more if it were recognized that relief of need belongs to their sphere. In this realm the international comity among countries calls for official aid only to meet unforeseeable and exceptional disasters.

As for economic development, the West can best promote this by reduction of its often severe barriers to imports from poor countries. External commerce is an effective stimulus to economic progress. It is commercial intercourse with the West which has transformed economic life in the Far East, Southeast Asia, part of Africa, and Latin America.

However, even removal of trade restrictions may well do little for the economic advance of some Third World countries and groups. Where the enlargement of external opportunities would not bring about the economic advance of particular societies, external donations to their governments would be even less likely to do so.

V.A.4. A Renewed Aid Mandate*

1. *Does aid any longer matter—even to its recipients—compared to other policy instruments?* Development assistance will continue to be enormously important to those very poor countries—broadly, the low-income countries with per capita incomes of $400 or less—which without it are not sufficiently creditworthy to finance the net imports they need in order to develop. Most of the job of building agricultural and other capacities, developing human and physical infrastructure, promoting exports, getting more of the benefits of growth to the poor, moderating population growth humanely, and achieving broader participation in the development process must be done by these countries themselves—and that is why . . . an essential, if difficult, aspect of aid in the 1980s will remain the maintenance of a dialogue with host governments concerning such self-help policies. But even with their own best efforts, these low-income countries for a long time to come will face real resource deficits which they cannot cover with the combination of their unassisted export capacity, savings capacity, and human capital-building capacity. Nor is any outside instrument but aid—not commercial borrowing (except in unsustainable spurts), not foreign private investment, and not private philanthropy on any imaginable scale—an adequate or viable answer to the real resource deficits of these very poor countries. . . .

All members of OECD should be concentrating on better trade access and more private investment—*but not instead of aid.* All three instruments can deliver net benefits to both developing and developed countries; when properly designed, they are not alternatives or competitors. And while aid of course can be (and *is*) helpful to a considerable array of middle-income developing countries, it is in the low-income countries

*From John P. Lewis, "Development Assistance in the 1980s," in Overseas Development Council, *U.S. Foreign Policy and the Third World: Agenda 1982,* 1982, pp. 102–8. Reprinted by permission.

that it has no close substitute—especially now, as we learn not only of the prospects . . . in the low-income countries of Africa but also of the continuing needs of the more populous, low-income nations of South Asia's poverty belt.

Therefore whether aid still matters to the United States in good part comes down to the issue of whether or not these low-income countries matter to the United States. This leads us to the next question, which concerns the purposes of aid from the donor's rather than the recipient's perspective.

2. *Is aid a sufficiently coherent instrument for advancing donor-country interests?* The U.S. Agency for International Development (AID) and the other development cooperation agencies and ministries that normally represent their governments on the Development Assistance Committee [of the OECD] are all charged with acting as if the promotion of Third World development were per se an important objective of their governments—and this is indeed the bent of their conscientious, professional staffs. This is of course the posture that OECD governments adopt when they participate in the World Bank and other multilateral, development-promoting agencies—or, for example, when they sign an International Development Strategy for the Third U.N. Development Decade. Yet in formal as well as realistic political terms, development promotion does not quite ring true as an ultimate or basic purpose of donor governments; for, in the usual view, the responsibility of the latter is to serve the interests of their own constituents, not to do good unto outsiders. Hence, viewed descriptively, development promotion is better understood as an intermediate objective toward which donor governments direct aid and other policy instruments in order to further certain of the basic goals that they expect development promotion to serve.

The aid programs of each donor country simultaneously pursue a variety of purposes.

The weightings given these purposes vary across the set and for individual donors from time to time. But all donor nations have mixed purposes; indeed, commonly even a donor's participation in a specific program or project is variously motivated. The purposes can be grouped into three categories.

First, economic aid to assist development often is given in part to further the donor's national self-interests as traditionally construed. These can include (a) strategic and defense purposes; (b) a variety of political and/or ideological purposes (e.g., to influence behavior in multilateral fora, to strengthen cultural and historic ties with particular regions, to propagate social modes and institutions on which the donor places intrinsic value); or (c) the donor's own economic and commercial interests, sought through expanded export, increased access to scarce materials, or new opportunities for private investors.

Second, aid is given—again by all donors—partly for humanitarian, moral, or ethical reasons. Whatever political theory posits against the credibility of external generosity by nation states, some of the latter's constituents (both outside governments and within the legislative and executive branches of governments) press for such action. This drive is clearest in response to sudden disasters, but it also includes abiding concern for the poorest of the poor. Its force is easy to underestimate. Humanitarian reasons have tended to dominate aid policy in DAC's front-runner countries for some time. . . .

A *third* rationale for aid—one whose importance is growing in the thinking of all donors—lies midway between these two rationales. It has picked up a confusing variety of names—"mutal interests," "the management of interdependence," and "world economic security." Whatever the nomenclature, . . . during the past ten or twelve years policymakers have been waking up to what a fragile and vulnerable system this planet is and how greatly its survival depends on solutions to a whole set of subsystem issues such as environmental degradation, population growth, balancing the world's food needs and supplies, finding the combination of conservation and renewable substitutes that will diminish the exhaustion of nonrenewable resources (particularly energy), and finding ways to make and keep the world's trade, financial, and monetary systems efficient and viable.

These are matters of the liveliest self-interest for the United States—and for every other country. Finding solutions clearly is a "positive sum" game; all or nearly all hands will benefit. But the difference, compared with matters of traditional national self-interest, is that in these cases the benefits cannot be sought unilaterally or be sliced up into country-by-country gains. They are joint benefits requiring joint pursuit.

The relationship of these nontraditional self-interest issues to an aid rationale is that development promotion is an inescapable part of any sensible strategy for global systems maintenance. The positive linkage between development and a number of the system's sectoral needs—for example, in the areas of food, energy, population, trade, and the maintenance of orderly commercial financial flows—is unmistakable. As for the broader linkage between development and global stability, . . . development, to be sure, tends to unseat traditional elites and is not a tranquil process. But in a Third World where change is already endemic—and in a Third World that is more immune than before to traditional instruments of power wielded from outside—those wishing to keep the level of turbulence manageable do well to bet on "development processes that succeed, without excessive delay, in coupling growth with gains in equity. . . . They are more likely than non-development to yield a set of responsible, self-reliant, national participants in the global system. . . ."

3. *Does aid work?* Development assistance is an awkward, difficult business. It operates in unfamiliar cultures and has to deal across the interface between sovereign states with indigenous governments that are jealous of their autonomy, often short on trained skills, weakly managed, and sometimes venal and repressive. . . . Donors can try to concentrate

their aid on countries making serious policy and reform efforts to help themselves, but there is no way they can bypass the host governments, which almost always are the effective as well as the formal centers of power and decision making in their systems. The aid input usually is a minor determinant of development outcomes; it can catalyze internal forces positively, but it can also fail to do so—or can be swamped by extraneous circumstances. Moreover, in times past, aid sometimes has had adverse side effects (although these are avoidable) that have dampened productive incentives, delayed self-reliance, or reinforced internal inequalities without contributing to a process that will eventually reduce them.

Thus it is obvious that the record of all development assistance by all donors up to now is mixed. It is easy enough to assemble a negative scorecard of mistakes, silly or counterproductive projects, and other failures. But there are some powerful counter points to be made.

First, there have been major and spreading achievements. Multifaceted aid from a number of donors was a catalyst—not the main force, but a strong, indispensable catalyst—for the remarkable improvement in South Asian food production that blossomed in the 1970s. In the case of South Asian agriculture, "success" (by no means complete) was achieved with a very thin spread of aid per capita. In other cases—South Korea and Taiwan, for example—very heavy concentrations of economic aid (in both cases, interestingly, for strategic reasons) have helped lay the base for burgeoning economic expansion. There also has been a good deal of progress—failures as well, but mainly significant, ramifying successes—in helping build such key development-promoting institutions as agricultural universities, technical institutes, and enterprise management training establishments in many countries. Directly and indirectly aid has contributed to the downward trend in birthrates that has begun to appear in certain countries, especially in Asia. Almost single-handedly—with the lead first coming from American foundations and then picked up by the World Bank and bilateral donors—aid has created a network of international agricultural research institutes comprising the apex of a system which, as it becomes further articulated at both the national and subnational levels, is injecting the most dynamic of all ingredients into the transformation of traditional agriculture.

The list of on-balance successes could be many times longer. It constitutes no scientific proof that aid, overall, has had positive and significant net benefits. But it fortifies a strong suspicion that without aid in the 1960s and 1970s, Third World growth (which on average was strong) would have been slower, the outcomes for the poor would have been worse, social and political turbulence would have been greater, and less groundwork would have been laid for further advances. In particular, without aid, the poorest countries, where growth was slower, would have lagged more.

Second on the positive side is the factor of experience—and the knowledge that has come with it. Development assistance is now in its fourth decade. . . . To anyone who has followed aid activity over an extended period, it is evident that the quality of aid operations has slowly continued to improve. Donor agencies have learned a great deal about the development process. They are doing better policy analysis. There is a keener appreciation of the importance of management in both their own operations and those of recipient countries and of the efficiencies that the latter countries can gain from greater reliance on decentralized (including free-market) modes of economic organization. There is more emphasis on incentives and on finding simpler, more flexible aid procedures without sacrificing accountability. Donors generally are now more sophisticated in dealing with recipients than they were in the past. They are rather better at not being counterproductively intrusive while at the same time promoting durable self-reliance and reinforcing internal (including redistributive and participatory) reforms. A good part of the operational gains are, moreover, attributable to the fact that many recipient governments are becoming more serious and businesslike development promoters. . . .

A *third* point about aid effectiveness relates to potential alternatives: Aid effectiveness compared with what? In the case of the low-income countries particularly, there is no good alternative to aid for meeting needs from which, as a matter of enlightened and broadened self-interest, the rest of the world cannot stand aside. The only rational course is to improve aid, not scuttle it. In the end, this is the answer to the spate of critics who assault the activity. A dozen years ago those who saw aid as a soft-headed enterprise were joined by critics on the New Left who, on the contrary, decried what they saw as neo-imperialist efforts to shore up repressive Third World elites. It was no surprise that, in the past two or three years—a period of strained geopolitics, troubled economies, beleaguered trade, and squeezed budgets, as well as slack leadership concerning aid—a chorus of criticism welled up from both these quarters. . . . However, these . . . critics. . . . do not address the larger question of alternatives but only score points on aid's conspicuous failings: aid trafficks with repressive and/or corrupt regimes; it implements self-serving purposes; it fails to implement the right models of development adequately; it gives either too much or too little attention to questions of equity. The critics are impatient; much of their quarrel seems to be with the nation-state system. If one posits that this system is likely to be around for some time, their criticism proposes no actionable options to aid, and their complaints are better read as a useful agenda for further aid *improvement* than a case for aid *abandonment*.

The conclusion is that if there are good reasons for a renewal of the . . . aid mandate, one need have no qualms about the instrument being so flawed as to be unworthy of use.

Comment

Although a persistent question is whether foreign aid is successful, it is difficult to reach a quantitative evaluation of the effectiveness of aid. To do so, the analysis at minimum would entail three steps. First, it would have to be recognized that aid has multiple objectives, and there would have to be as many separate assessments as there were identified purposes. It is, however, unlikely that there is a way of adding up the collective assessments of differently aimed activities into a single total. Second, it would be necessary to proceed, aimed activity by aimed activity, to assess benefits—sorting out the parts and pieces of achievement attributable to public aid flows, gauging the degree to which the established objectives had been attained, noting the efficiency with which inputs had been translated into outputs, and, if account were to be taken also of inadvertent or by-product benefits, then identfying as well the purposes against which these were to be measured. Finally, in order to arrive at activity-by-activity estimates of net achievement, one would have to take account of the costs—inescapably in the form of the alternative benefits foregone by doing this activity rather than some other, but also very commonly in the form of unwanted side effects produced by the activity undertaken.

These steps are proposed by the former chairman of the OECD's Development Advisory Committee. (See OECD, *1980 Review,* p. 54.) After reviewing the benefits and costs—even if the complexities introduced by multiple objectives are set aside and the only focus is on development promotion—the conclusion is that there is not "an unassailable, data-based proof of development's macro-effectiveness that will quiet all critics and skeptics" (*1980 Review,* p. 62). There are, however, a number of robust (albeit arguable) propositions that support aid, and it is the nature of these propositions that the burden of proof should be placed on those attacking them, not on the proponents of future aid efforts. The foregoing selection has been argued in this fashion. (See also, Chapter III of the OECD, *1980 Review.*)

V.A.5. Improving the Quality of Aid—Note

The donor nations as well as the recipients must now bear a responsibility for improving the aid relationship. Specifically, there are three major ways the donors might improve the quality of foreign assistance: by untying their aid, by giving more scope to program aid, and by operating more within a multilateral context.

Aid may be tied by both source and enduse: the recipient country may not have the freedom to apply the aid to imports from sources other than the donor country, and the use of aid may be restricted *via* specification of commodities or projects. Aid-tying has a cost to the recipient countries; if it is tied by project as well as by source, the switching possibilities in the use of the aid are severely limited, and the costs of tying can be quite significant to the recipient country. Aid-tying is essentially a protectonist device, reducing the real value. The direct costs of tying aid can be estimated as the difference between the cost of importing from the tied source and the cost of importing the same commodities from the cheapest source.

In addition to the direct costs incurred, tying of aid may have significant indirect costs for the recipient country by causing a distortion of development priorities. The distortion in the allocation of investment resources can be especially deleterious by biasing the recipient's development program toward those projects that have a high component of the special import content allowed for under the conditions of the tied aid and avoiding those projects with a large amount of "local costs" that cannot be covered by aid. "Double-tying"—by donor procurement and project restriction—can only too readily artificially alter the relative priority of different projects and bias investment toward import-intensive projects.

Although project-type loans have had most appeal to the donor countries, it can be argued that more development assistance should be on a general program basis. It is first of all illusory to believe that aid for a certain project is financing that particular project: it is impossible to limit the effects of aid only to the project to which aid is ostensibly tied. Aid is fungible, and the aid is actually financing the marginal project that would not have been undertaken but for the receipt of aid. Moreover, the efficacy of any one project is a function of the entire investment program; what ultimately matters is how the recipient country allocates its total investment expenditures. When aid is limited to specific projects, it becomes difficult to provide more aid for education, agriculture, small-scale industry, and administrative services which are not visible as large projects but which are extremely important for development. Most significantly, it should be noted that the subsequent uses of the income generated from a project are of more importance than the initial benefits from the project. To determine the effectiveness of aid, it is necessary to consider not only the initial increment of income resulting from the receipt of aid, but also whether the increment in income is subsequently used to relax one of the constraints on development, or is instead dissipated in higher consumption or used to support a larger population at the same low per capita level of income. Insofar as the most effective use of aid depends upon the operation of the whole set of development policies in the recipient country, program aid rather than project aid may be considered the more appropriate context from the start.[1]

The argument that the quality of development assistance can be improved by untying aid and shifting to nonproject aid is also an argument for extending the scale and range of aid efforts on a multilateral basis. In contrast to bilateral aid, multilateral aid has several distinct advantages: it is less influenced by the donor's interests; the undesirable effects of tying are more easily avoided; it can

[1]See Hans W. Singer, "External Aid: For Plans or Projects?" *Economic Journal*, September 1965, pp. 539–45.

more readily harmonize and improve the financial terms of aid (unlike bilateral aid, which allows one country to insist on hard terms while another offers aid on soft terms); it facilitates coordination of aid programs among the various aid sources and with the development priorities of the recipient countries; and it provides the opportunity for more aid consortia and consultative group arrangements to bring together the aid donors assisting a group of developing countries. If regional integration can contribute to development, then attention should also be given to the means of distributing aid through regional development institutions. Aid programs can then avoid being piecemeal and fragmentary, and there can be more opportunity for the active participation of recipient countries in the aid process.

What matters for securing the effective use of aid is not only its specific form or the terms on which it is rendered by the donor, but also the extent to which aid is successfully integrated by the recipient country into its development plan. Clarity on the objectives of foreign assistance is the necessary first step in determining how much aid is needed by a recipient country. The essence of capital assistance is the provision of additional resources, but external assistance should add to—not substitute for—the developing country's own efforts. If financial assistance from abroad is to result in a higher rate of domestic investment, it must be prevented from simply replacing domestic sources of financing investment or from supporting higher personal consumption or an increase in nondevelopmental current expenditures by the government.

When foreign aid is available on a general purpose basis, the allocation of the foreign capital is decisive in determining whether it contributes as much as possible to raising the growth-potential of the recipient country. The efficient allocation of investment resources then depends upon the application of investment criteria in terms of the country's entire development program, and domestic policy measures must be adopted to supplement the use of foreign assistance. Regardless of the amount of aid received, the for-

mation of capital depends, in the last resort, on domestic action.

It is appropriate therefore to emphasize the necessity of self-help measures: unless recipient governments adopt policies to mobilize fully their own resources and to implement their plans, the maximum potential benefits from aid will not be realized. As the record of foreign assistance in several countries shows, external aid may be incapable of yielding significant results unless it is accompanied by complementary domestic measures such as basic reforms in land tenure systems, additional taxation, investment in human capital, and more efficient government administration.

The success stories of foreign aid point up the case for "performance" as the criterion for allocating aid. The "performance criterion" would have a country qualify for aid according to its performance in accomplishing such objectives as raising its marginal rate of saving, lowering its incremental capital-output ratio, and reducing its balance-of-payments deficit.[2] The purpose of this criterion is to allow aid to exert positive leverage in having the recipient countries meet specified standards in their development policies and to ensure that the limited amount of aid is allocated to those countries where it will be most productive.

Several objections may be raised, however, against the "performance criterion" for aid allocation. It does not allow a country to qualify for aid simply on the basis of "need"; and yet, this may be an essential part of any foreign assistance program. The "performance criterion" is actually designed as a measure of the recipient country's progress toward a termination of external aid, but it may be argued that the transfer of resources from rich to poor countries should become a permanent feature of the international economy. Indeed, the performance criterion sidesteps questions of equity: a country may reach a state of self-sustaining growth and thus not qualify for additional aid, but still

[2]H. B. Chenery and A. M. Strout, "Foreign Assistance and Economic Development," *American Economic Review,* September 1966, pp. 728–9.

have a per capita real income lower than another country which has not yet reached self-sustaining growth and is still receiving aid even though it has a higher per capita income. Finally, the performance criterion might be interpreted as simply indicating that a country can absorb more capital, rather than that it needs aid: the fact that a country receives low marks on performance may be the very indication that it needs a larger component of aid in its capital inflow. It has been contended, for example, that many of the African countries require more aid proper.

Because the emphasis is now on the problems of absolute poverty, unemployment, and inequality, the performance criterion is less controlling of aid allocations than simpler evidence of need. Special consideration must now be given to the lowest income countries that are extremely vulnerable to foreign exchange needs.

The use of income distribution criteria and employment criteria may also improve the efficacy of foreign assistance. An expansion of lending activities in agriculture, education, and population sectors may support employment and income distribution objectives. More generally, the emphasis on these objectives now requires a shift in the orientation of aid away from capital-intensive projects, investments in urban rather than rural areas, projects in the modern rather than the traditional and informal sectors, and away from large rather than small projects.[3]

Instead of imposing a rigid and quantitative interpretation of the performance criterion, it is more appropriate to interpret it as simply reemphasizing the necessity of self-help measures and the requirement that foreign aid should avoid supporting domestic policies that turn out to be counterproductive to the recipient country's development. From this viewpoint, the granting of program aid, the insistence on self-help measures, and the concern over "performance," are all interdependent elements in the aid relationship—a relationship that is necessarily reciprocal with respect to donor and recipient behavior.

Just as the absence of complementary domestic policies may limit the effectiveness of aid, so too may its impact be neutralized by changes in the other components of the total flow of resources from rich to poor countries. The total flow is affected by private foreign investment, export earnings, and the terms of trade, as well as by foreign aid. It is therefore essential to recognize the relationships between capital assistance, private foreign investment, and international trade. The contribution of international assistance will be greater if public loans and grants are not competitive with, but instead stimulate, private foreign investment. Public aid for economic overhead facilities can create opportunities for private investment, and the private investment can, in turn, ensure fuller use of these facilities and raise their financial and economic return. Similarly, policies should be pursued that will bolster export earnings so that the inflow of development capital will be able to do more than simply offset a weak trend of export earnings or a deterioration in the recipient country's terms of trade. Of particular concern now is the need for policies that stabilize the poor countries' foreign exchange earnings; this problem is examined in section VIII.C, below.

Finally, attention should be given to ways of minimizing the burden of debt-service payments. When the return flow of interest and amortization payments exceeds the inflow of new capital assistance, the country confronts a transfer problem and must generate an export surplus. If the country is to accomplish this without having to endure the costs of internal and external controls, or currency depreciation, its development program must give due consideration to the country's debt-servicing capacity.

This becomes part of the problem of selecting appropriate investment criteria. To provide for adequate servicing of the foreign debt, the inflow of capital should increase productivity sufficiently to yield an increase in real income greater than the interest and amortization charges. If this is done, the economy will have the capacity to raise the necessary funds—either through a direct commercial return or greater taxable capac-

[3]ILO, *Time for Transition*, Geneva, 1975, p. 62.

ity. Moreover, to provide a sufficient surplus of foreign exchange to avoid a transfer problem, the capital should be utilized in such a way as to generate a surplus in the other items of the balance of payments equal to the transfer payments abroad. This does not mean that a project financed by foreign aid must itself make a direct contribution to the balance of payments, for the ability to create a sufficiently large export surplus depends on the operation of all industries together, not only on the use made of foreign investment.

As long as capital is distributed according to its most productive use and the excess spending associated with inflation is avoided, the necessary export surplus can be created indirectly. The allocation of foreign aid according to the criterion of productivity will also be the most favorable for debt servicing, since it maximizes the increase in income from a given amount of capital, thereby contributing to the growth of foreign exchange availabilities.

The problem of the growing burden of debt-servcing will also be eased for the aid-receiving country when capital assistance is offered at lower interest, for longer terms and with more continuity, and when the creditor country follows a more expansionary domestic policy and a more liberal commercial policy.

The problem of debt-servicing is discussed more fully in the next section—Note V.B.

Comment

Although the previous Note suggests ways by which the effectiveness of aid might be improved, the plea for more effectiveness should not be read as a substitute for a greater volume of aid. The net flows to the poorest of the poor countries are grossly inadequate relative to the needs posed by their lagging performance, and programs that are too small are also likely to be ineffective.

The case for a greater volume of aid has been presented by the chairman of OECD's Development Advisory Committe, the World Bank's president in arguing for replenishment of the International Development Association, and by the Brandt Commission.[1] The latter offered the following recommendations:

There must be a substantial increase in the transfer of resources to developing countries in order to finance:

1. Projects and programmes to alleviate poverty and to expand food production, especially in the least developed countries.

2. Exploration and development of energy and mineral resources.

3. Stabilization of the prices and earnings of commodity exports and expanded domestic processing of commodities.

The flow of official development finance should be enlarged by:

1. An international system of universal revenue mobilization, based on a sliding scale related to national income, in which East European and developing countries—except the poorest countries—would participate.

2. The adoption of timetables to increase Official Development Assistance (ODA) from industrialized countries to the level of 0.7 percent.

3. Introduction of automatic revenue transfers through international levies on some of the following: international trade; arms production or exports; international travel; the global commons, especially sea-bed minerals.

Lending through international financial institutions should be improved through:

1. Effective utilization of the increased borrowing capacity of the World Bank resulting from the recent decision to double its capital to $80 billion.

2. Doubling the borrowing-to-capital ratio of the World Bank from its present gearing of 1:1 to 2:1, and similar action by Regional Development Banks.

[1] *North-South: A Programme for Survival,* Report of the Independent Commission on International Development Issues, Willy Brandt, Chairman, 1980.

3. Abstaining from the imposition of political conditions on the operations of multilateral financial institutions.

4. Channeling an increasing share of development finance through regional institutions.

5. A substantial increase in programme lending.

6. The use of IMF gold reserves either for further sales, whose profits would subsidize interest on development lending, or as collateral to borrow for on-lending to developing countries.

7. Giving borrowing countries a greater role in decision-making and management.

Resource transfers should be made more predictable by long-term commitments to provide ODA, increasing use of automatically mobilized revenues, and the lengthening of the International Development Association (IDA) replenishment period.

Consideration should be given to the creation of a new international financial institution—a World Development Fund—with universal membership, and in which decision-making is more evenly shared between lenders and borrowers, to supplement existing institutions and diversify lending policies and practices. The World Development Fund would seek to satisfy the unmet needs in the financing structure, in particular that of programme lending. Ultimately it could serve as a channel for such resources as may be raised on a universal and automatic basis.[2]

A number of reviews provide excellent critical surveys of the Brandt Report: P. D. Henderson, "Survival, Development and the Report of the Brandt Commission," *The World Economy* (June 1980); Graeme S. Dorrance, "North-South: The Need for Discussion," *The Banker* (April–May 1980); Dudley Seers, "North-South: Muddling, Morality and Mutuality," *Third World Quarterly* (October 1980); H. W. Singer, "The Brandt Report: A 'Northwestern' Point of View," *Third World Quarterly* (October 1980). For a more radical view by a structural critic of the international order, see Teresa Hayter, *The Creation of World Poverty: An Alternative View to the Brandt Report* (1981).

[2]Ibid., pp. 254–5.

EXHIBIT V.5. Savings, Investment, and Balance of Payments (percent share of GNP)

Indicator	1960	1970	1975	1976	1977	1978
National Savings						
Developing countries						
Low income: Asia and Pacific	11.7	14.1	16.8	18.9	19.5	19.9
Africa south of						
Sahara	10.8	14.1	8.4	10.0	9.3	6.6
Middle income: Africa south of						
Sahara	15.5	16.8	23.9	24.4	25.0	26.3
North Africa and						
Middle East	20.6	17.7	20.8	22.1	22.6	22.4
Asia and Pacific	10.3	20.6	22.4	25.8	26.2	26.3
Latin America						
and Caribbean	19.4	20.0	20.6	21.8	22.8	21.8
Europe	21.1	22.5	20.2	20.1	20.9	19.7
Total	18.0	20.0	20.4	21.5	22.3	22.4
Capital surplus oil exporters	22.3	36.5	52.9	51.2	49.1	47.7
Industrialized countries	23.2	24.7	20.9	22.0	22.0	22.1
Investment, Including Stock						
Developing countries						
Low income: Asia and Pacific	14.5	16.7	20.6	20.9	20.3	21.3
Africa south of						
Sahara	12.2	16.8	17.9	16.5	15.5	16.7
Middle income: Africa south of						
Sahara	20.3	22.1	28.0	27.4	27.4	28.2
North Africa and						
Middle East	24.0	23.3	32.4	32.6	34.8	32.4
Asia and Pacific	15.1	25.0	28.6	27.2	27.2	28.9
Latin America						
and Caribbean	21.1	22.0	24.4	24.4	24.8	25.3
Europe	22.5	25.5	26.1	25.2	25.7	23.7
Total	20.2	23.1	25.8	25.3	25.7	25.5
Capital surplus oil exporters	30.8	19.3	26.1	29.3	31.6	30.9
Industrialized countries	22.3	23.8	20.9	21.8	21.9	22.4
Balance of Payments—Current						
Account Surplus/Deficit						
Developing countries						
Low income: Asia and Pacific	−2.0	−0.9	−2.2	−0.2	−0.6	−1.3
Africa south of						
Sahara	—	−1.6	−8.1	−2.7	−0.8	−3.2
Middle income: Africa south of						
Sahara	—	−3.6	−4.8	−3.4	−1.3	−2.3
North Africa and						
Middle East	−1.1	−2.4	−8.1	−7.6	−9.4	−9.7
Asia and Pacific	−0.2	−2.3	−5.5	−0.9	−0.3	−1.4
Latin America						
and Caribbean	−1.4	−1.8	−4.1	−3.1	−2.8	−3.4
Europe	0.8	−1.1	−4.6	−3.9	−3.8	−1.4
Total	—	−1.7	−4.4	−2.9	−2.5	−2.6
Capital surplus oil exporters	—	2.1	20.5	19.9	16.2	14.1
Industrialized countries	0.2	0.4	0.4	−0.1	−0.2	0.4

Source: World Bank; and IMF, *International Financial Statistics.*

EXHIBIT V.6. Non-Oil-Developing Countries: External Debt, 1973–1983[a] (in billions of U.S. dollars)

	1973	1974	1975	1976	1977	1978	1979	1980	1981	1982	1983
Total outstanding debt of non-oil developing countries	**130.1**	**160.8**	**190.8**	**228.0**	**278.5**	**336.3**	**396.9**	**474.0**	**555.0**	**612.4**	**664.3**
Short-term debt	18.4	22.7	27.3	33.2	42.5	49.7	58.8	85.5	102.2	112.7	92.4
Long-term debt	111.8	138.1	163.5	194.9	235.9	286.6	338.1	388.5	452.8	499.6	571.6
By type of creditor											
Official creditors	51.0	60.1	70.3	82.4	98.7	117.5	133.0	152.9	172.4	193.2	218.7
Governments	37.3	43.4	50.3	57.9	67.6	79.1	87.2	98.7	108.6	120.4	135.3
International institutions	13.7	16.6	20.3	24.8	31.0	38.4	45.8	54.2	63.8	72.8	83.3
Private creditors	60.8	77.9	95.1	114.8	137.3	169.1	205.1	235.6	280.4	306.4	353.0
Unguaranteed debt	29.3	36.0	40.8	45.9	51.4	56.4	67.3	77.5	96.7	103.9	113.7
Guaranteed debt	31.5	42.0	52.4	66.6	85.9	112.7	137.8	158.1	183.7	202.2	239.3
Financial institutions	17.3	25.6	36.7	49.0	59.1	79.5	102.9	121.6	144.5	159.5	193.8
Other private creditors	14.2	16.3	17.6	19.8	26.8	33.2	34.9	36.5	39.2	42.7	45.5
By analytical group											
Net oil exporters	20.4	26.0	34.1	42.4	53.3	61.2	70.5	79.4	96.5	108.1	129.0
Net oil importers	91.4	112.1	129.4	152.5	182.7	225.4	267.6	309.1	356.2	391.5	442.6
Major exporters of manufactures	40.8	51.7	60.9	73.1	85.2	108.1	127.7	145.2	170.6	184.3	212.4
Low-income countries	25.4	29.7	33.2	38.3	46.5	53.1	59.5	67.0	73.0	80.1	90.8
Other net oil importers[b]	25.2	30.6	35.3	41.1	51.0	64.2	80.4	96.9	112.7	127.1	139.4
By area											
Africa	14.2	17.7	21.9	26.9	35.0	42.1	49.6	55.1	60.5	67.1	75.0
Asia	30.0	34.6	39.8	46.4	57.9	67.4	76.1	88.4	100.8	115.1	131.7
Europe	14.5	17.2	20.0	23.4	28.7	38.2	49.0	57.5	63.4	69.2	73.8
Middle East	8.7	10.3	13.3	16.1	20.3	24.7	28.4	32.9	35.4	39.3	43.7
Western Hemisphere	44.4	58.2	68.6	82.0	94.0	114.3	135.1	154.7	192.6	208.9	247.4

Sources: World Bank, Debtor Reporting System; and Fund staff estimates and projections. IMF, *World Economic Outlook* 1983, p. 200.

[a]Excludes data for the People's Republic of China prior to 1977.

[b]Middle-income countries that, in general, export mainly primary commodities.

EXHIBIT V.7. Non-Oil-Developing Countries: Long-Term and Short-Term External Debt Relative to Exports and to GDP, 1973–1983[a] (in percent)

	1973	1974	1975	1976	1977	1978	1979	1980	1981	1982	1983
Ratio of external debt to exports of goods and services[b]											
All non-oil developing countries	115.4	104.6	122.4	125.5	126.4	130.2	119.2	112.9	124.9	143.3	144.4
By analytical group											
Net oil exporters	154.7	124.9	162.4	169.5	179.3	176.9	144.3	128.4	154.6	179.5	192.2
Net oil importers	109.4	100.9	115.4	117.5	116.8	121.8	114.1	109.5	118.3	135.1	134.3
Major exporters of manufactures	91.7	88.6	103.0	103.3	99.5	101.1	96.9	94.0	100.6	116.2	114.2
Low-income countries	227.9	214.5	226.1	225.1	217.8	226.3	209.8	201.4	231.1	254.1	262.9
Other net oil importers[c]	96.9	84.7	98.3	104.3	111.6	124.8	115.5	110.9	121.9	138.0	136.6
By region											
Africa	71.5	65.4	80.9	94.2	103.1	111.4	100.8	97.4	119.9	147.4	148.6
Asia	92.9	81.0	91.6	84.4	83.3	77.7	70.2	68.2	72.5	80.9	85.4
Europe	102.4	97.1	108.0	114.9	127.4	136.4	125.6	121.6	118.2	129.6	129.7
Middle East	145.4	105.2	131.5	137.5	140.4	142.4	133.8	113.1	112.6	134.3	133.1
Western Hemisphere	176.2	163.4	195.8	204.1	194.1	211.5	192.9	178.4	207.4	245.6	242.8
Ratio of external debt to GDP[b]											
All non-oil developing countries	22.4	21.8	23.8	25.7	27.4	285	27.5	27.6	31.0	24.7	34.7
By analytical group											
Net oil exporters	26.2	25.5	27.7	32.3	38.5	39.3	37.4	34.0	36.1	44.7	43.5
Net oil importers	21.7	21.2	23.0	24.4	25.4	26.6	25.8	26.3	29.7	32.1	32.7
Major exporters of manufactures	20.2	19.6	22.2	22.7	23.9	25.1	24.6	25.1	29.3	33.2	33.8
Low-income countries	20.1	20.1	20.9	24.4	24.9	24.0	24.4	23.6	24.7	26.2	26.5
Other net oil importers[c]	26.2	25.2	26.2	27.7	28.6	31.5	28.8	30.6	34.1	35.8	35.6
By region											
Africa	19.4	19.6	21.6	25.8	28.4	29.4	28.9	28.8	30.6	35.2	35.1
Asia	19.7	18.9	20.4	22.4	23.4	22.3	22.2	23.2	25.2	26.7	27.1
Europe	24.5	23.1	22.8	24.6	25.7	28.6	25.1	29.0	33.1	34.7	34.5
Middle East	36.2	34.0	39.0	42.3	45.4	48.3	56.0	52.6	51.3	50.3	47.4
Western Hemisphere	23.0	22.8	25.5	26.4	28.4	30.3	28.8	27.0	31.9	38.2	38.6
Memorandum items											
Ratios (including People's Rep. of China)[b]											
To exports:											
All non-oil developing countries	—	—	—	—	123.6	127.0	116.1	109.4	119.8	136.5	137.7
Low-income countries	—	—	—	—	169.0	170.0	152.0	137.7	140.0	148.7	155.5
To GDP:											
All non-oil developing countries	—	—	—	—	23.9	24.6	23.9	24.1	27.3	30.5	30.5
Low-income countries	—	—	—	—	14.3	13.5	13.4	13.2	14.3	15.1	15.3

Source: IMF, *World Economic Outlook* 1983, p. 201.

[a]Excludes data for the People's Republic of China, except where noted.

[b]Ratio of year-end debt to exports or GDP for year indicated.

[c]Middle-income countries that, in general, export mainly primary commodities.

V.B. EXTERNAL DEBT AND COUNTRY RISK ANALYSIS— NOTE

The increase in lending to governments of developing countries by private commercial banks has raised questions of country creditworthiness. When banks engage in cross-border lending they are obviously concerned about the capacity of the borrowing country to service the debt—that is, to pay interest and amortization in foreign currency. To appraise the creditworthiness of the borrower, lenders engage in country risk analysis to determine the borrower's ability to generate sufficient foreign exchange to meet debt service obligations. For this analysis there is no formula or one definitive approach: it depends on the analyst's perception of the country's development process and how this relates to the country's balance of payments. A debt service crisis—that is, the borrower cannot or will not repay on schedule—is in essence a balance-of-payments crisis, and this, in turn, is a development crisis.[1] Country risk analysis therefore depends on an understanding of the development process and how the course of development affects the balance of payments.

Even though the loan is ostensibly for a given project, it supports in reality the marginal project—the project that would not have been undertaken but for this loan. The loan helps to fill the savings gap and foreign exchange gap by making more resources available for capital formation and by increasing the country's capacity to import. Because capital is fungible, the loan actually supports the country's development program and balance of payments instead of being limited to some given project. So too is the debt service on the loan a charge on the economy as a whole—a charge against the total use of resources. Provided that the social rate of return to capital in the least productive project is greater than the interest rate on the most expensive loan, there should be no debt service problem.

In practice, however, it is not operationally feasible to find the "marginal project" and to calculate whether the marginal return is greater than the marginal cost of borrowing. To circumvent this difficulty, the analyst must shadow price the project and also undertake macroanalysis to analyze the ultimate effect of the loan on the total use of resources in the borrowing country.

When shadow pricing the project, the analyst corrects for price distortions to reflect true social costs—raising the rate of interest, lowering the wage rate, and increasing the cost of foreign exchange. Externalities are also calculated. Instead of focusing on simply the internal *financial* rate of return, the shadow pricing allows calculation of the internal *economic* rate of return. If, in addition, some judgment is made on the distribution of income, the internal *social* rate of return may be calculated. (This is explained later in Chapter X.) This process of shadow pricing for the rate of return is equivalent to determining whether the effective rate of interest (nominal rate of interest corrected for inflation, aid-tying, and changes in terms of trade) is greater then the accounting rate of interest (social return to capital).[2]

Even though a project meets the social efficiency criterion based on shadow pricing, there is still the problem of whether the country can transfer a portion of the increased output and income into foreign exchange for debt-servicing. To determine the capacity to service external debt, some analysts engage

[1] Cf. Goran Ohlin, "Debts, Development and Default," in G. K. Helleiner (ed.), *A World Divided*, 1976, pp. 207–22.

[2] For details of evaluating foreign capital inflows in a cost-benefit framework, see Deepak Lal, "The Evaluation of Capital Inflows," *Industry and Development*, No. 1, 1978, pp. 2–19. In Chapter X we consider project appraisal in greater detail.

in ratio analysis, examining such ratios as debt outstanding/GNP, debt service/exports, imports/international reserves, imports/exports, and so forth. If the numerator in the fraction increases relative to the denominator, a debt crisis might be indicated. Ideally, one would like an index that would show the *risk* of a sharp fall in any kind of foreign exchange inflow and a rise in import needs, compared with the *ability* to offset such risks by compressing imports rapidly, obtaining compensatory financing, or using international reserves. No one ratio captures this. Therefore, several ratios may need to be used as proxies. But again, neither the history of rescheduling cases nor the econometric analysis of default functions indicates a definitive number of ratios. A suggested list might include: debt service/exports, debt service/debt outstanding, debt outstanding/exports, net transfer/imports, rate of growth of debt/rate of growth of exports, and imports/reserves. Increases in these ratios might be warnings of a debt crisis. But in past renegotiation cases there has been large variance and dispersion in these ratios. Other factors must therefore be considered.

Beyond ratios, country risk analysis should monitor some "key performance indicators" that will indicate how national economic management is affecting the growth of the economy and the capacity to service the debt. The key performance indicators are (1) a rising ratio of savings to national income, (2) a rising ratio of taxes to income, (3) a decreasing incremental capital-output ratio (less unutilized capacity), (4) a decreasing current account deficit, (5) high employment elasticity—that is, the rate of growth in employment relative to the rate of growth in output, and (6) more equitable income distribution.

To realize positive changes in these performance indicators the debtor country may have to undertake a set of policies, reflecting a higher quality of policy analysis and implementation. Price distortions will have to be removed: real interest rates raised, overvalued foreign exchange rate corrected, wages brought closer to opportunity cost. The fiscal deficit must be reduced. Local capital markets may have to be deepened to mobilize local savings. The foreign trade regime may have to be liberalized and the bias against exports removed. All these policies will affect the debtor country's performance. These policies are frequently suggested when the IMF imposes conditionality on a member country's access to drawing rights in the higher credit tranches or in standby arrangements. When the Fund imposes conditionality, this may also encourage commercial banks to provide longer-term capital inflows.

This concentration on the policies necessary to improve the economy's performance in order to service the debt also illuminates other issues of debt-servicing that are frequently confused.[3]

What is meant by the "burden" of the debt? This is usually related to the debt-servicing problem. There would, of course, be no problem of debt service if capital flowed into the country in sufficient amount to allow the developing country to meet interest and amortization payments on foreign obligations and also to maintain its imports at a desired level. In reality, however, sooner or later—depending on the growth in new foreign borrowing, rate of interest, and amortization rate—the debt-servicing charges may require a net capital outflow from the debtor country. When the return flow of interest and amortization payments exceeds the inflow of new capital, the country becomes a "mature debtor" and confronts a transfer problem in servicing the debt. The country has to achieve sufficient self-sustaining growth to remove the resource gap and cover the net capital outflow. The country will have to generate an export surplus equal to its net outward transfer of interest on current account and amortization on capital account in its balance of payments.

The direct costs of debt service do not, however, constitute the burden of the debt—provided the social rate of return from the external capital exceeds the interest cost. True, part of the increased production from the use

[3]This section is drawn from Gerald M. Meier, *International Economics*, 1980, pp. 343–8.

of the external resource inflow has to be repaid abroad, and this is a reduction that would not be necessary if the savings had been provided at home. But the reality is that the savings have been provided from overseas, and the foreign savers must receive some return. Of most importance to the borrowing country is that its economy has realized additional investment, and the benefits from this should exceed the direct costs of the foreign savings that made possible the capital formation. The direct costs of servicing the foreign debt out of additional income should not be a cause for concern.

Of genuine concern are the indirect costs. These arise when the debt-servicing country has to undertake burdensome policies of balance-of-payments adjustment to acquire sufficient foreign exchange for debt service. Domestic savings in the developing country will have to become sufficient to finance all domestic investment and, in addition, the interest cost of accumulated debt and the repayment of the principal of its loans. In order to convert the surplus of savings into the foreign exchange it needs for debt-servicing, the developing country will have to generate an export surplus through expenditure-reducing and expenditure-switching policies so as to expand exports or reduce the demand for imports. This may require some combination of deflation, internal and external controls over resource allocation, and exchange rate depreciation. The adverse effects of these measures of balance-of-payments adjustment are the indirect costs of foreign borrowing, and they constitute the burden of debt-servicing.

It might be thought that this burden can be avoided if the investment of foreign capital creates its own means of payment by directly expanding exports or replacing imports. The lender might also believe that if it lends for a project that earns foreign exchange or saves foreign exchange there can be no transfer risk in debt-servicing. But this is again to adopt the myopic and illusory view of project financing. Once we appreciate the relationship between total resource availabilities and uses, the interdependence of investments, and the principle that debt service is

ultimately a charge on the economy as a whole, we can recognize that the transfer problem can still be solved without stipulating that the investment of foreign capital should create its own means of payment by directly expanding exports or by replacing imports. Instead of committing the fallacy of misplaced concreteness, we should realize that debt capacity cannot be determined without appraising the country's development program as a whole. Analysis of the entire program is necessary for an assessment of the conditions under which the competing claims on total resources, on savings, and on foreign exchange can be adjusted so as to release the amount required for debt service. In the last analysis, it is not a matter of whether "the project" that the foreign loan is ostensibly intended to finance will be able to carry the cost of the loan—but the return on the marginal project or the ultimate effect on the total use of resources. If it is realized that the ability to create a sufficiently large export surplus depends on the operation of all sectors together, not simply on the use made of foreign capital alone, it is then apparent that a project financed by foreign borrowing need not itself make a direct contribution to the balance of payments. Indeed, even if foreign capital were limited to financing projects that earn or save foreign exchange, developments elsewhere in the economy may at the same time be affecting the supply of foreign exchange so adversely that the debt service problem is aggravated even though the foreign capital has supposedly been directed to projects that ought to be able to carry the costs of the loans.

Instead of such a narrow balance-of-payments criterion for the allocation of investment, the basic test for the allocation of foreign capital, as for any investment, is that it should be invested in the form that yields the highest social marginal product. The allocation of capital according to its most productive use will also be the most favorable for debt-servicing, because it maximizes the increase in income from a given amount of capital and thereby contributes to the growth of foreign exchange availability. The export of particular commodities or services through which the interest is transferred abroad should then be determined by the principle of comparative costs. There are thus two principles determining debt capacity: the investment criterion of social marginal productivity and the trade criterion of comparative cost. To allocate foreign capital to a foreign exchange project is to do violence to the separation of these two basic principles, and it is to settle for the easier, but misleading, approach of project appraisal instead of country appraisal.

The elements that compose the analysis of a country's creditworthiness can be synthesized in a country risk matrix (see Table 1). The vertical scale illustrates the lender's appraisal of the borrowing country's balance-of-payments potential—that is, the country's potential to have a sufficient flow of foreign exchange to service its debt. Countries in the top row (numbered 1) have the highest potential, whereas countries at the lowest rating (numbered 5) have the least potential and can be expected to confront payment delays

or defaults. Underlying the evaluation of balance-of-payments potential is the assessment of the key performance parameters. And behind these, in turn, lie the policies that the borrowing country would have to undertake to raise these performance parameters and to realize its balance-of-payments potential.

In the columns of Table 1, countries are ranked according to their capacity for national economic management. This involves a judgment on the borrowing country's ability and willingness (often a political matter) to undertake the policies that will allow the country to achieve its balance-of-payments potential. Countries in column A have the highest policy capability to undertake the measures that would allow debt-servicing. All countries rated E or 5 would present the greatest country risk to the lender, whereas those rated A or 1 would be most creditworthy with the highest debt capacity. Japan and Zaire are simply illustrative of the relative ratings that the lender could make within the matrix. Ratings would of course change over time.

Comment

Several statistical and econometric studies have attempted to refine the methodology of country risk analysis. Using the statistical techniques of discriminant and logit methods, the studies attempt to develop a model that will predict debt reschedulings based on historical

TABLE 1. Country Risk Matrix

		High A	B	C	D	Low E
		High 1	Japan				
		2					
		3					
		4					
		Low 5					"Zaire"

Capacity for national economic management

Balance-of-payments potential

Policies

patterns. With varying degrees of predictive value, the studies attempt to establish econometric default functions.

See R. Z. Aliber "A Conceptual Approach to the Analysis of External Debt of the Developing Countries, *World Bank Staff Working Paper* No. 421 (October 1980); R. Z. Aliber, "Describing External Debt Situations: A Roll-Over Approach." *IMF Staff Papers,* Vol. XXII, No. 1 (1975); G. Feder and R. Just, "A Study of Debt Servicing Capacity Applying Logit Analysis," *Journal of Development Economics,* Vol. 4, No. 1 (1977); G. Feder, "Economic Growth, Foreign Loans and Debt Servicing Capacity of Developing Countries," *Journal of Development Studies* (April 1980); Charles R. Frank, Jr., and William R. Cline, "Measurement of Debt Servicing Capacity: An Application of Discrimination Analysis," *Journal of International Economics,* Vol. I, No. 3 (1971); Alice L. Mayo and Anthony G. Barrett, "An Early Warning Model for Assessing Developing Country Risk," in S. H. Goodman (ed.), *Proceedings of a Symposium on Developing Countries' Debt* (August 1977); K. Saini and P. Bates, "Statistical Techniques for Determining Debt-Servicing Capacity for Developing Countries," *Federal Reserve Bank of New York, Research Paper* No. 7818 (September 1978); Nicholas Sargen, "Economic Indicators and Country Risk Appraisal," *Federal Reserve Bank of San Francisco Economic Review* (Fall 1977).

The models all have Type I errors (failures to predict actual reschedulings) and Type II errors (prediction of reschedulings that did not in fact occur). Moreover, the default functions are derived from a historical sample, and their applicability to a different sample in the future is questionable.

V.C. THE INTERNATIONAL MONETARY SYSTEM AND DEVELOPMENT FINANCE— NOTE

What emerges from the preceding selections is that foreign aid has been declining just at a time when there is a greater capacity to use aid more effectively and when the need in many countries has become even more urgent. It is understandable that the LDCs have therefore sought new measures for the extension of foreign aid. If aid is not forthcoming in sufficient amounts in the traditional form of open aid explicitly granted by donor to recipient, then the transfer of resources from rich to poor countries must come via other policy instruments. Most prominent in UNCTAD discussions are the attempts to have aid increased in a "disguised" form through trade policy (i.e., through international commodity agreements and preferences on manufactures) and through reform of the international monetary system. In Chapter VIII we examine the scope for aid through trade policy. Here we consider the merits of introducing a stronger component of development finance into the international monetary system.

New international monetary arrangements have been evolving since August 15, 1971 when the United States suspended convertibility of the dollar into gold, and a regime of floating exchange-rates for most major currencies emerged. There has been official intervention in exchange markets, however, so that the floats have been "managed" within limits. Although rates were not fully flexible, the old par system of the IMF was dismantled, and a debate emerged over establishment of a new exchange-rate system to improve the balance-of-payments adjustment process. This debate was also closely related to the question of how payments imbalance might be settled more readily with greater international liquidity. And this, in turn, raised the issue of supplementing development aid

by linking the creation of additional international reserves with assistance to developing countries. The general position of LDCs, as represented by the Lima Action Program and statements of UNCTAD,[1] has been in favor of very limited flexibility or a return to a fixed exchange-rate system and the creation of additional international liquidity in the form of a fiduciary instrument like Special Drawing Rights (SDRs).

In the debate over flexible exchange-rates, some special arguments relate to LDCs with respect to whether (i) rates are fixed or flexible between developed countries (DCs) and LDCs, and (ii) rates are fixed or flexible among the DCs.

The LDCs may favor fixed rates among the DCs, but some management of a "crawling peg" between the LDC currency and DC currencies. Several LDCs have used some form of "crawling peg" to offset their differential rates of inflation and to leave their real effective exchange-rate fairly constant. These include Brazil (a "trotting peg"), Colombia, the Philippines, Korea, Malaysia, Morocco, Yugoslavia, and Indonesia.

In favor of greater flexibility, it is claimed that flexible rates depoliticize the problem of devaluation. LDCs tend to maintain overvalued disequilibrium rates, protected by trade and exchange restrictions, and are reluctant to devalue for political reasons; but this tendency to postpone adjustment would be overcome if depreciation of the deficit country's currency came about automatically under freely fluctuating rates. Although devaluations have not met with political favor, a study of some two dozen currency devalua-

---

[1] G. M. Meier, *Problems of A World Monetary Order,* 2nd ed., 1982, pp. 301–14.

tions in LDCs shows that the action has generally been successful in improving the balance of trade.[2]

Most of the LDCs, however, favor fixed rates between their currencies and those of other countries with which they have most of their trade and financial relations. Being generally a small open economy, the LDC believes it is advantageous to maintain convertibility at a fixed price into the currency of some major country with which the small LDC trades extensively or on which it depends for capital for investment.

Perhaps even more persuasive than the positive case for pegging to a major currency, is the negative case against flexible rates for LDCs. It is argued that flexible rates have several special disadvantages for LDCs. The problems of overcoming uncertainty and risk aversion may be especially severe for an LDC which does not have well-established forward exchange markets and which would have to diversify its reserve and debt portfolios to reduce exchange-rate risks. The facilities for a forward market between foreign currency and domestic currency are usually extremely thin in the LDC, and it is too facile to believe that forward cover can be provided the LDC's exporters by utilizing forward markets in the developed countries. Flexible rates intensify the complexity of portfolio management of reserves for LDCs, and reserves held in a depreciating currency would lose purchasing power. The creation of uncertainty for the foreign investor who wants to reconvert funds into the creditor's currency can also become a significant deterrent to capital inflow. The real value of the repayment burden of servicing external debt could also be severe if the debt is denominated in an appreciating currency.

Further, freely fluctuating rates tend to inhibit regional integration among LDCs unless the countries can agree to a joint float. Finally, exchange-rate depreciation for an

LDC would be ineffective as an adjustment mechanism to the extent that domestic inflation persists, the LDC's demand for imports is a function of its output and is unresponsive to price changes, the LDC's marginal propensity to save is a constant that cannot be readily altered by relative price changes, and the LDC's exports have a low price elasticity of demand (i.e., conditions of a "structural disequilibrium"). Thus, on grounds of both inefficacy and undue burden, the LDCs tend to reject fluctuating exchange-rates.

The strength of these arguments can only be assessed in comparison with what are the feasible alternatives to flexible rates. If rates are to change only infrequently, but the changes are very large, then the uncertainty and risk aversion may be even greater than under more frequent, but smaller, rate changes. If the alternative to adjustment through rate flexibility is the imposition of trade restrictions, or is a policy of national income contraction, then the alternative costs may be greater than any burden imposed by rate flexibility. It is therefore not sufficient simply to point out that there are costs involved in rate flexibility: in the absence of access to unlimited international liquidity, there will be some costs to any remedial policy for correcting a balance-of-payments deficit. The objective is to discover the least-costly remedial policy.

Even if it is granted that the LDC wants to peg its currency to a DC currency, the question still remains whether fixed or flexible rates among the DCs themselves would be of most advantage to the LDCs. Again, this depends on the feasible alternatives for the DCs. The dominant concern of the LDC should be expansion of its exports to the DCs. Trade with the DCs is by far the largest source of foreign exchange for the LDCs. It is therefore of utmost importance that the DCs refrain from imposing trade barriers on imports from the LDCs, and that the DCs promote a high rate of domestic expansion so that imports from LDCs will be maintained. If flexible rates among the DCs will provide an effective adjustment mechanism, so that

[2]Richard N. Cooper, *Currency Devaluation in Developing Countries,* Princeton Essays in International Finance, No. 86, June 1971.

trade controls or deflation can be avoided, then flexibility among DC-rates will be best from the viewpoint of the LDCs.[3]

With flexibility among DC-currencies, the LDC can then peg either to a key currency (dollar, franc, mark, yen), to a bundle of currencies, or to the SDR. Which is most desirable for the LDC will depend on the diversification of its trade and financial transactions with "the rest of the world." Technically, to reduce its loss of control over its effective exchange-rate, the small LDC should peg to a weighted average of key currencies. If the objective is to keep its domestic prices in line with the "world" price level, the weights will have to correspond to those of each major country contributing to such a price level. If the goal is to maintain balance-of-payments equilibrium by adjusting the effective exchange-rate, more complicated calculations of multiple-currency pegging will be necessary, involving price elasticities by countries and forecasts of future trade patterns. Because of the complicated calculations required to maintain some target trade-weighted exchange-rate (and how should financial flows be weighted, as compared with trade flows?), the LDCs are more likely to opt for pegging to the SDR. The SDR is defined in terms of a basket of five major currencies, and it is undoubtedly operationally simplest to peg to a "standard basket" SDR.

To the extent that the mechanism of adjustment is more effective through flexible rates and disabsorption policies, there is less need for the creation of additional reserve assets. But to the extent that countries are unwilling to bear the costs of adjustment, or countries welcome continual surpluses while corresponding deficits are much less readily tolerated, there will have to be an autonomous inflow of new reserve assets into the system.

In the course of discussions on international monetary reform it increasingly has been argued that the SDR should become the principal asset of settlement between central banks, and, in time, the principal reserve asset of the system. It is a common judgment that if countries must suffer deflation or impose restrictive measures on trade and capital movements in order to protect their international reserves, then there is a shortage of international liquidity. Even though one cannot specify the "right" amount of international liquidity,[4] one can certainly maintain that countries are revealing a shortage of international liquidity when the rate of international economic growth is retarded and there is a retreat from liberalization of trade in order to husband reserves. But how much liquidity should be created? Who is to control the creation of the additional liquidity? How is the increase to be distributed? And what are to be the benefits to the LDCs?

Even if the LDCs were not to share in the control of the creation of additional liquidity, or were not to receive directly any of the initial increase in liquidity, they would still benefit indirectly from any plan that expanded world reserves. For to the extent that such an expansion forestalls the developed countries from adopting beggar-my-neighbor policies, or allows a relaxation of such restrictive measures, the developing countries will benefit. If as a result of access to new reserves, a developed country can have a higher rate of domestic growth without encountering a balance-of-payments constraint, then the demand for imports from LDCs can rise. If a

---

[3]For a comprehensive discussion, see William R. Cline, *Interests of the Developing Countries in International Monetary Reform,* Brookings Staff Paper, 1975. Cline concludes that the empirical evidence of currency changes in the early 1970s indicates that the LDCs' fears of flexible rates have generally been unwarranted, and that the LDCs' gains from an improved monetary system should greatly exceed any external costs to them from flexibility in DC-rates.

[4]It is illusory and misplaced precision to specify an "optimum amount" of international liquidity by relating the "need" to such variables as imports, variations in foreign trade, imports and capital flows, past deficits, domestic money supply, or current liabilities. See Fritz Machlup, "The Need for Monetary Reserves," *Banca Nazionale del Lavoro,* September 1966, pp. 175–222.

developed country is enabled to remove restrictions on the outflow of private foreign investment, then again the LDCs may benefit. Or if monetary policy—previously kept "tight" out of consideration for the balance of payments—is eased, the LDCs and international institutions specializing in development assistance may have greater access to the capital markets of developed countries. And most importantly, if developed nations no longer have to plead that pressures on their balance of payments prevent an increase in foreign aid or the untying of aid, then the recipient LDCs will benefit.

Although these indirect benefits are of value, the LDCs have argued for more than this indirect assistance: they have wanted development finance to be linked with liquidity creation.[5] A scheme of international monetary reform would then be of direct benefit to the LDCs in that it would directly provide additional aid in the process of creating additional international liquidity.

Special Drawing Rights are a form of unconditional credit: they involve no fixed repayment schedule and require no statement of need by users. Developing countries would well prefer this to the conditionality imposed by the IMF on some types of drawings. Furthermore, since net users have to pay only interest and do not have to repay capital, payments on the net use of SDRs will tend to be lower than they would be for a commercial bank loan of similar size. The lowest-income countries that have not had access to the Eurocurrency market would tend to benefit most from the "link."[6]

The standard argument against linking liquidity creation and development finance is, of course, that the need for reserves and the need for development finance are two distinct issues and that therefore the LDCs are mixing up two separate questions. It is argued

that the need for reserves is to cover a temporary imbalance, while the need for long-term development finance is to cover a chronic balance-of-payments gap. If the amount of liquidity to be created is determined by development finance, then, it is argued, there will be too much liquidity. Moreover, it is contended that the developing countries would not conserve an addition to their reserves but would instead spend it, contrary to the notion that the creation of liquidity should meet the demand for liquid assets to hold as precautionary balances, not to spend as transaction balances.

Against this scepticism, proponents of a direct link between monetary reform and the provision of development finance offer several counter-arguments. In brief:

i. The need for more reserves by LDCs is especially acute. It is contended that there is a widening trade gap, primary product export earnings fluctuate widely, and the mechanism of adjustment to a balance-of-payments deficit operates more slowly in an LDC than in an advanced economy.[7] There is therefore a justification in initially distributing an increase in international liquidity to LDCs.

ii. As for the contention that an increase in reserves would allow the developing countries to escape from balance-of-payments discipline, it is replied that for an LDC the so-called "discipline of the balance of payments" does not in reality lead to deflationary (or disinflationary) monetary and fiscal policies but instead merely to import restrictions. An increase in reserves would therefore not actually have the undesirable effect of removing balance-of-payments discipline but rather the favorable effect of supporting the liberalization of trade.

iii. The argument that developing countries are incapable of conserving an increase in additional reserves is also denied. Contrary to the usual impression, the statistical evidence does not support the view that the typ-

[5]See Y. S. Park, *The Link Between Special Drawing Rights and Development Finance,* Princeton Essays in International Finance, No. 100, September 1973.

[6]Graham Bird, "SDR Distribution, Interest Rates and Aid Flows," *The World Economy,* December 1981, pp. 419–27.

[7]But cf. A. Kafka, "International Liquidity: Its Present Relevance to the Less Developed Countries," *American Economic Review, Papers and Proceedings,* May 1968, pp. 596–607.

ical or average LDC behavior is to increase overseas expenditure by an amount corresponding to any increase in reserves.[8]

iv. Finally, even if the developing country did choose to spend an increase in its reserves on additional imports, some would argue that this is quite legitimate. For if the additional liquidity has not been acquired subject to specific conditions on its use, then—as the owner of unconditional liquidity—the developing country should be able either to spend it or hold it.[9] From this standpoint, there is no reason why more severe provisions should be imposed on an LDC than on any other country that receives additional liquidity.

When the Special Drawing Account was established in the IMF in 1969, the emphasis was only on liquidity-creation, and a link to development finance was not incorporated in the facility for Special Drawing Rights. The establishment of this facility provided, through deliberate international decisions (an 85 percent majority vote of IMF members was required to create SDRs), a major new supplement to existing reserve assets, on a permanent basis, backed by the obligation of Fund members to accept the SDRs and pay a convertible currency in return. The first allocation of SDRs amounted to $9.5 billion over the period 1970–72. SDRs were allocated to each participating member country according to its quota in the IMF; such an allocation did not favor the LDCs and was criticized by those who advocate a direct or "organic" link between liquidity-creation and liquidity-distribution in favor of the LDCs. Since the SDR was redefined in terms of a "standard basket" of major currencies, it has been increasingly used as a numéraire in international transactions. Whether the SDR is to become the principal reserve asset will depend on the future volume of new SDRs that are created and their substitution for other reserve assets. SDRs are transferred by debiting the SDR account of the user and crediting the SDR account of the receiver, with the user country acquiring convertible currency from the receiving member.

In the initial creation of SDRs, there was no direct connection with foreign aid, but the LDC members of the IMF share along with other Fund members through additions to their reserves in proportion to their quotas, and they benefit indirectly to the extent that the SDRs allow an increase in aid expenditure and trade liberalization on the part of developed countries.

The LDCs still advocate, however, either an organic link through an increase in SDR allocations to the LDCs, or allocation of SDRs to development agencies that could use these funds for long-term loans to the developing countries, or a contribution by developed countries of a certain proportion of their SDR allocation to multilateral development agencies, or the transfer to development agencies of reserve currencies received by the IMF in exchange for a special issue of SDRs.[10] If the problem of liquidity-creation at first dominated the establishment of the SDR facility, the ensuing years of discussion about international monetary reform have raised more critical questions regarding the distribution of SDRs.

Although the SDR-aid link issue poses important questions for both the technical operation of the international monetary system and moral judgments of international distributional equity, the quantitative impact of any flexible SDR-aid link scheme will only be marginal relative to the foreign exchange that LDCs derive from trade and capital movements.

The LDCs must support policies that provide more aid and more trade and more capital inflow—not policies that entail any trade-offs among the sources of foreign exchange.

While the SDR-aid link may have only

[8]Report of the Group of Experts, *International Monetary Issues and the Developing Countries*, UNCTAD, 1965 (66.II.D.2) paragraphs 35–6; Paul P. Streeten, "International Monetary Reform and the LDCs," *Banca Nazionale del Lavoro*, June 1967, pp. 8–9.

[9]Streeten, "International Monetary Reform," p. 9.

[10]Details of proposals for an organic link are presented in Park, *Special Drawing Rights and Development Finance*, pp. 9–11.

marginal significance for the receipt of foreign exchange by the LDCs, as compared with expansion by the developed countries and greater market access in the developed countries, nonetheless the idea of linking reserve creation to development assistance has symbolic value in terms of distributional equity. If international poverty is a manifestation of international inequality, the channeling to LDCs of a part of the share of SDRs formerly going to industrial countries would be at least a welcome symbol of a deliberate effort to transfer resources from rich to poor countries.

It may also be argued that if "objective indicators" are introduced imposing international rules that limit a country's freedom regarding reserve composition, these rules should be more lenient for LDCs. A wider range for "objective indicators" might be permitted for LDCs than DCs, in view of the greater fluctuation in export earnings of LDCs than DCs, and in deference to the need of the LDCs to acquire liquidity at less cost than on private capital markets.

The report by the Brandt Commission argued that reform of the international monetary system should involve improvements in the exchange-rate regime, the reserve system, the balance-of-payments adjustment process, and the overall management of the system that should permit greater participation of developing countries in the decision making of the IMF.

The report argues that any serious reform must aim at greater stability of international currencies, particularly among key currencies. This can only be achieved if the reserve system and adjustment mechanism are reformed simultaneously. The SDR should become the principal means of increasing global liquidity, and "the distribution of such unconditional liquidity should favor the developing countries who presently bear high adjustment burdens."[11] There should also be pressure in the world economy:

[11] Willy Brandt, *North-South: A Program for Survival, Report of the Independent Commission on International Development Issues*, 1980, chapter 13.

The IMF should avoid inappropriate or excessive regulation of [the developing countries'] economies, and should not impose highly deflationary measures as standard adjustment policy. It should also improve and greatly extend the scope of its compensatory financing facility. Surplus countries should accept greater responsibility for payments adjustments, and IMF measures to encourage this should be considered.[12]

Furthermore, the report suggests that the bulk of the Fund's holdings of gold could be used as collateral for IMF borrowings from financial markets that would be lent primarily to middle-income developing countries. Another part could be sold and the profits used to subsidize interest rates on loans to low-income developing countries.

Although it may be unrealistic to expect that the international financial community would support the linking of development finance to liquidity creation, or that the IMF would depart from its fundamental principle of treating all member countries uniformly, there is still much that the IMF can do to play a more significant role in promoting development. To allow larger standby agreements with developing countries, and to offset the adverse repercussions of any international trade recession, the IMF's resources of quotas, SDRs, and compensation schemes should be increased. The IMF's imposition of conditionality for use of the Fund's resources and the stabilization programs associated with standby agreements are also of major importance to the LDCs. Actions by the IMF may also influence commercial banks to continue their lending operations to LDCs.

As Sir Arthur Lewis concluded about the importance to developing countries of an international monetary institution with wide responsibilities and powers:

[The] developed countries, with stronger economies, less dependence on international flows, and easy fraternal relations between central bankers, could get along fairly well without an international monetary institution; and having one, could manage quite well if its function was confined to discussing changes in exchange rates. To the less de-

[12] Ibid.

veloped countries, on the other hand, an institution which did not look beyond exchange rates to the wider context which determines international monetary flows could be a menace rather than a help. Given the difference in their immediate interests, the instinct of the developed countries will be to narrow the discussion, while the instinct of the developing will be to widen it. . . . [13]

[13]Quoted in *IMF Survey,* November 7, 1977, p. 349.

V.D. PRIVATE FOREIGN INVESTMENT

V.D.1. Benefits and Costs of Private Foreign Investment— Note

Considerable interest is now being shown in measures that might promote private foreign investment and allow it to make a greater contribution to the development of the recipient countries. In an attempt to promote a larger flow of private capital to developing nations, several capital-exporting countries have adopted a range of measures that include tax incentives, investment guarantees, and financial assistance to private investors. International institutions are also encouraging the international flow of private capital; the International Finance Corporation, for instance, cooperates directly with private investors in financing new or expanded ventures.

Of far greater influence, however, than the measures adopted by capital-exporting nations or international organizations are the policies of the capital-recipient countries themselves. Controls exercised by the host country over the conditions of entry of foreign capital, regulations of the operation of foreign capital, and restrictions on the remittance of profits and the repatriation of capital are far more decisive in determining the flow of foreign capital than any policy undertaken by the capital-exporting country.

Policies of the host country are now being adopted in the context of development planning, and their rationale and effects have taken on new dimensions in this light. No longer is it simply a matter of private investors dismissing investment prospects with the complaint that a "favorable climate" does not exist; nor need host countries contend that an inflow of private capital entails nothing but "foreign domination." The meaning of a "favorable climate" calls for reinterpretation in terms of development planning, and the effects of foreign investment in countries

that are newly independent should not be analyzed as if the undesirable features in the history of colonialism need be repeated. The central problem now is for the recipient country to devise policies that will succeed in both encouraging a greater inflow of private foreign capital and ensuring that it makes the maximum contribution feasible toward the achievement of the country's development objectives. The tasks of development require both more effective governmental activity and more investment on the part of international private enterprise. But the private investors must be aware of the developmental objectives and the priorities of the host country and understand how their investments fit into the country's development strategy. The contribution of private foreign capital has to be interpreted in terms beyond private profit. At the same time the government must recognize that if risks are too high or the return on investment is too low, international private investment will be inhibited from making any contribution at all. Development planning now requires the government to influence the performance of private foreign investment, but in doing this, the government should appreciate fully the potential contribution of this investment, and it should devise policies that will meet the mutual interests of private investor and host country. This calls for more intensive analysis of the consequences of private foreign investment and for more thought and ingenuity in devising new approaches that favor the mobilization of private foreign capital while ensuring its most effective "planned performance" in terms of the country's development program.

At present, the policies taken by the developing countries reveal a mixed picture of restrictions and incentives. On the one hand, the foreign investor's freedom of action may be restricted by a variety of governmental regulations that exclude private foreign investment from certain "key" sectors of the economy, impose limitations on the extent of foreign participation in ownership or management, specify conditions for the employment of domestic and foreign labor, limit the amount of profits, and impose exchange controls on the remission of profits and the repatriation of capital.

On the other hand, a progressive liberalization of policy towards private foreign capital has occurred during recent years. Many countries now recognize that an inflow of private capital may offer some special advantages over public capital, and a number of investment incentive measures have been recently adopted or are under consideration. These incentive devices include assistance in securing information on investment opportunities, the provision of supplementary finance, establishment of economic overhead facilities such as in industrial estates, protective tariffs on commodities that compete with those produced by foreign investors, exemptions from import duties on necessary equipment and materials, the granting of exchange guarantees or privileges, tax concession schemes for the encouragement of desired new investments, and special legislation for the protection of foreign investments.

To remove the ambivalence that characterizes these policies, it is desirable to reexamine the role of private foreign capital more systematically by appraising the prospective benefits and costs of private foreign investment. Such an appraisal may then provide a more rational basis for determining what type of policy is most appropriate for securing the maximum contribution from private foreign investment.

From the standpoint of national economic benefit, the essence of the case for encouraging an inflow of capital is that the increase in real income resulting from the act of investment is greater than the resultant increase in the income of the investor.[1] If the value added to output by the foreign capital is greater than the amount appropriated by the investor, social returns exceed private returns. As long as foreign investment raises productivity, and this increase is not wholly appropriated by the investor, the greater product must be shared with others, and there must be some direct benefits to other income groups. These benefits can accrue to (a) domestic labor in the form of higher real wages, (b) consumers by way of lower prices, and (c) the government through higher tax revenue. Beyond this, and most importantly in many cases, there are likely to be (d) indirect gains through the realization of external economies.

An increase in total real wages may be one of the major direct benefits from an inflow of foreign capital. This can be recognized in Figure 1 where the line EG illustrates the marginal productivity of capital in the capital-recipient country, given the amount of labor. If initially, the domestically owned capital stock is AB, the total output is $ABCE$. We assume that profits per unit of capital equal the marginal product of capital, and that total profits on domestic capital are $ABCD$, and total real wages are CDE. Let there now be an inflow of foreign capital in the amount BF. Total output then increases by the amount $BFGC$, and the profits on foreign capital are $BFGH$ of this amount. Since the profit rate on total capital has fallen, profits on domestic capital are reduced to $ABHI$. But the total real wages of labor are now GIE, with the increase in real wages amounting to $DCGI$. Although in this case, with a given marginal productivity of capital schedule, most of labor's gain—the amount $DCHI$—is merely a redistribution from domestic capitalists, there is still a net increase in the real incomes of domestic factors, represented by the rise in real wages in the amount CGH.

[1]Much of the following analysis is based on Sir Donald MacDougall, "The Benefits and Costs of Private Investment from Abroad: A Theoretical Approach," *Economic Record*, March 1960, pp. 13–35; Paul Streeten, *Economic Integration*, second edition, Leyden, 1964, chapter 5.

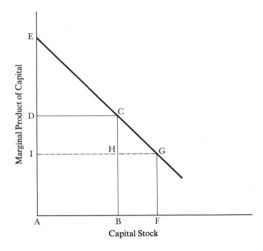

FIGURE 1.

For a developing country, the inflow of foreign capital may be significant in not only raising the productivity of a given amount of labor but may also allow a larger labor force to be employed. If, as was contended in the discussion of dualistic development in Chapter III, a shortage of capital in heavily populated poor countries limits the employment of labor from the rural sector in the advanced sector where wages are higher, an inflow of foreign capital may then make it possible to employ more labor in the advanced sector. The international flow of capital can thus be interpreted as an alternative to labor migration from the poor country: when outlets for the emigration of labor are restricted, the substitution of domestic migration of labor into the advanced sector becomes the most feasible solution. The social benefit from the foreign investment in the advanced sector is then greater than the profits on this investment, for the wages received by the newly employed exceed their former real wage in the rural sector, and this excess should be added as a national gain.

Domestic consumers may also benefit from direct foreign investment. When the investment is cost-reducing in a particular industry, consumers of the product may gain through lower product prices. If the investment is product-improving or product-innovating, consumers benefit from better quality products or new products.

In order that labor and consumers might enjoy part of their benefit from the higher productivity in enterprises established by foreign investors, the overseas withdrawal by the investors must be less than the increase in output. But even if the entire increase in productivity accrues as foreign profits, this requirement may still be fulfilled when the government taxes foreign profits. For many countries, taxes on foreign profits or royalties from concession agreements constitute a large proportion of total government revenue. The fiscal benefit derived from foreign investment is evident from the fact that the share of government revenue in the national product of countries that have received substantial foreign investment is considerably higher than in most of the other low-income countries.

The most significant contribution of foreign investment is likely to come from external economies. Direct foreign investment brings to the recipient country not only capital and foreign exchange but also managerial ability, technical personnel, technological knowledge, administrative organization, and innovations in products and production techniques—all of which are in short supply. This ensures in the first instance that a project involving private foreign investment will be adequately formulated and implemented, unlike the situation that has frequently confronted public economic aid when the recipient country has not had the talent or inclination to undertake adequate feasibility studies and formulate projects that might qualify for public capital. The preinvestment survey, act of investment, and operation of the investment project are all ensured in private foreign investment. One of the greatest benefits to the recipient country is the access to foreign knowledge that private foreign investment may provide—knowledge that helps overcome the managerial gap and technological gap. The provision of this knowledge can be interpreted as "private technical assistance." The private technical assistance and the demonstration effects that are integral features of private foreign investment may spread and have beneficial results in other sectors of the economy. The rate of technological advance in a poor country is highly dependent on the rate of capital inflow. New techniques accompany the inflow of private capital, and by the example they set, foreign firms promote the diffusion of technological advance in the economy. In addition, foreign investment may lead to the training of labor in new skills, and the knowledge gained by these workers can be transmitted to other members of the labor force, or these workers might be employed later by local firms.

Private foreign investment may also serve as a stimulus to additional domestic investment in the recipient country. This is especially likely through the creation of external pecuniary economies. If the foreign capital is used to develop the country's infrastructure, it may directly facilitate more investment. Even if the foreign investment is in one industry, it may still encourage domestic investment by reducing costs or creating demand in other industries. Profits may then rise and lead to expansion in these other industries.

Since there are so many specific scarcities in a poor country, it is common for investment to be of a cost-reducing character by breaking bottlenecks in production. This stimulates expansion by raising profits on all underutilized productive capacity and by now allowing the exploitation of economies of scale that had previously been restricted. When the foreign investment in an industry makes its product cheaper, another industry that uses this product benefits from the lower prices. This creates profits and stimulates an expansion in the second industry.

There is also considerable scope for the initial foreign investment to produce external investment incentives through demand creation in other industries. The foreign investment in the first industry can give rise to profits in industries that supply inputs to the first industry, in industries that produce complementary products, and in industries that produce goods bought by the factor-owners who now have higher real incomes. Similar effects may also follow from investment that is product-improving or product-innovating. A whole series of domestic investments may thus be linked to the foreign investment.

Against these benefits must be set the costs of foreign investment to the host country. These costs may arise from special concessions offered by the host country, adverse effects on domestic saving, deterioration in the terms of trade, and problems of balance-of-payments adjustment.

To encourage foreign enterprise, the government of the host country may have to provide special facilities, undertake additional public services, extend financial assistance, or subsidize inputs. These have a cost in absorbing governmental resources that could be used elsewhere. Tax concessions may also have to be offered, and these may have to be extended to domestic investment since the government may not be able to discriminate, for administrative and political reasons, in favor of only the foreign investor. Moreover, when several countries compete among themselves in offering inducements to foreign capital, each may offer more by way of inducement than is necessary: the investment may be of a type that would go to one country or another, regardless of inducements, but the foreign enterprise may "shop around" and secure extra concessions. Without some form of collective agreement among capital-receiving countries regarding the maximum concessions that will be made, the cost of "over-encouraging" certain types of foreign investment may be considerable.

Once foreign investment has been attracted, it should be expected to have an income effect that will lead to a higher level of domestic savings. This effect may be offset, however, by a redistribution of income away from capital if the foreign investment reduces profits in domestic industries. The consequent reduction in home savings would then be another indirect cost of foreign investment. But it is unlikely to be of much consequence in practice, for it would require that foreign investment be highly competitive with home investment. In a poor country, it is more probable that foreign capital will complement domestic investment and will give rise to higher incomes and profits in other industries, as already noted.

Foreign investment might also affect the recipient country's commodity terms of trade through structural changes associated with the pattern of development that results from the capital inflow. If the inflow of capital leads to an increase in the country's rate of development without any change in the terms of trade, the country's growth of real income will then be the same as its growth of output. If, however, the terms of trade deteriorate, the rise in real income will be less than that in output, and the worsening terms of trade may be considered another indirect cost of the foreign investment. Whether the terms of trade will turn against the capital-receiving country is problematical depending on various possible changes at home and abroad in the supply and demand for exports, import-substitutes, and domestic commodities. It is unlikely, however, that private foreign investment would cause any substantial deterioration in the terms of trade. For if an unfavorable shift resulted from a rising demand for imports on the side of consumption, it would probably be controlled through import restriction. And if it resulted, on the side of production, from a rising supply of exports owing to private direct investment in the export sector, the inflow of foreign capital would diminish as export prices fell, thereby limiting the deterioration in the terms of trade. Moreover, if the deterioration comes through an export bias in production, it is still possible that the factoral and the income terms of trade might improve even though the commodity terms of trade worsen, since the capital inflow may result in a sufficiently large increase in productivity in the export sector.

Of greater seriousness than the foregoing costs are those associated with balance-of-payments adjustments. Pressure on the balance of payments may become acute when the foreign debt has to be serviced. If the amount of foreign exchange required to service the debt becomes larger than the amount of foreign exchange being supplied by new foreign investments, the transfer mechanism will then have to create a surplus on current account equal to the debit items on account of the payment of interest, dividends, profits, and amortization on the foreign borrowings.[2] When a net outflow of capital occurs, a reallocation of resources becomes necessary in order to expand exports or replace imports. To accomplish this, the country may have to endure internal and external controls or experience currency depreciation. The adverse effects of these measures of balance-of-payments adjustment must then be considered as indirect costs of foreign investment, to be added to the direct costs of the foreign payments.

The direct costs in themselves need not be a matter of great concern. For even though part of the increased production from the use of foreign capital has to be paid abroad in profits or interest—and this is a deduction that would not be necessary if the savings were provided at home—this is merely to say that the country must not expect to get an income from savings if it does not make the savings.[3] What is fundamental is that the country does have additional investment, and the benefits from this may exceed the direct costs of the foreign savings that made possible the capital formation.

The indirect costs, however, are rightly a cause of concern, insofar as the capital-receiving country may be unable or unwilling to endure a loss of international reserves and

[2]The length of time which elapses before this occurs will depend on the growth in new foreign investment, rate of interest and dividend earnings, and the amortization rate. Cf. E. D. Domar, "The Effect of Foreign Investment on the Balance of Payments," *American Economic Review*, December 1950, pp. 805–26.

[3]Cf. J. R. Hicks, *Essays in World Economics*, Oxford, 1959, p. 191.

does not want to impose measures of balance-of-payments adjustment in order to find sufficient foreign exchange for the remittance of the external service payments. External measures such as import quotas, tariffs, and exchange restrictions may suppress the demand for imports, but they do so at the expense of productivity and efficiency. Internal measures of higher taxation and credit tightness involve the costs of reduced consumption and investment. And the alternative of currency devaluation may cause the country to incur the costs of a possible deterioration in its terms of trade, changes in income distribution, and necessary shifts of resources. To avoid, or at least minimize, these indirect costs, the role of private foreign investment must be related to the debt-servicing capacity of the host country. And this depends on the country's development program as a whole, since the ability to create a sufficiently large export surplus rests on the operation of all industries together, not simply on the use made of foreign investment alone (see section V.B).

In the past there has been a general tendency for poor countries to overestimate the costs of foreign investment and to discount the benefits, especially the indirect benefits. Now, however, there is a wider appreciation that within the context of a development program and with a careful appraisal of the prospective benefits and costs of foreign investment, policies may be devised to secure a greater contribution from the inflow of private capital. Instead of discouraging investment from abroad simply because it involves some costs, the developing countries are increasingly recognizing that they should attempt to devise policies that will encourage the maximum feasible contribution. Although the formulation of specific policies must depend on particular conditions in each country, we may at least suggest some of the principal considerations that might shape these policies.

In general, the attraction of private foreign investment now depends less on fiscal action, upon which most countries have concentrated, and more on other conditions and measures that guarantee protection of the investment and provide wider opportunities for the foreign investor. If private foreign investment is to be encouraged, it is necessary to allay the investor's concern over the possibilities of discriminatory legislation, exchange controls, and the threat of expropriation. Investment guarantees may be utilized more effectively to lessen the investor's apprehension of nonbusiness risks. Either unilaterally or through bilateral treaties, governments can offer some assurances designed to reduce the likelihood of expropriation or of impairments of investors' rights and to assure investors of an adequate recourse if such impairments should occur. It has always been difficult to secure agreement by both investing and recipient countries on a uniform set of substantive rules, as in a multilateral investment charter. The World Bank has, however, succeeded in establishing an International Center for Settlement of Investment Disputes, which provides facilities for the settlement, by voluntary recourse to conciliation or arbitration, of investment disputes arising between the foreign investor and the host government.

Finally, along with assurances against the occurrence of risk and measures for the adjustment of investment disputes, considerable attention is being given to the possibilities of providing guarantees under which the investors will be compensated for any loss they may suffer from other than normal business causes. Although such a guarantee is something of a measure of last resort, it does help to minimize the investor's risk and gives some advance assurance of a reliable "safety margin." Some capital-supplying nations have provided insurance coverage, but the insurance of investments in developing countries might be made more effective through the establishment of a multilateral investment insurance program as opposed to participation in a number of bilateral programs.

While investment guarantees may help in removing "disincentives" to foreign investment, the attraction of private capital depends even more on positive inducements in the form of greater opportunities for profit-making. The private investor's first concern is whether costs will be covered and a profit earned. Some developing countries offer special tax concessions that provide a tax holiday or reduce the rate of tax on profits, but these measures are not effective unless the investment yields a profit. The foreign investor is likely to be less interested in receiving an exemption after a profit is made than in being sure of a profit in the first instance. It is therefore most important to raise profit expectations. To do this, it may be necessary to undertake additional public expenditures, especially in developing the country's infrastructure and in ensuring a supply of trained labor. Yet rarely is a government willing to undertake expenditures expressly for the purpose of attracting foreign investment; instead of incurring the present cost of additional expenditures, most governments prefer to assist foreign investors through a future sacrifice in revenue. Though politically more feasible, tax concessions are not likely to be the most powerful inducements that the host country can offer to encourage a flow of investment.

At the same time, their use can be overdone. They involve a cost to the government not only in terms of a revenue foregone, but also in terms of equity and administrative costs. More importantly, the LDCs may offer excessive concessions in their efforts to attract foreign investment. If an investment is going to occur in one LDC or another (for example, in order to secure a raw material supply), but each LDC competes against the other in offering concessions, then the LDCs are likely to overconcede.[4] When tax concessions are granted to existing investments, in order not to discriminate, there is simply a

windfall. Moreover, the concessions are likely to attract the quick speculative type of foreign investment which is in the country only to take advantage of the concessions and leaves as soon as these are withdrawn. Finally, if the benefits of foreign investment are realized for the host country during the early years of the investment, there is no case for prolonging the concessions beyond the relatively short period.

Developing nations are now mainly interested in having foreign enterprises contribute to their industrialization, rather than following the historical pattern of being directed to agriculture or mining. In most cases, however, the size of the domestic market has remained too small to offer much attraction. As a development program proceeds, domestic markets may widen, and this limitation will be reduced. Much can also be done to widen markets and establish a more substantial base for industry by promoting regional markets through arrangements for a common market or a free trade association. The establishment of a customs union or free trade area may have considerable potential for attracting investment to the development of manufacturing industry.

Even more significant than regional preferential arrangements would be a general preferential system by which developed countries granted preferences to all LDCs on their exports of manufactures and semimanufactures. Such a system may offer considerable attraction to private foreign investment, especially by inducing the transfer of production facilities required from the developed preference-granting countries to the less developed preference-receiving countries in order to turn labor and raw materials into saleable products and obtain the dual advantages of tariff-free or preferential market access and lower labor costs.

In considering measures to encourage foreign investment, a developing country does not want, of course, to seek foreign capital indiscriminately. The objective is to ensure that the investment supports activities from which the recipient nation may derive maximum national economic gain, as assessed through benefits and costs. To achieve the most effec-

[4]Cf. Dudley Seers, "Big Companies and Small Countries," *Kyklos,* 1963, pp. 601–3; R. H. Green and Ann Seidman, *Unity or Poverty?,* Baltimore, 1968, pp. 99–131.

Several studies indicate that tax incentive programs have not been effective. See, for example, Jack Heller and Kenneth M. Kauffman, *Tax Incentives for Industry in Less Developed Countries,* Cambridge, 1963, pp. 60–6; M. C. Taylor, *Industrial Tax Exemption in Puerto Rico,* Madison, 1957, pp. 143–9; Peter Kilby, *Industrialization in an Open Economy: Nigeria,* 1945–66, Cambridge, 1969, pp. 132–4.

tive utilization of foreign investment in terms of its entire development program, the country may have to adopt policies, such as preferential tax treatment or other incentives, that will attract private capital into activities where it will have the maximum catalytic effect of mobilizing additional effort. From this standpoint, it is especially important that policies affecting the allocation of foreign capital be based on an awareness of the external economies that can be realized from different patterns of investment. Beyond a consideration of the direct increase in income resulting from the investment and other short-term criteria, it is important to look to the more indirect and longer-run possibilities—from the widening of investment opportunities to even the instigation of social and cultural transformations.

Finally, the recipient country may be well advised to emphasize a partnership arrangement betwen foreign and domestic enterprise. A joint international business venture that involves collaboration between private foreign capital and local private or public capital is a promising device for protecting international investment, integrating foreign investment within a development program and safe-guarding against an enclave type of investment, stimulating domestic management and investment, and reducing the transfer burden and balance-of-payments difficulties.

The alternatives of a 100 percent foreign-owned enterprise and a joint venture are, however, only two of a number of possible arrangements for securing a mix of foreign capital, management, and technology. The major question is whether there are other means of transferring scarce managerial and technical knowledge without having to be in joint supply with capital as in a foreign direct investment. As already noted, the cost for foreign equity capital is high, even post-tax. The host country may well consider this cost excessive for the foreign managerial and technical knowledge which it desires but which cannot be acquired through a direct foreign investment without the high payment for equity capital with which it is in joint supply. The new approach to foreign investment

has therefore been to focus on alternative arrangements for securing capital, management, technology, and marketing capabilities without the foreign ownership and control that has commonly been associated with foreign direct investment. It may be possible to "unwrap" the bundle of inputs that come in the package of direct foreign investment and secure inputs that are more appropriate for the needs of the recipient country, or that cost less when they are not tied to equity capital.

The problem for the host country is to evaluate the benefits and costs of alternative arrangements for importing the investing firm's capabilities, and then to secure by inducements and regulations the best feasible alternative. The alternative arrangements span an entire spectrum. At one end of the spectrum is the traditional form of direct investment involving 100 percent foreign equity ownership and no time-limit on the existence of the foreign-owned enterprise in the recipient country. This arrangement is appropriate for only those sectors where the joint mix of capital, technology, and management cannot be supplied in any other way and the investment continues to provide a properly discounted benefit-cost ratio greater than that of unity for an unlimited time period. Moving on from this arrangement, the host country may initially allow 100 percent ownership but then insist that any expansion of the enterprise occur through national participation. It may further limit the time of foreign control by requiring a national majority equity holding to emerge within a certain period. There may be a "fadeout" provision such as Decision 24 of the Andean Common Market, which requires multinational corporations to fade down from 100 percent to 49 percent ownership over a period of 15 or 20 years.[5] There may be other requirements and means for divestment over time.[6] Moving still further to a dilution of the foreign equity, the host coun-

[5]Andean Foreign Investment Code, Commission of the Carthegena Agreement, International Legal Materials, Vol. 2, 1972.

[6]Albert O. Hirschman, *How to Divest in Latin America, and Why,* Princeton Essays in International Finance, November 1969.

try may insist at the very outset on a joint venture and may also establish a limited time for any foreign equity participation. At the other end of the spectrum, the host country may exclude foreign equity altogether and seek the managerial and technological knowledge through other contractual arrangements that might allow the transfer of technical and managerial skills without being tied to equity capital. Licensing agreements, technical services agreements, engineering and construction contracts, management contracts, and co-production agreements can prove to be of considerable benefit to a developing country—supplying the needed foreign knowledge at a lower cost than must be paid when the knowledge comes with equity capital.[7]

Some doubts may, however, be expressed that the LDCs can indeed realistically expect to receive foreign technological and managerial knowledge without equity capital. This may prove difficult or impossible for the latest technology or research-and-development type of enterprise because the discoverer and owner of such technology normally wishes to retain control. But this does not apply to the older, more standardized types of technology. Assuming that the demand for such technical services should increase, then it can be expected that a supply of such services will be induced.

Similarly, it can be contended that a management contract is not an effective instrument for the discovery of investment opportunities as distinguished from simply the operation of an investment. This may be true, but in the LDCs the discovery of new investment opportunities is not as relevant as in more advanced countries, and the crucial

need is still much more for simply the adaptation, imitation, widening, and deepening of existing methods of investment.

Finally, it may be doubted whether there will be sufficient motivation when there is no equity interest. But managerial fees can be graduated according to profits, and even other objectives such as foreign exchange savings realized. Other incentive devices—short of ownership—can also be utilized.

In general, these contractual arrangements are extremely flexible devices for securing the transfer of the nonmonetary resources of management and technology; they may be adapted to widely diverse circumstances; and their utility in meeting a variety of objectives is becoming increasingly appreciated. Together with the fact of development planning, these new approaches to international investment are causing both the foreign investor and the recipient country to consider the benefits and costs of foreign investment in a newer light. This approach can be particularly efficacious when activities are reserved under a development program for public ownership or for majority ownership by local nationals, but there is still a need for seeking technical information or managerial services from abroad.

If the technical and managerial components of direct foreign investment can be secured through contractual nondirect investment devices without having to grant its supplier a controlling equity interest, and if financial aid is provided from foreign public sources of capital (either directly or indirectly through a development bank or development corporation), then the recipient LDC may benefit from an optimal mix of public financial aid and private technical assistance.

The potentialities for combining local public or private ownership with technical assistance from private foreign enterprise and capital assistance from public sources deserve considerable emphasis.

---

[7] A co-production agreement allows a national firm in the LDC to acquire imported equipment and technology in return for payment "in kind" by exporting its products for a number of years to the guaranteed market overseas.

Comment

Cost-benefit analysis as used in project appraisal has as much applicability to the assessment of private foreign investments as to domestic investment projects. Chapter X discusses in detail the techniques of project appraisal. See also A. K. Sen, *The Flow of Financial Re-*

sources: Methods of Evaluating the Economic Effects of Private Foreign Investment (Report
to UNCTAD, August 20, 1971).

Sen notes that the problem of negotiations on terms and conditions, including possible
concessions, is an important aspect of foreign private investment that requires special attention (pp. 20–21). He states:

Let a foreign firm F be in negotiation with the government of a developing country G. Consider a
series of contracts involving various proposals for concessions, e.g., combinations of tax benefits, repatriation facilities and exchange arrangements. If both F and G prefer one sort of contract to another,
then the latter can be rejected. After weeding out the non-starters, there will remain a sequence of
contracts, which can be labelled 1 to n, such that F always prefers a contract with a higher number and
G a contract with a lower number. Which particular contract will be chosen will depend on the bargaining power of the two parties.

How would the government G rank the alternatives? If the alternative projects are physically identical
and differ only in the extent of the concessions given to F, then ranking them may be no great problem.
G will prefer to make fewer concessions just as F will prefer more. But what if the alternative proposals
differ from each other in production structure and not merely in terms of concessions? Or what if one
proposal involves more concessions of one type (e.g., tax benefits) and less of another (e.g., repatriation
facilities)? Then the ranking procedure must be related to the present value estimations.

The theoretically satisfactory way of solving the problem is not far to seek though its practical applicability may be open to doubts. For the economy as a whole, alternative foreign investment proposals
including concessions represent alternative production possibilities. If the shadow prices are chosen ap-
popriately, no more than one alternative will have positive present value. For the evaluation of each
project the other projects are alternatives that are rejected and the maximum benefits thus foregone
must be counted as costs for the particular project under scrutiny. . . .

This procedure makes it possible to select the best alternative from a given set. By doing the exercise
again after eliminating the best project in the list, the second-best can be identified. And so on for the
whole lot, thereby obtaining the entire ranking.

In practice this procedure may be thought to be complex, though it is by no means infeasible given
the progress in computational facilities. Under a simplifying assumption a much easier procedure could
be applied. If the projects are so small that they are unlikely to alter the shadow prices for the economy
as a whole, except the shadow price of the option of selecting one of the alternatives, then the projects
could all be ranked in terms of their respective present values at given shadow prices, excluding the cost
of losing the option of doing one of the projects. Since this last cost item is not included, the "present
value" calculated this way can be positive for more than one alternative project. The rule in this case is
straightforward: choose the project with the highest "present value." (This applies only insofar as the
"present values" are positive. If a project has negative "present value," then its yield is negative even
without bringing in the cost of the option lost. Thus a negative "present value" is a ground for rejection,
though a positive "present value" is not necessarily a ground for acceptance.)

The distinction between the "present value," as calculated in this way, and the true present value of
net benefits is important. For the latter the rule is to choose all projects that yield positive present value,
while for the former the alternatives have to be ranked in terms of "present value" and the alternative
with the highest value is chosen. . . .

V.D.2. Transnational Enterprises and Linkages*

This paper reviews the literature on the relationships between transnational corporations (TNCs) in the manufacturing sector and domestic enterprises as well as industrial structures in host LDCs. There are two broad sets of relationships involved, both of which are of significance for understanding the effects of TNCs on host economies and to the formulation of policy. The "direct" relationships that TNCs strike up with local suppliers or purchasers (backward and forward "linkages" in the Hirschman sense) can constitute powerful mechanisms for stimulating (or retarding) economic, and particularly industrial, growth in LDCs. The "indirect" effects that the entry and operations of TNCs may have on local industrial structure, conduct, and performance may be equally important: TNCs may change the nature and evolution of concentration; they may affect the profitability and growth of indigenous firms; they may alter financing, marketing, technological, or managerial practices of the sectors that they enter; they may, by predatory conduct, drive domestic firms out of business; and so on.

DIRECT LINKAGES

Direct linkages may be defined to constitute those relationships between TNCs and domestic enterprises trading with them that have led the latter to respond, positively or otherwise, to technological, pecuniary, marketing, or entrepreneurial stimuli provided by the former.[1] A "linkage" in this sense is clearly different from a normal transaction in a competitive market; it refers essentially to *externalities* created for domestic industry by

the entry of TNC investment. The classic general discussion of the role of linkages in the development of LDCs is by Hirschman (1958), who proposes a deliberate strategy of creating imbalances to harness the forces of entrepreneurship and growth that lie latent in every economy. Particular investments are thus supposed to create such strong external economies in sectors that supply or buy from them that new investments are undertaken in order to exploit them; foreign investment is assigned a vital role "to enable and to embolden a country to set out on the path of unbalanced growth . . . [and] to take the first unbalancing steps in growth sequences.[2]

While it is obvious that TNC investments can create strong local linkages in this sense, and indeed the policies of many host LDCs to compel TNCs to maximize their purchase of local inputs have aimed at exploiting these linkages, it is far from clear how the actual experience of TNCs in LDCs is to be evaluated. The normal procedure, of using the proportion of local to total purchases by TNCs as an indicator of backward linkages, is inadequate, since it does not take account of externalities and does not enable us to assess the "efficiency" of linkage creation. Though it may serve as a crude approximation to the outer limits of the stimulus provided by TNCs to local enterprises, it does not, for instance, show (*a*) if the local enterprises would have been set up in the absence of TNC investments; (*b*) whether they gained or lost by having TNCs as major customers (where this is the case); (*c*) if the host economy could have created the same linkages at lesser cost, say by replacing the TNC by a local firm; (*d*) if the linked local enterprises are desirable from the social point of view (where the linkages are fostered behind heavy protective barriers); and (*e*) whether negative linkages were created by stifling potential local investment. The proper economic evaluation of

---

*"Transnationals, Domestic Enterprises, and Industrial Structure in Host LDCs: A Survey" by Sanjaya Lall. From *Oxford Economic Papers*, Vol. 30 (1978). Reprinted by permission of Oxford University Press.

[1]See Scitovsky (1954) and Hirschman (1958).

[2]Hirschman (1959), pp. 205–6.

linkages must be based on a case-by-case cost/benefit examination of actual situations and plausible alternatives, necessarily a difficult and impressionistic procedure; however, the existence and desirability of TNC linkages can only be judged by some such method.

Let us now consider how the existing literature has treated the issue. Our review is confined to *backward* linkages, since there appears to be hardly any empirical work on forward linkages created by TNCs: perhaps not a great omission, since forward linkages cannot be expected to be very strong. We may consider backward linkages for the two main forms of TNC investment—import-substituting and export-orientated—separately, as the issues raised are rather different.

Import-Substituting TNCs

The vast bulk of foreign manufacturing investment in LDCs has gone into protected import-substituting activities, where governments have been able, especially in the larger and more industrialized areas, to push firms into buying large proportions of their inputs from local sources. TNCs have, consequently, developed extensive and long-standing relationships with local enterprises in countries like India, Mexico, Brazil, Argentina, and so on. Despite the significance of the phenomenon, however, the existing work on TNCs has paid scant attention to examining the economic benefits and costs of the linkages created.

Most of the studies of foreign investment in LDCs have simply noted the extent of local purchasing by TNCs and sometimes remarked on the general difficulties of local procurement (due to technological backwardness, small scale, high cost, poor quality, or unreliability) without attempting to analyse the linkages created in any detail. Thus, a study of six developing countries commissioned by UNCTAD produced data on the import propensities of 159 firms, foreign and domestic, in Kenya, Jamaica, India, Iran, Colombia, and Malaysia, without going into

the economics of domestic purchase.[3] Similarly, studies of U.S. investment in LDCs in general,[4] Peru,[5] Iran,[6] South Korea,[7] Malaysia,[8] and some others,[9] have discussed the use of local inputs by TNCs. The general findings, that TNCs buy relatively few inputs within the less industrialized host economies but may be forced or persuaded to increase local content by the more advanced ones, add little to our understanding of the significance or desirability of the externalities created in LDCs.

There are three other studies which may

---

[3]For a summary see Lall and Sreeten (1977). This study found that over half the sample firms imported goods worth over 30 per cent of their total value of sales—over 65 per cent of India is excluded—but that this high degree of import dependence did not differ significantly between TNCs and other firms.

[4]See Mason (1967), who attempts to quantify the local linkages of U.S. foreign investments using aggregate industry data, measuring backward linkages simply by the "ratio of local expenditure to total sales" and forward linkages by the "ratio of local sales to total sales." See Hufbauer and Adler (1968) for estimates of local and foreign buying propensities of U.S. TNCs.

[5]Vaitsos (1976) gives comparative data on the import propensities of local and foreign firms in Peru for 1973, which show that foreign firms had higher imports in eleven out of twelve broad industry groups. He notes, however, that this does not necessarily imply that local firms created more linkages (p. 40); such aggregate data do not permit a detailed examination of the technologies and products involved.

[6]Daftary and Borghey (1976) provide rather sketchy data on local purchases by thirteen TNCs, and conclude that few of these have set up significant local linkages, except with the domestic packaging industry (pp. 75–6).

[7]See Jo (1976), who reports that foreign firms have higher import propensities than local firms, and that supply, cost, and quality problems limit the growth of local purchasing.

[8]Thoburn (1973), in the course of his study of the tin and rubber sectors, touches upon the role of foreign engineering firms in Malaysia. He finds that they helped in the development of local suppliers in processes of low capital intensity and few scale economies; "but in all cases the firms concerned were already in existence when the link with foreign firms was formed" (p. 113).

[9]See chapters 5 and 14 of the annotated bibliography on TNCs by Lall (1975) for other references on LDCs.

be mentioned separately because they tackle the issue of TNC linkages more directly. Reuber and associates (1973), using information provided by the head offices of TNCs, noted that import-substituting investments created far more local linkages than export-orientated ones, and found, for sixty-four sample firms, that 45 per cent of inputs in 1970 came from local sources. Parent companies were asked whether their operations had given rise to local suppliers or distributors, and their answers indicated that some one-third of the investments had directly given rise to such local activity. Reuber made no attempt to assess the costs and benefits of such linkages, and also qualified the estimates by noting that "such figures must be viewed with some suspicion both because of the many conceptual and practical difficulties in deriving estimates of this kind and because of the vested interest of respondents in presenting the spin-off effects of their activities in as favourable a light as possible" (p. 156).

Watanabe (1972 and 1974), in his examinations of subcontracting in LDCs, presents a general but useful analysis of this particular (and rather strong) form of linkage. Though he is not concerned exclusively with TNCs, he cites examples of foreign firms (like Singer in South East Asia) which have used subcontracting successfully, and concludes that such activity, "by stimulating entrepreneurship and encouraging industrial efficiency, can help to promote the industrialization of the less developed countries and thus create the additional employment opportunities they badly need."[10] He analyses the conditions for success of such linkages (which he terms "within-border industrial subcontracting"), briefly notes the contribution that TNCs may make by providing assistance with investment, technology and quality control, and recommends policies for increasing linkages; he does not, however, examine in detail any specific instances of subcontracting by foreign firms. In his 1974 paper he examines the problems of subcontracting in India (though without discussing

the role of TNCs), and compares its experience to the highly successful one of Japan.

A more pessimistic view of the virtues of local purchasing emerges from Baranson's study of the Cummin's diesel-engine project in India and his analysis of the automotive industry in LDCs generally.[11] He comments at length on the problems raised by the high cost, poor quality, and unreliability of local suppliers in cases where the government has forced the pace of buying local inputs,[12] and discusses the reasons for this state of affairs (protection, technological and skill shortages, lack of experience, small scale, and the like). We must not, however, draw unfavourable general conclusions about the desirability of linkages or the capabilities of local enterprises from this experience: there are several other industries (see below) where domestic linkages have been economically viable, and even for India the recent boom in exports of medium-to-high technology goods (including transport equipment, chemicals, and engineering goods) indicates that some of the problems described by Baranson for the 60s may have been the teething difficulties of launching new and complex industrial processes.

To return to TNCs, however, we find that we are left with very little empirical work on the process and value of creating linkages. The general impression conveyed by the literature is that TNCs establish relatively few linkages in small or industrially backward economies; that in larger economies they may create extensive linkages, mostly because of government pressure; and that a substantial part of these linkages in import-substituting industries may be excessively costly and uneconomical. This is all in line with a priori expectation, but it is sadly inadequate in explaining the specific nature of the linkages that have been created, and in providing the

[11]Baranson (1967, 1969).

[12]Lall (1977) notes that foreign automobile assembly plants in Malaysia have not created significant domestic linkages; despite the government's expressed desire to increase local content, the absence of statutory controls on imports has led the TNCs to continue to depend heavily on imports.

[10]Watanabe (1972), p. 425.

sort of evaluation of their social value that was described earlier.

Export-Oriented TNCs

The recent growth of manufactured exports from LDCs by foreign firms has attracted a great deal of attention, and the creation of linkages, especially by subcontracting, has often been mentioned in this context. In contrast to the inefficiency usually associated with linkages in import-substituting industries, it may be expected that linkages created by firms competing in world markets will be more efficient and beneficial for the host economies (at least in a narrow technical sense, without referring to distributional, social, or political effects). It would be useful to start by distinguishing four types of export-oriented TNCs which have different implications for the creation of domestic linkages.

First, there are TNCs which started by substituting for imports and have grown internationally competitive enterprises with substantial export interests (VW in Brazil or Singer in Asia may be good examples). Such activities usually involve technologies which are stable and not very sophisticated, and they are based in areas with a cheap but relatively skilled labour force and an experienced indigenous sector. The use of the TNCs' marketing networks and established brand names are important in such export activity. These TNCs may have established considerable domestic linkages in the early phases, though, of course, the extent and nature of these linkages may change as they gear themselves for world markets.

Second, there may be foreign firms which produce and export "traditional" products like footwear, textiles, processed foods, or sports goods. For those industries (like textiles) where technology is easily available and product differentiation is insignificant, the foreign firms involved may be buying groups, retailers, or small manufacturers (sometimes from other LDCs, like Hong Kong firms in Malaysia) rather than TNCs proper. For those (like food processing) where product

differentiation, marketing, or product innovation are important, however, large TNCs may predominate in production and export activity.[13] In both cases, there exists a vast potential for linkages with domestic producers, who may manufacture components or whole products for foreign firms.

Third, there are new TNC investments in "modern" industries in LDCs undertaken specifically for export, transferring fairly complex technologies to LDCs to service established world markets. A constellation of factors (labour and transport costs, the nature of the technology, need for short production runs, managerial requirements, and, of course, political stability)[14] influences the decision to locate such investments, good examples of which are the Philips and General Electric complexes in Singapore, or some "border industries" in Mexico; the availability of local components is not, however, one of the important factors attracting them. In most cases, such investments are tightly controlled from abroad, the components and processes may be quite advanced, and there may not be much scope for local linkages. It is possible, nevertheless, that local enterprises may be able to provide some products at the right price and quality, and a few linkages may develop in the more advanced of the host economies.[15]

Fourth, there are "sourcing" investments where only a particular (labour-intensive) process is transferred to LDCs, the more capital-intensive processes being retained in the home countries where the requisite equipment, skills, and R and D facilities exist. The best-known example of this is the electronics industry, especially the semiconductor sector, where the demanding specifications, the rapidly changing technology, and requirements

[13]See de la Torre (1974) and Helleiner (1976).

[14]For a detailed analysis of these factors see Sharpston (1975).

[15]UNCTAD (1975) notes that this is happening in South Korea, Taiwan, Hong Kong and Singapore. However, König (1975) finds that Mexico, despite its industrial development, is unable to provide "border industries" with even 1 per cent of their inputs; he places the full blame for this on inefficiencies caused by protection.

of cost minimization reduce the scope for domestic linkages to practically nothing.[16]

Of these four types of TNC investment, the first two are likely to create the most linkages, the third rather less, and the fourth least of all. The extent of linkages created in particular LDCs depends upon the stage of development of indigenous industry, the availability of local skills and technology, institutions and government policies, changes in demand and technology in world markets and their political attractiveness to TNCs.[17] The main benefits of such investment are generally supposed to be employment creation, export promotion (though net foreign exchange benefits may be very low for the third and fourth groups that depend heavily on imported components), skill and technology transfer (particularly in the first and second, sometimes the third, groups), and the stimulation of local linkages (see below). The main costs mentioned are the generous fiscal and infrastructural incentives that LDCs have to offer (especially for investments in the fourth category), the socio-political constraints of having to ensure a docile and low-cost labour force, the danger of losing "footloose" TNCs when costs rise, the risk of getting poor terms from monopsonistic buyers, and the instability of demand for exports. Of these, the danger of "footloose" behaviour does not seem to have been realized;[18] fiscal

concessions certainly have been generous; TNCs have clearly shown a marked preference for stable regimes with little or no labour problems; the incidence of "squeezing" local firms needs further investigation; and export market instability is not a particular feature of TNC exports. On the whole, the benefits seem to have outweighed the costs with LDCs, and many of them are now seeking to attract TNCs or foreign buying groups.[19]

Besides the general studies of this phenomenon mentioned above, a number of country studies have discussed export-oriented foreign investment (and subcontracting) for Mexico,[20] Hong Kong,[21] Singapore,[22] the Caribbean,[23] and Taiwan.[24] Nearly all of them—with the exceptions of Evers (1977) and Fernandez (1973)—have come to favourable conclusions about the net benefits of such activity to host LDCs, but their discussion of linkages as such has remained desultory and unsatisfactory. There are some impressionistic and anecdotal accounts[25] of the potential for creating beneficial linkages which confirm the general analysis given above, but none of these studies has attempted a systematic evaluation of the extent, costs, and benefits of linkages from the viewpoint of the host economy or the local enterprises. Of those which have touched on linkages, the following may be mentioned:

[16]See UNCTAD (1975), Change (1971), Finan (1975). U.S. Tariff Commission (1970) and Lim and Pang (1976). Some products of the electronics industry, mainly in consumer electronics, *are* amenable to local manufacture in their entirety, and so fall into the third group.

[17]For general discussions of the determinants of export-orientated foreign investments and their costs and benefits see Helleiner (1973, 1976), Adam (1972, 1975), Michalet (1977), de la Torre (1974); for an analysis of the significance of labour skills in trade see Hirsch (1975) and for a recent theoretical analysis of TNCs and trade see Hirsch (1975, 1976); for a description of the role of multinational buying groups see Hone (1974); and for an examination of the tariff provisions in developed countries which lead to "offshore assembly" see Finger (1975).

[18]Rising wage costs in Singapore have led TNCs to upgrade the skill content of their activities rather than leave the country. See Lim and Pang (1976) and Lall (1977).

[19]East European countries are also entering the field, and their use of "industrial co-operation agreements," under which Western firms provide technology, and usually also equipment and intermediate inputs, in return for processed goods, seems to have provided major benefits to their smaller establishments without incurring the problem of direct TNC investment. This arrangement, discussed by Hewett (1975), may serve as a model to the more advanced LDCs.

[20]See König (1975), Baerresen (1971), Walker (1969), Fernandez (1973), Sahagun (1976) and Watanabe (1974).

[21]Reidel (1974) and Evers et al. (1977), the latter concentrating on textiles.

[22]Lim and Pang (1976) on the electronic industry.

[23]Van Houten (1973).

[24]Reidel (1975).

[25]Especially in Helleiner (1976), Watanabe (1972) and Sharpston (1975).

1. Evers et al. (1977), on the textile and clothing industries in Hong Kong, discuss the role of trading companies in developed countries that subcontract to local manufacturers. They find that local linkages for clothing manufacture, in terms of the purchase of local cotton textiles, has weakened rather than strengthened in recent years with the growth of exports, for two reasons: discrimination in developed countries against cotton, and the demand for higher quality products, both leading to a greater dependence on imported textiles (often supplied by the buyers). The authors comment extensively on poor working conditions, use of child labour, excessive working hours (up to 105 hours per week for men), and low wages that support the success of the industry in Hong Kong, and draw unfavourable conclusions for the distribution of benefits resulting from such export-led growth. Conditions are apparently worse in small establishments, since large ones have themselves become multinational and gone to cheaper areas like Malaysia and Indonesia.

2. Lim and Pang (1976), who survey the electronic industry in Singapore, note that European firms buy a fair amount of their inputs (40–50 percent) locally, while U.S. (under 10 percent), and Japanese (about 20 percent) buy much less. This is due to the fact that U.S. firms are specialized in the semi-conductor sector and Japanese firms in high-technology components, beyond the technological capabilities of domestic firms, while European firms manufacture mainly consumer electronics where the scope for local purchase is higher. However, local products tend to be rather costly, and are purchased chiefly in order to qualify for GSP privileges in selling to Europe (a minimum local content is required for these exports). Local firms face the usual problems of quality, technology, high costs, and so on, and are sometimes assisted by the local TNCs from whom they subcontract by free technology transfers. Firms which subcontract to foreign buying groups seem to face greater problems; their wage costs are

higher than Hong Kong or Taiwan so that they are constantly threatened with losing their markets; they complain of little assistance from the government; and they are short of finance and new technology.

3. UNCTAD (1975) reviews the electronics industry in LDCs generally, and reaches optimistic conclusions about the effects and prospects for subcontracting. It finds that several finished electronic products can be successfully manufactured by local enterprises in South East Asia, and subcontracting has led to "a whole network of small manufacturers that were set up as a result of the backward linkages created" (p. 26).[26]

Clearly, much more evidence is needed on the experience of different industries in different LDCs before we can generalize about the impact of TNC linkages in export-based industries. It is obvious that substantial linkages have been created, and that in some sectors, like electricals, they have been beneficial to host countries; however, it is possible that in some other industries, like textiles, linkages have been weakening and have had undesirable effects on distribution and welfare. A related question which has been almost totally neglected is whether such exporting activity (perhaps excluding very high-technology products) could have been undertaken more economically by local firms in countries like India, where the bulk of "modern" manufactured exports are not in fact accounted for by TNCs, and whether this would have created more beneficial linkages. This whole area is of vital importance to policy-making, and cries out for detailed empirical research.

[26]As noted above, however, this has not occurred for "border industries" in the advanced but highly protected economy of Mexico, even in textiles, despite the efforts of some TNCs to increase local content in order to qualify for GSP (General System of Preferences) privileges. See König (1975), pp. 92–4.

References

Adam, G. (1972), "Some implications and concomitants of worldwide sourcing," *Acta Oeconomica*, pp. 309–23.

Adam, G. (1975), "Multinational corporations and worldwide sourcing," in H. Radice (ed.), *International Firms and Modern Imperialism* (Penguin).

Baerresen, D. W. (1971), *The Border Industrialization Program of Mexico* (D. C. Heath).

Baranson, J. (1967), *Manufacturing Problems in India: the Cummins Diesel Experience* (Syracuse University Press).

Baranson, J. (1969), *Automotive Industries in Developing Countries* (IBRD).

Chang, Y. S. (1971), *The Transfer of Technology: Economics of Offshore Assembly, the Case of Semiconductor Industry*, Report No. 11 (UNITAR).

Daftary, F., and Borghey, M. (1976), "Multinational enterprises and employment in Iran," World Employment Programme, Working Paper No. 14, ILO, mimeo.

De la Torre, J. 1974), "Foreign investment and export dependency," *Economic Development and Cultural Change*, pp. 135–50.

Evers, B., de Groot, G., and Wagenmans, W. (1977), "Hong Kong: development and perspective of a clothing colony," translated summary of Progress Report No. 6, Development Research Institute, Tilburg, Netherlands, mimeo.

Fernandez, R. A. (1973), "The border industrialization program on the U.S.–Mexico border," *Review of Radical Political Economics*, Spring, pp. 37–52.

Finan, N. (1975), "The international transfer of semiconductor technology through U.S. based firms," Working Paper No. 118, National Bureau of Economic Research, New York.

Finger, J. M. (1975), "Tariff provisions for offshore assembly and the exports of developing countries," *Economic Journal*, pp. 365–71.

Helleiner, G. K. (1973), "Manufactured exports from less-developed countries and

ployment in the less developed countries," *Economic and Political Weekly*, annual number, February, pp. 247–62. multinational firms," *Economic Journal*, pp. 21–47.

Helleiner, G. K. (1976), "Transnational enterprises, manufactured exports and em-

Hewett, E. A. (1975), "The economics of East European technology imports from the West," *American Economic Review*, May, pp. 377–82.

Hirsch, S. (1975), "The product cycle model of international trade," *Oxford Bulletin of Economics and Statistics*, pp. 305–17.

Hirsch, S. (1976), "An international trade and investment theory of the firm," *Oxford Economic Papers*, pp. 258–70.

Hirschman, A. O. (1958), *The Strategy of Economic Development* (Yale University Press).

Hone, A. (1974), "Multinational corporations and multinational buying groups," *World Development*, February, pp. 145–50.

Hufbauer, G. C., and Adler, F. M. (1968), *U.S. Manufacturing Investment and the Balance of Payments* (U.S. Treasury Department).

Jo, Sung-Hwen (1976), "The impact of multinational firms on employment and incomes: the case study of South Korea," World Employment Programme, Working Paper No. 12, ILO, mimeo.

König, W. (1975). "Towards an evaluation of international subcontracting activities in developing countries," U.N.

Lall, S. (1975), *Private Foreign Manufacturing Investment and Multinational Corporations: An Annotated Bibliography* (Praeger).

Lall, S. (1977), "Transfer pricing in assembly industries: a preliminary analysis of the issues in Malaysia and Singapore," Commonwealth Secretariat, London, mimeo.

Lall, S., and Streeten, P. P. (1977), *Foreign Investment, Transnationals and Developing Countries* (Macmillan).

Lim, L., and Pang, Eng-Fong (1976), "The electronics industry in Singapore: structure, employment, technology and linkage," Economic Research Centre, University of Singapore, mimeo.

Mason, R. H. (1967), "An analysis of benefits from U.S. direct foreign investments in less-developed areas," Ph.D. thesis, Stanford University.

Michalet, C.-A. (1977), "International subcontracting," in *OECD Development Centre's "Experts" Meeting on International Subcontracting and Reinforcing LDCs' Technological Absorption Capacity,* OECD, mimeo.

Reidel, J. (1974), *The Industrialization of Hong Kong* (Institut für Weltwirtschaft).

Reidel, J. (1975), "The nature and determinants of export-oriented direct foreign investment in a developing country: a case study of Taiwan," *Weltwirtschaftliches Archiv,* pp. 505–28.

Reuber, G. L. et al. (1973), *Private Foreign Investment in Development,* Oxford, Clarendon Press.

Sahagun, V. M. B. et al. (1976), "The impact of multinational corporations on employment and incomes: the case of Mexico," World Employment Programme, Working Paper No. 13, ILO, mimeo.

Scitovsky, T. (1954), "Two concepts of external economies," *Journal of Political Economy,* pp. 143–52.

Sharpston, M. (1975), "International subcontracting," *Oxford Economic Papers,* pp. 94–135.

Thoburn, J. T. (1973), "Exports and the Malaysian engineering industry: a case study of backward linkage," *Oxford Bulletin of Economics and Statistics,* pp. 91–117.

UNCTAD (1975), *International Subcontracting Arrangements in Electronics between Developed Market-Economy Countries and Developing Countries* (U.N.).

U.S. Tariff Commission (1970), *Economic Factors Affecting the Use of Item 807.00 and 806.30 of the Tariff Schedules of the United States* (Government Printing Office, Washington, D.C.).

Vaitsos, C. V. (1976), "Employment problems and transnational enterprises in developing countries: distortions and inequality," World Employment Programme, Working Paper No. 11, ILO, mimeo.

Van Houten, J. F. (1973), "Assembly industries in the Caribbean," *Finance and Development,* June.

Walker, H. O. (1969), "Border industries with a Mexican accent," *Columbia Journal of World Business,* January–February, pp. 25–32.

Watanabe, S. (1972), "International subcontracting, employment and skill promotion," *International Labour Review,* pp. 425–49.

Watanabe, S. (1974), "Constraints on labour-intensive export industries in Mexico," *International Labour Review,* pp. 23–45.

V.D.3. Multinational Enterprises in Developing Countries—Note

The multinational enterprise (MNE)—with facilities in many countries and responsive to a common management strategy—has gained increasing prominence as an instrument for private foreign investment in developing countries. While the capital, technology, managerial competence, and marketing capabilities of an MNE can be utilized for a country's development, there is also a fear that the MNE may dominate the host country or impose excessive costs.

Criticism of the MNE is but the latest attempt to dispel complacency over the relevance of the neoclassical theory of international trade for development problems. As we shall see in Chapter VIII, critics of the neoclassical trade theory first attempted to discredit the theory's power to explain historical development by arguing that international trade had actually operated historically as a mechanism of inequality. After the establishment of the postwar international economic institutions, the argument shifted to a criticism of the alleged biases and deficiencies of the international institutions comprising the Bretton Woods system. And now the MNE has become the object of criticism, with pessimistic warnings about future detriment to the developing countries if the MNE is not sufficiently regulated.

Does the evaluation of the operation of the MNE, however, call for more than a social benefit-cost type of analysis, such as outlined in selection V.D.1? Why should the MNE be analyzed differently from direct investment from one home country to a single host country? The essential question is what difference does the attribute of "multinationality" make to the analysis?

True, an MNE is likely to have the power of an oligopoly; but so too may some "simple" foreign enterprises or domestic independent companies. True, an MNE may be a vertically integrated enterprise that uses transfer prices for intrafirm trade; but so too may "simple" foreign investment. True, an MNE may be involved in the costly process of import substitution; but so too may a simple foreign enterprise or a national firm. True, an MNE may be depleting too rapidly a wasting asset; but so too may other forms of investment that are not multinational in character. In assessing the contribution of a foreign investment by an MNE, we have to be clear on whether what is being assessed is the *investment project* per se, the *foreignness* of the investment, or some *alternative* institutional arrangement for acquiring the ingredients of the direct investment package.

The distinguishing feature of an MNE is that the range of its major decisions (finance, investment, production, research and development, and reaction to governmental policies) is based on the opportunities and problems that the MNE confronts in all the countries in which it operates. In utilizing its "global scanning capacity" to determine its investment plan, worldwide sourcing strate-gies, and marketing based upon expectations of returns and risk factors, the MNE concentrates on the total net worth of the investor's interests, not that of an individual subsidiary alone.

Although these features of foreign investment associated with "multinationality" do not call for a different type of analysis from the general benefit-cost analysis already discussed, the multinational firm is characterized by some behavioral differences that broaden the reach and increase the intensity of both the benefits and costs of foreign investment. As Caves has indicated,[1] a national branch of a multinational firm might behave differently from an equal-sized independent company for three reasons:

(1) *Motivation.* The multinational firm maximizes profits from its activities as a whole, rather than telling each subsidiary to maximize independently and ignoring the profit interdependences among them. The multinational firm also spreads its risks, and could therefore behave quite differently in an uncertain situation from an independent having the same risk-return preference function.

(2) *Cognition and information.* Its corporate family relations give the multinational unit access to more information about markets located in other countries—or to information to which it can attach a higher degree of certainty.

(3) *Opportunity set.* The set of assets held by a multinational unit can differ from a national firm's in various ways—perhaps most notably in its skill in differentiating its product and its financial capacities.

Although Caves's analysis is concerned with the differences in market behavior between a national branch of a multinational firm and an equal-sized independent company, these behavioral differences are also relevant as between a multinational firm and a "simple" type of foreign enterprise in the developing country.

[1]Richard E. Caves, *International Trade, International Investment, and Imperfect Markets,* Princeton University Special Papers in International Economics, No. 10, November 1974, pp. 21-2.

These behavioral differences can be especially significant in: first, promoting foreign investment; second, allowing the MNE to act as a unit of real economic integration; and third, endowing the MNE with greater bargaining power.

The growth of MNEs tends to promote more foreign investment because the MNE is less of a risk-averter when it operates in a number of countries, produces a number of products, practices process specialization, and enjoys greater maneuverability with respect to marketing opportunities and conditions of production than does a firm with a narrower range of activities.

Emphasizing the interrelations between output and input flows in international trade, Baldwin has stated:

When the international firm becomes economically viable in a particular industry, not only is it possible to transfer knowledge, capital, and technical and managerial labor across borders more efficiently, but these transfers tend to be economically feasible with smaller product markets than is the case when the optimum size of productive units is small. Moreover, because of the pecuniary and technological externalities that exist among intermediate sectors in a vertical product line, it may not be economically profitable from a private viewpoint to add a new product to a country's production list unless the international firm mechanism is utilized.[2]

The MNE is also a unit of integration in the world economy. The transmission of factors (capital, skills, technological knowledge, management) via the MNE, together with the MNE's economies of scale in R&D and marketing, make it a unit of real international integration. By its multinational operations and intrafirm transactions, the MNE transcends the national barriers to commodity trade and impediments to international factor movements. As a planning unit that makes resource allocation decisions, the MNE becomes the mechanism for making effective the LDC's potential comparative advantage. The MNE provides the complementary resources of capital, technology, management, and market outlets that may be necessary to bestow an "effective" comparative advantage to the labor-surplus factor endowment in the host country.

This can also be evaluated as efficient international production. The MNE views production as a set of activities or processes, and the global strategy of the MNE amounts in essence to the solution of activity models of production, with production processes in many countries. A competitive equilibrium solution to the programming problem is imposed within the MNE when it operates efficiently as a planning unit, and each process is in the solution basis. Regulatory interference with the MNE will alter the equilibrium basis, and some processes formerly in operation may become inefficient to use. The likelihood for a labor-surplus economy is that labor becomes unemployed for lack of cooperating factors previously supplied by the MNE. Or if workers were formerly employed in a lower productivity occupation, there is a loss in real wages.

This interpretation of the MNE as an efficient technical and allocational unit of integration means that while intrafirm trade conforms to *corporate* advantage, it is also identical with the realization of *comparative* advantage. If the nation-state fragments the world economy through restrictions on commodity and factor movements and thwarts international economic integration, the MNE may serve a complementary—rather than competitive—function to the nation-state: the MNE may be the vehicle for evoking in practice the principle of comparative advantage in world trade, for trade in both outputs and inputs. The internal resource allocation in the MNE is a substitute mechanism for the market, but when it realizes comparative advantage in processes and activities, the resource allocation decisions of the MNE will be more efficient than those in unintegrated markets that are characterized by imperfections and uncertainty. For global technical efficiency, the world economy is the

[2]R. E. Baldwin, "International Trade in Inputs and Outputs," *American Economic Review, Papers and Proceedings,* May 1972, p. 433.

territorial unit of international production (not the nation-state, which is a unit of international politics).

What, however, is the distribution of gains between the MNE and host country? More pointedly, how might the net benefit for the host country be raised? This is the crucial question posed by the attribute of "multinationality." For multinationality instills foreign investment by an MNE with greater bargaining power because of its tendency to be of larger size, its capability to exercise wider options, and its capacity to avoid some forms of regulation that cannot reach beyond national jurisdiction.

These powers are especially suspect when they coalesce in the practice of transfer pricing. The host country may believe that transfer pricing allows the MNE to minimize taxes, escape from tariff charges, or be the means of remitting profits from a subsidiary to the parent company that would otherwise not be allowed by exchange restrictions.[3]

If the MNE is concerned with overall profit, not profit at any particular stage, then the dominant motivation behind the pricing structure in a vertically integrated operation is to gain maximum advantage vis-à-vis the different governmental rates of taxation and regulation of international capital flows. Transfer prices or cost allocation techniques then acquire an artificial quality in the absence of "arm's-length" transactions.

The developing country's desire to regulate transfer pricing is only a special instance of the general problem of how the bargaining process between the host government and MNE distributes the fruits of the foreign investment—more technically, the extent to which the developing country can capture from the MNE a greater share of the MNE's quasi-rents on its supply of technological knowledge, management, and capital. In the most formal terms, the problem is for the host government to devise an optimal welfare tax on foreign capital which improves the terms of foreign borrowing.[4]

The more general problems of bargaining between host government and MNE have been summarized as follows.[5]

For the transfer of a certain "package" of know-how, capital management and inputs there is a range of values which would be acceptable to both sides but which both sides have an interest in concealing. The ability to conceal the relevant values is however much greater for the MNE than for the host country.

In settling the bargain and in drawing up the contract, a large number of items may be for negotiation, in addition to income and sales tax concessions and tariff and nontariff protection of the product. Among these are:

1. specific allowances against tax liabilities, such as initial or investment allowances, depletion allowances, tax reporting techniques, loss offset provisions, etc.;
2. royalty payments, management fees and other fees;
3. duty drawbacks on imported inputs for exports;
4. content of local inputs;
5. profit and capital repatriation;
6. structure of ownership and degree and timing of local participation;
7. local participation in management at board level;
8. obligations to train local labour;
9. transfer pricing;
10. rules and requirements relating to exporting;
11. degree of competition and forms of competition; price control and price fixing;
12. credit policies (e.g., subsidized interest rates);
13. extent of capitalization of intangibles;
14. revalorization of assets due to currency devaluation;
15. subsidies, e.g., to energy, rent, transport, or export expenses such as insurance, freight, promotion;

---

[3]For an analysis of the adverse effects of the transfer pricing mechanism, see Constantine Vaitsos, *Intercountry Income Distribution and Transnational Enterprises,* Oxford, 1974, chapter 6; S. Lall, "Determinants and Implications of Transfer Pricing by International Firms," *Bulletin of the Oxford Institute of Economics and Statistics,* August 1973.

[4]W. M. Corden, *Trade Policy and Economic Welfare,* Oxford, 1974, pp. 339–40, 345–7, 355–64.

[5]Paul Streeten, "The Multinational Enterprise and the Theory of Development Policy," *World Development,* October 1973, pp. 8–9.

16. place and party of jurisdiction and arbitration;
17. time and right of termination or renegotiation.

A contract between the MNE and the host government will contain provisions under some of these headings. Such possible contracts can be ranked in an order of preference by the MNE and by the government. If both the MNE and the government prefer a certain contract to another, the latter can be eliminated. The only complication here is that either party has an interest in concealing the fact that its interest coincides with that of the other party. For by appearing to make a concession, when in fact no concession is made, it may be spared having to make a concession on another front where interests conflict.

But leaving this complication aside, amongst the contracts that remain when those dominated by others have been eliminated, the order of preference for the MNE will be the reverse of that for the government. If the least attractive contract from the point of view of the MNE is outside the range of contracts acceptable to the government, no contract will be concluded. But if there is some overlap, there is scope for bargaining. The precise contract on which the two partners will settle will be determined by relative bargaining strength.

E and D are ruled out because both the MNE

Ranking of Contracts in Order of Preference

MNE	Government F	
A	C	↑
B	(E)		
C	(D)	Range of bargaining
(D)	B	
(E)	A	↓
F		

and the government prefer C; F is ruled out because it is unacceptable to the MNE.

At the same time, in determining the relative value of the different contracts, the host government will find cost-benefit analysis useful. By comparing the present value of the stream of benefits with that of the costs the disparate components in the bargain can, at least in principle, be made commensurable. Cost-benefit analysis and bargaining-power analysis are not alternative methods of approach but are complementary. Cost-benefit analysis will not tell a government whether a particular project is acceptable or not, i.e., whether it falls within the acceptable bargaining range, but it will help it to rank those that are acceptable.

Comment

For an evaluation of the role of multinational enterprises in LDCs, the following may be consulted: Paul Streeten, "The Multinational Enterprise and the Theory of Development Policy," *World Development* (October 1973); Paul Streeten, "Costs and Benefits of Multinational Enterprises in Less Developed Countries," in J. H. Dunning (ed.), *The Multinational Enterprise* (1971); Stephen Hymer, "The Multinational Corporation and the Law of Uneven Development," in J. Bhagwati (ed.), *International Economics and World Order to the Year 2000,* (1972); Stephen Hymer, "The Efficiency (Contradictions) of Multinational Corporations," *American Economic Review* (May 1970); O. Sunkel, "Big Business and 'Dependencia,'" *Foreign Affairs* (April 1972); R. E. Caves, "International Corporations: The Industrial Economics of Foreign Investment," *Economica* (February 1971); H. G. Johnson, "The Efficiency and Welfare Implications of the International Corporation," in C. P. Kindleberger (ed.), *The International Corporation* (1970); A. O. Hirschman, *How to Divest in Latin America and Why* (1969); G. K. Helleiner, "Manufactured Exports from Less Developed Countries and Multinational Firms," *Economic Journal* (March 1973); Richard J. Barnet and Ronald E. Muller, *Global Reach* (1974); C. Fred Bergsten et al., *American Multinationals and American Interests* (1978); Raymond Vernon, *Sovereignty at Bay* (1971); Raymond Vernon, *Storm Over the Multinationals* (1977); E. Penrose, "'Ownership and Control': MNCs in LDCs," in Gerald Helleiner (ed.), *A World Divided* (1976); Richard Newfarmer, *Transnational Conglomerates and the Economics of Dependent Development* (1979); Peter Evans, *Dependent Development* (1979); Sanjaya Lall and Paul Streeten, *Foreign Investment, Transnationals and Developing Countries* (1977); Carlos Diaz-Alejandro, "The Less Developed Countries and

Transnational Enterprises," in Sven Grassman and Erik Lundberg (eds.), *The World Economic Order* (1981); Theodore H. Moran, "Multinational Corporations and Dependency," *International Organization* (Winter 1978); Sanjaya Lall, *The Multinational Corporation* (1980); Thomas G. Parry, *The Multinational Enterprise: International Investment and Host-Country Impacts* (1980); Thomas J. Bierstaker, *Distortion on Development: Perspectives on the Multinational Corporation* (1978); Isaiah Frank, *Foreign Enterprise in Developing Countries* (1980); For an excellent review article, see Paul Streeten, "Multinationals Revisited," *Finance & Development* (June 1979).

Comment

It is significant that the internationalization of LDC firms is growing relatively rapidly. Local firms in parts of Africa, Asia, Latin America, and the Middle East are moving in increasing numbers to establish manufacturing plants in other LDCs. As the LDC share of world industrial production and exports grows, so too will their share of international investment and transfer of technology.

The emergence of multinationals from developing countries is attracting more attention; for example, refer to the following: Dennis J. Encarnation, "The Political Economy of Indian Joint Industrial Ventures Abroad," *International Organization* (Winter 1982); Sanjaya Lall, "The Emergence of Third World Multionationals: Indian Joint Ventures Overseas," *World Development,* (February 1982); S. Lall, *Developing Countries as Exporters of Technology* (1982); Louis T. Wells, Jr., "The Internationalisation of Firms from Developing Countries," in Tamir Agmon and C. P. Kindleberger (eds.), *Multinationals from Small Countries* (1977); David A. Heenan and Warren J. Keegan, "The Rise of Third World Multinationals," *Harvard Business Review* (January–February 1979); K. Kumar (ed.), *Multinationals from Developing Countries* (1982).

V.E. TRANSFER OF TECHNOLOGY

V.E.1. Appropriate Technology*

Technology is often identified with the hardware of production—knowledge about machines and processes. Here a much broader definition is adopted, extending to all the "skills, knowledge and procedures for making, using and doing useful things." Technology thus includes methods used in non-marketed activities as well as marketed ones. It includes the nature and specification of what is produced—the product design—as well as how it is produced. It encompasses managerial and marketing techniques as well as techniques directly involved in production. Technology extends to services—administration, education, banking and the law, for example—as well as to manufacturing and agriculture. A complete description of the technology in use in a country would include the organisation of productive units in terms of scale and ownership. Although much of the discussion will be in terms of technological development in the hardware of technology, the wider definition is of importance since there are relationships between the hardware and the software—between, for example, mechanical process and managerial techniques and infrastructural services—which help determine the choice made in both spheres.

Technology consists of a series of techniques. The technology available to a particular country is all those techniques it knows about (or may with not too much difficulty obtain knowledge about) and could acquire, while the technology in use is that subset of techniques it *has* acquired. It must be noted that the technology available to a country cannot be identified with all known techniques: on the one hand weak communication may mean that a particular country only knows about part of the total methods known to the world as a whole. This can be an important limitation on technological choice. On the other hand, methods may be known but they may not be available because no one is producing the machinery or other inputs required. This too limits technological choice.

The actual technology in use is thus circumscribed first by the nature of world technology, then by the availability to the country of known techniques, and finally by the choice made among those available. If the technology in use is thought to be inappropriate, or because an inappropriate subset is available to the country, or because an inappropriate selection is made, or for some combination of the three reasons. Confusion is caused by failing to distinguish between the three.

Each technique is associated with a set of characteristics. These characteristics include the nature of the product, the resource use—of machinery, skilled and unskilled manpower, management, materials and energy inputs—the scale of production, the complementary products and services involved, etc. Any or all of these characteristics may be important in determining whether it is possible and/or desirable to adopt a particular technique in a particular country and the implications of so doing.

More formally, we may think of all the known techniques as $wT = \{Ta, Tb, Tc, Td, \ldots Tn\}$ (where "known" means known to the world) as constituting world technology. For a particular country, the technology available for adoption is that subset of world technology known to the country in question *and* available. Say, $cT = \{\overline{Ta} \ldots \overline{Tn}\}$, where c denotes the country and the bar indicates that only techniques known to the country and available are included. Thus $cT \subset wT$.

*From Frances Stewart, *Technology and Underdevelopment*, 2nd ed., New York, Macmillan, London and Basingstoke, 1977, pp. 1–3, and "International Technology Transfer: Issues and Policy Options," *World Bank Staff Working Paper* No. 344, July 1979, pp. 78, 82–88. Reprinted by permission.

Each of the techniques *Ta, Tb* . . . etc. is a vector consisting of a set of characteristics, ai, aii, aiii, bi, bii, biii. . . . Thus technology can be described in matrix form, with each column representing the characteristics of each technique, as shown in Table 1.

The technology in use in a particular country is that subset of the technology available to it that has been selected and introduced, or $uT = \{\overline{Ta} \ldots \overline{Tn}\}$ where $uT \subset cT \subset wT$.

The processes by which world technology is narrowed down to an actual set of techniques in use may be crudely described as shown in Figure 1.

The characteristics of technology are largely determined by the nature of the economies for which they are designed. The most significant determinants of the characteristics of new technology are the income levels, resource availability and costs in the society in and for which the technology is designed, and the system of organization of production, and the nature of the technology in use in the society. In each of these respects, societies of advanced countries differ from those of poor countries. Consequently, technology designed to suit advanced countries tends to be ill adapted (or "inappropriate") to the conditions prevalent in poor countries. The transfer of such technology to poor societies tends, as a result, to cause various distortions and inefficiencies.

In discussing "characteristics" of technology, one should include all the relevant features which determine its resource use, productivity, and impact on production and consumption patterns. These features include the nature and design of the product, the scale and organizational system for which the technology is designed, its resource use, including capital and labor intensity, materials and fuel use, skill requirements, and the infrastructural and complementary inputs it requires. The traditional economist's characterization of techniques according to their capital or labor intensity forms only one, and quite often a relatively insignificant, aspect of the total characterization.

Techniques designed for modern advanced countries tend to produce high-income products, require high levels of investible resources per employee, high levels of education and skills, be of a large scale and require sophisticated management techniques, be associated with high levels of labor productivity, and be linked, through inputs and outputs, with the rest of the advanced technology system. If these techniques are transferred unmodified to LDCs, the result will be a concentration of resources, of savings and expenditure on human resources and infrastructure, on a small part of the economy. Incomes will tend to be concentrated in this area, leading to markets for the high-income products the system produces. Resources available in the low-income country will tend to be underutilized, including raw materials as well as labor.

TABLE 1. Matrix of World Technology = wT

Characteristics	T_a	T_b	T_c	T_d	T_e
Product type					
Product nature					
Scale of production					
Material inputs					
Labor input:					
Skilled					
Unskilled					
Managerial input					
Investment requirements					

Many of the well-established characteristics of the dual economy can be seen as following from the characteristics of advanced country technology: the capital-intensity of productive techniques, the heavy reliance on imported managers, skill deficiencies, un- and under-employment and a relative (often absolute) deprivation of the economy outside the modern sector. Only economies which are growing very rapidly and are selective about the choice of techniques and adept at modifying them are able to overcome this dualism, by absorbing a growing proportion of their workforce into the modern sector. South Korea and Taiwan provide the obvious examples. In other economies, dualistic tendencies have been partially offset by a deliberate attempt to protect the non-modern sector, providing it with resources and protected markets to prevent it being undermined by the modern sector. This is the policy of "walking on two legs" pursued most extensively by China (and to a less marked extent by India). In China employment expansion in the modern sector has been similar to that in many other developing economies, lagging well behind growth in output, while the technology adopted has tended to be capital intensive. Overall employment policies have succeeded because of the absorption of labor in the agricultural and rural non-agricultural sectors.

There is a growing body of literature that questions the rather simplistic technological determinist argument advanced above. It is argued that in many industries a wide choice of efficient technologies has been established by empirical research. Recently, Pack has argued that countries could make significant gains at the macro-level in terms of employment, output and savings, by policies leading to the adoption of the most appropriate techniques in existence. [See selection V.E.3.] It has long been established that there is considerable potential for labor intensity in ancillary processes, even if the core technology is more fixed. Old techniques from advanced countries offer more labor-intensive and small-scale alternatives than the most recent techniques. While this sort of argument sup-

ports the view that there is a wider range of choice than the completely determinist view implies, other considerations suggest that the potential for selecting labor-intensive techniques may be exaggerated by calculations based on the micro-case studies. In the first place, many of the studies show that considerations of product standards/characteristics may rule out the labor-intensive technologies. Secondly, the labor-intensive techniques are often only economic at small scale. Thirdly, entrepreneurs do not have information about the complete "shelf" of techniques in existence; their access to information about different techniques depends on their channels of information. There tends to be a bias in channels of information towards technology currently in use in the supplying countries— i.e., the advanced countries. Appropriate techniques, which are often older techniques from advanced countries, or techniques recently developed in LDCs are less well promoted.

Fourthly, many of the studies neglect the determinants of choice or selection mechanisms. It is often assumed that the only relevant selection mechanism is the relative price of capital and labor, and that is in the control of government. In fact, the determinants of choice are far more complex. The nature and scale of the market is one critical determinant. Products sold on the international market or to high-income consumers may need to use the most recent technology in order to compete. Because scale of production and the nature of the market are of importance in determining choice of product and technique, the factors determining these are significant. Income distribution and trading strategy help determine the nature and scale of markets for different types of product. The distribution of investible resources between enterprises of different size and type is also of relevance. The very substantial wage differentials between enterprises of different sizes suggest that the real wage level may be outcome as well as (partial) cause of technological choice. Moreover, a number of recent studies of technological choice have shown that the most rational choices—both in terms of profit maximization and appropriateness of techniques—are sometimes rejected in favor of less profitable and less appropriate techniques. Thus investigation of the decision mechanisms involved is required if choice of technique is to be altered in a more appropriate direction.

Fifthly, the studies establishing a range of choice are essentially static, depicting the situation at the point in time when they were made. But the so-called "shelf" is moving as technical change proceeds, and some parts of the shelf are moving much faster than others. In particular, with the current world balance of Research and Development, the modern capital-intensive part of the shelf is moving forward, in terms of new products and efficiency of technique, as compared with the labor-intensive part; and the "modern" end is also getting increasingly capital-intensive, larger scale, and the products more sophisticated as incomes rise in the advanced countries. Thus while there may be scope for some push in the direction of labor intensity and other dimensions of appropriateness in some products, the aggregate effects are likely to be swamped by dynamic changes in the opposite direction.

More appropriate technology may be roughly defined as technology whose resource use is more in keeping with LDC resource availability, and whose products are more suited to low-income consumers. This means that more appropriate technology will be more labor-intensive, less skill intensive, smaller scale, use more local materials, and produce simpler low-income products than most of advanced country technology currently being transferred to low-income coun-tries. Technology may be more appropriate in one respect, and no more so in others; or more in some respects, less in others. It is then a matter of judgment as to whether it is to be preferred. More appropriate technology may be less efficient, either in the economic sense that it is less profitable (socially and/or privately), or in the stricter sense (which has been defined as technical inefficiency) that it uses more of all resources to produce the same output. If it is socially or technically inefficient as compared with the "inappropriate" alternative, then the economy would suffer from some output loss in adopting it. In such a situation it would only be worth-while adopting if it were believed that learning effects would be such as to outweigh initial inefficiency, or that income distribution and similar effects are such as to outweigh the loss in output. If we assume that these effects may be incorporated into the measure of social efficiency (and that we can give some meaning to this concept), then an economy should only adopt more appropriate techniques if they can be shown to be socially efficient. In discussing ways in which appropriate technology can be promoted, it is assumed that what is in question is the promotion of socially efficient appropriate technology.

Broadly, one may distinguish two types of appropriate technology: appropriate technology for the "modern" sector, which consists in the adaptation of modern sector advanced country technologies in more labor-intensive directions; and appropriate technology for the traditional sector, which upgrades and improves traditional technologies.

Comment

On the problem of "appropriate" technology, the following are noteworthy: the special issue on "Technology," *World Development* (March 1974); special issue on "Science and Technology in Development," *Journal of Development Studies* (October 1972); G. D. Helleiner, "The Role of Multinational Corporations in the Less Developed Countries' Trade in Technology," *World Development* (April 1975); Paul Streeten, "Technology Gaps Between Rich and Poor Countries," *Scottish Journal of Political Economy* (November 1972); Jack Baranson, *Industrial Technologies for Developing Countries* (1969); Jack Baranson, *Technology and the Multinationals* (1978); W. Berankek and G. Danis, *Science and Technology and Economic Development* (1978); A. S. Bhalla (ed.), *Technology and Employment in Industry*

(1975); A. S. Bhalla, *Toward Global Action on Appropriate Technology* (1979); C. Cooper (ed.), *Science, Technology and Development* (1973); Frances Stewart, *Technology and Underdevelopment* (1977); C. P. Timmer et al., *The Choice of Technology in Developing Countries* (1975); Charles Cooper, "Choice of Techniques and Technological Change as Problems in Political Economy," *International Social Science Journal* (1973); E. K. Y. Chen, *Multinational Corporations, Technology and Employment* (1982).

A series of reports by the United Nations Institute for Training and Research (UNITAR) is highly instructive; so too are the Industrial Planning and Programming Series of UNIDO, as well as the reports of UNCTAD.

V.E.2. Capital-Stretching Innovations*

First and foremost, it should be remembered that, unlike in an advanced country where technological change is viewed as rather automatic and routinized or as capable of being generated through R & D expenditures according to some rules of cost/benefit analysis, in the contemporary developing societies technological change cannot either be taken for granted or afforded through basic R & D allocations. In this situation, we cannot avoid the question of what, given the existence of a shelf of technology from abroad, is the pattern by which the typical less developed economy, in fact, manages to innovate. This question in turn forces us to look at least at the following dimensions more carefully: (1) the precise nature of that technology shelf, (2) the availability within the LDCs of required initial managerial and entrepreneurial capacity, and (3) the changing nature of that required managerial and entrepreneurial capacity in the course of transition to modern growth.

The technology shelf developed in the mature industrial economies abroad may be described by a set of unit activities following a smooth envelope curve as in Figure 1. A particular technology can be described by an L-shaped contour producing one unit of output

*From Gustav Ranis, "Industrial Sector Labor Absorption," *Economic Development and Cultural Change,* April 1973, pp. 392–7. Reprinted by permission.

with a given pair of capital and labor coefficients. The technology shelf is composed of the complete set of such activities or technologies which have been demonstrated to be feasible somewhere in the advanced countries at some historical point in time, including the present. Since there exists a number of technology-exporting countries—for example, the United States, Germany, the United Kingdom, and Japan—with continuous tech-

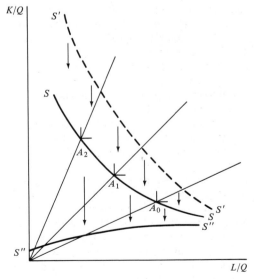

FIGURE 1.

nological transfers among themselves as well as with the LDCs, it is not unreasonable to postulate the existence of a single technological shelf for the lending world as a whole. For example, unit technology A_0 may have been generated in Germany in 1920, A_1 in the United States in 1920, and A_2 in the United States in 1950. In other words, as we move to the left along the shelf we run into more "modern" technology, that is, technology of more recent vintage and of higher capital intensity. As capital per head increases this means that the typical worker has learned to cooperate with more units of capital of increasing technical complexity. This capital-deepening process, in other words, is more complicated than the textbook version of "homogeneous" labor being equipped with more units of "homogeneous" capital.

At any point in time the typical LDC is, then, theoretically free to borrow a particular unit activity from anywhere along this shelf. What technology is chosen and what happens as an immediate and ultimate consequence of that choice, that is, what secondary processes and reactions are set off, is, of course, all part and parcel of the innovation process taken as a whole. The quality of the process, each step of the way, in turn depends on both the economic environment, that is, the nature of the relative price signals, and on the entrepreneurial, managerial, and skilled labor capacity of the borrower.

The role of innovation must therefore be seen as intimately related to the stage in which the developing economy finds itself. In other words, the role of technological change in output and employment generation must be viewed as sensitive to the same discernible phases of growth as the economy moves in transition from open agrarianism to Kuznets' modern economic growth. In the first post-independence or import-substitution phase previously mentioned, an effort is made to increase the supply of domestic entrepreneurship and the economy's learning capacity, partly through the importation of people via aid but mainly through the system of protection established by government policies. In fact, the most reasonable explanation for the

import-substitution syndrome is that it is a response to a real (or imagined) shortage of entrepreneurship and that it permits time, through informal learning by doing or more formal educational processes, for this entrepreneurial capacity to develop.

In terms of Figure 1, this means that, although the technological shelf may look as indicated by curve SS, the *actual* choices available to the developing country during the import-substitution phase are more aptly described by $S'S'$. In other words, due to the inadequate state of entrepreneurial capacity during the early postindependence period of physical controls, the efficiency of generating output per unit of capital in the borrowing country is likely to be substantially below that in the lending country. This is likely to be more true the more capital intensive the import, that is, the further removed from the cultural inheritance and experience of the borrower. Such technological imports are often accompanied by imported engineers, even managers and supervisors—adding up to what is called a "turn-key project." The most advanced and sophisticated technology can, of course, be made to "work," in the physical sense, even in the most backward developing economy. But a shiny new plant imbedded in a society many decades distant is bound to be substantially less efficient. This is true for a thousand direct reasons, such as the absence of even minimal skilled labor supplies, domestic subcontracting, and repair and maintenance possibilities, as well as for many more subtle sociological reasons which enter into the total milieu in which the plant is required to operate. The more sophisticated and removed from the rest of the economy is the technological transplant, the greater is the relative inefficiency, as indicated by the shape of the $S'S'$ curve.

If and when the economy then moves away from the import-substitution phase and enters into the second phase of liberalization and export substitution, a second important, if unintentional, type of innovation is likely to appear, namely, a reduction in the extent of the inefficiency of the original transplanted technology. Call it X efficiency if you like, but the cost of the pure transplantation is likely to be reduced, quite unintentionally, that is, largely as a result of factors external to the profit-maximizing behavior of the productive unit itself. This increase in productive efficiency over time will increase in quantitative significance as the import-substitution hothouse temperature is gradually turned down and a more competitive efficiency may be represented by the arrows tending, over time, to move $S'S'$ back toward the original SS position.

Another more conscious and quantitatively more important type of innovation begins to gather importance during this same second phase of transition. This phenomenon may be called innovational assimilation—innovating "on top of" imported technology in the direction of using relatively more of the abundant unskilled labor supply. As the economy shifts from a natural-resource-based growth pattern in the import-substitution phase to a human-resource-based system in the export-substitution phase, there is an increasing sensitivity to the continuously changing factor endowment, first in terms of the efficient utilization of the domestic unskilled-labor force, and later in terms of the incorporation of growing domestic skills and ingenuity. In other words, the appropriate type of technology finally in place must be one in which not only the initial choice from the shelf but also the adaptations and adjustments consciously made thereafter, in response to changing domestic resource and capability constraints, play an important role.

The more liberalized the economy, in terms of the government's performing a catalytic role through the market by indirect means rather than trying to impose resource allocation by direct controls, the better the chances that the millions of dispersed decision makers can be induced, by the sheer force of profit maximization, to make the "right" decision. As the gap between shadow and market prices narrows—coupled with the expectation of continued labor surpluses for years to come—we would expect transplantation choices to become more flexible, that is, labor intensive. However, since shelf choices are likely to continue to be severely constrained—partly by a lack of illumination of substantial portions of it, partly by such institutional inhibitions as prestige, aid tying, and so forth—we can realistically expect relatively less benefits from liberalization to accrue in the transplantation process. On the other hand, we can expect much more from the assimilation type of innovational behavior which now tends, for the same reasons, to be more slanted in a labor-using direction. In the typical labor surplus type of economy—for one likely to become one over the next decade (as is probably the case in much of Africa)—all this means a much greater possibility for the efficient accomodation of pure labor services.[1] Whether this will lead to a sectoral output shift in favor of labor-intensive export commodities or a mix change predominantly addressed to the domestic market, of course, depends on, *ceteris paribus*, income elasticities of demand, the government's fiscal prowess, and the type (e.g., size) of the economy. Moreover, no strong generalization as to the relative importance of shifts in output mix versus changes in technology for given mixes is likely to be valid. It should be clear, however, that the important issue is that the search for innovation can now be considered a conscious activity of the individual entrepreneur and—given the combination of more realistic relative price signals after liberalization plus greater entrepreneurial capacity—that it is likely to be mainly directed toward various forms of indigenous capital stretching on top of the imported technology. Such capital stretching can be represented by a reduction in the capital coefficient per unit of output. The effective post-assimilation set of unit technologies, that is *after* domestic assimilation, may thus be represented by curve $S''S''$ in Figure 1, with the strength of the indigenous labor-using innovative effort indicated by the

---

[1] It is important to emphasize the word "efficient" since I am not concerned here with the, possibly also legitimate, objective of employment creation as a separate social goal, to be weighed against output growth.

amount of the "downward" shift in the capital coefficient.

It should be noted here that a negatively sloped technology shelf, for example, SS, representing pure technological transplantation, permits, as we move to the left, higher labor productivity levels, but only at increasing capital cost. In a country characterized by capital scarcity this may mean increased technical unemployment (à la Eckaus) and hence a lower value of per capita income for the economy—in spite of the higher level of labor productivity achieved. Domestic capital stretching, however, can materially affect that situation by enabling more workers to be employed per unit of the capital stock. If the post-assimilation unit technology set, $S''S''$, for example, is upward sloping from left to right, higher labor productivity levels become consistent with lower capital/output ratios.

In summary, once the overall policy setting has turned more favorable and permitted the economy to enter the second phase of transition, it is this indigenous capital-stretching capacity which I consider to be of the greatest importance—especially for the contemporary developing economy facing the formidable labor force explosion predicted for the seventies and eighties. It is in this specific area also where the skepticism of planners, engineers, and aid officials generally is most pronounced—especially with respect to the full range of technological choice really available when all the dust has settled. Historical examples from the Japanese case, as well as contemporary evidence from Korea and Taiwan, permit us to demonstrate the existence and potential importance of such capital-stretching innovations for the labor surplus developing country.

V.E.3. Factor Intensity*

Though it is not our purpose to survey the literature on choice of techniques, a summary of some of the conclusions we have reached on the basis of recent literature is germane at this point.

1. In a large number of industrial activities a product is producible with a considerable range of alternate ratios of capital to labor. Much of the potential substitution of labor for capital stems from use of labor-intensive methods in "peripheral" production activities; labor, with little if any capital, can be used to transport material within the factory, to pack cartons, and to store the final product. The evidence for these statements is drawn from

observation of both DC and LDC factory operations and engineering specifications.

2. Evidence is also accumulating that the core production process itself, whether the cooking of food or the production of woven cotton cloth, offers efficient possibilities for using less expensive equipment and more labor per unit of output of *a given quality*, i.e., the more labor-intensive processes are not relegated to the production of inferior commodities. Adaptation of existing equipment, for example, changing the "normal" speed of operation, offers still further opportunities to save capital and increase the relative use of labor. Finally, extensive underutilization of industrial capacity provides considerable scope for increasing the effective labor-capital ratio.

3. There are some industries that probably offer limited possibilities for altering the capital-labor ratio compared with that prevailing in advanced economies. These

*Howard Pack, "Technology and Employment: Constraints on Optimal Performance," Reprinted by permission of Westview Press from *Technology and Economic Development: A Realistic Perspective,* edited by Samuel M. Rosenblatt. Copyright © 1979 by the International Economic Studies Institute.

are typically activities in which most LDCs have no comparative advantage and where the basic problem is to forestall their introduction (typically behind tariff walls) rather than to suggest methods of changing production in a more labor-intensive direction. Even these classical no-technical-substitution cases offer some choice, principally in the price of equipment which typically varies among the sources of supply.

To establish some orders of magnitude a set of numerical results derived from a number of recent studies are shown in Table 1. These figures measure the ratio of fixed capital per worker necessary to begin a new production operation using varying *existing* technologies. The underlying engineering analyses have been carried out by teams of engineers and economists. Variations in the capital-labor ratio reflect several factors: (1) different engineering principles used in the core process; (2) varying sources of supply of the same equipment as some firms or countries exhibit lower prices fairly consistently; (3) differences in the degree of mechanization of peripheral activities such as the bagging of fertilizer; and (4) minor adaptations in existing plants reflecting learning accumulated during the production process.

Thus, some of the most recent work suggests a rather substantial range of technical choice in modern manufacturing. It should

be noted that all of these studies consider substitution among plants of efficient size, in which no further scale economies are to be realized. The range of choice presented is almost surely to be more circumscribed than the options to be derived from a still more systematic search that would include machinery produced in the LDCs themselves in the set of available techniques. For example, the engineering data for the textile study do not take account of the additional labor intensity afforded by semiautomatic looms produced in Korea. These are no longer produced in the industrialized countries but are currently in wide use in Korean textile production, including that destined for export. Their inclusion would significantly widen the efficient range of choice in weaving.

If an LDC is planning the expansion of its industrial sector, its choices with respect to capital intensity are certainly not narrow. There need be no trade-off between output (in this case value added originating in manufacturing) and employment; as long as plentiful unskilled labor can be substituted for scarce capital both employment and output increase. The political authority has two dimensions of choice in view of the substitution possibilities. By providing a reasonably competitive atmosphere in product markets, particularly a liberal international trade regime, it will encourage the expansion of sectors which are not capital-intensive. The critical impotance of correct sector choice can read-

TABLE 1. Fixed Investment per Job Created (dollars)

		Alternative Technologies				
	Capacity per Year	1	2	3	4	5
Sugar refining	50,000 tons	2,869	3,480	3,869	5,987	6,204
Maize milling	36,000 tons	2,917	5,465	7,081	9,730	
Urea	528,000 tons	123,789	126,302	134,800	137,631	
Cotton yarn	1 ton	2,942	16,434			
Woven cotton cloth	1 million sq. yards	1,508	8,125	11,870	33,063	
Beer brewing	200,000 hectolitres	11,419	15,000			
Men's leather shoes	300,000 pair	760	1,042	2,157		

Source: For cotton yarn and woven cloth: H. Pack, "The Optimality of Used Equipment: Some Computations for the Cotton Textile Industry," *Economic Development and Cultural Change,* January 1978; all other studies at the University of Strathclyde; summaries appear in *World Development,* October 1977.

ily be seen in Table 1—compare the capital-labor ratio of the least capital-intensive fertilizer plant with that of the most capital-intensive shoe or cloth producing technology. If policies are pursued, whether by direct government investment or by allowing distorted factor and product prices to prevail, which systematically encourage the expansion of sectors whose lowest achievable capital cost per job created is $124,000 only a limited contribution to employment growth can be expected from that sector. Though careful attention to design can reduce the cost per job from $138,000 to $124,000, the latter remains considerably in excess of the capital available to equip new labor force entrants.

The second choice facing the government, assuming that reasonable balance in sectoral expansion is achieved, is, of course, appropriate choice of technique within a given sector. Interestingly enough, the amount of direct evidence demonstrating inappropriate choice of manufacturing technology is remarkably small. Though anecdotes abound about automated factories employing very few workers, little is known about the relative importance of very modern equipment in a typical LDC's annual investment. The conclusion that inappropriate technology is widely utilized is based primarily on the discrepancy between measured growth rates of real manufacturing output and employment. This discrepancy may, however, reflect increasing capital per worker or greater labor productivity with the same capital per worker, or some combination. We assume that at least some improvement in the employment-generating effects of new investment is possible; in the main, this assumption is based, not on inferences from the growth of average labor productivity in many LDCs, but on the level of exports of new capital goods from DCs to LDCs and the absence of any significant intra-LDC trade in capital goods, and the lack of substantial production except in a handful of countries.

In addition, some of the microeconomic work on choice of technique, particularly that comparing local and foreign companies in the same productive activity, has indicated some inappropriate production methods. At least two studies explicitly addressing the question of whether firms, given their realtive factor prices, have in fact chosen the cost minimizing techniques or a more capital-intensive one, have suggested that the latter is the case.

OBSTACLES TO CORRECT CHOICE OF FACTOR PROPORTIONS

Assuming that private *and* public firms often choose an inappropriate technology where alternatives are available, can such behavior be explained? The most obvious, and until recently the most widely emphasized, explanation was that of incorrect factor market prices facing producers; the cost of unskilled labor being above and that of capital below their respective opportunity costs. While these are undoubtedly important elements, they are unlikely to constitute the sole explanation.

Consider a firm undertaking an entirely new venture or expanding an existing one. The profit augmenting returns to a search for appropriate plant and equipment must be weighed against the increase in profits to be obtained by alternative uses of entrepreneurial and technician time. Once the scarcity of both management and staff time (in the larger firms) is taken into account, it is obvious that many activities exist to which an allocation of time may be profitable. Better inventory control; improved floor supervision; searching for lower cost suppliers; identification of new markets; coaxing better treatment from government in the form of higher protection, rebates, or tariffs on inputs; and exploiting the entire panoply of government measures may be better uses of one's time than choosing "the" correct technique, though it too could improve profits.

These possibilities suggest that, all other factors being equal (the country, sector, product mix, and relative factor prices), the firms facing lower costs of acquiring the information needed for implementing a cost-minimizing, labor-intensive technology are more likely to take that step than companies for whom the (explicit and implicit) information costs are very high. The adoption of a readily available capital-intensive technology may well be the profit-maximizing strategy for the latter. It is plausible to conjecture that MNCs have lower search costs than purely local companies involved in the same activity. They can easily identify and transfer equipment among subsidiaries, especially items that have become too expensive to utilize in higher wage countries because of their labor intensity. Indeed, the parent company may have established a new plant partly to utilize such equipment in the production of exports. Alternately, the local manager may ask the parent company's purchasing office for advice on the availability of used equipment if it is not available within the country. Given the well known difficulties of identifying reliable equipment such "costless" aid to the local manager (in both time and explicit costs) clearly increases the likelihood of his employing appropriate equipment in order to take advantage of the factor prices facing him. Not only can a purchasing office identify and physically evaluate the condition of the equipment, it also probably can obtain a better price, insofar as most studies of the used equipment market indicate that price setting in this market is one of bilateral monopoly rather than perfect competition.

Thus, if we observe the production of similar products in a country by both local firms and MNCs the preceding argument suggests that MNCs would utilize a more appropriate technology, given the relative factor prices facing the two types of firms. Put slightly differently, given the substitution opportunities in production, the MNC is more likely to approximate its cost-minimizing factor proportions than would a purely local firm.

This view, of course, contrasts strongly with the often polemical work that asserts, usually without evidence, that multinationals use excessively capital-intensive methods. Insofar as the logic of the argument can be separated from the hyperbole of the typical discussion, it appears that the major assumption is that MNCs utilize the same production process in the host country as in the country of origin, since this is the only technology with which they are familiar, i.e., the search costs are less. However, this begs the question of why these otherwise profit-maximizing entities (clever enough to set transfer prices to maximize global net profits) engage in no profitability calculus on the benefits and costs of adaptation despite the widely differing factor prices prevailing in the home country and the LDC.

It is often overlooked that an MNC which has been in operation for some length of time is likely to have various vintages of equipment in its worldwide plants. As wages rise in the richer of the countries where it operates, the quasi-rents to be earned on older equipment will decline. Rather than sell such equipment in the used equipment market in the DCs, firms can earn higher returns by moving it to a lower wage location. It is considerably easier for an MNC than for a local LDC company to identify this equipment and purchase it directly from the vendor in the DC. Intracompany transactions in the face of great uncertainty about the quality of the equipment are likely to result in more movement of equipment than in a market in which one important attribute of the commodity, its quality, is very difficult to determine.

Thus, the possession of a considerable range of vintages within its international operations may permit adaptive MNC behavior with respect to technology. Clearly this cannot be the case when the underlying production process offers virtually no substitution opportunities, for example, oil refining and other continuous process industries. Though the multinationals do utilize older vintage equipment, there is no evidence to suggest that they engage in research specifically designed to modify production techniques to better suit LDC factor availabilities. However, because most MNC production is in traditional branches such as food processing and hand soap, the use of traditional methods, twenty years out of date in the advanced countries, is almost surely the cost-minimizing strategy rather than the development of newer, labor-intensive techniques exhibiting improved productivity.

Comment

We may raise three basic questions regarding the choice of technique by multinational enterprises: (1) whether the technologies used by multinationals are adaptable to the low-wage labor-abundant conditions in LDCs, (2) whether multinationals do in fact adapt the technologies they transfer, and (3) whether multinationals adapt better or worse than local firms. An excellent review of the literature addressed to these questions is presented by S. Lall, "Transnationals, Domestic Enterprises, and Industrial Structure in Host LDCs: A Survey," *Oxford Economic Papers* (July 1978), pp. 217–21, with an extensive bibliography.

Other significant references on this subject include: R. H. Mason, "Some Observations on the Choice of Technology by Multinational Firms in Developing Countries," *Review of Economics and Statistics* (1973), pp. 349–55; Samuel Morely and Gordon Smith, "Limited Search and the Technological Choices of Multinational Firms in Brazil," *Quarterly Journal of Economics* (February 1976); William H. Courtney and Danny M. Leipziger, "Multinational Corporations in LDCs: The Choice of Technology," *Oxford Bulletin of Economics and Statistics* (November 1975); Danny M. Leipziger, "Production Characteristics in Foreign Enclave and Domestic Manufacturing: The Case of India," *World Development* (April 1976).

For additional readings on the micro-substitution possibilities in different industries in developing countries, see S. N. Acharya, "Fiscal/Financial Intervention Factor Prices and Factor Proportions: A Review of Issues," *Bangladesh Development Studies* (October 1975); H. Pack, "The Substitution of Labor for Capital in Kenyan Manufacturing," *Economic Journal* (March 1976); Y. Rhee and L. Westphal, "A Microeconomic Investigation of Choice of Technology," *Journal of Development Economics* (September 1977); G. Ranis, "Industrial Technology Choice and Employment: A Review of Developing Country Evidence," *Interciencia* (1977); L. J. White, "The Evidence on Appropriate Factor Proportions for Manufacturing in Less Developed Countries: A Survey," *Economic Development and Cultural Change* (October 1978); Samuel M. Rosenblatt (ed.), *Technology and Economic Development: A Realistic Perspective* (1979); A. S. Bhalla (ed.), *Technology and Employment in Industry,* 2nd ed. (1980).

Although these studies indicate a wide potential choice in both primary and secondary production operations and alternative commodity specifications, the empirical fact remains that the selections actually made in the developing countries still appear to be "inappropriate" by the standards discussed in the foregoing readings. It is therefore necessary to analyze why the problem of inappropriate technology persists and what policy measures might be undertaken to overcome the obstacles to the use of appropriate technology.

CHAPTER VI

Industrialization Strategy

This chapter should be read in conjunction with the next one on agricultural strategy. For a development program cannot afford to emphasize industrialization at the expense of agricultural development. Although the initial development plans of many LDCs focused on programs of deliberate industrialization, the role of industrialization is now being reappraised. It is not a question of concentrating resources on industry or on agriculture—as alternatives. Rather, it is increasingly realized that the mutually supportive interactions between agriculture and industry should receive prime attention.

Instead of industrialization via import substitution, which involved an output mix and choice of techniques that conflicted with other development objectives, there is now the advocacy of a simpler, more appropriate type of industrialization. As Streeten states,

The disenchantment with industrialization in recent writings and speeches has been based on a confusion: it is a disenchantment with the form that economic growth had taken in some developing countries and with the distribution of its benefits. . . . After a reorientation of goals, industrialization as the servant of development regains its proper place in the strategy. Industry should produce the simple producer and consumer goods required by the people, the majority of whom live in the countryside; hoes and simple power tillers and bicycles, not air conditioners and expensive cars and equipment for luxury flats. . . .

In simple mass consumption goods, often produced in a labour-intensive, capital saving way, the developing countries have a comparative advantage and could expand their trade among themselves. But all this depends upon countries opting for a style of development that gives priority to satisfying the simple needs of the large number of poor people. Industries producing clothing, food, furniture, simple household goods, electronics, buses and electric fans would thrive without the need for heavy protection in a society that had adopted this style of industrialization and development. Much of the recent criticism of inefficient, high-cost industrialization behind high walls of protection and quantitative restrictions should be directed at the types of product and of technique which cater for a highly unequal income distribution and reflect entrenched vested interests. It is in no way a criticism of industrialization for the needs of the people.[1]

---

[1] Paul Streeten, "Industrialization in a Unified Development Strategy," *World Development*, January 1975, p. 3.

The future of industrialization lies in a shift from industrialisation via import substitution to a different pattern of domestic output and industrialization via export substitution. As a corollary of this shift, the old dispute about whether to give priority to industry or agriculture is not a real issue. The question instead is how to achieve concurrently both agricultural and industrial development.

Section VI.A. indicates that industrialization offers substantial dynamic benefits that are important for changing the traditional structure of the less developed economy, and the advocacy of industrialization may be particularly compelling for primary export countries that confront problems of a lagging export demand while having to provide employment for a rapidly increasing labor force. Systematic support is given to the industrialization argument in Rosenstein-Rodan's emphasis on the external economies to be realized through industrialization, and his advocacy of a "big push" in the form of a high minimum amount of industrial investment in order to jump over the economic obstacles to development. Although the "balanced growth" doctrine is sometimes related to the big push theory, we should note that the principle of balanced growth is not a necessary component of the big push theory, and balanced growth need not be dependent upon a large amount of public investment or dominance of the public sector.

Selections VI.A.4 and VI.A.5 also summarize the much-discussed "balanced growth" versus "unbalanced growth" approaches to investment. By emphasizing that investment decisions are mutually reinforcing and that overall supply "creates its own demand," the balanced growth doctrine has considerable appeal as a means of initiating development. Critics of the doctrine, however, argue that a poor country does not have the capacity to attain balanced investment over a wide range of industries and that, moreover, the method of balanced growth cannot bring about as high a rate of development as can unbalanced growth. Instead of striving for balanced investment, proponents of unbalanced growth advocate the creation of strategic imbalances that will set up stimuli and pressures which are needed to induce investment decisions. As expressed by Hirschman, for instance, "our aim must be to keep *alive* rather than eliminate the disequilibria of which profits and losses are symptoms in a competitive economy. If the economy is to be kept moving ahead, the task of development policy is to maintain tensions, disproportions, and disequilibria."[2]

According to this view, the central task of a development strategy is to overcome the lack of decision-taking actions in the economy; for this purpose, unbalanced growth is necessary to induce investment decisions and thereby economize on the less developed economy's principal scarce resource, namely, genuine decision making.

It has now become clear that the phrases "balanced growth" and "unbalanced growth" initially caught on too readily and that each approach has been overdrawn. After much reconsideration, each approach has become so highly qualified that the controversy is now essentially barren. Instead of seeking to generalize either approach, we should more appropriately look to the conditions under which each can claim some validity. It may be concluded that while a newly developing country should aim at balance as an investment criterion, this objective will be attained only by initially following in most cases a policy of unbalanced investment. In operational terms, the crucial question has become how to determine what is the proper sequence of investment decisions in order to create the proper amount of imbalance in the right activities.

Section VI.B. focuses on recent experience with industrialization strategies that have been based on import substitution (VI.B.2) and on export substitution (VI.B.3). Policies that have encouraged industrialization through import controls and tariff protection have at the same time adversely taxed agricultural production and exports. To redress the previous bias in favor

[2]Albert O.Hirschman, *The Strategy of Economic Development,* New Haven, 1958, p. 66.

of import substitution, emphasis is now being given to the positive relationships between exports and industrialization. Several reasons are offered in section VI.B for the superiority of industrialization via export substitution. (Chapter VIII will offer a more detailed analysis of export-led development.)

Finally, the relationships between agriculture and industry are outlined in section VI.C. The view that agriculture can serve as a resource reservoir for industry is examined, but the shift in focus now seems to be on the mutual interactions between industry and agriculture. Without agricultural development, as formulated in the next chapter, there cannot be the realization of a positive industrial program, as outlined in this chapter.

VI.A. PATHS TO INDUSTRIALIZATION

VI.A.1. The Theory of the "Big Push"*

An institutional framework different from the present one is clearly necessary for the successful carrying out of industrialisation in international depressed areas. In what follows arguments are submitted tending to show why the whole of the industry to be created is to be treated and planned like one huge firm or trust.

The first task of industrialisation is to provide for training and "skilling" of labour which is to transform Eastern European peasants into full-time or part-time industrial workers. The automatism of *laissez-faire* never worked properly in that field. It broke down because it is not profitable for a private entrepreneur to invest in training labour. There are no mortgages on workers—an entrepreneur who invests in training workers may lose capital if these workers contract with another firm. Although not a good investment for a private firm, it is the best investment for the State. It is also a good investment for the bulk of industries to be created when taken as a whole, although it may represent irrecoverable costs for a smaller unit. It constitutes an important instance of the Pigovian divergence between "private and social marginal net product" where the latter is greater than the former. Training facilities (including transport and housing) of one million workers per annum would involve costs of certainly more than £ 100 million per annum—a sum which may be too great to be borne by the State (or the Eastern European national economy) if

taken *apart* from the costs of the 50% participation in its own "Eastern European Industrial Trust" that we shall propose. It should be counted as capital investment in the Eastern European Industrial Trust (E.E.I.T.).

That is not, however, the most important reason in favour of such a large investment unit.

Complementarity of different industries provides the most important set of arguments in favor of a large-scale planned industrialisation. In order to illustrate the issues involved, let us adopt the somewhat roundabout method of analysing two examples. Let us assume that 20,000 unemployed workers in Eastern and South-Eastern Europe are taken from the land and put into a large shoe factory. They receive wages substantially higher than their previous meagre income *in natura*. It would be impossible to put them into industry at their previous income standard, because they need more foodstuffs than they had in their agrarian semi-unemployed existence, because these foodstuffs have to be transported to towns, and because the workers have to pay for housing accommodation. If these workers spent all their wages on shoes, a market for the products of their enterprise would arise representing an expansion which does not disturb the pre-existing market, and 90% of the problem (assuming 10% profit) would be solved. The trouble is that the workers will not spend all their wages on shoes. If, instead, one million unemployed workers were taken from the land and put, not into one industry, but into a whole series of industries which produce the bulk of the goods on which the workers would spend their wages, what was not true in the case of one shoe factory would become true in the case of a whole system of industries: it would create its own additional market, thus

*From Paul N. Rosenstein-Rodan, "Problems of Industrialization of Eastern and South-Eastern Europe," *Economic Journal*, June-September 1943, pp. 204–7; "Notes on the Theory of the 'Big Push,'" in Howard S. Ellis (ed.), *Economic Development for Latin America*, Macmillan and Co. Ltd., London; St. Martin's Press, New York, 1961, pp. 57–8, 60–62, 65–6. Reprinted by permission.

realising an expansion of world output with the minimum disturbance of the world markets. The industries producing the bulk of the wage goods can therefore be said to be complementary. The planned creation of such a complementary system reduces the risk of not being able to sell, and, since risk can be considered as cost, it reduces costs. It is in this sense a special case of "external economies."

It may be added that, while in the highly developed and rich countries with their more variegated needs it is difficult to assess the prospective demand of the population, it is not as difficult to foresee on what the formerly unemployed workers would spend their wages in regions where a low standard of living obtains.

Two other types of "external economies" will arise when a system of different industries is created. First, the strictly Marshallian economies external to a firm within a growing industry. The same applies, however, (secondly), to economies external to one industry due to the growth of other industries. It is usually tacitly assumed that the divergence between the "private and social marginal net product" is not very considerable. This assumption may be too optimistic even in the case of a crystallised mature competitive economy. It is certainly not true in the case of fundamental structural changes in the international depressed areas. External economies may there be of the same order of magnitude as profits which appear on the profit and loss account of the enterprise.

The existing institutions of international and national investment do not take advantage of external economies. There is no incentive within their framework for many investments which are profitable in terms of "social marginal net product," but do not appear profitable in terms of "private marginal net product." The main driving-force of investment is the profit expectation of an individual entrepreneur which is based on experience of the past. Experience of the past is partly irrelevant, however, where the whole economic structure of a region is to be changed. An individual entrepreneur's knowledge of the

market is bound to be insufficient in this case because he cannot have all the data that would be available to the planning board of an E.E.I.T. His subjective risk estimate is bound to be considerably higher than the objective risk. If the industrialisation of international depressed areas were to rely entirely on the normal incentive of private entrepreneurs, the process would not only be very much slower, the rate of investment smaller and (consequently) the national income lower, but the whole economic structure of the region would be different. Investment would be distributed in different proportions between different industries, the final equilibrium would be below the optimum which a large E.E.I.T could achieve. In the international capital market the existing institutions are mostly used to invest in, or to grant credit to, single enterprises. It might easily happen that any one enterprise would not be profitable enough to guarantee payment of sufficient interest or dividends out of its own profits. But the creation of such an enterprise, e.g., production of electric power, may create new investment opportunities and profits elsewhere, e.g., in an electrical equipment industry. If we create a sufficiently large investment unit by including all the new industries of the region, external economies will become internal profits out of which dividends may be paid easily.

Professor Allyn Young's celebrated example elucidates our problem. He assumed that a Tube line was to be built in a district and that an accurate estimate was made of costs and receipts. It was found that the rate of profit would be below the usual rate of yield on investments obtainable elsewhere. The project was found not profitable and was abandoned. Another enterprising company bought up the land and houses along the proposed Tube line and was then able to build the line. Although the receipts from the passenger traffic would not pay a sufficient rate of profit, the capital appreciation on the houses and land more than made up the deficiency. Thus the project was realised; the Tube line was built. The problem is: Is it desirable—i.e., does it lend to an optimum allocation of resources and maximisation of national income—that this form of capital gain (external economy) be included as an item in the calculus of profitability, or is it not? Allyn Young hints that it is not desirable because the capital appreciation of houses and land along the Tube line due to an influx of people from other districts has an uncompensated counterpart in a capital depreciation of houses and land in districts out of which people moved into the Tube-line district. Agricultural land in Eastern and South-Eastern Europe will, however, not depreciate when the agrarian excess of population moves out. In this case external economies should be included in the calculus of profitability.

• • •

"There is a minimum level of resources that must be devoted to . . . a development program if it is to have any chance of success. Launching a country into self-sustaining growth is a little like getting an airplane off the ground. There is a critical ground speed which must be passed before the craft can become airborne. . . ."[1] Proceeding "bit by bit" will not add up in its effects to the sum total of the single bits. A minimum quantum of investment is a necessary, though not sufficient, condition of success. This, in a nutshell, is the contention of the theory of the big push.

This theory seems to contradict the conclusions of the traditional static equilibrium theory and to reverse its famous motto *natura non facit saltum*. It does so for three reasons. First, it is based on a set of more realistic assumptions of certain indivisibilities and "nonappropriabilities" in the production functions even on the level of static equilibrium theory. These indivisibilities give rise to increasing returns and to technological external economies. Second, in dealing with problems of growth this theory examines the path towards equilibrium, not the conditions at a point of equilibrium only. At a point of static equilibrium net investment is zero. The theory of growth is very largely a theory of in-

vestment. Moreover, the allocation of investment—unlike the allocation of given stocks of consumer goods (equilibrium of consumption), or of producers' goods (equilibrium of production)—necessarily occurs in an imperfect market, that is, a market on which prices do not signal all the information required for an optimum solution.[2] Given an imperfect investment market, pecuniary external economies have the same effect in the theory of growth as technological external economies. They are a cause of a possible divergence between the private and the social marginal net product. Since pecuniary, unlike technological, external economies are all-pervading and frequent, the price mechanism does not necessarily put the economy on an optimum path. Therefore, additional signalling devices apart from market prices are required. Many economists, including the author, believe that these additional signals can be provided by programming. Third, in addition to the risk phenomena and imperfections characterizing the investment equilibrium, markets in under-developed countries are even more imperfect than in developed countries. The price mechanism in such imperfect markets does not provide the signals which guide a perfectly competitive economy towards an optimum position. . . .

Indivisibilities of inputs, processes, or outputs give rise to increasing returns, that is, economies of scale, and may require a high optimum size of a firm. This is not a very important obstacle to development since with some exceptions (for instance in Central America) there is usually sufficient demand, even in small, poor countries, for at least one optimum scale firm in many industries. There may be room, however, only for one or a few firms with the obvious danger of monopolistic markets.

As Allyn Young pointed out, increasing returns accrue to a firm not only with the growth of its size but also with the growth of

[1]Massachusetts Institute of Technology, Center for International Studies, *The Objectives of United States Economic Assistance Programs,* Washington, D.C., 1957, p. 70.

[2]See P. N. Rosenstein-Rodan, "Programming in Theory and in Italian Practice," in Massachusetts Institute of Technology, Center for International Studies, *Investment Criteria and Economic Growth,* Cambridge, Mass., 1955.

the industry and with the growth of the industrial system as a whole. Greater specialization and better use of resources become possible when growth helps to overcome indivisibilities generating pecuniary external economies. The range of increasing returns seems to be very wide indeed.[3]

Social overhead capital is the most important instance of indivisibility and hence of external economies on the supply side. Its services are indirectly productive and become available only after long gestation periods. Its most important products are investment opportunities created in other industries. Social overhead capital comprises all those basic industries like power, transport, or communications which must precede the more quickly yielding, directly productive investments and which constitute the framework or infrastructure and the overhead costs of the economy as a whole. Its installations are characterized by a sizeable initial lump and low variable costs. Since the minimum size in these basic industries is large, excess capacity will be unavoidable over the initial period in under-developed countries.[4] In addition, there is also an irreducible minimum industry mix of different public utilities, so that an under-developed country will have to invest between 30–40 per cent of its total investment in these channels. Since over-all vision is required as well as a correct appraisal of future development, programming is undoubtedly required in this lumpy field. Normal market mechanisms will not provide an optimum supply.

Social overhead capital is characterized by four indivisibilities. First, it is indivisible (irreversible) in time. It must precede other directly productive investments. Second, its equipment has high minimum durability. Lesser durability is either technically impossible or much less efficient. For this and other reasons it is very lumpy. Third, it has long gestation periods. Fourth, an irreducible minimum social overhead capital industry mix is a condition for getting off the dead-end.

Because of these indivisibilities and because services of social overhead capital cannot be imported, a high initial investment in social overhead capital must either precede or be known to be certainly available in order to pave the way for additional more quickly yielding directly productive investments. This indivisibility of social overhead capital constitutes one of the main obstacles to development of under-developed countries.

Relatively few investments are made in the small market of an under-developed country. If all investment projects were independent (which they are not) and if their number grew, the risk of each investment project would decline by simple actuarial rules. The lower marginal risk of each investment dose (or project) would lead to either higher or cheaper credit facilities and these would thus constitute internal economies. In reality, however, various investment decisions are not independent. Investment projects have high risks because of uncertainty as to whether their products will find a market.

Let us restate our old example, at first for a closed economy. If a hundred workers who were previously in disguised unemployment (so that the marginal productivity of their labour was equal to zero) in an underdeveloped country are put into a shoe factory, their wages will constitute additional income. If the newly employed workers spend all of their additional income on the shoes they produce, the shoe factory will find a market and will succeed. In fact, however, they will not spend all of their additional income on shoes.

[3]The capital-output ratio in the United States has fallen over the last eighty years from around 4:1 to around 3:1, while income per head, wage-rates, and the relative importance of heavy industry were rising. This is due to technical progress (change in production functions), increasing returns on balance (increasing returns prevailing over decreasing returns), and to the rising demand for labour-intensive services characteristic of high-income economies. It is my conviction that increasing returns played a considerable part in it.

[4]We may distinguish in fact between the developmental social overhead capital which provides for a hoped for but uncertain future demand and the rehabilitation social overhead capital which caters to an unsatisfied demand of the past. The first with its excess capacity will necessarily have a big sectoral capital-output ratio (10–15:1); the second, through breaking bottlenecks, has a certain high indirect productivity and a much lower capital-output ratio.

There is no easy solution of creating an additional market in this way. The risk of not finding a market reduces the incentive to invest, and the shoe factory investment project will probably be abandoned. Let us vary the example. Instead of putting a hundred previously unemployed workers in one shoe factory, let us put ten thousand workers in one hundred factories and farms which between them will produce the bulk of the wage-goods on which the newly employed workers will spend their wages. What was not true in the case of one single shoe factory will become true for the complementary system of one hundred factories and farms. The new producers will be each other's customers and will verify Says' Law by creating an additional market. The complementarity of demand will reduce the risk of not finding a market. Reducing such interdependent risks naturally increases the incentives to invest. . . .

A high minimum quantum of investment requires a high volume of savings, which is difficult to achieve in low income, under-developed countries. There is a way out of this vicious circle. In the first stage when income is increased due to an increase in investment which mobilizes additional latent resources, mechanisms must be provided which assure that in the second stage the marginal rate of saving is very much higher than the average rate of saving. Adam Smith's dictum that frugality is a virtue and prodigality a vice has to be adapted to a situation of growing income. Economic history does not show that the proportion saved from the increase in income was higher than the previous average rate of saving.

A zero (or very low) price elasticity of the supply of saving and a high income elasticity of saving thus constitute the third indivisibility.

These three indivisibilities and the external economies to which they give rise, plus the external economies of training labour, form the characteristic pattern of models of growth of under-developed countries.

The economic factors discussed so far give only the necessary, but not the sufficient, conditions of growth. A big push seems to be required to jump over the economic obstacles to development. There may be finally a phenomenon of indivisibility in the vigour and drive required for a successful development policy. Isolated and small efforts may not add up to a sufficient impact on growth. An atmosphere of development may only arise with a minimum speed or size of investment. Our knowledge of psychology is far too deficient to theorize about this phenomenon. This does not make it a less important factor. It may well constitute the difference between necessary and sufficient conditions for success.

VI.A.2. Critique of the "Big Push" Argument*

. . .[T]he theories I am considering have several characteristics which warrant their being grouped together. For one thing, these theories are generally strongly interventionist, at least so far as concerns the assumption

*From Howard S. Ellis, "Accelerated Investment as a Force in Economic Development," *Quarterly Journal of Economics,* November 1958, pp. 486, 491–5. Reprinted by permission.

of responsibility by the state for a greatly increased rate of saving, and—extending out from this basis according to the predilections of the individual writer—to more or less, and generally more, control (and sometimes operation) of the specific lines of investment and production. Secondly, these "big push" theorists usually consider manufacture as inherently superior to primary production as a vehicle of development. These two characteristics are so general that I shall terminate the list with these alone for greater emphasis; but it would be tempting to point to the frequency also of an inflationary bias in writings of this sort, to autarkical leanings and to a fondness for general equilibrium planning as implied by linear or nonlinear programming. But the interventionist and other features of these theories, upon which I shall want to comment later, are their overtones rather than their substance.

The substantive bases for an accelerated rate of investment through state intervention are principally three: a demographic argument, a line of reasoning involving the propensity to consume, (or to save), and thirdly, conclusions reached from the technical discontinuities or "lumpiness" of investment. Let me say clearly in advance that in no case do I reject the reasoning completely; but that in all cases I attach much greater weight than do the proponents of these theories to the limits of possible gain, to the risks and costs of the proposed line of action, and to the merits of alternative policies. . . .

The chief basis upon which the "big push" of investment has been justified, since its original enunciation by Paul Rosenstein-Rodan a decade and a half ago, has been the possibility of realizing extensive external economies, and this ground is still a favorite with nearly all writers of this persuasion. But the great offset to the possibility that domestic development programs should give rise to further external economies has been definitely set forth by Professor Viner: foreign trade makes available to the developing country the much more substantial economies realized upon world markets, independently of home investment.[1] This fact is now recognized by Professor Rosenstein. But he fails to give overt recognition to the further fact adduced by Viner that the newly developing countries nowadays are chiefly primary producers, and, as such, investment for exports and for marginal import substitutes, where external economies are presumably negligible, occupies a very large part of total investment. For this entire sector, the "big push" loses its specific justification from external economies.

We are left then with that portion of production for the domestic market which does not substitute for imports. Still, this can be a very substantial field, embracing purely local consumer goods production and most public utilities—transportation, communication, power, water and sewerage facilities, and the like. Even here, however, there are limits to potential external economies. Viner points out that certain investments—presumably in the case of fairly inelastic demand—are cost-reducing rather than output-expanding. Since external economies depend upon expansion of output in the initial industry, they become negligible for this category of investment. I should like to call attention to two further limitations of considerable significance. In the field of purely domestic goods, a large fraction will be personal services and very light industry (a good deal of food and raiment production) in which the "chunkiness" of fixed investment is unimportant because fixed investment is itself a small fraction of costs. Since external economies are simply internal economies in adjacent industries, their significance is correspondingly small in these cases. It is furthermore worth remembering that, in the case of public utilities, potential external economies do not pertain to the cost of the equipment of these industries if it can be more cheaply imported.

Taken together, all of these limitations need not entirely remove the possibility of external economies. But they are neither as universal as often supposed nor, when they actually exist, as substantial. Furthermore and finally, though their existence does increase the productivity of the economy for given magnitudes of investment, they do not constitute a reason for a *concentration of investment in point of time* if—as would appear probable in any but the smallest countries—the "chunkiness" of individual investments levels out to a fairly full utilization of capacities in the aggregate for all capital facilities

[1]Jacob Viner, "Stability and Progress: the Poorer Countries' Problem," First Congress of the International Economic Association, Rome, September 6–11, 1956; mimeographed paper, pp. 27–31. [Reprinted in Douglas Hague (ed.), *Stability and Progress in the World Economy*, New York, 1958.]

together. This is a decidedly relevant consideration if "accelerated investment" is taken, not as simply synonymous with more investment continually, but as a "big push" followed by a lower rate.

Beyond its substantive theoretical basis in the population, savings, and external economies arguments, the doctrine of accelerated rates of investment has overtones for policy which its proponents, I am sure, would not be content to have ignored. One of these is the predilection for manufacturing over agricultural and other primary industries. In part this predilection may simply reflect a sentimental desire to see the country "independent" of its neighbors, particularly the richer ones; but in part it may rest on rational arguments, such as the improvement in labor morale which is supposed to attend factory production, the cultural and demographic effects of large cities, which are supposed to be favorable to economic progress, and the risks of primary production from the fluctuations of world markets. On the other hand, agricultural and primary types of production have in their favor that they utilize the relatively abundant factors of land and labor and economize capital; that characteristically in the less developed countries they provide two-thirds or more of the national income; and that, by the same token, they supply the chief wherewithal for industrial imports and investment in general.

It would scarcely seem necessary at the present stage of the debate concerning economic development to say that the merits of investment in agriculture versus industry have to be settled according to the peculiarities of each country. By consequence, whatever merits may inhere in crash programs of investment may just as well be associated with agriculture—irrigation, drainage, transportation facilities, reform of fragmented landholdings, etc.,—as with building industrial plants; in particular cases, indeed, more so.

Somewhat similar reflections would be germane to the penchant of the "big push" economists for planning, state direction of investment, and extensive controls. Linear programming, for example, is essentially an in-formation service, and the benefits of its information may just as well be made available to private as to public entrepreneurs. In and of itself, linear programming does not supply any rationale for accelerated investment. If it should appear desirable to supplement private voluntary savings by the fiscal arm of the state, the funds can be lent to private firms. The theoretical underpinning of accelerated investment programs pertains to a *rate* of investment, and not necessarily to government controlled investment. Ordinary economic motivations of the individual and the firm are a powerful engine of economic progress. It would be regrettable if the economists of the free world created an impression to the contrary.

What, in conclusion, may be said of the general merits of the "big push" philosophy of economic development? As a starting point for development some kind of impulse is of course, necessary; a change from stagnation is not likely to come by almost imperceptible degrees. Economic historians and cultural anthropologists have pointed to various prime movers in economic change: to the roles of the foreign trader and foreign capital, to immigration and the transfer of techniques, to the process of technical innovation itself, to cultural change, and to political revolution. Among these, intensive programs of state investment, as in the Japanese and Russian cases, should certainly take their place. But they are by no means the only or even the chief channel through which development can be achieved; and the demographic advantages, the capital accumulation, and the external economies to be expected from crash programs of government investment can easily be overrated.

A statistical summary of recent economic development throughout the world by John H. Adler reaches the important conclusion, among others, that "a relatively low level of investment 'pays off' well in the form of additional output."[2] The author emphasizes this conclusion most sharply in connection with

[2]John H. Adler, "World Economic Growth—Retrospect and Prospects," *Review of Economics and Statistics,* Aug. 1956, p. 279; cf. also p. 283.

India and Pakistan; but the chief reason for this conclusion, the prevailing low capital-output ratio, is also characteristic of many other of the less developed countries of Asia and Latin America as his statistics reveal. Thus it appears that it is far from generally true that a massive injection of capital is a precondition of growth.

A general weakness of the "big push" doctrine is that it frequently ignores the conditions for *evoking* the investment to which it ascribes such potency in the general picture of development, as well as neglecting the conditions under which investments, once made, can be fruitful. It is through the assumption of a *deus ex machina*, the state, which does all or most of the investing, that this theory is able to avoid the problems of securing not only the saving, but also the willingness to undergo risk, which is implied in investment. And it is only through a singular narrowness that the theory often implies that it tells the whole story of the successful operation of the economy, once the investment is made.

In point of fact, the conditions for the evoking of private investment and the conditions for the profitable use of capital are largely the same. I should place high upon this list the existence of stable and honest government, the absence of inflation, and the accessibility of the economy to the gains of foreign trade and commerce. But other factors, such as the improvement of general and technical education, the amelioration of agriculture (which bulks large in nearly all low-income countries), and progress along the family-limitation front would seem to be equally critical. Taken together, or in some cases even singly, we would seem to have identified a number of factors in economic progress which could outweigh a burst of state-engineered investmenet.

Some food for thought concerning programs of intensive investment would seem to be offered by certain points made recently by Simon Kuznets. His statistical and historical studies lead to the conclusion that "current international differences in *per capita* income are congealed effects of past differences in the rate of growth of *per capita* income." How far would it be necessary to go back into the history of the more advanced countries to reach levels comparable to the *per capita* incomes of the currently less developed countries? The answer is that we should have to go back about ten decades to reach the current income level of Latin American and about fifteen decades for that of Africa and Asia.[3] Thus, even at a very early stage in the industrialization of Western Europe, per capita incomes were probably as high as in Latin American today and certainly higher than in Asia and Africa. The economic development of the most advanced countries, at least, scarcely seems to be the result of crash programs.

[3]Simon Kuznets, "Quantitative Aspects of the Economic Growth of Nations," in *Economic Development and Cultural Change*, October 1956; see especially pp. 23–5.

VI.A.3. Linkage Effects and Industrialization *

[T]wo inducement mechanisms may be considered to be at work within the directly productive activities (DPA) sector:

*From Albert O. Hirschman, *The Strategy of Economic Development*, New Haven, Yale University Press, 1958, pp. 100–4, 109–13. Reprinted by permission.

1. The input-provision, derived demand, or *backward linkage effects*, i.e., every nonprimary economic activity, will induce attempts to supply through domestic production the inputs needed in that activity.

2. The output-utilization or *forward linkage effects*, i.e., every activity that does not by

its nature cater exclusively to final demands, will induce attempts to utilize its outputs as inputs in some new activities.

Development policy must attempt to enlist these well-known backward and forward effects; but it can do so only if there is some knowledge as to how different economic activities "score" with respect to these effects. Ordinarily economists have been content with general references to the advantages of external economies, complementarities, cumulative causation, etc. But no systematic effort has been made to describe how the development path ought to be modified so as to maximize these advantages even though the existence of input-output statistics supplies us with a few tools for an analysis of this kind.

First, a further note on the linkage concept itself. What do we imply when we speak of the linkage effects emanating from industry A toward industy B? Language can be quite ambiguous here, for we may have in mind the potential *importance* of the linkage effect in terms of, say, the net output of the new industries that might be called forth; or we may mean the *strength* of the effect, i.e., the probability that these industries will actually come into being. The total effect could be measured by the sum of the products of these two elements; in other words, if the establishment of industry W may lead, through linkage effects, to the establishment of n additional industries with net outputs equal to x_i ($i = 1, 2, \ldots n$) and if the probability that each one of these industries will actually be set up as a result of the establishment of industry W is p_i ($i = 1, 2, \ldots n$), then the total linkage effect of industry W is equal to

$$\sum_1^n x_i p_i$$

The probabilities can be interpreted as measuring the strength of the stimulus that is set up. For backward linkage, this strength can be roughly measured as follows: suppose industry W requires annual inputs of $y_1, y_2 \ldots y_n$ and suppose that the minimum economic size (in terms of annual productive capacity) of firms that would turn out these in-

puts is equal to $a_1, a_2 \ldots a_n$; then the strength of the stimulus or the probability that the setting up of industry W will lead to the setting up of industries producing the inputs is equal to the ratio of the y's to the a's.[1] Minimum economic size is not a technical concept, but is defined in economic terms relative to normal profits and efficient foreign suppliers. In other words, it is the size at which the domestic firm will be able both to secure normal profits and to compete with existing foreign suppliers, taking into account locational advantages *and* disadvantages as well as, perhaps, some infant industry protection. In this way comparative cost conditions are automatically taken into account.[2]

In the case of forward linkage, an interpretation of the p's is less straightforward. The concept of economic size is not helpful here, since the size of the market for the industries that might be brought into being through forward linkage does not depend on their suppliers. A clue can perhaps be found in the importance of the articles produced by industry W as inputs for the output of the to-be-linked industry. If these inputs are a very small fraction of the industry's eventual output, then their domestic availability is not likely to be an important factor in calling forth that industry. If, on the other hand, these articles are subjected to few further manufacturing operations, then the strength of the forward stimulus is likely to be substantial, provided demand is sufficient to justify domestic production.

In these cases, then, importance and strength—the x's and the p's—of the linkage

---

[1] The ratio is to be defined as having a ceiling of 1, i.e., the value of the ratio is equal to unity, whenever the y's are equal to or *larger than* the a's. Note also that the y's are equivalent to the gross output of the new industries or firms in physical terms whereas the x's are their net outputs in value terms.

[2] Data on the economic size of plants in different industries would be the starting point for determining minimum economic size in different countries. Research in this area in relation to economic development is surprisingly scant, except for the pioneering article of K. A. Bohr, "Investment Criteria for Manufacturing Industries in Underdeveloped Countries," *Review of Economics and Statistics*, Vol. 36, (May 1954), pp. 157–66.

effect are inversely correlated. Industries where the x's are small and the p's large are sometimes aptly called "satellite" industries. They are almost unfailingly established in the wake of industry W but are of minor importance in comparison to that industry. Thus defined, satellite industries can be established through backward or forward linkage. In the case of cement, for instance, the manufacture of multi-wall bags for packing purposes represents backward linkage while the establishment of a cement block industry represents satellite formation through forward linkage. A satellite industry usually has the following characteristics:

1. It enjoys a strong location advantage from proximity to the master industry;
2. it uses as principal input an output or by-product of the master industry without subjecting it to elaborate transformation, or its principal output is a—usually minor—input of the master industry; and
3. its minimum economic size is smaller than that of the master industry.

While satellite industries are almost certain to be established once the master industry is in place, the establishment of industry W also results in stimuli toward the setting up of nonsatellite industries. In these cases, the strength of the stimulus is infinitely weaker, but the stake is far bigger. Examples of such a situation are the stimulus that the setting up of a multi-wall bag factory gives toward the creation of pulp and paper industry or, for the case of forward linkage, the stimulus given by the establishment of an iron and steel industry to all the metal-fabrication industries. Here the establishment of one industry is a contributing factor which by itself is quite unlikey to result in the creation of the others; but when we speak of external economies and complementarities, we think at least as much of these uncertain linkages as of the far more certain, but also far less significant, satellites with which any industry of a certain size surrounds itself. The weakness of the stimulus in the case of nonsatellites can be explained by the absence of the three factors that define satellites. Linkage is

reduced to the fact that an input of the newly established industry is an output of the to-be-created industry or vice versa, but the established industry would not be the principal customer or supplier of the to-be-created industry; in fact, particularly in cases of backward linkage, minimum economic size of the to-be-created industry would frequently be larger than that of the industry where the linkage originates.[3]

In spite of the importance of the nonsatellite type of linkage, it seems necessary to provide for some arbitrary cut-off point for small probabilities. It is all very well to say that the establishment of a brewery sends out a stimulus in the direction of a paper industry because of the labels needed for the beer bottles, but by itself this stimulus is not likely ever to lead to the setting up of a paper mill. Thus, if we consider *in isolation* the linkage effects exclusively of the beer industry on further industrial or agricultural development, we should consider only those stimuli whose probability exceeds a certain critical value, say one-half.[4]

If we proceed in this way, the joint linkage effects of two industries, say beer and cement, considered as a unit, are likely to be larger than the sum of their individual linkage effects, since some of the xp products which are omitted in computing the individual effects because the p's are below the critical value will exceed this value if added together for both industries. Here we have an argument in favor of multiple development that we would consider convincing were it not that our principal argument against it is con-

[3]To the extent that the minimum economic size of an industry is larger the farther away one moves from the finished consumer or producer goods stage. This is, of course, by no means universally true as is shown, e.g., by the large minimum size of the motor vehicles makers.

[4]It is a good rule of thumb that an industry can properly be established in an underdeveloped but developing country as soon as existing demand is equal to one-half of the economic size of the plant as defined above. The additional demand needed to justify the investment can be expected to come from the growth of existing demand and from the development of new demand through forward linkage, once the plant is in existence.

cerned with its feasibility rather than with its desirability.

The fact that the linkage effects of two industries viewed in combination are larger than the sum of the linkage effects of each industry in isolation helps to account for the cumulative character of development. When industry *A* is first set up, its satellites will soon follow; but when industry *B* is subsequently established, this may help to bring into existence not only its own satellites but some firms which neither *A* nor *B* in isolation could have called forth. And with *C* coming into play some firms will follow that require the combined stimuli not only of *B* and *C* but of *A, B,* and *C.* This mechanism may go far toward explaining the *acceleration* of industrial growth which is so conspicuous during the first stages of a country's development.

BACKWARD LINKAGE AT WORK

The lack of interdependence and linkage is of course one of the most typical characteristics of underdeveloped economies. If we had homogeneous input-output statistics for all countries, it would certainly be instructive to rank countries according to the proportion of intersectoral transactions to total output; it is likely that this ranking would exhibit a close correlation with both income per capita and with the percentage of the population occupied in manufacturing.

Agriculture in general, and subsistence agriculture in particular, are of course characterized by the scarcity of linkage effects. By definition, all *primary* production should exclude any substantial degree of backward linkage although the introduction of modern methods does bring with it considerable outside purchases of seeds, fertilizers, insecticides, and other current inputs, not to speak of machines and vehicles. We may say that the more primitive the agricultural and mining activities, the more truly primary they are.

Forward linkage effects are also weak in agriculture and mining. A large proportion of agricultural output is destined directly for consumption or export; another important part is subjected to some processing industries that can be characterized as satellite inasmuch as the value added by them to the agricultural product (milling of wheat, rice, coffee, etc.) is small relative to the value of the product itself. Only a comparatively small fraction of total agricultural output of underdeveloped countries receives elaborate processing, which usually takes place abroad.

The case for inferiority of agriculture to manufacturing has most frequently been argued on grounds of comparative productivity. While this case has been shown not to be entirely convincing, agriculture certainly stands convicted on the count of its lack of direct stimulus to the setting up of new activities through linkage effects: the superiority of manufacturing in this respect is crushing. This may yet be the most important reason militating against any complete specialization of underdeveloped countries in primary production.

The grudge against what has become known as the "enclave" type of development is due to this ability of primary products from mines, wells, and plantations to slip out of a country without leaving much of a trace in the rest of the economy. Naturally hostility to the profits earned by foreign companies plays an important role in such attitudes; but the absence of direct linkage effects of primary production for export lends these views a plausibility that they do not have in the case of foreign investment in manufacturing. I say plausibility rather than validity, for while as such the primary production activities leading to exports may exert few developmental effects, they do finance imports which can become very powerful agents of development as we shall see below.

Since interdependence in the input-output sense is so largely the result of industrialization, we must now attempt to trace the various ways in which manufacturing and the accompanying linkage effects make their appearance. In this connection, we shall utilize another one of Chenery's findings, namely that more than ninety percent of all input-output flows can usually be arranged in a triangular pattern. Circularity—i.e., the fact that coal is needed for steel-making and steel for coal mining—is undoubtedly present in the structure of a country's production, but apparently to a much smaller degree than would be suspected upon looking at an input-output table that has not been "triangularized." In other words, there is no compelling *technological* requirement for the simultaneous setting up of various industries, an interesting complement to our case against the existence of such a requirement on economic grounds.

In a triangular arrangement of the input-output matrix, there is a "last" sector whose output goes entirely to final demand and which takes in inputs from a number of other sectors; the second-to-last sector sells its output to final demand and to the last sector and buys inputs from some or all other sectors except from the "last"; and so on, until we come to the "first" sector whose output goes to all the subsequent sectors and possibly also to final demand, but which does not use any inputs from other sectors.

Industrialization can of course *start* only with industries that deliver to final demand, since *ex hypothesi* no market exists as yet for intermediate goods. This means that it will be possible to set up only two kinds of industries:

1. those that transform domestic or imported primary products into goods needed by final demands;
2. those that transform imported semimanufactures into goods needed by final demands.

To the pioneer industrial countries only the first course was open, and this explains the towering importance of a few industries (textiles, iron and steel, pottery) during the early stages of the Industrial Revolution. In today's underdeveloped countries the textiles, food processing, and construction materials industries based on local materials are still of great importance, but, to a very significant extent, industrialization is penetrating these countries in the second manner, through plants that perform the "final touches" on almost-finished *industrial* products imported from abroad. Examples are the many con-

verting, assembly, and mixing plants, the pharmaceutical laboratories, the metal-fabricating industries, and many others. This trend has many advantages: it often provides an investment outlet for small amounts of capital that might not easily become available for ventures which require the pooling of the resources of many investors, and it makes it possible to start industrial undertakings without the heavy risk that comes in underdeveloped countries from having to rely on the output of unreliable domestic producers.

In this way underdeveloped countries often set up "last" industries first—i.e., these are "last" industries considering the input-output flow of the advanced countries: what in these countries are inputs from the other sectors are replaced in underdeveloped countries by imports. Such industries could be termed "enclave import industries," in analogy to the enclave export activities that were previously mentioned. For here again we have an undertaking that at least in its beginning is antiseptically linkage-free; materials are imported from abroad, some value is added to them through mixing, assembling, packaging, etc., and the finished product is rushed to the final consumers. The enclave nature of these industries is sometimes emphasized by the location of the plant at a point as close as possible to the most convenient port of arrival of the imported materials, and again this type of venture has proven particularly attractive to foreign capital—many of the branch plants owned by foreign corporations specialize in this kind of operation.

But there is a considerable difference between the enclave export and enclave import activities. The former have great trouble in breaking out of the enclave situation. Usually some forward linkage effects can be utilized—ores and cane sugar can be refined before being shipped. But the scope for such operations is strictly limited. With respect to import enclave industries, the situation is radically different: they set up backward linkage effects of practically infinite range and depth.

In fact, much of the recent economic history of some rapidly developing underdeveloped countries can be written in terms of industrialization working its way backward from the "final touches" stage to domestic production of intermediate, and finally to that of basic, industrial materials. In this way, industrialization has even proven to be a powerful stimulus to the development of agriculture. By providing a reliable market, processing industries originally based on imported agricultural materials such as cotton textiles and beer have stimulated in Colombia the domestic production of cotton and barley. . . .

In most of these cases, imported goods have been gradually replaced by domestic production which has been called forth by the existence of a large and stable market. Of considerable importance are the backward linkage effects that are the combined result of the existence of several "last stage" industries. The minimum economic size of many intermediate and basic industries is such that in small markets a variety of user industries needs to be established before their combined demand justifies a substitution of imports of intermediate and basic goods by domestic production.

Comment

Albert O. Hirschman has broadened his linkages approach in an important paper, "A Generalized Linkage Approach to Development, with Special Reference to Staples," in Manning Nash (ed.), *Essays on Economic Development and Cultural Change in Honor of Bert F. Hoselitz* (1977). This paper goes beyond production linkages of the input-output character to consider consumption and fiscal linkages. The analysis is applied to export-led growth based on staple exports. See also selections VI.B.3 and VI.B.4 for related discussions of export-led development.

VI.A.4. The Case for Balanced Growth*

It is no longer so certain that the less developed countries can rely on economic growth being induced from the outside through an expansion of world demand for their exports of primary commodities. In these circumstances reliance on induced expansion through international trade cannot provide a solution to the problem of economic development. It is not surprising therefore that countries should be looking for other solutions. It is important to keep these things in mind, because they form the background to

*From Ragnar Nurkse, "The Conflict Between 'Balanced Growth' and International Specialization," *Lectures on Economic Development,* Faculty of Economics (Istanbul University) and Faculty of Political Sciences (Ankara University), Istanbul, 1958, pp. 170–76. Reprinted by permission.

the case for balanced growth which is now so much in vogue.

The circumstances indicated do not apply to all underdeveloped countries today: Kuwait and perhaps Iraq have nothing to worry about. But in so far as these cicumstances do exist in reality it is clear that the poorer countries, even if they are only to keep pace with the richer, to say nothing about catching up with them, must expand production for their own domestic markets or for each others' markets. Now domestic markets are limited because of mass poverty due to low productivity. Private investment in any single industry considered by itself is discouraged by the smallness of the existing market.

The limits set by the small size of the local market for manufactured goods are so plainly visible to any individual businessman that we are fully justified in taking for granted conditions of imperfect competition, and not the pure atomistic competition which even in advanced economies does not exist to any significant degree, outside the economics textbooks.

The solution seems to be a balanced pattern of investment in a number of different industries, so that people working more productively, with more capital and improved techniques, become each others' customers. In the absence of vigorous upward shifts in world demand for exports of primary products, a low income country through a process of diversified growth can seek to bring about upward shifts in domestic demand schedules by means of increased productivity and therefore increased real purchasing power. In this way, a pattern of mutually supporting investments in different lines of production can enlarge the size of the market and help to fill the vacuum in the domestic economy of low income areas. This, in brief, is the notion of balanced growth.

Isolated advance is not impossible. A solitary process of investment and increased productivity in one industry alone will certainly have favorable repercussions elsewhere in the economy. There is no denying that through the normal incentives of the price mechanism other industries will be induced to advance also. But this may be a snail's pace of progress. The price mechanism works but it may work too slowly. That is one reason for the frequently observed fact that foreign direct investments in extractive export industries have created high productivity islands in low income areas and have had little impact on the level of productivity in the domestic economy.

Within the domestic economy itself, advance in one direction, say in industry A, tends to induce advance in B as well. But if it is only a passive reaction to the stimulus coming from A, the induced advance of B may be slow and uncertain. And B's slowness and passiveness will in turn slow down and discourage the initial advance of A. The ap-

plication of capital to one industry alone may therefore be subject to sharply diminishing returns. As a way of escape from slowness if not from stagnation, the balanced growth principle envisages autonomous advance along a number of lines more or less simultaneously.

Viewed in this way, balanced growth is a means of accelerated growth. Some economists treat the problem of achieving balanced growth as quite separate from the problem of speeding up the rate of advance in a backward economy. I admit that this may be a convenient distinction to draw on other grounds. But in my view, balanced growth is first and foremost a means of getting out of a rut, a means of stepping up the rate of growth when the external forces of advance through trade expansion and foreign capital are sluggish or inoperative.

In the existing state of affairs in low income areas the introduction of capital-using techniques of production in any single industry is inhibited by the small size of the market. Hence the weakness of private investment incentives in such areas. The balanced growth principle points to a way out of the deadlock. New enterprises set up in different industries create increased markets for each other, so that in each of them the installation or capital equipment becomes worth while. As Marshall said, "The efficiency of specialized machinery . . . is but one condition of its economic use; the other is that sufficient work should be found to keep it well employed" (*Principles,* p. 264). The techniques that have been developed in production for mass markets in advanced countries are not well adapted and sometimes not adaptable at all to output on a more limited scale. It is easy to see that the relationship between the size of the market and the amount of investment required for efficient operation is of considerable importance for the theory of balanced growth.

Frequently the objection is made: But why use machinery? Why adopt capital-using methods in areas where labor is cheap and plentiful? Why not accordingly employ techniques that are labor-intensive instead of capital-intensive?

The answer is obvious. As an adaptation to existing circumstances, including the existing factor proportions, the pursuit of labor-intensive production methods with a view of economizing capital may be perfectly correct. But the study of economic development must concern itself with changing these circumstances, not accepting them as they are. What is wanted is progress, not simply adaptation to present conditions. And progress depends largely on the use of capital, which in turn depends on adequate and growing markets, which in the absence of a strongly rising world demand for the country's exports means a diversified output expansion for domestic use.

Reference has been made to the importance of autonomous advance in a number of mutually supporting lines of production. How is this achieved? Autonomous advance in different branches simultaneously may come about through the infectious influence of business psychology, through the multiplier effects of investment anywhere which can create increased money demand elsewhere, or through deliberate control and planning by public authorities. According to some writers the balanced growth argument implies that the market mechanism is eliminated and that investment must be effected according to a coordinated plan. This opinion, which is widely held, seems to be dubious. There are many important reasons for government planning, but this is not necessarily one of them. As a means of creating inducements to invest, balanced growth can be said to be relevant primarily to a private enterprise system. State investment can and often does go ahead without any market incentives. Planning authorities can apply capital, if they have any, wherever they may choose, though if they depart too much from balance as dictated by income elasticities of demand they will end by creating white elephants and intolerable disproportionalities in the structure of production. It is private investment that is attracted by markets and that needs the inducement of growing markets. It is here that the element of mutual support is so useful and, for rapid growth, indispensable.

It is important to note that the doctrine under consideration is not itself concerned with the question of where the capital is to be found, for all the balanced investment which it envisages. I have tried to make it clear in my discussion of it that the argument is primarily relevant to the problem of the demand for capital; it takes an increased supply of capital for granted. In my presentation balanced growth is an exercise in economic development with unlimited supplies of capital, analogous to Professor Lewis's celebrated exercise in development with unlimited labor supplies.

In reality, of course, capital supplies are not unlimited. It may be that the case for state investment stems chiefly from the fact that capital is scarce and that government efforts are necessary to mobilize all possible domestic sources of saving. Measures to check the expansion of consumer demand may be necessary to make resources available for investment but may at the same time weaken the private inducement to invest. This is a famous dilemma to which Malthus first called attention in his *Principles of Political Economy*. A case for state investment may clearly arise if and when the mobilization of capital supplies discourages private investment activity and so destroys the demand for capital. But this case is entirely separate from the principle of balanced growth as such. It might only be added that the capital supply problem alone creates a strong presumption against relying on the indiscriminate use of import restriction which may reduce a country's real income and therefore make it harder to increase the flow of saving.

Elsewhere I have tried to explain how the balanced growth idea is related to the classical law of markets. Supply creates its own demand, provided that supply is properly distributed among different commodities in accordance with consumers' wants. An increase in consumable output must provide a balanced diet. Each industry must advance along an expansion path determined by the income elasticity of consumer demand for its product. This simple idea must be the starting point in any expansion of production of domestic markets in the less developed countries, in so far as external demand conditions do not favor the traditional pattern of "growth through trade." Yet, as often happens in economic discussion, critics have tended to dismiss this idea either as a dangerous fallacy or as an obvious platitude. It is hardly necessary to add that the pattern of consumable output cannot be expected to remain the same in successive stages of development. The content of a balanced diet of a man with a thousand dollars a year will differ from that of a man with a hundred dollars.

The relation between agriculture and manufacturing industry offers the clearest and simplest case of balance needed for economic growth. In a country where the peasantry is incapable of producing a surplus of food above its own subsistence needs there is little or no incentive for industry to establish itself: there is not a sufficient market for manufactured goods. Conversely, agricultural improvements may be inhibited by lack of a market for farm products if the non-farm sector of the economy is backward or undeveloped. Each of the two sectors must try to move forward. If one remains passive the other is slowed down.

It is important in this connection to make a clear distinction between two concepts that are frequently confused: the marketable surplus and investible surplus of the farm sector. The farm sector's marketable surplus of farm products determines the volume of non-farm employment in manfacturing and other activities. It reflects simply the farm sector's demand for non-agricultural commodities. This is the concept that is relevant to the balanced growth principle.

An investible surplus of farm products represents an act of saving in the farm sector. It can conceivably result from a transfer of surplus labourers from the farms to capital construction projects: a food surplus may then arise through forced or voluntary saving in the farm sector for maintaining the workers engaged on capital projects. This is the concept relevant to the problem of capital supply. It is obvious that even a large marketable surplus of food need not involve any saving by the farmers. It presents a very helpful inducement, but does not in itself create the means, for capital investment outside the agricultural sector. A fuller discussion of the interrelationship between marketable and investible surpluses would take us too far from our present subject. It seemed desirable to mention the distinction here merely for the sake of conceptual clarity. So much for the relation between agriculture and industry.

Within the manufacturing field alone the case for balanced investment implies a horizontal diversification of industrial activities all pushing ahead, though naturally at varying rates. The objection can be made that such diffusion of effort and resources over many different lines of activity must mean a loss of dynamic momentum in the economy. This is possible. The dispersal of investment over a variety of consumer-goods industries can undoubtedly be carried to excess. The balanced growth principle can be and has been interpreted far too literally. Producing a little of everything is not the key to progress. The case for balanced growth is concerned with establishing a pattern of mutually supporting investments over a range of industries wide enough to overcome the frustration of isolated advance, in order precisely to create a forward momentum of growth. The particular factors that determine the optimum pattern of diversification have to do with technology, physical conditions and other circumstances that vary from country to country. There can be no standard prescription of universal applicability. We are concerned with a point of principle and cannot deal with the precise forms of its implementation in practice. Just as it is possible for manufacturing industry as a whole to languish if farmers produce too little and are too poor to buy anything from factories, so it is possible for a single line of manufacturing to fail for lack of support from other sectors in industry as well as agriculture; that is, for lack of markets.

VI.A.5. Balanced versus Unbalanced Growth*

... Before we enter upon a discussion of the merits and faults of the doctrines of balanced growth (BG) and of unbalanced growth (UG), it is necessary to clarify two questions to which the contributors to the debate have not given clear and satisfactory answers. The first question, most relevant in the present context of our discussion, concerns the role of planning; the second question [concerns] the role of supply limitations and supply inelasticities.

In the controversy the role of government (or for that matter private) planning has not always been brought out clearly. In particular, it is not always clear whether the question under consideration relates to planning or whether it relates to an attempt to explain development that takes place without planning, or with only an initial impulse of planning in the form of an investment project, while things are thereafter left to take their own course with market forces responding to demand and supply.

Nurkse thought that BG is relevant primarily to a private enterprise economy. It is (he argued) private investment that needs market inducements. In his doctrine, the choice between public and private investment and betweeen direct controls and market incentives is mainly a matter of administrative expediency. But he seems to be wrong in this. The indivisibilities assumed in BG imply the need for coordination, i.e., planning, although it would, in principle, be possible to have either private or public coordination.

UG as propounded by Hirschman is consistent with, but does not require, initial *and* continued planning. His state administrators are—or should be—subject to the same kind of pressures as private entrepreneurs. The role of the state is both to induce and to repair disequilibria. Thus state action becomes a dependent, as well as an independent, variable. But again, on closer inspection it would seem that UG, to be most effective, does require planning and preferably state planning, because no private firm may want or be able to carry the surplus capacity and the losses, and because private horizons are too narrow.

It is not surprising that both BG and UG should, to be most effective, presuppose (each a different kind of) planning, for they are both concerned with lumpy investments and complementarities. Coordination is needed in order both to get things done that otherwise would not be done, and in order to reap the rewards of complementarities. Market forces look best after adjustments that can be made in infinitesimally small steps. This is why the concept "marginal" plays such an important part in neo-classical Western economic theory. It is also one of the important differences between developed and underdeveloped countries. In the former a new profitable investment project is normally small relative to the size of existing capital equipment (however measured), relatively to new investment, and relatively to the hinterland of facilities on which it can draw. In underdeveloped countries indivisibilities are more prominent and marginal adjustments rarer for at least four reasons.

First, both the existing stock of equipment and the additions to it are small compared with those in advanced countries with comparable populations. Since plant and equipment often have to be a minimum size for technical reasons, the addition of a plant or a piece of equipment makes a greater proportionate difference both to the stock of capital and to total investment.

Second, economic development is usually directed at moving people from agriculture to industrial enterprises. This normally implies an increase in the number of indivisible units.

Third, the necessary social overhead capital and the basic structure of industry (power, steel, transport, housing, government buildings) consist of large indivisible units.

*From Paul Streeten, "Balance versus Unbalanced Growth," *The Economic Weekly,* April 20, 1963, pp. 669–71. Reprinted by permission.

Fourth, complementarities between enterprises and activities are likely to be more important in the meagre economies of underdeveloped countries, so that a given investment is more liable to require complementary and supplementary investments. Both BG and UG give rise to external economies. A cost incurred by A creates profit opportunities for B. If steps are taken to seize these opportunities at once and in one type of sequence (BG), the results will be different than if they are seized later and in a different type of sequence (UG). But there is no guarantee that A will be induced by market forces to incur these costs, indeed there is a presumption that it will not be so induced.

We next turn to the role of supply limitations and supply inelasticities in the controversy. Nurkse explicitly confined his discussion to the demand side. He assumed supplies to be available and asked what would investment have to be like to justify them? He wrote:

There is no suggestion here that, by taking care of the demand side alone, any country could, as it were, lift itself up by its bootstraps. We have been considering one particular facet of our subject. The more fundamental difficulties that lie on the supply side have so far been kept off-stage for the sake of orderly discussion.[1]

Nevertheless, the position of this chapter in his book and the emphasis laid on it have led to misinterpretations. If BG stresses *markets* as the main limitation on growth, UG in the Hirschman version stresses *decisions*. The implication of Hirschman's theory is that supplies will be forthcoming with relative ease if only the lack of decision-taking can be overcome. This shift of emphasis to an attitude, usually assumed either constant or automatically adjusted to precisely the required extent, should be welcomed. Hirschman has been charged with excessive preoccupation with *investment* decisions. Much of his book indeed focuses attention on them, but it clear that he had a wider concept in mind, as is shown by his use of the terms "de-

velopment decisions" and "developmental tasks."

Insofar as BG is concerned with the creation of markets through complementary investment projects and the inducement to invest by providing complementary markets for final goods, it stresses a problem which is rarely serious in the countries of the region. Final markets can often quite easily be created without recourse to BG, by import restrictions and, less easily, by export expansion.

On the other hand, although UG is correct in pointing to the scarcity of decision-taking in some countries, it should not be contrasted, but it should be combined with the provision of more supplies. The contrast drawn by UG between scarcity of physical resources and scarcity of decision-taking can be misleading. Those who stress resources say that decisions will be taken as soon as resources are available; those who stress decision-taking say that resources will flow freely as soon as adequate inducements to take decisions are provided. The former group of experts go out on missions and advocate high taxation in order to "set resources free," the latter recommend low taxation in order to "encourage enterprise."

Both views reflect misplaced aggregation and illegitimate isolation, two types of bias introduced by the careless use of Western concepts and models. No general formula will serve. The correct division often cuts across these categories. The question is what combination of resource policy, reform of attitudes (including "incentives") and of legal, social and cultural institutions, is necessary in a particular situation.

Moreover, the tendency of both BG and UG to underplay supply limitations diverts attention from the fact that planning must be directed as much at restricting supplies in certain directions as at *expanding* them in others. The policy package presupposes a choice of allocating limited supplies, i.e., supplies growing at a limited rate, and in response to certain stimuli, to the most important uses, combined with inducements to decisions of all kinds (not only investment de-

---

[1] *Problems of Capital Formation in Underdeveloped Countries*, pp. 30–31.

cisions). These supply limitations are considerably less important in advanced industrial countries now and were less important in the early developing phase of many now advanced countries, like Sweden or the regions of recent settlement. These countries had almost unlimited access to capital at low interest rates, a reserve of skilled labour and plentiful natural resources. Again, certain underdeveloped regions in advanced countries (Southern Italy, the South of the USA) can draw on supplies but lack development decisions.

The models developed in the BG vs. UG controversy seem to have drawn on this kind of experience from "ceilingless economies" which is relevant to South America but not to the entirely different problems of South Asia. The two important differences between, on the one hand, advanced countries now and in their development phase, and, on the other hand, the underdeveloped countries of South Asia are:

1. that investments in advanced countries can more often be treated as marginal than in underdeveloped countries, and

2. that advanced countries are and were high supply-elasticity economies with responses and institutions already adapted to economic growth.

Both doctrines have certain faults. The trouble with advocating UG is that, for countries embarking on development, unbalance is inevitable, whether they want it or not, and governments and planners do not need the admonitions of theoreticians. All investment creates unbalances because of rigidities, indivisibilities, sluggishness of response both of supply and of demand and because of miscalculations. There will be, in any case, plenty of difficulties in meeting many urgent requirements, whether of workers, technicians, managers, machines, semimanufactured products, raw materials or power and transport facilities and in finding markets permitting full utilization of equipment. Market forces will be too weak or powerless to bring about the required adjustments and unless coordinated planning of much more than investment is carried out, the invest-

ment projects will turn out to be wasteful and will be abandoned.

Insofar as unbalance does create desirable attitudes, the crucial question is not whether to create unbalance, but *what* is the *optimum* degree of unbalance, *where* to unbalance and *how much,* in order to accelerate growth; which are the "growing points," where should the spearheads be thrust, on which slope would snowballs grow into avalanches? Although nobody just said "create any old unbalance," insufficient attention has been paid to its precise composition, direction and timing.

The second weakness of UG is that the theory concentrates on stimuli to *expansion,* and tends to neglect or minimise *resistances* caused by UG. UG argues that the active sectors pull the other with them, BG that the passive sectors drag the active ones back. While the former is relevant to South America, the latter is relevant to South Asia. It would, of course, be better, as Nurkse would have liked it, if *all* sectors were active, and the wish may have been father of the thought behind these models. But the problem is how to activate them. Activation measures must take the form both of positive inducements and of resistances of resistances.

The UG model in the Hirschman version has the great merit, in comparison with many other models, of including attitudes and institutions, and in particular investment incentives, normally assumed fully adjusted to requirements, and of turning them from independent variables or constants into dependent variables. In particular Hirschman's discussion of forward and backward linkages is provocative and fruitful. It brings out the previously neglected effects of one investment on investment at earlier and later stages of production. But the doctrine underplays obstacles and resistances (also in attitudes) called into being by imbalance. Shortages create vested interests; they give rise to monopoly gains; people may get their fingers burnt by malinvestments and may get frightened by the growth of competition. The attitudes and institutions evolving through development will arouse opposition and hostility. Some of these resistances may be overcome only by state compulsion, but the governments of the "soft states" are reluctant to use force and the threat of force. Once again, the absence of this type of reaction from the models is both appropriate for Western countries and is opportune to the planners in South Asia, but it introduces a systematic bias and neglects some of the most important issues.

Turning now to BG, we have seen that its main weakness is that it is concerned with the creation of complementary domestic markets as an inducement to invest, whereas markets in the countries of the region can usually be created by import restrictions, and, where possible, export expansion. This relates to final goods and principally to consumers' goods. As far as intermediate markets are concerned, Nurkse came out in favour of UG (vertical imbalance) in his second Istanbul Lecture.[2] Social overhead investment provides the conditions and inducements for consequential direct productive investment. As for horizontal balance, he believed that the case "rests on the need for a 'balanced diet.'"[3] But he later drew a distinction be-

tween BG as a method and BG as an outcome or objective.[4] What remains of the doctrine is the emphasis on the complementarity of markets for final goods as an ultimate objective for investment incentives. But not only is absence of markets not normally a serious obstacle to development; even where it is, it is by no means the main obstacle and, in any case, balanced growth cannot always remove it.

What is sound in BG is the stress on the investment package, on the need for coordination, on the structure of an investment complex. But investment is not the only component in this package: and there is too much stress on the complementarity of final markets. What is needed is a package of policy measures containing

1. complementary investments;
2. actions to reform attitudes and institutions, including the desire to invest, but also the ability and willingness to work, (which may involve raising *consumption*), to organise and manage and in particular to administer politically;
3. a carefully thought-out timetable showing the sequence of the various measures which would be determined by technological, political and sociological factors;
4. controls checking undesirable or less desirable investments; and
5. policies designed to weaken or eliminate obstacles and inhibitions to development, including resistances induced by measures 1 to 4.

[2]R. Nurkse, *Equilibrium and Growth in the World Economy*, pp. 259–78.

[3]"The difficulty caused by the small size of the market relates to individual investment incentives in any single line of production taken by itself. At least in principle, the difficulty vanishes in the case of a more or less synchronized application of capital to a wide range of different industries. Here is an escape from the deadlock; here the result is an over-all enlargement of the market. People working with more and better tools in a number of complementary projects become each others' customers. Most industries catering for mass consumption are complementary in the sense that they provide a market for, and thus support, each other. This basic complementarity

stems, in the last analysis, from the diversity of human wants. The case for 'balanced growth' rests on the need for a 'balanced diet.'" *Problems of Capital Formation in Underdeveloped Countries, pp. 11f.*

[4]Op. cit., p. 279.

VI.B. LESSONS OF RECENT HISTORY

VI.B.1. The Industrial Achievement*

The industrialized countries' manufacturing output has grown at an unprecedented rate in the last quarter century, but the developing countries manufacturing output has grown even more rapidly. Some developing countries have built up a manufacturing sector to the point at which, though they still have relatively low income, they may be regarded as industrialized; a dozen countries are clearly semi-industrialized; most of the developing countries are well into an industrializing stage; and for the most part only very small countries with a low population are still non-industrialized.... For some, very small developing countries, as for some very small high income countries, industrialization remains a limited objective because their comparative advantages lies in other sectors.

There have been several attempts at a typology of industrialization based on the changing share of value added in manufacturing in the GDP, the proportion of value added contributed by various manufacturing branches to value added in manufacturing as a whole, value added per unit of capital and labour employed, the share of exports in manufacturing output, and of manufactured exports in total exports. These and similar indicators all contribute to an understanding of the growth of manufacturing and its role in the economy, but they have different implications in varying circumstances. Two large, traditionally agricultural countries—China and India—have each developed a highly complex and relatively sophisticated industrial structure and they should be regarded as semi-industrialized although their shares of manufacturing value added in total GDP is

*From Helen Hughes, "Industrialization and Development: A Stocktaking," UNIDO, *Industry and Development,* No. 1, 1978, pp. 5, 13–18. Reprinted by permission.

still relatively low. Exports of manufactures cannot be regarded as an index of manufacturing development although the character of manufactured exports might be expected to change with industrial development. Small "city states" such as Hong Kong and Singapore, had a high level of manufactured exports from the beginning of their industrialization process because their size required a high degree of specialization to encompass adequate economies of scale and it would be unreasonable for them to develop a "balanced" industrial structure that included all sectors.

Statistical difficulties add to the conceptual problems. Countries with heavy protection for manufacturing over-value their manufacturing output in relation to non-protected activities and to other countries with lower protection. The underpricing of agricultural production to keep down the urban cost of living similarly tends to over-value manufacturing production. The difficulties, and ensuing differences in the measurement of the value added in service industries among countries, make the use of conventional ratios of value added in manufacturing to GDP particularly prone to error. Comparing the share of value added in manufacturing to value added in commodity production may be a more useful indicator, for it eliminates both the difficulties of measuring value added in service industries and the effects of changing weights of service industries in a growing economy. It corresponds fairly closely to the share of value added in manufacturing to GDP when the ratio of manufacturing to GDP is low, but the two indicators diverge when the ratio of manufacturing is relatively high because services, having declined in relative terms in the early stages of industrialization, grow quite rapidly at the high income levels that accompany a high level of industrialization. There are many difficulties in identifying export manufacturing data, and in reconciling such data with industrial production figures. The differences in the national accounts methodologies of centrally planned eonomies and market economy countries make for serious comparison difficulties. Finally, standardization of data in United States dollars at official rates introduces distortions.

The utilization of human and physical capital is an important aspect of industrial development. The ability to adapt and to innovate is critical to industrial progress and therefore entrepreneurial, managerial and technical capacities are perhaps the most important, and most elusive, equalities in the maturing of an industrial economy. Such capacities are in much more ample supply in the industrialized countries than in the non-industrialized developing countries, but at least to date they have not been meaningfully measured, Entrepreneurship, management and technical expertise require the support of adequate labour and capital resources. The supply of labour is not homogenous. Skills and skill potential are important. Indicators of educational levels, the only generally available proxy measurements of human capital, are thus poor reflections of actual human capital.

The measurement of physical capital is no less difficult. The availability and use of electric power is a generally used measure, but again it is a poor proxy of the complex of public utility facilities required in an industrialized economy and an even poorer measure of the capital in the sense of fixed investment used in manufacturing. "Capital" remains conceptually illusive and the problems of measuring it are too well known to require elaboration.

The commercial infrastructure—banking, import-export, wholesale and retail trade and such auxiliary services as market research and advertising—is also an important aspect of industrial development. Many of the external economies associated with industrial growth flow from interaction with appropri-ate commercial development. However, the difficulties of distinguishing between traditional commercial services that are sometimes inimical to industrial development, and those that complement industrial development, have thus far also precluded measurement.

A composite index of indicators of industrial progress would thus be difficult to calculate. The best single indicator of the maturity of industrialization seems to be the share of value added in manufacturing in commodity production.... The ensuing categorization remains artificial, making arbitrary demarcation lines in what is essentially a continuum of experience from countries barely beginning to industrialize to those with mature manufacturing capacity. In this context it is important to recognize that the differences between developing countries at the ends of the spectrum have become more important in many respects than the similarities between them.

SEMI-INDUSTRIALIZED COUNTRIES

(Share of manufacturing 40 to 60 per cent of value added in commodity production)

The semi-industrialized countries are concentrated in Latin America, the Republic of Korea is a leading example in East Asia, and there are developments in this direction in the Middle East. Hong Kong and Singapore have only recently graduated from this category and, as already suggested, China and India should also be included.

In general, the semi-industrialized countries have relatively well-established private or public enterprise/manufacturing sectors; they have also clearly overcome the acute early human and physical capital shortages. Their industrial structure is being determined by their resource bases, size, geographic location, and policies reflecting comparative advantages arising from these endowments rather than by progressive import substitution. This is particularly so where they have taken care not to lock themselves into an inward-oriented, import substituting, excessively protected framework. The export-oriented countries tend to be specialized, whereas countries that have followed largely import substituting policies tend to have 'balanced" industrial development patterns even though in the early days of industrialization this meant inadequate scales of production.

In relative terms, the geographic concentration of manufacturing is often greater than in industrialized countries, with most manufacturing plants in a handful of centres where physical infrastructure facilities are available. Other industrial "poles" are now being developed, but generally manufacturing-led urban concentration is a greater socio-economic problem in semi-industrialized than in industrialized countries because the semi- industrialized countries do not have the stock of infrastructure and levels of income that make rapid improvement in the urban structure economically, if not always politically, possible in high income countries.

INDUSTRIALIZING COUNTRIES

(Share of manufacturing 20 to 40 per cent of value added in commodity production)

The largest number of developing countries in Africa, Asia, and Latin America fall into the category of industrializing countries. Some countries' industrial production is heavily weighted by mineral processing, and in many cases high protection exaggerates the extent of industrial involvement.

These countries are well beyond their first steps towards industrialization. Most produce a substantial proportion of the consumer goods required by the local market; a significant range of intermediates, notably construction materials; and they have begun or are beginning to produce capital goods. Indonesia and Nigeria should probably come into this category although the value added in manufacturing falls short of 20 percent of value added in commodity production. Again, the agricultural sectors of these very large countries swamp the industrial sectors that have been established. Except for the large countries, a balanced industrial structure again tends to reflect inward-oriented import substitution strategies and unduly small scales of production rather than industrial maturity.

The countries in this category have also overcome the initial lack of human and capital resources for industrialization. A pool of indigenous enterpreneurs, managers and technicians has been established although it is not yet adequate for the rapid rate at which these countries wish to expand industrial production. The industrializing countries have also built up at least in some areas, some of the physical infrastructure—ports, land transport, water supply and power—necessary for industrial operations, but in most cases it is less adequate than in the semi-industrialized countries. Manufacturing industries still tend to be clustered in a capital city with perhaps one or two other centres, with concomitant socio-economic problems. Bangkok, Djakarta and Manila are typical cities with acute urban development problems. However, there are exceptions: in Colombia and Malaysia, for example, manufacturing has, for historical reasons, developed in several centres in each country, and the problems of urbanization are correspondingly less pressing.

EXHIBIT VI.1. Structure of Production

| GDP (millions of dollars) | | Distribution of Gross Domestic Product (percent) | | | | | | | |
| | | Agriculture | | Industry | | (Manufac-turing)[a] | | Services | |
1960	1981	1960	1981	1960	1981	1960	1981	1960	1981
Low-Income									
Economies		**48** w[b]	**37** w	**25** w	**34** w	**11** w	**16** w	**27** w	**29** w
China and India		**48** w	**33** w	**28** w	**39** w	—	—	**24** w	**28** w
Other Low-									
Income		**48** w	**45** w	**12** w	**17** w	**9** w	**10** w	**40** w	**38** w
1 Kampuchea, Dem.	—	—	—	—	—	—	—	—	—	—
2 Bhutan	—	—	—	—	—	—	—	—	—	—
3 Lao, PDR	—	—	—	—	—	—	—	—	—	—
4 Chad	180	—	52	—	12	—	4	—	36	—
5 Bangladesh	3,170	11,910	58	54	7	14	5	8	35	32
6 Ethiopia	900	3,870	65	50	12	16	6	11	23	34
7 Nepal	410	2,420	—	—	—	—	—	—	—	—
8 Burma	1,280	5,770	33	47	12	13	8	10	55	40
9 Afghanistan	1,190	3,230	—	—	—	—	—	—	—	—
10 Mali	270	1,120	55	42	10	11	5	6	35	47
11 Malawi	170	1,420	58	43	11	20	6	13	31	37
12 Zaire	130	5,380	30	32	27	24	13	3	43	44
13 Uganda	540	9,390	52	75	12	4	9	4	36	21
14 Burundi	190	880	—	56	—	16	—	9	—	28
15 Upper Volta	200	1,080	55	41	16	16	9	12	29	43
16 Rwanda	120	1,260	80	46	7	22	1	16	13	32
17 India	29,550	142,010	50	37	20	26	14	18	30	37
18 Somalia	160	1,230	71	—	8	—	3	—	21	—
19 Tanzania	550	4,350	57	52	11	15	5	9	32	33
20 Viet Nam	—	—	—	—	—	—	—	—	—	—
21 China	42,770	264,340	47	35	33	46	—	—	20	20
22 Guinea	370	1,670	—	37	—	33	—	4	—	30
23 Haiti	270	1,590	—	—	—	—	—	—	—	—
24 Sri Lanka	1,500	4,120	32	28	20	28	15	16	48	44
25 Benin	160	850	55	44	8	13	3	7	37	43
26 Central African Rep.	110	690	51	37	10	13	4	6	39	50
27 Sierra Leone	—	1,040	—	31	—	20	—	6	—	49
28 Madagascar	540	2,890	37	35	10	14	4	—	53	51
29 Niger	250	1,710	69	30	9	32	4	8	22	38
30 Pakistan	3,500	25,160	46	30	16	26	12	17	38	44
31 Mozambique	—	—	—	—	—	—	—	—	—	—
32 Sudan	1,160	7,540	—	38	—	14	—	6	—	48
33 Togo	120	880	55	24	16	27	8	7	29	49
34 Ghana	1,220	21,260	41	60	10	12	—	7	49	28

EXHIBIT VI.1. Structure of Production (*Continued*)

GDP (millions of dollars)			Distribution of Gross Domestic Product (percent)							
			Agriculture		Industry		(Manufac-turing)[a]		Services	
	1960	1981	1960	1981	1960	1981	1960	1981	1960	1981
Middle-Income										
Economies			24 w	14 w	30 w	38 w	20 w	22 w	46 w	48 w
Oil Exporters			27 w	13 w	26 w	40 w	15 w	17 w	47 w	47 w
Oil Importers			23 w	14 w	33 w	36 w	22 w	25 w	44 w	50 w
Lower Middle-Income			36 w	22 w	25 w	35 w	15 w	17 w	39 w	43 w
35 Kenya	730	6,960	38	32	18	21	9	13	44	47
36 Senegal	610	2,330	24	22	17	26	12	15	59	52
37 Mauritania	90	630	44	28	21	24	3	7	35	48
38 Yemen Arab Rep.	—	2,770	—	28	—	16	—	6	—	56
39 Yemen, PDR	—	570	—	13	—	28	—	14	—	59
40 Liberia	220	930	—	36	—	27	—	8	—	37
41 Indonesia	8,670	84,960	50	24	25	42	—	12	25	34
42 Lesotho	30	320	—	31	—	21	—	5	—	48
43 Bolivia	460	7,900	26	18	25	27	15	14	49	55
44 Honduras	300	2,380	37	32	19	25	13	17	44	43
45 Zambia	680	3,430	11	18	63	32	4	18	26	50
46 Egypt	3,880	23,110	30	21	24	38	20	32	46	41
47 El Salvador	570	3,550	32	26	19	20	15	15	49	54
48 Thailand	2,550	36,810	40	24	19	28	13	20	41	48
49 Philippines	6,960	38,900	26	23	28	37	20	25	46	40
50 Angola	—	—	—	—	—	—	—	—	—	—
51 Papua New Guinea	230	2,580	49	—	13	—	4	—	38	—
52 Morocco	2,040	14,780	23	14	27	34	16	18	50	52
53 Nicaragua	340	2,590	24	20	21	33	16	26	55	47
54 Nigeria	3,150	70,800	63	23	11	37	5	6	26	40
55 Zimbabwe	780	6,010	18	18	35	37	17	27	47	45
56 Cameroon	550	6,270	—	27	—	20	—	8	—	53
57 Cuba	—	—	—	—	—	—	—	—	—	—
58 Congo, People's Rep.	130	1,870	23	9	17	53	10	5	60	38
59 Guatemala	1,040	8,660	—	—	—	—	—	—	—	—
60 Peru	2,410	23,260	18	9	33	41	24	25	49	50
61 Ecuador	970	13,430	26	12	20	38	16	11	54	50
62 Jamaica	700	2,960	10	8	36	37	15	15	54	55
63 Ivory Coast	570	8,670	43	27	14	23	7	12	43	50
64 Dominican Rep.	720	6,650	27	18	23	27	17	15	50	55

EXHIBIT VI.1. Structure of Production (*Continued*)

GDP (millions of dollars)		Distribution of Gross Domestic Product (percent)								
		Agriculture		Industry		(Manufac-turing)[a]		Services		
1960	1981	1960	1981	1960	1981	1960	1981	1960	1981
65 Mongolia	—	—	—	—	—	—	—	—	—	—
66 Colombia	3,780	32,970	34	27	26	31	17	21	40	42
67 Tunisia	770	7,100	24	16	18	37	8	14	58	47
68 Costa Rica	510	2,630	26	23	20	28	14	20	54	49
69 Korea, Dem. Rep.	—	—	—	—	—	—	—	—	—	—
70 Turkey	8,820	53,910	41	23	21	32	13	23	38	45
71 Syrian Arab Rep.	890	15,240	—	19	—	31	—	26	—	50
72 Jordan	—	2,550	—	8	—	30	—	14	—	62
73 Paraguay	300	5,260	36	28	20	26	17	17	44	46
Upper Middle-Income			**18** *w*	**10** *w*	**33** *w*	**39** *w*	**23** *w*	**24** *w*	**49** *w*	**51** *w*
74 Korea, Rep. of	3,810	65,750	37	17	20	39	14	28	43	44
75 Iran, Islamic Rep. of	4,120	—	29	—	33	—	11	—	38	—
76 Iraq	1,580	—	17	—	52	—	10	—	31	—
77 Malaysia	2,290	24,770	36	23	18	36	9	18	46	41
78 Panama	420	3,490	23	10	21	21	13	10	56	69
79 Lebanon	830	—	12	—	20	—	13	—	68	—
80 Algeria	2,740	41,830	16	6	35	55	8	11	49	39
81 Brazil	14,540	210,660	16	13	35	34	26	27	49	53
82 Mexico	12,040	238,960	16	8	29	37	19	22	55	55
83 Portugal	2,340	21,290	25	12	36	44	29	35	39	44
84 Argentina	12,170	153,330	16	9	38	38	32	25	46	53
85 Chile	3,910	32,860	9	7	35	35	21	22	56	58
86 South Africa	6,980	74,670	12	7	40	53	21	23	48	40
87 Yugoslavia	9,860	63,350	24	12	45	43	36	30	31	45
88 Uruguay	1,110	9,790	19	8	28	33	21	26	53	59
89 Venezuela	7,570	67,800	6	6	22	45	—	15	72	49
90 Greece	3,110	33,390	23	17	26	31	16	20	51	52
91 Hong Kong	950	27,220	4	—	39	—	27	—	57	—
92 Israel	2,030	17,440	11	5	32	36	23	26	57	59
93 Singapore	700	12,910	4	1	18	41	12	30	78	58
94 Trinidad and Tobago	470	6,970	8	2	46	52	24	13	46	46
High-Income Oil Exporters			—	**1** *w*	—	**76** *w*	—	**4** *w*	—	**23** *w*
95 Libya	310	27,400	—	2	—	71	—	3	—	27
96 Saudi Arabia	—	115,430	—	1	—	78	—	4	—	20
97 Kuwait	—	24,260	—	( )	—	71	—	4	—	29
98 United Arab Emirates	—	30,070	—	1	—	77	—	4	—	22

EXHIBIT VI.1. Structure of Production (*Continued*)

	GDP (millions of dollars)		Distribution of Gross Domestic Product (percent)							
			Agriculture		Industry		(Manufacturing)[a]		Services	
	1960	1981	1960	1981	1960	1981	1960	1981	1960	1981
Industrial Market Economies			**6** *w*	**3** *w*	**40** *w*	**36** *w*	**30** *w*	**25** *w*	**54** *w*	**61** *w*
99 Ireland	1,770	16,590	22	—	26	—	—	—	52	—
100 Spain	11,430	185,080	—	7	—	36	—	29	—	57
101 Italy	37,190	350,220	13	6	41	42	31	29	46	53
102 New Zealand	3,940	25,010	—	11	—	31	—	23	—	58
103 United Kingdom	71,440	496,580	3	2	43	33	32	20	54	65
104 Japan	44,000	1,129,500	13	4	45	43	34	30	42	53
105 Austria	6,270	66,240	11	4	46	39	35	37	43	57
106 Finland	5,010	48,940	17	7	34	36	23	25	49	57
107 Australia	16,370	171,070	12	5	40	—	28	—	48	—
108 Canada	39,930	282,500	5	4	34	32	23	19	61	64
109 Netherlands	11,580	140,490	9	4	46	33	34	24	45	63
110 Belgium	11,280	96,940	7	2	41	37	30	25	52	62
111 France	60,060	568,560	10	4	39	35	29	25	51	61
112 United States	505,300	2,893,300	4	3	38	34	29	23	58	63
113 Denmark	5,960	58,260	11	4	31	32	21	19	58	64
114 Germany, Fed. Rep.	72,100	708,540	6	2	53	46	41	—	41	49
115 Norway	4,630	57,140	9	5	33	42	21	15	58	54
116 Sweden	13,950	112,420	7	3	40	31	27	21	53	66
117 Switzerland	8,550	94,260	—	—	—	—	—	—	—	—
East European Nonmarket Economies			—	—	—	—	—	—	—	—
118 Albania	—	—	—	—	—	—	—	—	—	—
119 Hungary	—	22,560	28	18	39	48	—	—	33	34
120 Romania	—	48,412	—	13	—	60	—	—	—	27
121 Bulgaria	—	—	—	—	—	—	—	—	—	—
122 Poland	—	—	—	—	—	—	—	—	—	—
123 USSR	—	—	—	—	—	—	—	—	—	—
124 Czechoslovakia	—	—	—	—	—	—	—	—	—	—
125 German Dem. Rep.	—	—	—	—	—	—	—	—	—	—

Source: World Bank *World Development Report*, 1983, pp. 152–3.

[a]Manufacturing is a part of the industrial sector, but its share of GDP is shown separately because it typically is the most dynamic part of the industrial sector.

[b]Indicates weighted average.

VI.B.2. Industrialization via Import Substitution—Note

In many LDCs—especially in Latin America and Asia—the dominant strategy of industrialization has been the production of consumer goods in substitution for imports. Given an existing demand for imported consumer goods, it was simple to base the postwar rationale for industrialization on the home replacement of these finished goods (in most industries by importing components and engaging in the final assemblying process, in the hope of proceeding to "industrialize from the top downwards" through the ultimate production of the intermediate products and capital goods). Besides allowing the home replacement of an existing market, import substitution also had considerable appeal by virtue of the common belief that it would help meet the developing country's balance-of-payments problem.

Although the widespread pursuit of import substitution has in practice been based mainly on the objectives of industrialization and balance-of-payments support, the policy has been rationalized by a number of protectionist arguments. Proponents of industrial protectionism have adduced several special arguments in the context of development— arguments that should be considered more seriously than the usual simple assertions about a "natural" inferiority of agriculture or the supposed necessity of industrialization to achieve a rising level of income.

Support for import replacement comes partly from an appeal to the experience of industrialized countries. Historical studies of some countries show not only that the share of industiral output rises with development, but also that the growth of industries based on import substitution accounts for a large proportion of the total rise in industry.[1] It is also true that "much of the recent economic history of some rapidly developing underdeveloped countries can be written in terms of industrialization working its way backward from the 'final touches' stage to domestic production of intermediate, and finally to that of basic, industrial materials."[2] At first, the country may import semifinished materials and perform domestically the "final touches" of converting or assembling the almost-finished industrial imports into final products. Later on, with the growth in demand for the final product, a point may be reached at which the import demand for intermediate components and basic goods is sufficiently high to warrant investment in their production at home; the market has become sufficiently large to reach a domestic production threshold.[3]

As with any interpretation of historical development, however, it is one thing to determine what has happened to make the course of development in one country a "success story" and quite another to infer from this experience that the same result could now be induced more rapidly in another country through deliberate policy measures. The historical evidence on the contribution of import substitution to industrialization applies only to some countries; in other countries, the replacement of imports was not significant. Moreover, we should recognize that the rise of industry through import replacement was in large part due to systematic changes in supply conditions, not simply to a change in the composition of demand with rising income.[4] The changes in factor supply—especially the growth in capital stock per worker and the increase in education and skills of all kinds—were instrumental in causing a systematic shift in comparative advantage as per capita income rose. But for a presently underdeveloped country there is no reason to

[1]For evidence, see H. B. Chenery, "Patterns of Industrial Growth," *American Economic Review,* September 1960, pp. 639–41, 651.

[2]A. O. Hirschman, *The Strategy of Economic Development,* New Haven, 1958, p. 112.

[3]Ibid., p. 114.

[4]Chenery, "Patterns of Industrial Growth," pp. 624–5, 628–9, 644.

expect that a tariff on industrial imports would cause the supplies of capital, human skills, and natural resources to change in a way that would favor the substitution of domestic production for imports. The changes in supply conditions that occurred in other countries cannot now be duplicated simply by a policy of industrial protection.

Nor is industrial protection justified by reference to the historical pattern of industrialization working its way backward from the "final touches" stage to domestic production of formerly imported materials. On the contrary, this pattern demonstrates that it is the growth of imports which subsequently induces domestic production; in offering proof that a market exists, the imports can fulfill the important function of demand formation and demand reconnaissance for the country's entrepreneurs, and the imports can act as a catalytic agent that will bring some of the country's underemployed resources together in order to exploit the opportunities they have revealed.[5] For the objective of eventually replacing imports with domestic production, it would thus be self-defeating to restrict imports at too early a stage and thereby forgo the awakening and inducing effects which imports have on industrialization.[6] An increase in imports—not their restriction—is the effective way to prepare the ground for the eventual creation of an import-replacing industry. Only after the domestic industry has been established can the country afford to dispense with the "creative" role played by imports, and only then would there be a case for protection of the domestic industry. Although in promoting the demand for import substitutes, restrictions on imports allow the country to bypass the difficulties of having to build up internal demand simultaneously with supply,[7] nonetheless such a protective commercial policy is designed merely to replace imports; this in itself is no guarantee of cumulative growth. Even though industriali-

zation may be initiated through import substitution, there still remains the problem of sustaining the industrialization momentum beyond the point of import replacement.

Another special argument for industrialization via import substitution rests on the contention that a peripheral country's demand for industrial imports increases much more rapidly than does the foreign demand for its exports, so that the country must supply all those industrial products which cannot be imported in view of the relatively slow growth of its exports. If we accept the contentions that there is disparity in the income elasticities of demand for imports and exports, that the industrial imports are essential and must be either imported or produced at home, and that the country has no other means of increasing its capacity to import, then there is *prima facie* a case for industrial protection to encourage import substitutes. What is relevant for individual primary exporting countries, however, is not the overall income elasticity of demand for primary products, but the prospects for their individual exports. It is unreasonable to believe that export prospects are equally unfavorable for foodstuffs, minerals, and raw materials, or for all commodities in each of these broad categories. Moreover, though the elasticity of demand for a commodity may be low on world markets it may be high for the commodity from a particular source of supply. Nor can the future demand of industrial countries for imports be inferred simply from their income elasticity of demand for imports. Their import requirements will also depend on their growth rates in income (a high growth rate may offset a low income elasticity of demand), on shifts of the long-term supply elasticities within the industrial countries (domestic output of certain minerals and fuels, for example, has not kept pace with demand, so that import requirements are rising relatively to income growth), and on the degree of liberalization in the importing countries' commercial policies. Without undertaking individual commodity and country studies, it is therefore difficult to gauge how applicable is the argument for indus-

[5]Hirschman, *Strategy of Economic Development,* p. 123.

[6]Ibid., p. 124.

[7]Cf. Gunnar Myrdal, *An International Economy,* New York, 1956, p. 276.

trialization because of a weak export position.

We should also allow for the fact that a developing country's capacity to import industrial products will depend not only on its export earnings, but also on the inflow of foreign capital, changes in the terms of trade, and the capacity to replace other imports (such as foodstuffs and raw materials) with domestic production. To the extent that these other factors may raise the capacity to import industrial products, there is less need for industrial protection.

The case is also weakened if in attempting to offset the limited demand for exports, the policy of import substitution should in turn give rise to limitations on the supply side and deter exports. Such a worsening of the export situation may occur when the country's scarce financial and human resources are concentrated on industrialization, resources are diverted from the export sector, home consumption limits the available export supply, or the industrialization program is inflationary.

Another facet of the argument for replacing industrial imports with domestic production is related to the objective of expanding employment outside of agriculture. It may be contended that industrialization is necessary to provide employment opportunities for the presently underemployed, to absorb manpower that would otherwise become redundant when agricultural productivity rises through the adoption of more advanced techniques, and to take up the increase in the size of the labor force as population grows.

The promotion of new employment opportunities is certainly a crucial component of development programming, and in this connection there is considerable point to the emphasis on industrialization. The relevant questions here, however, are whether investment should be directed toward import-replacing industries, and whether industrial protectionism is the most appropriate policy for facilitating the expansion of nonagricultural employment.

It is possible that the objectives of more employment and a more rapid rate of development are incompatible, and this conflict in

social objectives must first be resolved. A policy of industrialization through import substitution must also be compared with a policy of gradually inducing industrialization through agricultural improvement, or promoting industry through the production of manufactured exports (as discussed in VIII.B). There is also a tendency to exaggerate the amount of employment that could be provided by substituting home manufacture for imports; as country studies show, the direct employment which can be provided by replacing imports with domestic manufacture is generally limited for a poor country.

Further, it can be questioned whether industrialization through protection is the best remedy for underemployment. The effect of surplus labor in agriculture is low productivity, but the remedy for this is capital formation, not industrialization as such. Although the surplus labor constitutes an "investible surplus," this surplus can be applied in various investment outlets, and we cannot simply conclude that the optimum resource use is in import-competing industries. We should also recognize that other policies might be more effective in stimulating labor mobility than would protection. When occupational mobility is restricted by institutional and cultural barriers, the supply responses to the price and income stimuli of protection are necessarily weak, and extra-economic measures are required in such forms as education and training, land tenure reforms, and policies that foster cultural change. Finally, we must distinguish between the mere availability of surplus laborers and their actual transference into productive employment as efficient and fully committed industrial workers. This raises all the complex problems of creating and disciplining an industrial labor force.[8]

A more sophisticated version of the employment argument is that indsutry should be protected by a tariff in order to offset the effects of an excessively high wage rate for labor in the importable manufacturing indus-

[8]Cf. W. Galenson (ed.), *Labor and Economic Development,* New York, 1959; W. E. Moore and A. S. Feidman (eds.), *Labor Commitment and Social Change in Developing Areas,* New York, 1960.

tries.[9] It is claimed that the wage differential between the agricultural and industrial sectors overvalues labor for the industrial sector in the sense that industrial wage rates exceed the social opportunity costs of employing more labor in industry. This may be due to the alleged fact that industrial wages are based on agricultural earnings, which are determined by the average product of labor in agriculture rather than by the marginal product of labor which is lower (compare the discussion of Lewis's model in III.B.1 above); or it may be due to market imperfections that make the gap between agricultural and industrial wages greater than can be accounted for by "net advantages" as between agricultural and industrial work. In either case, there is a distortion in the labor market which raises the private cost of labor in industry above its social opportunity cost (the marginal product of labor in agriculture). This results in an inefficient allocation of labor between agriculture and industry, and it also understates the profitability of transforming agriculture into manufactures.[10] It is therefore concluded that protection of manufacturing industry may increase real income above the free trade level by making the relative price of manufactures higher and facilitating the redistribution of labor from agriculture to import-competing industries.

This conclusion, however, can be criticized

[9]For a detailed analysis of this argument, see E. E. Hagen, "An Economic Justification for Protection," *Quarterly Journal of Economics,* November 1958, J. Bhagwati, "The Theory of Comparative Advantage in the Context of Underdevelopment and Growth," *Pakistan Development Review,* Autumn 1962, pp. 342–5; J. Bhagwati and V. K. Ramaswami, "Domestic Distortions, Tariffs and the Theory of Optimum Subsidy," *Journal of Political Economy,* February 1963, pp. 44–50.

[10]In technical terms, the wage differential against industry causes the feasible production possibility curve to be drawn inwards within the maximum attainable production possibility curve based on a uniform wage. It also makes the commodity price ratio diverge from the domestic rate of transformation, so that the optimum conditions characterized by the equality of the foreign rate of transformation, domestic rate of transformation in production, and domestic rate of substitution in consumption are violated in the free trade case. See Bhagwati and Ramaswami, "Domestic Distortions," pp. 48–9.

in several respects. Insofar as it is concerned with absorbing underemployed agricultural labor into import-competing industries, this aspect of the argument is subject to the same qualifications raised previously for the general argument of expanding employment through industrial protection. More pointedly, with regard to the alleged distortion in the labor market, it can be questioned whether the mere existence of a differential between industrial and agricultural wages is proof of a distortion. To the extent that the wage differential might be explained entirely by rational considerations of differences in costs and preferences as between industrial and agricultural work, there is no genuine distortion.[11] Considering the other possible reason for a distortion in the labor market— that industrial wages are related to agricultural earnings, but these earnings exceed the marginal producitivity of agricultural labor—we must recognize that this result is based on the assumption of surplus agricultural labor and the ability of the worker to receive the average product because the supply of labor is the family which works on its own account and not for wages. This consideration is not relevant, however, for thinly populated countries or for plantation labor. And, regarding the concept of surplus labor and any estimate of its extent, we should recall all the reservations discussed in our earlier analysis of the labor surplus economy (III.A).

Even if we assume, however, that the wage differential does represent a genuine distortion, we must still recognize that the effects of this distortion may be better offset by domestic policies rather than a tariff on industrial imports. The difficulty with protection by a tariff is that it seeks to remedy the distortion by affecting foreign trade whereas the distortion is in a domestic factor market.[12] In this case, a policy of subsidization of produc-

[11]For a list of conditions under which wage differentials do not represent a genuine distortion, see ibid., pp. 47–8.

[12]A tariff could make the foreign and domestic rates of transformation equal, but it destroys the equality between the domestic rate of substitution and the foreign rate of transformation.

tion of the import-competing commodity, or of taxation of agricultural production, would be superior to a tariff.[13] A policy of subsidization on the use of labor in the import-competing industry, or a tax on its use in agriculture, would be an even better solution; since it directly eliminates the wage differential, this policy yields a higher real income than would a tariff, and an even higher real income than can be attained by tax-cum-subsidy on domestic production.[14] A tariff on industrial imports is thus the least effective way of offsetting a distortion in the labor market.

Although we have so far been skeptical about the validity of protectionist arguments for import substitution, there remain two arguments that have more merit—the infant industry case and the attraction of foreign investment argument.[15] Temporary tariff protection of an infant industry is generally ac-

[13]A policy of subsidization or taxation of domestic products could equate the domestic and foreign rates of transformation and the domestic rate of substitution. But since it does not eliminate the inefficiency of labor-use induced by the excessive wage differential, it achieves this equality along the production possibility curve that is within the maximum attainable production possibility curve.

[14]A policy of tax-cum-subsidy on the use of labor could achieve the equality of the domestic rate of transformation, foreign rate of transformation, and the domestic rate of substitution, and it can do this along the maximum attainable production possibility curve. For in this case, the wage differential against the industrial sector is directly removed, and both the inefficiency in labor allocation and the divergence of commodity prices from opportunity costs are simultaneously eliminated.

[15]We omit the more general external economies argument and the terms of trade case for protection. These arguments are analytically correct, but are not among the most relevant for import-substitution in a poor country. The external economies argument merges with the balanced growth doctrine. There is, moreover, no a priori reason why—among all possible alternative investment opportunities—we should expect the net external economies to be greatest in import-competing industries. And again, a policy of tax-cum-subsidy on domestic production may be shown to be superior to a tariff. Cf. Bhagwati and Ramaswami, "Domestic Distortions," pp. 45–7.

Although it is possible that a nation may succeed in improving its terms of trade by switching production from exportables to import-substitutes, this policy has little practical relevance for poor countries that cannot exercise sufficient monopoly or monopsony power in foreign trade.

cepted as a valid policy for establishing an industry that would eventually be able to produce at lower costs and compete favorably with foreign producers. Nonetheless, to justify government intervention, it is not sufficient to anticipate solely the realization of internal economies of scale. For if the future benefits were to accrue only to the firm, the investment might then still be made by a private firm without protection insofar as the firm can cover its earlier costs of growth out of its later profits. Protection should instead be based on the condition that the social rate of return exceeds the private rate of return on the investment. The social benefit is likely to exceed the private benefit in an infant industry for two special reasons that are particularly relevant for a newly developing country: the knowledge of new industrial protection techniques acquired in the protected industry may also be shared with other producers, and the training of the labor force may also redound to the benefit of other employers. When external economies are present, social benefits will exceed private benefits, and market forces would not yield the social optimum output. To gain the additional benefits, government aid may then be advocated.

It should be realized, however, that protection causes society to bear not only the losses that would be incurred by the industry during its period of infancy, but also the cost of consumption in the form of higher-priced import substitutes during this period. The ultimate saving in costs, therefore, ought to be sufficient to compensate the community for the excess costs during the "growing up" period.

Finally, when the social rate of return exceeds the private, the preferable policy, in a way analogous to the other cases of domestic distortions, would be a direct subsidy on facilities to further the "learning process" of new production methods, or provisions by the government for the training of labor. These subsidies are superior to a protective tariff, since they avoid the intermediate loss to consumption that occurs with protection.

Protection may, however, be an effective policy for fostering an import-replacing industry when its successful establishment depends on the acquisition of better technical knowledge and experience. For when the country imposes prohibitive tariffs, or other import restrictions, against foreign manufactures, the foreign manufacturer may be induced to escape the import controls against his product by establishing a branch plant or subsidiary behind the tariff wall. Although the protection would have little effect in attracting supply-oriented industries, the inducement may be significant for the creation of "tariff factories" in market-oriented industries. It may be particularly effective in encouraging the final stages of manufacture and assembly of parts within the tariff-imposing country when there is an import duty on finished goods while raw materials or intermediate goods remain untaxed. This assumes, of course, that a sufficiently high domestic demand exists for the product of the tariff factory. And in determining whether the attraction of additional private foreign capital provides a net gain, we must again recall the earlier discussion about the various costs and benefits of foreign capital.

From the foregoing appraisal of the various protection arguments, we may conclude that they must be highly qualified, the costs of protection not underestimated, and superior alternative policies not overlooked. Beyond these analytical considerations, the actual experience of many developing countries with industrial protectionist policies also confirms the conclusion that developing countries are likely to overemphasize the scope for replacement of industrial imports. A policy of import-substitution industrialization becomes increasingly difficult to follow beyond the consumer goods phase because with each successive import-substitution activity through the intermediate and capital goods phases, the capital intensity of import-substitution projects rises, resulting in a larger import content of investment. On the demand side, the projects tend to require increasingly large domestic markets for the achievement of a minimum efficient scale of production.[16]

[16]David Felix, "The Dilemma of Import Substitution—Argentina," in Gustav F. Papanek (ed.), *Development Policy—Theory and Practice*, Cambridge, 1968, pp. 60–61.

The limitations and deleterious effects that have resulted in practice from actual import-substitution policies will be discussed in greater detail in Chapter VIII. We may simply note now that in many instances, the protectionist policies have resulted in higher prices, a domestic product of inferior quality, excess capacity in the import-competing industries, and a restraint of agricultural output and on the expansion of exports. A number of country studies can now document the contention that overinvestment has occurred in import-replacing industry.

In some countries the promotion of import substitutes through tariff rates that escalate with the degree of processing (low on imported intermediate goods and high on final goods) has actually resulted in negative value added. Although high protection of final goods makes production of the import substitute privately profitable in local currency, the value of inputs at world prices exceeds the value of the final product at world prices; the process of import substitution is socially inefficient.

Not only has the actual process of import substitution been inefficient in resource use; it has also often intensified the foreign exchange constraint. At the same time as policies have subsidized import replacement, they have inhibited expansion of exports, but there has not been a net saving of imports since the replacement of finished import commodities has required heavy imports of fuels, industrial materials, and capital goods, as well as foodstuffs in cases where agricultural development has also suffered.

After a period of import-substitution industrialization, the problems of maldistribution in income and unemployment have also become more serious than they were in the first place. The use of subsidies, overvalued exchange rates, rationing of underpriced import licenses, high levels of effective protection, and loans at negative real interest rates have induced the production of import substitutes by capital-intensive, labor-saving methods and have resulted in industrial profits in the sheltered sector and high industrial wages for a labor elite, aggravating inequalities in income distribution. As noted repeatedly, employment creation in the urban im-port-replacement industrial sector has not kept pace with the rural-urban migration, and the unemployment problem has been aggravated by the transfer of the rural under-employed into open unemployment and underemployment in the urban sector.

Country studies provide some supporting evidence for the disenchantment with industrialization via import substitution, and at the same time they reinforce our conclusion that an LDC must now focus on the possibilities of inducing a gradual process of indus-trialization through agricultural develop-ment, and on the potential industrialization through the export of manufactured prod-ucts. Having realized the limitations of an in-ward-looking strategy of industrialization, many LDCs—as represented through the pronouncements of UNCTAD—have in fact recently changed their emphasis and are now seeking measures that will promote indus-trialization via the substitution of exports of processed primary products, semimanufac-tures, and manufactures instead of exports of primary commodities.

Comment

The import-substituion strategy of development has been critically examined by many economists. For an analysis of theoretical issues and empirical results, see B. Balassa, *The Structure of Protection in Developing Countries (1971);* M. Bruno, *"The Optimal Selection of Export Promoting and Import Substituting Projects."* in United Nations, *Planning the External Sector* (1967); M. Bruno, "Optimal Patterns of Trade and Development," *Review of Economics and Statistics,* (November 1967); A. O. Hirschman, "The Political Economy of Import Substituting Industrialization," *Quarterly Journal of Economics* (February 1968); K. H. Raj and A. K. Sen, "Alternative Patterns of Growth under Conditions of Stagnant Export Earnings," *Oxford Economic Papers,* (February 1961); H. Bruton, "The Import Substitution Strategy of Economic Development," *Pakistan Development Review* (Summer 1970); I. M. D. Little, T. Scitovsky, and M. FG. Scott, *Industry and Trade in Some Developing Countries,* 1970, chapters 2 and 3; Hollis Chenery, "Comparative Advantage and Development Policy," *American Economic Review* (March 1961); Joel Bergsman, "Commercial Policy, Allocative Efficiency and 'X-efficiency,'" *Quarterly Journal of Economics* (August 1974); I. M. D. Little, "Import Controls and Exports in Developing Countries," *Finance & Development* (September 1970); J. Bhagwati, *Anatomy and Consequences of Trade Control Regimes* (1978); Anne O. Krueger, *Foreign Trade Regimes and Economic Development: Liberalization Attempts and Consequesnces* (1978).

VI.B.3. Industrialization via Export Substitution—Note

In contrast with industrialization via import substitution, there is an increasing interest in the potentialities of an industrialization strat-egy that emphasizes export substitution. "Export substitution" is the export of nontra-ditional products such as processed primary products, semimanufactures, and manufac-tured goods in substitution for the traditional exports of primary products. Other selections have already indicated how some countries have reduced the share of traditional exports in total exports while diversifying into new exports made up largely of manufactured goods (see selections I.C.1 and I.C.2).

This Note considers why the export-substi-tution process has some distinct advantages over the import-substitution process. It might be though that in terms of relaxing a country's foreign exchange constraint, a unit of foreign exchange saved by import substitution is equivalent to a unit of foreign exchange earned by export substitution. But there are other indirect effects and dynamic considerations in favor of export substitution.

First, the domestic resource cost of earning a unit of foreign exchange tends to be less than the domestic resource cost of saving a unit of foreign exchange. This means that the resources used in import substitution could have earned a greater amount of foreign exchange through export expansion than the foreign exchange saved in import substitution, which relies on high effective rates of protection. Even though the import substitution is profitable in local currency because of the high protection, the economic costs in terms of real resource used is excessive. The value of exports that could be produced with a given use of scarce factors is greater than the value of imports that could be replaced.

Moreover, to the extent that it rests on exogenous world demand, the process of industrialization through export substitution is not limited to the narrow domestic market as is the import-substitution process. A developing economy must overcome the diseconomies of small size. And, as classical economists have emphasized, "the division of labor is limited by the extent of the market." If a country can export to a world market, it can enjoy economies of scale, learning effects, and the competitive gains of X-efficiency.[1] "X-efficiency" refers to forces that intensify motivation and competition that result in lower cost curves for the firm.

Furthermore, a pro-trade strategy may also attract foreign direct investment. An inflow of foreign capital to support export substitution is not dependent on home market protection but is induced by considerations of efficiency on the side of resource costs. Foreign investment for export substitution also tends to have more linkages to agriculture when it involves the processing of primary products. It also upgrades labor skills when it involves the production of labor-intensive manufactures.

Besides private foreign investment, other sources of foreign capital—such as commercial banks that syndicate Eurocurrency loans to the LDCs—may be more willing to lend to a country that promotes exports. This is because the debt-servicing problem is eased when the country has increasing export revenue, and the ratio of debt-servicing to export revenue is falling.

Most important, export substitution contributes more than does import substitution to the objectives of greater employment and improvement in the distribution of income. Being labor-intensive in production technique, and dependent on the demand of worldwide markets, the nontraditional exports may absorb more labor than import replacement. They may also reduce the cost of employment in terms of the complementary use of scarce factors of capital and imported inputs.

Export substitution also indirectly aids employment creation in the urban-industrial sector by avoiding an agricultural bottleneck that would otherwise handicap urban-industrial employment. By exporting manufactures and semimanufactures, the developing countries are able to import agricultural goods and thereby keep the real wage low as expressed in terms of industrial goods. If, on the contrary, there is a slow growth of agricultural production, and the price of agricultural goods rises relative to that of industrial goods, the real wage in terms of industrial goods would rise. This in turn would induce a substitution of capital for labor, and it would also reduce profit margins, thereby causing savings to decline and the rate of capital formation to decrease. Industrial employment would thereby be adversely affected.[2]

---

[1]Harvey Leibenstein, *General X-Efficiency Theory and Economic Development,* New York, 1978.

[2]Countries have adjusted to agricultural stagnation by expanding food imports by means of labor-intensive industrial exports. Contemporary examples are Korea and Taiwan, while historical cases include the repeal of the Corn Laws in the United Kingdom and Japanese food imports from her colonies after 1900.

The evidence from the past two decades does show that the range of labor-intensive manufactures exported from LDCs has indeed widened, and the number of LDCs engaged in export substitution has increased. In conformity with hypotheses about export-based development, the evidence indicates that export growth rates explain a significant portion of the variance in income growth rates, which cannot be explained by the growth in primary inputs; that generally the greatest increase in the GNP of various LDCs is better correlated with exports than any other variables; that the higher-income LDCs have a higher ratio of exports to GDP and a faster rate of growth; and that the higher rate of growth is correlated with a more diversified export base.

Recognizing the potential for a new industrialization strategy, an increasing number of LDCs desire to promote nontraditional exports.

The new industrialization strategy has not, however, gone unchallenged. Some analysts interpret the promotion of labor-intensive processes and component manufacturing as the replacement of a nineteenth-century "plantation society" with the twentieth-century creation of a "branch plant society," as involving undue bargaining power in favor of the foreign enterprise; or as resulting in an unequal international distribution of the gains from trade and investment. Thus, Helleiner cautions about the dependence effects:

Export-oriented labour-intensive industries selling to multinational firms, and totally unintegrated with the rest of the economies in which they are located, would seem to combine some of the most disagreeable features of outward orientation and foreign investment. Particularly where there are "export processing zones," the manufactured export sector constitutes an "enclave"—an "output of the mother country"—in as real a sense as any foreign-owned mine ever did. These disagreeable features, moreover, are combined in a manner which leaves the host country with a minimum of bargaining advantage.

Not only is the export manufacturing activity extraordinarily "foot-loose," dependent as it is on neither local resources nor local markets, but it is also likely to bind the host country both to sources of inputs and to market outlets over which it has

an absolute minimum of control. Bargaining strength is likely to be considerable less for a country manufacturing components or undertaking middle-stage processing than it is even for a raw material exporter; for copper or cocoa beans can, after all, be sold on a world market or bartered with socialist states or even used domestically. What is a country to do, however, with tuners designed to meet the particular specifications of Philco television receivers—other than sell them to Philco? Production for export within the multinational firm may indeed be a means for acquiring a share of the expanding markets in products for which world demand is income-elastic; but it may render the host country exceptionally "dependent" upon powerful foreign actors; foreign firms and/or governments may be in a strong position to influence the host countries' policies—both external and domestic—either directly or through their employees or local suppliers where they dominate so utterly particular sectors of their economies. The fundamental problem with this dependency relationship is that continuation or further development in the field of these manufactured exports is subject to the decision of foreign firms over which the host countries can have extraordinarily little influence—decisions over plant location, new product development, choice of techniques, market allocations, etc. One might therefore sensibly hesitate before committing oneself overly in this direction.[3]

To the extent that export substitution rests on foreign investment by vertically integrated transnational firms, it has been criticized by Vaitsos as constituting only "shallow development." Vaitsos analyzes the export-substitution activities of transnational enterprises as follows:

The basic attraction offered by developing countries to such export activities by transnational firms is obviously due to the very low wages of unskilled labor in such countries given minimum productivity rates. . . .

The development of this type of international sourcing by transnational firms has important repercussions for developing countries. Their comparative advantage in this case rests in specializing in unskilled labor whose wages have to stay comaratively low while importing a package of inputs (both physical and intangibles) from abroad. Since

[3]G. K. Helleiner, "Manufacturing for Export, Multinational Firms and Economic Development," *World Development,* July 1973, p. 17.

skills and technology, capital, components and other goods are mobile internationally while unskilled labor is not (or is preferred not to be, due to the heavy social costs involved), transnational firms will be induced to intensify such international sourcing, diversifying their sources of unskilled labor among different developing countries to assure a continuous availabilty of supply, or the products of that input.

The "shallowness" of such a development process is a result of the following reasons. The type of labor utilized represents generally the weakest and less organized part of the labor class, thus limiting possibilities for increasing labor returns unless a general shortage of labor takes place in the country, in which case opportunity cost considerations arise for the host economy. If wages increase foreign investors will tend to shift to other countries since their locational interests stem from the existence of low wages given some minimum productivity levels. The training necessary for local labor in such activities is generally very small, limiting spill-over effects. Of critical importance is the absence of marketing knowhow effects for the host country since the goods traded are within the captive markets of affiliates. Final product promotion is handled abroad by the foreign centers of decision making.

The concentration on low wage, unskilled-labor-intensive, export promoting activities has been compared to the older enclave structures in the extractive industry. The basic difference between them, though, is that in the former the foreign investor is not very much captive once he has committed his activities in a country since the investment is very low, the shifting of activities to other nations is easy to undertake since there is no uniqueness in the local supply of inputs and the tapping of local resources did not imply the expensive discovery of previously unknown resources (as in the extractive sector). Thus, the possibility of enhancing the bargaining power of the host government to share in a more equitable distribution of the surplus involved is minimal or non-existent.[4]

From the preceding quotations, it is clear that the issues raised by a strategy of industrialization via export substitution are controversial. They cannot be resolved in isolation. The efficacy of this industrialization strategy is dependent upon the performance of foreign investment, relations between multinational enterprises and host countries, and the trade policies of the developed importing countries. This topic should therefore be considered alongside the selections in V.D and V.E, above, and Chapter VIII.

[4]Constantine V. Vaitsos, "Employment Effects of Foreign Direct Investments," in Edgar O. Edwards (ed.), *Employment in Developing Nations*, New York, 1974, pp. 339–41.

VI.B.4. Interactions Between Industrialization and Exports*

Sustained economic growth requires a transformation of the struture of production that is compatible with both the evolution of domestic demand and the opprotunities for international trade. This transformation normally involves a substantial rise in the share of industry and—except for a few specialized mineral producers—a shift away from dependence on primary exports toward manufactured goods as a source of foreign exchange. There is considerable evidence that success in developing manufactured exports is critical to this process, and conversely that continued emphasis on import substitution will ultimately lead to a slowing down of growth.

Despite the amount of attention given to alternative strategies of trade and development since the work of I. M. D. Little, Tibor Scitovsky and M. FG. Scott, there has been

*From Hollis B. Chenery, "Interactions Between Industrialization and Exports," *American Economic Review, Papers and Proceedings*, Vol. 70, No. 2 (May 1980), pp. 281–7. Reprinted by permission.

little attempt to examine the underlying relationships in quantitative terms. A fuller understanding of the various mechanisms that have been posited requires that the internal and external aspects of industrialization be examined together in a framework that brings out the several interactions among them.

This paper is drawn from a comparative study of sources of industrial growth in selected semi-industrial countries that have followed policies ranging from the extremes of export promotion to import substitution. The core of the analysis is a set of input-output accounts that permits changes in the structure of demand, trade, and production to be analyzed in comparable terms over periods of fifteen to twenty years. I will compare the main effects of different types of trade and development strategy on industrial growth and structure. The methodology emphasizes interrelations on the demand side, which tend to be neglected in other approaches. Attention is focused on the effects of early or late development of manufactured exports, which is a major source of the differences among strategies.

THE TRANSFORMATION OF PRODUCTION AND TRADE

The structural transformation of developing countries is characterized by a period in which the rising share of manufacturing in GNP approaches that of primary production and a significant portion of manufactured goods begins to be exported. Countries that have reached this stage have been alternatively described as "semi-industrial" or "newly industrialized."[1] Depending on the criteria used, there were between twenty and twenty-five such countries by 1970.

The present sample consists of seven of the sixteen principal semi-industrial countries identified by Bergsman: Korea, Taiwan, Co-

lombia, Turkey, Yugoslavia, Mexico, and Israel (in ascending order of 1960 per capita income).[2] Japan and Norway, which had largely completed the transformation of production by 1960, are added for comparative purposes. The sample was selected primarily on the basis of the availability of input-output data covering fifteen years or more. Table 1 gives selected structural characteristics for the nine countries.

The Sources of Growth

An input-output model is used to provide a consistent framework for the analysis of growth and structural change. The same twenty-three-sector classification is used for each country, which leads to a comparable decomposition of output growth in each sector into the direct and indirect effects of increases in domestic demand, exports, and import substitution. For this purpose import substitution is defined for each sector by the reduction in the share of total supply that is provided by imports.

The model is based on the following accounting balances for each sector:

$$X_i = u_i(W_i + D_i) + E_i \qquad (1)$$
$$M_i = m_i(W_i + D_i) \qquad (2)$$

where X is total output, D is domestic final demand, W is intermediate demand, M is imports, E is exports, m_i is the share of imports in total supply, and u_i is the domestic share. Assuming that $W_i = \Sigma a_{ij}X_j$ the level of output can be expressed by the solution to the corresponding Leontief model as

$$X_i = \Sigma r_{ij}(u_jD_j + E_j) \qquad (3)$$

The coefficients r_{ij} are the elements of the inverse of a Leontief domestic matrix in which the coefficients (u_ia_{ij}) represent the amount supplied from domestic sources.

Equation (3) makes it possible to solve for the increase in output of each sector, ΔX_i, in

---

[1] Joel Bergsman identifies sixteen significant semi-industrial countries, ten of which are the subject of the recent OECD study of "The Impact of the Newly Industrialising Countries."

[2] The remaining nine countries identified by Bergsman are: Egypt, the Philippines, Brazil, Portugal, Hong Kong, Singapore, Greece, Argentina and Spain. Marginal cases include India, Uruguay. Chile, South Africa, Thailand and Malaysia.

TABLE 1. Indicators of Structure and Growth

			Per Capita GNP			Share of GDP	
		Population (millions)	Level (U.S.$ 1970)	Average Growth Rate[a]	Exports[a]	Manufactured Exports[a]	Value-Added in Industry[a,b]
Group A							
Korea	1955	22	131	—	1.6	0.2	13.1
	1963	27	149	1.6	4.9	1.2	16.9
	1973	33	323	8.0	31.8	24.3	29.7
Taiwan	1955	9	199	—	8.3	1.4	23.6
	1963	12	252	3.0	17.6	6.2	28.6
	1973	15	513	7.4	51.6	38.3	43.8
Israel	1955	2	950	—	11.5	4.9	31.6
	1963	2	1429	5.2	21.4	11.2	35.5
	1973	3	2374	5.2	28.3	15.1	36.7
Norway	1955	3	1244	—	40.7	10.4	35.2
	1963	4	2168	7.2	39.0	12.6	33.1
	1973	4	3179	3.9	43.4	19.1	30.4
Group B							
Yugoslavia	1955	18	329	—	6.6	2.0	41.7
	1963	19	510	5.6	15.6	11.8	40.8
	1973	21	813	4.8	22.3	12.5	41.4
Japan	1955	89	500	—	10.7	9.1	26.5
	1963	97	992	8.9	9.3	7.4	40.8
	1973	108	2349	9.0	10.3	8.8	42.5
Group C							
Colombia	1955	13	285	—	12.4	0.2	19.3
	1963	17	309	1.0	11.9	0.5	23.2
	1973	23	415	3.0	15.5	3.7	24.9
Turkey	1955	24	264	—	5.2	0.2	16.9
	1963	30	319	3.7	5.9	0.3	19.0
	1973	38	461	3.8	8.1	1.5	24.5
Mexico	1955	31	424	—	16.7	3.8	26.8
	1963	40	513	2.4	10.4	1.7	27.2
	1973	56	719	3.4	9.2	3.0	31.1

Source: See Kubo and Robinson.

[a]Shown in percent.

[b]Industry includes manufacturing and construction.

terms of increases in internal and external demand in all sectors (ΔD_j and ΔE_j) and changes in two sets of parameters (Δu_j and Δa_{ij}). The solution of ΔX_i can be expressed as the sum of four factors:[3]

[3]This formulation is discussed in the paper by Moises Syrquin and myself. The superscripts refer to time periods.

(a) The expansion of domestic demand in all sectors (DD):

$$\sum_j r_{ij}^1 u_j^1 \Delta D_j$$

(b) The expansion of exports in all sectors (EE):

$$\sum_j r_{ij}^1 \Delta E_j$$

(c) Import substitution in all sectors (IS):

$$\sum_j r^1_{ij} \Delta u_j (D_j^2 + W_j^2)$$

(d) Technological change (TC):

$$\sum_j r^1_{ij} u^1_j \sum_k \Delta a_{jk} X_k^2$$

The effects of trade policy are shown by terms (b) and (c), export expansion and import substitution. When there is no change in import proportions or in input-output coefficients, the last two terms vanish and sectoral growth is determined only by increases in internal and external demands.

The Role of Trade

Trade and development strategies are often characterized by a spectrum varying from inward to outward looking or from "import substituting" to "export led." The direct effects of these policy differences on production are shown most clearly by changes in the share of manufactured exports, which are given in Table 1. Since the sample illustrates a wide variety of development patterns, there is little difficulty in dividing the countries into three groups on this basis. *Group A:* Countries with high or rapidly rising manufactured exports: Korea, Taiwan, Israel, Norway. *Group B:* Intermediate cases: Yugoslavia and Japan. *Group C:* Countries with low manufactured exports: Colombia, Turkey, and Mexico.

In the two intermediate cases, manufactured exports rose rapidly before 1960 but maintained a relatively high and stable share of GDP thereafter.

The four sources of growth of all manufacturing for these three groups of countries are given in Table 2. The subperiods are five to ten years, depending on the availability of input-output data. They extend from the mid-1950s to the early 1970s, except for Japan where it was possible to make approximate calculations for the prewar period. In all countries except Norway, the data cover part of the initial period of import substitution, which is particularly notable in the analysis of Korea, Taiwan, and Colombia. Thereafter the patterns diverge substantially.

In the four countries in Group A, the growth of manufacturing is increasingly due to the continued expansion of exports, which accounts for 50 percent or more of the total increase in output. In Korea and Taiwan, export expansion led to a rapid acceleraton of industrial growth; but in Israel, Norway, and Yugoslavia the demand effects of export expansion were largely offset by import liberalization.

The countries in Group C are typical of a large group (which includes India, Brazil, Chile, Uruguay, and Argentina) whose development strategy has been based on import substitution for several decades (see my book with Syrquin, table 16). The decomposition of the sources of manufacturing growth shows that export expansion was the smallest of the four factors, accounting for less than 10 percent of the total increase. Colombia, the least industrialized of this group, illustrates the typical pattern of declining effects of import substitution with no offsetting rise in export effects. After import substitution is largely completed, manufacturing growth cannot exceed that of domestic demand and therefore tends to decline until there is a change in trade policy.

TRADE-DEVELOPMENT SEQUENCES

The previous section established a rough grouping of countries based primarily on the role of manufactured exports in the structural transformation of the economy. I will now examine the differences in development-trade sequences at a less-aggregated level to ascertain the extent to which they vary among countries and industries. Before doing so, some of the differences in trade policies will be noted.

The seven developing countries all experienced some degree of balance-of-payments disequilibrium during the 1950s, reflected in foreign exchange shortages and quantitative restrictions (QRs), and exacerbated by overvalued exchange rates. The trade and ex-

TABLE 2. Sources of Growth in Manufacturing Output

	Period	Average Annual Growth Rate	Percent of Total			
			Domestic Demand Expansion	Export Expansion	Import Substitution	Changes in Input-Output Coefficients
Group A						
Korea	1955–63	10.4	57	12	42	−11
	1963–70	18.9	70	30	0	0
	1970–83	23.8	39	62	−3	2
Taiwan	1956–61	11.2	35	28	25	12
	1961–66	16.6	49	44	2	5
	1966–71	21.1	35	57	4	4
Israel	1958–65	13.6	62	27	13	−2
	1965–72	11.3	71	49	−37	17
Norway	1953–61	5.0	65	36	−16	15
	1961–69	5.3	51	58	−19	10
Group B						
Yugoslavia	1962–66	16.6	74	25	−5	6
	1966–72	9.1	72	38	−22	12
Japan	1914–35	5.5	70	33	5	−8
	1935–55	2.8	71	−7	15	21
	1955–60	12.6	76	12	−3	15
	1960–65	10.8	82	22	0	−4
	1965–70	16.5	74	18	−1	9
Group C						
Colombia	1953–66	8.3	60	7	22	11
	1966–70	7.4	76	5	4	15
Turkey	1953–63	6.4	81	2	9	8
	1963–68	9.9	75	5	10	10
	1968–73	9.4	71	16	−2	15
Mexico	1950–60	7.0	72	3	11	14
	1960–70	8.6	86	4	11	−1
	1970–75	7.2	81	8	3	8

Source: See Table 1.

change-rate regimes of four of these countries—Korea, Israel, Colombia and Turkey—have been compared to a larger sample by Anne Krueger. While Korea and Israel show progressive liberalization and reduction of QRs by the early 1960s, Colombia and Turkey maintained high levels of protection and import substituting policies for most of the period. Both the latter had intervals of liberalization and export expansion in the late 1960s.

Yuji Kubo and Sherman Robinson have extended this comparison to the other countries in our sample. In Group A, Taiwan followed a sequence similar to Korea and liberalized trade even more fully by 1970. In Group C, Mexico followed a moderate form of import substitution strategy with relatively low levels of protection.

In summary, the trade policies of the countries in Group A (plus Japan) actively favored exports since the early 1960s, while those of Group C discriminated against them in varying degrees. In addition the transformation was affected by large inflows of foreign assistance to Korea, Taiwan, and Israel which made possible higher growth rates and more outward-looking trade and development policies.

To indicate the differences in trade-development sequences among sectors, the fourteen branches of manufacturing in our models have been aggregated into three groups: (a) light industry (food, textiles, clothing, wood products, etc.); (b) heavy industry (chemicals, metals, petroleum, etc.), and (c) machinery. Light industry includes sectors in which both demand and factor proportions favor early development while machinery typically develops at a relatively late stage. The three principal sources of growth, expressed as percentages of each sector's increase in output (as in Table 2), are shown in Figures 1, 2, and 3 for each of these sectors.

Outward-Looking Sequences. In Group A countries, each sector shows the same decline in import substitution and rapid rise of exports as a source of growth that was indicated in Table 2. This shift is earlier and more pronounced in light industry, where import substitution is only significant in the first period, and takes place last in machinery. These differences also persist at less-aggregated levels. There is a corresponding change in the pattern of exports in each country (not shown) with a growing component of heavy industrial products.

Despite these differences in degree, the major impression from these comparisions is a general similarity in the trade-development sequences of each sector in the three developing countries in Group A. After an initial period of strong import substitution, export expansion became the major sources of industrial growth in Korea and Taiwan in each major sector, and also led to an acceleration of growth in each. In Israel, however, exports predominated only in light industry.

A final phase of import liberalization in each sector is shown by Norway, Israel, and Yugoslavia. In this phase export expansion is partly offset by increased imports, so that the rate of sectoral growth is determined primarily by domestic demand.

Inward-Looking Sequences. Although there are some significant differences in timing, the inward-looking countries of Group C indicate the effects of the exhaustion of import substitution possibilities in all sectors. The failure to develop manufactured exports (except on a modest scale in light industry) has led to the decline of the rate of growth shown in both light and heavy industry, but not yet in machinery.

Even though Colombia, Turkey, and Mexico are relatively large countries and have had fairly rapid rates of growth, the expansion of the domestic market has not offset this failure. A more detailed analysis shows these countries lagging particularly in machinery and metal products, sectors in which the countries in Group A have had above average growth.

In summary, the general features of the inward-looking pattern carry over to each of the major sectors, as in the case of the export-led strategy. While the opportunities for import substitution persist longer in heavy industry and machinery and in light industry, its ultimate decline is similar.

CONCLUDING REMARKS

This paper illustrates an approach to the analysis of structural change in which internal and external factors are treated together in an interindustry framework. The method is adapted from techniques used in development planning and takes advantage of information collected for this purpose. It can be extended to encompass production functions and factor use by sector in order to provide a more complete analysis of the source of growth and structural change.

The effects of trade policy on industrial structures that are revealed by this analysis are quite striking. Although import substitution is an important feature of early stages of industrialization in all developing countries, it can be accelerated or retarded by trade policy. The later stage of expansion of manufactured exports is more susceptible to pol-

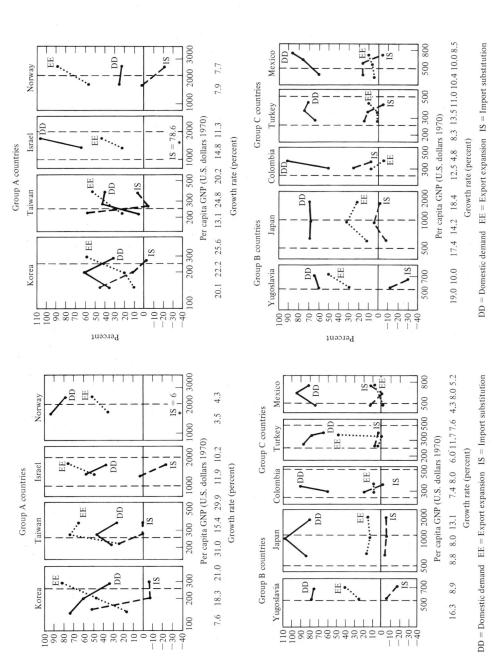

FIGURE 1. Sources of increase in light industry (percent).

FIGURE 2. Sources of increase in heavy industry (percent).

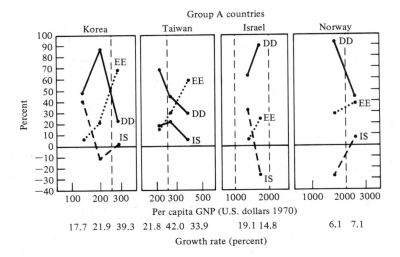

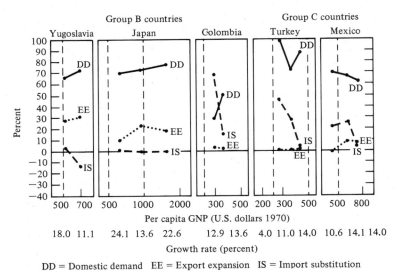

DD = Domestic demand   EE = Export expansion   IS = Import substitution

FIGURE 3. Sources of increase in machinery (percent).

icy influence and is shown to have a large effect on the subsequent course of industrial development.

To complete the linkage between industrialization and export growth, it would be necessary to examine the changes in comparative advantage that result from the acceleration of growth and learning by doing in successful export-led strategies. This process, which is explored in my paper with Donald Keesing, has been a major factor behind the growing share of the semi-industrial countries in world markets for manufactures. Their success in exporting manufactured goods has in turn contributed to more rapid industrial growth in a cumulative process.

References

J. Bergsman, "Growth and Equity in Semi-Industrialized Countries," *World Bank Staff Working Paper* No. 351, 1979.

H. B. Chenery and D. B. Keesing, "The Changing Composition of Developing Country Exports," *World Bank Staff Working Paper* No. 314, 1979.

Hollis B. Chenery and Moises Syrquin, *Patterns of Development 1950–1970*, London, 1975.

———— and ————, "A comparative Analysis of Industrial Growth," in R. C. O. Matthews, ed., *Measurement, History and Factors of Economic Growth*, New York, 1979.

Anne O. Krueger, *Foreign Trade Regimes and Economic Development: Liberalization Attempts and Consequences*, New York, 1978.

Y. Kubo and S. Robinson, "Sources of Industrial Growth and Structural Change: A Comparative Analysis of Eight Countries," mimeo, World Bank, 1979.

I. M. D. Little, Tibor Scitovsky, and M. FG. Scott, *Industry and Trade in Some Developing Countries: A Comparative Study*, Oxford, 1970.

VI.C. AGRICULTURE-
INDUSTRY INTERACTIONS

VI.C.1. Industrialization and
Agricultural Development*

The interrelationships between growth in manufacturing and that in other sectors of the economy are critical for industrialization as well as for overall development. Policymakers have long been conscious of the importance to manufacturing of investment in infrastructure. However, economic analysis has largely neglected intersectoral links, concentrating instead on either macroeconomic or sectoral and subsectoral issues. . . .

This "selection" focuses on what is generally the most important of the connections between industrialization and other sectors—the relationship with agriculture.

Agricultural economists usually analyze the role of agriculture in economic development in the context of models of closed economies. Foreign trade is absent, and final demand linkages and input-output relations ensure a perfect complementarity in production between agriculture and industry. International trade theorists, on the other hand, caution that when trade intervenes, demand interrelationships need not imply supply complementarities. Exports and imports may be large enough to offset the relation between domestic demand and domestic supply of major commodities. In the stylized view of agricultural economists, industry and agriculture produce only goods for domestic absorption which for one reason or another cannot be subject to international trade. In the simplified vision of international trade theorists, all agricultural and industrial goods are internationally traded. Empirically, the first view aptly describes the economy of large countries, but the second has more applica-

bility to countries of less than 15 million population, in which imports typically are 40 percent or more of the total supply of commodity consumption.

The position taken here is midway between the models of international trade theorists and the agricultural economists. [When we deal] with food supply, agricultural production is assumed not to be subject to international trade, whereas industrial commodities can be freely imported and exported. The analysis is conducted in terms of a dual economy where agriculture provides the growing urban sector with both workers and wage goods. Attention is focused on the problem of producing an agricultural surplus for the urban market and on the connections between economic growth and the agricultural terms of trade. [When we deal] with export agriculture, the roles are reversed: agricultural output is a traded commodity and industry a producer of domestic goods. Industrialization and export agriculture are discussed in terms of a simplified analysis of a foreign exchange-constrained economy, in which the industrial sector neither exports nor competes with imports. The discussion centers on the consequences of the pattern and rate of economic growth of the developing economy of a "squeeze" on agriculture through foreign exchange controls.

The purpose of these semi-open models is not to discuss the advantages or disadvantages of food self-sufficiency or autarkic industrialization, but rather to inquire into the policy issues that arise under such empirically relevant scenarios.

The difficulties associated with policies relying solely on the price mechanism to promote a "virtuous circle" of interactions between industry and agriculture are reviewed in the third and final section.

*From Edmar L. Bacha, "Industrialization and Agricultural Development," in John Cody et al. (eds.), *Policies for Industrial Progress in Developing Countries*, London, Oxford University Press, 1980, pp. 259–61, 263–6, 268–72. Reprinted by permission.

I. INDUSTRIALIZATION AND THE FOOD SUPPLY

In this section, two-sector models are used to study the interrelationships between industry and agriculture. While historically labor market linkages have been perhaps the first connection between the two, product markets eventually became the dominant focus of their interaction, as described below. The need to provide food for the growing urban labor force gives rise to so-called marketed surplus problems. Here these are analyzed in the context of the Soviet and the Japanese experiences. In the final part of this section, the thesis that agricultural growth in mixed market economies is causally linked to the agricultural terms of trade is discussed in terms of the induced innovation hypothesis proposed by Hayami and Ruttan.

The Dual Growth Models

The relationships between subsistence agriculture and manufacturing industry rarely fit the enclave growth model in which a modern export sector develops by importing labor, capital, food, and raw materials, with traditional agriculture remaining as a purely subsistence activity without any connection to the growth of manufacturing. Foreign-controlled plantation economies approximated this enclave model, as did some highly capital-intensive, foreign-dominated mining operations, until developing countries began to appropriate the economic rents accruing to such operations.

The first connection between agriculture and industry is established by the use of an unskilled labor force from agriculture in the industrial sector and its ancillary service activities. A stylized view of the labor market relationships between town and country in the early stages of economic development runs as follows. Industry is a labor-using activity which can draw freely from a pool of surplus agricultural labor. These labor resources are made available to industry at a constant wage in terms of industrial goods. Economic growth is defined as the transfer of

labor from subsistence agriculture to market-oriented industry. Implicitly, industry is defined as everything that is modern and growing, and agriculture everything that is traditional and stagnant. Intersectoral product flow are ignored because of two assumptions: (1) extended family systems in the rural sector supply urban workers with the required wage goods through nonmarket channels: or (2) wage goods are imported at constant prices in terms of domestic industrial goods.

Both assumptions are untenable. The latter leaves open the question of where the modern sector is going to obtain the foreign exchange to pay for the wage goods; it does not recognize that, culturally, wage goods may be specific to the local economy and hence not available from foreign sources; and it ignores that governments are usually adamantly opposed to letting a significant fraction of basic food consumption be imported from abroad.

The assumption that migrant workers provide for their own subsistence through informal rural connections is equivalent to saying that the terms of trade between agriculture and industry remain constant as workers move from country to town. The equivalence would follow because under fixed terms of trade it can be assumed that the urban wage is fixed in terms of industrial goods. In fact, the urban wage consists of a bundle of wage goods in which agricultural, not industrial, products predominate. The terms of trade will remain constant as labor is withdrawn from agriculture only if (1) the marginal product of labor in agriculture is zero, so that total agricultural output remains constant in spite of the labor transfer, and (2) the migrant worker consumes the same amount of agricultural goods as when he was a rural dweller. The second assumption ignores transport and commercialization costs, which are important, as well as the eventual need for a higher industrial wage to induce workers to migrate. The zero marginal productivity assumption has been the object of a long and heated debate in the development literature, with many experts suggesting that this is an acceptable presumption only for clearly overpopulated rural areas.

In the absence of informal subsistence mechanisms, the need to provide food for the industrial labor force establishes a product market relationship between agriculture and industry. As industrial employment grows and income per capita expands, the urban demand for agricultural products increases.

If it can indeed be presumed that under these conditions the terms of trade will not change, the policy implication is clear—policymakers need worry only about industrial growth. Agriculture will respond swiftly to the increasing urban demand by making better use of its partially idle labor and land resources.

There is a problem with the assumption that market-oriented agricultural growth is constrained only by lack of demand and that, if urban demand materializes, rural output will respond along a highly price-elastic supply curve. Historically this has been the case in only a few countries, and they had strongly market-oriented agricultural production. Several Southeast and East Asian countries, some African countries, and such areas in Latin America as Argentina and southern Brazil fit this pattern. In other countries the "benign neglect" of agriculture and even active policies were unable to avoid the grave difficulties that occasioned the voluminous literature on the marketed surplus problem.

The Marketed Surplus

The important question is how to guarantee a continuous supply of agricultural goods to the growing urban sector. The neoclassical answer is simple: raise agricultural prices. But this would mean paying more for farm products and would leave less resources for industrial accumulation. The higher the volume of industrial goods that has to be put aside to pay for agricultural inputs (both wage goods and raw materials), the lower will be the volume of industrial goods that can be added to the capital stock of the modern sector.

The Soviet industrialization debate of the 1920s showed the the dilemma is particularly acute in the case of a crash industrialization program. The issue was further complicated in the USSR because agriculture was based on private peasant farming, whereas industry was state-owned and run. Under these conditions, as Preobrazhensky noted, "an exchange of the smaller quantity of labor of the [socialist] economic system for the greater quantity of labor of the [nonsocialist] economic system" was needed to secure a rapid industrial advance from the low initial base.[1] This famous "law of primitive socialist accumulation" stands for the whole set of government market controls which serve one purpose: to bring about a shift of resources from the private to the socialized sector over and above the share the latter could obtain as a result of the operation of competitive economic relations.

The trouble with this scheme is that the relationships between a modern industrial sector and a backward peasant agricultural sector are not symmetrical. Food is indispensable for industry, while the peasants' need for industrial products is secondary, if not superfluous. Faced with dwindling supplies of industrial goods and increasing claims for their own products, peasants may simply refuse to play the game and step back to a closed subsistence economy. This was the situation in the USSR. The price squeeze that resulted from a policy of holding down food prices was met by the peasants' massive withdrawal from the market, which threatened to bring the Soviet economy to the brink of disaster. Stalin's solution was to step up forced collectivization of the peasantry. Through state farming, he managed to break the peasants' veto power over his decisions on economic policy and so managed to industrialize peasant Russia. However, the human costs were enormous (Preobrazhensky himself died in the great purge of 1937), and long-term agricultural productivity growth became, and still is, a bottleneck in Soviet economic development. The lesson seems to

[1] Evgeny Preobrazhensky, *The New Economics* (London; Oxford University Press, 1965), p. 91

be that developing countries not contemplating forced output by the rural sector will find it difficult to follow Preobrazhensky's recommendation to further industrialization by reducing the relative prices of agricultural products.

For an example of how to resolve the terms of trade dilemma, agricultural economists point to Japan from the Meiji revolution to World War I. Despite its meager endowment of land, Japan's agricultural and industrial development went forward concurrently. Farm output expanded within the existing framework of small-scale agriculture with remarkably low demands on foreign exchange resources. The major factors responsible for the high rate of growth in agricultural output were the increased productivity and greater utilization of existing land and labor made possible by the diffusion of new technology. While it has been argued that this process did not require major capital inputs, the Meiji period did see substantial investment in rural infrastructure. It is, however, true that rural-to-urban capital flows occurred. A policy of high land taxes was adopted, which drew a substantial share of the increased agricultural productivity for investment in the industrial infrastructure, while avoiding the disincentive effects of the Soviet experience before collectivization.

It is moot whether a similar option exists for contemporary developing countries. More important now are institutional and organizational reform, infrastructural investments, and research and development, all highly complementary inputs in the creation of new production potentials in agriculture. The complementarity between infrastructure investments and investment in research and development raises a serious question about the validity of the assumption that primary emphasis on scientific progress can provide a relatively inexpensive route to rapid growth of agricultural production during the early stages of development.

Where modernization of agriculture requires heavy initial investments, it is not possible a priori to anticipate the direction of intersectoral capital flows between agriculture and industry in a process of concurrent economic growth. But is not this question of intersectoral financial flows just a red herring? Should agriculture and industry be analyzed as separate entities, as if they were two independent countries? The answer might be in the affirmative in the USSR of the 1920s, where a socialized industrial sector confronted an antagonistic peasant society. But it should not be true for planning processes in politically integrated developing countries if planners are concerned with the welfare of the country as a whole rather than with the interests of specific social groups within it.

What this means is that, in principle, the sectoral location of an investment activity should not be an issue in planned investment decisions. However, the planning process of many developing countries has been characterized by a considerable degree of urban bias. Agriculture is often treated as inherently low in productivity, industry as high in productivity. Empirical misconceptions, ideological biases, and class interests mingle together to explain such an antirural attitude. Policy measures are sometimes designed to deliver subsidized inputs, credits, and extension activities to farmers to mitigate such bias, but in practice these measures largely tend to benefit medium- and large-scale farmers. This policymaking pattern has been criticized as one of the main reasons economic growth in developing countries since World War II has failed to reach the poorer groups in the population.

A pro-rural strategy has been advocated in its stead as part of a broad reconsideration of the development problem. The reasoning behind this is simple enough. Most of the poor are in the countryside. Given current rates of rural population growth and likely rates of urban labor absorption, it is argued that the poor will remain in the rural sector for a long time. If alleviation of poverty is the main objective of development policy, then it follows that the problem should be attacked at its root, without waiting for an eventual absorption of most of the labor force in the modern urban sector. Measures should be adopted to increase the productivity and income of the rural poor even if they result in less resources for urban industrial capital accumulation, which mostly benefits the middle- and upper-income groups. Such a strategy is of course in sharp contrast to the industrialization-first doctrine with which this analysis of the interactions between agriculture and industry began.

II. INDUSTRIALIZATION AND EXPORT AGRICULTURE

Viewed from the intersectoral perspective, the main difference between the analyses of the last section and those of this section lies in a redefinition of the role of agriculture. Earlier, it was described as that of supplying industry with food. Here its output is foreign exchange.

To facilitate the discussion, consider the case of a developing country with a budding, fully protected domestic-market-oriented industrial sector, the material inputs of which are indirectly supplied by domestic agriculture through the export of primary products to the rest of the world. The relevant policy issues are illustrated by reference to the historical experiences of Brazil and Argentina since the 1930s.

A triangular trade pattern is established between agriculture, industry, and the rest of the world, which can be visualized from the Brazilian growth process from the 1930s to the early 1960s. Agriculture (A) sells coffee to the world (W) and buys manufactured products from industry (I), which in turn acquires capital goods from foreign markets. (These relationships are illustrated in Figure 1.) In its role of foreign exchange supplier, agriculture in fact functions as the machine-producing sector of the economy. For the sake of the argument, take the dollar prices of coffee and imported machines to be given and assume that coffee production depends only on a specific input—say, land—the growth of which is exogenously determined. How can the growth rate of domestic industry be raised under these conditions?

One clear possibility is to increase the

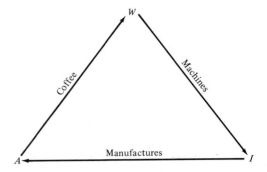

FIGURE 1. The trade pattern between agriculture, industry, and the rest of the world.

cruzeiro price of manufactures relative to the cruzeiro price of machines. If this is done, the industrial sector will have more of its own product—say, cement—left over after paying for the machines and can add that to its capital stock. In practice, the relative price change can be done by freezing the cruzeiro-dollar exchange rate at a time when the internal price of manufactures is being raised by domestic inflation. This certainly happened in Brazil from the immediate postwar period to the early 1960s. In fact, the price twist was carried to such an extreme that, by the end of the 1950s, the purchasing power of a unit of domestic industrial goods in terms of imported machinery was two and a half times higher than in the late 1940s. As the exchange rate lags behind industrial prices to increase the purchasing power of domestic manufactures over imports, the domestic price ratio of coffee to manufactures goes down. Domestic inflation increases the prices of industrial goods, while the cruzeiro price of coffee, under given world coffee prices, accompanies the more sluggish growth of the cruzeiro-dollar exchange rate.

This method of increasing industrial capital accumulation raises several issues. First, the assumption that the external terms of trade (the dollar price of coffee divided by the dollar price of machines) are given does not fit the facts. The amount of coffee exported by Brazil does affect the international coffee prices.

Second, the quantity of coffee that Brazilian farmers produce is a function of the domestic terms of trade (cruzeiro price of coffee divided by the cruzeiro price of manufactures). Abundant empirical evidence on the supply response of Brazilian coffee farmers indicates that the quantity produced cannot be taken as exogenously determined. Coffee production is a profit-making activity that shares with other sectors the available endowments of labor and capital. In the context of the two-sector model under discussion, this means that as the relative price changes, there is some substitution in production between coffee and manufactures. Again, this is true for agricultural production more generally.

Third, while a surplus is generated for the industrial sector through the relative price twist, the conclusion cannot be drawn that this surplus will be invested productively. It may be wasted as conspicuous consumption or else embodied in a form—say, cement—with very low marginal productivity indeed.

Consider the first two issues together. Since Brazil has a monopoly power in the international coffee market, it follows that up to a point it is to its advantage to turn the domestic terms of trade against the coffee sector in order to reduce exports and raise world coffee prices. In the determination of the optimal price policy from the national point of view, attention has to be paid to the fact that the long-run foreign demand curve is more price elastic than the corresponding short-run relation. As a consequence, to keep competition at bay and foreign consumers loyal, the optimal price will be found at a lower level than that which would maximize short-run earnings. Thus if a country has a monopoly power in international trade, turning relative domestic prices against exports would be, up to a point, not a squeeze on agriculture but a squeeze on foreigners. The latter could be justified in terms of national welfare.

Argentina more than Brazil provides a pure case where industrial development was achieved by a squeeze on domestic export agri-

riculture. Trade policies similar to those applied in Brazil were followed from the early 1940s to the mid-1950s. Argentina was certainly an important supplier of meat, wool, and grains in the world market, but, from a long-run perspective, foreign demand price elasticities for Argentinian products were high enough to justify the assumption of given world prices.

The degree of price discrimination in Argentina in favor of industry and against agriculture can be gauged by the evolution of the purchasing power of domestic manufactures over imports, as previously defined. According to Diaz-Alejandro, this quotient increased by an average of 54 percent between 1930–39 and 1945–55. Diaz-Alehandro submits that Argentina's slippage behind other countries of recent settlement since the 1930s was causally associated with the price shifts and related economic policies. He reasons, in terms of the relationships shown in Figure 1, that the industrial sector in Argentina during this period would be better described as a home-goods sector than as a truly import-substituting sector. Cement, for example, is not exported, and domestically it is only a poor substitute for imported machines. But this home-goods sector expands by drawing resources away from export agriculture, causing a reduction in the supply of foreign exchange to the economy. Additional investment in the industrial sector can only take the form of cement, to continue the example, because foreign exchange is not available to convert domestic savings into imported machines. Because cement substitutes poorly for machines, the incremental capital-output ratio is very high. Diaz-Alejandro concludes that in an economy with a severe foreign exchange bottleneck, not even a gross saving of 20 percent, as was the case in Argentina, will bring rapid growth. Under such conditions, the transformation of savings into tangible machinery and equipment becomes a difficult task.

From this example, it would appear that for most developing countries the capacity to transform smoothly ex ante savings propensities into nonconstruction capital goods requires either expansion of foreign exchange earnings or a balanced, in-depth program of industrialization.

The contrast in the 1940s and 1950s between the uncertain growth rates of Argentina, based on the development of light manufactures, and the vigorous expansion of Brazil, based on a better integrated industrial structure, seems to confirm Dìaz-Alejandro's argument that, given the decision not to promote exports of either rural or manufactured products, emphasis on light manufacturing is misplaced. A forward-looking policy should address primarily the more complex industries and key social overhead facilities for which state support is of greater strategic importance. Nevertheless, it may be argued that Brazil's strategy was excessively costly and that only the country's sheer size and diversity made it viable. Brazil eventually had to move to a less inward-oriented policy to sustain rapid industrial and overall growth. Similar policies have not proved effective in the very large countries of South Asia, and they have been costly and ineffectual in medium- and small-scale countries.

Comment

As the foregoing selection indicates, the interactions between industry and agriculture can be analyzed under either closed-economy or open-economy assumptions. For additional readings, see Bruce F. Johnston, "The Role of Agriculture in Economic Development," *American Economic Review* (December 1961); W. H. Nicholls, "An 'Agricultural Surplus' as a Factor in Economic Devlopment," (February 1963); W. Owen, "The Double Squeeze on Agriculture," *American Economic Review* (March 1966); M. June Flanders, "Agriculture versus Industry in Development Policy," *Journal of Development Studies* (April 1968); Bruce F. Johnston and Peter Kilby, *Agriculture and Structural Transformation* (1975), chapter 7. An excellent survey article is Bruce F. Johnston, "Agriculture and Structural Transformation in Developing Countries: A Survey of Research," *Journal of Economic Literature* (June 1970).

For analysis of the role of agriculture in the context of an economy open to international trade, see Hla Myint, "Agriculture and Economic Development in the Open Economy," in Lloyd G. Reynolds (ed.), *Agriculture in Development Theory* (1975).

Comment

The early dual sector models of Lewis, Fei and Ranis, and Jorgenson (Chapter III) interpreted economic development as involving a major transformation of the economy from one which is dominantly agricultural to one containing a large and growing urban-industrial sector. The inevitable relative decline in agriculture arises from (1) increased specialization in production, which transfers many nonagricultural production jobs from the farm household to urban centers; (2) relatively low-income elasticites of demand for agricultural as compared with nonagricultural commodities under conditions of rising incomes; (3) high transport costs of particular agricultural and nonagricultural commodities, which militate against extreme specialization in agricultural production; and (4) the inconsistency of normal input-output relationships in a high-productivity, high-income agriculture with the existing population density of many low-income countries. Such a transformation is emphasized as a means of relieving the burden of population growth and consequent fragmenting of farms and low incomes.

As labor moves from the agricultural to the nonagricultural sector, there is the problem of providing food supplies for the growing urban labor force. Creation of nonfarm jobs requires a large increase in capital in the urban sector. Agriculture may be an important source of such capital. The populous agricultural sector may also provide needed markets for industrial output of consumer goods. The agricultural sector also depends on inputs produced in the industrial sector.

These interactions between the agricultural and nonagricultural sectors are analyzed by John W. Mellor, "Toward a Theory of Agricultural Development," in Herman M. Southworth and Bruce F. Johnston (eds.), *Agricultural Development and Economic Growth* (1967) and Bruce F. Johnston, "Agriculture and Structural Transformation in Developing Countries: A Survey of Research," *Journal of Economic Literature* (1970), with an extensive bibliography. See also selection VII.A.1.

VI.C.2. Complementarity of Industry and Agriculture*

The case for rapid industrialisation in the West Indies rests chiefly on over-population. The islands already carry a larger population than agriculture can absorb, and populations are growing at rates of from 1.5 to 2.0 per cent per annum. It is, therefore, urgent to create new opportunities for employment off the land. . . .

However carefully the peasant may work his holding in staple crops—and, or course, at present he is very backward—he cannot make 2 or 3 acres yield him a reasonable standard of living. He cannot get from 2 or 3 acres even the 6 shillings a day or more which he hopes to earn in the town, so that it is not at all surprising that there is a continual drift to the towns. If peasant agriculture is to be put on its feet, the number of peasants must be reduced drastically, in relation to the land that they now occupy, so that each family may be able to have a reasonable acreage (more equipment to work the land will also be needed). . . .

In a word, if West Indian agriculture is to yield a decent standard of living, the number engaged in the present acreage must be drastically reduced—it must be something like halved, if current expectations of what is reasonable are to be fulfilled. But this is not

*From W. Arthur Lewis, "The Industrialisation of the British West Indies," *Caribbean Economic Review*, May 1950, pp. 1, 6–7, 16–17, 38. Reprinted by permission.

practicable unless new employments can be found for those who would be displaced in the process. Until new employments can be created, mechanisation and other increased use of capital equipment will be a doubtful boon, and major improvements in peasant agriculture will be impossible. . . .

If this impression is right, then agriculture in the islands will yield a decent standard of living only if the numbers engaged in it are drastically reduced, and this will be possible only if new employments can be created outside agriculture. The creation of new industries is an essential part of a programme for agricultural improvement.

This is not generally realized. There are still people who discuss industrialisation as if it were an *alternative* to agricultural improvement. In countries where agriculture is not carrying surplus population, industry and agriculture are alternatives. New Zealand, on the one hand, or England on the other, have to weigh carefully the respective merits of industry and of agriculture, and to decide on relative emphases. But this approach is without meaning in the West Indian islands. There is no choice to be made between industry and agriculture. The islands need as large an agriculture as possible, and, if they could even get more people into agriculture, without reducing output per head, then so much the better. But, even when they are employing in agriculture the maximum number that agriculture will absorb at a reasonable standard of living, there will still be a large surplus of labour, and even the greatest expansion of industry which is conceivable within the next twenty years will not create a labour shortage in agriculture. It is not the case that agriculture cannot continue to develop if industry is developed. Exactly the opposite is true: agriculture cannot be put on to a basis where it will yield a reasonable standard of living unless new jobs are created off the land. . . .

Two propositions follow from this. The first is that, if the West Indian market is itself to support a large manufacturing industry, then the standard of living must first be greatly increased. The way to increase the standard of living, as we have already seen, is to make it possible for each worker to have at his disposal the produce of a large acreage; i.e., greatly to reduce the number of persons in agriculture per 1,000 acres, without reducing the total output of agriculture. But this, as we have also seen, means putting more persons into manufacturing industry. Thus the full complementarity of industry and agriculture stands revealed. If agriculture is to give a higher standard of living, then industry must be developed. But equally, if industry is to be developed, then agriculture must give a higher standard of living, in order to provide a demand for manufactures. The agricultural and the industrial revolutions thus reinforce each other, and neither can go very far unless the other is occurring at the same time. Those who speak as if the choice in the West Indies lay between agricultural development and industrial development have failed completely to understand the problem.

The second proposition is that manufacturing industries cannot provide employment for an extra 120,000 in the next ten years unless the islands start to export manufactures to outside destinations. Neither their own growing demands, nor the replacement of imports, can provide a large enough market. The domestic market for manufactures is too small to support more than a fraction of what is needed. For, at the present standard of living, the local demand is for food, rather than for manufactures.

Now, if the islands were not short of good, cultivable land, the conclusion would be to put the surplus population on to the land to grow this food. Since they are short of land, they will have to depend for their food supplies increasingly on importing food, and on putting people instead into producing manufactures which will be exported to pay for imported food. . . .

The islands cannot be industrialised to anything like the extent that is necessary without a considerable inflow of foreign capital and capitalists, and a period of wooing and fawning upon such people. Foreign capital is needed because industrialisation is a frightfully expensive business quite beyond the resources of the islands. Light industries, based on imported materials, will require, say, £600 of capital or more, for each person employed, and heavy industries, using local materials, may easily demand £2,000 per head. To provide employment for 100,000 persons calls for an investment in manufacturing alone (i.e., excluding all the subsidiary activities that will bring employment up to 400,000) of something like £130,000,000. There is no prospect of the West Indies providing such a sum out of its own savings; it must be borrowed abroad. Then, some people may say, let it be borrowed by the government. Let the government set up the factories, and hire foreign technicians to run them. It is very doubtful if the governments could raise any such sum on their own credit. But even if they could, and even if they were able to hire technicians, the problem would still not be solved. For successful industrialisation on a big scale is possible only if the islands can export manufactures. And, since it is difficult and expensive to break into a foreign market by building up new distribution outlets, this is most likely to succeed if the islands concentrate on inviting manufacturers who are already well established in foreign markets. If an industry is to supply only the local West Indian market, it is quite feasible for the government to start and run it. But those industries which are to try to sell in Latin America, or in the United States, or in England, are better left to foreign capitalists.

EXHIBIT VI.2. Growth of Production, 1960–1981

	Average Annual Growth Rate (percent)									
	GDP		Agriculture		Industry		Manufac-turing		Services	
	1960–70	1970–81	1960–70	1970–81	1960–70	1970–81	1960–70	1970–81	1960–70	1970–81
Low-income economies	4.6 w^a	4.5 w	2.2 m^b	2.3 m	6.6 m	3.6 m	5.4 m	2.9 m	4.2 m	4.6 m
China and India	4.5 w	4.8 w	1.8 m	2.4 m	8.3 m	6.4 m	—	—	5.2 m	4.8 m
Other low-income	4.7 w	3.6 w	2.7 m	2.3 m	6.6 m	3.2 m	5.9 m	2.8 m	4.2 m	4.6 m
1 Kampuchea, Dem.	3.1	—	—	—	—	—	—	—	—	—
2 Bhutan	—	—	—	—	—	—	—	—	—	—
3 Lao, PDR	—	—	—	—	—	—	—	—	—	—
4 Chad	0.5	—	—	—	—	—	—	—	—	—
5 Bangladesh	3.7	4.2	2.7	2.4	8.0	9.0	6.6	11.2	4.2	5.3
6 Ethiopia	4.4	2.2	2.2	0.9	7.4	1.8	8.0	2.8	7.8	4.2
7 Nepal	2.5	2.1	—	—	—	—	—	—	—	—
8 Burma	2.6	4.8	4.1	4.7	2.8	5.6	3.4	4.6	1.5	4.7
9 Afghanistan	2.0	3.9	—	3.2	—	3.2	—	2.8	—	5.3
10 Mali	3.3	4.6	—	4.0	—	2.4	—	—	—	5.9
11 Malawi	4.9	5.6	—	—	—	—	—	—	—	—
12 Zaire	3.4	−0.2	—	1.5	—	−0.8	—	−2.3	—	−0.4
13 Uganda	5.6	−1.6	—	−0.8	—	−9.8	—	−9.3	—	−0.7
14 Burundi	4.4	3.2	—	2.2	—	8.5	—	5.9	—	3.5
15 Upper Volta	3.0	3.6	—	1.4	—	2.9	—	3.4	—	5.8
16 Rwanda	2.7	5.3	—	—	—	—	—	—	—	—
17 India	3.4	3.6	1.9	1.9	5.4	4.4	4.7	5.0	4.6	5.2
18 Somalia	1.0	3.9	−0.6	—	3.4	—	4.0	—	4.2	—
19 Tanzania	6.0	5.1	—	5.5	—	2.2	—	2.9	—	5.4
20 Viet Nam	3.8	—	—	—	—	—	—	—	—	—
21 China	5.2	5.5	1.6	2.8	11.2	8.3	—	—	5.7	4.4
22 Guinea	3.5	3.0	—	—	—	—	—	—	—	—
23 Haiti	0.2	3.4	−0.6	1.1	0.2	7.1	−0.1	7.6	1.1	3.5
24 Sir Lanka	4.6	4.3	3.0	3.0	6.6	4.2	6.3	2.1	4.6	5.0
25 Benin	2.6	3.3	—	—	—	—	—	—	—	—
26 Central African Rep.	1.9	1.6	0.8	2.3	5.4	4.0	5.4	−4.3	1.8	(·)
27 Sierra Leone	4.3	1.9	—	2.4	—	−3.6	—	3.7	—	4.5
28 Madagascar	2.9	0.3	—	0.3	—	0.3	—	—	—	0.4
29 Niger	2.9	3.1	3.3	−3.0	13.9	11.4	—	—	(·)	6.9
30 Pakistan	6.7	4.8	4.9	2.6	10.0	5.5	9.4	4.4	7.0	6.1
31 Mozambique	—	—	—	—	—	—	—	—	—	—
32 Sudan	1.3	4.1	—	2.3	—	3.2	—	1.5	—	6.0
33 Togo	8.5	3.2	—	1.5	—	6.2	—	−10.4	—	3.2
34 Ghana	2.1	−0.2	—	0.0	—	−2.2	—	−1.0	—	0.4
Middle-income economies	6.0 w	5.6 w	3.4 m	3.0 m	7.4 m	6.8 m	6.7 m	5.9 m	5.5 m	6.1 m
Oil exporters	6.3 w	6.2 w	3.3 m	3.4 m	7.4 m	7.6 m	7.4 m	8.7 m	4.8 m	7.2 m
Oil importers	5.8 w	5.4 w	3.5 m	2.9 m	7.0 m	5.9 m	6.5 m	5.6 m	5.7 m	5.7 m

EXHIBIT VI.2. Growth of Production, 1960–1981 (*Continued*)

	Average Annual Growth Rate (percent)									
	GDP		Agriculture		Industry		Manufac-turing		Services	
	1960–70	1970–81	1960–70	1970–81	1960–70	1970–81	1960–70	1970–81	1960–70	1970–81
Lower middle-income	5.0 w^a	5.6 w	3.0 m^b	3.2 m	6.8 m	7.4 m	7.1 m	5.8 m	5.3 m	6.0 m
35 Kenya	5.9	5.8	—	4.2	—	8.5	—	9.5	—	6.0
36 Senegal	2.5	2.0	2.9	2.6	4.4	4.1	6.2	2.0	1.7	0.9
37 Mauritania	6.7	1.7	1.4	3.1	14.1	−4.0	9.2	4.6	7.4	5.2
38 Yemen Arab	—	8.7	—	3.6	—	13.9	—	12.1	—	11.7
39 Yemen, PDR	—	—	—	—	—	—	—	—	—	—
40 Liberia	5.1	1.3	—	4.0	—	−0.7	—	5.6	—	1.4
41 Indonesia	3.9	7.8	2.7	3.8	5.2	11.2	3.3	13.9	4.8	9.5
42 Lesotho	5.2	8.4	—	4.3	—	12.9	—	9.6	—	9.2
43 Bolivia	5.2	4.4	3.0	2.9	6.2	3.7	5.4	5.3	5.4	5.2
44 Honduras	5.3	3.8	5.7	1.9	5.4	4.9	4.5	4.7	4.8	4.6
45 Zambia	5.0	0.4	—	1.8	—	−0.4	—	0.3	—	1.2
46 Egypt	4.3	8.1	2.9	2.9	5.4	7.6	4.8	8.7	4.7	11.8
47 El Salvador	5.9	3.1	3.0	2.3	8.5	3.3	8.8	2.4	6.5	3.3
48 Thailand	8.4	7.2	5.6	4.5	11.9	9.9	11.4	10.3	9.1	7.5
49 Philippines	5.1	6.2	4.3	4.9	6.0	8.4	6.7	6.9	5.2	5.3
50 Angola	—	—	—	—	—	—	—	—	—	—
51 Papua New Guinea	6.7	1.9	—	—	—	—	—	—	—	—
52 Morocco	4.4	5.2	4.7	()	4.2	5.8	4.2	5.4	4.4	6.4
53 Nicaragua	7.3	0.8	7.8	2.7	10.4	2.1	11.4	2.8	5.8	−0.8
54 Nigeria	3.1	4.5	−0.4	−0.4	14.7	6.0	9.1	12.4	2.3	7.4
55 Zimbabwe	4.3	1.8	—	—	—	—	—	—	—	—
65 Cameroon	3.7	6.3	—	3.9	—	9.4	—	5.3	—	6.8
57 Cuba	—	—	—	—	—	—	—	—	—	—
58 Congo, People's Rep.	2.3	5.1	1.8	2.1	7.4	13.6	7.4	−1.8	1.1	2.2
59 Guatemala	5.6	5.5	4.3	4.3	7.8	7.3	8.2	5.9	5.5	5.4
60 Peru	4.9	3.0	3.7	0.3	5.0	3.4	5.7	2.9	5.3	3.5
61 Ecuador	—	8.6	—	2.9	—	12.5	—	10.8	—	8.7
62 Jamaica	4.4	−1.2	1.5	0.5	4.8	−3.6	5.7	−2.6	4.6	()
63 Ivory Coast	8.0	6.2	4.2	4.7	11.5	9.3	11.6	5.8	9.7	5.8
64 Dominican Rep.	4.5	6.3	2.1	3.2	6.0	7.6	5.0	6.1	5.0	6.7
65 Mongolia	—	—	—	—	—	—	—	—	—	—
66 Colombia	5.1	5.7	3.5	4.7	6.0	4.7	5.7	5.7	5.7	6.8
67 Tunisia	4.7	7.3	2.0	4.1	8.2	9.3	7.8	11.7	4.5	7.5
68 Costa Rica	6.5	5.2	.57	2.2	9.4	7.4	10.6	7.1	5.7	5.2
69 Korea, Dem. Rep.	—	—	—	—	—	—	—	—	—	—
70 Turkey	6.0	5.4	2.5	3.2	9.6	6.1	10.9	5.5	6.9	6.2
71 Syrian Arab Rep.	4.6	10.0	—	8.2	—	9.8	—	8.2	—	10.8
72 Jordan	—	—	—	—	—	—	—	—	—	—
73 Paraguay	4.2	8.8	—	7.0	—	11.0	—	8.1	—	9.1

EXHIBIT VI.2. Growth of Production, 1960–1981 (*Continued*)

	Average Annual Growth Rate (percent)									
	GDP		Agriculture		Industry		Manufac-turing		Services	
	1960–70	1970–81	1960–70	1970–81	1960–70	1970–81	1960–70	1970–81	1960–70	1970–81
Upper middle-income	**6.4** w	**5.6** w	**4.0** m	**2.6** m	**8.8** m	**4.5** m	**7.8** m	**6.3** m	**7.1** m	**6.5** m
74 Korea, Rep. of	8.6	9.1	4.4	3.0	17.2	14.4	17.6	15.6	8.9	8.2
75 Iran, Islamic Rep. Of	11.3	—	4.4	—	13.4	—	12.0	—	10.0	—
76 Iraq	6.1	—	5.7	—	4.7	—	5.9	—	8.3	—
77 Malaysia	6.5	7.8	—	5.2	—	9.3	—	11.1	—	8.5
78 Panama	7.8	4.6	5.7	2.0	10.4	4.1	10.5	2.7	7.6	5.3
79 Lebanon	4.9	−5.4	6.3	—	4.5	—	5.0	—	4.8	—
80 Algeria	4.3	6.9	0.1	3.9	11.6	7.6	7.8	11.6	−1.1	6.4
81 Brazil	5.4	8.4	—	5.2	—	9.1	—	8.7	—	8.3
82 Mexico	7.6	6.5	4.5	3.4	9.4	7.4	10.1	7.1	7.3	6.6
83 Portugal	6.2	4.4	1.3	−0.8	8.8	4.4	8.9	4.5	5.9	6.0
84 Argentina	4.3	1.9	1.8	2.5	5.8	1.4	5.6	0.7	3.8	2.2
85 Chile	4.4	2.1	3.1	3.0	4.4	0.7	5.5	()	4.6	2.9
86 South Africa	6.3	3.7	—	—	—	—	—	—	—	—
87 Yugoslavia	5.8	5.7	3.3	2.6	6.2	6.8	5.7	7.1	6.9	5.6
88 Uruguay	1.2	3.1	1.9	1.2	1.1	3.5	1.5	4.3	1.0	2.9
89 Venezuela	6.0	4.5	5.8	3.4	4.6	2.7	6.4	5.3	7.3	5.9
90 Greece	6.9	4.4	3.5	1.7	9.4	4.5	10.2	5.5	7.1	5.2
91 Hong Kong	10.0	9.9	—	−3.0	—	—	—	10.1	—	—
92 Israel	8.1	4.0	—	—	—	—	—	—	—	—
93 Singapore	8.8	8.5	5.0	1.7	12.5	9.0	13.0	9.7	7.7	8.5
94 Trinidad and Tobago	4.0	5.5	—	−1.8	—	4.0	—	1.3	—	6.9
High-income oil exporters	—	**5.3** w	—	**7.1** m	—	**3.1** m	—	**9.2** m	—	**12.2** m
95 Libya	24.4	2.3	—	10.5	—	3.1	—	14.7	—	17.1
96 Saudi Arabia	—	10.6	—	5.3	—	10.2	—	6.5	—	12.2
97 Kuwait	5.7	2.3	—	7.1	—	−2.2	—	9.2	—	9.6
98 United Arab Emirates	—	—	—	—	—	—	—	—	—	—
Industrial market economies	**5.1** w	**3.0** w	**1.4** m	**1.6** m	**5.7** m	**2.9** m	**5.9** m	**3.1** m	**4.6** m	**3.6** m
99 Ireland	4.2	4.0	0.9	—	6.1	—	—	—	4.3	—
100 Spain	7.1	3.2	—	2.1	—	3.9	—	6.0	—	4.5
101 Italy	5.5	2.9	2.6	1.3	6.6	2.9	8.0	3.7	5.1	3.2
102 New Zealand	3.6	2.0	—	—	—	—	—	—	—	—
103 United Kingdom	2.9	1.7	2.2	1.6	3.1	0.4	3.3	−0.5	2.8	2.5
104 Japan	10.4	4.5	2.1	0.2	13.0	5.6	13.6	6.5	10.2	4.2
105 Austria	4.6	3.5	1.2	1.9	5.4	3.2	5.2	3.4	4.4	3.9
106 Finland	4.3	3.1	.05	0.0	5.2	3.3	6.1	3.7	5.0	3.6
107 Australia	5.6	3.3	2.0	—	5.9	—	5.5	—	4.0	—
108 Canada	5.6	3.8	2.5	1.8	6.3	2.9	6.8	3.2	5.5	4.3

EXHIBIT VI.2. Growth of Production, 1960–1981 (*Continued*)

	GDP		Agriculture		Industry		Manufacturing		Services	
	1960–70	1970–81	1960–70	1970–81	1960–70	1970–81	1960–70	1970–81	1960–70	1970–81
109 Netherlands	5.2	2.7	2.8	3.9	6.8	2.0	6.6	2.6	5.1	3.7
110 Belgium	4.7	3.0	−0.5	0.7	5.5	3.1	6.2	3.0	4.6	3.5
111 France	5.5	3.3	1.6	0.5	7.1	2.7	7.8	3.2	5.0	4.2
112 United States	4.3	2.9	.05	1.6	4.6	2.3	5.3	2.9	4.4	3.3
113 Denmark	4.5	2.1	0.1	2.6	5.2	1.1	5.2	3.1	4.6	2.5
114 Germany, Fed. Rep.	4.4	2.6	1.5	1.3	4.8	—	5.4	2.1	4.2	2.5
115 Norway	4.3	4.5	0.7	2.2	5.5	5.0	4.8	1.3	5.0	4.5
116 Sweden	4.4	1.8	0.8	−1.1	6.2	0.8	5.9	0.7	3.9	2.7
117 Switzerland	4.3	0.7	—	—	—	—	—	—	—	—
East European nonmarket economies	—	—	—	—	—	—	—	—	—	—
118 Albania	—	—	—	—	—	—	—	—	—	—
119 Hungary	5.3	5.0	3.2	2.9	6.3	5.8	6.5	5.9	5.8	5.0
120 Romania	8.6	9.1	1.7	4.9	12.8	9.2	—	—	—	—
121 Bulgaria	—	—	—	—	—	—	—	—	—	—
122 Poland	—	—	—	—	—	—	—	—	—	—
123 USSR	—	—	—	—	—	—	—	—	—	—
124 Czechoslovakia	—	—	—	—	—	—	—	—	—	—
124 German Dem. Rep.	—	—	—	—	—	—	—	—	—	—

Source: World Bank, *World Development Report*, 1983, pp. 150–51.

[a]Indicates weighted average.

[b]Indicates median value.

VI.C.3. Overcoming the Weakness of Agriculture*

Agriculture has been the weakest link in the development chain. Industry in LDCs has grown at around 7 percent per annum, the number of children in school has multiplied by four, the domestic savings ratio has risen by three percentage points—the picture is ev-

*From Sir W. Arthur Lewis, "Development Strategy in a Limping World Economy," *The Elmhurst Lecture, The International Conference of Agricultural Economists,* Banff, Canada, September 3–12, 1979 (processed), pp. 2–9. Reprinted by permission.

erywhere bright until one turns to agriculture, where the dominant fact is that, in LDCs as a whole, food production has failed to keep pace with the demand for food, thereby causing or aggravating a whole series of other problems.

The basic reasons for this failure are well known, so I will list but not dwell on them.

The first has been fast population growth. Population has grown at around 2.5 percent per annum, and per capita demand has pushed the growth of total demand well beyond three percent, while output has grown at significantly less than 3 percent, turning what used to be an export surplus into an import surplus of food.

Secondly, the technological revolution in tropical food production has only just begun, research in the colonial days having been confined almost but not exclusively to commercial crops exportable to the world market. We have made spectacular progress with maize, wheat for subtropical conditions, and rice for areas of controlled irrigation, but have still far to go with other rice, with sorghums, and millets, and with livestock management.

Third, even where there is new technology to impart, the agricultural extension services and the network for supplying modern inputs to the farmer—especially seeds, fertilisers and pesticides, are gravely deficient, and in many areas virtually non-existent.

Fourth, investment in rural infrastructure is inadequate. Road systems have improved immensely, and the penetration of the countryside by buses and trucks is altering the patterns of rural life. But not enough has been invested in irrigation, or in storage facilities.

Fifth, everyone speaks in favour of land reform, but very few governments have done it in any of its various forms, whether distributing land to the landless, or converting from rental to ownership tenures, or fixing rental ceilings. The case for some sort of land reform remains unquestionable from the standpoint of justice; the case from the standpoint of its effects on production is now stated with greater sophistication, recognising the extent to which higher output is tied to improved technology, extension and investment. Indeed several writers now speak not of land reform but of "the land reform package," to distinguish what they see as good land reform from bad land reform.

And finally to complete our list of factors that have inhibited agricultural output we must add poor terms of trade. The prices of agricultural commodities in world trade fell throughout the 1950s and most of the 1960s,

while industrial prices rose all the time. This was anomalous, since prosperity usually improves agriculture's terms of trade. The basic factor was the enormous increase in agricultural productivity in the United States, resulting in the build up of stocks of cereals; since agricultural commodities compete with each other either on the demand side or on the supply side, this depressed all other agricultural prices. Add to this that in several LDCs governments wanted to keep farm revenues low, whether by imposing taxes on exportable crops, or by placing price ceilings on food for the domestic market. This is at first sight a curious phenomenon. One would expect that farm populations, being more than half the nation (in most cases), would carry enough political clout to be able to defend themselves against such measures—and would on the contrary be manipulating the terms of trade in their favour, but this is not automatic. European farmers were doing this at the end of the nineteenth century, but the contemporaneous efforts of American farmers—though they were still in the majority—were a failure.

Let me now turn from the causes of the low level of agricultural output in the LDCs to some of its effects. Agricultural failure is not the sole cause of the problems I shall mention, but makes in each case a significant contribution.

Take first the probability that inequality of the income distribution has increased along with recent growth. This is not a novel phenomenon. Increased inequality is inherent in the classical system of economics because population growth keeps labour income down while profits and rents increase. Given the long and strident debate between economic historians as to what happened to the European living standards in the first half of the century, no modern economist should have assumed that economic growth would automatically raise the incomes of those at the lower end of the scale. Rapid population growth has also played its negative role in our day, restraining the wage level and farm income per head. Since the majority of the labour force in LDCs consists of farm people, who also have the lowest incomes, the standard of living of the great bulk of the population can be raised only by raising farm income. Decisions of the effects of growth on income distribution or income distribution on growth lead nowhere unless farm income is at the centre of the alleged relationship.

The worst effects of population growth combined with technological standstill are to be seen in the arid zones of the tropical world, where some 500 million people live, especially along the fringes of the African and Asian deserts. There we have the largest concentration of human poverty; the numbers continue to grow rapidly; and we have not yet had the technological breakthrough in dry farming that might promise higher productivity. To raise the living standards of these hundreds of millions is the greatest challenge to those who work for development.

Consider next the huge flow of migrants from the countryside into the towns. Central to this of course is the growth of population. Relatively under-populated countries can cope with population growth by opening up new land, as has been happening over much of Africa, but in less favoured countries population growth means smaller farms, more landless labourers and lower output per head. Unless a green revolution is set in motion, the natural reaction of farmers caught in this situation is to put pressure on the young to migrate to the cities, which they will do if the cities show signs of expanding employment. This is not a complete solution. The towns cannot provide employment for the whole of the natural increase in the countryside, not to speak of women now also leaving the family tasks and seeking wage employment; so unemployment mounts. The government is also trapped. The towns exert great pressure for expansion of the public services—of water, bus transport, schools, hospitals, and so on— eating up more funds than exist, and leaving nothing to spend in the countryside. So the differential in amenities between town and country widens all the more, and the stream of migrants is increased. Unemployment in the towns cannot be ended by spending more in the towns. The basic solution is rather to

make the countryside economically viable, with a larger cultivated area, with rising productivity on the farms, more rural industry, and better social amenities.

Note "the larger cultivated area." Development economists have been mesmerized by European experience into assuming that the development process always involves a decline in the number of persons in agriculture. This is true of relative decline, but it extends to an absolute decline only in the later stages of development. For example, around 1850 in Western Europe the agricultural population was only 50 percent of the whole, and the rate of natural increase about one and a quarter percent. So the agricultural population would decline absolutely if the non-agricultural population grew at over 2.5 percent a year. Whereas with 70 percent in agriculture and a rate of natural increase of 2.5 percent, an absolute decline of the agricultural labour force requires non-agricultural employment to expand at 8.3 percent per annum, which it cannot do.

An increase in the absolute numbers engaged in agriculture is therefore an essential item in coping with the current flood of population. The fact that the green revolution in cereals is labour-intensive helps, especially if the natural propensity of the more enterprising farmers to invest in labour saving machinery can be restrained. But there is no escaping the need to bring more land under cultivation, by opening up roads, irrigation, terracing, drainage, and other investment in infrastructure. Some governments are actively engaged in colonisation schemes of this sort, which, if highly planned to meet modern standards, are costly and troublesome. The subject is neglected in our textbooks. It needs more research and experimentation, leading to action.

A third consequence of the weakness of agriculture is that it is one of the reasons why so many LDCs have had balance of payments troubles, have incurred large external debts, or have found themselves defaulting on their obligations. It is not just that a larger output would earn more foreign exchange, or save on food imports. Indirectly it would reduce urbanization, the high cost of which is the prime cause of their needing so much capital and having to borrow so much. Also, in countries suffering from the two-gap disease, it would facilitate the translation of domestic saving into foreign exchange.

A fourth and final consequence of the weakness of agriculture has been to inhibit the growth of manufacturing industry because of the farmers' low purchasing power. The physical output of LDC commercial export crops grew rapidly, aided on the supply side by the expansion of internal transport, and on the demand side by the unusually rapid growth of the developed countries. But the prices at which these commodities sold were poor; exports are a small part of agricultural output, so their prices are linked on the supply side to the price of food, which as we saw earlier, was depressed by American surpluses. The individual LDC can do well out of exporting agricultural raw materials or tropical beverages; but for the group of LDCs as a whole the elasticity of supply of these commodities is so high, at prices yielding roughly the same incomes as domestic food production, that the factoral terms of trade stay much the same despite increases in demand or improvements in technology. The road to riches does not run in these directions.

At the same time farm incomes from domestic production were also low, for reasons which we have already considered. So import substitution of manufactures, which was the starting point of industrialization, was limited by the narrowness of the domestic market. LDCs soon discovered that if industry is to grow at 7 percent per annum, in the face of a peasantry with only a small marketable surplus, industry must look to foreign markets. By the year 1970 this lesson had been learnt, and nearly every LDC had begun exporting some manufactures to developed countries. Unfortunately this range was very narrow, dominated by textiles and clothing; broadening only as the protests and restrictions of MDCs forced the more advanced LDCs into light metals, electronics and other fields. The LDC effort was clearly successful, since LDC exports of manufactures were growing at ten percent a year, despite the barriers erected by the MDCs. Whether world trade will revive, and if so whether LDC exports of manufactures will again grow at ten percent are crucial questions for LDC development strategy. . . . But no matter how they may be answered, it will be to the advantage of LDCs to raise their agricultural productivity, since this would simultaneously raise the living standards of their farmers, create a domestic market for their manufactures, and improve their terms of trade.

Comment

The preceding two selections indicate a shift in the thinking of Lewis with respect to the role of agriculture vis-á-vis industry. The first of the two selections by Lewis (VI.C.2), written in 1950, focused on the labor surplus in agriculture and emphasized putting more persons into manufacturing industry. So too did Lewis's 1954 dual-sector model, examined in Chapter III. The last selection (VI.C.3) is written against the background of a fast population growth, the poverty of subsistence farmers, the migration from the countryside, and unemployment and underemployment. It emphasizes the necessity to absorb labor in agriculture.

Agriculture is also now emphasized in order to increase the productivity of food producers and thereby raise the export prices of commercial tropical crops, to increase the demand for domestically produced manufactures, and to reduce the balance-of-payments deficit by increasing export revenue from primary products and by saving foreign exchange through import substitution for food imports. As Lewis states, "the most important item on the agenda of development is to transform the food sector, create agricultural surpluses to feed the urban population, and thereby create the domestic basis for industry and modern services." For elaboration of his latest position, see W. Arthur Lewis, *The Evolution of the International*

Economic Order (1978); *Growth and Fluctuations 1870–1913* (1978); and "Development Strategy in a Limping World Economy," *The Elmhurst Lecture,* Banff, Canada, September 3, 1979.

The next chapter examines policies that might accomplish Lewis's objectives for agricultural development.

CHAPTER VII

Agricultural Strategy

We have repeatedly referred to the removal of the agricultural bottleneck as a strategic policy issue: the attainment of a proper balance between the establishment of industries and the expansion of agriculture is a persistently troublesome problem for developing nations. In the earlier days of development planning, deliberate and rapid industrialization was often advocated. Experience, however, has shown the limitations of overemphasizing industrialization, and it is increasingly recognized that agricultural progress must have a vital role in the development process. The earlier confrontation of industrial development *versus* agriculture has been shown to be a false issue, and the concern now is rather with the interrelationships between industry and agriculture and the contribution that each can make to the other.

Agricultural progress is essential to provide food for a growing nonagricultural labor force, raw materials for industrial production, savings and tax revenue to support development of the rest of the economy, to earn more foreign exchange (or save foreign exchange when primary products are imported), and to provide a growing market for domestic manufactures. As the theme of section VII.A emphasizes, the intersectoral relations between agriculture and industry will determine the course of structural transformation in a developing economy: if in the longer run, there is to be a diminishing share of agriculture in output, there first must be in the short run successful policies of agricultural development to facilitate this transformation.

Another theme in this chapter is the special effort that must be made to help the rural poor take advantage of the potential now provided by the green revolution. Section VII.B examines some of the issues raised by the new seed-fertilizer technology, especially policies that might increase yields among small-scale, low-income producers of traditional crops, and policies that might provide more employment for small farmers and landless labor. With the present concern over absolute poverty and unemployment, rural development takes on a new importance in its own right—and not simply for its instrumental value for industrial development. Agricultural development is now crucial for amelioration of absolute poverty and for labor absorption.

Even with allowance for the imprecision of the data, the general enormity of the problem can be sensed from the World Bank's estimates that, of the 800 million people in LDCs who are in absolute poverty, some 80 percent, or 640 million, are in the rural areas. Given the magnitude of the numbers in rural poverty and the incapacity to reduce significantly these numbers by any feasible amount of rural-urban migration, the rural proportion of those in poverty is likely to remain high in many LDCs.

Only about a third of the population in developing countries, however, live in countries that have had a satisfactory performance in agricultural production.

If past trends in food production and agriculture simply continue, the outcome by the year 2000 will be not only unsatisfactory but alarming. As a study of the Food and Agriculture Organization concludes, trend production performances in the majority of developing countries would perpetuate the weakness of the agricultural basis of economic development and would not provide the food supplies needed as a prerequisite to relieve many millions of people of their grossly inadequate nutritional conditions. Between 1980 and 2000, it is projected that the food and agricultural experience in a large part of the developing world will be characterized by semi-stagnation and a tendency to deficits in output with the majority of the countries showing little improvement in per capita production.[1]

For most of the developing countries, rural development on a massive scale will be needed for decades. But the progress of rural development will be crucially dependent on the outcome of the green revolution, measures of land reform, land settlement at the extensive margin, new forms of rural institutions, and various special programs designed to increase the productivity and incomes of the rural poor. The selections in section VII.C therefore focus on various components of a rural-based development strategy.

While the green revolution provides a potential for increasing farm output by technical innovations that increase the productivity of labor and land, it is necessary—from the standpoint of labor absorption—to realize the advantages of a labor-using and yield-increasing strategy of agricultural development. In this connection, the transformation of Japanese agriculture is instructive. The "Japanese model" has three important characteristics: first, agricultural output has been increased within the unchanged organizational framework of the existing small-scale farming system. This was possible because of increases in the productivity of the existing on-farm resources of land and labor, and was associated with small demands on the scarce resources of capital and foreign exchange. Second, the bulk of the nation's farmers have been involved in increases in agricultural productivity associated with the use of improved varieties of seeds, fertilizers, and other current inputs; and technological progress of this type has continually been the source of greater agricultural productivity. Third, agricultural and industrial development moved forward together in a process of "concurrent" growth.[2]

Emphasis is therefore placed in selection VII.C.1 on the relevance of a "unimodal strategy" such as occurred historically in the Japanese pattern of a small-scale farming system and the participation of the bulk of the nation's farmers in the increase of agricultural productivity. Such a strategy, however, must also be linked to changes in the land tenure system, technological development in agriculture, and persistent concern with the effects on employment generation.

[1]Food and Agriculture Organization of the United Nations, *Agriculture: Toward 2000*, 1981, chapter 2.

[2]Kazushi Ohkawa and Bruce F. Johnston, "The Transferability of the Japanese Pattern of Modernizing Traditional Agriculture," in Erik Thorbecke (ed.), *The Role of Agriculture in Economic Development*, 1969, pp. 277–8.

Higher per capita output must be realized. But to do this, the selections in section VII.C emphasize a number of requirements. It is necessary to use more "modern" inputs per unit of land, while also providing for an increasing total use of labor. There must also be improved incentives for farm producers, especially through pricing policies that do not overvalue inputs to farmers while undervaluing their output. Better distribution of ownership or access to productive resources is also required, especially for small landholders, and the distribution of income must be improved.

VII.A. IMPORTANCE OF AGRICULTURE

VII.A.1. Agriculture's Contribution to Development— Note

Ever since at least the time of Ricardo, the "theology" of development has emphasized that agricultural progress contributes to the support of greater productivity throughout the economy. In his *Principles of Political Economy and Taxation,* Ricardo viewed the problem of diminishing returns in agriculture as crucial. He believed that a limitation on the growth of agricultural output set the upper limit to the growth of the nonagricultural sector and to capital formation for economic expansion.

It is now customary to summarize in four ways how greater agricultural productivity and output contribute to an economy's development: (1) by supplying foodstuffs and raw materials to other expanding sectors in the economy; (2) providing an "investible surplus" of savings and taxes to support investment in another expanding sector; (3) selling for cash a "marketable surplus" that will raise the demand of the rural population for products of other expanding sectors; and (4) relaxing the foreign exchange constraint by earning foreign exchange through exports or by saving foreign exchange through import substitution.

Kuznets summarizes these contributions as the "market contribution" and the "factor contribution."

A given sector makes a contribution to an economy when it provides opportunities for other sectors to emerge, or for the economy as a whole to participate in international trade and other international economic flows. We designate this contribution the market type because the given sector provides such opportunities by offering part of its product on domestic or foreign markets in exchange for goods produced by the other sectors, at home or abroad. . . .

Thus agriculture makes a market contribution to economic growth by (1) purchasing some production items from other sectors at home or abroad; (2) selling some of its product, not only to pay for the purchases listed under (1) but also to purchase consumer goods from other sectors or from abroad, or to dispose of the product in any way other than consumption within the sector. In all these ways, agriculture makes it feasible for other sectors to emerge and grow and for international flows to develop; just as these other sectors and the international flows make it feasible for the agricultural sector to operate more efficiently as a producing unit and use its product more effectively as a consuming unit.[1]

The "factor contribution" occurs "when there is a transfer or loan of resources from the given sector to others. Thus if agriculture itself grows, it makes a product contribution; if it trades with others, it renders a market contribution; if it transfers resources to other sectors, these resources being productive factors, it makes a *factor* contribution."[2]

In this traditional interpretation, the development process is viewed as one of structural transformation from an economy in which agricultural employment and output dominate to a decline in the share of the labor force in agriculture and a decrease in the share of agriculture in GNP. But this structural transformation is itself dependent on agricultural progress. Industrial development will be cut short by lack of agricultural progress—unless the economy is in the exceptional situation of being able to export manufactures for imports of foodstuffs and raw materials (compare, Hong Kong). In Lewis' dual-sector model, we saw that if food supplies to the modern sector do not keep up with the modern sector's demand for labor, the modern sector will have to consume a

[1]Simon Kuznets, *Economic Growth and Structure,* New York, 1965, pp. 244–5.

[2]Ibid., p. 250.

larger share of its output in feeding its labor force, and this will leave a smaller surplus for capital accumulation. More generally, it is widely believed that "both in concept and in practice it is possible for the agricultural sector to make large net transfers of resources to other sectors. If these transfers are used productively, the rate of economic growth can be accelerated."[3]

Agriculture's contribution of foodstuffs— the "wage good" in classical terminology—is clear. If the labor force for manufacturing or another expanding sector is drawn from agriculture, the new workers must "take their lunch" with them when they leave the rural sector. A growing urban labor force must be supported by an expanding supply of foodstuffs. A growing population must also be supported with increased food supplies. The annual rate of increase in demand for food is given by $D = p + \eta g$, where p and g are the rate of growth of population and per capita income, and η is the income elasticity of demand for agricultural products.[4] As indicated by Johnston and Mellor,[5] not only are there high rates of population growth in the LDCs, but the income elasticity of demand for food in these countries is considerably higher than in high-income countries—probably on the order of .6 or higher in the low-income countries versus .2 or .3 in Western Europe, the United States, and Canada. A given rate of increase in per capita income therefore has a considerably stronger impact on the demand for agricultural products in the lower-income countries than in the economically advanced countries.

Johnston and Mellor observe that:

The increase in farm output in Japan between the 1880's and 1911–20, which seems to have been of about the same magnitude as the growth of demand during that period, corresponded to an annual rate of increase in demand of approximately 2 percent. With current rates of population growth and a modest rise in per capita incomes, the annual rate of increase of demand for food in a developing economy can easily exceed 3 percent, a formidable challenge for the agriculture of an underdeveloped country. Moreover, as a result of the expansion of population in cities and in mining and industrial centers dependent upon purchased food, the growth of demand for marketed supplies is a good deal more rapid than the overall rate of increase. Thus there are additional problems in developing transportation links and marketing facilities in order to satisfy the requirements of the nonagricultural population.

If food supplies fail to expand in pace with the growth of demand the result is likely to be a substantial rise in food prices leading to political discontent and pressure on wage rates with consequent adverse effects on industrial profits, investment, and economic growth. There is scant evidence concerning the price elasticity of demand for food in underdeveloped countries. At least in the case of an increase in prices as a result of demand outstripping supply, there is a strong presumption that the price elasticity for "all food" is extremely low, probably lower than in economically advanced countries. Cheap starchy staple foods—cereals and root crops—provide something like 60 to 85 percent of the total calorie intake in low-income countries, so there is relatively limited scope for offsetting a rise in food prices by shifting from expensive to less costly foods; and the pressure to resist a reduction in calorie intake is strong.

The inflationary impact of a given percentage increase in food prices is much more severe in an underdeveloped country than in a high-income economy. This is a simple consequence of the dominant position of food as a wage good in lower-income countries where 50 to 60 percent of total consumption expenditure is devoted to food consumption compared with 20 to 30 percent in developed economies.

Owing to the severe economic and political repercussions of a substantial rise in food prices, domestic shortages are likely to be offset by expanded food imports, provided that foreign exchange or credits are available.[6]

[3]John W. Mellor, "Accelerated Growth in Agricultural Production and the Intersectoral Transfer of Resources," *Economic Development and Cultural Change,* October 1973, p. 5.

[4]K. Ohkawa, "Economic Growth and Agriculture," *Annals Hitotsubashi Academy,* October 1956, pp. 45–60.

[5]Bruce F. Johnston and John W. Mellor, "The Role of Agriculture in Economic Development," *American Economic Review,* September 1961, pp. 571–81.

[6]Ibid., p. 573.

Through the transfer of capital and labor to nonfarm activities, agriculture may also provide an investible surplus. The transfer of labor has been repeatedly discussed in the context of the Lewis model and needs no further attention here. But it should be noted that agriculture can be a source of capital formation in ways other than the simple lending of voluntary savings. There may be a compulsory transfer from agriculture for the benefit of other sectors, ordinarily through taxation in which the burden on agriculture is greater than the governmental services provided to agriculture. Kuznets remarks:

The measurement of such forced contributions of agriculture to economic growth is not easy; the incidence of some indirect taxes is difficult to ascertain and the allocation of government expenditures in terms of benefits to agriculture and to economic growth elsewhere is far from simple. But this factor contribution by agriculture was clearly quite large in the early phases of economic growth in some countries. Thus in Japan in the last two decades of the nineteenth century the land tax was over 80 percent of central government taxation, and the direct tax ratio to income produced was between 12 and 22 percent in agriculture, compared with from 2 to 3 percent in the nonagricultural sectors. Forced extraction of surplus from agriculture by taxation, confiscation, and other measures also probably financed a considerable part of industrialization in the Soviet Union. Indeed, one of the crucial problems of modern economic growth is how to extract from the product of agriculture a surplus for the financing of capital formation for industrial growth without at the same time blighting the growth of agriculture, under conditions where no easy *quid pro quo* for such surplus is available within the country. It is only the open economy, with access to the markets of the more highly developed countries, both for goods and for capital loans, that can minimize this painful task of initial capital accumulation.[7]

Another way of transferring resources from the agricultural to the nonagricultural sectors is by the government turning the terms of trade against agriculture by imposing price controls on agricultural products, taxation, or the use of multiple exchange-rates that discriminate against agriculture. If the improvement in the terms of trade in the nonagricultural sectors raises nonagricultural incomes, and the beneficiaries save at a higher marginal rate than the decreased agricultural incomes, aggregate saving rates will increase, and agriculture will have made a net contribution to total saving in an indirect manner. The next selection gives some indication of what has actually occurred in recent years by way of income transfers from agriculture.

A "marketable surplus" from agriculture is needed not only to provide the wage good to industry, but also to widen the home market for the industrial products. The demand for industrial products depends on growth of farm cash income, unless the country can export its growing industrial output. Barring unlimited export possibilities, and with 70 to 90 percent of the home market in the rural sector, the nature of rural demand will affect the growth of non-farm employment and output. Increased agricultural productivity, a growing marketable surplus, and rising real income are necessary to raise the rural sector's demand for industrial output.

Finally, agriculture may be a major source of foreign exchange. It is clear that agricultural exports dominate in a country's early phase of development. But also important in relaxing the foreign exchange constraint is the possibility in several developing countries to save foreign exchange by replacing imports of foodstuffs with home production. Export promotion and import substitution are activities not only for the industrial sector but also for agriculture.

Considering these various contributions of agriculture, development economists have insisted that if there is to be in the longer run a structural transformation in output and labor force, there must first be in the short run "successful policies of agricultural development" to facilitate this transformation. But what specifically do "successful policies of agricultural development" entail? And is the purpose of agricultural development sim-

[7]Kuznets, *Economic Growth*, pp. 250–51.

ply to underwrite the expansion of nonagricultural sectors—even at the expense of an "agricultural squeeze"? Now, in view of the emphasis on absolute poverty and the employment problem, is it not necessary to concentrate on agricultural development for the sake of employment and a diminution in inequality? Even though the longer-term objective is structural transformation—the absorption of a larger fraction of the rural population in new income-earning opportunities—there remains the complex problem of the timing of this transformation and the intertemporal sequence of policies to accomplish it. The lessons of recent history have shown that an "urban bias" can discriminate against agriculture;[8] and that, as illustrated in the next selection, the net outflow of resources from agriculture may be excessive. Not only may there be an inefficient use of the resources transferred to the nonagricultural sectors, but the transfer may itself be at the expense of more employment and higher income in the agricultural sector. Should not the "growth-promoting interactions between agriculture and industrial development" mean more than that agricultural development should have simply instrumental value for industrial development?

In the early years of development planning, Viner wisely anticipated the answer to this question:

Let us now suppose that *real* incomes are lower in agriculture than in industry, and that by tariff protection or subsidies industry can be made to expand and to draw workers from the country into the cities. Is this sound economic policy?

The correct answer depends on why *per capita* real incomes are lower in agriculture than in manufacturing. There may be urban exploitation of agriculture, through monopolistic pricing by employers, or through labour monopolies in the factories which by forcing wages up force up also the prices which the agricultural population has to pay for urban products and services—including govern-

[8]Michael Lipton, "Strategy for Agriculture: Urban Bias and Rural Planning," in Paul Streeten and Michael Lipton (eds.), *The Crisis of Indian Planning*, London, 1968, chapter 4.

ment services. The tariff, supported as providing better employment opportunities for the agricultural population, may itself be a major instrument whereby agricultural real incomes are depressed. Government may also operate to depress agricultural real incomes by imposing its taxes, mainly or largely, directly or indirectly, on agriculture, and directing its expenditures mainly to the benefit of the urban population. Even though the rural population may have lower *per capita* incomes than the urban, it may nevertheless be the only economically healthy part of the population, the only part which gives good value to the community in ecxhange for what it gets from the community. Where the situation is one—as it often is—of urban exploitation of the rural population, to propose as a remedy the further subsidization of urban industry as a means of drawing rural workers to the city is equivalent to proposing to remedy the exploitation of worker bees by the drones by transforming the worker bees also to drones. It is obvious that it can work at all only as long as there still remain worker bees in the fields to be exploited.

The refutation of bad argument does not necessarily refute the conclusions reached by such argument. It is not my position that the path to economic progress is not, for many countries and even for most countries, by way of industrialization and urbanization. I have in fact conceded that as any country or any region becomes more prosperous it will normally tend to increase the ratio of its population which is non-agricultural. My position is a different one, and I will now state it frankly and positively for the first time. The real problem in poor countries is not agriculture as such, or the absence of manufactures as such, but poverty and backwardness, poor agriculture, or poor agriculture and poor manufacturing. The remedy is to remove the basic causes of the poverty and backwardness. This is as true in principle, and probably nearly as true in practice, for industrialized countries as for predominantly agricultural countries.

Misallocation of resources as between agriculture and manufactures is probably rarely a major cause of poverty and backwardness, except where government, through tariffs, discriminatory taxation and expenditure policies, and failure to provide on a regionally non-discriminatory pattern facilities for education, health promotion, and technical training, is itself responsible for this misallocation. Where there is such government-induced misallocation, it is today more likely to consist of the diversion of agrarian-produced resources to the support of parasitic cities than of overinvestment of resources in primary industries and in workers in such industries.

Economic improvement may call for greater industrialization, but this should be a natural growth, appropriately facilitated by government but not maintained under hot-house conditions. In many countries, the most promising field for rapid economic development lies in agriculture, and the measures needed are primarily such as will promote health, general education, technical training, better transportation facilities, and cheap rural credit for productive use. There are no inherent advantages of manufacturing over agriculture, or, for that matter, of agriculture over manufacturing. It is only arbitrarily in fact that the line separating the two can be drawn. The choice between expansion of agriculture and expansion of manufactures can for the most part best be left to the free decisions of capitalists, entrepreneurs, and workers. To the extent that there is need for government decision, it should be made on rational grounds, in the light of considerations of costs and of comparative returns from alternative allocations of scarce national resources, human and material. If direction is accepted from maxims and arbitrary dogmas and prejudices, from unsubstantiated and incredible natural laws of the inherent inferiority of one type of industry over another, then it is highly probable that the result will be the squandering of resources so scanty in supply that they need to be carefully husbanded, and the sore disappointment of the wishes of the great masses of population crying to be relieved of their crushing poverty.[9]

The emphasis on agricultural development now is not only for its instrumental value in sustaining expansion elsewhere in the nonagricultural sectors, but for its own absorption of labor and its own increase of real income among the rural poverty target groups of the small farmers and the landless laborers. The widely expressed view now is that the root of the employment problems lies in the fact that modern economic activity is not being diffused to the countryside. An agricultural strategy that would improve the rural-urban balance now requires the extension of planning, infrastructure, appropriate technology, and complementary resources to the rural sector.[10] If in earlier decades of development, agricultural development had instrumental value, in future decades it must have an intrinsic value of its own.

[9]Jacob Viner, *International Trade and Economic Development*, London, 1953, pp. 51–3.

[10]See, for instance, Edgar O. Edwards (ed.), *Employment in Developing Nations*, New York, 1974, pp. 30–31.

VII.A.2. Strategies for Transferring Agricultural Surplus*

The agricultural sector is of particular interest and concern with respect to capital accumulation in the early stages of economic development. The agricultural sector is initially dominant in the economy, containing the bulk of national income, labor and capital resources. In the long run, the nonagricultural sectors must grow at a substantially more rapid rate than the agricultural sector, gradually providing a transformation of the econ-

*From T. H. Lee, "Strategies for Transferring Agricultural Surplus under Different Agricultural Situations in Taiwan," Conference on Agriculture and Economic Development, Japan Economic Research Center, September 6–10, 1971, pp. 1–7, 12–15, 21–5; also in Lee, *Intersectoral Capital Flows in the Economic Development of Taiwan, 1895–1960*, Cornell

University Press, Ithaca, 1971, pp. 8–12, 131–4, 139–42. Reprinted from Teng-hui Lee: *Intersectoral Capital Flows in the Economic Development of Taiwan, 1895–1960*. Copyright © 1971 by Cornell University. Used by permission of the publisher, Cornell University Press.

omy from one dominated by agriculture to one dominated by other sectors. It is logical to presume that this process of economic transformation will proceed more rapidly if a net transfer of income and savings can be made from the agricultural sector to other sectors of the economy.

The recent literature on the role of agriculture in economic development has been enhanced by a number of essays on intersectoral capital flows in relation to the transformation of traditional agriculture in less developed countries. Two different viewpoints can be categorized from these papers. One is that agriculture does not require a large amount of capital for its transformation. Agriculture, therefore, is a great contributor of capital to industrialization. The other opinion is that the investment requirements for agricultural transformation are so large that capital may have net inflow from nonagriculture to agriculture. These views are based primarily on different emphases of how to modernize the traditional agriculture.

Obviously, there are many differences between countries in social-institutional arrangements with which to mobilize the resources from the agricultural sector to the nonagricultural sector. According to the initial level of agricultural productivity and resource endowment, capital requirement for transforming traditional agriculture will be different between countries.

Infusions of the new technology into traditional agriculture are gaining dramatic results in Southeast Asia. Several countries in this area have begun shifts in production as strategic moves toward agricultural development. There is a spreading optimistic belief that the transformation is already sufficient to lift away the spectre of famine and to postpone, at least, the materialization of the Malthusian trap. These gains have been most noticeable in basic food grains (rice, corn and wheat) and have been realized mainly from new high-yield varieties with adequate supplies of fertilizer, pesticides, water and modern implements. It is expected that the new technology will quickly spread within the na-

tions and across national boundaries. Therefore, provided that increased production is actually obtained by the presently developing countries, a new set of agricultural problems can be anticipated, for which new solutions must be discovered. How to maintain the current increase in agricultural production with more inputs and investment in agriculture, and how to effectively siphon off such gains in agricultural production for the nation's industrial development, are most important and urgent tasks in the Southeast Asian countries.

The experience of Taiwan in economic development is an example of a country with a traditional agricultural pattern successfully advancing and transforming its economy as a whole. . . .

FRAMEWORK FOR MEASUREMENT

The interrelationships between agricultural production and nonagricultural production are dealt with here by dividing the areas participating in the economic transactions of the national economy of Taiwan into six sectors: agricultural production, agricultural household, nonagricultural production, nonagricultural household, government, and foreign trade.

In the agricultural production sector, services of primary production factors such as land and labor flow from the agricultural household sector (D_a).[1] The sector also produces agricultural output (Y_a). The agricultural production sector consumes production goods such as chemical fertilizer, feed, and other material manufactured in the nonagricultural production sector (R_n^a). Agricultural products used in agricultural production are provided from the gross agricultural output within the sector. The net agricultural output is partially consumed by the agricultural

---

[1]The letters in brackets are the symbols used for the given item in the algebraic expression of these variables and relationships presented in equations below.

household sector (C_a^a). The remaining amount of net output is sold to the nonagricultural production sector as raw materials (R_a^n), to the nonagricultural household sector for consumption (C_a^n), and directly to foreign trade as exports (E_a). The total quantity of agricultural products sold amounts to the sum of $R_a^n + C_a^n + E_a$. In nonagricultural production, services of production factors flow from the nonagricultural household sector (D_n). The sector produces two products, consumer goods and capital goods. Consumer goods flow from the nonagricultural production sector to the nonagricultural household sector (C_n^n), to the agricultural household sector (C_n^a), (C_n^a), to the government sector (C_n^g), and to exports (E_n). Capital goods are distributed to the agricultural production sector as intermediate goods (R_n^a), as investment goods (I_a), and for investment in its own sector (I_n). No capital goods export is assumed in this case. The government sector collects taxes (G_a) from the agricultural household sector and (G_n) from the nonagricultural household sector, and allocates the revenue for consumption of industrial goods (C_n^g), and for government savings (S_g). In the foreign trade sector, the government exports agricultural products (E_a), and industrial consumer goods (E_n), in exchange for consumer goods (M_c), and capital goods (M_i). The balance of international trade represents an additional variable (F).

Income generation is represented by flows in the opposite direction from the commodity flows between sectors. In addition to the commodity transactions between sectors, income also flows from the agricultural household sector to the nonagricultural sector in the form of payment of land rent, wages, and interest. The agricultural household sector also receives income from the nonagricultural household sector.

These commodity and income flows can be summarized in the following accounting equations.[2]

[2] J. C. Fei and G. Ranis, *Development of the Labor Surplus Economy, Theory and Policy*, Homewood, 1964, p. 57.

Inflows		Outflows	
$D_a + R_n^a$	$= C_a^a + C_a^n + R_a^n + E_a$		(1)
$D_n + R_a^n + M_c + M_i$	$= C_n^n + C_n^a + C_n^g + R_n^a + I + E_n$		(2)
$C_a^a + C_a^n + S_a + G_a$	$= D_a$		(3)
$C_n^a + C_n^n + S_n + G_n$	$= D_n$		(4)
$C_n^g + S_g$	$= G_a + G_n$		(5)

Adding the five equations and cancelling out similar terms on both sides of the resulting equality, we have:

$$S_a + S_n + S_g = I + (E_a + E_n) - (M_c + M_i) \quad (6)$$

or

$$I_n = (S_a - I_a) + S_n + S_g + F \quad (7)$$

where $I = I_a + I_n$, and $F = (E_a + E_n) - (M_c + M_i)$. The terms S_a, S_n, and S_g in the above equations denote the savings of agricultural household, nonagricultural household, and government. Equation (6) is the financing equation indicating the relationship between savings and investment for the national economy as a whole. Equation (7) indicates the sectoral interdependence. The investment in the nonagricultural sector depends upon the amount of net capital flow from agriculture, size of savings in its own and government sectors, and the export surplus. Adding equations (1) and (3) for the agricultural sector, we have:

$$S_a = C_a^n + R_n^a + E_a - C_n^a - R_n^a - G_a \quad (8)$$

As government taxing on agriculture is not greatly in the form of commodities, the term (G_a) in equation (8) may be better included in the term (S_a) from equation (8) and the term ($S_a - I_a$) in equation (7); then we can draw the following cases, indicating the balance of commodity flows between agriculture and nonagriculture.

$$C_a^n + R_a^n + E_a - C_n^a - R_n^a \overset{>}{\underset{<}{=}} I_a \quad (9)$$

or

$$C_a^n + R_a^n + E_a - C_n^a - R_n^a - I_a = B \quad (9')$$

The terms on the left side of equation (9′) indicate the commodity transactions between two sectors, and the term B is the balance showing the physical aspect of capital outflow from agriculture. The term B is also the balance of capital accounting between two sectors.

Generally speaking, it is more common and more useful to set up both capital and current operating (income) accounts in order to investigate the sectoral commodity and financial transactions. Captial account shows the changes in assets and liabilities. An increase in assets or decrease in liabilities indicates the outflow of capital. A decrease in assets or an increase in liabilities indicates the inflow of capital. The term B can, therefore, be expressed as follows:

$$B = R + K \qquad (10)$$

The term R on the right side of the above equation is the balance of current financial transactions between sectors, including the net payments of land rent, wages, and interest, and government taxing and subsidies. The term K is the balance of the capital account between sectors, including the net changes in outstanding short-term and long-term loans and investment.

The above exposition of the accounting system of sectoral interdependence between agriculture and nonagriculture is based on commodity and income flows and the sectoral capital accounting. The important fact is that both of the above sectoral accounts of income and capital are related to the expense accounts of income, consumption, and savings-investment in the agricultural and the nonagricultural sector. This means that the above sectoral accounts can be derived statistically from the social income accounts including income, consumption, and savings-investment in a sector. When we construct the social income account for the agricultural sector, the sectoral accounts can be systematically derived from it.

Equations (9′) and (10) are generally valued at current prices of commodities and services in the transactions. The effects of changes in price ratios or sectoral terms of trade on sectoral capital flows are not reflected in equations (9′) and (10). The term B in the equations, therefore, should be adjusted for changes in the price ratios. The equation (9′) in real terms thus can be expressed:

$$(C_a^n + R_a^n + E_a) / P_a - (C_n^a + R_n^a + I_a) / P_n = B' \qquad (11)$$

where P_a and P_n are price indices for agricultural products and nonagricultural products bought by the agricultural sector. When capital flows out from the agricultural sector, the term B' can be expressed:

$$B' = B/P_a + (C_n^a + R_n^a + I_a) / P_n (P_n/P_a - 1) \qquad (12)$$

The first term on the right side of the equation is the financial amount of capital outflow from agriculture in real terms, and the second term is the amount of capital outflow caused by the change in the sectoral terms of trade between agriculture and nonagriculture. We call the former the visible net real capital outflow and the latter the invisible net real capital outflow. . . .

STRATEGIC MEASURES FOR AGRICULTURAL DEVELOPMENT AND CAPITAL TRANSFER

With a systematic examination of Taiwan's experience for the period 1895–1960, we set out to provide a statistical framework for empirical analysis of intersectoral capital flow between the agricultural sector and the nonagricultural sector. A statistical scale for measuring the intersectoral capital flows was developed by the social accounting system based on the definition of capital, and an effort was made to identify the determinants of the net capital outflow from the agricultural sector. Conclusions may be summarized as follows:

(a) The direction of the intersectoral net capital flow was identified as an outflow from the agricultural sector in Taiwan throughout the entire period. The amount of net capital outflow showed a slightly increasing trend in terms of real price up to 1940, but has tended to decline since 1950. Invisible net real capital outflow caused by terms of trade against agriculture was less important in the prewar period but increased in relative importance to more than 50 percent of the total net real capital outflow in the postwar period. Financially, current transfers of rent payment and taxes occupied the most important role in the financial accommodation of net agricultural surplus in the prewar period, and direct capital transfer of farmers' savings became increasingly important in the postwar period.

(b) The size of the intersectoral capital flow is dependent in part on the changes in the terms of trade, but it is also significantly dependent on the physical and financial measures by which development can be achieved. Certain measures and conditions significantly influenced the intersectoral capital outflow in Taiwan: (1) Under the Japanese administration a new system of government taxes and levies was imposed while the inherited system of agricultural squeeze was not abolished. Since institution of land-reform program in the postwar period, taxation and levies by means of both direct and hidden methods have been strenthened. (2) Despite the high-gross squeeze, agricultural productivity of land and labor in the sector was not affected. After the shift from traditional agriculture in the period 1926–1930, the increase in agricultural productivity was accelerated. Neither the initial resource endowment nor the level of agricultural productivity in Taiwan in 1895 was any more favorable than in countries presently developing. However, the successful transformation of traditional agriculture in Taiwan could be accomplished while maintaining a continuous net outflow of capital from the agricultural sector. A heavy investment in irrigation was initiated in the transformation period, yet it did not bring a net inflow of capital from the

nonagricultural sector with it. This important aspect of agricultural development particularly with reference to the role of government and technological progress in agriculture is discussed below.

(c) The empirical tests showed that Taiwan's experience departed appreciably from the conventional hypotheses regarding net capital outflow from agriculture. (1) Taiwan has maintained a continuous outflow of net capital from the agricultural sector under the high growth rate of agricultural population and labor force. This fact disproves the broadly held viewpoint that decelerating the rate of population growth is a necessary condition for accelerating the growth of agricultural surplus. (2) The agricultural wage rate or per capita consumption of farmers improved through time, despite the increase of population in agriculture. However, the proportion of total agricultural income going to agricultural labor has tended to decline relatively in contrast to the nonagricultural sector where the proportion of total income to labor increased. In the context of net capital outflow from the agricultural sector, the relative decline of the share of labor income in agriculture is thus a more important concept than that of constant institutional wage rate in agriculture. (3) Heavy investment in irrigation is necessary in order to transform traditional agriculture in the paddy farming areas. Intensive innovation in the use of capital has been witnessed in the period of transformation of traditional agriculture. This departs from the conventional viewpoint of a complementary relation between capital and labor in agricultural innovation. (4) As for the amount of net capital outflow, it is clearly shown by the statistical comparison in the text that the concept of "net agricultural savings" is not appropriate. (5) Financial adjustment of the net agricultural surplus is one of the important factors determining the magnitude of the net capital outflow from the agricultural sector. The problem of intersectoral capital flow can be discussed from the viewpoint of financial adjustment and the commodity transferring process as well as from the viewpoint of increase in agricultural productivity.

(d) Finally, agricultural development is primarily concerned with the feasiblity of increasing net agricultural surplus or net capital outflow from the agricultural sector. In less-developed countries like Taiwan, mobilization of internal capital must depend on agricultural development. The development of agriculture and the application of economic squeeze on agriculture are closely related to government strategies for agricultural development.

In relation to the intersectoral capital outflow from agriculture, four important government measures toward agricultural development can be derived: (1) allocation of capital to agriculture, (b) technological progress, (c) agricultural taxation, and (d) organizational improvements....

IMPLICATIONS OF TAIWAN'S EXPERIENCE

In considering the implications of the above discussion, it is important to gereralize the relationship between determinants of the intersectoral capital flow in order to provide a measurement of agricultural development. The resource endowment and the level of agricultural productivity determine the size of agricultural investment that can be undertaken to achieve a given rate of agricultural growth. Basically, land productivity and per capita land area or man-land ratio are the determinants of the level of agricultural productivity in terms of labor. Consequently, given the increase in population, limited land resource and heavy food requirements in a low income country, a big increase is required in irrigation and land improvements. For this reason, Ishikawa has concluded that the agricultural sector may require a net inflow of capital from the nonagricultural sector for the transformation of agriculture in Asia.[3] This obviously does not apply to Tai-

wan's experience, since a big push in irrigation and land improvement had not been undertaken in Taiwan before a surplus in the government budget and technological progress were realized. Two important factors need to be noted in this context: (a) determined government action, and (b) technological relation between the fixed capital input and biological technology. The former is related to the basic problem of capital allocation in the whole national economy. Since agriculture is generally considered the mainstay of the economy, better utilization of slack in agriculture is preferred to additional input of scarce capital funds. The latter is concerned with the availability of new varieties of seeds, with the farmers' skill in application of chemical fertilizer, and with the method of cultivation in relation to the heavy irrigation investment. The requirement for heavy irrigation investment seems to be large in the period of transition from extensive to intensive farming in paddy farming areas. With the high pressure of population, there is a general tendency for labor intensive cultivation in agriculture. To absorb more labor input in farming, expansion of productive capacity in terms of land is naturally necessary. However, the intensity of farming is greatly dependent on the demand for crops and livestock as well as the quantitative and qualitative relationships between inputs. Landowners, as receivers of large shares of land rent from the additional increase of output, will play some role in encouraging such intensive farming. In Taiwan, promotion of new varieties of seeds, chemical fertilizers, and irrigation investment represented such an effort on the part of landlords.

Agricultural transformation which simultaneously maintains a net capital outflow calls for a variety of strategies. The more important of these are: (a) the basic agricultural investment should be accompanied by technological improvement; (b) an appropriate investment scheme with large labor input and less input of capital goods should be selected, and (c) a capital transfer mechanism should be established. According to the dif-

[3]Shigeru Ishikawa, *Economic Development in Asian Perspective,* Tokyo, 1967, pp. 346–347.

ferent conditions or stages of agricultural development, the above strategic components will change in relative importance, as the experience of Taiwan has shown. . . .

VII.A.3. Urban Bias*

The most important class conflict in the poor countries of the world today is not between labour and capital. Nor is it between foreign and national interests. It is between the rural classes and the urban classes. The rural sector contains most of the poverty, and most of the low-cost sources of potential advance; but the urban sector contains most of the articulateness, organisation and power. So the urban classes have been able to "win" most of the rounds of the struggle with the countryside; but in so doing they have made the development process needlessly slow and unfair. Scarce land, which might grow millets and beansprouts for hungry villagers, instead produces a trickle of costly calories from meat and milk, which few except the urban rich (who have ample protein anyway) can afford. Scarce investment, instead of going into water-pumps to grow rice, is wasted on urban motorways. Scarce human skills design and administer, not clean village wells and agricultural extension services, but world boxing championships in showpiece stadia. Resource allocations, within the city and the village as well as between them, reflect urban priorities rather than equity or efficiency. The damage has been increased by misguided ideological imports, liberal and Marxian, and by the town's success in buying off part of the rural elite, thus transferring most of the costs of the process to the rural poor.

The disparity between urban and rural welfare is much greater in poor countries now than it was in rich countries during their

*From Michael Lipton, *Why Poor People Stay Poor*, London, Temple Smith, 1977, pp. 13, 16–7, 19–21, 23–4. Reprinted by permission.

early development. . . . This huge welfare gap is demonstrably inefficient, as well as inequitable. . . . It persists mainly because less than 20 percent of investment for development has gone to the agricultural sector . . . although over 65 percent of the people of less-developed countries (LDCs), and over 80 percent of the really poor who live on $1 a week each or less, depend for a living on agriculture. The proportion of skilled people who support development—doctors, bankers, engineers—going to rural areas has been lower still; and the rural-urban imbalances have in general been even greater than those between agriculture and industry. Moreover, in most LDCs, governments have taken numerous measures with the unhappy side-effect of accentuating rural-urban disparities: their own allocation of public expenditure and taxation; measures raising the price of industrial production relative to farm production, thus encouraging private rural saving to flow into industrial investment because the value of industrial output has been artificially boosted; and educational facilities encouraging bright villagers to train in cities for urban jobs.

Such processes have been extremely inefficient. For instance, the impact on output of $1 of carefully selected investment is in most countries two to three times as high in agriculture as elsewhere yet public policy and private market power have combined to push domestic savings and foreign aid into non-agricultural uses. The process has also been inequitable. Agriculture starts with about one-third the income per head of the rest of the economy, so that the people who depend on it should in equity receive special attention not special mulcting. Finally, the misallocation between sectors has created a needless and acute conflict between efficiency and equity. In agriculture the poor farmer with little land is usually efficient in his use of both land and capital, whereas power, construction and industry often do best in big, capital-intensive units; and rural income and power, while far from equal, are less unequal then in the cities. So concentration on urban development and neglect of agriculture have pushed resources away from activities where they can help growth *and* benefit the poor, and towards activities where they do either of these, if at all, at the expense of the other.

Urban bias also increases inefficiency and inequity *within* the sectors. Poor farmers have little land and much underused family labour. Hence they tend to complement any extra developmental resources received— pumpsets, fertilisers, virgin land—with much more extra labour than do large farmers. Poor farmers thus tend to get most output from such extra resources (as well as needing the extra income most). But rich farmers (because they sell their extra output to the cities instead of eating it themselves, and because they are likely to use much of their extra income to support urban investment) are naturally favoured by urban-biased policies; it is they, not the efficient small farmers, who get the cheap loans and the fertiliser subsidies. The patterns of allocation and distribution within the cities are damaged too. Farm inputs are produced inefficiently, instead of imported, and the farmer has to pay, even if the price is nominally "subsidised".... The processing of farm outputs, notably grain milling, is shifted into big urban units and the profits are no longer reinvested in agriculture. And equalisation between classes inside the cities becomes more risky, because the investment-starved farm sector might prove unable to deliver the food that a better-off urban mass would seek to buy.

Moreover, income in poor countries is usually more equally distributed within the rural sector than within the urban sector. Since income creates the power to distribute extra income, therefore, a policy that concentrates on raising income in the urban sector will worsen inequalities in two ways: by transferring not only from poor to rich, but also from more equal to less equal. Concentration on urban enrichment is triply inequitable: because countryfolk start poorer; because such concentration allots rural resources largely to the rural rich (who sell food to the cities); and because the great inequality of power *within* the towns renders urban resources especially likely to go to the resident elites.

However, urban bias does not rest on a conspiracy, but on convergent interests. Industrialists, urban workers, even big farmers *all* benefit if agriculture gets squeezed, provided its few resources are steered, heavily subsidised, to the big farmer, to produce cheap food and raw materials for the cities. Nobody conspires; all the powerful are satisfied; the labour-intensive small farmer stays efficient, poor and powerless, and had better shut up. Meanwhile, the economist, often in the blinkers of industrial determinism, congratulates all concerned on resolutely extracting an agricultural surplus to finance industrialisation. Conspiracy? Who needs conspiracy?

Thirdly, how far does the urban bias thesis go towards an agricultural or rural emphasis? It was noted that there is a rather low limit to the shifts than *can* swiftly be made in allocations of key resources like doctors or savings between huge, structured areas of economic life like agriculture and industry. In the longer run, if the arguments of this book are right, how high do they push the allocations that should go to agriculture in poor countries: from the typical 20 percent of various sorts of scarce resource (for the poorest two-thirds of the people, who are also those normally using scarce resources more efficiently, as will be shown) up to 50 percent, or 70 percent, or (absurdly) 100 percent? Clearly the answer will differ according to the resource being reallocated, the length of time for the reallocation, and the national situation under review. The optimal extra proportion of doctors for rural India, of investment for rural Peru, and of increase in farm prices for rural Nigeria will naturally differ. However, it remains true that pressures exist to set all these levels far below their optima. To acquire the right to advise against letting children go naked in winter, do I need to prescribe the ideal designs of babies' bonnets?

Linked to the question "Is there a limit to the share of resources agriculture ought to get?" is a more fundamental question. Does the need for a high share of rural resources last for ever? Does not development imply a move out of agriculture and away from villages? Since all developed countries have a very high proportion of resources outside agriculture, can it make sense for underdeveloped countries to push more resources *into* agriculture? And—a related question—as a poor country develops, does it not approach the British or U.S. style of farming, where it is workers rather than machines or land that are scarce, so that the concentration of farm resources upon big labour-saving farms begins to make more sense?

The best way to look at this question is to posit four stages in the analysis of policy in a developing country towards agriculture. Stage I is to advocate leaving farming alone, allowing it few resources, taxing it heavily if possible, and getting its outputs cheaply to finance industrial development, which has top priority. This belief often rests on such comfortable assumptions as that agricultural growth is ensured by rapid technical change; does not require or cannot absorb investment; and can be directed to the poor while the rich farmers alone are squeezed to provide the surpluses. Such a squeeze on agriculture was overtly Stalin's policy, and in effect (though much more humanely) the policy of the Second Indian Plan (1956–61) as articulated by Mahalanobis, its chief architect. The bridge between the two was the economic analysis of Preobrazhensky and Feldman. The underlying argument, that it is better to make machines than to make consumer goods, especially if one can make machines to make machines, ignores both the possible case for international specialisation, and the decided inefficiency of using scarce resources to do the right thing at the wrong time.

The second stage in policy for rural development usually arises out of the failures of Stage I. In Stage II, policy-makers argue that agriculture cannot be safely neglected if it is adequately to provide workers, materials, markets and saving to industry. Hence a lot of resources need to be put into those parts of agriculture (mainly big farms, though this is seldom stated openly) that supply industry with raw materials, and industrial workers with food. That is the stage that many poor countries have reached in their official pronouncements, and some in their actual decisions. Stage II is still permeated by urban bias, because the farm sector is allocated resources not mainly to raise economic welfare, but because, and insofar as, it uses the resources to feed urban-industrial growth. Development of the rural sector is advocated, but not for the people who live and work there.

In Stage III, the argument shifts. It is realised that, so long as resources are concentrated on big farmers to provide urban inputs, those resources will neither relieve need nor—because big farmers use little labour per acre—be used very productively. So the sequence is taken one step further back. It is recognised, not only (as in Stage II) that efficient industrialisation is unlikely without major growth in rural inputs, but also (and this is the distinctive contribution of Stage III) that such growth cannot be achieved efficiently or equitably—or maybe at all—on the basis of immediately "extracting surplus." Stage III therefore involves accepting the need for a transformation of the *mass* rural sector, through major resource inputs, *prior* to substantial industrialisation, except insofar as such industrialisation is a more efficient way than (say) imports of providing the mass rural sector with farm requirements or processing facilities. For development to "march on two legs," the best foot must be put forward first.

It is at Stage III that I stop. I do not believe that poor countries should "stay agricultural" in order to develop, let alone instead of developing. The argument that neither the carrying capacity of the land, nor the market for farm products, is such as to permit the masses in poor countries to reach high levels of living without a major shift to non-farm activities seems conclusive. The existence of a Stage IV must be recognised, however. Stage IV is the belief that industrialism degrades; that one should keep rural for ever. This is attractive to some people in poor countries because it marks a total rejection of imitativeness. Neither Western nor Soviet industrialism, but a "national path," is advocated. Other people, notably in rich countries, argue that environmental factors preclude an industrialised world where all consume at U.S. levels; that there would be too little of one or more key minerals, or that the use of so much energy would disastrously damage the world's air, water, climate or other aspects of the ecosystem. . . .

The learning process, needed for modern industrialisation, is sometimes long; but it is fallacious for a nation, comprising above all a promising but overwhelmingly underdeveloped agriculture, to conclude that, in order to begin the process of learning, a general attack on numerous branches of industrial activity should be initiated. A far better strategy is to concentrate first upon high-yielding mass rural development, supported (partly for learning's sake) by such selective ancillary industry as rural development makes viable. Rapid industrialisation on a broad front, doomed to self-strangulation for want of the wage goods and savings capacity that only a developed agricultural sector can provide, is likely to discredit industrialisation itself.

The arguments for rapid general industrialisation, prior to or alongside agricultural development, assume against most of the evidence that such a sequence is likely to succeed. But no national self-esteem, no learning-by-doing, no jam tomorrow, can come from a mass of false starts. If you wish for industrialisation, prepare to develop agriculture.

EXHIBIT VII.1. Growth Rates of Agricultural and Food Output by Major World Regions (excluding China), 1960–1980

Region and Country Group	Agricultural Output				Food Output			
	Total		Per capita		Total		Per capita	
	1960–70	1970–80	1960–70	1970–80	1960–70	1970–80	1960–70	1970–80
Developing countries	2.8	2.7	0.3	0.3	2.9	2.8	0.4	0.4
Low-income	2.5	2.1	0.2	0.4	2.6	2.2	0.2	−0.3
Middle-income	2.9	3.1	0.4	0.7	3.2	3.3	0.7	0.9
Africa	2.7	1.3	0.2	−1.4	2.6	1.6	0.1	−1.1
Middle East	2.5	2.7	0.0	0.0	2.6	2.9	0.1	0.2
Latin America	2.9	3.0	0.1	0.6	3.6	3.3	0.1	0.6
Southeast Asia	2.9	3.8	0.3	1.4	2.8	3.8	0.3	1.4
South Asia	2.5	2.2	0.1	0.0	2.6	2.2	0.1	0.0
Southern Europe	3.1	3.5	1.8	1.9	3.2	3.5	1.8	1.9
Industrial market economies	2.1	2.0	1.1	1.2	2.3	2.0	1.3	1.1
Nonmarket industrial economies	3.2	1.7	2.2	0.9	3.2	1.7	2.2	0.9
Total world	2.6	2.2	0.7	0.4	2.7	2.3	0.8	0.5

Note: Production data are weighted by world export unit prices. Decade growth rates are based on midpoints of five-year averages, except that 1970 is the average for 1969–71.

Source: *World Development Report, 1982.*

VII.B. FOODGRAIN REVOLUTION

VII.B.1. The Green Revolution: Seven Generalizations*

By the mid-1970s, a substantial body of empirical evidence had emerged that permits some clarification on the initial impact of the adoption of the new varieties on production and on the functional and personal distribution of income. The conclusions that emerge from these studies can be summarized in a series of seven generalizations. Broad generalizations of the type presented below are never able to capture the rich detail of the particular location specific investigations on which they are based. The net effect of this review of the literature does, however, add up to a quite different perspective on the impact of the green revolution than the views that dominate much of the earlier social sciences literature.

The new wheat and rice varieties were adopted at exceptionally rapid rates in those areas where they were technically and economically superior to local varieties. In the Indian Punjab, the proportion of total wheat area planted to the new high yielding varieties of wheat rose from 3.6 percent in the 1966–67 the year of initial introduction, to 65.6 percent in 1969–70. In three important wheat producing districts in the Pakistan Punjab, 73 percent of wheat acreage was sown with Mexican wheats during the 1969–70 rabi (winter) season.

In the Philippines, 95 percent of the farmers in the barrios and almost 60 percent of the farmers in the entire municipality where the new rice varieties were initially introduced had adopted the new varieties in 1969, four years after initial introduction. These rates compare favorably to the diffusion rates of new crop varieties in developed countries.

*From Vernon W. Ruttan, "The Green Revolution: Seven Generalizations," *International Development Review*, December 1977, pp. 16–22. Reprinted by permission.

The rate of adoption of the new wheat and rice varieties has declined since the early 1970s. In the case of the new wheat varieties the largest yield increments have been achieved in relatively arid areas where farmers have had access to effective tubewell or gravity irrigation systems. In the case of rice, the largest yield increments have been achieved on irrigated rice during the dry season in areas such as Central Luzon (Philippines) or Western Uttar Pradesh (India).

The agro-climatic regions where the wheat varieties developed at CYMMIT and the rice varieties developed at IRRI were best adapted have achieved relatively rapid and high level of adoption. Where diffusion of the CYMMIT and IRRI based varieties has depended on the adaptation or development of varieties suited to other environmental conditions, or on the modifications of environmental conditions, the rate of diffusion has been slower and the yield impact has been lower. Diffusion to other areas will depend, to a very substantial degree, on the development of varieties of wheat and rice suited to other ecological niches and on investment in irrigation and drainage in those areas where well adapted varieties are available. It will also depend on the successful development of high yielding varieties of other food grains, coarse grains and grain legumes.

Neither farm size nor tenure has been a serious constraint to the adoption of new high-yielding grain varieties. This is not to say that differential rates of adoption by farm size and tenure have not been observed. What the available data do seem to imply is that within a relatively few years after introduction, lags in adoption rates due to size or tenure have typically disappeared.

Neither farm size nor tenure has been an important source of differential growth in productivity. Sidhu's evidence from the Indian Punjab indicates that the new wheat technology has been approximately neutral with respect to scale—it has not been strongly biased in either a labor-saving or a capital-saving direction, and small and large farmers have achieved approximately equal gains in efficiency.

Azam interprets the data that are available from a number of studies in the Pakistan Punjab to indicate "that while the smaller farmers do face relatively more severe constraints of irrigation water and credit, the differences in the severity of these constraints is not serious enough to have caused any significant differences in the yields obtained by the small farmers as compared with the large farmers." Similar results have been reported from the Philippines by Mangahas and from Indonesia by Soejono.

The introduction of the new high yielding wheat and rice technology has resulted in an increase in the demand for labor. Sidhu's results indicated a very substantial shift to the right in the labor demand function on wheat producing farms, as a result of the introduction of the new wheat varieties in the Indian Punjab. . . . The net effect of the increase in demand for labor has been a significant rise in real wages in the Punjab at a time when real wages were constant or declining in most states in India.

HIGH-YIELDING VARIETY TECHNOLOGY

An extensive review of the literature by Bartsch indicates that the introduction of high yielding varieties into traditional wheat and rice production systems has typically resulted in substantial increases in annual labor use per hectare. The increase in labor use has been due to greater labor utilization per unit of cropped area, and in some cases, to higher cropping intensity.

Even mechanized farms typically were utilizing increased labor inputs per hectare although simulation results conducted by Bartsch and by Singh indicate that labor input per hectare might be expected to decline substantially under fully mechanized techniques combined with adoption of the high yielding variety technology.

At this stage it seems more accurate to view the growth of tractor mechanization, in areas such as the Punjab, as an economic response to the rising demand for labor associated with the intensification of crop production rather than as an autonomous source of technological change leading to labor displacement. This process was underway prior to the introduction of the new wheat varieties and has been reinforced by the more rapid growth in demand for labor since their introduction.

Landowners have gained relative to tenants and laborers from the adoption of the higher yielding grain varieties. Data assembled by Mellor indicate that although the percentage increase in labor earnings from increased employment and wages is often fairly large, the percentage of the increased output allocated to labor is relatively small. . . .

Much of the discussion about the income distribution effects of the green revolution has failed to distinguish between its absolute and relative effects on income distribution. Many authors who refer to the worsening position of the smaller owners and tenants or landless laborers are apparently referring to the widening absolute gap in the income distribution rather than to an actual decline in the income of those who occupy the lower end of the income distribution in rural communities. . . .

The effect of introduction of the new high yielding varieties has been to contribute to a widening of wage and income differentials among regions. As mentioned in the first generalization, the varieties have been developed to respond most favorably to those elements in the environment which are subject to man's control. They are more responsive than the varieties they replaced to higher levels of fertilization, to more effective irrigation and drainage; and more effective control of pathogens, insects, weeds. Reductions in sensitivity to certain natural variations such as day length and temperature make them more adaptable to intensive systems of crop production.

The contribution of the new varieties to productivity growth has, therefore, been greatest in those regions where there has been substantial investment in physical and institutional infrastructure development. This pattern is reinforced by the location specific character of agricultural technology. . . .

The contribution of the new seed-fertilizer technology to the widening of regional income disparities has apparently been greater than its impact on disparities in income within communities and regions. The associated changes in the regional distribution of political resources can be expected to become a more important source of institutional stress and institutional change than the stress at the community level which has received so much attention in recent literature.

The effect of the introduction of the new high yielding varieties has been to dampen the rate of increase in food grain prices at the consumer level. During the 1974–75 crop year the new higher yielding or modern varieties of wheat were planted on over 20 million hectares and the new high yielding varieties of rice were planted on close to 25 million hectares in Asia and the Near East.

In Asia over 60 percent of the wheat area and over one quarter of the rice area are planted to the modern varieties developed since the mid-1960s. Evenson has estimated that in crop year 1974–75, the supply of rice in all developing countries was approximately 12 percent higher than it would have been if the same total resources had been devoted to production of rice using only the traditional rice varieties available prior to the mid-1960s. . . .

The impact of a shift to the right in the supply of food grain is particularly significant for both the urban and rural poor. The distribution of grains among consumers depends primarily on the relative amount of a particular commodity consumed by each income stratum and on the price elasticity of demand in each stratum. The larger the quantity consumed and the higher the absolute value of the price elasticity of demand in the lower in-

come strata, relative to the higher income strata, the more favorable will be the distributional benefits.

This is illustrated quite dramatically by the impact of the new rice technology on consumer welfare in Colombia since the mid-1960s. Between 1966 and 1974 the percentage of the area planted to modern varieties rose from 10 percent to 99 percent. Yields on irrigated land rose from 3.1 to 5.4 metric tons per hectare, and total rice production increased from 600 thousand to 1,570 thousand metric tons. Most of the increased production was absorbed in the local market. The benefits were transmitted to consumers through both lower prices and increased per capita consumption.

The benefits were strongly biased in favor of low income consumers. The lowest income quartile of Colombian households, which received only 4 percent of household income, captured 28 percent of the consumer benefits resulting from the shift to the right in the supply curve for rice.

In most countries, increases in food grain production have generally not been adequate to prevent substantial increases in food grain prices, when measured in current dollars, in the face of the general inflationary pressures that have dominated world commodity markets between the late 1960s and the early 1970s. It is clear, however, that in the absence of the contribution of the new high yielding varieties, food grain prices would be even higher in many countries of Asia, Africa and Latin America. Part of the new income streams generated by the new varieties have been transferred from producers to consumers either through the market or through administered distribution schemes.

Thus while there may be some ambiguity regarding the distribution of the gains by size of farm or by economic or social class within the agricultural sector, there can be little question that the distributional effect on the consumption side has been positive. And among those who have gained on the consumption side have been the landless and near landless workers in rural areas.

Issues of the distribution of gains between

producers and consumers in the developing countries which have benefited from the new high yielding varieties have been given less attention than in developed countries. This may be in part because the rapid growth of demand stemming primarily from population growth has tended to equal or exceed the rate of growth in supply even when the growth in supply has been augmented by rapid technical change.

Perhaps the more important factor is that with relatively few exceptions the peasant producers of food crops in Asia are not effectively organized to reflect their economic interests at the policy level. Resistance to low price levels tends to take the form of attempts to adjust the crop mix to relative price shifts rather than to directly influence price policy.

CONCLUSION

The picture that emerges from this review of the evidence on the initial impact of the green revolution can be summarized as follows—a technology that is essentially neutral with respect to scale has been introduced into environments in which the economic, social and political institutions have varied widely with respect to their neutrality. This view has been eloquently expressed by Wolf Ladejinsky:

When all is said and done, it is not the fault of the new technology that the credit service doesn't serve those for whom it was originally intended; that the extension service is not living up to expectations; that the panchayats are essentially political rather than development bodies; that security of tenure is a luxury of the few; that rentals are exorbitant; that ceilings on land are merely notional; that for the greater part tenurial legislation is deliberately miscarried, or wage scales are hardly sufficient to keep soul and body together.

Where the technology has been introduced in areas characterized by a reasonable degree of equity in the distribution of resources, the effect has been favorable both in terms of productivity and equity. When the technology has been introduced in areas characterized by great inequality in the distribution of resources, the productivity impact has been

weak and the pattern of inequity has been reinforced. The differential impact of the technology on income growth has apparently been greater among regions than among economic factors and social classes within regions.

It is still premature to attempt a definitive evaluation of the impact of the green revolution technology on institutional change. Few attempts have been made to separate the effects of technical change from the other dynamic changes that have also impinged on the rural areas which are experiencing rapid productivity gains.

It does seem clear, however, that the contribution of the new seed-fertilizer technology to food grain production has weakened the potential for revolutionary change in political and economic institutions in rural areas in many countries in Asia and in other parts of the developing world. The green revolution has not turned red. In spite of widening income differentials, the gains from productivity growth, in those areas where the new seed-fertilizer technology has been effective, have been sufficiently diffused to reinforce interests of most classes in an evolutionary, rather than a revolutionary, pattern of rural development.

The most serious criticism that can be levelled at the green revolution is that it has not yet become sufficiently pervasive. The most disturbing evidence of failure in agricultural development in Asia over the last decade is the evidence of declining real wages in many areas where the impact of the new seed-fertilizer technology on productivity growth has been marginal.

Furthermore there is evidence that even in the more favored areas the productivity gains are coming more slowly and at greater cost than during the last decade. A combination of continued rapid growth in the rural labor force pressing against inadequate rate of growth in productivity is resulting in increasing immiserization of the landless and near landless in many areas in Asia. It is possible that this increasing immiserization may, in the next decade, induce the revolutionary changes in rural institutions which were anticipated in the 1970s by the radical critics of the green revolution.

References

Azam, K. M. "The Future of the Green Revolution in West Pakistan: A Choice of Strategy," *International Journal of Agrarian Affairs*, Vol. 5, March 1973.

Bartsch, William G. *Employment Effects of Alternative Technologies and Techniques in Asian Crop Production: A Survey of Evidence*. Geneva, International Labor Office, Provisional Draft, 1973.

Evenson, Robert E. "Comparative Evidence on Returns to Investment in National and International Research Institutions," in Thomas M. Arndt, Dana G. Dalrymple and Vernon W. Ruttan (eds.), *Resource Allocation and Productivity in National and International Agriculture Research*, Minneapolis, 1977, pp. 237–65.

Ladejinsky, Wolf. "The Green Revolution in the Punjab: A Field Trip," *Economic and Political Weekly*, Vol. 4, June 28, 1969, pp. A73–A83.

————. "Green Revolution in Bihar, The Kosi Area: A Field Trip," *Economic and Political Weekly*, Vol. 4, September 27, 1959, pp. 1–14.

Mangahas, Mahar. "Economic Aspects of Agrarian Reform under New Society," *Philippine Review of Business and Economics*, Vol. 11, December 1974, pp. 175–87.

Mellor, John W. *The New Economics of Growth: A Strategy for India*, Ithaca, 1976.

Sidhu, Surjit S. "Economics of Technical Change in Wheat Production in the Indian Punjab," *American Journal of Agricultural Economics*, Vol. 56, May 1974, p. 221.

————. "Relative Efficiency in Wheat Production in the Indian Punjab," *The American Economic Review*, Vol. 64, September 1974, pp. 742–51.

Singh, Srinath. *Modernization of Agriculture*, New Delhi, 1976.

Soejono, Irlan. "Growth and Distributional Changes in Paddy Farm Income in Central Jave," *Prisma—Indonesian Journal of Social and Economic Affairs*, May 1976, pp. 26–32.

Comment

Studies of the green revolution include: T. T. Poleman and D. K. Freebairn (eds.), *Food, Population, and Employment: The Impact of the Green Revolution* (1973); Clive Bell, "The Acquisition of Agricultural Technology," *Journal of Development Studies* (October 1972); B. F. Johnston and J. Cownie, "The Seed-Fertilizer Revolution and Labor Force Absorption," (September 1969); B. F. Johnston and Peter Kilby, *Agriculture and Structural Transformation* (1975).

J. W. Mellor, *The New Economics of Growth* (1976); C. Wharton, "The Green Revolution: Cornucopia or Pandora's Box?" *Foreign Affairs* (April 1969); W. Ladejinsky, *Agrarian Reform as Unfinished Business* (1978); Michael Lipton, "The Technology, the System, and the Poor: The Case of the New Cereal Varieties," in K. Post (ed.), *Developing Societies: The Next 25 Years* (1979).

Radical political economists have argued that the green revolution's technology tends to be monopolized by large commercial farmers who have better access to new information and better financial capacity. A large profit resulting from the exclusive adoption of modern varieties of technology by large farmers stimulates them to enlarge their operational holdings by consolidating the farms of small nonadopters through purchase or tenant eviction. As a result, polarization of rural communities into large commercial farmers and landless proletariat is promoted. See Harry M. Cleaver, "The Contradictions of the Green Revolution," *American Economic Review* (May 1972); Ali M. S. Fatami, "The Green Revolution: An Appraisal," *Monthly Review* (June 1972); Keith Griffin, *The Political Economy of Agrarian Change* (1974); Richard Grabowski, "The Implications of an Induced Innovation Model,"

Economic Development and Cultural Change (July 1979); Richard Grabowski, "Reply", *Economic Development and Cultural Change* (October 1981).

Comment

The green revolution is often compared to the "Japanese model" of increases in agricultural productivity associated with the use of improved varieties, fertilizers, implements, and other complementary inputs within the framework of Japan's small-scale farming system. For a comparative study of Japan's experience and what has been brought about by the green revolution, see Kazushi Ohkawa, *Differential Structure and Agriculture—Essays on Dualistic Growth* (1972).

Some other important studies of the Japanese case are: B. F. Johnston, "Agriculture and Economic Development: The Relevance of the Japanese Experience," *Food Research Institute Studies,* Vol. 5 (1966); W. W. Lockwood (ed.), *The State and Economic Enterprise in Japan* (1965), Chapters 2 and 6; Saburo Yamada, "Changes in Output and in Conventional and Nonconventional Inputs in Japanese Agriculture Since 1880," *Food Research Institute Studies,* Vol. 7 (1967); Lawrence Klein and Kazushi Ohkawa (eds.), *Economic Growth: The Japanese Experience Since the Meiji Era* (1968), part I; K. Ohkawa and B. F. Johnston, "The Transferability of the Japanese Pattern of Modernizing Traditional Agriculture," in E. Thorbecke (ed.), *The Role of Agriculture in Economic Development* (1969); M. Akino and Y. Hayami, "Agricultural Growth in Japan, 1880–1965," *Quarterly Journal of Economics* (August 1974).

VII.B.2. Generations of Problems*

In the regions of Asia where the production revolution has occurred, the impact on marketed surplus has been nothing short of phenomenal. Even with a moderately high on-farm demand from increased output, marketings have risen much more than proportionately to production. While the response of public and private sectors in a few regions has been good, the pace of change, the preoccupation with production, and the ability of policy makers to handle only a few issues simultaneously have meant that few policy actions were taken before crises erupted. Transportation bottlenecks often have been a problem, as an example from West Pakistan will illustrate. In Sind (the lower half of the hour-glass-shaped Indus Basin), rail marketings of rice in 1969 completely swamped the

*From Walter P. Falcon, "The Green Revolution: Second-Generation Problems," *American Journal of Agricultural Economics,* December 1970, pp. 701–9. Reprinted by permission.

system. Large, uncovered piles of rice accumulated at railheads, and prices to farmers fell substantially. Millers were working equipment at capacity and were running into severe inventory and working capital constraints. (As usual, they were blamed for the decline in price.) It nearly required a French-style, pitchfork rebellion to obtain more rail cars, to change government policy to permit trucks to deliver rice to the port, etc. In the meantime, however, farmers were "hurt," at least relative to what would have been the case with a better transport system and faster-moving government policy machinery.

Similar stories on milling, grading, storage, and transport can be told for other countries as well. The problem of limited, old-style mills, unable to handle increased supplies or to produce "export-quality" rice, is well documented in reports and government documents that I have seen for at least five Asian countries. These physical problems of marketing have been exacerbated by social factors in several countries of Southeast Asia, where specific ethnic or racial groups have traditionally controlled most of the commerce. Regardless of the efficiency of the marketing system, rural problems have tended to be blamed on these groups. Justly or unjustly, middlemen are an important factor in social and political unrest in these countries. This unrest, in turn, has posed the problem of either taking over milling in the public sector or developing a set of incentives and guidelines for the private trade that will protect the public interest as seen by the policy makers. Efficiency and ideology are often in conflict on this point, and the net result in many regions has been that the developments in marketing skills have lagged.

There have also been varietal-quality questions that have posed difficulties both domestically and internationally.... However important these difficulties may have been in the short run, they are clearly transitional in nature. New varieties are already being developed and introduced that will overcome many of the most severe quality problems.

In addition to the readily identifiable milling, transport, and grading questions, there are also formidable second-generation problems concerned with pricing and markets. There are economic and political dimensions to these questions, and both aspects must be incorporated into meaningful answers.

A number of the food-deficit countries have historically had a structure of relative prices that bore little relationship to world prices. Although in allocative efficiency terms such a structure has always had drawbacks, the problem takes on even more serious proportions when countries and regions close their food import gap and become potential exporters. Adjusting domestic support prices, which at the official exchange rate are often double or more the world price, is no easier politically in these countries than in the United States.

In addition to internal pricing difficulties an even larger problem looms ahead on the international side. For those regions "lucky" enough to emerge as surplus areas the problems of breaking into international grain markets have rarely appeared so difficult. The International Wheat Agreement appears to be seriously undermined, and there has been a considerable softening in rice prices, particularly in the lower-quality grades.

Several elements of the international dimension deserve mention. What happens to "world prices" for wheat and rice is obviously dependent on what happens to the green revolution in the developing countries as well as to the agricultural policies of the developed nations. As indicated previously, there are reasons to believe that portions of Indonesia, India, and East Pakistan are likely to be net importers for some time. On the other hand, the quantity traded internationally is so small relative to production—less than four percent in the case of rice—that increases in production in key countries such as India are likely to have important international price repercussions. Perhaps even more important than what happens in the developing countries is what happens to agricultural policy in the advanced countries. Unable to adapt to rapid technological advances and structural change themselves, these countries have instituted support systems that use commodity exports to solve sectoral income distribution problems. In short, less-developed countries breaking into export markets will be faced with three kinds of problems: (a) a tenacity among developed countries in fighting for shares of the commerical market and a willingness to cut prices to retain them; (b) an increasing amount of foodgrains being supplied by developed countries at concessional terms to countries that might "normally" be trading partners of developing countries; and (c) an inability, or at least difficulty, of the less-developed world to compete in "buyers'" markets in terms of specific grades, quality, deliverability, etc. This does not mean that the developing countries cannot sell in international markets. What it does mean is that planners in these countries must be hardheaded about the quantities and especially the prices at which wheat and rice can be exported and about the concomitant internal price adjustment (or export subsidy) that will be required at these levels.

The foregoing marketing and demand problems, any one of which could be the subject of a major paper, suggest several conclusions:

First, the production gains in certain regions have shown how rapidly second-generation marketing problems can arise. It is to be hoped that in the future policy makers will heed earlier the warnings given by marketing specialists and will react before crisis situations develop. Unless these milling and transport problems are solved, farm prices will decline steeply and the quality problems of exporting will be all the more difficult. What is particularly needed in several Asian countries is a marketing strategy that resolves the basic public/private/foreign investment question on marketing facilities. Also needed is an explicit recognition of the interaction of price support policies and techniques with the behavior and efficiency of marketing firms.

Second, planners must pay increasing attention to the adjustment and pricing problems attendant on the new varieties. The narrow focus on foodgrains and relative neglect of other crops must be reevaluated in a multicrop setting. In particular, the cropping patterns of many of the irrigated areas of Asia which can best use the new varieties are quite sensitive to profitability changes. What constitutes an appropriate incentive price for foodgrains in these areas with the new varieties has changed substantially; unfortunately, the rhetoric of the later 1950's and early 1960's regarding the need for ever higher agricultural prices has not changed. Vested interests in agriculture are already a fact of life in these countries, and economists concerned with agriculture must keep in mind the overall needs of development, not just the needs of the agricultural sector. Since most agricultural goods are tradable, what is especially needed in the less-developed countries is an assessment of the domestic costs of earning or saving foreign exchange from producing various agricultural

and nonagricultural commodities. The real tragedy would be for those countries to retain outmoded pricing policies which lead to great inefficiencies in resource use, stock accumulations, and/or highly subsidized agricultural exports—exports that were uneconomically grown in real terms in the first place. Unfortunately, experience in dealing with such problems in developed countries does not inspire confidence, nor do recent policies in a number of Asian countries.

Third, the advanced countries must consider more seriously the distorting effects of their dumping programs. The talk of *a* world market price for wheat or for rice is largely a fiction, and concessional pricing arrangements will be a sharp deterrent to the generation of third-country foodgrain exports.

Fourth, since there is little reason to have confidence in the developed countries' ability to deal with their sectoral income distribution problems without resort to concessional efforts, the developing countries should look increasingly to domestic markets for absorbing additional supplies. On this point there is some room for optimism. What has been seriously underestimated, I believe, is the investment and employment uses to which wheat and rice, the wage goods, can be put. The basic elements in this argument can be stated as follows: With significant increases in production, foodgrain prices in a closed economy would fall. However, given the fact that much of the increase came from cost-free technological change, prices could fall somewhat and still provide adequate incentives to farmers. In addition, with substantial supplies of grain, the government can have a much more expansionary fiscal and monetary policy. (Indeed, in India and Indonesia the lack of adequate food supplies and a fear of rising prices have been constraints on the size of the development budget.) The more expansionary monetary and fiscal policy—particularly if it is directed toward labor-intensive public projects—can shift the demand curve for grains, helping to counteract some of the decline in prices. Given the fact that the price of the wage good is a major development constraint in much of Asia, especially as seen by finance ministers, the increases in production from the green revolution can thus continue after initial import substitution has been exhausted. These increases can be converted into investible resources through fiscal and monetary expansion, and the country (perhaps even the agricultural sector, if the investments are rural) could be much better off. This should be one element of development strategy for countries moving into foodgrain surpluses; moreover, it seems especially important for countries who find themselves with seriously distorted internal prices. This approach should provide time both to solve the institutional problems of entering international trade and to make transitional changes in relative and absolute price levels without having to rely on stock accumulation or "excessive" subsidies to agriculture. Such a strategy also has much in common with a sensible P.L. 480 policy which can effect shifts in the demand curve through investment policies, thereby helping to counteract much of the decline in prices that would have resulted from increased supplies.

The first-generation production problems and the second-generation marketing and demand difficulties created by the green revolution are a formidable list. Nevertheless, they are largely short-run issues on which economists have worked for years. By contrast, the third-generation problems, having to do with equity, welfare, employment, and social institutions generally are questions that have received inadequate attention even in the developed countries. . . .

These third-generation factors arise from four principal sources: (a) population growth rates in excess of 2.5 percent annually in areas already extraordinarily densely populated; (b) very low average income levels, coupled simultaneously with great regional and personal disparities in income, wealth, and political power; (c) limited opportunities for nonfarm employment, even if the manufacturing and service sectors grow very rapidly; and (d) the possibility for technological leap-frogging with agricultural inputs and

techniques, which are often of a labor-displacing nature. The resulting dilemma can be baldly stated: The Asian countries need agricultural growth if ever they are to break the chains of poverty; but they need equity as well, for obvious humanitarian reasons and in order not to find themselves in a continuous cycle of violence and repression. The challenge of these forces is far greater in magnitude than the problems ever faced by the United States and most other presently developed nations. Moreover, the latter are not in a position to help. Although they are perhaps capable of exporting the growth technology, they have few institutional forms to export that can come to grips with the income distribution and employment questions that now plague Asia.

India, Pakistan, and Indonesia—three enormously large and regionally heterogeneous countries—present stark examples of the problems outlined above.

Perhaps even more important than the direct effects, and often neglected in discussions on employment, are the side effects of increased food supplies and lower food prices on public and private savings and investment generally. As noted earlier, the food-price constraint is an important one and has a pervasiveness that extends far beyond the agricultural sector. Here, too, the green revolution helps, provided that its potential for increasing savings is realized and is transferred into real investment.

Far more disturbing, however, are two other effects of the green revolution on employment, welfare, and stability. Both of these derive basically from the unequal regional growth that seems to be a concomitant of the new technology. The process is as follows: The regions with irrigation, such as the Punjab, have the ability to respond rapidly to the new technology. A combination of the resulting production plus an agricultural price policy that reflects concerns for nongrowing districts as well as vested agricultural interests will mean that incomes in the irrigated regions will grow at phenomenal rates. That is all to the good; the difficulty is that welfare, between regions as among people, is more a relative concept than an absolute idea. In this interregional sense, therefore, the green revolution is hardly a stabilizing influence.

Within a given region, the mechanism producing greater income inequality is much the same, and the form is even more virulent. Although in theory the new seeds and fertilizer are neutral to scale, in practice they are not. Under rationed conditions, and unfortunately these often prevail for inputs in Asia, it is the larger farmers who obtain the fertilizer and receive the irrigation water. Moreover, with the prices and technology now prevailing, agricultural incomes of large farmers have risen dramatically. This too is not "bad," but the side effects may be. Land prices are rising rapidly, as farmers seek to expand size and find new outlets for their increased incomes. Even more important is the drive that these windfall gains are providing for certain types of mechanization. Although this is a broad question, deserving also of a separate study, several points deserve mention. First, there are powerful forces that are pressing for mechanization of all kinds. Large farmers, foreign and domestic industrialists, politicians, and even aid agencies have vested interests in promoting various implements, including tractors. Some forms of mechanization may be labor-displacing, others not. However, large farms in wheat areas are an example of where tractors and combines will be introduced, barring strong government action to the contrary. The net result will be to make tenants into laborers and to increase the number of people displaced from agriculture. Just as in the interregional illustration, the intraregional effects of the green revolution are likely to increase the inequality of incomes within agriculture. There will indeed be agricultural growth in these areas, but probably increasing tension among classes as well. Perhaps the growth in service and supply industries in small towns can absorb this additional displacement. But the adjustment problems, with which the United States had trouble in coping under much more favorable demographic circumstances and over a century, must be dealt with in Pakistan in 20 years. This labor-displacement process was not "easy" in the United States; in Asia the situation is distressing even to contemplate. . . .

Several recommendations and reconsiderations are suggested in the light of these third-generation questions. First, as long as the new varieties remain limited to a few regions and as long as farm incomes are primarily dependent on acreage rather than people, it is naive to believe that the new technology for agriculture is likely to be a stabilizing influence. Growth generally is destabilizing, and this form of unequal agricultural development is particularly so. Even if the first borrowings of technology are neutral to scale (which in practice probably they are not), subsequent borrowings are likely to be labor-displacing unless strong policy measures are introduced. The magnitude of this phenomenon will vary by commodity and region, but the direction seems fairly clear. Second, some way must be found to close the gap between social and private benefits from certain forms of agricultural technology. It is not sufficient to appeal to the "Japanese method" of cultivation, to urge labor-intensive techniques for agriculture and industry, or to proclaim the virtues of small-scale industry. Such pronouncements must be transformed into instruments of direction and control: high taxes on tractors; a possible lowering of wheat and rice prices as a stimulant to the rest of the economy; much higher interest rates on capital and higher de facto rates for foreign exchange; progressive land taxes; and perhaps even ceilings on farm size so as to make uneconomical, from a private point of view, certain forms of technology. And in any Asian country, no one should discount the size and power of the forces that are likely to be against most of these policies.

Third, neither growth nor equity problems in Asia can be solved by the green revolution or even by the agricultural sector alone. The employment problem in particular is total-economy in character, whose solution requires increased savings, more foreign exchange, higher investment rates, altered factor- and product-pricing structures—in short, economic development. While agricultural policies should not aggrevate the situation, meangingful answers to these issues must look to other sectors as well.

Fourth, given the tearing effect that unequal regional growth has on the national fabric, there is need to stress again the importance of developing new technology for the monsoon/dryland areas.

Finally, while there is need to keep social and private benefits from diverging among the large farms, the oppostie side of the coin is to assist small farmers. . . . Given the resources available and the political interests that are involved, a broad-based welfare system does not seem to be the answer. Nor do special loan or credit arrangements to small farmers which are used for unproductive investments. There is reason to be even more skeptical, as amply demonstrated in the United States, about price support or input subsidies as an instrument. It is the large farmer who has the marketed surplus and who uses most of the inputs. (Nearly one-third of the farmers in Indonesia, Pakistan, and India, for example, are net purchasers of grains.) It is spurious to argue for higher farm prices or increased subsidies to "help the small farmer," for it would be hard to design a more inefficient system for reaching them. (Some rough calculations for India and Pakistan indicate that of $10 transferred via a price-support system, only about $1 goes to "small" farmers.) The small-farmer argument, which is always offered by the representatives of larger farmers whenever pricing is an issue, should be viewed very skeptically.

Except for the obvious and important point of assuming a ready supply of inputs such as fertilizer, the literature of agricultural development has little to offer in the way of positive suggestions for dealing with the agricultural production alternatives for millions of small Asian farmers. Providing credit in kind (as under the BIMAS program in parts of Indonesia) has worked in some circumstances, as have a few cooperative arrangements. The program at Comilla in East Pakistan, for example, has shown the merit of cooperative credit, marketing, and pump facilties at the village level. On the other hand, most of the cooperatives of South and Southeast Asia have been run as heavy-handed government agencies with little local support except among the rural elite who have benefited from them. Similarly, loan programs especially designed for small farmers have generally had little success because of prohibitively high transaction costs for issuing and monitoring small loans. Perhaps most promising as an aid to the smaller operator is the provision of adequate supplies of irrigation water. The employment effects from this type of infrastructure are substantial, and reliable water supplies may provide the flexibility for diversifying and intensifying output. On the whole, however, the outlook is far from bright for the smaller farmer.

CONCLUDING COMMENTS

The foregoing assessment of the green revolution is hardly one of wild enthusiasm. The purpose has not been to argue that it should not have happened or to deny its great production successes in certain regions. Rather, the intent has been to indicate how limited a solution the revolution is, given the broader development problems of South and Southeast Asia.

Four central themes stand out in the analysis. First, impressive as the gains to date have been, the term "revolution" can be applied correctly only to about 10 to 15 percent of Asia. One of the greatest second-generation obstacles is that set of individuals who believe, explicitly or implicitly, that the first-generation solutions have been found. Many additional answers are needed, and any complacency on varietal research would be most unfortunate both in terms of growth and regional equity. Clearly also, a real revolution will require greatly expanded investments in irrigation and substantial improvements in systems for pest control.

Second, the sudden increases in agricultural output have already or will soon necessitate basic pricing decisions on the parts of governments. It would be a great pity if the nations of Asia, in the face of remarkable productivity changes, maintained pricing structures that did not keep in mind the needs of the entire economy. As a result of the increased production from the green revolution, there is considerable potential for expanding the development effort with investment programs that are wage-good intensive. As regards exports, the developed countries could play a major facilitating role; however, their probable increased use of dumping programs will provide the most formidable kinds of competition for those developing nations who generate export surpluses. Hence, the internal market opportunities and the external market difficulties indicate the probable need for downward adjustments in relative grain prices in several Asian nations.

Third, the limited technological revolution in agriculture has permitted an easing of one critical development constraint. It has not, however, provided a panacea for the employment and equity problems, and indeed has probably been destabilizing in the sense that it has widened income disparities within and between regions. Lest this view be regarded as too bleak, it should also be emphasized that without the green revolution, the development situation in these countries would now be even more dire.

Finally, although it is important to recognize and understand what has happened in the past, the great challenge of the future will be to forge institutions that can deal simultaneously with the demographic explosion, rapid economic growth, and equality of income distribution. Certain obvious mistakes in policies can be avoided, such as the subsidization of tractors. However, there is little in the way of a broad, institutional blueprint in the history of the developed countries or in the general writings of agricultural economists that is now of much help on this issue. The Asian challenge of the future will be to encourage growth elements in the economy—such as the green revolution—while at the same time fostering equity so as to prevent an ascending spiral of violence and repression.

VII.C. Designing an Agricultural Strategy

VII.C.1. The Case for a Unimodal Strategy*

The historical experience in a number of countries, and the recent technical breakthroughs of the Green Revolution, justify major emphasis on increases in factor productivity. It is, however, the experience of Japan and Taiwan that is especially useful in demonstrating that an *appropriate* sequence of innovations based on modern scientific knowledge and experimental methods makes possible an expansion path for the agricultural sector that is characterized by large increases in factor productivity *throughout* the agricultural sector. Such a strategy enables a widening fraction of the working population in agriculture to be associated with increasingly productive technologies, based mainly on expanded use of purchased inputs that are divisible and neutral to scale. It is because the new inputs of seed and fertilizer, that are the essence of the Green Revolution, are complementary to the large amounts of labor and land already committed to agriculture that these increases in factor productivity can have such a large impact on total farm output. At the same time, by involving an increasingly large fraction of the rural population in the process of technical change, such a strategy means that the fruits of economic progress are widely shared.

The thrust of this argument is that it is possible and desirable to devise and implement agricultural strategies which are efficient in terms of a number of objectives, including but not confined to the objective of achieving desired increases in farm output at low cost. The following objectives, which are examined later in some detail, seem to be es-

*From Bruce F. Johnston, "Criteria for the Design of Agricultural Development Strategies," *Food Research Institute Studies in Agricultural Economics, Trade, and Development,* Vol. 11, No. 1, 1972, pp. 35–7, 42–54. Copyright 1972 by the Board of Trustees of Leland Stanford Junior University.

pecially relevant to the design of strategies for agriculture that are efficient in this broad sense:

(1) Contributing to the overall rate of economic growth and the process of structural transformation,

(2) Achieving a satisfactory rate of increase in farm output at minimum cost by encouraging sequences of innovations which exploit the possibilities for technical change most appropriate to a country's factor endowments,

(3) Achieving a broadly based improvement in the welfare of the rural population, and

(4) Facilitating the process of social modernization (including the lowering of birthrates, the extension and improvement of rural education, and the strengthening of entrepreneurial capacities) by encouraging widespread attitudinal and behavioral changes among farm households.

I believe that it is useful to assess the "total efficiency" of alternative agricultural strategies in terms of their relative success in achieving those four objectives.

The concept of total efficiency is, quite obviously, difficult to define operationally. That is inherent in the nature of the problem. But the problem must be confronted because only when a country's agricultural strategy is efficient in this broad sense is the trade-off between the goal of increased output and other objectives likely to be minimized. Indeed, it is my contention that with an agricultural strategy that is designed with those multiple objectives in view, the trade-off is likely to be small or nonexistent.

A country's overall strategy for agriculture is a composite of substrategies relating to research, education, water resources development, promotion of farmers' organizations, marketing and price policy, credit and the distribution of inputs, agricultural taxation, land tenure, policies affecting the nature and pace of mechanization, and other elements. The total efficiency of the strategy depends on the complementarities among those various activities and the quality of implementation as well as decisions with respect to the allocation of funds and personnel and policies for individual substrategies. . . .

THE CHOICE BETWEEN UNIMODAL AND BIMODAL AGRICULTURAL STRATEGIES

The most fundamental issue of agricultural strategy faced by the late developing countries is to choose between a bimodal strategy whereby resources are concentrated within a subsector of large, capital-intensive units or a unimodal strategy which seeks to encourage a more progressive and wider diffusion of technical innovations adapted to the factor proportions of the sector as a whole. The essential distinction between the two approaches is that the unimodal strategy emphasizes sequences of innovations that are highly divisible and largely scale-neutral. These are innovations that can be used efficiently by small-scale farmers and adopted progressively. A unimodal approach does not mean that all farmers or all agricultural regions would adopt innovations and expand output at uniform rates. Rather it means that the type of innovations emphasized are appropriate to a progressive pattern of adoption in the twofold sense that there will be progressive diffusion of innovations within particular areas and extension of the benefits of technical change to new areas as changes in environmental conditions, notably irrigation facilities, or improved market opportunities or changes in the nature of the innovations available enable farmers in new areas to participate in the process of modernization. Although a bimodal strategy entails a much more rapid adoption of a wider range of modern technologies, this is necessarily confined to a small fraction of farm units because of the structure of economies in which commer-

cial demand is small in relation to a farm labor force that still represents some 60 to 80 percent of the working population.

The late developing countries face a wide choice of farm equipment embodying large investments in research and development activity in the economically advanced countries. The performance characteristics of these machines are impressive, and representatives of the major manufacturing firms in the economically advanced countries are experienced and skillful in demonstrating their equipment. And they now have added incentive to promote sales in the developing countries to more fully utilize their plant capacity which is large relative to domestic demand (mainly a replacement demand since the period of rapid expansion of tractors and tractor-drawn equipment in the developed countries has ended). The availability of credit under bilateral and international aid programs temporarily eliminates the foreign exchange constraint to acquiring such equipment; and when such loans are readily available it may even appear to be an attractive means of increasing the availability of resources—in the short run. Within developing countries there is often considerable enthusiasm for the latest in modern technologies. But little attention is given to research and development activity and support services to promote the manufacture and wide use of simple, inexpensive equipment of good design, low import content, and suited to the factor proportions prevailing in countries where labor is relatively abundant and capital scarce. . . .

Under a bimodal strategy frontier firms with their high capital to labor ratio would account for the bulk of commercial production and would have the cash income required to make extensive use of purchased inputs. Inasmuch as the schedule of aggregate commercial demand for agricultural products is inelastic and its rightward shift over time is essentially a function of the rate of structural transformation, to concentrate resources within a subsector of agriculture inevitably implies a reduction in the ability of farm households outside that subsector to adopt new purchased inputs and technologies. In addition, the high foreign exchange content of many of the capital inputs employed in the frontier sector implies a reduction in the amount of foreign exchange available for imported inputs for other farm firms (or for other sectors). It is, of course, because of these purchasing power and foreign exchange constraints that it is impossible for the agricultural sector as a whole to pursue a crash modernization strategy. It might be argued that a proper farm credit program could eliminate the purchasing power constraint, but the availability of credit (assuming that repayment takes place) merely alters the shape of the time horizon over which the constraint operates. And capital and government revenue are such scarce resources in a developing country that government subsidy programs are not feasible means of escaping from this constraint. In brief, bimodal and unimodal strategies are to a considerable extent mutually exclusive.

Under the bimodal approach the divergence between the factor intensities and the technical efficiency of "best" and average firms is likely to become progressively greater as agricultural transformation takes place. Moreover, both the initial and subsequent divergences between the technologies used in the two sectors are likely to be accentuated because the factor prices, including the price of imported capital equipment, faced by the modern sector in contemporary developing countries typically diverge from social opportunity cost. This divergence is obvious when subsidized credit is made available on a rationed basis to large farmers and when equipment can be imported with a zero or low tariff at an official exchange rate that is overvalued. In addition, the large-scale farmers depend on hired labor rather than unpaid family labor. The wages paid hired labor may be determined by minimum wage legislation, and even without a statutory minimum the price of hired labor is characteristically higher than the opportunity cost of labor to small farm units. . . .

Under the unimodal strategy with its emphasis on highly divisible and scale-neutral innovations, the best firms in the agrarian sector display essentially the same factor intensities as average firms. Interfarm differences in performance will be large, especially during transitional periods as farmers are learning how to use new inputs efficiently, but this will reflect mainly differences in output per unit of input rather than major differences in factor proportions. Inasmuch as the expansion path for the agricultural sector associated with a unimodal strategy implies a level of capital intensity and foreign exchange requirements that are compatible with a late developing country's economic structure, more firms within the agricultural sector are able to expand their use of fertilizer and the other divisible inputs that dominate purchases under this strategy. Thus, the diffusion of innovations and associated inputs will be more broadly based, and the divergence in factor intensities between frontier firms and average firms will be moderate.

Although the foregoing has emphasized the contrast in the pattern of technical change, it is apparent that the two strategies will have significantly different impacts on many dimensions of economic and social change. Most obvious are the differences in the nature of demand for farm inputs, but the structure of rural demand for consumer goods will also be very different under a unimodal as compared to a bimodal strategy.

A major difference in income distribution is to be expected because of the likelihood that under a bimodal strategy the difficult problem of absorbing a rapidly growing labor force into productive employment would be exacerbated whereas under a unimodal strategy there is a good prospect that the rate of increase in demand for labor would be more rapid than the growth of the labor force. Underemployment and unemployment would thus be reduced as a result of wider participation of the rural population in improved income-earning opportunities. This improvement in income opportunities available to members of the rural work force would result in part from increased earnings as hired labor since rising demand for labor would tend to raise wage rates and the number of days of work available during the year for landless laborers and for very small farmers whose incomes derive to a considerable extent from work on farms that are above average size.

Most important, however, would be the increased incomes earned by farm households cultivating their own or rented land. The extent to which tenants would be able to share in the increased productivity resulting from yield-increasing innovations will be determined by forces related to land reform as an aspect of broadly based improvement in the welfare of the rural population. Basically, however, it will depend upon the rate of growth of the rural population of working age seeking a livelihood in farming or in nonfarm activities relative to the rate of expansion of income-earning opportunities. The latter will be influenced strongly by the demand on the part of landowners for labor "hired" indirectly through tenancy arrangements, or hired directly as laborers on owner-operated farms.

THE MULTIPLE OBJECTIVES OF AN AGRICULTURAL STRATEGY

In the paragraphs that follow I comment briefly on some of the reasons why the design of an efficient strategy for agriculture should be guided by explicit consideration of four major objectives of an agricultural strategy and the interrelationships among them. . . .

Contributions to overall economic growth and structural transformation. It is conventional when considering agriculture's role in economic development to catalog a number of specific "contributions." Several of these contributions imply a net transfer of factors of production out of the agricultural sector as the process of structural transformation takes place. Typically the farm sector provides foreign exchange, public and private investment resources, and labor to the more rapidly expanding sectors of the economy as well as increased supplies of food and raw materials to support a growing urban population and manufacturing sector.

These contributions are, of course, synonymous with the increased sectoral interdependence that characterizes a developing economy. Outward labor migration and increased farm purchasing power are synchronized with the growing importance of commodity flows between agriculture and other sectors: a flow of food and raw materials out of agriculture and a return flow of farm inputs and consumer goods from the manufacturing sector. Tertiary activities of government, transport, marketing and other service industries expand to meet the needs of individual sectors and to facilitate the linkages between them.

Agricultural exports have special significance here for two reasons. First, in countries that have experienced little structural transformation there are usually few alternative means of meeting the growing demands for foreign exchange that characterize a developing economy. Secondly, expanded production for export makes it possible to enlarge farm cash incomes when the domestic market for purchased food is still very small, and at the same time it provides a stimulus and the means to establish some of the physical infrastructure and institutions that are necessary for the creation of a national, market-oriented economy.

The structure of rural demand for farm inputs associated with alternative agricultural strategies exerts an important influence on the growth of local manufacturing as well as on the pattern of productivity advance within agriculture. I emphasize the composition of this demand because the capacity of the agricultural sector to purchase inputs from other sectors is powerfully constrained by the proportion of the population living outside agriculture. Pathological growth of population in urban areas only loosely related to the growth of off-farm employment opportunities is a conspicuous and distressing feature of many of the contemporary less developed countries, but basically this growth of urban population depends on the transformation of a country's occupational structure that is a concomitant of economic growth.

The nature of the linkages between agriculture and the local manufacturing sector and the seriousness of foreign exchange and investment constraints on development will be influenced significantly by the structure of rural demand for both inputs and consumer goods. Because of their differential effects on the sequence of innovations and on rural income distribution, a bimodal and a unimodal strategy will differ greatly in their aggregate capital and foreign exchange requirements.

The more capital-intensive bimodal strategy emphasizes rapid adoption of mechanical innovations such as tractors along with chemical fertilizers and other inputs essential for increasing crop yields. Even if that type of machinery is manufactured locally, the foreign exchange requirements for capital equipment and for components are high, and the production processes require a high level of technical sophistication, large plants, and capital-intensive technologies.

The unimodal strategy with its emphasis on mechanical innovations of lower technical sophistication and foreign exchange content, such as improved bullock implements and low-lift pumps, appears to offer greater promise for the development of local manufacturing which is less demanding in its technical requirements and which is characterized by lower capital-labor ratios and lower foreign exchange content. On the basis of experience in Japan and Taiwan as well as an analysis of the nature of the supply response to the two patterns of demand, it seems clear that a unimodal strategy will have a much more favorable impact on the growth of output and especially on the growth of employment in local manufacturing and supporting service industries. The reasons cannot be pursued here except to note the wider diffusion of opportunities to develop entrepreneurial and technical skills through "learning by doing" that leads to increasing competence in manufacturing. Progress in metalworking and in the domestic manufacture of capital goods are especially significant because they are necessary to the creation of an industrial sector adapted to the factor proportions of a late developing economy.

Increasing farm productivity and output. The differences in farm productivity between modern and traditional agriculture are, of course, to be attributed mainly to their use of widely different technologies. Those differences in turn are based on large differences in their use of fixed and working capital and associated differences in their investments in human resources that affect the level and efficiency of agricultural research and other supporting services as well as the knowledge, skills, and innovativeness of the farm population.

The importance of distinguishing between inputs and innovations that are mainly instrumental in increasing output per acre and those that make it possible for each farm worker to cultivate a larger area has already been noted. Biological and chemical innovations increase agricultural productivity mainly through increasing yields per acre. In general the effect on yield of farm mechanization *per se* is slight, although certain mechanical innovations, notably tubewells and low-lift pumps may be highly complementary to yield-increasing innovations. Indeed, for some high-yielding varieties, especially rice, an ample and reliable supply of water is a necessary precondition for realizing the genetic potential of the new varieties. This distinction between yield-increasing and labor-saving innovations is significant because the relative emphasis given to these two types of innovations largely determines whether development of agriculture will follow a unimodal or bimodal pattern.

The thrust of a unimodal strategy is to encourage general diffusion of yield-increasing innovations and such mechanical innovations as are complementary with the new seed-fertilizer technology. The bimodal strategy emphasizes simultaneous adoption of innovations that increase substantially the amount of land which individual cultivators can efficiently work in addition to the yield-increasing innovations emphasized in the unimodal approach.

For reasons discussed above, it is not possible for developing countries to pursue the unimodal and bimodal options simultaneously. In placing emphasis on reinforcing success within a subsector of large and capital-intensive farms, a bimodal strategy may have an advantage in maximizing the rate of increase in the short run because it bypasses the problems and costs associated with involving a large fraction of the farm population in the modernization process. In a longer view, however, a unimodal strategy appears to be more efficient, especially in minimizing requirements for the scarce resources of foreign exchange and loanable funds.

Policies and programs to ensure that the seed-fertilizer revolution is exploited as widely and as fully as possible are clearly of central importance. This emphasizes the importance of adaptive research and of training and extension programs to promote further diffusion of new varieties and to narrow the gap between yields at the farm level and the potential yields obtainable. Investments in infrastructure and in land and water development required to provide environmental conditions favorable to the introduction of more productive technologies are also priority needs....

The distribution of land ownership and, more particularly, the size distribution of operational units are highly important factors influencing the choice of technique and the factor proportions that characterize the expansion path of the agricultural sector. Both are influenced by policies and practices affecting land tenure which are discussed in the following section.

Achieving broadly based improvement in the welfare of the rural population. In a longer term view substantial improvement in the welfare of the rural population depends upon the process of structural change which, inter alia, makes possible a reduction in the absolute size of the rural population, a large increase in commercial demand for farm products, and large increases in the capital-labor ratio in agriculture. There are, however, some more direct relationships between strategies for agriculture and the improvement of rural welfare that need to be considered.

Rural works programs are probably the most frequently discussed measure aimed directly at improving the welfare of the poorest segments of the farm population. There is much to be said for such programs as a means of providing supplemental employment and income to the most disadvantaged members of the rural population and at the same time building infrastructure important to agriculture and other sectors. But because of the organizational problems and particularly the severe fiscal constraints that characterize a developing country, it seems doubtful whether this approach can have a very substantial effect on underemployment and unemployment in rural areas. ...

Other programs also merit attention because they offer the promise of substantial benefits relative to their cost, and some of them can also make a substantial contribution to the expansion of output by improving the health and productivity of the rural population. Public health programs such as malaria control are notable examples. The success of such programs is, of course, a major factor underlying the population explosion and the urgent need for policies and programs that will have both direct and indirect effects in encouraging the spread of family planning. Nutritional programs also deserve attention. The effects on well-being of increased farm productivity and incomes can be enhanced considerably if diet changes are informed by practical programs of nutrition education. ...

Although it is foolhardy to attempt to treat the complex and controversial subject of land tenure in a few paragraphs, the positive and negative effects on rural welfare of land reform programs cannot be ignored. In Asia the land tenure situation is dominated by the fact that the area of arable land is small relative to the large and growing farm population entirely or mainly dependent on agriculture for their livelihood. One implication of this, which is distressing but beyond dispute, is that for the agricultural sector as a whole in these countries the average farm size will become even smaller—or at least that the number of agricultural workers per acre of arable land will continue to increase for several decades until a structural transformation turning point is reached.

It is sometimes argued that because of the connection between size of holding and choice of technique, redistributive land reform is a necessary condition for a unimodal strategy. Indeed it is even claimed that the success of unimodal strategies in Japan and Taiwan is attributable to their postwar land reforms, notwithstanding the fact that in both countries the basic pattern of progressive modernization of small-scale, labor-intensive, but technically progressive farm units was established long before World War II.

I am persuaded that an effectively implemented land reform program that brings about a more equal distribution of landed wealth will not only contribute to the goal of equity but will also tend to facilitate low-cost expansion of farm output based primarily on yield-increasing innovations. Although such a program would appear to be desirable, there is reason to believe that for a good many Asian countries it is not a likely outcome. It therefore seems important to emphasize that historical evidence and logic both contradict the view that in the absence of land reform the pattern of agricultural development will inevitably accentuate the problems of rural underemployment and unemployment and the inequality of income distribution.

The critical factor determining the choice of technique and factor proportions in agriculture is the size distribution of operational (management) units rather than ownership units. Past experience, for example in prewar Japan and Taiwan, demonstrates that a highly skewed pattern of land ownership is not incompatible with a unimodal size distribution of operational units. To a considerable extent the widespread condemnation of tenancy, particularly of share tenancy, seems to stem from a tendency to confuse what is really a symptom with the root cause of the miserable existence that is the plight of so many tenant households in underdeveloped countries. The fact that tenants are prepared to accept rental arrangements that leave them such a meager residual income is fundamentally a consequence of the extreme lack of alternative income-earning opportunities. The proposition, briefly stated, is that bargaining between landowners and tenants will tend to result in equilibrium arrangements with respect to the rental share, the amount of land rented to individual tenants, the cropping pattern and other farm practices, and sharing of expenses of inputs. These arrangements will tend to maximize the landowner's rental income subject to the constraint that a tenant and members of his household must obtain residual income that represents a "wage" approximately equal to his best alternative earnings or they will not enter into the agreement. To the extent that the proposition is valid, it means that improvement in the welfare of tenants must depend primarily on improving the income-earning opportunities available, including the possibility of enlarging their own holdings by redistributive land reform as well as the increase in demand for labor within and outside agriculture.

The advantages of organizing agricultural production primarily on the basis of small-scale units appropriate to the unfavorable man-land ratios that characterize the agricultural sector in late developing countries are enhanced by the new technical possibilities resulting from the seed-fertilizer revolution. Although those advantages are to a considerable extent a function of the size of operational units, there are some specific advantages of owner cultivation related to productivity considerations as well as the more obvious effects on income distribution. Although in principle, investments in land improvement that are profitable will be made by the landowner, by the tenant, or under some joint agreement, the division of responsibility in decision-making is likely to delay or prevent investments even though they would be to the advantage of both parties. Owner cultivation also avoids the difficulties that arise when landlords, responding to higher yields, raise the percentage share of output that they demand as rent. But if redistributive land reform is not a realistic possibility, widespread renting of land seems clearly preferable to the further concentration of land in large operational units and the bimodal pattern which is thereby accentuated. . . .

Facilitating the processes of social modernization by encouraging widespread attitudinal and behavioral changes. The spread of economic and technical change among the rural population, buttressed by a network of institutions and communication links, undoubtedly has significant effects on the process of social modernization that go beyond their effects on economic growth. It seems likely that the broad impact of a unimodal strategy would have favorable effects in three areas important to this process of social change. First, the wide diffusion of familiarity with the calculation of costs and returns and of opportunities to acquire managerial experience would appear to provide a favorable environment for the training and recruitment of entrepreneurs. The same would apply, of course, to the wider diffusion of learning experiences in manufacturing which is associated with a unimodal strategy.

Secondly, a broadly based approach to agricultural development seems likely to generate strong support for rural education as well as the institutions more directly related to promoting increased agricultural productivity. It is sometimes argued that large-scale, highly commercialized farm enterprises are easier to tax than millions of small units. Because of the power structure maintained or created by a bimodal strategy, however, the greater administrative convenience may in practice mean very little. The fact that public education, and especially rural education, in most of South America seems to lag behind progress in other developing countries where average incomes are considerably lower seems to provide some support for this generalization.

Thirdly, and most important, the reduction in birthrates in the countryside, resulting from spontaneous changes in attitudes and behavior as well as behavioral changes induced by government population programs, are likely to be more widespread and have a greater effect on the national birthrate under a unimodal than a bimodal strategy. For reasons examined earlier, the bulk of the population in the late developing countries is going to be in the agricultural sector for several decades or more. Under those circumstances rapid reduction in a country's birthrate to bring it into tolerable balance with a sharply reduced death rate cannot be achieved unless family planning spreads in the countryside as well as in towns and cities. It seems probable that reasonably rapid changes in this domain of behavior are more likely to take place if the dynamic processes of economic and technical change affect a large fraction of a rural population involved to an increasing extent in formal and informal education and communication networks (including mass media). It also seems likely that the wider spread of improved income and educational opportunities will affect motivations in ways favorable to the practice of family planning. . . .

Comment

Considering the efficiency of farmer decision making, several studies have examined the allocational behavior of peasant producers from the viewpoint of efficiency across farm size groups, risk, pricing policy, credit, and marketing. See T. W. Schultz, *Transforming Traditional Agriculture* (1964); Amartya K. Sen, "Peasants and Dualism with or without Surplus Labor," *Journal of Political Economy* (October 1966); D. W. Hopper, "Allocational Efficiency in Traditional Indian Agriculture," *Journal of Farm Economics* (August 1965); M. Lipton, "The Theory of the Optimizing Peasant," *Journal of Development Studies* (August 1968); M. Schluter and T. Mount, "Some Management Objectives of the Peasant Farmer," *Journal of Development Studies* (August 1977).

VII.C.2. A Three-Pronged Strategy for Rural Development*

A general conclusion suggested by a policy analysis perspective is that we should focus on the more serious failings of rural development programs and on the most feasible and desirable opportunities for mitigating those failures. Our analysis of the constraints and opportunities relevant to today's low-income countries leads us to conclude that three areas of historical failure merit priority attention: (1) the failure to design and implement effective strategies for fostering broad-based agricultural development; (2) the failure to reduce excessive mortality and morbidity among infants and small children and the interrelated failure to slow the rapid growth of population and labor force; and (3) the failure to create effective problem-solving organizations at the local level to improve the performance of development bureaucracies.

This diagnosis is the basis for our advocacy of a three-pronged strategy for rural development. The first "prong" relates to the need for a broadly based, employment-oriented pattern of agricultural development. Expansion of opportunities for productive employment, both inside and outside agriculture, is of central importance. Fuller and more efficient utilization of the relatively abundant resource of human labor can facilitate the expansion of output while at the same time generating the incomes that enable the poor to raise their levels of consumption. This analysis and empirical evidence emphasize the importance of tightening the labor supply/demand situation if increases in returns to labor are to be achieved.

The second prong involves strengthening a very limited set of social services. This in-cludes education as is now generally recognized. Because of their importance and past neglect, we stress particularly the need for interventions directed at the interrelated problems of malnutrition and chronic ill-health among infants and small children. In addition to the high human and economic costs associated with impaired child development and the excessive mortality rates among those vulnerable groups, the risk that small children will not survive to maturity is also a major obstacle to the spread of family planning. Considerable attention has been given in the past few years to the decline in fertility in the developing world. A number of middle-income countries and two low-income countries—China and Sri Lanka—have indeed achieved remarkably rapid declines in fertility. It is hardly coincidental that virtually all of the countries that have realized significant declines in fertility since 1960 have also sharply reduced infant and child mortality rates.[1]

Our third prong concerns organization programs designed to strengthen the institutional infrastructure and managerial skills needed for rural development. The neglect of these problems is in part a consequence of the tendency for economists to focus on what to do while neglecting the "details" of how to do it. More than a decade and a half ago Hsieh and Lee asserted that "the main secret of Taiwan's development" was "her ability to meet the organizational requirements."[2] This lesson has, however been largely ignored in spite of the accumulating evidence that organizational requirements are not easily fulfilled and require serious and sustained attention. Success in implementing the first and

*From Bruce F. Johnston and William C. Clark, "Rural Development Programs: A Critical Review of Past Experience," paper prepared for the XVIII International Conference of Agricultural Economists, Jakarta, Indonesia, August 24–September 2, 1982 (processed), pp. 6–9. Reprinted by permission.

[1]Bruce F. Johnston and William C. Clark, *Redesigning Rural Development: A Strategic Perspective,* Baltimore, 1982, pp. 145–47.

[2]S. C. Hsieh, and T. H. Lee, *Agricultural Development and Its Contributions to Economic Growth in Taiwan,* Joint Commission on Rural Reconstruction, Taipei, 1966.

second "prongs" of an effective strategy for rural development is unlikely unless the organizational requirements are met.

Analysis of the interrelationships among activities in these three areas emphasizes that program interventions can have significant complementary as well as competitive impacts on each other. We have suggested that the components of a rural development strategy can be designed (and redesigned) in ways that maximize their capacity for mutual support and minimize the risk that action in one program area will compromise efforts in other areas. This is obviously a difficult challenge, especially since development specialists are far from being in agreement concerning the need for priority attention to simultaneous action in these three program areas.

The greatest danger of the three-pronged perspective described here is that it will be interpreted as a recommendation to adopt any and all programs which may be advocated in the production, consumption, or organization areas. No interpretation could be further from our actual intent. On the contrary, widespread and sustained progress towards improving rural well-being requires that only a very few of the highest priority, most mutually reinforcing programs should be undertaken at all. Strategic choice means choosing *not* to do a vast number of tactically attractive things. Our emphasis on the necessity of an appropriate balance between production- and consumption-oriented activities highlights this key requirement of strategic design.

The need to conserve scarce resources, to undertake only those tasks most central to the improvement of rural well-being, is equally acute when we consider the organizational components of a development strategy. A strategic perspective means using all available forms of social organization—including political, market, and traditional structures—for the tasks which they can be made to perform reasonably well, while preserving scarce administrative talent for focused intervention when and where it can do the most good. Effective production and consumption programs can be expanded only with the growth of organizational capacity for their effective implementation. This focus on the need to develop organizational competence directs attention at another major theme of our strategic perspective—the importance of time and timing.

Improving rural well-being is an inherently time-consuming process. Historical experience teaches that, at best, broadly based and sustainable progress will be measured in decades, not years. In part, the pace of development is limited by fundamental structural-demographic constraints: even under the most optimistic of assumptions, today's late-developing countries will remain predominantly rural societies into the twenty-first century. Perhaps even more significant for policy design, however, is that development is essentially a learning process: the growth of organizational competence and personal knowledge are as fundamental a requirement as the growth of capital in the conventional sense. Because most of the "answers" to development questions aren't known by anyone, because even those answers which are known by some must be laboriously passed on to others, because all answers must be adapted to specific places and times, the learning process of development necessarily entails a great deal of trial and error.

This much-needed persistence has too often been lacking in rural development strategies. The desire to bypass the errors, to teach answers instead of facilitating learning, is strong—and disastrous. Impatience for immediate results has often encouraged relief-and-welfare approaches to improving rural well-being. Such short-term activities, however, almost invariably lead to the neglect of more fundamental long-term tasks: building organizational and technical capabilities and strengthening the capacities of local people to meet their own needs. Failure to pursue rural development strategies that are focused on programs to strengthen indigenous capacities to accelerate the growth of output, expand employment, improve health and nutrition, and slow population growth will mean that the number of people suffering the deprivations of rural poverty will continue to increase.

Those of us who have emphasized the relevance of the experience of Japan and Taiwan have been guilty of teaching answers instead of stressing the need for a learning process leading to a continually improving sequence of program designs. In particular, we have been much too slow to take account of a major limitation of technology transfer based on their experience. Because of the relatively homogeneous character of agriculture in those two countries and the dominant importance of irrigated production, there was enormous scope for expanding farm productivity and output by relying mainly on improved seed-fertilizer combinations for rice and a few other major crops. In countries with different and more heterogenous conditions, including major reliance on rainfed production, it is necessary to confront the more difficult task of identifying a number of strategies adapted to a variety of agroclimatic conditions and crops. Experience at ICRISAT, for example, suggests that in areas where rainfall is variable and only marginally adequate, there is a need for improved methods of soil and water management in order to realize the yield potential of improved varieties and fertilizer. Little sustained and systematic attention has been given to the task of evolving equipment and tillage innovations for that purpose that meet the needs of smallholders with very limited cash income and purchasing power.

The development "failures" that we have noted are failures about which something can be done. It must not be forgotten that only a decade or two ago many of today's middle-income countries faced constraints and conditions comparable to those of today's low-income countries. A number of those countries have made substantial progress in improving the well-being of their people because they *did* pursue strategies for rural development emphasizing vigorous and sustained production, consumption, and organization programs similar to the three "prongs" of the strategy that we have advocated. China and Taiwan are only two of the specific examples in which these critical choices played a pivotal role.

We believe that the efforts of today's low-income countries to emulate such successes will be facilitated to the extent that the development debate within these countries and the international development community can be focused constructively on fundamental constraints and opportunities, on the longer term implications of strategic policy decisions, and on systematic efforts to learn from both successes and failures.

Comment

General theories of development, such as those of the dual sector variety, are concerned with trends of real rural wages over the long period. But such general models are silent on the behavioral and institutional features of the rural sector. More attention needs to be given to the labor relations and the mechanisms that determine wages, employment, and earnings in rural areas. For a critical review of the existing literature on labor and other factor markets in rural areas, see Hans P. Binswanger and Mark R. Rosenzweig, *Contractual Arrangements, Employment and Wages in Rural Markets* (1981). This monograph looks at the various models and theories of labor markets and tenancy with attention to the issues of absent markets, market failure, collusive power, and the interdependence of markets. A central conclusion is that an understanding of institutional arrangements or imperfections in any one market (e.g., the labor market) requires attention to the imperfections in or constraints on other markets (e.g., the land or credit markets).

Other important literature on rural labor markets may be cited: Pranab K. Bardhan, "Interlocking Factor Markets and Agrarian Development," *Oxford Economic Papers,* Vol. 32, (1980); P. K. Bardhan and T. N. Srinivasan, "Cropsharing Tenancy in Agriculture: A Theoretical and Empirical Analysis," *American Economic Review* (March 1971); Clive Bell, "Alternative Theories of Sharecropping," *Journal of Development Studies* (July 1977); S. N. S.

Cheung, *The Theory of Share Tenancy* (1969); Lloyd G. Reynolds (ed.), *Agriculture in Development Theory* (1975); Joseph E. Stiglitz, "Alternative Theories of Wage Determination and Unemployment in LDCs: The Labor Turnover Model," *Quarterly Journal of Economics* (May 1974); A. Braverman and T. N. Srinivasan, "Credit and Sharecropping in Agrarian Societies," *Journal of Development Economics* (December 1981); A. Braverman and J. E. Stiglitz, "Sharecropping and the Interlinking of Agrarian Markets," *American Economic Review* (September 1982).

VII.C.3. The New Rural-Based Development Strategy*

In low income countries agriculture occupies half to two-thirds of the labor force, produces on the order of half the gross national product, provides well over half the consumption goods (much more, of course, for the poor) and is geographically pervasive. A rural-based strategy emphasizes mobilization of labor for productive purposes, recognizes the importance of capital and attempts to reduce the capital per worker by turning to a labor intensive structure of production. Because the laboring classes spend the bulk of even increments to their income on food, mobilization of labor requires increased agricultural production. If employment increases without a commensurate increase in food supplies, inflationary pressure will mount and demand policies which reduce employment will be instituted. Thus accelerated growth in agricultural production is essential to the mobilization of labor.

Of course, the relation of agriculture to poverty abatement is as close as its relation to growth strategy. Increased food consumption is essential to improved welfare for the poor. The food needs of the massive numbers of the Third World poor are so great that

*From John W. Mellor, "The New Rural-Based Development Strategy," presented at the Joint UNITAR/EDI Seminar on Economic Development and Its International Setting, Washington, D.C., March 27, 1979, as a précis of the arguments documented in John W. Mellor, *The New Economics of Growth—A Strategy for India and the Developing World,* a Twentieth Century Fund Study, Cornell University Press, Ithaca, New York, 1976. Reprinted by permission.

they can only be met if there is a large increase in domestic food production. The need cannot be met by marginal redistribution of income from the more well off to the poor because of sharp differences in food consumption patterns. In India, for example, the lower 20 percent of the income distribution spend 60 percent of its increments to income on food grains alone and 85–90 percent on food and agricultural commodities in total. In sharp contrast, the top 10 percent of the income distribution spend only 5 percent of increments to income on grain and 35 percent on food and agricultural commodities in total. One dollar of income removed from the rich will only reduce demand for grain by 5¢. Given to the poor the same dollar increases the demand for grain by 60¢. Thus a fiscal policy balance of a dollar from the rich and a dollar to the poor brings about a twelvefold imbalance for food. With variation in the composition of the food basket these relationships hold broadly throughout the Third World.

The converse of these growth and equity relations is equally correct. If the rate of growth of food production is to be substantially increased on a sustained basis it must almost inevitably be accompanied by policies which succeed in providing higher rates of consumption growth by the poor. They are the people with the latent demand for increased quantities of food. In the short run, exports may be increased, often however only under subsidy, or storage stocks may be enlarged. In the longer run failure to match increased food production with increased domestic demand will cause depressed agricultural prices and hence loss of the production incentives essential to maintenance of high agricultural growth rates.

Thus we describe a two-way street. If employment is to increase, if labor is to contribute to growth, if the poor are to prosper, there must be increased food production. If there is to be increased food production there must be commensurate increase in the effective demand of the poor which may best be accomplished by employing them in productive processes.

THE KEY ROLE OF TECHNOLOGICAL CHANGE IN AGRICULTURE

Unfortunately, achieving accelerated growth in agriculture is not effortless. Annual growth rates of 2.5 percent, more or less keeping up with population growth, have generally been achieved by gradual increases in cultivated area and greater intensity of labor use inevitably accompanied by declining productivity and income. A dynamic role in development requires agricultural growth of 4 percent or even higher. That can rarely be achieved except by application of modern science to development of high yielding crop varieties and practices. New technology not only increases yields per acre, thereby circumventing the troublesome problem of rapidly approaching limits to expanding the cultivatable area, but also increases labor productivity and overall efficiency in resource use. The requisite new agricultural technology has two characteristics of importance to development planning.

First, because of the variability of agricultural conditions it is only infrequently that new technology can be transferred from one environment to another. There is a consequent need for a vast system of agricultural experiment stations covering a wide range of conditions. The development of trained personnel and the institutions to effectively utilize that personnel in creating effective new technology is one of the most important and difficult to meet features of agricultural development.

Second, modern agricultural technology requires an immense supply of purchased inputs such as fertilizers, pesticides and increased control of water as well as ready communications with sources of new technology. The consequent commercialization of agriculture calls for vast investment in roads and electrification while providing the basis for growth stimulating linkages with other sectors of the economy. Thus while agricultural development is essential to improve welfare for the poor, it will only occur when vast investments are made and large numbers of people trained, many to highly advanced levels. Primitive agriculture is no more the salvation of the poor than capital intensive industry.

CONSUMER DEMAND STIMULATED GROWTH

The new agricultural technology creates a prosperous peasantry and hence demand for production inputs such as pumps, improved tools and fertilizers as well as for consumer goods. The peasantry already with adequate calories wish more of vegetables and livestock products, travel, housing and furnishings, textiles, and electronics. These are largely goods and services which are efficiently produced by labor intensive processes. Thus the economic ring is closed. More food is produced, the producers exchange that food for goods and services from other sectors, employment is made in the other sectors for low income people who spend the bulk of those increments to income on food. Because demand patterns are skewed towards non-agricultural goods and services, those other sectors, when stimulated by agriculture will accelerate to 10-15 percent growth rates compared to the 4 percent considered remarkable in agriculture. Thus the overall growth rates accelerate as the faster growing sectors gradually become relatively more important. Industrial development is fundamental in the old and new strategies in growth. The difference lies in how industrial growth is achieved and its composition.

A rural led pattern of growth has the further advantage of being geographically diffused. While it requires large investments in roads and electrification, it thereby offers opportunity for manufacturing to be more widely diffused, jobs coming to the rural poor rather than the rural poor migrating to the megalopolis.

The rural based, high employment strategy depends on a delicate balance of sufficient demand for industrial goods and services to make it profitable to invest in their production (retained profits and induced savings being the engine of capital formation in this model) and sufficiently labor intensive production systems to provide increased employment to the low income people who will spend their income on food and thereby provide adequate demand and incentive prices for food production. Thus public policy must be sensitive to the needs for the measures to assist growth in industry on one hand and effective demand for food on the other.

A more basic difficulty arises if land ownership is highly concentrated in the hands of a small, wealthy, land owning class. Their consumption patterns may be oriented towards imported goods or very capital intensive goods. In that case, the strategy will fail from lack of domestic demand for agricultural production and inadequate employment growth. Participation in development will be limited to a small elite.

THE ROLE OF INTERNATIONAL TRADE

The new rural-based strategy is highly dependent on rapidly growing international trade. It is not a subsistence oriented approach. Trade is essential as a means of conserving scarce capital, providing an outlet for abundant labor and may even be needed to meet short run food needs.

The capital demands of the new strategy are immense, not only for modernizing agriculture but also to combine with the greatly increased labor supply that is mobilized by the strategy—all in the context of accelerated growth. Thus while every effort is made to raise savings rates, the capital intensity of

production processes must be held down as much as possible. A necessary component of this effort is to import those essential goods such as fertilizers, aluminum and even steel which are efficiently produced only by highly capital intensive processes. These goods are best paid for by export of labor intensive manufactures which serve to further increase employment, broaden distribution of income and raise the demand for food. Further, when the strategy is working at its best, growth in demand for food may temporarily outpace domestic production while inclement weather may reduce food production. In general, trade is a much cheaper way of meeting these problems than halting the strategy or building large food stocks.

If the industrial countries do not provide a favorable environment for trade, then the growth strategy for developing countries will have to be more autarkic—more capital to heavy industry and less to agriculture and consumer goods industries—and of course slower growth, less employment, and less amenities and food for the poor.

THE ACCEPTABILITY OF THE NEW STRATEGY

Why would a country fail to opt for the agricultural based, high employment strategy which probably gives faster growth than alternative strategies and certainly benefits the poor more? The strategy of course has little appeal to narrowly based elitist governments for it is, after all, a strategy which delivers to the bulk of the farmers and to labor. It is a strategy of broadly based governments. The dependence of the strategy on international trade may seem a dubious policy given the uncertainties of trade policy in the developed nations and the almost complete absence of Third World influence on world trade rules and regulations. Finally, the strategy gives little emphasis, at least initially, to the heavy industry on which military defense depends. Many governments may find this too uncertain a world for faith in an agrarian approach.

One may ask further, why might the developed nations choose to encourage the new strategy and thus provide trade and aid guarantees for the strategy? The developed nations have expressed much concern with the long term implications of population growth. It is the broad participation in the rural-based strategy that brings down population growth rates. The Western developed nations espouse broadly representative governments. Again it is the broad participation of farmers and labor in the rural-based strategy that offers the essential conditions for such political systems. Major groups in developed countries claim humanitarian concern for the eradication of poverty. It is the rural-based strategy that promises the food and employment essential to poverty abatement. Finally, the trade requirements of the strategy are in the long term economic interest of the developed nations even though they pose short term problems of economic and political adjustment.

Comment
Several major studies of strategies for agricultural development can be cited. Especially informative are: Bruce F. Johnston and Peter Kilby, *Agriculture and Structural Transformation* (1975); J. W. Mellor, *Economics of Agricultural Development*, ed. (1974); T. W. Schultz, *Transforming Traditional Agriculture,* (1964); T. W. Schultz, *Economic Growth and Agriculture* (1968); C. K. Eicher and L. W. Witt (eds.), *Agriculture in Economic Development* (1964); H. M. Southworth and B. F. Johnston (eds.), *Agricultural Development and Economic Growth* (1967); Clifton R. Wharton (ed.), *Subsistence Agriculture and Economic Development* (1969); Y. Hayami and V. W. Ruttan, *Agricultural Development: An Internatonal Perspective* (1971); Arthur T. Mosher, *Getting Agriculture Moving* (1966); Uma J. Lele, *The Design of Rural Development: Lessons from Africa* (1975); Sterling Wortman and Ralph W. Cummings, Jr., *To Feed the World* (1978); Bruce F. Johnston and William C. Clark, *Redesigning Rural Development: A Strategic Perspective* (1982); C. Peter Timmer, Walter P. Falcon, and Scott R. Pearson, *Food Policy Analysis* (1983).

International policies to stabilize commodity prices are analyzed in section VIII.C.

Comment
Special attention should be given to the problems of rural development in sub-Saharan Africa. Annual rates of increase of major staple food crops in sub-Saharan Africa in 1960 to 1975 were only about 2 percent, compared with almost 3 percent in Asia and over 3.5 percent in Latin America. Because of higher population growth, annual rates of increase in production required to meet consumption needs by 1990 are also estimated to be higher in sub-Saharan Africa, about 4.5 percent, compared with not quite 4 percent for Asia and less than 3 percent for Latin America. (International Food Policy Research Institute, *Food Needs of Developing Countries,* Research Report No. 3, December 1977).

For excellent analyses of agriculture in sub-Saharan Africa, see World Bank, *Accelerated Development in Sub-Saharan Africa: An Agenda for Action* (1981); Uma Lele, "Rural Africa: Modernization, Equity, and Long-Term Development," *Science* (February 1981); Uma Lele, *The Design of Rural Development: Lessons from Africa* (1975); K. Anthony et al., *Agricultural Change in Tropical Africa* (1979); Shankar N. Acharya, "Perspectives and Problems of Development in sub-Saharan Africa," *World Development* (Feburary 1981); Carl K. Eicher and Doyle C. Baker, *Research on Agricultural Development in Sub-Saharan Africa: A Critical Survey,* MSU International Development Paper No. 1 (1982), with an extensive bibliography and literature reviews.

VII.C.4. Land Reform*

If we compare the different forms of land tenure, three distinct patterns emerge, and we can say that from the standpoint of economic analysis there are really three distinct problems of reform. We can leave out some land systems altogether as irrelevant to our subject—the peasant systems, in which land ownership is more or less equally distributed, and communal tenure systems, in which the land is communally owned (mainly prevalent in Africa). These may need other types of reform—reforms of the agrarian structure—but they do not need redistribution of ownership. We can concentrate on the land systems in which the large estate is the predominant form of tenure.

We must, however, distinguish sharply between the different types of large estate. One of the great difficulties in the study of this subject is that we have no accepted vocabulary. Much confusion arises from lack of precise terminology. "Large estate" itself is an ambiguous term, referring to at least three different forms of tenure and three different types of economic organisation. The three types are:

1. The type of ownership characteristic of Asian countries, in which the land holding is only a property and not a large farm or large producing unit. The property is leased in small units to tenant cultivators, either on the basis of money rent or on a basis of sharecropping rents.

2. The large estate, characteristic of South European countries and of Latin America, which is both a large property and a large enterprise. This type of estate is managed by salaried officials and worked by labourers and people of indeterminate status, squatters or share-croppers. Estates of this kind are

*From Doreen Warriner, *Land Reform and Economic Development,* National Bank of Egypt Fiftieth Anniversary Commemoration Lectures, Cairo, 1955, Lecture II. (Corrected version reprinted in Carl Eicher and Lawrence Witt (eds.), *Agriculture in Economic Development,* New York, McGraw-Hill, 1964, pp. 280–90.) Reprinted by permission.

usually extensively cultivated, or used as cattle ranges. We may call them latifundia, since this is the term used in the countries where they prevail; they are the direct descendants of the slave-tilled ranches of the Roman Empire.

3. Plantation estates. These are also both large properties and large enterprises. They are usually owned by a company with foreign capital and foreign management, though estates of a plantation type may also be found in private ownership. The methods of cultivation are usually intensive.

Many countries have agrarian structures which include estates of two or even three of these types. The land system of Egypt in certain features resembles the Asian form of ownership, while in other features it is a plantation system.

These forms of ownership and enterprise have very little in common with the types of large-scale farming found in advanced countries, i.e., in countries with an industrialised economy and commercialised agriculture. The Asian system is found principally in subsistence economies, while latifundia and plantations produce mainly for export.

From the standpoint of economic analysis, the most obvious feature of all these types of ownership is the existence of an institutional monopoly. In Asian countries, where demographic pressure is high, the level of rents is determined not by the fertility of the land, but by the fertility of human beings. Land is a scarce factor of production, and would command a high price in terms of its produce, whatever the system of land tenure. The existence of institutional monopoly allows the landowner to raise rents to a still higher level. In latifundian systems and in plantation systems, the estate owner is a monopoly buyer of labour, controlling the use of land rather than its price, and he uses his monopoly power to keep wages low.

The main economic argument for land reform is the need for securing a more equal distribution of income by eliminating these monopoly elements. In the first case the aim is to reduce the price for the use of land, i.e., a reduction in rents, and in the second case, the aim is to subdivide big holdings and secure a fuller use of land, an increased demand for labour, and higher wages for the farm worker.

But, it may be objected, will not this redistribution of ownership reduce productivity by dividing up efficient large estates? If we wish to use this argument, we must consider in what sense these estates are to be regarded as efficient. The theory of the firm is always difficult to apply in agriculture, and as far as the under-developed countries are concerned, it seems to have very limited application.

The argument that the division of large agricultural enterprises will cause a decline in productivity is true on two assumptions: (1) that there is competition between the factors of production and (2) that there are economies of large scale production. These assumptions are generally valid in industrialised countries. In England, for example, a large farm has generally become large because it is a more efficient producer, i.e., it produces at lower costs; it can compete more effectively for the factors of production and combine them more efficiently, using more capital and using it more fully; it can also use more efficient management and more specialised labour. In such conditions there is a presumption that the size of farms is more or less adjusted to an optimum scale of output for certain types of farming. This optimum scale of output is difficult to define precisely, and in practice means the minimum area needed to utilise power-driven machinery. . . .

When we try to apply this argument about the scale of production to the under-developed countries, we shall find that over a very wide range of conditions it has no validity at all. In Asian land systems, large estates are not large producing units. Land reform in such systems simply means the transfer of ownership from the landowner to the cultivator of the existing small holding. The size of the farm is not affected, for there are no large farms. When the Governments of India and Pakistan speak of "uneconomic farms," they mean farms which fall below a subsistence minimum, not below a technical optimum. Nor does the argument about efficient large estates apply generally to latifundian systems. The haciendas in Mexico and many of the latifundia in Southern Italy were not efficient large estates on any standard. They wasted both land and labour.

So generally speaking, the argument about "efficient large estates" does not seem to apply to the first type or the second type of estates which we have distinguished. It does seem to apply to plantation estates which use intensive methods of cultivation and modern methods. Every plantation system is a special case. Where there is reason to believe that sub-division of the estate would lead to a decline in production, then the monopoly effect on labour must be tackled by a policy for raising wages, and taxing profits to secure reinvestment in other types of farming producing for local needs. Or the estate may be divided with safeguards for maintaining efficiency, as under the Egyptian Land Reform. . . .

Several other arguments used against land reform are false because they are based on projections of conditions in advanced countries, and do not take these basic differences into account. One argument frequently encountered in international discussions is that because tenancy works very well in England there can be no reason for Asian countries to abolish tenancy by redistribution of ownership: what they need is legislation to improve the security of tenure for tenants. This argument overlooks the monopoly influence in Asian countries. It is true that tenancy works well in England, because the conditions of tenancy are regulated by law, and also because land is only one of the many forms of holding wealth. If a landowner attempts to take too high a rent, the tenant will prefer to invest his capital in other ways. But in Asian conditions tenancy laws will never suffice to counteract the effects of monopoly ownership.

Another argument of this kind is that there is no need for expropriation by compulsion.

This argument runs as follows: "If governments wish to encourage ownership, they can do this by giving tenants special credit facilities enabling them to buy their holdings. In Switzerland (or Denmark or Sweden) the land system has evolved itself by gradual adjustment to modern conditions, and Asian countries should therefore adjust their systems gradually, without drastic legislation to expropriate owners of land." The logical fallacy in this argument is obvious. In advanced countries, an improvement in the economic position of agriculture will enable the tenant to buy his land, and special credit facilities can encourage the acquisition of ownership. In the United States, the proportion of ownership to tenancy rises when agriculture is prosperous, and special legislation aids farm purchase. In European countries, particularly in Scandinavia, governments have helped tenants to become owners by giving them easy credit terms. But in Asian countries, the market price of land is too high in terms of what it produces to allow the tenant to purchase his land. If agriculture becomes more prosperous, either as a result of higher prices or better harvests, the share-cropping tenant will not be able to buy his holding, because the landlord benefits equally from the increased income, and the tenant's position in relation to the landlord has not improved. There is no price which the tenant can afford to pay which the landlord will be willing to accept. If the tenant is to acquire ownership, the price of land must be fixed at a level which he can pay, and this will inevitably be much lower than the market value of the land. All land reforms involve expropriation to some extent for this reason.

In economic terms, there can be no ground for paying compensation at all, since the existing prices of land are monopoly prices. The price that is actually fixed in reform legislation is determined by political bargaining power.

We can conclude therefore that the existence of institutional monopoly creates a strong argument for land reform on the ground of equalizing incomes. We can conclude that in Asian systems and in latifundian systems the redistribution of ownership will not have adverse effects on production through the division of efficient large units, though in plantation systems sub-division may have bad effects, and other ways of equalizing incomes may have to be used.

These arguments, however, tell us nothing about the positive effects of reform on development. They are negative arguments which show it will not do harm. If we are to consider the effects on economic development, this is not enough, and it is the investment aspect that must be considered.

The general economic argument for land reform as distinct from the social argument for more equality is that these systems of ownership give rise to large incomes which are not reinvested in production. They give rise also to social attitudes inimical to investment. Landowners spend conspicuously; buy more land; or invest in urban house property; or lend at extortionate rates of interest to cultivators for non-productive purposes. This argument applies with great force to Asian tenancy systems and to latifundian systems. It does not apply generally to plantation systems. These may have bad social consequences, but whatever their defects may be, failure to invest productively is not one of them, or not generally one. (There are exceptions where plantations keep land out of cultivation, and these systems cause trouble.)

In general, the land systems of Asia and Latin America are strong deterrents to investment and aggravate the shortage of capital by draining capital from agriculture. They undervalue the future. The land owners' preference for land as a form of holding wealth can be explained simply as a result of the secure and high return on capital which results from institutional monopoly. . . .

The crucial question is whether land reform—the change to small ownership—will give better results in the future. Can it promote more investment? . . .

All we can say as to the investment effect is that results depend mainly on what can be done to give inducements to invest, through special credit facilities and special forms of village organisation. We cannot say that reform will *cause* more investment: but we can certainly say that it is a condition, for without more income in the hands of the cultivator, no investment programme for agriculture is likely to have much effect.

Can we say anything about the production

effects of reform, when there is actually subdivision of the land?

Here too we can only say that results will depend on how far the new owners can intensify farming, either by the use of more labour on the land, or by the use of more labour and more capital. . . .

Comment

The case for a small farm or reformed agricultural system claims several advantages—more employment, more equitable distribution of income, and a wider home market for the manufacturing sector. But the case for small holdings must also address itself to other requirements. It is also essential to consider the effects of land reform on agricultural production, both for exports and for increasing food production. Capital formation is also necessary in both agricultural and industrial sectors. And efficiency must be achieved, as well as employment and equity.

The economic gains to be had from a radical modification of land tenure patterns appear to be greatest during periods when rapid technical changes are opening up new production possibilities which are inhibited by existing tenure relationships. See Yujiro Hayami and Vernon W. Ruttan, *Agricultural Development: An International Perspective* (1971). In view of the technical revolution in grain production and the explosive rate of growth in the agricultural labor force, the authors conclude that the payoff to tenure reforms, involving a shift from share tenure, plantation, and collective tenure systems to smallholder owner-operator systems, may be greatly increased in the future.

On the need for and reform in connection with the development of agriculture, see D. Warriner, *Land Reform and Development in the Middle East* (1957); D. Warriner, *Land Reform in Principle and Practice,* (1969); D. Felix, "Agrarian Reform and Industrial Growth," *International Development Review* (October 1960); P. M. Raup, "The Contribution of Land Reforms to Economic Development," *Economic Development and Cultural Change* (October 1963); Anthony Y. C. Koo, *The Role of Land Reform in Economic Development—A Case Study of Taiwan* (1968); Dale Adams, "The Economics of Land Reform: Comment," *Food Research Institute Studies,* Vol. 12, No. 2 (1973); Peter Dorner, *Land Reform and Economic Development* (1972); R. Albert Berry, "Land Reform and Agricultural Income Distribution," *Pakistan Development Review* (Spring 1971); Folke Dovering, "Land Reform: A Key to Change in Agriculture," in Nurual Islam (ed.) *Agricultural Policy in Developing Countries* (1972); David Lehmann, *Peasants, Landlords and Governments* (1974).

VII.C.5. Price Incentives*

Most developing countries for the last quarter century have had policies designed to

*From Gilbert T. Brown, "Agricultural Pricing Policies in Developing Countries," Theodore W. Schultz (ed.), *Distortions of Agricultural Incentives,* Bloomington, Indiana University Press, 1978, pp. 84–89. Reprinted by permission.

lower the prices of food and other agricultural goods and to increase the prices of manufactured goods. Trade and foreign-exchange practices have been major instruments of these policies, along with tax, direct price, and other market-control measures. The conventional wisdom supporting this twisting of the terms of trade against agriculture has had four main pillars, based on the assumptions:

1. that aggregate agricultural production is not very responsive to price changes;
2. that the chief beneficiaries of higher prices would be the larger size farmers;
3. that higher food and other agriculture-related prices such as clothing would most adversely affect low-income consumers; and
4. that manufacturing provides a more rapid means of growth, and that achieving that growth depends upon large transfers of income (profits) and foreign exchange from agriculture to manufacturing.

Thus, policies that depress agricultural prices and increase manufacturing prices will result both in more rapid economic growth and in a more equal distribution of income.

Lagging agricultural production and overall economic growth in many developing countries that have followed such policies, however, have led to increasing concern about measures that reduce farm incomes and incentives. Argentina, Egypt, Kenya, the Ivory Coast, Pakistan, Peru, the Philippines, Thailand, and Uruguay are among the countries which have acted to significantly increase agricultural relative to nonagricultural prices in the last several years. Greater emphasis in the development literature on employment-led and rural-development strategies and on strategies to meet basic needs and to benefit persons in the lowest 40 percent of the income distribution, has also provided new intellectual support for price policies more favorable to agriculture, including lessened subsidies for capital goods, less over-valued exchange rates and protection for industry, and increased production of foodstuffs and other wage goods.

In contrast to those of the developing countries, price policies in the industrialized countries during this period have been distorted in favor of rather than against the farmer, and the typical problem has been overproduction rather than underproduction of agricultural commodities. Moreover, as pointed out by D.

Gale Johnson, greater agricultural productivity per hectare in industrialized than in developing countries is a phenomenon that has occurred largely since the 1930s, and within the period of differential price policies. In the period 1934–38, grain yields averaged 1.15 tons per hectare in industrial countries, and 1.14 tons (i.e., the same level) in developing countries. By 1975, however, grain yields in industrial countries were more than double those in developing countries, 3.0 tons versus 1.4 tons per hectare. This is not to argue, of course, that the more rapid growth in agricultural yields and production in the industrialized countries is due solely to differences in price policies. A plausible hypothesis is that both the more favorable farm prices and the more rapid growth of farm yields in industrial countries reflect efforts to support farm incomes and increase agricultural productivity, while developing countries have generally been much more concerned about increasing industrial incentives and production, and urban incomes.

The focus of this paper is not on the factors that explain the differences in growth rates between developed and developing countries, however, but on the effects of recent pricing policies on today's developing countries. My hypothesis is that agricultural production, income distribution, and economic growth would all benefit from reduction or elimination of distortions that reduce agriculture's domestic terms of trade. The relation of agriculture's domestic terms of trade to income distribution and economic growth particularly are problems whose complexities outrun our capacity to measure by formal models, but they are also problems that are too important to neglect.

Several general problems of terminology or analysis should be briefly mentioned. First, references to "free-market" prices are to those that would exist in absence of specific controls and policies that now distort the relation of agricultural to nonagricultural prices, including those relationships that magnify differences between domestic and world-market prices. This is not to imply that world-market prices are "free," or that policy should aim to equate domestic and world-market prices or price relatives at all times. Neither is it to imply that shadow free-market prices can be known with exactitude, or to ignore that we are dealing with neither a first nor even a second-best world. Rather, the comparison to probable prices "in the absence of controls" reflects only a judgment about approximate price relationships. Second, references to changes in prices are to changes from existing distorted price relations, not from the traditional equilibrium-price starting point of economic theory. Usually the discussion concerns what would happen if the distortion between existing prices and free-market or "equilibrium" (using that term loosely) prices were reduced. Thirdly, prices are an incomplete measure of incentives. If agriculture's relative productivity is increasing, it is possible for agricultural incomes and incentives to be growing at the same time that agricultural prices are declining. Fourthly, a fundamental distinction must be made between measures such as price controls, taxes, and subsidies that artificially lower food and agricultural prices and measures such as on-farm investment, technological advances, and rural infrastructure development (e.g., roads, electricity, and water) that lower prices by lowering the real costs of production. Reductions in real resource costs of production (i.e., increases in input yields) may benefit urban dwellers, farmers, and rural laborers alike.

EFFICIENT USE OF RESOURCES

Higher prices may stimulate agricultural production by (1) causing producers to move closer to their production-possibility frontier by better use of resources, (2) encouraging use of more labor and other variable resource inputs to reach higher production-function and output levels, or (3) inducing investment and the discovery and adoption of new agricultural technologies that result in new, lower-cost production functions.

The usual empirical basis of arguments that agricultural production is not very responsive to price changes rests upon multiple-correlation analysis of the acreage or output of a particular crop in relation either to the relative prices of that crop versus others, or to several presumably independent variables, such as output price and use of fertilizer, labor, and water. The price elasticity of aggregate agricultural production is less than for individual crops, of course, since substitution between crops may account for an important part of the response of a single crop to changes in its relative prices. This multiple-correlation methodology can be faulted on several grounds, including the lack of independence between prices on one hand and the level of use of fertilizer and other inputs. The use of acreage rather than output in most such studies underestimates the price elasticity of production by not taking account of changes in yields, which have been accounting for an increasingly large part (now more than half) of the annual growth in world food-grain production. Also, it is doubtful that yearly fluctuations in prices are an adequate proxy for changes in the income expectations that determine rates of investment in agriculture and its supporting infrastructure, labor inputs, and the adoption of new techniques. These decisions appear to depend more upon whether expected profitability is above or below a "threshold" level of acceptability, and may be little affected by yearly price fluctuations unless these cause longer-run expectations of profitability to change. Moreover, incentives are a function of net income and not just prices, and therefore a new technology may importantly change the incentive effect of a given set of prices as happened during the Green Revolution in wheat and rice.

Price incentives may cause farmers to use improved seeds, along with more fertilizer, pesticides, and other purchased inputs, to adopt improved cultural practices, and to apply more family or hired labor. All of these ways of increasing the efficiency of resource use may occur at once, for example, if a small farmer decides to reduce or give up his off-farm employment—or a son does not migrate to the city—in order to adopt the more labor-intensive techniques required to reap the benefits of new varieties. Generalities about most small farmers as "subsistence" farmers unaffected by agricultural prices are at best misleading.

Timmer and Falcon have found a close rank correlation between unhulled rice (paddy) prices and rice yields among Asian countries. For 1970, they found that rice yields varied from 5.64 and 4.53 metric tons per hectare in Japan and Korea to 2.1 to 1.7 tons per hectare in Indonesia, Thailand, the Philippines, and Burma. At the same time, the ratio of the price of a kilogram of rice to the price of a kilogram of fertilizer nutrients showed a similar wide variation, from 1.43 and 0.96 in Japan and Korea to 0.4 to 0.1 in Indonesia, Thailand, the Philippines, and Burma. This pattern of inter-country relationships between prices and yields cannot be explained as short-term elasticity response, but may well be indicative of the long-run responsiveness of production to incentives. While the price data used in this study were only for one year, the difference in national prices are very substantial, and reflect longstanding differences in price policies among these countries. It is noteworthy that the three countries with the highest yields—Japan, South Korea, and Taiwan—have some of the poorest soils among the nine countries studied. The high prices to farmers in these countries appear necessary to cover the costs of achieving these yields under the given climate, soil, and other conditions, even though the decisions to pay such high prices may have been primarily political. It is interesting to speculate to what levels rice yields and production would fall in Japan if farmers there received the same price as Thai farmers, or conversely the levels to which rice yields and production would climb in Thailand within a few years if Thai farmers faced the same rice and fertilizer prices as Japanese farmers.

SHIFTS IN THE PRODUCTION FUNCTION

The most important long-run effects of price incentives on production may be through price-induced shifts in the production function, rather than through greater efficiency of resource use with existing production functions. These long-run effects depend upon the extent to which the incentive structure has an important effect upon technological change (both on research and on adoption of new techniques by farmers), on public and private investment related to agriculture, and on institutional change affecting agricultural output (land reform, extension services, marketing, and distribution facilities).

Clear links have been demonstrated between pricing policy and both the discovery and nature of new technological discoveries, and the adoption of these techniques by farmers. The relationship between relative prices of land and labor in Japan and the United States, and the very different directions of technological change in these two countries in the last century, has been well documented. The late-1973 jump in oil prices has also presented ample evidence of the link between prices and research. Much of the agricultural research initiated since then is "energy saving," with heavy emphasis on reducing fertilizer requirements, for example, through nitrogen fixation, seed treatment, and placing a small amount of fertilizer close to the seed or seedling roots.

The link between price incentives and private investment in chemical inputs, labor, land leveling, irrigation, and other measures to increase farm output is almost axiomatic. Studies of diffusion of new techniques and of new investment in developing countries indicate that where profitability of adopting a new technique or investing, say, in a tube well is very high, that the new techniques will be rapidly adopted and the new investment quickly made. At the margin at least there are wealthy individuals who make choices between agricultural and nonfarm investments. A large proportion of upper and even middle-class individuals in South Asia reside in cities and have a profession, a business, or a government job, but own substantial farmland operated by a hired manager or tenant (sometimes a relative). For these individuals, as for the small farmer deciding how to divide his time between his own farm and other employment, the choice between farm and nonfarm investment (and employment) is a recurring one. Higher returns to farming certainly attract more labor and more investment (ceteris paribus) into farming. Moreover, the higher returns generate more income and saving, and, therefore, the ability to finance more investment in agriculture. Nearly all studies show high marginal saving rates among even poor farmers. Thus, an important part of the additional income accruing to farmers through higher prices is likely to result in greater savings and investment. In countries where farm yields are low and returns to additional investment in agriculture are high (e.g., where fertilizer use is well below optimal levels because farmers lack financial resources, as is true in much of South Asia and other food-deficit low-income coun-

tries) an important part of that saving is likely to be invested in farming.

Public investment and institutional changes may also be importantly affected by prices, but research on these topics is in its infancy. Evidence has been presented that public investment in irrigation in the Philippines has been closely correlated with the import price of rice. There has certainly been a tendency for some officials to think of nonagricultural development as somehow more important than progress in agriculture. Higher prices for agricultural products will make at least the nonshadow-priced value of agricultural projects more attractive. The more attractive financial return may induce highly productive institutional development, such as more effective agricultural research and extension systems, and input distribution and output-marketing systems.

Comment

The effects of government intervention in agricultural pricing have become a major concern to development economists. This concern is directed to an analysis of the interrelationships among agricultural prices and resource allocation, incentives, income distribution, and employment.

Nobel Laureate Theodore Schultz, among others, has argued strongly that the economic potential for agricultural development has been largely unexploited because of government intervention to suppress economic incentives by pricing agricultural products below competitive market equilibrium relative to inputs. These interventions are based on: (1) undervaluation of agriculture's contribution to growth derived from the misunderstanding of agriculture as an inherently backward sector incapable of innovation; (2) the false assumption that the market mechanism is an instrument for middlemen to exploit small farmers and poor urban consumers; and (3) the false assumption that there is a trade-off between agricultural efficiency and equity in income distribution, both within agriculture and between rural and urban sectors. See Theordore W. Schultz (ed.), *Distortions of Agricultural Incentives* (1978).

A number of studies also present evidence that agricultural pricing policies have had an adverse effect on (1) the gap between rural and urban income, (2) the incentive to produce food and export crops, (3) the ability of governments to establish and maintain food reserves, and (4) employment opportunities in farming, processing, and rural industries. These studies are surveyed by Carl K. Eicher and Doyle C. Baker, *Research on Agricultural Development in Sub-Saharan Africa: A Critical Survey*, M.S.U. International Development Paper No. 1 (1982).

There is also more attention being given to relative food prices as important determinants of change in the relative and absolute real income of low-income people. For a study of important trade-offs and conflicts among various direct short-run influences and indirect long-run effects of price policy on the real incomes of the poor, see John W. Mellor, "Food Price Policy and Income Distribution in Low-Income Countries," *Economic Development and Cultural Change* (October 1978).

Comment

A number of empirical studies offer evidence on the positive supply elasticity of agricultural production in response to price incentives. An excellent summary of empirical estimates of supply elasticities is presented by Hossein Askari and John T. Cummings, *Agricultural Supply Response: A Survey of the Econometric Evidence* (1976). See also Raj Krishna, "Agricultural Price Policy and Economic Development," in Herman M. Southworth and Bruce F. Johnston (eds.), *Agricultural Development and Economic Growth* (1967); T. W. Schultz (ed.), *Distortions of Agricultural Incentives* (1978); W. Falcon, "Farmer Response to Price in a Subsistence Economy," *American Economic Review, Papers and Proceedings,* (May 1964); K. Bardhan, "Price and Output Response of Marketed Surplus of Foodgrains," *American Journal of Agricultural Economics* (February 1970).

VII.C.6. Food Prices*

Two very different views of the role of food prices in the economic development process have dominated thinking in academic and decisionmakers' circles since the Second World War. General development economists, following the implications of the classic economic growth model developed by Arthur Lewis and others, argued that food prices should be kept low to keep real wages low and thus promote rapid industrialization. A variant of this argument emerged primarily in the Latin American context, where the structural analysts argued that food prices are irrelevant to the long-run development process since both producers and consumers are insensitive to changes in prices. Consequently, political leaders can feel free to manipulate food prices for whatever short-run political effect is desirable. Usually this manipulation takes the form of keeping urban food prices low to satisfy workers, politically active students, and the urban middle class.

The second, or neoclassical view, holds that food prices are a critical factor in farmers' decisions about which crops to grow and how intensively to grow them, even in fairly

traditional peasant economies. In the presence of new biological and chemical technologies that offer significantly higher yields for basic food crops when used properly, price incentives become the major factor in determining yields. As empirical evidence has been gathered over the past decade demonstrating a dramatic long-run response to price, this neoclassical view has increasingly been pushed on Third World leaders who are urged to set their prices carefully.[1]

This article attempts to reconcile these two views of the role of food prices. It does this by examining the role of prices in the production sector, where the evidence for impact in both the short run and long run is quite persuasive. In other words, as far as it goes the neoclassical view has increasingly been

*C. Peter Timmer, "Food Prices and Food Policy Analysis in LDCs," *Food Policy,* Vol. 5, No. 3, pp. 188–93, 197–99, Butterworth Scientific Ltd, Journals Division, Guildford, August 1980.

[1]The empirical evidence is reviewed in C. P. Timmer, "Fertiliser and Food Policies in LDCs," *Food Policy,* Vol. 1, No. 2, 1976, pp. 143–154. More detailed discussions are in C. P. Timmer and W. P. Falcon, "The Impact of Price on Rice Trade in Asia," in G. Tolley and P. Zadrozny (eds.), *Trade, Agriculture and Development,* 1975; and Willis Peterson, "International Farm Prices and the Social Cost of Cheap Food Policies," *American Journal of Agricultural Economics,* Vol. 61, No. 1, February 1979, pp. 12–21. The production-oriented neoclassical policy advice is most clearly argued in T. W. Schultz (ed.), *Distortions of Agricultural Incentives,* Indiana University Press, Bloomington, 1978.

pushed on Third World leaders important roles that neoclassical analysis has largely ignored on an empirical basis:

The differential impact on levels of food consumption (and hence on nutritional status) by poor and rich households. Serious constraints on data and on modelling methodology have prevented significant empirical investigation of this important issue.

The mechanisms by which short-run and long-run food prices determine the distribution of household income levels.

When these two added dimensions of the impact of food prices are included in the neoclassical analysis, the policy advice to "get prices right" becomes much more complicated than assuring farmers prices determined by world markets and realistic foreign exchange rates. Indeed, the income distribution and differential consumption effects of food price changes legitimize much of the short-run political concern over urban food prices, even if the advice based on the classical growth model or structuralist analysis is faulty on empirical grounds. The article concludes, then, with a discussion of the role of food prices in the policy process and the type of analysis modern political economies need to cope with the complex trade-offs in an interrelated multi-staple food system.

THE PRODUCTION SECTOR

Direct Roles

Traditional economic theory and more than half a century of empirical investigation confirm three important direct roles for prices in the production sector: in the choice of crops to be grown; in the choice of technologies used to grow the crops; and, in the choice of input levels needed to produce output levels, i.e., to aggregate agricultural output.

The evidence is overwhelming that farmers are quite sensitive to changes in relative output prices between alternative feasible crops. Where permitted (and frequently even where they are not), farmers change the crops they plant in close correspondence to their relative

profitability which, for given technologies and input prices, will depend directly on the relative farm gate prices. Krishna's review of estimated price elasticities for long-run acreage response reports values greater than one for cotton and jute in pre-war India and Pakistan, and values exceeding 0.5 for important food crops for much of the developing world.[2] Clearly, the composition of agricultural output is largely determined by the relative prices farmers receive for their produce....

The type of technology used by farmers and within the food system more generally also depends on food prices. The issue here is the nature of the production process itself and particularly whether it should be capital or labour intensive. With low food prices in poor countries, few peasants are able to afford modern agricultural equipment; the level of food prices determines whether capital-intensive agricultural techniques are feasible without government subsidy. The choice between capital- and labour-intensive farming depends on the relative factor prices, i.e., how expensive capital is relative to farm labour in the face of their differential contribution to output. Barker has shown that four-wheeled tractors make relatively small productivity contributions for much of Asian agriculture and need subsidies to compete with labour in most settings.[3] Similarly, the appropriate choice of rice milling technology in Java is neither hand-pounding nor large rice mills. Small rice mills are optimal under a fairly wide range of factor and output price conditions likely to prevail in Indonesia.[4]

[2]Raj Krishna, "Agricultural Price Policy," in H. M. Southworth and B. F. Johnston (ed.), *Agricultural Development and Economic Growth*, Cornell University Press, 1967.

[3]Randolph Barker, "Barriers to Efficient Capital Investment in Agriculture," in T. W. Schultz, (ed.), *Distortions of Agricultural Incentives*, Cornell University Press, Ithaca, N.Y., 1967.

[4]The evidence is presented in C. Peter Timmer, "Choice of Techniques in Rice Milling on Java," *Bulletin of Indonesian Economic Studies*, Vol. 9, No. 2, 1973, and in C. P. Timmer et al. *The Choice of Technology in Developing Countries: Some Cautionary Tales*, Harvard Studies in International Affairs, No. 32, 1975.

Again, prices are the crucial variables in the socially desirable choice once the technical productivities of the alternatives are understood. It must be emphasized, however, that improving technical productivities of inputs is at least as important for raising the profitability of food production as manipulating the relative prices of inputs and outputs. . . .

Evidence from the Stanford Project on the Political Economy of Rice in Asia indicates a yield elasticity for rice production (with constant rice and other cropped areas) of 0.14 when varieties and cultivation techniques are kept constant, and 0.33 when these can also change in response to price incentives. The strikingly positive relationship between the relative price of rice to fertilizer and per hectare rice yields for ten important Asian rice producers and the USA is shown in Figure 1.

Indirect Roles

The long-run impact of prices on agricultural production depends partly on letting the direct effects discussed above accumulate and gradually take hold. But three areas of indirect impact also contribute to a more significant long-run price response: on the rate of adoption of new technology; on agricul-

tural research directions and its social payoff: and, on the directions and effectiveness of institutional change.

The factors determining the rate of diffusion of new agricultural technology have been studied quite intensively for several decades. The profitability of the new technology relative to existing varieties or techniques is the most powerful factor explaining the speed and magnitude of its impact on national agricultural productivity. Given the risks of experimenting with new techniques and varieties in traditional agricultural settings, this price impact works more slowly than farmers' adjustments in fertilizer use when prices change.

Vernon Ruttan has been the leading proponent of a long-run role for prices in the agricultural sector that is ultimately more powerful than any discussed so far. The induced innovation hypothesis grows out of the recognition of severe limits to agricultural growth from factors of production in abundant supply such as labour in many Asian countries. The nature of the agricultural production process is such that strongly diminishing returns are likely when any single factor is used very intensively. Consequently, few growth opportunities exist using tradi-

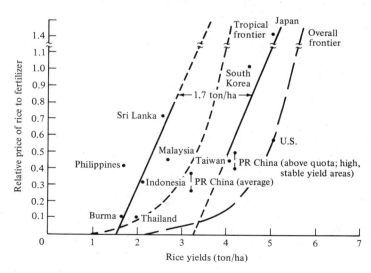

FIGURE 1. Relationship between rice yields and the rice price to fertilizer price ratio in selected countries, 1970.

tional agricultural techniques for countries with unbalanced factor endowments.[5]

In response to food prices rising relative to the prices of the abundant factors of production, societies find it profitable to invest in research that supplements the availability of scarce factors of production, such as land in Asia, while being complementary to the abundant factors. Thus, Japan invested heavily in biological and chemical innovations to raise yields per hectare in the face of severe land constraints and rising agricultural land prices. The fertilizer-responsive seeds developed by Japanese scientists thus extended the productivity potential of Japan's scarcest agricultural resource while complementing its abundant labour supply. . . .

THE CONSUMPTION SECTOR

Ample economic analysis and business evidence confirm that consumers substitute between various commodities as their relative prices change. This is increasingly true as the commodity becomes more narrowly defined and, hence, as the scope for substitution increases. Consumers may find it quite difficult to substitute between food and non-food items, although they shift quite flexibly between chicken and turkey when the relative prices shift significantly. But farmers do not grow food or non-food and the scope for consumption changes of particular commodities is extremely important for agricultural policy purposes. Traditionally this was the major reason for analysing consumption patterns, to determine how much and which crops farmers should be encouraged to grow.

The overall market changes in consumption induced by price changes are composed of changes from thousands and millions of individual households, and each household reacts to price changes according to its own circumstances. These circumstances depend on a host of individual factors including tastes, household composition, knowledge,

and social background. Most important, consumption response to food price changes depends critically on the household's income level.

Understanding the extent to which consumers at different income levels change their food intake as food prices change is extremely important, for only with such information is it possible to trace the impact of food price changes on nutritional status of at-risk populations. The impetus to do this comes from economic planners concerned about guaranteeing basic needs and from nutritionists concerned about the nutritional status of populations at risk. This broader food policy analysis is just now receiving serious methodological and empirical treatment.

Policy impact is traced through one of three mechanisms: price effects, exogenous income effects, and endogenous income effects. Pinstrup-Anderson, et al. have investigated the impact of a shift in food supply curves (a possible food supply policy) on the calorie and protein intake of various income strata of urban households in Cali, Colombia. This is the simplest of all possible policy effects to trace out because there is a single chain of causation from food supply policy through price effects to nutritional (i.e., consumption) impact on the urban households. Even so, the methodology requires a full own- and cross-price elasticity matrix by income strata to translate food price changes into income-strata-specific consumption changes and a full set of market equations to translate neutral supply shifts into price changes.

Extending the analysis to broader policies (food marketing or economic development policies) or to other vulnerable groups (the landless rural poor or subsistence-oriented small farmers) adds entirely new dimensions to the complexity of the impact. Exogenous income effects via changed employment patterns or opportunities and endogenous income effects for farmers due to output or price changes must be added to the price effects. Income-strata-specific income elasticities will be needed to translate the income changes into consumption changes. Much

[5]The most important presentation of this perspective is in T. W. Schultz, *Transforming Traditional Agriculture,* Yale University Press, 1964.

more difficult will be the corresponding functional relationships that translate the policy changes into income-strata-specific income changes. For the exogenous income effects it will be necessary to specify any changes in employment and/or wages (by income class) caused by the policies under analysis. The endogenous income effects are especially difficult to specify because they depend on both output and price components. Both of these, but especially the output component, are likely to vary systematically by income strata.

More important, the translation of policy change into resulting effects on prices and incomes must necessarily be done in the specific political, social, and economic context of the change itself. For instance, any price changes due to a shift in supply will depend on whether the country is an importer or exporter, the state of the marketing sector, and existing institutional mechanisms of price formation. Similarly, the income effects of a marketing change will depend on the extent of open or disguised unemployment, choice of technique in processing and distribution, and mechanisms of wage formation. It is difficult to generalize about these in the absence of a significant number of reliable agricultural sector models able to trace through price and income effects by income class. No such models exist at present although several models are able to trace these effects without disaggregating income. . . .

Substitution of one basic foodstuff for another as relative prices change promotes efficiency in an economy, encouraging consumers to buy the relatively more abundant, and hence cheaper commodity. Does such substitution have any welfare costs? In particular, are some basic foods nutritionally better than their substitutes, and does any significant substitution of food in general take place when overall food prices rise and fall in real terms?

The first question is more difficult to answer than would first appear since the nutritional value of foods depends on what is relatively least adequately supplied in the diet. Although protein deficiencies have received much attention in the past thirty years as a focus of nutrition policy concern, most experts now view the primary nutritional problem in the Third World as inadequate energy intake from traditional foods. Protein tends to be supplied in adequate amounts from such foods when calorific needs are met, with perhaps the important exceptions of weaning and toddler children and in areas with high reliance on tropical roots as the main calorific source. In most environments, substitutions which maintain or improve calorific intake, even if cassava is substituted for rice, will not result in serious deterioration of nutritional status if high protein foods such as legumes and fish continue to be consumed with starchy roots in their traditional pattern. Certainly, little nutritional harm arises from substituting equal calories of sorghum or millet for wheat or rice.

The second question is analogous to asking whether aggregate agricultural output is responsive to the terms of trade between agricultural and non-agricultural goods. Just as that question must be answered positively on the basis of long-run evidence drawn from cross-section data, so too must the consumption equivalent. On the basis of data from 16 developing countries for an average of 10 years each, Weisskoff estimated the overall price elasticity of demand for food at -0.87, a figure that is predictably much larger in absolute terms than the -0.16 that Houthakker derived with similar methodology for European countries. At the level of national aggregates, consumers do substitute food for non-food and this substitution is more responsive in poor countries than in rich.

The evidence is similar for cross-section analysis of consumers within countries, with an intriguing twist. Indonesian data. . . . indicate significant price elasticities for calories from rice, maize, and cassava (providing on average three-quarters of Indonesian calorific intake), but the lowest income group has a smaller absolute price response than the higher income groups. There is a real physiological constraint below which poor consumers cannot go, and nearly all the budget must be devoted to calorie purchases.

The final role of food prices in determining consumption patterns relates to the formation of long-run tastes. Although economists usually assume that tastes are given, the duality between equilibrium quantities and equilibrium prices that derives from formal planning models provides the framework for a new interpretation of mechanisms of taste formation that rely on natural climatic advantage and physical availability of particular crops as the basis for a society's basic food tastes. The dual of such factors is the (implicit) relative price of, say, rice to wheat, or potatoes to corn, and if these prices were consciously manipulated for long periods of time then tastes would similarly be changed. Japan's new taste for wheat products may be a case in point.

INCOME DETERMINATION

The impact of food prices on the level and distribution of incomes is the least understood of the three major areas discussed here. Much of what is known quantitatively about these relationships draws from a major research project at Cornell University directed by John Mellor, and heavily oriented toward India.[6] The project looked at the four basic topics of most relevance to the impact of food prices: the direct impact on the real income of consumers: the direct impact on producers; the impact on the level of food production; and, the impact on employment.

The obvious point about food prices and the real income of consumers is the differential budget shares of poor versus rich consumers devoted to food purchases. Higher food prices have a disporportionately large impact on the poor although the absolute impact—the total real loss in income—may be

larger for the middle and upper classes. The direct impact on producers tends to have a similarly skewed effect. Farmers producing significant market surpluses who will benefit from higher food prices are typically in the upper income strata of rural societies and the direct effect of higher food prices will tend to skew further the rural income distribution. This effect will be further exacerbated if significant numbers of rural landless workers must purchase most of their food from the market.

It is only with the impact on food production that the income distribution consequence of higher food prices tends to reverse. Given the high marginal propensity of the poor to buy food from additional income, economic development strategies aimed at raising the income of the poor often run afoul of inadequate food supplies. If higher food prices can promote technical change in agriculture and significantly larger food supplies in the future, a growth strategy aimed at reaching the poor may become economically and politically feasible.

The impact of food prices on employment is the most complicated area of the four. Employment is affected indirectly through national food consumption patterns because of varying employment intensities of different foods (vegetables require more labour than wheat). Employment is also affected via price impact on the total level of agricultural production and hence on demand for farm labour in general; through cropping patterns that may include crops grown for export or industrial use (groundnuts in India require nearly twice as much labour per acre as cotton); and through the choice of inputs used to produce food. Obviously, mechanized equipment may affect employment, although very careful attention to the mechanical requirements of double or triple cropping is important. However, more subtle employment changes are also caused by input choices. Fertilizer, for example, may substitute indirectly for labour if similar aggregate output could be achieved by more extensive cultivation with higher labour input per unit of output.

[6]The most succinct statement of the project results appears in John Mellor, "Food Price Policy and Income Distribution in Low-Income Countries," *Economic Development and Cultural Change,* October 1978. More of the earlier conceptual analysis for the project is contained in John Mellor, *The New Economics of Growth: A Strategy for India and the Developing World,* Cornell University Press, Ithaca, N.Y., 1976.

The major impact of food prices on employment, discussed in the economic development literature, is through the level of real wages. The classic Lewis model of development with unlimited supplies of labour relies almost entirely on keeping food prices low as a mechanism for rapidly expanding both wage employment and the capitalist surplus for reinvestment in the modern industrial sector. The strategy appears to have worked well for Japan, Taiwan, South Korea, and perhaps now for China. . . .

The best that can be said now is that the answers are likely to be country-specific and will require careful integration of detailed micro level studies with a sensitive macro model capable of capturing income-distribution effects, commodity substitution in production and consumption, and price determination mechanisms in both open and closed economies.

THE POLICY PROCESS

Many food deficit countries urgently need higher real food prices as an incentive to millions of small farmers to raise the agricultural productivity through adoption of modern technology. But those same higher, incentive food grain prices will have a disproportionate impact on food consumption of the poor. Many of these people are already suffering from inadequate protein-calorie intake, and further reduction in their food consumption may mean serious malnutrition or death.

This dilemma has been resolved historically in two ways. First, food grain imports can be used to fill the gap between inadequate domestic production and consumption levels generated by low food prices. Second, in some countries prices of the preferred food grain have been raised as an incentive to domestic farmers while secondary grains and root crops have been kept cheap, or subsidized, to protect the poor. The substitute opportunities increase policy flexibility to deal with this fundamental dilemma of modern political economies.

Policy analysis in multi staple-food econo-

mies is obviously much more complicated than in single food grain economies. The consumption picture becomes more complicated because of the need to know multiple own-price effects by income class, and cross-price effects also become important. The production side is made more complicated by the substitute possibilities if they are produced domestically. Planning intensification programmes for rice, for example, when maize, wheat, or barley are alternatives, requires a complex balancing of output price incentives, input subsidies, credit programmes, and development of suitable seed and production technologies. Attempts to raise rice prices to increase production, while keeping maize prices low to protect poor consumers, may simply be frustrated by the production substitution options and the level of alternative technologies, unless dual price systems with extensive subsidies can be implemented.

The complications extend to the import and domestic marketing arenas. Planning food grain imports, especially if much of the grain will be available under food aid terms, is far more complicated if several grains are being imported (or some exported) and changes at the margin in their rate of substitution are being attempted. On the domestic side, the marketing structure for the preferred grain, typically rice or wheat, is usually much more fully developed than for secondary grains and root crops. The latter are usually viewed by government planners as inferior foods produced primarily for subsistence which deserve little government attention to production, marketing, or consumption issues.

A number of important countries with large populations now seem to be facing the prospect of inadequate internal or external resources to increase availability of favoured food grains fast enough to meet market demand at constant prices, not to mention the latent nutritional demand that would be forthcoming at significantly lower prices. In the absence of massive food aid transfers, these countries will have to seek food grain substitutes for the poorest parts of their populations until long-term investment in agricultural infrastructure, made profitable by higher incentive prices for the preferred food grain, begins to transform the domestic production outlook.

A differential price policy by commodity, even if it includes direct subsidies on those foodstuffs such as cassava and maize that are consumed primarily by the poor as a means of implementing the policy, offers the potential to target the nutritional impact without many of the associated enforcement costs and leakages of target-oriented programmes using more preferred foods. Such a strategy relies on self enforcement. The desire, or necessity, of the poor to eat staple foodstuffs no longer attractive to the more wealthy presents an opportunity to deal with inadequate protein-calorie intake without subsidizing the consumption of the entire population and hence bankrupting the nation. Such a strategy calls for high political commitment to increasing the access of the poor to adequate food. It may also be the only financially feasible way of coping with protein-calorie malnutrition over the next several decades.

The analytical costs of such a multi-commodity price policy are quite high. But these high analytical costs must be compared with the costs of subsidizing food consumption for much of the population or attempting to enforce target-oriented food distribution. The combination of high analytical and political costs is not attractive, but neither are the alternatives.

CHAPTER VIII

Trade Strategy

This chapter concentrates on the problems connected with the transmission of development through trade. It is especially concerned with whether there is a conflict between market-determined comparative advantage and the acceleration of development—whether in pursuing the gains from trade, a country might limit its attainment of the gains from growth.

Materials in the first section present opposing views on this question. Some economists argue that the accrual of the gains from trade is biased in favor of the advanced industrial countries, that foreign trade has inhibited industrial development in the poorer nations, and that—contrary to what would be expected from classical trade doctrine—free trade has in reality accentuated international inequalities. In contrast, others maintain the traditional position that foreign trade can contribute substantially to the development of primary exporting countries and that the gains from international specialization merge with the gains from growth. A more eclectic approach attempts to identify the various conditions that favor—or inhibit—a process of export-led development.

Phenomena associated with a changing international division of labor may also exert strong influence on the rate and structural pattern of a country's development. The concern over the role of the LDCs in a new international economic order is connected with problems of facilitating a new international division of labor: To what extent can primary-producing countries exercise "resource bargaining power"? What is the scope for import substitution? What are the potentials for export of manufactured products?

The trade policy of a developing country is closely related to the problems raised by the foreign exchange constraint on the country's development. A number of theoretically sophisticated arguments support a protectionist trade policy for a developing country. In actual practice, however, protectionist policies have rarely been adopted out of a reasoned consideration of how protectionism might improve the terms of trade, raise the savings ratio, take account of external economies, or overcome distortions in the labor market. On the contrary, it has been the persistent shortage of foreign exchange that has dominated considerations of trade policy, and protectionist policies have been much more in the nature of ad hoc responses to recurrent balance-of-payment crises.

These policies have, however, been disappointing in most countries. The policies have not succeeded in reducing the foreign exchange constraint; indeed, in some cases, it can be claimed that import-substitution policies have actually intensified the shortage. Nor have the policies of import replacement succeeded in achieving any widespread degree of industrialization beyond the immediate replacement of the final imported consumer goods; nor has there been the expected progression from import replacement to production for export markets (as in the earlier Japanese case); nor has industrial protection been an effective means of ameliorating the labor absorption problem. Nonetheless, import-substituting policies have become self-justifying in LDCs as their trade gap has widened, and the countries have resorted to yet another round of import restrictions to meet the balance-of-payments problem. These disappointing results of import substitution in practice are reviewed in section VIII.B.

There is now a notable shift of emphasis away from import-replacing policies to the outward-looking policies of export promotion, particularly of semimanufactured and manufactured exports. This requires consideration of a variety of policies—not only the granting of tariff preferences for exports from the LDCs but, even more important, a reduction of the effective rates of protection as well as a removal of nontariff barriers. If their nontraditional exports are to be promoted, the LDCs will also have to pursue policies to take advantage of the new opportunities provided by the underlying real forces of a changing international division of labor.

There has now been considerable experience of inward-oriented and outward-oriented development strategies. Section VIII.B reviews the lessons of this experience, emphasizing policies that liberalize the foreign trade regime and promote exports. Some of the selections also look to the future, asking about the future growth in world trade and whether the success stories of East Asian countries can be generalized to a larger group of countries.

In demanding the reform of international trading arrangements, the LDCs in UNCTAD are seeking not merely more trade, but more trade at higher export prices. In essence, the trade proposals of UNCTAD attempt to internationalize protection or invert protection in the sense of having it practiced by developed importing countries in favor of the less developed exporting countries. Both international commodity agreements for primary products and preferences for manufactured exports have the objective of improving the LDCs' terms of trade by raising export prices, thereby effecting a transfer of real resources from consumers in developed countries to producers in LDCs. If balance-of-payments and budgetary considerations make it unlikely that more resources can be transferred through taxpayers in the developed countries in the form of "open aid," then the transfer may have to come more covertly through implicit taxation of consumers in the developed importing countries. The selections in section VIII.C discuss how the character of trade in primary products might be changed through the use of "producer power" and international commodity agreements.

Proposals for regional integration, as a means of lessening the dependence on primary exports and accelerating development, have also gained increasing favor. With slower growth in the more developed countries and the slow down of trade between the LDCs and MDCs, there is also now more consideration of how LDC-LDC trade might be promoted. The Note in section VIII.D appraises the contributions that regional integration, in the form of a customs union or free trade area, might make to the development of its member nations.

The issues raised in this chapter tend to cut across the objectives of international efficiency in resource allocation, international stabilization of primary export revenue, and international redistribution of income. In the more orthodox view of trade theory, these objectives are kept quite separate, and different policy instruments are advocated as being "first-best" policy for each objective. In international policy discussions, however, the problems become only too easily intermixed. And just as there is a political controversy over whether the international monetary system should be linked to development finance, so too there is political disagreement over "aid through trade policy," over the sacrifice of efficiency in international resource allocation for the sake of an international transfer of resources, and over the burden that must be shared as a result of adjustments to a changing international division of labor.

VIII.A. INTERNATIONAL TRADE AND INTERNATIONAL INEQUALITY

VIII.A.1. Trade as an "Engine of Growth"—Note

An overriding issue in the relations between trade and development is the ultimate question of whether there is a conflict between the gains from trade and the gains from growth.[1] Can foreign trade have a propulsive role in the development of a country? Or, on the contrary, are the dictates of comparative advantage incompatible with the requirements of accelerated development?

The orthodox interpretation as expounded by classical and neoclassical economists is that foreign trade can be a propelling force in development. Adam Smith's model of foreign trade postulates the existence of idle land and labor before a country is opened to world markets. The excess resources are used to produce a surplus of goods for export, and trade thereby "vents" a surplus productive capacity that would otherwise be unused. In Smith's words,

Between whatever places foreign trade is carried on, they all of them derive two distinct benefits from it. It carries out that surplus part of the produce of their land and labour for which there is no demand among them, and brings back in return for it something else for which there is a demand. It gives a value to their superfluities, by exchanging them for something else, which may satisfy a part of their wants, and increase their enjoyments. By means of it, the narrowness of the home market does not hinder the division of labour in any particular branch of art or manufacture from being carried to the highest perfection. By opening a more extensive market for whatever part of the produce of their labour may exceed the home consumption, it encourages them to improve its pro-

duction powers, and to augment its annual produce to the utmost, and thereby to increase the real revenue and wealth of the society.[2]

This idea of "vent for surplus" assumes that resources are not fully employed prior to trade, and that exports are increased without a decrease in domestic production, with the result that trade raises the level of economic activity.

More generally, classical economists considered comparative advantage as determining the pattern of trade. Not the use of surplus resources but resource reallocation allowed trade to benefit a country by promoting a more efficient international allocation of resources. Without any increase in resources or technological change, every trading country is able to enjoy a higher real income by specializing in production according to its comparative advantage and trading. The exports have instrumental significance as the intermediate goods used for the "indirect production" of imports: exports allow the country to "buy" imports on more favorable

[1]This Note is an abbreviated version of Gerald M. Meier, "External Trade and Internal Development," in Peter Duignan and L. H. Gann (eds.), *Colonialism in Africa 1870–1960*, Vol. 4, New York, 1975. See also Gerald M. Meier, *The International Economics of Development*, New York, 1968, chapter 8.

[2]Adam Smith, *An Inquiry into the Nature and Causes of the Wealth of Nations*, Edwin Cannan (ed.), 1937, p. 415. For more detailed discussion of Smith's theory, See Hla Myint, "The Classical Theory of International Trade and the Underdeveloped Countries," *Economic Journal*, 1958, Vol. 68, pp. 317–31. Myint indicates that Smith's concept of surplus productive capacity is not merely a matter of surplus land by itself but surplus land combined with surplus labor; and the surplus labor is then linked with his concept of "unproductive labor" (p. 323). This interpretation allows Smith's vent-for-surplus model of trade and growth to be consistent with W. Arthur Lewis's model of development with unlimited supplies of labor. See R. E. Caves, "'Vent for Surplus' Models of Trade and Growth," in R. E. Baldwin et al., *Trade, Growth, and the Balance of Payments: Essays in Honor of Gottfried Haberler*, 1965, pp. 95–115.

terms than if produced directly at home. The gain from trade is on the import side; and it is significant that the gains are also mutual, realized by all the trading countries. By specializing in commodities for which its costs are comparatively lowest, a trading nation would, in Ricardo's words, increase "the sum of commodities and mass of enjoyments"; in modern jargon, trade optimizes production.

Although specialization according to comparative advantage yields the direct benefits of international exchange, there are in addition dynamic aspects of trade that are relevant for the growth-transmitting effects of trade above and beyond the static gains. Classical and neoclassical economists did not make the dynamic aspects of trade central to their thought; but to the extent that they did consider the effects of trade on development, they saw no conflict between a country's conformity with its comparative advantage and the acceleration of its development. Indeed, John Stuart Mill stated that trade, according to comparative advantage, results in a "more efficient employment of the productive forces of the world," and that this might be considered the "direct economical advantage of foreign trade. But there are, besides, indirect effects, which must be counted as benefits of a high order." A most important "indirect" dynamic benefit, according to Mill, is

the tendency of every extension of the market to improve the processes of production. A country which produces for a larger market than its own, can introduce a more extended division of labour, can make greater use of machinery, and is more likely to make inventions and improvements in the processes of production.

Widening the extent of the market, inducing innovations and increasing productivity through foreign trade allow a country to overcome the diseconomies of being a small country.

Another important consideration, according to Mill, "principally applicable to an early age of industrial advancement," is that

a people may be in a quiescent, indolent, uncultivated state, with all their tastes either fully satisfied or entirely undeveloped, and they may fail to put forth the whole of their productive energies for want of any sufficient object of desire. The opening of a foreign trade, by making them acquainted with new objects, or tempting them by the easier acquisition of things which they had not previously thought attainable, sometimes works a sort of industrial revolution in a country whose resources were previously undeveloped for want of energy and ambition in the people: inducing those who were satisfied with scanty comforts and little work, to work harder for the gratification of their new tastes, and even to save, and accumulate capital, for still more complete satisfaction of those tastes at a future time.[3]

Further, Mill stated that trade benefits the less developed countries through

the introduction of foreign arts, which raises the returns derivable from additional capital to a rate corresponding to the low strength of accumulation; and the importation of foreign capital which renders the increase of production no longer exclusively dependent on the thrift or providence of the inhabitants themselves, while it places before them a stimulating example, and by instilling new ideas and breaking the chain of habit, if not by improving the actual condition of the population, tends to create in them new wants, increased ambition, and greater thought for the future.[4]

The indirect benefits of trade on development are therefore of three kinds: (1) those that widen the extent of the market, induce innovations, and increase productivity; (2) those that increase savings and capital accumulation; and (3) those that have an educative effect in instilling new wants and tastes and in transferring technology, skills, and entrepreneurship. This emphasis is on the supply side of the development process—the opportunity that trade gives a poor country to remove domestic shortages, to overcome the diseconomies of the small size of its domestic market, and to accelerate the "learning rate" of its economy.

For these several reasons, the traditional

[3]John Stuart Mill, *Principles of Political Economy*, 2 vols., London, 1848, Vol. II, book III, sec. 5, chapter 17.

[4]Ibid., Vol. 1, book 1, sec. 1, chapter 13.

conclusion has been that the gains from trade do not result merely in a once-over change in resource allocation, but are also continually merging with the gains from development: international trade transforms existing production functions and increases the productivity of the economy over time. If trade increases the capacity for development, then the larger the volume of trade, the greater should be the potential for development.

More recently, various export-based models of growth have been formulated to present a macro-dynamic view of how an economy's growth can be determined by expansion in its exports. One version of the export-based model is that of the staple theory of growth.

The term "staple" designates a raw material or resource-intensive commodity occupying a dominant position in the country's exports. It has a structural similarity to the vent-for-surplus view insofar as "surplus" resources initially exist and are subsequently exported. It also has some affinity with Lewis's model of development with an unlimited supply of labor when the surplus to be vented through trade is one of labor and not natural resources.

The staple theory postulates that with the discovery of a primary product in which the country has a comparative advantage, or with an increase in the demand for its comparative advantage commodity, there is an expansion of a resource-based export commodity; this in turn induces higher rates of growth of aggregate and *per capita* income. Previously idle or undiscovered resources are brought into use, creating a return to these resources and being consistent with venting a surplus through trade. The export of a primary product also has effects on the rest of the economy through diminishing underemployment or unemployment, inducing a higher rate of domestic saving and investment, attracting an inflow of factor inputs into the expanding export sector, and establishing linkages with other sectors of the economy. Although the rise in exports is induced by greater demand, there are supply

responses within the economy that increase the productivity of the exporting economy.

The staple theory has some relation also to Rostow's leading-sector analysis insofar as the staple-export sector may be the leading sector of the economy, growing more rapidly and propelling the rest of the economy along with its growth. In Rostow's analysis, however, a primary-producing sector can be a leading sector only if it also involves processing of the primary product.

A more general analysis of the effects of trade on the rate of growth has been considered by Corden.[5] Instead of the "demand-motored" model of the staple theory, Corden analyzes a "supply-motored" model that emphasizes growth in factor supplies and productivity. After a country is opened to world trade, five different effects may be distinguished. First is the "impact effect" corresponding to the static gain from trade: current real income is raised. Then there may be the "capital-accumulation effect": an increase in capital accumulation results when parts of the static gain are invested. This amounts to a transfer of real income from the present to the future instead of an increase in present consumption. Third may be the "substitution effect." This may result from a possible fall in the relative price of investment goods to consumption goods if investment goods are import-intensive. This would lead to an increase in the ratio of investment to consumption and an increase in the rate of growth. The fourth possibility is an "income-distribution effect": there will be a shift in income toward the factors that are used intensively in the production of exports. If the savings propensities differ between sectors or factors, this will have an effect on the overall savings propensity and hence on capital accumulation. Finally, there is the "factor-weight effect." This considers the relative productivity of capital and labor and recog-

[5]W. Max Corden, "The Effects of Trade on the Rate of Growth," in *Trade, Balance of Payments and Growth*, Jagdish N. Bhagwati et al. (eds.), Amsterdam, 1971, pp. 117–43.

nizes that if the rate of growth of output is a weighted average of capital and labor growth rates (with a consant returns-to-scale aggregate production function), then if exports rise, and exports use the faster-growing factor of production, the rate of growth of exports will rise more rapidly. These effects are all cumulative, and intensify the increase in real income over time as a result of opening a country to foreign trade.

The positive view of trade and development thus emphasizes the direct gain that comes from international specialization plus the additional support to a country's development through a number of spread effects within the domestic economy.

Comment

Critics of the view that trade will transmit development often deny the relevance of the conclusions of neoclassical trade theory. Some claim that the theory of comparative advantage is static and misses the essence of change in the development process. But the conclusions derived from the theory of comparative advantage need not be limited to a "cross section" view and a given once-for-all set of conditions. The comparative cost doctrine still has validity among countries undergoing differential rates of development. For a simple exposition of how to incorporate different types of factor growth, technological progress, and changes in the structure of demand into the neoclassical theory of comparative advantage, see G. M. Meier, *International Trade and Development* (1963), chapter 2. For some illustrations of the changing international division of labor, see "A 'Stages' Approach to Comparative Advantage," in Irma Adelman (ed.), *Economic Growth and Resources,* Vol. 5, *National and International Issues* (1979).

Another criticism is directed against the "factor-price equalization theorem" derived from neoclassical theory. This theorem states that, under certain conditions, free trade is a perfect substitute for complete international mobility of factors and is sufficient to equalize, in the trading countries, not only the prices of products but also the prices of factors. Against this proposition, however, critics argue that, in reality, the international distribution of income has become more unequal. Some, like Myrdal, would contrapose against the factor-price equalization theorem a theory of "cumulative causation" or a "cumulative process away from equilibrium in factor proportions and factor prices, engendered by international trade." See Gunnar Myrdal, *An International Economy* (1956) and *Rich Lands and Poor* (1957), chapter 11.

This criticism is, however, highly overdrawn. The critics attribute much more importance to the theorem than did its expositors who recognized its highly restrictive assumptions and hence never maintained that equalization will actually occur. The very special set of assumptions are: identical production functions in all countries; constant returns to scale exist in the production of each commodity; and factor and product markets are perfectly competitive. Insofar as these restrictive conditions have been violated in reality, it should not be surprising that factor returns have not been equalized between rich and poor countries. See P. A. Samuelson, "International Factor-Price Equalization Once Again," *Economic Journal* (June 1949).

Although the factor price equalization theorem cannot be claimed to be a valid empirical generalization, the fundamental contention of neoclassical trade theory does hold—the real income of each country will be higher with trade than without trade.

VIII.A.2. Patterns of Trade and Development*

[It is] instructive to take a look at past experience and see how economic growth in certain areas was induced through international trade in the nineteenth century. The areas involved in this process of growth through trade were chiefly the so-called regions of recent settlement in the temperate latitudes outside Europe. These areas, in which the United States may be included, received a large inflow of labour as well as capital from Europe, but a basic inducement that caused them to develop was the tremendous expansion of Western Europe's, and especially Great Britain's, demand for the foodstuffs and raw materials which they were well suited to produce. Growth at the periphery was induced, through trade, by growth in the rising industrial centre.

Alfred Marshall referred to "the splendid markets which the old world has offered to the products of the new."[1] He forgot to mention the crucial point that these were growing markets, but this he probably assumed as a matter of course. The penultimate chapter of his *Principles* is entitled "General Influences of Economic Progress" and begins as follows: "The field of employment which any place offers for labour and capital depends, firstly, on its natural resources; secondly, on . . . knowledge and . . . organization; and thirdly, on . . . markets in which it has a superfluity. The importance of this last condition is often underrated; but it stands out prominently when we look at the history of new countries."[2]

It was under the impression of this experience that Marshall made the following pronouncement: "The causes which determine the economic progress of nations belong to the study of international trade."[3] In the second half of the twentieth century this may seem to us a curious statement. It can be understood only in the light of certain historical conditions, and it embodies the particular experience of Britain's economic relations with the new countries overseas. Economic growth in these areas was due not to international specialization alone but more particularly to the fact that the character of trade was such that the rapid growth which was taking place in the centre was transmitted to the outlying new countries through a vigorous increase in the demand for primary products.

Trade in the nineteenth century was not simply a device for the optimum allocation of a given stock of resources. It was that too, but it was more than that. It was above all "an engine of growth." This profoundly important observation is one which we owe to Sir Dennis Robertson.[4]

It helps us to see things in perspective, but in doing so it serves also to limit the significance of classical trade theory to its proper sphere. The conventional tendency has been to credit international specialization as such with the spectacular growth of the new countries in the nineteenth century. In the light of Robertson's remark it may perhaps be suggested that classical specialization theory, which in the nature of the case is a static analysis, has derived more prestige from nineteenth-century experience than it has deserved. The dynamic nature of trade as a transmitter of growth was overlooked during an era in which progress was taken for granted, like the air we breathe.

There is no doubt that international trade was peculiarly important in the conditions of the nineteenth century. In real volume it increased tenfold between 1850 and 1913, twice as fast as world production. Imperialism had very little to do with the expansion

*From Ragnar Nurkse, "Trade Theory and Development Policy," in H. S. Ellis (ed.), *Economic Development for Latin America,* Macmillan and Co. Ltd., London; St. Martin's Press, New York, 1961, pp. 236–45. Reprinted by permission.

[1]Alfred Marshall, *Principles of Economics,* 8th ed., London, 1920, pp. 668–9.

[2]Ibid., p. 668.

[3]Ibid., p. 270.

[4]D. H. Robertson, *Essays in Monetary Theory,* London, 1940, p. 214.

of trade. As was shown by J. A. Hobson himself,[5] the tropical colonies took a minor share in the growth of British trade. Continental Europe and the new countries outside as well as within the British Empire took the major share. The regions of recent settlement were high-income countries from the start, effective markets as well as efficient producers. Their development was part of the growth of international trade itself.

So much for the new countries. Elsewhere, in the truly backward areas, economic growth induced through international trade in some cases carried with it certain features that were, and still are, regarded as undesirable. It sometimes led to a lopsided pattern of growth in which production of primary products for export was carried on with the aid of substantial investment of foreign capital, while the domestic economy remained far less developed, if not altogether primitive. This picture applies especially to tropical areas. It is the familiar picture of the dual economy resulting from trade and from foreign business investment induced by trade. Areas of outpost investment producing for foreign markets often showed a lack of social as well as economic integration internally. Moreover, their export activities were subject to the familiar hazards of cyclical instability.

Nevertheless, even unsteady growth through foreign trade is surely better than no growth at all. Mr. Bauer has given impressive examples of progress resulting from peasant production for export in some parts of West Africa during the early half of the twentieth century.[6] Elsewhere foreign capital working for export has usually led to an additional demand for local labour, increased wage incomes, expenditures on local materials, new sources of taxation, and, in the case of mineral concessions, lucrative profit-sharing arrangements. All these benefits have helped to promote expansion in the domestic economy.

The traditional pattern of development through production for expanding export markets is not to be despised and ought not

to be discouraged. Indeed, I should like to assume that all opportunities in this direction are fully exploited. The trouble is that in the mid-twentieth century, with a few notable exceptions, conditions for this type of growth do not, by and large, appear to be as promising as they were a hundred years ago.

Since 1913 the quantum of world trade has increased less than world production. To be sure, in the last five or six years we find the volume of trade in the non-communist world increasing at just about the same pace as production. But when we look at it more closely we find that it is chiefly among the advanced industrial countries that international trade has been expanding in the recent past. These countries, including above all the United States, are themselves efficient primary producers, especially for food. Their demand for exotic raw materials like crude rubber, silk, nitrates, jute, vegetable oils, hides, and skins has been, and will probably continue to be, affected by the growth of the chemical industry in the twentieth century. . . . Professor D. D. Humphrey in his voluminous study, *American Imports*,[7] attaches great importance to the technological factor. He estimates that, in its effect on total United States imports, the displacement of imported raw materials by synthetic products has more than offset the 75 per cent reduction in the American tariff which has taken place in the last twenty years partly through duty reductions and partly through the effect of price inflation on the burden of specific duties. While tariff changes have mainly affected imports of manufactured goods from other industrial countries, technological displacement has particularly affected United States imports from the less developed countries.

Only for minerals are conditions generally favorable, although even here it should be noted that, first, the demand for metals is affected by the increasing efficiency of scrap collection and recovery in the industrial countries. Second, mineral deposits are gifts of nature, and if a country does not happen to have any, it can do nothing in response to

[5] J. A. Hobson, *Imperialism,* 3rd ed., London, 1938, ch. 2.

[6] P. T. Bauer, *West African Trade,* Cambridge, 1955.

[7] D. D. Humphrey, *American Imports,* New York, 1955.

the rise in world demands. Some countries that have deposits fail to exploit them. Nevertheless, the point remains that while Guatemala, for example, can at least try to grow chicle, she cannot try to grow nickel. Third, the export of minerals involves in an obvious sense an element of living on capital.

The growth of synthetic materials is undoubtedly one explanation of the findings which Professor Kindleberger reaches in his book on *The Terms of Trade: A European Case Study.* This study lends some support to the view that the poorer countries' terms of trade have shown a tendency to deteriorate. Kindleberger has calculated industrial Europe's terms of trade separately for various parts of the world, including in particular two groups of countries overseas, the areas of recent settlement, not including the United States, and the poorer countries (the rest of the world in his grouping). Difficulties due to quality changes and transport costs apply to both groups. Both the new countries and the poor countries are exporters of primary products and importers of manufactured goods. From 1913 to 1952, according to these estimates, Europe's terms of trade with the areas of recent settlement showed a 20 per cent improvement, while in trade with the poorer countries Europe's terms seem to have improved by as much as 55 per cent.[8]

Other recent studies have provided evidence that world demand for the poorer countries' export products has tended to rise much less than in proportion to the production and incomes of the advanced countries.[9]

[8]C. P. Kindleberger, *The Terms of Trade: A European Case Study,* New York, 1956, p. 234.

[9]For the post-war period this conclusion is documented in United Nations, *World Economic Survey, 1956,* and also in the annual report of the Contracting Parties to the General Agreement on Tariffs and Trade, *International Trade, 1955,* Geneva, 1956.

For a longer period, Professor Cairncross has made a careful statistical study of world exports of manufactured goods since 1900 showing that the manufactured goods which the industrial countries export to each other have constituted a steadily increasing proportion of their total exports of manufactured articles; A. K. Carincross, "World Trade in Manufactures since 1900," *Economia Internazionale,* November 1955.

It is therefore not surprising that, according to the report of the Contracting Parties to the General Agreement on Tariffs and Trade, we find the following distribution of international trade in the non-communist world in 1955. The exports of twenty advanced industrial countries (United States, Canada, Japan, and Western Europe) to each other constitute as much as 40 per cent of total exports. Exports from these twenty countries to all less developed countries outside the communist orbit amount to 25 per cent of the total. Exports from the less developed to the advanced countries represent another 25 per cent. Only 10 per cent of the total are exports of the less developed countries to each other, even though the more than hundred countries in this group contain two-thirds of the total population of the non-communist world.[10] Why is it that so little of the coffee, tea, rubber, and tin produced in these countries goes to other countries in the same group? Obviously the main explanation is the low purchasing power of people in these countries, which in turn is a reflection of their low productivity.

The fact that the economically advanced countries are each others' best customers is now more than ever a central feature of world trade. It is chiefly within this small circle of countries that international trade is now expanding. With the leading exception of petroleum and a few other minerals, it can hardly be said that primary producing countries are enjoying a dynamic expansion in world demand for their exports. . . .

Professor T. W. Schultz in his paper on "Economic Prospect of Primary Products" shows that the demand for all raw materials, whether imported or domestically produced, has lagged far behind the increase in output in the United States. What we are considering therefore is merely the international aspect of a fairly general tendency. In a country amply supplied with capital and technical know-how, it seems a perfectly natural ten-

[10]*International Trade,* 1955. The figures given in this report exclude trade within the communist orbit. For the sake of comparability I have adjusted them so as to exclude trade between communist and non-communist countries as well.

dency for investment in research and development to displace crude materials with synthetic products made from a few basic elements of mostly local origin. These trends are not confined to the United States. They are affecting the trade of other advanced areas as well.[11]

If this is the situation of the mid-twentieth century, the mental habits which economists have inherited from the mid-nineteenth may no longer be altogether adequate. It will be recalled that Professor Hicks' analysis of the long-run dollar problem was based on what he described as "a change in economic atmosphere between the nineteenth and twentieth centuries."[12] His analysis in regard to the dollar problem was open to criticism, yet I believe that in emphasizing the varying incidence of productivity changes on international trade he made an important point, a point that had been noted some years earlier by Professor Haberler.[13] While Britain's ratio of imports to national income showed a rising tendency during most of the nineteenth century, the United States import ratio has been practically halved in the last five decades.[14] This has happened in spite of the fact that in short period comparisons the United States typically shows a rather high income elasticity of imports. There seems to have been a long-run downward shift in the United States import function, resulting from changes in economic structure. It is not certain that tariff policy provides the major part of the explanation. It seems very likely that the incidence of technological advance has had a good deal to do with it.

The slight increase which has occurred in the last few years in the United States import ratio has been due to increased imports of finished and semi-finished manufactures. This has meant increased trade with other industrial countries, Canada, Western Europe, Japan. Imports of crude materials, largely from under-developed areas, have not regained their pre-war position in relation to United States gross national product. All this does not mean that the absolute volume of United States imports has failed to expand. It increased by 44 per cent from 1929 to 1955[15] But notice two things. This increase is much less than proportional to the growth of United States output. Moreover, it is much less than the rate of growth of British imports in the nineteenth century, which during any comparable period showed a two to threefold increase in volume.

It is useful to keep in mind these elementary facts about American imports because the United States is now the dominant economy not only in world production but also in world trade. Some economists are more inclined to stress the future prospect of expansion in United States imports, but that is a debatable matter. It is never quite safe, and for present purposes really unnecessary, to engage in predictions. The facts for the recent past are sufficient to indicate a change in the economic atmosphere of international trade between the nineteenth and twentieth centuries.

It will be remembered that in Hicks' analysis of the dollar shortage, the balance of payments problem resolves itself into a terms of trade problem. This seems a plausible sim-

[11]A. K. Cairncross and J. Faaland, "Long-Term Trends in Europe's Trade," *Economic Journal*, March 1952, pp. 26-7.

[12]J. R. Hicks, "An Inaugural Lecture," *Oxford Economic Papers*, June 1953, p. 130.

[13]G. Haberler, "Dollar Shortage?" in S. E. Harris (ed.), *Foreign Economic Policy for the United States*, Cambridge, Massachusetts, 1948, pp. 438-9.

[14]United States exports as a percentage of gross national product fell from 5.7 per cent in the period 1896-1914 to 2.97 per cent in 1955. See W. Lederer, "Major Developments Affecting the United States Balance of International Payments," *Review of Economics and Statistics*, May 1956, p. 184.

[15]The quantum of crude material imports, as already stated, increased by only 23 per cent. The other commodity groups showed the following percentage increases from 1929 to 1955: crude foodstuffs, 33 per cent; manufactured foodstuffs, 55 per cent; semi-manufactures, 76 per cent; finished manufactures, 52 per cent. Is it not possible, however, that the relatively small rise in imports of crude commodities may be due, not to a low rate of growth of United States demand, but rather to a deficiency on the supply side? The answer is in Professor Schultz's paper, where the strategic role of demand is clearly demonstrated.

plification. Any country in foreign exchange difficulties can normally restore its balance of payments by accepting a worsening in its terms of trade. In Hicks' model external balance is maintained by changes in terms of trade.

But can we not go a step further? There has been a tendency, in Britain and elsewhere, to exaggerate both the actual extent and the economic significance of changes in the terms of trade. We are sometimes apt to think of these changes as if the resources of each country were for ever committed to the existing export industries. This view may be all right for the short run, but in the longer run labour and capital within each country can usually move to other occupations, and do in fact move. If the relationship of export prices to import prices undergoes a marked increase or decline, it is entirely natural that factors of production should tend to move from export industries to import-competing industries or vice versa. This may involve simply changes in the allocation of *increases* in factor supplies rather than movements of existing factors. In any event, the point is that a change in the terms of trade tends to induce shifts in production and in the distribution of resources, which will tend to reverse or counteract the change in the terms of trade. What remains is growth and change in the volume of productive activity induced through international trade. On this view, changes in the terms as well as in the balance of trade are a transient and relatively insignificant element in the mechanism by which processes of economic growth (or decline) may be transmitted from one country to others.

This does not imply that shifts in external demand do not matter. Fortunate indeed is the country with an expanding export market for the commodity in whose production it has a comparative advantage; for it can then draw increasing supplies in limitless variety from the outside world. The suggestion is merely that, because of the possibility of internal factor shifts in response to varying price relationships, long-term trends in external demand conditions need not be reflected fully, if at all, in changes in the terms of trade.

In considering the international mechanism of development it is necessary at any rate to admit the possibility of variation in the conditions of growth transmission through trade. Just as the limited extent to which the United States economy transmits its own growth rate to primary producing countries is fully understandable in the light of its own abundant natural resources combined with its ample capital supplies and technical know-how, so the nineteenth century experience was conditioned by the fact that the industrial revolution happened to originate on a small island with a limited range of resources, at a time when the chemical industry was yet unborn.

As a result, the rate of growth in the import demand of the dominant economy of the twentieth century seems different from that of the nineteenth. If this is so, it is not certain that the less developed countries can rely on economic growth being induced from the outside through an expansion of world demand for their exports of crude materials.[16] In these circumstances reliance on induced expansion through international trade may not be able to provide the main solution to the problem of development. It is not surprising, therefore, that countries should be looking for other types of solution. It will be useful to keep these things in mind, because they form the background to the case for balanced growth which is now so greatly in vogue.

[16]To ask the less developed countries to increase their export quantities of primary products in the face of a price-inelastic and not an upward-shifting demand schedule would be to ask, in effect, for an income transfer from poor to rich countries though a change in the terms of trade in favour of the latter. If one of several countries exporting the same primary commodity were to cut its export costs and prices, its export proceeds could indeed increase, but only at the expense of a fall in the other countries' export proceeds. The balance of payments adjustment process alone (whether through exchange rate variations or domestic price changes) would lead the latter to cut their export prices too, and all will be worse off at the end than they were at the start.

VIII.A.3. Trade as a Mechanism of International Inequality*

Our inherited economic theory would ... lead us to expect that international inequalities should not be so large as they are and not be growing. In any case this theory does not furnish us with an explanation in causal terms of these inequalities and their tendency to increase.

"The fact that many under-developed countries do not derive the advantages from modern transportation and commerce that theory seems to demand is one of the most pertinent facts in the present international situation and cannot be easily dismissed"—I am quoting from a recent paper by a Swedish economist, Mr. Folke Hilgert.[1] ...

Hilgert points out that huge movements of labour and capital from Europe have transformed the plains in the temperate belts into "white man's land" with high, rapid and sustained economic development and rising levels of living. "Yet the gradual filling of the 'empty spaces' has not reduced the pressure of population in, for instance, Asia's overpopulated regions where labour is most abundant."

Let us remember, however, that according to the classical doctrine movements of labour and capital between countries would not be necessary for bringing about a development towards equilisation of factor prices and, consequently, earnings and incomes; in fact, the theory of international trade was largely developed on the abstract assumption of international immobility of all factors of production. That trade itself initiated a tendency towards a gradual equalisation of factor prices was implicit already in the expositions by the classical authors, though their method

of stating the law of comparative costs in terms of only a single factor, labour—which, however, could have different "qualities" or degrees of "effectiveness"—turned the emphasis in other directions.

After Eli F. Heckscher's paper on the equalising influence of trade on factor prices and Bertil Ohlin's restatement of the classical theory of international trade in terms of a general equilibrium theory of the Lausanne school type,[2] trade appeared more clearly as a substitute, or an alternative, to factor movements in permitting an adjustment of industrial activity to adapt itself to the localisation of natural and population resources with the result that the relative scarcity of labour and capital became less different. Upon this foundation there has in recent years been a lively discussion between the econometricians elaborating, under specific, abstract and static, conditions, the relative effectiveness of this tendency to equalisation of factor prices as a result of international trade.[3]

The inadequacy of such theories for explaining reality cannot be accounted for by pointing to the relative breakdown of the multilateral trading system as it functioned prior to the First World War, a change which is related as both effect and cause to the increase of national trade and payments restrictions. For, as Hilgert observes, a similar confrontation of the facts of international inequality with the theory of international

*From Gunnar Myrdal, *Development and Underdevelopment*, National Bank of Egypt Fiftieth Anniversary Commemoration Lectures, Cairo, 1956, pp. 9–10, 47–51. Reprinted by permission.

[1]"Uses and Limitations of International Trade in Overcoming Inequalities in World Distribution of Population and Resources," *World Population Conference*, Rome, 1954.

[2]Eli F. Heckscher, "The Effect of Foreign Trade on the Distribution of Income," *Readings in the Theory of International Trade*, selected by a committee of the American Economic Association, Allen & Unwin, London, 1950 (translation from the Swedish original 1919); Bertil Ohlin, *Interregional and International Trade*, Harvard University Press, Cambridge, Mass., 1933.

[3]The recent discussion of the problem of factor price equalisation as a result of international trade was initiated by Professor Paul A. Samuelson in two articles in the *Economic Journal*, 1948 and 1949; for fuller reference see Svend Laursen, "Production Functions and the Theory of International Trade," *American Economic Review*, 1955, pp. 540 ff.

trade for the period before 1914 reveals the same discord. And I would add that it is not self-evident but, indeed, very much up to doubt whether today a freer trade would necessarily lead to less of international inequality or whether in general trade between developed and (densely populated) under-developed countries has ever had that effect. . . .

Contrary to what the equilibrium theory of international trade would seem to suggest, the play of the market forces does not work towards equality in the renumerations to factors of production and, consequently, in incomes. If left to take its own course, economic development is a process of circular and cumulative causation which tends to award its favours to those who are already well endowed and even to thwart the efforts of those who happen to live in regions that are lagging behind. The backsetting effects of economic expansion in other regions dominate the more powerfully, the poorer a country is.

Within the national boundaries of the richer countries an integration process has taken place: on a higher level of economic development expansionary momentum tends to spread more effectively to other localities and regions than those where starts happen to have been made and successfully sustained; and inequality has there also been mitigated through interferences in the play of the market forces by organised society. In a few highly advanced countries—comprising only about one-sixth of the population in the non-Soviet world—this national integration process is now being carried forward towards a very high level of equality of opportunity to all, wherever, and in whatever circumstances they happen to be born. These countries are approaching a national harmony of interest which, because of the role played by state policies, has to be characterized as a "created harmony"; and this has increasingly sustained also their further economic development.

Outside this small group of highly developed and progressive countries, all other countries are in various degrees poorer and mostly also less progressive economically. In a rather close correlation to their poverty they are ridden by internal economic inequalities, which also tend to weaken the effectiveness of their democratic systems of government in the cases where they are not under one form or another of oligarchic or forthright dictatorial rule.

The relations between relative lack of national economic integration and relative economic backwardness run, according to my hypothesis of circular cumulative causation, both ways. With a low level of economic development follow low levels of social mobility, communications, popular education and national sharing in beliefs and valuations, which imply greater impediments to the spread effects of expansionary momentum; at the same time the poorer states have for much the same reasons and because of the very fact of existing internal inequalities often been less democratic and, in any case, they have, because they are poorer, been up against narrower financial and, at bottom, psychological limitations on policies seeking to equalise opportunities. Inequality of opportunities has, on the other hand, contributed to preserving a low "quality" of their factors of production and a low "effectiveness" in their production efforts, to use the classical terms, and this has hampered their economic development.

On the international as on the national level trade does not by itself necessarily work for equality. A widening of markets strengthens often on the first hand the progressive countries whose manufacturing industries have the lead and are already fortified in surroundings of external economies, while the under-developed countries are in continuous danger of seeing even what they have of industry and, in particular, their small scale industry and handicrafts outcompeted by cheap imports from the industrial countries, if they do not protect them.

It is easy to observe how in most underdeveloped countries the trading contacts with the outside world have actually impoverished them culturally. Skills in many crafts inherited from centuries back have been lost. A city like Baghdad, with whose name such glorious associations are connected, today does not harbour any of the old crafts, except some silver smithies, and they have adopted patterns from abroad requiring less craftsmanship; similarly it is only with the greatest difficulties that one can buy a book of Arabic literature, while cheap magazines in English or Arabic are in abundance.

If international trade did not stimulate manufacturing industry in the under-developed countries but instead robbed them of what they had of old-established crafts, it did promote the production of primary products, and such production, employing mostly unskilled labour, came to constitute the basis for the bulk of their exports. In these lines, however, they often meet inelastic demands in the export market, often also a demand trend which is not rising very rapidly, and excessive price fluctuations. When, furthermore, population is rapidly rising while the larger part of it lives at, or near, the subsistence level—which means that there is no scarcity of common labour—any technological improvement in their export production tends to confer the advantages from the cheapening of production to the importing countries. Because of inelastic demands the result will often not even be a very great enlargement of the markets and of production and employment. In any case the wages and the export returns per unit of product will tend to remain low as the supply of unskilled labour is almost unlimited.

The advice—and assistance—which the poor countries receive from the rich is even nowadays often directed towards increasing their production of primary goods for export. The advice is certainly given in good faith and it may even be rational from the short term point of view of each under-developed country seen in isolation. Under a broader perspective and from a long term point of view, what would be rational is above all to increase productivity, incomes and living standards in the larger agricultural subsistence sectors, so as to raise the supply price of labour, and in manufacturing industry. This would engender economic development and raise incomes *per capita*. But trade by itself does not lead to such a development; it rather tends to have backsetting effects and to strengthen the forces maintaining stagnation or regression. Economic development has to be brought about by policy interferences which, however, are not under our purview at this stage of the argument when we are analysing only the effects of the play of the market forces.

Neither can the capital movements be relied upon to counteract international inequalities between the countries which are here in question. Under the circumstances described, capital will, on the whole, shun the under-developed countries, particularly as the advanced countries themselves are rapidly developing further and can offer their owners of capital both good profits and security.

There has, in fact, never been much of a capital movement to the countries which today we call under-developed, even in earlier times—except tiny streams to the economic enclaves, mainly devoted to export production of primary products which, however, usually were so profitable to their owners that they rapidly became self-supporting so far as investment capital was concerned and, in addition, the considerably larger but still relatively small investments in railways and other public utilities which had their security in the political controls held by colonial governments. The bulk of European overseas capital exports went to the settlements in the free spaces in the temperate zones which were becoming populated by emigration from Europe. After the collapse of the international capital market in the early 'thirties, which has not been remedied, and later the breakdown of the colonial system, which had given security to the foreign investor, it would be almost against nature if capital in large quantities were voluntarily to seek its way to under-developed countries in order to play a role in their economic development.

True, capital in these countries is scarce. But the need for it does not represent an effective demand in the capital market. Rather, if there were no exchange controls and if, at the same time, there were no elements in their national development policies securing high profits for capital—i.e. if the forces in the capital market were given unhampered play—capitalists in under-developed countries would be exporting their capital. Even with such controls and policies in existence, there is actually a steady capital flight going on from under-developed countries, which in a realistic analysis should be counted against what there is of capital inflow to these countries.

Labour migration, finally, can safely be counted out as a factor of importance for international economic adjustment as between under-developed and developed countries. The population pressure in most under-developed countries implies, of course, that they do not need immigration and the consequent low wages that immigrants are not tempted to come. Emigration from these countries would instead be the natural thing. For various reasons emigration could, however, not be much of a real aid to economic development, even if it were possible.

And the whole world is since the First World War gradually settling down to a situation where immigrants are not welcomed almost anywhere from wherever they come; people have pretty well to stay in the country where they are born, except for touristing by those who can afford it. And so far as the larger part of the under-developed world is concerned, where people are "coloured" according to the definition in the advanced countries, emigration is usually stopped altogether by the colour bar as defined by the legislation, or in the administration, of the countries which are white-dominated and at the same time better off economically.

If left unregulated, international trade and capital movements would thus often be the media through which the economic progress in the advanced countries would have backsetting effects in the under-developed world, and their mode of operation would be very much the same as it is in the circular cumulation of causes in the development process within a single country.... Internationally, these effects will, however, dominate the outcome much more, as the countervailing spread effects of expansionary momentum are so very much weaker. Differences in legislation, administration and *mores* generally, in language, in basic valuations and beliefs, in levels of living, production capacities and facilities, etcetera make the national boundaries effective barriers to the spread to a degree which no demarcation lines within one country approach.

Even more important as impediments to the spread effects of expansionary momentum from abroad than the boundaries and everything they stand for is, however, the very fact of great poverty and weak spread effects within the under-developed countries themselves. Where, for instance, international trade and shipping actually do transform the immediate surroundings of a port to a centre of economic expansion, which happens almost everywhere in the world, the expansionary momentum usually does not spread out to other regions of the country, which tend to remain backward if the forces in the markets are left free to take their course. Basically, the weak spread effects as between countries are thus for the larger part only a reflection of the weak spread effects within the under-developed countries themselves.

Under these circumstances the forces in the markets will in a cumulative way tend to cause ever greater international inequalities between countries as to their level of economic development and average national income *per capita*.

Comment

Some assessments of colonialism and neocolonialism are also relevant in considering the argument that international trade has operated as a mechanism of international inequality. Many writers have traced forces of dependency through history, and the legacy of imperialism is often referred to in explaining underdevelopment.

Studies that emphasize features of imperialism or "exploitation" are: R. Rhodes (ed.), *Imperialism and Underdevelopment* (1970); H. Magdoff, *The Age of Imperialism* (1969); K. Boulding and T. Mukerjee (eds.), *Economic Imperialism* (1972); P. A. Baran, *The Political*

Economy of Growth (1962), chapters 6–8; K. T. Fann and D. C. Hodges (eds.), *Readings in U.S. Imperialism* (1971); Walter Rodney, *How Europe Underdeveloped Africa* (1972); D. S. Landes, "Some Thoughts on the Nature of Economic Imperialism," *Journal of Economic History* (December 1961); A. Emmanuel, *Unequal Exchange* (1972); S. Hymer and S. Resnick, "International Trade and Uneven Development," in J. Bhagwati (ed.), *Trade, Balance of Payments, and Growth* (1971); B. J. Cohen, *The Question of Imperialism* (1973); R. J. Owen and R. B. Sutcliffe (eds.), *Studies in the Theory of Imperialism* (1972); D. K. Fieldhouse (ed.), *The Theory of Capitalist Imperialism* (1967); Johan Galtung, "A Structural Theory of Imperialism," *Journal of Peace Research* (1971); B. Warren, *Imperialism: Pioneer of Capitalism* (1980). An extensive bibliographic essay is presented by Gavin Williams, "Imperialism and Development: A Critique," *World Development* (July–August 1978).

The literature on dependency, as listed in Chapter II above, is also relevant.

Comment

During the 1950s and 1960s, the United Nation's Economic Commission for Latin America (ECLA) was influential in formulating ideas on development that contradicted orthodox, neoclassical thought. In doing so, ECLA was in many respects a precursor of the dependencia school and also the North-South dialogue.

The main ECLA document is entitled *The Economic Development of Latin America and Its Principal Problems* (1950). ECLA publications offer a critique of the neoclassical theory of international trade and emphasize the tendency for international trade to reproduce the inequality among nations through relations between the center and periphery. Special emphasis is given to the consequences of differential technical progress and the worsening of the periphery's terms of trade. In development programming, ECLA's early objectives were industrialization of the periphery, "healthy protectionism," programming of import substitution, foreign currency allocation policies, and the avoidance of a reduction in real wages.

See Fernando Henrique Cardoso, "The Originality of the Copy: The Economic Commission for Latin America and the Idea of Development," in *Toward a New Strategy for Development*, A Rothko Chapel Colloquium (1979), chapter 2.

Comment

The terms of trade issue remains very much alive—despite the many critical questions raised about the empirical evidence, its welfare significance, and policy implications. The Singer-Prebisch thesis on the alleged tendency for the long-term movement of terms of trade to be against developing countries is still prominent in discussions of the distribution of gains from trade, and its implications for "distributive justice" carry over to demands for a New International Economic Order. For an account of the emergence of this thesis, see Joseph Love, "Raúl Prebisch and the Origins of the Doctrine of Unequal Exchange," *Latin American Research Review* (November 1980).

The empirical evidence has recently been reviewed more closely by John Spraos, "The Statistical Debate on the Net Barter Terms of Trade between Primary Commodities and Manufactures," *Economic Journal* (March 1980); Michael Michaely, "The Terms of Trade between Poor and Rich Nations," *Institute for International Economic Studies,* University of Stockholm, Seminar Paper No. 162 (November 1980); Irving B. Kravis and Robert E. Lipsey, "Prices and Terms of Trade for Developed-Country Exports of Manufactured Goods," *National Bureau of Economic Research Working Paper* No. 774 (September 1981).

The theory of "unequal exchange," as presented recently in A. Emmanuel's *Unequal Exchange: A Study of the Imperialism of Trade* (1972), stems from Marxist theory and contends that there is a transfer of reinvestible surplus (surplus value) from the low-wage developing country to the high-wage industrial country via the terms of trade. Trade is believed to be unequal to the "South" because their terms of trade are lower than they would be under a

Pareto efficient trade arrangement, which would allow perfect international labor mobility. This argument relates to the absolute level of the terms of trade rather than to secular deterioration or cyclical fluctuations. For a discussion of Emmanuel's analysis, see Edmar L. Bacha, "An Interpretation of Unequal Exchange from Prebisch-Singer to Emmanuel," *Journal of Development Economics* (December 1978); David Evans, "Unequal Exchange and Economic Policies," *Economic and Political Weekly* (February 1976). Another Marxist analysis of unequal exchange is offered by Samir Amin in three works: *Accumulation on a World Scale* (1974), *Unequal Development* (1976), and *Imperialism and Unequal Development* (1977).

The influence of a developing country's agricultural productivity on its terms of trade should be emphasized. Sir Arthur Lewis has argued that so long as the bulk of tropical peoples are food farmers with relatively low productivity, their tropical export products are available to the rest of the world on an essentially low-wage basis. Since farmers can grow cash crops for export or foods, the prices of these two must tend to move together. The newer trade in light manufactures from the tropics is essentially of the same kind; it is an additional opportunity to sell low-wage labor. The low factoral terms of trade derive from the low productivity of the bulk of tropical producers—the food farmers. If the terms of trade are to improve, it is necessary to raise the productivity of food farmers who constitute the source of wage labor into the export sector. See selection VI.C.3 and W. A. Lewis, *The Evolution of the International Economic Order* (1978).

Lewis also concludes that

It is easy to exaggerate the potential contribution of foreign trade to development. To take an extreme example, India's exports are only 5 per cent of her national income. If as a result of a new international economic order India were paid five times as much for exports (without an increase in prices of imports) her national income would be raised only by 20 per cent in the first instance, say from $100 to $120 per head. The basic cause of India's poverty is not her terms of trade but the fact that an Indian farmer produces only one-eleventh as much food as an American farmer. Other countries depend on foreign trade to a greater extent than India, and would benefit more directly from better terms of trade. One must also take into account the indirect effects. But the main points remain: the poverty of the tropical countries is due mainly to their low productivity and only secondarily to their terms of trade. Their productivity is not low because their terms of trade are poor; their terms of trade are poor because their agricultural productivity is low (*Growth and Fluctuations 1870-1913*, 1978, p. 244).

VIII.A.4. Conditions of Export-Led Development—Note

The foregoing materials raise a central question: Under what conditions can a process of export-induced development follow upon an expansion of the export sector? How can export expansion also act as an engine of domestic development? Notwithstanding the possibility of lagging exports in more recent decades, most of the underdeveloped countries have experienced long periods of export growth. In most cases, after a country was exposed to the world economy, its exports grew markedly in volume and in variety. Yet, despite their secular rise, exports in many countries have not acted as a key propulsive sector, propelling the rest of the economy forward. Although the classical belief that development can be transmitted through trade has been confirmed by the experience of some countries that are now among the richest in the world, trade has not had a similar stimulating effect for countries that have remained underdeveloped. Why has not the growth in exports in these countries carried over to other sectors and led to more widespread development in the domestic economy?

As noted above, some critics of the classical position contend that the very forces of international trade have been responsible for inhibiting development. They argue that the development of the export sector by foreign capital has created a "dual economy" in which production has been export-biased, and the resultant pattern of resource utilization has deterred development. This argument, however, tends to contrast the pattern of resource utliization that actually occurred with some other ideal pattern. More relevant is a comparison between the actual pattern and the allocation that would have occurred in the absence of the capital inflow. There is little foundation to the assertion that if there had been no foreign investment, a poor country would have generated more domestic investment; or that, in the absence of foreign entrepreneurs, the supply of domestic entrepreneurs would have been larger. Contrary to what is often implied by the critics of foreign investment, the real choice was not between employing the resources in the export sector or in domestic production, but rather between giving employment to the surplus resources in export production or leaving them idle.[1] It is difficult to substantiate the argument that foreign investment was competitive with home investment, or that the utilization of resources in the export sector was at the expense of home production.

Another contention is that trade has impeded development by the "demonstration effect": the international demonstration of higher consumption standards in more developed countries has allegedly raised the propensity to consume in the less developed countries and reduced attainable saving rates. By stimulating the desire to consume, however, the international demonstration effect may also have operated on incentives and been instrumental in increasing the supply of effort and productive services—especially as between the subsistence sector and the exchange economy.[2] This positive effect on the side of factor supply may have more than offset any negative effect on saving.

More serious is the argument that international market forces have transferred income from the poor to rich nations through a deterioration in the terms of trade of the less developed countries. The significance of this argument is also overdrawn, and it can be questioned on both theoretical and empirical grounds. The alleged trend is not based on the measurement of prices within the poor countries, but rather on inferences from the United Kingdom's commodity terms of trade or the terms of trade between primary products and manufactured products.[3] This does not provide a sufficiently strong statistical foundation for any adequate generalization about the terms of trade of poor countries.[4] The import-price index conceals the heterogeneous price movements within and among the broad categories of foodstuffs, raw materials, and minerals; no allowance is made for changes in the quality of exports and imports; there is inadequate consideration of new commodities; and the recorded terms of

---

[1]Cf. Hla Myint, "The Gains from International Trade and the Backward Countries," *Review of Economic Studies,* Vol. 22, No. 58, 1954–55; "The 'Classical Theory' of International Trade and the Underdeveloped Countries," *Economic Journal,* June 1958, pp. 317–37.

[2]For an instructive analysis of the general process by which the money economy has developed through expansion of export production induced by the growth of new wants for imported consumers' goods, see Hla Myint, *The Economics of Developing Countries,* London, 1964, Chapters 1–5.

[3]United Nations, Department of Economic Affairs, *Relative Prices of Exports and Imports of Under-Developed Countries,* New York, 1949, pp. 7, 13–24; W. A. Lewis, "World Production, Prices, and Trade, 1870–1960," *Manchester School,* May 1952, p. 118.

[4]For detailed criticisms, see R. E. Baldwin, "Secular Movements in the Terms of Trade," *American Economic Review, Papers and Proceedings,* May 1955, pp. 267ff.; P. T. Ellsworth, "The Terms of Trade Between Primary Producing and Industrial Countries," *Inter-American Economic Affairs,* Summer 1956, pp. 47–65; T. Morgan, "The Long-Run Terms of Trade Between Agriculture and Manufacturing," *Economic Development and Cultural Change,* October 1959, pp. 6–17; Gottfried Haberler, "Terms of Trade and Economic Development," in H. S. Ellis (ed.), *Economic Development for Latin America,* New York, 1961, pp. 275–97; Jagdish Bhagwati, "A Skeptical Note on the Adverse Secular Trend in the Terms of Trade of Underdeveloped Countries," *Pakistan Economic Journal,* December 1960; G. M. Meier, *International Economics of Development,* New York, 1968, Chapter 3.

trade are not corrected for the substantial decline in transportation costs. The introduction of new products and qualitative improvements have been greater in manufactured than in primary products, and a large proportion of the fall in British prices of primary products can be attributed to the great decline in inward freight rates. The simple use of the "inverse" of the United Kingdom's terms of trade to indicate the terms of trade of primary producing countries involves therefore a systematic bias which makes changes appear more unfavorable to the primary exporting countries than they actually were.

Even if it were true that the less developed countries experienced a secular deterioration in their commodity terms of trade, the question would still remain whether this constituted a significant obstacle to their development. The answer depends on what caused the deterioration and whether the country's factoral terms of trade and income terms also deteriorated. If the deterioration in the commodity terms is due to increased productivity in the export sector, the single-factoral terms of trade (commodity terms corrected for changes in productivity in producing exports) can improve at the same time. As long as productivity in its export industries is increasing more rapidly than export prices are falling, the country's real income can rise despite the deterioration in the commodity terms of trade: when its factoral terms improve, the country benefits from the ability to obtain a greater quantity of imports per unit of factors embodied in its exports. Also possible is an improvement in the country's income terms of trade (commodity terms multiplied by quantity of exports) at the same time as its commodity terms deteriorate. The country's capacity to import is then greater, and this will ease development efforts. When due weight is given to the increase in productivity in export production and the rise in export volume, it would appear that the single-factoral terms and income terms of trade actually improved for many poor countries, notwithstanding any possible deterioration in their commodity terms of trade.

Having rejected the view that international

trade operated as a mechanism of international inequality, we must look to other factors for an understanding of why trade has not had a more stimulating effect in underdeveloped countries. If the export sector is to be a propelling force in development, it is essential that the export sector not remain an enclave, separate from the rest of the economy; instead, an integrated process should be established, diffusing stimuli from the export sector and creating responses elsewhere in the economy. A more convincing explanation of why export-led development has occurred in some countries, but not in others, would therefore distinguish the differential effects of the integrative process by focusing on the varying strength of the stimuli in different countries from their exports and on the different response mechanisms within the exporting countries.[5]

Different export commodities will provide different stimuli, according to the technological characteristics of their production. The nature of the export good's production function has an influence on the extent of other secondary changes elsewhere in the economy, beyond the primary increase in export output.[6] With the use of different input coeffi-

[5]The following paragraphs draw upon G. M. Meier, "External Trade and Internal Development," in Peter Duignan and L. H. Gann (eds.), *Colonialism in Africa 1870–1960*, Vol. 4, *The Economics of Colonialism*, New York, 1975, Chapter 11.

[6]Although more empirical research is needed, some illustrative cases are suggested by D. C. North, "Location Theory and Regional Economic Growth," *Journal of Political Economy*, June 1955, pp. 249–51; Dudley Seers, "An Approach to the Short-Period Analysis of Primary-Producing Economies," *Oxford Economic Papers*, February 1959, pp. 6–9; R. E. Caves and R. H. Holton, *The Canadian Economy*, Cambridge, 1959, pp. 41–7; J. V. Levin, *The Export Economies*, Cambridge, 1960; R. E. Baldwin, "Export Technology and Development from a Subsistence Level," *Economic Journal*, March 1963, pp. 80–92; M. H. Watkins, "A Staple Theory of Economic Growth," *Canadian Journal of Economics and Political Science*, May 1963, pp. 141–58; V. D. Wickizer, "The Plantation System in the Development of Tropical Economics," *Journal of Farm Economics*, February 1958, pp. 63–77; Dudley Seers, "The Mechanism of an Open Petroleum Economy," *Social and Economic Studies*, June 1964, pp. 233–42; M. J. Herskovitz and M. Horwitz, *Economic Transition in Africa*, Evanston, 1964, pp. 312–18.

cients to produce different types of export commodities, there will be different rates of learning and different linkage effects. The degree to which the various exports are processed is highly significant in the determination of external economies associated with the learning process; the processing of primary-product exports by modern methods is likely to benefit other activities through the spread of technical knowledge, training of labor, demonstration of new production techniques that might be adapted elsewhere in the economy, and the acquisition of organizational and supervisory skills.

In contrast, growth of the export sector will have a negligible carry-over if its techniques of production are the same as those already in use in other sectors, or if its expansion occurs by a simple widening of production without any change in production functions. If the introduction or expansion of export crops involves simple methods of production that do not differ markedly from the traditional techniques already used in subsistence agriculture, the stimulus to development will clearly be less than if the growth in exports entailed the introduction of new skills and more productive recombinations of factors of production. More favorable linkages may stem from exports that require skilled labor than from those using unskilled labor. The influence of skill requirements may operate in various ways: greater incentives for capital formation may be provided through education; on-the-job training in the export sector may be disseminated at little real cost through the movement of workers into other sectors or occupations; skilled workers may be a source of entrepreneurship; skilled workers may save more of their wage incomes than unskilled workers.[7] The level of entrepreneurial skill induced by the development of an export is also highly significant. The level will be expanded if the development of the export commodity offers significant challenge and instills abilities usable in other sectors, but is not so high as to require the importing of a transient class of skilled managerial labor.

Although the processing of a primary product provides forward linkages in the sense that the output of one sector becomes an input for another sector, it is also important to have backward linkages. When some exports grow, they provide a strong stimulus for expansion in the input-supplying industries elsewhere in the economy. These backward linkages may be in agriculture or in other industries supplying inputs to the expanding export sector, or in social overhead capital. The importance of linkages has been stressed by Hirschman.[8]

The notion is emphasized also by Perroux, who refers to a developing enterprise as a "motor unit" when it increases its demands on its suppliers for raw materials or communicates new techniques to another enterprise. The "induction effect" that the motor unit exerts upon another unit may be considered in two components that frequently occur in combination: (1) a dimension effect that is the augmentation of demand by one enterprise to another by increasing its supply; and (2) an innovation effect that introduces an innovation which for a given quantity of factors of production yields the same quantity of production at a lower price and/or a better quality. When a motor unit is interlinked with its surrounding environment, Perroux refers to a growth pole or a development pole.[9] The emphasis on generating new skills, innovations in the export sector or other sectors linked to exports, and technical change are important in determining the learning rate of the economy.

Beyond this, the nature of the production function of the export commodity will also

[7]Richard E. Caves, "Export-led growth and the new economic history," in *Trade, Balance of Payments and Growth*, J. N. Bhagwati et al. (eds.), Amsterdam, 1971, pp. 403–42.

[8]Albert O. Hirschman, *The Strategy of Economic Development*, New Haven, 1958, Chap. 9.

[9]Francois Perroux, "Multinational Investment and the Analysis of Development and Integration Poles," in *Multinational Investment in the Economic Development and Integration of Latin America*, Bogotá, Inter-American Development Bank, April 1968, pp. 99–103.

determine the distribution of income, and, in turn, the pattern of local demand and impact on local employment. The use of different factor combinations affects the distribution of income in the sense that the relative shares of profits, wages, interest, and rent will vary according to the labor intensity or capital intensity of the export production and the nature of its organization—whether it is mining, plantation agriculture, or peasant farming. If the internal distribution of the export income favors groups with a higher propensity to consume domestic goods than to import, the resultant distribution of income will be more effective in raising the demand for home-produced products; and to the extent that these home-produced products are labor-intensive, there will be more of an impact on employment. In contrast, if income is distributed to those who have a higher propensity to import, the leakage through consumption of imported goods will be greater. If income increments go to those who are likely to save large portions, the export sector may also make a greater contribution to the financing of growth in other sectors.

If the export commodity is subject to substantial economies of scale in its production, this will tend to imply large capital requirements for the establishment of enterprises, and hence extra-regional or foreign borrowing. This may then lead to an outward flow of profits instead of providing profit income for local reinvestment. But this is only part of the impact of the foreign investment. For a full appraisal, it would be necessary to consider all the benefits and costs of the foreign investment. And these too will vary according to the nature of the export sector in which the foreign investment occurs.

Finally, the repercussions from exports will also differ according to the degree of fluctuation in export proceeds. Disruptions in the flow of foreign exchange receipts make the development process discontinuous; the greater the degree of instability, the more difficult it is to maintain steady employment, because there will be disturbing effects on real income, government revenue, capital formation, resource allocation, and the capacity to import according to the degree of amplitude of fluctuation in foreign exchange receipts. To the extent that different exports vary in their degree of fluctuation, and in revenue earned and retained at home, their repercussions on the domestic economy will also differ. Depending on the various characteristics of the country's export, we may thus infer how the strength of the integrative process, in terms of the stimulus from exports, will differ among countries.

In summary, we would normally expect the stimulating forces of the integrative process to be stronger under the following conditions: the higher the growth-rate of the export sector, the greater the direct impact of the export sector on employment and personal income, the more the expansion of exports has a "learning effect" in terms of increasing productivity and instilling new skills, the more the export sector is supplied through domestic inputs instead of imports, the more the distribution of export income favors those with a marginal propensity to consume domestic goods instead of imports, the more productive is the investment resulting from any saving of export income, the more extensive are the externalities and linkages connected with the export sector, and the more stable are the export receipts that are retained at home. Some exports fulfill these conditions more readily than others, and countries specializing on these exports will enjoy greater opportunities for development.

Even with a strong stimulus from exports, however, the transmission of growth from the export-base to the rest of the economy will still be contingent upon other conditions in the economy. The weak penetrative power of exports in underdeveloped countries can be explained not only by a possibly weak stimulus from a particular type of export, but also by the host of domestic impediments that limit the transmission of the gains from exports to other sectors even when the stimulus may be strong.

After analyzing the character of a country's export base for an indication of the strength of the stimulus to development provided by its export commodities, we must go on to examine the strength of the response or diffusion mechanism within the domestic economy for evidence of how receptive the domestic economy is to the stimulus from exports. The strength of the integrative process, in terms of the response mechanism to the export stimulus, will depend on the extent of market imperfections in the domestic economy and also on noneconomic barriers in the general environment. The integrative forces are stronger under the following conditions: the more developed the infrastructure of the economy, the more market institutions are developed, the more extensive the development of human resources, the less are the price distortions that affect resource allocations, and the greater is the capacity to bear risks. Our view of the carry-over should stress not only the mechanical linkages but also a more evolutionary (and hence biological rather than mechanical) analogy that recognizes societal responses. What matters is not simply the creation of modern enterprise or modern sectors but modernization as a process. This involves not simply physical production or mechanical linkages but a change in socioeconomic traits throughout the society, and an intangible atmosphere that relates to changes in values, in character, in attitudes, in the learning of new behavior patterns, and in institutions.

In sum, the effects of a strong integrative process will be the following: (1) an acceleration in the learning rate of the economy; (2) an enrichment of the economic and social infrastructure (transportation, public services, health, education); (3) an expansion of the supply of entrepreneurship (and a managerial and administrative class); and (4) a mobilization of a larger surplus above consumption in the form of taxation and saving. These effects constitute the country's development foundations. Once these foundations are laid, the country's economy can be more readily transformed through diversification in primary production and the service industries, new commodity exports, and industrialization via import substitution and export substitution.

It follows that if a more extensive carry-over from exports is to be achieved, it is necessary to remove the domestic impediments that cut short the stimulus from exports. Many of the policy recommendations in this book refer to the need for reducing the fragmentation and compartmentalization of the economy by overcoming the narrow and isolated markets, ignorance of technological possibilities, limited infrastructure, and slow rate of human-resource development. To accomplish this, alternative forms of economic and social organization are required, and policy measures must aim at diminishing the prevalence of semimonopolistic and monopolistic practices, removing restraints on land tenure and land use, widening and expanding financial markets, promoting market facilities and increasing investment in economic and social infrastructure, and in promoting human-resource development.

It also follows that the stimulus from the export-base should be as strong as possible. While domestic limitations and impediments may have accounted for the weak carry-over of exports in the past when export markets were expanding, it may be contended (as Nurkse does, VIII.A.2) that exports no longer enjoy a strongly rising world demand and do not now provide a sufficient stimulus for development in the first instance. If exports are confined to a slow rate of growth, then there can be little scope for development through trade even if the domestic obstacles are removed. To counter this "export pessimism," it is all the more necessary for underdeveloped countries to raise productivity in agriculture in order to ensure that their primary exports are competitive on world markets, and to prevent home consumption from causing a limitation of their export supplies. Further, it is important that the less developed countries pursue policies that will ensure that they specialize as much as they can in exports with the highest growth prospects. To do this, a country must have the capacity to reallocate resources—to shift, for instance, from exporting a foodstuff which may have only a slowly growing demand, to the export of an industrial raw material or a mineral for which the demand may be rising more rapidly. Of special significance is the country's potential for taking advantage of new export opportunities in manufactured goods. The exportation of manufactured commodities may play a strategic role in transmitting development to some poor countries that have a favorable factor endowment and can gain a comparative advantage by utilizing labor-intensive methods. In selection VIII.B.4, we shall consider more fully the issue of export stimulation, giving particular attention to the opportunity for exporting manufactures. Efforts at regional integration may also promote trade in manufactures among the developing nations themselves, as will be discussed in section VIII.D below.

Export prospects may also be improved by a more liberal importation policy on the part of advanced countries. A removal of trade restrictions is beneficial not only for the more traditional primary exports, but also for encouraging new manufactured exports. The export market for primary products might also be expanded if industrialized nations avoided artificial supports for the substitution of primary products by synthetic materials. And along with the liberalization of trade, it is vitally important that the LDCs should be able to look forward to the maintenance of high rates of growth in the advanced countries to which they export.

Finally, advanced countries can contribute by supporting policies to stablize export proceeds. High and stable levels of employment in industrial nations will help reduce the short-term fluctuations in export proceeds; but in addition, national and international measures might be advocated to achieve greater short-run stability in international commodity markets.

Comment

The following readings offer various interpretations of the potentials and limitations of development through trade: R. E. Baldwin, "Patterns of Development in Newly Settled Regions," *Manchester School* (May 1956); R. E. Baldwin, "Export Technology and Development from a Subsistence Level," *Economic Journal* (March 1963); K. Berrill, "International Trade and the Rate of Economic Growth," *Economic History Review* (April 1960); J. Bhagwati, "Immiserizing Growth: A Geometrical Note," *Review of Economic Studies* (June 1958); J. Bhagwati, "Growth, Terms of Trade, and Comparative Advantage," *Economia Internazionale* (August 1959); J. Bhagwati, *Foreign Trade Regimes and Economic Development* (1978); H. B. Chenery, "Comparative Advantage and Development Policy," *American Economic Review* (March 1961); G. Haberler, *International Trade and Economic Development* (1959); J. R. Hicks, *Essays in World Economics* (1959), chapter 8; H. G. Johnson, *International Trade and Economic Growth* (1958), chapter 3; D. Keesing, "Outward-Looking Policies and Economic Development," *Economic Journal* (June 1967); Hla Myint, "The Gains from International Trade and the Backward Countries," *Review of Economic Studies*, Vol. 22, No. 58 (1954–55); Hla Myint, "The 'Classical Theory' of International Trade and the Underdeveloped Countries," *Economic Journal* (June 1958); Hla Myint, *Economics of the Developing Countries*, London (1964), chapters 2–5; Hla Myint, "Inward and Outward-Looking Countries of Southeast Asia," *Malayan Economic Review* (April 1967); R. Nurkse, "Some International Aspects of the Problem of Economic Development," *American Economic Review* (May 1952); R. Nurkse, *Patterns of Trade and Development* (1956); H. W. Singer, "The Distribution of Gains Between Investing and Borrowing Countries," *American Economic Review* (May 1950); W. A. Lewis, *Aspects of Tropical Trade 1883–1965* (1969); H. W. Singer, *The Evolution of the International Economic Order* (1978); I. Kravis, "Trade as a Handmaiden of Growth," *Economic Journal* (December 1970); Anne O. Krueger, *Foreign Trade Regimes and Economic Development: Liberalization Attempts and Consequences* (1978).

VIII.B. INWARD- VERSUS OUTWARD-ORIENTED DEVELOPMENT STRATEGIES

VIII.B.1. Trade Policy as an Input to Development*

My topic is the question: what difference does the set of commercial policies chosen by a developing country make to its rate of economic growth? Three points are salient. First, in its present state, trade theory provides little guidance as to the role of trade policy and trade strategy in promoting growth. Second, the empirical evidence overwhelmingly indicates that there are important links between them. Third, a number of hypotheses as to the reasons for these links have been put forward, but there is not as yet sufficient evidence to enable us to estimate their relative importance.

Turning first to theory, there are many static propositions but few useful theorems about the effects of alternative trade policies on growth. Clearly there are gains to be achieved through trade in the development process. Even the trade and growth models along Corden-Johnson lines are based upon differential rates of change in capital-labor ratios in two-country, two-commodity worlds under assumptions of free trade. They provide little indication of the quantitative importance of trade as a contributor to growth, and still less insight into the probable orders of magnitude of the losses in attainable growth rates that may be incurred with departures from free trade.

To be sure, once the assumption that there are only two goods is abandoned, theory suggests that activity in production of tradables should be undertaken to the point where the international marginal rate of transformation $(IMRT)$ equals the domestic marginal rate of transformation $(DMRT)$, with no production

*From Anne O. Krueger, "Trade Policy as an Input to Development," *American Economic Review, Papers and Proceedings,* May 1980, pp. 288–92. Reprinted by permission.

in lines where domestic opportunity cost exceeds the international price ratio. An allocation of resources satisfying this criterion would be optimal in the absence of any dynamic considerations.

Theory does not, however, indicate how many activities are likely to be undertaken. Nor does it suggest the relative importance of exporting and import-competing activities in an optimum allocation, or how that allocation would change with growth. Worse yet, there is nothing in theory to indicate why a deviation from the optimum should affect the rate of economic growth. Most growth models suggest that there are once-and-for-all losses arising from nonoptimal policies with lower levels of income resulting from them but no change in growth rates.

Turning from theory to practice, developing countries' trade policies have fallen into two distinct categories. One group of developing countries has adopted trade policies which diverge from the optimality criterion, often by a large amount, by protecting their domestic industries. These "import substitution" policies have been employed to stimulate domestic production on the theory that nonagricultural sectors must grow at a rate above the rate of growth of domestic demand, and can do so only insofar as additional production substitutes for imports. The other category, "export promotion," has consisted of encouragement to exports, usually beyond the extent that would conform to the $IMRT = DMRT$ criterion. Countries adopting an export-oriented trade strategy have generally experienced rapid growth of traditional exports, but even more rapid growth of nontraditional exports.

Experience has been that growth performance has been more satisfactory under export promotion strategies (meant as a general bias toward exports and not as a package of specific measures to encourage selective exports of particular items themselves induced by a bias toward import substitution) than under import-substitution strategies. While it is impossible to specify a particular model of growth process that will simultaneously satisfy all observers, the relationship between export performance and growth is sufficiently strong that it seems to bear up under many different specifications of the relationship. It has been tested over many countries for: (1) rates of growth of real *GNP* and of exports (see Michael Michaely); (2) for real *GNP* net of exports and exports (see Bela Balassa); and (3) for rates of growth of *GNP* as a function of rate of capital formation, aid receipts, and export growth (see Constantine Michalopoulos and Keith Jay). Time-series and cross-section data have been pooled, so that deviations of countries' growth rates from their trends have been estimated as a function of the growth of export earnings (see my book, p. 271ff). In all of these specifications, rate of growth of exports has turned out to be a highly significant variable. While the "success stories" of Korea, Taiwan, and Brazil are well known, there are enough other observations, both for different time periods in the same country (as for example Turkey and the Philippines) and of countries (including on the positive side Ivory Coast, Colombia, and Malaysia and on the negative side India, Argentina, and Egypt), so that there is little doubt about the link between export performance and growth rates.

Moreover, it seems clear the export performance is a function in large part of governmental policies. While an export promotion strategy will not always be successful in generating more export growth (especially if policies affecting the domestic market are inappropriate), certainly policies adopted to encourage import substitution, especially when they include overvalued exchange rates and quantitative restrictions upon imports, retard the growth of exports. . . .

The central question, then, is why such a difference in growth performance should be associated with export promotion contrasted with import substitution. There are three major hypotheses, and each undoubtedly contains some explanatory power. . . .

The first hypothesis is that technological-economic factors imply an overwhelming superiority for development through export promotion. These factors include such phenomena as minimum efficient size of plant, increasing returns to scale, indivisibilities in the production process, and the necessity for competition. According to this hypothesis, failure to take advantage of the opportunities to exploit these phenomena through trade significantly impairs the attainable rate of growth. A second hypothesis is that differences in growth rates have resulted, not from the choice of trade strategy per se, but rather from excesses in the ways in which import substitution policies were administered. The third hypothesis is that policies adopted in pursuit of an export promotion strategy are generally far closer to an optimum, both in the $DMRT = IMRT$ sense and with respect to the domestic market, than are those adopted under import substitution. Under this interpretation, the role of trade policy is to constrain policymakers in such a way that they do not impede the growth rate as much as they otherwise would.

Both the first and second hypotheses are consistent with the notion that the nonagricultural sector of most developing countries is, in some sense, an "infant industry," and requires some stimulus for growth. The third, by contrast, essentially takes the negative view, that markets would function well and provide satisfactory growth if only policymakers would abstain from counter-productive intervention.

The first hypothesis really amounts to an assertion that the gains from trade, especially for developing countries, are so sizable that the losses associated with import substitution significantly reduce the rate of return on factor accumulation. On the negative side, domestic markets are extremely small in most developing countries, and attempts to replace imports result in the construction of plants of less-than-efficient minimum size, while simultaneously generating an oligopolistic or monopolistic market structure. As import substitution proceeds, new activities are increasingly capital intensive and inefficiencies from below-minimum-efficient size increase. On the positive side, so the argument runs, export promotion permits entrepreneurs to base their plans on whatever size plant seems appropriate: size of domestic market is no longer a virtually binding constraint, as it is when the activity is profitable only because of very high rates of effective protection. Moreover, monopoly positions arise less frequently under export promotion, as exporters face competition from abroad as well as from other domestic producers.

Export promotion may also be more efficient in permitting rapid expansion of profitable activities; by contrast, under import substitution, most activities are constrained to expanding at approximately the same rate: inefficient firms and sectors expand approximately as rapidly as efficient ones. In this view, potential export lines consist of a number of industrial products (girls' sneakers, wigs, tennis rackets, engine parts, plywood, and so on) and it is as much a matter of the right entrepreneur, and the right specialized product, as choosing the "right industry" that is necessary for rapid growth. To be sure, factor proportions and comparative advantage may result in greater profitability of relatively labor-using industries, but the basic notion is that there are thousands of industrial products, and that, among relatively labor-intensive activities, the ones which will develop into exports will be those in which there are firms with good management and an ability to utilize factors of production efficiently.

A final aspect of the technology-related view of the advantages of export promotion has to do with factor proportions. Given the vast disparity in capital-labor ratios of the industrial sectors of the developed and developing countries, the opportunity for trade represents a means for shifting the demand for labor outward more rapidly than the import-substitution strategy permits. If there are differences of, say, two-to-one and six-to-

one in capital-labor ratios between activities at the prevailing wage-rental ratio, while the rate of capital accumulation is the binding constraint on expansion of employment in the urban sector, an allocation of additional capital to the labor-intensive activity for export will permit an upward shift in the demand for labor three times as great as that which would occur if import substitution dictates the start of the more capital-intensive activity. To be sure, the expectation is that the more rapid rate of growth of demand for industrial labor would drive up the urban wage once the demand for labor was rising more rapidly than the labor force, but this is precisely a desired outcome of policy. . . .

The second hypothesis focuses upon the costs of import substitution policies as in fact carried out, and suggests that alternative means of achieving import substitution might have avoided them. According to this view, the failure of import substitution resulted from the excesses of the particular ways in which domestic industries were encouraged: extreme currency overvaluation combined with quantitative restrictions provided the equivalent of prohibitive tariff protection; techniques of allocating import licenses were employed which prevented competition among domestic firms and rewarded entrepreneurs for license-getting abilities rather than their cost-minimizing performance; and excessive and detailed quanitative controls were employed over many aspects of economic activity. One of the costs was the failure of export earnings to grow as much as they would have under "better" import-substitution policies; that in turn led to "stop-go" patterns with their attendant costs. Simultaneously, the emerging "foreign exchange bottleneck" had both direct and indirect impacts upon the structure and growth of the economy. In particular, efforts at "import substitution" stopped being geared toward development of economic new industries, and became focused upon "foreign exchange saving," often in highly irrational and indiscriminate ways, which further distorted the system.

The third view denies the need for any bias

toward exports and implicitly or explicitly asserts that growth would be optimal in the absence of intervention. A bias toward exports is therefore better than one toward import-substitutes only because policies are less distortive. In this view, an export-oriented strategy imposes constraints on policymakers, both in what they can attempt to do, and in making them aware of the costs of mistakes. Policymakers receive feedback in a relatively short time period as to the costs of their policies. Also, it is infeasible to rely upon quantitative controls: the international price, at least, cannot be administered and to that extent, more generalized forms of incentive, including a relatively realistic exchange rate, must be employed. Indeed, it is argued that incentives cannot be as biased toward export promotion as they can be toward import substitution. This is precisely because to do so would require either export subsidization (whose costs would be immediately evident through the drain on the budget) or such a degree of currency undervaluation that a current account surplus would absorb much of the country's savings potential.

According to this third line of argument, constraints upon policymakers go well beyond the inability to impose too great a bias toward exports. For example, it is virtually impossible to administer any highly protective system for intermediate and capital goods imports if exporters are expected to compete in international markets: they must be permitted ready access to imported raw materials, intermediate goods, and capital equipment. To impose any comprehensive system of licensing or controls would entail delays and other costs, inconsistent with the export strategy. Thus, the commitment to an export-oriented development strategy implies a fairly liberal and efficient trade regime, and thus prevents paperwork, delays, bureaucratic regulation, and other costs that can arise under import substitution. This in turn limits the restrictions that can be imposed on capital account. More generally, under an export promotion strategy, there is an international market in the background: it functions as a constraint upon economic behavior,

both of entrepreneurs and of government officials, and simultaneously provides feedback to them as to the success or failure of policies in terms of their objectives.

Undoubtedly, all three approaches to the differential in economic performance contain elements of truth. There are export opportunities that are passed up under import substitution where indivisibilities or increasing returns within a range would permit sizable gains in output. There are also high-cost import substitution activities which, if never undertaken, would have freed resources for considerably more productive use, even within an import-substitution strategy. Likewise, the international market has served to constrain policymakers and induce them to abandon uneconomic policies sooner than they otherwise would have done. Knowledge is not yet far enough advanced to determine the relative importance of the alternatives. It will not be until we have far more information than is currently available about the order of magnitude of indivisibilities and minimum size plant contrasted with size of markets in *LDCs*, and also about the determinants of politicians' and bureaucrats' behavior. Moreover, it is certain that the primary sources of growth are internal, and that there is no magic formula, or single policy change, that can by itself account meaningfully for differences in economic performance.

Nonetheless, experience has clearly demonstrated the importance of access to international markets in providing a means of permitting more rapid growth than would otherwise be feasible. Given the enormous difficulties and costs of achieving the institutional and other changes that economic growth requires, it is probable that trade policy changes have a higher rate of return to *LDCs* than most other feasible policy changes. It is, of course, to be hoped that protectionist pressures in the developed countries do not result in fewer opportunities for the *LDCs*. If such protectionist measures are taken, they will lower the rate of return to outward-oriented trade strategies. They will however, for the foreseeable future, still leave that rate distinctly above the returns from a policy of persisting with inward-oriented growth.

References

B. Balassa, "Exports and Economic Growth: Further Evidence," *Journal of Development Economics,* June 1978, Vol. 5, pp. 181–89.

W. M. Corden, "The Effects of Trade on the Rate of Growth," in Jagdish Bhagwati et al. (eds.), *Trade, Balance of Payments, and Growth,* Amsterdam, 1971.

H. G. Johnson, "The Theory of Trade and Growth: A Diagrammatic Analysis," in Jagdish Bhagwati et al. (eds.), *Trade, Balance of Payments, and Growth,* Amsterdam, 1971.

I. Kravis, "Trade as a Handmaiden of Growth: Similarities between the Nineteenth and Twentieth Centuries," *Economic Journal,* December 1970, Vol. 80, pp. 850–72.

Anne O. Krueger, *Foreign Trade Regimes and Economic Development: Liberalization Attempts and Consequences,* Cambridge, Mass., 1978.

———— et al., *Alternative Trade Strategies and Employment,* Chicago, 1981.

M. Michaely, "Exports and Growth: An Empirical Investigation," *Journal of Development Economics,* March 1977, Vol. 4, pp. 49–53.

C. Michalopoulos and K. Jay, "Growth of Exports and Income in the Developing World: A Neoclassical View," disc. paper No. 28, A.I.D., November 1975.

VIII.B.2. Phases in Exchange Control Regimes*

[We may delineate] exchange control regimes into certain basic types or, what we term, Phases that have a broadly differentiated impact on economic efficiency and performance.

This notion of Phases, shortly to be defined but essentially based on the restrictionist content and associated blend of control and price instruments, reflected initial familiarity with the evolving exchange control regimes in specific countries and the strongly suggested hypothesis that these regimes went through a sequencing. These Phases in the exchange control regimes were designed essentially as a classificatory and descriptive device to capture meaningfully the evolution of the exchange control system in terms of its restrictionist content and the dimensions and

pattern of its use of control and price instruments.

A. PHASE I

This Phase is characterized by the systematic and significant imposition of Quantitative Restrictions (QR). It might start in response to an unsustainable payments deficit resulting from intense or sustained prior inflationary pressure (due, for example, to the initiation of a large-scale development plan and consequent extraordinary increases in government expenditures) or from a sharp drop in world prices for some major exports (as in 1953). These reasons for instituting controls are of interest in ascertaining the logic of the evolution of exchange control regimes but are not critical to the definition of Phase I.

Throughout Phase I (which, of course, can be of varying duration) controls are generally maintained and often intensified. This continuation of increased severity might result

*From J. Bhagwati's *Foreign Trade Regimes and Economic Development: Anatomy and Consequences of Exchange Control Regimes,* copyright © 1978, National Bureau of Economic Research. Reprinted with permission from Ballinger Publishing Company, pp. 56–9.

from any of several interrelated factors: (1) the continuation of initial controls might be necessary to contain an *ex ante* unsustainable payments deficit; (2) the initial set of controls might result in evasions of the system through illegal transactions that negate any possible impact on the balance of payments; (3) once controls are instituted, policy-makers may perceive the new instruments as handy for a variety of purposes in addition to controlling the payments situation and begin employing them for such purposes; and (4) policy-makers may perceive their actions as freed from a balance of payments constraint and adopt policies that in fact require restrictiveness afresh to offset further adverse effects on the balance of payments.

B. PHASE II

This phase is characterized by continued reliance upon quantitative restrictions and, indeed, generally increased restrictiveness of the entire control system. However, Phase II is distinguished by two additional and related aspects of the QR system, both relatively unimportant during Phase I: (1) for a variety of reasons, indicated below, the detailed workings of the control system become increasingly complex; and (2) price measures are adopted to buttress the functioning of the control system. Both of these characteristics of Phase II stem from dissatisfaction with the results of an undifferentiated system and are often the result of many small decisions rather than an overall policy design.

1. Although neither term is quite appropriate, Phase I decision-making and policies may be characterized as "crude" and "unsophisticated." Quantitative restrictions are applied with relatively few rules, and treatment of competing claims to import licenses tends to be relatively undifferentiated in the sense that rules for allocation tend to be of an "across the board" nature, such as allocating to everyone a certain percentage of this person's imports over a specified number of earlier years or allotting licenses pro rata with applications. The major motivation for changes in the control system during Phase I

is a concern with evasions, both legal and illegal, of the system. Thus, export licensing may be adopted to ensure that exporters do not succeed in their attempts at capital flight; controls over tourist and other invisible transactions are aimed at preventing the emergence of a black market, and so on.

In Phase II, however, the rules of the regime have become more complex and differentiated. The growth of the bureaucracy to administer the allocations and the inevitable tendency to differentiate increasingly among alternative end uses and claimants as the control regime is perceived to be a continuing state of affairs interact to produce a complex system.

2. The other major feature of Phase II is an increasing resort to price measures to supplement the QR regime. This generally occurs with respect to both exports and imports. The continuation or intensification of foreign exchange shortage leads to recognition that additional export earnings would be desirable. Rebate schemes, import replenishment schemes, special credits for exporters, and a variety of other devices may be instituted that offset part or all of the discrimination against exports implicit in an overvalued exchange rate. Like the quantitative restrictions discussed above, however, export incentives tend to be adopted in a piecemeal and fragmented fashion. As for imports, price measures are also adopted to absorb part of the excess demand for imports. Tariffs may be increased or surcharges added to the cost of importing. Guarantee deposits are generally required on various categories of imports. These and other measures tend to reduce (but hardly eliminate) the windfall gain or premium accruing to the recipients of import licenses.

The following aspects of the price situation in Phase II are then evident: (1) the exchange parity is "overlaid" by tariffs and subsidies, levied in lieu of formal parity change; (2) the effective exchange rate for exports, on the average, is rarely as high as the effective exchange rate for imports, implying a bias against the (relative) incentive to export; (3) the domestic currency is overvalued at the current parity plus trade tariffs and subsidies, implying a premium (on the average) on imports; and (4) this import premium varies across different activities, implying differential incentives to produce and invest in these different activities.

C. PHASE III

Phase III is entered against the backdrop just defined, and it can take various forms. It may consist of a mere "tidying-up" operation directed at replacing the diverse import premiums by reasonably uniform tariffs such that the differential incentive effects caused by diverse premiums on different imports are greatly reduced or virtually eliminated. Alternatively, the tidying-up operation may replace the existing tariffs and export subsidies with a formal parity change, the result being that the (average) effective exchange rates on exports and imports do not change much but the dispersion of tariffs is replaced by the uniform devaluation—an action again of rationalization in this instance. On the other hand, Phase III may be substantially ambitious and take the form of what might be described as a devaluation cum liberalization package. Such a package may have a gross devaluation large enough to leave a net devaluation despite the removal of the trade tariffs and subsidies, with accompanying grants by donors of additional credits to facilitate early expansion of imports, debt rescheduling, and similar measures aimed at quick and easy liberalization of imports.

D. PHASE IV

Phase IV is entered when Phase III has resulted in *continued* liberalization. This means that the average import premium has fallen, the bias against exports has substantially diminished (the effective exchange rate for exports having come closer to the effective exchange rate for imports), and the degree of dispersion in the incentives to expand different activities has diminished through greater uniformity in these incentives via the foreign trade sector.

Needless to say, this outcome can only be anticipated from a Phase III episode when the latter takes the ambitious form of a concerted effort of the kind presupposed in a devaluation cum liberalization package.

E. PHASE V

The transition from Phase V occurs when the exchange regime is virtually liberalized in the sense that there is full convertibility on current account and quantitative restrictions are not employed as a means of regulating the balance of payments. Thus, an economy in Phase V is not an exchange control regime in the usual sense of the term, and Phase V represents a total alternative to the QR regimes of Phases I and II. The pegged exchange rate is at its equilibrium level, a flexible exchange rate policy is in operation, or monetary and fiscal policies are employed as the instruments to achieve payments balance in contrast to a reliance on the exchange control mechanism.

VIII.B.3. Inward-Oriented Strategies*

Industrial development generally begins in response to domestic demand generated in

*From Bela Balassa, *The Process of Industrial Development and Alternative Development Strategies,* Princeton University, International Finance Section, Essays in International Finance No. 141, December 1980, pp. 4–11. Reprinted by permission.

the primary sector that also provides investible funds for manufacturing industries. Demand for industrial products and investible savings represent possible uses of the surplus generated in agriculture, or in mining. The surplus is generated as primary output comes to exceed subsistence needs and, more often than not, it is associated with export expansion.

At the same time, the effects of primary exports on industrial development depend to a considerable extent on input-output relationships and on the disposition of incomes generated in the export sector. Infrastructure in the form of ports, railways, and roads are often important inputs for primary exports, and their availability may contribute to the development of industrial activities.

The disposition of incomes generated in the export sector is affected by ownership conditions. In the case of foreign ownership, a substantial part of the surplus may be repatriated, albeit taxing the earnings of foreign capital does add to domestic incomes. There are leakages in the form of investing and spending abroad, as well as consuming imported luxuries, in the case of domestic ownership in a system of plantation-type agriculture and large-scale mining, too. And, as Douglas North noted, plantation owners have little incentive to finance human investment in the form of general education.

By contrast, in cases when family-size farms predominate, demand is generated for the necessities and the conveniences of life as well as for education. Such demand contributes to the development of domestic industry that enjoys "natural" protection from imports in the form of transportation costs. It further contributes to the accumulation of human capital that finds use in manufacturing industries.

The process of industrial development may be accelerated if natural protection is complemented by tariff or quota protection. This last point, in turn, leads me to the discussion of the next step in the industrialization process: the first, or "easy" stage of import substitution.

THE FIRST STAGE OF IMPORT SUBSTITUTION

With the exception of Britain at the time of the Industrial Revolution, and, more recently, Hong Kong, all present-day industrial and developing countries protected their in-

cipient manufacturing industries producing for domestic markets. There were differences, however, as regards the rate and the form of protection. While the industrial countries of today relied on relatively low tariffs, a number of present-day developing countries applied high tariffs or quantitative restrictions that limited, or even excluded, competition from imports.

At the same time, high protection discriminates against exports through the explicit or implicit taxation of export activities. Explicit taxation may take the form of export taxes while implicit taxation occurs as a result of the effects of protection on the exchange rate. The higher the rate of protection, the lower will be the exchange rate necessary to ensure equilibrium in the balance of payments, and the lower the amount of domestic currency exporters receive per unit of foreign exchange earned.

The adverse effects of high protection are exemplified in the case of Ghana, where import prohibitions encouraged inefficient, high-cost production in manufacturing industries: taxes on the main export crop, cocoa, discouraged its production: and other crops were adversely affected by the unfavorable exchange rate. Ghana's neighbor, the Ivory Coast, in turn, followed a policy encouraging the development of both primary and manufacturing activities. As a result, it increased its share in cocoa exports, developed new primary exports, and expanded manufacturing industries.

Differences in the policies applied may largely explain that, between 1960 and 1978, per capita incomes fell from $430 to $390 in Ghana, in terms of 1978 prices, as compared to an increase from $540 to $840 in the Ivory Coast. This has occurred notwithstanding the fact that the two countries have similar natural resource endowments and, at the time of independence, Ghana had the advantage of a higher educational level and an indigenous civil service corps.

Indeed, there is no need for high protection at the first stage of import substitution, entailing the replacement of the imports of nondurable consumer goods, such as clothing, shoes, and household goods, and of their inputs, such as textile fabrics, leather and wood, by domestic production, since these commodities suit the conditions existing in developing countries that are at the beginning of the industrialization process. The commodities in question are intensive in unskilled labor; the efficient scale of output is relatively low and costs do not rise substantially at lower output levels; production does not involve the use of sophisticated technology; and a network of suppliers of parts, components, and accessories is not required for efficient operations.

The relative advantages of developing countries in these commodities explain the frequent references made to the "easy" stage of import substitution. At the same time, to the extent that the domestic production of these commodities generates external economies in the form of labor training, the development of entrepreneurship, and the spread of technology, there is an argument for moderate infant industry protection or promotion.

THE CHOICE OF SECOND-STAGE IMPORT SUBSTITUTION

In the course of first-stage import substitution, domestic production will rise more rapidly than domestic consumption, since it not only provides for increases in consumption but also replaces imports. The rate of growth of output will however decline to that of consumption, once the process of import substitution has been completed.

Maintaining high industrial growth rates, then, necessitates turning to the exportation of manufactured goods or moving to second-stage import substitution. This choice, in fact, represents alternative industrial development strategies that may be applied after the completion of the first stage of import substitution.

Second-stage import substitution was undertaken in the postwar period in several Latin American countries, some South Asian countries, in particular India, as well as in the European socialist countries. In Latin America, it responded to the ideas of Raúl Prebisch, in whose view adverse foreign mar-

ket conditions for primary exports and lack of competitiveness in manufactured exports would not permit developing countries to attain high rates of economic growth by relying on export production. Rather, Prebisch suggested that these countries should expand their manufacturing industries oriented towards domestic markets. This purpose was to be served by industrial protection that was said to bring additional benefits through improvements in the terms of trade.

Similar ideas were expressed by Gunnar Myrdal. Myrdal influenced the policies followed by India, which were also affected by the example of the Soviet Union that chose an autarkical pattern of industrial development. And, the European socialist countries faithfully imitated the Soviet example; they attempted to reproduce the Soviet pattern in the framework of much smaller domestic markets and also lacking the natural resource base of the Soviet Union.

Second-stage import substitution involves the replacement of the imports of intermediate goods and producer and consumer durables by domestic production. These commodities have rather different characteristics from those replaced at the first stage. Intermediate goods, such as petrochemicals and steel, tend to be highly capital-intensive. They are also subject to important economies of scale, with efficient plant size being large compared to the domestic needs of most developing countries and costs rising rapidly at lower output levels. Moreover, the margin of processing is relatively small and organizational and technical inefficiencies may contribute to high costs.

Producer durables, such as machinery, and consumer durables, such as automobiles and refrigerators, are also subject to economies of scale. But, in these industries, economies of scale relate not so much to plant size as to horizontal and to vertical specialization, entailing reductions in product variety and the manufacture of parts, components, and accessories on an efficient scale in separate plants.

Reducing product variety will permit longer production runs that lower production costs through improvements in manufacturing efficiency along the "learning curve," savings in expenses incurred in moving from one operation to another, and the use of special-purpose machinery. Horizontal specialization is however limited by the smallness of domestic markets in the developing countries. Similar conclusions apply to vertical specialization that leads to cost reductions through the subdivision of the production process among plants of efficient size.

Given the relative scarcity of physical and human capital in developing countries that completed the first stage of import substitution, they are at a disadvantage in the manufacture of highly physical capital-intensive intermediate goods and skill-intensive producer and consumer durables. In limiting the scope for the exploitation of economies of scale, the relatively small size of their national markets also contributes to high domestic costs in these countries. At the same time, net foreign exchange savings tend to be small because of the need for importing materials and machinery.

The domestic resource cost ratio relates the domestic resource cost of production, in terms of the labor, capital, and natural resources utilized, to net foreign exchange savings (in the case of import substitution) or net foreign exchange earnings (in the case of exports). In the absence of serious distortions in factor markets, the domestic resource cost (DRC) ratio will be low for exported commodities. It is also relatively low for consumer nondurables and their inputs, in the production of which developing countries have a comparative advantage. However, for the reasons noted beforehand, DRC ratios tend to be high in the manufacture of intermediate goods and producer and consumer durables.

Correspondingly, the establishment of these industries to serve narrow domestic markets is predicated on high protection. Also, rates of protection may need to be raised as countries "travel up the staircase," represented by DRC ratios, in embarking on the production of commodities that less and less conform to their comparative advantage.

This will occur as goods produced at earlier stages have come to saturate domestic markets. High protection, in turn, discriminates against manufactured and primary exports and against primary activities in general.

CHARACTERISTICS OF INWARD-ORIENTED DEVELOPMENT STRATEGIES

In the postwar period, several capitalist countries in Latin America and in South Asia and the socialist countries of Central and Eastern Europe adopted inward-oriented industrial development strategies, entailing second-stage import substitution. Capitalist countries generally utilized a mixture of tariffs and import controls to protect their industries whereas socialist countries relied on import prohibitions and on industry level planning.

Notwithstanding differences in the measures applied, the principal characteristics of the industrial development strategies applied in the two groups of countries show considerable similarities. To begin with, while the infant industry argument calls for temporary protection until industries become internationally competitive, in both groups of countries protection was regarded as permanent. Also, in all the countries concerned, there was a tendency towards what a Latin American economist aptly described as "import substitution at any cost."

Furthermore, in all the countries concerned, there were considerable variations in rates of explicit and implicit protection among industrial activities. This was the case, first of all, as continued import substitution involved undertaking activities with increasingly high domestic costs per unit of foreign exchange saved. In capitalist countries, the generally uncritical acceptance of demands for protection contributed to this result, when, in the absence of price comparisons, the protective effects of quantitative restrictions could not even be established. In socialist countries, the stated objective was to limit imports to commodities that could not be produced domestically, or were not available in sufficient quantities, and no attempt was made to examine the implicit protection the pursuit of this objective entailed.

In both groups of countries, the neglect of intraindustry relationships further increased the dispersion of protection rates on value added in processing, or effective protection, with adverse effects on economic efficiency. In Argentina, high tariffs imposed on caustic soda at the request of a would-be producer made the theretofore thriving soap exports unprofitable. In Hungary, the high cost of domestic steel, based largely on imported iron ore and coking coals, raised costs for steel-using industries and large investments in the steel industry delayed the substitution of aluminum for steel, although Hungary had considerable bauxite reserves.

Countries applying inward-oriented industrial development strategies were further characterized by the prevalence of sellers' markets. In capitalist countries, the size of national markets limited the possibilities for domestic competition in industries established at the second stage of import substitution while import competition was practically excluded by high protection. In socialist countries, the system of central planning applied did not permit competition among domestic firms or from imports and buyers had no choice among domestic producers or access to imported commodities.

The existence of sellers' markets provides little inducement for catering to the users' needs. In the case of industrial users, it led to backward integration as producers undertook the manufacture of parts, components, and accessories in order to minimize supply difficulties. This outcome, observed in capitalist as well as in socialist countries, led to higher costs, since economies of scale were foregone.

Also, in sellers' markets, firms had little incentive to improve productivity. In capitalist countries, monopolies and oligopolies assumed importance, and the oligopolists often aimed at the maintenance of market shares while refraining from actions that would invoke retaliation. In socialist countries, the existence of assured outlets and the emphasis

on short-term objectives on the part of managers discouraged technological change.

The managers' emphasis on short-term objectives in socialist countries had to do with uncertainty as to the planners' future intentions. In capitalist countries, fluctuations in real exchange rates (nominal exchange rates, adjusted for changes in inflation rates at home and abroad) created uncertainty for business decisions. These fluctuations, resulting from intermittent devaluations in the face of rapid domestic inflation, aggravated the existing bias against exports as the domestic currency equivalent of export earnings varied with the devaluations, the timing of which was uncertain.

In countries engaging in second-stage import substitution, distortions were further apparent in the valuation of time. In capitalist countries, negative real interest rates adversely affected domestic savings, encouraged self-investment, including inventory accumulation, at low returns, and provided inducements for the transfer of funds abroad. Negative interest rates also necessitated credit rationing that generally favored import-substituting investments, whether it was done by the banks or by the government. In the first case, the lower risk of investments in production for domestic as compared to export markets gave rise to such a result; in the second case, it reflected government priorities. Finally, in socialist countries, ideological considerations led to the exclusion of interest rates as a charge for capital and as an element in the evaluation of investment projects.

There was also a tendency to underprice public utilities in countries following an inward-oriented strategy, either because of low interest charges in these capital-intensive activities or as a result of a conscious decision. The underpricing of utilities benefited, in particular, energy-intensive industries and promoted the use of capital.

In general, in moving to the second stage of import substitution, countries applying inward-oriented development strategies de-emphasized the role of prices. In socialist countries, resources were in large part allocated centrally in physical terms; in capitalist countries, output and input prices were distorted and reliance was placed on non-price measures of import restrictions and credit allocation.

EFFECTS ON EXPORTS AND ON ECONOMIC GROWTH

The discrimination in favor of import substitution and against exports did not permit the development of manufactured exports in countries engaging in second-stage import substitution behind high protection. There were also adverse developments in primary exports as low prices for producers and for consumers reduced the exportable surplus by discouraging production and encouraging consumption.

In fact, rather than improvements in the external terms of trade that were supposed to result, turning the internal terms of trade against primary activities led to a decline in export market shares in the countries in question. Decreases in market shares were especially pronounced in cereals, meat, oilseeds, and nonferrous metals, benefiting developed countries, in particular, the United States, Canada, and Australia.

The volume of Argentina's principal primary exports, chiefly beef and wheat, remained, on the average, unchanged between 1934–38 and 1964–66 while the world exports of these commodities doubled. In the same period, Chile's share fell from 28 percent to 22 percent in the world exports of copper, which accounts for three-fifths of the country's export earnings.

Similar developments occurred in socialist countries where the allocation of investment favored industry at the expense of agriculture. In Hungary, the exports of several agricultural commodities, such as goose liver,

fodder seeds, and beans, declined in absolute terms and slow increases in production necessitated the imports of cereals and meat that were earlier major export products.

The slowdown in the growth of primary exports and the lack of emergence of manufactured exports did not provide the foreign exchange necessary for rapid economic growth in countries pursuing inward-oriented industrial development strategies. The situation was aggravated as net import savings declined because of the increased need for foreign materials, machinery, and technological know how. As a result, economic growth was increasingly constrained by limitations in the availability of foreign exchange, and intermittent foreign exchange crises occurred as attempts were made to expand the economy at rates exceeding that permitted by the growth of export earnings.

Also, the savings constraint became increasingly binding as high-cost, capital-intensive production at second-stage import substitution raised capital-output ratios, requiring ever-increasing savings ratios to maintain rates of economic growth at earlier levels. At the same time, the loss of incomes due to the high cost of protection reduced the volume of available savings and, in capitalist countries, negative interest rates contributed to the outflow of funds.

In several developing countries, the cost of protection is estimated to have reached 6–7 percent of the gross national product. At the same time, there is evidence that the rate of growth of total factor productivity was lower in countries engaging in second-stage import substitution than in the industrial countries. Rather than reducing the economic distance vis-à-vis the industrial countries that infant industry protection was supposed to promote, then, there was a tendency for this lag to increase over time.

Comment

Although policymakers tend to view import substitution and export promotion as alternative strategies, a rational trade policy would pursue both strategies until the last unit of domestic resources devoted to each yields the same return in terms of foreign exchange saved through import substitution or earned through exports. Export promotion does not mean that there should be no import-substitution industries, and import substitution does not mean that no new products should be produced for export. A rational policy implies no bias in favor of either strategy.

Appropriate domestic policies, the exchange rate, and trade policies should allocate resources efficiently to internal and external opportunities. As a condition of optimal resource allocation, policies should equate the marginal domestic resource cost of saving foreign exchange with the marginal domestic resource cost of earning foreign exchange.

If in many countries the bias has in the past been too heavily in favor of import substitution, why cannot the bias now become too great in favor of exports in a country that adopts an export-promoting strategy? The possibility does exist, but excessive export bias is less likely than excessive import bias. This is because an export promotion regime usually begins after a preceding period of import substitution that has already been so biased against exports that incentives for exports can be considerable before they reach a point of oversubsidizing exports. Moreover, export-promoting measures tend to rely on price incentives while import-substitution regimes are usually administered through quantitative controls that are characterized by considerable dispersion and unpredictability. Export promotion measures are also subject to more public scrutiny to the extent that they involve budgetary measures rather than quantitative restrictions. Exporting firms must also face price and quality competition in international markets, and the exporting firms are more likely to realize economies of scale than are import-substitution industries producing for only a narrow domestic market.

A number of country studies indicates that the economic cost of incentives distorted toward export promotion has been less than the cost of those distorted toward import substitution. Most notable is the research project sponsored by the National Bureau of Economic Research (NBER), now published in ten country volumes. Two synthesis volumes are: J. Bhagwati, *Foreign Trade Regimes and Economic Development: Anatomy and Consequences of Exchange Control Regimes* (1978) and Anne O. Krueger, *Liberalization Attempts and Consequences* (1978). Other relevant empirical evidence is provided by Bela Balassa in *The Newly-Industrializing Countries in the World Economy* (1981) and *Development Strategies in Semi-Industrial Countries* (1981).

VIII.B.4. Trends and Prospects for Export of Manufactures— Note

As preceding selections indicate, developing countries frequently utilize trade policy to promote their industrialization. If the promotion of import-substitution industrialization (ISI) was the earlier attempted strategy of industrialization, there is now a new hope that industrialization might be more successfully based on the processing of the LDCs' primary materials for export and on the export of other semimanufactures and manufactures in which LDCs might become competitive. Arguments in favor of an export substitution strategy of industrialization were presented in selection VIII.B.1. But

what are the prospects for making such a strategy actually effective?

This question might first be explored against the background of some of the statistical trends. Although the developing countries' share of world GNP from manufacturing was still less than 10 percent, manufacturing output has been growing faster in the LDCs than in the more developed countries (MDCs). Growth rates have been especially high in LDCs relative to MDCs in metal products, including machinery and equipment, basic metals, and clothing and footwear. Advances in supply capability cannot be denied. Exports of manufactures have also grown faster in the developing countries than in the developed countries. Real growth rates in exports of manufactures from developing countries exceeded an average annual growth rate of 12 percent from 1960 to 1976, while the rate was approximately 8.8 percent for developed countries. Some rates of export growth are given in Table 1. Growth in exports of manufactures by regions can be noted in Table 2. Table 3 offers a comparison of the growth in

TABLE 1. Past and Projected Rates of Export Growth by Broad Product Groups (in constant 1975 prices)

	World 1960–75	LDCs 1960–75	World 1975–85	LDCs 1975–85	Percent of LDC Exports			Percent Share of Increase	
					1960	1975	1985	1960–75	1975–85
Fuel and energy	6.3	6.2	3.6	3.4	39	40	30	42	18
Agricultural products	4.2	2.6	4.4	3.1	43	27	20	16	12
Non-fuel minerals	3.9	4.8	4.2	5.8	7	7	7	6	6
Manufactures	8.9	12.3	7.8	12.2	11	26	43	36	64
Total merchandise	7.1	5.9	6.4	6.4	100	100	100	100	100

Source: World Bank, *World Development Report, 1978*, tables 13 and 25.

TABLE 2. Exports of Manufactures—Absolute Value, Growth, and Relationship to Exports and to Gross Manufacturing Output

Region and Group	Value (billion current U.S. dollars)				Real Growth Rate 1965–74	Manufactures as a Percent of All Exports 1973	Exports as a Percent of Manufacturing Output 1973
	1965	1973	1974	1975			
Developing	4.6	24.3	32.5	33.2	16.3	21.5	10
Latin America	0.63	4.09	6.41	6.55	21.1	14.9	4
East Asia	1.75	13.65	17.52	17.83	20.9	48.9	30
Turkey and Yugoslavia	0.63	2.14	2.86	3.11	10.7	51.3	8
South Asia	1.00	2.35	2.87	2.90	12.4	49.6	10
Middle East and North Africa	0.33	1.47	2.1	2.0	15.0	4.2	6
Sub-Saharan Africa	0.25	0.6	0.7	0.8	4.9	4.8	5
Developed	84.5	289.0	386.0	419.0	10.8	71.3	15
Transitional	1.06	6.22	8.56	8.26	18.0	70.8	14
Other Western Europe	55.23	188.22	244.61	268.56	10.4	76.2	25
North America	19.73	56.51	77.42	85.73	8.9	59.1	8
Japan	7.66	34.58	51.30	52.63	15.6	93.6	11
Australia, New Zealand, South Africa	0.84	3.43	4.05	3.92	11.4	22.3	8
Centrally planned	12.7	32.8	38.7	46.7	5.9	56.7	3
World total	101.8	346.1	457.2	498.9	10.6	60.0	12

Source: "World Trade and Output of Manufactures: Structural Trends and Developing Countries' Exports," *World Bank Staff Working Paper* No. 314, January 1979, p. 12.

TABLE 3. Growth of the Value of Exports and Imports in Selected Developing Countries (average annual growth rates)

	Argentina	Brazil	Chile	Colombia	India	Israel	Korea	Mexico	Singapore	Taiwan	Yugoslavia
Manufactured goods											
1953–60	−11.7	9.9	3.2	0.0	1.3	18.0	14.0	5.6	n.a.	29.5	28.0
1960–66	14.6	27.5	15.6	35.0	6.7	15.3	80.0	12.7	24.5	36.5	21.5
1966–73	33.5	38.5	0.0	27.5	7.7	17.5	50.0	20.0	42.0	47.0	14.9
Traditional primary products											
1953–60	0.7	−5.3	4.3	−4.5	2.4	16.8	−17.5	−0.3	—	−3.2	3.6
1960–66	6.7	2.0	9.5	−0.5	0.3	15.2	26.5	3.8	—	8.0	11.6
1966–73	6.9	7.6	5.1	6.5	0.2	16.7	16.0	1.7	—	1.2	12.5
Nontraditional primary products											
1953–60	−3.4	5.4	−5.6	11.9	5.6	47.0	7.1	12.2	n.a.	12.7	19.6
1960–66	3.6	9.6	11.3	5.9	9.2	16.8	22.5	10.3	29.5	36.5	2.3
1966–73	14.0	26.5	7.6	25.5	10.4	16.9	35.5	6.3	19.5	25.0	11.1
Primary products together											
1953–60	0.2	−3.1	2.5	−3.5	3.7	20.5	−5.4	3.8	n.a.	−1.2	12.4
1960–66	6.3	4.7	9.7	0.3	4.5	15.5	24.0	6.9	29.5	17.3	5.7
1966–73	7.8	17.0	5.5	10.7	6.5	16.8	26.0	4.3	19.5	17.0	9.8
Part of which, agricultural goods											
1953–60	0.2	−3.5	−9.0	−4.8	3.9	18.3	−3.2	5.4	n.a.	−2.1	14.5
1960–66	6.2	4.5	22.5	1.0	3.7	9.5	25.2	7.7	2.9	15.6	6.7
1966–73	7.9	16.7	2.7	11.1	9.5	11.7	29.5	5.7	19.2	16.3	9.8
Total exports											
1953–60	−0.6	−2.8	2.6	−3.4	2.6	19.6	−3.2	3.9	n.a.	2.2	17.2
1960–66	6.7	5.4	10.1	1.5	5.5	15.3	40.0	7.8	28.5	23.5	13.6
1966–73	10.8	19.9	5.3	12.7	7.0	17.0	44.0	8.1	28.5	35.5	−13.8

Source: B. Balassa, "Export Incentives and Export Performance in Developing Countries: A Comparative Analysis," *World Bank Staff Working Paper* No. 248, March 1977, p. 18a, table 1.

exports of manufactures and primary products from several developing countries.

Keesing lists the following reasons for the especially rapid growth in exports of manufactures from developing countries:

1. Export incentives and industrial policies have been improved in many developing countries, shifting away from excessive emphasis on import substitution and production only for the domestic market;
2. Exporting of manufactures is so new that it has expanded from a small base with much benefit from learning and cumulative experience;
3. Supply capabilities have leaped forward through transfer of technology and borrowing of production methods from developed countries, aided by rapid build-ups of skilled manpower, know-how, and investment in some developing countries;
4. Trade liberalization in developed countries has been favorable to imports from developing countries;
5. Businesses in developed countries—retail chains, other large buyers, trading firms, and multinational manufacturing corporations—have played an active and crucial role while seeking low-cost sources of supply based on low-cost labor. Their efforts, which have greatly accelerated export growth, have been spurred by slow labor force growth and rising real wages in developed countries as well as by declining transport costs, technological and organizational innovations, and a favorable international policy environment.[1]

The bulk of manufactured exports still comes from a fairly small number of relatively advanced industrial LDCs, as shown in Table 4. However, an increasing number of LDCs have been able to participate in the growth of manufactured exports. More than 40 LDCs had exports worth over $100 million in 1979, compared with 22 in 1970. Countries with exports of manufactures over $1 billion increased from 3 in 1965 to 12 in

[1]Donald B. Keesing, "World Trade and Output of Manufactures," *World Bank Staff Working Paper* No. 316, January 1979, pp. 6–7.

1975. In 1975, 9 countries were each exporting more than $2 billion of manufactures, whereas a decade earlier no countries were.

The range of exports has also widened. In almost any year in the 1960s through 1976, real growth rates have been over 10 percent, not only in clothing and electronic assembly, but also in machinery, transport equipment, textile yarn and fabrics, steel, chemicals, and almost every other major group of manufactured exports. Although exports have been built initially around labor-intensive, technologically standardized, "older" products such as textiles, clothing, and footwear, several countries have graduated to the subsequent generation of exports that are more skill-intensive and capital-intensive. Other newcomers to the export of manufactures have then replaced the more advanced LDCs with exports of the older labor-intensive products. Table 5 shows the increasing diversification in the exports of developing countries.

In examining the imports of the industrial countries from the non-OPEC developing countries, the largest increases have been in the specialized machinery and the road motor vehicles categories; the ratios of 1978 to 1973 exports are 4.5 and 4.8, respectively, as compared to an overall average of 2.7. The next largest increases, with the ratio of 1978 to 1973 imports being 3.7 and 3.4, took place in the other categories of machinery and transport equipment and household appliances. All in all, the industrial countires' imports of engineering products from the non-OPEC developing countries shows above-average increases, with the ratio of 1978 to 1973 imports being 3.4.

The developing countries have made little progress in exporting commodities that are highly intensive in physical capital, require sophisticated technology, or necessitate the availability of precision-engineered parts, components, and accessories. Several of the LDCs, however, have made progress in exporting skilled, labor-intensive commodities, such as ships and TV sets, as well as parts, components, and accessories of engineering products to the industrial countries. Growth

TABLE 4. Leading Developing-Economy Exporters of Manufactures in 1965 and 1975

Country or Territory	Value (millions current U.S. dollars)		Percent 1965	Share 1975	Cumulative Share 1975
	1965	1975			
Hong Kong (including reexports)	989	5,590	21.5	15.8	15.8
Excluding reexports	n.a.	4,464	—	—	—
Taiwan	187	4,303	4.1	12.2	28.0
Korea	104	4,136	2.3	11.7	39.7
Yugoslavia	617	2,903	13.4	8.2	47.9
Singapore (including reexports)	300	2,233	6.5	6.3	54.2
Excluding reexports	n.a.	1,286	—	—	—
Brazil	124	2,192	2.7	6.2	60.4
India	809	1,961[a]	17.6	5.6	66.0
Mexico (including border)	166	2,090	3.6	5.9	71.9
Argentina	84	723	1.8	2.0	73.9
Malaysia	68	664	1.5	1.9	75.8
Pakistan	190[a]	571	4.1[a]	1.6	77.4
All developing countries	4,590	35,280	100.0	100.0	100.0

Sources: United Nations and national trade statistics.

[a]Including what is now Bangladesh (exported 178 in 1975).

TABLE 5. Composition of LDC Trade in Manufactures by Destination, 1975 (percent)

	Trade among LDCs[a]	LDC Exports to MDCs	LDC Imports from MDCs	Share of Inter-LDC Trade in Total LDC Imports
Machinery and transport equipment	31	18	55	6
Textiles	14	10	4	28
Clothing	5	19	1	39
Chemicals	13	7	12	11
Iron and steel	6	5	10	7
Other manufactures	31	41	19	15
Total	100	100	100	10

Source: United Nations, *Yearbook of International Trade Statistics*, various issues.

[a]Includes significant reexports, notably in machinery and transport equipment.

has also been rapid in the exports of other consumer goods that require average skill intensity and are relatively intensive in unskilled labor.[2]

[2]Bela Balassa, "Structural Change in Trade in Manufactured Goods Between Industrial and Developing Countries," *World Bank Staff Working Paper* No. 396, June 1980, pp. 19–21.

Table 5 illustrates the compositional differences between manufactures exported to MDCs and to other LDCs in 1975. In the aggregate, nearly two-thirds of LDC manufactured exports go to MDCs, nearly one-third to other LDCs, and only limited amounts to the central planned economies. A more comprehensive view of world trade in manufactures can be gained from the matrix presented in Table 6.

One can see that about 60 percent of world trade in manufactures takes place among developed countries, that developing countries' imports of manufactures are more than three times as large as their exports of manufactured goods, and that nearly 85 percent of their manufactured imports come from developed market economies.

The important question now is: What is the potential for future growth in exports of manufactures from the LDCs? The answer will depend on the changing pattern of comparative advantage in the process of economic development, protectionism in the MDCs, growth in the MDCs, and LDC policies with respect to an outward-looking strategy of development. We may now explore the first two factors, leaving the other factors to be analyzed in the following two selections.

Once we appreciate the fact of changing comparative advantage, we can recognize a greater potential for the export of manufactures. Comparative advantage proceeds through "stages" within a developing country according to which the structure of exports changes with the accumulation of physical and human capital.[3] A developing country's

intertemporal pattern of comparative advantage proceeds roughly from unskilled, labor-intensive to skill-intensive to physical, capital-intensive, and so on, to the high-technology products in more advanced economies.

Beyond the initial capacity to acquire a comparative advantage in resource-based or labor-intensive commodities, there are other forces that may widen the basis of exports of manufactures from the DCs. Some of the effects of technological change, for example, may go in this direction. Technological change is usually interpreted as promoting more trade in new manufactured commodities that embody a high degree of research and development or are intensive in highly skilled labor. Although it is true that much of the trade in manufactures is composed of products embodying advanced scientific and technical knowledge and that the LDCs lack the necessary basis for producing and exporting these products, it must nonetheless be recognized that technological information is eventually diffused and that a breakthrough achieved in one country stimulates emulation in other countries. More significantly, with the lapse of time, a new product will pass through a "product cycle" in the course of which the technology becomes more standardized and thus more readily transferable to an LDC.

As a product passes through its "new" and "growth" phases into its "mature" phase, its production process tends to become more

[3]Bela Balassa, "A 'Stages' Approach to Comparative Advantage," in Irma Adelman (ed.), *Economic Growth and Resources: National and International Issues*, Vol. 5, 1979, pp. 121–56.

TABLE 6. Matrix of World Trade in Manufactures, 1976 (billion U.S. dollars)

Exports From/To	Developed	(Part to) Europe	Developing	Centrally Planned	World Total
Developed	321	(224)	121	27	469
(of which Western					
Europe)	(226)	(193)	(61)	(20)	(307)
Developing	28	(10)	14	3	45
Centrally planned	9	(8)	7	34	50
World total	358	(242)	142	64	564

Source: "World Trade and Output of Manufactures: Structural Trends and Developing Countries' Exports," *World Bank Staff Working Paper* No. 316, January 1979, p. 17.

standardized, requiring less of skilled management and less of scientific and engineering know-how, and thus makes more use of relatively unskilled labor and standardized machinery, which are easily obtainable and maintainable. The production process of a mature product may therefore be more easily adopted by a newly developing country (hence the early introduction of the textile industry into industrializing countries). Insofar as the mature products are standardized manufactures, their export marketing is also relatively easier because specifications and prices for these nondifferentiated products are easily available and their markets are highly price sensitive.

It may be expected that eventually a given technological advantage will be dissipated and will give way to conventional factor-cost advantages, so that the new line of production may become more accessible to developing countries.

As technological conditions and factor endowments change in a developing country, so too will its comparative advantage in different manufactured goods. The country may progress up the export ladder from an early generation of exports to a higher generation. At the same time as comparative advantage changes within a country, the commodity composition of trade changes among countries. As a country graduates into exports with greater domestic value added, its lower-value exports are taken over by another newly emerging exporting country that has been in the queue. Thus, exports of manufactures may initially consist largely of textile yarn and fabrics and other standardized intermediate goods, such as leather, plywood, and cement. Later, consumer goods and then capital goods may contribute a rising share of exports. Ultimately, the leading developing countries may export technically complex products, such as supertankers, aircraft, and heavy machinery. Through this continually evolving process of upgrading and diversification of manufactured exports within a developing country, and the movement of developing countries through the queue, the potential is raised for the expansion of man-

ufactured exports from newly industrializing countries.[4]

The potential, however, will not be realized if the MDCs impose import restrictions. The trade policies of the MDCs are therefore important in determining whether exports of manufactures from the LDCs are to grow more rapidly and include a wider range of products.

Greater access to the markets of the developed countries requires that the policies of MDCs condone trade liberalization. Although the "average" nominal tariff rate on manufactured goods in the major industrial countries has been reduced considerably through successive rounds of trade negotiations, there is still a wide dispersion of tariffs over the range of manufactures and semi-manufactures of potential interest to the LDCs, and in some cases even the nominal tariff rates are very high. There is still a strong degree of protectionism in the tariff structures of the major industrial nations: nominal tariff rates still tend to rise with the degree of labor-intensiveness; effective rates of protection tend to be much higher than nominal tariff rates; and effective tariffs on the products of special interest to developing countries are generally higher than those on other products, so that the tariff structure in the major developed countries remains strongly protected against imports of labor-intensive manufactured goods from the LDCs.

Even more restrictive are the nontariff barriers—especially quotas—placed on imports from LDCs. Textiles are, for example, the most important manufactured commodities now exported by the LDCs, but textiles confront severe quota limitations. The original negotiation of the Arrangement Regarding International Trade in Cotton Textiles was based on the concept of "market disruption." Members of GATT may place "restraints"

---

[4]For an empirical study of prospective changes, see Bela Balassa, "Prospects for Trade in Manufactured Goods Between Industrial and Developing Countries, 1978–1990," *Journal of Policy Modeling,* Vol. 2, No. 3, 1980, pp. 437–55.

on particular categories of cotton textile imports if increased imports constitute "market disruption," defined as: (1) a sharp and substantial increase in imports of a particular item; (2) import prices substantially below domestic prices in the importing country; and (3) serious damage to domestic producers or threat thereof. Not only does the invocation of "market disruption" allow severe restrictionist measures on textiles (the major export of more developing countries than any other class of manufactured goods), but it also sets an undesirable precedent for other manufactures that might receive similar treatment. No policies promoting manufactured exports will be effective if the concept of "market disruption" is invoked to restrict the entry of manufactures into advanced markets. This contradicts any attempt to grant preferences to LDCs. If a preference system is qualified by the imposition of tariff quotas,[5] then the efficacy of preferences is clearly diminished. If developed countries are to be receptive to imports from LDCs, they must provide adjustment assistance measures to move resources out of displaced industries in which the comparative advantage of developed countries has been lost to new, more efficient, higher technology product lines. Market

[5]Under a system of tariff quotas, the importing country specifies the quantity of imports of a product it is prepared to import at the preferential duty rate, with all imports greater than this amount being subject to the full most-favored-nation rate.

access on a broader front through trade liberalization can be more significant for LDC exports than preferences subject to safeguards.

After prolonged but unsuccessful attempts to secure actual effective preferential treatment, the LDCs may be better advised to emphasize market access across the most-favored-nation tariffs. Such tariff reductions and removal of nontariff barriers would allow greater access to developed markets than any feasible preference system. This requires, however, some liberal safeguard system and adjustment assistance to raise the import-absorption capacity of the developed importing countries. The basic problem is that of reducing the adjustment costs entailed by a changing international division of labor in order that the real sources of comparative advantage might operate to change the structure of trade. Unless the MDCs can move out of stagflation to high rates of growth and adopt industrial policies and adjustment assistance programs that will facilitate the movement out of declining industries, the forces of protectionism might react against imports from LDCs.

At the same time that the MDCs must remove their trade restrictions, the LDCs must pursue policies to take advantage of wider opportunities. If new exports are to be supported, the LDCs will have to undertake export promotion policies. These policies are considered in the next selection.

Comment

Given their concern about the labor absorption problems in the LDCs, policymakers have given special attention to the employment impact of a more rational trade policy. Some studies examine the employment effect through intercountry or intertemporal comparison of trade patterns and the transformation of the industrial structure of the labor force. See, for example, Hollis B. Chenery and Moises Syrquin, *Patterns of Development 1960–1970* (1975); Hollis B. Chenery, "Interactions between Industrialization and Exports," *American Economic Review* (May 1980).

Other studies compare the labor intensity of import-substituting and export industries at each point in time. Under an export promotion strategy, export industries grow faster, as do import-competing industries under import substitution. If employment per unit of output and value added are greater in one set of industries than the other, then employment growth will be faster under the trade strategy that allows the labor-intensive industries to grow relatively faster.

EXHIBIT VIII.1. Growth of Merchandise Trade

	Merchandise Trade (millions of dollars)		Average Annual Growth Rate (percent)				Terms of Trade (1975 = 100)	
			Exports		Imports			
	Exports 1981	Imports 1981	1960–70	1970–81	1960–70	1970–81	1978	1981
Low-income economies	42,444 t^a	60,117 t	4.9 m^b	−0.7 m	5.3 ma	2.4 m	109 m	87 m
China and India	29,624 t	36,567 t	—	—	—	—	—	—
Other low-income	12,820 t	23,550 t	5.0 m	−0.8 m	5.4 m	1.9 m	110 m	88 m
1 Kampuchea, Dem.	—	—	—	—	—	—	—	—
2 Bhutan	—	—	—	—	—	—	—	—
3 Lao, PDR	9	85	—	—	—	—	—	—
4 Chad	141	137	5.9	−7.2	5.1	−3.8	111	101
5 Bangladesh	791	2,594	6.5	−0.7	7.1	5.1	99	79
6 Ethiopia	374	738	3.6	−0.8	6.2	(.)^c	158	69
7 Nepal	63	195	—	—	—	—	—	—
8 Burma	455	373	−11.6	1.3	−5.7	−2.8	110	123
9 Afghanistan	263	484	1.5	5.3	0.8	8.9	107	112
10 Mali	154	370	2.9	7.1	−0.4	7.4	110	102
11 Malawi	284	359	11.6	5.9	7.6	2.4	108	82
12 Zaire	662	672	−1.8	−3.1	5.5	−11.9	100	74
13 Uganda	317	395	4.9	−9.8	6.2	−9.1	144	106
14 Burundi	71	167	—	—	—	—	—	—
15 Upper Volta	75	338	14.6	7.3	8.0	7.6	106	98
16 Rwanda	147	191	15.8	0.4	8.0	10.7	180	107
17 India	8,064	15,001	3.2	4.6	−0.9	3.2	108	66
18 Somalia	200	199	2.4	6.7	2.6	3.2	109	98
19 Tanzania	566	1,410	3.4	−8.1	6.0	−1.2	121	113
20 Viet Nam	153	791	—	—	—	—	—	—
21 China	21,560	21,566	—	—	—	—	—	—
22 Guinea	428	351	—	—	—	—	—	—
23 Haiti	333	587	—	—	—	—	—	—
24 Sri Lanka	1,036	1,803	4.6	−1.5	−0.2	1.4	151	80
25 Benin	36	886	5.0	−7.0	7.5	5.0	101	84
26 Central African Rep.	136	88	8.1	1.9	4.5	−1.9	116	104
27 Sierra Leone	277	238	0.4	−4.4	1.9	−1.6	112	73
28 Madagascar	335	494	5.4	−2.5	4.1	−3.1	117	87
29 Niger	297	449	6.0	23.4	11.9	13.4	106	88
30 Pakistan	2,880	5,342	8.3	3.0	5.3	4.0	97	75
31 Mozambique	457	774	6.0	−15.0	7.9	−16.7	84	77
32 Sudan	658	1,529	2.2	−5.2	0.6	4.2	86	88
33 Togo	344	597	10.5	1.5	8.5	10.3	97	63
34 Ghana	878	1,184	0.2	−7.1	−1.5	−5.0	193	75
Middle-income economies	337,172 t	403,729 t	5.4 m	4.1 m	6.4 m	4.8 m	98 m	87 m
Oil exporters	146,227 t	148,221 t	3.9 m	2.5 m	2.8 m	9.5 m	95 m	133 m
Oil importers	198,945 t	257,508 t	7.0 m	4.3 m	7.- m	3.2 m	101 m	73 m

EXHIBIT VIII.1. Growth of Merchandise Trade (*Continued*)

	Merchandise Trade (millions of dollars)		Average Annual Growth Rate (percent)				Terms of Trade (1975 = 100)	
			Exports		Imports			
	Exports 1981	Imports 1981	1960–70	1970–81	1960–70	1970–81	1978	1981
Lower middle-income	98,497 *t*	122,588 *t*	5.2 *m*	3.0 *m*	6.5 *m*	4.1 *m*	98 *m*	77 *m*
35 Kenya	1,144	1,946	7.2	−1.9	6.5	−1.8	144	99
36 Senegal	416	1,035	1.2	−1.4	2.3	2.5	97	68
37 Mauritania	259	265	50.6	−0.3	4.6	3.2	81	72
38 Yemen Arab Rep.	39	1,699	—	—	—	—	—	—
39 Yemen, PDR	421	1,096	—	—	—	—	—	—
40 Liberia	531	448	18.4	1.2	2.9	−1.5	88	63
41 Indonesia	22,259	13,271	3.4	6.5	2.0	11.9	95	154
42 Lesotho	—	—	—	—	—	—	—	—
43 Bolivia	909	825	9.6	−1.9	8.0	7.0	129	153
44 Honduras	760	949	10.7	4.2	11.6	1.9	102	75
45 Zambia	1,044	1,032	2.3	−0.2	9.8	−6.8	89	67
46 Egypt	3,233	8,839	3.2	0.4	−0.9	9.4	83	86
47 El Salvador	792	986	5.5	0.7	6.3	2.3	129	80
48 Thailand	6,918	10,014	5.2	11.8	11.4	4.9	87	62
49 Philippines	5,722	7,946	2.2	7.7	7.2	2.6	98	68
50 Angola	1,744	1,640	9.0	−12.7	11.5	0.2	103	152
51 Papua New Guinea	851	1,116	—	—	—	—	—	—
51 Morocco	2,242	4,356	2.5	2.2	3.4	5.4	74	63
53 Nicaragua	529	731	9.7	0.2	10.5	−1.3	113	76
54 Nigeria	18,727	18,776	6.5	0.5	1.7	17.8	102	190
55 Zimbabwe	663	704	—	—	—	—	81	94
56 Cameroon	1,079	1,428	7.0	4.9	9.3	6.9	168	90
57 Cuba	1,128	1,897	4.0	1.2	5.4	1.6	72	65
58 Congo, People's Rep.	1,040	791	5.1	16.8	−1.0	6.7	82	96
59 Guatemala	1,281	1,774	9.0	5.0	7.1	5.2	134	77
60 Peru	3,255	3,803	2.0	4.6	3.8	0.5	90	72
61 Ecuador	2,562	2,332	2.9	5.7	11.6	9.3	107	136
62 Jamaica	974	1,473	4.6	−6.7	8.1	−6.5	107	75
63 Ivory Coast	2,586	2,434	8.7	5.1	9.7	5.7	150	78
64 Dominican Rep.	1,188	1,450	−2.3	3.8	10.0	2.2	49	49
64 Mongolia	3,190	5,181	2.2	1.6	2.5	6.5	145	127
66 Colombia	2,209	3,924	4.2	4.0	2.3	9.2	81	104
67 Tunisia	2,209	3,924	4.2	4.0	2.3	9.2	81	104
68 Costa Rica	968	1,198	9.5	4.0	10.0	2.2	125	87
69 Korea, Dem. Rep.	—	—	—	—	—	—	—	—
70 Turkey	4,703	8,911	—	1.2	—	2.0	95	67
71 Syrian Arab Rep.	2,103	4,663	3.3	5.2	4.1	12.6	99	130
72 Jordan	732	3.149	10.1	21.2	3.6	13.9	74	61
73 Paraguay	296	506	5.4	6.8	7.6	6.6	110	72

EXHIBIT VIII.1. Growth of Merchandise Trade (*Continued*)

	Merchandise Trade (millions of dollars)		Average Annual Growth Rate (percent)				Terms of Trade (1975 = 100)	
			Exports		Imports			
	Exports 1981	Imports 1981	1960–70	1970–81	1960–70	1970–81	1978	1981
Upper middle-income	238,675 *t*	283,141 *t*	5.4 *m*	7.0 *m*	5.9 *m*	4.7 *m*	97 *m*	89 *m*
74 Korea, Rep. of	21,254	26,131	33.4	22.0	20.6	10.9	105	67
75 Iran, Islamic Rep. of	10,169	12,634	12.5	−13.4	11.6	10.5	94	217
76 Iraq	9,372	18,907	5.4	−2.1	1.4	23.6	94	209
72 Malaysia	12,884	13,132	5.8	6.8	2.3	7.1	109	101
78 Panama	315	1,540	10.2	−1.9	10.5	−4.3	93	93
79 Lebanon	1,107	3,946	14.4	1.9	5.1	3.3	101	88
80 Algeria	14,056	11,505	3.5	1.0	−1.1	12.0	96	196
81 Brazil	23,172	24,007	5.0	8.7	4.9	2.9	108	56
82 Mexico	20,033	24,168	2.8	15.3	6.4	9.5	92	89
83 Portugal	4,147	9,799	9.6	—	14.2	—	—	—
84 Argentina	6,304	9,425	3.5	9.4	0.4	3.2	77	71
85 Chile	3,952	6,364	0.7	9.8	4.8	3.5	88	61
86 South Africa	22,670	21,485	5.4	7.2	8.2	−1.4	80	73
87 Yugoslavia	10,929	15,817	7.7	4.5	8.8	4.6	104	99
88 Uruguay	1,215	1,599	2.2	4.3	−2.9	3.6	124	87
89 Venezuela	20,959	10,645	1.1	−7.0	4.4	9.6	92	212
90 Greece	4,292	8,677	10.8	10.8	10.8	4.7	98	88
91 Hong Kong	21,737	24,680	12.7	9.7	9.2	12.1	103	100
92 Israel	5,416	7,777	10.8	9.6	8.8	2.2	101	68
93 Singapore	20,967	27,608	4.2	12.0	5.9	9.9	102	—
94 Trinidad and Tobago	3,725	3.115	4.9	−4.9	3.2	−5.8	96	129
High-income oil exporters	174,131 *t*	68,249 *t*	11.0 *m*	−1.5 *m*	11.0 *m*	20.8 *m*	94 *m*	208 *m*
95 Libya	16,391	15,414	67.5	−7.5	15.4	15.7	94	213
96 Saudi Arabia	120,240	35,244	11.0	4.5	11.2	33.5	94	205
97 Kuwait	16,561	8,042	5.2	−9.4	10.7	16.0	92	210
98 United Arab Emirates	20,939	9,549	—	4.5	5.5	25.6	96	189
Industrial market economies	1,210,104 *t*	1,290,415 *t*	8.5 *m*	5.4 *m*	9.5 *m*	4.4 *m*	100 *m*	90 *m*
99 Ireland	7,706	10,603	7.1	8.4	8.3	6.4	104	90
100 Spain	20,337	33,159	11.5	—	18.5	—	99	87
101 Italy	72,215	91,022	13.6	6.7	9.7	3.6	101	86
102 New Zealand	5,563	5,684	4.6	3.9	2.9	1.7	114	107
103 United Kingdom	102,807	101,991	4.8	6.6	5.0	3.6	107	105
104 Japan	152,016	143,287	17.2	9.0	13.7	3.9	112	79
105 Austria	15,845	21,048	9.6	7.3	9.6	6.7	97	88

EXHIBIT VIII.1. Growth of Merchandise Trade (*Continued*)

	Merchandise Trade (millions of dollars)		Average Annual Growth Rate (percent)				Terms of Trade (1975 = 100)	
			Exports		Imports			
	Exports 1981	Imports 1981	1960–70	1970–81	1960–70	1970–81	1978	1981
106 Finland	14,015	14,202	6.8	4.8	7.0	2.5	92	84
107 Australia	21,767	23,768	6.5	3.8	7.2	5.2	92	92
108 Canada	69,907	66.010	10.0	4.2	9.1	5.5	93	95
109 Netherlands	68,732	65,921	9.9	5.0	9.5	3.5	100	96
110 Belgium	55,705	62,464	10.9	4.6	10.3	5.3	96	90
111 France	100,497	120,924	8.2	6.6	11.0	6.5	101	90
112 United States	233,739	273,352	6.0	6.5	9.8	4.4	95	86
113 Denmark	16,317	17,874	7.1	4.9	8.2	2.5	101	87
114 Germany, Fed. Rep.	176,043	163,934	10.1	5.8	10.0	5.5	101	86
115 Norway	18,220	15,652	9.1	7.0	9.7	4.3	92	129
116 Sweden	28,630	28,824	7.7	2.2	7.2	4.2	93	87
117 Switzerland	27,043	30,696	8.5	4.2	9.0	4.5	108	102
East European nonmarket economies	150,270 *t*	146,968 *t*	9.4 *m*	6.7 *m*	8.6 *m*	6.1 *m*	—	—
118 Albania	—	—	—	—	—	—	—	—
119 Hungary	8,893	8,854	9.7	8.2	9.1	6.1	98	96
120 Romania	12,610	12,458	9.4	—	8.8	—	—	—
121 Bulgaria	1,848	2,633	14.4	11.6	12.9	8.7	—	—
122 Poland	13,182	15.224	−0.3	6.7	−0.4	6.0	101	98
123 USSR	79,003	72,960	9.7	5.6	7.1	8.3	—	—
124 Czechoslovakia	14,876	14,658	6.7	6.4	7.0	5.1	—	—
125 German Dem. Rep.	19,858	20,181	8.3	—	8.6	—	—	—

Source: World Bank, *World Development Report, 1983,* pp. 164–65.

[a]Indicates a total.

[b]Indicates a median value.

[c]Indicates a value substantially less than one.

A number of studies indicate that the creation of employment is greater from export expansion than import substitution. Westphal found that the labor-capital ratio for manufactured exports in Korea in 1966 was 3.24 compared with 2.67 for domestic production and 1.98 for import substitution; see Larry E. Westphal, "The Republic of Korea's Experience with Export-Led Industrial Development," *World Development,* Vol. 6, No. 3 (1978). Krueger's calculations of the ratio of labor per unit of domestic value added in exportable and import-competing industries for several countries also indicated that exportables are in general more labor-intensive than import substitutes; see Anne O. Krueger, "Alternative Trade Strategies and Employment in LDCs," *American Economic Review* (May 1978).

When resources are switched from import substitution to export promotion, employment is created for two reasons: (1) because of the greater degree of labor intensity in exportables, and (2) because of the higher overall rate of return to investment in the economy and the

EXHIBIT VIII.2. Structure of Merchandise Exports

	Percentage Share of Merchandise Exports									
	Fuels, Minerals, and Metals		Other Primary Commodities		Textiles and Clothing		Machinery and Transport Equipment		Other Manufactures	
	1960	1980	1960	1980	1960	1980	1960	1980	1960	1980
Low-income economies	9 w^a	18 w	70 w	37 w	15 w	18 w	(.) w	4 w	6 w	23 w
China and India	—	20 w	—	30 w	—	18 w	—	5 w	—	27 w
Other low-income	8 w	9 w	83 w	62 w	4 w	21 w	(.) w	2 w	5 w	6 w
1 Kampuchea, Dem.	0	—	100	—	0	—	0	—	0	—
2 Bhutan	—	—	—	—	—	—	—	—	—	—
3 Lao, PDR	—	—	—	—	—	—	—	—	—	—
4 Chad	3	—	94	—	0	—	0	—	3	—
5 Bangladesh	—	(.)^b	—	34	—	49	—	(.)	—	17
6 Ethiopia	0	8	100	92	0	(.)	0	(.)	0	(.)
7 Nepal	—	(.)	—	69	—	24	—	0	—	7
8 Burma	4	—	95	—	0	—	0	—	1	—
9 Afghanistan	(.)	—	82	—	14	—	3	—	1	—
10 Mali	0	—	96	—	1	—	1	—	2	—
11 Malawi	—	(.)	—	90	—	5	—	4	—	1
12 Zaire	42	—	57	—	0	—	0	—	1	—
13 Uganda	8	—	92	—	0	—	0	—	(.)	—
14 Burundi	—	(.)	—	99	—	(.)	—	(.)	—	1
15 Upper Volta	0	(.)	100	89	0	2	0	2	(.)	7
16 Rwanda	—	—	—	—	—	—	—	—	—	—
17 India	10	7	45	34	35	22	1	7	9	30
18 Somalia	0	1	88	98	0	(.)	8	(.)	4	1
19 Tanzania	(.)	10	87	74	0	8	0	1	13	7
20 Viet Nam	—	—	—	—	—	—	—	—	—	—
21 China	—	25	—	28	—	16	—	5	—	26
22 Guinea	42	—	58	—	0	—	0	—	0	—
23 Haiti	0	—	100	—	0	—	0	—	0	—
24 Sri Lanka	(.)	16	99	65	0	11	0	1	0	7
25 Benin	10	—	80	—	7	—	(.)	—	3	—
26 Central African Rep.	12	(.)	86	74	(.)	(.)	1	(.)	1	26
27 Sierra Leone	15	—	20	—	0	—	0	—	65	—
28 Madagascar	4	9	90	84	1	2	1	2	4	3
29 Niger	—	—	100	—	0	—	0	—	0	—
30 Pakistan	0	7	73	43	23	37	1	2	3	11
31 Mozambique	0	—	100	—	0	—	0	—	0	—
32 Sudan	0	1	100	96	0	1	0	2	0	(.)
33 Togo	3	58	89	32	3	4	0	3	5	3
34 Ghana	7	—	83	—	0	—	0	—	10	—

EXHIBIT VIII.2. Structure of Merchandise Exports (*Continued*)

	Percentage Share of Merchandise Exports									
	Fuels, Minerals, and Metals		Other Primary Commodities		Textiles and Clothing		Machinery and Transport Equipment		Other Manufactures	
	1960	1980	1960	1980	1960	1980	1960	1980	1960	1980
Middle-income										
economies	30 *w*	36 *w*	59 *w*	27 *w*	3 *w*	9 *w*	1 *w*	10 *w*	7 *w*	18 *w*
Oil exporters	48 *w*	78 *w*	48 *w*	15 *w*	1 *w*	2 *w*	(.) *w*	2 *w*	3 *w*	3 *w*
Oil importers	15 *w*	12 *w*	68 *w*	34 *w*	5 *w*	13 *w*	2 *w*	14 *w*	10 *w*	27 *w*
Lower middle-income	20*w*	44 *w*	76 *w*	38 *w*	1 *w*	5 *w*	(.) *w*	2 *w*	3 *w*	11 *w*
35 Kenya	1	34	87	50	0	1	0	3	12	12
36 Senegal	3	39	94	46	1	1	1	3	1	11
37 Mauirtania	4	—	69	—	1	—	20	—	6	—
38 Yemen Arab Rep.	—	(.)	—	49	—	6	—	25	—	20
39 Yemen, PDR	—	75	—	25	—	(.)	—	(.)	—	(.)
40 Liberia	45	59	55	38	0	(.)	0	1	0	2
41 Indonesia	33	76	67	22	0	1	(.)	(.)	(.)	1
42 Lesotho	—	—	—	—	—	—	—	—	—	—
43 Bolivia	—	86	—	11	—	(.)	—	1	—	2
44 Honduras	5	7	93	81	0	2	0	(.)	2	10
45 Zambia	—	—	—	—	—	—	—	—	—	—
46 Egypt	4	67	84	22	0	0	(.)	(.)	3	2
47 El Salvador	0	5	94	59	3	13	(.)	3	3	20
48 Thailand	7	14	91	57	0	9	0	6	2	14
49 Philippines	10	21	86	42	1	6	0	2	3	29
50 Angola	—	—	—	—	—	—	—	—	—	—
51 Papua New Guinea	0	46	92	52	0	(.)	0	(.)	8	2
54 Nigeria	8	95	89	4	0	(.)	0	(.)	3	1
55 Zimbabwe	71	—	25	—	1	—	(.)	—	3	—
56 Cameroon	19	33	77	64	0	1	2	(.)	2	2
57 Cuba	2	5	93	90	1	0	(.)	0	4	5
58 Congo, People's Rep.	7	86	84	7	(.)	(.)	5	(.)	4	7
59 Guatemala	2	6	95	70	1	6	0	1	2	17
60 Peru	49	64	50	20	0	6	0	2	1	8
61 Ecuador	0	56	99	41	0	1	0	1	1	1
62 Jamaica	50	23	45	14	2	1	0	3	3	59
63 Ivory Coast	1	5	98	87	0	3	(.)	2	1	3
64 Dominican Rep.	6	3	92	73	0	(.)	0	1	2	23
65 Mongolia	—	—	—	—	—	—	—	—	—	—
66 Colombia	19	3	79	77	0	6	(.)	2	2	12
67 Tunisia	24	56	66	8	1	18	1	2	8	16

EXHIBIT VIII.2. Structure of Merchandise Exports (*Continued*)

	Percentage Share of Merchandise Exports									
	Fuels, Minerals, and Metals		Other Primary Commodities		Textiles and Clothing		Machinery and Transport Equipment		Other Manufactures	
	1960	1980	1960	1980	1960	1980	1960	1980	1960	1980
68 Costa Rica	0	1	95	65	0	5	0	4	5	25
69 Korea, Dem. Rep.	—	—	—	—	—	—	—	—	—	—
70 Turkey	8	8	89	65	0	16	0	3	3	8
71 Syrian Arab Rep.	0	74	81	18	2	4	0	1	17	3
72 Jordan	0	29	96	35	0	4	0	9	4	23
73 Paraguay	0	(.)	100	88	0	(.)	0	(.)	0	12
Upper middle-income	38 w	32 w	46 w	23 w	4 w	10 w	2 w	13 w	10 w	22 w
74 Korea, Rep. of	30	1	56	9	8	29	(.)	20	6	41
75 Iran, Islamic Rep. of	88	—	9	—	0	—	0	—	3	—
76 Iraq	97	—	3	—	0	—	0	—	0	—
77 Malaysia	20	35	74	46	(.)	2	(.)	11	6	6
78 Panama	—	24	—	67	—	3	—	(.)	—	6
79 Lebanon	—	—	—	—	—	—	—	—	—	—
80 Algeria	12	99	81	1	0	(.)	1	(.)	6	(.)
81 Brazil	8	11	89	50	0	4	(.)	17	3	18
82 Mexico	24	39	64	22	4	3	1	19	7	17
83 Portugal	8	7	37	21	18	27	3	13	34	32
84 Argentina	1	6	95	71	0	2	(.)	7	4	14
84 Chile	92	59	4	21	0	(.)	0	1	4	19
86 South Africa	29	23	42	23	2	1	4	5	23	48
87 Yugoslavia	18	9	45	18	4	9	15	28	18	36
88 Uruguay	—	1	71	61	21	16	—	4	8	18
89 Venezuela	74	98	26	(.)	0	(.)	0	(.)	(.)	2
90 Greece	9	25	81	28	1	17	1	3	8	27
91 Hong Kong	5	2	15	5	45	34	4	19	31	40
92 Israel	4	2	35	16	8	8	2	13	51	61
93 Singapore	1	28	73	18	5	4	7	26	14	24
94 Trinidad and Tobago	82	93	14	2	0	(.)	0	1	4	4
High-income oil exporters	—	98 w	—	(.) w	—	(.) w	—	1 w	—	1 w
95 Libya	100	100	0	(.)	0	(.)	0	(.)	0	(.)
96 Saudi Arabia	95	99	5	(.)	0	(.)	0	(.)	0	1
97 Kuwait	—	89	—	1	—	1	—	3	—	6
98 United Arab Emirates	—	—	—	—	—	—	—	—	—	—

EXHIBIT VIII.2. Structure of Merchandise Exports (*Continued*)

	Percentage Share of Merchandise Exports									
	Fuels, Minerals, and Metals		Other Primary Commodities		Textiles and Clothing		Machinery and Transport Equipment		Other Manufactures	
	1960	1980	1960	1980	1960	1980	1960	1980	1960	1980
Industrial market economies	11 *w*	13 *w*	23*w*	15 *w*	7*w*	5 *w*	29 *w*	35 *w*	30 *w*	32 *w*
99 Ireland	5	3	67	39	6	8	4	19	18	31
100 Spain	21	8	57	20	7	5	2	26	13	41
101 Italy	8	7	19	8	17	11	29	33	27	41
102 New Zealand	(.)	7	97	72	0	3	(.)	5	3	13
103 United Kingdom	7	18	9	8	8	4	44	35	32	35
104 Japan	11	2	10	2	28	4	23	55	28	37
105 Austria	26	5	22	12	10	9	16	28	26	46
106 Finland	3	8	50	22	1	7	13	18	33	45
107 Australia	13	28	79	44	(.)	1	3	7	5	20
108 Canada	33	28	37	23	1	1	8	26	21	22
109 Netherlands	15	26	34	23	8	4	18	17	25	30
110 Belgium*a*	15	15	9	11	12	7	13	22	51	45
111 France	9	8	18	18	10	5	25	34	38	35
112 United States	10	9	27	23	3	2	35	40	25	26
113 Denmark	2	5	63	38	3	5	19	24	13	28
114 Germany, Fed. Rep.	9	7	4	7	4	5	44	45	39	36
115 Norway	22	59	34	9	2	1	10	12	32	19
116 Sweden	10	9	29	12	1	2	31	40	29	37
117 Switzerland	2	5	8	4	12	6	30	33	48	50
East European nonmarket economies	18 *w*	—	33 *w*	—	3 *w*	—	34 *w*	—	21 *w*	—
118 Albania	—	—	—	—	—	—	—	—	—	—
119 Hungary	6	9	28	25	7	7	38	32	21	27
120 Romania	—	—	—	—	—	—	—	—	—	—
121 Bulgaria	3	—	75	—	12	—	6	—	4	—
122 Poland	—	20	—	9	—	6	—	36	—	29
123 USSR	24	—	28	—	1	—	21	—	26	—
124 Czechoslovakia	20	7	11	9	(.)	5	45	50	25	29
125 German Dem. Rep.	—	—	—	—	—	—	—	—	—	—

Source: World Bank, *World Development Report, 1983*, pp. 166–67.

*a*Indicates a weighted average.

*b*Indicates a value substantially less than one.

larger national income, the rate and level of investment will also be increased. Employment rises with the switch to a more labor-intensive mode of production and from an expansion in the capital stock.

The most comprehensive study is Anne O. Krueger et al., *Trade and Employment in Developing Countries, I. Individual Studies* (1981). See also Juergen B. Donges, "A Comparative Survey of Industrialization Policies in Fifteen Semi-Industrial Countries," *Weltwirtschaftliches Archiv* (1976); C. Hsieh, "Measuring the Effects of Trade Expansion on Employment," *International Labour Review* (January 1973); William G. Tyler, "Manufactured Exports and Employment Creation in Developing Countries," *Economic Development and Cultural Change* (January 1976); Yves Sabolo, "Industrialisation, Exports and Employment," *International Labour Review* (July-August 1980).

Comment

Trade policies of the MDCs are obviously of extreme importance in determining whether the LDCs will have market access for their exports. These policies are being increasingly determined by the industrial countries' concern with "domestic injury" from LDC imports and the requests for "market safeguards" to reduce market penetration. In recent years, there has been a spread of neoprotectionism in industrial countries, as evidenced by the imposition of quantitative restrictions on imports, "voluntary export restrictions," and "orderly marketing agreements." In their imposition of these trade barriers, countries have bypassed the provisions of the General Agreement on Tariffs and Trade (GATT).

A major shortcoming of the Tokyo Round of GATT trade negotiations completed in 1979 was its failure to reach agreement on a code of "market safeguards" that would bring international order to the enactment of quotas and voluntary export restrictions. See Bela Balassa, "The Tokyo Round and the Developing Countries," *Journal of World Trade Law,* Vol. 14 (1980); Donald B. Keesing and Martin Wolf, *Textile Quotas Against Developing Countries* (1980); G. M. Meier, "Externality Law and Market Safeguards: Applications to the GATT Multilateral Trade Negotiations," *Harvard International Law Journal* (Summer 1977); G. M. Meier, "The Tokyo Round of Multilateral Trade Negotiations and the Developing Countries," *Cornell International Law Journal* (Summer 1980).

VIII.B.5. Export Promotion: Lessons of Experience—Note

An increasing number of countries have promoted their manufactured exports and reached the status of newly industrializing countries (NICs) or semi-industrialized countries (SICs).[1] Outstanding performers

[1] J. Bergsman, "Growth and Equity in Semi-Industrialized Countries," *World Bank Staff Working Paper* No. 351, 1979. Bergsman identifies 16 principal SICs: Korea, Taiwan, Colombia, Turkey, Yugoslavia, Mexico, Israel, Egypt, Philippines, Brazil, Portugal, Hong Kong, Singapore, Greece, Argentina, and Spain. Marginal cases include India, Uruguay, Chile, Thailand, and Malaysia.

have been the Republic of Korea, Taiwan, Hong Kong, Singapore, and Brazil. The record of some of these "success stories" has been noted in Chapter 1. They have achieved the promotion of industry through an outward-looking policy rather than through the protection of an inward-looking industrial structure. These countries exemplify the structural transformation of an open dualistic economy. As successful export performers, they demonstrate that this transformation involves a substantial rise in the share of manufacturing in GNP and a significant shift away from dependence on primary exports toward manufactured goods as a source of foreign exchange. There is considerable evidence that success in promoting manufactured exports is critical to the course of industrial development.[2]

What are some of the lessons to be learned from the experience of these countries and the manner in which they promoted the export of their manufactured goods?

On the demand side, conditions were highly favorable during the 1950s and 1960s up to the slowing down of growth in the world economy after 1973. The earlier two decades were unique for the high rate of growth in the more developed countries (MDCs)—an historical record period—and for the growth in world trade. The demand for imports was high and rising in the MDCs, and the high growth rate of the MDCs fostered trade liberalization and weakened the case for protection. Of course, as growth occurs in the MDCs, their pattern of demand has to match the actual or potential comparative advantage of the exporting LDCs to create opportunities for exports. This is likely to be more true for exports of manufactured goods than primary products.

On the supply side, however, the LDCs varied in their international competitiveness and in their capacity to take advantage of export markets. In large part, the differences in performance are to be explained by differences in governmental policies—especially as related to the entire set of policies that determined the foreign trade regime and the bias between import substitution and export promotion in the different countries. To promote exports, governmental policies have to accomplish an outward-oriented policy shift that removes the bias in favor of import substitution. As long as an import-substitution bias exists, exports will suffer from the implicit taxation and quantitative restrictions, from the cost of inputs being above free trade prices, and from the diversion of resources to the sheltered and capital-intensive import-substitution industries.

When government policies are biased against exports in favor of import substitution, the effective exchange rate for imports (EER_m) is higher than the effective exchange rate for exports (EER_x). The term EER_m equals the number of units of domestic currency that would be paid for a dollar's worth of imports, taking into account tariffs, surcharges, interest on advance deposits, and other measures that affect the price of imports. The term EER_x is defined as the number of units of domestic currency that can be obtained for a dollar's worth of exports, taking into account export duties, subsidies, special exchange rates, input subsidies related to exports, and other financial and tax measures that affect the price of exports.

An outward-looking policy shift must reduce the bias against exports by changing the ratio of EER_x/EER_m from less than unity to equal to unity. This is illustrated in Figure 1, where the international price ratio changes from PP under a foreign trade regime that is biased in favor of import substitution to $P'P'$ in a regime that is neutral and represents free trade conditions. The policy objective should be to remove the bias against exports and establish an unbiased "free trade" regime for

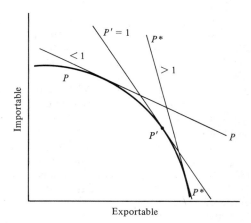

FIGURE 1. Definition of import-substituting and export promoting strategies. (Source: Adapted from J. Bhagwati, *Anatomy and Consequences of Exchange Control Regimes*, 1978, p. 208.)

[2]See Hollis B. Chenery, "Interactions between Industrialization and Exports," *American Economic Review*, May 1980, pp. 281–7.

exports. If the regime were to raise the ratio of EER_x/EER_m above unity (P*P*), it would be oversubsidizing exports and protecting exports instead of promoting exports by simply removing the bias against exports and establishing a neutral trade regime.

There is evidence that oversubsidization of exports is less likely to occur than oversubsidization of import substitution (see selection VIII.B.1). Although an outward-oriented industrial development strategy does not mean favoring exports over import substitution, it does mean that similar incentives are provided to production for domestic and for export markets. The creation of such a free trade regime for exports provides incentives that improve export performance. A devaluation of the country's overvalued exchange rate will stimulate the demand for the country's exports. If, at the same time, tariffs and quantitative restrictions are removed from imports, the devaluation will be compensated on the import side.

If the EER_m is initially greater than EER_x, the exchange rates can be realigned by raising their EER_x. This can be done through a number of policy measures that increase gross export receipts, reduce the cost of exports, or reduce profit tax liability through such measures as export exchange rates, subsidies to export value, tax and duty concessions, foreign exchange retention schemes, and preferential credits.

In Korea, for example, various export promotion schemes have been followed: tariff exemptions on imports of raw materials and spare parts, tariff and tax exemptions granted to domestic suppliers of exporting firms, domestic indirect tax exemptions, reduction in direct taxes on income earned in exporting, accelerated depreciation, import entitlement linked to exports, reduced taxes on public utilities, monopoly rights granted in new export markets, direct export subsidies, credit subsidies through lower interest rates, and preferential access to loans. When these incentives are included in the computation of effective exchange rates for exports, the effective exchange rate becomes considerably higher than the nominal or official exchange

rate.[3] In 1975, for instance, Korea's official exchange rate was 485 won per dollar, but when export subsidies (internal tax exemptions, customs duty exemptions, and interest rate subsidies) were added, the EER_x became 566 per dollar.

It is not sufficient, however, simply to graft export subsidies onto the preexisting import structure. If protection against imports remains high, the incentive to sell domestically is likely to remain greater than the incentive to export. Those policies that bring the ratio of EER_m and EER_x closer to unity characterize what Bhagwati and Krueger term Phases III and IV in their typology of exchange control regimes. (See selection VIII.B.2.)

Much of the success of Korea, Singapore, and Taiwan has been written in terms of Phases III and IV policy reforms. In these countries, a free trade regime was applied to exports. Exporters were free to choose between domestic and imported inputs; they were exempted from indirect taxes on their output and inputs; and they paid no duty on imported inputs. The same privileges were extended to the producers of domestic inputs used in export production. These incentives ensured that in the manufacturing sector, on average, exports and import substitution received similar treatment. Nor was there discrimination against primary exports and primary production in general.[4]

Experience also shows that these export incentives will not be effective unless the policies can be expected to last for the duration of investments in the export sector. A long-term commitment to these policies is essential; the political and economic risks can be reduced only if there is policy stability.

[3]Anne O. Krueger, *The Developmental Role of the Foreign Sector and Aid: Studies in the Modernization of The Republic of Korea, 1945–1975,* 1979, chapters 4 and 5; Larry E. Westphal, "The Republic of Korea's Experience with Industrial Development," *World Development,* 1978.

[4]For a comparison with other countries, see Bela Balassa, *The Process of Industrial Development and Alternative Development Strategies,* Princeton Essays in International Finance No. 141, December 1980, pp. 12–16.

Four principles of an outward-oriented development strategy have been summarized by Professor Balassa:

The experience of developing countries in the postwar period leads to certain policy prescriptions. First, while infant-industry considerations call for the preferential treatment of manufacturing activities, such treatment should be applied on a moderate scale, both to avoid the establishment and maintenance of inefficient industries and to ensure the continued expansion of primary production for domestic and foreign markets.

Second, equal treatment should be given to exports and to import substitution in the manufacturing sector, in order to ensure resource allocation according to comparative advantage and the exploitation of economies of scale. This is of particular importance in the case of intermediate goods and producer and consumer durables, where the advantages of large plant size and horizontal and vertical specialization are considerable and where import substitution in the framework of small domestic markets makes the subsequent development of exports difficult. The provision of equal incentives will contribute to efficient exportation and import substitution through specialization in particular products and in their parts, components, and accessories.

Third, infant-industry considerations apart, variation in incentive rates within the manufacturing sector should be kept to a minimum. This amounts to the application of the "market principle" in allowing firms to decide on the activities to be undertaken. In particular, firms should be free to choose their export composition in response to changing world market conditions.

Fourth, in order to minimize uncertainty for the firm, the system of incentives should be stable and automatic. Uncertainty will also be reduced if the reform of the system of incentives necessary to apply the principles just described is carried out according to a timetable made public in advance.[5]

The transition to a liberalized unbiased trade regime has, however, proved difficult for a number of countries. Economists have proposed that a country start with a compensated devaluation—that is, a devaluation coupled with the removal of quotas and tariffs in order to bring the exchange rate to its long-run equilibrium level and to adjust tariffs and export subsidies so that domestic relative prices remain the same.[6] Quotas should be replaced by tariffs to allow price incentives.

This is the first step of rationalization. The next step should be to reduce the variance in effective rates of protection and to reduce home-market bias—including *additional liberalization, variance reduction, and bias reduction.* But the transition period to the liberalized trade regime will take a number of years, and a successful transition requires a whole sequence of changes over several years. During this transition period, the government must have the determination and political support to remove existing distortions and achieve the reallocation of resources in the face of resistance by affected interest groups. Political stability and commitment are essential to provide strong signals and strong incentives to exporters. Furthermore, the country must have some safety net that provides foreign exchange to support import liberalization before the export promotion becomes sufficient to earn foreign exchange. An inflow of foreign capital, or the ability to utilize foreign reserves, has been of critical importance in cases of successful liberalization. From a study of several countries, Krueger concluded that "In many of these instances, import liberalization could not have begun without receipt of new lines of credit. Of those liberalizations that were possible because of credits, many terminated when the credits were exhausted."[7] If import liberalization cannot be supported by a capital inflow, then the redesign of import protection will have to be delayed until export growth

---

[5]Bela Balassa, *The Process of Industrial Development and Alternative Development Strategies,* Princeton, p. 24.

[6]See I. M. D. Little, T. Scitovsky, and M. Scott, *Industry and Trade in Some Developing Countries,* 1970, chapter 10; B. Balassa, *Policy Reform in Developing Countries,* 1977, pp. 25–27; A. O. Krueger, *Synthesis,* National Bureau of Economic Research, Vol. 9. For a good discussion of the processes and problems in several cases of transition, see Donald B. Keesing, "Trade Policy for Developing Countries," *World Bank Staff Working Paper* No. 353, August 1979, pp. 220–52.

[7]Krueger, chapter 8, p. 67.

has begun and the balance-of-payments situation has eased.

Once a country succeeds in shifting to an outward-oriented policy, it must continue to follow monetary and fiscal policies that will avoid inflation. For if inflation were to ensue, the domestic currency would again become overvalued in terms of foreign currency, and tariffs and quantitative restrictions would be reimposed. A combination of protection for domestic sale of final goods and a declining real effective exchange rate or the purchasing-power-parity-adjusted effective exchange rate (say, EER_x deflated by general consumer prices) will make it less profitable, relatively and absolutely, to export than to sell domestically.

At the micro level, the competitiveness of export firms will depend on their cost competitiveness and product or nonprice competitiveness.[8] Cost competitiveness is determined by factor productivity, factor prices, factor proportions, and location relative to export markets. Especially significant is the relationship between wages and labor productivity for the labor-intensive exports that tend to dominate in the early period of export promotion. Although money wages in the LDC may be low, exports will not be competitive if the efficiency of labor is so low that the wage costs per unit of output are actually high. Product competitiveness will also depend on such nonprice determinants of export success as design, quality control, punctuality in delivery, and service. A close relationship with Western trading companies has often helped to improve models and design, and to overcome marketing problems.

Furthermore, the supply of entrepreneurship is obviously important in improving both cost competitiveness and product competitiveness. There has not, however, been a uniform need for foreign entrepreneurship or the resources of the multinational enterprise. In Korea and Taiwan, for example, only a small percentage of the exports is produced by firms with any foreign equity participation. Nor has it always been necessary to first produce for the home demand before being able to export. For a number of countries exporting manufactures, the new export industries have been quite different from their old import-substitution industries.

What can we expect in future? Can the success stories continue their success, and can other nations also become newly industrializing countries via an outward-oriented industrial policy? The crucial issue now is: If the MDCs in the future do not exhibit the rapid growth of the 1950s and 1960s, can the experience of the successful export performers be repeated for other LDCs? The next selection considers this issue.

[8]For an illustration of this in Colombia, see David Morawetz, *Why the Emperor's New Clothes Are Not Made in Colombia*, New York, 1981.

Comment

Successful as the newly industrializing countries were in promoting exports of manufactures during the past two decades, there is now a resurgence of export pessimism. Can the East Asian model of export-oriented development be generalized to other developing countries? Can developing country exports keep growing? Will slow growth in the MDCs and the spread of protectionism limit imports from the LDCs?

A number of studies examine these questions. Some statistical projections are offered by Bela Balassa, "Prospects for Trade in Manufactured Goods between Industrial and Developing Countries, 1978–1990," *Journal of Policy Modeling*, Vol. 2, No. 3 (1980). Another simulation exercise concludes that generalization of the East Asian model of export-led development across all developing countries would result in untenable market penetration into industrial countries, but the author, William R. Cline, concludes that

the findings of the study should not be interpreted to favor a closed-economy strategy of discouragement of exports. On the contrary, in many developing countries trade liberalization still has far to go. Several

EXHIBIT VIII.3. Exports of Manufactures from Developing Countries

	All Developing Countries	Low-Income Developing Countries	Middle-Income Developing Countries
Value of exports, 1980 (1978 billion U.S. dollars)	97.4	6.0	91.4
Annual growth of exports,			
1970–80 (%)	12.9	6.9	13.4
Destination, 1977 (%)	n.a.	100.0	100.0
Industrial countries	n.a.	51.0	58.0
Developing countries	n.a.	27.0	30.0
Centrally planned economies	n.a.	12.0	6.0
Capital-surplus oil exporters	n.a.	10.0	6.0

Source: *World Development Report, 1981*, New York, Oxford University Press, 1981.
Note: n.a. = not available

Latin American countries in particular could raise their manufactured exports substantially without even reaching cross-country norms, let alone export dimensions of the East Asian variety, and one strongly suspects that in many such cases liberalization of the trading and exchange rate regimes would lead to more rapid export growth.

See William R. Cline, "Can the East Asian Model of Development Be Generalized?" *World Development,* Vol. 10, No. 2 (1982).

EXHIBIT VIII.4. Growth of Industrial Output, Employment, and Exports in Selected Countries

	Thailand	Malaysia	Korea	Singapore
Average annual growth (%)				
Industrial output				
1960–70	11.6	—	17.2	12.5
1970–79	10.4	9.9	16.5	8.6
Industrial employment				
1960–70	5.3	5.0	11.2	5.7
1970–77	12.1[a]	6.9	7.7	4.5
Merchandise exports				
1970–79	12.0	6.5	25.7	11.0
Percentage of manufactures in merchandise exports				
1960	2	6	14	26
1978	25	21	89	46
Percentage of labor force in industry				
1960	4.4	11.7	9.3	23.0
1970	6.0	14.6[b]	20.1	30.3
1977	14.3[c]	20.1[b]	27.5	33.2

Source: *World Development Report, 1981; ILO Yearbook of Labour Statistics, 1978;* and *ILO Labour Force Estimates and Projections, 1970–2000,* Geneva, 1977.
[a]1970–76.
[b]World Bank estimates.
[c]1976.

EXHIBIT VIII.5. Exports, Imports, Manufactured Output, and GNP in Selected Developing Countries (percent)

	Argentina	Brazil	Chile	Colombia	India	Israel	Korea	Mexico	Singapore	Taiwan	Yugoslavia
Share of manufactured exports in manufactured output											
1960	0.8	0.4	3.0	0.7	9.7	7.9	0.9	2.6	11.2	8.6	10.8
1966	0.9	1.3	4.1	3.0	9.4	12.8	13.9	2.9	20.1	19.2	13.8
1973	3.6	4.4	2.5	7.5	8.6	14.1	40.5	4.4	42.6	49.9	16.9
Incremental ratio of manufactured exports to manufactured output											
1960–66	1.0	3.6	5.5	7.7	8.9	23.9	24.8	3.2	28.4	24.8	15.8
1966–73	6.5	5.6	0.0	11.4	7.7	14.9	45.7	5.5	47.5	56.4	19.5
Share of manufactured imports in total utilization of manufactured goods											
1960	14.6	10.8	26.3	30.8	19.3	28.5	24.4	19.6	56.2	28.5	22.0
1966	6.3	7.5	21.6	28.0	16.5	32.8	26.5	16.2	53.2	29.3	17.3
1973	5.4	13.0	17.5	21.5	9.5	41.2	35.9	15.2	64.3	38.9	24.0
Incremental ratio of manufactured imports to utilization of manufactured goods											
1960–66	−3.9	−3.0	14.1	20.5	10.4	42.5	31.9	11.7	49.2	30.5	13.6
1966–73	4.4	15.7	10.8	14.2	−0.4	45.1	40.4	14.4	67.0	42.2	29.4
Ratio of total exports to GNP											
1960	8.9	6.1	12.6	11.3	4.2	8.4	1.5	6.4	9.9	9.5	22.4
1966	7.3	7.1	15.7	9.5	4.2	12.8	6.5	5.4	26.6	17.1	14.2
1973	8.1	9.8	7.6	11.8	4.3	15.5	26.1	4.3	44.6	47.8	14.5
Incremental ratio of total exports to GNP											
1960–66	5.3	12.3	23.0	3.4	4.1	20.4	13.0	4.3	52.0	24.7	10.7
1966–73	9.0	11.5	3.3	14.5	4.3	17.4	34.8	3.3	52.0	63.3	14.8
Ratio of total imports to GNP											
1960	10.3	7.1	12.9	12.6	7.5	20.1	16.0	9.0	65.4	18.9	32.8
1966	5.2	6.1	13.5	12.6	7.4	21.2	18.7	7.2	62.5	19.9	18.3
1973	5.5	11.1	6.8	10.6	4.5	30.8	34.3	8.6	91.5	40.5	22.0
Incremental ratio of imports to GNP											
1960–66	1.3	0.9	14.9	12.4	7.3	23.0	22.2	5.1	57.9	20.8	12.3
1966–73	6.0	14.2	2.4	8.4	0.3	37.3	41.3	9.7	103.6	50.8	26.4

Source: Bella Balassa, "Export Incentives and Export Performance in Developing Countries: A Comparative Analysis," *Weltwirtschaftliches Archiv* 114 (1978).

Note: In the absence of manufactured output figures for 1960, these have been derived from the 1966 figures by utilizing growth rates of value added in manufacturing and inflation in prices of manufactured goods for the period 1960–66. The same method has been applied in cases where 1973 manufactured output figures are not available.

EXHIBIT VIII.6. Distribution of Merchandise Exports by Economic Sector, 1960 and 1977–78 (percent)

	Industrial Products and Materials									
	Agricultural Commodities		Fuels, Minerals, Metals		Textiles and Clothing		Machinery, Transport Equipment		Other Manufactures	
Country Group	1960	1978	1960	1978	1960	1978	1960	1978	1960	1978
Low-income countries	69	38	13	32	13	12	(.)	3	5	15
Middle-income countries	60	29	27	35	3	9	2	12	8	17
Industrial market economies	23	15	11	8	7	5	29	38	30	34
Capital-surplus oil exporters	4	(.)	96	98	0	(.)	0	1	0	1
Nonmarket industrial economies	33	11	18	25	3	3	25	34	21	27
	1960	1977	1960	1977	1960	1977	1960	1977	1960	1977
Developing countries by region										
Africa, south of the Sahara	73	32	14	65	a	a	1	(.)	12	3
Middle East and North Africa	24	6	71	89	a	a	0	1	5	4
East Asia and the Pacific	58	26	18	22	a	a	4	13	20	39
South Asia	66	40	5	7	a	a	1	5	28	48
Latin America and the Caribbean	47	41	48	43	a	a	1	5	4	11
Southern Europe	55	27	10	7	a	a	8	20	27	46

Sources: *World Development Report, 1981* and *World Tables, 1980.*
Note: (.) indicates a value substantially less than 1.
[a]Included in other manufactures.

VIII.B.6. The Slowing Down of the Engine of Growth*

Let me begin by stating my problem. For the past hundred years the rate of growth of output in the developing world has depended on the rate of growth of output in the developed world. When the developed grow fast, the developing grow fast, and when the developed slow down, the developing slow down. Is this linkage inevitable? More specifically, the world has just gone through two decades of unprecedented growth, with world trade growing twice as fast as ever before, at about 8 percent per annum in real terms, compared with 0.9 percent between 1913 and 1939, and less than 4 percent per annum between 1873 and 1913. During these prosperous decades, the less developed countries (LDCs) have demonstrated their capacity to increase their total output at 6 percent per annum, and have indeed adopted 6 percent as the minimum average target for LDCs as a whole. But what is to happen if the more developed countries (MDCs) return to their former growth rates, and raise their trade at only 4 percent per annum: Is it inevitable that the growth of the LDCs will also fall significantly below their target? My purpose is not to predict what is going to happen, but to explore existing relationships and how they may change.

The extraordinary growth rates of the two decades before 1973 surprised everybody. We knew that the world economy experiences long swings in activity; that world trade, for example, grew faster between 1830 and 1873 than it grew between 1873 and 1913, that is to say, between 4 and 5 percent before 1873, compared with between 3 and 4 percent after 1873. But a jump to 8 percent was inconceivable. . . .

The fast pace of world trade played havoc

*From W. Arthur Lewis, "The Slowing Down of the Engine of Growth," *American Economic Review,* September 1980, pp. 555–7, 559–64. Reprinted by permission.

with development theory. The collapse of international trade in the 1930's had seemed irreversible, so much so that Keynes had even declared that we didn't need much of it anyway. So in the 1940's and 1950's we created a whole set of theories which make sense if world trade is stagnant—balanced growth, regional integration, the two-gap model, structural inflation—but which have little relevance in a world where trade is growing at 8 percent per annum. Also many countries, basing their policies on the same assumption, oriented inwards mainly towards import substitution. The fact that world trade was growing rapidly was not universally recognized until the second half of the 1960's. Then nearly every country discovered the virtues of exporting. Now we are in danger of being caught out again. Since 1973 the growth rate of world trade has halved, and nobody knows whether this is temporary or permanent. But most of our economic writing continues to assume implicitly that a return to 8 percent is only just around the corner.

Let me come back to the relationship between MDCs and LDCs. The principal link through which the former control the growth rate of the latter is trade. As MDCs grow faster, the rate of growth of their imports accelerates and LDCs export more. We can measure this link. The growth rate of world trade in primary products over the period 1873 to 1913 was 0.87 times the growth rate of industrial production in the developed countries; and just about the same relationship, about 0.87, also ruled in the two decades to 1973.[1] World trade in primary products is a wider concept than exports from developing countries, but the two are sufficiently closely related for it to serve as a proxy. We need no elaborate statistical proof that trade depends on prosperity in the in-

[1]For data, see my *Growth and Fluctuations 1870–1913,* pp. 175–76.

dustrial countries. More interesting is the evidence that the relationship was quantitatively the same over a hundred years, so that the two-thirds increase in the rate of growth of exports of primary products from *LDC*s was no more or less than could be predicted from the increased rate of growth of *MDC* production.

Most interesting is that the coefficient is less than one, viz. 0.87. This means that if the engines of growth were industrial production in *MDC*s and exports of primary products in *LDC*s, then the *MDC* engine was beating slightly faster than the *LDC* engine. The effects of equal beating would not necessarily be exactly the same. And there are side effects that strengthen the connection. When the beat is faster the terms of trade are expected to be more favorable to the *LDC*s (though that did not happen this time). The domestic market prospers, so *LDC* industrialization for the domestic market is speeded; this happened. The *MDC*s relax their barriers to imports of manufactures, so this trade accelerates as well. Foreign capital flows into minerals, manufactures, and infrastructure. And foreign countries take more migrants, so that the homeward flow of remittances to *LDC*s is larger in prosperous times.

Putting it all together, including the fact that industrial production grew faster in *LDC*s than in *MDC*s, it is not surprising that the rate of growth of gross domestic product was just about the same in *LDC*s and in *MDC*s over the quarter of a century ending in 1973, namely about 5 percent per annum. Since *LDC* population was growing faster than *MDC* population, there is a big gap in the growth rates of output per head, about 4 percent in *MDC*s, against 2.5 percent in *LDC*s. The performance of *LDC*s was remarkable in absolute terms, but the gap between *MDC*s and *LDC*s in income per head continued to widen rapidly.

Now we come to our dilemma. The objective of most people who are concerned with these matters is to narrow the per capita gap between *MDC*s and *LDC*s. But how is one to do this if they are linked to equal growth of

total output? One might perhaps conceive a lower rate of growth of *MDC*s. Many *MDC* voices are calling for this—the environmentalists, the persons who fear exhaustion of exhaustible resources, the advocates of greater grace and leisure in our lives, and others. But if the *MDC* growth rate falls, the *LDC* growth rate will fall too, and *LDC*s will get the worst of it, since the terms of trade will move against them. Given the link, it is in the interest of *LDC*s that the *MDC*s should grow as rapidly as they can.

Three questions come to mind. First, what is likely to happen to the speed of MDC growth? Secondly, can LDCs maintain fast growth even in face of a decline of MDC growth? And thirdly, is it desirable that LDC development depend on rapid growth of exports to MDCs? . . .

In what follows I shall assume that industrial production in *MDC*s grows more slowly than it was growing before 1973, and that the imports of these countries grow only at 4 percent a year, over the next twenty years. This is not a prediction; it is merely the assumption whose consequences we are seeking to analyze.

I shall also assume that *LDC*s want their *GDP* to grow at 6 percent per annum, and that this requires thier imports to grow at 6 percent. This linkage follows from the further assumption that the individual *LDC* will not become more self-sufficient, perhaps because it is too small; though *LDC*s as a group will have to be more self-sufficient. No importance attaches to whether the figure for imports is the same as the figure for the growth of gross domestic product; all that matters is that the growth rate of exports from *LDC*s is assumed to be significantly higher than the rate of growth of imports of *LDC* commodities into *MDC*s. The *LDC*s will continue to pay for some of their imports out of proceeds of transfers, including foreign aid and private foreign investment, but we shall assume that this still leaves *LDC*s needing, say, a 6 percent growth rate for exports, while *MDC*s are assumed to increase their imports from *LDC*s only at 4 percent a year.

The problem is how to reconcile these two growth rates.

There could theoretically be a simple way, namely for *LDC*s to have an ever increasing share of *MDC* imports, but we have closed this door. The main link between *MDC* and *LDC* economies has been the *MDC* demand for *LDC* primary commodities. This has been a link in terms of physical volume, not much affected by prices. The *LDC*s could not sell significantly more primary produce by reducing prices; on the contrary, they would earn substantially less purchasing power as the terms of trade deteriorated. The *LDC*s could earn more by reducing the volume or by joining together in raising prices. The direct effect of these actions would be to reduce output, but this could be offset by investing the extra earnings judiciously. However none of this seems to be in the cards; so we shall assume that our problem cannot be solved by accelerated or decelerated production of primary commodities normally exported to *MDC*s.

What about manufactures? These are now nearly 40 percent of the exports of the non-OPEC *LDC*s, and are still their fastest growing export. Could the whole problem be solved simply by increasing the growth rate of manufactured exports to *MDC*s, in substitution for primary products? I shall assume that this cannot be done, since if it can be done my paper ends abruptly. Also I do not think that it can be done. The *MDC*s are willing to let in manufactured exports when they are prosperous, since they then have many growing industries that can take in people displaced by imports. Our assumption that the *MDC* growth rate is low rules out this possibility. It would indeed be more appropriate to assume that *MDC*s will take less manufactures from *LDC*s rather than more.

Our basic assumptions therefore are that *LDC*s need to have their exports grow at 6 percent a year, but *MDC*s will increase their imports from *LDC*s only at 4 percent a year. What is to happen to the growth of *LDC* output?

Let me concede at once that from the standpoint of the individual *LDC* it matters not at all what the *MDC* growth rate may be. Given resources and flexibility, it can always sell more to *MDC*s. However, it thereby displaces some other *LDC*'s trade. What one can do cannot be done by all.

At the level of arithmetic this problem now has only one solution. If total sales from *LDC*s increase at 6 percent, while sales to *MDC*s increase at 4 percent, sales to the rest of the world (given weights of seven to three) must increase initially at about 11 percent per annum. Ignoring the socialist countries, which could help by buying much more from *LDC*s but won't, the *LDC*s can solve the problem only by accelerating sharply their trade with each other.

Inter-*LDC* trade is still rather small—about 19 percent of the exports of non-OPEC *LDC*s.[2] The percentage did not change significantly over the two decades to 1973 despite all the effort that was put into creating and servicing regional trade institutions. Can this trade take up the slack left by *MDC*s as *MDC*s slow down?

The answer is in the affirmative. Currently the *LDC*s depend on the *MDC*s for food, fertilizers, cement, steel, and machinery. Taken as a group, *LDC*s could quickly end their dependence for the first four, and gradually throw off their dependence for machinery. They also import a considerable quantity of light manufactures for which they are not in any sense dependent (some $31 billion in 1977, compared with $47 billion of engineering products). They could quickly rid themselves of these, and more gradually throw off their dependence for machinery.

The *LDC*s are capable of feeding themselves now, if they adopt appropriate agrarian policies and, as our eleven new international tropical agricultural research institutes give us better varieties and improved technology, output should more than keep up with population. The problem is to get through the period while the birth rate re-

[2]Trade data in this and the next two paragraphs are from GATT, *International Trade 1977–78*.

mains obstinately high to the less-frightening times when the birth rate will have dropped below twenty per thousand. It may be a near thing, but we should make it.

As for fertilizers, cement, and steel, these are made by applying standard technology to raw materials that are widely available outside the *MDC*s. Machinery is more bothersome because important parts of this trade involve economies of scale, continually improving technology, and patented or secret knowledge. However, several *LDC*s are moving into this field, and already machinery is 15 percent or more of the output of manufactures in at least eight *LDC*s (India, Brazil, Singapore, Chile, Korea, Argentina, Mexico, and Israel)[3] The *LDC* exports of engineering products are also growing rapidly, and contrary to popular belief, already exceed *LDC* exports of textiles and clothing in value. There is no reason why *LDC*s as a group should not become nearly self-sufficient in standard types of equipment. . . .

It follows, therefore, that in the situation we are analyzing, where world trade decelerates, customs unions would be more highly prized and would be made more effective, especially in regard to large-scale industries with region-wide economies of scale. But even so, the leading commodities that *LDC*s would now have to produce to a greater extent for each other cannot be shared out between next door neighbors on a political basis. Food, fertilizers, cement, steel, and fule pick their locations more in terms of raw material availability, and machinery will come in the first instance from those *LDC*s that already have a substaintal industrial base. This new *LDC* trade would be worldwide, just as European and U.S. trade are worldwide.

I am therefore arguing that it is physically feasible for *LDC*s to maintain a high rate of growth even if *MDC*s decide otherwise for themselves. How does physical feasibility translate into an effective economic framework?

One way would be to follow the customs union route, with *LDC*s giving preferential treatment to imports from other *LDC*s. The nucleus of this exists already in the Protocol Relating to Trade Negotiations among Devoloping Countries which came into force in 1973, with the blessing of GATT, and which provides for negotiated preferential arrangements among sixteen of the bigger and more advanced *LDC*s. The philosophy of such an arrangement is in line with the spirit of Bretton Woods, which recognized the rights of countries to impose restrictions on other countries which were tending persistently to run balance-of-payments surpluses, as would be the situation if the *LDC*s were growing faster than the *MDC*s. One may doubt however whether such different countries will get very far along the route of preferential concessions. If they are to prefer each other's goods, this will have to be because they are competitive in price with those of *MDC*s.

In the economist's model this competitiveness would come about automatically. The *LDC*s would run a balance-of-payments deficit because of the *MDC* slowdown, yet persist in their own rapid growth instead of slowing down themselves. Adjustment comes in the old gold standard version through an outflow of gold that reduces their price levels; or in the modern versions by devaluation, which has the same effect. The real world is more complicated. Inflation is universal, but aggressive sellers of manufactures have to keep their prices down; so this set of *LDC*s would need special emphasis on inflation controls. Devaluation cannot be avoided when prices cease to be competitive, but is palliative rather than curative in situations when it triggers further increases in domestic costs that reinstate the differential that it was meant to eliminate. The *LDC*s have the same problem as the *MDC*s: the domestic price level can no longer be controlled merely by twirling general controls such as the rate of interest, or the supply of money, or the rate of exchange for the currency. They too now

[3]Share of machinery in manufactures calculated from United Nations, *Yearbook of Industrial Statistics 1976*.

experience the cost-push element in price determination for which the only remedy is some sort of incomes policy. We expect more from the economic system than our grandparents did in the nineteenth century, by way of full employment and faster growth, and should not be surprised that the economic system requires more from us by way of supporting institutions.

These new aggressive LDCs, exporting machinery to each other, may also have problems in financing their trade. Nearly every LDC has a separate currency. We are envisioning Nigeria selling cereals to India for rupees, with which it buys machinery from Brazil. Some kind of clearing agreement may become necessary; otherwise LDC traders will tend to do business with each other in one or more MDC currencies, and will be constrained by the relative scarcity of such currencies. Perhaps the International Monetary Fund would straighten this out. A more serious problem will be to finance the export of capital goods from one LDC to another, since the seller is expected to help finance the buyer. It is not likely that the LDC exporters can do this on their own. We must assume that they will be allowed to raise untied loans in the MDC financial markets, perhaps using the regional development banks as intermediaries to a greater extent than is now the case.

But the real problem is not whether LDCs can become competitive and hold their own in each other's markets. Problems of pricing and foreign exchange can work themselves out in the world market. The real problem is whether LDCs will persist in rapid growth despite the slowdown of the MDCs. If the economy is still dependent, the balance-of-payments weakness will pull it down; but if it has attained self-sustaining growth, the weakness in the foreign exchanges merely launches a drive to export to other LDCs, and the weakness in the balance of payments is then only transitional.

If a sufficient number of LDCs reach self-sustaining growth, we are into a new world. For this will mean that instead of trade de-termining the rate of growth of LDC production, it will be the growth of LDC production that determines LDC trade, and internal forces that will determine the rate of growth of production. Not many countries are ready to make this switch. India is an obvious possibility, along with some of the other subscribers to the Protocol of 1973. It is not possible for all LDCs to make this switch and neither is it necessary, for if leading LDCs grow fast and import heavily, they will substitute to some extent for the former rapid growth of MDCs. For those who use the language of center and periphery, this means that a number of countries leave the periphery and join the center. Or if they are specially linked to each other by preferential trade and currency arrangements, one may even speak of the creation of a new center consisting of former peripheral nations that have built a new engine of growth together.

The shadow on this picture is what happens to those LDCs whose best option has been to export raw materials to MDCs. Our exercise starts from the assumption that the growth rate of MDC demand is reduced, so these face surpluses and unfavorable terms of trade. We have provided an escape for LDCs that can turn to exporting food or manufactures, but we have not assumed that the new core LDCs will substitute for the MDCs by drinking more coffee or tea, or using more rubber and jute. This solution therefore involves some hardships for the less adaptable LDCs, constrained by climate or by the small size of their markets. A framework for helping them exists already in the IMF's compensatory financing, and in the EEC's STABEX support; but these are meant for temporary fluctuations. Bigger and more persistent support would be required.

Transnational corporations would probably play some part in the establishment of this new inter-LDC trading network. The cadre of domestic entrepreneurs is adequate in the more advanced industrial LDCs to manage most of the range of light consumer goods and light engineering products. One of our main concerns, however, is to diminish reliance on *MDC*s for heavy machinery and such, and this extends into fields where experience is limited. Since we are assuming that the market will send out price signals favoring production in *LDC*s, whether because of tariffs or of currency adjustments, transnational corporations will be eager to preserve their markets by establishing subsidiaries behind the protective barrier. Hostility to such corporations is universal and their influence is diminishing in most sectors, especially in mining, public utilities, distribution, and finance; but not in manufacturing, where judging by advertisements in the *New York Times* and the financial press, *LDC* governments are only too anxious to invite the participation of transnational corporations. There are plenty of restrictions—on the hiring of expatriate staff, on percentages of equity owned by foreigners, on borrowing in the local market, on technology, and so on. Also, in many cases joint ownership with local capitalists or with government agencies is prescribed. A government anxious to promote industrialization and a corporation anxious to preserve or extend its market find common ground.

The awkward part of the exercise is to sustain the momentum of 6 percent growth through the transition from dependence on *MDC* trade to dependence on *LDC* markets. During this transition the leading industrial *LDC*s must establish their footholds in each others' markets, as well as those of other *LDC*s; also the agrarian changes must occur which both feed the urban population and present a growing market for its goods and services. It is possible that some of the leading *LDC*s can take this in their stride, just as German industrialists launched their trade drive in the 1880's, followed by the United States after 1895, by Japan in the 1930's, and more recently by Brazil. They do not have to begin with machinery, since *LDC*s still import so much light manufactures from *MDC*s. They can start here and move more gradually into machinery.

At the other extreme, it is also possible that there is simply not yet enough entrepre-

neurial steam in the leading *LDC*s to make this transition without a supporting framework. I have already mentioned the main international elements of such a framework, namely preferential tariff and currency arrangements. The domestic element consists of the maintenance of home demand in the face of stagnant world trade in primary products, so that the economy can continue to go forward instead of collapsing. Much of the responsibility for maintaining momentum then falls on the government, given its large share of the cash economy, and also the extent to which it regulates or supports the private sector. It has to carry the responsibility for a large investment program (private and public) in human and physical capital. This responsibility could not be carried without external aid. The *MDC*s would have to be in a mood to say: we will not give you more trade; here for a while is more aid instead.

The recession that started in 1974 has now lasted long enough for *LDC*s to consider the possibility that *MDC*s intend to maintain rates of *GNP* growth which will allow world trade to expand only at around 4 percent a year. This would be a major blow to *LDC* growth aspirations, unless new steps were taken to support rising participation of *LDC*s in *LDC* trade. I have been trying to analyze what these steps might be. They ought to figure prominently in current North–South negotiations, but in fact they do not, since these negotiations tacitly assume that high *MDC* growth rates will soon be resumed. Perhaps this assumption will turn out to be correct; economics does not foretell the future. For the least, *LDC*s should be discussing among themselves in what directions they would wish to go, prior to negotiations with the *MDC*s.

Of course, the problems tackled in this paper would not arise at all if *MDC*s were willing to allow *LDC*s a greater share of *MDC* markets. This would be the logical evolution of a situation where *LDC*s grow faster than *MDC*s; trade with *LDC*s should become an ever-increasing portion of *MDC* trade. We live in a strange world. Through the 1960's and 1970's, *MDC*s have been dismantling their barriers to each other's trade while increasing their barriers to *LDC* trade. Since imports of manufactures from developing countries are only two percent of the consumption of manufactures in OECD countries, this indicates exceptional sensitivity to minor change. Lack of sensitivity, on the other hand, characterizes the failure of developed countries to recognize that dependence is mutual, in that the non-OPEC *LDC*s take 20 percent of OECD exports, and could

therefore by their prosperity help a little to sustain OECD prosperity. It can hardly be an OECD interest to force the *LDC*s into discriminating against OECD sources.

Nor would these problems arise if the *MDC*s would return to the attack on mass poverty within their own borders which they launched so successfully in the 1950's and 1960's, and have now abandoned; since what we all really need is that world trade recapture its growth rate of 8 percent a year. But that is a different story.

VIII.C. TRADE IN PRIMARY PRODUCTS

VIII C.1. Techniques of Price Raising*

The traditional approach to price raising has been to negotiate an agreement to control the quantity of a commodity coming on the world market. Export restriction schemes can be effective in the short run, but they also create their own problems, particularly if they are not sufficiently flexible in allowing increasing market shares for newer, or low cost, producers. This was a major reason, for example, for the breakdown of the International Coffee Agreement in 1973. Market sharing conflicts have also caused great difficulties in the renegotiation of other commodity agreements based on export quotas.

There are, however, other possible techniques which can be considered which avoid the market sharing problem, at least overtly. One possibility for some commodities would be the establishment of an intergovernmental joint marketing agency, which would act as sole buyer from developing producing countries, and as sole seller to developed importing countries. The agency could maintain its own stock which could, in effect, be used in the same way as the traditional type of international buffer stock to smooth out excessive short term price variations. But, by its monopoly position, the agency would also be in a position to raise the level of prices as and when appropriate. The operational principles of such a marketing agency, and its mode of financing, would need to be elaborated in some detail.

Joint marketing agencies would be easier to operate for minerals than for agricultural commodities, since mineral output is more

*From Alfred Maizels, "A New International Strategy for Primary Commodities," in G. K. Helleiner (ed.), *A World Divided: The Less Developed Countries in the International Economy,* London, Cambridge University Press, 1976, pp. 41–4. Reprinted by permission.

amenable to regulation designed to prevent the accumulation of excessive stocks, either in the hands of the marketing agency or in the producing countries themselves. In the case of an agricultural crop, if the marketing agency is obliged to purchase the entire exportable output of producing countries, it would also need the power to dispose of excess stocks either by selling the commodity (at relatively low prices) for non-traditional uses and/or by destruction. Alternatively, a ceiling on the marketing agency's stocks of an agricultural commodity could be agreed, so that producing countries would themselves have to hold or destroy some stocks in years of good harvests.

A classic example of this type of operation, in this case by a private company, is afforded by the Central Selling Agency, a subsidiary of De Beers, which has virtually a monopoly of the world supply of diamonds. The technique is probably applicable to a number of other commodities, particularly minerals.

Further alternatives arise in the field of fiscal policy. One possibility for certain commodities would be the enforcement by all producing countries of an agreed minimum price for their exports. An informal arrangement among the governments of Algeria, Italy, and Spain, to take a recent example, forced up the price of mercury by about one-third between 1973 and mid 1974.

A minimum export price scheme would have similar effects on the aggregate revenue of exporting countries as would a corresponding export quota scheme, but the distribution of gains among the exporting countries is likely to differ insofar as the enforcement of a price minimum results in a shift in the pattern of demand (e.g., away from low price varieties of the commodity).

Another fiscal approach would be the imposition of a uniform *ad valorem* export tax by all producing countries. The more elastic is the aggregate supply, and the more inelastic the aggregate demand, the greater will be the proportion of the tax borne by the consumer. The export tax approach has the advantage of simplicity insofar as it avoids the problem of classifying different varieties or grades, as well as that of negotiating export quotas. An important recent example is the decision of certain banana producing countries to impose a tax on banana exports; though strenuously resisted by the transnational corporations concerned, it seems that this would be a viable technique in suitable circumstances for achieving a fairer share of the benefits of trade for the producing countries.

Where transnational corporations are producers as well as traders, the possibility exists of increasing the net return to the producing countries from the productive activities of these corporations in developing countries by increases in local taxes and royalties. Apart from the well known OPEC case, action on these lines has recently been taken by certain developing countries (Jamaica, Guyana and Haiti) to increase their tax and royalty revenue from bauxite production. An interesting feature of these new tax arrangements is that they aim to relate government tax revenue from bauxite mining to the open market value of the end product (i.e., aluminum) where that is processed. This is a special case of the principle of "indexation," which might well be applicable to a number of other minerals also.

Indexation, in its more general form, relates to measures designed to maintain the commodity export prices received by developing countries in terms of the prices they have to pay for their imports (or their imports of manufactures) from developed countries. Such measures clearly presuppose the evolution of effective market control techniques: once these are established, the indexation of commodity prices to the prices of, say, manufactures exported by developed countries would not be a difficult technical

problem. It would, of course, have important economic effects on both the developing and the developed countries.

As regards the latter, indexation would have certain feedback effects on the rate of inflation, though this is not likely to be a major element in the whole range of inflationary pressures in the developed market economy countries. There would also be a positive element insofar as these various measures to maintain an adequate unit return, in real terms, for the exports of developing countries would be very largely balanced by a greater volume, and certainly a smoother flow, of purchases of capital equipment and other development goods from the industrialised countries.

As regards the impact on the developing countries, much would depend on national action to prevent an excessive expansion in production following an increase in the world price of a particular commodity. Without such action, a price rise could result in the accumulation of excessive stocks, as well as being a disincentive to invest in other sectors, such as in manufacturing industry. Where the monetary benefits of the price rise are channelled into government revenue (as with an export tax), it would be administratively easier to divorce the world price from the net return to the domestic producer. In other cases, internal fiscal measures may be required, according to circumstances, to regulate the growth of output, to increase the efficiency of commodity production and/or to finance diversification programmes as appropriate.

There may thus be scope for effective producer action to regulate the level of world prices of a number of important export commodities. Detailed examination of the circumstances of each commodity market will be required to determine the possibilities. In any event, producer action in one set of commodity markets would not rule out joint producer-consumer action in other markets should that prove feasible and desirable for both groups of countries. Cooperation with consumer countries would be important where such countries can improve the effectiveness of an agreement, e.g., by "policing" the quotas under an export restriction scheme (as in the coffee and cocoa agreements), or where they are important producers of the commodity concerned (as for wheat).

However, joint producer-consumer agreements of the traditional type are likely to involve constraints on the price objective of international action, for the reasons discussed earlier. Such agreements would need to incorporate, *inter alia,* supply commitments by exporting countries at the maximum of a price range as a *quid pro quo* not only for purchasing commitments by importing countries at the minimum of the price range, but also for greater flexibility by these latter countries on the level of the price range itself.

There should, however, be increasing scope also for long term agreements between commodity importing and exporting countries, on either a bilateral or a multilateral basis. Such agreements could specify annual quantities to be traded (where this can reasonably be done), or annual quantitative targets. To the extent that prices can also be specified in such long term agreements, this would help in reducing instability in one sector of the commodity export trade of developing countries. However, price clauses in long term agreements would normally require provi-

sions for annual review in the light of changing market circumstances.

Bilateral long term agreements of this type are usual in the trade between the foreign trade enterprises of socialist countries of Eastern Europe and national trading corporations of individual developing countries. Long term agreements covering commodity trade between market economy countries are normally undertaken between private companies. The greater part of Japanese imports of iron ore, for example, are purchased under long term contracts of up to twenty years' duration from mining companies in Australia and in a number of developing countries.

The negotiation of long term contracts, on a government to government basis, would also allow for the provision of indexation clauses for the adjustment of prices of the commodities covered in line with changes in the prices of manufactured goods. Insofar as such indexation is related to imports of commodities by developed countries, it would enable developing countries to import the same commodities at (lower) world market prices.

The wider use of long term contracts, both bilateral and multilateral, would allow developing countries to plan investments in new capacity with much greater assurance of profitable returns from their commodity exports than they have had hitherto.

VIII.C.2. International Resource Bargaining—Note

The control of the price of oil by the Organization of Petroleum Exporting Countries (OPEC) has posed in dramatic form the question of whether the exercise of "producer power" in commodities can be generalized to other primary producers. Can there be additional producer monopoly agreements that effectively control future supplies or prices of minerals, food, and other primary products

so as to create artificial scarcities and raise export prices above competitive market levels? Is oil a special situation, or can effective producer power be exercised also for bauxite, copper, tin, phosphates, coffee, tea, rubber, and other primary products?

The answers to these questions rest in the outcome of a complex process of international resource bargaining. But we might identify various conditions in this process that will determine the relative bargaining strengths of different producing and consuming countries. First, primary production in the LDCs must be disaggregated—at the least, into such categories as oil, non-fuel minerals, tropical agricultural products, cereals. Secondly, it should be recognized that market intervention can assume various forms: a cartel of exporters that takes collusive action to set production and export quotas or to raise export prices, or one producer acting as a price leader with others following, or by export controls over the flow of exports through imposition of quantitative limitations or export taxes. Whether a particular form of market intervention will be successful in raising the export price and revenue for a particular primary product will depend essentially on the existence of three conditions: (1) a dominant position by a producer country in export markets or the capacity for effective collusion by a group of producer nations; (2) an inelastic demand for the product in consumer countries; (3) a low elasticity of supply of alternative materials for consumer countries.

The economic prospects for successful market intervention must ultimately be determined by detailed econometric studies on an individual commodity basis.[1] Opposing conclusions of a general nature, however, may be summarized here.

The "threat from the Third World" has been emphasized by Bergsten, who states:

Four countries control more than 80 percent of the exportable supply of world copper, have already organized, and have already begun to use their oligopoly power. Two countries account for more than 70 percent of world tin exports, and four countries raise the total close to 95 percent. Four countries combine for more than 50 percent of the world supply of natural rubber. Four countries possess over one-half the world supply of

bauxite, and the inclusion of Australia (which might well join the "Third World" for such purposes) brings the total above 90 percent. In coffee, the four major suppliers have begun to collude (even within the framework of the International Coffee Agreement, which includes the main consuming countries) to boost prices. A few countries are coming to dominate each of the regional markets for timber, the closest present approximation to a truly vanishing resource. The percentages are less, but still quite impressive, for several other key raw materials and agricultural products. And the United States already meets an overwhelming share of its needs for most of these commodities from imports, or will soon be doing so.

A wide range of Third World countries thus have sizeable potential for strategic market power. They could use that power against all buyers, or in a discriminatory way through differential pricing or supply conditions—for example, to avoid higher costs to other LDCs or against the United States alone to favor Europe or Japan.

Supplying countries could exercise maximum leverage through withholding supplies altogether, at least from a single customer such as the United States. Withholding is a feasible policy when there are no substitute products available on short notice, and when the foreign exchange reserves of the suppliers become sizeable enough that they have no need for current earnings.

The suppliers would be even more likely to use their monopoly power to charge higher prices for their raw materials, directly or through such techniques as insisting that they process the materials themselves.[2]

Considering whether oil and OPEC represent a unique case which cannot be duplicated, Bergsten states that

it is very doubtful that oil is different in any qualitative sense. Indeed, many other OPECs look much *easier* to organize and maintain. OPEC had to pool twelve countries to control 80 percent of world oil exports, but fewer countries are usually involved in production of other primary products. Most OPEC countries are heavily dependent on oil, and cartelization was especially risky for them. Other commodity producers are more diversified. OPEC could politicize oil and threaten the world economy; its successors will have an easier task because their products are less important. And eco-

[1]Political prospects are as crucial as economic prospects, but they are not amenable to such systematic empirical study. That is why the problem of international resource bargaining might be characterized more aptly as a problem of international resource *diplomacy.*

[2]C. Fred Bergsten, "The Threat from the Third World," *Foreign Policy,* Summer 1973, pp. 107–8.

nomic and political differences among OPEC countries seem much sharper than those among other potential cartelizers. So new OPECs seem at least as likely as OPEC itself.[3]

In contrast with Bergsten's view, a prominent report by economists from Japan, the European Community, and North America states that

the frequent portrayal of a future world of primary commodities divided up into cartels of developing country producers, as in the Organization of Petroleum Exporting Countries (OPEC), dictating prices and turning the supply on and off to achieve political or other ends, is vastly overdrawn. Primary products are produced by many countries, imports are not everywhere a major proportion of total consumption, and industrial rather than developing countries are the leading suppliers of many internationally traded commodities. Furthermore, many primary commodities can be substituted for each other, depending on price and availability. New collusive attempts by exporters to exploit markets are entirely possible—the more so because governments now intervene more actively in setting the conditions for production and sale, because the issues have become heavily politicized, and because the prospects for short-term gains are sometimes attractive. Also, following the example of OPEC is tempting. The crucial point, however, is that the number of commodities on which collusion would be feasible or effective is small, the economic impact is likely to be limited and isolated rather than pervasive as with oil, and the prospects for sustained success over the medium term, to say nothing for the long term, are dim.[4]

On the particular prospects for market manipulation in the markets for tropical agricultural products, the report recalls that

past attempts by exporting countries to maintain prices of coffee and cocoa above competitive levels have met with only limited and temporary success, as individual exporting countries either would not observe or could not enforce export quotas without the cooperation of importing countries.... Cane

sugar does not lend itself to producer cartelization because of the large number of suppliers and the competition from beet sugar and substitute sweeteners. For other tropical products, such as natural rubber and fibers, attempts to rig prices would be self-defeating because of competition from synthetics. . . .

In the case of cereals, experience with the International Grains Arrangement suggests how difficult it is for exporters, even when their number is limited, to maintain world prices above competitive levels for any significant length of time. Pressure is building up for greater price stability, however, and a renewed international effort to reduce the range of price fluctuations for grains and possibly for oil seeds as well seems bound to be given consideration. But if such a negotiation does take place, it must have as participants both exporters and importers. The end result of a successful negotiation would be a joint commodity agreement rather than a producers' cartel.[5]

It is also questioned whether cartels in mineral industries can be effective.

First, rarely do the major producers and exporters of a mineral adhere to the same political and economic objectives.... Second, many of the producing nations depend heavily on mineral exports for their foreign exchange earnings, so the costs to them of withholding supplies are high.... Third, mineral production involves high fixed costs which continue whether production takes place or not. Thus, pressure mounts to cut prices during downswings in the business cycle to keep capacity utilization from falling drastically.

All this strongly suggests that attempts by producing countries to form cartels in the mineral industries are unlikely to succeed for any extended period. In time members will find the demand for their exports falling as producers outside the cartel boost their supplies and consumers switch to substitute materials. Eventually, they will have to abandon artificially high prices to avoid losing their markets entirely.[6]

Another study reaches similar conclusions:

Even the strongest political urge, or the most adroit management, cannot alter certain basic factors that, in our judgment, severely limit the possible accomplishments of producers' alliances in non-fuel minerals.

[3]C. Fred Bergsten, "The New Era in World Commodity Markets," *Challenge,* September–October 1974, p. 40.

[4]*Trade in Primary Commodities: Conflict or Cooperation?,* A Tripartite Report, The Brookings Institution, Washington, D.C., 1974, pp. 1–2.

[5]Ibid., p. 32.

[6]Ibid., pp. 30–31.

The key economic fact is that, while demand for most non-fuel minerals is price-inelastic in the short run . . . , this is not necessarily true over the long run, certainly not to the extent that holds for oil. Calculations based on historic experience for tin, aluminum and copper, for example, suggest strongly that in the long run the drop in demand more than offsets any price increase, so that the total return to the producers eventually becomes less than before the price change. Although the econometric measurement of price elasticities is a tricky process leading to differing estimates of individual cases, there is little disagreement on the broad point about short-term and long-term price elasticity.

The reasons are threefold—stockpiles, recycling possibilities, and the use of substitutes—none of which, of course, applies to oil in anything like the same way as yet.[7]

The foregoing clearly represent different views on the prospect of OPEC-like cartels being effective in various primary commodity markets. The major purpose of the cartel might be interpreted as the improvement in the producing country's terms of trade—more precisely, not simply the commodity terms of trade $\frac{P_x}{P_m}$, but rather the income terms of trade $\frac{P_x Q_x}{P_m}$, where P_x is an export price index, Q_x is an export volume index, and P_m is an import price index. This is an attempt to raise the primary country's share in the gains from trade and to increase its "capacity to import" (Q_m) derived from a given Q_x (as distinguished from the capacity to import based on a capital inflow). Thus, issues of international distributional equity and the size of a country's development program (as determined by the foreign exchange constraint), become intertwined with the process of international resource bargaining.

But to the extent that cartels and other measures to control export prices succeed, they impose real costs on the international community by inducing the production of costlier sources of supply, aggravating inflationary pressures, slowing down the rate of growth in consuming countries, and inviting retaliatory measures.

The deleterious effects on the "Fourth World" countries that are in the "resource-poor" category—that is, agricultural countries without mineral resources—should be of special concern to the international community. The problem of acquiring minerals (and the derivatives of fertilizer and foodstuffs) at a price they can afford became in the 1970s a major handicap to the realization of development plans in resource-poor developing countries. Special arrangements that will provide these countries with the means of financing these imports or that will provide them with additional export revenue may impose additional costs on the world economy.

It is also noteworthy that most primary products are actually produced in high-income countries. At the same time as several rich countries are substantial exporters of primary products, some poor countries are heavy importers of foodstuffs and industrial raw materials. Price-raising commodity agreements would therefore not offer a straightforward transfer of resources from rich to poor countries. On the contrary, as Professor Cooper notes, they would generate

a quite arbitrary distribution of gains and losses among both developed and less developed countries. Moreover, the less developed countries that would benefit tend to be those that are better off; with minor exceptions, the poorest countries would not benefit, and often would lose, from raising commodity prices. Such an action would thus not contribute much to the alleviation of world poverty.[8]

From the standpoint of world economic welfare, the policies of trade liberalization, additional aid, and foreign investment (with a benefit-cost ratio greater than unity) are first-best policies in comparison with cartels

[7]Bension Varon and Kenji Takeuchi, "Developing Countries and Non-Fuel Minerals," *Foreign Affairs,* April 1974, pp. 505–6. For similar views, see also Raymond F. Mikesell, "More Third World Cartels Ahead?" *Challenge,* December 1974, pp. 26–7.

[8]Richard N. Cooper, "Developed Country Reactions to Calls for a NIEO," in *Toward a New Strategy for Development,* A Rothko Chapel Colloquium, 1979, p. 259.

and related price fixing undertakings that have costly side effects and are hence second-best as policies for increasing the gains from trade and raising the capacity to import.

The discussion of the control of trade in primary products has raised other issues that deserve attention. The use of export controls that impede access to supplies imposes costs on the world economy that are similar to those of import controls. But GATT has been concerned only with the latter. Bergsten has therefore proposed new rules to govern export controls:

Like those existing GATT rules which seek to govern the use of import controls, a set of rules on export controls would have four immediate goals:

1. To deter producing countries from erecting export controls except in clearly defined and justified circumstances.

2. To reinforce that deterrent by providing a basis for concerted response by the world trading community.

3. To limit the scope and duration of those controls which are actually applied.

4. To provide an international framework into which disputes triggered by export controls can be channeled when they are actually applied, to reduce the likelihood of unilateral reactions and emulation/retaliation cycles. . . .

The proposed set of rules would permit the use of export controls for national security purposes and "infant industry" protection, and to avoid serious injury (or the threat thereof) to national economies. But they would otherwise be proscribed.

The proscription would be backed by the requirement that any country adopting an unjustified export control had to provide adequate compensation or, more likely, accept any of a number of types of economic retaliation. Nonsignatories of the agreement could be subjected to such retaliation, broadening the scope of the deterrent, although every effort would be made to maximize membership in the new regime. Retaliation would also be authorized against "reverse dumping" and against import subsidies, in the form of import duties and "countervailing export controls," respectively.

When controls were justified, their application would be subject to agreed time limits and, for longer-term controls, the presentation of an acceptable domestic adjustment program. And they would require advance notification and consulta-tion, undergo multilateral surveillance both at their initiation and throughout their subsequent application, have to be administered through export taxes rather than quotas whenever possible, and apply on a most-favored-nation basis. Such a regime would seem to provide a reasonable chance that export controls could be relatively depoliticized, and avoid unilateral reactions and emulation/retaliation cycles.

Any comprehensive arrangements to "assure access to supplies" must probably encompass commodity agreements as well as rules limiting the use of trade controls. Buffer stocks, agreed production levels and perhaps other arrangements to preserve agreed volumes of trade and price ranges would be needed. The nature of the decision-making machinery on all these issues would be a central concern to all negotiating parties.

Thus, from an intellectual standpoint, commodity agreements and new trade rules must be viewed together in dealing with the problem of access to supplies. But they msut also be viewed in tandem from a negotiating standpoint, because together they might provide the basis for a package which served the interests of the several different groups of countries.[9]

International commodity agreements are also frequently proposed to reduce price fluctuations and stabilize foreign exchange earnings.

Finally, the problem of international resource bargaining relates to two other issues discussed in previous chapters. Another objective of the exercise of "commodity power" is to increase the domestic value added from the primary commodity by inducing domestic processing of the commodity (bauxite into alumina, crude oil into refined petroleum products, etc.). This relates to the process of industrialization via export substitution, as discussed in selection VI.B.3 above. An additional objective is to exercise more national control over foreign investment in primary products and to capture more of the rents from that investment. This relates to the problem of private foreign investment, as discussed in section V.D, above.

[9]C. Fred Bergsten, *Completing the GATT: Toward New International Rules to Govern Export Controls*, British-North American Committee, Washington, D.C., 1974, pp. 23, 51–2.

Thus, the exercise of "producer power" raises not just one issue—that of improvement in the terms of trade—but also other related issues: (1) the stability of export prices and foreign exchange receipts in order to increase the developing country's capacity to import; (2) domestic processing of primary commodities; and (3) an increase in the benefit-cost ratio of foreign investment. For the longer-run period that is relevant to the outcome of development programs, the resolution of these other issues may well be more crucial than the shorter-run use of "producer power" to improve the terms of trade.

Comment

The feasibility of international arrangements to stabliize commodity prices is highly dependent on the characteristics of individual commodity markets. For different commodities, see Walter P. Falcon and Eric A. Monke, "International Trade in Rice," *Food Research Institute Studies,* Vol. XVII, No. 3 (1979–80); International Maize and Wheat Improvement Center, *World Wheat Facts and Trends* (1981). The problems associated with buffer stocks are analyzed by Shlomo Reutlinger, "Evaluating Wheat Buffer Stocks," *American Journal of Farm Economics,* (February 1976); Anne E. Peck, "Implications of Private Storage of Grains for Buffer Stock Schemes to Stabilize Prices, *Food Research Institute Studies,* Vol. XVI, No. 3 (1977–78); David M. G. Newbery and Joseph E. Stiglitz, *The Theory of Commodity Price Stabilization: A Study in the Economics of Risk* (1981).

VIII.D. REGIONAL INTEGRATION AND DEVELOPMENT—NOTE

The possibilities for South-South cooperation are now being considered more seriously—whether in deference to Lewis's concern about the slow growth of the MDCs, or to other implications of dependency, delinking, and collective self-reliance. A major effort at South-South cooperation could come from regional integration schemes. As a close student of the North-South dialogue observes,

The weakness of most proposals for South-South cooperation has been that they tended to build grand designs on the basis of an aggregated, mythical South. . . . It may be far more productive to follow up on avenues of cooperation on a regional or sub-regional level and in certain specific areas of action. The perspective for cooperation may often be functional and geopolitical, rather than global and "idealized."[1]

Various degrees of integration are possible, but most interest centers on the potential role of customs unions and free trade areas. Although both a customs union and free trade area provide for across-the-board trade liberalization for all or most products among the member countries, a customs union also adopts a common external tariff.

At a level less general than a customs union or free trade association, regional integration might be directed simply toward "sectoral integration"—that is, the removal of trade restrictions on only a selected list of commodities, or the treatment of the problems of some one industry as a whole on a regional basis.

Beyond free trade in goods, a more comprehensive economic union might allow for the free movement of factors of production, a common monetary system, and the coordination of economic policies among the member countries. It is still unrealistic to expect this of developing countries; therefore, we will be concerned here with only the implications of free trade in goods.

As a basis for appraising specific proposals, we consider in this Note the benefits that might be derived from economic groupings among developing countries and the difficulties that are likely to be encountered in their formation.

Advocates of an economic union believe that its formation will accelerate the development of the member countries by (1) stimulating the establishment and expansion of manufacturing industries on a more rational basis, (2) increasing the gains from trade, and (3) providing benefits from intensified competition.

We have seen that many countries have adopted a policy of deliberate import substitution in consumer goods. When each country restricts its imports, however, and attempts to substitute home production, industrialization becomes unduly compartmentalized, and the uneconomic multiplication of import-competing industries is wasteful. In contrast, if manufacturing industry can be encouraged in the context of a customs union or free trade area, it may attain a higher level of productivity than results from industrial protection in each country. Greater specialization within the region can increase the share of exports and imports in manufacturing and reduce the excessive number of products manufactured in an excessive number of protected firms.

To reach an efficient scale of output, a modern manufacturing plant may have to produce a larger output than the low level of home demand in a single underdeveloped country can absorb. By pooling markets through the removal of internal trade barriers, a free trade union might thus provide a sufficiently wide export market to make economies of scale realizable. Within a union, secondary industry can become more efficient

[1]Mahbub ul Haq, "Beyond the Slogan of South-South Cooperation," in Khadija Haq (ed.), *Dialogue for a New Order*, New York, 1981.

as specialization occurs in the member country that acquires a comparative advantage. At the same time, the other constituent countries may now replace their imported manufactures from outside the union and thereby be able to spend a higher proportion of their foreign exchange on outside imports that are essential but cannot be produced efficiently within the union. A more rational pattern of production and trade within the region may therefore be an important result of integration.

It is frequently argued that because of similar levels and patterns of consumption in the LDCs, there should be more scope for inter-LDC trade than for trade with developed countries. As Frances Stewart states,

Consumption patterns among South (i.e., developing) countries should be much more similar to each other than those of North (i.e., developed) countries: the sort of goods—for consumption and investment—developed for one country in the South should be more appropriate, both for production and consumption, to other South countries than to North products they currently import. . . . A coordinated policy to encourage South-South trade would provide the South innovators with the markets they require, and hence, in the end, would be likely to prove self-justifying.[2]

The extension of the market, together with the inducement to get behind the external tariff wall, may also be particularly effective in attracting direct private foreign investment in manufacturing. And over time, there is the further possibility that new industries can become increasingly competitive on world markets and eventually be able to export manufactured goods to nonmember countries. But this depends first on establishing a sufficiently wide market within the union to allow operation of a manufacturing industry on a large enough scale.

An expansion of trade among the member countries is also expected to result from the removal of trade barriers. If this takes the form of replacing high-cost producers within

the region by lower-cost producers, the effect is one of "trade creation."[3] The gains from trade are then increased, since the international division of labor is improved as resources shift into more efficient production. On the other hand, some of the intraunion trade may merely replace trade that formerly occurred between members and nonmembers. When the formation of an economic union has this "trade-diverting" effect, the international division of labor will be worsened if the outside source of supply is actually a low-cost source, and its product now becomes higher priced within the union because of the external tariff. In this case, there is an uneconomic diversion of output from the low-cost outside source to the high-cost supplier within the union, and the gains from trade are diminished.

In considering whether trade creation or trade diversion is likely to dominate in a particular union, we have to take into account the preunion level of tariff rates among the members, the level of the postunion external tariff compared with the preunion tariff levels of each member country, the elasticities of demand for the imports on which duties are reduced, and the elasticities of supply of exports from the members and foreign sources. Conditions are more propitious for trade creation when each member's preunion duties are high on the others' products, the members are initially similar in the products they produce but different in the pattern of relative prices at which they produce them, the external tariff of the union is low compared with the preunion tariff levels of the members, and the production within the union of commodities that are substitutes for outside imports can be undertaken at a lower cost.

The formation of a free trade union might also result in an improvement—or at least the forestalling of a deterioration—in the region's commodity terms of trade. This is possible if there is a reduction in the supply of exports from the union, or the demand by members of the union is reduced for imports

[2]Frances Stewart, "The Direction of International Trade: Gains and Losses for the Third World," in G. K. Helleiner (ed.), *A World Divided*, New York, 1976, pp. 98–9.

[3]Jacob Viner, *The Customs Union Issue*, New York, 1950, pp. 48–52.

from outside, or the bargaining power of the members in trade negotiations is strengthened. But unless the members of the union are the chief suppliers on the world market or constitute a large part of the world market for their imports, they are unlikely to be able to exercise sufficient monopolistic or monopsonistic power to influence their terms of trade by raising duties on their trade with the outside world or by inducing outsiders to supply their goods more cheaply. Moreover, when free trade is confined only to the region, there is the risk of retaliation through the formation of other economic blocs. A union may thereby inhibit the realization of the more extensive gains from the "universal" approach to free trade.

Finally, regional integration might be beneficial in encouraging competition among the member countries. Technical efficiency in existing industries might then be improved as marginal firms are forced to reduce their costs, resources are reallocated from less efficient to more efficient firms, and monopolies that had previously been established behind tariff walls are no longer in a sheltered position. Further, the stimulation of competition within each country may yield not only a better utilization of given resources, but may also raise the rate of growth of productive resources. This may result from stronger incentives to adopt new methods of production, to replace obsolete equipment more rapidly, and to innovate more rapidly with more and better investment.

In practice, however, a number of objections have been raised against proposals for regional integration, and actual negotiations have encountered serious difficulties. As is true for a union among even advanced countries, political problems take precedence, nations will guard against a sacrifice of their sovereignty, and the administration of the union may be extremely complex. For underdeveloped countries, these problems tend to be especially acute since many have only recently gained political independence, newly established national governments may be excessively concerned with their own national interests and needs, and the administrative

requirements may be beyond their present capacity. Aside from the political and administrative difficulties, there are also several economic objections to a union.

To begin with, it may be argued that the case for an economic union is in reality weak when the constituent countries have not yet established many industries. Limitations on the supply side may be more of a deterrent to the creation of an industry than is the narrow market on the side of demand. If production conditions do not also improve, the mere extension of the consumer market will not be sufficient to create industries. Moreover, when manufacturing industry is only at a rudimentary stage in the member countries, there is not much scope for eliminating high-cost manufacturers within the region. Nor is there much scope for realizing the benefits of increased competition when there are not yet similar ranges of rival products, produced under different cost conditions, in the several member nations. A union will not cause substantial improvement in the utilization of resources unless industries have already been established but need wider markets than the national economy can provide for the realization of economies of scale, and the member countries have been protecting the same kinds of industry, but have markedly different ratios of factor-efficiency in these industries to factor-efficiency in nonprotected branches of production.

It has been pointed out that the case for a union is strongest among countries that have little foreign trade in proportion to their domestic production, but conduct a high proportion of their foreign trade with one another.[4] When these conditions prevail, there is less possibility for introducing, within each member country, a distortion of the price relation between goods from other member countries and goods from outside the union, and more of a possibility for eliminating any

[4] R. G. Lipsey, "The Theory of Customs Unions: A General Survey," *Economic Journal*, September 1960, pp. 507–9. This conclusion rests, however, on the assumption that there are no productive economies of large scale.

distortion by tariffs of the price-relations between domestic goods and imports from other member countries. There is therefore greater likelihood that the union will improve the use of resources and raise real income.

A union among underdeveloped countries, however, is unlikely to conform to these conditions. The ratio of foreign trade to domestic production is generally high for these countries, and the actual volume of intraregional trade is normally only a small proportion of the region's total foreign trade. The gain from regional integration would therefore be small. The basic difficulty is that, with existing trade patterns, the formation of a union is likely to cause a considerable amount of wasteful "trade diversion." Over the long run, comparative costs and trade patterns may change, and economies of scale may give rise to competitive advantages as development proceeds, so that the scope for "trade creation" will become greater within the union. But the immediate gain is small, and the longer-run prospects for the creation of new trade are not likely to influence current decisions to join a union.

The case for regional preferential trading arrangements is stronger than that for a general preference scheme if the regional arrangement allows the avoidance of trade diversion. GATT (Article 24) insists that tariffs among members of a customs union or free trade area be reduced to zero; it can be demonstrated, however, that in some cases, less trade diversion will result if the members reduce their internal tariffs below the external tariff but not necessarily to zero.[5] In this respect, a partial preferential arrangement has merit.

Besides the possibility of "trade diversion," other undesirable consequences may result from a union. The member countries are unlikely to benefit equally, and some members may feel that others are gaining at their expense. A country may have a strong compar-

ative advantage in only primary products and will sell to other members only goods that it could as readily export to outside countries. At the same time, the location of manufacturing industry and ancillary activities may become localized within one member country, and "polarization" results. Other members may then contend that if they too had been able to adopt tariff protection against their partners, they would have also been able to attract industry. A nonindustrialized member country may further complain that in buying from an industrialized partner, instead of importing from the outside, it is losing revenue equal to the duty on outside manufactures. And, with a common external tariff, member countries no longer have the discretionary power to use variations in the tariff for the purpose of adjusting their national revenues to their own requirements. The internal strains that arise from uneven development among the member countries may thus make it extremely difficult to preserve a regional grouping. As one study states

Surprising as it may appear to some, one of the main obstacles lies in the *differences* among the developing countries which form a union. These disparities of size and stage of economic development cause problems so far as the equitable sharing of costs and benefits are concerned. In fact, this emphasis on "equity" might well prove the rock on which all such schemes founder. If indeed customs unions are instituted to take advantage of a larger market, to shift production to optimum localities and, in general, to stimulate economic efficiency, *some* sectors in *some* geographical areas will undoubtedly be adversely affected. Theoretically, it should be possible, if the customs union leads to a rate of growth higher than would otherwise have been the case, to compensate the losers *and* have a net surplus. But the technical implementation of compensation schemes is fraught with practical difficulties.

Basically, what has to be provided for the disadvantaged members, if they are to stay in the union, is one or more of the following preferential measures:

1. Balance-of-payments support through financial institutions of the union or external institutions (e.g., the IMF). A credit system organised by

[5]Ibid., pp. 506–7; W. M. Corden, *Recent Developments in the Theory of International Trade*, Princeton, 1965, p. 54.

a Regional Payments Union (perhaps initially funded externally) might be one way by which countries could be assisted if *intra*-union trade were to lead to balance-of-payments problems.

2. Fiscal policy support measures. Import duties, particularly for small countries, often form a large part of total government revenue. These are slated to disappear with the union and so alternative fiscal means must be developed for substituting lost receipts. Fiscal policy may also have to be used to encourage new industry to locate in the disadvantaged member but, of course, if this means a *permanent* subsidy, the advantage of the customs union is lost.

3. Commercial policy might be especially geared to the needs of the least developed of the group. For example, a longer transition period to the zero tariff situation might be provided for.

4. Credits for new investment.[6]

The most important lesson to be learned from efforts at regional integration is that, if the potential benefits of integration are to be fully realized, the regional association must be a strong one and must be capable of coordinating trade policies, including exchange-rate policy among the member countries, and must provide some means for an equitable distribution of the costs and benefits among members. Most proposals for regional integration do not yet show promise of sufficient cohesion and policy coordination.

Although a comprehensive form of free trade area or full customs union may not yet be practicable for most of the developing countries, there are still substantial advantages that can be derived from more ad hoc functional types of regional cooperation short of comprehensive integration. Measures of "partial integration" may help to avoid the costs of "micro-states" and national development along compartmentalized lines. In particular, the complementary development of specific industries through a regional investment policy has considerable potential. The realization of markets of sufficient size,

avoidance of duplication, and better location of projects might result. There are a few outstanding examples of multinational investment projects, and there should be scope for many more.

It is also possible for more to be accomplished by way of partial liberalization of regional trade for certain products or sectors. Countries might identify specific sectors or individual products for which they could commit themselves not to erect trade barriers with each other. Products that are not yet fabricated in a particular group—that is, new products for the region—might be singled out as a particularly suitable object of such a commitment, especially if supplemented by some commitments regarding a regional investment policy.

A regional agreement might also be effective in bargaining over the entry of foreign investment and the import of technology into the region. Instead of individual countries having to engage in their own bargaining with the foreign investor or foreign supplier of technology, a regional bargaining unit may have more power and may be able to harmonize conditions of entry to greater advantage for the recipient members.

Finally, an important area of regional cooperation—and one that could be used to support other areas—is that of channeling aid through regional integration banks or development corporations. The more this is done, the more influential might the regional institutions be in promoting the regional investment policies and regional trade liberalization policies that are necessary to avoid uncoordinated duplicative national development policies.

Until the risks of joining a free trade union are diminished, this less ambitious approach involving efforts to secure sectoral integration may be the most feasible alternative. Even though a customs union may be the ultimate objective, it will still be a sizable accomplishment in the immediate future to secure the mutually supporting measures of regional investment policies, regional trade liberalization, and regional aid institutions.

[6]Derek T. Healey, *Integration Schemes among Developing Countries: A Survey*, Sixth Conference of Economists, Hobart, 1977, pp. 31–2.

Comment

There have been several efforts to secure economic integration among developing countries. Most notable are the Latin American Free Trade Association (LAFTA), the Central American Common Market (CACM), the Andean Common Market (ACM), the Caribbean Community (CARICOM), the East African Community (EAC), and the Association of Southeast Asian Nations (ASEAN). These integration schemes, however, have generally not lived up to expectation, and most have undergone major modifications. Problems have generally been encountered in determining the scope for profitable specialization, the creation or strengthening of appropriate production structures, and the equitable distribution of the benefits of integration among member countries.

For an appraisal of the experience with regional integration schemes, see J. B. Nugent, *Economic Integration in Central America* (1974); David Morawetz, *The Andean Group* (1974); Peter Robson, *The Economics of International Integration* (1972); Martin Carnoy (ed.), *Industrialization in a Latin American Common Market* (1972); UNCTAD, *Economic Cooperation and Integration among Developing Countries* (1976); Bela Balassa and E. J. Stoutjesdijk, "Economic Integration among Developing Countries," *Journal of Common Market Studies* (September 1975); Constantine V. Vaitsos, "Crisis in Regional Cooperation among Developing Countries: A Survey," *World Development,* Vol. 6 (1978); Peter Robson, *Integration, Development and Equity: Economic Integration in West Africa* (1983).

CHAPTER IX

Human-Resource Development

Another strategic policy issue is the development of human resources. If the earlier faith in development through the accumulation of material capital has waned, it has in recent years been replaced by a new creed of investment in human capital. It is now widely believed that improvement in the quality of people as productive agents must be a central objective of development policies. But how are the abilities and skills of people to be improved, and their motivations and values modified so as to be more suitable for developmental efforts? This is clearly one of the most difficult questions we have encountered, and yet, on its answer is likely to depend a country's success in achieving self-sustaining development.

Part of the difficulty in formulating policy to improve the "human infrastructure" within a less developed country is that economists have only recently begun to analyze this question systematically. Perhaps the greater part of the difficulty, however, is that an answer to the question entails not only economic analysis but also sociological, psychological, and political considerations. The inherently multidisciplinary character of the answer has caused each discipline to acknowledge the question but to fall short of a satisfactory answer. This chapter, in concentrating on the economics of the problem, will not be immune to this same criticism, but it will at least attempt to fashion the economic analysis so that it might suggest some links with other disciplines.

Before considering policy measures related to the quality of the population we should first gain some perspective on the quantitative problem of population pressure. Section IX.A examines the nature of the population explosion and its importance from the standpoint of its effects on the quality of population. Population is growing much faster in the LDCs than in the MDCs, and the urban population is growing especially rapidly. By the end of this century, about 80 percent of the world's population will be in the developing countries, and human-resource policies have to be considered in the context of this rapid population growth. The exacerbation of the employment problem is direct. The effects of population growth on the quality of health facilities, nutrition, educational programs, and public services also make it necessary to acquire a better understanding of demographic problems. It is now especially apposite to investigate whether population growth worsens absolute poverty and the maldistribution of income. Do absolute poverty and the maldistribution of income contribute, in turn, to high rates of fertility? Furthermore, what are the socioeconomic correlates of declining fertility, and how might policy interventions affect these correlates in order to reduce the rate of population growth? If public policies can reduce mortality rates, can they also reduce fertility rates? These questions are examined in section IX.A.

Section IX.B outlines some policies to improve health and nutrition conditions among the world's poor. Among the first to suffer from shortages or inadequacies of food are the children—a country's investment in the future. And children, along with their mothers, are numerically dominant in developing countries. In these areas one-fifth of the population is under the age of 5 years, two-fifths are below the age of 15 years, while mothers and children together account for over two-thirds of the total population. The children are the most vulnerable group.

Especially tragic is the ill-health brought on or aggravated by malnutrition. Malnutrition adversely affects mental progress, physical growth, productivity, and the working life span. In cost-effectiveness terms—let alone fundamental human rights—there can be high returns from programs to reduce the incidence of malnutrition.

Poverty is the major cause of disease in developing countries, and more than medical facilities is needed to improve health conditions. Health policies must be related much more to the environment and to the ecological, cultural, and nutritional situation which permits disease to thrive in poverty areas. As with technology, so too is there a need for an "appropriate" transfer of medical knowledge and medical technology: health programs have been only too often biased toward a small section of the urban population, and to oversophisticated "curative" treatment rather than more basic, widespread "preventive" treatment.

As analyzed in section IX.C, formal and informal education and training in both the modern and traditional sectors are clearly necessary for the development of human resources. Any cost-benefit analysis of the "returns" to education must incorporate the interactions between education and the economy, giving particular attention to education as an investment, the importance of rural education in a developing economy, and the interdependence between education, manpower requirements, and development. Although each individual commonly views his or her own education as a consumption good, it is more appropriately viewed from the standpoint of the economy's development as an investment good: to the economist, human beings can be conceptualized as human capital or embodied savings. It is then an economic problem to determine how much the economy should invest in human capital, and of equal importance, what the composition of that investment should be. The selections in section IX.C therefore consider both the quantitative growth of education and the character of education needed in a developing economy.

Although this chapter considers population growth, health, nutrition, and education each as separate topics, it should be realized that all of these elements of human-resource development are interrelated. And while fertility, health, nutrition, and education affect one another, so too does each, in turn, affect income. Much of our earlier discussion of basic human needs is also relevant to the topics of this chapter.

IX.A. POPULATION

IX.A.1. Population and Poverty—Note

Few developmental problems evoke as much pessimism as does the rapid increase in population in poor countries. If economists value a higher rate of development, they still fear, as John Stuart Mill did, a growth in population that "treads close on the heels of agricultural improvement, and effaces its effects as fast as they are produced." It is not difficult to find a basis for this fear—in that a large part of the gain in aggregate income has been used simply to support a larger population at the same low per capita level of income.

This pessimistic outlook on population growth is as old as academic economics itself.[1] Long ago economics was designated the "dismal science." Originally this was because of the view of classical economists who, when considering the long-run development of an economy, could see only the eventual advent of a dismal "stationary state" in which the springs of economic progress would have evaporated, growth in output would no longer outstrip population growth, and wages would be at subsistence levels. So far, however, this pessimism has proved unfounded for industrial nations: the economic histories of these nations represent the success stories of economic progress—of the achievement of a high rate of increase in real income, so that population and per capita real income have both been able to increase. Indeed, when some economists thought that the Great Depression of the 1930s might indicate a state of secular stagnation in mature industrial nations, they were concerned lest population growth in these countries actually be too slow. But although capital accumulation, technical progress, and the phenomenon of

increasing returns to scale may have dispelled the shadow of Malthus from the few rich industrial countries, that shadow still hovers over the many poor agrarian countries.

In these countries, per capita income has remained pitifully low, and the alarming prospects of population growth have revived neo-Malthusian fears. Once again there is widespread concern that economic betterment will be thwarted by excessive population pressure and that, unless acceptable means are found for checking population growth, the "revolution of rising expectations" must remain unfulfilled. It has become common to hear the development problem summarized as one of "increasing the fertility of the soil and reducing the fertility of human beings."

Most development economists argue against the Malthusian view that population will eventually be limited by food production. They point to the fact that apart from drought areas, population nowhere appears yet to have approached the capacity of the land to support it. Whether or not adequate food production is achieved, however, depends a great deal on government making resources available, pursuing appropriate pricing policies, ensuring necessary research, and developing an infrastructure for transport, storage, and marketing.

Regarding the problem of malnutrition and hunger, this is, as noted in Chapter VII, more a problem of poverty and inadequate income than a matter of inadequate global food supplies. In many countries where malnutrition is extensive, food availability would meet the food needs of all if it were distributed according to need and not according to income. The population-food problem is solved when incomes suffice to buy adequate food at prices that provide adequate incen-

---

[1]The history of thought on population growth and development is traced by Lord Robbins, *The Theory of Economic Development in the History of Economic Thought,* New York, 1968, Lecture II.

tives to producers. From the viewpoint of global food policy, the rich countries are capable of generating surpluses of food for export. But to meet their increased demand for food grains by increased imports, the developing countries would need to export more, receive foreign aid, or borrow overseas. The great majority of developing nations will therefore have to satisfy most of their own production needs most of the time. To this end, cost-reducing innovations must continue to occur sufficient to outweigh the limitations of fixed land resources.

It is extremely important, however, to realize that the population problem is much more than a food problem: it has wider ramifications that make it a general development problem. A high rate of population growth not only has an adverse effect on improvement in food supplies, but also intensifies the constraints on development of savings, foreign exchange, and human resources. Rapid population growth, which stems from high birth rates, tends to depress savings per capita and retards growth of physical capital per worker. The need for social infrastructure is also broadened, and public expenditures must be absorbed in providing these facilities for a larger population rather than in providing directly productive assets. Population pressure is also likely to intensify the foreign exchange constraint by placing more pressure on the balance of payments. In some cases, the need to import foodstuffs will require the development of new industries for export expansion and/or import substitution. Possibly the most serious disadvantage to a high rate of population growth in a poor country is that it makes the human resources constraint more difficult to remove. Larger numbers militate against an improvement in the quality of the population as productive agents. The rapid increase in school-age population and the expanding number of labor force entrants put ever-greater pressure on educational and training facilities and retard improvement in the quality of education. Similarly, too dense a population aggravates the problem of improving the health of the population. With the concern over unemploy-

ment and inequality, students of population are now also asking whether population growth intensifies the extent of absolute poverty and the maldistribution of income.

In most developing countries, the working-age population has roughly doubled in the past 25 years. At expected growth rates, it will double again in the next 25 years. This growth clearly intensifies pressure on employment and the amount of investment available per labor market entrant.

That these disadvantages have become very real for many LDCs can be recognized if we contrast the demographic patterns of rich and poor countries. One striking difference is that a much higher percentage of the total population in poor countries is in younger age groups, and life expectancy is much lower than in rich countries. In most of the LDCs, 40 to 50 percent of the population is below fifteen years of age, whereas in developed countries the corresponding percentage is about 25 percent. If the economically productive age bracket is taken as fifteen to sixty-five years, the percentage of population in this category is considerably less in poor countries than in rich. This "bottom heavy" age structure of population results in a high ratio of dependents to adult workers, which means the differentiation and productive power of the labor force are limited. Even worse, it means greater consumption and constitutes a major obstacle to an increase in savings in many LDCs. This high dependency ratio requires the economy to divert a considerable part of its resources, that might otherwise go into capital formation, to the maintenance of a high percentage of dependents who may never become producers or, if so, only for a relatively short working life.

Not only do most of the people in the world live in the less developed areas, but the concentration is increasing. In many LDCs, the populations are of the high-growth potential type. In these countries the simple application of modern public health measures has allowed the death rate to fall spectacularly to the low levels of the rich country, while birth rates have remained very high and resistant to change. If, as its true for many LDCs, the birth rate remains at a high level of about 40 per thousand while the death rate is reduced to about 10 per thousand, then the population will double within a generation. With the declining death rates, the rates of natural increase have risen in the LDCs to 2, 3, or even 4 percent a year in regions of persistently high fertility. While the population in the rich countries, constituting 30 percent of the world's population, is growing at an average of only 1 percent or less, the population in the poor countries, amounting to 70 percent of the world's population, is growing at an average rate of 2.5 percent. Almost all the doubling times for populations in poor countries are more rapid than the world average. The next selection outlines the demographic situation for the rest of the century.

The population explosion that has been experienced during the last two decades in most of the LDCs is in marked contrast with the history of the presently rich industrial nations when they were in earlier phases of their development. In their nineteenth-century preindustrial phase, the countries of western Europe had a population growth that was generally less than half the rate now existing in the poor countries. Moreover, in the past the decline of the death rate in industrialized countries was mainly due to the development process itself—through such factors as improved diet, better housing, sanitation. The death rates declined as part of the general evolution of Western society—induced by improvements in economic conditions and accompanied by changes in social attitudes that allowed birth rates to begin falling before death rates reached their low levels. Now, however, mortality rates are falling in poor countries not because of development, but because modern medical knowledge and scientific techniques of death control can be readily transferred from the rich countries and applied in nonindustrial areas. Modern medical and public health advances have stimulated declines in mortality independently of economic development and social change.

A crucial question now is whether population control policies can also stimulate declines in fertility,[2] without having to wait for higher levels of economic and social development to bring about a "normal" decline in fertility. Can family planning programs be effective in the face of traditional beliefs and social institutions that have sustained fertility at a high level? Or can an adjustment of birth rates to the fall in death rates be induced only by long-run forces of development and the resultant changes in the traditional culture? Is the future of population growth essentially a question of the future of development?

This Note has reversed the last question and emphasized that the very future of development is itself dependent upon a reduction in heavy population pressures, lest it be increasingly difficult to remove the shortages of capital, foodstuffs, foreign exchange, and skills that now limit the rate of development. But the total discussion of this book can be interpreted as claiming that the potential for economic development is greater than the potential for population growth. To realize this potential as rapidly as possible, we must therefore recognize the beneficial effects that can come from declining fertility, and consider the inclusion of policies of family planning as a complement to other policies of development planning. We must also give due weight to the belief that rapid population growth is a consequence as well as a cause of poverty. Declining fertility is highly correlated with a reduction in unemployment, improved status of women, better health care, more education, and greater income.

Many demographers believe the time is dropping rapidly for the demographic transition from high to low birth and death rates. One major study of recent trends in natality in the LDCs concludes the following.

The data support the following conclusions about recent changes in natality in less developed regions:

1. A rapidly growing number of countries have been entering the demographic transition on the natality side especially since 1970.

---

[2]A general fertility rate is number of births per 1000 women in reproductive ages 15–49.

2. Once a sustained reduction of the birth rate has begun, it proceeds at a much more rapid pace than it did historically in Europe and among Europeans overseas.
3. The "new" countries may reduce birth rates quite rapidly despite initially higher levels than existed historically in Western Europe.
4. Where available, the more refined measures of fertility, standardizing for differences in age structure, yield results similar to those for crude birth rates.
5. There is no direct evidence yet that current fertility reductions will terminate at levels significantly higher than those achieved in European countries and Japan.

Above observations are now based on the experience of many countries, though the precise extent of fertility decline is often clouded by defective data. There is now clear evidence of fertility reduction in the largest countries, dramatically rapid in China, and measurably in India and in Indonesia. Fertility reduction is now general in East Asia and in Latin America. As yet there is little evidence of this in tropical Africa or in the Moslem Middle East and Pakistan and Bangladesh.

The relationship between socioeconomic variables and fertility is clearly different within the different major cultural regions of the less developed world; quite different levels and kinds of development are associated with fertility reductions, for example, in East Asia and in Latin America. This confirms common sense and explains why efforts to relate socioeconomic measures and fertility "across the board" for all less developed countries have sometimes led to confusing results.

Finally, is there indeed a new or renewed demographic transition? The evidence suggests that there is. A rapidly growing number of countries of diverse cultural background have entered the natality transition since World War II and after a 25-year lapse in such entries. In these countries the transition is moving much faster than it did in Europe. This is probably related to the fact that progress in general is moving much faster in such matters as urbanization, education, health, communications and often per capita income. If progress in modernization continues, notably in the larger countries, the demographic transition in the less developed world will probably be completed much more rapidly than it was in Europe.

It would be foolhardy, however, not to end on a word of caution. On any assumptions concerning the reduction of fertility that may occur with socioeconomic progress, it still follows that one may anticipate and must accommodate an enormous increase in the world population and that these increases will be greatest precisely in those countries economically least well-equipped to absorb the increase in numbers.[3]

[3]Dudley Kirk, "A New Demographic Transition?" in Study Committee, National Academy of Sciences, *Rapid Population Growth,* Baltimore, 1971, pp. 145–6. Revised by the author for this edition.

IX.A.2. The Demographic Momentum*

First, we indicate the likely demographic situation for the remainder of the century "in the natural course of events." Then we indicate the possible developments and options

*From Bernard Berelson et al., "Population: Current Status and Policy Options," *The Population Council Center for Policy Studies, Working Paper* No. 44, May 1979, pp. 32–6. Reprinted by permission.

with regard to (a) the technology of fertility regulation and (b) the programmatic interventions on fertility, mortality, and migration. We then conclude with some overall observations.

What can be said with considerable certainty is that from now to the year 2000—absent a great catastrophe, virtually of nuclear dimensions—*only more population is ahead for the developing sector and for the world.* As the reader knows, the demographic momentum inherent in a young age structure will carry waves of population growth into the new century even if replacement fertility were to be achieved everywhere tomorrow—which is of course unthinkable under any realistic consideration. Even if fertility continues to decline moderately in the developing world and does not rise much in the developed, and even if mortality declines more slowly, *substantial demographic momentum will still be carried over into the next century—at that time at the doubling rate of approximately 40–50 years.*

The latest projections of the world's population in 2000, as against about 4.2 billion now, range from a low of 5.9 billion to a high of 6.6, *or an increase in the 40–60 percent range.* Most of that increase is of course in the developing world: from 3 billion now to from 4.5 to 5.2 billion, for an increase in the 50–70 percent range. The projected annual growth rates at that time range from 0.9 percent to 1.7 percent, with crude death rates from 8 to 10 and crude birth rates from 18 to 25.

Given the present state of the art, it does not seem warranted to go into the details of the matter since there is no scientific way to choose among the projections anyway: India and China could rebound upward, some large high-fertility countries could stay that way, some countries with improved health could increase their fertility. Suffice it to say that the lower projections extrapolate the most recent declines . . . or stress the impact of family planning programs . . . or rest on expected social trends like entry of women into the labor market, urbanization, and shortages of commodities . . . and that the higher ones take more pessimistic views in general.

But there are three main points on which such work seems to agree, all of considerable importance: (1) *the trend in fertility and growth is now down, probably on an historical scale,* although the age structure will be a retarding burden for the rest of the century on the order of, say, a 5–10 percent drag on fertility reduction in countries experiencing declines;* (2) *there is still a long way to go be-*fore the world and its major areas will achieve the comfortable state of low fertility, low mortality, and low growth that is desirable in the short run and required in the long run; and (3) *rapid urbanization will continue in most developing countries.*

Now let us break down the population growth situation for the larger developing countries—29 countries with 10 million or more population and about 85 percent of the developing sector. How close are they likely to come to a target of CBR 20, or roughly a two-and-one-half-child family, by the year 2000, and thus to a rate of natural increase close to 1 percent (assuming the U.N. projection of a crude death rate of 8 to 10 at that time)? *A current analysis classifies the countries by their prospect of reaching that goal* on the basis of their present demographic trends, their status on presumed basic determinants of fertility (like literacy and education, life expectancy and infant mortality, GNP and nonagricultural employment, female status and age at marriage), and their programmatic efforts, *into four categories:*

The Certain: South Korea, Taiwan, Chile

Their CBRs are now in the low 20s, they have low mortality and infant mortality, they already have favorable social settings with improvement continuing, they have no major retarding effect from ethnic traditions, they have the requisite family planning program effort, they are riding substantial downward trends in fertility of at least 15 years' duration. As of now, this group has only 2 percent of the population of the developing world.

The Probable: China, Brazil, Mexico, the Philippines, Thailand, Turkey, Colombia, Sri Lanka, Venezuela, Malaysia

These countries now have CBRs in the 30s or below, their crude death rates are in the 6–11 range, they have favorable social settings with advances in progress almost everywhere, only one (Moslem Turkey) has a high-fertility ethnic tradition and that country is rapidly modernizing, only six have the requisite program effort but Mexico is now vitalizing its program and Brazil, Turkey, and Venezuela have the administrative potential to do so, all appear to be on a downward trend which in some cases is quite sharp although their recency leaves a few somewhat suspect. This group has 42 percent of the total developing population. They will come close to the target, or could if they would.

The Possible: India, Indonesia, Egypt, Peru

Here is a mixed picture: India and Egypt are in the upper 30s in CBR, India, Indonesia, and Egypt had impressive fertility declines recently, India had and Indonesia has a good family planning program for its setting but the former is now in a relapsed position from which it may not soon recover. On the other hand, death rates are still high, social factors are mixed to unfavorable, and two countries are Moslem. This group has 28 percent of the developing population. They have a chance of reaching the target, but it will take some doing, and given the difficulties in the two large countries, a CBR of 25 for this group would be a signal achievement.

The Unlikely: Bangladesh, Pakistan, Nigeria, Iran, Zaire, Afghanistan, Sudan, Morocco, Algeria, Tanzania, Kenya, Nepal

In these countries, all the indicators are unfavorable: birth rates from the mid-40s up and stable so that the initial break in fertility is still to come, death rates still high, an unfavorable and only slowly changing socioeconomic setting, Moslem and/or African high fertility traditions, no real family planning effort in recent years. This group, with 13 percent of the population, has no discernible chance to achieve the stipulated target under expectable circumstances, and by present indications would do well to reach CBR 35 by the end of the century.

Actually, if the Certain and the Probable were to average CBR 20 by the end of the century, the Possible CBR 25, and the Unlikely CBR 35—with the remaining countries at CBR 30—the birth rate for the developing sector would then be about CBR 25 (identical with the U.N.'s low variant) and a growth rate still about 1.6 percent. Naturally, in any such projection a great deal depends upon China, India, and Indonesia (with 54 percent of the developing population), and upon a few other large countries (over 50 million)—Brazil, Bangladesh, Pakistan, Nigeria, and Mexico—that all together make up two-thirds of the developing world. But *as of now, CBR 20 and a population growth rate of one percent in the developing sector by 2000 seem out of reach short of heroic efforts,* and perhaps not even then. As a rough rule of thumb, *in the modern era it takes an average of about 20–25 years— say, one generation—for a country to move from CBR 35 to CBR 20.* Of the Possible and Unlikely countries, all but the four sub-Saharan Africa countries (Nigeria, Zaire, Tanzania, Kenya) will be at or below CBR 35 by century's end, according to the U.N. medium projection. Meanwhile, the demographic momentum continues.

Comment

An excellent review of population trends in the major regions of the developing world is presented by Robert H. Cassen, "Current Trends in Population Change and Their Causes," *Population and Development Review,* Vol. 4, No. 2 (1978). It indicates the importance of socioeconomic, cultural, and environmental factors in explaining fertility differences not only among countries but also within countries. It suggests that the factors commonly associated with fertility decline—such "correlates of fertility decline" as education, urbanization, improved status of and wider employment opportunities for women, mortality declines, and increased practice of family planning—contribute to fertility differentials within countries even in those instances in which the prevailing culture appears to give a disposition to high fertility.

An additional survey is presented in Robert H. Cassen, "Population and Development: A Survey," *World Development,* Vol. 4, Nos. 10/11 (1976). This considers the macro-aspects of the effects of population growth on the economy, on real output, food, employment, income distribution, health, education, and urban development. An extensive bibliography is also included.

EXHIBIT IX.1. Estimated Age Structure of the Population by Region, 1975

Age	0–4	5–14	15–64	Percentages 65+
Eastern Africa	18.5	26.4	52.4	2.7
Middle Africa[a]	17.0	25.6	54.5	2.9
West Africa	18.4	26.4	52.7	2.5
Southern Africa	17.5	23.5	55.1	3.9
North Africa	17.1	27.2	52.5	3.3
Middle East (incl. Turkey)	17.1	26.0	53.0	3.9
South Asia (incl. Iran)	16.5	26.4	54.1	2.9
Southeast Asia (incl. Burma, Philippines)	17.0	26.6	53.4	3.0
East Asia (excl. China, Taiwan, Japan)	13.3	24.8	58.3	3.6
Caribbean	14.5	26.2	54.2	5.1
Central America (incl. Mexico)	17.9	27.9	50.9	3.4
Tropical South America	16.5	26.6	53.8	3.1
Temperate South America	10.6	19.8	62.3	7.3
North America	7.9	17.6	64.3	10.2
Europe	7.7	16.2	63.8	12.9
Japan	9.1	15.4	67.7	7.8

Source: United Nations, *Selected World Demographic Indicators by Countries, 1950–2000,* May 1975.

[a]Includes Angola, Central African Empire, Chad, Congo, Equatorial Guinea, Gabon, Cameroon, and Zaire.

EXHIBIT IX.2. The Demographic Transition

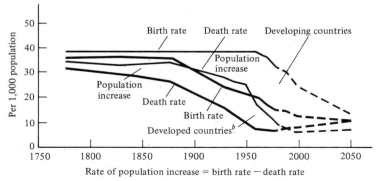

Rate of population increase = birth rate − death rate

[a] Crude birth and death rates. The projected increases in death rates after about 1980 reflect the rising proportion of older people in the population.
[b] Includes industrialized countries, the USSR, and Eastern Europe.

Source: *World Development Report, 1982.*

EXHIBIT IX.3. Fertility in Relation to Income: Developing Countries, 1978

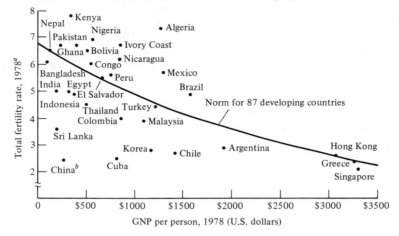

^{a}The total fertility rate indicates the average number of children that
would be born to each woman in a population if each were to live through
her childbearing years (usually considered ages 15–49) bearing children
at the same rate as women of those ages actually did in a given year.
^{b}Estimated fertility and GNP for China are for 1979.

IX.A.3. Fertility Determinants *

Certain variables have emerged as consistently important in their relationship to fertility. A critical few describe characteristics of the socioeconomic environment that can be altered through public policy: infant mortality, female education and labor force participation, availability of family planning services, and, possibly, income distribution. The strength and direction of the effect on fertility of these policy variables is very different for countries at different stages of development and with different cultural environments.

INFANT MORTALITY AND FERTILITY

Almost all studies of the determinants of fertility indicate a positive effect of infant

*From Nancy Birdsall, "Analytical Approaches to the Relationship of Population Growth and Development," *Population and Development Review,* March and June 1977, pp. 85–90. Reprinted by permission.

mortality on fertility, that is, countries with high rates of infant mortality on the whole have high rates of fertility. (Infant mortality is an important component of overall mortality, particularly in developing countries.) There is *no* country with high mortality and low fertility, taking high mortality as annual death rates above 15 per thousand and low fertility as annual birth rates below 30 per thousand.

What is the causal mechanism that links high fertility and high infant mortality? On the one hand, high infant mortality results in high fertility because parents who experience child loss early ultimately may more than replace lost children, and parents in high-mortality communities may insure themselves against future child loss by having more children than they would want. On the other hand, high fertility contributes to high infant (and child) mortality because close spacing of births and many births may deplete the mother's physical resources and reduce the family's per capita financial resources; a commonly noted phenomenon is the death of a child when, on the birth of a subsequent child, the mother ceases breastfeeding the older child.

The major point in the present context is that the relationship between infant mortality and fertility differs by country and by prevailing economic conditions within countries. For example, high fertility is most likely to contribute to high mortality among the poorest groups and is most likely to show up on a country basis in the poorest countries, as indeed it does in Africa. There kwashiorkor is "the disease that kills the child whose mother carries another child in her womb"; it is often related to malnutrition exacerbated by early or sudden weaning.

Opinion differs as to whether the poorest countries, even with a strong replacement effect, end up with more or fewer people as mortality falls. Studies that have dealt with the timing of the relationship, however, indicate that the response of lower fertility to lower mortality is maximized when the incidence of infant and child mortality is lagged two to four years. This tends to support the opinion that reduced infant mortality will in the long run reduce fertility enough so that the rate of natural increase will go down. This view would be strengthened if studies were better able to incorporate the indirect effect of reduced mortality: lower death probabilities induce parents to invest more in their children, which in turn leads them to lower their desired fertility. They replace a large quantity of children with fewer children of higher quality. In other words, lower mortality not only assists parents to achieve desired family size with fewer births; it may lead parents to reduce their desired family size.

Reduction of infant mortality is an important policy objective on its own merits. Because countries with high average levels of infant and child mortality also have high levels of fertility, the policy objectives of reducing both mortality and fertility can be mutually reinforcing. (Countries with the highest rates are primarily in Africa and south Asia; most countries of Latin America now have much lower mortality and fertility rates.) Where political and cultural barriers to the advocacy of family planning and other fertility-reduction efforts exist, reducing infant mortality can be expected to lay the groundwork for later efforts concentrating on fertility.

FEMALE EDUCATION AND LABOR FORCE PARTICIPATION

Female education bears one of the strongest and most consistent negative relationships to fertility for a variety of reasons: through its effect on raising age of marriage; because it may improve the likelihood that a woman has knowledge of and can use modern contraceptives; and because it has some intangible effect on the woman's ability to plan, her interest in nonfamilial activities, and so on. No need to invoke fertility reduction to justify improving educational opportunities for women: better educated women will be more productive workers, better parents, and better-informed citizens; however, where male/female student ratios indicate that women suffer some schooling disadvantage, fertility effects provide additional justification for rectifying the imbalance. The fertility-reducing effect of women's education holds true even for the highest levels of education; women who obtain secondary and higher education marry later, and increasing the age at marriage has a pronounced effect on a country's fertility rate.

But female labor-force participation appears to have an independent effect on fertility only for those women who work in high-prestige, modern-sector jobs. High rates of female labor-force participation, like virtually all other variables, are neither a necessary condition for fertility decline (consider Korea, Turkey) nor a sufficient condition for it (consider countries of West Africa). On the other hand, increasing opportunities for women to work in the modern labor force can accelerate a fertility decline; where women may desire more children than their husbands (as is possible in the Middle East and

Pakistan, where custom deprives most women of opportunities in other endeavors), offering women some other avenue of activity than child rearing may reduce family size. Good earning opportunities, like higher education, can increase the age of marriage for women.

From the point of view of policy, an important conclusion emerging from these analyses is the highly tentative nature of the effect of "status of women" on fertility. But "status of women" does not define an area where public intervention is possible; education and jobs for women do. Improving women's opportunities for education and for modern jobs, like reducing infant mortality, has its own justification; piggybacking its fertility-reducing benefit onto programs and projects geared to improving women's lives increases the measured benefits of such projects relative to their given costs.

FAMILY PLANNING SERVICES AND FERTILITY

Do family planning services reduce fertility more efficiently and more effectively than general development programs? The wide range of estimates of the cost of averting a birth ($1–$400) and its benefits ($100–$900) illustrates the difficulty of answering such a question. Estimating the costs of averted births requires estimating the number of births averted because of a family planning program, itself a complicated task; some births might have been averted anyway if some couples are substituting publicly provided contraceptives for private efforts. And "costs per acceptor" is an unreliable measure since acceptors may make repeated visits in different areas, change contraceptives, and otherwise muddy the attendance statistics. Even where the existence of a family planning program is correlated over time with a decline in fertility, assurance that the program itself caused the decline requires the systematic elimination of such other possible causes as increases in income, changes in occupational structure, and increases in education. Few studies of the effect of programs

have adequately controlled for the probable effect of these nonprogram changes on fertility.

Advocates of family planning programs argue that: many programs are still in their infancy and have been poorly run; they have absorbed tiny proportions of national budgets and of foreign aid expenditures; they provide many secondary benefits—improved health for mothers and infants, increased control by women over their own bodies, and greater control by families over their own future. Moreover, support of voluntary family planning programs is one of the few widely accepted direct interventions governments have made to reduce their rates of population growth; the immediate question is not whether support is warranted, but how much and in what form. What is the effectiveness of spending on family planning relative to other expenditures that also have both general development and fertility-reducing effects? Only investigations on a country basis can begin to answer such a question.

INCOME DISTRIBUTION AND FERTILITY

Will an improvement in the distribution of income within a country reduce its fertility rate? In an analysis of 1960–1965 data on 64 countries, Repetto reports an elasticity of the general fertility rate with respect to the share of income received by the poorest 40 percent of households of −.36, compared to an elasticity of the general fertility rate with respect to increase in average per capita income of −.20.

Income distribution data are notoriously poor, and Repetto's result suffered in a subsequent estimation in which he omitted several East European countries (which have both low fertility and relatively equal income distributions); the income distribution variable was no longer statistically significant in explaining the fertility variable. Moreover, whether such cross-section results should be used to predict the pattern of a relationship over time is highly questionable.

There is thus no real indication that individuals' fertility behavior is affected by their relative income per se, over and above their absolute income; the income distribution-fertility link found is more probably the result of a coincidence over the period since World War II between improvements in the level of absolute income of the poorest and increases in their relative share. In any event, insofar as "income distribution" is used to mean some nexus of programs, including income increases, to alleviate the poverty of the poorest, an inverse relationship to fertility seems to hold. Fertility-reducing effects can be added to the other benefits of raising income levels of the poorest groups.

Highlighted above are four areas of public policy intervention. All may contribute to reducing fertility at tolerable cost; all provide benefits in addition to fertility reduction. Careful design of policy in these areas can accelerate the fertility decline that general improvement in standards of living inaugurates.

Comment

The major lines of research on the multiple relationships between population growth and economic development have been directed to the determinants and consequences of fertility. The research can be further divided into macro- and micro-type research. An excellent survey of several research studies is presented by Nancy Birdsall, "Analytical Approaches to the Relationship of Population Growth and Development," *Population and Development Review* (March 1977; June 1977).

Of particular interest in the macro-consequences studies is the attempt to compare costs of a family planning program to the projected savings realized in health or education costs. Usually the savings in the latter are shown to "pay" for the former in this form of analysis. Such comparisons, however, necessitate assumptions regarding costs of launching family planning programs, acceptor rates, and the relationship between acceptor rates and actual births averted, as well as assumptions about future costs in health, education, or other areas, and about the society's welfare function, which may value children per se in addition to capital goods.

A number of studies have considered the benefits and costs of poopulation control programs: A. J. Coale and E. M. Hoover, *Population Growth and Economic Development in Low-Income Countries* (1958); P. M. Hauser (ed.), *The Population Dilemma* (1963); Bernard Berelson (ed.), *Family Planning and Population Programs* (1966); Goran Ohlin, *Population Control and Economic Development* (1967); Dudley Kirk and Dorothy Nortman, "Population Policies in Developing Countries," *Economic Development and Cultural Change* (January 1967); J. E. Meade, "Population Explosion, The Standard of Living, and Social Conflict," *Economic Journal* (June 1967); J. Spengler, "The Economist and the Population Question," *American Economic Review* (March 1966); R. A. Easterlin, "Effects of Population Growth on the Economic Development of Developing Countries," *The Annals,* (January 1967); Harvey Leibenstein, "Socio-Economic Fertility Theories and Their Relevance to Population Policy," *International Labour Review* (May–June 1974); Harvey Leibenstein, "An Interpretation of the Economic Theory of Fertility: Promising Path or Blind Alley," *Journal of Economic Literature* (June 1974); Harvey Leibenstein, "Pitfalls in Benefit-Cost Analysis of Birth Prevention," *Population Studies* (June 1969); Timothy King et al., *Population Policies and Economic Development* (1974); Philip M. Hauser (ed.), *World Population and Development* (1979); R. A. Easterlin (ed.), *Population and Economic Change in Developing Countries* (1980).

Comment

Besides the macro-research involving benefit-cost analysis, there has been more research on how individual fertility decisions are affected by environmental changes. The "new economics of the household" treats the child as both a produced (investment) and consumer good. Fertility is the result of rational economic choice within the household.

This economic model concludes that, for poor families in developing countries, children entail low net costs and, in the extreme case, may actually be a net benefit. In contrast, the literature dealing with macro-consequences concludes that high fertility entails a high net cost to poor societies. This theoretical gap between the low private and high social costs of children has been a principal justification for government policies to reduce fertility. On the micro-models, see Theodore W. Schultz (ed.), *Economics of the Family: Marriage, Children and Human Capital* (1974).

IX.A.4. Economics of Population Quality*

While land per se is not a critical factor in being poor, the human agent is: Investment in improving population quality can significantly enhance the economic prospects and the welfare of poor people. Child care, home and work experience, the acquisition of information and skills through schooling and in other ways consisting primarily of investment in health and schooling can improve population quality. Such investments in low-income countries have, as I shall show, been successful in improving the economic prospects wherever they have not been dissipated by political instability. Poor people in low-income countries are not prisoners of an iron-clad poverty equilibrium that economics is unable to break. There are no overwhelming forces that nullify all economic improvements, causing poor people to abandon the economic struggle. It is now well documented that in agriculture poor people do respond to better opportunities. . . .

I now turn to measurable gains in the quality of both farm and nonfarm people (Schultz 1979*b*, 1979*c*). Quality in this context consists of various forms of human capital. I have argued elsewhere (Schultz 1974) that, while a strong case can be made for using a

*From Theodore W. Schultz, "Nobel Lecture: The Economics of Being Poor," *Journal of Political Economy*, Vol. 88, No. 4, 1980, pp. 643, 645–8. Reprinted by permission.

rigorous definition of human capital, it will be subject to the same ambiguities that continue to plague capital theory in general and the capital concept in economic growth models in particular. Capital is two-faced, and what these two faces tell us about economic growth, which is a dynamic process, are, as a rule, inconsistent stories. It must be so because the cost story is a tale about sunk investments, and the other story pertains to the discounted value of the stream of services that such capital renders, which changes with the shifting sands of growth. But worse still is the capital homogeneity assumption underlying capital theory and the aggregation of capital in growth models. As Hicks (1965) has taught us, the capital homogeneity assumption is the disaster of capital theory. This assumption is demonstrably inappropriate in analyzing the dynamics of economic growth that is afloat on capital inequalities because of the differences in the rates of return, whether the capital aggregation is in terms of factor costs or in terms of the discounted value of the lifetime services of its many parts. Nor would a catalog of all existing growth models prove that these inequalities are equals. But why try to square the circle? If we were unable to observe these inequalities, we would have to invent them because *they are the mainspring of economic growth*. They are the mainspring because they are the compelling economic signals of growth. Thus, one of the essential parts of economic growth is concealed by such capital aggregation.

The value of additional human capital depends on the additional well-being that human beings derive from it. Human capital contributes to labor productivity and to entrepreneurial ability. This allocative ability is valuable in farm and nonfarm production, in household production, and in the time and other resources that students allocate to their education. It is also valuable in migration to better job opportunities and to better locations in which to live. It contributes importantly to satisfactions that are an integral part of current and future consumption.

My approach to population quality is to treat quality as a scarce resource, which implies that it has an economic value and that its acquisition entails a cost. In analyzing human behavior that determines the type and amount of quality that is acquired over time, the key is the relation between the returns from additional quality and the costs of acquiring it. When the returns exceed costs, the stock of population quality will be enhanced. This means that increases in the supply of any quality component are a response to a demand for it. It is a supply-demand approach to investment behavior because all quality components are here treated as durable scarce resources that are useful over some period of time.

My hypothesis is that the returns to various quality components are increasing over time in many low-income countries: the rents that entrepreneurs derive from their allocative ability rise, as do the returns to child care, schooling, and improvements in health. Furthermore, the rates of return are enhanced by the reductions in the costs of acquiring most of these quality components. Over time the increases in the demand for quality, in children and on the part of adults in enhancing their own quality, reduce the demand for quantity; that is, quality and quantity are substitutes, and the reduction in demand for quantity favors having and rearing fewer children (Becker and Tomes 1976; Rosenzweig and Wolpin 1978). The move-

ment toward quality contributes to the solution of the population "problem."

INVESTMENT IN HEALTH

Human capital theory treats everyone's state of health as a stock, that is, as health capital and its contribution as health services. Part of the quality of the initial stock is inherited and part is acquired. The stock depreciates over time and at an increasing rate in later life. Gross investment in human capital entails acquisition and maintenance costs. These investments include child care, nutrition, clothing, housing, medical services, and the use of one's own time. The flow of services that health capital renders consists of "healthy time" or "sickness-free time," which are inputs into work, consumption, and leisure activities (Grossman 1972; Williams 1977).

The improvements in health revealed by the longer life span of people in many low-income countries have undoubtedly been the most important advance in population quality. Since about 1950, life expectancy at birth has increased 10 percent or more in many of these countries. People of western Europe and North America never attained so large an increase in life expectancy in so short a period. The decline in mortality of infants and very young children is only part of this achievement. The mortality of older children, youths, and adults is also down.

Ram and Schultz (1979) deal with the economics of these demographic developments in India. The results correspond to those in other low-income countries. In India from 1951 to 1971 life expectancy at birth of males increased by 43 percent and that of females by 41 percent. Life spans over the life cycle after age 10, 20 and on to age 60, for both males and females in 1971, were also decidedly longer than in 1951.

The favorable economic implications of these increases in life span are pervasive. Foremost are the satisfactions that people derive from longer life. While they are hard to measure, there is little room for doubt that the value of life expectancy is enhanced.

Measurement, however, is not impossible. Usher (1978) devised an ingenious extension of theory to determine the utility that people derive from increases in life expectancy. His empirical analysis indicates that the additional utility increases substantially the value of personal income.

Longer life spans provide additional incentives to acquire more education as investments in future earnings. Parents invest more in their children. More on-the-job training becomes worthwhile. The additional health capital and the other forms of human capital tend to increase the productivity of workers. Longer life spans result in more years of participation in the labor force and bring about a reduction in "sick time." Better health and vitality of workers in turn lead to more productivity per man hour at work.

INVESTMENT IN EDUCATION

Education accounts for much of the improvements in population quality. But reckoning the cost of schooling, the value of the work that young children do for their parents must be included. Even for the very young children during their first years of school, most parents forego (sacrifice) the value of the work that children perform (Rosenzweig and Evenson 1977). Another distinctive attribute of schooling is the vintage effect by age over time. Starting from widespread illiteracy, as more schooling per child is achieved the older adults continue through life with little or no schooling, whereas the children on entering into adulthood are the beneficiaries.

The population of India grew about 50 percent between 1950–51 and 1970–71. School enrollment of children ages 6–14 rose over 200 percent. The rate of increase in secondary schools and universities was much higher (Government of India 1978). Since schooling is primarily an investment, it is a serious error to treat all schooling outlays as current consumption. This error arises from the assumption that schooling is solely a consumer good. It is misleading to treat public expenditures on schooling as "welfare" expenditures and as a use of resources that has the effect of reducing "savings." The same error occurs in the case of expenditures on health, both on public and private account.

References

Becker, Gary S., and Tomes, Nigel, "Child Endowments and the Quantity and Quality of Children," *J.P.E.* Vol. 84, No. 4, August 1976, S143–S162.

Government of India, Planning Commission, *Draft Five Year Plan 1978–83,* New Delhi, 1978.

Grossman, Michael, *The Demand for Health,* National Bureau of Economic Research, Occasional Paper No. 119, New York, Columbia University Press, 1972.

Hicks, John R, *Capital and Growth,* Oxford, Clarendon Press, 1965.

Ram, Rati, and Schultz, Theodore W., "Life Span, Health, Savings, and Productivity," *Economic Development and Cultural Change,* Vol. 27, April 1979, pp. 399–421.

Rosenzweig, Mark R., and Evenson, Robert F., "Fertility, Schooling and the Economic Contribution of Children in Rural India: An Econometric Analysis," *Econometrica,* Vol. 45, July 1977, pp. 1065–79.

Rosenzweig, Mark R., and Wolpin, Kenneth I. "Testing the Quantity-Quality Fertility Model: The Use of Twins as a Natural Experiment," mimeographed, New Haven, Conn., Yale University, Econ. Growth Center, October 1978.

Schultz, Theodore W., *Transforming Traditional Agriculture,* New Haven, Conn., Yale University Press, 1964. (Reprint: New York, Arno, 1976.)

———, "Human Capital: Policy Issues and Research Opportunities," in *Human Resources,* New York, Columbia University Press (for National Bureau of Economic Research), 1972.

——— (ed.), *Economics of the Family: Marriage, Children and Human Capital,* Chicago, University Chicago Press, 1974.

———, "The Value of the Ability to Deal with Disequilibria," *Journal of Economic Literature,* Vol. 13, September 1975, pp. 827–46.

———, "On Economics, Agriculture, and the Political Economy," in Theodore Dams and Kenneth E. Hunt (eds.), *Decision-Making and Agriculture,* 16th International Conference of Agricultural Economists, Nairobi, Kenya, Oxford, Alden, 1977.

————, "On Economics and Politics of Agriculture," in Theodore W. Schultz (ed.), *Distortions of Agricultural Incentives,* Bloomington, Indiana University Press, 1978. (*a*)

————, "What Are We Doing to Research Entrepreneurship?" in *Transforming Knowledge into Food in a Worldwide Context,* Minneapolis, Miller, 1978. (*b*)

————, "Concepts of Entrepreneurship and Agricultural Research," Kaldor Memorial Lecture, Agricultural Economic Workshop, University Chicago paper No. 79, p. 26, Ames, Iowa State University, 1979 (*a*)

————, "Investment in Population Quality throughout Low-Income Countries," in Philip M. Hauser (ed.), *World Population and Development: Challenges and Prospects,* Syracuse, N.Y., Syracuse University Press, 1979. (*b*)

————, "Reckoning the Economic Achievements and Prospects of Low Income Countries," Snyder Memorial Lecture, West Lafayette, Ind., Purdue University, 1979. (*c*)

————, "The Value of Higher Education in Low Income Countries: An Economist's View," Paris, International Institute of Educational Planning, 1979. (*d*)

————, "On the Economics of the Increases in the Value of Human Time over Time," R. C. O. Matthews (ed.), in *Measurement, History and Factors of Economic Growth,* Fifth World Conference of the International Economic Association. (London: Macmillan, 1980.)

Usher, Dan, "An Imputation to the Measure of Economic Growth for Changes in Life Expectancy," in Milton Moss (ed.), *The Measurement of Economic and Social Performance,* New York, Columbia University Press (for National Bureau of Economic Research), 1978.

Welch, Finis, "Education in Production," J.P.E., Vol. 78, No. 1, January–February 1970, pp. 35–59.

————, "The Role of Investments in Human Capital and Agriculture," in Theodore W. Schultz (ed.), *Distortions of Agricultural Incentives,* Bloomington, Indiana University Press, 1978.

Williams, Alan, "Health Service Planning," in Michael J. Artis and A. R. Nobay (eds.), *Studies in Modern Economic Analysis,* Edinburgh, Blackwell, 1977.

IX.B. HEALTH AND NUTRITION

IX.B.1. Intercountry Variations in Health*

Health conditions vary more among the less developed countries than between more and less developed ones. Life expectancy varies from about 40 years (Mali, Angola, and Upper Volta) to about 70 years (Sri Lanka, Singapore, and Argentina). Life expectancy generally rises with per capita incomes, thus lending credence to the old notion that economic development is good medicine. But the high levels of health in a few very poor areas (Sri Lanka and the Indian state of Kerala, for example) and the low life expectancy in a smaller number of relatively wealthy areas (Brazil and Nigeria) demonstrate that the relationship is neither simple nor inescapable. Moreover, the pattern of disease and the scale of morbidity both vary widely across geographic areas. The differences reflect not only variations in income levels, environmental sanitation, access to health care, levels of education, etc., but also such uncontrollable factors as climate. The following paragraphs attempt to highlight the conditions prevailing in selected regions of the world.

The highest rates of infant and early childhood mortality and the lowest life expectancies are reported by the countries of sub-Saharan Africa. Life expectancy ranges from 39 years to 54 years (lower than the average for India). It is estimated that at least a million African children die each year without reaching the age of five. In much of Africa, half of all deaths occur among children under five. [See Table 1.]

The countries of Southeast Asia and the South Pacific face the second most grave health problems. The region is characterized by population pressures, borderline nutritional status, and difficult water supply and waste management problems. On the other hand, it is relatively literate, its communities are often highly organized, and its public administration is generally fairly well developed. Wide intercountry variations are found not only in health but in income, education, and climate. Life expectancy for the region, excluding China, is about 51 years—somewhat below the average for all developing countries. Singapore, Malaysia, Hong Kong, and Korea are industrializing rapidly and have life expectancies at birth between 63–72 years, whereas Laos People's Democratic Republic has a very low life expectancy at birth (42 years) and a very high crude death rate (2 per 1,000). [See Table 2.]

In South Asia, Sri Lanka and the State of Kerala in India differ significantly from the remaining areas of the region. Life expectancy is 69 years in Sri Lanka as compared to only 43 years in Nepal. More accessible health services, higher literacy, good transportation and communications, and more equitable distribution of food seem to account for these two exceptional areas.[1] Kerala reports especially high health status, even though incomes are significantly lower than Indian national averages.[See Table 3.]

The goal of the ten-year health plan (1970–1980) for the Americas was to increase life expectancy at birth by five years in those countries where it was below 65 years in 1970. More than one-third of all Latin American countries had surpassed this goal by 1977, and all are expected to gain at least three years by 1980. Temperate South America is expected to reach 70 years of life expectancy by 1980; tropical South America, with the exception of Bolivia, should reach 65

*From Frederick Golladay and Bernhard Liese, "Health Issues and Policies in the Developing Countries," *World Bank Staff Working Paper* No. 412, August 1980. Reprinted by permission.

[1]Gwatkin, Davidson, "Nutrition Planning and Physical Well-being in Kerala and Sri Lanka," *Overseas Development Council,* Washington, D.C. January 1978.

TABLE 1. Health Indicators for Selected African Countries

Country	GNP per Capita in U.S. Dollars 1978	Births per Thousand Population 1978	Deaths per Thousand Population 1978	Deaths per Thousand Infants Aged 0–1 1978	Life Expectancy at Birth 1978
Ethiopia	120	49	45	—	39
Mali	120	49	22	120	42
Somalia	130	48	20	—	43
Burundi	140	47	20	138	45
Chad	140	44	21	—	43
Rwanda	180	51	19	133	46
Upper Volta	160	48	22	—	42
Zaire	210	46	19	—	46
Malawi	180	52	20	142	46
Mozambique	140	46	19	93	46
Niger	220	51	22	162	42
Sierra Leone	210	46	19	—	46
Tanzania	230	48	16	—	51
Benin	230	49	19	—	46
Lesotho	280	40	16	116	50
Madagascar	250	45	19	53	46
Central African Republic	250	44	19	—	46
Kenya	330	51	14	51	53
Mauritania	270	50	22	—	42
Uganda	280	45	14	—	53
Sudan	320	45	18	132	46
Angola	300	48	23	24	41
Cameroon	460	42	19	—	46
Ghana	390	48	17	63	48
Liberia	460	51	18	159	48
Nigeria	560	50	18	163	48
Senegal	340	49	22	158	42

Source: Infant death rates from World Bank, *Health Sector Policy Paper,* second edition, February 1980, annex 1; other data from *World Development Report, 1980.*

years; Caribbean countries, excluding Dominican Republic and Haiti, have surpassed 70 years of life expectancy.

Deaths per 1,000 population in Latin America decreased from around 11 in 1960 to around 8 in the early 1970s. Although there were 18 Latin American countries with crude death rates greater than 10 per 1,000 in 1960, only 6 countries continued to experience this rate by 1975. The ratio of percent decreases of deaths under 1 year of age to present decreases of deaths 1–4 years of age between 1968 and 1974 was approximately 1:1 in North America, 1:4 in Central America, and 1:2 in South America. Thus, greater achievement has been attained in reducing deaths of 1- to 4-year-olds in Latin America during this period.[2]

Table 4 below presents selected health indicators for countries in the Latin America region.

[2]Pan American Health Organization, *Health Conditions in the Americas, 1973–1976,* Scientific Publication No. 364, Washington, D.C., 1978.

TABLE 2. Health Indicators for Selected Countries in Southeast Asia and the Pacific

Country	GNP per Capita in U.S. Dollars 1978	Births per Thousand Population 1978	Deaths per Thousand Population 1978	Deaths per Thousand Infants Aged 0–1 1978	Life Expectancy at Birth 1978
Lao People's Democratic Republic	90	45	22	—	42
Indonesia	360	37	17	—	47
China	230	18	6	—	70
Thailand	490	32	8	68	61
Philippines	510	35	9	65	60
Papua New Guinea	560	41	16	—	50
Korea, Republic of	1,160	21	8	37	63
Malaysia	1,090	29	6	31	67
Hong Kong	3,040	19	6	12	72

Source: *World Development Report, 1980.*

TABLE 3. Health Indicators for Selected Countries in South Asia

Country	GNP per Capita in U.S. Dollars 1978	Births per Thousand Population 1978	Deaths per Thousand Population 1978	Deaths per Thousand Infants Aged 0–1 1978	Life Expectancy at Birth 1978
Bangladesh	90	46	18	139	47
Nepal	120	45	21	—	43
India	180	35	14	—	51
Pakistan	230	45	15	—	52
Sri Lanka	190	29	6	—	69

Source: *World Development Report, 1980.*

HEALTH RESOURCES

Problems of health infrastructure development and health personnel availability in developing countries vary among regions and between rural and urban areas within countries. The following describes, by region, the current status of physical resources in the health sector in terms of both quantity and distribution.

Africa

Access to health facilities in rural areas of African countries is inadequate. On the av-erage, ratios of population to hospital beds are 15 to 20 times those in developed countries.[3] Moreover, these few facilities often must cover wide geographic expanses and large numbers of people. Inadequate transportation systems and the cost of transport and lodging further limit actual rural coverage. In Kenya, for example, 40 percent of the outpatients coming to rural health centers lived within 8 km; 30 percent lived 8 to 16 km

[3]World Health Organization, *WHO Quarterly Reports,* Geneva, 1979, p. 696.

TABLE 4. Health Indicators for Selected Latin American Countries

Country	GNP per Capita in U.S. Dollars 1978	Births per Thousand Population 1978	Deaths per Thousand Population 1978	Deaths per Thousand Infants Aged 0–1 1978	Life Expectancy at Birth 1978
Honduras	480	47	12	118	57
Bolivia	510	44	15	158	52
Colombia	850	31	8	98	62
Paraguay	850	39	9	—	63
Ecuador	880	44	10	66	60
Guatemala	910	41	12	77	57
Nicaragua	840	45	13	37	55
Mexico	1,290	38	8	60	65
Panama	1,290	31	6	47	70
Costa Rica	1,540	28	5	28	70
Brazil	1,570	36	9	92	62
Uruguay	1,610	20	9	46	71
Argentina	1,910	21	8	—	71
Venezuela	2,910	36	7	40	66

Source: *World Development Report, 1980.*

away; and 30 percent lived more than 16 km away.[4]

The distribution of facilities favors urban areas. In Borno State, Nigeria, for example, where 80 percent of the population lives in villages, only 50 percent of health clinics are in rural areas.[5] There are only 233 persons per dispensary in the semiurban areas surrounding Lagos, whereas in outlying, rural states there are between 25,000 and 60,000 persons per dispensary.[6]

Africa has a severe shortage of medical personnel, with between 20,000 and 40,000 persons per physician. Moreover, medical personnel are poorly distributed. The overwhelming majority of physicians practice in urban areas where 10 percent to 20 percent of the population lives, while rural areas are left virtually unserved. In Senegal, for example, 76 percent of the nation's physicians are concentrated in the capital (Dakar) area, where only 17 percent of the population lives.[7] Yet expanding the supply of physicians is prohibitively expensive for most African nations; medical training alone costs more than $25,000 per physician exclusive of the capital costs of medical schools and teaching hospitals.[8] Health personnel other than physicians are also in short supply. On the average, Africa has only 4 to 8 nurses/midwives per 10,000 persons, compared to 63 in North America.[9] Such shortages impede expansion of health care systems to currently underserved populations.

Table 5 presents data on health facilities and personnel for selected African nations.

[4]Ministry of Health, Kenya, *Rural Health Strategy,* 1973.

[5]Derived from *Facilities and Manpower Survey,* Federal Ministry of Health, Lagos, Nigeria, 1978.

[6]*Facilities and Manpower Surveys,* Federal Ministry of Health, Lagos, Nigeria, 1978.

[7]Robin J. Menes, M.H.S., *Syncrisis: The Dynamics of Health: Vol. XIX, Senegal.*

[8]U.S. Department of Health, Education and Welfare, *Public Health Services,* Division of Program Analysis, June 1976, p. 96.

[9]World Bank, *Health Sector Policy Paper,* March 1975, p. 34. Deprived from World Health Organization, *WHO Annual Statistics, 1973–76,* Vol. III, table 2.5.

TABLE 5. Health Resources in Selected African Countries

Country	Population		
	Per Hospital Bed	Per Physician	Per Nurse/ Midwife
Ethiopia	3,080	69,340	22,320
Niger	1,200	55,420	6,790
Mauritania	2,320	15,150	1,580
Burundi	810	45,430	5.420
Sudan	1,110	12,680	980
Togo	680	20,770	2,530
Ghana	600	10,510	2,530
Nigeria	1,170	14,810	1,620

Source: World Bank, *Health Sector Policy Paper*, 1980.

South Asia

South Asia has more abundant health manpower than Africa but a similar lack of facilities. The major exception is Sri Lanka, where a determined program of development of infrastructure and personnel has resulted in ratios of population to resources that are among the lowest in the developing world.

South Asia averages 3,000 to 4,000 persons per hospital bed, but only about 30 percent of private medical facilities compensates to some degree for public sector maldistribution. Health centers and clinics, or subcenters in rural areas, are often understaffed and so do not adequately serve their catchment areas which often exceed 100,000 persons each. In India, for example, only 58 percent of rural health centers operate with full staff complement.[10]

Although the supply of physicians is greater in South Asian countries such as India than in other developing regions, population/physician ratios are about 2,000:1 in urban areas and 12,000:1 in rural regions.[11] Ratios of population to nursing personnel av-

[10]Montek S. Ahluwalia et al., "India: Occasional Papers," *World Bank Staff Working Paper* No. 279, May 1978, p. 198.

[11]Ahluwalia, op cit.

erage 455:1 with Bangladesh and Nepal having the greatest shortages.[12] Table 6 presents comparative infrastructure and personnel data for countries of South Asia.

Southeast Asia and Pacific

The health facilities in South Asia and the Pacific are relatively well developed, particularly at the hospital level. Ratios of population per hospital bed for Thailand, the Philippines, and Papua New Guinea are among the lowest in the developing world outside of Latin America. Major programs of expansion of rural health centers have been undertaken recently by countries in this region. In Indonesia, for example, the major goal of the health plans from 1969 to 1979 was to ensure one health center per rural administrative unit; by 1977 this goal had been exceeded. However, underutilization of public health facilities is a serious problem throughout this region, due either to poor staffing and management as in Thailand, or due to competition with highly complex systems of traditional medicine as in Indonesia.[13]

Countries in the Southeast Asia and Pa-

[12]Policy Paper No. 80, *Nepal Project Paper, Integrated Health Services*, USAID, May 1976, p. 22.

[13]World Bank, "Indonesia: Health Sector Overview," East Asia and Pacific Regional Office, unpublished.

TABLE 6. Health Resources in Selected South Asian Countries

Country	Population		
	Per Hospital Bed	Per Physician	Per Nurse/ Midwife
Bangladesh	5,640	15,050	38,540
India	1,620	4,100	3,960
Pakistan	2,070	3,920	5,680
Sri Lanka	330	4,010	1,300
Nepal	6,630	36,450	17,420

Source: World Bank, *Health Sector Policy Paper*, 1980.

cific region have pursued vigorous programs of training for health personnel. Thailand, for example, nearly doubled the number of nurses between 1968 and 1975.[14] In Indonesia, the second national plan (1974–1979) sought to double the number of nurses and nearly to double the number of health assistants.

Except in Indonesia, physicians are in relatively plentiful supply in the region. However, Korea, Malaysia, the Philippines, and Thailand face major problems of physician emigration due to greater opportunities abroad for specialization and economic advancement. However, the distribution of physicians remains a problem for most countries. In Indonesia about 60 percent of physicians are concentrated in urban areas. In Thailand there are three times as many physicians in Bangkok as in the remainder of the country. In Korea there is eight times as much physician time available per capita in Seoul as in the rural provinces.[15]

Thus, the region faces problems of poor access and underutilization of health facilities, and of maldistribution and emigration of health personnel. Table 7 presents comparative physical resources data for selected countries in the region.

Latin America

Latin America has the most developed and best distributed health infrastructure of any region of the developing world. Ratios of population to infrastructure often compare favorably to those of developed countries. Argentina, for example, has a lower population per hospital ratio than does Spain. Exceptions to this relatively bright picture, however, are found in Bolivia, Peru, and Ecuador.

The population per health worker fell from

TABLE 7. Health Resources in Selected Countries in Southeast Asia and the Pacific

Country	Population		
	Per Hospital Bed	Per Physician	Per Nurse/ Midwife
Indonesia	1,560	18,160	4,730
Thailand	800	8,460	1,530
Philippines	640	3,150	1,050
Papua New Guinea	170	—	2,350
Korea, Republic of	1,510	2,020	1,240

Source: World Bank, *Health Sector Policy Paper*, 1980.

500 to about 360 from 1970 to 1976. The population per physician decreased from 1,800 in 1964 to 1,300 in 1976.[16] Wide variations are found throughout the regions. In 1976, Central America had 1,400 people per physician, whereas tropical South America had 1,600 and temperate South America had 600—a ratio similar to that of the United States.[17] But the urban-rural distribution of physicians remains skewed, with two-thirds of physicians located in large cities, where only one-third of the population resides.[18] In North America there were 248 nurses and 411 nursing auxiliaries for every 100 physicians. In Central America there were 80 nurses and 132 nursing auxiliaries per 100 physicians. The relative scarcity of nurses is largely a function of their lower social status in Latin America but also reflects the emigration of some 20 percent of nurses to North America.

Problems of structure, distribution, and emigration characterize health personnel in Latin America. Rather than a pyramid with

[14]Ellen Schaengold, "Preliminary Review of the Health Sector in Thailand," in *World Bank: Income Growth and Poverty Alleviation in Thailand: Some Special Studies,* East Asia and Pacific Programs Department, June 22, 1979, annex IV, p. 14, table 5.

[15]World Bank mission data.

[16]Pan-American Health Organization, *Health Conditions in the Americas, 1973–1976,* Scientific Publication No. 364, Washington, D.C., 1978, p. 118.

[17]*Health Condtions in the Americas,* p. 119.

[18]*Health Conditions in the Americas,* p. 126.

TABLE 8. Health Resources in Selected Latin American Countries

Country	Population		
	Per Hospital Bed	Per Physician	Per Nurse/ Midwife
Honduras	660	3,300	1,170
Bolivia	490	2,120	3,520
Paraguay	690	1,190	1,570
Peru	510	1,800	2,370
Chile	270	2,320	420
Costa Rica	260	1,550	570
Brazil	270	1,660	4,070

Source: World Bank, *Health Sector Policy Paper*, 1980.

a broad base of auxiliary personnel, a body of technicians and an apex of professionals, the structure of health manpower in Latin America resembles a sand clock with a slip neck of technicians and two receptacles representing a relatively small cadre of auxiliaries and a much larger cadre of professionals.

Table 8 presents comparative data for Latin America.[19]

Middle East

The level of development of health infrastructure and personnel in the Middle East varies widely due primarily to vast income and environmental differences. The oil exporting nations of the Arabian Peninsula have per capita incomes among the highest in the world. Some of their problems of infrastructure and personnel development are serious, especially as regards access to services by nomadic populations. Nonetheless, they have made very significant progress in recent years.

Health infrastructure in the Middle East generally is poorly distributed. In Syria, for example, 45 percent of the health clinics are located in Damascus and Aleppo. The population per hospital bed in Damascus is one-

[19] *Health Conditions in the Americas*, p. 124.

tenth that in the rural provinces of Al Hasakeh or Al Rakka.[20] In Jordan 71 percent of the hospital beds are located in Amman, which has 57 percent of the population.[21]

In Afghanistan, on the other hand, basic health centers outside of urban areas are well distributed, but fall far short of the needed numbers. Similarly, in the People's Democratic Republic of Yemen (PDRY) 95 percent of health clinics and centers are located outside of Aden, but total numbers are inadequate, resulting in insufficient rural access.[22] Egypt has developed a well-distributed rural system with sufficient numbers of rural health units to ensure that there is a health care facility within three kilometers of every village. However, problems of management and supplies limit utilization.[23]

Shortages and maldistribution of some categories of health personnel characterize Mid-

[20] Raymond Ueber, M. Susan, *Health and Policymaking in the Arab Middle East*, Center for Contemporary Arab Studies, Georgetown University, Washington, D.C., 1978, appendix G, pp. 51–52.

[21] John F. Gallivan, M.P.A., *Syncrisis: The Dynamics of Health*, Vol. XXI, The Hashemite Kingdom of Jordan, U.S. Department of Health, Education and Welfare, May 1977, p. 44.

[22] See tables 3.42 in WHO/PDRY, *People's Democratic Republic of Yemen Primary Health Care Programme*, Aden, 1979, pp. 95–96.

[23] World Bank mission information.

TABLE 9. Health Resources in Selected Middle East Countries

Country	Population		
	Per Hospital Bed	Per Physician	Per Nurse/ Midwife
Egypt	470	4,630	1,870
Yemen, PDR	660	32,380	1,940
Jordan	940	2,550	3,820
Syria	1,070	3,060	3,430
Iraq	480	2.470	2,130
Iran	650	2,570	1,630

Source: World Bank, *Health Sector Policy Paper*, 1980.

dle Eastern countries. Nursing, laboratory and technician staff are generally in short supply. Cultural and religious traditions require that women be attended only by females, yet all countries in the region have a critical shortage of female personnel. Since this problem is in part a result of the lack of women with the prerequisite educational levels, many of the countries in the region have turned to training traditional midwives to ensure access to services for women and children. These and other shortages are often characteristic of national personnel. In the Yemen Arab Republic, for example, 47 percent of physicians and 20 percent of nurses are expatriates.[24]

Maldistribution also characterizes health manpower in the region. In Syria, 65 percent of the midwives practice in Damascus, leaving only 300 midwives to serve the rest of the country. In PDRY, 73 percent of physicians practice in Aden, and in Jordan, 76 percent practice in Amman.[25]

Table 9 indicates the variations in the region in the availability of health facilities and personnel.

[24]Yemen Arab Republic, Ministry of Health, *National Health Programme,* 1976/77–1981/82, Sana'a, August 1976, p. 51.

[25]Primary Health Care Program, WHO/PDRY, table 3.43, pp. 97–8; Gallivan Jordan, *Syncrisis:* The Dynamics of Health, U.S. Department of Health, Education and Welfare, May 1977, p. 48.

IX.B.2. Nutrition Objectives*

The mathematically precise economic growth models that have been in vogue since the 1940s seldom take explicit account of the notion of investment in human beings. Increases in tomorrow's income are assumed to result primarily from today's additions to material capital, and since consumption displaces capital investment, it becomes an enemy of growth, not a handmaiden. Consumption in the form of educational services, clothing, and eating of course have an instrumental impact on productivity, but since the effects of such consumption are difficult to identify, all growth in income is imputed to those more easily measurable factors included in the model. Expenditures on health and nutrition are also classified as consumption and thus fail to show up as factors affecting national growth.

Recently, however, the concept of capital has been extended to human beings. Development of the new theory was prompted by the discovery that "increases in national output have been large compared with the increases of land, man-hours, and physical reproducible capital. Investment in human capital is probably the major explanation for this difference." A significant part of economic growth in the United States and Western Europe, for example, has been attributed to education, and any residual growth to "knowledge."

In similar attempts to begin to measure economic returns to health investment, the cost of preventing a death is compared with the worker's future income, had he lived. Or the investment in human capital—the health, food, clothing, housing, education, and other expenditures necessary to enable a person to develop his particular skills—is measured against his loss through death any time prior to retirement. Those costs can also be measured against debility, where death is not a factor. Whether an illness results in temporary loss of work days or some temporary or permanent reduction in work capacity, the estimated loss in output added to the cost of medical care can be compared with proposed expenditures for preventing the occurrence of the illness in the first place.

*From Alan Berg, *The Nutrition Factor,* Brookings Institution, Washington, D.C., 1973, pp. 16–29.

Similar comparisons can be made of the benefits to be gained from expenditures on nutrition. Improved nutrition that returns an absent worker to the active labor force, or helps lengthen his working life span, or overcomes a debility that is reducing his productive capacity, or that enables a child to return to school or to improve his understanding or retention of things taught, or that enables an adult to absorb more effectively in-service training or the advice of an agricultural extension agent clearly raises the flow of earnings above what it would hve been in absence of the improvement in well-being.

Once a person's well-being is stabilized, nutrition costs become a maintenance expenditure. Increments of nutrition no longer lead to increases in productivity. An improvement in nutrition thus can help to improve or maintain the productivity level of an active member of the labor force, or it can take the form of an investment—for example, helping to push up the expected lifetime earnings of a two-year-old child.

SAVINGS ON MEDICAL COSTS

One measure of the benefits of a nutrition program is in the medical costs saved through reduced demand for medical services. In Caribbean hospitals, 20–45 percent of the pediatric beds are filled by nutrition cases; in India, 15 percent; in Guatemala, 80 percent. Nearly half a million hospital inpatients from thirty-seven developing countries were officially registered for malnutrition in 1968 (actual numbers may be higher due to classification of nutritional ailments under other diseases). At an average cost of $7.50 a day for ninety days for each case,[1] costs for treating malnutrition are on the order of $340 million a year to the thirty-seven countries. If treatment were provided to the approximately 10 million preschoolaged children

who need it[2]—without it, severe (third degree) protein-calorie malnutrition is generally fatal—annual costs would be on the order of $6.8 billion.

Clearly it is cheaper to prevent malnutrition than to cure it. However, as long as the elimination of, say, a case of kwashiorkor frees a bed and other medical resources for treatment of some other sick person who was otherwise unable to gain entry into the system, total hospital costs will not go down. Since unsatisfied demand for curative services is typical in low-income countries, reduction of malnutrition is not likely to bring about either a net reduction in medical expenditures or a slowing of the rate of growth in medical system investment. Adequate nutrition, however, would enable the medical system to increase the welfare and restore the productivity of all those persons in the queue who would be able to replace malnutrition patients in the system.

Reducing Productivity Losses

Another potentially large nutrition benefit for developing countries is the reduction in productivity losses caused by the debility of a substantial portion of the labor force. Unfortunately, medical data of the kind needed for calculating debility seldom are available for poor countries, and even if clinical data are accessible, they do not include many of the sick who never enter the statistics because of the excess demand on the medical system. In any case, the synergistic interaction of malnutrition with much prevailing illness makes it difficult to pin down the exact contribution of each factor. Often malnutrition itself does not put sufferers into the queues.

An alternative approach to measuring productivity losses is through use of aggregative data on food supply and the occupational distribution of the labor force. From estimates of daily caloric need in different occupations,

---

[1]Cost of hospitalization in Guatemala is $7.31 a day; in Uganda, $7.84 a day. This compares to national per capita health budgets in many countries of between $1 and $2 a year.

[2]An estimated 3 percent of the 325 million pre-school-aged group in developing countries need such treatment; that is twenty times the number of medical facility costs available for children for all diseases.

shortfalls in work capacity can be calculated for different levels of shortfall in caloric intake. Comparison of a country's average caloric need to average national caloric consumption then yields national working capacity shortfalls. For low-income countries these shortfalls are almost always very substantial, often as high as 50 percent. While this means of linking individual productivity to national productive capacity is conceptually useful, it relies on such aggregative data that its utility in estimating the cost of malnutrition is limited.[3]

Extending Working Years

Another cost of malnutrition is the reduced number of working years resulting from early death. For the majority of the developing countries, increases in the life expectancy of adults would add years to the working lives (rather than retirement years) of most adults. In countries where life expectancy at ten or twenty is particularly short, the added working years would be those when healthy adults would be at the peak of their powers and earning capacity.

Other things being equal, a lengthening of working life reduces the country's dependency ratio—the proportion of those in the population (largely the young) who produce no income to those who work. . . . Lower dependency ratios, of course, increase per capita income and, potentially, per capita savings as family incomes are required to support fewer numbers.

The age structure and life expectancy rates

[3]The example given here is based on the work of Hector Correa, who recognizes that because of data limitations many of his assumptions are heroic. A more refined model would offer finer breakdowns of the labor force, adjustment of work factors for local conditions and of caloric requirements by occupation and local conditions, and estimates of daily intake by income level and by season. It would still fail to take account of such important factors as employment opportunities, intra-family food distribution, the impact of cooking habits on nutrient content, the problems of efficiency of absorption, and the productivity impact of early malnutrition on mental and physical capacity.

of developing countries indicate that reductions in adult mortality would not only add years to income-generating lives and reduce dependency ratios, but increase the "yield" on education and other investments society makes in workers during their formative years. The advances are only potential, however, because they depend on productive employment being available.

The Problem of Surplus Labor

Restoring a worker to good health adds nothing to national production if no job exists for him. The apparent slow growth of employment opportunities compared with the growth of the labor force in poor countries is a common source of development economists' skepticism that better health and nutrition will bring economic benefits. Many countries have a substantial labor surplus in the form of seasonal idleness in agriculture, open urban unemployment, and part-time or work-sharing employment which has been called disguised unemployment. Hence the case for seeking productivity benefits from better nutrition, especially for the masses of the unskilled, would seem weak.

Yet, in rural areas of low-income countries, labor is more commonly in short supply than in surplus during harvest and other periods of intense activity. Do farm workers try to feed themselves seasonally to higher capacity, like draft animals? In fact, can they do so during the weeks preceding harvest, when cash income is at the lowest annual point and grain prices are at their peak? What happens to the productivity of workers who undergo alternating periods of well-being and malnourishment?

Open unemployment does not necessarily mean that production problems can be solved merely by hiring additional workers. Many functions impaired by a worker's malnourishment cannot be satisfactorily corrected by added hands. Most machine-paced operations have precisely defined needs for which the human work input cannot be divided among more workers to compensate for inefficiency. If a job is strictly machine paced, the worker would have narrow scope for reducing his performance below the machine's automatic demand. Malnutrition might then be reflected in shoddy output, particularly if the work is dependent on the worker's manual precision or strength. Malnutrition also is reflected in accident rates and poor work attendance. (In numerous instances, factories that have introduced feeding programs have experienced lower accident and absenteeism rates.) . . .

The quality of labor. Productivity is of course more than a function of human energy, of numbers of workers. Energy loss is a limited basis for calculating the effect of malnutrition on national production. As development proceeds, human energy is replaced by machine energy; human quality becomes more important than sheer physical capacity. Demands on human physical energy output decrease as the proportion of the work force in agriculture declines. (Although this may sound like a long-term description of the development process, it is already happening in some developing countries.) In agriculture, timely initiative, physical dexterity, and comprehension of increasingly sophisticated techniques all become critical to the successful exploitation of new technologies. In cultivating the new high-yielding grain varieties, farmers fall short of maximum returns because they fail, in varying degree, to apply the recommended practices. Some constraints, like inaccessibility or high cost of credit, are beyond the farmers' control. But errors of planting depth and timing, pesticide application, and fertilizer application rates and timing are not economic; they may reflect such factors as education, mental performance level, dexterity, and attention.

The small farmer exemplifies the problem. His decision making on the use of his own resources is not divisible. If malnutrition during his childhood limited his learning opportunity and undernourishment as an adult is compounding his disadvantages, his potential efficiency in making decisions is not increased by the presence of unemployed labor in the neighborhood.

Given the gross unemployment picture—

and clearly this is one of the major challenges facing many countries—an economic, as distinct from welfare, case cannot be made for special expenditures merely to upgrade the potential productivity of those masses of unskilled, landless, adult workers who have dim prospects of gainful employment. There are, of course, other limiting factors in the picture besides malnutrition—poorly functioning extension and credit services, inadequate transport systems, inadequate equipment (perhaps exacerbrated by policies encouraging capital rather than labor intensive technologies), illiteracy, and so on. Any presumption that improvements in nutritional status are a sufficient condition for realizable improvements in productivity would therefore be simplistic.

Yet, it would be equally simplistic to dismiss the productivity value of nutrition because of the existence of idle adults. To do so is to assume that underemployed labor is available (or can be made available) in the vicinity of an activity at the right time, that it possesses required skills, that it can be hired in fact, and that the work is technically capable of being divided among more workers than are currently employed. Often this is not the case. Much of the unemployed and underemployed today turns out to be a diverse and complex group that needs to be sorted out before conclusions are reached about the value of nutritional improvements. Moreover, recognizing the increasing importance of skilled manpower and general labor quality for future national growth, investment in large numbers of malnourished children today can improve the quality of a significant fraction of the future labor force. This is probably the area in which nutrition will prove critical to development in the long run. . . .

Other Economic Benefits

Nutrition programs promise a number of economic benefits in addition to the direct productivity benefits:

As the incidence of communicable diseases among the adequately nourished is lowered, the exposure of others to these diseases will be reduced.

The increased income of well-nourished workers (or well-nourished children when they enter the labor force) should improve the living standards of their dependents, thereby raising both their current consumption and their future productivity.

Housewives, whose activities are not measured in a market economy, should when better nourished improve performance on a number of economically important functions, not least of which is the quality of care for the young.

Returns may be raised on other investments closely related to human well-being, particularly education. (Low-income countries now spend nearly 4 percent of their gross national products on education, almost a third more than in 1960. The efficiency of the education systems they support may be reduced as much as 50 percent by the dropout and repeater rates to which malnutrition contributes heavily.)

Benefits Compared with Costs

Even where opportunities for returns to better nutrition appear to be significant, the costs must be weighed. Will the nutrition expenditure be less than the value of the expected increase in production? How will it compare with returns to alternative investments? The answers will depend on whose malnourishment is to be corrected, what increments in their productivity can be expected, how much the program will cost, whether its effects will be immediate or delayed, and what discount rate is applied to determine present value if benefits are delayed.

Productivity payoffs from nutrition investment can be anticipated for workers employed in machine-paced occupations in modern manufacturing sectors, students for whom malnutrition limits the potential joint returns from education and health expenditures, and small farmers facing the more exacting demands of new agricultural technol-

ogies. The widest and most lasting impact, however, probably would come from providing adequate nutrition to mothers in the last trimester of pregnancy—the critical period for fetal growth—and to children six months through two or three years of age (most of the needs before six months can be met through breast feeding). The greatest physiological need and greatest growth occur in the early years: 80 percent of eventual brain weight, for example, is reached by age two. During this time children require, relative to body weight, two and one-half times as much protein as adults; without adequate nourishment, they are susceptible to severe consequences of childhood infections such as measles and whooping cough and to diarrheal diseases. Even if a child's diet is fully adequate only in utero and during the critical early years of life, he probably will be brought closer to his growth potential. If, during adulthood, his energy intake level falls short of some desirable norm, his productivity will already have been ratcheted to a higher level—more relevant to a modern economy—than a life time at his current nutrition level could achieve.

Payoff on Child Nutrition Investments

An institutional feeding program designed to meet all nutritional deficiencies of a child from six months through his third year can cost roughly $8 a year or a total of $20.[4] (This *annual* cost to prevent malnutrition is approximately the same as the *daily* cost to treat it in a number of countries.) Suppose that the program averts a disability in a child's later performance. Assume also that if the disability were not avoided, the child would be able to produce (or earn) an annual

---

[4]The $8 would meet deficiencies of a diet that currently satisfies three-fourths of a child's protein need and two-thirds of his caloric need. The estimate is based on the production and distribution costs of Bal Ahar, used in India's child feeding programs (the child feeding program is being used here only for illustrative purposes, and is not being suggested as the lowest cost means of achieving the nutrition goal).

income of $200 over a thirty-five-year period starting at the age of fifteen. How much of an increase above $200 would be required to make the nutrition investment break even?

Of course, returns beginning twelve years after an investment is made are remote, and they should be adjusted to account for the long waiting period. If a discount rate of 10 percent is used to convert future benefits to present value, an improvement of only 4 percent ($8) in annual earning capacity is needed to break even—the annual productivity increase is about the same as the annual cost of the feeding. Both the time stream and the discount rate are on the conservative side, however. In developing societies a child often turns worker at eight or ten. Though a discount rate of 10 percent is commonly used for developing countries, it is probably too high for important irreversibilities—for assets or opportunities that once forgone can never be restored. The irreversibility of the human condition or opportunity resulting from malnutrition would place nutrition investments at the lower end of any discount range, increasing their competitive strength as investments.

Nonetheless, an increase in future productivity of 4 percent is a modest reflection of higher levels of performance. The actual rate of return will depend on a number of factors. The higher the initial income of the worker, the smaller proportionately need be the break-even increase in productivity. The larger his shortfall in working capacity due to malnutrition, the greater will be the increase in his performance from better nutrition. If his improvement in performance can move him upward in occupational groups, the gains may be more significant. Increased productivity ought also to include side benefits and enhanced returns to other investments. In a study that compared nutrition levels and IQ differences of Chilean children with IQ and productivity (or wages) of Chilean workers, the potential increase in earnings from child feeding that would offset protein-calorie deficiencies during the critical periods of early growth was estimated to range from 19 percent to 25 percent. Those rates are quite competitive with returns to education; in India, for example, education returns have been estimated in the range of 9 percent to 16 percent.

It would be hard to find a more favorable investment opportunity than avoidance of vitamin A blindness. Poverty-stricken societies where such blindness is considerable have few facilities for training the blind for productive occupations. The upkeep of the blind, minimal as it is, represents a total burden to their families or the society. Assuming that the average blind person could be sustained at a subsistence cost as low as $25 a year, the cost is 1,250 times the annual ingredient cost of the vitamin A needed for prevention. If vitamin delivery techniques should raise the cost several times, the arithmetic would still be highly favorable. The average blind person need only be in a position, if sight loss were avoided, to produce a modest fraction of this annual consumption for the investment in his sight to yield an enormous return. For India the consumption burden (at $25 a year per person) of one million people blind from vitamin A deficiency will cumulate to $1 billion over their lifetimes. . . .

Many of the links between diet, performance potential, and economic returns are poorly understood and may remain so, given the complexities of human development and behavior. Little is known, for example, about the relative damage caused by different degrees of malnutrition at different ages and of varying durations. The major benchmark provided by medical science is the concept of "minimum daily requirements" of specified nutrients. Any sustained diet below the minimum daily requirement implies damage, especially in environments where widespread diarrhea and other ailments lead to heavy nutrient losses. Although it is known that the extent of damage increases as the level of nutritional deprivation falls—as a child moves from first to third degree malnutrition—the shape of the curve relating deprivation to loss of physical, motor, and mental development, and to the severity of nutrition-related diseases, is unknown. The threshold beyond which the extent of loss becomes serious cannot be defined, nor can the degree of mental or physical shortfall or other resulting damage that separates the serious from the inconsequential be calculated.

Although it may never be possible to separate the mass of the world's malnourished children into neat groups whose potential performance can be forecast from specific investments in varying nutritional supplements, a clear line can be drawn between those who will live and the significant number of those who will die of malnutrition or related causes. Before children born today in developing countries reach their fifth birthdays, approximately 75 million youngsters will die of malnourishment and associated illnesses. The known numbers of those whose lives will be marked by illnesses that seriously strike the malnourished are so great, and the effects of malnutrition on educational and productive capacity so apparent, that investment in nutrition programs can almost be undertaken as an act of faith. . . .

IX.B.3. Nutrition Actions *

It may be fair at this point to offer the following conclusions about the nutrition problem:

· Malnutrition is a problem of major proportions.
· The nutritional condition of the poor is no better than it was a decade ago. In many countries it is worse.
· The nutrition problem is not likely to be resolved in most countries within a generation by increasing incomes and agricultural production.
· The basic problem is food-energy insufficiency, sometimes complicated by deficiencies of specific nutrients.
· The principal victims are the very poor, especially the rural poor. Most governments are not reaching them with the benefits of nutrition; few have central ministries with the outreach to do so.

Commonly expressed goals to eradicate malnutrition in the near future are unrealistic. The aim should be to overcome malnutrition in those areas, forms, and population groups in which it exerts the greatest drag on development. The problem exists in almost all countries, but within countries it differs significantly among various income groups, occupations, and regions. Malnutrition in Northeast Brazil, for example, is as severe as it is in parts of South Asia. The largest problem in sheer numbers is the Indian subcontinent. The largest problem by proportion of population in needs is in Sahelian Africa, Bangladesh, and parts of Central America. In most parts of the world, supply of food has kept ahead of population growth. In sub-Saharan Africa, however, food production per capita has been declining for a decade. Life expectancy is fifteen years less than in Asia and may well become worse.

The need for nutritional help exists among people of all ages and both sexes, not just small children and pregnant and lactating women. The problem is particularly serious among families of landless agricultural laborers, farmers with small landholdings that rural development programs do not reach, small-scale fisherman, and the urban unemployed. Together they constitute more than half the malnourished in most countries. Their nutritional condition reflects inadequacies in the availability of food, in economic and sometimes physical access to the food that is available, in knowledge of the best way to use the available resources, and in

*From Alan Berg, *Malnourished People: A Policy View,* Washington, D.C., 1981, pp. 47–52. Reprinted by permission.

health practices that affect biological use of the food that is consumed.

Accordingly, nutrition efforts should be designed to expand food supplies—increasing production and reducing food losses—in ways that will benefit the poor, with attention focused on what is grown, who grows it, and what is stored; to increase the incomes of the poor, to improve their access to food by improving the marketing system and adjusting price policies in ways that benefit consumers without creating a disincentive to producers and by setting up special feeding programs; to try through education to bring about changes in food preferences, in the distribution of food within families, and in hygiene; to improve health and environmental conditions—water, sanitation, immunization, and management of diarrhea—and to attack specific problems of micronutrient deficiencies with mass-dose capsules or through fortification of food staples. Some changes can best—or perhaps only—be brought about through changes in government policies; others can be attacked directly through nutrition projects.

The effectiveness of different nutrition efforts and the relative importance of various determinants of malnutrition under differing conditions are now better understood than they were five years ago. Although increasing income is fundamental to increasing food consumption, for example, it is now seen to be less efficient than lowering food prices. From tightly controlled field studies it has been learned that, in addition to equity benefits, increasing the amount of food consumed and improving nutrition in other ways can significantly increase the weights and heights of total populations of children and improve their nutritional status—or at least prevent or retard its rate of deterioration. It is possible to suggest what it costs through nutrition services to avert death at an early age, to avert a day of illness, to gain an extra centimeter in growth, and to increase psychomotor development scores by a percentage point. Even some general effects of broad nutrition programs can be predicted.

PRIORITIES

Despite the high degree of variability in nutritional needs among countries and in the causes of and appropriate responses to those needs, there are certain strategies that merit high priority in most countries. Accelerated growth in the incomes of the poor and--with few exceptions—in food production continue to be of primary importance. Attention needs to be given to the development of nutrition-oriented agricultural production policies and programs. And to ensure that food reaches those in need, food-demand programs, including the strong possibility in many instances of food subsidies, are required. Broad programs, such as general consumer food subsidies, may under some circumstances be as effective in reaching target groups as narrow efforts, such as institutional feeding programs designed to reach children of pre-school age. Clearly, however, subsidy programs should concentrate on low-income groups instead of all income groups, on regional rather than countrywide programs, and on seasonal rather than year-round aid. Most of the larger developing countries already have sizable subsidy programs. Concentration should be on increasing their effect on nutrition, imporoving their efficiency in the process.

These are new areas of emphasis that can complement the well-known direct programs—nutrition education, fortification of staples with micronutrients, incorporation of nutrition-related actions into health services. The priorities that public officials assign to these various actions will depend on their countries' nutrition problems and the causes of them, the distribution of malnutrition between rural and urban areas, the extent to which the rural malnourished are small-farm families, the probable cost-effectiveness of possible programs, the institutional strength and funding capacity to mount programs, and political constraints.

The actions selected should have the aim of causing a specific improvement in specific nutritional deficiencies of a specific population within a stated period. They should be well defined as to content, costs, timing, location, and means of execution. When information to determine all this is not sufficient, projects can be developed for laying the groundwork. Action should not be limited to the gathering of data, but every operational program should include a track for evaluation and for learning from experience. Nutrition work in a country with an information base and experience in nutrition programs, such as Costa Rica, India, or the Philippines, would be very different from work in a country that had previously given little attention to nutrition.

The complexity of the nutrition problem and the multiplicity of potential nutrition actions should not be allowed to dictate complex projects. Projects should be broadly conceived with regard to content, but they should not be expected to address the many factors that affect nutritional status. Complex projects have generally been found difficult to implement effectively. Whenever it is feasible, there should be a sharp focus on a small number of critically needed actions.

Nutrition actions should be designed in ways that limit the need for managerial skills, of which many countries have a shortage. Similarly, there needs to be a clear focal point for administration of projects—multiministerial coordinating mechanisms have not proved to be particularly promising in accelerating actions. Generally a single agency should be made responsible for nutrition projects—whether an agriculture, health, or social welfare ministry, or a planning agency will depend on the nature of the project and the practices and preferences of government.

NUTRITION IN AGRICULTURE

In countries where actions involving agriculture can make a significant contribution to meeting chronic needs in nutrition—urban as well as rural—specific agriculture projects designed to have an effect on nutrition should be considered. Nutrition should also be inserted as an explicit objective in agricultural

and rural development projects aimed at improving the well-being of low-income groups whenever it is feasible. Malnutrition sometimes is used as a justification for such projects, but nutrition goals are not explicitly included in project objectives, and any nutritional gains occur largely by coincidence. Improvements in nutrition must be accepted as an important objective of these projects and the costs of possible actions must be taken into account. Nutrition actions should not be undertaken if their negative effects on other project goals would more than offset the gains from other actions. But modest reorientation of project designs can sometimes have significant nutritional effects without causing unacceptable changes in the achievement of other goals. When benefits of various goals are conflicting, the tradeoffs among the various goals should be weighed.

In certain agricultural and urban projects the addition of nutrition objectives might improve project design. The importance of nutrition to objectives and design will differ among projects. In Nepal, for example, a rural development project was based on an understanding of the way food consumption in the region was related to need; designation of project components, including the selection of crops, flowed from this understanding. A project in the Southern Highlands in Papua New Guinea, involving a shift from subsistence crops to cash crops, was modified to provide extension services that would help increase production in family food gardens and to include other assurances that the modernization effort would not be nutritionally negative. In Malaysia the design for a resettlement project in south Kelantan provided means for settlers to meet their nutritional needs during the first seven years, before rubber trees could be tapped. The government thus withheld a portion of the land for food crops, helped to build and stock community fish ponds, and provided nutrition education.

Often the steps required to incorporate nutritional goals are relatively easy to plan and implement—as, for example, in the choice of crops to emphasize in agricultural research projects—and need not be administratively or analytically complex. . . .

Projects in agriculture and rural development must not be allowed to cause a deterioriation of nutritional status. Quite unintentionally they could have harmful effects on food supply, food prices, or incomes. Both policies and projects should be routinely examined for their nutritional effects, including, if possible, their effect on groups that are not their direct beneficiaries. Where potentially deleterious effects are discerned, the offending portions of the projects should be reoriented or nutritional components should be added to offset the negative effects.

In agriculture and rural development projects that call for evaluation, nutritional status should, whenever it is feasible, be a key measure of project performance.

NUTRITION IN HEALTH

The interaction of malnutrition and infection has a far more serious effect on individuals than the combined effect of the two working independently. Consequently, the effects of nutrition actions and health programs undertaken simultaneously are greater than the sum of their effects on the same populations would be if the actions were undertaken separately. Since integration of nutrition with health services is a particularly efficient way of using limited resources, improved nutrition should be considered an explicit objective in all relevant health work. Problems associated with acute forms of malnutrition and vitamin and mineral deficiencies can be much more productively attacked through health services than can the low levels of performance associated with chronic food deprivation.

IMPLICATIONS FOR DEVELOPMENT-ASSISTANCE AGENCIES

Malnutrition is a major development problem that calls for development-assistance agencies to broaden both their perspective on their nutrition work and their view of their policies and lending in other sectors, particularly in agriculture. Especially within agencies involved in general development work, improved nutrition, like reductions in poverty levels, needs to be seen as an overall objective. Much of the policy and project work of development institutions affects the nutrition of low-income groups, but these agencies are not always aware of the extent and sometimes even the direction of that effect. Furthermore, they sometimes miss cost-free or low-cost opportunities for strengthening positive nutrition effects in their work in other sectors. External agencies can only make a substantial contribution to improved nutrition if they adopt it as an explicit and sustained objective. This does not demand massive budgets for nutrition projects, though identifiable nutrition projects may be the best response to the nutrition problem in some countries. What is needed primarily is a nutrition dimension in development-assistance programs, particularly in agriculture, and the systematic incorporation of food consumption issues in economic dialogues and sector work.

Development institutions and the governments of developing countries can work together to do this by:

- making a substantial effort to improve understanding of the nature and extent of the problem, of where in the chain of nutrition events the weakest links are, and of ways in which nutrition issues can be better integrated into operations;
- incorporating nutrition concerns explicitly in agricultural and rural development project work by
- developing projects that respond to the nutrition findings of economic and sector work,
- analyzing the nutritional consequences of projects in agriculture and rural development, and
- adding nutrition components to increase the benefits of projects or neutralize their possible negative effects;

- including improvement of nutritional status as an objective and part of the design of appropriate health projects; and
- setting up free-standing nutrition projects when they are the most appropriate mechanisms for achieving stated nutrition objectives.

External-assistance agencies should continue to emphasize food production, but with increased attention to those foods consumed by low-income groups and further support to projects that help to strengthen the purchasing power of the poor. They can also help government bodies fill gaps to their knowledge. Unknowns abound in this complex field. Much remains to be learned about the precise nature of nutritional deprivation, the relative importance of its causes, its consequences, and the cost-effectiveness of remedial action. A sizable gap in knowledge that the agencies should fill is on the nutritional effects of their projects, especially in agriculture and rural development. They need particularly to work on the design and implementation of simple, low-cost monitoring and evaluation systems. Increased emphasis on nutrition is a logical extension of the effort to increase production of food, to assure consumption by those who need it. The food-policy approach can complement and broaden other work of development-assistance agencies.

Comment

The special problem of famines is analyzed by Amartya Sen, *Poverty and Famines* (1981). Sen develops an exchange entitlement approach to explain the causation of starvation in general and of famines in particular. For an informative commentary on this topic, see Kenneth Arrow's review of Sen's book in *New York Books,* Vol. XXIX, No. 12 (1982). Also refer to selection I.C.6 for a discussion of the relationship between entitlements and poverty, and to T. N. Srinivasan, "Malnutrition: Some Measurement and Policy Issues," *Journal of Development Economics,* Vol. 8 (March 1981).

EXHIBIT IX.4. Life Expectancy in Relation to Per Capita GNP, 1978

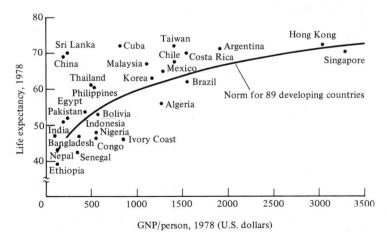

Source: Nancy Birdsall, "Population Growth and Poverty in the Developing World," *Population Bulletin,* Vol. 35, No. 5, Washington, D.C., Population Reference Bureau, 1980.

EXHIBIT IX.5. Trends in Life Expectancy, Child Mortality, and Literacy, 1950–1979

Country Group	Life Expectancy (years)				Child Mortality[a]				Literacy Rate (percent)			
	1950	1960	1970	1979	1950	1960	1970	1979	1950	1960	1970	1979
All developing countries	43	48	54	58	28	22	16	12	33	38	46	36
Low-income	41	47	53	57	28	22	16	12	20	27	29	51
Africa	35	39	43	46	44	38	32	27	—	17	17	29
Asia	41	48	53	58	27	21	13	11	20	28	31	52
Middle-income	46	50	55	59	28	22	16	11	48	49	64	68
Africa	37	41	46	50	42	35	27	22	16	22	37	—
Asia	42	47	53	59	28	22	14	9	54	54	69	75
Latin America	51	56	60	64	23	17	12	8	37	63	72	78
North America	42[b]	47	52	57	40[b]	36	27	13	19[b]	19	24	40
Middle East	—	48	53	57	—	30	18	16	—	17	35	49
Southern Europe	39	62	66	68	10	7	5	3	75	80	85	85
High-income oil exporters	—	46	51	57	—	35	20	11	—	14	26	32
Industrial market economies	68	70	71	74	3	2	1	1	95	97	98	99

Source: *World Development Report, 1982.*
[a]Deaths per thousand children aged 1 to 4 years.
[b]The 1950 data for North Africa include the Middle East.

EXHIBIT IX.6. Comparative Social Indicators, 1978

Country	GNP per Capita		Population and Vital Statistics				Health and Nutrition			Education[b]		
	1978 ($)	Growth Rate (%) 1970-78	Population 1978 (mill)	Population Growth Rate (%) 1970-78	Crude Birth Rate (per 1000)	Crude Death Rate (per 1000)	Life Expectancy at Birth (years)	Child Death Rate (per 1000)[a]	Calorie Supply (% per capita required)[a]	Primary School Enrollment Ratio (%)	Female Enrollment Ratio (primary)	Adult Literacy Rate (% of total)
Low-Income Asia and Pacific												
Afghanistan	240	2.7	14.6	2.2	48	22	42	27.0	110	20	6	12
Bangladesh	90	0.5	84.7	2.5	46	18	47	23.0	78	81	58	26
Bhutan	100	—	1.2	2.1	44	23	41	28.0	—	11	7	—
Burma	150	1.6	8.6	2.2	39	14	53	15.0	106	80	78	67
Cambodia (Kampuchea)	—	—	—	—	33	15	46	—	78	—	—	—
India	180	1.4	643.9	2.0	35	14	51	18.0	91	80	64	36
Indonesia	360	5.6	136.0	1.8	37	17	47	20.0	105	86	81	62
Lao P.R.	90	-2.2	3.3	1.3	45	22	42	27.0	94	92	84	—
Maldives	150	—	0.2	3.0	44	18	47	21.0	80	36	—	82
Nepal	120	2.3	13.6	2.2	45	12	43	23.0	91	71	32	19
Pakistan	230	1.0	77.3	3.1	45	15	52	17.0	99	51	32	21
Sri Lanka	190	1.8	14.3	1.7	26	6	69	2.0	96	86	82	78
Vietnam	170	—	51.7	2.9	37	9	62	6.0	83	141	142	87
Low-Income Africa South of Sahara												
Angola	300	-3.8	6.7	2.3	48	23	41	34.0	91	—	—	—
Benin	230	1.1	3.3	2.8	49	19	46	27.0	98	58	37	11
Burundi	140	0.9	4.5	2.0	47	20	45	28.0	97	23	18	25
Cape Verde	160	—	0.3	2.1	26	9	60	—	—	—	—	—
Central African Rep.	250	1.0	1.9	2.2	42	19	46	27.0	99	81	57	—
Chad	140	-0.7	4.3	2.2	44	21	43	30.0	74	41	21	15
Comoros	180	-5.4	0.4	3.9	40	18	46	17.0	81	85	71	20
Equatorial Guinea	—	—	0.3	2.2	42	19	46	—	—	26	—	—
Ethiopia	120	0.3	31.0	2.2	49	25	39	37.0	75	26	—	10
Gambia, The	230	4.9	0.6	3.0	48	23	41	34.0	97	41	27	10

EXHIBIT IX.6. Comparative Social Indicators, 1978 (Continued)

Country	GNP per Capita		Population and Vital Statistics				Health and Nutrition			Education[b]		
	1978 ($)	Growth Rate (%) 1970–78	Population 1978 (mill)	Population Growth Rate (%) 1970–78	Crude Birth Rate (per 1000)	Crude Death Rate (per 1000)	Life Expectancy at Birth (years)	Child Death Rate[a] (per 1000)	Calorie[a] Supply (% per capita required)	Primary School Enrollment Ratio (%)	Female Enrollment Ratio (primary)	Adult Literacy Rate (% of total)
Guinea	210	2.3	5.1	2.9	46	21	43	30.0	84	—	—	—
Guinea-Bissau	290	—	0.6	1.6	41	23	41	34.0	101	113	74	—
Kenya	330	1.0	14.7	3.3	51	14	53	14.0	88	104	98	40
Lesotho	280	9.3	1.3	2.3	40	16	50	21.0	99	119	139	55
Madagascar	250	−2.4	8.3	2.5	45	19	46	27.0	115	92	86	50
Malawi	180	3.2	5.7	2.9	52	20	46	27.0	90	62	50	25
Mali	120	1.8	6.3	2.5	49	22	42	32.0	90	28	20	10
Mauritania	270	−0.8	1.5	2.7	50	22	42	32.0	86	31	21	17
Mozambique	140	−4.6	9.9	2.5	46	19	48	27.0	81	—	—	—
Niger	220	−0.6	5.0	2.8	51	22	42	32.0	91	23	16	8
Rwanda	180	1.4	4.5	2.9	51	19	46	27.0	98	61	57	23
Senegal	340	−0.9	5.4	2.6	49	22	42	32.0	95	47	37	10
Sierra Leone	210	−1.5	3.3	2.5	46	19	46	27.0	93	37	29	15
Somalia	130	−1.3	3.7	2.3	48	20	43	31.0	88	44	32	60
Sudan	320	1.4	17.4	2.6	45	18	46	31.0	93	41	34	20
Tanzania	230	2.1	16.9	3.0	48	16	51	20.0	89	70	60	66
Togo	320	5.7	2.4	2.7	50	19	46	27.0	90	106	78	18
Uganda	280	—	12.4	2.9	45	14	53	17.0	91	53	44	—
Upper Volta	160	2.0	5.6	1.6	48	22	42	32.0	79	16	12	—
Zaire	120	−2.2	26.8	2.7	46	19	46	27.0	104	93	78	15
Middle-Income Africa South of Sahara												
Botswana	620	14.4	0.8	2.0	51	17	48	23.0	94	105	114	35
Cameroon	460	1.2	8.1	2.2	42	19	46	27.0	89	119	106	—
Congo, P.D.R.	540	0.1	1.5	2.5	45	19	46	27.0	103	155	143	—
Djibouti	450	−3.1	0.3	8.2	—	—	45	—	—	—	—	—
Gabon	3,580	6.0	0.5	0.9	33	22	44	30.0	104	202	197	14

Ghana	390	−2.3	11.0	3.0	48	17	48	23.0	86	74	64	30
Ivory Coast	840	1.4	7.8	5.6	50	19	46	27.0	105	92	69	20
Liberia	460	1.1	1.7	3.3	51	18	48	23.0	104	57	40	30
Mauritius	830	6.7	0.9	1.3	25	7	67	4.1	114	104	108	80
Namibia	1,080	0.4	1.0	2.8	44	15	51	—	—	—	—	—
Nigeria	560	4.3	80.6	2.5	50	18	48	24.0	83	42	33	—
Reunion	3,060	−1.6	0.5	1.8	28	7	65	—	—	—	—	—
Sao Tome and Principe	490	—	0.1	1.3	—	—	—	—	—	—	—	—
Seychelles	1,110	3.9	0.1	2.1	28	8	66	13.0	—	95	—	—
South Africa	1,480	0.7	27.7	2.7	38	10	60	10.0	116	92	—	65
Swaziland	590	5.3	0.5	2.5	48	19	46	27.0	99	95	91	39
Zambia	480	−0.8	5.3	3.0	49	17	48	23.0	87	98	87	—
Zimbabwe	480	−1.1	6.9	3.3	48	14	54	16.0	108	—	90	—
Middle-Income North Africa and Middle East												
Algeria	1,260	2.2	17.6	3.2	48	14	56	16.0	99	90	75	37
Bahrain	4,100	—	0.4	7.1	44	8	65	6.0	—	—	—	—
Egypt	390	6.2	39.9	2.2	37	13	54	18.0	109	72	56	44
Jordan	1,050	9.0	3.0	3.3	46	13	56	16.0	62	63	79	70
Lebanon	—	—	3.0	2.5	33	8	65	6.0	101	—	—	—
Morocco	670	4.1	18.9	2.9	45	13	55	17.0	105	68	50	28
Syrian Arab Rep.	930	5.4	8.1	3.2	45	13	57	14.0	108	103	85	53
Tunisia	950	6.2	6.0	2.0	32	12	57	15.0	112	100	81	55
Yemen A.R.	529	—	5.6	1.9	48	25	39	31.0	91	25	6	13
Yemen, P.D.R.	420	—	1.8	1.9	48	21	44	31.0	81	77	54	27
Middle-Income Asia and Pacific												
American Samoa	7,400	7.0	0.03	2.1	—	—	—	—	—	—	—	—
Brunei	10,640	7.2	0.2	3.4	—	—	—	—	—	—	—	—
Fiji	1,420	3.2	0.6	1.8	27	4	71	1.0	99	109	109	75
French Polynesia	5,270	1.9	0.2	3.1	—	—	—	—	—	—	—	—
Guam	7,130	5.5	0.1	1.0	—	—	—	—	—	—	—	—

EXHIBIT IX.6. Comparative Social Indicators, 1978 (*Continued*)

Country	GNP per Capita		Population and Vital Statistics				Health and Nutrition			Education[b]		
	1978 ($)	Growth Rate (%) 1970–78	Population 1978 (mill)	Population Growth Rate (%) 1970–78	Crude Birth Rate (per 1000)	Crude Death Rate (per 1000)	Life Expectancy at Birth (years)	Child Death Rate (per 1000)[a]	Calorie Supply (% per capita required)[a]	Primary School Enrollment Ratio (%)	Female Enrollment Ratio (primary)	Adult Literacy Rate (% of total)
Hong Kong	3,040	6.3	4.6	1.9	19	6	72	1.0	126	119	117	90
Kiribati	690	3.2	0.06	1.6	—	—	—	—	—	—	—	—
Korea, Rep. of	1,160	7.9	36.6	1.9	21	8	63	5.0	119	111	111	93
Macao	1,460	15.9	0.3	2.4	—	—	—	—	—	—	—	—
Malaysia	1,090	4.8	13.3	2.7	29	6	67	3.0	117	93	91	60
New Caledonia	4,650	−5.5	0.2	3.3	—	—	—	—	—	—	—	—
New Hebrides	540	1.9	0.1	2.6	—	—	—	—	—	—	—	—
Papua New Guinea	560	2.2	2.9	4	41	16	50	19.0	85	60	49	32
Philippines	510	3.7	45.6	2.7	35	9	60	7.0	97	105	108	87
Singapore	3,290	6.5	2.3	1.5	17	6	70	1.0	134	110	107	75
Solomon Islands	430	2.1	0.2	3.5	49	12	—	—	81	73	59	—
Taiwan	1,400	−5.8	17.1	2.0	21	5	72	1.0	120	100	—	82
Thailand	490	4.3	44.5	2.7	32	8	61	6.0	105	83	79	84
Tonga	430	0.9	0.1	1.9	—	—	—	—	—	—	—	—
Trust Terr. of Pacific	1,230	1.5	0.1	3.3	—	—	—	—	—	—	—	—
Western Samoa	—	—	0.2									
Middle-Income Latin America and Caribbean												
Antigua	950	−3.1	0.1	1.3	20	7	—	—	85	80	—	—
Argentina	1,910	1.3	26.4	1.3	21	8	71	3.0	126	110	111	94
Bahamas	2,520	−6.5	0.2	3.9	27	5	69	4.0	96	—	—	—
Barbados	1,960	2.5	0.3	0.6	19	8	71	3.0	129	112	114	99
Belize	840	4.7	0.1	0.9	41	6	—	—	125	85	—	—

Bermuda	9,260	2.3	0.05	0.5	—	—	—	—	—	—	—	—
Bolivia	510	2.5	5.3	2.6	44	15	52	22.0	83	80	72	63
Brazil	1,570	6.1	119.5	2.8	36	9	62	9.0	107	90	90	76
Chile	1,420	−1.1	10.7	1.7	22	7	67	5.0	109	117	116	88
Colombia	850	3.8	25.6	2.1	31	8	62	9.0	102	103	105	81
Costa Rica	1,540	1.1	2.1	2.5	28	5	70	3.0	114	111	110	90
Dominica	440	−3.3	0.1	1.2	21	5	—	—	87	—	—	—
Dominican Republic	910	4.1	5.1	2.9	37	9	60	10.0	93	102	103	67
Ecuador	880	5.8	7.8	3.3	44	10	60	10.0	92	101	100	74
El Salvador	660	2.0	4.3	2.9	39	9	63	8.0	90	77	75	62
French Guinea	2,340	0.6	0.06	3.0	—	—	—	—	—	—	—	—
Grenada	530	−2.0	0.1	1.6	25	7	69	4.0	88	—	—	99
Guadeloupe	2,850	3.0	0.3	0.1	29	6	69	—	—	—	—	—
Guatemala	910	3.3	6.6	2.9	41	12	57	15.0	98	65	60	47
Guyana	560	—	0.8	1.8	28	8	67	4.0	110	99	98	—
Haiti	260	2.2	4.8	1.7	43	17	51	23.0	93	71	—	23
Honduras	480	0.5	3.4	3.3	47	12	57	14.0	89	89	88	57
Jamaica	1,110	−1.9	2.1	1.7	29	6	70	3.0	119	97	98	86
Martinique	3,950	5.7	0.3	0.1	30	7	69	—	—	—	—	—
Mexico	1,290	1.0	65.4	3.3	38	8	65	6.0	114	116	114	76
Netherland Antilles	3,150	0.9	0.3	1.2	—	—	—	—	—	—	—	—
Nicaragua	840	1.8	2.5	3.3	45	13	55	17.0	109	92	88	57
Panama	1,290	−0.6	1.8	2.6	31	6	70	3.0	101	86	84	—
Paraguay	850	4.6	2.9	2.8	39	9	63	8.0	122	102	98	81
Peru	740	1.0	16.8	2.7	39	12	56	16.0	97	110	106	72
Puerto Rico	2,710	0.2	3.2	2.8	23	6	72	—	—	87	86	—
St. Kitts-Nevis	660	1.2	0.1	1.0	24	10	—	—	129	—	—	—
St. Lucia	630	1.0	0.1	2.3	33	7	—	—	91	95	—	—
St. Vincent	380	−1.3	0.1	2.3	31	8	—	—	89	85	85	—
Suriname	2,110	8.4	0.4	−1.4	37	7	68	5.0	118	101	97	80
Trinidad and Tobago	2,910	2.0	1.1	1.2	66	6	70	3.0	111	81	81	95
Uruguay	1,610	1.6	2.9	0.3	20	9	71	3.0	114	95	94	94
Venezuela	2,910	3.3	14.0	3.3	36	7	66	5.0	99	104	103	82
Virgin Islands (U.S.)	5,350	−0.2	0.1	3.5	—	—	—	—	—	—	—	—

EXHIBIT IX.6. Comparative Social Indicators, 1978 (*Continued*)

	GNP per Capita		Population and Vital Statistics					Health and Nutrition			Education[b]		
Country	1978 ($)	Growth Rate (%) 1970–78	Population 1978 (mill)	Population Growth Rate (%) 1970–78	Crude Birth Rate (per 1000)	Crude Death Rate (per 1000)	Life Expectancy at Birth (years)	Child[a] Death Rate (per 1000)	Calorie[a] Supply (% per capita required)	Primary School Enrollment Ratio (%)	Female Enrollment Ratio (primary)	Adult Literacy Rate (% of total)
Middle-Income Europe													
Channel Islands	4,170	0.6	0.1	0.9	—	—	—	—	—	—	—	—
Cyprus	2,120	1.4	0.7	0.6	19	9	72	2.0	136	70	70	—
Faroe Islands	8,080	4.2	0.04	1.4	—	—	—	—	—	—	—	—
Gibraltar	3,660	4.8	0.03	1.4	—	—	—	—	—	—	—	—
Greece	3,250	3.8	9.4	0.7	15	9	73	1.0	136	105	103	—
Greenland	6,760	5.7	0.05	0.9	—	—	—	—	—	—	—	—
Isle of Man	3,360	−1.1	0.06	1.5	—	—	—	—	—	—	—	—
Israel	4,120	1.5	3.7	2.7	26	7	72	1.0	122	97	98	—
Malta	2,170	11.8	0.3	0.3	17	10	71	0.4	129	106	108	—
Portugal	1,990	3.0	9.8	1.0	18	10	69	2.2	126	130	127	70
Spain	3,470	3.1	37.1	1.2	18	8	73	1.0	128	114	115	—
Turkey	1,200	4.2	43.1	2.5	32	10	61	10.0	115	98	90	60
Yugoslavia	2,380	5.1	22.0	0.9	18	8	69	2.0	136	100	99	85
Capital Surplus Oil Exporters													
Iran	—	—	35.8	2.9	40	14	52	14.0	130	98	77	50
Iraq	1,860	7.3	12.2	3.3	47	13	55	17.0	89	100	76	—
Kuwait	14,890	−0.4	1.2	6.1	47	5	69	2.0	—	93	87	60
Libya	6,910	−3.0	2.7	4.1	47	13	55	17.0	126	148	140	50
Oman	2,570	3.7	0.8	3.2	49	19	47	47	—	44	—	—
Qatar	12,740	−2.6	0.2	9.3	45	19	48	29.0	—	—	—	—
Saudi Arabia	7,690	12.4	8.2	3.5	51	15	53	28.0	88	47	35	—
United Arab Emirates	14,230	—	0.8	14.8	44	19	48	29.0	—	—	—	—
Industrialized Countries													
Australia	7,990	1.5	14.2	1.6	16	8	73	1.0	128	92	92	100
Austria	7,030	3.6	7.5	0.2	11	12	72	0.7	134	100	100	99

Country											
Belgium	9,090	3.3	9.8	0.3	12	11	72	1.0	136	105	104	99
Canada	9,180	3.2	23.5	1.2	16	8	74	0.8	127	102	102	98
Denmark	9,920	2.1	5.1	0.4	12	10	74	1.0	127	103	103	99
Finland	6,820	2.5	4.8	0.4	14	9	72	0.6	114	88	88	100
France	8,260	3.0	53.3	0.6	14	10	73	1.0	136	108	110	99
Germany, Fed. Rep. of	9,580	2.3	61.3	0.1	9	12	72	1.0	127	90	—	99
Iceland	8,390	2.7	0.2	1.3	19	7	75	0.7	110	101	101	100
Ireland	3,470	2.3	3.2	1.2	21	11	73	1.0	141	109	109	98
Italy	3,830	1.9	56.7	0.7	13	9	73	1.0	136	105	105	98
Japan	7,280	3.8	114.9	1.2	15	6	76	0.8	126	100	99	99
Luxembourg	10,540	3.9	0.4	0.7	11	12	72	1.0	141	102	103	100
Netherlands	8,410	2.1	13.9	0.8	13	8	74	0.7	124	102	102	99
New Zealand	4,790	0.5	3.2	1.6	17	8	73	1.0	127	111	110	99
Norway	9,510	3.9	4.1	0.6	13	10	75	0.6	118	101	101	99
Sweden	10,210	1.0	8.3	0.4	12	11	75	0.4	120	96	97	99
Switzerland	12,100	0.2	6.3	0.1	11	9	74	0.7	130	85	86	99
United Kingdom	5,030	1.6	55.8	0.1	12	12	73	1.0	132	105	105	99
United States	9,590	2.1	221.9	0.8	15	9	73	0.7	135	99	—	99
Centrally Planned Economies												
Albania	740	4.1	2.6	2.5	30	6	69	2.0	113	—	—	—
Bulgaria	3,230	5.7	8.8	0.5	16	11	72	1.0	144	96	96	—
China	230	4.5	952.2	1.6	18	6	70	1.0	105	127	129	—
Cuba	810	−1.2	9.7	1.6	19	6	72	5.0	118	122	119	96
Czechoslovakia	4,720	4.2	15.1	0.7	18	11	70	1.0	138	96	97	—
German Dem. Rep.	5,710	4.8	16.7	−0.2	13	13	72	1.0	139	94	95	—
Hungary	3,450	5.0	10.7	0.4	16	12	70	0.8	134	98	98	98
Korea, Dem. Rep. of	730	4.5	17.1	2.6	33	8	63	5.0	121	113	112	—
Mongolia	940	1.5	1.6	2.9	37	8	63	5.0	104	108	105	—
Poland	3,670	5.9	35.1	0.9	19	9	71	0.8	140	101	99	98
Romania	1,750	9.6	21.9	0.9	19	9	70	1.0	130	102	101	98
USSR	3,700	4.3	261.0	0.9	18	10	70	1.0	135	97	97	100

Source: World Bank.

[a] 1977 data.

[b] 1977 or earlier data, as available.

IX.C. EDUCATION

IX.C.1. Investment in Human Capital—Note

Although the objective of adding to the stock of physical capital has dominated investment discussions, it has now become evident that a high priority must also be assigned to investment in human capital.

Many studies of economic growth in advanced countries confirm the importance of nonmaterial investment. These statistical investigations indicate that output has increased at a higher rate than can be explained by an increase in only the inputs of labor and physical capital. The "residual" difference between the rate of increase in output and the rate of increase in physical capital and labor encompasses many "unidentified factors," but a prominent element is the improvement in the quality of inputs. Although some of this progress may be incorporated in physical capital, the improvements in intangible human qualities are more significant.

For purposes of measurement, capital formation is usually identified with the net increase of land, structures, durable equipment, commodity stocks, and foreign claims. But the capital stock should be interpreted more broadly to include the body of knowledge possessed by the population and the capacity and training of the population to use it effectively. Expenditures on education and training, improvement of health, and research contribute to productivity by raising the quality of the population, and these outlays yield a continuing return in the future. If these expenditures are considered as capital expenditures, then the proportion of capital formation in national income in the rich countries would be much larger than is conventionally indicated in national accounts that treat these expenditures under the flow of goods to ultimate consumers rather than under capital. But since poor countries do not make many such investments in the formation of human capital, this broad interpreta-

tion of capital would not increase significantly the proportion of their national incomes devoted to capital formation.

While investment in human beings has been a major source of growth in advanced countries, the negligible amount of human investment in underdeveloped countries has done little to extend the capacity of the people to meet the challenge of accelerated development. The characteristic of "economic backwardness" is still manifest in several particular forms:[1] low labor efficiency, factor immobility, limited specialization in occupations and in trade, a deficient supply of entrepreneurship, and customary values and traditional social institutions that minimize the incentives for economic change. The slow growth in knowledge is an especially severe restraint to progress. The economic quality of the population remains low when there is little knowledge of what natural resources are available, the alternative production techniques that are possible, the necessary skills, the existing market conditions and opportunities. and the institutions that might be created to favor economizing effort and economic rationality. An improvement in the quality of the "human factor" is then as essential as investment in physical capital. An advance in knowledge and the diffusion of new ideas and objectives are necessary to remove economic backwardness and instill the human abilities and motivations that are more favorable to economic achievement. Although investment in material capital may indirectly achieve some lessening of the economic backwardness of the human resources, the direct and more decisive means is through investment in human beings.

Emphasizing the weight that should be

[1]Hla Myint, "An Interpretation of Economic Backwardness," *Oxford Economic Papers*, June 1954, pp. 132–63.

given to the growth in the quality of human resources, Professor Schultz illustrates the possible implications of the quality component as follows:

Suppose there were an economy with the land and physical reproducible capital including the available techniques of production that we now possess in the United States, but which attempted to function under the following restraints: there would be no person available who had any on-the-job experience, none who had any schooling, no one who had any information about the economy except of his locality, each individual would be bound to his locality, and the average life span of people would be only forty years. Surely, production would fall castastrophically. It is certain that there would be both low output and extraordinary rigidity of economic organization until the capabilities of the people were raised markedly by investing in them. Let me now take a Bunyan-like step and suppose a set of human resources with as many but no more capabilities per man than existed as of 1900 or even as of 1929 in the United States. The adverse effects on production in either case would undoubtedly be large. To continue the speculations, suppose that by some miracle India, or some other low-income country like India, were to acquire as it were overnight a set of natural resources, equipment, and structures including techniques of production comparable per person to ours—what could they do with them, given the existing skills and knowledge of the people? Surely the imbalance between the stock of human and non-human capital would be tremendous.[2]

Recent experience with attempts to accumulate physical capital at a rapid rate in poor countries bears out the necessity of due attention to human capital. It has become evident that the effective use of physical capital itself is dependent upon human capital. If there is underinvestment in human capital, the rate at which additional physical capital can be productively utilized will be limited since technical, professional, and administrative people are needed to make effective use of material capital. In many newly developed countries the absorptive capacity for physical capital has proved to be low because the ex-

tension of human capabilities has failed to keep pace with the accumulation of physical capital.[3]

While the case for investment in human resources is gaining wider acceptance, the means of attaining an increase in this type of investment have still received only superficial consideration compared with the intensive investigations that have been made of the problems of investment in physical goods.

It is not difficult to identify the more important categories of activities that improve human capabilities. As Professor Schultz suggests, a typical list would be:

(1) health facilities and services, broadly conceived to include all expenditures that affect the life expectancy, strength and stamina, and the vigor and vitality of a people; (2) on-the-job training, including old-style apprenticeship organized by firms; (3) formally organized education at the elementary, secondary, and higher levels; (4) study programs for adults that are not organized by firms, including extension programs notably in agriculture; (5) migration of individuals and families to adjust to changing job opportunities.[4]

Underlying each of these activities, however, are a number of questions that should be studied more seriously.[5] At the outset, the problem of measurement presents several difficulties: Is it possible to separate the consumption and investment part of expenditures on these activities? Can the particular resources entering into each of these components be identified and measured? And can the rate of return on investment in education

[2]T. W. Schultz, "Reflections on Investment in Man," *Journal of Political Economy*, Supplement, October 1962, pp. 2–3.

[3]For strong arguments that "the experience of planning seems to suggest that knowledge (and certainly not investment resources) is the most important scarce factor in underdeveloped countries with otherwise favorable social climate," see B. Horvat, "The Optimum Rate of Investment," *Economic Journal*, December 1958, pp. 751–3.

[4]T. W. Schultz, "Investment in Human Capital in Poor Countries," in P. D. Zook (ed.), *Foreign Trade and Human Capital*, Dallas, 1962, pp. 3–4, 11–12.

[5]The remainder of our discussion concentrates on education and training. For a consideration of human capital formation through health services, see Selma J. Mushkin, "Health as an Investment," *Journal of Political Economy*, Supplement, October 1962, pp. 129–57.

be compared with the rate of return on investment in some other alternative use? As yet, no completely satisfactory empirical procedure for answering these questions has been devised. Although a few studies have recently made noteworthy steps in the direction of measuring some consequences of an increase in tangible capital,[6] no empirical study of investment in human capital is yet free from some arbitrary elements, and more statistical evidence is needed.

Another problem of particular importance to a country engaged in development programming is to determine at what phase of development the formation of intangible capital is most significant. It can be argued that a high rate of increase in the demand for improvements in the quality of inputs appears only at a fairly advanced phase of development. The early industrialization in Western Europe, for example, appears to have been accomplished without requiring as prerequisites marked improvements in skills and knowledge and health of workers.[7] And the contribution of education to American growth has been most pronounced in the more recent decades, while capital investment was more important in earlier decades.[8] Unlike the earlier historical situation, however, it may now be necessary to have a relatively high level of skill and much more knowledge to take advantage of the more complex equipment and techniques that may be obtained from advanced countries.

There are additional questions to be raised concerning what types of education should be emphasized, to what degree, and how soon. Some economists have such questions in mind when they criticize—from the viewpoint of the economic, though not social or moral, value—proposals for mass education or extensive systems of higher education in newly developing nations. They contend that these countries do not yet have an effective demand for large numbers of educated workers; it will take considerable time to raise the presently limited absorptive capacity of the economy for educated persons; and a poor country cannot afford to pay for as much education as can rich countries.[9] Since educational outlays compete for resources that have an alternative use in directly productive investment, it is essential to determine what proportion of national income should be devoted to education. And within the education system itself it is necessary to establish priorities for the various possible forms of education and training.

From the standpoint of accelerating development, the immediate requirements may call for emphasis on vocational and technical training and adult education rather than on a greatly expanded system of formal education. Considering its high cost and the problems of absorption that it raises, even the case of universal primary education is questionable. Professor Lewis expresses such skepticism in the following comments on African proposals:

The limited absorptive capacity of most West African economies today—especially owing to the backwardness of agriculture—makes frustration and dislocation inevitable if more than 50 percent of children enter school. This, coupled with the high cost due to the high ratio of teachers' salaries to average national income, and with the time it takes to train large numbers of teachers properly, has taught some African countries to proceed with caution; to set the goal of universal schooling twenty years ahead or more, rather than the ten years ahead or less associated with the first flush of independence movements. Such a decision is regarded as highly controversial by those for whom literacy is a universal human right irrespective of cost.... On the other hand, considering that in most African territories less than 25 per cent of

---

[6]For example, Mary Jean Bowman, "Human Capital: Concepts and Measures," in *Money, Growth, and Methodology,* Essays in Honor of Johan Akerman, Lund, 1961, pp, 147–68.

[7]Cf. Schultz, "Investments in Human Capital," pp. 3–4, 11–12.

[8]Edward F. Denison, "Education, Economic Growth, and Gaps in Information," *Journal of Political Economy,* October 1962, p. 127.

[9]These arguments are cogently presented by W. Arthur Lewis, "Education and Economic Development," *International Social Science Journal,* Vol. 14, No. 4, 1962, pp. 685–99; Thomas Balogh, "Misconceived Educational Programmes in Africa," *Universities Quarterly,* June 1962, pp. 243–9.

children aged six to fourteen are in school, a goal of 50 per cent within ten years may be held to constitute revolutionary progress.[10]

More immediately serious than the lack of universal primary education is the deficiency in secondary education. The most critical manpower requirement tends to be for people with a secondary education who can be managers, administrators, professional technicians (scientists, engineers, agronomists, doctors, economists, accountants, etc.), or subprofessional technical personnel (agricultural assistants, technical supervisors, nurses, engineering assistants, bookkeepers, etc.). Lewis characterizes the products of secondary schools as "the officers and noncommissioned officers of an economic and social system. A small percentage goes on to university education, but the numbers required from the university are so small that the average country of up to five million inhabitants could manage tolerably well without a university of its own. Absence of secondary schools, however, is an enormous handicap.... The middle and upper ranks of business consists almost entirely of secondary school products, and these products are also the backbone of public administratiion."[11]

Also deserving of high priority is the infusion of new skills and knowledge into the agricultural sector. In order to achieve a system of modern agriculture, the quality of labor in agriculture needs to be improved as an input in its own right and also to allow the use of better forms of nonhuman capital (equipment, seeds, insecticides, etc.). In many countries that have experienced substantial increases in agricultural production, the key factor has not been new land or land that is superior for agriculture; nor has it been mainly the addition of reproducible capital. More importantly, the agricultural transformation has been based predominantly upon new skills and useful knowledge required to develop a modern agriculture.[12] Educational

facilities for agriculture may also provide a way of encouraging rural school-leavers to take up work in the rural sector rather than migrating to the towns, and the special training of young school-leavers may allow them to act as the agents for introducing new and improved agricultural techniques.

For the broader problems of educational requirements, the making of "manpower surveys" (as discussed in selection IX.C.3) may furnish a useful basis for determining the principal skill shortages and what types of training activities should be emphasized. At least for the short term, the provision of agricultural extension services, training in mechanical and technical skills, and training in supervisory and administrative skills may contribute the most to fulfilling manpower requirements. After overcoming the immediate bottlenecks of scarce personnel in specific key occupations, the education system should then be devised to provide a balance between general education, prevocational preparation, and vocational education and training.

We may conclude that the recent attention to investment in human capital should prove salutary in cautioning against an overemphasis on physical capital to the neglect of the more intangible factors. When considered for a poor country, however, investment in human capital calls for new approaches and special emphases that differ from those in advanced economies. An extensive system of formal education is a commendable objective—but it must necessarily be a distant objective. Instead of attempting to imitate the educational system of an advanced country, newly developing countries may more suitably concentrate, at least in the early phases of their development programs, on methods of informal education and on the objectives of functional education. These efforts are less time-consuming, less costly, and more directly related to manpower requirements than is a formal educational system. As such, they are likely to prove most effective in improving the economic quality of human resources.

[10]Lewis, "Education and Economic Development," p. 689.

[11]Ibid., pp. 688–90.

[12]Cf. Schultz, "Investment in Human Capital," p. 9.

Comment

References to the literature on human capital theory are included in a number of selections in this chapter. For a comprehensive survey of the subject, see Mark Blaug, "Human Capital Theory: A Slightly Jaundiced Survey," *Journal of Economic Literature* (September 1976). Also significant is M. J. Bowman, "The Human Investment Revolution in Economic Thought," *Sociology of Education,* Vol. 39 (1966).

For a comprehensive survey of the state of knowledge about the effects of education on incomes, see Timothy King (ed.), "Education and Income," *World Bank Staff Working Paper* No. 402 (July 1980).

A critique of social cost-benefit analysis in educational planning is offered by G. S. Fields, "Assessing Educational Progress and Commitment," *Report for the U.S. Agency for International Development* (October 1978). See also World Bank, *Education* (1980); Ronald Dore, *The Diploma Disease* (1976); M. Selowsky, "On the Measurement of Education's Contribution to Growth," *Quarterly Journal of Economics* (August 1969); Dean T. Jamison and Lawrence J. Lau, *Farmer Education and Farm Efficiency* (1981).

IX.C.2. Educational Investment*

The educational product, in the context of economic development. . . not only includes the components of education usually distinguished as consumption (i.e., enjoyment of the fuller life permitted by education) and as direct investment (with the gains accruing "internally" in the form of increased earnings to the educated person), but also education as investment in the functioning of the economic and social system at large. These latter gains accrue "externally," not only to those in whom the educational input is invested, but also to other members of the community.

The theory of investment planning may be looked at from the micro or macro level. In macro terms, the problem is to determine the alternative growth path available to the economy, assuming the best structure of capital formation to apply in each case, and then to choose the optimum path on the basis of the community's time preference. In micro terms, the problem is one of rating alterna-

*From Richard A. Musgrave, "Notes on Educational Investment in Developing Nations," in OECD Study Group in the Economics of Education, *Financing of Education for Economic Growth,* Paris, 1966, pp. 31–9. Reprinted by permission.

tive investment projects and of deciding which one is to be included within a given level of overall capital formation. There is no reason why investment in human resources by education should not be included in such an analysis. However, education investment has certain characteristics—quite apart from the previously noted factor of externality—which pose special problems and should be noted at the outset.

CHARACTERISTICS OF EDUCATIONAL INVESTMENT

The product of education outlays, to begin with, carries joint features of consumption and investment. For this reason, the share of resources allocated to education cannot be considered wholly an investment outlay. The consumption component has to compete with alternative forms of consumption, while the investment component must compete with alternative forms of capital formation. To the extent that the two parts are inseparable, the proper allocation of resources to education should leave the rate of return thereon (computed as ratio of the present value of additional earnings to investment cost) below that of alternative investments which do not carry joint consumption components.

This distinction between the consumption and capital formation aspects of education outlays, however, is somewhat misleading. The consumption product of education may be divided into current consumption (the delights of attending school) and the future consumption (the ability to appreciate life more fully later on). Since the latter is much the major element, the consumption component is largely in the nature of a durable consumer good and hence investment. The essential distinction, thus, is not between the consumption and investment aspects of education output, but between education investment which generates imputed income (the fuller life later on) and education investment which generates increased factor earnings to the labour supplied by the educated person.

What weight is to be given to the two components in the development context, and how is this to be reflected in the pattern of the education programme? Recent writers have pointed to the extension of secondary education as being the primary goal of education policy in countries with a low level of educational capital stock, with extension of elementary education and technical training at the subsequent level of capital stock, and expansion of higher education at a more advanced stage.[1] While this priority is derived from the projected needs for various types of skill and training, it also suggests that the imputed-income component of the education mix tends to be of particularly great importance at the early stages.

Secondly, investment in education is characterized by a gestation period which is substantially longer than that of many other types of capital formation. Indeed, education seems the time-consuming, Boehm-Bawerkian type of investment par excellence. Periods of ten to twenty years may be involved, depending on how far the education process

is carried, and even longer spans must be allowed for if teacher-training is taken into consideration. Even though certain skills may be acquired fairly rapidly, especially if a previous foundation is laid, the educational capital stock cannot be changed quickly, particularly for the more advanced type of education. This introduces a constraint in investment planning and demands a correspondingly longer planning horizon which in turn points to the need for public policy guidance seen in the context of a long-term development perspective, if not development plan.

A similar consideration relates to a further feature of investment in education, i.e., the relatively long useful life of the education asset. Consideration of returns over, say, a thirty-year period, lends great weight to the importance of the discount factor in assessing the relative productivity of investment in education. Since the useful life for competing investments tends frequently to be shorter, the relative case for investment in education is low if the appropriate rate of discount is high. Thus, the selection of the appropriate rate of discount is of particular importance in assessing the proper share for education in total capital formation. There being no developed capital markets which provide a clear indicator of this rate, its determination becomes essentially a matter of public policy. Investments should be ranked by a present value rather than an internal rate of return criteria. Moreover, there may well be a difference between the government's and the private investor's evaluation of present, relative to future, needs. To the extent that public policy takes a longer view, it will also tend to require a larger share for education in investment outlays.

The relatively long, useful life, moreover, makes it necessary that the type of education be chosen in order to meet future demands in particular skills. This applies less to general and elementary education, which lays a more flexible basis, but becomes of great importance for specialized and technical types of training that do not permit easy conversion. As already noted, educational planning in the

[1] See Frederick Harbison and Charles A. Myers, *Education, Manpower and Economic Growth,* New York, 1964, Chapters 4–6.

context of a longer-term development view is essential.

Finally, a word regarding the resource cost of education. Recent discussions of the economics of education[2] emphasize, and rightly so, that this cost not only includes teachers' salaries, buildings and equipment, but also the opportunity cost of lost income on the part of the student. Depending on the structure of the developing country, this latter component may be of varying significance. Where there is a general surplus of labour supply, the opportunity cost of forgone earnings will be small or non-existent. Under other conditions, customary use of child labour may produce the opposite situation. While the former is the more typical case, other components of education cost (school teachers' salaries in particular) tend to be relatively high in underdeveloped countries.[3] Even though the income stream from a given factor input into education will be large (educated workers are needed to take advantage of modern techniques, and education is highly complementary to other types of capital formation) the rate of return on educational investments (relative to that on other investments) is therefore not as high as suggested by the income stream alone.

EXTERNALITIES

The standard procedure for determining the value of investment in education is to estimate the future stream of incremental earnings which accrue to the student, and to discount it to obtain the present value. This present value is then related to the cost of investment in obtaining the rate of return. This procedure excludes additions to output which accrue externally and to the benefit of others rather than to the educated person alone. Such oversight may be acceptable in assess-

ing the value of education for a developed economy, but hardly for the underdeveloped country, where external benefits constitute a substantial part of the total gain.

Perhaps the most important aspect of the external benefits of education lies in the change in the social and cultural climate, incident to the widening of horizons, which education entails. As has been pointed out many times, such a change is an essential condition of success for many developing nations. At the same time, this benefit result is not an automatic consequence of education at large, but only of the proper type, quality and quantity of education. Supply of professional people who cannot be absorbed into appropriate positions may readily become an external dis-economy and source of instability.

As noted previously, different types of investments in the early stages of development tend to be highly complementary, and this holds par excellence for the proper combination of investment in education and capital equipment. Without a capable labour force modern capital equipment cannot be operated, and it is precisely the access to superior techniques that is the one hopeful factor in the development picture. Now it is true that the existence of such complementarity need not, per se, constitute an externality which would fail to be recorded in a perfectly functioning pricing system. If tractors can be substituted for oxen only if trained drivers are available, this will be reflected in corresponding higher wages for the driver. The trouble, however, lies in the fact that in an economy where there are as yet no tractors, the supply of drivers is unlikely to be forthcoming, and vice versa. The generation of growth (whether "balanced" in an overall Nurkse sense or not) requires a concerted effort to provide a chain of investments, thereby reducing the risks of individual investments and making it possible for an investment programme to succeed where individual investments would fail.

This necessity for investment planning exists even for investments which, given the necessary supply of entrepreneurial talent,

[2]For a survey of this literature, see Chapter I in William J. Bowen, *Economic Aspects of Education,* Princeton, 1964.

[3]See W. Arthur Lewis, "Priorities for Educational Expansion," *Policy Conference on Economic Growth and Investment in Education,* OECD, Washington, 1961, Part III, p. 37.

would be appropriately undertaken privately. It exists par excellence for investment in education. Left to household decisions, neither the market knowledge, foresight or financial requirements are present which are needed to secure adequate supplies. This is especially the case in underdeveloped countries where the whole attitude towards education has to overcome conventional barriers and become reoriented to the development process. . . .

Sensible education targets, therefore, must be developed by considering the needs of the particular economy and the demands posed by its specific plans. This raises a question of the rate at which the system needs to, or can absorb additional supplies of educated manpower. Arthur Lewis stresses the fact that absorption capacity is limited by the high cost of education in developing countries. To quote:

The main limitation on the absorption of the educated in poor countries is their high price, relative to average national output per head. . . . In consequence, all production . . . which depends on using educated people is much more expensive, in relation to national income, in poor than in rich countries. The poor countries may need the educated more than the rich, but they can even less afford to pay for or absorb large numbers. . . . In the long run, the situation adjusts itself because the premium for education diminishes as the number of educated increases. . . . As the premium for education falls, the market for the educated may widen enormously.

And he further notes that

to give eight years of primary education to every child would cost at current prices about 0.8 per cent of national income in the USA, 1.7 per cent in Jamaica, 2.8 per cent in Ghana and 4.0 per cent in Nigeria. The main reason for this difference is that, while the average salary of a primary school teacher is less than one and a half times per capita national income in the USA, a primary school teacher gets three times per capita national income in Jamaica, five times in Ghana, and seven times in Nigeria.[4]

The fact that school teachers' wages are high relative to average wages in the under-

[4]W. A. Lewis, op. cit., pp. 37–38.

developed country need not mean that the absorptive capacity, as we understand it, is low. The rate of return on education equals the ratio of present value of wages, or earnings due to education, to the cost of producing it. The high relative wage of the educated person may merely express the extreme scarcity of the education factor, and hence its ability to command a high return at the given cost of producing it. The high wage might be an indicator of under- rather than over-supply, as demand may prove elastic if only increased supplies could be made available. At the same time, the cost of producing education may be high at early stages of development, relative to that of producing other capital goods, say tractors. If so, the rate of return on education (relative to that on tractors) will not be as high as suggested by the high income stream (wages) accruing to the educated factor alone. The cost of producing education must be lowered before increased investment in education is profitable. This, however, is subject to the previously noted condition that education is highly complementary to other forms of capital formation.

In addition to genuine scarcity, the high salaries demanded for work in positions requiring education reflect conventional factors and the desire to absorb the status previously held by the colonial official. As a result, there is frequently a "minimum wage structure" for high-level work which exceeds the economic return on such work, and prices educated services out of the market. Such rigidities need to be broken down to permit an effective education policy, and to the extent that they are permitted to prevail, appropriate allowance must be made in formulating realistic education targets. A policy which results in a supply of education that cannot be absorbed is obviously inefficient.

A further aspect of the cost problem which deserves special attention is the extent to which the educational effort involves a need for foreign exchange. Capital formation in the developing countries is frequently limited by the fact that capital goods cannot be produced at home, and that the foreign exchange available for acquiring them abroad is scarce. The question arises whether investment in education is more or less capital intensive than are other, and to some extent alternative, forms of capital formation. The answer depends on the level of education. While the exchange component of elementary education cost tends to be relatively low, it rises at the middle level, and for higher education it becomes extremely high. At later stages, this pattern may fit the needs and resources of the country but at the earlier stages, where emphasis is on middle-level education, the match tends to be an unfortunate one and points to the need for an all-out effort in domestic teacher-training.

PRIORITIES

The matter of educational priorities is obviously of vital importance. Unless the right kind of education is provided, setting overall targets has little meaning. Educated people who are unable to find suitable jobs, not only fail to add to the national product but become a source of political instability. Since the cost of various types of education (primary versus secondary versus advanced; liberal arts versus technical, and so forth) differs greatly, the very setting of overall targets has to be derived from the structural composition of the education supply.

Comment

Posing the question—"Why Isn't the Whole World Developed?"— Richard A. Easterlin answers that the worldwide spread of modern economic growth has depended chiefly on the diffusion of a body of knowledge concerning new production techniques. The acquisition and application of this knowledge by different countries have been governed largely by whether their populations have acquired traits and motivations associated with formal schooling. See his paper "Why Isn't the Whole World Developed?," *Journal of Economic History* (March 1981).

The World Bank's *Education Sector Policy Paper* (1980) concludes that "Studies have shown that economic returns on investment in education seem, in most instances, to exceed returns on alternative kinds of investment, and that developing countries obtain higher returns than the developed ones."

For an extensive bibliography on education and development, see Mark Blaug, (ed.), *Economics of Education,* Vols. 1 and 2 (1968, 1969). Several writings by T. W. Schultz are highly instructive on the role of education in development: "Capital Formation by Education," *Journal of Political Economy* (December 1960); "Investment in Human Capital," *American Economic Review* (March 1961); "Education and Economic Growth," in N. B. Henry (ed.), *Social Forces Influencing American Education* (1961); "Investment in Human Capital in Poor Countries," in P. D. Zook (ed.), *Foreign Trade and Human Capital* (1962). The special supplement of the *Journal of Political Economy* (October 1962) also contains a number of pertinent papers covering particular aspects of the problem of "Investment in Human Beings."

Rigorous models of educational planning are presented by S. Bowles, "A Planning Model for the Efficient Allocation of Resources in Education," *Quarterly Journal of Economics* (May 1967); G. Correa and J. Tinbergen, "Quantitative Adaptation of Education to Economic Growth," *Kyklos* (1962); R. G. Davis, *Planning Human Resource Development* (1966); J. Tinbergen and H. C. Bos, *Econometric Models of Education* (1965).

Also informative are: Marcelo Selowsky, "A Note on Preschool-Age Investment in Human Capital in Developing Countries," *Economic Development and Cultural Change,* Vol. 24 (July 1976) and M. R. Rosenzweig and R. E. Evenson, "Fertility, Schooling and the Economic Contribution of Children in Rural India," *Econometrica,* Vol. 45 (July 1977).

EXHIBIT IX.7. Enrollment Ratios by Region, 1960–75 (percent)

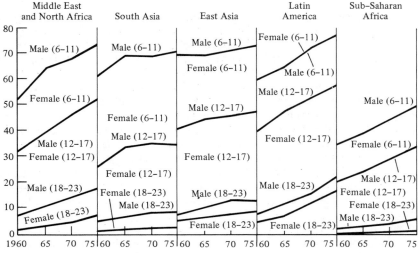

Source: UNESCO.

EXHIBIT IX.8. Rates of Return to Education (percent)

Country Group	Primary	Secondary	Higher	Number of Countries
All developing countries	24.2	15.4	12.3	30
Low income/adult literacy rate under 50 percent[a]	27.3	17.2	12.1	11
Middle income/adult literacy rate over 50 percent	22.2	14.3	12.4	19
Industrialized countries	—	10.0	9.1	14

Source: World Bank.

Note: In all cases, the figures are "social" rates of return: the costs include forgone earnings (what the students could have earned had they not been in school) as well as both public and private outlays; the benefits are measured by income before tax. (The "private" returns to individuals exclude public costs and taxes, and are usually larger.) The studies refer to various years between 1957 and 1978, mainly in the latter half of the period.

[a]In this sample of 30 developing countries, those countries with low incomes also had literacy rates below 50 percent (at the time the studies were done). All the middle-income countries had literacy rates above 50 percent.

IX.C.3. Approaches to Human-Resource Development*

Most modernising economies are confronted simultaneously with two persistent, yet seemingly diverse, manpower problems: *the short-age of persons with critical skills* in the modernising sector and *surplus labour* in both the modernising and traditional sectors. Thus,

*From Frederick H. Harbison, "Human Resources Development Planning in Modernising Economies," *International Labour Review,* Vol. 85, No. 5, May 1962, pp. 435–38, 440–1, 456–58; "A Systems Analysis Approach to Human-Resource Development Planning," in UNESCO, *Manpower Aspects of Educational Planning,* Paris, 1968, pp. 57–8, 59–64. Reprinted by permission.

the strategy of human resources development is concerned with the twofold objective of building skills and providing productive employment for unutilised or underutilised manpower. The shortages and surplus of human resources, however, are not separate and distinct problems; they are very intimately related. Both have their roots in the changes which are inherent in the development process. Both are related in part to education. Both are aggravated as the tempo of modernisation is quickened. And, paradoxically, the shortage of persons with critical skills is one of the contributing causes of the surplus of people without jobs. Although the manpower problems of no two countries are exactly alike, there are some shortages and surpluses which appear to be universal in modernising societies.

The manpower shortages of modernising countries are quite easy to identify, and fall into several categories:

1. In all modernising countries there is likely to be a shortage of highly educated professional manpower such as, for example, scientists, agronomists, veterinarians, engineers, and doctors. Such persons, however, usually prefer to live in the major cities rather than in the rural areas, where in many cases their services are most urgently needed. Thus, their shortage is magnified by their relative immobility. And, ironically, their skills are seldom used effectively. In West Africa and also in many Asian and Latin American countries, for example, graduate engineers may be found managing the routine operation of an electric power substation or doing the work of draughtsmen. Doctors may spend long hours making the most routine medical tests. The reason is obvious.

2. The shortage of technicians, nurses, agricultural assistants, technical supervisors, and other sub-professional personnel is generally even more critical than the shortage of fully qualified professionals. For this there are several explanations. First, the modernising countries usually fail to recognise that the requirements for this category of manpower exceed by many times those for senior professional personnel. Second, the few persons who are qualified to enter a technical institute may also be qualified to enter a university, and they prefer the latter because of the higher status and pay which is accorded the holder of a university degree. Finally, there are often fewer places available in institutions providing intermediate training than in the universities.

3. The shortage of top-level managerial and administrative personnel, in both the private and public sectors, is almost universal, as is the dearth of persons with enterpreneutrial talents.

4. Teachers are almost always in short supply, and their turnover is high because they tend to leave the teaching profession if and when more attractive jobs become available in government, politics, or private enterprise. The scarcity is generally most serious in secondary education, and particularly acute in the fields of science and mathematics. This shortage of competent teachers is a "master bottleneck" which retards the entire process of human resources development.

5. In most modernising countries there are also shortages of craftsmen of all kinds as well as senior clerical personnel such as bookkeepers, secretaries, stenographers, and business machine operators.

6. Finally, there are usually in addition several other miscellaneous categories of personnel in short supply, such as, for example, radio and television specialists, airplane pilots, accountants, economists and statisticians.

I shall use the term "high-level manpower," or alternatively "human capital," as a convenient designation for the persons who fall into categories such as those mentioned above. The term "human capital formation," as used in this paper, is the process of acquiring and increasing the numbers of persons who have the skills, education, and experience which are critical for the economic and political development of a country.

The analysis of human capital formation is thus parallel and complementary to the study of the processes of savings and investment (in the material sense). In designing a strategy for development, one needs to consider the total stock of human capital required, its rates of accumulation, and its commitment to (or investment in) high-priority productive activities.

The rate of modernisation of a country is associated with both its stock and rate of accumulation of human capital. High-level manpower is needed to staff new and expanding government services, to introduce new systems of land use and new methods of agriculture, to develop new means of communication, to carry forward industrialisation, and to build the educational system. In other words, innovation, or the process of change from a static or traditional society, requires very large "doses" of strategic human capital. The countries which are making the most rapid and spectacular innovations are invariably those which are under the greatest pressure to accumulate this kind of human capital at a fast rate. Here we may make two tentative generalisations:

First, the rate of accumulation of strategic human capital must always exceed the rate of increase in the labour force as a whole. In most countries, for example, the rate of increase in scientific and engineering personnel may need to be at least three times that of the labour force. Sub-professional personnel may have to increase even more rapidly. Clerical personnel and craftsmen may have to increase at least twice as fast as the labour force, and top managerial and administrative personnel should normally increase at a comparable rate.

Second, in most cases, the rate of increase in human capital will need to exceed the rate of economic growth. In newly developing countries which already are faced with critical shortages of highly skilled persons, the ratio of the annual increase in high-level manpower to the annual increase in national income may need to be as high as three to one, or even higher in those cases where expatriates are to be replaced by citizens of the developing countries.

The accumulation of high-level manpower to overcome skill bottlenecks is a never-ending process. Advanced industrial societies as well as underdeveloped countries are nor-mally short of critical skills. Indeed, as long as the pace of innovation is rapid, the appetite of any growing country for high-level manpower is almost insatiable.

As indicated above, no two countries have exactly the same manpower problems. Some have unusually serious surpluses, and others have very specialised kinds of skill bottlenecks. Politicians and planners, therefore, need to make a systematic assessment of the human resources problems in their particular countries. Such assessment may be called "manpower analysis."

The objectives of manpower analysis are as follows: (1) the identification of the principal critical shortages of skilled manpower in each major sector of the economy, and an analysis of the reasons for such shortages; (2) the identification of surpluses, both of trained manpower as well as unskilled labour, and the reasons for such surpluses; and (3) the setting of forward targets for human resources development based upon reasonable expectations of growth. Such forward targets are best determined by a careful examination and comparison, sector by sector, of the utilisation of manpower in a number of countries which are somewhat more advanced politically, socially and economically.

Manpower analysis cannot always be based on an elaborate or exhaustive survey. It is seldom possible to calculate precisely the numbers of people needed in every occupation at some future time. But, whether statistics are available or not, the purpose of manpower analysis is to give a reasonably objective picture of a country's major human resources problems, the inter-relationships between these problems, and their causes, together with an informed guess as to probable future trends. Manpower analysis is both qualitative and quantitative, and it must be based upon wise judgment as well as upon available statistics. In countries where statistics are either unavailable or clearly unreliable, moreover, the initial manpower analysis may be frankly impressionistic. . . .

Once the manpower problems of a newly developing country are identified, a strategy must be developed to overcome them effectively. The essential components of such a strategy are the following: (1) the building of appropriate incentives; (2) the effective training of employed manpower; and (3) the rational development of formal education. These three elements are interdependent. Progress in one area is dependent upon progress in the other two. The country's leaders should not concentrate on only one or two of them at a time; they must plan an integrated attack on all three fronts at once.

The argument has been made that investments in formal education alone are not likely to solve either critical skill shortages or persistent labour surpluses in modernising societies. Investments in education are likely to contribute effectively to rapid growth only (1) if there are adequate incentives to encourage men and women to engage in the kinds of productive activity which are needed to accelerate the modernisation process; and (2) if appropriate measures are taken to shift a large part of the responsibility for training to the principal employing institutions. The building of incentives and the training of employed manpower, therefore, are necessary both as a means of economising on formal education and as a means of making the investment in it productive. . . .

The third component of the strategy is wise judgment and prudent investment in building the system of formal education. This calls for giving priority to investment in and development of broad secondary education. It requires that the costs of universal primary education be kept as low as possible by applying new technologies which can make effective use of relatively untrained teachers and which can multiply the contribution of a very small but strategic group of highly trained professionals. Finally, in the area of higher education, the strategy stresses the need for giving priority to investment in intermediate-level training institutions and the scientific and engineering faculties of universities. But this does not mean that the production of liberally educated persons should be neglected.

The three essential components of the strategy are interdependent, and call for a well-designed and integrated attack on all three fronts at once. And it is imperative that the strategy of building and utilising human resources be an integral part of a country's national development programme.

The major thesis of this paper is that the manpower approach should encompass much more than a tabulation of "heads and hands" in precise occupational categories. It must go far beyond the construction of purely quantitative forecasts, projections, or targets for formal education. It should be related to a broad strategy of human-resource development rather than to a narrow concept of education planning.

Without questioning the usefulness and importance of the kind of quantitative analysis which is characteristic of most manpower surveys, I suggest that it may now be appropriate to use in addition a systems analysis concept. It should be possible to look at the various constituent elements of human-resource development as a system which is somewhat analogous to a system for the generation and distribution of electric power. In using this frame of reference, one can identify skill-generating centres, such as, for example, universities, training institutes, and employing organizations, which develop people on the job. The linkages between such centres are analogous to transmission lines. The manpower problems, such as skill shortages and labour surpluses, encountered by developing countries may be thought of as attributable to power failures in particular generating centres, ineffective linkages between these centres, or faulty design resulting in the failure of the total system to carry the loads expected of it. A system of human-skill generation should be designed to carry varying loads; it must have built-in flexibility to meet such loads; it must be adequate in size; and above all its components must be properly balanced. The systems-analysis approach makes it easier to identify in operational terms major problem areas, and it compels the analyst to examine the critical inter-relationships between various manpower, education, and economic-development programmes. It provides a logical starting-point for building a strategy of human-resource development.

HUMAN-RESOURCE PROBLEMS IN DEVELOPING ECONOMIES

The major human-resource problems in developing societies are: (a) rapidly growing population; (b) mounting unemployment in the modern sectors of the economy as well as widespread underemployment in traditional agriculture; (c) shortage of persons with the critical skills and knowledge required for effective national development; (d) inadequate or underdeveloped organizations and institutions for mobilizing human effort; and (e) lack of incentives for persons to engage in particular activities which are vitally important for national development. There are obviously other major human-resource development problems such as nutrition and health, but these lie for the most part in other technical fields and are thus beyond the scope of this paper.

The manpower analyst, of course, is particularly interested in the present and future size of the labour force, its growth rates in both the traditional and modern sectors, and the factors which determine labour-force participation of various groups. Of necessity he must also be concerned with the consequences of policies to limit population growth. For example, a reduction in birthrates will not immediately lead to a reduction in the labour force, but at the same time it would probably increase a country's propensity to save and to invest in productive activities. Population control, therefore, in addition to its other obvious benefits, may contribute directly to greater labour productivity. Certainly, the human-resource development strategist should give very close attention to population problems and assume greater responsibility for proposing population-control measures.

Mounting unemployment in urban areas is probably the most serious and intractable problem facing today's newly developing countries....

Although he might wish that somehow or other the problem would "go away," the human-resource development planner cannot escape responsibility for considering ways and means of absorbing surplus manpower and directing it into productive activities.

The evaluation of occupational needs and skill-generating capacity has been a traditional concern of manpower specialists. Here, unlike the situation with unemployment, it is possible to suggest viable solutions for rather clearly defined problems. Manpower requirements can be determined; appropriate programmes of formal education and on-the-job training can be devised; and progress toward achievement of goals can be measured.

In setting targets for education and training programmes, the analyst is concerned with two related but distinct concepts— "manpower requirements" and "absorptive capacity." "Manpower requirements" may be defined as clearly evident needs for persons with particular education, training, and experience. The assumption here is that such persons are necessary, if not indispensable, for the achievement of a programme of national development. "Absorptive capacity" is a looser term which refers to a country's capacity to provide some kind of useful employment for persons with certain educational qualifications. In effect, "manpower requirements" should express *minimum* or essential needs; "absorptive capacity" should express the *maximum* number of persons who can be employed without encountering redundancy or serious under-utilization of skill. The skill-generating centres, therefore, should produce trained manpower within this range between the maximum and the minimum; otherwise the skill-generation system is distorted or unbalanced.

The "demand" for education or training must be distinguished from the allowable range between manpower requirements and absorptive capacity. Demand stems from social and political pressures for various kinds of education as well as from the willingness of people to pay fees to acquire it. Thus, for example, the demand for university education may be very high because of the status, prestige, and pay enjoyed by graduates; but, in many countries, this results in the production of graduates who cannot be effectively absorbed in the economy. When demand is clearly out of step with requirements or absorptive capacity, the country's educational system is clearly distorted or out of balance with the needs for national development. In using the systems analysis approach, a major task of the human-resource planner is to detect actual and potential distortion and to consider measures for achieving a proper balance.

Another type of distortion in many countries is the underdevelopment, if not outright neglect, of appropriate measures of training persons in employment. A great deal of money is wasted in formal pre-employment craft or technical training which could be provided more efficiently and cheaply by employing establishments. Also the efficiency of skill-generating systems could be greatly improved by closer linkages between schools and universities and the employing institutions. For some reason, education planners have been inclined to think that on-the-job development lies beyond their legitimate concern, and at the same time they appear to have ignored the task of building the necessary bridges between formal education and in-service training. The systems-analysis approach helps to highlight this underdeveloped area of concern.

In the past, manpower analysis has centred on measurement of needs for various categories of high-level manpower, and in doing so it has usually overlooked the vital problem of organization and institution building. Successful development requires the building of effective government organizations, private enterprises, agricultural extension forces, research institutions, producer and consumer co-operatives, education systems, and a host of other institutions which mobilize and direct human energy into useful channels. Organization is a factor of production, separate from labour, high-level manpower, capital, or natural resources. The essence of organization is the co-ordinated effort of many persons toward common objectives. At the same time the structure of organization is a hierarchy of superiors and subordinates in which the higher levels exercise authority over the lower levels.

The successful leaders of organizations, or more accurately the "organization builders," are in any society a small but aggressive minority committed to progress and change. They feed the aspirations, give expression to the goals, and shape the destinies of peoples. They play the principal roles on the stage of history, and they organize the march of the masses.

A major problem in many developing countries is "organizational power failures." Often government ministries, commercial and industrial organizations, or educational institutions simply fail to "deliver the goods." Usually, the trouble may be traced to a dearth of "prime movers of innovation."

Who then are these prime movers of innovation? Certainly the entrepreneur who perceives and exploits new business ventures belongs to this group, as does the manager or top administrator in public establishments. He may not always have new ideas of his own, but his function is to organize and stimulate the efforts of others. He structures organizations, and either infuses hierarchies with energy and vision or fetters them with chains of conformity. But effective orgnizations also need other creative people. The agronomist who discovers better measures of cultivation, and the agricultural assistants who teach the farmers to use them, belong to the innovator class, as do public-health officers, nurses, and medical assistants. Engineers are in essence designers of change, and engineering technicians and supervisors put the changes to work. And last but not least, professors, teachers, and administrators of educational institutions in many countries may constitute the largest group of prime movers of innovation, as they are the "seedcorn" from which new generations of manpower will grow.

Some innovators are "change-designers" who make new discoveries, suggest new methods of organization, and plan broad new strategies. Others are "change-pushers" who are able to persuade, coach and inspire people to put new ideas to work. Some innovators, of course, are at the same time change-designers and change-pushers. But whether they are designers, pushers, or a combination of the two, the prime movers of innovation must have extensive knowledge and experience. Thus, for the most part, they are drawn from the ranks of high-level manpower. But they need more than proven intelligence and thorough technical training. They should have in addition keen curiosity, a capacity for self-discipline, and an unquenchable desire for accomplishment. They should be adept at asking questions. They should have the knack of stimulating others to produce ideas and to activate the ablest minds about them; and they should be able to sell ideas to superiors, subordinates, and associates. The prime mover of innovation must be convinced that change can occur as a result of individual action, and he must have the drive within him to bring it about. This may stem from a desire to rise in social status, to build up material wealth, to acquire political influence, or to preserve an already established prestige position.

Many of the persons holding commanding positions in organizations are conformists or even obstructors of innovation. They must be systematically replaced by more creative innovators. The human-resource development planner should be able to locate the critical points of power loss in organizational structures and to suggest remedial measures.

A final problem area in human-resource development is incentives. It is one thing to estimate the needs for manpower of various qualifications but quite another to induce persons to prepare for and engage in occupations which are most vital for national growth. In most developing countries, it is incorrect to assume that relative earnings and status reflect the value of the contribution of individuals to development. Pay and status are often more related to tradition, colonial heritage, and political pressures than to productivity. Characteristically, for example, the rewards of subprofessional personnel and technicians are far from sufficient to attract the numbers needed—the pay of teachers is often inadequate; the differentials in compensation between the agricultural officer and agricultural assistant are too great; and the earnings of scientists and engineers, in comparison with administrative bureaucrats in government ministries, are too low. The preferences for urban living, the forces of tradition, and historical differentials all tend to distort the market for critical skills. It follows then that the demand for certain kinds of education, particularly at the university level, is inflated relative to the country's absorptive capacity. The human-resource development planner must therefore consider deliberate measures to influence the allocation of manpower into high-priority activities and occupations. Such measures may include major changes in the wage and salary structure, scholarship support for particular kinds of education and training, removal of barriers against upward mobility, and in some cases outright compulsion. As many developing countries have learned to their chagrin, investments in education can be wasted unless men and women have the will to prepare for and engage in those activities which are most critically needed for national development.

These then are the problems and tasks which face the human-resource development planner—the consequences of population increases and the measures for controlling them; underemployment and unemployment in both the traditional and modern sectors; skill shortages and the processes of developing high-level manpower to overcome them; organizational weakness and the need to find prime movers of innovation for institutional development; and provision of both financial and non-financial incentives in order to direct critically needed manpower into productive channels. Some of these are subject to quantitative analysis; others are purely qualitative; and a few are subject only to intuitive judgment. But, they are all interrelated. The systems approach forces the analyst to examine them simultaneously as he searches for the weak spots—the points of power failure or the major areas of distortion—in a country's overall effort to effectively develop and utilize its human resources.

Comment

The activity of entrepreneurship is also essential for the development process. An interdisciplinary approach—combining economic, psychological, and social factors—may best analyze the factors determining the supply of entrepreneurship. Especially significant is David McClelland's analysis of achievement motivation as a psychological determinant of entrepreneurship; see *The Achieving Society,* 2nd ed. (1976). It may be suggested, however, that successful entrepreneurship depends not only on an individual's motivation, but also on his or her abilities and a permissive environment that provides incentives and opportunities for entrepreneurs. Economists have tended to emphasize a favorable economic environment, but according to McClelland, whenever economic growth begins, some tiny community within the larger society which has played the major entrepreneurial role can nearly always be identified. The theory of achievement motivation predicts that those in the population who will take greater advantage of increased opportunities are precisely those relatively few individuals who have a high need to achieve. The policy implication, therefore, is that efforts must be undertaken to instill a higher need to achieve in a larger segment of the population. This conforms to the more general view expressed throughout this chapter that the key to development is human resources, and that the abilities, values, and attitudes of people must be changed in order to accelerate the process of development.

An extensive bibliography on accelerating economic development through psychological training is presented by D. C. McClelland and D. G. Winter, *Motivating Economic Achievement* (1969). Critiques of the influences of achievement motivation on entrepreneurship are offered by S. N. Eisenstadt, "The Need for Achievement," *Economic Development and Cultural Change* (July 1963) and S. P. Schatz, "*n* Achievement and Economic Growth," *Quarterly Journal of Economics* (May 1965).

Other instructive studies of entrepreneurship are F. H. Harbison, "Entrepreneurial Organization as a Factor in Economic Development," *Quarterly Journal of Economics* (August 1956); E. Hagen, *On the Theory of Social Change* (1962); W. P. Glade, "Approaches to a Theory of Entrepreneurship Formation," *Explorations in Entrepreneurial History* (Spring–Summer 1967); Peter Marris, "The Social Barriers to African Entrepreneurship," *Journal of Development Studies* (October 1968); G. F. Papanek, *Pakistan's Development* (1967), chapter 2; Peter Kilby (ed.), *Entrepreneurship and Economic Development* (1971); H. Leibenstein, *General X-Efficiency Theory and Economic Development* (1976); T. W. Schultz, "Investment in Entrepreneurial Ability," *Scandinavian Journal of Economics* (1980).

An important work on sociological and psychological modernization is Alex Inkeles and D. H. Smith, *Becoming Modern* (1975). For an annotated bibliography, see John Brode, *The Process of Modernization* (1975).

IX.C.4. Education and Employment*

Although the linkages between education and employment are complex and, in the past, often analyzed with simplistic notions of causality, recent research results have yielded new insights about the nature of these linkages.[1] A number of international organi-

*From Edgar O. Edwards and Michael P. Todaro, "Education, Society and Development: Some Main Themes and Suggested Strategies for International Assistance," *World Development,* January 1974, pp. 27–30. Reprinted by permission.

[1]For the most recent and comprehensive analysis of the interrelationships between education and employment, see Mark Blaug, *Education and the Employment Problem in Developing Countries,* Geneva, 1973.

zations, including the ILO and the Ford and Rockefeller Foundations, have been engaged in intensive analyses and have conducted numerous conferences and meetings on the employment topic over the past two years.[2] The authors have participated in a number of these activities and the following represents a condensed statement of our current thinking about the principal relationships between education and employment. In the interests of brevity, the argument is put forward as a series of major propositions and derivative strategies relating to the education-employment nexus.

SEVEN BASIC PROPOSITIONS ABOUT EDUCATION AND EMPLOYMENT

Proposition 1. *Pressures outside the educational system will force it to overproduce in terms of the real manpower needs of development, giving rise to the phenomenon of educated unemployment.*

An educational system in any society both reflects and adapts itself to the political and economic circumstances of that society. Economic signals or incentives and socio-political constraints operative in the society are the primary factors determining the employment aspirations of individuals and hence the level and composition of the aggregate private demand for education. This demand in turn influences the supply, composition, and academic standards of educational opportunities, both public and private. Political pressures force the public educational system to attempt to meet quantitatively the aggregate demand for school places. In the event that the number of these places is limited by public financial constraints or policy decisions, the private sector will tend to find alternative ways of meeting unmet educational demand.[3]

The educational composition of the system's output also will accord with the dictates of aggregate demand with the private system once again meeting needs unmet by the public system. Since aggregate private demand will normally exceed job opportunities and since this demand will tend to be satisfied either politically (through the public system) or privately, educational systems in LDCs are likely to overproduce in terms of the real manpower needs of the nation. Moreover, this divergence between the output of the educational system and the number of new job opportunities is likely to grow over time. Given these inexorable pressures to overproduce, major modifications in the educational system must depend primarily on changes in economic incentives and social constraints and *not* on isolated initiatives taken within the educational system itself.

Proposition 2. *Education, in conjunction with the development of a modern sector, transforms various kinds of underemployment into open unemployment, primarily through rural-urban migration.*

In traditional societies it has been customary for members to share among themselves the work which the community considered necessary to perform. Even in feudal landlord-tenant settings, the landlord often regarded it as his responsibility to share available work among all of those who accepted his patronage. In most LDCs the development of a modern sector has introduced very different working arrangements such as the discipline of a standard work-week and minimum wages. The modern sector has also been characterized by an urban, industrial bias and a need for a new set of specialized occupational skills. Educational systems responded quickly to these modern sector needs, focusing curricula on modern-sector educational requirements and strengthening urban schools more quickly than those in rural areas. These several contemporaneous

[2]Edgar O. Edwards (ed.), *Employment in Developing Nations,* New York, 1974; and ILO, *Scope, Approach and Content of Research Oriented Activities of the World Employment Programme,* Geneva, 1972.

[3]Some examples of private-sector initiatives in response to unsatisfied, aggregate demands include the Harambee school movement in Kenya and the proliferation of private colleges and universities in India and the Philippines.

events have meant that many young people previously underemployed in rural areas have flocked to the cities in search of education or jobs in numbers substantially in excess of the opportunities available. Many, indeed growing numbers, have become openly unemployed, a vivid and visible transformation of widely dispersed rural underemployment into the far more troublesome and potentially explosive problem of open urban unemployment. Recent LDC research on rural-urban migration has demonstrated that the propensity to migrate increases with increasing educational attainment and that the ranks of the urban unemployed are increasingly being swelled by the more educated.[4]

Proposition 3. *Limited job opportunities tend to be rationed by educational certification with the more educated replacing the less well educated, even though higher qualifications may not be needed to perform the task adequately.*

Given the chronic tendency of educational systems of LDCs increasingly to overproduce in terms of available employment opportunities, the problem of rationing limited modern-sector jobs assumes growing importance. Typically these jobs are allocated to those with higher levels of educational attainment regardless of whether that education is really necessary for satisfactory job performance. The educationally less fortunate are relegated to the ranks of the unemployed and underemployed on the fringes of the urban sector. This rationing device has the appealing political merit of being apparently objective, relatively untainted by obvious favor, and patently dependent for its operation on many private as well as public decisions. But its operation does not relieve unemployment or improve the allocation of resources beyond insuring that those most over-educated are indeed eventually employed. So the magnitude of the problem is left to grow and an apparently fair rationing mechanism is unlikely

to provide continuing political cover for an increasingly explosive situation.[5]

Proposition 4. *Rising unemployment, distorted wage differentials, and excessive education must be taken into account if social rate-of-return and benefit/cost calculations are to play a role in educational planning.*

Although political factors are dominant in LDC government decisions with regard to the supply of educational opportunities, economic analyses of social and private rates of return to investment in various levels of education remain a tool of considerable potential importance in assessing the wisdom of educational investment decisions, both for local governments and donor agencies. This analytical tool has been much maligned, sometimes justifiably so and other times as the result of a critic's misunderstanding of the legitimate, albeit limited, role which these calculations can play.[6] For the most part, however, rate-of-return calculations have not taken account of factors such as educational displacement, rising unemployment among the more educated, the distorted wage and price signals in the economy as a whole. We believe that many manpower plans based on these calculations would be considerably modified, especially with respect to their projections of needed quantitative expansion among the highly educated, if the above factors were taken into account. In particular, the apparent discrepancy between rates of return to investment in education as compared to alternative investment in other sectors of the economy would not be nearly so wide if the factors mentioned above were given adequate treatment.

[5]For a more detailed discussion of the job rationing by educational certification phenomenon, see E. O. Edwards and M. P. Todaro, "Educational demand and supply in the context of growing unemployment in less developed countries," *World Development,* March/April 1973.

[6]For a further exposition of the role of cost-benefit analysis in a political setting, see Edgar O. Edwards, "Investment in education in developing nations: Conflict among social, economic, and political signals," paper presented at IBRD conference on *The Economics of Education: Alternative Strategies for Investment,* Washington, D.C., October 1973 (mimeo).

[4]See, for example, M. P. Todaro, "Education, migration and fertility," paper presented at IBRD conference on *The Economics of Education: Alternative Strategies for Investment,* Washington, D.C., October 1973 (mimeo).

Proposition 5. *Public subsidies to education, especially at the higher levels, contribute to the widening gap between "private" and "social" benefit/cost calculations and thus lead to excessive levels of aggregate private demand for higher education; these subsidies also limit financially the ability of the public sector both to supply educational opportunities and to create jobs.*

In many LDCs both the percentage and absolute amount of educational costs borne privately tend to decrease with increasing levels of educational attainment. This phenomenon, in combination with the positive relationship between educational attainment and expected income from employment, creates an explosive private demand for higher levels of education. In order to satisfy this demand, primary and secondary facilities must be expanded by some multiple of the demand for higher education to take account of the large percentage of students who will not make it to the higher levels. The irony of the situation is that the wider the gap between *perceived* "private" benefits and costs of secondary versus primary and tertiary versus secondary education and the more unprofitable a given level of education becomes as a *terminal point* (e.g., primary education), the more demand for it increases as an *intermediate stage* or precondition to the next level of education! This puts increased pressure on the government in conjunction with donor agencies to expand lower-level facilities in order to meet the demand for higher-level education.[7]

Public subsidies not only stimulate the demand for education; they also limit the ability of governments to create both educational and job opportunities. Reducing these subsidies would release government funds for job-creating investments, raising the economy's capacity to absorb educated man-power in productive employment. Such an increase in the demand for educated man-power would itself justify a more rapid growth in educational opportunities. Thus a reduction in public subsidies should (a) reduce the excess demand for education, (b) increase employment opportunities and (c) provide developmental justification for a larger educational system than would otherwise be the case.

Proposition 6. *Constraints on upward mobility in the labor market force many of those discriminated against to seek social and economic advancement through the educational system, thus increasing the already heavy burden carried by it.*

Those who expect that without substantial education their employment and promotion opportunities will be limited because of caste, race, creed, tribe, or the simple lack of over-valued exit credentials from the educational system, may seek to circumvent these obstacles through further education. This implies, of course, that educational systems are on the whole characterized by fewer discriminatory practices than the labor market itself. In these circumstances, the existence of substantial social and political biases in hiring and promotion practices may contribute to the overloading of the educational system. If, on the other hand, such labor-market constraints can be reduced, some resources of the educational system will be freed for the improved performance of its other essential functions.

Proposition 7. *Employment, in addition to providing income, is also a major means for disseminating work-related knowledge.*

Employment is often regarded by those seeking it in developing countries as a reward for the successful completion of a continuous segment of the educational process. Education is regarded as a preparation for work; work is seldom seen as a learning experience in its own right or even as a useful basis for further education. Unfortunately, this view is frequently reinforced by hiring practices of employers and incentive schemes supported by policy-makers, and it reflects a rather common underevaluation of the learning which can be obtained through participation in the labor market. Moreover, the learning potential inherent in employment opportunities does not seem to be significantly realized in practice. For example, the wider sharing of

[7]See Edwards and Todaro, op. cit. and Blaug, op. cit.

available work among members of the labor force would spread the associated learning experience over a larger number of beneficiaries; social and economic policies which promoted variety in an individual's work experiences, whether with one or several employers, rather than narrow, routine specialization would enrich his life and his potential for contributing to a nation's development; and the use of information on an individual's degree of success in work settings as a means for evaluating his potential to gain from further education would add an important dimension to the criteria currently in common use in determining who progresses in the educational system.

SOME STRATEGIES FOR IMPROVING EDUCATION AND EMPLOYMENT

In the light of the above propositions, the following strategies for improving the relationship between education and employment are offered:

1. *Minimizing imbalances, incentive distortions, and socio-political constraints will improve both education and employment.*

Policies which tend to remedy major economic imbalances (e.g., those between rural and urban areas), to correct distortions in incentives (e.g., in income and wage differentials), and to alleviate social and political constraints on upward mobility will have the multiple beneficial effect of increasing job opportunities, modifying the accelerated rate of rural-urban migration, and facilitating development-related modifications of educational systems.

2. *Where politically feasible, educational budgets should grow more slowly and be more oriented towards primary education.*

In the light of growing unemployment among the educated, educational budgets should grow more slowly than in the past to permit more funds to be used for the creation of employment opportunities. Moreover, a larger share of educational budgets should be allocated to the development of primary, as opposed to secondary and higher, education as a basis for self-education and work-related

learning experiences. If a slowdown in subsidized public higher education is off-set by expansion of the private sector, there is at least the favorable incentive effect that the beneficiaries must pay more of the cost of their education.

3. *Work-sharing arrangements should be encouraged.*

In the absence of full employment, policies should be explored which will encourage a wider sharing of available work as a means of dispersing income, spreading work-related learning experiences, and reducing the numbers openly unemployed. It is not, however, a simple task to identify appropriate incentive mechanisms which will induce the private sector to assume the additional managerial costs which might be required in order to realize the social benefits of work sharing. This need not be a constraint on public-sector employment practices where social benefit calculations can enter directly into employment decisions.[8]

4. *Job-rationing by educational certification must be modified.*

In order to break the vicious circle in which overstated job specifications make overeducation necessary for employment, policies are needed which will induce or require both public and private employers to seek realistic qualifications even though the task of job rationing may be made somewhat more difficult as a result.[9]

5. *Subsidies for upper-level education should be reduced.*

As a means of overcoming distortions in the aggregate private demand for education induced by excessive subsidies to education especially at higher levels, policies should be promoted by which the beneficiary of education (as opposed to his family or society as a whole) would bear a larger and rising proportion of his educational costs as he proceeds through the system—either directly,

---

[8]For some theoretical arguments in support of work-sharing arrangements, see Edgar O. Edwards, "Work effort, investable surplus, and the inferiority of competition," *Southern Economic Journal,* October 1971.

[9]The ILO Ceylon Report, op. cit., makes extensive recommendations along these lines.

through loan repayments, or by service in rural areas.[10]

6. *Inequities and discrimination in both education and employment should be minimized.*

In order to reduce the burden on the educational system and to improve the performance of its essential functions, policies should be pursued which (1) reduce social

---

[10]See Edwards and Todaro, op. cit., for further discussions of the distributive implications of current methods of post-primary education in the context of rising levels of unemployment among the educated.

and educational discrimination in hiring and promotion in labor markets, (2) encourage greater reliance on job-related learning experiences as a basis for occupational advancement and (3) stimulate the use of successful work experience as a criterion for advancement in the educational system.

Insofar as possible, donor agencies should ensure that their policies of support for public education reinforce strategies, such as those listed above, which tend to make education appropriate, quantitatively and qualitatively, for the employment opportunities likely to emerge in the coming decade.

IX.C.5. Development as a Generalized Process of Capital Accumulation*

The contemporary interest in the economics of education, and more broadly in the economies of all processes connected with the augmentation and application of knowledge, represents a confluence of interests derived from concerns with widely divergent problems. These problems include such matters as the economic value of education, the contribution of education to past economic development in advanced countries, and the role of education and expenditure on increased education in the planned development of underdeveloped countries.[1]

The formulation of concern with the economics of education (in a broad sense) in these particular terms, while appropriate to the current state of economic research and thinking, is for this very reason both restric-

---

*From Harry G. Johnson, "Towards a Generalized Capital Accumulation Approach to Economic Development," in OECD Study Group in the Economics of Education, *The Residual Factor and Economic Growth*, Paris, 1964, pp. 219–25. Reprinted by permission.

[1]Cf. T. W. Schultz, ed., "Reflections on Investment in Man," *Journal of Political Economy, Supplement*, October 1962, pp. 1–8.

tive in its implications and likely to appear before much more time has passed as a transient stage in the evolution towards a more comprehensive formulation of economic development problems in terms of a broadly conceived concept of capital accumulation. . . .

Concentration on the role of human capital has already proceeded far enough to generate the beginnings of a counter-revolution. The general outlines of the counter-revolution are indeed already apparent. On the one hand, the recent emphasis on human capital formation in growth accountancy is based on the recognition that conventional measures of labour input fail to take account of improvements in the quality of labour and aims primarily at more accurate measurement of labour inputs. Application of the same criteria to inputs of capital suggests that the contribution of capital may also have been grossly underestimated, as a result both of understatement of the flow of capital services into production by the conventional equation of service flow with the depreciated value of capital stock, and of failure to measure accurately improvements in the performance characteristics ("quality") of capital equipment.[2] On the other hand, the evidence on rates of return to educational investment in the United States does not suggest that there has been serious general underinvestment in education there, while both casual empirical observation of under-developed countries and some detailed research on the relative returns to investments in education and material capital in them[3] suggest that at least in some cases the proportion of resources devoted to human capital formation may be too high rather than too low.[4] A rehabilitation of investment in material capital as a potent source of economic growth may therefore be in prospect. What is more important, while the process of increasing economic knowledge proceeds in phases of exaggerated concentration on one or another aspect of a problem, both the effect and the intent are to arrive at a unified and more powerful synthesis of explanations of economic phenomena. The contemporary phase, in which the concepts of human capital and of investment in it figure as corrections of emphasis in a system of economic ideas dominated by material capital, is bound to merge into one in which human and nonhuman capital are treated as alternative forms of capital in general. The desirability of achieving such a synthesis is not merely a matter of scientific economy and elegance, it is also a pre-requisite for rational discussion and formulation of policy for economic growth in both advanced and underdeveloped countries. The purpose of this paper, accordingly, is to sketch the outlines of

such a synthesis, in the form of a generalised capital accumulation approach to economic development, and to discuss some of its implications for social and economic policy.

The essential elements of a generalised capital accumulation approach to economic development are already present in the literature of economics, and at least some applications of the approach (for example, the explanation of wage differentials) have been familiar to economists ever since economics became established as a separate subject of study. The foundations of it were explicitly laid in Irving Fisher's classic work on capital and income, and carried forward by F. H. Knight's work on the theory of capital; and the approach is exemplified, and its potency demonstrated, in the recent research of T. W. Schultz, Gary Becker, and others on human capital.[5] The essence of it is to regard "capital" as including anything that yields a stream of income over time, and income as the product of capital. From this point of view, as Fisher pointed out, all categories of income describe yields on various forms of capital, and can be expressed as rates of interest or return on the corresponding items of capital. Alternatively, all forms of income-yielding assets can be given an equivalent capital value by capitalising the income they yield at an appropriate rate of interest. By extension, the growth of income that defines economic development is necessarily the result of the accumulation of capital, or of "investment"; but "investment" in this context must be defined to include such diverse activities as adding to material capital, increasing the health, discipline, skill and education of the human population, moving labour into more productive occupations and locations, and applying existing knowledge or discovering and applying new knowledge to increase the efficiency of productive processes. All such activities involve incurring costs, in the form of use of current resources, and investment in them is socially worth while if the rate of return over cost exceeds the general rate of interest, or the capital value of

---

[2]Cf. Zvi Griliches, "The Sources of Measured Productivity Growth: U.S. Agriculture, 1940–1960," *Journal of Political Economy,* August 1960.

[3]Cf. Arnold C. Harberger, *Investment in Man Versus Investment in Machines: The Case of India,* a paper prepared for the Conference on Education and Economic Development, University of Chicago, April 4–6, 1963. Harberger finds the rate of return on real investment in India to be substantially higher than the rate of return on investment in education.

[4]This proposition becomes almost a truism if the concept of investment in human capital formation is extended to include expenditures on improved health, whose effects on the rate of population increase constitute one of the major economic problems of underdeveloped countries.

[5]See T. W. Schultz, op. cit.

the additional income they yield exceeds the cost of obtaining it. From the somewhat different perspective of planning economic development, efficient development involves allocation of investment resources according to priorities set by the relative rates of return on alternative investments.

The conception of economic growth as a process of accumulating capital, in all the manifold forms that the broad Fisherian concept of capital allows, is a potent simplification of the analytical problem of growth, and one which facilitates the discussion of problems of growth policy by emphasising the relative returns from alternative investments of currently available resources. The Fisherian concept of capital, however, and the approach to the analysis of production and distribution problems associated with it, are not as yet characteristic of the work and philosophical approach of the majority of economists, and to some the implications of the approach for policy with respect to human beings appear to be positively repugnant. Must economists instead employ a narrower concept of capital that identifies capital with material capital goods and equipment used in the production process, and distinguishes it sharply from labour? . . .

As already mentioned, the limitations of accumulation of material capital as an explanation of a prescription for growth have prompted the contemporary interest in human capital formation, and suggest a generalisation of the concept of capital accumulation to include investment in all types of capital formation. An important obstacle to such a generalisation is that the treatment of human beings as a form of capital, even if only conceptually, seems offensive to some economists as being contrary to democratic political philosophy. This reaction, however, involves a confusion of analytical approach and normative recommendations unfortunately only too common in discussions of economic problems with policy connotations. To recognise that important areas of socio-economic policy involve decisions analytically identical with decisions about investing in machines is not at all to imply that people

should be regarded as no different from machines; on the contrary, refusal to recognise the investment character of a problem because people are involved may result in people receiving worse treatment than machines. One might, indeed, hazard the generalisation that democratic free-enterprise economies tend to make wasteful use of their human resources, precisely because people are not sufficiently regarded as socially productive assets.

Conception of economic growth as a generalised process of capital accumulation provides a unifying principle for the statistical explanation of past growth and the formulation of policy for future growth or plans for economic development. It does not, however—and cannot be expected to—dispose of any real problems, though it does clarify understanding of them. Instead, it transforms these problems into problems of the special characteristics of particular types of capital, or of the specification of efficient investment programmes.

From the point of view of economically relevant differentiations, items of capital can be classified in a variety of ways. One fundamental distinction to be drawn relates to the nature of the yield or contribution to economic welfare—the distinction between consumption capital, which yields a flow of services enjoyed directly and therefore contributing to utility, and production capital, which yields a flow of goods the consumption of which yields utility. The returns from production capital are directly observable, and therefore more amenable to measurement than the returns on consumption capital.

Another fundamental distinction relates to the form in which capital is embodied—here it seems necessary not only to distinguish capital embodied in human beings from capital embodied in non-human material forms, but also to distinguish between capital embodied in both human and non-human physical forms and capital embodied in neither, the latter category comprising both the state of the arts (the intellectual production capital of society) and the state of culture (the intellectual consumption capital of society). The significance of this distinction is closely related to a third distinction—one which is particularly relevant to policy problems—between types of capital according to whether the returns to investment in capital accumulation accrue to the investor or to others. Here it seems necessary to distinguish: (a) capital goods which render specific services to production or consumption by the owner; (b) human capital, the distinguishing characteristic of which is that, both inherently and by legal tradition, control over the use of the capital is vested in the individual embodying the capital, regardless of the source of finance of the investment in it; (c) social capital or collective capital, the distinguishing characteristic of which is that for reasons of inherent necessity or administrative convenience its services to production or consumption are not charged to individual users but are paid for by taxation of the community at large; (d) intellectual capital or knowledge, the distinguishing characteristic of which is that, once created it is a free good, in the sense that use of it by one individual does not diminish its availability to others.

All forms of capital other than capital goods rendering specific services to production or consumption raise serious problems for economic analysis measurement and policy formation. The fusion of human capital with the personality of its owner raises among other things the problem of how far expenditure on the creation of human capital should be accounted as investment, and how far it should be classed as consumption; while the vesting of control over the use of capital in the individual invested in, given the imperfection of markets for personal credit, poses the problem of how far education should be provided at public expense. The divergence of private and social costs and benefits inherent in free or subsidised education raises some particularly difficult problems in conjunction with the fact that educated people are especially mobile interregionally and internationally, so that resources devoted to education in poor countries may run substantially to waste in unilateral transfers of human capital to richer countries.[6] Social capital investment involves a similar separation of costs of investment from benefits, and a similar mixture of equity and efficiency considerations. Investment in knowledge raises the thorniest of all problems, since the zero marginal cost of knowledge to additional users implies that no system of recouping the cost of investment in knowledge-creation by charging for its use can be economically efficient. . . .

The distinctions discussed above do not include a distinction between natural resources (natural capital) and man-made capital. For most economic purposes, such a distinction is unnecessary—natural resources, like capital goods, can be appropriated, transferred, and invested in. Natural resources do, however, raise two sorts of special problems. First property rights in some range of natural resources are typically vested in society or the state; this poses the problem of ensuring efficient exploitation of these resources through appropriate accounting and charging for the use of the state's natural capital, a problem particularly important at the time when resources are first brought into use. Secondly, some kinds of natural resources, which are likely to be of particular importance to developing countries, are nonrenewable, and pose the problems of efficient depletion and exhaustion—of efficient capital decumulation, rather than accumulation. The prob-

[6]Brinley Thomas has emphasised the economic absurdity of the contemporary migration pattern between advanced and underdeveloped countries, in which the advanced countries cream off the professional talent of the underdeveloped countries by immigration and attempt to replace it by their own experts supplied at great expense as part of development aid. See Brinley Thomas, "International Factor Movements and Unequal Rate of Growth," *The Manchester School of Economic and Social Studies,* January 1961. The ease of migration of educated people from underdeveloped countries, especially those in which English is the language of instruction, to advanced countries is a serious limitation on the potentialities of achieving economic development by educational investment and suggests the social desirability of devising means of obliging either the emigrants themselves or the countries receiving them to repay the social capital invested in them to their countries of origin.

lems of achieving economic development through the exploitation of depleting natural resources become particularly acute and politically highly charged when such exploitation is dependent on the participation of foreign capital and enterprise.

Conception of economic development as a generalised process of capital accumulation, in conjunction with recognition of economically significant differences between various types of capital, has important implications for the efficient programming of investment of economic development. These implications centre on the relationships of complementarity and substitutability in both production and consumption that may exist between types of capital provided by different investment processes, and the consequent desirability of aiming at both balanced investment in the production of complementary types of capital and the selection of the most efficient combinations of types of capital in the light of the relative costs of different kinds of investment. The complementarity between modern equipment and technology, a skilled labour force, and social overhead capital in the transportation and distribution systems is by now sufficiently recognised for development planning to aim at producing integrated investment programmes comprising investment in education and vocational training (manpower programmes) as well as investment in industrial and social overhead. For such comprehensive development investment programmes to maximise the contribution of investment to economic growth, however, recognition of complementarity must be allied with recognition of substitutability and analysis of rates of return on the total investment of capital in alternative programmes involving investment in capital goods, human capital, social capital and the acquisiton of new knowledge.

Much of the literature on economic development assumes far too easily that low-wage labour is necessarily cheap industrial labour, ignoring the magnitude of the investments in human and social capital that may have to be made to convert rural workers into skilled industrial labour, and the possibility that investment of the same capital in agricultural improvement might yield far higher returns. On the other hand, there is a strong possibility, exemplified by the successful development of exports of some technologically fairly advanced products from otherwise underdeveloped countries, that the greatest comparative advantage for such countries lies in skilled-labour-intensive products, for the reason that a generally low-wage level makes the cost of investment in human capital low (especially forgone earnings and the cost of instruction and educational structures) by comparison with comparable costs in advanced countries. In addition, such countries may be able to catch up with the advanced countries far more rapidly in the accumulation of knowledge than in the accumulation of material capital.

Apart from its implications for planning for economic growth, a generalised capital accumulation approach to economic development points to the potential fruitfulness of research into and analysis of the efficiency of a wide range of processes and policies that involve the allocation of capital but are not usually thought of as concerned with investment. It has, for example, been amply demonstrated by empirical research that rates of return on investment in education vary widely between different levels of the education system; and there is good reason for doubting that existing educational systems are very efficient when considered as an industry producing extremely long-lived capital assets. The field of public health and medical care, viewed as an industry concerned with the repair and maintenance of human capital, also offers scope for economic analyses of rates of return on alternative investments. Institutional arrangements for supporting and rewarding fundamental and applied research, considered as an industry producing intellectual capital, provide an even greater challenge to economists. Within the traditional scope of economics, labour mobility, unemployment policy, and policy respecting the location of industry all demand the application of capital theory. Perhaps the most important area requiring rationalisation in terms of a broadened concept of capital accumulation, however, is the theory and practice of public finance. Not only do income tax systems typically make a very poor adjustment for the capital investment element in personal income, but the necessity of recouping by income and profits taxation the costs of investments in human capital customarily provided free or at a subsidised price to the people invested in creates disincentives to the efficient use and accumulation of capital of all kinds.

CHAPTER X

Project Appraisal

Having considered in earlier chapters the overall contribution of capital to development, and the various ways of financing a higher rate of investment, we now turn to the remaining problem of how to determine the allocation of investment resources. When investment resources are as scarce as they are in a poor country, the rational allocation of capital is of the greatest importance.

How can a developing country be assured that the investment resources used in a given project would not have any better alternative use in terms of the country's objectives? To answer this question is to engage in the practice of project appraisal.

National governments guide the pattern of investment either by direct investment in the public sector or by controls on private investment. To provide rational guidance, the government must formulate and evaluate investment projects in such a way as to be able to compare and evaluate alternative projects in terms of their contribution to the objectives of the nation. So too must an international lending agency such as the World Bank engage in project appraisal. Even a private foreign investor may have to negotiate with a host government on the basis of the real worth of the foreign investment to the economy as a whole.

A private firm typically invests according to commercial profitability. But national profitability or social profitability may differ from commercial profitability. National benefits and costs may differ from benefits accruing to a firm and costs incurred by the firm. The techniques of project appraisal have been designed to evaluate projects when the social benefits and costs differ from the private benefits and costs. In assessing social benefits, one may consider issues of income distribution, public goods, and merit wants.

To provide an introduction to project appraisal, this chapter highlights some central issues that must be considered when a project analyst attempts to deal systematically with the divergences between private and social values. The selections concentrate on the theory of project appraisal, not on actual computation.

The Note at the outset (section X.A) presents the rationale underlying project appraisal, emphasizing that it is applied welfare economics in a world of the second best. After examining measures of private profitability (X.B.1 and X.B.2), subsequent selections introduce other considerations that are necessary for the calculation of social benefits and costs. Section X.C explains shadow pricing, with particular attention to the key shadow prices of foreign exchange, wages, and opportunity costs of capital. In addition, other important objectives, for example, the designation of beneficiaries of the project and the placing of a premium on investment, are discussed in X.D.

X.A. GENERAL RATIONALE OF PROJECT APPRAISAL—NOTE

Project appraisal does not rest on a set of techniques that can be applied mechanically, but is an approach that must be interpreted analytically. Interpretation becomes necessary because in reality investment resources are not allocated in a first-best world of perfect competition with no externalities. Instances of market failure and distortions are especially widespread in a developing economy. The distortions that prevail in a developing economy are commonly in foreign trade prices, factor markets, the nonoptimal income distribution, and in the use of nonoptimal taxes and subsidies. In correcting for these distortions, the practice of project appraisal is an exercise in the theory of the second-best.

A "first-best" economy would fulfill the marginal conditions of perfectly competitive equilibrium in all product and factor markets, with no uncertainty, no externalities, and a given income distribution. The perfectly competitive solution to resource allocation would then be equivalent to a Pareto-efficient allocation, reached by voluntary exchange in a market price system. Market prices of goods and factors would equate and equal the marginal social cost (MSC) of producing and the marginal social value (MSV) of using the relevant goods and factors. For a marginal investment project, the values of the outputs and inputs at market prices would then provide the correct values to be used in calculating the net present value (NPV) of the project. Economic costs and benefits would not differ from financial costs and benefits, and calculations of private commercial profitability would then be equivalent to social economic profitability.

Once conditions in a developing economy diverge, however, from those of the ideal first-best world, we enter a second-best world—a world in which the development practitioner must live. The development economist must be concerned with the existence of monopolies, taxes and subsidies, externalities, and price distortions. When market prices are not honest prices, reflecting real value, or prices do not exist for public goods, or do not value the social benefit of merit wants, then the market prices will no longer equate and equal the MSC and the MSV of the commodities.

To remove price distortions, neutral fiscal devices of lump-sum taxes and subsidy would constitute the best remedial policies, restoring the equivalence of the MSC and the MSV with market price. But this is not feasible and is rarely undertaken. The problem then is to correct for the price distortions in the practice of project appraisal through shadow pricing, using a cost-benefit analysis based on imputed values—that is, on the real economic values of costs and benefits—instead of relying on the market price data used in calculating private commercial profitability. The divergence between the MSC and the MSV has to be taken as a constraint, and the shadow prices corresponding to this constrained or "second-best" welfare optimum will need to be computed. Shadow pricing involves efficiency prices, and the calculation of a project's rate of return proceeds from the internal rate of *financial* return to the internal rate of *economic* return. Similarly, calculations of the project's NPV proceed onward from the discounted value of private net benefits (private receipts minus private costs) to the value of social net benefits (social benefit minus social cost), discounted at a social rate of discount. If consideration is also given to who the beneficiaries of the project are—to valuation of the resultant income distribution—then "social prices" that weight the income distribution are used to calculate the internal *social* rate of return. The social rate of return may also reflect the country's valuation of the distribution of income between consumption and investment that results from the project.[1]

A World Bank analyst has summarized the context of project analysis as follows:

In essence, project analysis assesses the benefits and costs of a project and reduces them to a common denominator. If benefits exceed costs—both expressed in terms of this common denominator—the project is acceptable: if not, the project should be rejected. As such, project analysis may appear divorced from both the fundamental objectives of the economy and the possible alternative uses of resources in other projects. The definition of benefits and costs, however, is such that these factors play an integral part in the decision to accept or reject. Benefits are defined relative to their effect on the fundamental objectives; costs are defined relative to their opportunity cost, which is the benefit forgone by not using these resources in the best of the available alternative investments that cannot be undertaken if the resources are used in the project. The forgone benefits are in turn defined relative to their effect on the fundamental objectives. By defining costs and benefits in this fashion we try to ensure that acceptance of a project implies that no alternative use of the resources consumed by this project would secure a better result from the perspective of the country's objectives.

Economic analysis of projects is similar in form to financial analysis in that both assess the profit of an investment. The concept of financial profit, however, is not the same as the social profit of economic analysis. The financial analysis of a project identifies the money profit accruing to the project-operating entity, whereas social profit measures the effect of the project on the fundamental objectives of the whole economy. These different concepts of profit are reflected in the different items considered to be costs and benefits and in their valuation. Thus, a money payment made by the project-operating entity for, say, wages is by definition a financial cost. But it will be an economic cost

only to the extent that the use of labor in this project implies some sacrifice elsewhere in the economy with respect to output and other objectives of the country. Conversely, if the project has an economic cost in this sense that does not involve a corresponding money outflow from the project entity—for example, because of environmental effects or subsidies—this cost is not a financial cost. The two types of cost need not coincide. Economic costs may be larger or smaller than financial costs. Similar comments apply to economic and financial benefits. Economic costs and benefits are measured by "shadow prices," which may well differ from the market prices appropriate for financial costs and benefits.

Shadow prices are determined by the interaction of the fundamental policy objectives and the basic resource availabilities. If a particular resource is very scarce (that is, many alternative uses are competing for that resource), then its shadow price, or opportunity cost (the foregone benefit in the best available alternative that must be sacrificed), will tend to be high. If the supply of this resource were greater, however, the demand arising from the next best uses could be satisfied in decreasing order of importance, and its opportunity cost (or shadow price) would fall. Market prices will often reflect this scarcity correctly, but there is good reason to believe that in less developed countries imperfect markets may cause a divergence between market and shadow prices. Such divergences are thought to be particularly severe in the markets for three important resources: labor, capital, and foreign exchange. . . .

Resource availabilities, however, need not be the only constraints operating in the economy: political and social constraints may be equally binding. The alternatives open to the government in pursuing its development objectives can be limited by these noneconomic constraints to a narrower range than that implied by the basic resource availabilities. If the tools of general economic policy—that is, fiscal and monetary policy—cannot break these constraints, project analysis should take account of them by means of appropriate adjustments in shadow prices. For example, if the government is unable to secure a desired redistribution of income through taxation, it can use the allocation of investment resources as an alternative method of redistributing income. If in project analysis higher values were to be attached to increases in income accruing to the poorer groups within society, investment would be biased in favor of these groups. In other words, all available policy tools should be working jointly toward the same

---

[1]Sometimes what we have termed the internal economic rate of return is called the internal social rate of return, and some selections that follow refer to what we have called efficiency prices as social prices. But we wish to distinguish among the internal *financial* rate of return at market prices, the internal *economic* rate of return at efficiency prices, and assuming all units of income are equally valuable, and the internal *social* rate of return with social prices that include the distributional aspects between consumption and investment and between rich and poor.

goals. If one instrument is inoperative or blunted, other instruments may be used to achieve the same end.

Project analysis is designed to permit project-by-project decision-making on the appropriate choices between competing uses of resources, with costs and benefits being defined and valued, in principle, so as to measure their impact on the development objectives of the country. In many cases, however, a more direct link is necessary with the sector and economy as a whole: for example, the merit of a project characterized by economies of scale cannot be judged without making an estimate of the demand for its output, and this in turn requires placing the project in its sectoral and country context.

Furthermore, in practice, many shadow prices (for land and natural resources, for example) are difficult to determine independent of the project appraisal process, because they depend on the alternative projects that have been rejected. This is the basic reason why a systematic scrutiny of plausible alternatives is at the heart of the appraisal process: it is not sufficient in practice to select an acceptable project whose benefits appear to exceed costs; it is necessary to search for alternatives with a larger surplus of benefits over identified costs. If such projects are found, it means that the opportunity cost of using, say, land in the project originally considered acceptable has been underestimated or wholly neglected.[2]

If project analysis is to make its maximum contribution to a better allocation of resources, it is clear that social cost-benefit analysis must underlie each stage of project preparation—from project identification to feasibility studies of technical possibility and economic viability, to final calculations of present net social value.

Social cost-benefit analysis in the context of the development process therefore raises

the following issues that will be considered in the remainder of this chapter: (1) specification of costs and benefits; (2) valuation of costs and benefits; (3) choice and formulation of constraints; (4) treatment of risk and uncertainty; (5) choice of the rate of interest for discounting future costs and benefits; and (6) choice of a decision rule for accepting or rejecting projects.

The concept of a cost or a benefit has meaning only in relation to objectives of the country's development program. Various objectives might be relevant: higher consumption or real income; better distribution of consumption or income; employment; national prestige or independence; changes in skills, attitudes, and institutions. Because project appraisal in the context of a development plan is an exercise in constrained maximization, the choice of the objective function and the selection of the relevant constraints are crucial. The shadow price of a given resource is the increase in the maximum value of the objective when ceteris paribus the economy is endowed with a unit more of the resource. As such, it is the "marginal product" of the resource, the "product" being reflected in the value of the objective function. The choice of shadow prices will therefore depend on the objective function and the nature of the constraints that the economy faces.

In practice, the shadow prices used can only be "approximately right," given the complexity of objectives and constraints in any actual economy. Although the perfectionist may be left unsatisfied, the practice of project appraisal is an improvement over simple reliance on calculations of private commercial profitability. The need is clear, progress has been made, and a broad consensus on proper techniques of project appraisal has emerged.

[2]Lyn Squire and Herman G. van der Tak, *Economic Analysis of Projects,* Baltimore and London, (1975), pp. 15–17.

Comment

The leading sources on project appraisal techniques are UNIDO, *Guidelines for Project Evaluation* (1972), reinterpreted by John R. Hansen, *Guide to Practical Project Appraisal: Social Benefit-Cost Analysis in Developing Countries* (1978); and I. M. D. Little and J. A. Mirrlees, *Project Appraisal and Planning for Developing Countries* (1974). Also significant for a review of the basic issues raised by the various methods of project evaluation are Deepak

Lal, *Methods of Project Analysis: A Review* (1974); A. Harberger, *Project Evaluation* (1976); E. V. K. Fitzgerald, *Public Investment Planning for Developing Countries* (1978). For an extension to distributional issues, see L. Squire and H. G. van der Tak, *Economic Analysis of Projects* (1976).

More empirical studies include the "Symposium on the Little-Mirrlees Manual," *Bulletin Oxford Institute of Economics and Statistics* (February 1972); Michael Roemer and Joseph J. Stern, *The Appraisal of Development Projects* (1975); I. M. D. Little and M. FG. Scott, *Using Shadow Prices* (1976); M. FG. Scott et al., *Project Appraisal in Practice* (1976). A useful volume focusing on benefit-cost techniques for agricultural investment is J. Price Gittinger, *Economic Analysis of Agricultural Projects,* 2nd ed. (1982).

For general background readings on benefit-cost analysis, see R. Sugen and A. Williams, *The Principles of Practical Cost-Benefit Analysis* (1978); G. Irvin, *Modern Cost-Benefit Methods* (1978); R. Layard (ed.), *Cost-Benefit Analysis* (1972); E. J. Mishan, *Elements of Cost-Benefit Analysis* (1976); A. R. Prest and R. Turvey, "Cost-Benefit Analysis: A Survey," *Economic Journal* (December 1975), which includes an extensive bibliography.

It is indicative of how recent the application of cost-benefit analysis is to projects in developing countries that the first published cost-benefit analysis of any investment in an LDC was in 1972—I. M. D. Little and D. G. Tipping, *A Social Cost Benefit Analysis of the Kulai Oil Palm Estate* (OECD, 1972).

X.B. BENEFITS AND COSTS
X.B.1. Plans and Projects*

A sound development plan requires a great deal of knowledge about existing and potential projects. This is obvious enough for a short-term operational plan (3–5 years) which should, among other things, contain firm and realizable plans for Government expenditure in different sectors. But it is just as true for a perspective plan, which covers a period of, say, 10–15 years.

Such a perspective plan will lay down target rates for gross national production, consumption, and also for investment and its financing by both domestic and foreign savings. For this to be done, it is clear that a relationship has to be assumed between the level of investment during the plan period (and also for several years prior to the plan period) and the rate of growth of domestic product which depends more or less closely on that level of investment.

This connection between investment and the rate of growth cannot be properly estimated without a great deal of knowledge about actual and potential investment projects. . . .

In principle, there are an infinite number of feasible plans, only one of which is the best of all. One can never hope to arrive at this optimum plan. But unless one strives continually to direct one's investment to those sectors where it would yield the most benefits to the economy, and within sectors to projects which yield most, one will certainly end up with a plan which is very far short of what could be achieved. Thus, if the division of investment between different sectors of the economy is to be rational, it is essential that the costs and benefits of many different projects in each sector should be assessed on a comparable basis. Here, one must admit that

*From Ian M. D. Little, "Project Analysis in Relation to Planning in a Mixed Economy," in OECD Development Center, *Development Problems,* Summary of Papers at the Colombo Seminar, Paris, 1967, pp. 47, 49–52, 54–65. Reprinted by permission.

there are limits to what economic analysis can achieve. No matter the sector of activity, costs are relatively easy to estimate on a comparable basis. But this is not always true of benefits. For instance, although there is by now a considerable body of work concerned with estimating the benefits of education and medical expenditure, one cannot be proud of, or place much confidence in, the results as yet. But no such strong reservations need be made in the important spheres of economic infrastructure, industry proper, and agriculture. In these spheres, although it is of course true that formal estimates of cost and benefit always go wrong, nevertheless it would be highly obscurantist to suggest that one should not try to peer into the future at all. And, if one is going to peer into the future, it is important to make sure that the manner in which it is done does not lead to biases as between different sectors and different projects. . . .

I have laboured the point that realistic plans cannot be formulated in the absence of a great deal of project planning, and without proper economic appraisal of projects. But it is also true that a good economic appraisal of projects often cannot be made without a plan.

Project appraisal obviously requires an estimate of the demand for the product. But how can one estimate the domestic product unless one has some idea of how the economy will develop? And how the economy develops in turn depends at least partly on the long-range plans and policies of the Government. . . .

In presenting the twin propositions that "plans require projects" and "projects require plans," it may seem that an insoluble chicken and egg dilemma has been posed. If good plans cannot be formulated without a proper economic appraisal of projects, and if the real value of projects cannot be properly ascertained, except within the framework of a plan, where does one start? But the chicken and egg analogy is false, as one is never totally devoid of knowledge. Inadequate plans are first formulated using inadequate methods of project appraisal. These in turn should permit improvements in project analysis and appraisals, and so on. Macro-economic planning can be gradually improved in the light of improvements in micro-economic planning, and vice versa. By such iteration and re-iteration, one gradually tries to come near to optimum planning.

PROFITABILITY ANALYSIS

In principle, one can approach an optimum investment plan only if all new projects are compared with each other with a view to seeing that none are rejected which are superior to any of those selected. In principle, of course, this implies that public sector projects are compared with those in the private sector, both being evaluated in the same manner. But in this section, I shall neglect the special problems which arise from trying to compare public and private projects, and I shall speak *as if* all projects were in the public sector.

In this section also, I shall concern myself only with the analysis of gross profits, that is, profits before depreciation is subtracted. Or to use another terminology, with pre-tax cash flows. Of course, decisions in the public sector should not necessarily be based on profitability, since there are many reasons for thinking that profits are not always a good measure of the net benefit to society. Nevertheless, profitability analysis and social cost-benefit analysis have much in common, and it is therefore convenient, first, to set out the proper principles for the former, and then to modify it in such a way as to turn it into a social cost-benefit analysis. This helps to bring out the differences between the two, differences which are important in that the private sector will make its own decisions on the basis of profits alone (albeit net of tax).

A. The Basic Predictions. The basic figures required for economic appraisal, whether or not the appraisal limits itself to considering only actual cash flows, consists of a prediction of

1. all receipts from the sale of outputs of the project for each year of the life of the project, these including the sale of any buildings and equipment remaining at the end of the life of the project, and
2. all expenditures on goods and services according to the year in which they are made, from the date of the first expenditures until the end of the life of the project. These expenditures include capital expenditures, whether for initial equipment or for replacement, as well as all current costs.

Current expenditures may be subtracted from current receipts. One then has two streams, the first consisting of net current receipts (gross profits), and the second consisting of capital expenditures, whether for initial equipment or replacement. . . .

So far, it has been assumed that a single well-defined project is up for consideration. But, in principle, no such finalized version of the project should come forward without much consideration having been given to alternative ways of doing more or less the same thing. First, there is always the question of whether it would not have been better to design the project on a larger or a smaller scale. Secondly, given the scale, there are usually numerous alternative techniques which might have been employed. Each of these many alternatives arising out of possible differences of scale and techniques is in principle another project, which has been rejected. Each of these will have had technical, managerial, and economic aspects. Were these alternatives properly assessed from these different angles before rejection? Naturally, one cannot fully evaluate a myriad of different possibilities before one of them is put forward for final consideration. Perhaps the most one can say is that those responsible for putting forward the final project, should be as aware as those who exercise the final choice of the need for proper appraisal and of the methodology which the final choosers operate. But, also, where important and feasible

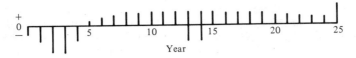

FIGURE 1.

variants present themselves, and the economic choice is not obvious, the initiating departments should be encouraged to consult with the central project evaluators.

B. The Profitability Criterion. I can now turn to describing the kind of analysis which the evaluators should conduct upon the basic figures already described. A diagram may be helpful here—see Figure 1.

- Above the line is measured the current cash flow (gross profits before depreciation). The exception is the last year, where the positive amount includes the disposal value of the terminal equipment.
- Below the line we have investment expenditures including replacement.
- The sum of the positive and negative items is the cash flow.
- Twenty-five years are included in the diagram. This is arbitrary, but unless the discount rate (see below) is extremely low, what happens after 25 years is very unlikely to make a significant difference.

Now suppose that the project can borrow any sums of money required at a fixed rate of interest. Using this market rate of interest, the next step is to discount all the net current receipts, and the investment expenditures back to the present, and add up.[1] This result is known as the *Present Value.* In symbols,

$$\sum_{t=1}^{t=25} \frac{X_t}{(1 + r)^t}$$

where X_t is the cash flow in year t, and r is the rate of interest.

Ignoring risk it is logical to make any investment which results in a positive present value.

[1]Discounting simply means working compound interest backwards. For instance, £100 cumulated for two years at 10% interest becomes £121. £121 discounted at 10% for two years is £100.

A closely allied, but nevertheless different, procedure is to experiment until one has found that rate of discount which makes the present value equal to zero.

In symbols one solves the equation

$$\sum_{t=1}^{t=25} \frac{X_t}{(1 + y)^t} = 0$$

for y. The solution (y) is called the *"Internal Rate of Return."* In a riskless situation, it pays to invest if the internal rate of return exceeds the rate of interest (if $y > r$).

The present value method is technically superior, since the internal rate of return can give an incorrect result in special circumstances. I shall not go into this. The only, but not unimportant, advantage of the internal rate of return (given that it does give the correct result) is that it is more familiar to administrators and businessmen. It is in fact the proper way to calculate what is familiarly and loosely known as the "yield."

Either of these methods is known as *"discount of cash flow analysis."* The point of using cash flow, rather than profits, is that replacement expenditures are explicitly accounted for, and the usual rather arbitrary methods of allowing for depreciation of capital are thereby avoided. The annual figures are gross of depreciation, but the final result is a *net* present value or *net* yield. The logic of the method is impeccable. It is now used by the most sophisticated firms in making their investment decisions, although the great majority still use much more rudimentary methods.

I have so far dealt with riskless cases only. There is no one correct method of allowing for risks. Two methods of approaching the problem are discussed briefly below.

First, one can use a higher rate of interest than the market rate for discounting purposes, or require that the internal rate of return substantially exceeds the market rate before embarking on an investment. The advantage of this is that the reduction of expected net receipts is greater the further in the future they are (and risks presumably increase with time). But it is rather mechanical, and leaves open the choice of how great the risk discount should be, and also the question of whether and how this risk discount should be varied between different classes of projects. While uniformity has advantages in preventing unconscious and irrational preferences from biasing the result, there is the corresponding disadvantage that risks do differ between projects, and that they can to some extent be broken down for separate consideration instead of being lumped together in an overall risk allowance.

The second method is to try to make a high and a low estimate for each expenditure and receipt, and so produce a high and a low estimate of the present value, or the internal rate of return. The final step consists of some subjective evaluation of the result—and choice!

What I have said about risk is, of course, quite inadequate. But the subject had to be mentioned, if only because private entrepreneurs certainly make some allowance, however informal, while the subject is often not even mentioned where public sector projects are concerned.

SOCIAL COST-BENEFIT ANALYSIS

Three modifications may be made to the gross profitability discussed above in order to turn it into a social cost-benefit analysis. They are as follows:

1. Other prices than those actually reigning may be used to value the inputs and outputs of the project.

2. An allowance may be made for benefits or costs which arise elsewhere in the economy as a result of the operation or construction of the project.

3. The annual benefits and costs may be differently treated in a social cost-benefit analysis, as compared to a profitability analysis, in order to arrive at an investment criterion. Thus neither "present value" nor "the internal rate of return" may be appropriate. It is in fact necessary to introduce a new concept, the *"benefit-cost ratio."*

X.B.2. Measures of Profitability*

The profits of an enterprise equal the difference between its earnings and its costs. For a project the stream of future profits and losses may be calculated period by period. The main complications in the concept of profitability arise from the necessity to convert this stream of profits and losses into some simple measure expressed as a number, e.g., the "rate of return" or "the present value" of the project.

If the stream of profits is $P_0, P_1, P_2, \ldots, P_n$,

*From UNIDO, *Guidelines for Project Evaluation,* United Nations, 1972, pp. 18–26. Reprinted by permission.

with a positive figure standing for net profits and a negative figure for a net loss, or the net expenditure, the "present value" of the stream is simply the discounted sum of this stream, the discounting being done at the appropriate rate of interest, i. Representing the present value of the project at interest rate i as $V(i)$, we get:

$$V(i) = \sum_{i=0}^{n} \frac{P_t}{(1 + i)^t} \qquad (1)$$

What kind of measure of profitability is the present value? It is a fairly good measure, since it converts the entire stream of profits into one number representing the total amount of profits today that would be equivalent to the entire stream of profits. The equivalence is defined as that given by the appropriate rate of interest. For the evaluation of commercial profitability, the appropriate rate of interest is the rate that rules in the market for borrowing and lending. If a person can lend and borrow at 10 per cent, he would have no reason to choose a project that costs £100 today and yields only £109 next year. Similarly, he would have no reason to reject a project that yields £111 one year from now and costs only £100 today. Even if he does not have the money, he can borrow it at 10 per cent and make a net profit of £1 by next year.

What it may be asked, if the person in question has a personal rate of discount that is different from 10 per cent? What if he finds £115 next year to be equivalent to £100 today? Would he then not be justified in rejecting a project that yields £111 next year and costs £100 this year? He would be, but the question that arises in this case is: Why does he have a personal rate of discount of 15 per cent when he can borrow and lend at 10 per cent? If there were this difference, should he not proceed to borrow a large quantity of money, since he pays only £110 next year for £100 this year while he considers £115 next year to be just as satisfactory as £100 this year? He should thus make use of the market by borrowing, and this he should continue to do until his personal rate of discount comes down to the level of the market rate of interest of 10 per cent. (Another possibility is that the market rate of interest will rise, thanks to his borrowing, but this would be unlikely in a large market, since any individual would tend to be a small operator compared with the enormity of the entire market.) Similarly, if the person initially has a personal rate of discount lower than the market rate (e.g., if he thinks that £100 this year is equivalent to £108 next year), then he should use the market as a lender. He can get £110 by lending £100 this year, and clearly it is worth his while to do this, since he regards £108 to be enough compensation for losing £100 this

year. As he lends more and more he will tend to shift his preference in favour of money now; this rise in the rate of discount will continue until it equals the market rate of interest.

Thus, for a private operator, the correct discount rate is the market rate of interest, at least if we accept the conventional assumptions of economic rationality. And this he can use for calculating the present value of a project. It is, of course, possible that the interest rate would vary from period to period, and the calculation of the present value need not be based on the assumption of an unchanging interest rate. Suppose that the interest rate between year 0 and year 1 is i_1, and that between year 1 and year 2 is i_2 (and so on), then the present value of the project is given as:

$$V(i_1, i_2, \ldots, i_n)$$
$$= \sum_{t=0}^{n} \frac{P_t}{(1 + i_1) \ldots (1 + i_t)} \quad (2)$$

It is clear that (1) is a special case of (2) when $i_1 = i_2 = \cdots = i_n$.

A relevant question to ask is the following: At what rate of interest, constant over time, would the present value of a project be exactly zero, i.e., for what i would we have $V(i) = 0$? This is not unduly complicated to calculate. An interest rate for which the present value of a project is zero is called the "internal rate of return" of the project. It is perfectly possible in principle that the present value of a project may become zero at more than one rate of interest, e.g., the stream $(100, -500, 600)$ has two internal rates of return, namely, 100 per cent and 200 per cent. This problem, while somewhat intriguing, is perhaps not very important for a variety of reasons. For one thing, this multiplicity of the internal rate of return would never occur if a project yielded losses up to a certain point in time and thereafter yielded profits (e.g., after it comes into operation). In such a case, the higher the interest rate the lower will be the present value (as in Figure 1), and the internal rate of return must be unique (OA in Figure 1).

While we cannot spend time on the ques-

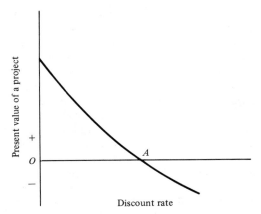

FIGURE 1. Present value at alternative discount rates.

tion of multiplicity of the internal rate of return, the question of the relative significance of the internal rate of return and of the present value is an important one and should engage our attention. The present value at the market rate of interest and the internal rate of return are both measures which convert the stream of profits into one number, and it is relevant to know which one is a better guide. Do they, in fact, conflict? In choosing projects we may follow the rule that all projects with an internal rate of return higher than the market rate of interest should be chosen. Alternatively, we may recommend that all projects with a positive present value should be selected. Does it make any difference which of the two rules we follow? The answer is "No, not at all," so long as the present value always goes down as the discount rate is raised, as in Figure 1. If the market rate of interest is less than $0A$, the project represented in Figure 1 should definitely be chosen according to both criteria, while if it is more than $0A$ it should be rejected by both tests. There is no conflict whatever in all this.

The real conflict arises when the rule of choosing all projects satisfying either of these criteria cannot be followed. There may be certain specific constraints. For example, the choice of one project may rule out another, e.g., projects A and B may be two variants of

a dam on a certain river, and the construction of one would eliminate the possibility of having the other. Suppose that A yields a higher internal rate of return (say, 20 per cent rather than 10 per cent) and a lower present value at the market rate of interest of 5 per cent (say, £1 million rather than £2 million), which should we choose? The conflict arises with the question of ranking the two projects in terms of their relative desirability. Figure 2 represents this and also illustrates that such a conflict can arise even though the present value of each project declines with the discount rate.

One can say that, in a significant sense, the present value is a better guide than the internal rate. It yields a measure of total gains which the latter does not. If 5 per cent is the market rate (and also the rate at which a person is ready to discount future earnings), project B yields twice as much return as project A, and clearly this is a good thing for B. The fact that the rate of return is higher with A than with B is not very compelling so long as the choice is between having project A and having project B. To take an extreme case, a person may get a return of 500 per cent on a penny and a return of only 20 per cent on $1,000. The latter is likely to be more attractive if the market rate of interest and the person's rate of discount are 10 per cent. The present value gives a measure of total gains, which the internal rate does not. In what follows, the present value of the commercial returns of a project at the market rate of interest will be taken as a measure of the profitability of a project.

The present value is a good framework also for public choice even though the rate of discount to be used should not necessarily be the market rate of interest but the appropriate social rate of discount; also, the profits should be social profits as measured from the point of view of the society and not commercial profits as normally defined. The reason for preferring the present-value formulation in this case is the same as in the case of a commercial evaluation, that is, the present value gives a measure of total gains (in this case social gains and not commercial gains).

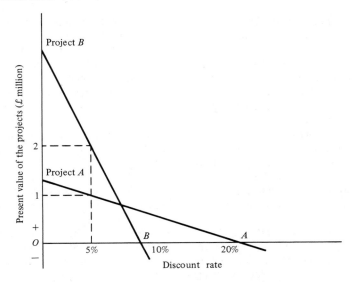

FIGURE 2. Conflict between present value and discount rate.

LIMITATIONS OF COMMERCIAL PROFITABILITY

In what respects does a measure of commercial profitability differ from that of national economic profitability? Why is it that commercial profits are often treated as a bad guide to social gains? If the framework is one of "present value" in both cases, clearly the distinction must lie in the divergence between commercial profits and social gains in any year and that between the market rate of interest and the appropriate social rate of discount.

Commercial profits measure the difference between the value of earnings and costs in a certain period. The earnings are direct money earnings of the firm at market prices and the costs are money costs, again at market prices.... Social benefit-cost analysis must go deeper and ask what is the meaning of market prices, that is, what do they represent? If a person is ready to offer £1 for something, he expects to get at least £1 worth of satisfaction from it. Does this mean that the social value is also worth £1? Not necessarily.

First, how much money a person is ready to offer depends on his income level. A rich man may offer a good deal of money for trivia, while a very poor person may find it difficult to spend even very small amounts of money on essentials. The price offered in the market is, thus, not a good guide to social welfare, for it includes the influence of income distribution on the prices offered.

One could, of course, retort by asking why, if the guardians of public policy do not like the income distribution (e.g., if they disapprove of the existing inequality), they do not reform it directly. Once the distribution is reformed, the project evaluator can simply treat the money prices offered as guides to welfare without worrying about income distribution. This retort, while not uncommon, is somewhat hollow, since there are constraints—political, economic and social—that prevent such reforms of income distribution, and given these limitations the exercise of project evaluation cannot be based on the notion that all appropriate income redistributions have already been carried out.

Further, one of the simpler means of income redistribution may, in fact, be project selection. For example, the choice may be between project *A* to be located in a poor region or project *B* to be placed in a rich area, or between project *X,* which uses a large amount of poor, unskilled labour, which might otherwise be unemployed, and project *Y,* which uses factors of production supplied by rich people. Project choice has distributional implications, and sometimes it may be politically or socially more feasible to redistribute income this way rather than through taxes or other direct means. We have, therefore, quite a legitimate reason to consider distributional questions in evaluating social gains from a project. This immediately takes one beyond commercial profitability.

Second, a project may have influences that work outside the market rather than through it. For example, a particular industrial project may produce a great deal of smoke and foul air in the town in which it is located. Or a firm may train the labour force in the region. While the first impact may be undesirable and the second laudable, the firm's profits may not reflect either. The cost of bad health or the unpleasant life of neighbours may not depress commercial profits, and the reward for training may not go to the firm, since, after training, the workers are free to leave.

The effects that work outside the market are called "externalities." These do not enter calculations of commercial profits, since these are made at market prices. Externalities are obviously relevant for social choice and provide a sufficient argument for rejecting commercial profitability as a guide to public policy. Externalities can arise in the process of production (e.g., industries causing water pollution), in the process of consumption (e.g., additional private cars adding to the crowding of the roads), and also in the process of sales and distribution (e.g., garish shop display or advertising affecting the tranquillity of the community). Externalities are often most pervasive.

Third, even in the absence of externalities and considerations of income distribution, commercial profitability may still be misleading. If a consumer is ready to pay £1 for a good, he expects to get at least £1 worth of

satisfaction from that particular good; but he could expect to get more, conceivably much more. If we look at the market value of a good produced by a project, we get a measure of a floor to expected satisfaction. But in fact the consumer may expect more and get more. If we try to go into the question of total satisfaction from a project, we would have to examine the excess of what consumers are willing to pay for its products and what they actually pay. This difference is sometimes called the "consumers' surplus." In Figure 3, the line *AB* represents the maximum a consumer is ready to pay for each unit of a good. If the market price is *BC,* he will then buy *OC* units of it. The total expenditure he will make on it is *ODBC,* which will represent the earnings of the producer from him. But the value of the satisfaction that he anticipates is more, namely, *OABC.* The difference, *ABD,* represents the surplus that he enjoys. While commercial profitability takes no account of it, it is clearly a relevant consideration for public-project evaluation.

It is worth noting that for the last unit purchased there is no surplus, since the price paid, *BC,* is no lower than the price the buyer is ready to pay. Thus, the question arises not for variations near point *B,* but for the choice between bulky projects. In ascertaining the social gains from one sizable project rather than another, it is relevant to know the respective magnitudes of the consumers' surplus.

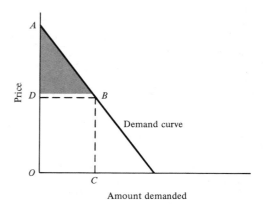

FIGURE 3. Consumers' surplus.

Considerations of income distribution, externalities and consumers' surplus are among the factors that distort commercial profits as a measure of national gains. There are other factors also, but the considerations discussed should have been sufficient to illustrate the difference between social and private gains.

Another ingredient of present-value estimates is the social rate of discount. Given any series of profits (private or social) the size of present value depends on the rates of discount. The social rates of discount may differ from commercial rates of interest for many reasons. An individual may expect to live only a certain number of years and the discounting of the future that springs from this limitation may not be appropriate for social choice, since the planners may wish to take a longer view and give greater importance to the welfare levels of future generations. Even the general public of today (as distinct from policy makers) may feel that for public projects, where all are forced to save simultaneously, a lower rate of discount may be appropriate than would be reflected in the market behaviour of individuals. Individuals may be ready to sacrifice for the future only if others are ready to do the same, and while such a joint action is possible through public policy, there is no way of bringing it about in individualistic market behaviour. Deep problems are involved here. . . . Suffice it to note now that there are no compelling reasons to believe that the market rate of interest must be the appropriate rate at which to discount future benefits. This is still another reason for commercial profitability to differ from measures of social gain.

PROFIT MAXIMIZATION AND EFFICIENCY

The usual defence of commercial profit maximization as a criterion is based on the implicit assumption of "perfect competition." Perfect competition is a case where there are many sellers and many buyers so that no one has any monopoly power; each person has perfect knowledge; there are free entries into the market; the product is homogeneous, i.e., there are no variations in quality. It can be proved that if there are no externalities (and a few other relatively minor conditions are satisfied), an equilibrium in a perfectly competitive market must achieve "economic efficiency," which is defined as a state where no one can be made better óff without making someone else worse off. Economic efficiency is also sometimes called "Pareto optimality" after the economist Pareto. Each firm maximizing its profits at given prices helps to achieve this type of optimality for the society.

Is this result—which is made much of in the formal economic literature—a compelling reason for recommending that public-project evaluation be guided by profit maximization at given market prices? The answer is a decided "no." First, the absence of externalities is a very dubious assumption, since they are quite widespread. In the presence of externalities, even perfect competition may not achieve economic efficiency. Second, economic efficiency is a very limited requirement. It tells us nothing whatever about income distribution. Some people may be terribly poor and others extremely rich, and still if no poor person can be made better off without making someone else worse off, the situation will still be called economically efficient. As a criterion it does not go very deep.

A no less disturbing consideration is the recognition that the result is based on all markets being perfect. Suppose some are and some are not. There will then be no reason for believing that one would move closer to economic efficiency by maximizing profit at given market prices, and indeed such a policy might conceivably take one further away from economic efficiency. The rule in question works only if all units are in competitive equilibrium. It does not give much guidance to an individual enterprise if imperfections exist in the rest of the economy.

Thus, it should be clear that the relationship between efficiency and profit maximization under competitive conditions does not really establish any very strong reason for basing project selection on commercial profit maximization at given market prices.

X.B.3. Social Cost-Benefit Analysis*

In offering guidelines for the use of cost-benefit analysis in developing countries we pay special attention to industry and agriculture, as well as to infrastructural projects where the output has a market price. Education, health, and defence are neglected. This is not meant to imply that useful work is not going on in these fields. Certainly, cost-effectiveness analysis can be applied. But it is still very controversial whether full cost-benefit analysis in such sectors, where benefits are particularly difficult to measure, is as yet sufficiently soundly based to be a good guide for policy makers.

Thus we are concerned with the application of cost-benefit analysis precisely in fields in which it is considered unnecessary in developed economies. The justification for this can only be that it is felt that within such sectors of more advanced economies the price mechanism works in such a way that profits are a reasonable measure of net benefit, but that this is not true of most developing countries.

Why should one start with the presupposition that actual prices are very much worse reflectors of social cost and benefit than is the case in advanced economies? The main reasons are briefly adumbrated below.

Inflation

Very rapid inflation is more common in developing countries, particularly in South America. This is no accident. The very urgency of the desire to develop rapidly results in a constant tendency for demand to outrun supply: furthermore, lagging supply in the sectors which are most resistant to change, particularly agriculture, results in sectoral price rises which tend to transmit themselves

*From I. M. D. Little and J. A. Mirrlees, *Project Appraisal and Planning for Developing Countries,* Heinemann, London, 1974, pp. 29–37. Reprinted by permission.

across the board. and may virtually force the monetary authority to increase total money demand if a recession of activity is to be avoided.

If inflation proceeded uniformly so that relative prices were unaffected, it would not be a reason for prices to be a poor measure of real costs and benefits. But this, for institutional and political reasons, is seldom the case. For example, governments in such circumstances will often use price controls in selected fields where they can in practice be operated. This makes activity in these fields relatively or absolutely unprofitable, without regard to the net benefit of such activities.

A particular case of such control concerns the price of foreign exchange, which brings us to the next reason.

Currency Overvaluation

In almost all countries, the government "manages" the price of foreign exchange. With inflation, if the exchange rate is unaltered, domestic prices get out of line with world prices. This implies that, on average, the rupee[1] prices of imports and exports are too low relative to those of goods which are not traded. So long as the currency is not devalued to rectify the situation, the demand for foreign exchange for imports and other purposes will exceed the supply, and the government will be forced to restrict imports, often in ways which open up gaps between the market prices of goods and the real cost of procuring them. But some governments faced with a price inflation do not resort to import controls in order to maintain the domestic currency overvaluation, but devalue

[1]We use 'rupees' to stand for the domestic currency unit, and 'dollars' to stand for a unit of foreign exchange. This is solely because it is awkward not to have a short familiar expression for these units: forced to choose, we selected rupees and dollars as being the units of the largest noncommunist developing and developed countries, respectively.

more or less frequently. If inflation is rapid and the government devalues periodically but not very frequently, then it is inevitable that the currency will be alternatively underval- ued and overvalued. If the inflation is slow, the government usually tries to avoid deval- uation, and long periods of overvaluation are likely.

Wage Rates and Underemployment

It has been seen that the theory of com- petition requires that the marginal product of labour (the extra output resulting from the employment of a small extra amount of la- bour) be equal to the wage paid.

Because of monopoly power, and immobil- ity, there are undoubtedly serious imperfec- tions in the labour markets of many indus- trialized countries. But these imperfections are not usually thought to cause major inter- sectoral distortions of the pattern of produc- tion (regional distortions may be an excep- tion, and here wage subsidies have been used). On the other hand, it is often argued that this is the case in many developing countries.

In "modern" sectors of the economy—in- cluding modern industry and commerce, gov- ernment, and plantations—it is common to find that unskilled workers earn three or four times as much as casual rural labour, a dif- ference far greater than can be accounted for by the difference in the cost of living; and therefore that the cost of employing people in these sectors is apparently much greater than the loss of rural production, assuming that such rural earnings are a fair measure of la- bour's marginal contribution to production. It has been argued that the earnings of casual labour overstate the marginal product of la- bour. This is because, in most developing countries, the greater part of rural labour is family labour. Since a dependent member of the family cannot be sacked, he may "earn" (i.e., consume) as much as a hired man but yet have a lower marginal product. As against this, in some places it is probable that the marginal product of a hired man is greater than his earnings because the em- ploying farmers exercise some monopsonistic power.

That men by working are unable to con- tribute as much to production as they con- sume is what is meant by underemployment. The extended family system permits under- employment in the towns as well as the coun- tryside. If relief were given institutionally, via unemployment benefits, the very low pro- ductivity urban activities—petty trading, car-watching, etc.—would largely disappear and more people would become openly and wholly unemployed, a circumstance which would, of course, imply that wages did not re- flect the social cost of employment.

The real cost of employing a man in the modern sector is still a subject of controversy, mainly because insufficient is known about the effects on the traditional sectors including agriculture, and because these effects will vary widely from country to country, and perhaps from region to region, or even town to town. However, there is rather wide agree- ment that modern sector wages almost every- where overstate, perhaps greatly overstate, the social cost of employment.

Imperfect Capital Markets

Where risks are equal, interest rates on loans should be equal, if profits are to mea- sure net social benefits. Interest rates have such an enormous range in many developing countries, that it is implausible to suggest that this is just a measure of differential risks. Other factors operate, such as govern- ment intervention, ignorance, and monopoly elements in the supply of capital, to widen the range from low to almost astronomical rates.

Large Projects

It is more common in developing coun- tries—especially in small countries with, as yet, little development—that a project will be so large as to have important repercussions on profits elsewhere in the economy. In these circumstances, as we have seen, the profita- bility of the project itself cannot be regarded as a good measure of net social benefit.

Inelasticity of Demand for Exports

In a number of developing countries, a large part of export receipts is accounted for by one, two, or three export commodities. Where a country also accounts for a considerable part of total world production, then it can influence, within limits, the price it obtains by restricting sales—which is, of course, an abrogation of the conditions of perfect competititon. The free market price cannot then correctly measure the benefit, because, like any monopolist, the country would gain if it exported less at a higher price.

This, in turn, implies that the country would gain by devoting rather less resources to producing these primary commodities, and rather more to others, or to industrialization. This situation can be best rectified by suitable export taxes on the commodities, together with other policies (including use of the revenue thus raised) which encourage the transfer of resources. Some countries recognize this situation and do in fact use export taxes. But the situation has also been used as an argument for encouraging industry by protection—which brings us to our next section.

Protection—Import Quotas, Tariffs, Export Disincentives

The protection of domestic industry may be a deliberate interference with the price mechanism designed to make it operate in a manner more conducive to society's benefit than would a laissez-faire commercial policy. A well-designed interference, in the shape of special encouragement of industrialization, may well make industrial profits a better guide to social advantage than they otherwise would be, either for the reasons given above, or for other reasons.

The main way in which industry is specially encouraged is by tariffs and import quotas. Thereby, the domestic price of the output is kept above the import price. But the outputs of one industry are often the inputs of another. Consequently, when an industry contemplates exporting, it finds that the very system which protects it in its home market puts it at a positive disadvantage in export markets; whereas reason suggests that if industrial production is worth special encouragement, then it is worth special encouragement, and not actual discouragement, in producing for export. Thus tariff protection, like currency overvaluation, implies that the rupee price obtainable for an export underestimates the social value of that export. Some developing countries have taken measures to offset this effect, but such measures are often insufficient, and not very scientifically devised in such a way as to make the rupee price measure the benefit to the country.

Apart from the fact that protection discourages exports of both industrial and agricultural products, it is also the case that different industries receive enormously different degrees of protection, usually for no apparently rational economic reason. This situation has arisen partly because countries have selected industries or plants (or have agreed to protect private initiatives) without the kind of economic appraisal being advocated here. Protection has followed the establishment of industries, rather than itself being used as a screening device.

Another reason why the relative gap between domestic and world prices is highly divergent as between industries is the extensive use of import quotas. A country runs into balance of payments problems. The situation is brought under control by restricting imports and, naturally, the least essential goods are most restricted. The result may be a growth of domestic industry, behind protective quotas, which bears little relation to the long-run comparative advantage of the country. If a wrong industry gets established it handicaps any other industry which uses its output. For instance, steel-using industries will be handicapped by a high-cost local steel plant, unless the latter is subsidized so that it can supply at prices no higher than the import price. It is our belief that bad management of foreign trade or foreign exchange is one of the principal reasons why internal prices get highly distorted, and hence lead to industrial investments which are of little or no benefit to the country concerned.

We have now outlined seven important and fairly non-controversial reasons why the price mechanism and the profit motive may not work as closely for the social advantages as in developed countries. Other more general reasons could be adduced, such as ignorance of opportunities and techniques, inertia, short-sightedness, lack of a market economy, and greater fragmentation of markets leading to local monopoly power; but these have relatively little direct bearing on project evaluation especially in the public sector. We turn now to a further three reasons, which may be more controversial.

Deficiency of Savings and Government Income

Two projects may have the same net profit, but a different effect on the relative amount of extra consumption, savings, and taxation.

As we saw, economic theory often treats savings and investment as of equal value. This is really a facet of the principle of consumers' sovereignty. It is assumed that it can make no difference to benefit whether some extra income is consumed, or saved and hence made available for investment. This is reasonable for an individual who freely chooses whether to spend or not. For him, an extra dollar of savings is worth the same as an extra dollar of consumption. But is it true for society?

To cut a long story short, if the government believes that rather more savings and rather less current consumption would be good for society, there may be a conflict. The point is that savings can be transformed into investment, and investment can produce extra future consumption for a sacrifice of present consumption: and the government may put a relatively higher value on the consumption of people in the future than do private persons. Furthermore, private persons may be inhibited from saving by income and other taxes which have the effect of double-taxing savings. We have already referred to these problems above, where it was argued that the rate at which society ought to discount the future may differ from the rate at which a firm can borrow. Thus, if the government chooses a discount rate for projects which is lower than the market rate of interest,[2] this is in effect to say that it considers future consumption to be more valuable than is indicated by the aggregate choices of private individuals. If the public saved more, interest rates would be lower, and the government pleased. In other words, the government considers present savings to be more valuable than present consumption.

Governments can reduce aggregate private consumption, and thus increase savings, by taxation. On the other hand, taxation has administrative and political costs. So perhaps it is money in the hands of the government which should be considered to be more valuable than private consumption: this view is strengthened by the fact that a rational government should see to it that the value of its expenditure at the margin is equal in all lines, whether it be defence, agricultural extension, education, or investing in industry. Many people will be rather unwilling to accept that money in the hands of the government is more useful than many kinds of private expenditure, especially when governments are seen to waste money and promote silly investments. But the project evaluator may in any case have to take a government view. This is a difficult and controversial matter, which will be taken up again.

Finally, it should be noted that although discussion of this problem has arisen mainly in the context of developing countries, it seems to us that it arises also in the case of rich countries.

The Distribution of Wealth

The preceding section was largely concerned with the distribution of benefits, as between the present and future. But there is

---

[2]'The market rate of interest' may be quite a wide band in developing countries, even if we restrict the meaning of 'the market' to that for medium and large scale industrial borrowing.

also a problem of the distribution of benefits today—the problem of inequality, to which we have already referred. There is a dilemma here, for inequality tends to promote savings, and help future generations. This is especially true of corporations: company profits belong mainly to the rich, but are one of the main sources of saving. The dilemma can be made less acute insofar as public savings can, by increased taxation, take the place of savings of the rich; but there is a limit to this, and some element of dilemma remains.

The extent to which project selection should concern itself with different kinds of inequality will come up again. There is the additional important question of how far a practicable criterion for project selection can take proper account of inequalities.

External Effects

Some economists believe that external economies are of special importance in developing countries: that some industries have important beneficial effects on others in ways which cannot be, or anyway are not, reflected in the price obtainable for the output of the industry, or in the price it pays for its inputs. There has been much speculation and debate on this subject. But there is very little positive evidence. Certainly there has been much naive wishful thinking—for instance, that the provision of electricity, steel, or transport, would somehow create its own demand.

It was already shown that many of the more obvious external effects can be allowed for by a suitable definition of the project to be considered. But others will remain.

SOCIAL OBJECTIVES AND THE NOTION OF ACCOUNTING PRICES

A rather strong case has now been presented for saying that a project's anticipated receipts and expenditures cannot be relied upon to measure social benefits and costs in most developing countries. It is believed that this is true also of more developed economies, but to a lesser extent. There is therefore a strong *prima facie* case for the use of cost-benefit analysis.

We have seen that the basic idea of such an analysis is to use hypothetical rather than predicted actual prices when evaluating a project. The rate of discount may also not correspond to any actual interest rate. These 'shadow' prices, as they are often called, are chosen so as to reflect better the real costs of inputs to society, and the real benefits of the outputs, than do actual prices.

The name 'shadow price' is perhaps unfortunate. It suggests to many, even to some economists, that an analysis based on them is remote from reality, and therefore academic and highbrow, and so is to be distrusted. Of course, shadow prices may be unreal in that they are not the current prices of goods in a market. But then no price in a project analysis can ever be an actual price—for every price assumed in such an analysis necessarily lies in the future. The whole point of a shadow price is indeed that it shall correspond more closely to the realities of economic scarcity and the strength of economic needs than will guesses as to what future prices will actually be. From now on we shall use the term "accounting prices."

It is worth emphasis that if any input or output is valued at a different price from that actually expected to be paid or received by the project, then, in our terminology, a social accounting price is being used. In this sense, most project appraisals have made use of accounting prices. For instance, it is widely accepted in project analysis that indirect taxes on inputs should not be counted as costs. Or again, for some years now, direct imports and exports of projects have often been valued at c.i.f. or f.o.b. prices (border prices, as we shall term them) by, among others, consultants working for the IBRD. Some evaluators may think that they are not using shadow prices when they make such adjustments. That is a matter of terminology. What we want to make clear is that, in our terminology, they are using accounting prices.

While accounting prices have been in use for some time, they have seldom been used in a comprehensive and systematic way, but rather haphazardly. This is dangerous. Once some important prices become badly distorted—e.g., the price of labour or foreign exchange—the repercussions are widespread. Every price is then liable to need adjustment. What we are primarily concerned with in this book is to show how a whole set of accounting prices can be systematically and logically estimated and applied, yielding a practical method of analysis which can be expected to measure net social benefit better than ordinary profitability analysis. Being practical precludes perfectionism. We make no claim that accounting prices can be exact reflections of social costs and benefits—merely much better reflections than actual prices for many projects in many countries. Nor, of course, is it claimed that the use of accounting prices is a very satisfactory method of dealing with distortions. Many of the distortions can be fully dealt with only by removing them—that is, by adopting policies which lead to proper correspondence of prices and costs and benefits. There may be yet others which, because of the difficulty of measuring them in a reasonably objective way, cannot be satisfactorily allowed for in a usable and politically acceptable criterion. These have to be left to the judgment of the politician and his advisers.

X.C. SHADOW PRICING

X.C.1. Distortions in Factor Markets*

It is appropriate to begin by stating the obvious: cost-benefit analysis is undoubtedly the most used, and arguably the most useful, form of *applied welfare economics*. Its theoretical basis as well as its limitations are therefore necessarily those of its parent, *theoretical welfare economics*. This paper is not for those who deny any practical use for theory, but for those who whilst recognizing the limitations of theoretical welfare economics nevertheless feel that in our present state of knowledge it provides the only basis for making an economic assessment of investment plans and proposals.

The purpose of any project selection procedure must be to provide a decision rule for accepting or rejecting a project. The net present value *(NPV)* or the internal rate of return *(IRR)* of the project is the index usually used. Our chief concern in this paper will be with, first, what should be included in the time stream of benefits and costs; secondly, what are the relevant values of the various cost-benefit components; and thirdly, how the discount rate (or rates) needed for determining the *NPV*, or the cutoff *IRR* at which projects are accepted, should be chosen. Most of the differences in the alternative procedures relate to apparently differing prescriptions in these three respects.

It will be repeatedly emphasized in this paper that any substantive differences among the alternative procedures are in large part dependent upon differing assumptions about the relevant aspects of the economic environment in which the investment decisions are being made. One of the basic purposes of this paper will be to demonstrate that, *in principle,* most of the suggested procedures are

*From Deepak Lal, *Methods of Project Analysis: A Review,* World Bank Staff Occasional Papers No. 16, Johns Hopkins University Press, Baltimore, 1974, pp. xiii–xvii, 24–38. Reprinted by permission.

equivalent, if the same assumptions are made about the economic environment, though naturally there are differences in *emphasis* as to which set of assumptions is more relevant for LDC's in general, and more importantly in the *practical* problems of estimating the relevant values to be included in the *NPV/IRR* index, with accuracy and ease.

The reason why *in principle* most of the methods are equivalent, given the same basic assumptions about the economic environment, is their common lineage—theoretical welfare economics. One of its basic results is that in a perfectly competitive economy (with no uncertainty about future tastes and technology), allocation of resources on the basis of market prices of goods and factors (for which markets exist) would result in Pareto optimality for a given income distribution.[1] Market prices of goods and factors would equate and equal the marginal social cost *(MSC)* of producing and the marginal social value *(MSV)* of using the relevant goods/factors. For a truly marginal investment project (in the sense that it does not alter the *MSV*

---

[1]Pareto optimality necessitates that for a given distribution of income:

   (i) the marginal rates of transformation in production of different commodities are equal to their marginal rates of substitution in consumption.

   (ii) the marginal rates of substitution between any pair of factors are the same in all the industries in which they are used.

   (iii) the marginal rates of substitution of any pair of commodities is the same for all individuals consuming both goods.

Given that the above conditions hold, a Pareto optimum will exist, such that for the given income distribution it will not be possible to make one person better off without making someone else worse off. Treating the same physical commodity at different dates as many different commodities, equivalent intertemporal marginal equivalences for an efficient intertemporal program can be derived. See Dorfman, Samuelson and Solow [2].

and *MSC*'s of the output it produces and inputs it uses as a result of its operation), the values of the output and inputs at market prices would provide the correct values to be used in determining the net present value of the project.[2] Market prices would be the "shadow" prices to be used in project selection.

If the investment project being considered is not marginal (or if there are externalities), and does affect the *MSV* and *MSC*'s of its output and inputs, then the relevant measures of the social benefits and costs of the project will be the change in the consumers' and producers' surpluses caused by the project. This, in principle, will be the procedure recommended by *all* the project selection procedures we shall consider. In the case of the perfectly competitive model, valuation of the changes in producers' and consumers' surpluses, at market prices, will provide the correct indication of the net social benefits of the project.

To the extent, however, that the perfectly competitive paradigm does not hold—for example due to the existence of monopolies, taxes and subsidies, externalities, and/or increasing returns—market prices will no longer indicate the *social* costs and benefits of using and producing different commodities. The social cost to be included in the *NPV/IRR* index of social profitability, properly defined, will still be the marginal social cost of the various inputs used, and the social benefit will be the marginal social value of the output produced. However, the breakdown of the perfectly competitive assumptions results in market prices no longer equating and equaling the *MSC* and *MSV* of the relevant commodities. The market price will not equal either the *MSV* or *MSC*—and in some cases of rationing may not equal either. The problem then is to adjust the market price to obtain the relevant "shadow" prices,

which are therefore generally needed in investment appraisal because of the divergence between the *MSC* and *MSV* of the relevant commodities.

If neutral fiscal devices (lump-sum taxes and subsidies) are feasible, then a full Pareto optimum could still be achieved if the government eliminates the divergence between *MSC* and *MSV* by suitably corrective tax-subsidy measures, thereby restoring the equivalence of *MSC* and *MSV* with the market price of the commodity. However, for obvious reasons it will not be possible, in most cases, to cure the divergence in this manner. In that case, the divergence between the *MSC* and *MSV* of the commodity may have to be taken as a datum (or a constraint) and the "shadow" prices corresponding to this constrained (or "second-best") welfare optimum will need to be computed. A large number, if not most, of the shadow prices which we shall consider are of this "second-best" kind.

Second, even if the government can eliminate the divergence between *MSC*'s and *MSV*'s by suitable tax-subsidy policy, it may take time for the divergence to disappear. Then current market prices will not equate the *MSC* and *MSV* of the relevant commodities, but it is expected that future market prices will. As investment takes time and its effects are extended into the future, it is clearly the *MSC*'s and *MSV*'s of the relevant inputs/outputs appropriately dated which will be relevant in working out the project's social profitability. If it appears likely that in the future an existing divergence between *MSC* and *MSV* will be corrected, the appropriately dated price which reflects the social cost/benefit of the project will not be the current market price, nor the current *MSC* and *MSV* of the commodity, but rather the "equilibrium" price which is expected to prevail in the future. In this sense, even when an economy is moving towards an optimal set of market prices, from a distorted current set, it may be necessary to use "shadow" prices corresponding to the *future* optimal market prices, rather than the *current* market or shadow prices for pricing inputs and outputs

[2]The net benefits being discounted at the optimal discount rate which equates the marginal rate of transformation (*mrt*) in production of present into future consumption, to its marginal rate of indifferent substitution (*mrs*) in consumption, determined in a perfect market for intertemporal consumption.

which form the time stream of benefits and costs of the investment project.

Third, even for a perfectly competitive economy, there will be different Pareto optima associated with different income-distributions. Judging between these different Pareto optima will necessarily involve normative judgments about the desirability of particular income distributions.[3] Even if agreement can be reached on the desired income-distribution, there will still be the problem of legislating this "optimal" distribution. Again if neutral fiscal devices in the form of lump-sum taxes and subsidies are feasible, the government would be able to achieve a Pareto optimum with the optimal distribution of income. If however, as is more likely, neutral fiscal instruments are not available, then the distributional effects of investment projects will also have to be computed, and judged against and along with their purely "production" or "efficiency" effects. These problems open up other areas where there may possibly be conflicting judgments, and hence prescriptions for project selection procedures.

Practical Problems

These theoretical problems are compounded by practical ones. First, even though there may be agreement about the nature of the correct prices to be used in project selection, there may, nevertheless, be disagreement as to whether or not the existing divergences between *MSV*'s and *MSC*'s which affect these prices will continue into the future or whether they will change. Depending on what assumption is made about the future course of the economy, the "second-best" or "first-best" shadow price will be the relevant one to choose.[4] In a sense, this is an empirical

question; but to the extent that future government policies are normally unknown, the element of judgment involved in deciding which of these alternative assumptions is relevant, when considering existing distortions in commodity and factor markets, will be of paramount importance in deciding which is the correct "shadow" price to use. Hence it is important to remember that differing prescriptions on alternative evaluation procedures will most often be due to differing implicit assumptions about the current and, more importantly, the future economic environment.

Second, though we have been discussing the evaluation of a particular project and the social valuation of its inputs and outputs in what may appear to be a partial equilibrium framework, in principle, any proper investment criteria must take account of the total (direct and indirect) or what are termed the general equilibrium effects of the investment project. Thus for instance if an industrial project employs some seemingly underemployed labor in the urban sector, the ultimate effects via the impact on rural-urban migration could be a significant change in total output of the economy. The shadow wage rate will then in this case have to incorporate both the direct and indirect (via migration) effects of increasing industrial employment. The *MSC*'s and *MSV*'s which are taken as the "shadow" prices in determining the social profitability of the investment project, must therefore be the general equilibrium "shadow prices." This might appear to be an impossible task, but the relative merits of alternative investment appraisal procedures will depend upon their success in taking account of the general equilibrium effects of projects, which will in turn, if the procedures are to be *practical,* necessitate making certain simplifying assumptions about the economic environment. Once again, these assumptions, though empirical in nature, require judgment, and hence there can be disputes as to whether or not the simplifying assumptions are "realistic" or relevant or both.

For all the above reasons, even though all the procedures we will consider start from

[3]It being noted that investment projects affect both the intratemporal as well as the intertemporal distribution of income; the former by the distribution of their net benefits amongst contemporaries at a point in time, and the latter by the distribution of net benefits as between generations, over a period of time.

[4]The second-best shadow price is that associated with continuing divergences, the first-best, that with no divergence, between *MSV* and *MSC*.

the same theoretical foundations, and hence are identical if equivalent assumptions are made, they may nevertheless differ to the extent that, in practice, they emphasize one set of assumptions about the economic environment rather than another. Hence, the continuing charges and countercharges that a particular procedure has ignored or assumed away an important aspect of reality, and is hence invalid; as well as the impression conveyed to neutral observers of shadow pricing on the part of different protagonists, and bafflement at the conflicting claims and counterclaims that are made for different procedures. This, however, does not imply that in practice certain procedures are not more general and easier to apply than others. However, it may be more important to begin by realizing that the similarities amongst the procedures are far greater than the differences. . . .

DISTORTIONS IN FACTOR MARKETS

In this part we relax the assumption made that factor markets are perfectly competitive. We now introduce factor market distortions but, for simplicity and clarity, assume away all other distortions. Thus the domestic market prices of the two primary factors will no longer be taken to equal their *social* opportunity costs, as we had hitherto assumed. Distortions in both the markets for labor and capital have been discussed in the project evaluation literature. The two fully fledged evaluation procedures, the UNIDO and Little-Mirrlees procedures, identify the same distortions and, except for some differences in assumptions about the likely future changes in some of the divergences, provide identical rules in principle, except for a difference in numeraire. The UNIDO procedures take current consumption as their numeraire, the Little-Mirrlees current savings.[5]

Note that current savings generate the time stream of future consumption. As consumption, following the practice in theoretical welfare economics, is identified as the source of economic welfare, this means that the net benefits will be dated consumption, and there will be the problem of making commensurable present consumption and future consumption. As long as the same relative price between present and future consumption is used to "add up" the intertemporal net benefits of the project, it does not matter which of the two relevant "commodities" (present consumption or future consumption [savings]), we take as our numeraire.[6]

We turn first to examine the adjustments necessary to take account of the distortions in the market for capital.

Capital

Savings and investment are the means for changing the time shape of the intertemporal consumption stream which is feasible given resource and technological transformation constraints. The capital market intermediates between those making savings and investment decisions. In a perfect capital market, the social return from one unit of current savings (the net present value of the consumption stream made possible by one unit of current savings) at the margin, is equal to the social value of one unit of current consumption. The former will depend upon the opportunities open to society in production, to convert one unit of present consumption into future consumption—that is, the social productivity of investment—the latter on the weight society places on one unit of future consumption in terms of present consumption—the social rates of time preference. In a perfect capital market, the rate of interest R will equal and equate the marginal rate of transformation (mrt) of present into future consumption, and the marginal rate of indifferent substitution (mrs) of present and fu-

[5]More precisely the *LM* numeraire is "uncommitted social income measured at border prices." It need not be saved, but could be spent on uses (like administration, health, law and order, et cetera) which are considered as useful as savings by the government.

[6]The only difference will be the "cosmetic" one that the appropriate discount rate to be used with savings as the numeraire will generally be *higher* than that to be used with consumption as the numeraire.

ture consumption. That is, $R = mrt = mrs$, of the two "commodities" present and future consumption. Distortions in the capital market will drive a wedge between the components of the above marginal equivalence, so that $mrt \neq mrs$. Moreover, the rate of interest may not equal either the mrt or mrs. Furthermore, if the capital market is segmented, there may be a multiplicity of rates of interest.

Two basic sources of distortion have been identified as causing the divergence between the mrt and mrs of present and future consumption. One is due to the presence of externalities, the other to the presence of monopolistic or fiscal distortions or both in the capital market. We will consider the causes and adjustments for the former type of distortion, the causes of the latter type being self-evident, and the remedies being similar to those suggested for the former type.

The source of the externality in the capital market is due to the interdependence and the mortality of private savers. Being mortal, they cannot be expected to extend their altruism to the infinite generations which are properly the concern of a society, which at least in principle, is immortal. As a result, the savings (future consumption) generated, *ceteris paribus*, as a result of the decisions of private savers is likely to be less than socially optimal. Furthermore, *if* private savers knew that everyone else was going to save at the socially optimal rate, then they too would agree to save at this rate. Hence, the externality. The result is that the private rate of time preference is higher than the social. Under laissez faire, a perfect capital market would insure that enough savings would be invested until the social return to investment (savings) fell to the private rate of time preference. That is, the private marginal rate of substitution (mrs_p) in consumption would be equated to the private and *ex hypothesi, social*, marginal rate of transformation (mrt) in production, of present into future consumption. However, as the externality causes the marginal *private* rate of substitution to be higher than the marginal *social* rate of substitution (mrs,) we have $mrs_p = mrt > mrs$.

Once again the first best solution would be to cure the above divergence, by appropriate tax-subsidy policy; in this case by using fiscal policy to raise the savings rate in the economy till mrs_p and mrt had become equal to mrs. Note that as the savings level is raised toward the optimal level, mrs will rise and mrs_p and mrt will fall.

However, the government may have imperfect control over savings in the economy, and may not be able to legislate the optimal savings rate by direct fiscal means. In that case, it will be necessary to take account of the divergence in the mrt and mrs in the capital market. As long as the divergence exists, current savings are socially more valuable than current consumption. Hence, if the government can indirectly, through its choice of projects, influence the savings rate, this "savings constraint" may be overcome over time till savings and consumption are considered to be equally socially valuable. The way in which the government could influence the savings-consumption balance of the economy through project choice is by influencing the choice of techniques and by choosing projects whose benefits tend to be saved and reinvested rather than consumed.

The way in which both the UNIDO and *LM* [Little-Mirrlees] procedures take account of the divergence is by differentially weighting the project's net benefits which are consumed and those which are saved. *The only difference between the procedures in principle is the difference in numeraires.* Whereas (a) the UNIDO procedures use *present consumption* as the numeraire, and put a *premium on savings*, (b) the *LM* procedures use *current savings* as the numeraire, and *penalize consumption*. To see this, consider the following simple algebraic example.

Algebraic Example: First, consider the procedure adopted in the UNIDO *Guidelines*, which take *consumption as its numeraire*. Assume that the net benefits from a project in any year (t) are Bt, and that of these 0 percent in any year are saved and reinvested and $(1 - 0)$ percent are consumed. The social rate of time preference today is d_0, and the social return to investment today is

r_0 ($r_0 > d_0$). Moreover, over time, the divergence between r and d is likely to diminish, till T years from today the divergence will disappear (the level of savings will be optimal). Finally, the project incurs capital costs of K in the base year, yielding the stream of net benefits for N years.

To obtain the social profitability of the project we first note that the opportunity cost of the capital costs K is the present value of the future consumption which would have resulted if Rs K of present investment were made at the current social rate of return to investment, r_0. Thus, if Rs 1 of current investment, which is assumed to remain intact forever, leads to net output of Rs 1.1 in the next period, $r_0 = 1.1/1 = .1$. Part of this return (θ) will be saved and invested. Hence, the increase in investment next year ($t = 1$) will be $[1\ (1 + r_0) - 1]\theta = r_0\theta$. Total investment next year will therefore be $(1 + r_0\theta)$. The year after next ($t = 2$) investment will increase by $[(1 + r_0\theta)(1 + r_1) - (1 + r_0\theta)]\theta = (1 + r_0\theta)r_1\theta$. Total investment in year $t = 2$ will therefore be $[(1 + r_0\theta)r_1y\theta + (1 + r_0\theta)] = (1 + r_0\theta)(1 + r_1\theta)$. Hence, by year T, when the savings constraint ceases to operate, total investment would have accumulated to: $(1 + r_0\theta)(1 + r_1\theta)\ldots(1 + r_{T-1}\theta)$. To get the present value of this accumulated investment which, *ex hypothesi*, is as valuable as an equal amount of consumption at T, we have to discount its value back to the present ($t = 0$) at the changing social rates of time preference ($d_0, d_1, d_2, \ldots d_T$), period by period. This present value is:

$$(1 + r_0\theta)(1 + r_1\theta)\ldots(1 + r_{T-1}\theta)/ \atop (1 + d_1)(1 + d_2)\ldots(1 + d_T) \qquad (1)$$

In addition to this accumulated investment, the initial Rs 1 of investment will have resulted in consumption of $(1 - \theta)(1 + r_0\theta)$ in $t = 1$; of $(1 - \theta)(1 + r_0\theta)(1 + r_1\theta)$ in $t = 2$; and hence in year t of $(1 - \theta)(1 + r_0\theta)(1 + r_1\theta)\ldots(1 + r_{t-1}\theta)$. The present value of this stream of consumption is:

$$\sum_{t=0}^{T} \frac{(1 - \theta)(1 + r_0\theta)\ldots(1 + r_{t-2}\theta)(1 + r_{t-1}\theta)}{(1 + d_1)\ldots(1 + d_{t-1})(1 + d_t)} \qquad (2)$$

Confining our time horizon to T, the present value of the stream of consumption made possible by Rs 1 of investment today (s_0) is then:

$$s_0 = (1) + (2) \qquad (3)$$

The social opportunity costs of capital expenditure of K today are therefore s_0K.

The benefits are B_t in year (t), of which θB_t will be saved and invested. The value of this saving in terms of consumption at date t will be given by the social opportunity cost of investment in year t, which on an analogous argument to that for deriving s_0, will be s_t. The rest of the benefits $(1 - \theta)B_t$ will be consumed in year t. Hence, the present value of the stream of net benefits will be given by:

$$\sum_{t=0}^{N} \frac{(1 - \theta)B_t + s_t\theta B_t}{(1 + d_1(1 + d_2)\ldots(1 + d_t)} \qquad (4)$$

and the *NPV* of the project will be given by:

$$NPV = (4) - s_0K \qquad (5)$$

Thus on the "generalized" UNIDO procedures[7] it is necessary to know both the changing social return to investment (the r_t's) as well as the changing social rates of discount (the d_t's). Moreover, the discount rate used to obtain the *NPV* of the project will be the social discount rates d_t's.

The alternative *LM procedure* takes *savings as its numeraire*, and uses the own rate of return on investment (called the accounting rate of interest, *ARI*) as the discount rate. However, as we will show, it is identical to the "generalized" UNIDO procedures, except for the change in numeraire. Following the same argument as before, and making the same assumptions, we found that Rs 1 of investment yielded a present value of total future consumption generated by the investment of s_0. That is, Rs 1 of current savings

---

[7]"Generalized" because, as the next section explains, the way in which s is calculated on the UNIDO *Guidelines* assumes that its value remains constant over time. This, in practice, is likely to be an implausible assumption. But as the above account suggests, the UNIDO approach can be generalized, so that it is identical to the *LM* one, except for the change in numeraire.

(investment) is worth s_0 of present consumption. Consumption therefore has $(1/s_0)$ the value if the same resources had been invested. In year 1, therefore, the value of $(1 - \theta)(1 + r_0\theta)$ consumption generated is $(1 - \theta)(1 + r_0\theta)/s_1$. In year t, the value of the consumption generated from the net benefits of the project will be $B_t(1 - \theta)/s_t$.

In each year there will also be yB_t savings generated, and these will be valuable at par, as savings is our numeraire. The total value, in terms of savings of the net benefits in any year, will then be:

$$B_t(1 - \theta)/s_t + \theta B_t$$

These total savings benefits in each year have then to be discounted back to the present at the accounting rate of interest, $(ARI)(p_t)$[8] in each period to get the present savings value of the project. Hence, the NPV of the project on the LM procedures will be given by:

$$NPV = \sum_{t=0}^{N}$$

$$\frac{B_t(1 - \theta)/s_t + \theta B_t}{(1 - p_1) \ldots (1 + p_{t-1})(1 + p_t)} - K$$

(6)

Note that, as savings is our numeraire, the capital costs K incurred in year 0 are valued at par.

Moreover, the LM Manual derives a relationship between p_t, s_t, and d_t. It is:

$$s_t/s_{t+1} = (1 + p_t)/(1 + d_t) \qquad (7)$$

Now consider a two period case, that is from $t = 0$ to $t - 1$. For the project to be acceptable on the LM criterion, the NPV given by (6) should be positive, that is:

$$\frac{B_1 [(1 - \theta)(1/s_1) + \theta]}{(1 + p_1)} \geq K \qquad (8)$$

[8]Thus, if say Rs 1 of investment today leads to a net return of Rs 0.1 tomorrow, of which half (.05) is saved and invested, and if consumption has no social value in terms of the numeraire savings, then the ARI is $.05/1 = .05$. If on the other hand, consumption and savings are considered socially equally valuable, then the ARI would be $.1/1 = 0.1$. In general if the value of one unit of consumption in terms of savings is $1/s$, the ARI in this example will be $(.05 + .05/s)$.

Multiplying both sides of (8) by s_1, and then dividing both sides by $s \sqrt{s_0}$, we get:

$$\frac{B_1 [(1 - \theta) + \theta s_1]}{s_1/s_0 \cdot (1 + p_1)} \geq s_0 K \qquad (9)$$

From (7) the denominator of the LHS of (9) is equal to $(1 + d_1)$, hence, we get (9) equal to:

$$\frac{B_1 [(1 - \theta) + \theta s_1]}{(1 + d_1)} \geq s_0 K \qquad (10)$$

as the criterion for accepting a project on the LM procedure.

But now consider the same two period case on the UNIDO procedures; the acceptance criterion is that the NPV given by (5) be positive; and it can be seen from (4) and (5) that this gives the identical result (10) as the criterion of acceptability. Hence, the two procedures LM and UNIDO are identical in terms of the information needed to take account of suboptimal savings. The differences in the discount rates on the two procedures (the ARI on the LM, the social rate of discount on the UNIDO) merely reflect a change in numeraire.

LM and UNIDO in Practice: To show the equivalence in principle of the two procedures, in the above algebraic example, we had assumed that the value of s is calculated on the UNIDO procedures on the LM assumption that savings and consumption will be equally valuable T years from today. In practice, however, the formula given by UNIDO to calculate the value of s assumes that the divergence in the relative social value of aggregate consumption and savings, and hence the value of s, remains constant till infinity. Thus the UNIDO formula for calculating s is:

$$s = (1 - \theta)r/(d - \theta r),$$

where s = marginal propensity to save
r = rate of return on investment
d = social rate of discount of consumption

This equation will only provide meaningful values if $d > \theta r$, otherwise the social value of investment (s) will be infinite. There is no plausible economic reason why d must necessarily be greater than θr.[9] Moreover, the actual value of s given by the formula will be very sensitive to the values chosen for d, θ and r, and small differences in the values of these variables could lead to large differences in the value of s.

The assumption of a constant divergence in the relative social values of aggregate consumption and savings, and hence a constant s, must therefore be rejected in favor of the more plausible LM assumption that this divergence disappears after T years and hence s will typically fall over time to a value of unity at T.[10]

Finally, it should be emphasized that both procedures require information on the social rate of discount and the social rate of return to investment in the economy. We therefore next examine how these parameters can be estimated.

Estimating the Intertemporal Parameters:[11] The LM Manual gives a formula[12] relating the ARI_0 (p_0), and the social discount rate (d_0) to s_0 and T. This is:

$$s_0 = [1 + \tfrac{1}{2}(p_0 - d_0)]^T \qquad (11)$$

Given the definition of the ARI:

$$p_0 = r_0 [\theta + (1 - \theta)/s_0] \qquad (12)$$

Hence, substituting (12) into (11) we have:

$$s_0 = \{1 + \tfrac{1}{2}[r_0 (\theta + (1 - \theta)/s_0) - d_0]\}^T \qquad (13)$$

This formula succinctly expresses the various intertemporal parameters we need to estimate. These are r_0, d_0, T and θ; and given these s_0 will be determined.

The social return to investment is r_0 and θ is the percentage of this return saved; r_0 will thus be the return at accounting prices from marginal current investments. On certain plausible assumptions,[13] this return can be derived as a weighted average of social rates of profits on existing investments in the economy. θ, can be estimated from data on savings propensities and tax rates.

This leaves d_0, the social discount rate, and T the date when savings and consumption are expected to be equally valuable, to be estimated.

The social discount rates (d_t) reflect the distributional weighting given to income (consumption) transfers between generations. In determining these weights it is plausible to assume that as a result of the normal processes of growth, future generations will in any case be richer than present ones. Just how much richer will depend upon the expected rate of growth in per capita consumption over the future. Suppose the latter rate is g. Further assume that the elasticity of social marginal utility (defined as the percentage change in social utility resulting from a percentage change in consumption) with respect to per capita changes in consumption is e. Then it can be shown[14] that

$$d_t = (1 + g_t)^e - 1 \qquad (14)$$

This leaves T, which is rather harder to determine. However, from projections of expected growth rates of national income and savings, it may be possible to arrive at some estimate of the likely date by which savings are likely to be sufficient to give an adequate long term growth rate. This date can then be taken to be T.

---

[9]Thus Maurice Scott points out that "one could argue that d should be zero in Mauritius (with per capita consumption roughly constant) while s and r are both positive."

[10]Another consequence of assuming a constant s ($s_t = s_t + 1$) is that from (7) above the discount rate ($p_t = d_t$) is the same on both LM and UNIDO procedures.

[11]A fuller discussion is contained in Lal [11].

[12]See Little and Mirrlees [14], p. 179, and Lal [10], Appendix 11.

[13]See Lal [11] for the derivation of such a rate from a heterogenous capital dual economy model which avoids the capital theoretic problems arising from derivations based on aggregate production functions. This method is also similar to that advocated by Harberger; see his *Project Evaluation: Collected Papers*, Chicago, 1972. For an application of the method, see Lal [10], Appendix 11.

[14]Assuming a constant elasticity social utility function (U) which has per capita consumption (C) as one of its arguments, then $U = C^e$, and $d_t = (U_t^t / U_{t+1}^t)C$, and $g = (C_{t+1} - C_t)/C_t$. Hence $d_t = (1 + g)^e - 1$.

Labor[15]

One of the most common forms of distortion identified in the project evaluation literature is in the labor markets of surplus labor economies, such that the wage rate does not equal the social opportunity cost of labor in the economy.

Two components have been traditionally identified in the social opportunity cost of labor in surplus labor economies. The *first* is the output foregone elsewhere in the economy, as a result of employing labor on the project. The *second* are the costs in terms of increased aggregate consumption that may result as more labor (which consumes most of its income) is employed on the project. If, due to the nonoptimality of savings (discussed above), present consumption is socially less valuable than current savings, then any increase in aggregate consumption, caused by increasing employment as a result of the project, will not be as valuable as the equivalent amount of savings. This factor will have to be reflected in the measure of the social opportunity cost of labor.

To concretize this, consider a particular formulation of the social opportunity cost of labor, that is, the shadow wage rate *(SWR)*, due to *LM.* Except for a change in numeraire, which *LM* take to be "savings" rather than consumption, their analysis is similar to other well-known ones due to Sen and Marglin, and which have been incorporated in the UNIDO procedures.

Assume first that the wage paid to a laborer in his new job, *c,* is above the value of the output foregone elsewhere by moving him from his previous employment, *m.* Second, given the nonoptimality of savings, and taking savings as the numeraire, one unit of current consumption is socially worth $(1/s)$ units of current savings. *The s factor is the same as in the discussion of capital in the previous section.* Then, the costs of employing one more person in the economy (in terms of savings) are given by:

$$SWR = m + (c - m)$$
$$- (c - m)/s \quad (15)$$

[15]This section is based on Lal [9], where a fuller treatment of the subject may be found.

The first term on the *RHS* is the output foregone elsewhere in the economy, which has been traditionally identified with the marginal product of labor in agriculture. In addition, assuming that workers in both industry and agriculture consume all their incomes, the economy will be committed to providing them with extra consumption of $(c - m)$ as $c > m$. This increase in aggregate consumption must be at the expense of aggregate savings given the well-known Keynesian national income identities. But given the non-optimality of savings, this increase in aggregate consumption (decrease in savings) must represent a social cost. As, *ex hypothesi,* society values s units of consumption as equal in social value to one unit of savings, the net social cost of the increase in consumption (in terms of the numeraire, savings) will be

$$(c - m) - (c - m)/s$$

which are the second and third terms of (15). The above expression reduces to:

$$SWR = c - (c - m)/s \quad (16)$$

We now turn to the determination of the output foregone (m), and various other complications in determining the *SWR,* in the following sections.

Output Foregone: In most conventional analyses the output foregone m, in the above *SWR* formulation, has been identified with the marginal product of the relevant labor in its previous employment. While this would, given certain other assumptions to be discussed, be correct for labor which was previously in wage employment, it may not in general be correct for labor which was previously self-employed. This is an important consideration, in view of the fact that in most developing countries a substantial portion of the labor force is self-employed.

Moreover, in most conventional analyses it was also assumed that the marginal product of the laborer withdrawn from the traditional sector, agriculture, would be zero and hence $m = 0$. In a definitive analysis of dualism and surplus labor within a model of family farms on which there is equal work and income sharing, and which explicitly incorporated leisure as an argument in the individual peasant's utility function, Sen demonstrated that zero marginal productivity was not a necessary condition for the existence of surplus labor. [See selection III.A.3.] The necessary and sufficient conditions are given by a constant disutility of effort, which implies a constant marginal rate of substitution between income and leisure over the relevant range of hours worked per man, in the traditional sector. Given this, output in the traditional sector would not fall with the withdrawal of workers, and hence for them $m = 0$, even though the marginal productivity of labor was positive in the traditional sector. Thus, in general, for a family farm worker withdrawn from a farm without any hired labor, the change in output will not equal his marginal product.

Divergence Between Average and Marginal Costs: Certain writers have noted that the conventional analysis may *understate* the extra consumption cost of industrial labor. This is due to the assumption made in these analyses that "agricultural" workers can be hired by the "industrial" sector at a constant real wage *(Wi),* which is either given by a constant institutional wage, or else by a constant supply price of labor to the industrial sector. Dixit [1] suggests that this assumption may be unrealistic, especially if there are terms of trade effects following a withdrawal of labor from agriculture. Then, if the industrial labor market is competitive, the supply price of labor to industry and hence the industrial wage will rise with increased industrial employment.[16] This will create a diver-

gence between the *average* (c) and *marginal* $(c + \Delta c)$ cost of hiring industrial labor. The extra consumption the economy will be committed to will then be given by the difference between the *marginal* cost of hiring $(c + \Delta c)$ and output foregone, m.

Hence:

$$SWR = (c + \Delta c) - (c + \Delta c - m)/s \quad (17)$$

and if the premium placed on savings is very high $(s \to \infty)$, the *SWR* will be higher than the market wage (c). Note, however, that if there is a constant institutional wage in the industrial sector, then $c = 0$, and the *SWR* will be given as before by (16).

Rural-Urban Migration: As certain models of the labor market in developing countries have emphasized, the impact on net output in the economy cannot be deduced from the impact effects on output in the sector from which the new worker may be withdrawn. Hence, to obtain the value of m, it will be necessary to trace through all the indirect effects, in terms of the rural-urban migration that may ensue, as the result of creating one new job in, say, the industrial sector. Thus, if, for instance, we have, say, a laborer A moving to the project and his wage in his previous employment was $\$w$, and on his moving to the project his previous job is filled by someone else, B, who in turn moves from a job which paid him $\$Y$ $(w > Y)$, then the change in output (assuming that the two wage rates are determined in competitive markets for hired labor) by employing A on the project is not $\$w$ but $\$Y$, as now the first round effect of A's migration—a fall of output of $\$w$ in his previous employment—is offset by a rise in output in his previous activity by an equivalent amount when the other worker B replaced him, but which now results in the loss of output as a result of B's movement from his initial job to A's previous job of $\$Y$.

Furthermore, as a result of creating one more job in the "industrial" sector, more than one migrant may move from rural areas. If N people migrate, and the change in agricultural output as a result of one person's mi-

---

[16]In the simple closed economy two-sector model analyzed by Dixit [1], the supply price of industrial labor is equal to the income foregone by agricultural family workers moving to industrial jobs. In short run equilibrium their income foregone is determined by the average physical product of labor in agriculture (assuming equal income sharing among family farm workers) and the relative price of agriculture output. With the withdrawal of an agricultural worker, the average product of labor in agriculture rises, while total agricultural output (assuming no surplus labor) falls. This last factor leads to a rise in the relative price of agricultural output. The net effect is to raise the average value product of labor in agriculture and hence the supply price of labor to the industrial sector.

gration is Y, then the

$$SWR = c - (c - NY)/s \qquad (18)$$

Harberger [5] has used one particular model of rural-urban migration due to Harris-Todaro [7], to derive the SWR as always equal to the market wage c. This is obtained as follows. Harris-Todaro assume that there is *no* surplus labor in agriculture. The migrants come to the cities because the expected income in the urban sector is just equal to the income they forego in agriculture. The expected urban income is determined by the probability (P) of finding urban employment at the industrial wage c, which, in the Harris-Todaro model, is determined by the equilibrium ratio of employed to the total labor force in the cities, say P.[17] Furthermore, it is assumed that agricultural workers receive their marginal product (say a). At the margin, therefore, migrant workers will equate their marginal product (incomes) in agriculture, a, to the expected wage in towns, Pc (that is, $a = Pc$). When one more man is hired by the industrial sector the expected wage Pc rises as P rises. This induces rural-urban migration of $1/P$ workers, which restores the probability of finding a job in the urban sector to P, and the expected income to the equilibrium level Pc—when rural-urban migration ceases. Hence in expression (18) $N = 1/P$. Moreover, the "equilibrium" value of P is a/c (given the migration function $a = Pc$), and as the output foregone per

migrant on Harris-Todaro assumptions is the marginal product a, we have:

$$m = NY = (1/P)a = c$$

Substitution in expressions (16) or (18) yields $SWR = c$, the industrial wage. However, as has been pointed out above, in general it cannot be assumed that the change in output in the agricultural sector will equal the marginal product of labor. In that case, the change in output m within the Harris-Todaro migration model will be given by Y/P, where Y is the change in output in agriculture when one worker is withdrawn. As before we have $a = Pc$ (where a is the income the worker received in agriculture, which on a family farm would be equal to the average product of the farm if we assume equal income and work sharing on family farms). Hence $m = Y/P = Y$. Then c/a and the SWR given a Harris-Todaro-type migration function will be:

$$SWR = c - c(1 - Y/a)/s$$

From this it is obvious that, on the special Harris-Todaro assumption that $Y = a$, the SWR will equal c, the industrial wage. This is the Harberger derivation of the SWR, in his "Panama" example (see [6], p. 568 and following). More important, however, the Harris-Todaro-Harberger migration model is also restrictive in many other respects, some of which are more serious than others. First, it implicitly assumes that industrial wage earners have tenure, as the rate of labor turnover in industry does not figure in their determination of P. Empirically, this assumption may not be too inaccurate, as the rate of labor turnover does not seem to be very high in the industrial sector in most developing countries. Second, they consider the migration decision as a one-period decision, whereas strictly it should be a multi-period decision in which the present value of the costs of migration should at the margin be equal to the present value of the benefits from migration.[18] If, however, as seems likely, most migrants have a fairly high subjective

---

[17]See Harris and Todaro [7], p. 128. This is also the assumption made by Harberger [5], p. 570. This formulation of P is unrealistic. A more likely determinant of P is given by the number of vacancies occurring per unit of time divided by the number of candidates for those vacancies, that is, the urban unemployed. The latter in fact was the determinant of P in the earlier Todaro formulation (see [18], p. 142). But note that while these differing determinants of P will affect the "equilibrium urban unemployment" rate (which is the chief concern of other writers on rural-urban migration), the *"equilibrium" value* of P will be invariant to these alternative formulations of its determinants, as it will be determined by the rural-urban income differential. (In our formulation above, the equilibrium $P = a/c$.). For a fuller discussion see Lal [9].

[18]Todaro [18], p. 143, fn. 10, notes this.

rate of time preference (fairly short time horizon), then the use of a single period migration decision function may not be invalid. Third, Harris-Todaro do not incorporate any of the costs of migration (real and/or "psychic")[19] nor the relatively higher costs of urban living which the migrant would have to incur in their migration function. Finally, and most important, their migration model fails to take account of the existence of a fairly competitive "unorganized" (services and small industry) sector urban labor market with high labor turnover and easy entry for new workers, which is typical of many developing countries, and which provides some income to the migrants while they are searching for an "organized" (industrial) sector job at the high institutional wage c.

Thus it is essentially the last two features which need to be incorporated into a more general migration function. To derive the SWR for this more general migration model, we continue to assume that industrial wage earners can be taken to have tenure, and that a one-period decision model is a fair approximation to reality. However, we now assume that in addition to the agricultural income foregone, a, the migrant has to incur migration costs of d, which include both the real and "psychic" costs of migrating. Furthermore, if the migrant does not succeed in obtaining an industrial sector job at the high institutional wage of c, he can nevertheless find some employment in the "unorganized" urban labor market and derive an income w. Finally, we assume that by living in the town the migrant has to incur a relatively higher cost of living than in rural areas of u to maintain the same standard of living as he enjoyed in the countryside. If the chances of getting an "organized" (industrial) sector job are as before P, then at the margin the migrant will equate the costs of migration, which are given by $(a + d + u)$ with the expected benefits, $[Pc + (1 - P)w]$; that is, in equilibrium:

$$a + d + u = Pc + (1 - P)w$$

[19]Though Harris-Todaro note the existence of these costs, see their [7], p. 129, fn. 8.

This yields the "equilibrium" value of $P = (a + d + u - w)/(c - w)$.

As before, with the creation of an extra industrial sector job $N = 1/P$ migrants will move from agriculture, and as the output foregone per migrant in agriculture is Y, we have the total output foregone, $m = Y \cdot (c - w)/(a + d + u - w)$, and the

$$SWR = c - [c - Y \cdot (c - w)/(a + d + u - w)]/s \quad (19)$$

and in this more general and more realistic migration model, the conclusion drawn by Harberger that the institutionally given industrial wage c, is the shadow wage, will not be valid.

Disutility of Effort: Finally, in addition to changes in output, there will also be changes in the aggregate disutility of effort (E) with increased employment. To evaluate these, assume initially that there are no imperfections in the labor market. Then, at the margin, utility maximizing workers will equate the disutility of increased effort with the utility from the increased incomes (which we assume are all consumed) this extra work makes possible. That is, the extra disutility of effort (E) must equal the change in workers' consumption (including those left behind on the farm) which is given by $(c - m)$—the difference between the industrial wage (assuming the new job is in industry, and the worker moves to it from agriculture) and the total output foregone by employing one more man in the industrial sector. The value in terms of savings of this change in disutility of effort (which so far is in terms of consumption equivalents) is $(c - m)/s$. If the value society places on the disutility of effort is λ, then the SWR incorporating the costs of the disutility of effort will be:

$$SWR = c - (c - m)/s + \lambda(c - m)/s \\ = c - (c - m)(1 - \lambda)/s \quad (20)$$

Next relax the assumption that all labor markets are competitive, and assume that there is an institutional wage, c, in the sector to which the labor is moving which is above the supply price of labor L. The latter term includes all the private disutilities that may attach to the new job. Our earlier expression for the consumption equivalent of the net change in disutility $(c - m)$ will now be overstating the true change in disutility by $(c - L)$, which is the difference between the institutional wage c, and the supply price of labor L. The net change in disutilities in this more general case will therefore be given by $(c - m) - (c - L) = (L - m)$, and as before the value in terms of savings will be $(L - m)/s$, and the

$$SWR = c - (c - m)/s \\ + \lambda(L - m)/s \quad (21)$$

If $\lambda = 0$, that is, society places no value on the change in the private disutilities of effort, we get the traditional SWR as in (16) above. If, however, it is assumed that society should value disutilities of effort at their private costs, then $\lambda = 1$, and the

$$SWR = L + (c - L)(1 - 1/s) \quad (22)$$

The first term is the supply price of labor, the second is the value in terms of savings, of the extra consumption generated by the excess of the institutional wage over the supply price of labor. Thus, when $\lambda = 1$, we get the standard neoclassical result, that the SWR will be the supply price of labor, if there is no divergence between the social value of present consumption and savings, that is $s = 1$; and furthermore, that if $c = L$, that is, if labor markets are competitive, the SWR will equal the market wage c, no matter what the value of s, and irrespective of any divergence between m (the output foregone elsewhere in the economy) and the industrial wage c.

Alternative Formulations of the SWR: We can now, very succinctly, compare the various alternative SWR's that have been suggested in the literature.[20]

First, there is the view due to Galenson-Leibenstein [4] and Dobb [3] that the SWR *is the market wage;* that is, $SWR = c$. For

this to be the case, *either $c = m = L$, or $m = 0$, $s \to \infty$, $\lambda = 0$, or $E = 0$.*

Second, there is the view associated with Kahn [8] and Lewis [12] that the $SWR = 0$. For this to be the case: $m = 0$, $s = 1$, $\lambda = 0$, or $E = 0$.

Third, for Sen [17], Marglin [15] and to some extent UNIDO [19], the $SWR = c - c/s$. For this to be valid: $m = 0$, $\lambda = 0$, or $E = 0$.

Fourth, the LM [14] SWR is given by (16) above, $SWR = c - (c - m)/s$. For this to be valid: $\lambda = 0$. As they assume a positive marginal product in agriculture, E cannot be zero.

Finally, for Harberger [6], the *SWR is the supply price of labor L;* that is, $SWR = L$. For this to be valid: either $\lambda = 1$, $c = L$, or $s = 1$.

Part of the differences relate to empirical matters, that is, the value of m and E. But, in part, the differences relate to two value parameters, s and λ. The reasons why it may be necessary to take $s > 1$ have been given in the section on capital above. A number of reasons have been advanced by the present author, why it may also be desirable to assume that $\lambda = 0$, for developing countries.[21] However, the values assigned to these parameters must be in the nature of value judgments, and hence the possibility of conflicting advice on the different procedures. However, as this section has tried to show, if the same assumptions and value judgments are made, the alternative procedures will give identical answers, based upon the general expression for the SWR provided by (21) above.

References

[1] A. K. Dixit, "Short-Run Equilibrium and Shadow Prices in the Dual Economy." *Oxford Economic Papers* 23 (1971):384–400.

[2] R. Dorfman, P. A. Samuelson, and R. M. Solow, *Linear Programming and Economic Analysis,* New York: McGraw Hill (Rand Series), 1958.

---

[20]As most writers have not included rural-urban migration in their models for determining the SWR, this aspect is neglected in this section. The previous section has already dealt with the SWR's derived or derivable from the Harris-Todaro-Harberger-type models and a model developed in Lal [9].

[21]See Lal [9].

[3] M. H. Dobb, *An Essay on Economic Growth and Planning.* London: Routledge & Paul, 1960.

[4] W. Galenson and H. Leibenstein, "Investment Criteria, Productivity and Economic Development." *Quarterly Journal of Economics* LXIX (1955): 343–70.

[5] A. C. Harberger, "Survey of Literature on Cost-Benefit Analysis for Industrial Project Evaluation" in *Evaluation of Industrial Projects.* New York: United Nations (UNIDO), 1968.

[6] A. C. Harberger, "The Social Opportunity Cost of Labour." *International Labour Review* 103 (1971): 559–79.

[7] J. R. Harris and M. P. Todaro, "Migration, Unemployment and Development: A Two-Sector Analysis." *American Economic Review* LX (1970): 126–42.

[8] A. K. Kahn, "Investment Criteria in Development Programs." *Quarterly Journal of Economics* LXV (1951): 38–61.

[9] D. Lal, "Disutility of Effort, Migration and the Shadow Wage Rate." *Oxford Economic Papers* 25 (1973): 112–26.

[10] D. Lal, *Wells and Welfare.* Paris: Organization for Economic Cooperation and Development, 1972.

[11] D. Lal, "On Estimating Certain Intertemporal Parameters for Project Analysis." IBRD mimeograph. Washington, D.C., 1973.

[12] W. A. Lewis, "Economic Development with Unlimited Supplies of Labour." *Manchester School of Economics and Social Sciences* 22 (1954): 139–91.

[13] I. M. D. Little and J. A. Mirrlees, *Manual of Industrial Project Analysis in Developing Countries, Volume II: Social Cost-Benefit Analysis.* Paris: Organization for Economic Cooperation and Development, 1968.

[14] I. M. D. Little and J. A. Mirrlees, "A Reply to Some Criticisms of the OECD Manual." *Bulletin of Oxford University Institute of Economics and Statistics* 34 (1972): 153–68.

[15] S. A. Marglin, *Public Investment Criteria,* Cambridge, Mass.: MIT Press, 1967.

[16] A. K. Sen, "Peasants and Dualism With and Without Surplus Labor." *Journal of Political Economy* LXXIV (1966): 425–50.

[17] A. K. Sen, *Choice of Techniques, An Aspect of the Theory of Planned Economic Development.* 3rd ed. Oxford: B. Blackwell, 1968.

[18] M. P. Todaro, "A Model of Labor Migration and Urban Development in Less Developed Countries." *American Economic Review* LIX (1969): 138–48.

[19] United Nations Industrial Development Organization [P. Dasgupta, A. Sen, and S. Marglin], *Guidelines for Project Evaluation.* New York: United Nations, 1972.

X.C.2. Derivation of Shadow Prices*

In many economies market prices do not reflect the real scarcity values of the goods and services that are being produced. Monopolies, decreasing cost industries, taxes, exter-

nalities, foreign exchange and capital scarcities, unemployment and underemployment, government fixation of prices and wages, inflation, and so on, are common in most of the developed as well as the developing countries.

Is it at all possible, in view of the many difficulties, to determine all the relevant shadow prices? It has been suggested that they should be derived from general programming

*From F. L. C. H. Helmers, "Cost-Benefit Analysis," paper prepared for IMF Seminar, June 9, 1980, Washington, D.C. (processed). Reprinted by permission.

models. Such models can generate Lagrangean multipliers that represent in economic terms the shadow prices, which, given the constraints incorporated in the model, will result in an allocation of resources that will satisfy the postulated objective function. Such models should, in principle, be able to produce the real scarcity prices of the goods and services. However, although the models can provide valuable insights concerning the structural relations that exist in an economy, we seriously question on practical grounds whether all the shadow prices obtained from the models can be used for operational work. First, the models are still highly aggregated so that most of the duals they generate—the shadow prices—are extremely crude. Second, it must seriously be doubted whether the models can really depict the real world situation. It is not only that there are many distortions but also, to formulate the models, all cost and demand functions should be known. Obviously it is impossible to collect all these data. We feel, therefore, that in addition to the models approach a more practical approach must be followed.

In fact, this approach—the opportunity cost doctrine—has existed for a long time. Consider an economy where only two goods—X and Y are produced. Then the calculation of the costs of an output expansion would not pose a difficult problem. For instance, if the production of X is to be increased, the cost of producing the additional quantity of X is to be found by measuring the value of the Y goods that the community will have to give up in order to increase the production of X. Analysis of the production and demand functions for goods X and Y should readily provide the required data. The situation is more complicated when a multiplicity of goods is being produced, since it will obviously be impossible to analyze the production functions and demand curves of all the different goods. The opportunity cost doctrine therefore takes as a starting point the inputs which X uses rather than the displaced Y goods and defines the costs of these inputs as the returns that they would earn in the next best alternative elsewhere.

The opportunity cost approach is necessarily a detailed approach. The project analyst must investigate from where the resources for a project will be withdrawn and what their values are in those uses. As long as resources with low valued uses can be transferred to higher valued uses, the change is beneficial. This, in a nutshell, is what the theory of project planning is all about.

Without any claim for comprehensiveness, we may now illustrate how the shadow prices can be found in practice. When a project needs a certain input, then it is likely that to some extent demand elsewhere will be curtailed as well as that some additional quantities will be produced to satisfy the additional demand generated by the project. Thus the opportunity cost of the input consists of the weighted average of the value foregone in the alternative use and the resource cost of the additional production, the weights being the fractions of demand displaced and supply induced to additional demand. What will happen in practice depends on the shape of the demand and cost functions and theoretically the analyst needs therefore to investigate these functions in detail. In real life, however, it often suffices to make some rough estimates as the project may not be sensitive to the value of the input in question.

Foreign exchange is for many countries such a scarce resource that it can be treated as a separate production factor. To determine the shadow price of foreign exchange, we apply the same analysis as for an input. We should thus consider how an additional dollar of foreign exchange can be obtained and then determine the real resource values in the foregone uses. In principle, there are two ways to obtain foreign exchange: curtail imports or increase exports.

In case of a curtailment of imports, the shadow price of foreign exchange can be found by comparing the domestic value of the import with its c.i.f. value converted at the official exchange rate. Hence, if there are no quantitative restrictions, this value will be higher than the official exchange value by the amount of the import duties. Thus if the official exchange rate is U.S. $1.00 = Rs 2.00

and the import duties are 30 percent, the domestic value of U.S. $1.00 of foreign exchange is Rs 2.60.

If exports are to be increased, then the resources otherwise used to produce homegoods will be used to produce export goods. Hence, the shadow price of foreign exchange consists then of the resource value of the foregone homegoods. If there are no restrictions on exports, the level of the export duties or subsidies will provide us with a good indicator of the domestic value. For instance, if export duties average 10 percent of f.o.b. value of Rs 0.20 per U.S. $1.00 exported, then this means that exports are Rs 0.20 more expensive than the homegoods that could be produced with the same resources. Hence, the domestic value of the exports and the shadow price of foreign exchange would then be Rs 1.80 = U.S. $1.00.

As in all cases where a resource is used, there are thus two shadow prices corresponding to whether the resource comes from a displaced use or is additionally produced. As in reality there will be some combination of the two possibilities, the correct shadow price will be a weighted average of the two shadow prices. Now, with respect to foreign exchange it is, of course, extremely difficult to determine by how much exports will be increased and imports reduced if additional foreign exchange is needed. A short-cut method is to work with a normal average of the two shadow prices and, in our example, this would be the average of 2.60 and 1.80, so that the base estimate can be set at Rs 2.20. Further refinements can be made by considering whether one or the other possibility of earning foreign exchange is the more likely one. For instance, if in our country import curtailment is easier than increasing exports, then the foreign exchange shadow rate can be estimated at somewhere between Rs 2.20 and Rs 2.60. On the other hand, if it is easier to increase exports, then the shadow rate could be set at somewhere between Rs 1.80 and Rs 2.20. Whatever value one chooses, in all cases sensitivity tests should be applied.

As regards the shadow price of labor, many developing countries have still a short-age of skilled labor so that market wages can often be taken to represent the real scarcity values of this production factor. In several developing countries, however, unskilled labor is available in abundant supply. The determination of its shadow price is distinct from all other production factors because of the fact that the laborer's services are tied to the laborer. This means that if a laborer is withdrawn from existing employment to work in a new job, then not only the foregone product of the laborer but also the disutility of his extra effort should be taken into account to determine the shadow price. Thus, even if the foregone product of a hired unskilled worker is negligible, the shadow price must be set at the price which will induce him to work in the new job.

In many cities in the developing countries, we see that the influx of rural workers is greater than the job openings in the formal well-paid sector. In such cases, more than one person migrates to the cities when one person is hired. What this means is that in order to find the shadow price of labor, we must add to the opportunity cost of the hired laborer the opportunity cost of the workers who have migrated, but who cannot find a job in the formal sector. The shadow price of labor in the cities may thus be a multiple of the rural shadow price of labor. It is, of course, very difficult to determine precisely what the exact migration function is as often no reliable data will be available. The best one can do in such cases is to assume that the shadow price of urban labor lies somewhere between the institutional and the rural wage rate adjusted for cost-of-living differences. The use of both values will show whether the project is sensitive to the shadow wage rate and in cases where the shadow rate appears to be important, a range of rates of return can then be calculated to help the decision-making process.

Finally, a few remarks about the shadow price of capital. As a general principle, the rate of return of the project should be higher than the rate of return which the capital resources would have in their next best alternative.

Let us assume that the resources consist of displaced investment. Then there is the problem that the earnings of many enterprises are subject to corporation taxes and that some of these earnings include rewards for risk taking. Furthermore, the dividends and interest payments accruing to the investors will often be subject to income taxes. Should the shadow price of capital be calculated gross or net of such taxes and risk premiums? From the point of view of society as a whole, it is the foregone yield that is the relevant one. Hence, the correct shadow price should be the rate of return gross of taxes and risk premiums. That different parts of that rate of return accrue to the Government is not important since these are mere transfer payments. But what if part of all of the capital resources for the proposed project come from displaced consumption rather than displaced investment? If the income distribution in the country is not optimal, then there may indeed be a case to evaluate this consumption component differently from the displaced investment component.... In case, however, that the income distribution is considered roughly optimal, consumption may be considered as valuable as investment, and the shadow price of capital consists then of the weighted average rate of return on capital in the economy. In this respect it is perhaps of interest to mention that Harberger, after detailed investigation, arrived at rates of return on capital in India ranging from 17.2 to 21.3 percent. Lal made a similar investigation of the opportunity cost of capital in India and found rates of return ranging from 12 percent to 19 percent. It needs no elaborations that in a country with an abundance of capital resources, such as for instance in Saudi Arabia, the shadow price of capital will be much lower.

THE CALCULATION TECHNIQUES

After having imputed the correct scarcity values to all the inputs and outputs of a project, including negative values for harmful effects on the environment, the task at hand is to determine whether the project is worth undertaking. Two criteria have become common: the net present value and the internal rate of return criterion.

Under the net present value criterion all the costs and benefits of the project are discounted at the opportunity cost of capital to present values, and the project is considered worthwhile if it has a positive net present value. The criterion amounts thus to the calculation of the present value of the surplus the project generates over and above the opportunity cost of capital.

The internal rate of return criterion consists of calculating by trial and error the discount rate at which a project has a net present value of zero—the project's internal rate of return—and accepting the project only if its internal rate of return is larger than the opportunity cost of capital.

Is the internal rate of return criterion a theoretically correct criterion? The answer is negative, and the criterion may lead to wrong results if projects are to be ranked by priority. The reason for this is that the internal rate of return criterion assumes incorrectly that the benefits of the project under scrutiny will be reinvested at the internal rate of return instead of at the opportunity cost of capital as assumed under the net present value criterion. It is intuitively clear that the two criteria will therefore result in a different ranking of projects. If budgetary constraints play a role, so that a choice must be made out of a series of projects, then the only correct criterion is the net present value criterion. The way to proceed then is to calculate for each project the present value of the surplus it generates per dollar of current investments, and to choose those projects that have the highest surplus ratios.

The problem with the net present value criterion is, however, that the opportunity cost of capital, which serves as the discount rate, is difficult to estimate. One may attempt to calculate net present values by using a minimum and a maximum value for the opportunity cost of capital, but where one can only estimate that the opportunity cost of capital lies between some very extreme values, this procedure is not very meaningful. In such a case, the internal rate of return method may be used to establish a tentative ranking order of projects. As projects with high internal rates of return will be accepted in any case, one can then spend extra time on projects with low rates of return—those at the margin

of acceptability—in order to sharpen the accept-reject decision. This may be done for instance by calculating probability distributions of the costs and benefits. We feel, therefore, that the internal rate of return is an important tool in practical work despite its theoretical limitations.

X.C.3. Guide to Little-Mirrlees*

A FIRST APPROXIMATION

The *Manual*'s central message can be simply stated.[1] A valid assessment of an industrial project's worth to an economy often requires the use of values that differ from the values used in the normal kind of business or financial appraisals. Economic appraisals frequently must be done with "shadow" prices, i.e., any assumed prices that differ from those that will actually be realized in the company's own books ("market" prices). The particular shadow prices which Little and Mirrlees believe should be used are "world prices"; these represent a country's actual trading opportunities. The resulting streams of annual costs and benefits should then be weighted (discounted) to reflect the differing times when they will occur. The discounting operation has the effect of translating future values into their present worth, allowing the streams of future costs and benefits to be summed into single figures. You then subtract the single cost figure from the benefit figure. If there is a surplus the project is said to have a favorable present social value, and is worth doing. Economists will at once recognize that Little and Mirrlees are relying on the familiar discounted cash flow method,

using shadow prices, to test for a project's net present worth.

Thus the basic approach of the *Manual* is not new. For those to whom the basic concepts may be hazy or unfamiliar, the *Manual* provides an admirable introductory explanation, free of mathematics or jargon. But the major innovation put forward by Little and Mirrlees—their big idea that has stirred up most of the interest and most of the dust—is their notion that *all* prices used in project calculation should be world prices. They are not satisfied with the procedure followed by many institutions (including, normally, the World Bank Group) whereby partial use is made of international values, e.g., applying them to major inputs and outputs that are or easily could be traded. They argue in favor of valuing all inputs at world prices, even the so-called nontraded inputs that normally cannot possibly be imported (i.e., electricity, construction, local transport and labor). The reason Little and Mirrlees want to go "all the way" in using world prices for every input and output is to avoid the distortions which they feel creep into the calculations if only partial use is made of world prices. A cost-benefit calculation based partly on world prices and partly on domestic prices has to be put into a single currency through the use of an exchange rate. Little and Mirrlees don't like exchange rates, not even "shadow" exchange rates based on "correcting" unrealistic official rates. In their view, no exchange rate, no matter how good, can overcome the distortion in relative values which arises

---

*From G. B. Baldwin, "A Layman's Guide to Little-Mirrlees," *Finance & Development,* Vol. 9, No. 1, 1972, pp. 16–21. Reprinted by permission.

[1]The Little-Mirrlees manual is Volume II of the Organisation for Economic Co-operation and Development's two-volume *Manual of Industrial Project Analysis in Developing Countries.*

whenever you combine values taken from different sets of prices (such as world prices and domestic prices). The use of one set of prices—world prices—bypasses this problem and, by taking all prices from one common pool, achieves a more valid ordering of the relative values used in constructing costs and benefits.[2]

If by some miracle of wisdom a country had developed its economic structure under conditions of free trade and free exchange rates, its investment decisions would continuously have been made in the light of worldwide trading opportunities; consequently, the relative values of home prices and world prices would today stand in an undistorted relationship to each other. This is hardly the world as we find it. Protection and other trade restrictions are everywhere, investment decisions have often been made outside the discipline and opportunities of world prices, and many exchange rates now serve to distort rather than to preserve true relationships between domestic and world values. Little and Mirrlees want to prevent this bad history from contaminating investment decisions. They want to avoid using some good prices (world prices of traded items) and some not-so-good prices (the domestic prices of non-traded inputs), which must then be merged by use of a (frequently bad) exchange rate. If all values can be measured in world prices, the problem is solved. In a neat display of inventiveness, Little and Mirrlees have "solved" this problem. But some of their critics say the cure is worse than the disease. This point is far and away the most controversial part of the *Manual:* just how much trouble is it worth to avoid using a foreign exchange rate, official or shadow?

With this summary introduction we can take a closer look at some of the main features of the Little-Mirrlees approach.

[2]The key value of labor is brought into this system of world prices at its proper relative value by first giving it a hypothetical or shadow price in terms of its domestic scarcity and then translating this into its world-price equivalent.

SOCIAL PROFITABILITY AND PRIVATE PROFITABILITY

Little and Mirrlees begin by pointing out the many similarities between the calculation of an industrial project's private and its economic or social profitability. Both calculations start with the problem of estimating future income (i.e., "benefits") and costs (capital and operating). The cost and benefit estimates are both made up of two elements: (1) the number of physical units involved plus (2) the price used to value each physical element. "The essence of a cost-benefit analysis is that it does not accept that actual receipts adequately measure social benefits, and actual expenditures social costs. But it does accept that actual receipts and expenditures can be suitably adjusted so that the difference betweeen them . . . will properly reflect the social gain" (pp. 22–3).

A second but less crucial feature of their system is the emphasis given to savings. Little and Mirrlees feel that resources for investment are so often a critical constraint that they deserve to occupy a central role in evaluating projects. Their handling of this problem, by converting a project's cash flow into a pure savings flow stripped of all consumption elements, is neat, and deserves discussion. But not until we look further at what they have to say about the use of world prices.

WHY WORLD PRICES?

"If you can get more refrigerators by exporting bicycles to pay for them, than by diverting resources from making bicycles to making refrigerators at home, it is clearly right to make and export the bicycles and import the refrigerators. But whether this is in fact the case, requires a knowledge both of the relative costs of production at home, and of world prices and market conditions" (p. 85). The reason for relating everything to world prices is not because they are "more rational" than domestic prices but simply because "they represent the actual terms on which the country can trade" (p. 92). So it is logical to argue that all internationally traded goods—i.e., those which the country actually imports or exports, regardless of whether the project itself will do so—should be valued at their c.i.f. (for imports) or f.o.b. (for exports) prices. But what should we do with nontraded inputs and outputs? (The main nontraded inputs are domestic transportation, construction, electricity, land, and labor; other minor ones can be thought of, e.g., water and waste disposal, telecommunications, advertising, banking services, maintenance and repair services.)

Little and Mirrlees say that since traded goods are valued in world prices, nontraded goods must be similarly valued; "only thus can we ensure that we are valuing everything in terms of a common yardstick." Note that a "common yardstick" may refer either to use of a common currency (e.g., all values expressed in either dollars or rupees), or to the use of a common source of values (e.g., world prices, instead of a mixture of world prices and domestic prices). All methods of project appraisal require the use of a common currency, but only Little-Mirrlees require the use of both a common currency and a common source for all values used. The problem of trying to express all values in a single currency where they will stand in a right relationship to each other can be solved either by using "a special accounting price for foreign exchange" (a shadow exchange rate) or by revaluing domestic resources in terms of world prices; the latter is the method recommended in the *Manual*. Once all values are established in terms of world prices, it does not matter whether they are left in U.S. dollars or converted into domestic rupees (the two illustrative currencies used in the *Manual*). If *a complete set* of costs and benefits are converted from dollars into rupees any exchange rate can be used, since all values will retain a constant relationship to each other. But this is *not* true if some values are taken from world prices and some are taken from domestic prices and the two sets are then put into a single currency by using an exchange rate. This will change the relationships among different values and distort the estimate of the relationship between foreign and domestic resources.

USING INPUT/OUTPUT ANALYSIS TO CHASE DOWN TRADED ITEMS

Little and Mirrlees advance both pragmatic and theoretical reasons for wanting to anchor all cost-benefit values in world prices. Their pragmatic reason is that world prices represent actual trading opportunities, which heavily influence domestic investment decisions. Every industrial investment decision involves the "make or buy" decision involved in the refrigerator and bicycle quotation cited earlier. The development process involves a steady expansion of the demand for imports, and the only way to pay for them, in the long run, is to produce for export only those things a country can produce best. To make the most of its opportunities a country must deploy its resources (fundamentally, its land and its labor force) in ways which give it the most for its money, i.e., the most foreign exchange (either earnings or savings) for domestic resources used. And the only way to do this in a complete and theoretically consistent manner is to chase down all the inputs used by a project, direct and indirect, until all the potentially tradable items have been valued in world prices, leaving only land and labor. Land is dismissed as relatively unimportant in most industrial projects. But in valuing labor, Little and Mirrlees argue that even labor's own inputs (i.e., its consumption) should be valued in terms of world prices (they give us some help by suggesting how this refinement might be achieved).

It is not easy to value the nontraded inputs in world prices. The general procedure is to take each such input (power, construction, transport, or labor) and break it down into its own inputs; these in turn will consist of items that are traded and items that are nontraded. The latter are in turn broken down into traded and nontraded items, etc. etc. The only way this chain can be followed back very far is through a detailed input/output table for the economy as a whole. Few less developed countries have in existence a table that is detailed enough to permit the needed calculations for more than a few simple industries. If no such table is available, rough-and-ready approximations to world values can be used. These approximations or "conversion factors" are based on the ratio of domestic costs of a representative sample, of, say, construction items (wood, cement, steel, fuel, etc.) to the world price of these items. This ratio is based on using the official exchange rate; the reciprocal of the ratio is then used to adjust the domestic cost of nontraded inputs to values closer to what they would be if the complete input/output method had been rigorously followed. This conversion factor is in effect a way of correcting for the overvaluation of an exchange rate; however, it does it on an average basis and not with the precision theoretically achievable if all nontraded inputs could be decomposed into their ultimate traded elements which could then be valued in world prices.

THE PRICE OF LABOR

There is nothing particularly new or distinctive in the Little-Mirrlees treatment of this much-discussed question. Most of the labor used in industry comes from a labor-surplus rural sector, and its departure involves little or no loss of agricultural production, i.e., its opportunity cost (equal to its marginal productivity) is typically very low. However, industrial labor is usually paid considerably more than the agricultural subsistence wage. Some of this excess over what labor could earn in agriculture is a necessary cost of making it available at industrial locations; but some of the excess is an artificial creation of trade union policies, needlessly high minimum wages, or employer "softness" in relation to what he could pay if he wanted to pay no more than a competitive wage. So the proper domestic price for valuing labor is a shadow wage that lies somewhere between its actual market rate and an agricultural subsistence wage. A good deal of judgment is involved in settling on a figure (since the cost

stream stretches over many years, there is no reason for using a constant shadow price throughout the project life if there is any reasonable basis for varying it).

But Little and Mirrlees do not let the domestic shadow price of labor determine its value in project costs. A domestic shadow price reflects only labor's relative scarcity in the domestic economy; once this has been estimated, this domestic value must then be converted into a world price. In theory this can be done—as explained above—by decomposing labor's consumption into traded items; but in practice either a specific conversion factor or the standard conversion factor would almost always be used.

ADJUSTING FOR A PROJECT'S "COMMITMENT TO CONSUMPTION"

With nations, as with individuals, there is a neverending tug-of-war between consumption and savings. The ultimate purpose of all economic activity is to raise living standards, which means raising consumption. But it is nonconsumption out of present income (savings) which provides the resources for the investment necessary to assure higher consumption tomorrow. Hence the battle between consumption today and consumption tomorrow. Little-Mirrlees have an unusually clear discussion of this classical problem, although their operational advice seems unnecessarily complicated.

Obviously a dollar's worth of future consumption is never worth a full dollar to us today. Future values always stand at a discount compared to the present, and the more distant the future, the greater the discount. The specific rate at which future consumption is discounted is called the consumption rate of interest (economists often call this the social discount rate, a more ambiguous term). This is not the discount rate Little and Mirrlees use in discounting cost-benefit streams. Why not? Because projects generate future savings as well as future consumption. Indeed, Little and Mirrlees believe that savings are so difficult to generate, and so important to future consumption, that the main test of a project's economic merit in almost all less developed countries should be its ability to generate savings. There is no reason why future savings should carry the same discount rate as future consumption. So it may look at first as though future consumption will have to be discounted at one rate and future savings at another. To avoid this, Little-Mirrlees revalue future consumption in terms of savings: this gives us a unified benefit stream, a "cash flow" stripped of its consumption elements so that it represents only savings. These can then be discounted at a single rate; the rate at which savings are discounted is called the "accounting rate of interest" (ARI). This is the discount rate to use in calculating the present worth of a project's cost and benefit streams.

The social income stream (consumption plus savings) to be generated by a project is stripped of its consumption element by taking the consumption element out of both labor income and returns to capital. On the labor side this adjustment is made automatically by defining labor's cost in terms of its consumption only. Since only this consumption cost is deducted from project income, anything labor saves remains in the net benefit stream. The elimination of consumption from the returns paid to the owners of capital is accomplished by applying to the project's estimated incremental capital income an estimate of the general marginal propensity to consume of those who receive interest and dividends (for some reason no offsetting allowance is made for any extra government consumption which may result from tax revenue generated by a project).

Thus the use of a shadow price for labor increases the benefit stream while the adjustment for consumption out of profits reduces the stream: one wonders how near the truth one would be if neither of these offsetting adjustments were made! But at least Little-Mirrlees give us a complete, easy-to-understand lesson in why a "commitment to consumption" is "bad" and how they think it ought to be eliminated from the cost-benefit calculation.

WHAT DISCOUNT RATE TO USE?

As noted, in the Little-Mirrlees system (as in many others) the investment test used is a project's present social value—the difference between the present values of the benefit and cost streams. These present values are, of course, critically dependent on the discount rate used; different rates can change not only the size of the present social value but can make a positive value turn negative. So the specific ARI is important. The Little-Mirrlees rule for choosing the right discount rate is the same as that used by many others, including the World Bank Group: " . . . the accounting rate of interest should be kept as high as possible consistent with there being as much investment as savings permit" (p. 96). ("Savings" here means domestic plus foreign savings, the latter being net capital inflow.) If a too low ARI is chosen there will be excessive investment, a balance of payments deficit, and underuse of resources. Recognizing these limits and choosing a rate that will steer the right course between them is a matter of good judgment. Little and Mirrlees think most developing countries ought to use a rate around 10 per cent in real terms, i.e., after inflation; some countries might use even 15 per cent. Rather than worry about the exact correctness of the ARI, Little and Mirrlees sensibly suggest the trial use of three rates—high, low, and medium—to sort out the "obviously good" and the "obviously bad" projects, with marginal ones to be put off until the authorities see how large the investment program will be and whether any clearly better projects come along to displace the marginal candidates.

A PROJECT'S BALANCE OF PAYMENTS, EMPLOYMENT, AND FUTURE CONSUMPTION EFFECTS

One of the attractive features claimed for the Little-Mirrlees approach is that it provides a comprehensive project evaluation test. Once it is determined that a project has a positive PSV when world prices are used, one can be confident that it will fulfil all important economic objectives for which projects are often specifically tested. This applies to a project's impact on the balance of payments, on employment, and on society's claims for future consumption. By valuing all project inputs and outputs at world prices (i.e., in terms of their foreign exchange value), "import-substitution and exporting is encouraged to the maximum desirable extent." Once the authorities have persuaded project appraisers to use correct values (i.e., world prices) in their cost-benefit studies then "the right way to control the balance of payments is to concentrate on high-yielding projects, and not to try to do more investment than saving, tax policies, and foreign aid, allow." By valuing labor's shadow wage also in terms of foreign exchange (which may put a lower value on labor's consumption inputs than domestic prices do) "producers are encouraged to use labor, instead of imported inputs, to the maximum desirable extent." Finally, as we have seen, the problem of balancing consumption today against consumption tomorrow is handled by use of a shadow wage rate—e.g., a low shadow wage encourages labor-intensive projects, the main expression of consumption today over consumption tomorrow.

CONTROVERSIAL POINTS

Toward the end of the Little-Mirrlees volume one comes upon this self-description:

The methods of project appraisal described in this *Manual,* depending as they do on relatively crude methods of estimating accounting prices, can be thought of as a first step in the harnessing of the whole range of production decisions to social ends. . . . The methods suggested do not depend upon the prior analysis of reliable and sophisticated planning models. They are practicable, and are likely to be accurate enough to exclude all definitely bad projects, and allow all definitely good ones. Small mistakes on marginal projects are less important (p. 188).

Admirable goals for any appraisal method— reliability, simplicity, feasibility. At most points, the *Manual* meets these tests; at a few points it fails them.

Little and Mirrlees do not expect their *Manual* to give individual project analysts everything they need to go out and make valid cost-benefit studies of industrial projects. They acknowledge that they have really written a textbook of appraisal theory, not a how-to-do-it manual for men on the firing line. Furthermore, the textbook is meant for the education and guidance of a small group of high-powered economists who, the authors hope, will be found presiding over development planning at the center of things in every country. They urge every country to prepare a much shorter manual of its own, telling ministries and development banks how to do economic cost-benefit studies and giving them the necessary accounting prices.

The weakest—and certainly the most contentious—of the various steps recommended by Little-Mirrlees is the extent to which they go in using world prices. They want us to use them for *all* cost and benefit values, not just for important items that are actually traded, or could be. To do this involves a lot of trouble for a doubtful advantage. It is a lot of trouble because of the need to use input/output data that usually do not exist with nearly the accuracy needed to yield accurate results—and there seems little advantage in substituting the distortions of bad input/output data, or the approximations of conversion factors, for those arising from overvalued exchange rates. It is not even true that Little and Mirrlees get rid of exchange rates entirely, since some world prices will be in U.S. dollars, some in deutsche mark, some in yen, etc., and these can be merged only by using exchange rates. So part of the exchange rate problem is simply pushed outside the country. In most countries, it appears far simpler and sufficiently accurate to use:

1. World prices for the *actually traded* major capital and current inputs, and for the outputs;
2. Domestic factor costs (at either shadow or market prices as judged appropriate) for the *nontraded* inputs; and then to
3. Convert these foreign and domestic values into a single currency by resort to an ex-

change rate (again, using any reasonable rate if the official rate is felt badly out of line).

In a majority of industrial projects distortions in the values of nontraded inputs simply will not be important. Electricity rarely comprises more than 4–5 per cent of manufacturing costs, so a 20 per cent distortion of its value will affect total costs by only 1 per cent. Distortions in internal transport costs for capital and operating costs are unlikely to run more than the same order of magnitude. The construction element in plant capital costs is larger and may run 15–30 per cent; at least half of this will consist of labor costs which, as with operating labor costs, can be adjusted to an "economic" value through the use of a shadow wage. The distortion arising from using domestic currency to price labor's shadow wage is likely to be less than the margin of error inherent in deciding what shadow wage to use. Thus, when one looks at the relative unimportance of all the nontraded inputs, except labor, in a majority of industrial projects, refinements in these values begin to look relatively unimportant. Cost-benefit analysis simply does not work to the order of precision to which Little and Mirrlees want to take us.

Labor operating costs, which are important in most industrial or agricultural projects, can be handled satisfactorily by sensitivity analysis, i.e., by trying two or three different values to see how much difference it makes to the final result. There is no point in going to a lot of trouble to establish a doubtful accuracy for values that do not change a conclusion reached with more easily established, well-reasoned values. Little and Mirrlees make a good case for using sensitivity analysis when discussing the "fuzziness" surrounding the ARI; they might well have extended its use to other cost-benefit values. I cannot help concluding that this particular feature of the Little-Mirrlees methodology—the world-pricing-of-nontraded-inputs feature that has caused so much argument—is a tempest in a teapot. I doubt it will catch on, and it will not matter much if it doesn't. There is plenty of wisdom in the basic Little-Mirrlees approach without trying to make everything depend on their controversial method of valuing a project's nontraded inputs.

X.C.4. Foreign Exchange Rate*

Since the UNIDO method uses domestic currency as the *numeraire,* the project's foreign exchange impact must be identified so that the project's net present economic value may be adjusted by an appropriate premium, assuming of course that foreign exchange is more valuable than indicated by the exchange rate.[1] This process increases those economic-efficiency values that were measured in border rupees (border prices in dollars multiplied by the market exchange rate)

*From UNIDO, *Guide to Practical Project Appraisal: Social Benefit-Cost Analysis in Developing Countries* (John R. Hansen edition), 1978. Reprinted by permission.

[1]Foreign exchange may, of course, be less valuable than indicated by the market exchange rate, a situation that might prevail in a relatively open economy that had just undertaken a major (and essential) devaluation. In this case, the adjustment factor would simply assume a negative value. *In practice,* however, in most less developed countries that are not oil producers, it is generally safe to assume that there will be a premium on foreign exchange.

by the percentage premium on foreign exchange, a factor that roughly indicates the level of protection in the economy, i.e., the difference between average market and average border prices. This adjustment makes the prices established with reference to border prices compatible with prices based on domestic consumer willingness to pay in the protected market.[2] If the foreign exchange impact is positive, the net present value before adjustment will be increased by the adjustment; conversely, if it is negative, the net present value will be reduced.

In principle, all inputs and outputs are either tradables that can be valued directly in terms of foreign exchange or non-tradables whose inputs can be disaggregated in terms of tradables, non-tradables and labour. If the non-tradables identified in the first round of disaggregation are further disaggregated in a similar manner, and so on, theoretically any non-tradable can be valued in terms of its foreign exchange, domestic labour and capital content. Thus, it is impossible to say that the project analyst should count only the direct foreign exchange impact of the project in this part of the UNIDO analysis; the line between direct and indirect is too arbitrary to be of any help to the analyst.

In practice, the foreign exchange premium needs to be applied only to those goods that were valued at border prices, since inputs and outputs shadow priced with reference to domestic consumer willingness to pay or cost of production already implicitly include a premium on foreign exchange. Goods shadow priced "at the border" would generally include (*a*) all major inputs and outputs; and (*b*) any major non-traded inputs with a substantial foreign exchange component (e.g., electricity produced from imported oil).

Once an appropriate decision has been made about the inputs and outputs for which the foreign exchange impact will be evaluated, these impacts must be quantified separately for each input or output category so that an adjustment can be made to the net present economic value of the project.... Whether this adjustment is done on year-by-year values or on present values as recommended above depends on the assumption made about (*a*) the shadow price for foreign exchange over time; and (*b*) the foreign exchange content over time.

In practice, it may not be unreasonable to assume that both of these values are constant. The first assumption is widely made; few writings recommend that this value be changed over time, for there is usually little evidence to guide such differential shadow pricing of foreign exchange.[3] The second assumption is open to more challenge, but generally is reasonable. Even if there is a reduction in the direct foreign exchange content of a major non-tradable input (e.g., electricity now produced from oil that later will be replaced by indigenous hydroelectric power), the hydro facility will almost certainly involve some direct or indirect foreign exchange expenditures. The assumption of constant foreign exchange content for any specific input or output is especially reasonable in agricultural and industrial projects, where, aside from labour, the inputs and outputs are generally tradable.

Without these assumptions, it is necessary to calculate the foreign exchange impact of

---

[2]In the Little-Mirrlees system, a reverse but equivalent approach is used. Instead of increasing border prices to the domestic-market level with the premium on foreign exchange, domestic prices are decreased to border-price levels by the standard conversion factor.

[3]If there is strong evidence, however, that a given country is moving purposefully towards a free-trade policy, the precision of the analysis could (perhaps usefully) be increased by estimating the years until free trade is reached, then reducing the premium on foreign exchange each year by the present premium divided by the number of years to free trade. Conversely, if a country has recently undergone a substantial devaluation so that there is currently little or no economic premium over the official rate for foreign exchange, but if it is expected that fundamental problems will make another devaluation necessary in the near future (not an uncommon situation), it may be reasonable to apply a gradually rising premium. More refined non-linear estimations would probably be pointless given the uncertainties surrounding international trade and trade policies. *In practice,* it may be sufficient to set up a limited number of periods and hold the premium consistent during each period, which would simplify the calculations.

each input and output in each year of the project, calculate the premium, discount it back to the present to obtain a net present economic adjustment value of the foreign exchange impact and add it to the basic net present economic value.[4] The use of these assumptions greatly simplifies the valuation of the foreign exchange impact in the UNIDO method, for then this impact can be calculated on the basis of net present economic values. The present value of each input and output is multiplied by a weighted adjustment factor to obtain its foreign exchange adjustment value. These adjustment values are then added up . . . and used to modify the respective net present values. The weighted adjustment factors are the product of the foreign exchange content of each item and the adjustment factor for foreign exchange. All the year-by-year computations are thus avoided.

The premium to be attached to foreign exchange is important. . . . The *Guidelines* uses a foreign exchange shadow price based on marginal social value as revealed by the consumer willingness to pay for it in the form of imported goods. Without going into details, the derivation is based on the average of the percentage by which the domestic market price of the last unit of each good imported by the country exceeds its c.i.f. price expressed in domestic currency weighted by the share of each good in the actual marginal import bill.[5] Assuming a freely competitive domestic market for the good, this approach to valuing foreign exchange implicitly uses the domestic willingness to pay a premium above the "official" price for the foreign exchange needed to purchase these goods. If it can be assumed that the average premium on foreign exchange with an increase in economic activity will remain about the same, an adjustment factor based on a formula for average shadow exchange rates will be approximately equal to one based on a formula for a marginal shadow exchange rate.

In practice, the approach outlined in the preceding paragraph should give a usable estimate of the shadow price of foreign exchange. If the data are available, however, a more accurate indication of the shadow price of foreign exchange can be obtained. The approach proposed in the *Guidelines* is, as indicated above, based on the assumption that, in the case of a project that is a net user of foreign exchange, the amount it uses may be taken from other users and thus falls under the shadow pricing category of "consumer willingness to pay."[6] However, the use of foreign exchange by the project may also encourage the "production" of foreign exchange through manufacture for export or import substitution, in which case a somewhat different approach is required. This "production" will be stimulated if demand for foreign exchange by the project changes the incentive to other potential producers of export or import substitutes. The incentive to undertake foreign exchange earnings or saving activities depends on the "effective price" of foreign exchange, the "rupee" benefit received by domestic producers of goods who, on balance, earn or save a dollar of foreign exchange. For example, if the official exchange rate is Rs 10/$1, the c.i.f. price of an import-substituting good is $3 and the do-

[4]If the year-by-year adjustments are to be made, it would be advisable to set up the financial income statement and/or financial cash-flow table for the commercial-profitability analysis in stage one so that there is a double column under each year, one for the basic price and one for the foreign exchange content of this price.

[5]A simple formula for calculating an average shadow exchange rate (*SER*) similar to the UNIDO approach and based on a given year's data is:

$$SER = OER \left[\frac{(M + T_i) + (X + S_x)}{M + X} \right]$$

where OER = official exchange rate; M = c.i.f. value of imports; X = f.o.b. value of exports; T_i = import tax revenues; and S_x = export subsidies. (Export taxes should be regarded as negative subsidies.) Where quantitative restrictions are important, their tariff equivalents should be included, and if there are other sources of difference between border and domestic ex works prices (e.g., transport costs and importing profits), these should also be considered. Furthermore, any prohibitive quantitative restrictions or tariffs should be taken into account as well, if feasible.

[6]The converse of the following applies to projects that are net producers of foreign exchange.

mestic manufacturer, because of protection, can charge Rs 45, the "effective" rate is Rs 45/$3, or Rs 15/$1. This incentive will remain unchanged only if the effective foreign exchange price remains constant. If the effective rate does remain constant, the demand for foreign exchange by the project would fall on other uses, for there would be no inducement to the new production of foreign exchange, and all would have to share the present supply. The effective price is, however, very unlikely to remain constant, for that would require much more than a stable official exchange rate. It would require that there be no change in tariffs, quantitative restrictions, capital-movement regulations or any other protective device, despite increased demand for foreign exchange by the project and by other users. Such a situation would almost never occur, except in the short term, for it would deplete the country's foreign exchange reserves, which few governments could allow for long. Instead, given an increased demand for foreign exchange, the government would, for example, devalue the domestic currency, increase trade restrictions or increase export subsidies, which in turn would increase the incentives to produce import substitutes and exportables to earn foreign exchange and would reduce the incentives to produce non-tradables.

Given these predictable impacts of an increased demand for foreign exchange, it becomes important to examine the cost of producing additional foreign exchange and the value of such to the users. The relative importance of these two aspects—cost and supply and value and use—will depend, of course, on the relative responses of the supply and demand for foreign exchange given changes in its effective price.

Probably the best known approach to determining the cost of producing foreign exchange is the domestic resource cost method proposed by Michael Bruno.[7] While this ap-

[7]Michael Bruno, "Domestic Resource Costs and Effective Protection: Clarification and Synthesis," *Journal of Political Economy*, Vol. 80, No. 1, (January–February 1972), pp. 16–33.

proach is oriented to the cost of producing foreign exchange by a single project, the same principles apply at the macro level. However, at the macro level the analysis becomes more complex in that the elasticities of alternative sources of foreign exchange and of the demand for imports become important. Examination of this aspect of the shadow price of foreign exchange[8] would be a logical extension of the UNIDO method, although *in practice* it is unlikely to have a major impact on the relative ranking of projects.

Once the shadow price of foreign exchange has been determined, the adjustment factor for foreign exchange (AF_f) should be calculated. It is the premium on foreign exchange over the market rate and is equal to the shadow exchange rate divided by the market exchange rate, minus one. For example, if the shadow rate vis-à-vis the dollar is Rs 23 and the market rate is Rs 20, the AF_f is 23/20 − 1, or 15 per cent. The AF_f is weighted by the foreign exchange content of each item, and the weighted AF_f is used to determine the foreign exchange adjustment, which is then added up and used to adjust the economic net present value as discussed above. The adjustment for the value of foreign exchange puts the shadow prices fully on the basis of domestic accounting rupees.

The foreign exchange adjustment factor is next used ... to adjust the financial cash flows to reflect the differences between what the project paid for foreign exchange used in financial transactions and what the foreign

[8]See Bela Balassa, "Estimating the Shadow Price of Foreign Exchange in Project Appraisal," *Oxford Economic Papers*, Vol. 26, No. 2, July 1974, pp. 147–168. Balassa's formula for the premium on foreign exchange in a situation where trade restrictions are expected to continue (his second-best shadow exchange rate) is (implicitly):

$$AF_f = \frac{\sum e_f X_i (1 + S) + \sum_i n_m M_i (1 + 7)}{\sum_i e_f X_i + \sum_i n_m M_k} - 1$$

where AF_f = adjustment factor for foreign exchange; e_f = elasticity of supply of foreign exchange; n_m = elasticity of demand for imports; X_i = exports; M_i = imports; T = import taxes and S = export subsidies.

exchange is really worth. Similar adjustments are made with respect to foreign exchange the project received and the value of what it gave out in return.

X.C.5. Opportunity Cost of Capital*

The capital costs of a project can usefully be viewed from two perspectives for shadow pricing. For lack of better terms, let us call them the asset and the rent components. When Rs 100,000 is invested in project X, for example, two things happen. First, Rs 100,000 of financial resources is converted into real physical assets. Secondly, the investor removes this Rs 100,000 worth of financial resources from the national pool of savings that might be used for investment in alternative projects. Once invested in project X, therefore, these assets should yield a benefit, or rent, at least equal to what they would have otherwise earned.

The shadow pricing of capital thus presents two problems: (a) how to measure the value of the physical assets per se; and (b) how to measure the rental value or opportunity cost of capital—the benefits forgone by freezing investable resources as assets in project X instead of using them somewhere else.

Pricing of the asset component is exactly the same as for any other resource. If it is a fully traded good, the value is its border price. If it is partially traded or non-traded, its shadow price is its economic cost of production if the project induces increased domestic production, or its economic value measured in terms of consumer willingness to pay if the project takes it away from alternative users. The labour involved in the construction of the physical facilities is likewise valued according to the guidelines. In each case, the adjustment factor is calculated, and

*From UNIDO, *Guide to Practical Project Appraisal: Social Benefit-Cost Analysis in Developing Countries* (John R. Hansen edition), 1978. Reprinted by permission.

an appropriate economic adjustment is added to or subtracted from the net present values of the capital investments at market prices. . . . *In practice, capital costs with roughly similar adjustment factors can be grouped together to minimize the work.*[1]

The second part of the capital cost, its rent component, is the opportunity cost, or forgone productivity of the capital in other uses. The analysis here is strictly parallel to that for other resources:

1. The economic cost of capital is the cost of generating capital resources through additional savings;
2. Its economic value is the value of additional production in alternative uses.

[1]Some authors argue that if capital for a project comes from abroad and is available only to the project, the assets purchased with these funds should not be recorded as a cost until the capital is repatriated. This argument assumes that, in the case of a mineral-exploitation project, for example, the foreign mining company would not have invested in the country in the absence of the project, and therefore no other investment or production is given up in order to use the capital for the mining project. Under such circumstances, the country would incur a real capital cost only when it had to repay the foreign firm's original investment. This approach tends to increase the net present value and rate of return on projects because at least part of the total investment cost is discounted over more years than if it had been counted as a cost at the time of actual investment. While this treatment is theoretically correct, there are few instances of projects subject to economic evaluation by national authorities in which it can truly be said that the capital would not otherwise be available to the economy. Thus, *in practice* capital costs should usually be counted at the time the physical investment is made. The most likely exception to the latter is a project involving a private foreign investor who would not invest in the country in the absence of the project.

To the extent that capital for the project is generated from additional savings, its economic cost is the price or rent savers must be paid to forgo an additional unit of present consumption, the consumption rate of interest (CRI). To the extent that the capital is taken away from competing investments, its economic value is its marginal product at shadow prices in the "marginal investments,"[2] the investment rate of interest.[3] *In practice,* it is not necessary in the *Guidelines* to figure out where the capital came from, and thus the blend of interest rates that should be used, because stage three in this *Guide* converts the value of all inputs and outputs into their "consumption equivalents." It is therefore sufficient to use the CRI as the discount rate.

There are serious problems related to determining the CRI empirically.[4] *In practice,* however, two approaches can simplify the task considerably. The first is to use the "accounting rate of interest" or opportunity cost of capital as a crude first estimate of the

CRI. The second is to treat the discount rate as a budgetary device rather than as an economic reality that can be verified empirically: if the first estimate of the discount rate indicates that more projects are "acceptable" than can be financed with the available funds, the discount rate should be raised. Conversely, if the investment implied by the "acceptable" projects (including investing the money abroad) leaves excess investment funds, the cut-off point for the discount rate should be lowered.

Because of the problem of determining empirically an appropriate CRI, the *Guidelines* recommends treating it as an unknown to be determined later as a "switching value," that is, the value at which a project becomes acceptable. The graphical approach outlined above is very useful in this connection, for a switching value for one project is the value of the CRI that leaves a zero net present value for the project; it is the discount rate at which the net present value switches from positive to negative. Therefore, the switching value can also be regarded as the internal rate of return of the project. When more than one project is being considered, the switching value of the CRI is the discount rate at which one alternative comes to have a higher net present value than the other, a point also widely known as the cross-over discount rate. Another major practical advantage of the graphical approach in this connection is that the discount rate can be selected after the discounting is completed, provided, of course, that the rate chosen lies between 0 per cent and the upper "plotting point" discount rate.

These concepts can be demonstrated with Figure 1, which plots the net present economic values of projects A and B against discount rates of up to 25 per cent. If project A is considered in isolation, its switching value is 14 per cent, the maximum discount rate at which A is acceptable. Whether 14 per cent is the CRI is unknown, as indicated above, the *Guidelines* suggests determining that by what it calls the "bottom-up" procedure. The project analyst "at the bottom" can prepare the project appraisal indicating that the internal rate of return is 14 per cent and pres-

---

[2]The marginal investment is the last that would be undertaken if all possible investments were ranked according to their economic profitability and available funds were distributed accordingly.

[3]If savings are more valuable than consumption, the investment rate of interest theoretically should be further adjusted for the additional value to the economy of the part of the product that will be saved and will thus produce further rounds of additional consumption and investment.

[4]A theoretical formula exists for calculating the CRI:

$$CRI = ng + p$$

where:

g = elasticity of marginal utility of consumption with respect to changes in *per capita* income.

g = annual growth of average *per capita* income; and

p = pure time preference.

In practice, because of the inherently subjective nature of n and p, it makes more sense to follow the "bottom-up" approach suggested in the *Guidelines;* there is little point in having two areas of subjective judgment instead of one.

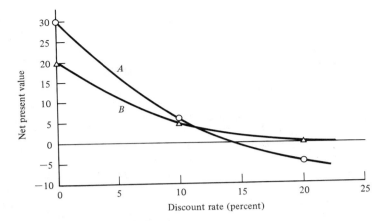

FIGURE 1. Switching values.

ent it to the ministers or planners "at the top."

If the ministers or planners accept the project, the analysts can assume that the planners judge the CRI to be less than 14 per cent; if they reject the project on the basis of the rate of return, the analysts know that the CRI is higher than 14 per cent. A repetition of this process, provided that the planners at the top are consistent, will gradually narrow the estimated CRI in the country to an acceptable range.

If projects A and B in Figure 1 are both under consideration as mutually exclusive alternatives, and if the planners choose project A, the analysts can assume that the CRI is less than 11 per cent, for at discount rates higher than this switching value the net present value of project B becomes more attractive. The converse conclusion is reached if project B is preferred by the ministers or planners, and again the actual value can be narrowed down by repetition of the process.

Comment

For a more detailed analysis of shadow exchange rates, see the following: Edmar Bacha and Lance Taylor, "Foreign Exchange Shadow Prices: A Critical Review of Current Theories," *Quarterly Journal of Economics* (May 1971); Bela Balassa, "Estimating the Shadow Price of Foreign Exchange in Project Appraisal," *Oxford Economic Papers* (July 1974); M. FG. Scott, "How to Use and Estimate Shadow Exchange Rates," *Oxford Economic Papers* (July 1974).

Shadow wage rates are analyzed by Deepak Lal, "Disutility of Effort, Migration and the Shadow Wage Rate," *Oxford Economic Papers* (March 1973); D. Mazumdar, "The Rural-Urban Wage Gap, Migration, and the Shadow Wage," *World Bank Staff Working Paper* No. 197 (1974).

Shadow interest rates are discussed by M. S. Feldstein, "The Social Time Preference Discount Rate in Cost-Benefit Analysis," *Economic Journal* (June 1964); Charles R. Blitzer, "On the Social Rate of Discount and Price of Capital in Cost-Benefit Analysis," *World Bank Staff Working Paper* No. 144 (1972); Deepak Lal, "On Estimating Certain Inter-temporal Parameters for Project Analysis," *World Bank* (processed, 1973).

Elements of risk and uncertainty in project appraisal are examined by Shlomo Reutlinger, "Techniques for Project Appraisal under Uncertainty," *World Bank Staff Working Paper*

No. 10 (1970); Louis Y. Pouliquen, "Risk Analysis in Project Appraisal," *World Bank Staff Working Paper* No. 11 (1970).

Also useful are the works by I. M. D. Little and M. FG. Scott, *Using Shadow Prices* (1976); M. FG. Scott et al., *Project Appraisal in Practice* (1976); A. C. Harberger, *Project Evaluation* (1974).

One of the most complex aspects of the exercise of project appraisal is the precise identification of the project evaluator's areas of control. This will affect the nature of the exercise that the evaluator has to solve and the shadow prices that will be relevant in the evaluation. How one assesses the government's ability to control different policies will alter markedly the nature of the appropriate shadow prices that are selected in project appraisal. This is illustrated, especially in the choice of shadow wage rates, by A. K. Sen, "Control Areas and Accounting Prices," *Economic Journal* (March 1972). To determine the appropriate shadow price of labor, Sen emphasizes that it is important for the project evaluator to consider the extent of influence that the government exercises over such relevant variables as the premium on savings over consumption, weights based on income distributional considerations, valuation of efforts by the peasant family and laborers, and the impact of employment creation on migration.

X.C.6. Social Prices *

The following paragraphs contain an outline of the general rationale for the inclusion of income distribution weights in project selection and broadly describe the manner in which this aspect of the analysis can be introduced into the standard appraisal methods.

The proposed use of distribution weights in project appraisal raises the question of the circumstances in which such weights are necessary. If, for example, the government values all income equally regardless of its distribution—either between the public and private sector or within the private sector—the need for distribution weights disappears. The weights themselves, however, only apparently disappear; in reality they are still there, but the implicit value judgments made are such that the social cost of each resource transfer is exactly offset by the resulting social benefit.

Many people would consider it rather extreme not to assign different values to marginal increments in consumption accruing to different income groups. Another point of

view, however, argues for excluding distribution weights. If the government, through its control of fiscal policy, is able to redistribute income costlessly, no need exists to include distribution weights in project selection; project selection should under such circumstances aim to maximize income and allow the fiscal system to redistribute it in a desirable fashion.

It is argued here, however, that, in general, redistribution can never be costless and that, in particular, redistribution in developing countries may be so costly as to be prohibitive. With regard to the general argument, all fiscal measures have an administrative cost and, at least in principle, a cost resulting from an unfavorable effect on incentives. With regard to the particular argument, the very unequal distribution of income-consumption in most developing countries and the difficulty of raising additional revenue indicate severe constraints on the government's use of the fiscal system. These constraints typically reflect an inability to raise sufficient revenue because to do so is not administratively feasible and an inability to tax the rich sufficiently because of that group's political power. Moreover, the general fiscal system of

*From Lyn Squire and Herman G. van der Tak, *Economic Analysis of Projects,* Baltimore, Johns Hopkins University Press, 1975, pp. 51–56. Reprinted by permission.

most developing countries (and, in fact, most developed countries) cannot possibly reallocate the benefits and costs of projects as varied and geographically dispersed as those usually found in these countries. If these arguments are accepted (rejected), distribution weights are (are not) required for project selection.

When distribution weights are considered necessary, they may be introduced into the standard economic analysis of projects in the following fashion. Assume that a project lasts one year and results in a net increase of E in real resources available to the economy.[1] If interest lies only in efficiency, the increase in real resources is an adequate measure of project benefits. But if there is interest in income distribution as well, the distribution of resources among different groups in society must also be examined. The resources accruing to each group can then be weighted in accordance with the appropriate concept of social welfare and summed to obtain the measure of the project's social worth.

To determine the distribution of real resources, the distribution of financial net benefits must be examined, because this will determine who has control over the increase in real resources. Obviously, the financial benefits will accrue either to the public sector or to the private sector, and, within the private sector, they will accrue either to the rich or to the poor. Assume, for example, that as a result of the project the income of one particular group in the private sector is increased by C and that all other net financial benefits accrue to the public sector. Assume further that the private sector allocates the entire increase in income to consumption.[2] The increased consumption will comprise various commodities or services that will have a cost in real resources, which may or may not equal C. Given the many distortions in the product and factor markets of less developed countries, it may be necessary to adjust C,

the financial measure of the increase in consumption, to obtain its real resource cost. Let the adjustment factor be β, so that the private sector enjoys an increase in real resources of $C\beta$, and the public sector retains control over the remainder: that is, $E - C\beta$.

To measure the social value of these changes reference must be made to the social welfare function. Assume that the increase in social welfare resulting from a marginal increase in the availability of real resources to the public sector is W_g, and that the social welfare resulting from a marginal increase in the availability of consumption to the particular income group is W_e. The measure of social benefits is then: $(E - C\beta)W_g + CW_e$. Although W_g is defined for real resources, W_e is defined for consumption at market prices. This simply reflects the fact that the public sector is concerned primarily with increases in real resources, whereas the private sector derives its utility from consumption possibilities as determined by market prices.[3]

NUMÉRAIRE

Social benefits then should be expressed in a common yardstick, or numéraire. Any commodity or resource may be chosen as this unit of account, but, once it has been chosen, all values must consistently be expressed in that numéraire. It is recommended that as numéraire the value of real resources that are freely available to the public sector be used: that is, we want to set the weight assigned to $(E - C\beta)$ equal to unity. To do this and to maintain all price relativities, we divide throughout by W_g, so that the measure of social benefits (S) in the chosen numéraire is:

$$S = (E - C\beta) + C_w, \qquad (1)$$

$$\begin{bmatrix} Net\ social \\ benefits \end{bmatrix} = \begin{bmatrix} Increase\ in\ real \\ resources\ in \\ public\ sector \end{bmatrix}$$
$$+ \begin{bmatrix} Social\ welfare \\ from\ increased \\ private\ sector \\ consumption \end{bmatrix}$$

[1] For a definition of symbols, see the Glossary of Symbols [the last section of this paper].

[2] An increase in private savings is treated separately: that is, for the moment it is assumed that there is no saving out of private income.

[3] W_c, however, will express the social value of the increase in private welfare.

where W_e/W_g has been replaced by ω. Thus, a unit of private consumption expressed in domestic prices (for example, C) has to be revalued by, in this case, ω to express it in the numéraire. This may appear tedious, but, if consumption expressed in domestic prices were used as numéraire, the reverse process would have to be gone through in order to express $(E - C\beta)$ in the consumption numéraire.[4]

EFFICIENCY AND SOCIAL PRICES

For practical purposes, it is more convenient to rewrite equation (1) in the following manner:

$$S = E - C(\beta - \omega) \qquad (2)$$

$$\left[\begin{array}{c} \text{Net social} \\ \text{benefits} \end{array}\right] = \left[\begin{array}{c} \text{Net efficiency} \\ \text{benefits} \end{array}\right]$$

$$- \left[\begin{array}{c} \text{Net social} \\ \text{cost of increased} \\ \text{private sector} \\ \text{consumption} \end{array}\right]$$

This has the advantage of separately identifying the efficiency benefits, E. Thus, the project economist-analyst can begin by estimating efficiency benefits as has been done in the past. The only other item he must estimate is the increase in net income accruing to the various income groups in the private sector who are affected by the project. The other elements of equation (2)—β and ω—will then either be provided by the national planning office or else be derived from a standard table.

Thus, the mechanics of this approach are fairly simple. Alternatively, but equivalently, the distributional element of projects can be included in the definition of shadow prices on

the grounds that all financial benefits must accrue to the factors of production employed by the project. For example, assume that the increase in income, C, generated by the project actually accrues as a result of increased wage payments to labor. The efficiency cost of employing labor—that is, forgone marginal product of labor—is netted out in obtaining the net increase in resources, E. In addition, employing labor involves a net social cost of increased consumption. Thus, the social cost of the labor input can be defined as: social cost = efficiency cost + $C(\beta - \omega)$. And if the increase in consumption per worker is c, then the social price per worker is: social price = efficiency price + $c(\beta - \omega)$.[5] This latter method may be useful for some factors such as unskilled labor, for which it is convenient to have an all-inclusive price for purposes of decentralized decision making, and may be essential for at least one price, the discount rate. For other factors this may not be particularly interesting, in which case the first method could be used. Although both methods may be used in any single project, they must not be used for the same factor payment because this would involve double counting. . . .

Some general implications of the approach outlined above can be considered at this stage. First, if the increase in consumption, c, is zero, the social price equals the efficiency price.[6] This might occur in a perfect labor market in which the transfer of labor involves no change in income or consumption. Second, if the wage earner spends all his income on, say, duty-free imports or, more generally, in nondistorted markets, then β equals unity. In other words, β can be viewed as a factor that corrects for market distortions, especially those caused by trade tariffs. β may vary for different consumers depending on the actual

[4]If account is to be taken of the distribution of consumption, the numéraire would have to be defined as the value of consumption at a particular level of consumption. The public income numéraire is used in I. M. D. Little and J. A. Mirrlees, *Project Appraisal and Planning for the Developing Countries*, 1974, the general format of which has been followed here. The consumption numéraire is used in United Nations Industrial Development Organization, *Guidelines for Project Evaluation*.

[5]Efficiency price is used in the traditional sense of opportunity cost: that is, the foregone marginal product per worker. The terms "shadow" and "accounting" are used indiscriminately to refer to both efficiency and social price.

[6]Throughout this paragraph comments applying to social and efficiency prices also apply to social and efficiency benefits as defined by equation (2).

composition of their consumption basket. Third, if the government is interested in income distribution, ω will tend to be low for the rich and high for the poor, and at some consumption level the situation $\omega = \beta$ would obtain, so that the real resource cost incurred by the government, $c\beta$, and the social benefit enjoyed by the worker, $c\omega$, as a result of a marginal increase in consumption are exactly offsetting. This level of consumption is known as the "critical consumption level": the social price equals the efficiency price at the critical consumption level. Fourth, as has been seen, the government may not wish to include distribution weights in project selection, in which case the social price always equals the efficiency price.

In presenting the economic analysis of a project, it will be instructive to indicate the project's worth at market, at efficiency, and at social prices. The first evaluation will correspond to the financial appraisal of the project. The second will be similar to that traditionally used by the Bank and other agencies: that is, all incomes will be considered equally valuable, there will be no premium on public income or investment, the discount rate will be the opportunity cost of capital, and other factor prices will be based on opportunity cost. In other words, the evaluation at efficiency prices corrects for the distortions in factor and product markets but does not assume any constraint on the government's ability to redistribute income or to invest. The third evaluation will include the project's distributional impact [see Equation (2)] if it is thought that the economy does suffer from a fiscal constraint.

GLOSSARY OF SYMBOLS

E = Net efficiency benefits

C = Private sector consumption

β = Consumption conversion factor

W_g = Marginal social value of foreign exchange in the public sector

W_c = Marginal social value of private sector consumption at consumption level c

S = Net social benefits

ω = Value of private sector consumption at consumption level C relative to the numéraire

X.D. OBJECTIVES AND RELATIVE WEIGHTS

X.D.1. Objectives of Planning *

The evaluation of investment projects should be carried out within the broad framework of the objectives of planning. The projects chosen from among the feasible alternatives should be those that contribute most towards the achievement of the planning goals. Therefore, good project analysis requires a clear statement of the planning objectives.

There are usually a number of objectives that the planners would like to achieve. Raising the standard of living, improving the distribution of income, achieving economic independence, reducing unemployment, etc., may all be regarded as desirable and the question is what relative weights to attach to these different goals. If one project fulfils one goal more and no goal less than another project, then we can choose the first project without much ado. But frequently one project will fulfil one goal better and another project will achieve more in terms of another goal, and then the conflict between the two can be resolved only by the relative weighting of the divergent achievements.

CONSUMPTION GOALS

Raising the standard of living is a basic aim of development planning. One measure of this standard is the level of average consumption per head evaluated at constant market prices. This is a rough measure but may be easier to handle than more sophisticated measures. If prices change over time, the rise in the money value of consumption will have to be corrected by the choice of an appropriate price index.

Evaluation at market prices does, however, leave out what economists call the "con-

sumers' surplus." A consumer may expect satisfaction worth $2 from a good but if the market price is $1 only, he need pay no more. So the market price does not fully measure the benefits that the consumers receive from a good. Corrections for this may be important in some cases and may be made by the usual method of estimating the demand curve for the good.

FUTURE CONSUMPTION AND GROWTH RATES

The planners will be interested not merely in the present consumption level but also in the future level. One method of bringing the future in is to attach a weight to the growth rate that is achieved today. But this cannot give an account of the future beyond the next period since growth rates may vary over time. A more satisfactory alternative is to estimate the consumption levels at different points of time in the future, to discount them at chosen rates of interest, and then to arrive at a total discounted sum of consumption. The interest rate used for discounting will reflect what relative weights the planners wish to attach to consumption today vis-à-vis that next year, the year after, and so on.

What considerations are relevant for the choice of these discount rates? That will depend on the objectives of planning. Presumably, if the consumption level is rising over time and people are getting richer, the importance of an additional unit of consumption today may be greater than that in the future. A 5 per cent discount will mean that the planners regard 105 units of consumption next year to be equivalent to 100 units this year. The planners will have to choose the discount rates after considering the expected growth rates of total consumption and of population.

*From Amartya K. Sen, *The Flow of Financial Resources,* United Nations Conference on Trade and Development TD/C/C.3/94/Add.1, August 20, 1971, pp. 6–10. Reprinted by permission.

DISTRIBUTION OF INCOME

Improvement of the distribution of income can be an important objective of planning especially in economies with much inequality. There are many ways of bringing income distribution into the cost-benefit evaluation. One of the simplest is to attach an additional weight to the consumption gains of the poorest sections of society. Depressed regions may be given preferential treatment through a premium attached to consumption accruing there, e.g., consumption of region A may get a weight of, say, 1.10 in comparison with a general weight of 1 per unit of average consumption.

It is sometimes argued that improvements in income distribution should be brought about not through project selection, which may interfere with production efficiency, but by fiscal means, e.g., taxation and subsidies. There is, obviously, some advantage in effecting redistribution through taxation, but there are limits to what can be achieved this way, given the political and administrative constraints. If, after tax reform, the planners still find the income distribution to be unsatisfactory, an improvement in the distribution may quite properly figure as a specific consideration in the choice of investment projects.

MERIT WANTS

It is not uncommon for the government to attach a degree of importance to certain types of needs in excess of that which these needs get in terms of market prices. For example, there may be a case for attaching greater importance to education than the market value of education would suggest. Other examples of such "merit wants" (as they have been called) include self-reliance in modern industrial technology, wider dissemination of modern science, or the employment of female labour in regions where women's emancipation is a felt need. In such cases, the planners may give an additional weight to what they regard as especially "meritorious" expenditure.

EMPLOYMENT OBJECTIVES

Reduction of unemployment is frequently an important objective of planning. If expansion of employment is thought to be an objective in its own right, then a weight may be given to the additional employment generated. The weight should reflect the amount of average consumption today that the planners are ready to sacrifice for generating an additional unit of employment.

It is worth considering whether employment is regarded as an objective in itself or as something that is desired as a means to other ends such as a better distribution of income. If the latter is the case the planners may prefer to give a special weight to the consumption of low-income groups, thereby permitting comparisons with other means of achieving the same end, e.g., paying doles or providing free rations. However, if greater employment is desired for its own sake, assigning a weight directly to employment may be the better procedure.

BALANCE OF PAYMENTS

Projects are sometimes judged in terms of their balance-of-payments impact. This is, undoubtedly, an important consideration, but its use in cost-benefit analysis requires some caution.

Foreign exchange is not desired for its own sake. It is not a basic objective of planning. In fact, it is more useful to view the foreign exchange balance as a constraint that restricts the freedom of resource allocation than as an objective in its own right. On this view, ultimate goals such as consumption creation, improvement of income distribution, etc., should motivate planning and the balance of payments should come in only as a constraint that must be met in achieving these other objectives.

Even if the earning of foreign exchange is not an objective in itself, it is likely to be a valuable means for achieving other objectives. Earning $1 more in foreign exchange will then have to be valued in terms of its impact on the fulfilment of the other objectives. If it is thought that having an additional dollar of foreign exchange will permit policies that lead to an additional $1.50 worth of present consumption (or its equivalent in terms of other objectives), then $0.50 is the premium to be placed on foreign exchange earning.

Many developing countries have chronic balance-of-payments problems and the nominal exchange rates of their currencies do not reflect the real scarcity of foreign exchange. If such a situation prevails, the case for putting a premium on foreign exchange is a straightforward one, since the nominal value requires an upward correction.

An additional dollar of foreign exchange can be valued for the purpose of cost-benefit analysis in terms of its maximum contribution to social welfare related to the objectives of planning. One has to compare its alternative uses, viz., expansion of imports and reduction of exports, and choose the feasible alternative that yields the highest return in terms of social welfare in units of present consumption. That return represents the social value of the expenditure.

EXTERNALITIES AND NON-QUANTIFIABLES

Not all the effects of a project work through the market. A factory that contrib-utes to the training of the local labour force performs a service that is not fully reflected in its profits. On the other hand, the profits of the individual firm also do not reflect any damage done to the environment, for example, through pollution. These non-market effects, known as "externalities," may be very important for project selection.

Some of these effects are, however, not easy to quantify. The value of "learning by doing" in modern industrial enterprises may be recognized as important without being susceptible of precise quantitative measurement. The valuation of the impact on the environment is also not easy.

There are two ways of dealing with this problem. One is to ignore non-quantifiable effects altogether. The other is to give some value to non-quantifiables in line with the general goals of planning without pretending to accuracy. The second approach seems preferable. To ignore the non-quantifiables altogether is to give them the value zero. That option is in any case open under the second approach as well, but if the planners feel that they have a better guess than zero, they may use that guess. Even market value estimates, especially those involving the future, involve considerable elements of guess work, and the valuation of externalities does not therefore differ in principle from the rest of the exercise.

X.D.2. Choice of Technology as a Problem of "Second Best"*

Before one can enter the debate on the complex question of the choice of technology in the context of development planning, certain preliminary issues have to be cleared up.

*From A. K. Sen, "Choice of Technology: A Critical Survey of a Class of Debates," in UNIDO, *Planning for Advanced Skills and Technologies,* Industrial and Planning Programming Series No. 3, New York, 1969, pp. 45–9. Reprinted by permission.

These include the concept of technical efficiency, which is one of the dominant concepts in the field of policy-oriented economics.

Suppose we are considering some technical choice i which permits the production of an output combination x using an input combination y. If it is possible to produce the same bundle of commodities x with less of at least one, and no more of any, of the inputs, then the technical choice i is not efficient. This is simply because efficiency implies producing a given quantity of output with as few inputs as possible. Similarly, if with that collection of inputs y, an output combination can be produced which exceeds x in at least one, and is no less in terms of any, of the outputs, then again the technical choice i must be regarded as inefficient. This is because efficiency also implies that for any given collection of inputs we should try to get the maximum of outputs.

In fact, we can combine the two criteria together by treating inputs as negative outputs.[1] Thus defined, what efficiency requires is that no more of any one output can be obtained given the amount of the others.

This takes us a certain distance, but not very far. If a certain technical choice leads to a greater output of a given commodity and a lower output of some other commodity than a different technical choice would do, the criterion of technical efficiency does not help us at all. Both these technical choices may satisfy the test of efficiency and yet we may be left with a problem still to be solved.

The concept of technical efficiency is often applied at a given point of time, but there is no difficulty in extending it over time. All we need to do is treat a certain commodity today as different from the same commodity tomorrow. In other respects the definitions, concepts and criteria need not be altered. The same problem of incompleteness persists, naturally, even in this extended view of technical efficiency, embracing more than one point in time. In fact, in comparing two alternative technological possibilities, we might face a possibility of having more of a certain commodity at point of time t and less of some commodity at a point of time $(t + 1)$. Once again the criterion of technical efficiency cannot solve this problem.

The main usefulness of the criterion of efficiency is that it permits a preliminary sorting out. A number of technological possibilities may be eliminated on grounds of inefficiency, and then we shall be left with a

set of efficient technological possibilities, the choice between which must be made on the basis of some other criterion. Efficiency is like a test applied in the "qualifying round," and it needs to be supplemented by some other criterion to determine which is the winner amongst those alternatives that have qualified.

This is where the notion of optimality comes in. This is one of the basic concepts used in economics: an optimum choice represents the "best" among the feasible alternatives. Naturally, if we are to choose the optimum combination we must have some criteria for discrimination between the various alternatives.

A preliminary point of logic may be cleared up at this stage. We can distinguish between two conditions for rational choice: the existence of either a "complete ordering" or a "choice set." The former requires that any two alternatives should be consistently comparable with each other in terms of some ordering relation, such as "being at least as good as . . . ." This property is sometimes called "connectedness." Another required condition is "transitivity," which demands that if x is regarded as being at least as good as y, and y is regarded as being at least as good as z, then x should be regarded as at least as good as z.[2] When these conditions are satisfied, a complete ordering exists over the relevant conditions.

The existence of a choice set is somewhat different. This requires the existence of some alternative which is regarded as at least as good as every alternative in the available set. This simply means that a "best" alternative

---

[1]See Debreu, p. 56. A good introduction to the problems of efficiency can be found also in Koopmans.

[2]On the logic of ordering, see Arrow and Debreu. It may be noted that the way we have defined any two alternatives being comparable not only guarantees "connectedness" but also yields "reflexivity" which requires that every alternative be regarded as "at least as good as" itself. When the alternatives considered are the same, what was defined as "connectedness" is in fact a condition of "reflexivity." By and large in optimal policy decision, reflexivity is not a major source of worry; in fact, a minimal degree of sanity seems to be sufficient. The real problem arises with connectedness and transitivity. On this, see in particular Arrow.

exists. The existence of a choice set may be regarded as sufficient for the purposes of choosing an optimal policy.

It is important to note that the existence of a complete ordering is neither a sufficient, nor a necessary condition for the existence of a choice set. It is not sufficient because, although we may be able to order alternatives in a certain fashion, if there is an infinite number of them, it is possible that no best alternative may exist. For example, alternative 2 may be preferred to 1, alternative 3 to 2, alternative 4 to 3, and so on, *ad infinitum.* It is not a necessary condition because, although we may be able to compare some alternative with all the others and find it to be at least as good as them all, there may, nevertheless, be intransitivities, or a lack of connectedness. For example x may be regarded as better than y and also better than z; but we may not be able to compare y and z by the criterion we are using. Even so, we may feel safe in choosing x, since it is the best alternative, although we cannot compare its two inferiors y and z.

In spite of this difference between the conditions for the existence of a choice set and those for the existence of a complete ordering it is clear that there is an intimate relationship between these two aspects of rational choice. In fact, most of the discussions on optimality have been concerned with obtaining a criterion for a complete ordering, and it has been supposed that this in itself will guarantee the identification of a best alternative. This presupposition makes eminently good sense when the number of alternatives is finite, when a consequence of the existence of a complete ordering is the existence of a choice set. When, however, the number of alternatives is infinite, this consequence may or may not follow. Furthermore, even when a complete ordering does not exist we may still be able to find what is the best thing to do. Although we shall not be concerned very much in this paper with this contrast it is important for us to bear in mind the difference between these two requirements of rational selection. Indeed, in some problems the distinction can be extremely important.

Whether we prefer a choice set or a complete ordering, we need some method of ordering, a criterion to tell whether a certain alternative x is better or worse than, or indifferent to, another alternative y. The concept of technical efficiency can be used partly for this purpose, and we may find that x is more efficient than y and simply eliminate y. However, as we noted before, this does not help when x and y are both efficient. Much of the debate on the choice of techniques is concerned with supplementing the criterion of technical efficiency by some other criterion that will permit us to choose between the efficient alternatives. In the discussion that follows we shall be concerned with a choice among a set of efficient alternatives, and shall assume that the inefficient ones have already been pruned away.

We shall thus have no further use for the concept of efficiency as such, which (it will be assumed) has done its job, and the discussion will concentrate on some supplementary criteria to take us beyond efficiency. The lively debate on technological choice which has taken place over the last two decades has been concerned with methods of supplementing the relatively uncontroversial criterion of technical efficiency. To this range of problems we now turn.

SUBOPTIMALITY OF SAVINGS RATE AND CHOICE OF TECHNOLOGY AS A PROBLEM OF "SECOND BEST"

Investment decisions can be classified into various types, according to whether they depend on the optimum size of investment, the optimum capital-intensity, or the optimum sectoral allocation. While it is important that we recognize these investment decisions to be different, we cannot regard them as independent. Indeed, much of the controversy on the choice of technology concerns the dependence of the amount of savings on the factor proportions selected.

A simple illustration may bring out the difference between some of the schools of thought. It may be argued that wage earners tend to have a higher propensity to consume than profit earners. This is likely to be spectacularly true in a socialist economy, where the profits are earned by the state, but it may hold good even in the case of a privately-owned enterprise. Given this assumption, it appears that the proportion of additional income that is saved will depend on the distribution of that additional income between the wage earners and the profit earners. And this distribution, in its turn, depends on the choice of technology, since a more labour-intensive technique will (other things being equal) tend to lead to a higher share of wages.

A special case of this has been much discussed: the assumption that the wage earners have a propensity to consume of 1 and profit earners have a propensity to consume of 0. This is, however, a rather limited case, and the problem with which we are concerned relates to much more general conditions, viz., the propensity to save of profit earners is systematically higher than that of wage earners. Given this assumption a direct link would be established between the degree of labour intensity chosen and the proportion of the additional income that will be saved.

Situations often occur in which one technique will lead to a higher amount of total output and another technique will generate a higher amount of total savings. If we wish to attach additional weight to the savings generated, over and above the weight that is attached to all output (be it saved or consumed), then clearly this will affect our decisions regarding which techniques to choose.

For the purpose of this discussion total output and total savings may be regarded as two separate commodities, even when they are assumed to be physically homogeneous, as in some simple models. The question of economic efficiency discussed in the last section may be applied to such a case. Any technique which generates less of either total savings or total output and no more of the other may be simply rejected as inefficient. But after this preliminary pruning operation had been carried out, we would be left with a set of techniques that could not be compared purely on

efficiency grounds. We should then have cases in which a higher amount of total savings results in a lower amount of total output. What our choice is in such a situation will depend crucially on the additional weights to be attached to savings as against output.

At this stage we might ask: Why must we attach any additional weight to savings as such? After all, savings involve a certain sacrifice of present in favour of future consumption, and what reason is there for us to believe that it is always better to sacrifice present consumption for a corresponding future amount? Indeed there is no such compelling reason in general. What the debate on choice of technology did was to assume (often implicitly) a suboptimal rate of savings, some outside constraint preventing the savings rate from rising to the optimal level. As a consequence there was always reason to look kindly on any policy which led to a higher proportion of savings.

Why this suboptimality should arise is itself a complex question. In the case of private-enterprise economy it can certainly be argued that the rate of savings may be considerably below optimal.[3] In particular, it has been argued that people might be willing to sign a contract forcing everyone to save a certain amount for the future, even when they may not do it individually under the market mechanism: a situation of this kind has been christened the "isolation paradox".[4]

There seems to be considerable agreement at a practical level regarding the need for raising the rate of saving in many underdeveloped countries. Indeed one has only to look through the planning documents of a variety of countries to see that one of the persistent themes is the need for a higher rate of saving and a higher rate of growth.[5] These documents are clearly based on certain assumptions, usually implicit, about the objectives to

[3]See Pigou, Ramsey, Baumol, Dobb, Sen (1961, Feb. 1967), Marglin (Feb. 1963, May 1963), Feldstein, and others.

[4]Sen (1961). See also Baumol, Marglin (Feb. 1963), Harberger, Lind, Phelps, and Sen (Feb. 1967).

[5]See R. F. Kahn for a review of some of the planning documents in this context.

be achieved by the economy, in terms of which the existing rates of saving appear to be below optimal. Sometimes the arguments are fairly sophisticated,[6] sometimes not.

Whatever the reasons for the suboptimality of the savings rate, it seems to be clear that this is a persistent diagnosis for most under-developed economies. In the presence of such suboptimality it is not difficult to see why additional weight has to be attached to the part of the additional income that is saved and invested as against the part that is consumed. It is in this context that much of the controversy on the problem of choice of technology in recent years become fully clear.

Essentially the problem is that of choice of technology in a world of suboptimal savings. It can also be viewed as a problem in the theory of "second best."[7] Since misallocation at the margin of choice between savings and consumption is due to some specific constraint, this will be reflected in the choice of the degree of labour intensity implicit in the technological selection. The problem would have been totally different if the case had been one of allocating an optimal amount of savings among techniques with varying degrees of labour intensity.

A distinction should be made in this context between

1. a general equilibrium formulation where the amounts of savings, the degrees of labour intensity, and the pattern of investment are to be simultaneously selected; and

2. a partial equilibrium formulation where the technical choice is confined to finding an optimal labour intensity for a marginal project.

In the former case the inoptimality of the savings rate should not be assumed although it may result from the allocational exercise.

In the latter case an over-all suboptimality of savings may be taken as given, since the project in question is too small to affect the over-all inoptimality of savings.

Some kind of an objective function may be given which depends on technical choice and the proportion of savings. In the absence of any constraint on savings, our choices should lead to an optimal situation with the usual marginal equalities, if the exercise is of the former kind: in the absence of a specific constraint on the rate of savings, the rate of transformation between consumption at time t and the consumption at time $(t + 1)$ will equal the rate at which we are ready to substitute the one for the other.[8] There will then be no need for a marginal preference in favour of future consumption, implying additional weight on the savings generated. Even in the general-equilibrium framework, if some outside constraint is imposed which prevents the rate of saving from rising above a certain level, a suboptimality of savings can result. It will then be appropriate to attach additional weight to savings as against the part of the income immediately consumed.

Such constraints can arise for a variety of reasons, including political difficulties in taxation. The planners may want a higher rate of saving in terms of the objectives assumed by them, but fail to achieve this for fear of political reactions.[9] Given this political constraint the suboptimality of the savings rate that may be generated will tend to influence the optimal technical choice in the direction of relatively more capital-intensive techniques, as implying a relatively higher rate of savings.

This is precisely where a different school of thought may make itself heard, arguing that such political constraints do not in fact occur,

---

[6]Optimum savings models have generally tended to yield extremely high rates of savings, very much in excess of the usual rates observed anywhere in the world. See, among others, Tinbergen (1957, 1962), Goodwin, Chakravarty, and Sen (1967).

[7]See Lancaster and Lipsey.

[8]This is on the assumption of smooth differentiability. When there is only a limited number of basic alternatives, with resultant "kinks" in the transformation surfaces, the corresponding rule will take the form of a set of inequalities. See Dorfman, Samuelson, and Solow.

[9]Whether this range of problems can arise in a fully socialist economy is a matter for discussion. For some indications that they do, see Pajestka and Marglin (Jan. 1966).

that the total amount of income to be saved can be determined by the planner in any way he likes, and that he can then see that this decision is executed through the machinery at his disposal, such as wages and incomes policy, taxation policy and monetary policies. If this is true then the link snaps between the choice of techniques and the proportion of income saved. Then technical choice may be made with the main purpose of maximizing the amount of output,[10] and the proportion of the output to be invested can be decided at a separate stage.

In the context of such an assumption it will be right to argue that the amount of income generated in a surplus-labour economy ought to be maximized even at the expense of savings. This argument could spring from the assumption either that there is no suboptimality of savings or that the proportion of income that can be saved, even if constrained, is not dependent on the distribution of income. Various elaborations of these arguments can be found in economic literature.

Having commented on what appear to be some of the major issues that divide the different schools of thought in the debate on technical choice, we may now proceed to discuss the controversy itself in some greater detail. We develop a general framework in the next section and then express the various criteria in terms of comparison and contrast. This general framework uses a very simple model with one homogeneous commodity, which nevertheless illustrates almost the entire controversy that has taken place in recent years on choice of techniques for an under-developed economy. At a later stage, in the context of a model on concave programming, we shall discard this assumption, and discuss the problem in a multi-commodity context.

A GENERAL FRAMEWORK

Let there be a production function relating output (Q) to labour (L) and capital (K).

[10]The implicit framework here is that of a one-commodity model, but the corresponding conditions for a multi-commodity model are easy to obtain.

$$Q = Q(L, K) \qquad (1)$$

We assume this to be homogeneous of the first degree, i.e., with constant returns to scale. Let the wage rate be given by w, the propensity to consume of wage earners by c_1 and the propensity to consume of profit earners by c_2. The amount of the income that is saved is represented as S, which is expressed by the following relationship:

$$S = L\,w(1 - c_1) + (Q - L\,w)(1 - c_2) \qquad (2)$$

We assume that the supply of labour is unlimited.[11] The object of the exercise is to maximize a certain weighted sum of output and savings.[12] It is to be remembered that savings S is a part of output Q, so that the weight attached to S is in the nature of a premium, i.e., it is an additional weight, over and above the weight that S receives as a part of Q. Let this premium on savings be given by λ, which we have taken to be positive, since we have assumed the savings rate to be suboptimal.[13] The object, therefore, is to maximize the following welfare function

$$V = Q + \lambda S \qquad (3)$$

Given the amount of capital the problem of the choice of techniques is simply to find the right amount L, which will determine the appropriate degree of capital intensity (K/L). Due to the assumption of constant returns to scale, it does not matter how we choose K, for the discussion is all in terms of ratios per unit

[11]For a contrast of views on the empirical acceptability of this assumption, see Nurkse, Lewis (1954, 1955, 1958), Eckaus, Mellor and Stevens, Rosenstein-Rodan, Leibenstein, Viner, Haberler, Oshima, Fei and Ranis, Schultz, Jorgenson (1966), Marglin (1966), Sen (Oct. 1966, Feb. 1967), and Mehra.

[12]In a general equilibrium framework the weights should vary with the choice of techniques, and the objective function should be "non-linear." However, in the case of a small project, the total savings and the consumption for the economy as a whole may not be much affected by the marginal choice. There the weights can be taken as given, much as the perfectly competitive firm takes prices as given.

[13]The choice discussed here is for a marginal project. A wider exercise should take λ as a variable. The optimality conditions, however, will remain the same for appropriate values of λ.

of capital. It is clear that the first order condition of maximization of the objective function is given by the following when K is given:

$$\frac{\partial V}{\partial L} = 0 \qquad (4)$$

Given the equation (1), (2) and (3) it can be seen that the conditions of maximization given by equation (4) requires the following:

$$\frac{\partial Q}{\partial L} [1 + \lambda(1 - c_2)] = \lambda w(c_1 - c_2) \qquad (5)$$

As a condition on the marginal productivity of labour we can re-write relationship (5) as follows, defining that magnitude to which the marginal product of labor is to be equated as "the real cost of labour" (w^*):

$$w^* = \frac{\partial Q}{\partial L} = \left[\frac{(c_1 - c_2)\lambda}{1 + (1 - c_2)\lambda} \right] w \qquad (6)$$

Much of the controversy on the choice of technology for an under-developed economy with surplus labour can be seen to be variations on the theme represented by equation (6). With this general framework we can sort out the different contributions in this controversial field.

One clarifying remark should be made before we proceed further. The evaluation of alternative techniques depends crucially on the value of λ, i.e., on the additional weight to be attached to investment as against consumption. The value of λ in its turn depends on the relative weights to be attached to consumption today as against that in the future. What we are really attempting, therefore, is to provide a one-period model which tries to catch the essence of comparison of the relevant sets of time series of consumption representing alternative technological possibilities.

That the problem of choice of techniques cannot be solved except in terms of making explicit value judgments about alternative sets of time series has been discussed by Sen[14] who also argued that the different criteria

proposed really boil down to doing this very thing in a highly implicit manner.[15] . . .

References

K. J. Arrow, *Social Choice and Individual Values*, New York, 1951.

W. J. Baumol, *Welfare Economics and the Theory of the State*, London, 1952.

S. Chakravarty, "Optimum Savings with Finite Planning Horizon," *International Economic Review*, Sept. 1962.

G. Debreu, *The Theory of Value*, London, 1959.

R. Dorfman, P. A. Samuelson, and R. M. Solow, *Linear Programming and Economic Analysis*, New York, 1958.

M. H. Dobb, *An Essay on Economic Growth and Planning*, London, 1960.

R. S. Eckaus, "Factor Proportions in Underdeveloped Countries," *American Economic Review*, Vol. 45, Sept. 1955.

C. H. Fei and G. Ranis, *Development of Labor Surplus Economy: Theory and Policy*, Homewood, 1964.

M. S. Feldstein, "The Social Time Preference Discount Rate in Cost-Benefit Analysis," *Economic Journal*, June 1964.

R. M. Goodwin, "The Optimum Path for an Underdeveloped Economy," *Economic Journal*, Dec. 1961.

G. Haberler, "Critical Observations on Some Current Notions on the Theory of Economic Development," *L'Industria*, Vol. 2, 1957.

A. C. Harberger, "Techniques of Project Appraisal," National Bureau of Economic Research, Conference on Economic Planning, 1964.

D. W. Jorgenson, "Testing Alternative Theories of the Development of a Dual Economy," in I. Adelman and E. Thorbecke (eds.), *The Theory and Design of Economic Development*, Baltimore, 1966.

———, "Subsistence Agriculture and Economic Growth," *Oxford Economic Papers*, 1967.

[14]Sen (1957).

[15]Explicit attempts at making these comparisons can be found in Sen (1957, 1968). This problem has been penetratingly studied by Marglin (Jan. 1966).

R. F. Kahn, "The Pace of Development," in Hebrew University, *The Challenge of Development*, Jerusalem, 1958.

T. C. Koopmans, *Three Essays on the State of Economic Science*, New York, 1957.

K. Lancaster and R. G. Lipsey, "The General Theory of Second Best," *Review of Economic Studies*, Vol. 24, 1956.

H. Leibenstein, "The Theory of Underemployment in Backward Economies," *Journal of Political Economy*, Vol. 65, Apr. 1957.

W. A. Lewis, "Economic Development with Unlimited Supplies of Labour," *Manchester School*, May 1954.

———, *The Theory of Economic Growth*, London, 1955.

———, "Unlimited Labour: Further Notes," *Manchester School*, Jan. 1958.

R. C. Lind, "The Social Rate of Discount and the Optimal Rate of Investment: Further Comment," *Quarterly Journal of Economics*, May 1964.

S. A. Marglin, "The Social Rate of Discount and the Optimal Rate of Investment," *Quarterly Journal of Economics*, Feb. 1963.

———, "The Opportunity Costs of Public Investment," *Quarterly Journal of Economics*, May 1963.

———, *Industrial Development in the Labour-Surplus Economy*, mimeographed, Jan. 1966.

———, "Mr. Jorgenson Against the Classics," in I. Adelman and E. Thorbecke (eds.), *The Theory and Design of Economic Development*, Baltimore, 1966.

S. Mehra, "Surplus Labour in Indian Agriculture," *Indian Economic Review*, Apr. 1966.

J. W. Mellor and R. D. Stevens, "The Average and Marginal Product of Farm Labor in Underdeveloped Economies," *Journal of Farm Economics*, Vol. 38, Aug. 1956.

R. Nurkse, *Problems of Capital Formation in Underdeveloped Countries*, Oxford, 1953.

H. T. Oshima, "Underemployment in Backward Economies: An Empirical Comment," *Journal of Political Economy*, Vol. 66, June 1958.

J. Pajestka, "Some Problems of Economic Development Planning," in Oscar Lange (ed.), *Problems of Political Economy of Socialism*, New Delhi, 1962.

E. S. Phelps, *Fiscal Neutrality toward Economic Growth*, New York, 1965.

A. C. Pigou, *Economics of Welfare*, 4th ed., London, 1932.

F. P. Ramsey, "A Mathematical Theory of Saving," *Economic Journal*, Dec. 1928.

P. N. Rosenstein-Rodan, "Disguised Unemployment and Underemployment in Agriculture," *Monthly Bulletin of Agricultural Economics and Statistics*, Vol. 6, July–Aug. 1957.

T. W. Schultz, *Transforming Traditional Agriculture*, New Haven, 1964.

———, "Significance of India's 1918–1919 Losses of Agricultural Labour—A Reply," *Economic Journal*, Vol. 77, Mar. 1967.

A. K. Sen, "Some Notes on the Choice of Capital-Intensity in Development Planning," *Quarterly Journal of Economics*, Nov. 1957.

———, "On Optimizing the Rate of Saving," *Economic Journal*, Vol. 71, Sept. 1961.

———, "Peasants and Dualism with or without Surplus Labour," *Journal of Political Economy*, Oct. 1966.

———, "Terminal Capital and Optimal Savings," in C. H. Feinstein et al. (ed.), *Capitalism, Socialism and Economic Growth, Essays in Honour of Maurice Dobb*, Cambridge, 1967.

———, "Isolation, Assurance and the Social Rate of Discount," *Quarterly Journal of Economics*, Feb. 1967.

———, *Choice of Techniques*, Oxford, 1960; 2nd ed., 1962; 3rd ed., 1968.

J. Tinbergen, "The Optimum Rate of Saving," *Economic Journal*, Dec. 1957.

———, "Optimum Savings and Utility Maximization over Time," *Econometrica*, Apr. 1962.

J. Viner, "Some Reflections on the Concept of 'Disguised Unemployment,'" *Contribucoes a Analise do Desenvolvimento Economico*, 1957.

X.D.3. Social Importance of Employment Creation*

It was noted earlier that one reason why employment is valued is because of its impact on income distribution. An unemployed person does not have a source of income; although it is possible to give him some income through a dole, this practice may be difficult to follow. In most developing countries a dole for the unemployed is not provided. Undoubtedly part of the reason is that with a large volume of surplus labour a poor country can ill-afford a dole system, and productive employment even with low output is preferable. Partly also, with disguised unemployment it is not very easy to identify those to whom a dole should be paid. Under these circumstances, an expansion of employment in spreading the real income very widely may contribute efficiently to the redistribution objective. As was noted earlier, many of the desirable aspects of employment creation, its impact on nourishment, on education etc. really relate to the fact that employment creates a source of livelihood for the family.

This being the case, it is worth considering whether employment should be valued separately in project selection in the light of its impact on income distribution, or whether income distribution should be given a specific value and employment treated as a means to it. Fundamentally, this is not a crucial question, since which way we do the calculation makes little difference so long as the link between employment and redistribution is clearly recognized and realistically calculated. However, from the point of view of the convenience of calculation this is a question of some importance.

If, on the one hand, we treat the income level of the poorer classes as the relevant item to which value is attached, that value will simply reflect the planners' idea of the rela-

tive importance of channelling consumption to the poor. The planners' evaluation need not be concerned with the precise calculation of the impact of employment on the consumption of the poor classes; this would be left to the project evaluator. If, on the other hand, the central policy makers attach precise value to employment, in estimating this value the policy makers will have to take into account the impact of employment on the consumption of the poor classes, and the value will have to be determined by considering this in conjunction with the innate importance of giving consumption opportunities to the poor. The second procedure is less direct than the first, and there are obvious advantages in following the first procedure. The project evaluator himself is in a better position to judge the precise impact of employment and other factors on income distribution, and it seems best to do this calculation directly and to leave the central policy makers in fixing social weights unencumbered by this complex detail. By valuing redistribution the division of labour between the project evaluator and the over-all policy maker will be more appropriate, and this is the procedure we follow in these Guidelines.

A more fundamental issue is why employment should be regarded as a vehicle of income distribution and why income cannot be redistributed more directly through taxation and fiscal policy. In principle there is no difficulty in paying a person a certain amount of money even without employing him in a project. Employment may be quite extraneous to the act of payment. The objection that paying someone without employing him will be unethical need not detain us; since we are considering the role of employment in income distribution, our real concern is with getting income to the poor person, whether or not he is employed. In fact, to the extent that work is regarded as unpleasant and leisure is regarded as valuable, paying people without making them work may well be considered a

---

*From UNIDO, *Guidelines for Project Evaluation,* Project Formulation and Evaluation Series No. 2, New York, 1972, pp. 91–7. Reprinted by permission.

superior means of income redistribution than employment.

The picture is, however, not so simple. Payment without work may have important political and social repercussions. If the Government decides to give a number of people some income without work, the question would naturally be raised why these people rather than others are selected for such support. This question of selection arises even for employment when unemployment is widespread, and charges of favouritism in job giving are not uncommon. However, in the case of employment creation, there are at any rate some possible criteria for suitability for jobs and also some definite procedure for giving employment. Also, getting paid for one's job is considered a compensation for one's effort, even though the institutional wage rate may be regarded as very much in excess of the unpleasantness of work in a country with unemployment. However that may be, politically the question of arbitrariness in job distribution, while important, is not likely to be such an explosive issue as the giving out of income without work.

In some situations income may be redistributed better through a direct payment than through giving employment. In dealing with people with some crying need, e.g., medical facilities, it may be simpler to give income than to give jobs. It is not being suggested that employment giving is always the best means of redistributing income. It need not be so at all. But often employment will be an important vehicle of income redistribution and the fact that its political feasibility is somewhat greater than pure distribution of money, except in very special situations, cannot be overlooked.

It might be mentioned in this context that the possibility of corruption is perhaps also less when income is redistributed through employment rather than through subsidies. It has been found, for example, that in giving famine relief in countries like India, the system of paying wages to labour in specially devised work programmes is less open to misuse than the system of a direct dole. There are clearer records of employment and also less

possibility of distributing money to nonexistent persons, which is not uncommon in the context of a pure dole in a country with a defective administrative system. This is another reason why employment may be an important means of redistribution.

Be that as it may, in considering project selection we should have to see the redistributional impact of employment creation as a possible part of the objectives of some projects. There is nothing strange about this. Basically, this is another reflection of a phenomenon we have outlined in several places in these Guidelines: the best economic possibilities are not the same as political feasibilities. The redistribution of income through employment may be feasible when pure redistribution without employment may not be, even when the latter may be economically perfectly possible.

What we are mainly concerned with is an understanding of how employment may affect income distribution. This will vary from project to project. One has to see to what extent additional employment will provide income to particularly depressed groups. We have already discussed earlier how the redistribution objective can be formulated in a variety of ways. One of the ways is to attach an additional weight to the consumption of depressed groups or classes. Sometimes when a whole region is known to be economically depressed, income generating in that region may be given a special weight. Quite clearly this will include the impact of employment because in estimating the income generated in that region, note must be taken of employment and wages paid out. If we are concerned with such broad considerations, no special efforts need be made to see that the effects of employment are reflected in the income-distribution objective; the procedure already suggested will do it very well. However, sometimes we may wish to attach a special importance to income accruing to depressed groups within a specific region, and we may then wish to attach a special weight to the wages paid to that group. Regions very often are internally unhomogeneous, and it may be important to distinguish between the depressed and the not-so-depressed classes in a certain region.

While such a distinction requires a fairly detailed calculation, it does not really affect the principles. On the one hand, the work should consist of making precise estimates of the income generated that will be enjoyed by these specific depressed groups. On the other hand, the policy makers must indicate the additional value to be attached to the income thus generated. For most of these really depressed groups, income and consumption are practically identical, so that we shall not be far wrong if we treat the accrued income of these groups as equivalent to their present consumption. In determining the value to be attached to the present consumption of these poorer groups, the policy makers must note that consumption to these groups will, on redistributional grounds, be regarded as more important than the consumption of the average citizen of the country. As part of aggregate consumption, consumption of these depressed groups will receive a weight in any case in the system of evaluating benefits of the projects. The additional weight to be attached to the consumption of these groups may be reflected through putting a positive value on the consumption of this group over and above the value of aggregate consumption.

For assessing the impact on employment and sectional income, the precise pattern of disbursement between different categories of expenditures would have to be examined. Very often project data are provided in such an aggregate manner that the expenditures on wages are not separated, nor is it specified where the additional people to be employed would be found. In the context of the objective of redistribution in relation to employment it would be important to obtain this breakdown, and to check what part of the disbursement reflects the additional wage bill and also to whom these wages are to be paid, i.e., whether the workers come from particularly depressed classes on whose income we would like to place an additional weight.

Compromises in project evaluation would, of course, have to be struck between the demands of perfection and the constraints of practicability. In principle it would be best to determine the precise income level of each employed person and attach a variable weight to his respective consumption; the weight will go up as the average income level goes down. This will not, however, be possible to do in any detail. The calculation would have to be done in terms of broad categories.

SOCIAL COST OF LABOUR

So far we have concentrated on the benefit side of employment, making only passing references to costs. In a country with full employment the cost of employment of labour is fairly easy to calculate. A person can be employed in a certain project only if he is withdrawn from employment somewhere else. From the point of view of this project, therefore, the cost of employing him may be thought to be equal to what he would have produced had he been employed elsewhere. This measure of what he would have alternatively produced is sometimes called "the social opportunity cost" of labour, a term that is often used in project-evaluation literature. By employing the person here the society is foregoing the opportunity of employing him elsewhere, and thus the social opportunity cost measures the value of the alternative opportunity that the society is losing by putting him to work in the project under discussion.

Defined this way, the opportunity cost of labour will be positive when there is full employment, but if there is unemployed labour it should be possible to employ labour in this project without having to withdraw it from elsewhere. Thus, the opportunity cost of labour as defined above may well be zero in the context of an economy with unemployment. Does this mean that employment of labour is costless for an economy with unemployment? The answer is "not at all," since along with employment come other changes in the economy that may or may not involve specific costs from the social point of view.

A few of the simpler considerations may be mentioned first, followed by a more complex problem. Although labour may be unemployed, it does not follow that there is no unpleasantness of work, especially since working conditions in developing countries often tend to be extraordinarily bad. The unpleasantness of work for those who would have otherwise been idle cannot be dismissed. This point assumes particular importance when there is a transfer of labour from the rural areas to the harsh living conditions of the growing towns and cities in the poor countries. The conditions of living, including the sanitary facilities and other social amenities in some of the urban areas of the developing countries, are often miserable, and it must be assumed that there is some loss in making people work under such conditions. It is possible to feel that this is an unimportant consideration, since the worker in question prefers to take the job rather than be unemployed. However, this is not a convincing argument. The worker prefers this job because he is paid a certain wage, and while this wage may overcompensate him for the inconvenience of bad working and living conditions, this does not mean that the working and living conditions do not involve some suffering. Therefore, just as we must calculate the benefits from employment in terms of output creation as well as of income redistribution and other objectives, we must also take into account the social costs, if any, of additional employment, especially when it involves migration.

From the social point of view, a further consideration may arise because the Government may have to construct housing and other facilities in an area to which the workers may be moving, and these costs may not be borne, at any rate not fully, by the workers themselves. Because a large proportion of the capital expenditure of a project lies in the cost of townships, this could be an important cost related to employment. If the benefits from new houses and good working conditions are provided, they may be included among the benefits of the project, but the cost of townships and housing must be counted as part of the cost of employment creation of the project.

A more complex consideration relates to the impact of employment on the distribution of the current income between consumption and investment. When an additional person is employed, drawn from the pool of the unemployed, and he is paid wages, some additional purchasing power is generated, and this will reflect itself in an increase in consumption. Of course, increased consumption is desirable, and indeed, aggregate consumption is the first objective that we examined in the context of cost-benefit calculation. However, an increase in immediate consumption may be achieved, under most circumstances, only through a reduction in investment. If the policy makers feel that, on balance at the margin, consumption and investment are equally attractive from the point of view of the society, it makes no difference whether investment is cut a little to increase immediate consumption correspondingly or whether immediate consumption is somewhat reduced for the sake of expansion of a corresponding amount of investment. If, however, we are dealing with an economy where the policy makers feel that the over-all rate of investment is deficient, a reduction in investment for the sake of an expansion of immediate consumption may be regarded as a loss. One way of viewing this problem is to regard the price of investment in terms of immediate consumption to be greater than one. . . . The shadow price of investment, $P^{\text{inv}}(t)$, is a crucial factor in assessing the social cost of employment, since the expansion of employment means a shift from investment to consumption, and the loss involved in this per unit is equivalent to the value of $[P^{\text{inv}}(t) - 1]$. If investment and consumption are already optimally distributed, i.e., there is neither underinvestment nor overinvestment, then the value of $P^{\text{inv}}(t)$ should be equal to 1 and the loss involved would be precisely 0. However, as is common in most developing countries, if the planners believe that the level of investment is too low, there will be a loss, since $P^{\text{inv}}(t)$ exceeds 1. The social cost of labour depends not merely on the social opportunity cost of labour but also on the shadow price of investment.

We may seem to be contradicting ourselves in some ways by regarding additional consumption generated through additional employment (a) to be a good thing because it leads to a better distribution of income, and (b) to be a bad thing because it leads to a shift from investment to consumption. This is, however, not a contradiction, and both facts are correct and relevant, though they work in opposite directions. A unit of income that accrues to a worker in a project rather than accruing to the project authorities can be viewed in one of two ways. To the extent that it reflects workers' consumption as opposed to average consumption of the community, it can be regarded as more valuable; to the extent that it reflects consumption rather than investment it must be regarded as less valuable if the country is suffering from a shortage of investment vis-à-vis consumption. The latter is the comparison of consumption with investment and the former is the comparison of consumption by a poorer group vis-à-vis that by a richer group. In making a detailed calculation of benefits and costs of a project both these considerations are relevant, but they will come into our estimation under different objectives and will work in different directions.

Under the broad hat of aggregate consumption would come the question of the relative weight of investment vis-à-vis average consumption today, since the impact of investment on future consumption is fully reflected in our estimation of the aggregate-consumption benefit. On the other hand, the special weight to be attached to the consumption of the poorer groups vis-à-vis average consumption today must come under the heading of the redistribution objective. Employment creation will, therefore, come in both the benefit and the cost side under these two sets of objectives; additional employment will involve a cost through the "aggregate-consumption objective" and a benefit through the "redistribution objective."

Comment

Previous selections argue that market savings tend to be below optimal, and that project appraisal should attach a premium on investment. In putting an extra weight on savings in the determination of the shadow price of labor, the project evaluator is raising the savings rate through control of project selection and the choice of capital-intensive investment.

A more general analysis of intertemporal optimality can be studied using the theory of optimal growth paths. Although the theory has been devised for advanced economies, some aspects of the theory relate to efficient capital accumulation and may be suggestive for the optimal allocation of investment between consumption and capital goods in a developing economy. An excellent survey article is F. H. Hahn and R. C. O. Matthews, "The Theory of Economic Growth: A Survey," *Economic Journal* (December 1964). Among the many growth models, the following may be of special interest: M. Dobb, *An Essay on Economic Growth and Planning* (1960); R. Findlay, "Optimal Investment Allocation Between Consumer Goods and Capital Goods," *Economic Journal* (March 1966); L. Johansen, "Some Theoretical Properties of a Two-Sector Model of Optimal Growth," *Review of Economic Statistics* (January 1967); L. G. Stoleru, "An Optimal Policy for Economic Growth," *Econometrica* (April 1965); S. Bose, "Optimal Growth and Investment Allocation," *Review of Economic Statistics* (October 1968); A. K. Dixit, "Optimal Development in the Labour-Surplus Economy," ibid. (January 1968); H. Uzawa, "Market Allocation and Optimum Growth," *Australian Economic Papers* (June 1968); Jaroslav Vanek, *Maximal Economic Growth* (1968); R. R. Nelson and S. G. Winter, "Neoclassical versus Evolutionary Theories of Economic Growth: Critique and Prospectus," *Economic Journal* (December 1974).

CHAPTER XI

Development Planning and Policymaking

All the preceding chapters have had some relevance for development planning, and we have already related specific aspects of development planning to several substantive problems. But we now want to examine the nature and scope of development planning in a more integrated fashion. By appraising the effectiveness of development planning in light of the development record and the analyses and policy proposals that have emerged in preceding chapters, this final chapter may also serve as a summary evaluation of the leading issues in development economics.

Just beneath the surface of practically all the preceding analyses has been the issue of planning versus the price system. We now focus directly on this, with some of the materials in this chapter arguing against the effectiveness of the price system for attaining the objectives of development. The market mechanism is criticized as being either ineffective, unreliable, or irrelevant for the problems now encountered by developing nations. It is contended that the price system exists in only a rudimentary form in many of the LDCs and that market forces are too weak to accomplish the changes needed for accelerated development. Even a fairly well-defined price system may be considered unreliable, it is claimed, when market prices of goods and factors are not a true reflection of the opportunity costs to society. Above all, it is contended that the price system must be superseded insofar as the determination of the amount and composition of investment are too important to be left to a multitude of individual investment decisions, and the tasks of the economy entail large structural changes over a long period ahead instead of simply marginal adjustments in the present period.

On the other hand, it can be argued that the objections to the market system are relatively unimportant compared with the essential functions of the market and that the disadvantages of detailed planning by a central authority are far more serious than the deficiencies of the market system. The market is extremely valuable in the context of development as an administrative instrument that is relatively cheap to operate (XI.A.2). For this reason and others outlined in XI.A, development policy might be better devoted to improving and strengthening the market system than to supplanting the market with detailed administrative controls.

To the extent, however, that there has been a large measure of government direction over the rate and pattern of development, we should appraise the techniques and applicability of development planning. Taken together, the materials in sections XI.B and XI.C indicate the nature of the available programming techniques, some operational problems, and the significance of their effects in practice. Although section XI.B considers general principles of model building and provides some introduction to the theory of development planning, it does not pretend to offer a detailed exposition of modeling techniques. Development programming has become a specialized subject in its own right, requiring more familiarity with mathematical and econometric techniques than can be provided here. We also slight the administrative aspects of development planning, leaving for more specialized courses in public administration or development management the consideration of the organizational problems of policy implementation.

We are, however, most interested in moving beyond the theory of development to a review of planning practice in order to distinguish between the techniques discussed in development literature and those that have actually been used in various countries. Although planning models have been useful in improving the formulation of development plans, their application is still beset with practical difficulties, and it is essential to recognize their possible abuse in development planning.

The Note in section XI.C submits some general conclusions on the present state of development planning and the modifications necessary to improve its future effectiveness. This Note and other selections in this chapter may appear critical of specific plans, but it should be realized that there can be considerable value to the planning process itself. The active process of planning may indeed be of more benefit than the actual plan, for it can demonstrate the need for the collection and use of more empirical information, promote the dissemination of knowledge, clarify objectives and choices, and indicate the political and administrative preconditions necessary for implementing policies.

What ultimately matters is the benefit that can come from a dialogue between the model-builder and policymaker. While a model cannot provide a final answer, it can illuminate choices and indicate to the policymaker the consequences of alternative decisions. The implementation of mathematical planning is, however, dependent on the degree of maturity of non-mathematical planning. It is only clear what aims are worth striving for when there has already been established an organized institutional, nonmathematical form of planning.

In a single model only a few hundred relationships and constraints can be considered. But people working in the central planning agencies and lower-level institutions and enterprises "sense" hundreds of thousands of further constraints and relations, and they can give expression to these in their own estimates. Mathematical planning will develop successfully only when it develops as one element of well-prepared and well-oriented institutional planning, connected by many threads with real economic life in developing countries.[1]

This chapter closes with a Note on international policymaking and the New International Economic Order (NIEO). Recognizing the futility of a North-South confrontation and the unrealism of many of the South's demands, the Note proposes instead that the North-South issues be factored into a cooperative solution of the several conflicts that the internationalization process has created for rich and poor countries alike.

---

[1]Janos Kornai, "Models and Policy: The Dialogue between Model Builder and Planner," in C. R. Blitzer et al., *Economy-Wide Models and Development Planning*, New York, 1975, chapter 2.

XI.A. PLANNING AND THE MARKET

XI.A.1. The Flaw in the Mechanism of Market Forces *

The free and unimpeded mechanism of market forces would lead to a maximum national income according to the liberal classical doctrine. Disregarding an ethical value-judgment about personal income distribution and special cases of increasing returns to scale the maximum would also be an optimum national income. Any conscious deliberate active economic policy designed to influence the amount and the composition of investment could not, according to this school, raise national income in the long run. It is the contention of this paper that the opposite is true, that an economic policy designed to influence the amount and composition of investment can raise the rate of economic growth and increase national income.

Maximization of national income would be reached, according to the "liberal" school, by the working of the mechanism of supply and demand on assumption of competitive conditions and of small changes per unit of time, in four stages or "equilibria": (1) allocation of given stock of consumers' goods, (2) allocation of production on assumption of given stock of equipment, land, and labor, (3) allocation of investment, on assumption of given stock of labor, land and capital. A fourth equilibrium condition is provided by Say's law.

It is true that the price mechanism works perfectly under those assumptions in the first stage, i.e., in allocation of given stocks of consumers' goods. It works less perfectly, but tolerably well, in the second stage, when we replace the assumption of given stocks of

consumers' goods by flows of supply of these goods from given stocks of equipment, raw materials, and labor.

The price mechanism does not work in this sense, however, in the third equilibrium when we drop the assumption of given fixed capital and assume that the amount and composition of investment is to be determined by a multitude of individual investment decisions.

The individual investment decision may lead to nonoptimum allocation of resources for the following reasons:

a. The investor maximizes the private, not the social net marginal product. External economies are not sufficiently exploited. Complementarity of industries is so great that simultaneous inducement rather than hope for autonomous coincidence of investment is called for.

b. The lifetime of equipment is long (say ten years) so that the investor's foresight is likely to be more imperfect than that of the buyer and seller or of the producer. The individual investor's risk may be higher than that confronting an over-all investment program. The costs of an erroneous investment decision are high; punishment in the form of loss of capital afflicts not only the investor but also the national economy.

c. Because of the indivisibility (lumpiness) of capital, large rather than small changes are involved. Yet the price-mechanism works perfectly only under the assumption of small changes.

d. Capital markets though often well organized are notoriously imperfect markets, governed not only by prices but also by institutional or traditional rationing quotas.

The investment theory is indeed the weakest link in the "liberal" theory.

It is finally recognized even by the strongest advocates of a free economy that an equi-

*From Paul N. Rosenstein-Rodan, "Programming in Theory and in Italian Practice," in Massachusetts Institute of Technology, Center for International Studies, *Investment Criteria and Economic Growth*, Cambridge, 1955; Asia Publishing House, Bombay, 1961, pp. 19–22. Reprinted by permission.

librium between aggregate demand and aggregate supply (i.e., the dynamic monetary equilibrium) cannot itself be ensured by trusting to the automatic responses of a free economy. This task can only be discharged by a deliberate policy. Without an equilibrium of aggregate demand and aggregate supply, however, prices cease to be reliable parameters of choice and the price mechanism breaks down.

The automatic responses of the market economy do not ensure an optimum allocation in two out of four markets. They allocate efficiently stocks of consumers' goods, and supplies of these goods flowing from stocks of equipment, but they do not function efficiently in the fields of investment and monetary equilibrium.

Programming is just another word for rational, deliberate, consistent, and coordinated economic policy. It is only spelling out explicitly what was always attempted implicitly in any monetary (fiscal and commercial) policy. Like Mr. Jourdain who talked prose all his life, programming at least in the field of monetary policy was always practiced, though it used shorthand rules of thumb or the "practical man's flairs, hunches, instincts and insights" rather than fully spelled out "White Papers" on output and employment. Neutral Government is as unrealistic an assumption as Neutral Money.

Monetary (fiscal and commercial) policy is a form of programming using indirect means for the achievement of its aims and targets. In its first pre-Wicksellian stage its only aim was equilibrium between aggregate demand and aggregate supply without distinguishing too clearly between investment and consumption. It became more purposeful in its second post-Wicksellian stage differentiating between and choosing its impact effects on various sectors of national income. In its third post-Keynesian stage it aims not only at *a* monetary equilibrium but at one which assures full employment and more and more also one (not necessarily the same) which assures the optimum rate of growth. In this third stage programming concerns not only the amount but also the composition of investment.

The *aim* of programming is to assure the maximum national income through time. For this purpose it tries to maximize the amount and to optimize the composition of investment. The *means* employed may be either indirect (monetary, fiscal and commercial policy as well as providing information on economic trends besides other incentives and disincentives) or direct (public investment). Even if no direct means were to be employed programming would be necessary in order to inform investors of short- and long-run trends, notably of intersectoral demands resulting from complementarity of industries (revealed by a periodically revised input-output table) and of indirect effects of investment on future demand of domestic, imported, or so far exported goods. Such information might guide and favorably influence the composition of investment.

The need for an active economic policy, even if it were to employ only indirect means, can hardly be denied. Agreement on this point may conceal, however, two different conceptions. The "liberal" considers State intervention as an occasionally necessary medicine. "Nobody denies that clean living is the best way to good health, but this is really not a sufficient reason to deny that it is sometimes necessary to take medicine." This view is based on the assumption that private investment decisions normally lead to an optimum position. The other view considers that a continuous active economic policy, beyond measures to assure an equilibrium between aggregate demand and aggregate supply, is necessary, since the multitude of dispersed individual uninfluenced decisions will not lead to the maximization of national income. The real question is how far programming should extend, what it should cover, what degrees of "freedom" it should leave between and within the various economic sectors. . . .

XI.A.2. The Market Mechanism as an Instrument of Development*

In recent times, there has been a retreat both in economic theory and in economic policy from the nineteenth-century ideal of the unfettered market as a principle of economic organization. But the economic pros and cons of this retreat have been fully debated, and the economist consequently has a great deal to say about the relative merits of the market as contrasted with other methods of economic organization, and the circumstances appropriate to each.

The subject of planning and the market in economic development is, therefore, one which falls definitely within the field of the economist. Before I go on to discuss it, I must define more precisely what I mean by it. "Planning and the market" may be interpreted in two different ways. First, it may refer to the contrast between direction of the economy by Government and the policy of *laissez-faire*. This is not my subject, though in a wider philosophical and historical context it offers much to discuss. For example, though *laissez-faire* and direction are often regarded as opposites, if one looks to the history of economic development one finds (as Professor Easterbrook has shown[1]) that economic development is almost invariably a process in which planning and direction on the one hand and freedom of enterprise on the other play their part, and are mixed. There is almost no case in which economic development has been entirely planned or entirely unplanned. The usual pattern is one of some framework of control by Government, within which the entrepreneur provides his

*From Harry G. Johnson, *Money, Trade and Economic Growth,* George Allen & Unwin Ltd., London, 1962, pp. 152–3, 156–9, 160–63. Reprinted by permission.

[1]Professor Easterbrook's analysis was presented in the Marshall Lectures at Cambridge University in the spring of 1956. Unfortunately these lectures have not been published, but some of the ideas are available in W. T. Easterbrook, "Long Period Comparative Study: Some Historical Cases," *Journal of Economic History,* XVII, No. 4. December 1957, pp. 571–95.

services—a mixture of bureaucracy and enterprise, in which bureaucracy takes care of the major risks of development and enterprise faces and overcomes the minor ones. Another relevant point that Easterbrook makes is that an economy which succeeds in finding a formula for growth tends to repeat that pattern after it has become inappropriate. For example, Britain has gone on trying to work the internationally-oriented pattern for her nineteenth-century development; Russia has been very successful in developing heavy industry but has not yet solved the problem of agriculture.

The alternative interpretation takes planning, in the sense of a general direction of the economy, as an established principle, and considers the market as an alternative to other and more direct means of detailed control. Given the general framework of economic planning, there is still a choice between two alternative methods of looking after the details. One is by direct detailed planning by a central authority, the other is by leaving the working out of details as far as possible to the operation of the market. (There is a third alternative, in which the Government is itself the entrepreneur and investor, which I shall consider later.)

This alternative interpretation is the one I shall be using: I shall discuss the question of the market mechanism as against detailed planning as an instrument of economic development. I should like to make it clear from the start that I am going to make a strong case for the market, as the preferable instrument of economic development, on two main grounds. The first is that the achievement of the desired results by control methods is likely to be especially difficult and inefficient in an underdeveloped economy; at this point I should like to remind you that a large part of Adam Smith's argument for *laissez-faire* was the inefficiency and corruption he saw in the Governments of his time. The second is that the remedies for the main fault which can be found with the use of the market mechanism, its undesirable social effects, are luxuries which underdeveloped countries cannot afford to indulge in if they are really serious about attaining a high rate of development. In particular, there is likely to be a conflict between rapid growth and an equitable distribution of income; and a poor country anxious to develop would probably be well advised not to worry too much about the distribution of income.

I am going to make a fairly strong case for the market, because the market figures relatively little in the literature of economic development, and the theoretical analysis which economics has developed in relation to markets is often overlooked or disregarded. . . .

I now want to recapitulate briefly the various economic functions of the market and the price system as a method of economic organization. I shall be brief, as the argument is a familiar one.

In the first place, the market rations supplies of consumer goods among consumers; this rationing is governed by the willingness of consumers to pay, and provided the distribution of income is acceptable it is a socially efficient process. Secondly, the market directs the allocation of production between commodities, according to the criterion of maximum profit, which, on the same assumption, corresponds to social usefulness. Thirdly, the market allocates the different factors of production among their various uses, according to the criterion of maximizing their incomes. Fourthly, it governs the relative quantities of specific types of labour and capital equipment made available. Fifthly, it distributes income between the factors of production and therefore between individuals. Thus it solves all the economic problems of allocation of scarce means between alternative ends.

These are static functions; but the market also serves in various ways to provide incentives to economic growth. Thus the availability of goods through the market stimulates the consumer to seek to increase his income; and access to the market provides an opportunity for inventors of new goods and technical improvements to profit from their exploitation. Moreover, the market serves particularly to provide an incentive to the accumulation of capital of all kinds: first to the accumulation of personal capital in the form of trained skill, since such skill earns a higher reward; and second to the accumulation of material capital, since such capital earns an income.

The argument, then, is that a properly functioning market system would tend to stimulate both economic efficiency and economic growth. And it is important to note that the market does this automatically, while it requires no big administrative apparatus, no central decision-making, and very little policing other than the provision of a legal system for the enforcement of contracts.

All this sounds very impressive; but it is clearly not the whole of the story. What, then, are the objections to the market, how serious are they, and what should be done about them in the context of economic development? I shall discuss these questions in some detail. But first I shall state briefly the central theme of my discussion. It is that in many cases the objections to the market can be overcome by reforming specific markets, so as to bring them closer to the ideal type of market; and that to overcome other objections to the market may be very expensive and may not prove to be worthwhile—in other words, the defects of the market mechanism may on balance be more tolerable than they look at first sight.

Now, what are the objections to the market? They can, I think, be classified into two main types. One type of objection is that the market does not perform its functions properly. The other type of objection is that the results produced by the functioning of the market are undesirable in themselves.

I begin with the first type of objection, that the market does not perform its functions properly. Here it is useful to draw a distinction between two quite different sorts of cases—those in which the market operates imperfectly, and those in which a perfectly functioning market would not produce the best results.

Imperfect operation of the market in an underdeveloped country may be attributable to ignorance, in the sense of lack of familiarity with market mechanisms and of awareness of relevant information, or to the prevalence of other modes of behaviour than the rational maximization of returns from effort. In the first case, the appropriate Governmental policy would seem to me to be, not to assume from the market the responsibility for allocative decisions, but to disseminate the knowledge and information required to make the market work efficiently and provide the education required to use it. The second case implies a more fundamental obstacle, not only to the use of the market but also to economic development itself, and suggests that successful economic development requires a basic change in social psychology. To my mind, it raises a serious question of fact. Is it really true that people in underdeveloped countries are strangers to the idea of maximizing gains? The idea that they are is very common in the literature and policy-making of economic development; one of its manifestations is the implicit assumption that both supplies and demands are completely price-inelastic. I am very sceptical about this, partly because of Bauer's work and partly because at least some of the actions of Governments in underdeveloped areas presuppose that even the poorest producers are susceptible to price incentives. I personally do not think one is justified in assuming as a general proposition that ignorance and illiteracy necessarily imply that men are not interested in making money. If it is true, there will be serious difficulties in the way of economic development; but again, the appropriate Governmental policy would seem to be to educate the people in the practice of rational economic behavior.

Even if the market functions perfectly, it will not produce the best possible results by its own criteria if there is a difference between social and private benefit or cost. This type of case may be particularly relevant to economic development; it includes the case of increasing returns to scale, and can be extended to include the possibility that technical progress or capital accumulation tend to proceed more rapidly in industry than in agriculture. But it raises an immediate question of fact—whether divergences between social and private benefit or cost are numerous and important or not. This is an important question, but one on which we do not know very much for certain. The theory of increasing returns is logically intriguing, but the influence of increasing returns still has to be disentangled from that of technical progress in historical growth. Again, it is a fact that few advanced countries are not industrial; but this by itself does not establish the wisdom of a policy of forced industrialization in an underdeveloped country. Aside from the question of fact, the existence of divergences between social and private returns does not necessarily indicate a need for the government to replace the market mechanism; instead, the operation of the market can be perfected by the use of appropriate taxes and subsidies to offset any divergences between social and private returns.

I now turn to the second type of objection to the market, the point of which is not that the market does not work in the way it should, but that the results produced are undesirable in themselves. Here, I think, there are two major objections to the market. The first is that the income distribution produced by the market is unjust and socially undesirable. The distribution of income through the market depends on the wealth and talents of different individuals, and on their individual skill in seeing a profitable opportunity of employing their money or labour. If they make a wise or lucky choice, they may obtain a much higher income. The objection is that this method of determining the distribution of income is not just. But if you attempt to intervene in the distribution of income, you immediately encounter the problem that such intervention interferes with the efficiency of the market system. If people are not allowed to enjoy the income they could obtain by their decisions, their decisions in turn will be affected, and the efficiency of the system will be impaired. There is, therefore, a conflict between economic efficiency and social justice. The extent and importance of this conflict is likely to vary according to the state of economic development. The more advanced a country is, the more likely are its citizens to have consciences about the distribution of income, and to accept the high taxation necessary to correct it without disastrously altering their behaviour; and on the other hand, the higher the level of income reached, the less serious will be any slowing down of the rate of growth brought about by redistribution policies. An advanced country can afford to sacrifice some growth for the sake of social justice. But the cost of greater equality may be great to any economy at a low level of economic development that wishes to grow rapidly, particularly as it is evident that historically the great bursts of economic growth have been associated with the prospect and the result of big windfall gains; it would therefore seem unwise for a country anxious to enjoy rapid growth to insist too strongly on policies aimed at ensuring economic equality and a just income distribution. I should add that the problem may not be in fact as serious as I have made it out to be, since in the course of time rapid growth tends in various ways to promote a more equal distribution of wealth. . . .

I have been discussing the objection to the results of the market system on the grounds that it produces an undesirable distribution of income. A second objection of the same sort is that the free market will not produce as high a rate of growth as is desirable. I think there is a strong case for this objection, because people's actions in regard to saving and investment depend very much on their guesses about the future. Now people are likely to know their own current requirements better than the Government. But the requirements of the future have to be looked at not from the individual or family point of view or that of the nation as a collection of individuals, but from the point of view of the ongoing society. The needs of society in the future, many economists agree, tend to be underprovided for by the free market.

Even if the conclusion that state action is desirable to raise the rate of growth is ac-

cepted, this conclusion nevertheless does not carry with it a number of corollaries which are often attached to it. In particular, it does not necessarily imply that the state ought to undertake development saving and investment itself. Private enterprise may be more efficient than the Government in constructing and operating enterprises, so that the best policy may be to stimulate private enterprise by tax concessions, subsidies, and the provision of cheap credit. Similarly, it may be preferable to stimulate private saving by offering high interest rates, rather than by forcing savings into the hands of the state by taxation or inflation. One argument against a policy of low interest rates and forced saving is that it may in the long run contribute to the inequality of income distribution. The reason is that the poor or small savers are mainly confined to low-yielding fixed-interest investments, directly or indirectly in Government debt, because these are safe and easily available, whereas the larger savers can invest their money in higher-yielding stocks and shares or directly in profitable enterprises. There is, therefore, an opportunity here for Government both to stimulate saving for development and to improve the distribution of income.

There is another reason for being wary of the proposition that the state should undertake development investment itself—the danger that if the Government undertakes investment itself, especially if its administrators are not too clear on their objectives, the result will be the creation of vested industrial interests inimical to further development, and resistant to technical change.

To summarize the foregoing argument from the point of view of development policy, it seems to me that much of development planning could usefully be devoted to the improvement and strengthening of the market system. This does not imply the acceptance of all the results of *laissez-faire,* especially with respect to the rate of growth; but there are reasons for thinking that too much emphasis on a fair or ethical distribution of income can be an obstacle to rapid growth.

The argument I have presented has been

concerned mainly with one side of the case for the market. The other side concerns the costs and difficulties of controls, in terms of the manpower costs of the administration they require, and their effects in creating profit opportunities which bring windfall gains to some members of the community and create incentives to evasion which in turn require policing of the controls. I have touched on that side of the argument sufficiently frequently to make it unnecessary to elaborate on it further.

Instead, I shall comment briefly on international markets in relation to economic development, since so far I have been implicitly concerned with internal markets. Economic development planning inevitably has a strong autarkic bias, by reason both of its motivation and of the limitation of the scope of control to the national economy. Nevertheless, international trade can play an important part in stimulating and facilitating the development process. Access to foreign markets for exports can permit an economy with a limited domestic market to exploit economies of scale, and the potentiality of such exports can serve as a powerful attraction for foreign capital and enterprise. Similarly, the capacity to import provided by exports can give a developing economy immediate access to the products of advanced technology, without obliging it to go through the long and perhaps costly process of developing domestic production facilities. Economic nationalism and excessive fear of the risks of international trade, by fostering aversion to exploiting the advantages of the international market, can therefore retard economic development unnecessarily.

One further comment on the international aspects of the market and economic development seems to me worth making. Discussion of the international side of development has been mostly concerned with commodity trade and commercial policy. But in fact one of the most important ways in which the world market system is imperfect is with respect to the international mobility of capital and labour. The problem of international capital movements has received a fair amount of attention, labour mobility and immobility much less. Now, the process of economic development in the past, especially in the nineteenth century, was characterized by vast movements, not only of capital, but also of labour, about the world. The mass movement of labour between countries has now been more or less shut off by the growth of nationalism. I believe it is important to recognize this restriction on international competition, and its implications for programmes of economic development. It means—looking at the world economy as a whole—that the solution to the problem of maximizing world output cannot be approached directly, by bringing labour, capital, technology, and natural resources together at the most efficient location; instead, the other productive factors have to be brought to the labour. To a large extent, "the economic development of underdeveloped countries" is a second-best policy,[2] in which gifts of capital and technical training by advanced to underdeveloped countries are a compensation for the unwillingness of the former to consider the alternative way of improving the labour to resources ratio, movement of the labour to the resources. The fact that development is a second-best policy in this respect may impose severe limitations on its efficiency and rapidity.

To conclude, I have been concerned with the role of the market in economic development; and I have aimed at stressing the economic functions of the market, in automatically taking decisions about various kinds of allocations of economic resources, and the place in economic development programmes of improvements in market organization and methods. I have been advocating, not a policy of *laissez-faire*, but recognition of the market as an administrative instrument that is relatively cheap to operate and may therefore be efficient in spite of objectionable features of

[2]See J. E. Meade, *The Theory of International Economic Policy, Volume II: Trade and Welfare*, London, Oxford University Press, 1955, and R. G. Lipsey and Kelvin Lancaster, "The General Theory of Second Best," *Review of Economic Studies*, XXIV (1), No. 63 (1956–57), pp. 11–33.

its operations. The general assumption on which I have been arguing is that economic development is a process of co-operation be-tween the state and private enterprise, and that the problem is to devise the best possible mixture.

XI.A.3 The Fragmented Economy*

While economists can usefully divide their labor as monetary theorists, tax experts, for-eign trade specialists, project evaluators, and so on, a unified view of the development pro-cess is a great analytical convenience. Why is public intervention so pervasive and generally so unsuccessful? Intervention is usually prompted by the perception—sometimes cor-rect—that a particular market is functioning badly, so that authorities feel pressed to "do something." An infant textile firm is helped by a tariff; or the price of an agricultural product may be raised to permit farmers to use a new fertilizer-intensive technology; or a tax exemption may be granted to a foreign firm for automobile assembly. This pressure for public intervention is the result of severe fragmentation in the underdeveloped economy.

THE FRAGMENTED ECONOMY

The economy is "fragmented" in the sense that firms and households are so isolated that they face different effective prices for land, labor, capital, and produced commodities and do not have access to the same technol-ogies. Authorities then cannot presume that socially profitable investment opportunities will be taken up by the private sector, be-cause prevailing prices need not reflect true economic scarcity—at least not for large seg-ments of the population. There is historical justification for this view in the nineteenth and early twentieth centuries. In Asia, Latin America, and Africa, primary commodity export enclaves were controlled by foreign-ers, and much of the general population re-mained outside of the market economy. In-digenous entrepreneurs had limited access to capital, no means of acquiring advanced technologies, and little skilled labor.

Thus in the determination of where in the vast new areas of the overseas world the raw material export industries were to be established, the pre-existing domestic supply of labor, capital, and en-trepreneurship played a minimal role. Where they did exist in areas of potential export production, these factors were highly immobile and could not be counted upon to engage in export industry operation.[1]

Newly independent governments quite properly felt compelled to act as agents of change to offset economic and political colo-nialism. In the past twenty or thirty years, poor countries have succeeded in introducing some new industrial activities—particularly the manufacture of goods previously im-ported—and in mobilizing some domestic factors of production. Their governments chose to do so, however, by manipulating commodity prices in a variety of ways and by intervening directly to help some individuals or sectors of the economy at the expense of others.

Consider the extraordinary lengths to which import tariffs have been used in Latin America, with rates of several hundred per-

*From Ronald I. McKinnon, *Money and Capital in Economic Development*, Brookings Institution, Washington, D.C., 1973, pp. 5–8. Reprinted by permission.

[1]Jonathan V. Levin, *The Export Economies: Their Pattern of Development in Historical Perspective*, Cambridge. 1960, p. 169. For a good description of how small farmers, who are strongly motivated to-ward economic efficiency, can nonetheless be locked into a backward agricultural technology, see Theo-dore W. Schultz, *Transforming Traditional Agricul-ture*, New Haven, 1964, pp. 36–48.

cent on some goods and absolute prohibitions on the import of others, while still others enter freely. The situation on the Indian subcontinent is no different. Price and quantity controls on foreign trade and domestic commerce make licensing and rationing commonplace. Byzantine patterns of industrial taxes and subsidies complicate government budgetmaking. Consequently, the market mechanism has become no better, and perhaps even worse, as an indicator of social advantage.

Modern fragmentation, therefore, has been largely the result of government policy and goes beyond the old distinction between the export enclave and the traditional subsistence sector. One manifestation is the often-noted existence of small household enterprises and large corporate firms—all producing similar products with different factor proportions and very different levels of technological efficiency. Continuing mechanization on farms and in factories in the presence of heavy rural and urban unemployment is another. Excess plant and equipment with underutilized capacity are commonly found in economies that are reputed to be short of capital and that do suffer from specific bottlenecks. In rural areas, tiny landholdings may be split up into small noncontiguous parcels, with inadequate incentives for agricultural land improvements.

While tangible land and capital are badly used, fragmentation in the growth and use of human capital can be more serious and no less visible. Learning-by-doing and on-the-job training in the "organized" economy are confined to narrow enclaves—export-oriented in the past but now increasingly inward-oriented toward "modern" manufacturing—whose employment growth may be less than the growth in general population. Unemployment among the highly educated coexists with severe shortages in some labor skills.

Indigenous entrepreneurship is narrowly based and is supported by heavy government subsidy. Tariff protection, import licenses, tax concessions, and low-cost bank finance commonly go to small urban elites and create great income inequality between the wealthy few and the poverty-stricken many. This income inequality has failed to induce high rates of saving in the classical manner, but governments remain reluctant to reduce the disposable income of well-to-do investors whose unique access to investment opportunities is guaranteed by the web of official controls and by the endemic fragmentation.

LIBERALIZATION AND THE CAPITAL MARKET

How does one begin to loosen the Gordian knot? The incredibly complex distortions in commodity prices now prevailing are the unplanned macroeconomic outcome of specific microeconomic interventions. But substantial fragmentation in the markets for land, labor, and capital provided the initial motivation for public authorities to "do something" and continues to pressure governments to intervene. Thus an explicit policy for improving the operation of factor markets is necessary to persuade authorities to cease intervening in commodity markets. Carefully considered liberalization in all sectors can then move forward—not merely as a reaction to the more obvious mistakes of the immediate past, but in ways that allay legitimate fears of pure laissez-faire.

However, the knot needs to be loosened further. To say that there are "imperfections in factor markets" is distressingly vague and often signals the end of formal economic analysis. But further systematic inquiry can proceed if the neoclassical approach of treating labor, land, and capital symmetrically as primary factors is dropped. It is hypothesized here that fragmentation in the capital market—endemic in the underdeveloped environment without carefully considered public policy—causes the misuse of labor and land, suppresses entrepreneurial development, and condemns important sectors of the economy to inferior technologies. Thus appropriate policy in the domestic capital market is the key to general liberalization, and particularly to the withdrawal of unwise public intervention from commodity markets. . . .

XI.A.4. Planning and Cost-Benefit Analysis*

The market is an indispensable element of every modern society based on labor division. Experience has shown that it will not disappear even after the revolutionary transformation of capitalist conditions rooted in the private ownership of production means. The market also functions in a socialist economy.

It is true that (as has already been mentioned) the scope of the market changes in history. Its regularities are deeply influenced by the actual social, economic, and political environment: the functioning of the other components of the economic control system. Yet whatever the conditions in which it functions, its importance lies in that it is a *real* market and not just a shadow market existing only on the paper of economic calculations. The market is a real market if the buyer spends money and the seller receives money. The buyer's interest is to spend less money for the article, while the seller's interest is to receive more for it. The real market functions in the framework of this contradiction.

I have no illusions about the market. I know very well that it is not "perfect." A real market price does not express exactly "how much a certain product is worth to society." The rent paid for resources does not reflect exactly their "relative scarcity." There may be not only small and temporary but also large and permanent deviations between the real market price and the so-called social valuation. If we think that the price wrongly orients those who make their choices relying on the price signal, we may try to change the actual price. This may be done in various forms: by government price fixation, taxation and subsidies, support or hindering of cartel formation, etc. It is not within the scope of the present study to take a stand on these questions, but the following principle must be

*From Janos Kornai, "Appraisal of Project Appraisal," in Michael J. Boskin (ed.), *Economics and Human Welfare: Essays in Honor of Tibor Scitovsky,* New York, Academic Press, 1979, pp. 91–96. Reprinted by permission.

stated: those who do not like the actual price should try to achieve a *change* in the *actual* price. The problem cannot be avoided by replacing the actual price we do not like with a shadow price we prefer. Shadow prices may play a useful role, but only as analytical tools in the hands of the planner. We cannot expect, however, as already discussed, that microunits (firms, local authorities, etc.) will base their *actual* decisions on financially nonbinding *accounting* prices.

In my opinion, the market should not be left to itself. The government may intervene in it, and does in fact in every modern society.[1] Besides, the market may be supplemented by planning and other government control activites of a nonmarket character. But within the sphere of market action, it should be a *real market* with real prices.

Planning is, in the vision of the CB school, a faint repetition of the market: a kind of ghost market with ghost prices and wages which are more advantageous than the real ones.

The CB school's "planning" is a language whose grammar and basic vocabulary are identical with those of the market, and which differs from the market only in its accent. Yet the real historical role of planning is not just that. Planning is a "separate language" with its own vocabulary and grammar.[2] It is not a faint repetition of the market, but a

---

[1] The study of shadow prices and their comparison with actual prices may help to correct the latter and to determine government price policy.

[2] In his classical article on externalities, Scitovsky (1954) underlined the complementary character of market and planning: "The proper co-ordination of investment decisions, therefore, would require a signaling device to transmit information about present plans and future conditions as they are determined by present plans; and the pricing system fails to provide this. Hence the belief that there is need either for centralized investment planning or for some additional communication system to *supplement* the pricing system as a signaling device.

"It must be added that the argument of this section applies with a special force to underdeveloped countries."

supplement with its own purpose. A *living* market must be supplemented by *living* planning.

The main aspect of planning is the *primal* aspect, if I may express it in the language of mathematical programming. The targets of production, investment, consumption, and domestic and foreign trade must be known beforehand. One must try to coordinate all these closely related processes. In parallel with the physical processes, their accompanying monetary processes, i.e., the flows of incomes and expenditures, must also be coordinated. All this, of course, must be completed by the *dual* aspect: the planning of future prices and wages. But these are not hypothetical prices either. The planning of prices means that there is consideration beforehand of what changes could be and ought to be achieved in future *actual* prices, wages, exchange rates, and interest rates.

Planning is therefore a wide prognosis and organized exchange of information on the one hand, and a preliminary coordination of interests and activities on the other hand. All this, if well done, will improve the economic efficiency and reduce the frictions of adaptation. However, the whole thing is but an *ex ante* coordination which will later be exposed to the test of practice. In the market sphere it is the actual market, and in the nonmarket sphere it is the other allocation processes (e.g., allocation by authorities, administrative selection, etc.) that will realize actual coordination and adaptation. They will do it either by faithfully following the plan or by correcting it. It may also happen that forces active in society will resist the plan and therefore the goals included in the plan will not be adhered to.

In real planning, as later in the real market and in other real nonmarket allocation processes, the representatives of different interests meet. It is true that this usually takes place in a very "professional" form: with economic and technical argumentation. If, however, one takes a closer look at the arguments, it is found that big enterprises, ministerial planners, ministers, the leaders of geographical regions, trade unions, etc., all try to assert in planning the "interests" of the

segment "represented" by them. This may seem alarming to those who believe that planning is a stricly impartial process which deduces its figures from facts independent of human interests. In reality, however, planning is a social process in which human beings take part. Finally, the plan is obtained out of this clash of interests.

THE TWO INTERPRETATIONS OF PLANNING

The various views on planning and project appraisal are summarized in Figure 1. Figure 1*a* shows the neoclassical (welfare economics) ideal of planning. According to this, planning is nothing else but the solution of the "economic problem" (i.e., allocation of scarce resources to attain maximum utility) on an economy-wide level. It presumes the existence of a social welfare function. The objective is to reach the maximum social welfare.

While this fundamental starting point is shared by all those holding the neoclassical view, there are differences between them regarding methods. This is shown by the branching in Figure 1. According to some, the "economic problem" can be solved only by an optimization mathematical model, or, at least, the solution can be approached only in this way (Figure 1*a*, lower left rectangle). Others hold the view that the problem must be solved exclusively by isolated project appraisal, i.e., by cost-benefit analysis (Figure 1*a*, lower right rectangle). There are also intermediate opinions, recognizing the usefulness of both procedures, but laying more stress on one or the other.

The basic conception of welfare economics accepted, the various views harmonize quite well with each other. Arguments are restricted to opinions about the best means or combination of means for "planning technology," which is, finally, not a very fundamental question.

In Figure 1*b*, I show the concept of planning that I accept, together with many other economists. As can be seen, it is not the "planning technology" that makes this concept different from the other concept, since

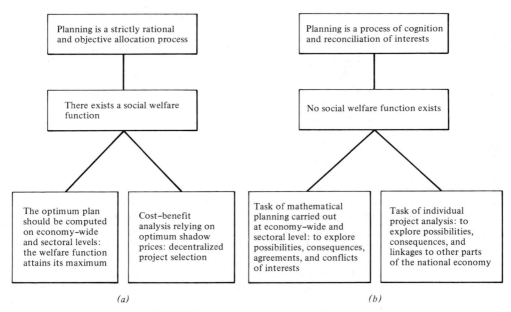

(a)   *(b)*

FIGURE 1. Two interpretations of planning.

both mathematical planning and project analysis also appear in this scheme, i.e., in the procedures. The point of difference is in the interpretation of the social function of planning. It does not begin with the sterile ideal of "rationality." The question here is not about the just, fine, and good planning, with every participant a "Homo oeconomicus." Instead, it approaches planning in the realistic way and poses the empirical question: What is planning in practice? First, it is a *cognitive* process; its participants try to explore possibilities and to state in advance what the consequences of effectuating this or that possibility would be. The task is, therefore, to enrich this exploration process as much as possible. Second, planning is a process of *reconciliation of interests*. It tries in advance to coordinate activities that would otherwise adjust to each other through conflicts. Planning may help in overriding the interests of particular groups to enforce more general goals of the political decision-makers and planners. Planning can fulfill these functions well if it clearly reveals the tensions and contrasting interests to be expected.

The fulfillment of both functions may be promoted by mathematical planning on economy-wide and sectoral levels (and within it by optimization models, nonoptimizing simulation examinations, and input-output analysis) as well as by project appraisal. The latter is—without sectoral and economy-wide analysis—by no means sufficient for planning. On the other hand, it may be a useful supplement to plan calculations of a wider scope.

The final question to be posed in this study is: What then is the place of cost-benefit analysis in planning? I think it has an important role to play—although much less important than the one assigned to it by the most ardent followers of the CB school.

THE PLACE OF COST-BENEFIT ANALYSIS

Before directly answering the question just mentioned, let us see objectively what has been the actual role of cost-benefit analysis up to now. I think that, as has been pointed out already, it has not fundamentally influenced actual decisions. If it has exerted an advantageous effect, it has not been expressed so much in the choice of certain projects as in the education of planners and decision-makers. It has accustomed preparers of decisions concerned with projects, and planners in general, as well as specialists of international organizations, to examine each project within comprehensive social interrelationships: to consider not only direct profitability counted at current prices, but to try to examine thoroughly the whole series of expectable direct and indirect effects. What will be the consequence of the project from the aspects of employment, foreign trade, and, in general, the economic growth of the developing country? Cost-benefit analysis virtually develops in those who practice it "conditioned reflexes" to such complexity of analysis. I see its main future role in this educational and disciplinary effect. A carefully carried out cost-benefit analysis enforces the regular collection of data in connection with all positive and negative effects, and thus supplies rich material for decision preparation.

Beyond this educational effect asserting itself, in the long run cost-benefit analysis has also a direct use. If it is carried out in several variants under alternative economic assumptions and maybe alternative numerical hypotheses, it may facilitate the many-sided comparison of the advantages and disadvantages of projects to be considered. No one unique salutary cost-benefit indicator is necessary. Instead, a set of indicators which describe in detail the economic and social consequences of the choice should be fixed in advance. The indicator vector should not be too big. I shall mention only for illustration that 15–30 indicators are already apt to demonstrate effects widely and in detail. In a project appraisal, the numerical value of these indicators must be determined. Their determination and comparison should be the main task of cost-benefit analysis (more exactly, of the cost-benefit analysis *interpreted in a wider sense* in accordance with the study). Within these limits, cost-benefit analysis may successfully promote the tasks of planning: cognition and reconciliation of interests.

Comment

The literature on the general topic of planning and the price system is extensive, but the following references may be cited for the particular problem of assessing the relative merits of the market mechanism and planning in the context of development: Hugh C. J. Aitken (ed.), *The State and Economic Growth* (1959); P. T. Bauer, *Dissent on Development* (1972), chapter 2; A. K. Cairncross, *Factors in Economic Development* (1962), chapter 19; Elliot J. Berg, "Socialism and Economic Development in Tropical Africa," *Quarterly Journal of Economics* (November 1968); Maurice Dobb, *An Essay on Economic Growth and Planning* (1960), chapter 1; A. O. Hirschman, "Economic Policy in Underdeveloped Countries," *Economic Development and Cultural Change* (July 1957); E. S. Mason, *Economic Planning in Underdeveloped Areas* (1958); R. M. Solow, "Some Problems of the Theory and Practice of Economic Planning," *Economic Development and Cultural Change* (January 1962); Raymond Vernon, "Comprehensive Model-Building in the Planning Process: The Case of the Less Developed Countries," *Economic Journal* (March 1966); Gustav Ranis, "Planning for Resources and Planning for Strategy Change," *Weltwirtschaftliches Archiv* (Summer 1965); H. B. Chenery, "The Structuralist Approach to Development Policy," *American Economic Review*, (May 1975); Charles Blitzer et al. *Economy-Wide Models and Development Planning* (1975); M. Cave and P. Hare, *Alternative Approaches to Economic Planning* (1981).

Outstanding general introductions to development planning are provided by W. Arthur Lewis, *Development Planning* (1966); Jan Tinbergen, *Development Planning* (1967); K. Griffin and J. Enos, *Planning Development* (1971); M. P. Todaro, *Development Planning* (1971); Mike Faber and Dudley Seers (eds.), *The Crisis in Planning* (1972): G. Ranis (ed.), *Govern-*

ment and Economic Development (1971); G. Pyatt and E. Thorbecke, *Planning Techniques for a Better Future* (1976).

An excellent survey article on development policymaking and planning is D. T. Healy, "Development Policy: New Thinking about an Interpretation," *Journal of Economic Literature* (September 1972).

XI.B. POLICY MODELS
XI.B.1. Planning Models*

Models are needed to analyse the interaction among elements in a social system. A purely theoretical formulation allows some useful deductions to be made as to the direction of changes in specified variables in response to particular policy measures. In this way we can predict that a devaluation of the currency will tend to raise exports and lower imports of each commodity. We cannot determine the magnitude of these changes without quantitative estimates of the more important structural relations involved in this model.

Intuitive planning is based on guesses as to the orders of magnitude of the parameters in the model that most directly affect a given economic response. Such guesses are derived either from similiar situations in the country in the past or from the experience of other countries. Intuitive planning includes the use of statistical trends and simple accounting relations to test the balance of supply and demand for different commodities. This common sense approach is likely to be most valid for short-term projections for which the underlying relations do not change greatly.

Greater rigour has been introduced into planning in the past decade by a more systematic use of statistical information both in testing the underlying theories and in applying them to particular problems. This procedure involves two different types of economic model:

1. An *econometric model,* which is used as a basis for estimating past structural relationships,
2. A *planning model,* which is used to determine the relationships between desired social objectives and the policy instruments that are proposed to achieve them.

*From Hollis B. Chenery, "Notes on the Use of Models in Development Planning," in M. Faber and Dudley Seers (eds.), *The Crisis in Planning,* Chatto & Windus, 1972, p. 129–34. Reprinted by permission.

The former type provides a quantitative test of theoretical assumptions about the behaviour of key elements, such as the rate of savings, the requirements for capital in each sector, the response of agricultural producers to changes in prices, etc. The latter combines these separate estimates into a coherent framework for planning. Planning models that are not based on statistical estimates must be used with great caution. It is not the use of models per se but the tendency to take the results of an inadequately tested planning model too seriously that has brought some disrepute to formal planning in several countries.

Econometric Models

Probably three-quarters of the overall quantitative analysis of underdeveloped economies has been carried out in the past dozen years. The rapid increase in statistics on sectoral output, employment, consumption, investment and national income has made possible a growing body of comparative studies of key aspects of the economic structure. These studies provide a basis for testing development theories, rejecting some hypotheses and refining and extending others. For example, capital formation has been shown to have greater importance in explaining the sources of growth in developing countries than in advanced countries in a number of recent studies. Conversely, there are no known cases of rapid growth being achieved in underdeveloped countries through technological change not accompanied by substantial investment. Studies have been made of other basic elements of planning models, such as the determinants of savings, the requirements for skilled labour, the price and income elasticities of demand for major commodities, etc. The next ten years will doubtless see a great increase in econometric studies, which furnish the building blocks from which planning models can be constructed.

The main limitation to the use of econometric models has been the short period of time for which usable statistical information is available for their estimation. There are probably twenty underdeveloped countries for which the major series are available since 1950 and another twenty or thirty for which they were started in the following decade. In the next five to ten years, it will be possible to carry out more extensive tests of development theories by using a mixture of cross-country and time series analysis covering periods long enough to have considerable statistical validity. The availability of such studies will help the individual planner by providing him with reference points to judge estimates for his own country.

Planning Models

A planning model specifies the relationships between the goals of the society and the instruments that the government has available to achieve them. The main advantage of a more formal analysis as compared to a more intuitive approach lies in the ability of the former to determine the indirect effects of given policies. However, the intuitive approach can take some account of variables such as administrative competence, political will and other factors that cannot be readily quantified. I assume, therefore, that both approaches will be used and will merely illustrate the areas in which formalization is particularly needed.

The growth of poor countries depends at least as much on their ability to reallocate resources to new uses and thus to change their economic structures as on an increase in total investment and other resource inputs. The instruments of development policy are more likely to be specific to particular sectors of the economy than is typically the case in advanced countries, where less change is needed and resources move more readily in response to market forces. A formal model of resource allocation focuses on the interaction among different types of productive activity both as competitors for limited resources and as suppliers of desired goods and services.

The simplest planning models that can perform this function are derived from Leontief's input-output approach to describing a system of general interdependence. Experiments have been carried on with this type of model in most of the developing countries having any interest in formal planning. Initially, these experiments were designed to test the possibilities for constructing such a model and to train a few technicians in its use. Since any comprehensive model requires estimates of a large number of economic relations, these early experiments were often based on rather rudimentary statistics. Solutions to such models are of value mainly in illustrating the interdependence of development policies in general terms.

Despite its conceptual simplicity, the input-output framework has the great virtue of forcing the analyst to consider the working of the economy as a whole. More complex formulations of individual demand and supply conditions can replace the initial crude approximations, and sectors can be further disaggregated as data become available. In this way a dozen or more countries have now developed a sufficient empirical base and enough experience in the use of intersectoral models so that they can be considered a practical planning tool. In the next decade several dozen more countries are likely to develop a usable inter-industry framework for their plans, while leaders in this field will have progressed to the use of more complex representations of the economic system.

THE CONTRIBUTION OF PLANNING MODELS

Although the past decade has been largely devoted to research and development on formal planning techniques, some practical results have already been achieved. The following examples illustrate the type of problem for which quantitative models can provide a notable improvement over more intuitive methods.

Protection and Import Substitution

One of the most common methods of stimulating industrial growth and reducing import requirements is to give tariff or quota protection to new industries. The level of such protection is set in relation to the cost structure of the domestic manufacturer and the cost of imports. Indirect effects on the rest of the economy are typically ignored in this pragmatic approach to policy.

A number of countries have recently assessed the cumulative effects of protectionist policies by means of interindustry analysis. Since the protection of an industry increases the cost of its products to its domestic customers, it is necessary to trace the effects of protection throughout the economy in order to find out the total economic costs and benefits of this policy. This has been done by measuring the total cost of domestic resources used throughout the economy to earn or save a dollar of foreign exchange in different types of production. Such studies typically show that:

1. The resource cost of protection is much greater than is indicated by the nominal tariff.
2. There is a large and irrational variation among sectors of industry and agriculture.
3. There is usually a systematic bias against exports and in favour of import substitution in industry as a means of earning foreign exchange.

Once this type of analysis has been made, a planning version of the model can be used to redesign the system of tariffs and subsidies so as to come closer to the ideal of equating the productivity of marginal resource uses in different areas. Applications of this kind have been made in Israel, Pakistan, India, Korea, Chile, Argentina and elsewhere.

Educational Planning

Education is another aspect of resource allocation which is difficult to analyse without taking account of repercussions throughout the economy. Until recently, education policy was typically determined with little regard for future needs for specific types of skill and without comparing the return on investment in human capital to other forms of investment.

A number of countries have recently experimented with a variety of models designed to integrate educational policy into general planning procedures. Rates of return to different levels of education have been computed from simple econometric models of production and used to determine the types in which expansion is most desirable. In more comprehensive studies, skilled labour is treated as an input needed for production in each sector, and future needs for education are derived as part of an overall projection of the economic structure. The results obtained are often quite different from those of intuitive planning procedures, which tend to prescribe the same educational structures for all countries at a given income level.

Employment Versus Other Objectives

One area in which both planners and policy makers have failed to produce satisfactory results is in the creation of new jobs. There is notable inconsistency between the asserted social goal of achieving full employment and the policies that governments adopt. The latter are designed primarily to increase total income within the limits of available investment and balance of payments constraints. Employment creation does not feature prominently in most development strategies and is usually assumed to be a corollary of high growth rates.

The present generation of planning models does not deal with this problem very well because the basic econometric and technological information on alternative factor proportions is not yet available. Existing models therefore tend to assume fixed relations between labour inputs and commodity output and to ignore the possibility of substitution either in production or by changing the composition of consumption. This overly rigid representation of the economy can be readily modified, however, once the empirical basis for doing so has been developed.

In an economy that is threatened with excess labour as well as balance of payments difficulties, an individual investment project should be judged by its contribution to at least three objectives:

1. Raising the national product,
2. Increasing employment,
3. Earning or saving foreign exchange.

The logical framework for making this type of assessment is that of linear (or nonlinear) programming, which determines an optimal allocation of resources for the whole economy under specified limitations. Solutions to such a model provide a basis for weighing the criterion of employment creation against other benefits and costs. The "shadow prices" of a linear programming model provide some of the needed links between sector plans and project evaluation in different parts of the economy.

Economy-wide linear programming models have been constructed for this purpose in at least a dozen countries. While most of them are still in an experimental stage, they offer a promising approach to the reconciliation of employment creation, foreign exchange savings and other objectives of development planning.

PLAN FORMULATION

The formulation of a development plan requires that a number of separate studies of individual sectors and types of policy be reconciled in a consistent framework. This can be done by starting from the projections of an aggregate model and using them as a basis for input-output solutions. These are compared to the sectoral studies and the assumptions of each adjusted until they are mutually consistent. This procedure results in a conssitent family of models, each of which is suited to a different type of policy analysis. In this way, the indirect effects of alternative policies at either the sector or the economy-wide level can be worked out.

An overall model that incorporates the main elements of alternative strategies can be particularly useful in the early stages of plan formulation. It should first be adjusted to include elements of intuitive judgement as to the range of political and administrative feasibility of alternative policy measures. Feasible solutions can then be determined under a series of alternative assumptions as to the principal objectives. Tests can also be made of the effect of alternative values of exogenous variables, such as export demands or weather conditions. This exploration of alternatives is a pragmatic aporoximation to the formal optimization procedures of mathematical programming.

The calculation of feasible alternatives provides a practical basis for the discussions between planners, administrators and politicians that are necessary to formulate a development plan. Political judgements can be elicited much better by considering concrete alternatives rather than abstract goals. Since each policy has a cost, the specification of goals and limitations can hardly be made in the absence of some knowledge of comprehensive alternative allocations of resources.

XI.B.2. A Model of Development Alternatives *

Current growth models have serious deficiencies as a basis for development policy. In fo-

*From H. B. Chenery and M. Bruno, "Development Alternatives in an Open Economy: The Case of Israel," *Economic Journal,* Vol. 77, No. 285, 1962, pp. 79–103. Reprinted by permission.

cusing on the savings-investment relationship and the possibilities of substitution between capital and labour, they exclude questions of equal concern to policy makers, such as the changing structure of demand, the role of foreign trade and the allocation of resources.

As a result, formal growth theory fails to clarify the relations among the several instruments of development policy, which should be one of its major functions.

As Tinbergen (1956) has taught us, a policy model should contain variables reflecting the economic goals of the society and the main instruments of government policy, and it should specify the more important structural relations connecting them. The degree of complexity required of a policy model for a developing economy is suggested by the following list of typical objectives, instruments and structural limitations.

1. Objectives: maximum income, full employment.
2. Instruments: capital imports, tax policy, trade policy, investment allocation.
3. Limitations: composition of demand, balance of payments, labour supply and requirements, capital supply and requirements.

The omission of several of these instruments and limitations may make the use of simpler models seriously misleading.

REQUIREMENTS OF A POLICY MODEL

The functions of a policy model are to determine consistent sets of economic policies and to facilitate the choice among them. The nature and results of development policies are represented by the variables in the model. The model must also include in some form the principal elements affecting the rate of growth, which were discussed in the preceding section.

Tinbergen (1956) and Theil (1958) have distinguished several types of variables in policy models:

1. Predetermined or exogenous variables.
2. Instrument variables (i.e., those subject to government control).
3. Objective variables (i.e., those reflecting the aims of policy).
4. Other endogenous variables (i.e., those that are irrelevant for policy analysis).

In Tinbergen's approach the objective variables are taken as given; the problem is to find that best combination of values for the instrument variables. Theil's approach is more general. He assumes that the social welfare depends on values of both instrument and objective variables. The optimum programme is that which produces a maximum of welfare consistent with the restraints on the system. In the absence of a quantifiable welfare function, however, the practical problem of setting values for the objective variables still remains.

Since a single optimum programme cannot be determined by economic analysis alone when there are several objective variables, our approach will be to establish a set of alternative programmes that includes the feasible degree of variation in all of the relevant variables. In cases where the Government has established a fixed policy goal, such as full employment or a specified defence expenditure, we follow Tinbergen in setting this as a fixed objective of the programme. Otherwise we follow Theil in considering a range of values for the objective variables. In this second category are consumption, the total productive capacity of the economy and the foreign debt. These together are assumed to determine the social welfare . . .

In order to determine the range of feasible programmes we include two types of controlled variables. The first are instruments of government policy, as defined by Tinbergen; they are subject to more or less direct control by the Government, as in the case of the exchange rate or the level of foreign borrowing. The second type may vary within limits set by institutional factors, but may or may not be directly influenced by government policy. The institutional limits must be included in determining realistic programmes, however.

These four categories are not mutually exclusive; an instrument variable can also be an objective or be subject to institutional limits, for example. Several combinations are shown in the following classification of the policy variables that will be included in the model [see Table 1].

The institutional limits provide a crude

TABLE 1. Classification of Policy Variables

Variables	Objectives		Policy Instruments	Institutional Limits
	Fixed	Variable		
1. Gross national product (V)		×		
2. Private consumption (C)		×		
3. Public consumption (G)	×			
4. Foreign capital inflow (F)		×	×	×
5. Unemployment rate (u)	×			
6. Savings rate (s)			×	×
7. Exchange rate (r)			×	
8. Rate of increase in labour productivity (l)				

substitute for a more complete welfare function, since they can be used to exclude values of any variable that are clearly in conflict with welfare maximization in the particular society.[1] They can also be used to allow for uncertainty as to the nature of a particular structural relation, as in the determinants of increased productivity.

Since many factors affect growth, some of which can only be adequately represented in a multi-sectoral model, it is useful to divide the analysis into two parts. To start with, an aggregate model can be used to determine the main development alternatives. The most promising of these can then be subjected to a more detailed analysis, which is not feasible until the range of possibilities has been narrowed down. The detailed results can in turn be used to revise the initial estimates of the aggregate model.

The main problem in designing an aggregate model for this purpose is to identify in advance the factors that may prove to be effective limits to growth. When a particular restriction—such as the composition of demands—is omitted from a model it is implied that whatever changes take place in this element will not significantly affect the parameters in the model. In some cases it will be necessary to subject this assumption to a quantitative test in order to determine its validity. The model can be built up in this way by adding those relations that prove to have a significant effect.

The idea of separate and conflicting limits to growth is a basic element of Harrod's (1939) pioneering work. Although he is primarily concerned with the cyclical aspects of differences between the limits set by the supply of capital and the supply of labour, his relations can be reinterpreted as a simple policy model of development alternatives. As is shown in equations (13) and (14) below, the Harrod model thus interpreted contains two equations, corresponding to the supply-demand balances for capital and labour. If all the parameters are fixed the maximum rate of growth will be determined by one of the two equations, and either labour or capital will be in excess supply.[2] In a policy model, however, some of the parameters become variables, and these equations determine the value of any two variables, as, for example, the savings rate and growth rate at full employment.

It has been argued above that there is a third general limitation to growth on a par with the two considered by Harrod: the balance of payments. As a policy problem, the balance-of-payments limitation is quite similar to the savings-investment limitation. An increase in the rate of growth often requires a change in the structure of income use in order to reduce the proportion going to con-

---

[1] Instead of treating the rate of unemployment as a fixed objective, we might assign institutional limits to it.

[2] In Harrod's terminology the labour-determined solution gives the "natural" rate of growth and the capital-determined solution the "warranted" rate.

sumption and hence to increase savings. It may also require a change in the structure of production in order to reduce the ratio of imports to total output. It is not clear a priori, either in Israel or in other countries, which of these structural relations is more likely to limit growth or which is harder to change. The parallelism between the two is completed by the fact that a foreign capital inflow plays a dual role in adding to both investment and foreign exchange resources.

STATEMENT OF THE MODEL

The model of development alternatives proposed here incorporates these three limits. They are described by means of ten endogenous variables, including the two variable objectives (V and C). The variables used in the model are as follows:[3]

Endogenous (Uncontrolled) Variables:

V_t	Gross national product[4]
C_t	Private consumption[4]
I_t	Total investment net of replacement
R_t	Replacement
E_t	Exports of goods and services
M_t	Imports of goods and services
S_t	Gross domestic savings
K_t	Total capital stock
N_t	Labour supply
L_t	Labour demand

Instrument and Controlled Variables:

G_t	Government current expenditure[4]
F_t	Foreign capital inflow[4]
u_t	Unemployment rate[4] $\left(\dfrac{N_t - L_t}{n_t}\right)$
s	Marginal propensity to save $\left(\dfrac{\Delta S}{\Delta V}\right)$
r	Effective exchange rate
l	Annual increase in labour productivity

---

[3]The subscript t refers to the year. In the base year $t = 0$, and in the final year of the planning period $t = n$.

[4]V_t, C_t, G_t, F_t and u_t are also objective variables.

Exogenous (Predetermined) Variables: Initial values of all variables

t	Time
P_{ei}	Export price in sector i
$\bar{K}_0$	Initial unused capital stock
$\bar{I}_n$	Final unused capital stock

In its initial form, the model consists of twelve equations, of which seven describe the structure of the economy, three specify the resource limitations and two are definitional. The model is later reduced to four equations in eight variables by eliminating the eight irrelevant endogenous variables—all except V and C. A development programme can then be specified by assigning values to four of the variables and determining the values of the remaining four from the model.

Since it is assumed that decisions on development strategy can be based on the values of the policy variables at the end of a planning period of n years, solutions are only needed for a single period. The equations are presented first in general form; estimates of the parameters are then given for the Israeli economy for a five-year planning period of 1959/60 to 1964/5. The aggregate model will be supplemented by an inter-industry analysis in order to take account of the composition of demand and of supply limitations in estimating the parameters.

The aggregate production function. Although the Harrod-Domar model has been criticized for its omission of substitution between labour and capital, it is generally recognized that substitution can only take place over a period of time and depends to a large extent on the installation of new equipment. We shall therefore treat the labour-capital ratio as a function of time, but shall assume that both inputs are required in fixed proportions at any moment. For simplicity, a trend will be assiciated only with the labour input, which is consistent with the experience of the past decade.

With complementary inputs, output is limited by whichever one is exhausted first. In Israel, as in most of the less-developed economies, this factor is more likely to be capital. We therefore write the production function as dependent on the stock of capital and the effectiveness of its utilization:

$$V_n = V_0 + \overline{\beta}(\overline{K}_0 - \overline{K}_n)$$
$$+ \beta(K_n - K_0) \quad (1)$$

where β represents the average product per unit of increase in the capital stock. The second term of this equation allows for the possibility of reducing the level of excess capacity, $\overline{K}$, which is a significant factor in Israel and elsewhere.

More important than the direct substitution between labour and capital is the effect of a change in the composition of output on capital requirements. This will be allowed for by estimating β from an inter-industry analysis so that it becomes a weighted average of the output-capital coefficients in each sector. Any substantial departure from the assumed composition of the increase in output will therefore require a recalculation of β.[5]

Labour demand. This demand for labour depends on the level of output and the increase in average labour productivity:

$$L_t = \lambda_0(1 - l)^t V_t \quad (2)$$

where λ_0 is the average labour input per unit of output at the beginning of the period and l is the annual rate at which it decreases. The estimate of l should also take account of the anticipated composition of output. As estimated statistically from past trends, l includes effects of both substitution and technological change.

Since we assume complementarity between capital and labour, equation (2) may be restated as a production function by solving for V_t if labour should become the factor limiting growth.

Import demand. The demand for imports depends on the five components of total demand:

$$M_t = \mu_c^r C_t + \mu_g^r G_t + \mu_i^r(I_t$$
$$+ R_t) + \mu_e^r E_t \quad (3)$$

Each import coefficient μ^r is derived from a solution to an input-output model containing specified proportions between domestic supplies and imports in each sector. The coeffi-

cient μ^r therefore represents the total imports required directly and indirectly per unit of each type of demand. The future import proportions are derived from the anticipated effective exchange rate, r. Use of a higher exchange rate will result in additional import substitution and a fall in the import coefficients.[6]

Replacement. The replacement of capital depends on the age and estimated life of the capital stock in different sectors of the economy. In aggregate form, this relationship may be indicated by:

$$R_t = R_t(K_t, K_{t-1}, K_{t-2}, \ldots) \quad (4)$$

although in practice R_t is estimated on a sector basis.

As Domar (1957) has emphasized, the replacement of worn-out equipment is substantially less than the conventional allowance for depreciation in a growing economy. We therefore define net investment I_t as gross investment less replacement. Part of net investment is covered by the excess of depreciation allowances over actual replacement.

Savings. Gross domestic savings depends on the level of *per capita* income, its functional distribution and the Government's tax policy. In the absence of an adequate basis for estimating the separate effects of these factors, an aggregate relation of the following form will be assumed:

$$S_n = S_0 + s(V_n - V_0) \quad (5)$$

where the marginal propensity to save out of increased GNP (s) is taken as an instrument variable. It represents the combined effects of tax policy, changes in income distribution and other policy measures that affect savings.

Labour supply. The supply of labour is determined from the natural increase of the existing population plus net immigration. For simplicity, the combined result is assumed to take an exponential form:

$$N_t = N_0(1 + \gamma)^t \quad (6)$$

---

[5]The coefficient β similarly depends on the sectors in which excess capacity is reduced.

[6]Import substitution as a result of a higher exchange rate may also produce a lower productivity of capital, but this can only be taken account of explicitly in more detailed models.

Exports. The level of total exports is the sum of the individual commodities and services exported; each is assumed to depend on the effective exchange rate and on foreign prices:

$$E_t = \sum_i E_i(r, P_{ei}, t) \qquad (7)$$

The time period is also assumed to affect achievable export levels because of the time needed to penetrate new markets and to establish export organizations for new products.

Savings-investment equilibrium

$$S_t + F_t = I_t + R_t \qquad (8)$$

Balance-of-payments equilibrium

$$M_t = E_t + F_t \qquad (9)$$

where M_t, E_t and F_t are all measured at constant domestic prices.[7]

Employment equilibrium

$$L_t = (1 - u)N_t \qquad (10)$$

where the proportion unemployed (u) is an objective variable.

Total net capital formation

$$\sum_{t=0}^{t=n-1} I_t = (K_n - K_0) \qquad (11)$$

In order to express the model in terms of initial and final-year values only, an approximation of the form

$$I_n = \rho(K_n - K_0) \qquad (11a)$$

may be substituted for equation (11); ρ depends on the rate of growth of investment and the length of the planning period. Some assumption of this sort is needed to make I_n determinate.

[7]The foreign capital inflow is normally given in current-value dollar terms. If we denote the latter by $F't$ we have $F_t = rF'_t/p_f$, where r is the exchange rate and p_f is an implicit price index defined by the expression

$$p_f = \frac{p_m M_t - p_e E_t}{M_t - e_t}$$

p_m and p_e are the respective import and export prices (indices) on foreign markets. In the Israeli case import prices are assumed constant and export prices are assumed to fall. Hence $p_f > 1$ and $F_t < rF'_t$.

Gross national product

$$V_t = C_t + G_t + I_t + R_t + E_t - M_t \qquad (12)$$

Reduced form of the model. The reduced form of a policy model is a set of equations involving the policy variables only, with all the irrelevant endogenous variables eliminated.[8] In the present case we eliminate eight variables and eight equations, so that the model is reduced to the following four equations in eight variables (the terms in square brackets are constants):

$$V_n = \left[\frac{N_0(1 + \gamma)^n}{\lambda_0} \right] \frac{(1 - u)}{(1 - l)^n} \qquad (13)$$

$$V_n = \frac{[\rho/\beta \overline{V}_0 + S_0 - R_n] - sV_0 + F_n}{\rho/\beta - s} \qquad (14)$$

$$V_n = \frac{\begin{array}{l}(1 - \mu_e)E_n + (1 - \mu_c)F_n \\ + (\mu_c - \mu_g)G_n + [(\mu_i - \mu_c)(\rho/\beta \overline{V}_0 - R_n)]\end{array}}{\mu_c + (\mu_i - \mu_c)\rho/\beta} \qquad (15)$$

$$C + G = (1 - s)V_n + (s - s_0)V_0$$

where

$$S_0 = s_0 V_0 \text{ and } \overline{V}_0 = \overline{\beta}(\bar{\kappa}_0 - \bar{\kappa}_n) + V_0 \qquad (16)$$

Equations (13), (14) and (15) correspond to the three equilibrium conditions for labour, capital and foreign exchange. When no limit is placed on F the labour-force equation (13) provides the ultimate limit to growth because the other two equations can be satisfied by increased foreign borrowing. With a given F, there are three separate limits.

Equation (14) corresponds to the Harrod-Domar equation, as can be seen by assuming a one-year period, no excess capacity, and equal marginal and average (net) savings rates. The equation then becomes:

$$\frac{\Delta V}{V} = \beta s + \beta \frac{F}{V} \qquad (14a)$$

or

$$V_n = \frac{V_0 + \beta F_n}{1 - \beta s} \qquad (14b)$$

[8]The concept is discussed by Theil (1958, chapter 7) under somewhat different assumptions.

The meaning of the balance-of-payments limit can be clarified by assuming that all of the import coefficients μ_l are equal and again taking a one-year period. The result is:

$$V_n = \left(\frac{1 - \mu}{\mu}\right)(E_n + F_n) \qquad (15a)$$

References

Domar, E. D., "Depreciation, Replacement and Growth, and Fluctuations," *Economic Journal* (December 1957).

Harrod, R. F., 1939, "An Essay in Dynamic Theory," *Economic Journal* (March 1939).

Theil, H., 1958, *Economic Forecasts and Policy,* North-Holland Publishing Co.

Tinbergen, J., 1956, *Economic Policy: Principles and Design,* North-Holland Publishing Co.

XI.B.3. Policy Instruments and Development Alternatives *

There has been little systematic analysis of the relative merits and defects of the policy instruments available to underdeveloped countries. Since control of international trade is administratively simpler than many other types of policy, there has been a tendency to rely heavily on it as a way of influencing the pattern of domestic production, without recognizing the drawbacks to exclusive reliance on this set of instruments. Colonial areas have been forced to devise other measures, since protection was denied to them, but they have rarely pursued overall development policies. The need for a greater variety of measures to promote development has now been widely recognized, but there is still inadequate consideration of the range of alternatives available.

In its need to change the pattern of resource use over a relatively short period of time, the promotion of development resembles (in lesser degree) the problem of mobi-

*From Hollis B. Chenery, "Development Policies and Programmes," *Economic Bulletin for Latin America,* Vol. 3, No. 1, March 1958, pp. 55–60; "A Model of Development Alternatives," Vol. 8, United States Papers Prepared for the United Nations Conference on the Application of Science and Technology for the Benefit of the Less Developed Countries, Washington, D.C., 1962, pp. 82–6. Reprinted by permission.

lization for war. The suitability of various instruments for the latter purpose has been widely discussed, and the experience of the United States and other countries has been analysed in some detail. A similar study of the actual effects of development policies is needed before very firm recommendations can be made to the underdeveloped countries, but some general comments may be in order.

CHARACTERISTICS OF INSTRUMENTS

Policy instruments may be classified in various ways: by the sectors of the economy on which they operate, by their use of prices or quantities as variables to be manipulated, by the extent to which they can be effectively controlled by the government, by the effect that they have on private incentives and freedom of choice, etc. In Table 1 representative instruments are classified according to the extent of their application (general versus specific) and their mode of operation (through prices or quantities). The general instruments act on broad aspects of the economy—the money supply, the government budget, investment, consumption—and are widely used in developed and underdeveloped countries alike. The specific instruments are applied differentially to individual sectors of the economy, as illustrated by subsidies, tariffs, or Government investment.

To achieve a given effect on production, or use of any commodity, there is a choice between controlling a price and controlling a quantity. In this respect, tariffs are an alternative to quotas, differential interest rates are an alternative to capital rationing, and subsidies to private producers are an alternative to production by the government. These measures differ in their effects on prices and consumer choices, in administrative convenience, in the predictability of their results, and in other respects. A choice between quantity and price variables as instruments must therefore be made by balancing the advantages and disadvantages in each case.

Some of the main issues of economic policy are concerned with the choice between general and specific instruments and between using prices and quantities as control variables. There is a strong case to be made for using general instruments rather than specific ones. The rates of interest, taxation, and exchange are the orthodox means of exerting Government influence in a *laissez-faire* economy. Their immediate objectives are stability in prices and the balance of payments and the prevention of unemployment. Growth is left to free market forces. The manipulation of interest rates and exchange rates allow market forces in each sector to determine where expansion or contraction of production and consumption will take place. These instruments therefore interfere less with the choices of producers and consumers than do measures which discriminate by sector. They also require a less detailed analysis for their use and do not substitute Government judgment of what is desirable for the action of market forces.

The need for specific instruments to supplement general measures derives from the deficiencies in the price mechanism which apply primarily to specific sectors of the economy. When these factors prevent the achievement of a satisfactory rate of growth, the problem is to devise policy measures which will improve on the working of the competitive economy without losing the advantages of private initiative and the automatic adjustment of the price system.

In designing policies for specific sectors, there is an argument for using price rather than quantity instruments which is based on reasoning similar to the case for general over specific instruments. Taxes and subsidies distort the choices open to producers and users of a commodity less than do allocation systems or other quantitative restrictions and hence are conducive to greater flexibility and over-all economic efficiency. Furthermore, the administrative requirements for price intervention of this type are generally less than for quantitative controls.

Despite the general case in favour of using the price system, there are several situations in which quantitative measures may be needed:

i. When it is necessary to limit consumption of an essential commodity in short supply (e.g., imported goods), the tax needed to bring about a given reduction in use might result in such high prices that the burden of the reduction would fall on lower income groups. In this case, price controls and rationing may be preferable on welfare grounds.

ii. Where a minimum increase in production is essential to production in other sectors—as in the case of power, transport and various auxiliary facilities—the price needed to ensure adequate private investment may be too high or the response of private investors too uncertain. In this case, quantitative measures, such as Government investment, may be more efficient because the cost to the society is less or the outcome more predictable.

iii. In general, where controls are needed for only a short period, as in the case of temporary shortages, it may be desirable to allocate supplies to more essential uses rather than upset the general price structure and distort investment decisions by allowing prices to rise. Quantitative measures are also likely to have more predictable effects in this case.

TABLE 1. Classification of Policy Instruments

Area of Policy	Price Variables		Quantity Variables	
	Instrument	Variables Affected[a]	Instrument	Variables Affected
General				
Monetary	Interest rate	(1) Level of investment (2) Cost of production	Open market operations	(1) Money supply (2) Prices
Fiscal	Personal income tax Corporate income tax	Consumption and saving (1) Profits (2) Investment	Government expenditure	(1) National income (2) Price level
Foreign trade	Exchange rate General tariff level	(1) Cost of imports (2) Price of exports (3) Balance of payments	Exchange auctions	Exchange rates
Foreign investment	Taxes on foreign profits	Level of foreign investment	Foreign loans and grants	(1) Investment resources (2) Exchange supply
Consumption	General sales tax	Consumption	Social insurance, relief, other transfers	(1) Consumption (2) Income distribution
Labour	Wage rates	(1) Labour cost (2) Profits and investment (3) Labour income	Emigration and immigration	Labour supply

734

Specific

Production	Taxes and subsidies Price control	(1) Profits and production (2) Investment	Government production Government research and technical assistance	Level of production Cost of production Level of investment
Investment	Interest rates Tax exemptions	(1) Profits (2) Investment by sector	Government investment capital rationing Restrictions on entry	(1) Prices and profits (2) Level of investment
Consumption	Specific sales taxes	Consumption by commodity	Government services (health, education)	(1) Consumption (2) Income distribution
Trade	Export subsidies Tariffs	(1) Price to consumer (2) Profits on domestic production (1) Profits and investment	Import quotas and prohibitions Exchange controls	(1) Level of imports (2) Domestic prices
Labour	Wage subsidy	(1) Labour cost and use (2) Profits and investment	Labour training	Supply of skilled labour
Natural resources	Taxes and subsidies	(1) Cost of production (2) Rate of exploitation	Surveys, auxiliary investment, etc.	Rate of development

[a]All taxes affect Government revenue and saving in addition to the variables cited.

In these examples, it is the dynamic elements in the situation and the deviation from a desirable income distribution which provide the principal arguments for using quantitative measures of control.

SPECIFIC MEASURES FOR INVESTMENT ALLOCATION

Although the specific measures listed in Table 1 affect both current production and the allocation of investment resources, it is the latter aspect that is crucial for the future course of development. The various instruments affect investment decisions through the availability and cost of primary inputs (labour, natural resources, imported commodities); through the supply of inputs from other sectors (raw materials, overhead facilities); through the demand for output (sales taxes, export subsidies); through profits (taxes, subsidies); and through measures directly related to the process of investment (interest rates, capital rationing, restrictions on entry, direct Government investment). There is therefore a considerable variety of choice between quantity and price instruments and among measures more or less directly related to a particular investment.

The a priori arguments concerning some of the principal measures for influencing investment decisions run somewhat as follows:

1. *Measures of Protection.* As indicated earlier, protective devices are perhaps the most common instruments for influencing the pattern of investment. For this purpose, tariffs are generally preferable to quantitative restrictions—quotas, prohibitions, exchange controls, etc.—for reasons already indicated. Quantitative restrictions prevent competition with domestic producers regardless of price, raise prices to users and limit demand, and require an elaborate administrative mechanism and detailed economic analysis to be effective. Quotas also involve a loss of revenue to the Government, as compared with the use of tariffs, unless the profits of importers can be recovered through taxes.

The cases where quantitative measures may nevertheless be needed derive from the principles given in the previous section. In cases of extreme shortage of foreign exchange, tariffs (or devaluation) may be too uncertain in their results and quotas or exchange restrictions may be adopted as emergency measures.

The effect of quantitative restrictions on investment in domestic substitutes for imports or in sectors using imported commodities is generally less certain than that of tariffs. Allocations are subject to variation according to the amount of exchange available, and the profitability of domestic production is harder to determine than in the case of a tariff.

As instruments for inducing investment in new types of production, subsidies may be preferable to either quantitative restrictions or tariffs because the price is not raised above the level of world prices. Total demand is therefore greater and using sectors are not penalized in export markets. The cost of this technique in Government expenditure must be weighed against its benefits, however.

Protection from foreign competitors is only one factor in the expansion of domestic production. Also required are entrepreneurs, capital, skilled labour, raw materials, etc. When some of these are lacking, the restriction only serves to reduce imports and raise prices to consumers. Trade restrictions are therefore a rather uncertain method of directing investment unless combined with other measures affecting factor supply, and they frequently have undesirable secondary effects.

2. *Government Investment versus Incentives to Private Investment.* Although the arguments concerning trade restrictions are based mainly on economic considerations, the choice between Government investment and incentives to private investors involves social and political factors to a large extent. In countries that do not have strong ideological preferences for either private or Government enterprise, the usual approach is to rely on private investment except in cases where it cannot be expected to work in the public interest (e.g., monopoly) or in which its performance has been demonstrably deficient.

Since the reaction of investors to various incentives (tax reduction, guaranteed markets, low interest rates, etc.) is subject to considerable uncertainty, such incentives are more likely to be adequate when a general objective is to be achieved—e.g., import substitution, increase of industrial employment—than when increases in output in specific sectors are required. Because of this uncertainty, the extent to which reliance on private investment is desirable can be determined only by an actual trial of specific measures.

Another alternative for securing investment in given sectors when tax incentives are thought to be inadequate or too costly to the treasury is the intervention of a Government agency as entrepreneur but not as a long-term producer. This may be done through development corporations, which sell their investments to private enterprises as they become profitable, or through mixed corporations, in which the role of the Government declines as the enterprise becomes established.

The assumption underlying all these measures is that it is bad for the Government to continue permanently as a producer in most fields. There is a widespread view (shared by the present writer) that the lack of incentives to efficiency in Government operations makes private operation preferable even where conditions are not favourable to the initial undertaking of the investment by private enterprise. In the absence of more objective evaluations of the experience with Government and private enterprise in various countries, it is impossible to support this conclusion empirically, and it is by no means universally held among democratic Governments. In countries such as India, for example, an attempt is made to ascertain the relative merits of public and private investment in specific fields rather than starting from this premise. Even in these cases, however, the sectors that are chosen for Government investment are limited in number and characterized by specific structural features (economies of large scale production, importance of the product, tendency to monopoly, etc.).

The possibility of attracting foreign investment adds a further element to the problem. To the argument against Government investment must be added the loss of additional investment resources, while the argument against private foreign investment must include the removal of profits from the economy and the future burden on the balance of payments. A purely economic evaluation would probably weigh the value of the additional investment resources and managerial talents more heavily than the cost of obtaining them (particularly where there are unemployed labour and natural resources because of lack of these factors), but the decision is infrequently made on purely economic grounds.

QUANTITATIVE ANALYSIS AND CHOICE OF INSTRUMENTS

The preceding discussion has been entirely in qualitative terms, which at best leads to the establishment of certain cases to which particular policies apply. The identification of an actual situation with the relevant case often depends on the results of quantitative analysis. Such factors as the extent of the excess demand for imports, the future amount of unemployed labour, the magnitude of the shift in resources needed in particular sectors, and the importance to the rest of the economy of a given investment, can only be determined from such an analysis. The initial study of development possibilities should be designed to permit a choice of policy instruments in different fields. Once this has been done, the long-term programme can be formulated in more specific terms which take account of the instruments chosen.

The importance of a quantitative analysis for the choice of policy instruments will be determined in part by the presence or absence of the following factors:

1. Economies of scale in production;
2. The possibility of imports and exports;
3. The use of the product in other sectors of production;
4. The predictability of demand.

In the production of consumer goods, the main objective of the development programme is likely to be a certain degree of substitution of domestic production for imports, but the choice of sector can be left to market forces. Quantitative analysis may be needed to determine the amount of employment and exchange saving which should be aimed at in the consumer goods industries, but not to determine the choice of sector.[1]

At the other extreme, the amount and distribution of investment in overhead facilities must be determined entirely from a quantitative analysis of future production because the alternative of imports is not available and output is needed to permit investment and production in other sectors. In some cases the choice between public and private investment will also depend on the amount of output required.

Choices among policy measures in the intermediate goods sectors are more affected by the outcome of the quantitative analysis than are those in consumer goods because demands derive from the planned outputs of the using sectors. Economies of scale are also more prevalent, and there is thus more interdependence among investment plans in earlier and later stages. While imports provide alternative sources of supply for many intermediate goods, some investments will not be undertaken unless there is a domestic supply of materials available. To ensure the carrying out of several interconnected projects, Government intervention in some form is likely to be necessary because the risk to private investors would be too great. Investments centering on steel production—ore, transport, power, iron and steel, fabricating—provide a good example. Once the initial investments have been made, however, most of them will prove suitable for private ownership and operation.

The advantage to the economy—in terms of the social productivity of the total investment—of inter-related projects of this type cannot be accurately determined from a partial analysis of each investment taken separately because the profitability of one may understate its contribution to the total. This dynamic type of external economy (as opposed to the technological external economies of static analysis) can only be taken account of adequately in the framework of an overall analysis.

TYPES OF DEVELOPMENT PROGRAMMES

A development programme is an analysis which provides a basis for designing and carrying out development policy. There is, however, no sharp distinction between programming and policy making, since each influences the other. The main function of a programme is to make different policies consistent with each other. Ideally, it should go further and help to select the best policies and the best means of carrying them out. The decision to make a development programme does not constitute an endorsement of increased Government intervention, or of any other particular set of policy instruments, therefore.

The nature of the analysis contained in a development programme is determined in part by the information available and in part by the instruments which are being considered. For simplicity, three general types can be distinguished, which I will call aggregate programmes, sector programmes, and overall programmes.

Aggregate programmes consist mainly of national accounts analyses and projections of other magnitudes such as industrial production, labour force, average productivity, etc. These projections are often combined with a more detailed anlaysis of certain aspects of the economy, such as the balance of payments, the sources of Government revenue, etc. . . .

Aggregate programmes provide a fairly adequate basis for the use of general policy instruments, but they do not furnish a check on the consistency of the results in specific

---

[1]This statement is not true where economies of scale are important as in the case of automobile production, because then the profitability of investment depends on an estimate of the quantity that would be demanded at the expected level of income.

sectors nor on the balance of payments. They are more likely to be adequate when the composition of production and consumption does not change too much as income increases, and when the market mechanism works well in directing investment and production decisions. . . .

Sector programmes are analyses of the demands and investment prospects in individual branches of production. Their main function is to determine the relative priority of investments within the sector. Investment programmes for the whole economy (or for all resources controlled by the Government) are sometimes constructed by merely adding up the high priority projects in each sector.

The sector approach is generally recognized to be inadequate as a basis for development policy because it does not provide a test of the consistency of the decisions made in each sector, nor a way of comparing high priority projects in one sector with those in another. It has nevertheless been the principal basis for development policy in Latin America and in most under-developed countries until quite recently. The defects in the sector approach are less serious in primary-producing economies than in those which have reached a high degree of industrialization and hence have a greater amount of inter-dependence among the various sectors.

Over-all programmes combine the elements of aggregate programmes and sector programmes in varying degrees. The analysis may start from over-all projections or from sector analyses, but in the final result they must be reconciled. It is only by some check of this kind that the consistency of the simpler models used in the two partial approaches can be tested. . . .

The need for over-all development programmes is most acute when large structural changes are required to establish or restore a process of balanced growth. Large balance of payments deficits, unemployment, bottlenecks in over-all facilities, and lack of growth may each be evidence of such conditions. These conditions may of course be merely symptoms of an excess or deficiency of total demand, and the diagnosis of structural dis-

equilibrium must try to identify the problems which would exist if inflationary (or, less often, deflationary) forces were offset. The design of policy in such circumstances is likely to call for an over-all analysis, however, whether the policy measures selected are general or specific in nature.

ELEMENTS OF POLICY ANALYSIS

General Scope. A policy model is designed to determine whether proposed economic policies are mutually consistent and to facilitate the choice among them. To fulfill these functions the model must: (a) incorporate the principal limits to achieving social objectives and (b) contain variables that indicate the nature of the policies implied by a given solution. To avoid becoming unwieldy, the model may omit variables which do not significantly affect the type of problem being considered or which can be handled in a separate analysis.

These considerations suggest that models designed to analyze long-run policy in the less developed countries should be significantly different from the models now used for the analysis of primary short-run policies in the advanced countries. Certain features will be emphasized, for example:

1. Long-term supply limitations, both in the aggregate and by sector, should be specified.
2. Since the less-developed country is typically quite dependent on foreign trade, exports and imports must be explicitly included.
3. The model should allow for the inflow of foreign capital as a significant element of development policy.

Objectives. The objectives of economic development are not adequately described as the maximization of any single measure of welfare, such as per capita output or consumption. All societies recognize the need to take account of a number of other social objectives, such as reduced unemployment, greater equality of income, and reduced economic instability. Some of these objectives can properly be taken as limitations on the economic system by assigning a given value or target to the appropriate variable. In most cases, however, it will be desirable to consider a range of alternative values in order to discover the opportunity cost or "trade off" between this and other objectives.

Variables. In his pioneering work on policy models, Tinbergen divides all variables into four categories.

1. *Objectives,* which reflect the aims of policy;
2. *Instruments,* which measure the direct effects of policy;
3. *Exogenous variables (data),* which are taken as given;
4. *Other endogenous* (irrelevant) *variables,* which do not directly affect either the choice of policy or the social welfare.

The first two types of variables—objectives and instruments—are the main concern of policy analysis, and I shall call them *policy variables.* Formally, the analyst's task is to maximize some (unknown) function of the objective variables. As Theil has emphasized, the social welfare is also affected by the values assumed by some of the instrument variables, such as taxes or income distribution, which thus take on some of the welfare characteristics of the objectives. Although a few policy variables, such as the exchange rate, are "pure" instruments which have no welfare implications per se, it will be convenient to assume that the desirability of a given type of policy is determined by the values of all the policy variables. A set of values for the policy variables may be called a *program.*

The Choice of Programs. In order to arrive at a political decision on the nature of the development policies to be followed, it is useful to focus attention on a few strategic variables having wide economic and social implications. These variables are primarily those which apply to large segments of the economy and occur in aggregate models, although a few sector decisions may be of the same degree of importance.

The formal model contributes to the choice of policy by determining *alternative feasible programs*—i.e., combinations of the strategic policy variables that are consistent with the social and economic structure of the economy. A feasible program is determined primarily by a solution to an aggregate model, supplemented by whatever elements of sector or inter-industry analysis may be necessary.

The range of programs to be considered should cover values of the policy variables that are politically as well as technically attainable. The solutions produced by the planners should indicate the possibility of achieving the several social objectives in varying degrees. In the absence of prior knowledge of the relative valuation of these objectives, the economist cannot determine an *optimum program.* At best, he can present the alternatives in such a way as to focus political attention on the problem of determining a social choice among a limited number of relevant alternatives. This is likely to be much easier than solving the larger problem of describing social preferences in general terms.

STRUCTURE OF THE MODEL

A policy model should specify the various factors limiting growth and the ways in which they can be modified by the instruments of government policy. The limits to be included depend on the present structure of the economy, the extent of the possible changes in the structure, and the data available for estimating economic relationships.

Since the economic structure may change rapidly in an underdeveloped economy, even a general planning model must pay some attention to the sector composition of demand and supply, which will affect both trade patterns and capital requirements. Once sector analyses have been made, however, their results can be incorporated into an aggregate model, which can then be used to study variations from the initial solution. This procedure will be followed here.

In designing econometric models for less developed countries, it is useful to start from the experience in advanced countries, making allowance for the differences noted above. An examination of aggregate models by Chenery and Goldberger concluded that the long-term model developed for the Netherlands by the Central Planning Bureau came closest to fitting the needs of the less developed economies. Features of this model that are particularly relevant to the choice of development policy are:

1. The inclusion of a number of policy instruments: the savings rate, import substitution, the relation of domestic to foreign prices, migration.
2. Explicit analysis of foreign trade.
3. Incorporation of the results of inter-industry analysis into the aggregate model by an iterative procedure.

These elements are utilized in the policy model designed by Goldberger to analyze existing data available for Argentina. The model was further developed by Chenery and Bruno to determine development alternatives in Israel. These models explicitly recognize four limits to growth:

1. The supply of capital.
2. The supply of labor.
3. The supply of foreign exchange.
4. The composition of internal and external demand.

The first three limits are reflected in the basic equations of the aggregate model. The composition of demand at different income levels, together with the possibilities for imports and exports, determines the capital requirements and import demands. . . .

A policy model is characterized by having more variables than equations. . . . This excess of variables constitutes the number of degrees of freedom of the model. . . . To solve the model, the values of a number of variables equal to the number of degrees of freedom must be fixed in advance. In general, the planner can assign consistent values to any combination of policy variables—objectives or instruments—equal to the number of degrees of freedom and then solve for the values of the remaining variables.

The process of solution is facilitated by first eliminating some or all of the irrelevant endogenous variables—i.e., those that are not selected to represent policy objectives. In the Israel case, for example, it was found convenient to reduce the model to four equations in eight variables, of which five are instruments and three are objectives.

These two models both allow for the anticipated composition of demand in estimating import requirements. The coefficients μ_c, μ_g, μ_i, μ_e, represent the total import requirements per unit increase in the four components of final demand: private consumption, government consumption, investment, and exports. The differences in the coefficients show the importance of allowing for changes in the composition of final demand. . . .

In designing the model, the analyst has a considerable choice of variables to represent government policy. It is sometimes feasible to use a variable that directly reflects the effects of government actions, such as the exchange rate. More often there will be several intermediate links between the actual policy measures, which may affect individual sectors of the economy, and the summary measure that it is convenient to use in the general model.

The range of choice is illustrated by the alternatives proposed for the analysis of savings in Argentina. On theoretical grounds, the following set of equations was suggested:

(1) *Net domestic saving*

$$S = \alpha_1 W + \alpha_2 R + T - G$$

(2) *Taxation*

$$T = tY$$

(3) *Income distribution*

$$W = w(R + W)$$

where

W = Disposable wage income
R = Disposable non-wage income
T = Taxes
G = Government current expenditure
t = Tax rate
w = Share of wages in disposable income

This formulation shows the several effects of government policy on savings by using three instruments: government expenditure (G), the tax rate (t), and the share of wages (w). Since information was not available to estimate the parameters in the savings and tax functions, the formulation was first simplified to:

(4) $S = \alpha^* Y - G$

and finally to:

(5) $S = \alpha Y$

In the last form, α reflects all the government policies that influence the rate of savings. A similar range of alternatives could be shown for other instrument variables which are less directly connected to the actions of the government.

THE DETERMINATION OF ALTERNATIVE POLICIES

Procedures. The greater value of a formal model is its ability to determine consistent sets of alternative policies. The weakness of the model approach is its oversimplification of many of the individual features of the economy in order to bring out their inter-relations. This drawback can be minimized by starting from a trial program in which additional elements of detailed analysis and judgment have been introduced. The model structure should be adjusted to be consistent with these added elements.

Given a realistic starting point, the model can then be used to explore a range of solutions in which the policy variables vary within predetermined limits. This range, which I shall call the *feasible area of choice,*

should cover all the consistent programs that might be of interest to policy makers.

The specified limits for each policy variable must be determined from outside sources. For example, the limits to increased saving may be set by feasible improvements in the tax structure and administration and the probable distribution of income. An optimistic estimate of these factors would set an upper limit to the savings rate that it is worth considering.

This approach demands less precision and detail in the model than would a mechanical application of a formal optimizing procedure. Additional information is used both in establishing the starting point for the analysis and in setting the range over which the equations in the model must hold. The use of linear approximations to non-linear functions can be quite accurate for a limited range when it would not be acceptable for the whole range of values.

Having specified the starting point and the allowable range for each policy variable, the analyst's next step is to fix values for a number of policy variables equal to the number of degrees of freedom in the model. If it is desired to determine the limits to the feasible area of choice, this can be done by setting the instrument variables and the objective variables alternately at their minima or maxima. A set of solutions will determine the range of values that is consistent with all the restrictions. . . .

The last step in the analytical procedure is to narrow the range of choice and finally to present a few of the leading alternative programs to the political authorities for decision. . . .

Comment

In advanced studies of planning models of development, attention is given to macroeconomic, multisectoral, optimizing, and control theory models. For studies of the design and use of econometric models and planning models, see H. B. Chenery (ed.), *Studies in Development Planning* (1971); C. R. Blitzer et al., *Economy-Wide Models and Development Planning* (1975). An excellent survey article is A. S. Manne, "Multi-Sector Models for Development Planning" *Journal of Development Economics* Vol. 1, No. 1 (1974). Other useful references are: S. Chakravarty, *Capital and Development Planning* (1969), chapters 1–5; E. Malinvaud and M. D. L. Bacharach (eds.), *Activity Analysis in the Theory of Growth and Planning* (1967), chapter 7; H. B. Chenery, "The Use of Interindustry Analysis in Development Programming," in T. Barna (ed.), *Structural Interdependence and Economic Development* (1956); H. B. Chenery and K. S. Kretschmer, "Resources Allocation for Economic Development," *Econometrica* (October 1956); H. B. Chenery and P. Clark, *Interindustry Economics* (1959), chapters 1–3; L. Johansen, *A Multi-Sectoral Study of Economic Growth* (1960); Roy Radner, *Notes on the Theory of Economic Planning* (1963); J. K. Sengupta and G. Tintner, "On Some Economic Models of Development Planning," *Economia Internazionale* (February 1963); J. Tinbergen and H. C. Bos, *Mathematical Models of Economic Growth* (1962); S. Chakravarty and L. Lefeber, "An Optimizing Planning Model," *Economic Weekly* (February 1965); I. Adelman and E. Thorbecke (eds.), *The Theory and Design of Economic Development* (1965); M. Bruno, "Experiments with a Multi-Sector Programming Model," (November 1967); Russell Ackoff, "Operations Research and National Planning," *Operations Reserach* (August 1957); Charles Hitch, "A Dissent," *Operations Research* (October 1957); M. Bronfenbrenner, "A Simplified Mahalanobis Development Model," *Economic Development and Cultural Change* (October 1960); Amartya Sen, "Interrelation Between Project, Sectoral and Aggregate Planning," *Economic Bulletin for Asia and the Far East* (June–September 1970); G. M. Heal, *Theory of Economic Planning* (1973); G. Pyatt and E. Thorbecke, *Planning Techniques for a Better Future* (1976); Leif Johansen, *Lectures on Macroeconomic Planning* (1977 and 1978), parts I and II.

XI.C. PLANNING EXPERIENCE

XI.C.1. The Crisis in Planning*

Although planning occurs in many types of decision-making units and is often defined to cover any attempt to select the best means to achieve desired ends, this paper focuses more narrowly on comprehensive development planning in low-income countries (although the discussion is also relevant to the "special case" of industrial countries). Advocates of comprehensive development planning typically propose that plans should meet the following specifications:

1. Starting from the political views and goals of the government, the plan should define policy objectives, especially as they relate to the future development of the economy.

2. It should set out a strategy by means of which it is intended to achieve the objectives, preferably translated into specific targets.

3. It should present a centrally co-ordinated, internally consistent set of principles and policies, chosen as optimal means of implementing the strategy and achieving the targets, and intended to be used as a framework to guide subsequent day-to-day decisions.

4. It should cover the whole economy (hence it is "comprehensive" as against "colonial" or "public sector" planning).

5. In order to secure optimality and consistency, it should employ a more-or-less formalized macro-economic model (which, however, may remain unpublished), employed to project the intended future performance of the economy.

6. It typically covers a period of, say, five years and finds physical expression as a medium-term plan document, which may, however, incorporate a longer-term perspective plan and be supplemented by annual plans.

*From Tony Killick, "The Possibilities of Development Planning," *Oxford Economic Papers*, Vol. 28, No. 2, July 1976, pp. 161–6. Reprinted by permission.

Most of the time, most low-income countries have development plans which apparently endeavour to meet all or most of these specifications; we are thus examining a highly significant aspect of applied economics, and the characteristics listed are chosen to identify what is common to most comprehensive development plans rather than to draw attention to any special features or eccentricities.

The economic case for development planning, while sometimes taken as axiomatic, is generally made out in terms of the failings of an unregulated market economy. Perhaps the chief of the arguments views planning as a superior means of arriving at investment and other decisions affecting the future, with the market seen as supplying information which is a poor guide for such decisions, leading to avoidable uncertainties and myopia. Thus, Scitovsky and others drew attention to the interdependence of investment decisions and alleged that aggregate investment made up of atomistic decisions would be less than that which would result from "centralised investment planning" providing more realistic signals of present plans and future conditions. In other ways, too, planning is seen as a means for correcting discrepancies between private and social valuations, for example, the market's tendency to over-value unskilled labour. Under the influence of the "big push" school of thought, it has also been seen as the only way to mobilize resources on the scale necessary for a successful development effort, and as the only practical means of weaving the various threads of economic policy into a consistent whole.

THE CRISIS IN PLANNING: EXPLANATIONS; SOLUTIONS

Although it is not a matter that can be reduced to any simple demonstration, there would probably be little disagreement today that the practice of planning has generally failed to bring many of the benefits expected from it. Waterston's study of the lessons of experience concluded that "there have been many more failures than successes in the implementation of development plans";[1] Seer's keynote paper for a 1969 conference on "The Crisis in Planning" was entitled "The Prevalance of Pseudo-planning";[2] and Healey is surely accurate in claiming that the results "have been sadly disillusioning for those who believed that planning was the only way."[3]

None of this, of course, is to deny individual successes nor some genuine benefits. The creation of planning agencies and preparation of plan documents has surely had an educational effect among politicians and administrators, helping to define, and raise the understanding of, major policy issues. Planners do not spend all their time dressing windows and have certainly helped to raise the standard of policy decisions on matters such as project selection. Nevertheless, there has been a vast gap between the theoretical benefits and practical results of development planning. It is doubtful whether plans have generated more useful signals for the future than would otherwise have been forthcoming; governments have rarely, in practice, reconciled private and social valuations except in a piecemeal manner; because they have seldom been operational documents, plans have probably had only limited success in mobilizing resources (although they probably have induced larger aid flows) or in co-ordinating economic policies.

The profession cannot be criticized for being unresponsive to this situation. Much thought has been given to the sources of poor plan performance, with the most commonly mentioned causes listed below:[4]

1. Deficiencies in the plans: they tend to be over-ambitious, to be based upon inappropriately specified macro-models, to be insufficiently specific about policies and projects, to overlook important non-economic considerations, to fail to incorporate adequate administrative provision for their own implementation.

2. Inadequate resources: incomplete and unreliable data; too few economists and other planning personnel.

3. Unanticipated dislocations to domestic economic activity: adverse movements in the terms of trade; irregular flows of development aid; unplanned changes in the private sector.

4. Institutional weaknesses: failures to locate the planning agency appropriately in the machinery of government; failures of communication between planners, administrators, and their political masters; the importation of institutional arrangements unsuited to local circumstances.

5. Failings on the part of the administrative civil service: cumbersome bureaucratic procedures; excessive caution and resistance to innovations; personal and departmental rivalries; lack of concern with economic considerations. (Finance Ministries are a particularly frequent target, often said to undermine the planning agency by resisting the co-ordination of plans and budgets.)

There is certainly ample evidence that each of these tendencies has contributed to the planning crisis, the precise combination varying over time and from country to country. But there seems to be a growing consensus among economists that yet another set of factors is the most important explanation: that "lack of government support for the plans is the prime reason why most are never carried out successfully."[5] Seers, while also finding fault with administrators and economists, argues that "political forces encourage the production of pseudo-plans";[6] Tinbergen sees as one of the difficulties "that among politicians, probably as a consequence of our educational system, a preference exists for

---

[1] Waterston, 1966, p. 293.

[2] Seers, 1972.

[3] Healey, 1972, p. 761.

[4] To avoid a wearisome number of detailed references, the reader is referred for examples of the following points to Waterston, 1966, chapters VI to IX, and Faber and Seers (eds.), 1972, passim. See also Powelson, 1972; Tinbergen, 1964; and Myrdal, 1968, chapter 15.

[5] Waterston, 1966, p. 340.

[6] Seers, 1972, p. 24.

thinking in qualitative terms only";[7] and Myrdal refers to "rivalries between parties or ministers" as one of the major problems.[8]

In the face, presumably, of the futility of advocating reformed political systems, most proposals for improving plan performance tend to the administrative or organizational. Frisch, for example, has developed an administrative decision model intended to secure "optimal implementation."[9] Myrdal perhaps comes closest to advocating a political solution in arguing for "democratic," or decentralized, planning.[10] Helleiner also tries to grasp the political nettle, with the prescription that "those engaged in planning activities must be sufficiently close to the seat of political power to be relevant to the actual process of political decision making . . ." but sees the practical application of this largely in terms of "new institutions and personnel."[11] Consistent with his views on the baneful influence of traditional education, a U.N. committee headed by Tinbergen advocates "Intensified training of many persons involved";[12] and Waterston's proposal for an "operational approach" to planning emphasizes the use of annual plans tied into budgetary procedures and supplemented by "multi-annual sector programmes."[13]

Some large questions have, however, gone unasked in these attempts to respond to the planning crisis, leaving some doubt whether the resulting prescriptions have been radical enough. The inclination to see politicians as the spoilers leaves one wondering why it would not be in their own interests to support their planners, if planning is viewed as a way of raising the rationality and effectiveness of public policies. Might it be that the concept of development planning is one that could not, with the best will in the world, be built into the process of government because "politics isn't like that"? Might it even be that a government really committed to the full execution of a plan could end up making worse rather than better decisions? It might similarly be asked of those advocating administrative-type reforms, what makes them think these solutions to be attainable through precisely those political processes which are blamed for past failings? Are not deficient institutions and procedures an expression of the political system itself, not to be remedied without first or simultaneously instituting political changes? For example, the respective roles of the planning agency and the finance ministry reflect, in substantial part, a distribution of political power; is it useful, then, to make proposals for raising the relative influence of the planning agency while remaining silent on the distribution of power?

Economists have generally failed to ask such questions and, significantly, it was a political scientist who, on reviewing explanations for plan failures similar to the list given above, was led to observe that it "rather plainly adds up to the conclusion that planning is more or less bound to fail, given the probability that many of these factors will be present in any situation of underdevelopment," and to urge that "Any useful conceptualisation of the planning process must start from a model of politics."[14] The record of past performance suggests the possibility that effective planning may simply not be feasible, so the next step is to take up Leys's point and examine the model of politics upon which the notion of development planning appears to have been built.

References

Faber, Mike, and Seers, Dudley (eds.), *The Crisis in Planning,* London, 1972 (2 vols.).

Frisch, R., "Optimal Implementation," *Revista Internazionale di Scienze Economiche e Commerciali,* Milan, 1966, No. 1.

Healey, Derek T., "Development Policy: New Thinking about an Interpretation,"

[7]Tinbergen, 1964, p. 43.

[8]Myrdal, 1968, p. 732.

[9]Frisch, 1966, passim.

[10]Myrdal, 1968, chapter 18 passim.

[11]Helleiner, 1972, pp. 354 and 347.

[12]Tinbergen, 1972, p. 160.

[13]Waterston, 1972, passim.

[14]Leys, 1972, pp. 56 and 60. The discussion of his paper, summarized in the same volume, certainly seems to justify Leys's complaint about how difficult other social scientists find it to communicate with economists (p. 79).

Journal of Economic Literature, September 1972.

Helleiner, G. K., "Beyond Growth Rates and Plan Volumes—Planning for Africa in the 1970's," *Journal of Modern African Studies,* October 1972.

Leys, Colin, "A New Conception of Planning?" in Faber and Seers (eds.), 1972, Vol. 1, chapter 3.

Myrdal, Gunnar, *Asian Drama,* Twentieth Century Fund, New York, 1968.

Powelson, John P., *Institutions of Economic Growth,* Princeton, N.J., 1972.

Seers, Dudley, "The Prevalence of Pseudo-Planning," in Faber and Seers (eds.), 1972, Vol. 1, chapter 1.

Tinbergen, Jan, *Central Planning,* New Haven, 1964.

Tinbergen, Jan, "The United Nations Development Planning Committee," in Faber and Seers (eds.) 1972, Vol. 1, chapter 7.

Waterston, Albert, *Development Planning: Lessons of Experience,* London, 1966.

————, "An Operational Approach to Development Planning," in Faber and Seers (eds.), 1972, Vol. 1, chapter 4.

Comment

The author of the foregoing selection suggests that instead of adopting a "rational actor" model of politics, economists should view politics and political decision making from the behavioral standpoint. The rational actor model

would have us see governments as composed of public-spirited, knowledgeable, and role-oriented politicians; clear and united in their objectives; choosing those policies which will achieve optimal results for the national interest; willing and able to go beyond a short-term point of view. Governments are stable, in largely undifferentiated societies; wielding a centralized concentration of power and a relatively unquestioned authority; generally capable of achieving the results they desire from a given policy decision (Killick, p. 171).

Opposing this view as being unrealistic and hence lacking relevance, Killick argues that governments do not and could not function in the manner implied by the economists' conceptions of development planning. The behavior of governments is far from the economists' idealization of the optimization process, and the rationality of government policies may be far different from the norms of economic rationality. (See Killick, "The Possibilities of Development Planning," *Oxford Economic Papers* (July 1976), pp. 161–81.)

Also relevant on the nature of political decision making are: Graham T. Allison, *Essence of Decision* (1971); Raymond A. Bauer and Kenneth J. Gergen (eds.), *The Study of Policy Formation* (1968); David Braybrooke and Charles E. Lindblom, *A Strategy of Decision* (1963); Herbert Simon, *Models of Man* (1957); Albert O. Hirschman, "Policymaking and Policy Analysis in Latin America—A Return Journey," *Policy Sciences,* Vol. 6 (1975); Guillermo O'Donnell, *Modernization and Bureaucratic-Authoritarianism* (1973); David Collier, *The New Authoritarianism in Latin America* (1979).

XI.C.2. Planned Development in India*

The structure of our economic policies in the last two decades of planned development was founded on six major premises:

(1) The only sensible long-term way of eradicating poverty must be to create more jobs by investing and growing faster; hence,

*From Jagdish N. Bhagwati, *India in the International Economy,* Lal Bahadur Shastri Memorial Lectures, Institute of Public Enterprise, Hyderabad, 1973, pp. 3–12. Reprinted by permission.

redistributive measures which would tend to use up investible resources in current consumption were undesirable.

(2) In consequence, the Government must direct its major effort at raising the domestic savings rate and securing external aid to supplement domestic savings until such time as the domestic savings rate had been raised to levels adequate to do away with foreign aid altogether and achieve rapid growth with self-reliance.

(3) The industrial sector, which would grow with investment and income, had to be planned and controlled *in depth:* towards this end, very detailed targeting and regulatory licensing of industrial establishments was considered necessary and resulted in the Industries (Development and Regulation) Act of 1951.

(4) The external accounts, i.e., the balance of payments, had also to be regulated, not via exchange rate adjustments and the use of protective tariffs, but by resort to comprehensive exchange control so that the use of imported raw materials, capital goods and other supplies was to be regulated by an elaborate administrative mechanism.

(5) Alongside these four basic premises of economic policy was the objective of an increasing role for the public sector in the ownership of the country's resources. As the succeeding Industrial Policy Resolutions and the pronouncements of our Prime Ministers underlined, this was a political objective but also one which reflected certain economic axioms. Thus, we thought that the public sector would invest where the private sector would not invest (e.g., steel in the Second Plan); and, in particular, the public sector would generate surpluses for investment, obviating the need to raise savings exclusively via the politically-difficult budgetary process of taxation. These dual economic objectives in expanding the public sector went alongside with the envisaged role of the expanding public sector in conjunction with the industrial licensing policy in controlling the concentration of private economic power. There was also the additional political objective of securing public control over the so-called

"commanding heights" of the economy, the "basic" or "key" sectors.

(6) Finally, while these policy instruments embraced directly the non-agricultural sector of our economy, though in turn influencing no doubt the agricultural sector, the Plan programmes repeatedly urged land reforms to transform the institutional structure in the rural economy and urged rural works programmes so that expanding production would go hand in hand with better income distribution.

Experience has now shown that these premises of our policies have been either misguided or inadequate or unrealistic in our political framework. In short, a serious restructuring of our policies is called for. Indeed, many of the more dramatic measures of recent years, especially the nationalization of banking and wholesale wheat trade, are evidence that a restructuring is either being intentionally designed or being forced by the complex of political and economic circumstances on the government. Hence a realistic appraisal of where our policy premises fell short is necessary to examine the optimal policy mix for our economy and to judge, in perspective thereof, the present and prospective governmental actions and programmes. To this task, I shall now turn.

(1) The estimates of increasing poverty in India have underlined the lesson that growing incomes do not necessarily trickle down to the bottom deciles. Even if they did, the process would be so slow that it would be intolerable in the time it would take: it is morally difficult and politically impossible to ask those in poverty to wait until perhaps the next millennium for significantly improved incomes. The early faith in the ability of growing incomes and investments to take care of the poor within the foreseeable future, in any significant fashion, is no longer with us.

(2) The failure of the income-generation mechanism to make an impact on poverty, in turn, must be traced to the inappropriateness of the other policy premises I listed earlier. The policy premise that domestic savings should be stepped up steadily and the level of

external aid should be tapered off as the domestic savings took its place has been only partially fulfilled: ironically, aid has substantially fallen for exogenous reasons since the mid-60's but domestic savings which increased steadily through the first three Five-Year Plans, have stagnated since then! (It is tempting to argue, as some radical economists have recently argued elsewhere, that over the long haul the presence of foreign aid in fact may have reduced our domestic savings effort; but systematic economic analysis does not support such a charge.) The Indo-Pakistan War, the refugee relief burden and the outflow of significant net resources to Bangladesh have undoubtedly contributed their share to this continuing failure to resume the rate of increment in the domestic savings rate. Nonetheless, since the mid-60's even our traditional strategy of increasing the rates of saving, investment and job-plus-income-creation has not been pursued with any degree of success.

(3) But the efficacy of this developmental strategy has been undoubtedly impaired also by the inefficiency which has resulted from our framework of industrial and foreign trade policies. Even while we heroically raised our domestic rate of saving through successive budgets, our policies which defined the *use* of these savings and accumulated capital stock have left us with intolerable inefficiencies and diminished returns to our efforts.

There are so many inefficiencies inherent in these policies that one could write volumes cataloguing them, as indeed I have! But let me highlight a few of the most obvious ones, focusing first on the industrial policy framework and next on the foreign trade regime, though the conjunction of both has disproportionately accentuated some of the unfortunate consequences of either taken by itself.

The detailed industrial targeting cannot possibly take into account costs and benefits at a micro-level. Industrial licensing has either buttressed this targeting or made the non-targeted industrial development none-the-less go through a series of substantially meaningless bureaucratic scrutinies for which no rational economic criteria have ever been defined or at least discovered. Import licensing, in combination with the principle of indigenous availability, has conferred "automatic protection" to domestic industry regardless of costs. The pro-rata-to-capacity allocations of imported (and other) materials to licensed units have, in combination with automatic protection and licensing restrictions on domestic entry, eliminated virtually all effective foreign and domestic competition, and in consequence also the incentive to efficiency and cost-reduction. The practically-assured markets for licensed units (in view of the elimination of foreign and domestic competiton) and the guaranteed share in the available imputs as soon as capacity is licensed have also meant that, even when there was excess capacity in an industry or a product, there could still be adequate incentive to add to capacity: there is little doubt that, while we have been eager to blame aid-tying to project imports for much of our phenomenal underutilisation of capacity, it is very much a result of our own licensing and allocation policies which make the addition of yet more capacity to underutilized-capacity industries ever so profitable.

This pattern of "bureaucratic capitalism" is reminiscent of the "bureaucratic socialism" from which the Soviet Union is busy disengaging itself in its Liebermannist reforms; but we have stuck to it, with occasional Ministerial and Prime Ministerial exhortations to improve it—exhortations which are no longer amusing—never facing up to the stark and compelling fact that it is one of the supreme examples of counterproductive and ill-conceived economic policy-making. Adam Smith discovered the Invisible Hand; and economists have correctly argued, in Joan Robinson's colourful phrasing, that the Invisible Hand may often work by strangulation. But the maze of meaningless controls that we continue to work with, so that the Invisible Hand is nowhere to be seen, represents a regression, a *reductio ad absurdum* that does our intelligence little credit and our economy much harm.

Indeed, one must ask why this policy

framework continues and answer that it is not merely a product of misguided thinking on the part of our intellectual Left—for several of us who are on the Left have already rejected this travesty of radicalism. It surely has to be explained, in the ultimate political analysis, as the most obvious and ideal instrument for creating an elaborate facade to delude the masses into the belief that socialism is being practised while, in reality, the policy merely serves to create political power and patronage, essentially leading to shared economic power in the urban areas between the private sector and the politicians, and to spawn ever more, in Shakespeare's phrase, "caterpillars of the Commonwealth": the economic agents whose function is to seek out the "rents," the monopoly profits which the system itself creates through the endless generation of licensed allocations, and the bureaucratic agents, with whom they have a symbiotic relationship, whose function is to allocate these rent-earning privileges among the competing claimants.

(4) Let me turn now to the foreign trade and exchange rate policies which, as I have already indicated, have critically reinforced this inefficient policy framework.

The automatic protection mindless of the cost of import substitution and the elimination of virtually any competitive spur to efficiency, which I have already noted, were the product of the comprehensive exchange control that we settled down to as a long-term way of managing our balance of payments.

The overvalued exchange rate has also implied a continuing discrimination against exports: a phenomenon that has become so obvious that the government has repeatedly sought to offset it by special subsidies to exportation. But the several export subsidy programmes have been generally chaotic in their selectivity and have reproduced on the export front the irrationalities and inefficiencies that have afflicted the import substitution mechanism. The multiplicity of effective exchange rates for exports, necessitated by the adherence to overvalued exchange rates, is a serious source of waste and must inevitably reduce the returns to our economic sacrifices.

Compounding these inefficiencies has been our peculiar attachment, only slightly diminished through the years, to making all import allocations generally non-transferable. The resulting bottle-necks and inflexibility are a totally gratuitous source of additional, and significant, waste in the system; they must also seriously impede exports where the ability to grasp sudden opportunities and to produce with predictable and rapid access to materials without red tape is surely critical.[1]

And let us not forget the simple but critical fact that the attempts to offset the ill-effects of over-valuation of the exchange rate on export performance through greater reliance on export incentives are also an additional source of the corruption which has now become almost endemic to our scene—and again, this is totally unnecessary as the most effective and efficient incentive to export is provided by eliminating the over-valuation of the exchange rate as some developing, and many developed, countries have now come to understand and practice.

Let me stress again that the objection to the energetic use of flexibility in setting the exchange rate has little justification in a radicalism that is concerned with socialist objectives as distinct from so-called socialist instruments of economic policy. In fact, not merely in India, but in many other developing countries which went through a phase of comprehensive exchange control in the three decades since the War, the exchange control regime has made a mockery of income distributional objectives by creating profits and privilege. And it is only the unthinking segment of intellectual opinion, which is mechanically wedded to obsolete and defunct notions, which would want to stick to overvalued exchange rates as a matter of *principle....*

Finally, I must reject the widespread notion that somehow, in Indian conditions, exchange rate flexibility would be unworkable. In this regard, the experience of the June

[1]These and other consequences of our trade and exchange rate policies were extensively discussed in J. Bhagwati and Padma Desai, *India: Planning for Industrialization,* London, 1970.

1966 devaluation has been widely misunderstood. The 1966 devaluation turned out to have been badly planned and timed, from a political and psychological standpoint: the extreme pressure exerted by the Aid India Consortium in favour of the devaluation produced a perfectly natural nationalist reaction which put the devaluation into a politically unacceptable strait-jacket; and the second major agricultural drought that followed it led to major price increases and export supply difficulties which swamped the effects of the devaluation. Careful analysis, which is necessary to separate out the effects of the drought from the effects of the devaluation, and which Prof. T. N. Srinivasan and I have just concluded, strongly indicates that the latter were favourable; and that, in the absence of the devaluation, the economy would have been in yet worse shape thanks to the drought.[2]

(5) Turning next to the economic objectives to which the public sector was supposed to contribute, I am afraid that the outcome, while not as unfortunate as in the case of our trade and industrial policy framework, has been less than satisfactory. For one reason or another, the contribution made by the public sector enterprises to public saving has fallen considerably short of our early optimism. Brilliant economists, of whom we now have a growing number, can readily construct rational reasons why a public investment may be run at a private loss and yet contribute to social gain. But these reasons have as little to do with the actual occurrence of inadequate profits, and resulting savings, in the public sector as do the sophisticated reasons for selective taxing and subsidising of foreign trade with the situation actually obtaining and described by me earlier in this Lecture.

As for the role of the expanding public sector investments, in conjunction with industrial licensing, in restraining the growth of the concentration of economic power, the growth of the Large Industrial Houses has

amply shown that we were not fully successful. At the same time, the stagnation in the rate of industrial investment, under the later policy of confining the Large Industrial Houses to the so-called "core" industries, suggests strongly that neither the public sector nor the small-scale sector has been able to fill the vacuum: so that we have run into the additional problem that a policy which seeks to confine the growth of the Large Houses to only the supposedly socially necessary "core" industries is also contributing, given the failure on the part of the public and the limited capacity of the small-scale sectors, to stagnation in industrial investments. At the same time, one cannot suppress the thought that there is little that is more than symbolic in a policy framework which leaves the Large Industrial Houses at their greatly-augmented capital stock and accompanying politico-economic power and seeks to convince the masses that somehow the prevention of a purely marginal addition to this capital stock is tantamount to ushering in socialism.

Indeed, it is somewhat ironic that we have now shifted from viewing the "core," the "basic," the "key" sectors as essentially the preserve of the public sector, in its exclusive or dominating domain, to viewing the "core" industries as the particularly choice investment field for what appear to be unsympathetic and uninvesting Large Industrial Houses. It is almost as if the attainment of the "commanding heights of the economy," that colourful phrase we learnt to use in progressive circles, had produced, not bliss but, vertigo!

(6) And let me turn finally to the sixth and last policy premise: that agricultural growth would be accompanied by improved income distribution via land reform and expanding rural works programmes. It is only an urban intelligentsia which needs to be reminded that, in a country such as ours, with the bulk of its population and its poor on land, socialist programmes cannot be formulated meaningfully except in so far as they involve the agricultural sector. The utmost importance attaches therefore to our agricultural land reforms. And yet, our progress on this front has

[2]Cf. J. Bhagwati and T. N. Srinivasan, *Foreign Trade Regimes and Economic Development: India,* National Bureau of Economic Research, Amsterdam, 1974.

been slow despite volumes of legislation on the subject. The readiness and ease with which the modern, non-agricultural sector has been subjected to the extensive pseudo-socialist regulation and control I have just discussed contrasts starkly with the lack of genuine socialist transformation in our agricultural economy, so that we have to-day an economy which is like an iceberg whose tip has the glossy look of socialism but whose bulk underneath has diverse capitalist and quasi-capitalist elements.

Nor have our rural works programmes ever become substantial or effective enough to make for a real impact on the agricultural economy. We have repeatedly built them into our Plans and talked of the numerous tasks that the "surplus" rural labour could be mobilized to perform. But, in the absence of organizational input and financial resources, we have had few results that would match our self-exhortations. Again, China has succeeded admirably here by being able to use its abundant labour in the communes, thus automatically providing the organizational framework and obviating the need to make budgetary allocations to compensate the "hired" labour.

We thus find ourselves in a situation where few of our original policy premises can be regarded as acceptable if we are to get the economy moving in the direction of rapid growth, self-reliance and social justice.

The present trade and industrial policies have reduced the returns to our investments. There are no mitigating "beneficial" effects such as increased savings in the economy or increased inducement to invest or enhanced R and D which can plausibly be cited, with supporting evidence. In our study of India's foreign trade regime,[3] Professor T. N. Srinivasan and I have examined these aspects at

[3]Bhagwati and Srinivasan, ibid.

length, only to conclude that there is no escape from the unpleasant evidence of the harmful effect of our policies on industrial efficiency and thence on the overall performance and growth of our economy.

These policies have also increased our external dependence—a paradox only if you believe that comprehensive exchange controls and licensed allocations must necessarily eliminate such dependence. But by adversely affecting our export performance, and by reducing the value added and hence increasing the consequent demand for external resources, *ceteris paribus,* corresponding to any investment in import substitution, we have compounded our dependence on foreign aid beyond what our early planners envisaged as the period during which we could take "aid to end aid". . . .

And finally let me stress the unpleasant but incontrovertible fact that our policies have been inadequate to the task of bringing social justice to our society. By reducing efficiency and the rate of growth, our trade and industrial policies have in fact cut into even the small but probable improvement in the incomes of the poor that we had hoped for. And as for their direct impact on income distribution, they have essentially redistributed income from the rich to the *nouveau riche:* the poor have indeed no way of asserting themselves in the marketplace but, in our policy framework, they equally cannot afford to wait in queues for licences nor do they have the position, privilege and resources to push past the line. Nor has our targeting and industrial licensing diminished the continuing and increasing use of resources to satisfy the needs of the rich, and the not-so-rich. And, as I noted earlier, our rural programmes and halting land reforms have left us with only increasing numbers below the poverty line in the last two decades.

A restructuring of our policy framework is, therefore, called for.

Comment

In all developing countries, the management of the public sector has become a prime concern. A major task of that management must relate to state-owned enterprises. As state-owned enterprises have increased markedly in numbers, more attention is being given to policies that might improve their efficiency. See Leroy Jones, *Public Enterprise and Economic Development* (1975); A. H. Gantt and Giuseppe Dutto, "Financial Performance of Government-Owned Corporations in Less Developed Countries," *IMF Staff Papers* (May 1968); Hamlin Robinson, "Public Corporations in Malaya," *Development Administration Review* (January 1973); Richard A. Musgrave et al., "Public Enterprises and the Fiscal System," chapter 8, in Musgrave et al., *Fiscal Reform for Bolivia,* vol. II (1977); A. Choksi, "State Intervention in the Industrialization of Developing Countries: Selected Issues," *World Bank Staff Working Paper* No. 341 (July 1979); William J. Baumol (ed.), *Public and Private Enterprises in a Mixed Economy* (1980); Leroy Jones et al., *Public Enterprises in Developing Countries* (forthcoming).

Comment
A large number of case studies are now available for an appraisal of development planning in practice. A selected list of readings follows: I. G. Patel, "Strategy of Indian Planning," in P. Chaudhuri (ed.), *Aspects of Indian Economic Development* (1971); J. N. Bhagwati and S. Chakravarty, "Contributions to Indian Economic Analysis: A Survey," *American Economic Review* (September 1969), supplement, part 2; R. S. Eckaus and K. Parikh, *Planning for Growth* (1967); R. S. Eckaus, "Planning in India," in M. F. Millikan (ed.), *National Economic Planning* (1967); B. S. Minhas, *Planning and the Poor* (1974); Pranab K. Bardhan, "India," in Hollis Chenery et al., *Redistribution with Growth* (1974); Deepak Lal, *Prices for Planning: Toward the Reform of Indian Planning* (1980); Ursula Hicks, "Thirty Years of Planning: The Indian Experience," *Malayan Economic Review* (October 1979); Gustav F. Papanek, *Pakistan's Development* (1967); W. P. Falcon and G. F. Papanek (eds.), *Development Policy: The Pakistan Experience* (1971); A. MacEwan, *Development Alternatives in Pakistan* (1971); G. T. Brown, *Korean Pricing Policies and Economic Development in 1960s* (1973); D. C. Cole and P. N. Lyman, *Korean Development: The Interplay of Politics and Economics* (1971); Wolfgang Stolper, *Planning Without Facts* (1966); Andrew Kamarck, *Economics of African Development,* rev. ed. (1971); Paul G. Clark, *Development Planning in East-Africa* (1965); R. H. Green, "Four African Development Plans," *Journal of Modern African Studies,* Vol. 3, No. 2 (1966); George B. Baldwin, *Planning and Development in Iran* (1967); Bertram M. Gross (ed.), *Action under Planning: The Guidance of Economic Development* (1967); Albert Waterston, *Development Planning: Lessons of Experience* (1969); Louis M. Goreaux, *Interdependence in Planning: Multilevel Programming Studies of the Ivory Coast* (1979); Nural Islam, *Development Planning in Bangladesh* (1977).

XI.C.3. The Future of Development Planning—Note

After all the discussion of the preceding chapters, we are left with the ultimate question of why the success stories of development planning have been so few and the disappointments so many. In this Note, it may be most appropriate to concentrate on the limits of development planning, instead of its accomplishments, because concerted attention in the immediate future must be given to those countries with a dismal development record even after experiencing two or more decades of planning. To this end, it is necessary first to isolate the reasons why development planning has not succeeded in coping more effectively with the strategic policy issues discussed in this book. We may then consider ways to improve the practice of development planning.

Many economists would suggest that the reasons for past failures are to be found mainly in an inability or unwillingness to implement development plans. Planning agencies in the developing countries are now capable of approximating the elements of a well-formulated plan in a creditable fashion. And yet we are left with the disconcerting question: has the ability to implement a development plan improved *pari passu* with the ability to formulate a plan? It can be maintained that the record of development planning reveals that problems of implementation now need more attention than problems of formulation.

In this vein, Sir Arthur Lewis prefaces his book *Development Planning* with the observation that "The economics of development is not very complicated; the secret of successful planning lies more in sensible politics and good public administration."[1] The implication of this statement is that the major problems of development planning center upon implementation—that the secret of successful planning lies essentially in policital stability and political leadership and in competent and effective public administration of the policy instruments by which the goals of development can be reached. But this has additional implications—namely, that economists know why poor countries have remained poor and that they also know what policy measures would accelerate their development.

Before placing so much emphasis on implementation, we should raise, however, the logically prior question of whether economists really do know what is wrong and how to put it right. In answering this question, we might reasonably argue that a major difficulty with development planning has been the economists' inadequate understanding of the development process, and that the secret of successful planning is not only—nor even mainly—a matter of implementation.

[1]W. Arthur Lewis, *Development Planning*, London, 1966, preface.

From the foregoing chapters we can identify three areas about which we need fundamental understanding before there can be a more intelligent basis for development planning. One area is that of the "unexplained residual factor." To the extent that our knowledge of the sources of economic development remains inadequate, we must also remain ignorant of relevant policy variables. This constitutes a severe limitation on the efficacy of development planning. Even if we were to succeed in disaggregating the residual into recognizable elements (such as advances in technical, managerial, and organizational knowledge), it would still be difficult to specify exactly how these elements are to yield to planning. Planning may operate effectively on the supply of inputs, but it is quite a different matter to bring the techniques of planning to bear on the income-raising forces constituting the residual.

Similarly, it is uncertain by what means a development plan can have an impact on population growth. And yet in many countries, a major challenge to development planning is the control of the income-depressing forces associated with heavy population pressures. The record of development planning in this area has so far been disappointing, but many development practitioners would now contend that it is of prime importance to acquire new meaningful sociological and scientific knowledge of the determinants of the birth rate and to institute as an essential element of development planning a set of policies aimed at birth control.

This brings us to the third set of factors with which it is difficult for development planning to cope—namely, the sociocultural and other noneconomic factors that have an effect on the process of development. If we are to improve our understanding of the two problem areas already discussed—the residual factor and population growth—we must also be able to evaluate more thoroughly the noneconomic factors in the development process. It is now stating the obvious to say that economic, social, and political change are all interrelated. Nonetheless, we do not yet know under what conditions and by what mechanisms it is possible to have the types of socio-cultural and political changes that will be most favorable for development. Without such knowledge, we cannot expect development planning to be very successful. Exactly how is planning to bring about cultural change? Are attitudes, motivations, and institutions amenable to change by planning? Or is planning actually counterproductive, inhibiting the emergence of the favorable sociocultural factors? If policymakers cannot identify the functional relationships among economic and noneconomic factors, and their quantitative significance, how can they determine whether to operate on economic incentives, or attitudes, or organizational structure, or social relations, or any of the many other factors that connect economic and noneconomic change? Despite the countless assertions that the interaction between economic and noneconomic variables is of utmost importance, the past emphasis has been on *economic* planning. The planning of social or political change has been negligible. But the future success of economic planning may depend upon an understanding of how to plan social and political transformations. And to achieve this, more than "sensible policies and good administration" are required.

At the same time as (and possible because) policymakers have remained ignorant about these fundamental aspects of the development process, a number of biases have been revealed within the actual planning process.[2] What has been unfortunate about these biases is that some of them have actually intensified the constraints on development and others have kept the actual rate below the attainable rate of development.

If we may refer to a characteristic style of development planning, three types of bias have been prominent: a bias toward macro-models in plan formulation to the relative neglect of the microeconomic aspects of planning (such as project analysis); a bias toward the quantitative aspects of planning to the relative neglect of other development forces that are not quantifiable but are of crucial importance (for instance, many aspects of human-resource development and sociocultural and political changes for which no data exist); a bias toward concentration on the formulation of a development plan without due regard for its implementation (even though formulation and implementation should be inseparable).

The quantitative bias in the theory of development planning tends to reinforce the other biases in development planning. Intersectoral programming models and other planning models are generally national planning models because the locus of industrial policy and the sources of data are usually national.[3]

Data accessibility also reinforces the macro bias, an emphasis on physical rather than human capital, and a focus on a few large projects rather than many small projects. Plans for industrial development also tend to dominate insofar as the outputs of industry are more easily measured and industrial inputs are more readily specified than in agriculture.[4]

As for their substantive content, many development plans have until recently emphasized inward-looking policies to the relative neglect of outward-looking policies; the development of the urban industrial sector with much less concentration on rural development; and the simple imitation of the advanced countries' institutions at the expense of innovation and adaptation.

In our previous discussions of the need to mobilize domestic and external resources, promote agricultural development, encourage foreign trade, and invest in human capital, we have repeatedly encountered arguments in support of those very policies that have actually been ignored by many of the past development plans. Recognizing the past

---

[2]These are biases in the sense of both statistical skewness and unwarranted valuations. Cf. Gunnar Myrdal, *Asian Drama,* New York, 1968, appendix 4.

[3]See Don Humphrey, "Some Implications of Planning for Trade and Capital," in Max F. Millikan (ed.), *National Economic Planning,* New York, 1967.

[4]Cf. Michael Lipton, "Urban Bias and Agricultural Planning," in Paul Streeten and Michael Lipton (eds.), *The Crisis of Indian Planning,* London, 1968.

biases in development planning, many development economists now maintain that the time has come to rethink the nature and scope of development planning. It has been increasingly recognized that the comprehensive "heavy-type" of central planning is still premature for most of the LDCs.

The plea is not, however, for a reversal to laissez-faire—but a plea for *competent* planning. To achieve this, students of development must devote more research to determining the appropriate range and forms of planning for a developing country (for instance, indicative versus controlling, or formal versus informal planning). The problem is to identify and institutionalize the most appropriate way of planning for the particular country at a particular period. An evolution of the planning approach itself would therefore be expected as the country develops.

More immediately, some major revisions of development planning can be suggested to remove the biases and secure more benefits from planning in the future. These revisions amount, on the one side, to making greater use of the market mechanism as an instrument of development policy within the domestic economy, while encouraging, on the other side, an extension of multinational planning in the international economy.

Many economists have come to believe that in order to overcome past deficiencies in planning and undertake policies that conform more closely to their present needs and capabilities, the majority of LDCs should retrench to a lighter type of planning. This would rely more on decentralized decisions operating through the market mechanism, and greater attention would be given to devising policies that might make private action more effective.

The advocacy of greater use of the market mechanism should not be interpreted as a call for a diminished role for the government, but rather a different role. Governmental policies are needed to strengthen the market system, and a stronger market system is in turn needed to allow public policy to operate more effectively through the market. Thus, in a sense, more planning is actually required to overcome the results of inadequate planning in the past: improved planning is now necessary to remove the distortions caused by arbitrary direct administrative controls that have produced a disequilibrium system and a set of trade, fiscal, financial, industrial, and wage policies that are often contradictory and self-defeating.

The case for a high degree of planning, with a large amount of public investment and deliberate industrialization constituting the core of the plan, may remain strong for countries that suffer seriously from the pressure of population on the land but have the potential for large domestic markets (such as India or China). For other countries, however, in which there are underutilized natural resources but only small internal markets, it can be persuasively argued that the basic problem is one of creating a favorable social and economic environment which will lead to expansion of private activity, more effective use of the underutilized resources, and capitalization on the existing opportunities for international trade.

If the private sector is to be enlarged, how is this now to be accomplished? Instead of allowing any economic resources to be left unemployed, governmental policies must try to mobilize through positive economic incentives and inducements the latent skills and capital in the private sector. Fundamentally, the stimulation of multiple centers of initiative depends on the establishment of markets and encouragement of market institutions. Economic and social overhead capital can help to establish the physical conditions for a market to exist and can support the interdependence of markets. The government also has a crucial role in building institutions such as a banking system, a money and capital market, agricultural cooperatives, labor organizations, rural credit institutions, and training institutes. It must also be recognized that many policy measures that can affect individual action by altering the economic environment are not of the usual monetary or fiscal type of policy, but rather of a kind that involve the legal and institutional framework, such as land tenure legislation, commercial law, and property rights.

Once market imperfections are reduced and the structure of markets improved, the market mechanism can itself be used as an instrument of development—promoting governmental policies as well as more effective private activity. Instead of relying on comprehensive and detailed administrative controls, the government can alter prices to execute policy and can provide price and income stimuli for an expansion in private output, an increase in exports, and a widening of domestic markets. These price changes may extend to foreign exchange rates, interest rates, tariffs, taxes, and subsidies. Subsidy and tax schemes can be especially relevant in inducing firms to value inputs according to their social opportunity costs, to exploit external economies, or to introduce new techniques of production.

Of most importance is the need to remove the distortions in internal price relations which have resulted from the use of numerous specific controls. We have repeatedly noted criticisms that interest rates are artificially low in the urban sector, exchange rates are overvalued, unskilled wages are too high in labour surplus economies, subsidization of import-substitutes has become suboptimal, exports and agriculture are being discriminated against. Accordingly, there are now more proponents advocating the adoption of flexible exchange-rates to avoid currency overvaluation, the removal of price controls on foodstuffs, and the liberalization of foreign trade controls with the substitution of domestic subsidy and tax schemes. It is argued that a more realistic price structure would remove the need for detailed investment planning and would induce additional private activity.

Although there are good reasons why the market mechanism should have a large role within the LDC's domestic economy, there is at the same time a need for more multinational planning for development within the international economy, as outlined in the next Note.

Comment

Many commentaries have been offered on the proposals for a New International Economic Order (NIEO), advocated by the developing countries in the United Nations and its agencies during the mid-1970s. The proposals emphasize the importance of reforming the international environment to ensure successful development planning. The basic themes of the NIEO can be noted in the document of UNCTAD. *New Directions and Structures for Trade and Development* (1976) and in the *Declaration and Program of Action of the NIEO,* presented at the Sixth Special Session of the General Assembly of the United Nations in 1974.

For a discussion of the issues raised by the NIEO, see Jagdish N. Bhagwati (ed.), *The New International Economic Order: The North-South Debate* (1977); Edward P. Reubens (ed.), *The Challenge of the New International Economic Order* (1981); Albert Fishlow et al., *Rich and Poor Nations in the World Economy* (1978); Robert W. Cox, "Ideologies and the New International Economic Order," *International Organization* (Spring 1979); Lance Taylor, "Back to Basics: Theory for the Rhetoric in the North-South Round," *World Development* Vol. 10, No. 4 (1982); Hans Singer, "The New International Economic Order: an Overview," *Journal of Modern African Studies,* Vol. 16, No. 4 (1978); Mordechai E. Kreinen and J. M. Finger, "A Critical Survey of the NIEO," *Journal of World Trade Law* (1976); Jurgen B. Donges, "The Third World Demand for a NIEO," *Kyklos* (1977); W. Loehr and J. Powelson, *Threat to Development: Pitfalls of the NIEO* (1983); United Nations, *The NIEO: A Selective Bibliography* (1980). Especially noteworthy is W. M. Corden, *The NIEO Proposals: A Cool Look* (1979).

XI.D. INTERNATIONAL POLICYMAKING AND THE NIEO—NOTE

For many developing countries, the quality of national economic management has distinctly improved. At the international level, however, policymaking shows little improvement and may actually have deteriorated in several problem areas. The world order is now less responsive to the needs of the LDCs than a decade ago. Although many of the preceding selections have argued that the market mechanism should have a larger role within the LDC's domestic economy, it can also be maintained that there is a need for more effective international policymaking in the interests of development. Improved policymaking at the international level would not be a substitute for necessary internal reforms, but it would be complementary and would extend the effectiveness of the internal reforms.

To plead for improved international policymaking is not, however, necessarily to endorse the call for a New International Economic Order (NIEO). The NIEO is subject to different interpretations. The proposals for an NIEO, as adopted at the Sixth Special Session of the United Nations General Assembly, included the following:

(a) An "integrated" program of price supports at levels higher than historic trends for a group of commodities exported by developing countries.

(b) The indexation of prices of exports of developing countries to prices of their imports from developed countries.

(c) The attainment of the target of 0.7 percent of gross national product (GNP) of developed countries for official development assistance.

(d) The linkage, in some form, of development aid to the creation of international reserves in terms of special drawing rights (SDRs) on the International Monetary Fund (IMF).

(e) The so-called Lima target for shifting manufacturing capacity from the developed to developing countries to the extent of 25 percent of world industrial output by the year 2000.

(f) Mechanisms for the transfer of technology to developing countries and codes of conduct for multinational enterprises.

Following the United Nations declaration, some proponents of the NIEO interpreted the new order as providing exemptions for LDCs from established rules, thereby granting some important short-term concessions such as more aid, debt relief, and trade concessions. Others identified a NIEO with long-term structural changes in the international system that would alter biases in income, wealth, and power distributions between LDCs and MDCs. As one proponent of a NIEO stated,

The basic purpose of the current demand for a new international economic order is to restructure the prevailing market rules, largely fashioned by the financial power of the rich nations and their multinationals; to obtain a greater voice in international financial institutions; and to break the age-old patterns of economic and political dependency of the poor nations on the goodwill of the rich nations. The main objective, however politely or skillfully stated, is restructuring of *power;* whether political, economic, financial, or intellectual.[1]

This interpretation sees in the post-colonial power structure a continuation of domination and dependence, caused not only by rules, procedures, and institutions designed by the rich countries, but also by the totality of economic, political, and even cultural relations among nations. This view stems from the earlier analyses of Singer, Prebisch, and Myrdal that see polarization or backwash effects as the causes of failure in LDCs.[2] According to this interpretation, the rules of international relations must be changed by removing biases in the present rules, by the exercise of countervailing power where at present the

[1]Mahbub ul Haq, "Beyond the Slogan of South-South Cooperation," in Khadija Haq (ed.), *Dialogue for a New Order,* New York 1981.

[2]See Chapters II, VIII.

distribution of power is felt to be unequal, and by counteracting biases that arise not from rules but from the nature of economic processes that inflict cumulative damage on the LDCs. Although a change in only the economic relations among nations may allow scope for positive-sum games, the emphasis on national power relations among sovereign states necessarily involves the relative concept of power, and hence entails a zero-sum game. The demand for greater participation in international decision making and for corrections in the basis of the international power distribution are bound to diminish the power of the richer countries.[3]

Others have pointed out that there is really nothing "new" to the NIEO. Some of its provisions were already advocated in the 1950s by Singer, Prebisch, and Myrdal. Moreover, the NIEO is not "international," "economic," nor "an order." On the contrary, many of its objectives are highly nationalistic and of a zero-sum game character, favoring the LDCs instead of emphasizing mutual gains for all actors in a positive-sum game. Furthermore, the policy objectives and policy instruments are as much political as economic. And, finally, given the lack of unanimity and the willingness of some countries for North-South confrontation, the measures are more likely to produce disorder than order.

Economists may criticize the ill-designed measures of the NIEO, but there is still validity in some of the objectives sought by the NIEO. The crucial question, however, is: How can these objectives be realized? It is unrealistic to believe that the MDCs will simply grant the demands of the LDCs out of a sense of altruism or humanitarianism or morality. Nor can UNCTAD be relied on to be an effective interest group for the poor countries. A more promising possibility lies in the enlistment of interest alignments among nations. Multinational and transnational firms are, for example, important ad-

vocates of better market access in the industrial countries and can form strong pressure groups.

Another view is that a NIEO is not to emerge through the benevolent generosity of the rich nations but only through the efforts of the South in restructuring domestic political and economic power and in organizing greater collective bargaining at the international level.

For many LDCs, however, the acquisition of countervailing power remains remote, and the tactic still smacks of an adversary position. A more cooperative approach might build on the enlightened self-interest of the MDCs and their sharing with the LDCs of some mutual needs for international economic management. Mutual needs are often analyzed in terms of an interdependent world economy. Much has been written recently about interdependence, especially from the viewpoint of energy, resource balances, and the global food/population equation. But interdependence is not a new phenomenon; for centuries, world economic integration has been increasing, and the international spread of development is only a continuation of the process. In the past two or three decades, however, the consequences of interdependence have become more pronounced; the duration of international economic conflicts has lengthened; the extent of economic gains and losses has grown; and the inadequacy of policy measures to resolve conflicts has increased.

This might be better interpreted as the result of the internationalization of the economic system. Outstanding features of this internationalization process have been the increases in the international flows of commodities, factors of production, management, technology, and financial capital, which have become ever more responsive—or more elastic—to differences between domestic and foreign variables. To an economist, this internationalization of markets is commendable because it promotes efficiency, specialization, and competition. To a national policymaker, however, internationalization has a negative side: it heightens the vulnerability of a nation

[3]Paul Streeten, "The New International Economic Order," *World Development* (January 1982), pp. 1–17.

to external developments. Domestic autonomy in policymaking is subordinated to international policy considerations. International economics is opposed by national politics. When the economic objectives of two or more nations clash, international tension and conflict result.

The conflicts can be grouped into three categories: (1) those that arise because a nation seeks to acquire a larger share of the gains from trade or foreign investment; (2) those that arise when a country tries to avoid being damaged by developments in another country; and (3) those that arise because a country wants to maintain its domestic autonomy in policymaking when confronted with an international event.

More specifically, the major conflicts tend to concern the following issues:

1. *Markets:* The attempt of each nation to have greater access for its exports to the markets of other countries and ready access to imports of needed resources from the markets of other countries.
2. *Terms of trade:* The attempt of each country to improve its terms of trade by raising export prices relative to import prices.
3. *Terms of foreign investment:* The attempt by host governments to raise the benefit-cost ratio of foreign capital inflows.
4. *Adjustment costs to imports:* The attempt of each nation to minimize market disruption or domestic injury from greater imports.
5. *Costs of balance-of-payments adjustment:* The attempt of each nation to minimize the cost of adjusting to a disequilibrium in its balance of payments by avoiding remedial policies or by trying to place some of the burden of adjustment on other countries.
6. *Stabilization policies:* The attempt of each nation to exercise national economic autonomy in stabilizing its own economy without subjecting its policies to external conditions.

The proper response to these conflicts does not lie in succumbing to the rhetoric of the New International Economic Order. The more realistic approach is to recognize that the demands for a NIEO reflect the consequences of the internationalization process with its attendant tensions and conflicts. But the adversary national interests are being given a particular North-South coloration. The problems of development must therefore be factored into the solutions of the problems of conflict that arise from the internationalization process. This means that economic independence cannot simply be legislated in response to the demands of UNCTAD or the NIEO as if the metropolitan country were legislating political independence. Economic independence must be attained through a structural transformation of the developing economies in which industrial production becomes a large proportion of total exports.

The disarray of the international economy has had adverse effects on development. Neither market forces, as would be represented by free trade or freely floating exchange rates, nor international codes of conduct now prevail in establishing world economic order. There is always the danger that the regulation of international economic conduct will be abandoned to either simple unilateral action or ad hoc negotiation dependent on bargaining power. In such an environment, the traditional beliefs of economists in a harmony of interest, mutual gains from trade, foreign investment as a nonzero-sum activity—all the beliefs that support internationalism over nationalism—would be submerged. To avoid the dangers of nationalism and policy competition among nations, more international coordination of policies is needed. Many of the policies recommended in this book depend on such coordination for their effectiveness. The liberalization of foreign trade regimes, promotion of outward-looking policies, mobilization of resources, coordination of international monetary policies, and cooperation between IMF, World Bank, and commercial banks, all require a diminution in competition among national policies and more cooperative international action.

Although for some problems the quality of policymaking might be improved at the national level by greater use of the market system, the more complex problems of development may require for their correction an extension of planning at the higher international level. Jan Tinbergen has emphasized the series of levels at which decisions have to be taken.[4] In order that the decisions regarding necessary policy instruments ("action parameters") be optimal, there must not be "external" effects—that is, the influences exerted on the well-being of groups outside the jurisdiction of those who make the decision should be weak. The area in which the impact of the instrument will be felt determines what decision level will be optimal. The level should be high enough to cover the area in which the impact is nonnegligible. Thus, while the newly developed "nation state" is a political unit and a cultural unit, it is an inappropriate economic decision-making unit for many developmental issues. Decisions made at the national levels are often at far too low a level to be optimal. Trade liberalization and access to markets in the developed countries, the monitoring of export controls and access to resources from primary-producing countries, more multilateral aid programs, harmonization of aid terms, compensatory financing measures, international stabilization policies, supplementary financial measures, coordination of international monetary policies—all these policies depend on cooperative international action.

After the development experience of the past quarter-century, the central question for the next quarter-century will be: Can national programs of development succeed

without the supportive existence of an international public sector? In the domestic economy, the public sector is charged with the maintenance of full employment, redistribution of income, and correction of market failures. But where is the responsibility for the performance of analogous functions in the world economy? The absorption of surplus labor requires an international full-employment policy. An international redistribution of income requires a more effective mechanism for transferring resources from rich to poor countries. The pervasiveness of international market imperfections—whether expressed as price distortions, transfer of inappropriate technology, or as "backwash effects"—requires for their correction some international authority that can transcend the limits of national jurisdiction.

The task ahead is to realize the potentialities of more extensive international governance. Although we can discern only the rudiments of an international public sector, we may submit that the future economic development lies in overcoming the fragmentation in policymaking that has characterized development policies within the poor countries and between rich and poor countries. This ad hoc piecemeal approach to policy has left a distorted policy framework that is third, or fourth—or nth best.

A student of international development has conveniently summarized the services that international agencies may be required to perform; most likely, these agencies will be:

(i) Providing a framework for the resolution of conflicts between member states.

(ii) Promoting joint activities between member states, which reap the advantages of scale, e.g., under complementarity or production sharing agreements.

(iii) Providing assistance in the mobilization of resources.

(iv) Providing advice in fields which require specialized technical skills.

(v) Providing assistance in the recruitment of personnel or organizations to perform specified tasks, e.g., engineering contractors, or managing agents.

[4]Jan Tinbergen, "Building a World Order," in J. N. Bhagwati (ed.), *Economics and World Order from the 1970s to the 1990s*, New York 1972, pp. 145–7; see also Martin McGuire, "Group Segregation and Optimal Jurisdictions," *Journal of Political Economy*, Vol. 82, January–February 1974, pp. 112–32.

(vi) Acting on member countries' behalf in negotiations with external organizations, e.g., foreign private investors, or aid agencies.[5]

To promote these services more effectively, some international economic institutions may have to be reformed, and the specialized international agencies will have to coordinate their programs more fully. In particular, a number of proposals have been made for changes in world trade institutions.[6] Improvements in development policy are likely to come ultimately from more cooperation among the international specialized agencies, regional agencies, and national governments of rich and poor countries alike. If instead of supporting an international order for development policy, each LDC simply pursues narrow national policies, we will have to expect a continued deterioration in development performance. So too will the potential to meet mutual needs be lost if in the quest for a new international order nations assume adversary positions.

It is hoped that the basic economic principles emphasized in this book, together with the lessons of recent development history, might provide a basis for future progress toward more effective development policymaking. This book has sought to bring out the issues at stake. If improved policymaking can follow, there is hope for a NIEO in which the "new" emphasizes the mutual interests of rich and poor countries alike, in contrast to national interests, and provides the means of conflict resolution so that the "order" can allay the disorderly conflicts of the internationalization process. Even if a perfect set of policies cannot be formulated and implemented, better policymaking can do much to reduce the disorder of the world economy, and to mitigate absolute poverty, to improve the distribution of income, and to provide more productive employment—for the benefit of both rich and poor countries.

[5]John White, "International Agencies: The Case for Proliferation," in G. K. Helleiner (ed.), *A World Divided,* New York 1976, p. 288.

[6]American Society of International Law, *Remaking the System of World Trade: A Proposal for Institutional Reform,* 1976; Atlantic Council, *GATT Plus: A Proposal for Trade Reform,* 1975; Miriam Camps, *Collective Management,* New York 1981.

INDEX